Principles of Macroeconomics

Richard W. Tresch

BOSTON COLLEGE

WEST PUBLISHING COMPANY

Minneapolis/Saint Paul   New York   Los Angeles   San Francisco

With love to
Alayne, Kimberly, Sara
and
my parents

and with special thanks to
Ken Felter

PRODUCTION CREDITS

COPYEDITING   Sherry Goldbecker
TEXT DESIGN   Kristin Weber
TEXT ILLUSTRATIONS   Randy Miyake, Miyake Illustration
PAGE LAYOUT   David Farr, ImageSmythe, Inc.
COMPOSITION   Parkwood Composition
INDEX   E. Virginia Hobbs
COVER DESIGN   David Farr, ImageSmythe, Inc.
PART-CHAPTER OPENING ART/COVER IMAGE   Maxine Masterfield, AWS, NWS, from *In Harmony with Nature*, by Maxine Masterfield, published by Watson Guptill, New York

Production, prepress, printing, and binding by West Publishing Company.

Chapter 22 of this text was written by Jonathan Wight, University of Richmond.

WEST'S COMMITMENT TO THE ENVIRONMENT

In 1906, West Publishing Company began recycling materials left over from the production of books. This began a tradition of efficient and responsible use of resources. Today, up to 95 percent of our legal books and 70 percent of our college and school texts are printed on recycled, acid-free stock. West also recycles nearly 22 million pounds of scrap paper annually—the equivalent of 181,717 trees. Since the 1960s, West has devised ways to capture and recycle waste inks, solvents, oils, and vapors created in the printing process. We also recycle plastics of all kinds, wood, glass, corrugated cardboard, and batteries, and have eliminated the use of Styrofoam book packaging. We at West are proud of the longevity and the scope of our commitment to the environment.

01 00 99 98 97 96 95 94   8 7 6 5 4 3 2 1 0

Library of Congress Cataloging-in-Publication Data

Tresch, Richard W.
    Principles of macroeconomics / Richard W. Tresch.
        p.   cm.
    Includes index
    ISBN 0-314-02847-1
    1. Macroeconomics.   I. Title.
HB172.5.T74   1994
339—dc20

93-36015
CIP

TABLE OF CONTENTS

PART V

THE ROLE OF PRICES AND THE PROBLEM OF INFLATION   543

CHAPTER 18

AGGREGATE SUPPLY AND AGGREGATE DEMAND   545

CHAPTER 19

CONTROLLING INFLATION AND OTHER POLICY ISSUES   577

PART VI

INTERNATIONAL ECONOMIC ISSUES   613

CHAPTER 20

INTERNATIONAL TRADE AND BARRIERS TO TRADE   615

Principles of Macroeconomics is the product of over twenty years of experience teaching the economic principles course at Boston College. It is a mainstream text that provides in-depth analysis, with examples, of the standard topics in macro principles. Nonetheless, the text contains a number of distinctive content and pedagogical features that, I believe, distinguish it from other mainstream texts.

CONTENT FEATURES

In my opinion, the fundamental problem in teaching macroeconomics is to present the controversy that exists between the new Keynesian and new classical economists over the operation of the macro economy in the short run, and to do so in a way that is fair to both schools yet does not hopelessly confuse our students.

CONTINUED FOCUS ON THE MACROECONOMIC POLICY GOALS I attempt to confront this fundamental difficulty by tightly structuring the presentation around the four macroeconomic policy goals—long-run economic growth, full employment, price stability, and stability in economic relations with foreign nations. The macro chapters begin with an extended discussion of the four macroeconomic policy goals, after which I ask the central policy question for the course: to what extent can the national government's fiscal and monetary policies help to achieve these goals? The government's policy problem is discussed repeatedly throughout the macro chapters, with hypothetical exercises and real-world examples showing what the government is trying to do. The analysis of the controversy between the two schools remains focused on this question throughout.

BALANCED PRESENTATION OF THE NEW KEYNESIAN AND NEW CLASSICAL VIEWS   I strive for a balanced presentation of the new Keynesian and new classical views of the macro economy, stressing areas of agreement and disagreement between the two schools. In my opinion, this requires an approach different from the one found in most existing texts. The standard story that students are told as economics texts move early on into the Keynesian cross is that the Keynesian consumption function is a major building block of the demand side of a broader macro model, a model on which macro economists generally agree. In my view, this story is not just a matter of some innocent hand waving that might be appropriate for a principles course. I think the story is wrong. The real business cycle model is now the prevailing model within the new classical school. In that model, any short-run output response to, say, a productivity shock is to be found in the supply of labor, not in the Keynesian consumption function.

In my opinion, a balanced presentation of the two schools requires three things:

a) A more detailed explanation of the Life Cycle Hypothesis than the paragraph or box to which it is relegated in most texts (if it is mentioned at all). The LCH, not the Keynesian consumption function, is the main component of the demand side of the real business cycle model.

b) An analysis of the market for labor from the new classical perspective including, most importantly, the relationship between interest rates and the supply of labor.

c) A comparison of the data that convinces new Keynesian economists that product and factor markets are riddled with imperfections, and the data that convinces new classical economists that the economy is essentially competitive and ought to be modeled as such.

The first analytical macro chapter, Chapter 9, meets the controversy head-on. Centered around the question of how best to model the macro economy, the chapter indicates the basic choices that new Keynesian and new classical economists make in building a simple model of the economy, and why they make them. Students learn the reasons for the controversy, namely, that the data are not entirely conclusive on either side and that each of the models has strengths and weaknesses in terms of explaining features of the macro economy. When I move on to the Keynesian cross in Chapter 10, students know that they are proceeding under the new Keynesian assumptions of sticky wages and prices, and unemployed resources. They also know that there is a very different view of the macro economy to which the text will return.

CONCLUDING EMPHASIS ON AREAS OF AGREEMENT
Fortunately, the new Keynesian and new classical economists have reached a consensus on the operation of the macro economy in the long run. We can speak with some confidence, therefore, about long-run issues such as the burden of running large structural budget deficits, how to control inflation, the need for credible policies, and the effects of tax policy on saving and investment in the long run. I highlight the areas of agreement in Chapter 19, the concluding macro chapter (and elsewhere, whenever appropriate).

FLEXIBLE PRESENTATION OF THE TWO VIEWS The presentation of the two views is flexible enough so that instructors who lean toward one school or the other can emphasize the material that is compatible with their own beliefs. I suppose this will be somewhat easier for new Keynesians, simply because much of the standard material in a macro principles course still retains a very definite new Keynesian bias. But new classical economists will find the building blocks of the real business cycle spelled out in sufficient detail for their needs, and I do not believe many of the existing principles texts can make that claim.

Additional Features

FULL DEVELOPMENT OF AS/AD MODEL DELAYED The full development of the Aggregate Supply-Aggregate Demand (AS-AD) model in terms of prices is delayed until the final chapters. This has two advantages. It avoids the confusion of carrying both the Keynesian cross and AS-AD models along simultaneously. The new Keynesian/new classical controversy is difficult enough for students to absorb without their being burdened early on with the full development of two analytical techniques. It also allows me to present the topic of money before developing the AD curve, an essential prerequisite.

FOCUS ON THE CIRCULAR FLOW OF ECONOMIC ACTIVITY The concept of the circular flow of economic activity reappears frequently as a motivational and organizational device. Fiscal and monetary policies are presented in terms of their attempt to influence the level and composition of the circular flow.

INTERNATIONAL ASPECTS OF THE MACRO ECONOMY THROUGHOUT International aspects of the macro economy are woven into the analysis throughout, beginning with the examination of macroeconomic policy goals and running through national income accounting, the development of the Keynesian model, automatic stabilizers, the twin budget and trade deficits, net export crowding-out, and the effects of fiscal and monetary policy. The macroeconomic analysis concludes with three chapters on international trade, international finance, and developing nations that focus on the key international issues of the day.

EMPHASIS ON THE PRACTICAL DIFFICULTIES IN THE CONDUCT OF FISCAL AND MONETARY POLICY Students are made aware of the practical considerations and difficulties in the conduct of fiscal and monetary policy.

INTUITIVE PORTFOLIO APPROACH TO MONEY AND MONETARY POLICY I have chosen an intuitive and uncluttered portfolio approach to money and its effects on the economy. The portfolio approach is extended to show how fiscal policy, and aggregate demand generally, affects interest rates.

PEDAGOGICAL FEATURES

The text contains a large number of pedagogical features designed to stimulate student interest, to help students learn and apply the material, to help students review material once they have studied a chapter, and to reinforce the coherence of the presentation. These features, which were carefully developed based on input from scores of economics professors, are designed and crafted to avoid cluttering the text and interrupting the flow of learning.

Within-Chapter Pedagogy

OPENING SCENARIO Each chapter opens with a scenario that draws students into the chapter and sets the stage for the concepts and material to follow.

MARGIN COMMENTS Occasional margin comments, printed in blue, ask students to reflect on the concepts being discussed, most often by requiring them to relate those concepts directly to their own experiences. The margin comments are also used to offer insightful historical notes and comments on current issues or to elaborate on a theoretical point.

LISTS OF CONCEPTS TO LEARN AND TO RECALL   Each chapter title page contains a list of Concepts to Learn that presents the learning objectives for the chapter. The Concepts to Learn list is immediately followed by a list of Concepts to Recall that alerts students to concepts from preceding chapters that they will need in order to understand the new material, and indicates where the concepts have appeared earlier.

MARGIN DEFINITIONS   Definitions of key terms appear in the margins.

DETAILED FIGURE CAPTIONS   Each figure contains a detailed caption that guides the student carefully through the figure and summarizes its key point.

CONCEPT SUMMARY TABLES   Concept Summary tables are used where appropriate to pull together key concepts and show their overall relationship to the topic.

END-OF-CHAPTER MATERIAL   End-of-chapter material includes a summary that reviews the architecture of the chapter and also provides a numbered list of key points, a list of key terms and concepts from the chapter, and questions and problems to test the student's understanding, ranging from questions calling for straight feedback to problems requiring analysis and synthesis.

Additional Special Features

CASES AND ECONOMIC ADVISOR'S REPORTS   An Economic Advisor's Report at the end of each main section places students in the role of economist by requiring them to apply concepts and theories to realistic consulting situations. These cases ask students to make recommendations and provide advice to "clients," based on the chapter material. Each case has an international aspect to it.

LOGO SECTIONS ON THE SPENDING MULTIPLIER IN THE UNITED STATES   Occasional sections in the chapters indicate how certain features of the macro economy affect

the value of the simple spending multiplier in the United States. They are identified with the logo

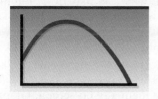

SUPPLEMENTARY MATERIALS

The text is accompanied by an impressive array of supplements for instructors and for students.

For Instructors

INSTRUCTOR'S MANUAL   (Charles G. Leathers, University of Alabama-Tuscaloosa) The Instructor's Manual contains teaching objectives and a teaching outline, other organizational options, teaching hints, alternate examples (including numerical examples), answers to end-of-chapter and between-part cases, additional essay and discussion questions, and teaching notes for the graphing supplement. The Instructor's Manual also includes a special note on where and how Tresch's text differs from other economics texts and a guide to using the supplement package that includes, for the graphing supplement, a set of teaching notes and, for the alternate topics, a set of objectives, teaching notes, an outline, teaching hints, supplemental readings (formatted on perforated pages), discussion questions, additional suggested readings, and transparency masters.

TEST BANK   (Richard Long, Georgia State University) The Test Bank contains over 5,000 multiple choice, true/false, fill-in-the-blank, short answer, and essay questions. Questions are classified as easy, medium, or hard and are categorized as analytical or factual. A chapter-opening matrix directs instructors to specific content areas, should they wish to test more heavily on particular topics. Questions are also provided for the alternate topics.

TRANSPARENCY MASTERS   Transparency masters are available for all the figures in the text. Acetates for the key figures are also available.

WESTEST 3.0   Westest 3.0 is a computerized testing program for DOS, Windows, or Macintosh that allows instructors to create, edit, store, and print exams. Instructors can prepare exams by copying questions to an exam window individually, as part of a sequential range, by using a numerical select, or by generating question lists randomly. Features similar to those of word processing programs enable instructors to add and edit questions directly on-screen. Exam questions can be arranged randomly, automatically by type (*e.g.*, true/false, multiple choice, etc.) or manually on-screen. Graphics are visible in the flow of the text.

WEST'S CLASSROOM MANAGEMENT SOFTWARE   West's Classroom Management software, included in Westest 3.0, lets instructors record and store student data and keep track of homework and project assignments and scores, exam scores, and class grades and rankings. Instructors can generate individual reports which graph a student's scores against the class average; document missing assignments by assignment or student; generate class summaries that show grade distribution; and produce class listings of students according to I.D. numbers, average scores, and overall grades.

ASTOUND PRESENTATION SOFTWARE   Astound Presentation Software is perfect for economics classes. Astound allows instructors to manipulate graphs live during class, showing the actual movement of shifts to illustrate changes due to economic factors. Bruce McClung (Southwest Texas State University) has created electronic transparency masters for use with Astound that include the teaching outlines and all major graphics in the text.

WEST'S VIDEODISC FOR ECONOMICS   West's Videodisc for Economics provides quick access to key illustrations and animated graphics and photographs, as well as footage from the Economics U$A series by Annenberg CPB. The videodisc format allows instructors to present graphs in a series of steps, allowing for a more gradual and easy-to-follow presentation.

WEST'S VIDEO LIBRARY FOR ECONOMICS   West's Video Library for Economics includes critical thinking videos that challenge students to apply economic terms to other aspects of their world, and a series of thematic videos that deal with the deficit, the global economy, and the economics of the natural environment. An instructor's manual for the Video Library includes lecture notes on the videos.

For Students

STUDY GUIDE   (Lynda Rush, California State Polytechnic University-Pomona) The Study Guide includes learning objectives, chapter reviews, hints and cautions for the student, concepts to recall, pre- and post-tests with answers, demonstration problems, true/false, multiple choice, and short answer questions, and guides to specific problems for individual improvement in particular areas of weakness.

SPANISH GLOSSARY   (Carol Clark, Guilford College, and Dr. Alejandro Velez, Professor of Economics and Coordinator of Latin American Studies, St. Mary's University, San Antonio, Texas) A Spanish Glossary will help Spanish-speaking students to understand the key terms crucial to economics.

GRAPHING SUPPLEMENT (Colin Linsley, St. John Fisher College, and Gary E. Maggs, St. John Fisher College) The graphing supplement, which comes shrink-wrapped with the text, is an extensive supplement that shows students how to read graphs, describes how graphs are used in economic analysis, and explains the algebra behind the graphs. It also includes exercises through which students test their knowledge of the material.

ALTERNATE TOPICS AND CASES BOOKLET   The booklet covers key topics in both micro and macro.

ALTERNATE TOPICS

- Khosrow Doroodian, Ohio University
    IMF Stabilization Policies in Developing Countries
- Barbara M. Fraumeni, Northeastern University/ Harvard University
    Productivity and Economic Growth
- Patrick D. Mauldin, Emory University
    An Economic Perspective on Health Care Expenditures
- Joseph Pelzman, George Washington University
    Building a Market Based System: The Case of the Former Soviet Union
- David R. Schlow, Pennsylvania State University
    A Historical Perspective on Discretionary Fiscal Policy and Monetary Policy: 1930–1993
- Peter M. Schwarz, University of North Carolina at Charlotte
    The Great Depression: What Caused It and Why Did It Last So Long?

- Paul M. Taube, University of Texas-Pan American
  Defense Cuts and Their Economic Impact
- By the author (with a macro orientation)
  Defense Contracting
  Noneconomic Factors and the Distribution
    of Income and Wealth
  Some Pitfalls in Interpreting Data on the
    Distribution of Income
  Tax Loopholes
  The Trade-off between Efficiency and Equity in
    Taxation
  Fiscal Federalism: The Economic Functions of
    the National, State, and Local Governments
  The Lucas Price Surprise Model
  Forward Exchange Rates, Interest Rates, and
    Speculation

ALTERNATE CASES (ECONOMIC ADVISOR'S REPORTS)

- Manfred W. Keil, Northeastern University
  Unemployment in Canada
  Macroeconomic Policy and Political Interactions
  Is Inflation Bad? International Evidence
  Convergence across States to Assess the Likelihood
    of Convergence across Countries
- James J. McLain, University of New Orleans
  2001: A Case Odyssey—In Investment
- George Plesko, Northeastern University
  Turning Swords into Plowshares??
  How Much Should Americans Pay for Gasoline?
  Why Pay More?
  Should Gillette Be Allowed to Buy Parker?
  How Much Should Water Cost?
  Can Government Affect Savings?

ECONOMIC$ STUDY WIZARD SOFTWARE 2.0   This software package contains graphics tutorials for both micro and macro that allow students to see the development of a graph from start to finish; terms and definitions; a review for the final exam; a special module that introduces the students to leading economists and their theories and ideas; and Quizmaster, an interactive-format review that randomly generates multiple choice, true/false, or completion questions. Study Wizard runs on IBM PCs and compatibles. Graphics tutorials require a color monitor.

ACKNOWLEDGMENTS

A Principles text is truly a joint product. I wish to acknowledge the contributions of the following people, and express to them my thanks and deepest gratitude.

JONATHAN WIGHT, UNIVERSITY OF RICHMOND, who brought closure to the text with a marvelous final chapter on The Developing Countries. Jonathan has set down the major economic problems facing these countries in clear and lively text that both students and their instructors will enjoy reading.

THE EXCELLENT GRADUATE STUDENTS AT BOSTON COLLEGE who helped with the preparation of the text:

- Those who assisted me with the background research: James Bathgate, Sirhan Ciftcioglu, Thomas Duggan, Elizabeth Hill, and Sr. Beth Anne Tercek.
- Those who assisted me in developing the end-of-chapter questions and the margin definitions: Basma Bekdache, Scott Browne, James Fetzer, Gurcan Gulen, Michael Kozy, Meral Karasulu, Brendan Lowney, David Richardson, Niloufer Sohrabji, and Gulcan Unal.

MY FACULTY COLLEAGUES AT BOSTON COLLEGE, who were a ready and willing source of expert advice on so many topics. Without meaning to slight anyone, I want to acknowledge the following for their advice and support: James Anderson, Kit Baum, David Belsley, Frank Gollop, Peter Gottschalk, Frank McLaughlin, Bob Murphy, and Steve Polasky.

THE PROFESSIONALS AT WEST PUBLISHING COMPANY, and to those associated with West, who helped with the production of the text. Many thanks to:

- Richard Fenton and Nancy Hill-Whilton, my editors, who gave me the greatest gift a Principles author can have—they let me write the book I wanted to write. They also have wonderful instincts for useful pedagogical and supplemental materials for an introductory text, and I followed their advice on these matters without exception. I look forward to working with Sharon Adams, who joined the project near the end and who will now be my editor.
- Thomas Modl, my production editor, who somehow brought all the elements of this complex project together under an extremely tight production schedule. I am moved to say that Nancy Hill-Whilton and Tom Modl worked harder on this project than I could possibly have imagined, and certainly harder than I had any right to expect.
- Sherry Goldbecker, my copy editor, whose suggestions improved the original manuscript immeasurably.
- Randy Miyake, the artist who, working from my wretched hand drawings, produced the beautiful figures for the text.

■ John Tuvey, my promotion manager, who developed a thoroughly professional marketing campaign, and who kept writing such nice things about me and the text.

THE ECONOMISTS WHO PRODUCED SUCH EXCELLENT SUPPORTING MATERIAL FOR THE TEXT. In addition to those who provided the supplements listed above, I am grateful to those who provided the Cases and Economic Advisor's Reports that appear in the text:

■ David Denslow, University of Florida
    Hard Times in California
    What Caused the Inflation of the 1970s?
■ K. K. Fung, Memphis State University
    A Free Ride to Cross-border Shopping
    The "Flipper" Factor in International Trade
■ Manfred W. Keil, Northeastern University
    An International Comparison of Unemployment
      Rates
■ James J. McLain, University of New Orleans
    The Accord of 2006: The End of Fiscal Policy?

THE ACCURACY REVIEWERS to whom I owe a special dept of gratitude:

■ Robert Gillette, Texas A & M University, who reviewed the figures.
■ Roy Van Til, University of Maine-Farmington, who checked all numerical data, calculations, and exercises.

THE MANUSCRIPT REVIEWERS who without exception read the chapters carefully and offered many sensible comments, criticisms, and suggestions. Although I could not incorporate all their ideas, I followed closely the thrust of their comments and the book is much better for my having done so:

Glen Atkinson, University of Nevada-Reno
Chris A. Austin, Normandale Community College
Werner Baer, University of Illinois at
    Urbana-Champaign
Klaus G. Becker, Texas Tech University
Roberto Bosnifaz, Babson College
Kathleen K. Bromley, Monroe Community College

Maureen Burton, California State Polytechnic
    University-Pomona
Carol Clark, Guilford College
Paul A. Coomes, University of Louisville
Joyce Cooper, Boston University
Joanna Cruse, Miami Dade Community College
David Denslow, University of Florida
Burton W. DeVeau, Ohio University
John Eckalbar, California State University-Chico
Robert Evans, Brandeis University
Michael J. Ferrantino, Southern Methodist University
Rodney Fort, Washington State University
Andrew W. Foshee, McNeese State University
K. K. Fung, Memphis State University
Robert Gillette, Texas A & M University
Edward C. Koziara, Drexel University
Charles G. Leathers, University of Alabama-Tuscaloosa
Stephen E. Lile, Western Kentucky University
Colin A. Linsley, St. John Fisher College
Richard Long, Georgia State University
Bruce McClung, Southwest Texas State University
Diana L. McCoy, Truckee Meadows Community
    College
Bruce McCrea, Lansing Community College
James J. McLain, University of New Orleans
Andrew Morrison, Tufts University
Kathryn A. Nantz, Fairfield University
Patrick B. O'Neill, University of North Dakota
Jan Palmer, Ohio University
George Plesko, Northeastern University
James E. Price, Syracuse University
Robert C. Puth, University of New Hampshire
Christine Rider, St. John's University
Lynda Rush, California State Polytechnic
    University-Pomona
P. Snoonian, University of Massachusetts-Lowell
James A. Stephenson, Iowa State University
Jack W. Thornton, East Carolina University
Gerald D. Toland, Southwest State University
Charles Tontar, Merrimack College
Alice Trost, University of Massachusetts-Boston
David A. Wells, University of Arizona
Jonathan B. Wight, University of Richmond
William D. Witter, University of North Texas

Introduction

1

The First Principles of Economics

LEARNING OBJECTIVES

CONCEPTS TO LEARN

The three-part economic problem

Opportunity cost

The three key players in the economy

Economic exchange

Interdependence

ou are about to begin the study of economics, a subject that has achieved a commanding presence in U.S. society. When the polling organizations ask people each year what the most pressing problem facing the nation is, they most often name inflation or unemployment, both economic problems. Bill Clinton and Ross Perot kept the 1992 presidential campaign tightly focused on economic issues. They knew that elections are often won and lost on the performance of the economy and that President Bush was vulnerable on that score. Both during and after the 1992 election, President Clinton promised that economic issues would occupy center stage in his administration. The president made this promise to a nation that is bombarded daily with economic news: THE NATIONAL DEBT EXCEEDS $4 TRILLION— UNEMPLOYMENT RISES FOR THE THIRD STRAIGHT MONTH— ANOTHER LARGE THRIFT INSTITUTION FAILS—U.S.-JAPANESE TRADE DEFICIT WORSENS—MORTGAGE RATES ON THE RISE—FED CHAIRMAN TO EASE UP ON THE MONEY SUPPLY—Details at 11:00.

The general interest in economic events has swept economists into the public limelight. They are interviewed regularly on television, and they write feature columns in many of the major city newspapers. A Nobel Memorial Prize in economics has been awarded annually since 1969; no other social science has been so honored.

What is economics that it should command so much attention?

Economics, first of all, is classified as a social science because it is concerned with the structure of society and the activities and interrelationships of individuals and groups within society. Anthropology, law, political science, psychology, and sociology are also classified as social sciences for the same reason. How is the discipline of economics distinct from these other disciplines?

Alfred Marshall, the leading economist of the early 1900s, said that economics is primarily concerned with the material requirements of personal well-being attained through the ordinary business of life. He was referring to such everyday matters as how we earn a living, what goods and services we buy, what products business firms choose to produce and how they produce them, and what services we want our governments to provide. Marshall believed that the study of these issues distinguished economics from the other social sciences, and most people today no doubt think of economics just as Marshall did. But the dividing line between economics and the other social sciences has become increasingly blurred since Marshall's day. The economic journals of the past year contain articles on welfare dependency, voting patterns in legislatures, divorce, language as a basis for discrimination, the selection of arbitrators in labor disputes, placement of a dollar value on the loss of life, and how information flows through government bureaucracies. These subjects hardly constitute what Marshall had in mind by the ordinary business of life. They seem more closely associated with what is commonly understood to be law, political science, psychology, and sociology, as the case may be. In fact, economics and the other social sciences are increasingly addressing similar issues; they are no longer so easy to distinguish on the basis of what they study.

If economics retains a distinctive identity among the social sciences, it is more by virtue of *how* it studies society and social relationships than by *what* it studies. Economists have contributed a systematic approach to the analysis of human behavior that has proved to be extremely useful and enlightening in a wide variety of applications. This approach, and the undeniable fact that most people have an abiding interest in their personal well-being and the ordinary business of life, goes far in explaining the current interest in economics.

For the beginning student, then, the key to understanding economics lies in understanding its fundamental principles of analysis. These principles are so important that the first four chapters will serve as an introduction to them. They need not be mastered at this point, but it is essential to meet the fundamental principles before attempting to analyze and interpret the important economic events and issues of the day. They appear time and again throughout the text and serve as the threads that tie economics together. Perhaps the best gauge of your progress in the course is whether you believe you are becoming more familiar with these principles as you proceed through the text from topic to topic.

THE ECONOMIC PROBLEM

The first principle of economic analysis is that every economic problem has an identical three-part structure consisting of *objectives*, *alternatives*, and *constraints*. Each part of the economic problem is equally necessary. Take away any one of them and the economic problem disappears.

Objectives: People must have **objectives,** or goals, to have an economic problem; they must care about the consequences of their decisions. Of course, we do have objectives in all aspects of our lives. We care about what goods and services we buy, how we earn our living, what kind of education we receive, how we spend our free time, and so forth. We want to do as well as we can in whatever we do.

Zonker Harris in the "Doonesbury" comic strip offers a striking contrast to the rest of us. Zonker appears to go through life without a care in the world, which makes him one of the happiest characters on the comic strip pages. More power to him. He is happy in large part because his carefree attitude frees him from ever having an economic problem. We are not so fortunate.

Alternatives: The term **alternatives** refers to the necessity of making choices. We must have more than one way of reaching our objectives. There can be no problem without choice because then there is no decision to be made. We would simply do the best we can by following the single available option.

Traditional peasant societies are tightly ruled by customs handed down through the ages. The people behave as they do largely because that is how their ancestors behaved. They face a limited range of economic problems as a result. In modern industrialized societies each generation is far more likely to set out on its own because economic development gives people the freedom to make new choices. Increased choice does not necessarily bring increased happiness, however, as any number of social scientists have noted. One consequence of our freedom to choose is that we are forced to confront the economic problem more frequently.

Constraints: **Constraints** that people face in trying to achieve their objectives form the final pillar in the structure of all economic problems. The idea of being constrained has a very precise meaning in economic analysis: No matter how cleverly we choose among the alternatives open to us, we cannot fully achieve our objectives. We always come up a little short when trying to solve our economic problems, which explains why confronting the economic problem is not usually a happy experience.

THE ECONOMIC PROBLEM
A three-part problem consisting of objectives, alternatives, and constraints.

OBJECTIVES
The part of the economic problem that refers to the goals that economic agents try to achieve.

ALTERNATIVES
The part of the economic problem that refers to the necessity of making choices.

CONSTRAINTS
The part of the economic problem that refers to the limitations that prevent economic agents from achieving their objectives.

We often do achieve particular objectives, of course. You will soon earn that college degree. Some people who want the good life do eventually buy that mansion high on the hill. Whenever we achieve a particular objective, we no longer have an economic problem relating to it because we are no longer constrained in pursuing it. No one fully escapes the economic problem, however. We always want more out of life than we are able to achieve.

The most common way of describing the notion of constraints is to say that we have limited, or scarce, resources. The **Law of Scarcity** is a fundamental principle of economics. It says that resources are scarce in the sense that they are not sufficient to achieve the stated objectives, or goals. For instance, suppose that you aspire to all the trappings of the good life: fine cars, a beautiful home, stylish clothes, Caribbean vacations, and the like. The Law of Scarcity applies to you so long as you cannot afford all the things you want. In other words, you continue to have an economic problem.

The three-part economic problem—objectives, alternatives, constraints—is so central to economics that it provides the most widely accepted short definition of economics itself. Economics is the study of how best to allocate scarce resources. In the definition, "allocate" refers to choosing among the alternatives, "scarce resources" refers to the constraints, and "best" implicitly captures the idea that people are trying to achieve various objectives, or goals.

THE KEY PLAYERS IN THE ECONOMY

The key players in an economy are the individual, the business firm, and the government. We will begin with the individual and the business firm because they define the roles that economic actors or agents can have in any economy. Government agencies play both parts, sometimes acting as individuals do and sometimes acting as business firms do.

Individuals perform two basic economic functions. On the one hand, they purchase most of the final goods and services produced by business firms. ("Final" goods and services are those that require no further processing, such as bread, shirts, and automobiles.) Economists refer to individuals in this role as **consumers** because people consume goods and services as they use them. On the other hand, individuals supply resources that they own to the business firms, which the firms then use to produce goods and services. Economists refer to these resources as **factors of production** because they serve as inputs into the production process. Individuals supply the three *primary* factors of production: labor, land, and capital.

Labor is a catch-all term referring to all the different kinds of skills and occupations found in the work force—blue-collar employees such as manual laborers; white-collar employees such as clerks, secretaries, and managers; professionals such as lawyers, doctors, and teachers; and **entrepreneurs,** those imaginative individuals who bring new ideas to the business world and are willing to take the risk of starting new ventures or businesses.

Individuals own and supply the **land** on which business firms build their factories and offices. *Land* also refers to the contents of the land, the fertile soil and the natural resources—minerals, natural gas, and oil—which are themselves important factors of production.

Capital refers primarily to plant and equipment, that is, the factories, buildings, and machinery that all firms require for the production of goods and services. Capital inputs have to be produced themselves, and business firms buy them directly from other business firms. But individuals supply the funds,

LAW OF SCARCITY
The principle that resources are not sufficient to achieve all the objectives, or goals, of an economic problem.

REFLECTION: Test your understanding of the economic problem by thinking about the economic problem of your college or university. What are some of its objectives, alternatives, and constraints?

CONSUMERS
Economic agents who consume goods and services and who supply the primary factors of production—labor, capital, and land—to producers.

FACTORS OF PRODUCTION
The resources or inputs that producers use to produce goods and services, consisting of labor, capital, land, and material inputs.

LABOR
A catch-all term referring to all the different kinds of skills and occupations found in the work force; one of the primary factors of production.

ENTREPRENEURS
Imaginative individuals who bring new ideas to the business world and who are willing to take the risks of starting new ventures or businesses.

through their savings, that enable business firms to purchase the plant and equipment.

Business firms occupy the other side of these transactions. Economists often refer to business firms as **producers** because their role is to produce the final goods and services that individuals consume. In order to do this business firms must receive factors of production from individuals and other business firms, and then decide how best to turn these inputs into goods and services. The only transactions firms engage in that do not directly involve individuals are the purchases by firms of semi-finished products, called **material inputs,** from other firms. Examples of material inputs include the grain used to make bread, the cloth used to make shirts, and the glass used in a car's windows. These material inputs are the most important factor of production for most firms. They are combined with the three primary factors of production supplied by individuals and brought to ever-higher stages of "finish." The last stage in the production hierarchy is the final good or service—the bread, shirt, and automobile.

Governments are both consumers and producers of goods and services. When the Department of Defense buys intercontinental ballistic missiles, it is engaging in an act of public consumption on behalf of all citizens. The missiles are final goods whose sole purpose is to deter foreign countries from acts of aggression against the United States. We may or may not like these missiles, but we are all forced to consume the service they provide. Governments are more often producers of goods and services. Public education, mass transportation systems, public utilities, the postal service, and the nation's highway system are all examples of goods and services that are produced and maintained by government agencies for the benefit of private individuals or business firms. Governments become involved in consuming and producing goods and services in a market economy because the market cannot always be relied on to provide the goods and services that people want. For example, individual citizens cannot easily provide for the security of an entire nation. The national government is in a much better position to formulate and carry out national security policy. Similarly, a complete network of highways is essential to any nation, yet private business firms could not profitably construct and maintain most of the highway network.

The government performs one other important function in an economy. It redistributes resources among individuals, most often to protect people from becoming impoverished or to help the less fortunate who have become impoverished. The leading example in the United States is the Social Security System, a $300 billion federal program that taxes workers through a payroll tax and transfers the proceeds to retired workers and their families in the form of monthly cash payments and hospital benefits. The result is a massive redistribution of income from the younger generations to the elderly, undertaken so that the elderly do not become wards of the state.[1]

The Economic Problems of the Key Players

Before leaving the key players, let's take a brief look at some of the economic problems that they face. Understanding the economic problems of individuals, business firms, and government agencies is one of the primary goals of economic analysis.

LAND

The property on which business firms build their factories and office buildings; includes the fertile soil and natural resources contained within the land; one of the primary factors of production.

CAPITAL

The plant and equipment required to produce goods and services; one of the primary factors of production.

PRODUCERS

Economic agents who produce goods and services by receiving factors of production from consumers and other producers.

MATERIAL INPUTS

Semi-finished products purchased by firms and used as a factor of production.

---

[1]The Social Security System also provides monthly cash payments and hospital benefits to disabled workers and their families. The disabled are a much smaller population than are the retired elderly.

UTILITY

The value that a consumer derives from the consumption of goods and services.

THE INDIVIDUAL   We have all experienced the individual's role as a consumer of goods and services. What is the nature of our economic problem in that role, which economists refer to as the consumer's economic problem? To begin thinking about the consumer's economic problem, suppose that all decisions relating to the earning of income have been made, so that the individual has a fixed amount of income to spend. What are the consumer's objectives, alternatives, and constraints, given a fixed income?

Objectives: We consume goods and services for a variety of reasons, some noble, some less so. A number of motives—survival, comfort, pleasure, learning, status, and greed—come easily to mind. Economists lump all of these motives under the single term **utility,** or satisfaction. Our goal as consumers is to achieve the highest possible utility, or satisfaction, from the goods and services we purchase.

Alternatives: Consumers make thousands of economic decisions every year of their lives. We have a bewildering variety of goods and services to choose from, and different people certainly choose very different ways of achieving satisfaction. The choices we make depend in part on our tastes or preferences, which determine how much satisfaction we receive from the goods and services we consume. Some people like fast cars, nice clothes, and dining in fine restaurants. Other people have little interest in fast cars or nice clothes and prefer to eat at home.

Constraints: The constraints, or scarce resources, that limit the amount of utility we can attain have two distinct components. On the one hand, everyone has limited income from which to purchase goods and services (wealth, the accumulation of all past saving, can be included along with income). On the other hand, all goods and services come with prices that reflect the costs of producing them. The combination of limited income and prices means that our purchases of goods and services must ultimately come to an end. Moreover, when consumers have made all their purchases they are not entirely satisfied, with rare exceptions. They would like to have bought even more. This is the test that consumers are effectively constrained, subject to the Law of Scarcity; they have not escaped the economic problem.

We have ignored all decisions related to the earning of income to this point. Once these are brought into the picture, the consumer's economic problem changes in both structure and complexity.

Consider the decision to work. To keep matters simple, suppose the individual will only work at one type of job and is deciding how much time to spend working at that job. The job pays an hourly wage. Notice how the economic problem changes form. Income is no longer a part of the constraint. Rather, deciding how much income to earn becomes one of the alternatives. Time is now the limited resource—there are only so many hours in the day to be spent working or not working. Also, the wage rate offered on the job becomes an important price. It is essentially the price or cost of time because it determines the dollars of income sacrificed for each hour the individual chooses not to work.

REFLECTION: Students understand as well as anyone that time is a scarce resource. Do you feel constrained more often by limited income or limited time?

A final complication in the consumer's economic problem arises whenever individuals decide to save some income, instead of consuming all of it. The decision to save introduces a time element into the consumer's decision process because saving is essentially a decision to forego current consumption for consumption sometime in the future. Saving changes both the objective and the alternatives as consumers think about purchasing goods and services over a number of years, not just one year. Saving also changes the consumer's constraint by providing additional income from the returns to the saving. It introduces a whole new set of prices in the form of interest rates and other rates of return that determine how much future consumption can be obtained for each dollar of current consumption sacrificed by saving.

THE BUSINESS FIRM   Although we are all consumers, most of us have not had experience managing a business firm. Nonetheless, even the most casual knowledge of business is enough to appreciate that "doing business" involves solving the economic problem.

Objectives: The objective that comes immediately to mind when thinking about the business firm operating in a market economy is **profit,** the difference between the revenue obtained from selling goods and services and the cost of producing them. In fact, much economic analysis of business behavior assumes that making a profit is the only objective of the firm. This is surely an overstatement, however. Managers of firms are also concerned with market share, sales growth, and even good will within the community. Nonetheless, profit is certainly the predominant goal of U.S. business.

Alternatives: Business firms face three distinct choices. They must decide *what* goods and services to produce, and then *how many* of each to produce. They must also decide *how* to produce their products. Most products can be produced in many different ways, and similar products are often produced quite differently in different parts of the world, and even within the same country. Some firms choose highly skilled labor operating the newest, most sophisticated machinery. Other firms choose older equipment and employ less skilled labor to operate it.

Constraints: Finally, all business firms encounter constraints in their pursuit of profit. On the revenue side, consumers will buy only so much of any one firm's product, no matter what the price. Consumers' budgets are limited, and they can often buy a similar product from another firm. Therefore, the total revenue from sales is naturally limited. On the cost side, a given amount of inputs can only produce so much output, no matter how efficient the firm is. Also, all inputs come with prices, so that input costs rise as firms expand their production. Therefore, attempts to increase profit by expanding production are squeezed on both the revenue and the cost sides: Revenues are limited, but costs continue to rise. The result of the revenue-cost squeeze is that business firms cannot escape the economic problem either. After the managers have made all their decisions as best they can, they still wish they had earned a larger profit.

GOVERNMENT AGENCIES   All government agencies, from the smallest town department to the giant Department of Defense, must confront the economic problem. Consider briefly the objectives, alternatives, and constraints of the Department of Defense.

Objectives: The broad goal of achieving national security has a number of specific components. The United States wants to deter acts of aggression against it. It also wants the flexibility to respond to aggression in the Middle East, Western Europe, and the Western Hemisphere, at the very least.

Alternatives: The Defense Department has a number of options in pursuing each of its objectives. For starters, it must decide what role each branch of the armed services should play in the different parts of the world and how best to equip the armed services for their missions.

PROFIT

The difference between the revenue obtained from selling goods and services and the cost of producing them.

Constraints: Even the mighty Defense Department is given a fixed budget by the administration and Congress. It is certainly constrained in trying to meet its numerous objectives. The ultimate constraint on all government agencies is the need to raise taxes to finance government activity. Citizens are willing to pay taxes, but only to a certain extent.

Other Examples of the Economic Problem

The economic problem appears in all walks of life, which explains why economic analysis extends beyond the ordinary business of life into areas traditionally associated with the other social sciences. Think about a politician trying to gain election. The objective is victory in the election. The alternatives are the essence of campaign strategy. How much time should the candidate spend on the campaign trail and in which parts of the state or country? How much of the budget should be allocated to media advertisements, how much to mailers and other campaign literature, how much to dinners, parties, and other social engagements? What portions of the advertising budget should go to television, to radio, and to the newspapers and magazines? The constraints are limited time, limited campaign funds, and the costs of the various options.

Students also feel the pressures of the economic problem, most obviously at exam time. It is Thursday, and you have five final exams next week—two on Monday, two on Tuesday, and the last one on Wednesday. You figure that you will have 30 hours available to study for the five tests. A common objective is to maximize your grade point average by scoring as well as you can on the five tests combined. The alternatives include the choices you must make regarding how to study for each subject, how much time to allocate to the study of each subject, and in what order to study the subjects. The constraints are time and your limited knowledge of the five subjects. Few students are able to score 100 on every exam; the Law of Scarcity applies to nearly every student.

A moment's reflection should be enough to appreciate how pervasive the economic problem is. A key point to derive from our examples is that an economic analysis of any problem begins by defining the structure of the problem in terms of three main components: What are the objectives? The alternatives? The constraints? What is the relationship between the alternatives and both the objectives and the constraints? How will a particular choice help in meeting the objectives? To what extent will it use up scarce resources? Once a problem is described in this fashion, the same set of economic principles can be applied to solving it. The actual issue or context does not really matter because all problems that can be structured as the economic problem are analytically equivalent. This is why we will begin each new topic area in this text with a discussion of its structure in terms of objectives, alternatives, and constraints. Understanding an issue as an economic problem is the first step toward understanding how to analyze it.

TWO PRINCIPLES STEMMING FROM THE ECONOMIC PROBLEM

Two important principles apply to all economic problems: interdependence and the meaning of cost as opportunity cost. Each follows directly from the structure of the economic problem.

Interdependence

The principle of **interdependence** says that economic decisions are interrelated. The consequences of a decision always spread beyond the immediate objectives of the decision. The structure of the economic problem guarantees this principle simply because any decision uses scarce resources. Whenever scarce resources have been expended, a decision to do something necessarily implies a decision not to do something else. As a result, any one decision always has at least two consequences: the benefit, in terms of the objectives, of the decision to do something; and the loss, also in terms of the objectives, of the decision not to do something else.

The principle of interdependence will be clear if the structure of the economic problem is kept firmly in mind. For example, voters have learned to discount the promises of politicians seeking election. "If I am elected, we will have better schools, smoother highways, expanded recreational facilities, and no new taxes." People know that something has to give because they recognize the principle of interdependence. If we do get better public services, then we will almost certainly pay higher taxes. Or we might get better schools and no new taxes, but then watch out for the potholes. Regarding your own economic problem as a consumer, you know when you are buying those new winter clothes that you will probably have to cut back on entertainment for awhile. When you are studying for final exams, the principle of interdependence is also evident, sometimes painfully so. You may choose to study hard for the biology final and pray that the history final will be easy.

Opportunity Cost

What does something cost? The answer to this question depends on the context in which it is being asked. Cost is usually defined as an absolute concept in everyday conversation, the purchase price of an item. For example, suppose that you are wearing a watch and someone asks you how much the watch cost. Your natural response would be to state the price of the watch, say, $75.00.

Sometimes, though, we add a relative sense to the notion of cost. If you happen to be a millionaire, you might respond: "Not much, only $75." If you happen to have only a small annual income, you might respond: "The watch was very expensive. It cost me $75." The words "not much" and "very expensive" are defining the cost of the watch in a relative sense. You are implicitly comparing the price of the watch relative to the resources that you have.

The relative meaning of cost is the one used in economic analysis. Economists always compare the prices of goods and services with the resources that are available to pay for them. The relative nature of cost in economic analysis follows directly from the structure of the economic problem and the associated principle of interdependence.

According to the principle of interdependence, the decision to purchase the watch ultimately prevents you from purchasing something else. For example, suppose you were choosing between the watch and a $75 sweater, knowing that you could afford only the watch or the sweater, but not both. Therefore, the decision to buy the watch is simultaneously a decision not to buy the sweater. Under these circumstances the true *cost* of the watch can only be accounted relative to the value to you of the sweater. The value of the sweater is said to be the opportunity cost of the watch, since the sweater is the alternative or opportunity foregone by choosing the watch.

OPPORTUNITY COST
The economic meaning of cost; the value, in terms of the objectives, of the next best alternative.

In general, economists define the true economic cost, the **opportunity cost,** of any decision A as the value, in terms of the objectives, of the next best alternative B. Notice that B must be the *next best* alternative among all the possible choices because only the next best alternative determines the value of what is being sacrificed by decision A. In other words, the answer to the question "Is A worth its cost?" is yes only if the value of A in terms of the objectives exceeds the value of the next best alternative B.

The following examples illustrate the notion of opportunity cost and how it differs from common everyday notions of cost. Each example assumes that the objective is to have as much income as possible.

EXAMPLES ILLUSTRATING OPPORTUNITY COST   Suppose that your rich uncle dies and leaves you the open-air parking lot he owned and operated in downtown San Francisco. After operating the parking lot yourself for a year, you discover just how nice a gift it was. It brought in $500,000 in parking revenue, with an out-of-pocket cost of only $50,000 for operators' salaries and routine maintenance and repairs. The parking lot appears to have brought you a profit of $450,000.

Is $450,000 the true profit, however? The answer from an economic point of view is certainly no because there is a large, hidden opportunity cost of using the land as a parking lot. Land in downtown San Francisco is extremely valuable as a site for office or apartment buildings. Suppose that a developer were willing to offer you $10 million for the land. Selling the land and placing the $10 million in a bank account that offers a 5 percent rate of interest would bring an annual income of $500,000, $50,000 more than the profit from operating a parking lot on the land.

By an economic accounting, then, the parking lot actually loses $50,000 per year: The value of the land as a parking lot is $50,000 less than the value in its next best alternative. Your tax accountant, however, will have to record a profit on the parking lot of $450,000, or you may wind up in jail. Cost for tax purposes in this example is the $50,000 you spent to operate and maintain the lot. The point is that the appropriate definition of cost depends on the circumstances in which it is being used. An economist includes the $500,000 opportunity cost because the relevant economic question is "What is the best use of the land among various alternatives?" In this example using the land for an office or apartment building is more valuable than using the land as a parking lot. The tax authorities, however, do not allow you to add the $500,000 of opportunity cost to the $50,000 you spent to operate and maintain the parking lot.

Your college education is another good example illustrating the concept of opportunity cost. Suppose that you think of your education strictly as an investment, as a means to better jobs and higher earnings for the years after college. What should be included in the annual cost of your education? The principal *out-of-pocket costs* are tuition, fees, books, room and board, supplies, other incidental living expenses, and, in some schools, a personal computer. But these are not the true economic costs, the opportunity costs.

The out-of-pocket costs and the opportunity costs of your education differ in two ways. First, the list of out-of-pocket costs misses a large opportunity cost, the wages that you could have earned had you not attended college. For students who do not work, a minimum value of those opportunity costs each year would be the minimum wage, $4.25 per hour, times 40 hours per week for 50 weeks, giving an annual sum of $8,500. And this amount understates what most young adults could actually earn today if not in college. It probably more closely represents the opportunity cost of students who are working part-time while attending college, instead of working full-time if they had not attended college.

Second, some of the out-of-pocket costs of an education, particularly room and board and incidental living expenses, would have been incurred anyway, even without attending college. True, a resident student might have lived at home for awhile if he or she had not attended college, but someone is still bearing the costs of the room and board. Since these out-of-pocket costs occur whether you attend college or not, they should be excluded from the true economic costs of obtaining the education.

Understanding the notion of cost as opportunity cost is central to proper economic analysis. It takes some practice because, as these examples illustrate, common notions of cost often differ from the economic meaning of cost. In particular, opportunity costs (for example, the $500,000 annual income from selling the parking lot to developers and the wages forgone by attending college) may differ from out-of-pocket costs, and some out-of-pocket costs (for example, payment of room and board by resident students) may not be opportunity costs.

There is only one sure way to make an accurate accounting of true economic cost. Describe as accurately as possible all elements of the economic problem under consideration, especially all relevant choices or alternatives for meeting the objectives. Economists always ask "What are the alternatives?" because the alternatives to any course of action determine the cost of that action. The playwright George Bernard Shaw understood this point regarding the difficulties of old age. When asked on his 80th birthday how it felt to be 80, he replied, "Not bad, considering the alternative."

EXCHANGE

Individuals, business firms, and government agencies do not solve their economic problems in isolation. They engage in **exchanges** of goods, services, and factors of production with one another in all possible combinations: individuals with businesses, businesses with businesses, government agencies with businesses, and so forth. The study of these exchanges is the second main theme in economic analysis, every bit as central to economic analysis as the study of the economic problem itself. A second expanded short definition of economics combines the two main themes of the discipline. **Economics** is often defined as the study of the allocation of scarce resources through the process of exchange.

The number of economic exchanges is truly staggering in a large, modern economy such as that of the United States, with its more than 250 million people, 18 million business firms, and 89,000 government agencies. The total value of economic exchange in the United States each year is measured in trillions of dollars.

Economists are interested in the incentives that motivate exchanges of goods and services and factors of production. How do individuals use these exchanges to increase their utility, firms to increase their profit, and government agencies to meet their objectives? No one has to tell individuals, business firms, and government agencies to engage in exchange. They are naturally drawn into

EXCHANGE

The trading of goods, services, and factors of production among the key players in the economy.

ECONOMICS

The study of the allocation of scarce resources through the process of exchange.

REFLECTION: What kinds of economic exchanges have you made in the past week in your role as a consumer? In your role as a supplier of primary factors of production?

economic exchanges with one another for all manner of items. Indeed, the urge to exchange is so strong that some people are quite willing to risk the consequences of engaging in illegal exchanges. The commonplace occurrence of economic exchanges can happen only because both parties typically gain from an exchange. We want to understand how the purchase and sale of goods and services can simultaneously benefit both consumers and producers by helping each of them solve their economic problems.

Economists are also interested in the results of economic exchanges, particularly whether they promote the interests of society as a whole. The results of exchanges very much depend on the conditions under which they take place. Some exchanges involve large numbers of participants, such as the sale of milk to millions of consumers by thousands of grocery stores. Other exchanges involve only a few participants, such as the bargaining between union representatives and business managers over the union wage. Governments often intervene in exchanges between individuals and firms. Very few goods, services, and factors of production escape taxation by some government in the United States, and governments try to influence the prices at which exchanges occur through such devices as minimum wage laws, rent controls, and quotas on goods imported from other countries. We want to understand how the number of participants and the nature of government intervention can affect the benefits of economic exchanges from society's point of view.

The economic problem and the process of exchange are the two main themes in economic analysis. We will return to the principles and issues of economic exchanges in Chapter 4. Chapters 2 and 3 continue to focus on the economic problem.

SUMMARY

Chapter 1 has provided an introduction to the two main themes of economic analysis: the economic problem and the process of exchange.

1. The economic problem has a three-part structure consisting of objectives, alternatives, and constraints.
2. The Law of Scarcity says that people are constrained in trying to solve their economic problems. They never have enough resources to meet all their objectives.
3. A widely accepted short definition of economics follows directly from the structure of the economic problem. Economics is the study of how best to allocate scarce resources.
4. The three key players in an economy are individuals, business firms, and government agencies. Individuals have the dual role of consuming goods and services and of providing factors of production to business firms. Business firms have the dual role of buying factors of production from individuals and other business firms and of producing goods and services for sale. Government agencies act as both consumers and producers in a market economy. They purchase some goods and services such as missiles on behalf of the citizens, and they produce a variety of goods and services such as public utilities and mass transit systems. Government agencies also redistribute income among individuals and business firms. All three players must confront the economic problem.

5. The principle of interdependence says that the consequences of economic decisions spread beyond the immediate concern of the decisions. The principle follows directly from the structure of the economic problem, which implies that a decision to choose one alternative is simultaneously a decision not to choose another alternative.
6. Because economic decisions are interdependent, the true economic cost of any decision is defined as an opportunity cost. The cost of any decision A is the value in terms of the objectives of the next best alternative B.
7. Individuals, business firms, and government agencies solve their economic problems by engaging in exchanges with one another.
8. A common expanded short definition of economics incorporates the two main themes of economic analysis: the economic problem and the process of exchange. Economics is the study of the allocation of scarce resources through the process of exchange.

KEY TERMS

consumers
the economic problem
economics
exchange

factors of production
interdependence
Law of Scarcity
opportunity cost

producers
profit
utility

QUESTIONS

1. You tell your friends that you are studying economics, and they ask, "What's economics about?" How would you answer them?
2. Give three examples of how the Law of Scarcity will affect you while taking your Principles of Economics class.
3. a. How are the principles of interdependence and opportunity cost related?
   b. Why does each principle follow directly from the three-part economic problem?
4. Name a well-known entrepreneur in the United States today, and indicate why that person is considered an entrepreneur.
5. Explain how consumers and producers are both "buyers" and "sellers" in the marketplace.
6. Suppose that you buy a ticket to a concert a month ahead of time for $20. Then you find out a week before the concert that your friends are having a big party at the same time. How will you decide whether to go to the concert or to the party? In particular, what is the opportunity cost of going to the party? Of going to the concert?
7. Look through your newspaper, and find one article that is discussing the government in its role as a producer and another article that is discussing the government in its role as a redistributor of income. Can you identify some or all of the three components of the government's economic problem in each article?
8. Describe the economic problem of buying a car in terms of its objectives, alternatives, and constraints.

2

Solving the Economic Problem

LEARNING OBJECTIVES

CONCEPTS TO LEARN

Efficiency

Process equity: equality of opportunity

End-results equity: horizontal equity

An economic model

The margin in economic analysis

Positive and normative economics

Microeconomics and macroeconomics

CONCEPTS TO RECALL

The three-part economic problem [1]

Opportunity cost [1]

Interdependence [1]

*A*ll students are keenly aware of the economic problem during final exams, when the problem of how to study effectively hits with full force. You may have four or five exams in one week and little time left to study for them. Some of your subjects come easily to you; others are quite difficult. The atmosphere during finals is also highly charged and stressful. Everyone is anxious, no one gets much sleep, and outside distractions such as telephone calls or stereos blaring are especially annoying. How should you go about studying for your exams with all these factors playing on your mind? What is the best solution to your studying problem?

Chapter 2 discusses the concepts and methods that economists use to analyze and solve the economic problem wherever it appears. We will often use the economic problem of studying for exams to illustrate the material in the chapter simply because you are so familiar with it.

SOLVING THE ECONOMIC PROBLEM: EFFICIENCY AND EQUITY

Economic analysis rests on a fundamental assumption about human nature: that people are always striving to find the best possible solutions to their own economic problems. In other words, economists assume that people are self-interested, that they try to squeeze every last personal advantage from any given situation. Although this may not seem like a terribly uplifting assumption about the human condition, it is really the only assumption that can support a unified theory of economic behavior. Economists are trying to understand and predict patterns of human behavior that apply generally to a broad range of situations. The only hope of finding such patterns rests on the assumption that people seek the best possible solutions to their economic problems. Suppose, instead, that people do not care enough about their objectives to try their best to achieve them. What, then, does motivate their behavior? No obvious answer comes to mind, and economists cannot build a consistent theory of economic behavior without knowing what motivates that behavior. In truth, people are primarily self-interested in much of what they do, which goes a long way toward explaining why economists have been fairly successful in describing their behavior.

What properties characterize the best possible solution to the economic problem? Economists judge solutions by means of two criteria, efficiency and equity, or fairness. Of the two, efficiency is the more widely applicable because it applies to all economic problems. Equity, or fairness, enters in only when the objectives of the economic problem involve the well-being of two or more people. For example, business firms want to be efficient in producing their products, and students want to be efficient in studying for their exams. Neither business firms nor students have reason to be concerned about equity in these matters. By contrast, parents may want to be both efficient and equitable (fair) in providing for their children, and a society may want to be both efficient and equitable in providing for its citizens.

Let's look closely at the criteria of efficiency and equity. They are central to the study of economics.

Efficiency

In the broadest sense, *efficiency* means that people have made the choices that best meet their objectives. This is why the efficiency criterion applies to all economic problems and would appear to be what solving the economic problem is all about. The notion of "best meeting objectives" is deceptive, however. It is an unambiguous criterion only if the economic problem has a single objective. To see this, think about the economic problem of studying for tests.

EFFICIENCY WITH A SINGLE OBJECTIVE   Suppose that you have a history test tomorrow. Your *objective* is to get 100 on the test. The *alternatives* are the various ways of studying for the test: Go over class notes, read the textbook a number of times, discuss the main issues and concepts with your friends, and so forth. The *constraints* are two-fold: You have a limited amount of time to study for the test and a limited knowledge of the subject matter. If this is truly an economic problem, then the constraints must prevent you from reaching your objective. The Law of Scarcity applies: No matter how well you study for the test, you cannot get 100. Instead, your (single) objective is to get as close to 100 as possible.

Figure 2.1 illustrates inefficient and efficient solutions to your economic problem. The possible test scores are listed on the vertical axis, with 100 the maximum possible score. The two bar graphs show the test scores you can achieve with each of two study strategies, labeled 1 and 2. Strategy 1 might involve spending most of your time discussing the issues and concepts with your friends, and strategy 2 might involve spending most of your time memorizing class notes. According to the figure, strategy 1 earns you 75 on the test, and strategy 2 earns you 85. Notice that neither strategy allows you to score 100 on the test; scoring 100 is impossible, given the nature of your economic problem.

Figure 2.1 indicates that strategy 1 is inefficient because it does not best satisfy your objective. Strategy 2 does better. (Perhaps your study group wandered too often from the course material.) Strategy 2 may or may not be efficient; we cannot tell from the information given in the figure. However, sup-

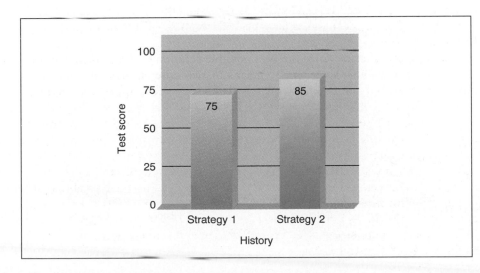

FIGURE 2.1

Studying for a History Test

The bar graphs show the scores achieved on a history test with two different studying strategies. Strategy 1 is inefficient; it does achieve the objective of getting as close to a 100 as possible. Strategy 2 may or may not be efficient. It is efficient if no other studying strategy can achieve a test score above an 85.

pose that you could somehow determine that no other study strategy would earn you as high a score as 85 on the test. If so, then strategy 2 is efficient— it best satisfies the single objective of scoring as close to 100 as possible.

The only wrinkle in defining efficiency when the economic problem has a single objective occurs when the objective does not have a natural limit. Consumers seek utility or satisfaction from their purchases of goods and services without any limit to the amount of utility they desire. Similarly, business firms strive to earn profits without any limit to the amount of profits they desire. In these cases, best meeting the objective means maximizing utility or profit, achieving the largest possible amount of utility or profit. The notion of maximizing the objective as the test of efficiency when the economic problem has a single objective is perfectly general. It also applies to cases in which the objective has a natural limit. In the study example, strategy 2 is efficient if 85 is the maximum possible test score that you are able to achieve.

EFFICIENCY WITH MULTIPLE OBJECTIVES   The notion that a set of choices best meets objectives becomes ambiguous, however, when the economic problem has two or more objectives. To see why, suppose that you have two tests tomorrow, one in history and one in calculus. You want to do well in both subjects, so now you have two objectives, to get 100 on each test. The choices that apply to studying history apply to calculus as well, as do the constraints of limited time and knowledge. However, the second test adds a new choice to the set of alternatives, how much time to spend studying for each test. Also, the constraints of limited time and knowledge are binding: You cannot get 100 on both exams no matter how well you study. In this example, though, we will assume that you can get 100 on one of the tests if you spend enough time studying the subject and study effectively.

Figure 2.2 illustrates the ambiguity of best meeting two (or more) objectives. Each graph illustrates a possible study strategy for meeting your objectives. Now there are two objectives, getting 100 on each test.

In the first strategy you have decided to concentrate on history and let calculus slide. You study long enough to get 100 on the history test, but then you only have enough time left for calculus to get 70 on the calculus test. Remem-

FIGURE 2.2

Studying for a History Test and a Calculus Test

The bar graphs show the scores achieved on a hisotry test and a calculus test with three different studying strategies. No strategy allows you to score 100 on both tests. Each of the studying strategies is efficient if the Law of Substitution holds: In order to achieve a higher score on one of the tests your score on the other test must decrease.

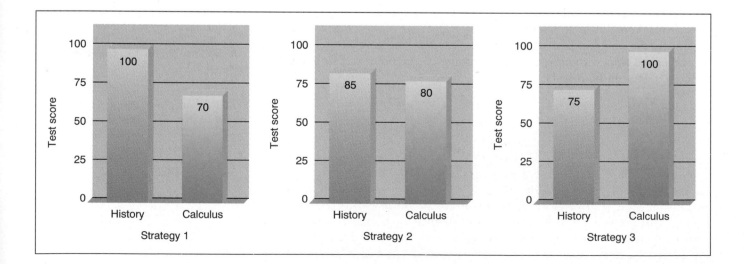

ber, getting 100 on both tests is impossible, given the structure of the economic problem. Assume for now that no other study strategy allows you to get above 70 on the calculus test, given that you get 100 on the history test. In this sense you have done as well as possible following this strategy. The third graph represents the opposite strategy, concentrating on calculus and letting history slide. This strategy allows you to get 100 on the calculus test and 75 on the history test. The second graph represents a more "balanced" strategy in that you allocate your studying time so you do fairly well on both tests. This strategy allows you to get 85 on the history test and 80 on the calculus test.

Which of these strategies best meets your objectives of getting 100 on both tests? The question has no answer without additional information on the relative worth you attach to the two subjects. All you do know is that both objectives are desirable and that you have insufficient time and knowledge to meet both of them. The notion of an efficient choice as one that best meets the objectives must be modified. Therefore, when there are two (or more) objectives, economists define **efficiency** as follows: An allocation (set of choices) is efficient if moving closer to any one objective is not possible without moving away from at least one other objective.

To see what efficiency now implies, consider the strategy 2 in Figure 2.2, which gives you 85 on the history test and 80 on the calculus test. Suppose that you rethink your studying strategy and discover another strategy that would allow you to (1) increase your test score in history to 89, while maintaining your test score in calculus at 80; or (2) increase your test score in calculus to 84, while maintaining your test score in history at 85; or (3) increase both test scores, to 88 in history and 82 in calculus. The new study strategy is clearly better. Therefore, the original study strategy pictured in the middle graph of Figure 2.2 is shown to be inefficient—it does not best meet the objectives of getting 100 on both tests.

You may discover even better study strategies, but eventually such easy gains must end. At some point different study strategies will be able to increase one test score only at the expense of the other test score. You can do better on the history test only if you are willing to accept a lower score on the calculus test, or you can do better on the calculus test only if you are willing to accept a lower score on the history test. Whenever this situation occurs, a study strategy is efficient. The **Law of Substitution** holds: Moving closer to one objective can be achieved only by moving farther away from another objective. Efficiency, then, best meets multiple objectives in the narrow sense of achieving an absence of slack. In our example, slack means being able to score higher on one of the tests without reducing your score on the other test or being able to score higher on both tests.

LIMITATIONS OF THE EFFICIENCY CRITERION   Finding efficient allocations is important because living with inefficient choices wastes scarce resources. When the economic problem has multiple objectives, however, the efficiency criterion is limited in the broader sense that it cannot solve the economic problem. It cannot determine the best allocation of resources. Return again to our study example and Figure 2.2. All three strategies pictured there could be efficient. Referring to the first graph, you may not be able to score above 70 in calculus without reducing your score in history below 100; the same may be true for the other strategies. Also, many other efficient study strategies may exist that

EFFICIENCY

A criterion for judging the solution to an economic problem that refers to making the choices that best meet the objectives; if the economic problem has a single objective, then efficiency means coming as close to the objective as possible; if the economic problem has more than one objective, then efficiency means that the Law of Substitution holds. A solution is efficient if moving closer to one objective requires moving farther away from at least one other objective.

LAW OF SUBSTITUTION

A test of efficiency with more than one objective that says that moving closer to one objective is possible only by moving farther away from at least one other objective.

produce combinations of test scores different from those pictured in the three graphs. If all these study strategies are efficient, which is best?

The efficiency criterion alone cannot answer this question. Study strategies in our example are either efficient or inefficient, and the efficiency criterion recognizes all efficient study strategies as equals. To reach a final solution requires an additional step. You must somehow assign a relative value, or weight, to your performance on each test and then judge which among all the efficient study strategies yields the highest weighted value of the two tests. The weighting scheme of relative values turns the two objectives into a single objective. For instance, you may be far more concerned with your history test score than with your calculus test score because history is your major. In that case you would place a relatively high weight on the history test score and a relatively low weight on the calculus test score. This, in turn, might lead you to prefer study strategy 1 in Figure 2.2 over the other two study strategies, even if all three study strategies are efficient. If, instead, you were concerned only with your overall grade point average, then you would give equal weight to both tests. In this case you would prefer the study strategy 3 in Figure 2.2 over the other two study strategies because its total score of 175 (175 = 100 + 75) exceeds the total scores of the other two study strategies (170 in the first graph and 165 in the second graph). Notice, though, that selecting a best strategy among a number of efficient strategies depends on whatever criterion you use to assign weights to the two test scores. You must be able to refine your objectives beyond the simple ideal of wanting to get 100 on both tests so that you turn the two objectives into a single objective, such as achieving the highest combined score.

Equity

The limitation of the efficiency criterion is particularly distressing when analyzing broad social issues that are concerned with the economic well-being of individual citizens. Figure 2.3 provides an example. The bar graph in the figure illustrates the average income levels of two groups of people within a poor, primarily agricultural country such as Haiti. Group 1 consists of the landed aristocracy, a small minority of the population. They have an average annual income of $50,000 according to the figure, which allows them to enjoy a lavish lifestyle. Group 2 consists of the peasants who work the land, the vast majority of the population. Their average annual income is only $500 according to the figure, which allows them to achieve little more than a subsistence lifestyle, to purchase only the barest necessities of food, clothing, and shelter. Although the average income numbers in Figure 2.3 are hypothetical, they are representative of the huge disparity in income between the landed aristocracy and the peasant farmers in many poor countries.

Suppose that an economist could demonstrate that the economy of this country is efficient: The income of the peasants cannot be increased without decreasing the income of the aristocracy. The efficiency of the economy may not be a terribly compelling criterion in this instance. A number of people may well favor redistributing income from the aristocracy to the peasants, even if some inefficiencies arise in the process of redistributing. Such people are using an entirely different criterion for judging solutions to economic problems, one based on their sense of equity, or fairness.

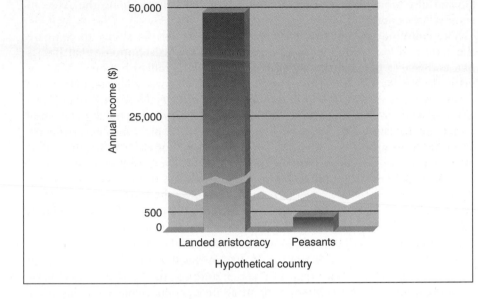

FIGURE 2.3

Income Distribution in a Poor Agricultural Country (Hypothetical Data)

The bar graphs show the distribution of income that is typical in poor agricultural countries. The landed aristocracy enjoy high incomes; the peasants who farm the land have meager incomes. The economy may be efficient. However, many people might not consider the distribution of income to be fair, and would be willing to redistribute income from the landed aristocracy to the peasant farmers.

The concern for equity in economic analysis expresses itself along two dimensions, equity in terms of economic outcomes or end results and equity in terms of the process that generated the end results. The end-results dimension of equity asks if the outcome is fair. Our hypothetical example in Figure 2.3 illustrates this concern. Should a small minority of the people be allowed to enjoy a lavish lifestyle while the vast majority of the people suffer a subsistence lifestyle? The process dimension of equity asks if the rules under which the economy operates are fair. Regardless of the outcome, did each individual in our hypothetical country have an equal chance of achieving a high standard of living?

END-RESULTS EQUITY   The concern for **end-results equity,** or fair outcomes, is not limited to the poorer countries of the world. Even the richest countries have some people who enjoy very high incomes and other people who are desperately poor. Every society must decide if the government should redistribute income from the rich to the poor and, if so, how much income it should redistribute. The decision to redistribute income is never an easy one because the rich lose from a redistribution of income and the poor gain. This begs a very difficult question: How should society value the losses of the rich against the gains of the poor? Philosophers, theologians, natural and social scientists, people from all walks of life have wrestled for centuries with the issue of comparing the gains and losses of different people without arriving at a convincing answer. All we have are various suggestions based on highly personal interpretations of what constitutes a just distribution of resources.

Economists tend to avoid the question altogether. According to economic Nobel laureate Wassily Leontief, economists agree on only two principles relating to end-results equity. The first principle is **consumer sovereignty:** Individuals are best able to judge their own self-interests. In particular, individuals can best determine how much they gain or lose in any given situation. The second principle is the efficiency principle applied to individuals: A policy

END-RESULTS EQUITY

A criterion for judging the solution to an economic problem that asks whether economic outcomes are fair.

CONSUMER SOVEREIGNTY

The principle that individuals are best able to judge their own self-interests.

or event is desirable if it makes at least one person better off without making anyone else worse off. Neither principle is helpful in resolving the issue of comparing gainers and losers.[1]

The consumer sovereignty principle casts doubt on the ability to compare the gains and losses experienced by different individuals. Suppose that Bob is rich and Sue is poor, so the government proposes a redistributional policy of taxing Bob $100 and transferring the $100 to Sue. Can we really compare Bob's loss in utility or satisfaction from the tax *as determined by Bob himself* with Sue's gain of utility or satisfaction from the transfer *as determined by Sue herself?* They might not measure their utility in the same way. People's incomes are commonly used to measure utility in economic studies, but everyone realizes that income is a very inaccurate measure of utility. Worse yet, Bob (and others who are taxed) may overstate his losses to try to persuade the politicians to scrap the redistributional policy. Sue (and others who receive transfers) may overstate her gains to try to convince the politicians to adopt the policy. For these reasons most economists are skeptical of being able to compare gains and losses of different individuals *as the individuals themselves perceive them.*

Society may decide that a dollar taken from the rich and given to the poor has more value to the poor than to the rich and use this judgment as a basis for redistributing income. Most economists are uncomfortable with this justification, however, because the idea that additional dollars of income are more useful to the poor is based on personal value judgments, not scientific inquiry. No one can prove it is true. Also, the justification is imposed from outside; it does not honor the principle of consumer sovereignty. When a society decides to redistribute income, it is not necessarily weighing the losses and gains of the rich and the poor as the rich and the poor themselves perceive them. Nonetheless, many societies do justify their redistributional programs on the grounds that additional dollars of income are more useful to the poor.

The efficiency principle is especially compelling in a social context: Why not adopt a policy that makes some people better off without harming anyone else? But the efficiency principle is no help at all in resolving the fundamental question of end-results equity because it does not apply to situations involving gainers and losers. The efficiency principle cannot be used to compare Bob's losses with Sue's gains in the tax-transfer example. Moreover, we saw in the hypothetical example illustrated by Figure 2.3 that even the most extreme situation of wealth and poverty could be efficient. The efficiency criterion is satisfied whenever the Law of Substitution holds; that is, whenever giving more to one citizen will mean giving less to another. As such, it simply avoids all the difficult issues in society's quest for end-results equity.

The fundamental question of comparing gainers and losers arises in all social issues because economic events and government policies invariably benefit some people and harm others. A new superhighway from the city to the country benefits vacationers and all businesses that need to transport goods between city and country. At the same time it forces people who live along the route of the highway to relocate to other homes. Do the benefits of the vacationers and businesses outweigh losses of those who are forced to move? Also, does the answer to this question change depending on the incomes of the gainers and losers? Suppose that rich Bob is a vacationer who benefits from the highway and poor Sue is a homeowner who is forced to relocate. Alternatively,

---

[1]W. Leontief, *Essays in Economics: Theories and Theorizing* (New York: Oxford University Press, 1966), 27.

suppose poor Sue is the vacationer and rich Bob the homeowner. Should society feel the same about the gains and the losses in the two situations? No one has ever been able to resolve these difficult questions of end-results equity.

Perhaps the only consensus that has arisen in the area of end-results equity is the principle of **horizontal equity,** which requires that equals be treated equally. If two people are identical in every respect that is relevant to economic activity—if, for example, they have the same tastes, the same abilities, and the same desire to work hard—then they should achieve the same level of economic well-being. Horizontal equity is the economic equivalent of the legal principle that all people should be equal in the eyes of the law.

The principle of horizontal equity begs the question of whether two people are ever truly identical in every respect. Nonetheless, the principle is universally appealing because it rules out discrimination in economic affairs. Differences in economic well-being that are based on economically irrelevant characteristics such as sex, or race, or religious beliefs are inherently unfair. People should not be allowed to gain an economic advantage simply because they are male rather than female, white rather than black, or Protestant rather than Roman Catholic. Notice, though, that the principle of horizontal equity has nothing to say about how to treat unequals, for instance, the gifted versus the not-so-gifted. The treatment of unequals is the far tougher question in deciding whether economic outcomes are fair.

PROCESS EQUITY   The concern for **process equity** in economic affairs is most closely associated today with the philosopher Robert Nozick. Nozick argues that any economic result is fair so long as the process generating the result is fair. Nozick's position has broad appeal, especially in the United States where the notion of fair play is a time-honored tradition. Americans hold dear the principle of **equality of opportunity**: Individuals should have equal access to whatever economic opportunities they are willing and able to pursue. This allows them to develop their economic potential to the fullest. Would most Americans go as far as Nozick and say that society should grant equal access to economic opportunities to all its members and let the chips fall where they may? Probably not, but a survey of U.S. business and political leaders by two professors at the Harvard Business School suggests that Americans do care more about process equity than end-results equity. The survey found that the business and political leaders are far more concerned about equality of opportunity than equality of results in economic affairs.[2]

When economists express a concern for equity in their professional writings, they are more likely to appeal to the process ideal of equality of opportunity than to any one ideal based on end-results equity. Equality of opportunity as a standard of equity will appear frequently throughout this text. Nonetheless, many economists would argue that end results matter, too. The most troubling aspect of Nozick's position is that the results of the economic game depend very much on the resources that people are able to bring to the game. Equal opportunity may not be enough. People lucky enough to be born with exceptional intelligence, or athletic ability, or competitive drive, or to have received a huge inheritance are far more likely to do well than are people without these advantages, no matter how the economic game is played. Society might be

HORIZONTAL EQUITY

A principle of end-results equity that requires that equals receive equal treatment.

PROCESS EQUITY

A criterion for judging economic activity that asks whether the rules under which the economy operates are fair.

EQUALITY OF OPPORTUNITY

A principle of process equity that requires that individuals have equal access to whatever economic opportunities they are willing and able to pursue so that they can develop their economic potential to the fullest.

[2]R. Nozick, "Distributive Justice," *Philosophy and Public Affairs* 3 (Spring 1973): 45–126; S. Verba, G. Orren, *Equality in America: the View from the Top* (Cambridge, MA: Harvard University Press, 1985), chapter 1

REFLECTION: Do you think that by and large people are treated fairly in the U.S. economy? If not, do you believe that the problems lie with end-results or with process, or with both?

quite willing to help people who fall behind because they were not so blessed from the start. Indeed, a society might be willing to help its poor simply because they are poor, whatever the reason.

The twin goals of end-results equity and process equity are not entirely independent of one another. The process equity principle of equality of opportunity is closely linked to the end-results principle of horizontal equity. Identical people who have equal access to economic opportunities should be able to achieve the same level of economic well-being. In other words, equality of opportunity tends to produce horizontal equity. The inverse is also true. Equals do not usually reach the same level of economic well-being when they do not have equal access to economic opportunities, either because of outright discrimination or for some other reason. The link between equality of opportunity and horizontal equity is another theme that appears throughout this text.

ECONOMISTS AS MODEL BUILDERS

Economists analyze social phenomena much as natural scientists analyze natural phenomena. When scientists study the natural environment, they often construct a portion of the environment in their laboratories so they can focus on the problem that interests them and conduct controlled experiments. A **controlled experiment** is a method of analysis that allows scientists to study the effects of changing one element in the environment at a time while holding all other elements in the environment constant. This is the way that scientists determine cause-and-effect relationships. If changing element A, but only element A, produces effect B, then A must cause B, since all other elements that might have caused B are being held constant in the controlled experiment and cannot influence B.

CONTROLLED EXPERIMENT

The scientific method of analysis for determining cause-and-effect relationships that studies the effects of changing one element in an environment at a time while holding constant all the other elements in the environment.

Economists believe that the controlled experiment is the proper way to study economic behavior. They operate under a handicap, however, because controlled experiments do not occur in society and economists cannot easily bring portions of society into a laboratory setting. Instead, they must confront economic events as they exist in the real world, and real-world environments are highly complex with many variables changing simultaneously. None of the conditions necessary for a controlled experiment are satisfied.

Economists respond to the complexities of actual events by *conceptualizing* a controlled experiment, even though they cannot actually conduct one. They construct a **model,** which is nothing more than a simplified description of some real-world situation. A model isolates one particular aspect of the situation so economists can study the effects on that one aspect as they change different elements of the model, one at a time. In other words, an economic model imitates the natural scientist's controlled experiment. Economic models can be expressed verbally, graphically, or mathematically. All three types of models will appear in this text, although the vast majority will be verbal or graphical.

MODEL

A simplified description of some real-world situation that isolates one particular aspect of the situation and studies the effects on that one aspect as different elements are changed one at a time.

Working with models takes some getting used to. Economic models have no intention of capturing every facet of reality, and this often bothers beginning students. Rather, the whole idea of building a model is to simplify, to capture the essence of a particular problem or event and take whatever insights come from the exercise. The test of a model is whether it tells us something useful about the real world.

A model can never describe all the complexities of the real world. Even if such a model existed, it would be as complicated as reality itself and utterly incomprehensible. No one claims to be able to understand human behavior and social interactions completely; this is why economists build models in the first place.

Modeling the Studying Problem

Let's return to the problem of how best to study for final exams in order to see how economists use models to analyze economic problems. Determining the absolute best study strategy for your exams is clearly a difficult problem. It is hard enough just to know where to begin! You have many exams and, no doubt, much catching up to do. Time is limited, everyone is stressed out, and the campus is filled with annoying distractions. The studying problem during final exams is so difficult that no one can ever tell you exactly how you should study. Still, we have to think about the problem in some way.

The economist's approach is to simplify the problem. We will build a model of the studying problem that captures just a few of its essential elements and see what the model can tell us about how to study. In order to build a model, economists make a number of simplifying assumptions about the nature of the problem. Here we will make six assumptions about studying for exams that will simplify the studying problem as much as it can be. Taken together, these six assumptions constitute a model of the studying problem. Our model is so simple that we will be able to determine a best studying strategy.

Assume that

1. You have four two-hour exams next Monday at 8:00, 10:00, 12:00, and 2:00 in history, calculus, Russian, and astrology.
2. You figure that you will have 30 hours of time available for studying before the exams. Studying occurs in units of one hour each; studying a subject for less than an hour is useless.
3. If you do not study at all, you will receive a failing grade of 50 on each exam.
4. You know how much your score will improve in each subject for every hour spent studying the subject. The information is contained in Table 2.1. For instance, the first hour spent studying your easiest subject, astrology, improves your test score by 10 points, the second hour by 9 points more, the third hour by 7 points more, and so forth. The first hour spent studying Russian, your most difficult subject, will improve your test score by 4 points, the second hour by 3 points more, and so on.
5. Knowledge learned is never forgotten, and each subject is totally independent of the others. There is no extra gain in knowledge from spending a number of consecutive hours on one subject, and no loss in knowledge as you switch from subject to subject.
6. No matter how you decide to study, you cannot achieve 100 on all four exams. There is not enough time for that.

Your problem is to devise a studying strategy that assures you the highest total score on all four tests combined, in other words, the highest grade point average. What should you study during each of the 30 study units?

Before thinking about the proper strategy, be sure you can identify the objectives, alternatives, and constraints of this economic problem.

Objective: You want to achieve the highest total test score on all four subjects combined. (This study problem has a single objective, unlike the study problem described earlier in the chapter in which you cared about your performance on each of the tests.)

Alternatives (Choices): You must choose which subject to study in each of the 30 one-hour study units.

Constraints: Limited time and limited knowledge prevent you from scoring 100 on every test.

You have no doubt noticed that our model or description of the study problem assumes away a number of real-world complications. No one has to take four exams in one day. In real life, you may not be allowed to fail any of the exams, although you can in this problem. Knowledge learned is forgotten, so that switching your studying from subject to subject could be costly. No one knows exactly how much a test score will improve for each hour spent studying. The various stresses experienced during final exams are also ignored. Remember, an economic model captures the essence of a problem by simplifying it.

The Margin in Economic Analysis

MARGIN

Refers to the effects of a small change in an economic variable.

What is the best studying strategy in this stylized situation? The key to the answer lies on the margin. The **margin** in economic analysis refers to the effects of a small change in an economic variable. In our study problem the only variable that can change is the amount of time spent studying a particular subject, and the smallest unit of time it can change is one hour. The improvement in the test score is the effect of changing the amount of studying by one hour. Therefore, each entry in Table 2.1 is defined as the marginal grade for a particular subject. The marginal grade indicates how much your test score changes (improves) for each additional hour of study.

The best studying strategy is easily stated in terms of marginal grades: *During every hour select the subject with the highest marginal grade.* That is, choose to study the subject each hour that yields the greatest improvement in the test score.

Apply the study strategy rule to the numbers in Table 2.1. You should spend the first hour studying astrology. Its 10-point improvement exceeds that for any other subject. The second hour should also be spent on astrology because the 9-point improvement is the best you can do that hour. Switch to calculus in the third hour to pick up 8 points. In the fourth and fifty hours study history and astrology in either order. You gain 7 points for studying either subject during those hours. Next, switch to calculus in the sixth hour to earn an ad-

TABLE 2.1   Improvement in Test Scores for Each Additional Hour of Study

HOUR	HISTORY	CALCULUS	RUSSIAN	ASTROLOGY
1st	7	8	4	10
2nd	5	6	3	9
3rd	5	4	3	7
4th	5	4	2	5
5th	4	4	2	5
6th	3	4	2	4
7th	3	3	1	3
8th	3	3	1	3
9th	2	2	1	2
10th	2	2	1	2

ditional 6 points. Continuing in this manner until the 30 hours are exhausted guarantees you the highest total score. You do not even have to keep track of your total score. To allocate your scarce time efficiently simply ask: What is true on the margin? Then select the highest marginal grade each time.

What is true on the margin is the single most important issue in economic analysis. It will appear time and again in our study of economics. Looking at the margin is the essence of all controlled scientific experiments because these experiments are specifically designed to study the effects of making small changes in a variable. Since economic models are conceptualized controlled experiments, the margin is central to economic analysis as well. In particular, our study problem shows that the key to solving the economic problem lies in the margin. We will see that nearly all efficient strategies for allocating scarce resources are described by rules involving the margin that are as simple as our studying rule.

Does the Model Pass the Test?

Our model of studying for exams is simple enough to yield a precise and simple studying strategy. Now let's put our model to the test. Does this admittedly simplified model tell us anything useful about the real-life problem of studying? Yes, it does. It yields an important insight that applies both to studying for exams and to taking exams: Do not waste precious time spinning your wheels on subjects or problems that are overly difficult. Study your easier subjects first because that will improve your overall grade point average the most. In our problem, spending hour upon hour trying to learn Russian is exactly the wrong thing to do. Our model suggests that when taking exams, you should always begin with the questions you know best. Earn points right away, rather than staring blankly at a difficult question for most of the exam period. (Starting with what you know has the additional advantage of relaxing you.)

The studying problem becomes more complicated if you cannot fail any one subject (or any one question on a test). You may have to spend much of your time on more difficult material in this case. But then our model highlights something you already know. The stricture against failing a subject has a very high opportunity cost in terms of your grade point average because it drags down other subjects as well. This is one reason why students drop subjects they are in danger of failing. Our simplified model tells us quite a bit about the student's economic problem after all. It passes the test of being a good model.

REFLECTION: How do you go about studying for a number of final exams? What assumptions about the economic problem of studying for exams lie behind your studying strategy?

NORMATIVE AND POSITIVE ANALYSIS

Economic analysis is traditionally divided into normative analysis and positive analysis. **Normative economic analysis** is the study of what *ought to be*. It attempts to determine appropriate norms or criteria for judging the results of economic behavior and activity. Normative statements cannot be shown to be true or false by testing them against real-world data and behavior. Instead, they rely on fundamental value judgments that people may choose to accept or reject. They are not subject to proof. **Positive economic analysis** refers to the study of what *is*. It attempts to determine what actually exists out there in the real world. All positive statements are testable. In principle, real-world data

NORMATIVE ECONOMIC ANALYSIS

The study of what ought to be; attempts to determine appropriate norms or criteria for judging the results of economic behavior and activity.

POSITIVE ECONOMIC ANALYSIS
The study of what is; attempts to determine what actually exists in the real world and to describe the consequences of economic decisions.

can prove whether a positive statement is true or false. Both normative analysis and positive analysis have important roles to play in the two broad subject areas of economics, the study of the economic problem and the study of exchange.

Analyzing the Economic Problem

Regarding the economic problem, the first task falls upon normative analysis to describe the objectives on the basis of individual or social norms. What are the goals to be achieved, and why? Once normative analysis has described the objectives, positive analysis then determines the alternatives and the constraints of the problem and describes the effects of various choices on both the objectives and the constraints. Normative analysis reappears to judge the solution to the economic problem on the basis of efficiency and equity. Is the solution efficient? And, in some contexts, is the solution equitable? The following example illustrates the interplay of normative analysis and positive analysis in solving an economic problem.

Suppose that the officials of a local community decide that they want to improve the academic quality of the high school. They believe that a better high school education will give the town's children better job opportunities and allow them to lead more cultured and examined lives. The normative basis of their decision is the value judgment that economic well-being, culture, and living the examined life are all worthwhile objectives. The choice to pursue these objectives by improving the high school is one of the alternatives and the beginning of the positive analysis of the problem. There are other ways to achieve these objectives, but the officials made this choice based on their own experiences and on studies about the actual relationship between a high school education and the objectives.

Positive analysis has more to add about the alternatives and the constraints. What are the choices for improving the quality of the high school? The officials can recruit more, and better, teachers; increase the length of the school day, or school year; de-emphasize the nonacademic parts of the curriculum; improve classroom facilities; and use more computerized instruction. What are the constraints: Is the budget for the high school set, or might it be increased by raising taxes, or applying for state or federal aid, or reducing other areas of the town's budget?

Positive analysis is also needed to determine the effect of the various alternatives on both the objectives and the constraints. What do we know about the effectiveness of the various options for improving quality? Do better teachers, longer school days, better facilities, and smaller class sizes really improve the quality of education? What does each of these options cost? How much must salaries rise to attract better teachers? And so forth.

Once positive analysis has described the structure of the problem, normative analysis judges whether the officials have achieved an efficient solution to their problem. Have they achieved the maximum improvement in educational quality, given the resources available to them? If not, what different choices would improve quality more for the same costs? The efficient solution depends on the effectiveness of the various options in improving educational quality and on their respective costs. Equity may also be an issue. Suppose that one set of choices lets the brightest students reach their full academic potential, but leaves the average students behind. Another set of choices improves the education of all students to some extent, but leaves the brightest students far short of achieving their full academic potential. The town will have to appeal to its sense of what is fair to determine which set of choices is better (assuming they cost the same).

Analyzing Economic Exchange

Regarding economic exchange, normative analysis establishes the norms for judging the effectiveness of economic exchanges. Economists judge economic exchanges using the norms of efficiency and equity, the same norms used to judge the solutions to economic problems.

The positive analysis of exchange describes the actual conditions under which exchange takes place and determines the implications of those conditions. Exchange occurs in a number of different environments. Wheat is produced by thousands of farmers and turned into a wide variety of products that reach hundreds of millions of consumers each day. The consumers and farmers never actually meet. Airplanes, in contrast, are produced by a handful of business firms and sold to a small number of other firms and to governments. The buyers and sellers are in close contact with each other. What results can be expected in each of these environments? What will the prices be? The quantities exchanged? Will the exchanges be orderly? The norms of efficiency and equity complete the analysis. Will the exchanges generate an efficient allocation of resources? Will they be even-handed and fair to all parties.

Positive analysis also describes how economic exchanges respond to government policy initiatives. How will individuals and business firms react to a 1 percent increase in a state's sales tax? If the federal government adds $5 billion to its educational grant-in-aid programs for state and local governments, will state and local spending for education increase by $5 billion? By more than $5 billion? By less than $5 billion? Positive analysis of this kind is obviously central to the conduct of effective government policy. The best of intentions can easily go awry if governments misjudge the responses to their policies.

MICROECONOMICS AND MACROECONOMICS

The study of economics is traditionally divided into microeconomics and macroeconomics. This text follows that tradition.

Microeconomics

As the name suggests, **microeconomics** studies the economy "in the small." Microeconomics takes snapshots of tiny sections of the economy and magnifies them. It focuses on (1) the economic problems of individual consumers, business firms, and government agencies; (2) the incentives that motivate them to engage in economic exchanges with one another; and (3) the results of their economic exchanges for particular products and factors of production, such as automobiles or labor. The vast majority of economic exchanges take place in

MICROECONOMICS

The study of the economy "in the small"; analyzes the economic problems of individual economic agents and the exchanges between them.

organized markets in the U.S. economy. Therefore, our study of microeconomics will concentrate on how markets work in the United States.

Microeconomics attempts to answer the following kinds of questions: Why do markets form so easily? What causes the prices of individual products to rise and fall? Should the government give poor families food stamps as well as cash? Is good weather necessarily good for farmers? Does minimum wage legislation prevent teen-agers from finding jobs? Why do 30 million Americans live in poverty? How do large corporations use their market power to increase their profits? To what extent does discrimination explain the fact that women receive lower wages than men? Are U.S. markets generally efficient or inefficient? Will the job prospects of college graduates improve over the next five years? Do taxes destroy people's incentives to work?

You will be better able to answer these questions when you have completed the microeconomic chapters.

Macroeconomics

MACROECONOMICS

The study of the economy "in the large"; analyzes the overall performance of the economy.

FULL EMPLOYMENT

The condition when all people who want to work have a job.

UNEMPLOYMENT

The condition when people are actively looking for work, but are unable to find a suitable job.

PRICE STABILITY

Prices in general are neither rising nor falling.

PRICE INFLATION

A persistent increase in the prices of most goods and services.

LONG-RUN ECONOMIC GROWTH

A continuing process in which the economy is able to produce ever-increasing amounts of goods and services year after year.

STABLE DOLLAR

The value of the dollar remains constant relative to the currencies of other nations.

Macroeconomics studies the economy "in the large," that is, the overall performance of the economy. It focuses on aggregate data such as the total consumption by all consumers, the total investment in plant and equipment by all business firms, the combined spending of all government agencies, the entirety of U.S. economic interactions with the other nations of the world, the total employment in all labor markets, and the total income earned and output produced by all factors of production.

Economists judge the overall performance of an economy on the basis of four broad objectives called the macroeconomic policy goals: full employment, price stability, long-run economic growth, and stability in a nation's international economic relations.

- **Full employment** exists whenever there is a job for all people who want to work. **Unemployment** exists whenever people are actively looking for work, but are unable to find a suitable job.
- **Price stability** occurs whenever prices in general are neither rising nor falling. Most nations today wrestle with the problem of **price inflation,** which is a persistent increase in the prices of most goods and services.
- **Long-run economic growth** is taking place whenever the economy is able to produce ever-increasing amounts of goods and services year after year.
- **Stability in international economic relations** has two dimensions. One is achieving an equality between the value of the nation's imports from other countries and the value of its exports to other countries. The other is achieving a stable dollar. A **stable dollar** exists whenever the value of the dollar remains constant relative to the currencies of other nations, such as the Japanese yen or French franc.

Pursuing the first three macroeconomic policy goals is a matter or law in the United States. Both the Employment Act of 1946 and the Humphrey-Hawkins Act of 1978 require the federal government to formulate economic policies that promote maximum employment, production (growth), and purchasing power (stable prices). No U.S. laws require an equality between imports and exports or a stable dollar, but even the most casual observer of economic events knows that the United States is deeply concerned about each of these issues.

The United States does not usually attempt to achieve the macroeconomic policy goals directly. National, state, and local governments do not routinely employ all the unemployed. Governments directly control only a very few prices. No government can dictate the rate of economic growth. The federal government does place some direct controls on international trade and makes some attempts to influence the value of the dollar, but by and large trade is free, and the value of the dollar is set in the marketplace. The federal government's macroeconomic policies are directed instead toward the overall level of economic activity. The idea is to try to achieve the macroeconomic policy goals indirectly by influencing the performance of the entire economy.

The macroeconomic policy record over the past twenty years has not been especially impressive. Unemployment averaged 6.1 percent of the labor force in the 1970s, 7.2 percent in the 1980s, and 6.5 percent in the first three years of the 1990s. These percentages are higher than the American public, and many economists, are willing to accept. Prices have not been stable. They rose an average of 7.1 percent per year in the 1970s, 5.6 percent per year in the 1980s, and 4.1 percent in the first three years of the 1990s. Since 1973 the rate of economic growth has been far below its trend for the entire twentieth century. The United States has not been able to achieve equality between its imports and exports. The value of imports has greatly exceeded the value of exports since 1981. Finally, the dollar has been very unstable. The value of the dollar fell steadily relative to most foreign currencies throughout most of the 1970s, rose sharply in the early and mid-1980s, and then fell again in the late 1980s and into the 1990s.

REFLECTION: Which of the four macroeconomic policy goals does the Clinton administration seem to be most concerned about? The least concerned about?

The macroeconomic chapters will explain how the government's macroeconomic policies attempt to achieve the macroeconomic policy goals and why they often do not succeed.

SUMMARY

The first section of Chapter 2 discussed the two criteria that economists use to judge the solutions to economic problems, efficiency and equity.

1. The meaning of efficiency depends on whether the economic problem has one or more objectives.
   a. If the economic problem has a single objective, then efficiency means coming as close to the objective as possible. If the objective has no natural limit, then efficiency means maximizing the objective. For example, a firm is efficient if it is maximizing its profit.
   b. If the economic problem has more than one objective, then efficiency means that the Law of Substitution holds: A solution is efficient if moving closer to one objective requires moving farther away from at least one other objective.
2. Equity has two dimensions, end-results equity and process equity. End-results equity judges whether economic outcomes are fair. Process equity judges whether the rules under which the economy operates are fair.
3. Economic events and policies invariably help some people and harm others. The fundamental question of end-results equity is how to evaluate and compare the benefits of those who gain against the losses of those who lose. The only consensus that has emerged on this question is the principle

of horizontal equity: equal treatment of equals. When horizontal equity exists, two individuals who are identical in every relevant economic aspect achieve the same level of utility or satisfaction.

4. A widely embraced principle of process equity is equality of opportunity, that people should have equal access to whatever economic opportunities they are willing and able to pursue.

5. Process equity and end-results equity are linked by the principles of equality of opportunity and horizontal equity because equality of opportunity tends to produce horizontal equity.

The second section of the chapter described the use of models in economic analysis.

6. A model is a simplified description of reality that tries to capture the essential features of real-world issues and events. Economic models are conceptual versions of the natural scientist's controlled laboratory experiment. Like controlled experiments, economic models are useful for discovering cause-and-effect relationships because they allow the economist to study the effects of changing one economic variable while holding all other variables constant.

7. Economists always ask: What is true on the margin? The margin refers to the effects of small changes in an economic variable. Looking at the margin is important because it points the way to efficient solutions of the economic problem.

The third section of the chapter described the distinction between normative and positive economic analysis.

8. Normative analysis studies what ought to be. It develops the norms or criteria for judging the solutions to economic problems and the results of economic exchanges. The two norms in economic analysis are efficiency and equity. Normative analysis also determines the objectives of an economic problem. All normative statements are based on value judgments; they cannot be proved or disproved.

9. Positive analysis studies what is. It describes the alternatives and constraints of the economic problem and indicates how the alternatives relate to both the objectives and the constraints. Positive analysis also describes how the conditions under which economic exchanges take place determine the results of the exchanges. Positive statements can be tested with real-world data; in principle, they can be shown to be true or false.

The final section of Chapter 2 discussed the distinction between microeconomics and macroeconomics.

10. Microeconomics studies the economy "in the small." It focuses on the economic problems of individual consumers, business firms, and government agencies; the incentives that motivate them to engage in economic exchanges with one another, and the results of their economic exchanges for particular products and factors of production.

11. Macroeconomics studies the economy "in the large." It focuses on the overall level of economic activity. Economists use four objectives to judge the performance of an economy: full employment, price stability, long-run economic growth, and stability in a nation's international economic relations.

KEY TERMS

consumer sovereignty
efficiency
end-results equity
equality of opportunity
full employment
horizontal equity

Law of Substitution
long-run economic growth
macroeconomics
the margin
microeconomics
model

normative economic analysis
positive economic analysis
price inflation
process equity
stable dollar

QUESTIONS

1. Economists are often criticized because their economic models do not fully and accurately describe the "real world." How might economists defend themselves against this charge?
2. a. What is the distinction between end-results and process equity?
   b. President Clinton has expressed concern that the wealthiest people in the United States gained relative to everyone else during the 1980s. Is his concern one of end-results equity or process equity?
3. What is the main difference between microeconomics and macroeconomics?
4. Many firms in the United States today are "downsizing," reducing the number of employees to lower their production costs. Why does the downsizing phenomenon fall within the realm of both microeconomics and macroeconomics?
5. What is the Law of Substitution, and how does it relate to the concept of efficiency?
6. Suppose that a farmer can grow either corn or wheat on his land. He thinks about different ways of planting the land and comes up with the following possible combinations of corn and wheat output. The numbers are in thousands of bushels.

CORN	WHEAT
100	0
75	60
50	50
45	75
35	60
0	95

Are any of these possibilities clearly inefficient? Why?

7. Which of the following statements are normative, and which are positive?
   a. Baseball players make too much money.
   b. The price of computer equipment usually starts to fall after it has been on the market for a long time.
   c. A 50-cent-a-gallon gasoline tax will cause some commuters to shift from using automobiles to public transportation.
   d. Charging a toll on the turnpike is fair because those who use the turnpike pay for its construction and maintenance.
8. Suppose Brenda knows the exact value that she derives from eating "buffalo wings" (chicken wings) in terms of money.

NUMBER OF WINGS EATEN	BRENDA'S TOTAL VALUE
1	$1.00
2	2.00
3	2.90
4	3.70
5	4.30
6	4.60
7	4.55

   a. What is the marginal value to Brenda of eating the fourth buffalo wing? Of eating the sixth buffalo wing?
   b. *Extra credit:* If buffalo wings cost $.50 each, how many will Brenda buy? How many will she eat if they are free?

3

Society's Economic Problem

LEARNING OBJECTIVES

CONCEPTS TO LEARN

Society's economic problem

The four fundamental economic questions

1. The what or output question

2. The how or input question

3. The for whom or distribution question

4. The now versus the future question

The production possibilities frontier

Long-run economic growth

The elements of an economic system

Pure market capitalism

Centrally planned socialism

CONCEPTS TO RECALL

The three-part economic problem [1]

Interdependence [1]

Opportunity cost [1]

Efficiency [2]

Equity [2]

n 1989 the seven Eastern European countries of Bulgaria, Czechoslovakia, East Germany, Hungary, Poland, Romania, and Yugoslavia quite literally stunned the world. They declared their freedom from decades of Soviet political and economic domination, completely rejected communism, and announced that they were going to abandon their current economic systems in favor of a completely different type of system. The only modern example of such an abrupt and total transformation of such large economies occurred in the former Soviet Union following the Russian Revolution in 1917. The Soviet example does not offer much of a guideline for the Eastern European countries, however, because the Soviets adopted an economic system that was tightly controlled by the national government. The Eastern European countries chose to go in the opposite direction. They cast off the tight reigns of centrally planned socialism in favor of a decentralized market economy.

Events since 1989 have shown that the transformation to capitalism will not come easily. West Germany immediately offered to serve as a benefactor to the East Germans as part of the reunification of Germany. The other countries were not so lucky. The tragic war among Croats, Serbs, and Muslims tore apart the former Yugoslavia, and Czechoslovakia split in two. The world watches anxiously as the great social and economic experiments in Eastern Europe unfold.

The economic problem is not limited to individuals, business firms, and government agencies. Society as a whole faces the standard economic problem with its objectives, alternatives, and constraints. Chapter 3 describes society's economic problem and the difficult choices that all societies have to make as they try to find the best solution to their respective economic problems.

Each of the seven Eastern European countries named above concluded in 1989 that market capitalism would do a far better job of solving its economic problem than centrally planned socialism had done. We will return to their prospects for success in transforming their economies after describing society's economic problem.

SOCIETY'S ECONOMIC PROBLEM

Modern economies are incredibly complex. Billions of exchanges of goods and services and factors of production take place every day, themselves the results of billions of economic decisions by individuals, business firms, and government agencies. No one can possibly comprehend the workings of an entire economy. The best we can do is gain a broad perspective on what is taking place within the economy and what is being accomplished. An excellent way to gain this perspective is to think of society as facing a giant economic problem consisting of objectives, alternatives, and constraints. Then we can view all economic activity as an attempt to solve society's economic problem, for better or worse. Using the economic problem to organize your thinking about an economy is especially helpful in understanding what a society expects from its economy. It is also helpful in judging whether an economy is performing anywhere near to its potential.

What is the structure of society's economic problem? What are the principal economic objectives, alternatives, and constraints for society as a whole?

Objectives

Humanism, the intellectual and philosophical movement that swept through Europe during the Middle Ages and gave rise to the Renaissance, stressed the interests of individuals over religion or the natural world. Those of us living in the Western Hemisphere have been raised in the humanist tradition. We take for granted that the primary goal of a nation's economy is to improve the economic well-being of its citizens. What exactly does this goal mean, however?

A humanistic society would undoubtedly like to make each of its members as well off as possible, or at least try to ensure that all people can develop their full economic potential. Uplifting as these goals may be, neither can serve as an economic objective for society, nor even as an ideal to strive for. These objectives are not merely unattainable; they are meaningless.

An overall economy is subject to the Law of Scarcity, just as are all its individual consumers, business firms, and government agencies. The Law of Substitution must eventually apply, no matter what choices are made among the various alternatives, simply because resources are limited. Giving more resources to some people so they can be better off necessarily means that other people must sacrifice—they are made worse off. Resources used to help me achieve my full economic potential are not available to help you achieve your full economic potential.

If societies cannot maximize each person's economic well-being or potential, then what economic objectives can they pursue? The answers are the two objectives discussed in Chapter 2, efficiency and equity.

Although a humanistic society cannot try to make everyone as well off as possible, it can strive to be efficient, to ensure that the Law of Substitution does hold. A society would not want to waste its scarce resources by being able to improve the economic well-being of some of its members without sacrifice to any other members. Economic efficiency is a fundamental objective of all humanistic societies.

Most economics generate fairly wide disparities in income. Some people are poor, and others are quite rich, with the remainder filling up the middle. A humanistic society will be moved to ask whether this situation is fair and, if not, what should be done about it. A society can never be content unless it perceives that people are being treated fairly in economic matters. Equity is also a fundamental economic objective of all humanistic societies.

Alternatives

A society is confronted with innumerable economic choices in its pursuit of efficiency and equity. Economists divide these choices into four broad categories, posed as the four fundamental questions that every society must answer: What? How? For Whom? Now versus the Future? These questions incorporate the two objectives of efficiency and equity along with the alternatives.

WHAT OR OUTPUT QUESTION
Asks what goods and services the economy will produce and in what quantities; one of the four fundamental economic questions that every society must answer.

THE *WHAT* OR *OUTPUT* QUESTION   What goods and services will the economy produce, and in what quantities? The output question refines the efficiency and equity objectives by recognizing that people's economic well-being ultimately depends on what goods and services they consume. Different people have different tastes. A teen-ager and an elderly person with the same incomes undoubtedly want to consume different kinds of goods and services. Tastes also change over time. For instance, American consumers as a whole are now spending a much higher percentage of their incomes on health care and a much lower percentage on food than they did in 1950. To be fully efficient and equitable, therefore, an economy must be responsive to individual preferences.

Consumers ultimately answer the What question in a market economy such as the United States, even though business firms produce the goods and services. The pursuit of profits leads firms to respond to consumers' desires as they decide what, and how much, to produce. Firms try to guess what consumers want to buy. If they guess right, they do well; if not, they lose. Business firms do try to influence consumers' purchases through advertising and related sales techniques, and they no doubt succeed to some extent. For the most part, however, firms respond to the demands of consumers. Consumers in the United States buy what they want within the limitations of their budgets.

HOW OR INPUT QUESTION
Asks how the economy produces its goods and services; one of the four fundamental economic questions that every society must answer.

THE *HOW* OR *INPUT* QUESTION   Once business firms decide what goods and services to provide, how will they produce each one of them? There are usually many different ways to produce any one good or service, and, in fact, similar products tend to be produced very differently throughout the world, even in different regions within a country. The Japanese use robotics in manufacturing their automobiles far more than the U.S. auto makers do. Textiles are produced very differently worldwide, the techniques varying from hand weaving to the use of extremely sophisticated machinery. Methods of farming also vary considerably throughout the world. There are nearly as many examples as there are products.

PRODUCTION TECHNOLOGY
A blueprint or method for transforming inputs into outputs.

Answering the How question involves choosing a **production technology,** which is a blueprint or method for transforming inputs into outputs. The inputs are the factors of production: labor, land and natural resources, capital, and semi-finished material inputs. The outputs are the goods and services. Technologies are products of people's minds. Scientists, engineers, and other people directly involved in production processes are continually inventing new materials, different machinery, and more effective ways of utilizing already existing resources. Most production technologies become widely known soon after they have been invented; keeping ideas a secret is very difficult.

Even so, the choice of technology is an economic problem, not just a scientific or an engineering problem of using the latest technologies hot off the drawing board. The reason for this is that different technologies require different kinds of resources, and similar kinds of resources are not at all equally available worldwide. Some countries have lots of capital and a highly skilled labor force. Other countries have relatively little capital and mostly unskilled labor. If the resources that are readily available are not particularly well suited to the latest technology, then using an older technology that the resources are suited for makes good *economic* sense. All societies have an economic interest in producing each unit of output with the least expenditure of their scarce resources. They have no particular interest in using the latest technologies.

THE *FOR WHOM* OR *DISTRIBUTION* QUESTION   The For Whom question asks: Who will receive the various goods and services produced in answer to the What question? As such, it recognizes the fundamental importance of equity in the presence of scarce resources and is therefore as much one of the objectives as it is one of the alternatives.

The For Whom question is determined primarily by the quantity and quality of the resources that each individual owns in a market economy. Labor, land, and funds supplied to firms for purchasing capital are the sources of income, and people's incomes determine in large part what they are able to consume. Are you willing to work long hours? Are you highly educated or relatively unskilled? Is there much demand for whatever skills you do possess? Do you own land that is valuable to farmers or mining companies or developers? Have you inherited vast amounts of wealth that can be lent to business firms for them to buy plant and equipment? The answers to such questions determine whether you number among the haves or have-nots in a market economy.

The For Whom question is not just a matter of equity. It also has an important efficiency dimension to it in a market economy. The incomes people earn for their labor, land, and capital reflect how scarce their resources are relative to the demand for them. People have an incentive to supply more of the resources that are relatively scarce and thus earn high incomes. At the same time, high incomes translate into high input prices from the point of view of the business firms, so firms have an incentive to use less of the resources that are relatively scarce. The opposite incentives apply when resources earn low incomes. We shall discover in later chapters why both of these incentives are crucial to the efficient operation of a market economy.

The What, How, and For Whom questions are closely interrelated in a market economy. For example, large numbers of people decided during the 1980s that they would rather rent movies and watch them at home on their VCRs than attend movie theaters. This choice was made possible, of course, through the introduction of new technologies associated with the video cassette and the VCR, an example of a change in answering the How question. Firms responded to the consumers' desires as expected, VCR and video cassette production expanded rapidly, as did the number of stores that rent video cassette movies. At the same time, a number of movie theaters closed. A decided change occurred in answering the What question. Finally, resources specific to video cassette production and distribution found their incomes increasing, whereas resources specific to the movie theaters lost income. Some of the answers to the For Whom question changed as well.

THE *NOW* VERSUS THE *FUTURE* QUESTION   Should society favor the current generation at the expense of future generations, or the reverse? At issue here is long-run economic growth, the rate of growth of income or output over time. As a general rule, faster rates of growth favor future generations over the current generation and slower rates of growth favor the current generation over future generations. We will consider the economic issues associated with the growth question in the next section of this chapter.

FOR WHOM OR DISTRIBUTION QUESTION
Asks who will receive the various goods and services that are produced; one of the four fundamental economic questions that every society must answer.

NOW VERSUS THE FUTURE QUESTION
Asks whether society will favor the current generation over future generations, or the reverse; one of the four fundamental economic questions that every society must answer.

Constraints

PRODUCTION POSSIBILITIES

The economy's capacity for producing goods and services, assuming that it produces them efficiently.

The level of economic well-being that a nation can enjoy is ultimately limited by its **production possibilities,** defined as its capacity for producing goods and services. The production possibilities, in turn, depend on (1) the quantity and quality of a nation's primary factors of production and (2) the technologies available for turning these resources into goods and services.

Regarding the factors of production, larger countries can produce more than smaller countries can simply because they are larger, other things equal. Their business firms have access to more labor and more funds to purchase capital. Larger quantities of land, other things equal, support more agricultural activity and supply more natural resources. But other things might not be equal. The quality of a nation's resources matters as well. Are workers literate and well educated? Are they healthy? Are they industrious, inventive, and interested in self-improvement? Is the plant and equipment modern? Is much of the land suitable for farming—level, well drained, rich in nutrients, and located in temperate climates? Does the land contain high-grade natural resources that are easily accessible? Nations that can answer yes to most of these questions invariably rank among the world's richest countries. Particularly important are the quality of the labor force and the total amount of capital in place for the labor to work with. Size alone is not enough for economic well-being.

For instance, China and India are the two most populous nations and rank second and eighth in land area. Because they are so large, their economies produce large quantities of goods and services, but they are both among the world's poorest countries in terms of income *per person,* the most commonly used measure of economic well-being. China and India are held back by the quality of their labor. Their workers are generally poorly educated and unskilled, not at all well suited to work with modern production technologies. Also, neither China nor India has been able to provide their workers with enough capital to make them highly productive.

Japan is a relatively small country compared with China or India. It ranks seventh among the world's countries in population and is only one-tenth the size of India and one-thirtieth the size of China in land area. It also has relatively few natural resources. But Japan ranks fourth among the world's countries in income per person. In contrast to China and India, its workers are highly skilled and able to adapt to modern technologies, and the Japanese economy has provided relatively large amounts of capital to each worker.

The production technologies that are available to business firms clearly affect a nation's production possibilities. Innovations such as the steam engine in the early 1800s, electricity in the late 1800s and early 1900s, and the modern, high-speed computer over the past 30 years each had obvious and dramatic effects on production possibilities worldwide. As noted above, however, technology and the quality of a nation's resources are closely interrelated. The latest advances in technology may be well known to a nation's business firms, but they will have little actual impact on production if the nation's resources are unsuited for them.

PRODUCTION POSSIBILITIES FRONTIER

A graphical representation of the economy's capacity for producing goods and services, assuming that it produces them efficiently.

THE PRODUCTION POSSIBILITIES FRONTIER   The notion that a society is constrained by its production possibilities can be represented by a simple diagram

FIGURE 3.1

The Production Possibilities Frontier

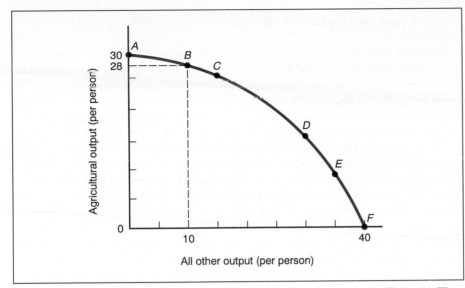

The solid line is the production possibilities frontier for the hypothetical data in Table 3.1. The frontier shows the combinations of agricultural output and all other output, per person, that the economy is able to produce, assuming that production is efficient. At point A, society puts all its resources into agriculture and is able to produce 30 units of agricultural output. At point F, society puts all its resources into all other goods and services and is able to produce 40 units of all other output. Points B, C, D, and E show different combinations of agricultural output and all other output that the economy is able to produce as it transfers some resources from agriculture to all other goods and services, or vice-versa.

known as the **production possibilities frontier.** To construct the frontier, everything that is produced must be placed into one of two categories so that production can be represented in two dimensions. Let's begin by dividing all production into agricultural output and all other output of goods and services. Represent the quantity of agricultural output per person on the vertical axis and the quantity of all other output per person on the horizontal axis, as in Figure 3.1. The figure corresponds with the data in Table 3.1. These data are completely hypothetical and are only meant to illustrate some of the properties of the production possibilities frontier. The data do not even have well-defined

TABLE 3.1   **Production Possibilities for a Hypothetical Economy**

POINTS	AGRICULTURAL OUTPUT PER PERSON	ALL OTHER OUTPUT PER PERSON
A	30	0
B	28	10
C	25	15
D	17	30
E	9	35
F	0	40

units because they represent combinations of many different kinds of goods and services.

Suppose, first, that society devotes all its resources to the production of agricultural output, using the farming technologies best suited to its resources. There would be some maximum amount of agricultural output attainable, 30 units according to our hypothetical data, represented by distance $0A$ in Figure 3.1. Alternatively, imagine that society devotes all its resources to the production of all other non-agricultural output, choosing the most suitable technology in each instance. There would be some maximum amount of all other output attainable, 40 units according to our hypothetical data, represented by distance $0F$ in Figure 3.1. Notice that the end points of the production possibilities frontier have different values. There is no necessary relationship between the distances $0A$ and $0F$, since different kinds of goods (and services) are being produced at each point.

To determine the other points on the frontier, return to point A. Imagine taking a few resources out of agricultural production and using them to produce all other output. Do so in a manner that provides the best possible answer to the How question. That is, take the resources that are best suited to all other production and least suited to farming. Also, combine the resources now available to each category of output such that they can produce the maximum possible agricultural and all other output. Suppose that production moves to point B, with agricultural production dropping to 28 units and all other production increasing from zero to 10 units. The 28 units of agricultural output and 10 units of all other output at point B represent the maximum possible production of agricultural and all other output, given the resources allocated to each category. Continuing to transfer resources from agriculture to all other goods and services in like manner, always providing the best possible answer to the How question, we locate points C, D, E, and so forth. When we have transferred all resources to all other output, production again takes place at point F. The curve $ABCDEF$ is society's *production possibilities frontier*. A number of its properties are worth noting.

THE PRODUCTION POSSIBILITIES FRONTIER AND THE CONSTRAINTS   The distance of the frontier from the origin is the most direct representation of the underlying constraints that limit how well off a society can be. Figure 3.2 depicts the relative positions of the production possibilities frontiers for a resource-rich country and a resource-poor country. The resource-rich country is endowed with large quantities of high-quality resources that can be adapted to the very latest production technologies. Its frontier is relatively far from the origin. The resource-poor country is less fortunate. Its production choices lie well inside those of the resource-rich country, and its frontier is relatively close to the origin.

INCREASING OPPORTUNITY COSTS ALONG THE FRONTIER   Notice that the production possibilities frontiers depicted in Figures 3.1 and 3.2 are bowed outward from the origin. As such, they are said to represent *increasing cost* production, in the sense of *increasing opportunity cost*. To see why a bowed-out frontier represents increasing opportunity cost, refer to Figure 3.3, which reproduces Figure 3.1.

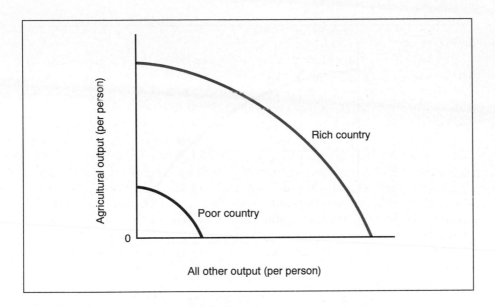

FIGURE 3.2

Production Possibilities Frontiers: Rich versus Poor Countries

The production possibilities frontier of a rich country is much farther away from the origin than the production possibilities frontier of a poor country. The rich country can produce many more goods and services per person than the poor country can because it has more high-quality resources and can use more productive technologies.

Note, first, that the Law of Substitution holds at all points along the frontier. Increasing production of all other output can occur only by reducing agricultural output, and vice versa. Since both goods are desirable, the cost of producing additional amounts of all other output is defined as the quantity of agricultural output that must be foregone. In other words, the cost of increasing all other output is an opportunity cost. In Figure 3.3 the opportunity cost of increasing all other output from 10 units at point B to 15 units at point C is the 3 units of agricultural output sacrificed in moving from B to C ($3 = 28 - 25$).

When the frontier is bowed outward from the origin, the opportunity cost of producing all other output increases as resources continue to be transferred out of agriculture into all other output. To see this, compare the move from points D to E with the move from points B to C. All other output increases by 5 units in each instance [$5 = (15 - 10) = (35 - 30)$]. But the opportunity cost in terms of lost agricultural output is 8 units in moving from D to E ($8 = 17 - 9$), whereas it was only 3 units in moving from B to C. The opportunity costs of increasing all other output have increased from point B to point D.

Increasing opportunity cost almost certainly applies to actual economies because some resources are better suited to certain activities than to others. At point B in Figure 3.3 most of society's resources are being used to farm. No doubt many of those resources are not very productive in farming—perhaps because of hilly terrain, infertile soil, or people who have neither the talent nor taste for farming. Much of this land and many of these people would be far more productive in producing other goods and services. If these resources are transferred in order to increase all other output from B (10 units) to C (15 units), it is possible to increase all other output with very little cost at all in terms of lost agricultural output. At point D, however, many of society's scarce resources are already producing all other output. Presumably only those resources better suited to agricultural production remain in the agricultural sector. Now, if society wishes to increase the production of all other goods and services, it can do so only at relatively great sacrifice of agricultural production.

FIGURE 3.3

The Increasing Cost Production Possibilities Frontier

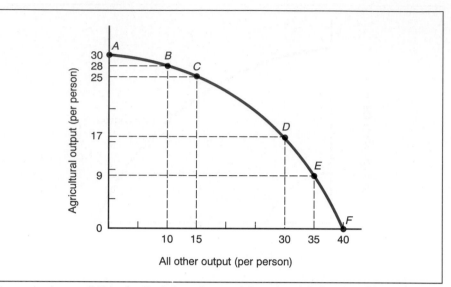

The production possibilities frontier is bowed outward from the origin because of increasing opportunity costs of production. Society must sacrifice ever increasing amounts of agricultural output for each additional unit of all other output that it produces as it increases production of all other output. The opportunity costs increase along the frontier because some resources are better suited to certain activities than to other activities.

This example is hardly unrealistic. History long ago taught us that farmers often have great difficulty leaving the farm to work in factories in a more urban environment. The slogan "women and children first" did not originate on a sinking ship. It was the hiring policy of the English textile mills at the beginning of the Industrial Revolution. Mill operators discovered very quickly that men did not take well to the long hours and dull routine of the factories. They became restless, irritable, and destructive. Women and children had fewer alternatives for work and were relatively more docile and productive as factory workers. Many of them had previously been domestics of various kinds in the feudal society of pre-Industrial England, if they had worked outside the home at all. Many farmers who left their farms in England journeyed to the New World to continue farming, rather than work in the English mills.

THE PRODUCTION POSSIBILITIES FRONTIER AND EFFICIENCY   All points along the production possibilities frontier represent efficient combinations of agricultural outputs and all other outputs. Society would like to produce more of each kind of output than it is able to. In a production context, therefore, efficiency requires that in order to have more of one kind of output, society must sacrifice some of the other output. But this is always true along the frontier, where the Law of Substitution holds.

Which is most efficient among points *A, B, C, D, E,* and *F* in Figure 3.1? The question has no meaning. These points each satisfy the requirements of production efficiency; they each represent the best possible resolution of the How question, given the resources allocated to each output. Nothing more can be said. Only if we bring in the desires of consumers for each product can a

FIGURE 3.4

**Efficient, Inefficient, and
Unattainable Production Points**

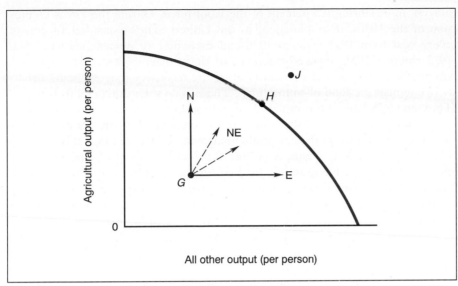

All points such as point *H* on the production possibilities frontier are efficient because the Law
of Substitution holds: To produce more of all other output society must reduce its production of
agricultural output, and vice-versa. All points such as *G* that lie inside the frontier are possible
but inefficient. By reallocating its scarce resources, society can move north, east, or northeast of
G, producing more of one kind of good without reducing its production of the other kind of
good, or producing more of both kinds of goods. Points such as *J* beyond the frontier are
unattainable given the quantity and quality of the nation's resources and the available
production technologies.

best point be determined. But this would be decided on the basis of efficiency
defined in terms of individuals' well-being, not simply in terms of production.

All points inside the production possibilities frontier are inefficient, however.
Consider point *G* in Figure 3.4. Since *G* lies inside the frontier, it is possible
to move north, east, or northeast of *G* on the graph by reallocating resources
to better answer the How question. A move to the north brings more agricultural output without sacrificing any output of all other goods and services.
Similarly, a move to the east increases all other output without sacrificing any
agricultural output. A move to the northeast brings more output of both goods.
Since both goods are desirable, presumably any of these reallocations would
be preferred to *G*. If possible, society should keep reallocating resources until
it hits the frontier. Only then are these free gains of output exhausted. In other
words, there is always some point on the frontier that dominates a given point
under the frontier.

Why might an economy be producing beneath its production possibilities
frontier? There are two possible causes. Either society is not using all of its
scarce resources, or it is not allocating the scarce resources it is using in the
best possible manner. The latter problem always exists to some extent, since
no society can hope to allocate every last resource exactly as required for production efficiency. But when market economies produce far below their potential, as the U.S. economy did in the early 1980s, the primary culprit is
unused resources. In the depths of the 1981–82 recession, industrial production
sank to 75 percent of its capacity, and over 10.6 million workers were unem-

ployed, representing 9.5 percent of the labor force. During the Great Depression of the 1930s, unemployment in the United States exceeded 14 percent every year from 1931 through 1940 and exceeded 20 percent annually from 1932 through 1936. Unused resources of these magnitudes clearly dominate any inefficiencies caused by misallocating the resources that are being used.

Economists are fond of counseling: "There is no such thing as a free lunch." They are referring to the principle of opportunity cost, that a decision to do something implies some other opportunity foregone. But the comparison between efficient and inefficient production points illustrates that this advice is somewhat misleading. There is no free lunch only if decisions are made efficiently. There are, for example, no free lunches along the production possibilities frontier. Free lunches abound, however, whenever decisions are made inefficiently. We saw that production increases can be made from point G in Figure 3.4 in any number of ways without any cost whatsoever. Indeed, an economist's particular expertise lies in discovering free lunches by advising people how to allocate their resources more effectively. Without free lunches economists would go hungry!

Here is a final thought along these same lines. Employing a worker who would otherwise be unemployed at a point such as G is costless from a social perspective, a "free lunch," *even if the worker draws a salary*. The output produced by the worker "pays" for the salary, and nothing has been sacrificed in the process.

PRICE INFLATION AND THE FRONTIER   Finally, what can be said about points beyond the frontier, such as J in Figure 3.4? A society would certainly prefer J to a point on the frontier such as H because it would mean an increase in both kinds of output. But J is unattainable, given current resources and technologies. The frontier defines the limits of what is possible.

Countries do occasionally try to reach beyond their means, however. When a market economy such as the United States attempts to do this, it suffers price inflation. The typical scenario is as follows. The government prints more money and places it in the economy so that consumers, business firms, and the government itself can spend more on goods and services. Once the economy reaches its production possibilities frontier, however, all the extra money does is drive up prices. The economy cannot produce any more goods and services. The *dollar value* of the goods and services continues to rise, but only because their prices, not the quantities themselves, are rising. Economists call this **demand pull inflation**, inflation resulting from the attempt to purchase more goods and services than the economy is capable of producing.

A more interesting problem for market economies is that prices can rise even if the economy is operating well below its production possibilities frontier. We will have to wait until the macroeconomics section of this text to understand how this can happen. The production possibilities frontier cannot explain why an economy can experience inflation with lots of unemployed resources. This is not a knock against the production possibilities frontier; it merely underscores the uses and limitations of economic models. The production possibilities frontier is a highly simplified description or model of an economy that yields many useful insights. We have seen how it helps us understand the concepts of production efficiency, full employment, and demand pull inflation. We will see in the next section how it helps us understand the process of

DEMAND PULL INFLATION
Price inflation resulting from the attempt to purchase more goods and services than the economy is capable of producing.

HISTORICAL NOTE: The last time the United States consciously tried to live beyond its means was in 1966 as a result of the Vietnam War. President Johnson increased the defense budget by $30 billion (over $120 billion in today's dollars) to fight the war without increasing taxes at a time when the economy was already operating on its production possibilities frontier. The predictable result was a significant increase in inflation over the next few years.

economic growth. But it definitely has its limitations as a model of the economy; it is not at all helpful in understanding why inflation and unemployed resources can exist at the same time. We need a different model to understand this problem.

LONG-RUN ECONOMIC GROWTH

The production possibilities frontier is an extremely useful device for illustrating the Now versus the Future question that all societies must address, the question of long-run economic growth. The frontier pictures the constraints on production in a given year. But societies do not have to accept the same frontier year after year. They can undertake policies to push the frontier out over time so that they can produce, and consume, ever-increasing amounts of all goods and services.

Long-run economic growth is defined as a *persistent* increase in the economy's *potential* for producing goods and services, with emphasis on the words *potential* and *persistent*. Potential refers to production possibilities, to the maximum possible quantities of goods and services that the economy can produce each year. The potential for producing goods and services must be distinguished from the actual production of goods and services, which may or may not be on the frontier. The increases in the economy's potential must also persist. Long-run economic growth is a continuing process. In terms of the production possibilities frontier, long-run economic growth refers to a persistent march of the frontier away from the origin.

Interest in economic growth is a fairly recent phenomenon in the broad sweep of history, dating back no further than the late 1700s. Until that time poverty, hunger, and disease were simply accepted as the fate of humankind. People had no hint of the vast improvement in living standards that would occur in a few countries over the next hundred years, made possible by sustained economic growth. Once these few countries showed the way, however, all countries wanted to follow. Long-run economic growth is a principal objective of all the world's nations.

LONG-RUN ECONOMIC GROWTH
A persistent increase in the economy's potential for producing goods and services.

The Growth Scorecard

Unfortunately, most countries have not been very successful. The World Bank divides the world's countries into four categories on the basis of their annual income per person in 1990: (1) low-income countries ($610 or less per person), (2) lower middle income countries (between $611 and $2,465 per person), (3) upper middle income countries (between $2,466 and $7,619 per person), and (4) high-income countries ($7,620 or more per person). Table 3.2 lists the number of countries in each category and the average dollar value of income per capita for each category as of 1990. As the table shows, living standards in most of the world's countries are very low. Citizens of the United States would have trouble imagining how anyone could survive on an average income of $610 per year or less, and even the $7,619 maximum income per person of the upper middle income countries is just about at the poverty level in the United

HISTORICAL NOTE: The United States, Japan, and (West) Germany have become the true giants among the world's economies. Together they account for 50 percent of all output produced for markets worldwide. In 1988 the United States was far and away the largest economy, producing 27 percent of the world's output, followed by Japan at 16 percent and West Germany at 7 percent.

TABLE 3.2   Classification of Countries by Stage of Development

COUNTRY CLASSIFICATION	NUMBER OF COUNTRIES	AVERAGE INCOME PER PERSON (1990)
Low Income	51	$610 or less
Lower Middle Income	56	Between $611 and $2,465
Upper Middle Income	39	Between $2,466 and $7,619
High Income[1]	40	$7,620 or more

[1]Includes the 21 large developed market economies of Asia, the Pacific, Western Europe, and North America, which are members of the Organization for Economic Cooperation and Development (OECD), and nineteen smaller, non-OECD countries. Among the smaller countries are many of the oil-exporting countries.

SOURCE: The World Bank, *Social Indicators of Development, 1991/92* (Washington, DC: Johns Hopkins University Press, 1992), Table B.1, pp. 378–379.

States. Economic growth has clearly proved to be an elusive target for all but a relatively few countries.

Achieving vigorous long-run economic growth is a complex process requiring just the right blend of social, cultural, demographic, political, and economic factors. At this point we want to concentrate on the most important economic determinants of growth.

Strategies for Economic Growth

The general strategies for achieving long-run economic growth are easily described in terms of the production possibilities frontier. The position of the frontier in any one year depends on the quantity and quality of a nation's primary factors of production and on the set of technologies available. These are the fundamental constraints underlying the frontier. Therefore, expanding the frontier necessarily involves (1) increasing the quantity of the primary factors of production, (2) improving the quality of these resources, or (3) inventing and employing new production technologies. Sustained economic growth is impossible without these changes.

Of the three primary factors of production—labor, capital, and land—labor and capital are far more important to the process of growth than is land. The total amount of land in a country is essentially fixed. Moreover, exploiting the resources contained in the land, through either farming or mining, requires applications of both labor and capital. So we can safely restrict our attention to increases in the quantity and quality of labor and capital when considering the role of resources in the process of growth.

INCREASING THE LABOR SUPPLY   Growth in the supply of labor is the single most important contributor to growth in a nation's *total* income or output for the simple reason that labor is by far the most important primary factor of production. In the United States, labor receives nearly 80 percent of all income paid by firms to primary factors of production. But increasing the supply of labor does not usually contribute very much to the growth of income or output *per person*, the key to improving a nation's economic standard of living. The problem is that increases in the labor supply typically result from increases in the overall population. When both output and population increase, the ratio of output to population, or output per person, does not increase very much.

Vigorous growth in output per person is possible if a country experiences an increase in **labor force participation,** the percentage of population that joins the labor force. Labor force participation has been increasing rapidly in the United States over the past 40 years, as ever more women have decided to work outside the home. In 1950 only 34 percent of all women were part of the labor force; by 1992 the percentage had grown to 57.8 percent. But such dramatic changes in labor force participation are unusual—they were unprecedented in the United States. And increases in labor force participation cannot continue indefinitely. Over the long run, increases in labor supply and increases in population tend to go hand in hand.

LABOR FORCE PARTICIPATION
The percentage of the population that joins the labor force.

INCREASING THE AMOUNT OF CAPITAL   Increasing the amount of capital is the key to increasing output per person. The single most important *economic* difference between the developed and the developing countries is that the former have been able to amass a large amount of capital per person, whereas the latter have not. Table 3.3 presents a recent estimate of the value of capital per person in 1980 for a sample of 10 countries that range from very low to very high income. With the exception of Korea (and Keyna, to a minor extent), there is a very high correlation between national output per person and capital per person: The more capital available per person, the higher the output produced per person. The table also indicates that increasing the amount of capital remains essential to economic growth long after a country passes through the early stages of development. These data are exactly what economists would expect, for a number of reasons. Some definitions are in order, however, before developing the point.

TABLE 3.3   **Output and Stock of Capital per Person for Selected Countries (1980 $)**

COUNTRY	OUTPUT PER PERSON	STOCK OF CAPITAL PER PERSON
INDIA	$ 244	$ 242
KENYA	412	1,272
INDONESIA	473	1,162
KOREA	1,607	4,028
BRAZIL	1,996	1,990
PORTUGAL	2,431	3,233
MEXICO	2,612	3,904
GREECE	4,302	5,653
SPAIN	5,616	5,133
UNITED STATES	11,998	29,741

SOURCE: K. M. Dadkhab and F. Zahedi, "Simultaneous Estimation of Production Functions and Capital Stocks for Developing Countries," *Review of Economics and Statistics* 3 (August 1986). Data were converted to dollars using exchange rates for 1980 reported in the *International Financial Statistics Yearbook, 1986* (Washington, D.C.: International Monetary Fund, 1986).

INVESTMENT

A flow variable that refers to the increase in the stock of capital during the year.

FLOW VARIABLE

A variable that can be measured only with reference to a period of time.

STOCK VARIABLE

A variable that can be measured at a given point in time.

LABOR PRODUCTIVITY

The amount of output produced per worker.

Capital refers to the amount of plant and equipment in place at any given time in private businesses and government-run enterprises, plus buildings used as residences. The nonresidential capital is most directly relevant to economic growth. **Investment** refers to increases in the amount of capital. It is a **flow variable,** meaning that it can only be measured with reference to a period of time, usually a year. In contrast, capital is a **stock variable;** it can be measured at a given point in time. For example, investment in plant and equipment in the United States in 1992 totaled $770.4 billion, meaning that firms added $770.4 billion to the nation's stock of plant and equipment during 1992. By December 1992 the U.S. Department of Commerce estimated that the United States had a stock of capital totaling $8.8 trillion of nonresidential capital and $14.0 trillion including residences. Thus, saying that continued increases in the stock of capital are the key to economic growth is equivalent to saying that sustaining a high level of investment is the key to economic growth.

Investment promotes economic growth because it simultaneously pursues all the possible strategies for growth. First, capital is one of the primary factors of production. Increasing the stock of capital directly increases a nation's productive capacity. Moreover, the gains in output are per-person gains because no corresponding increase in population occurs.

The increased quantity of capital in and of itself is only a small part of investment's contribution to growth, however. Far more important is the quality dimension of the new capital. New plant and equipment is improved plant and equipment. Growth in output per person could not continue if the new capital were not different from the capital already in place. To see why, imagine a farming situation in which three workers share one shovel. The shovel is the capital in this example. Adding new shovels should increase output, but only to the point at which each worker has a shovel. Adding more than three shovels cannot increase output because a worker can only use one shovel at a time. For growth to continue the shovels have to be replaced with better hand tools or machines such as tractors that increase **labor productivity,** defined as the output produced per worker.

What improved capital can do for labor productivity it can do for all other factors of production. New, and better, equipment in farming and mining improves the productivity of land. New and better equipment also improves the productivity of other capital, such as existing factories. In other words, investment acts to improve the *quality* of all factors of production by making them more productive.

NEW TECHNOLOGIES   We noted earlier that developing new technologies is essential for long-run economic growth. New technologies are only ideas or blueprints, however. To increase production they must actually be incorporated into production processes. Here, again, investment is a key because new technologies typically become incorporated into production through new capital. New machines are better machines precisely because they embody scientific and engineering advances.

HUMAN CAPITAL   Finally, investment has a direct effect on the quality of labor in addition to providing workers with new and better machinery. Economists distinguish between investments in physical and human capital. Investment in physical capital is the purchase of new plant and equipment that we have been referring to so far. **Investment in human capital** refers to investment in education, both the general education received in primary and secondary schools and in colleges and the more specialized forms of education such as graduate education and on-the-job training within businesses. The value of **human capital** is the market value of all accumulated knowledge and skills. Human capital is extremely difficult to evaluate, but economists believe that the value of human capital is about twice as large as the value of physical capital in the United States.

Investment in human capital may well be the single most important determinant of long-run economic growth. It contributes to growth in a number of ways. Scientific and engineering knowledge is essential for the development of new technologies. A high level of general education is also extremely important to sustaining economic growth. Only a highly literate, well-educated labor force can adapt itself easily to working with new equipment that embodies the latest technologies. For instance, learning the skills necessary to function in a modern computerized working environment is extremely difficult without a good general education. Finally, production processes and business organizations become ever larger and more complex as an economy grows. The managerial skills learned in a nation's business schools are needed to manage large-scale businesses effectively. Human capital contributes to growth in so many ways that it is virtually impossible to imagine a modern industrial economy arising without the benefit of a highly educated, highly skilled labor force.

The Sources of Economic Growth

Empirical studies of the sources of economic growth confirm that both physical and human capital are very important to the growth process. Table 3.4 reports the factors contributing to growth in total output for the United States from 1929 to 1982. The estimates come from Edward Denison, long considered one of the foremost authorities on U.S. economic growth.

Notice that the growth in the labor supply is the largest single contributor to growth in total output, which reflects the importance of labor in the production process. But remember that some of the growth in labor supply resulted from the natural growth in population, so that 32 percent overstates labor's contribution to growth in output per person. The direct and indirect

INVESTMENT IN HUMAN CAPITAL
Expenditures on education, both formal education received in school and on-the-job training provided by business firms.

HUMAN CAPITAL
The market value of all accumulated knowledge and skills.

TABLE 3.4   **Factors Contributing to U.S. Growth of Output, 1929–82**

FACTOR	CONTRIBUTION
GROWTH IN LABOR SUPPLY	32%
TECHNOLOGICAL ADVANCE	28
GROWTH IN CAPITAL STOCK	19
EDUCATION AND TRAINING	14
ALL OTHER	7

SOURCE: E. F. Denison, *Trends in American Economic Growth, 1929–1982* (Washington D.C.: Brookings Institution, 1985), 300.

TABLE 3.5   Investment and Growth in Labor Productivity in Six High-Income
Market Economies, 1971–80

COUNTRY	AVERAGE ANNUAL INVESTMENT/OUTPUT RATIO	AVERAGE ANNUAL GROWTH IN OUTPUT PER MAN-HOUR
JAPAN	34.0%	7.4%
FRANCE	24.2	4.8
GERMANY	23.7	4.9
ITALY	22.4	4.9
UNITED KINGDOM	19.2	2.9
UNITED STATES	19.2	2.5

SOURCE: *Economic Report of the President, 1983* (Washington, D.C.: U.S. Government Printing Office, February 1983).

effects of growth in the nation's capital stock account for 61 percent, or nearly all, of the remaining contributions to U.S. economic growth. Moreover, these percentages apply to growth in output per person as well as to growth in total output. Denison's estimates also underscore the importance of investment in human capital. Technological advance and education and training, both aspects of human capital, accounted for 42 percent of U.S. output growth. In contrast, growth in the stock of physical capital in and of itself contributed only 19 percent of the growth in output.

The data in Table 3.5 provide another indication of the close connection between increases in capital and economic growth. The table compares rates of growth in output per man-hour in manufacturing, a common measure of labor productivity, with investment as a percentage of domestically produced output for six of the high-income market economies for the period 1971–80. Japan's growth in labor productivity was by far the highest during the 1970s; so was its percentage of output devoted to investment goods. In contrast, both the United States and Great Britain lagged well behind the other countries in labor productivity growth, and they also had the lowest investment/output ratios.

The Opportunity Costs of Growth

If investment is the key to long-run economic growth, why don't the low- and middle-income developing countries simply increase the percentage of their resources devoted to investment? The problem is one of opportunity cost. Providing more resources for the production of investment goods means that fewer resources will be available for the production of consumer goods. When *total* output produced per person is only $1,500 per year (and in many countries it is far less than that), sacrificing consumption for investment can be very costly indeed. It can mean widespread starvation. Moreover, those who sacrifice, and survive, may not enjoy the benefits of their sacrifice. The returns to investing may not occur for a generation or more.

The necessary trade-off between investment and consumption can be explained in one of two ways. The production possibilities frontier provides the

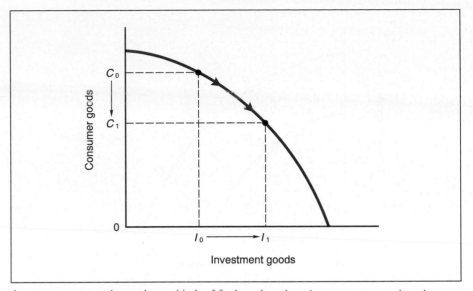

FIGURE 3.5

The Opportunity Cost of Economic Growth

An economy can produce only two kinds of final goods and services, consumer goods and investment goods. The figure illustrates the production possibilities frontier for consumer goods and investment goods. In order to increase investment from I_0 to I_1 to promote long-run economic growth, society must sacrifice, $(C_0 - C_1)$ of consumer goods. The sacrifice of consumer goods today is the opportunity cost of economic growth.

most direct approach. This time we will divide all output produced into consumer goods and investment goods. Referring to Figure 3.5, the vertical axis represents the quantity of consumer goods (C) produced, and the horizontal axis represents the quantity of investment goods (I) produced. This is a legitimate two-way division of total output because all final goods produced are either consumer goods or new capital sold to businesses (and government enterprises). All other produced goods are semi-finished products that are sold to other businesses as material inputs for further processing.

The trade-off between investment and consumption is immediately apparent in Figure 3.5. An increase in investment from I_0 to I_1 involves a sacrifice of consumption from C_0 to C_1. If C_0 is barely enough for survival, the increase in investment may well not be forthcoming.

The investment-consumption trade-off can also be explained by looking at how income flows through factor markets. Individuals receive the total income that flows through the factor markets in one of three forms: as wages and salaries for offering labor services to firms, as interest payments and profits in return for offering firms the funds for investment, and as rents in return for the use of their land. Once individuals receive income, they can use it in only one of two ways: They can either save it or use it to purchase consumer goods and services. The savings in turn become the source of funds that firms use to buy new plant and equipment. For example, people save by purchasing corporate bonds or stocks that firms offer as a means of raising funds. Or they deposit some of their income in bank accounts, and banks then loan the funds to business firms to be used for investment. Whatever the channels, the amount of income that individuals save in any one year must exactly equal the

FIGURE 3.6

The Strategy for Long-run Economic Growth

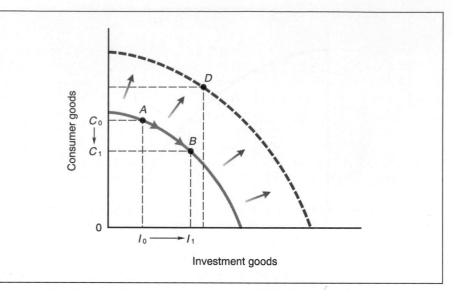

An economy is initially at point A on its production possibilities frontier, producing C_0 of consumer goods and I_0 of investment goods. In order to grow, society moves from point A to point B, increasing production of investment goods to I_1 and decreasing production of consumer goods to C_1. If growth takes, the production possibilities frontier moves out over time. Society can eventually move to a point such as D, producing more investment goods *and* more consumer goods than was possible before economic growth occurred.

amount of investment by firms because total income must match total spending on final output, consumer goods plus investment goods. So, in order to invest more, individuals must be willing to save more, which necessarily leaves less income available for purchasing consumer goods.

Every country must sacrifice some consumption for investment if only to maintain the existing stock of capital. All capital goods wear out over time. If there were no investment at all, the stock of capital would diminish and, with it, the nation's production capacity. The production possibilities frontier would march steadily inward to the origin. A level of investment just sufficient to maintain the existing stock of capital keeps the frontier more or less constant. Sustained economic growth is possible only by increasing investment beyond the replacement level, both now and in the future.

The strategy for economic growth, then, is depicted in Figure 3.6. An economy begins at point A, investing I_0 and consuming C_0. I_0 is just sufficient to maintain the capital stock and the economy's production possibilities. Growth is made possible by an initial move to point B, with investment increasing to I_1 at the cost of reducing current consumption to C_1. The idea is not to remain at point B, however. If growth occurs, the production possibilities frontier begins to move outward. Eventually, as it moves out far enough, the economy will be able to produce at points such as D, consuming more *and* investing more than when it began. Continued growth becomes ever less painful; the opportunity costs decrease. The problem for the low-income developing countries, though, is starting the process of economic growth. They may well need help from the developed nations in order to avoid the extreme sacrifices of consumption that would otherwise be necessary.

The Economic Health of a Nation

Our discussion of the production possibility frontier has revealed the two key determinants of the overall economic health of a nation: long-run economic growth and full employment of a nation's resources. In order to prosper, a nation must first increase its potential or capacity for producing goods and services. Its factors of production must become increasingly productive, which requires a high level of investment in both physical and human capital. Countries that are able to push their production possibilities frontiers out rapidly and continuously over time enjoy a high standard of living. Countries that cannot extend their production possibilities frontiers suffer low standards of living.

A nation must also realize its increased potential in order to prosper. Actual production must occur on or very near the production possibilities frontier, which requires efficient answers to the How question. A nation must use all its scarce resources and use them well. With reference to Figure 3.6, the increase in potential well-being created by moving the frontier out from the solid line to the dotted line does no good at all if the economy actually remains at point *B*. Societies must chase their frontiers as they move out over time.

CHOOSING AN ECONOMIC SYSTEM

Our discussion of society's economic problem has ignored one essential decision that must be made prior to addressing the four fundamental economic questions: What economic system will society choose to structure its economic activities? An **economic system** is the set of decision-making mechanisms, organizational arrangements, and rules for allocating society's scarce resources and determining the appropriate distribution of income. In short, it is the institutional setting in which society pursues the four economic questions.

Societies usually do not consciously choose an economic system. Rather, economic systems tend to evolve slowly over a long period of time in a manner consistent with a nation's cultural, social, and political mores. This is why the seven Eastern European nations stunned the world in 1989 with their intention to completely transform their economies in short order. History offers no precedent for what they are attempting. Let's take a closer look at what constitutes an economic system before discussing the prospects of the Eastern European economies.

People have a tendency to label economic systems with various forms of "isms"—capitalism, socialism, communism, and the like. Such labels are possible, but not especially helpful, because no actual economic system meets all the attributes of any one "ism" in its pure form. Economists want to understand how different economic systems affect the performance of the economy. For this purpose they have found it far more useful to identify the characteristics of economic systems that are most likely to differ from country to country and that have a direct bearing on how the economy performs. Four such characteristics stand out above all others: who has the decision-making authority within the economy, what methods are used to process and coordinate economic information, who owns the capital and land, and what incentives are used to motivate economic behavior.

ECONOMIC SYSTEM

The set of decision-making mechanisms, organizational arrangements, and rules for allocating society's scarce resources and determining the appropriate distribution of income.

Characteristics of Economic Systems

DECISION-MAKING AUTHORITY   Who makes the economic decisions? The answer to this question turns on the delegation of authority throughout the economy and how economic information is obtained and utilized. The spectrum runs from a completely centralized economy to a fully decentralized economy. In a **centralized economy** an agency of the national government has authority over all economic decisions and full access to all relevant economic information. Lower-level decision-making units, including consumers and business firms, receive only limited information, just enough to carry out the wishes of the central authority. In a **fully decentralized economy** individuals and business firms make all economic decisions and are responsible for generating and processing all relevant economic information.

No actual economic system is completely centralized or decentralized. Individuals, business firms, and government agencies always have some decision-making authority and share economic information. But nations do exhibit definite tendencies toward centralization or decentralization. Cuba and the People's Republic of China have chosen a centralized approach to their major economic decisions. So did the countries of Eastern Europe and the Soviet Union prior to 1989. The high-income market economies of Western Europe, the United States, Canada, and Japan, among others, lean just as heavily toward a decentralized approach.

INFORMATION PROCESSING AND COORDINATION   How does the economy process and coordinate economic information? Two mutually exclusive options are available for processing and coordinating information: the national economic plan and the market. A **national economic plan** goes hand in hand with centralized decision making. The central authority develops a plan that sets national economic objectives regarding the four fundamental economic questions and simply instructs lower-level decision-making units on how to carry out the plan. The plan also provides an incentive structure to ensure that lower-level units, especially individuals and business firms, follow the central agency's directives. The plan carries the force of law.

A market system is the opposite of central planning and goes hand in hand with a decentralized decision-making strategy. A **market** is any institutional arrangement through which buyers and sellers engage in the free exchange of goods, services, and factors of production. "Free" exchange does not mean that goods and services are traded free of charge. Rather, it implies that buyers and sellers enter into exchanges voluntarily and in pursuit of their own self-interests. Markets, in other words, honor the principle of consumer (and producer) sovereignty.

Prices process and coordinate all economic information in a market economy. The interaction of buyers and sellers in markets determines the prices at which the goods, services, and factors of production are exchanged. The prices established by their interaction incorporate all relevant economic information, such as which resources are abundant and which are scarce, which goods are costly to produce, and which goods and services consumers want to buy. We will take a closer look at markets and prices in Chapter 4.

CENTRALIZED ECONOMY

An economic system in which an agency of the national government has authority over all economic decisions and full access to all relevant economic information.

FULLY DECENTRALIZED ECONOMY

An economic system in which individuals and business firms make all economic decisions and are responsible for generating and processing all relevant economic information.

NATIONAL ECONOMIC PLAN

A plan developed by the central authority that sets national economic objectives regarding the four fundamental economic questions and instructs lower-level decision-making units on how to carry out the plan.

MARKET

Any institutional arrangement through which buyers and sellers engage in the free exchange of goods, services, and factors of production.

A national economic plan is also an institutional arrangement for exchanging goods and services, but, in contrast with the market, it honors the preferences of the central authority, not of individuals and business firms. This is why the market and the plan are mutually exclusive.

PROPERTY RIGHTS: THE OWNERSHIP OF FACTORS OF PRODUCTION   Who owns the factors of production, and how is the income associated with them to be distributed? The assignment of **property rights,** that is, deciding who owns the factors of production, is one of the more important issues that a society must resolve. It far transcends narrow economic concerns. The determination of property rights has a direct effect on all social interactions, including the amount of freedom that people enjoy.

Virtually all societies believe that people should own their own labor services and are entitled to the income derived from them. Therefore, the question of property rights applies to capital and land, not to labor.

The property rights to capital and land may be private, or public, or cooperative (collective). Private ownership means that individuals are granted all rights associated with ownership, including the right to transfer the property and the rights to receive all income generated by the property. Private ownership of capital and land, "private property," is a hallmark of capitalism. Public ownership means that the government owns the capital and land and receives all the income earned by these factors. Therefore, the government decides how to dispose of the income from capital and land. The income is often earmarked for investment, but not always. Public ownership is the defining characteristic of **socialism.** Collective ownership is a variant of public ownership under which the property rights to capital and land are held collectively by the citizens. They vote on how to use and distribute the earnings from these factors.

The assignment of property rights to capital and land has its most direct impact on the For Whom or Distribution question, but it can be expected to affect the allocation of these resources as well. In answering the How question, private owners offer their capital and land to whoever pays them the highest return. Although capital and land may be allocated on the same basis under public (or collective) ownership, broader social concerns are likely to come into play.

INCENTIVES   What incentive mechanisms will be used to encourage individuals and firms to engage in economic activity consistent with society's objectives? Economic systems may operate with either moral or material incentives. **Moral incentives** encourage behavior for the good of society and may be enforced with legal sanctions if such behavior is not forthcoming. **Material incentives,** in contrast, appeal to economic self-interest by allowing individuals and business firms to keep the gains from their exchanges. Material incentives are necessarily the primary incentive in a market economy because markets operate on the principle that individuals and business firms enter into market exchanges to pursue their own economic objectives. They must be allowed to keep the gains from their exchanges for the system to work.

Material incentives are also used in centrally planned economies. Since people own the rights to their own labor, material incentives are a natural way of

---

PROPERTY RIGHTS

The ownership of the factors of production.

SOCIALISM

An economic system with public ownership of capital and land.

MORAL INCENTIVES

Incentives that encourage behavior for the good of society and may be enforced with legal sanctions.

MATERIAL INCENTIVES

Incentives that appeal to economic self-interest by allowing individuals and business firms to keep the gains from their exchanges.

encouraging lower-level managers and workers to meet the plan's directives and to match labor supplies to the requirements of the plan. They may also use material incentives to reward and punish political behavior, as when the central planners reserve the highest paid jobs for those who are loyal to the ruling political party. Nonetheless, centrally planned economies are likely to rely heavily on moral incentives as well.

Pure Market Capitalism and Centrally Planned Socialism

PURE MARKET CAPITALISM

An economic system characterized by fully decentralized decision making, the use of markets to process economic information and coordinate exchange, private ownership of capital and land, and the use of material incentives.

CENTRALLY PLANNED SOCIALISM

An economic system characterized by centralized decision making, the use of a national economic plan to process information and coordinate exchange, public ownership of capital and land, and the use of both moral and material incentives.

The choices that a society makes regarding these four characteristics essentially define its economic system. Many different economic systems are possible. They can be thought of as lying along a spectrum whose endpoints are two stylized economic systems, pure market capitalism and centrally planned socialism. All of the world's economies are mixtures of these two paradigms.

The four principal characteristics of **pure market capitalism** are (1) decentralized decision making, (2) the use of markets and prices for processing and coordinating all economic information, (3) private ownership of capital and land, and (4) the exclusive use of material incentives. The government has only one necessary economic function to perform. It must ensure that market exchanges proceed in a free and even-handed manner. Beyond this, government economic activity may be justified if markets perform sufficiently badly in some areas. For example, markets cannot be relied on to provide for the national security; this is a task for the government. But the citizens, not the government, determine when government involvement in the economy is justified.

The four principal characteristics of **centrally planned socialism** are (1) centralized decision making within an agency of the national government, which sets all national objectives; (2) the use of a national economic plan designed by the central authority to process and coordinate all economic information and binding on all lower-level units, including all individuals and business firms; (3) public ownership of capital and land, with the central planning authority determining the disposition of all returns to the capital and land; and (4) the use of both moral and material incentives to implement the national plan. In its purest form, centrally planned socialism leaves no role at all for a free market system.

Pure market capitalism and centrally planned socialism each have their advantages relative to the other. The foremost advantage of pure market capitalism is the freedom it gives to its citizens to pursue their own economic self-interests. One immediate consequence of this freedom is that pure market capitalism is highly responsive to the wishes of individual consumers. Business firms respond to consumers' desires, so that consumers are able to buy what they want within the limits of their resources. Freedom and responsiveness to consumers are very big advantages in a humanistic society, since the whole purpose of an economic system is to promote individual well-being. Centrally planned socialism, in contrast, severely limits the personal freedom of its citizens and creates a privileged class of managers and government bureaucrats.

Pure market capitalism also has a decided advantage in promoting economic efficiency. Nothing comes close to matching the market as an efficient allocator of society's scarce resources. The market generally does a fine job of processing and coordinating economic information so that resources are directed to their most productive and valued uses. In the 1960s central planners in the former Soviet Union and the other socialist economies had hoped that the advent of powerful computers would allow them to model the economy in great detail and thereby allocate resources more efficiently. Their hopes were never realized, however. A modern economy has proved much too complex for even the most powerful computers to model effectively. The result is that national plans remain very poor processors and coordinators of economic information. Also, individuals without property rights to capital and land or the freedom to pursue their own self-interests have little incentive to conserve scarce resources and use them efficiently. Moral incentives that urge people to follow the dictates of the national plan for the good of society have not been very effective substitutes for self-interested material incentives. Centrally planned socialism proved to be grossly inefficient.

Centrally planned socialism is not without its advantages relative to pure market capitalism, however. It is better able to formulate and pursue national objectives simply because of the top-down nature of the decision-making authority. To cite one example, following the Russian Revolution the Soviet planners wanted to direct the nation's saving and investment toward the heavy manufacturing industries such as steel and were able to do so. In contrast, both political parties in the United States have been urging higher levels of saving and investment to promote economic growth for the past 20 years without any effect whatsoever. One can argue that centrally planned socialism's advantage in promoting national objectives is not worth much if the objectives do not reflect the will of the people. Perhaps U.S. citizens just do not want to save more. In any event, the market has been generating low levels of saving and investment in the United States, and the government has not been able to override this result despite the apparent political will to do so.

Centrally planned socialism also has a decided advantage in resolving the For Whom or Distribution question if society's preferences lean toward equality. The centrally planned socialist economies generally have a much more equal distribution of economic well-being than do the market economies. One reason relates to the income from capital. The government receives all income from capital under centrally planned socialism, whereas individuals receive the income from capital under pure market capitalism. The ownership of capital tends to become highly concentrated in the hands of a few in pure market economies. For instance, 70 percent of the capital in the United States is held by less than 10 percent of the population. Consequently, nearly all the income from capital is earned by a small percentage of the population, which is one reason why the distribution of income is far from equal in the United States. Also, central planners dictate the wages for different occupations, so they can avoid large disparities in wage income if they want to. Wage income is generally much more evenly distributed in the centrally planned socialist economies. Finally, the centrally planned socialist economies can, and typically do, ensure that everyone is provided with the basic necessities—food, clothing, shelter, medical care, even education. These items are either heavily subsidized or provided directly through government agencies. For example, energy in Poland was virtually free to consumers from 1960 to 1989. In contrast, many of the poor who are left behind in the market economies cannot afford even the most basic necessities.

A final advantage of centrally planned socialism is its ability to avoid having resources lie idle. The national plan dictates the allocation of all resources, so it can virtually guarantee that labor is fully employed and that capital and land are fully utilized. Pure market capitalism, in contrast, often experiences periods of high unemployment and underutilized capital and land.

Both economic systems, then, are prone to inefficiencies and are destined to operate below their production possibilities frontiers. The chief problem under centrally planned socialism is that scarce resources are badly misallocated. The chief problem under market capitalism is that resources lie idle at times. Overall, though, the efficiency advantage lies with pure market capitalism, as noted above. Resources are not always idle in the market economies, whereas resources are almost always badly misallocated in the centrally planned socialist economies.

The Eastern European Economies

The economic transitions under way in Eastern Europe are all the more remarkable because these countries are not just seeking small adjustments in their economic systems. Instead, they are trying to jump the entire length of the economic spectrum, replacing economies that were close to the ideal of centrally planned socialism with economies that are close to the ideal of pure market capitalism. When these countries began to transform their economies in 1989 fully 80 to 90 percent of their businesses were owned and operated by the government. They intend to make all these businesses private in short order and to dismantle the central planning bureaucracy. The world has never witnessed economic reforms quite like these.

What are their prospects of succeeding? In truth, they each face a formidable set of obstacles in trying to transform their economies.[1] Foremost among them are the crushing inefficiencies inherited from the old centrally planned system. Western economists estimated in 1989 that 30 to 40 percent of their businesses were not competitive in the world's marketplace. For this reason alone the move to market capitalism must proceed slowly, or these countries will face massive bankruptcies and unemployment that they simply cannot cope with.

Given the existing inefficiencies, another difficult problem is how to turn over their businesses from public to private ownership. Here the countries face a nasty Catch 22. Private investors will want to know the extent to which the businesses are competitive before they buy them, in other words, how much they should pay to become the owners. The competitiveness and value of the government-owned businesses are difficult to determine, however, because they had been buying their inputs and selling their products at completely artificial prices set by the central planners. The true value of the businesses cannot be determined until they become private and are forced to buy their inputs and sell their products at established market prices. But private investors will not buy the businesses and open them up to competition until they know their true values. Hence, the Catch 22. Furthermore, even if the businesses'

---

[1]The former East Germany is obviously something of an exception, since it has unified with West Germany, and the West Germans have agreed to help ease the transition. Nonetheless, the economy and citizens of East Germany face many of the obstacles listed below. The transformation of the East German economy will not be painless.

true values were known, the citizens of these countries do not have anywhere near enough wealth to buy the businesses themselves. The government could allow foreign investors to buy the businesses, but countries are always leery of foreign ownership. A final option is simply to give the businesses away to the citizens. This is likely to be viewed as very unfair, however. One family could receive stock in a viable, highly competitive business and become rich. Another family could receive stock in one of the noncompetitive businesses that quickly goes under, and so the family would remain poor. People are unlikely to tolerate such uneven outcomes generated simply by the luck of the draw. The question of how to privatize the government-owned businesses has economists stumped. No one is quite sure how best to do it.

The example of the luck of the draw points to a more general problem. These countries began the transformation of their economies with a fairly even distribution of income, and their citizens have an ingrained belief in equality. Also, they are accustomed to a system of government-owned capital and land in which no one profits directly from these resources, and they have been taught to distrust the profit motive. As the market economy evolves, one can only wonder how people will react to entrepreneurial citizens who own and manage profitable businesses and become well-to-do from the receipt of profits. Income from capital (and land) will almost certainly become highly concentrated, just as it is in the existing market economies. Wide disparities in income arising from profits could generate enormous social tensions throughout Eastern Europe.

An equally difficult problem will occur at the other end of the income distribution. Many firms will fail if the government-owned businesses are as inefficient as Western economists estimate. Unemployment will be high, and the governments will have to provide a huge safety net of public transfers to prevent widespread poverty. Will these countries be able to afford the safety net? This is an open question for all but the East Germans who have been promised support from the West Germans. The other countries will undoubtedly require aid from abroad to provide an adequate safety net for the unemployed and their families.

The final major obstacle in changing to a market economy is a legal one. The Eastern European countries do not have legal systems in place that can support a market economy. These countries must draft new laws that, at a minimum, clearly define the property rights to capital and land, are able to enforce private contracts, and can adequately resolve the inevitable rash of bankruptcies that will occur. The transformation to a market economy cannot proceed until these laws are passed and are being enforced.

Can the Eastern European countries overcome these obstacles? Economists are divided on this question. The pessimists believe that the obstacles are simply too great to permit anything approaching a smooth transition to a market economy. They doubt that the United States, Japan, and Western Europe will provide the aid required to avoid widespread poverty and deep social unrest. They see the distinct possibility of a populist counterrevolution to retain centrally planned socialism, driven by the belief in equality and the distrust of the profit motive. They also fear that deep-seated enmities among ethnic groups will resurface as the central governments lose their grips, a fear that was realized so immediately and tragically in Yugoslavia. Finally, the pessimists see the entrenched managers of the government enterprises as fighting the move to privatization at every turn so they can maintain their privileged positions.

Worse yet, few people besides the public managers have any managerial training or experience. The current managers will be difficult to replace if they resist privatization.

The optimists point to three factors that they believe will facilitate the transformation to a market economy. The first is simply a very strong will to succeed within some of the countries. Hungary, Poland, and the former Czechoslovakia are determined to join the European Economic Community in the near future, and they know they must achieve viable market economies to do so. The jury is still out on the will to succeed within Bulgaria and Romania and, of course, among the Croats, Serbs, and Muslims in the war-torn former Yugoslavia. Second, the countries all rely heavily on international trade. The optimists see this as a plus because trading in international markets forces businesses to set proper prices for inputs and outputs in order to compete at all. They argue that the resulting price discipline will cause their businesses to become competitive more quickly. Finally, the optimists believe that the Western market economies will provide the necessary financial assistance during the transition period. They point out that the West very much wants market capitalism to succeed in Eastern Europe. Also, the Eastern European countries have size working in their favor. The combined national output of the original seven countries (including the former East Germany) is only one-quarter as large as the national output of West Germany alone. The West can easily provide the aid required during the transition. The optimists concede that the obstacles listed above are serious and that the Eastern Europeans will need to be patient. Even the most optimistic economists believe that the transformation will take at least 15 years to complete.

We should note in closing that many of the economists who are optimistic about the prospects of the Eastern European countries are quite pessimistic about the more modest market reforms being undertaken in the countries of the former Soviet Union. The will to succeed does not appear to be very strong. The former Communist bureaucracy was much larger and far more entrenched there than in any of the Eastern European countries, and the popular support for market reforms is still very shaky. The countries of the former Soviet Union are also much less dependent on international trade than are the economies of Eastern Europe, so the disciplining force of the international marketplace is missing. In summary, the former Soviet countries face the same obstacles as the Eastern Europeans in trying to move to a more market-oriented economy, but they seem less well positioned to overcome them.

REFLECTION: Do the news reports from Eastern Europe suggest that any of the original seven countries are well on their way to transforming their economies into successful market economies?

SUMMARY

Chapter 3 began with a discussion of society's economic problem, consisting of objectives, alternatives, and constraints.

1. The economic objectives of a humanistic society are efficiency and equity.
2. Economists express the alternatives as four fundamental economic questions that all societies must answer. These questions also incorporate the objectives of efficiency and equity.
   a. The What or Output question: What goods and services should society produce and in what amounts?

   b. The How or Input question: How should firms produce each of the goods and services, and what factors of production and production technologies should they use?
   c. The For Whom or Distribution question: Who will receive the goods and services?
   d. The Now versus the Future question: Should society favor the current generation at the expense of future generations, or vice versa? This is the question of long-run economic growth.

3. The constraints that ultimately limit how well off a society can be consist of the quantity and quality of the nation's resources and the production technologies available for turning inputs into outputs.
4. The production possibilities frontier is a two-dimensional diagram representing the constraints of society's economic problem. The frontier shows the combinations of goods and services that the society is potentially able to produce, assuming that production is efficient.
5. An economy operates under its production possibilities frontier if its resources are either misallocated or unused. No society can operate beyond its frontier.
6. The production possibilities frontier exhibits increasing opportunity cost because some resources are better suited to produce particular goods and services. Increasing opportunity cost means that producing more of one output requires ever-increasing sacrifices of the other output.

   The second section of the chapter described the process of long-run economic growth.

7. Long-run economic growth refers to persistent increases in the potential of an economy to produce goods and services. It is represented as a continuing shift of the production possibilities frontier away from the origin.
8. Long-run economic growth requires a change in the quantity or quality of a nation's resources or the introduction of new production technologies.
9. Investment in physical and human capital (education) is the key to economic growth because it meets all three requirements for growth. Capital is an important factor of production, new capital tends to make all factors of production more productive, and new production technologies are usually embodied in new capital.
10. The opportunity cost of growth is that more investment comes at the expense of consumption. The sacrifice of consumption is very costly for poor countries, making the growth process difficult to start.

   The final section of Chapter 3 discussed society's choice of an economic system to solve the economic problem.

11. The four principal characteristics of an economic system that determine how an economy performs are the delegation of the decision-making authority, the way in which economic information is processed and coordinated, the ownership of capital and land, and the incentives used to encourage consumers and producers to pursue society's objectives.
12. Pure market capitalism and centrally planned socialism are stylized economic systems that lie at the endpoints of the spectrum of economic systems. All real-world economies are blends of these two systems.

13. Pure market capitalism decentralizes the decision-making authority to individuals and business firms, uses markets and prices to process and coordinate economic information, allows private ownership of capital and land, and relies entirely on material incentives. Its principal strengths are individual freedom, responsiveness to consumers' desires, and efficiency in the allocation of scarce resources.

14. Centrally planned socialism centralizes the decision-making authority in an agency of the national government, uses a national plan to process and coordinate economic information, has public ownership of capital and land, and relies on both material and moral incentives. Its principal strengths are the ability to formulate and pursue national objectives, a fairly equal distribution of income, and a virtual guarantee of full employment.

15. In 1989 seven Eastern European countries (Bulgaria, Czechoslovakia, East Germany, Hungary, Poland, Romania, and Yugoslavia) announced that they were going to transform their economic systems. They would replace systems designed along the lines of centrally planned socialism with systems designed along the lines of pure market capitalism. They face a number of obstacles in transforming their economies. Foremost among them is the fact that 30 to 40 percent of their companies were not competitive in 1989. The transformations of their economies will probably take at least 15 years under the best of circumstances.

KEY TERMS

centrally planned socialism
economic system
for whom or distribution question
how or input question
human capital

investment
long-run economic growth
market
national economic plan

now versus the future question
production possibilities frontier
pure market capitalism
what or output question

QUESTIONS

1. What is the production possibilities frontier, and which components of society's economic problem does it illustrate?

2. Suppose that an economy produces only two goods, X and Y.
   a. Draw a reasonable production possibilities frontier for the economy. Why did you draw it as you did?
   b. Suppose that a new technological advance makes the economy much more productive in producing good Y. Show how this discovery might affect the production possibilities frontier that you drew. Explain.
   c. Does this technological change permit society to consume more of good X?
   d. Pick a point on the original production possibilities frontier and label it A. After the technological change occurs, is A an efficient production point? Why or why not?

   e. Explain what the opportunity cost of producing more X is at point A before and after the technological change occurs.

3. How do the four fundamental questions that any society must answer relate to the components of society's economic problem?

4. Explain why the following statement is true: The *production possibilities frontier* illustrates the concepts of the *Law of Scarcity*, *efficiency*, and *opportunity cost*.

5. Suppose that an economy produces only two goods: baseball bats and 2 × 4s. Also, the only input needed to make these goods is trees. Here 1 tree makes 10 baseball bats, and 1 tree makes 20 2 × 4s. If there are 50 trees in the economy, draw the production possibilities frontier for this economy. Does this frontier illustrate the principle of increasing opportunity cost?

6. a. Why do economists believe that investment is the key to long-run economic growth?

   b. The poorer nations of the world understand that investment is the key to long-run economic growth, yet they are often reluctant or unable to increase investment significantly. Why is this?

7. President Clinton argues that the United States needs to improve formal education and also train workers who lack basic skills if it hopes to have a rapidly growing economy. Does this argument make sense?

8. What are the four principal characteristics that determine how an economic system operates? Describe the features of pure market capitalism and centrally planned socialism in terms of these characteristics.

9. Discuss the relative strengths and weaknesses of pure market capitalism and centrally planned socialism.

10. Describe some of the problems that the Eastern European countries will face as they attempt to convert from centrally planned economies to market-based economies.

4

Markets, Prices, and the U.S. Economy

LEARNING OBJECTIVES

CONCEPTS TO LEARN

A market	The circular flow of economic activity
The economic function of prices	Highlights of the U.S. economy
The principle of comparative advantage	

CONCEPTS TO RECALL

Economic exchange [1]	Pure market capitalism [3]
Interdependence [1]	

he U.S. economy is incomprehensibly large. Over 250 million individuals, 18 million business firms, and 89,000 government agencies engage in billions of market exchanges every day. The annual value of final goods and services produced in the United States passed the $6 trillion mark in 1993. How large is $6 trillion? Imagine the following exercise. Take 100 one-dollar bills, and tie them into a bundle one inch high. Keep doing this until you have bundled $6 trillion worth of dollar bills. Then pile all the one-inch, $100 bundles one on top of another. How tall would the stack be? The answer is tall enough to reach the moon and return to earth—twice!

The miracle of a modern decentralized market economy is that it works at all because capitalism would appear to be a recipe for chaos. The millions of individuals and business firms interact in thousands of markets without any direction whatsoever. Moreover, the market system says to each of them, in effect, "Do your own thing. Pursue your own self-interest as much as you possibly can. Forget about anyone else. Let others look out for themselves." Yet market exchanges are nearly always orderly, not chaotic, and markets are the most effective mechanism yet devised for promoting economic efficiency. One of the main goals of a first course in economics is to understand how this can be.

The two main themes in economic analysis are the economic problem and the exchange of goods and services and factors of production. Chapters 1 through 3 discussed the economic problem as it relates to individual economic agents and to society as a whole. Chapter 4 completes the introductory part of the text with a discussion of some fundamental issues related to exchange in a modern market economy. It provides the background information that we will need for our study of how markets operate in the U.S. economy. The natural place to begin is with a description of what a market is.

MARKETS

The thousands of markets in which buyers and sellers exchange products and factors of production are the heart and soul of a capitalist economy. What exactly is a market? In Chapter 3 we defined a market in a very general way as any institutional arrangement that permits the voluntary exchange of a good, service, or factor of production between buyers and sellers. Defining the concept of a market more precisely than this is difficult because markets take many different forms. Market exchanges occur in a variety of institutional settings, and markets have distinctive product and geographic dimensions that vary considerably from market to market.

The Institutional Setting

Think for a moment about the many different ways in which exchanges of consumer goods and services take place. The majority of transactions involving consumer goods occur in retail outlets, both large and small. But agricultural produce is often sold at roadside stands and open air markets. Other goods are sold through the mail or door to door. Many financial securities are traded electronically over phone lines. The dollar amounts of these telephone exchanges are transferred from one computer's memory to another without anything tangible changing hands. Some exchanges involve direct contact between the buyer and the seller. This is particularly true of services such as those provided by electricians, hairdressers, and restaurants. In contrast, manufactured goods are more often exchanged indirectly through intermediaries. For instance, retail outlets are usually intermediaries between the consumers and the producers. Retailers buy the goods from the manufacturers and then resell them to the consumers.

The same variety of institutional settings exists in factor markets. Many professional and skilled blue-collar labor services are exchanged by means of a formal contract that stipulates the salary and the requirements of the job. People can negotiate their own contracts, or they can be represented by intermediaries such as agents or union negotiators. Other occupations do not use formal contacts. Many white-collar jobs operate under implicit contracts in which the salary and the job requirements are well understood, even though nothing is put in writing. Exchanges involving unskilled labor are sometimes even more casual and intermittent. On some construction jobs laborers are hired daily on a first come–first hired basis and paid at the end of the day. Whether workers show up for work on any one day does not affect their chances of being hired on any subsequent day.

Transactions involving land can also occur in a variety of ways. Parcels of land can be sold directly from buyer to seller or through intermediaries such as real estate agents. Two wealthy doctors in Los Angeles may exchange 1,000 acres of Iowa farmland that neither has ever seen.

These examples illustrate why you cannot associate the concept of a market with any one particular institutional setting.

Market Boundaries

Markets have both product and geographic dimensions. Economists define individual markets by product or factor of production, as in the market for orange juice, or four-year liberal arts colleges, or computer scientists, or professional baseball players. But the boundaries between individual products and factors of production are not often clear-cut from either the buyers' or the suppliers' perspective. Consider product markets by way of example.

Economists first attempt to distinguish individual products from the buyers' perspective. Do buyers view the product as reasonably distinct? Are close substitutes available? How "close" is a close substitute? These are sometimes difficult questions to answer. Consider various writing implements as an example. Do consumers view felt-tipped pens as substitutes for ball point pens? Are pens and pencils substitutes for each other? Are they two products or one essentially interchangeable product? Consumers undoubtedly think of pens and electronic typewriters as reasonably distinct products, but do they consider electronic typewriters and word processors to be distinct products?

INDUSTRY

The collection of all firms producing the
same product.

The supplier's perspective enters into the determination of individual product markets as well. Products are produced by business firms, and an **industry** is the collection of all firms producing the same product. Particular industries may not be clearly defined, however. For example, even if consumers view felt-tipped and ball point pens as distinct products, business firms might see them as virtually identical because they can easily switch production from one to the other as demand dictates. If so, then a firm producing only felt-tipped pens at the moment is still very much in the market for ball point pens. The felt-tipped pen and ball point pen *industries* are not distinct. But are there distinct *markets* for the two kinds of pens? The buyers and sellers may reach different conclusions in this case.

Geography is yet another factor that determines what constitutes a distinct market. Economists do not typically use the term *market* as market researchers do when they speak of the Minneapolis–St. Paul "market." Market researchers use a geographic definition of a market because they are primarily interested in the sales potential of a particular geographic area. Economists define a market in terms of an individual product or factor of production because they are primarily interested in the exchanges of particular products and factors between buyers and sellers. Nonetheless, geography can create distinct local markets for otherwise identical products or factors of production because of the transportation costs between different regions of the country.

A blue-collar construction worker in Miami is in a market distinct from that of a blue-collar construction worker in Atlanta because it is costly to transport workers between the two cities. A construction worker in Miami cannot replace a construction worker in Atlanta, even if the workers have identical abilities and are performing the same tasks. Cement is bought and sold nationwide, but the exchanges occur in numerous distinct local markets, again because of the high costs of transporting cement over long distances.

At the other extreme, the markets for a large number of financial securities are virtually worldwide, with exchanges occurring 24 hours a day. National boundaries create no important transaction costs for electronic exchanges, and financial markets are always open in some time zones around the clock. Money managers can easily move funds from Tokyo to New York to London. Similarly, the markets for ever more manufactured products are becoming international in scope, as large multinational corporations set up offices and factories throughout the world. For example, there may no longer be a separate U.S. market for automobiles, given that nearly 40 percent of all new cars sold in the United States are produced by foreign firms. Some of the foreign auto makers operate factories in the United States. At the same time, Chrysler, General Motors, and Ford each produce cars in Europe. In sum, the geographic dimension makes it difficult to determine the proper extent of a market from an economic perspective, that is, the numbers of buyers and sellers to include when analyzing a market.

These difficulties notwithstanding, defining and analyzing individual product and factor markets is a useful way to understand how a market economy operates. We will analyze individual markets throughout the text on the assumption that the markets are well defined, and in many cases they are reasonably well defined.

REFLECTION: How would you describe
the institutional arrangements of the
market that brought you to your college or
university? Is this market national or
international in scope?

CHARACTERISTICS OF MODERN MARKET ECONOMIES

Analyzing the behavior of prices is a central focus of economics because markets function by means of prices. Economists think about prices somewhat differently than most people do. Whenever people stop to think about prices, their typical concern is that prices are too high or too low, for instance, that their salaries are too low or that the price of medical care is too high. Economists also describe instances in which prices can be said to be too high or too low. But their main interest in prices is how they process economic information and coordinate economic decisions. The fundamental economic question about market exchange is this: How do prices coordinate market exchanges and thereby allocate society's scarce resources?

Why are market exchanges orderly rather than chaotic, and why are markets such an effective mechanism for promoting economic efficiency? The answers must lie in how prices work. We have seen that individuals and business firms enter into market exchanges with completely different economic problems: They have different objectives, different alternatives, and different constraints. They share only one piece of information in common, the price to be paid for a good or service or a factor of production. Therefore, prices act as the signals that bring buyers and sellers together, and they must incorporate all the economic information that is necessary for exchange to take place. As such, prices bear the burden of making a market economy function smoothly and efficiently—nothing else can do this. Markets and prices are so closely tied together that a market economy is sometimes referred to interchangeably as a price system.

Subsequent chapters will describe how prices coordinate market exchanges in various market settings. In this introductory chapter we simply want to gain an appreciation for the enormous amount of work that prices are required to do in a modern, highly developed market economy such as that of the United States.

Three characteristics of the modern market economy place special burdens on prices. The first is that production is highly specialized. Specialization in production separates economic agents from one another and increases the number of market exchanges they must engage in. The second is that market exchanges do not occur in isolation. An economy is essentially a giant closed circle in which all markets are necessarily interrelated. As a result, prices must do more than bring buyers and sellers together in each individual market. The smooth and efficient functioning of a market economy requires that prices in different interrelated markets bear particular relationships to one another. The third characteristic is simply the sheer size and diversity of a developed market economy. Prices have to coordinate a huge number and variety of exchanges. Let's take a look at each of these characteristics.

Specialization

Each of us consumes a wide variety of goods and services. But we are typically involved in the production of only a very few goods and services, perhaps only one, or perhaps none at all. Indeed, most of us have no idea how to produce many of the products that we consume. This disparity between consumption and production is true in all but the most primitive economies. As economies develop, people become generalists in consumption and specialists in production.

Specialization in production and economic development go hand in hand: Neither can proceed without the other. Once an economy begins to grow and business firms become larger, factors of production tend to become ever more specialized, performing highly specific tasks associated with only one small part of the production process. The process of specialization is called the **division of labor,** but it applies to capital as well. Workers performing specific tasks use capital that is also designed just for those tasks. The automobile assembly line is a classic example. One worker bolts the right-hand side of the engine block to the chassis. Farther down the line another worker mounts the left front tire, and all the workers along the assembly line have their own sets of tools and machines.

The division of labor is profitable because it generates a phenomenon called **economies of scale,** which describes the relationship between the cost of production and the output as the scale of an operation is increased. Economies of scale arise whenever production costs rise proportionally less than output as output increases, so that the costs of producing each individual unit of output fall. Once again the automobile assembly line is a perfect example. Before Henry Ford introduced the assembly line to automobile manufacturing, cars were assembled in small garages by a few mechanics performing a large number of different tasks. Ford discovered that he could produce cars much more cheaply if they were manufactured in huge quantities on a highly specialized assembly line. The largest assembly lines today produce hundreds of thousands of cars each year.

The division of labor and resulting economies of scale in turn promote further economic growth. With lower unit costs, firms can sell their products at lower prices, which encourages people to buy more of the products. As firms sell more output, they employ more factors of production and generate more income that can be used to buy even more products. The economy develops and creates new possibilities for cost-cutting economies of scale through ever greater division of labor. With still greater specialization comes further economic growth, and the interaction of specialization and economic growth continues onward. At the level of the firm the process of specialization and economic growth culminates in the giant corporation, in which production occurs on a massive scale and uses large amounts of sophisticated capital. All functions within the corporation, including production, marketing, finance, and management, are highly specialized.

With specialization comes separation of consumers and producers. People have to engage in market exchanges with producers for almost all the goods and services that they consume. Separation also occurs within production. More and more firms produce intermediate, semi-finished products, which they sell to other firms for further processing in a hierarchical chain of production. This necessitates the development of still other markets to facilitate exchanges between the firms. Market exchanges, and prices, become ever more important to the operation of the economy as it continues to grow.

DIVISION OF LABOR

As an economy grows and as business firms become larger, the process by which factors of production tend to become ever more specialized, performing highly specific tasks associated with only one small part of the production process.

ECONOMIES OF SCALE

A characteristic of production in which production costs rise proportionately less than output as production increases, so that costs per unit of output fall.

HISTORICAL NOTE: In the early 1900s Henry Ford ran ads claiming that his cars were cheaper to purchase and maintain than good ol' Dobbin the horse.

The use of money, such as dollar bills and checks written against checking accounts, is an essential ingredient of the process of specialization and economic growth. This is why all but the most primitive societies use money to facilitate exchange. Without money all exchanges would be **barter** arrangements in which goods exchange directly for other goods. Two people would only engage in exchange if they each had something that the other wanted. For instance, economists who want new suits would have to find tailors who want economic advice; both are likely to go wanting. Barter is no longer necessary with the use of money. Economists can offer economic advice to people who want it, accept money in return, and exchange the money for suits. Tailors will accept the money, knowing that they, too, can exchange it for the things they want. So the use of money permits the specialization and the separation required for economic growth. At the same time the use of money requires the existence of prices so that people know how much money they must exchange for any good or service.

BARTER

An exchange of goods directly for other goods.

INTERNATIONAL SPECIALIZATION AND TRADE: THE PRINCIPLE OF COMPARATIVE ADVANTAGE

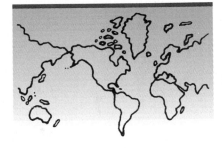

The gains from the division of labor and specialization in production extend well beyond national borders. Entire nations can gain by specializing their production in some goods and trading them for the goods that other nations specialize in producing. Moreover, a nation does not necessarily have to be the best at producing anything to benefit from international trade. The gains from specialization and international trade result from differences among nations in their opportunity costs of producing goods and services, and not necessarily from any absolute productivity advantages they may have.

David Ricardo, a London stockbroker who dabbled in economics and became the leading English economist of the early 1800s, was the first to demonstrate the potential gains from international trade on the basis of differences in opportunity costs. He was a staunch advocate of international trade among nations, and his argument in support of free trade became known as the principle of comparative advantage.

One country is said to have a **comparative advantage** over another in the production of a good if it can produce it with lower opportunity costs. Ricardo showed that two countries can *each* gain from trade if they specialize their production in the goods in which they have a comparative advantage and trade them for the goods in which they have a comparative disadvantage. Since every country is virtually certain to have a comparative advantage is something, specialization and international trade can benefit all countries.

The following simple example illustrates Ricardo's principle of comparative advantage. Suppose that the United States and England each use only labor to produce two goods, food (F) and clothing (C). In the United States 1 unit of labor can produce either 4 units of food or 3 units of clothing. In England 1 unit of labor can produce either 2 units of food or 2 units of clothing. The following summarizes the productivity of 1 unit of labor in each country:

COMPARATIVE ADVANTAGE

The principle that a country should specialize its production in those goods that it can produce with lower opportunity costs than can other countries and trade for those goods that other countries can produce with lower opportunity costs.

United States: 4F   3C
England: 2F   2C

Notice that labor in the United States is more productive than is labor in England in producing both goods; the United States has an absolute productivity advantage in both food and clothing. Nonetheless, both the United States and England can gain from specialization and trade because the opportunity costs of producing food and clothing differ in each country.

The opportunity costs of food. Producing 4 more units of food in the United States entails an opportunity cost of 3 units of clothing. Producing 4 more units of food in England entails an opportunity cost of 4 units of clothing. Therefore, the opportunity cost of producing food is lower in the United States than in England; the United States has a comparative advantage in producing food.

The opportunity costs of clothing. Producing 3 more units of clothing in the United States entails an opportunity cost of 4 units of food. Producing 3 more units of clothing in England entails an opportunity cost of only 3 units of food. Therefore, the opportunity cost of producing clothing is lower in England than in the United States; England has a comparative advantage in producing clothing.

Both countries can increase their consumption possibilities if the United States specializes in the production of food, England specializes in the production of clothing, and they trade U.S. food for English clothing. They both gain so long as they trade food for clothing somewhere between the ratios of 4F for 3C and 1F for 1C. Receiving more than 3C for 4F reduces the opportunity cost of clothing in the United States. At the same time, receiving more than 1F for 1C reduces the opportunity cost of food in England. The simultaneous reduction of opportunity costs is what allows both countries to increase their consumption possibilities through trade.

Here is one example illustrating the possibility of mutual gains through specialization and trade. Suppose that each country has 100 units of labor, and without trade they produce (and consume) the following:

- The United States allocates 55 units of labor to food and 45 units of labor to clothing, producing 220F and 135C (220 = 55 * 4; 135 = 45 * 3).
- England allocates 72 units of labor to food and 28 units of labor to clothing, producing 144F and 56C (144 = 72 * 2; 56 = 28 * 2).

The countries understand Ricardo's principle of comparative advantage, so they specialize and trade. The United States puts all its labor into food, producing 400F (400 = 100 * 4). England puts all its labor into clothing, producing 200C (200 = 100 * 2). They then trade 175 U.S. food units for 140 English clothing units, a trading ratio of 5F for 4C (175F/140C = 5F/4C). Thus, the trading ratio 5F for 4C is between the U.S. ratio of 4F for 3C and the English ratio of 1F for 1C, as required.

The United States consumes the remaining 225F (225F = 400F − 175F) and the 140C received in trade.

England consumes the 175F received in trade and the remaining 60C (60C = 200C − 140C).

Both countries have increased their consumption through specialization and trade:

United States: (225F, 140C) versus (220F, 135C)
England: (175F, 60C) versus (144F, 56C)

Ricardo's principle of comparative advantage is one of the more important principles in economics. It shows that *relative* cost advantages/disadvantages motivate people and countries to exchange goods and services. In our example the superior productivity of the United States does not prevent England from enjoying the benefits of exchange. The principle of comparative advantage is also a powerful argument against tariffs, quotas, and other means of "protecting" nations from foreign competition. Free trade, not protection from trade, increases a nation's economic well-being.

The Circular Flow of Economic Activity

The principle of interdependence that we described in Chapter 1 does not apply just to the economic problem. Interdependence is also a fundamental principle of market exchange. The entire economy of a nation is essentially a closed, interdependent circle along which all markets are interrelated. This principle is fundamental to economics and will appear again and again throughout the text.

Recall that individuals and business firms each have two economic roles to play. Individuals purchase goods and services from firms and supply them with the three primary factors of production, labor, land, and the funds to buy capital. Business firms purchase the factors of production to produce the goods and services that they then sell to individuals. Hence, individuals and business firms meet each other twice—and in such a way as to create a closed circle.

The flow of goods and services and factors of production throughout the economy from their interactions is called the **circular flow of economic activity** and is illustrated by the **circular flow diagram** in Figure 4.1. At the top of the circle are the markets for goods and services, in which the individuals are the buyers and the business firms are the suppliers. At the bottom of the circle are the markets for the factors of production: labor, land, and capital. Here the roles are reversed; the individuals are the suppliers, and the business firms are the buyers. The reversal of roles in each set of markets makes the flow of economic activity circular. The solid inner line indicates the direction of the flow of physical, or real, quantities of goods, services, and factors (for example, physical units of labor supplied to firms in the labor markets and actual units of goods and services going from firms to consumers in the product markets). The dotted outer line indicates the flow of dollars in a market economy. Consumers offer dollars to firms in exchange for goods and services, and they receive dollars from firms in exchange for their factors of production. The total dollar value of the flow of activity in the product markets defines the **national product** of a country. Similarly, the total dollar value of the flow of activity through the factor markets defines the **national income** of a country.

CIRCULAR FLOW OF ECONOMIC ACTIVITY

The flow of goods and services and factors of production through the product and the factor markets of the economy that results from the interactions of individuals and business firms; the flow is circular because firms sell products to individuals in the product markets and individuals sell factors of production to firms in the factor markets.

CIRCULAR FLOW DIAGRAM

A graphical representation of the circular flow of economic activity through the nation's product and factor markets.

NATIONAL PRODUCT

The total dollar value of the flow of economic activity through the product markets of a nation.

NATIONAL INCOME

The total dollar value of the flow of economic activity through the factor markets of a nation.

FIGURE 4.1

The Circular Flow of Economic Activity

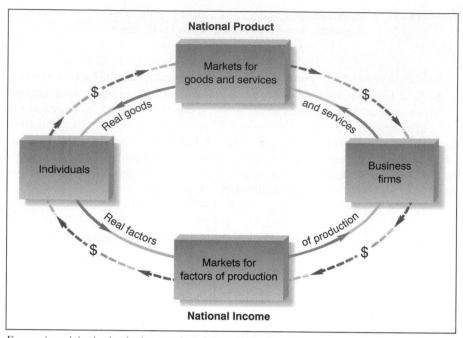

Economic activity is circular because individuals and business firms meet each other twice, in the markets for goods and services and in the factor markets, with their roles reversed. In the markets for goods and services, individuals are the buyers and the business firms are the suppliers. In the factor markets, individuals are the suppliers and the business firms are the buyers. The inner circle shows the flow of real goods and services and factors of production through the two sets of markets. The outer circle shows the flow of dollars through the two sets of markets. The government plays both roles of consumer and producer. The only breaks in the circular flow of economic activity are the exports to other countries and the imports from other countries.

IMPORTS

Goods and services, and factors of production, purchased from foreign individuals and business firms for domestic use.

EXPORTS

Domestically produced goods and services, and factors of production, sold to foreign individuals, businesses, and governments.

Figure 4.1 appears to ignore a key player in the economy, the government. Where do the national, state, and local governments fit into the circular flow of economic activity? The answer is that governments play both roles of buyer and supplier. When the Department of Defense orders military aircraft from Boeing to provide for the national security, the government is acting as a consumer on behalf of the citizens. When the national government delivers our mail and hires men and women to operate military bases or when local governments educate our children, these governments are acting as business firms, producing public goods and services on behalf of the citizens. So the presence of governments does not change the nature of the circular flow of economic activity.

There is only one exception to the concept of an economy as a giant, closed circle, the imports from and exports to foreign countries. Individuals, businesses, and governments purchase some of their goods and services and factors of production from foreign individuals and business firms. These purchases are **imports** from foreign countries. Similarly, individuals, businesses, and governments in foreign countries purchase goods and services and factors of production from domestic individuals and business firms. These purchases are **exports** to other countries. Because imported goods and services are not produced domestically, they represent a flow through the product markets for which there is no corresponding flow through the domestic factor markets. Imports appear as part of the flow of national income through other countries' factor markets. Similarly, when firms produce goods for export, they increase individuals' incomes because they purchase domestic factors of production to produce the goods. But the corresponding purchases of the exports appear as part of the flow of national product through other countries' product markets. Notice, though, that the circular flow of economic activity is maintained for the world's economy taken as a whole. The total amount of imports from other countries worldwide must equal the total amount of exports to other countries worldwide.

Imports and exports are important for virtually all countries, but thinking about economic activity as a circular flow is often a reasonable approximation. For most countries the value of imports approximately equals the value of exports, which means that the dollar values of domestic national product and national income are equal as well. The United States is an exception to this rule. Recently, U.S. imports have exceeded exports by a wide margin. Even so, the difference between U.S. imports and U.S. exports has only been about 1 percent of national product in recent years, so that the notion of the U.S. economy as a closed circle is not too far wide of the mark.

Interdependence of Economic Events

Markets are naturally interrelated because the flow of economic activity is circular. The effects of an important economic event always spread beyond the immediate impact of the event.

For instance, OPEC (Organization of Petroleum Exporting Countries) lost its control over the price of oil in the early 1980s, with the result that the price of a barrel of crude oil plummeted from $34 in 1981 to $10 by mid-decade. The market for oil felt the immediate consequence of the oil price decrease. On the one hand, factors of production associated with the oil industry suffered. People who worked in the oil industry either lost their jobs or were forced to take cuts in pay, and the returns to capital and land in the oil industry also declined. On the other hand, consumers of oil and oil-related products gained because of the price cuts.

The consequences spread far beyond the market for oil, however. States such as Texas that rely heavily on the income from oil suffered widespread economic losses. Because many of the citizens of Texas had less income, they could not spend as much as before on goods and services. Retailers soon felt the pinch as their businesses suffered. The real estate market also collapsed as more people were unable to afford houses and businesses did not need as much office and factory space, given their declining sales. As business suffered generally, people who had no direct connection with the oil industry also lost their jobs or received lower incomes, which contributed even further to the downward spiraling of the Texas economy. What started as a collapse in one market spread quickly throughout the entire Texas economy.

The experience was just the opposite in Massachusetts, an oil-consuming state. The Massachusetts economy was booming throughout the 1980s. The decline in the price of oil certainly helped to sustain the boom, as both consumers and businesses were able to buy fuel at lower prices. Massachusetts consumers could spend more of their incomes on other goods and services.

The oil price decrease had still further implications. One of the more notable was the comeback of the larger, heavier luxury automobiles. Large, gas-guzzling cars had fallen out of favor in the 1970s following oil price increases that were just as dramatic as the oil price declines of the 1980s.

The repercussions of major economic events are virtually endless as they work their way through the circular flow of activity. This must be so because as market events cause different people to have different incomes or cause different goods to be more or less expensive, people want to buy different kinds and amounts of goods and services. Businesses adjust their production accordingly to meet the new demands, which causes prices and incomes to adjust again, leading to still further changes in demands and in production. Prices and incomes continue to change indefinitely. These interdependent repercussions are part of what makes economic events so interesting—and often quite unpredictable.

The Size and Diversity of Modern Economies

The process of specialization and economic growth culminates in the modern, highly developed market economy such as that of the United States. Modern economies generate vast amounts of economic information, and innumerable economic decisions must be coordinated. Furthermore, modern economies are forever changing—they move through periods of expansion and contraction; new technologies and new products appear, while old technologies and old products disappear; clever new arrangements for exchanging goods and services evolve over time; and so on, endlessly. Prices must continually update economic information, and markets must be flexible enough to accommodate ever more and different kinds of economic decisions.

How many markets are there in the United States? No one knows. The annual Census of Manufacturers undertaken by the U.S. Department of Commerce identifies approximately 11,000 products within the manufacturing sector alone. But 11,000 far understates the number of manufactured goods that consumers would identify as distinct products. For example, under the product class "grape wines" the census lists only three products: red wine, white wine, and rose wine. Ernest and Julio Gallo would certainly hope that consumers distinguish between their varietal red jug wines and their limited reserve Zinfandels, and, of course, consumers do. How many service markets are there? How many markets for factors of production? So far as we know, no one has ever tried to count either of them.

THE U.S. ECONOMY

The U.S. economy provides a good example of the enormous size and diversity of modern developed market economies and of how much modern economies change over time. Let's look briefly at some of its highlights. This will give us some useful background information for our study of how markets operate in the U.S. economy.[1]

Size and Diversity

Thinking about a $6 trillion economy becomes somewhat more manageable if it is divided into its four major subsectors suggested by the circular flow of economic activity: the household sector, the business sector, the government sector, and the rest-of-the world sector. Figure 4.2 indicates the relative importance of each sector as a user and a producer of the final goods and services that pass through the nation's product markets.

THE HOUSEHOLD SECTOR   The **household sector** consists of all individuals in their dual roles as consumers of final goods and services and as suppliers of factors of production to business firms. It is by far the largest user of the final goods and services produced by the economy, accounting for 69 percent of all purchases.

This sector derives its name from the fact that individuals are organized into residences, or households, consisting of one or more people. In fact, when a government or private agency collects data on individuals, it often surveys by residence, so that many economic data are available only for households or families, not for individuals. (A family refers to related individuals, whereas a household may consist of unrelated individuals.) Grouping data by household or family is entirely appropriate, however, if the household or family is the relevant decision-making unit.

No matter how they are counted, an enormous number of decision-making units comprise the household sector. In 1992 the total population of the United States was 255.4 million people. In 1990, when the population was 251.4 million, they were organized into 94.3 million households, of which 66.3 million were family households and 65 million consisted of a single person.

INCOME   People earn income primarily through their labor. Approximately 80 percent of all income received in factor markets is wage and salary income. In 1992, 66.3 percent of all people aged 16 and older were in the civilian (nonmilitary) labor force, meaning that a total of 127 million people were working

HOUSEHOLD SECTOR

The sector of the economy that consists of individuals in their dual roles as consumers of final goods and services and as suppliers of factors of production to business firms.

---

[1]The data in this section come from three sets of sources that economists keep close at hand for information on the U.S. economy:

1. *The Economic Report of the President* (annual), prepared by the President's Council of Economic Advisers. The place to start, it includes data on all sectors of the economy. Also *Economic Indicators*, a monthly.
2. Three publications of the U.S. Department of Commerce:
   a. *The Statistical Abstract of the United States* (annual). The next place to turn, it is a compendium of economic, social, and demographic data.
   b. *Current Population Reports, Series P 60, Consumer Income* (approximately annual). A number of reports with detailed data on earnings and poverty are issued each year.
   c. The *Survey of Current Business*. Contains voluminous monthly data on the U.S. economy.
3. Two publications of the Board of Governors of the Federal Reserve Banking System, the nation's central bank:
   a. *Balance Sheets for the U.S. Economy (Publication C.9)* (annual). This publication provides data on U.S. wealth holdings, including capital and land.
   b. *Flow of Funds Accounts (Publication Z1)* (quarterly). This publication traces the flow of funds through the nation's financial markets.

FIGURE 4.2

The Composition of Final Output by Sector in the United States in 1992.

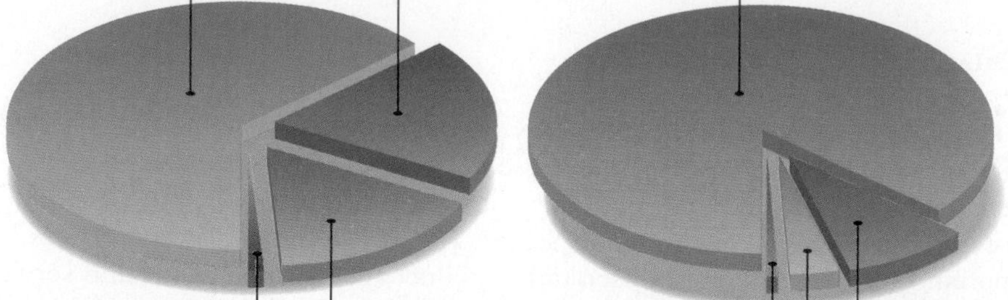

a. Purchases of Final Output by Sector   b. Production of Final Output by Sector

The pie-charts show the purchases and production of final output in the United States during 1992, by each of the four sectors of the economy—the household sector, the business sector, the government sector, and the rest-of-world (foreign) sector. The household sector is by far the largest purchaser of goods and services and the business sector is by far the largest producer of goods and services.

or actively seeking employment. That year 75.6 percent of all males and 57.8 percent of all females were in the labor force. Most of the remaining income represents income from saving, to be discussed below.

Not all the income received by households in the factor markets is available for their own consumption and saving. For instance, some income is taken by governments through taxation. Households consume the vast majority of income that is available to them, between 90 and 95 percent in most years. The remaining 5 to 10 percent of available income is saved.

CONSUMPTION Economists distinguish three kinds of consumer goods and services: consumer durables, consumer nondurables, and services. **Consumer durables** are manufactured goods that typically last more than one year, primarily motor vehicles, furniture, and household appliances. In 1992 they represented 12 percent of all consumption expenditures. **Consumer nondurables** are the remaining manufactured goods and include such items as food, clothing, gasoline, and heating fuels. They accounted for 31 percent of total consumption in 1992. The purchase of **services,** as from plumbers and electricians, airlines and rental car companies, and physicians and hospitals, accounted for the majority of consumer expenditures, 57 percent of total consumption in 1992.

SAVING AND WEALTH The act of saving is a decision to postpone consumption to some future date. Households hope to earn a return on their savings that will allow them to consume more goods and services in the future than they have sacrificed by not consuming today. Saving occurs in one of two forms. Households can purchase real, or tangible, assets such as a home or a parcel of land. They can also purchase financial assets such as corporate stocks and bonds, insurance of various kinds, pensions that will provide an income during retirement, and a variety of bank accounts and deposits. A household's **wealth,**

CONSUMER DURABLES

Manufactured goods that typically last more than one year.

CONSUMER NONDURABLES

Manufactured goods that typically last less than one year.

SERVICES

Purchases by consumers that are not manufactured, but that provide them with something useful.

WEALTH

For a household, the accumulation of all savings over time; also called *net worth.*

REFLECTION: Would you say that your own pattern of consumption during the past year was roughly in line with the national average: 12 percent consumer durables, 31 percent nondurables, and 57 percent services?

or net worth, is the accumulation of all its saving over time. Despite fairly low savings rates, U.S. households have accumulated on enormous amount of wealth. In 1992 the net worth of the United States totaled $17.7 trillion, an average net worth of $69,000 per person.

THE BUSINESS SECTOR   The **business sector** consists of all the private business firms. In 1988, the last year for which data are available, there were 18.9 million business firms in the United States (excluding over 2 million farms). The business sector is the major producer of final goods and services in the United States, accounting for over 87 percent of total production in 1992.

Business firms are distinguished by their size, their legal structure, and the kinds of products they produce.

FIRM SIZE   Most businesses in the United States are small businesses. In 1988, 78.8 percent of the 18.9 million firms had total receipts of less than $100,000. A relatively few large firms dominate in terms of value goods and services produced, however. Only 3.8 percent of the firms, about 730,000, had receipts greater than $1 million, but these firms accounted for 88.4 percent of total business receipts in 1988.

LEGAL STRUCTURE   Nearly all businesses in the United States are structured as single proprietorships, partnerships, or corporations. Table 4.1 shows the percentage of firms that have each kind of legal structure.

The **single proprietorship** is the simplest form of business. It has a single owner, or proprietor, who has complete freedom to transfer funds into and out of the business and total control over the operation of the business. Proprietorships are often service-oriented, individual- or family-run businesses such as family restaurants, neighborhood variety stores, carpenters, and dry cleaners. The proprietorship structure is appropriate only for relatively small businesses, since it is limited by the owner's ability to raise funds. Also, proprietorships are quite risky, since the business's assets are not legally distinct from the owner's personal assets. Therefore, owners must be prepared to cover any business losses out of their personal wealth. As indicated in Table 4.1, although

BUSINESS SECTOR

The sector of an economy that consists of all the private business firms and is the major producer of final goods and services.

SINGLE PROPRIETORSHIP

A form of business in which a single owner has total control over the operation of the business and has complete freedom to transfer funds into and out of the business.

TABLE 4.1   Comparison of U.S. Business Firms by Legal Type of Organization, 1988

TYPE OF FIRM	NUMBER OF FIRMS (THOUSANDS) (PERCENTAGE OF TOTAL)	VALUE OF RECEIPTS (MILLIONS) (PERCENTAGE OF TOTAL)
Proprietorships	13,679 (72.4)	$672 (6.1)
Partnerships	1,654 (8.8)	464 (4.2)
Corporations	3,563 (18.8)	9,804 (89.6)
Totals	18,896	10,940

SOURCE: U.S. Department of Commerce, Bureau of the Census, *Statistical Abstract of the United States, 1992* (Washington, D.C.: U.S. Government Printing Office, 1993).

most businesses are proprietorships, they generate only a small percentage of total business receipts.

A **partnership** is the next step up in complexity. It has two or more owners, or partners, who jointly determine how to transfer funds into and out of the business and who have total control over the operation of the business. Law firms and investment banks are commonly organized as partnerships. Overall, though, relatively few business firms are structured as partnerships, and they generate an even smaller percentage of total business receipts. Partnerships suffer the same two handicaps that proprietorships do as a legal structure suitable for large businesses. The partners' ability to raise funds is somewhat limited, and their own personal wealth is at risk in the business.

Corporations generate the overwhelming percentage of total receipts, as indicated in Table 4.1. The dominance of corporations is hardly surprising because the principles underlying the corporate structure are virtually essential to the efficient operation of any large-scale enterprise over a long period of time. There are five main principles of incorporation: (1) The corporation is recognized as a legal entity distinct from the owners of the firm; (2) owners have the right to transfer their shares of stock, which are their certificates of ownership; (3) the owners (stockholders) may delegate authority and responsibility to a group of managers; (4) the corporation has a potentially unlimited life; and (5) corporations enjoy limited liability for business losses, meaning that the financial liability of the owners is limited to the assets of the corporation. It does not extend to their personal assets.

These five principles give the corporate structure many advantages over the other two forms of business structure. People can easily supply funds to a corporation by purchasing stock without becoming involved with the firm in any essential manner and without risking personal bankruptcy. If they wish, owners can easily sever their financial ties to the firm by selling their stock. Funds for capital can therefore be raised easily and in great quantities. Furthermore, the life of the corporation continues beyond the lives of any of its owners. The corporate structure permits the separation of ownership from management, so that the terms of ownership and the identities of the owners need not have any effect on the operation of the business.

The main disadvantage of the corporate structure is that U.S. tax laws recognize the corporation as a separate identity subject to its own set of taxes. As a result, income earned by corporations is taxed twice, first by corporation income taxes and then by personal income taxes when the owners receive income from the profits of the corporation. Without this tax treatment, many more businesses would be likely to incorporate.

TYPE OF PRODUCT The third characteristic that distinguishes business firms from one another is the type of product or service they produce. The U.S. Department of Commerce divides all final goods and services produced into 10 major product, or industry, subgroups. Table 4.2 lists each subgroup, along with the percentage of total final output accounted for by each in 1988. The business sector includes all product categories except agriculture, government and government enterprises, and rest-of-world.

The table suggests the diversity of the U.S. economy; no one industry is dominant. Agriculture, mining, construction, and rest-of-world are all relatively minor; each produces less than 5 percent of the total output. The other in-

PARTNERSHIP

A form of business with two or more owners who have total control over the operation of the business and who jointly determine how to transfer funds into and out of the business.

CORPORATION

A form of business that is a recognized legal entity distinct from the owners of the firm, allows owners to transfer their shares of stock, allows owners to delegate authority and responsibility to a group of managers, has a potentially unlimited life, and has limited liability for business losses.

TABLE 4.2   Production of U.S. Final Output by Major Industry Group, 1988

INDUSTRY	PERCENTAGE OF TOTAL
Agriculture	2.3%
Mining	3.2
Construction	4.4
Manufacturing	23.0
Transportation	9.7
Wholesale and Retail Trade	17.2
Finance, Insurance, Real Estate	14.5
Services	15.3
Government, Government Enterprises	10.5
Rest of World	1.0

NOTE: Totals add to slightly more than 100 percent because of rounding error.

SOURCE: *Economic Report of the President, 1991* (data series discontinued after the 1991 *Report*) (Washington, D.C.: U.S. Government Printing Office, February 1991).

dustries produce from 9.7 percent (transportation) to 23.0 percent (manufacturing) of total output.

A final point relates to the economists' traditional division of final output into goods and services. The two components are roughly equal, with services having a slight edge. In 1992, 46 percent of total U.S. output consisted of manufactured goods (including structures) and 54 percent consisted of services. The service component has been steadily increasing throughout the post–World War II period. Services were only about 40 percent of final output in 1950.

THE GOVERNMENT SECTOR   The **government sector** in the United States includes the economic activities of the federal government, the 50 state governments, and over 89,000 local governmental jurisdictions. These governments are significant purchasers and producers of final goods and services. In 1992 they accounted for about 19 percent of total purchases and over 11 percent of total production of final output. One-sixth of all workers are employed in the government sector.

When people refer to "the government," they usually mean the federal government. But the state and local governments are important components of the government sector as well. They are actually more important than the federal government as purchasers of final goods and services, and they are far more important as producers of final output. The federal government accounted for only 40 percent of all government purchases in 1992, and roughly 75 percent of these goods and services were purchased for defense or defense-related activities. No one category of expenditures is nearly so dominant at the state and local level. State and local governments purchase, and produce, a variety of public goods and services, including primary, secondary, and higher education; highways and public transportation; health and hospitals; and public safety. They produce 70 percent of all government output and account for 84 percent of all government employment. The state and local portion of the government sector clearly has a great impact on the daily lives of many U.S. citizens.

GOVERNMENT SECTOR

In the United States, the economic activities of the federal government, the state governments, and all local governments.

Although governments have the power to raise funds through taxation, government decision making is an integral part of the market system. With rare exceptions such as an occasional military draft, governments do not commandeer inputs for public production. They purchase factors of production in the marketplace and are therefore in direct competition with the business sector for these resources. Military personnel and teachers for local school systems must be paid a high enough wage to bid them away from alternative employment in the private sector. Similarly, governments purchase many goods and services from the private sector, including military hardware and supplies of all types. As with employees, the prices for these goods and services must be high enough to make it profitable for firms to sell to the government. In competing with the business sector for goods and services and for factors of production, the governments add to the information that must be processed and coordinated by the market economy.

The data on government purchases and production in Figure 4.2 significantly understate the overall impact of the federal, state, and local governments on the U.S. economy. Government spending far exceeds government purchases of final output. In 1992 government expenditures totaled $2.1 trillion, whereas government spending on goods and services and on factors of production was only $1.1 trillion. The difference, approximately $1 trillion, was **transfer payments.** Unlike government expenditures on goods and services, transfer payments do not use up scarce resources. A government transfer payment is simply a transfer of existing income to another economic agent. Therefore, transfer payments are not included as part of the purchases or production of the government sector.

TRANSFER PAYMENT

The redistribution of existing income from one economic agent to another.

Transfer payments fall into one of three categories. The largest category is transfers to individuals as part of a legislated government program. These transfers are based on who the people are rather than on any services they have provided to the government. The two largest transfers to individuals are transfers to the aged under the Social Security System in the form of retirement pensions and medical insurance (Medicare) and transfers to individuals and families with low incomes through public assistance programs (Medicaid, Aid to Families with Dependent Children, Food Stamps, and numerous other programs). Interest payments on the government debt (discussed below) make up the second largest category of transfer payments. Grants-in-aid from one government to another comprise the third important category of transfer payments. Examples include federal transportation grants to states to help them pay for highway construction and maintenance and for public transit and state grants to their localities to help pay for local school systems. These transfers obviously have an important impact on many peoples' lives. In fact, in 1992 approximately two-thirds of the federal government's expenditures were transfer payments, and these federal transfer payments accounted for almost 90 percent of all government transfer payments.

A final characteristic of the government sector to consider is taxes. Governments collect an enormous amount of revenue, just over $1.8 trillion in 1992. The federal government relies primarily on a personal income tax and a payroll tax on wage income that is earmarked for the Social Security System. Sales taxes and personal income taxes are the chief revenue raisers at the state level, and the property tax is the most important source of tax revenue for local governments.

The revenues from all these taxes have not been sufficient to cover government expenditures in recent years. Recall that government expenditures were $2.1 trillion in 1992, nearly $300 billion more than tax revenues. When expenditures exceed revenues, government budgets are in **deficit** and governments finance their deficits by borrowing from the other sectors. The federal government was responsible for the revenue shortfall in 1992. It ran a $298 billion deficit, while the state and local governments ran a $16 billion **surplus** of revenues over expenditures. This has been typical of most years since 1981, when the federal government began to run annual deficits at levels unprecedented in U.S. history during times of peace. The federal debt was just under $1 trillion in 1980; by 1990 the federal debt exceeded $3.2 trillion, and by 1993 it exceeded $4 trillion. The continuing federal budget deficits are one of the leading economic issues of the 1990s, and reducing these deficits is one of President Clinton's top priorities.

BUDGET DEFICIT

A situation in which a government's expenditures exceed its revenues.

BUDGET SURPLUS

A situation in which a government's revenues exceed its expenditures.

THE REST-OF-WORLD SECTOR   The **rest-of-world sector** summarizes a nation's economic relationships with other countries. The purchase of final output by the rest-of-world sector is the difference between a nation's exports to other countries and its imports from other countries. This difference vastly understates the extent of a nation's international economic relationships, however. For example, the data in Figure 4.2 appear to suggest that economic relations with other countries are unimportant for the United States, but this is simply not true. The United States is an integral part of the world economy; U.S. exports and imports are each very important to the United States and to many other nations, and the United States has a major influence on capital markets throughout the world.

REST-OF-WORLD SECTOR

The sector of an economy that consists of a country's economic relations with foreign countries.

In 1992, 11 percent of all final goods and services purchased by the other three sectors were purchased as imports from other countries. Similarly, 11 percent of all final output produced that year was exported to other countries. The majority of U.S. exports and imports, 60 to 65 percent, are exchanged with the high-income capitalist countries such as Canada, Japan, and the Western European nations. Also, U.S. trade is concentrated in three product categories: industrial supplies and materials, capital goods, and automobiles. These three categories accounted for 74 percent of all exports and 68 percent of all imports in 1992. Trade in industrial and capital goods suggests that a substantial portion of U.S. trade consists of U.S. producers and foreign producers in the developed market countries exchanging factors of production with one another. The automobile trade is primarily with these same countries as well.

Only two other products are of any great significance in U.S. trade. The United States is the world's largest exporter of agricultural products. In 1992 agricultural products accounted for 9 percent of U.S. exports. The United States is also a major importer of petroleum and petroleum products. They accounted for 10 percent of all U.S. imports in 1992.

Today U.S. and foreign capital markets are also highly integrated, and funds for capital move easily across national borders. In 1992 U.S. asset holdings abroad totaled $2.2 trillion, of which $1.9 trillion were held by private U.S. citizens and businesses. Foreign asset holdings in the United States were even larger, $2.6 trillion, of which $2.2 trillion were held by foreign private citizens and businesses.

Thirty years ago domestic policy issues could safely be analyzed without paying much attention to international repercussions, but this is no longer true. Economic conditions in the United States have long had a significant impact on many other countries. The difference today is that economic conditions and policies in other countries now have a significant impact on the U.S. economy.

Changes in the U.S. Economy

The U.S. economy is hardly a static entity; it changes continually, sometimes even dramatically. The changes throughout the economy greatly increase the amount of information that prices must process and coordinate if they are to allocate resources properly. Here is a brief sampling of the more important changes over the past 40 to 50 years.

ECONOMIC CHANGES   Economic growth has been the rule rather than the exception for the United States throughout its history, and the same has been true in the last half of the twentieth century. The circular flow of real goods and services through U.S. markets increased in every decade since 1950. As a result, the flow of real goods and services was roughly 3.5 times larger in 1992 than in 1950, which generated a significant increase in overall economic well-being. Consumption per person of goods and services more than doubled, despite a 66 percent increase in the U.S. population.

The leading growth sectors in the period from 1950 to 1992 were the government and rest-of-world sectors. Government expenditures on final goods and services increased by 260 percent, and transfer payments increased by 840 percent (correcting for price changes). The growth in exports and imports was even more dramatic. Exports grew by 1100 percent and imports by 1240 percent, which underscores the substantial internationalization of the U.S. economy since World War II.

Economic growth is never constant in market economies. At times the economy is booming, and the circular flow of economic activity grows vigorously; at other times the economy is mired in a recession, and the circular flow of economic activity actually declines. For example, the U.S. economy grew at an average rate of 3.1 percent per year from 1950 to 1992. But the actual annual rates of growth varied considerably during this period, from a high of 10.3 percent in 1951 to a low of -2.5 percent in 1982. Why market economies experience periods of boom and bust is one of the outstanding puzzles in macroeconomics.

A final indication of the amount of economic change in the U.S. economy relates to the business sector. Each year large numbers of new firms come into being, while others fail and pass from the scene. In 1990, for example, Dun and Bradstreet estimated that there were 647,000 new incorporations and 60,432 business failures. These numbers are typical of recent years.

DEMOGRAPHIC CHANGES   The United States has undergone tremendous demographic changes since World War II. Significant demographic changes always have important economic consequences.

There was an unprecedented baby boom that lasted from 1947 through 1964, followed by an equally unprecedented baby bust from 1965 through the 1970s. Consequently, during the first half of the post-World War II period the average age of the population declined, and the proportion of youth swelled, despite continuing increases in the life expectancy of elder Americans. Since 1970, however, the population has been aging, and it will continue to age well into the twenty-first century. In 1970, 38 percent of the population was 20 and under, and 9.8 percent was 65 and older. By 1990 the percentage of youth declined to 28.8 percent, while the percentage of elderly rose to 12.4 percent. The average age of the population has increased by more than four years since 1970.

Demographic changes of this magnitude have an enormous impact on the composition and productivity of the labor force, on savings behavior, on the type of goods and services demanded, and on government transfer programs such as public assistance and Social Security. In short, these changes have an impact on virtually every aspect of the economy. The aging of the population as it continues into the next century may well be the single most important determinant of how the U.S. economy will perform.

The work experiences of American women have changed radically since 1950. Recall that 57.8 percent of all women aged 16 and older were in the labor force in 1992. The percentage was 33.9 in 1950. Throughout this period record numbers of women began trading hours of work in the home for hours of work in the market. Meanwhile, men began moving out of the market and into the home. The percentage of men in the labor force has dropped by 10 points since 1950. The American stereotype of the traditional two-parent family—husband working, wife staying at home—has been a myth for some time now.

Entry into the labor force has not been easy for women. They have had difficulty obtaining good, high-paying jobs, and they still shoulder most of the responsibility for managing the household. The economic status of working women is one of the leading concerns in the United States today.

Along with the increase in women working, the number of female-head-of-family households with no male present has increase substantially, especially among blacks. From 1970 to 1990 the number of such families grew from 7.2 percent to 17 percent of all families. For black families the percentages increased from 21.8 percent to 45.9 percent. Single-parent families headed by females are particularly vulnerable to poverty. They are three to four times more likely to be impoverished than are two-parent families.

The number of single-person households has increased even more dramatically—from 13.1 percent of all households in 1960 to 25 percent of all households by 1990. If the household is the relevant decision-making unit, then the number of such units in the household sector has been increasing much more rapidly than the growth in population would suggest.

The U.S. population is becoming ever more urbanized and concentrated. The percentage of the population living in urban areas increased from 69.9 percent in 1960 to 77.5 percent in 1990. The decline in the farming population has been especially dramatic. One of every eight workers was employed in agriculture in 1950. The ratio had declined to 1 in 40 workers by 1992. The influx of population to the cities has created some very difficult social and economic problems. Most of the nation's major cities are suffering from a lack of affordable housing, high crime rates, severely strained social services, deteriorating public school systems, and dangerously high levels of pollution.

Our survey of the economy concludes with two themes that have long been at the forefront of U.S. economic policy concerns: the concentration of wealth and power, and economic discrimination against nonwhites and women.

Concentrations of Income, Wealth, and Power

Many people worry that concentrations of income, wealth, and power in the U.S. economy undermine equality of economic opportunity. There is evidence of significant concentration in both the household and the business sectors. Income is highly concentrated: Over 46 percent of all income is earned by 20 percent of the families. Wealth is even more concentrated. According to the federal government's 1983 survey of wealth, 72 percent of all the nation's wealth is held by 10 percent of the nation's families. The richest 0.5 percent of families holds 35 percent of all wealth.

Within the business sector, the largest 100 corporations accounted for 75 percent of total manufacturing assets in 1991. The largest of these corporations are truly enormous. In 1982 Exxon's sales exceeded the total production of final goods and services of all but 19 *nations*.

To what extent do size and wealth confer unfair advantages in the marketplace and in the political arena? Should the government attempt to break down concentrations of income and wealth? Americans have struggled with these questions throughout the twentieth century.

Economic Discrimination

Racial and sexual discrimination appear to be serious problems in the United States, perhaps more so than in any of the other high-income market economies. A brief look at the data certainly suggests that nonwhites and whites, and men and women, have very different economic opportunities.

Whites fare much better economically than do blacks. For example, in 1990:

MEDIAN INCOME

The income of the family in the middle of the income distribution (half the families have incomes higher than the median and half have incomes lower than the median).

■ The median income of white families was $36,915; the median income of black families was $21,423, only 58 percent of white family income. (The **median income** is the income of the family in the middle of the income distribution. Half of the families have incomes higher than the median income, and half of the families have incomes lower than the median income.)

■ Only 10.7 percent of all whites lived in poverty compared with 31.9 percent of all blacks.

■ The unemployment rate for whites was 4.7 percent; the black unemployment rate was 11.3 percent.

■ Of all white families, 68.2 percent owned their own homes; only 43.4 percent of black families owned their homes.

■ Of white children 18 years old and younger, 79 percent lived with both parents, and 17 percent lived with their mother only; 38 percent of black children lived with both parents, and 51 percent lived with their mother only.

Women who work fare much worse than do men in the labor market. In 1990, for example:

- Women earned two-thirds as much as men, on average, a ratio that has not changed much since 1939. As one consequence of their lower wages, women are more vulnerable to poverty than are men.
- The average earnings of female *college* graduates were less than the average earnings of male *high school* graduates.
- Of all women who work, 70 percent were nurses and health technicians, elementary and secondary school teachers, retail sales clerks, clerical workers, apparel and textile workers, or service workers.
- To make matters worse, when both husband and wife work, the wife bore two-thirds of the responsibility for the household chores on average.

Not all of the economic differences between nonwhites and whites, and between men and women, are due to discrimination. Other factors such as differences in educational background and job experience partially explain these differences. Economic research has left little doubt, however, that economic discrimination against nonwhites and women is partly responsible for their economic disadvantages. The only area of disagreement among economists is what proportion of their disadvantages is due to discrimination.

Looking Ahead

Having completed our overview of the U.S. economy in these first few chapters, we are now prepared to see how markets operate in the United States. We will make our first pass at understanding market exchanges. The pages just ahead describe how markets function when they are highly competitive and operate according to the Laws of Supply and Demand.

SUMMARY

Chapter 4 began by discussing the nature of markets in a highly developed market economy.

1. A market is an institutional arrangement that permits the voluntary exchange of goods and services and factors of production between buyers and sellers.
2. Markets take on many different forms because market exchanges occur in many different institutional settings. Markets also have distinct product and geographic dimensions. Economists define markets by product or factor of production. A market for a single product becomes more distinct the fewer substitutes the product has in consumption and the less easily firms can switch their production from the product to another product. The transaction costs of engaging in exchange help determine the geographic extent of a market, from local to worldwide.

Markets function by means of prices. The second section of Chapter 4 discussed three characteristics of highly developed market economies that place a special burden on the work that prices have to perform: specialization in production, the circular flow of economic activity, and the size and diversity of modern market economies.

3. As an economy grows, firms engage in a division of labor in which factors of production are assigned ever more specialized tasks. The division of labor is profitable because it generates economies of scale, which lower the costs of producing each unit of output as the business expands. Lower costs and lower prices encourage more expansion and growth, which in turn lead to even more specialization and further economies of scale. Growth and specialization go hand in hand and are made possible by the use of money. Without money, all market exchanges would have to be barter arrangements. The number of market exchanges increases with the degree of specialization and economic growth.

4. Entire nations can gain from specialization and international trade by following Ricardo's principle of comparative advantage, which is based on differences among nations in the opportunity costs of production. Two countries can *each* gain from trade if they specialize their production in the goods in which they have a comparative advantage and trade them for the goods in which they have a comparative disadvantage. Since every country is virtually certain to have a comparative advantage in something, specialization and international trade can benefit all countries.

5. Individuals and business firms meet each other twice, in both the product and the factor markets. Individuals supply firms with factors of production and buy the products that firms produce. Firms buy the factors of production and use them to produce the products that they sell to consumers. The result of their interactions is a circular flow of economic activity through the product and the factor markets. Governments act as both consumers and producers of goods and services. The only exceptions to the circular flow are exports to other countries and imports from other countries. Because economic activity is circular, all markets are interrelated.

6. The final burden on prices is the sheer size and diversity of modern market economies. Prices have to coordinate billions of market exchanges in these economies.

The third section presented an overview of the U.S. economy, which emphasized the size and diversity of the economy and discussed some of the more important economic and demographic changes that have occurred since 1950.

7. The economies have four main subsectors: the household sector, the business sector, the government sector, and the rest-of-world sector. The household sector consists of individuals in their dual roles as consumers of goods and services and as suppliers of factors of production. The business sector consists of the more than 18 million private business firms in the United States. The government sector includes the economic activities of the federal government, the 50 state governments, and over 89,000 local governmental jurisdictions. The rest-of-world sector consists of the nation's economic relationships with other countries.

KEY TERMS

barter
business sector
circular flow of economic activity
comparative advantage

division of labor
economies of scale
government sector
household sector

industry
national income
national product
rest-of-world sector

QUESTIONS

1. State whether each of the following is a good or service. If the commodity is a good, state whether it is a durable or a nondurable good.
   a. Ford Taurus
   b. rare bottle of wine
   c. children's clothing
   d. four-bedroom house
   e. haircut
   f. Principles of Economics course
   g. toaster oven
2. a. List the principal characteristics of a corporation.
   b. What are the advantages and disadvantages of the corporate form of business?
   c. How does a corporation differ from a partnership? Give examples of each.
3. Group the following products by industry. (*Hint:* Products may belong to more than one group)
   a. wooden baseball bat
   b. tennis racquet
   c. two-person tent
   d. down parka
   e. fur coat
   f. Harley-Davidson motorcycle
   g. mountain bike
   h. Lincoln Town car
   i. Honda Accord
   j. catcher's mitt
4. Consider the following seven-person economy. The data are for 1994.

PERSON	INCOME	CONSUMPTION
1	$ 20,000	$ 19,000
2	18,000	18,000
3	45,000	43,000
4	5,000	5,000
5	70,000	53,000
6	30,000	20,000
7	150,000	145,000

   a. What is the median income in the economy?
   b. How much did each person add to net worth (wealth) during 1994?
5. Describe the circular flow of economic activity. What role do prices play in the circular flow?
6. a. List and discuss three characteristics of modern market economies.
   b. Discuss the roles that the four sectors of the economy play in modern market economies.
7. Define *national product* and *national income*. How do they differ?
8. List some of the economic areas in which the U.S. government is an active participant. What social objectives might the government be trying to fulfill in each of these areas?
9. Two countries, A and B, use only labor to produce food and clothing. In country A, 1 unit of labor can produce 2 units of food and 3 units of clothing. In country B, 1 unit of labor can produce 1 unit of food and 2 units of clothing.
   a. Which country has the comparative advantage in the production of food? Which country has the comparative advantage in the production of clothing?
   b. Suppose that each country has 100 workers. Without trade, A devotes 50 workers to the production of food and 50 workers to the production of clothing. Without trade, B devotes 80 workers to the production of food and 20 workers to the production of clothing. Show with an example how both countries can gain by specializing their production in one of the goods and trading for the other.
   c. How would your answer to part a change if, in country B, 1 unit of labor can produce 4 units of food and 6 units of clothing?

CASE

Growth Through International Trade

A number of the major oil exporting countries—Bahrain, Brunei, Kuwait, Libyan Arab Republic, Oman, Qatar, Saudi Arabia, and United Arab Emirates—are a decided exception to some of the general principles of economic growth discussed in Chapter 3. They have fairly limited production possibilities for most goods and services, yet their incomes per person are among the highest in the world. Moreover, they achieved their lofty positions relatively painlessly, with low opportunity costs. They were able to play the growth game by different rules because they are blessed with large supplies of oil, a natural resource in very great demand, and they were able to exploit this advantage through international trade. By trading oil for goods and services, these countries created a set of **consumption possibilities** that greatly exceeded their production possibilities. The result was instant riches and the possibility of relatively painless sustained economic growth. They played David Ricardo's principle of comparative advantage to the hilt.

Their strategy of growth through international trade is depicted in Figure CS1.1. The two goods this time are oil (horizontal axis) and all other goods and services (vertical axis). The production possibilities frontier, represented by the solid inner line, shows that these countries are particularly good at producing oil and not so good at producing all other goods and services. Without trade they would be forced to produce along their frontier at a point very close to the maximum of all other goods and services. They need very little oil for themselves and would simply do the best they could in producing everything else.

International trade offers them the opportunity of exporting oil and in return importing all other goods and services produced elsewhere. They *produce* mostly oil and relatively few of all other goods and services. The production point is represented by point B in Figure CS1.1, with oil production equal to $0B_1$ and all other production equal to $0B_2$. They still need very little oil for themselves—say, an amount equal to $0D_1$. The remainder, D_1B_1, is exported to other countries, which trade all other goods and services for the oil. In 1980, for example, oil production in Saudi Arabia was nearly 78 percent of total output produced, and over 95 percent of the oil produced was exported.

The price of oil on the world oil market determines how many of all other goods and services the oil-exporting coun-

FIGURE CS1.1
Growth Through Trade

The oil exporting countries produce at point B on their production possibilities frontier. They then trade D_1B_1 barrels of oil for B_2D_2 of all other goods and services that they are not so good at producing themselves. Trading oil for other goods and services allows them to expand their consumption possibilities far beyond their production possibilities; they consume at point D on their consumption possibilities frontier. The price of oil determines how many other goods and services they can receive in trade for their oil. Some of the other goods and services that they trade for are investment goods, which help them expand their production possibilities frontier over time.

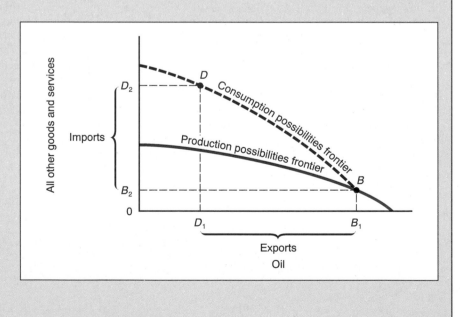

tries will be able to buy in exhange for their exported oil. Figure CS1.1 assumes that they can trade D_1B_1 of oil for B_2D_2 of all other goods and services. Hence, they end up *consuming* $0D_1$ of oil and $0D_2$ of all other goods and services, point D in the figure. D is a point on the **consumption possibilities frontier**, the dotted line in Fig. CS1.1, which shows how much oil and all other goods and services these countries are able to consume after trade has occurred. The consumption possibilities frontier pictured in the figure represents every consumption combination of oil and all other goods and services attainable by producing $0B_1$ of oil and trading increasing quantities of it for all other goods and services.

The ability to expand a nation's consumption possibilities beyond its production possibilities through international trade is available to all countries, although to a far lesser extent than is the case for the oil-exporting countries. It pays all countries to specialize their production in those things they produce relatively more effectively than others and to trade for those goods that other countries produce more effectively. For most countries, however, the constraints underlying their production possibilities are truly binding. International trade can expand consumption possibilities somewhat beyond the production possibilities frontier, but it cannot transform a poor country into a rich country by itself. The oil-exporting countries are truly exceptions in this respect.

Nevertheless, the oil-exporting countries have to increase their production possibilities if they hope to enjoy continued prosperity because the ability to trade oil for goods must eventually come to an end. The supply of oil is finite, and, in any event, new technologies will probably reduce the world's dependence on oil long before the supply of oil is exhausted.

Furthermore, instant riches do not produce a modern economy overnight. The oil-exporting countries will have to invest in both physical and human capital, just like all other developing nations, in order to increase their production possibilities. Their incomes may be high, but they still exhibit many of the same social and economic characteristics that the middle- and low-income developing countries do. For example, compare the following indicators of social well-being for Saudi Arabia with those of the United States in 1988 as estimated by the World Bank. The U.S. figures are in parentheses.

- Adult literacy: 51.1 percent (96 percent)
- Life expectancy: Male—62 (72); female—65 (79)
- Infant mortality per 1,000 births: 70 (10)

Achieving the U.S. social indicator rates will take the Saudis a generation or two, just as it would all developing countries.

The oil-exporting countries still have an enormous opportunity cost advantage over the other developing countries of the world, however, because they do not have to sacrifice nearly as much to achieve economic growth. By purchasing a mix of consumption and investment goods with their oil exports, they can build the capital base necessary for growth while enjoying a high level of consumption. The price of crude oil will determine how painless growth will be for them. The 1980s and 1990s have not been as kind in that regard as the 1970s were.

ECONOMIC ADVISOR'S REPORT

Suppose you are hired as an economic advisor to the government of Saudi Arabia. Answer the following questions.

1. The leaders ask you what Saudi Arabia should buy from other countries with its oil money. Would you advise the Saudis to buy only consumer goods, only capital goods, or a mixture of consumer goods and capital goods?
2. The leaders tell you that they would like to expand their country's production possibilities frontier to match their consumption possibilities frontier and to do this very rapidly, within five years. They ask you how they can do this. What would you say to them?

5

The Laws of Supply and Demand

LEARNING OBJECTIVES

CONCEPTS TO LEARN

The Laws of Supply and Demand

Market equilibrium

Factors that shift the demand and the supply curves

The elasticity of demand and supply

CONCEPTS TO RECALL

The consumer's and firm's three-part economic problems [1]

Opportunity cost [1]

The margin in economic analysis [2]

A market [4]

hapter 5 offers a first look at the operation of a market economy as background for our study of macroeconomics. The chapter describes how markets function when they operate according to the Laws of Supply and Demand. Supply and demand analysis is one of the more useful models for understanding market exchanges. It is very simple, yet it does an excellent job of explaining and predicting the pattern of prices and quantities in the vast majority of markets.

What will be the price of compact discs next year, and how many will be sold? What will the job market be like for this year's graduating seniors? When health-conscious Americans began eating fish and chicken instead of beef, the price of fish skyrocketed, but the price of chicken hardly increased at all. Why is this? Technological change has driven down the price of personal computers and driven up the price of medical care. Why has price responded so differently to technological change in these two markets? The Laws of Supply and Demand help us answer these questions.

Chapter 5 proceeds by analyzing demand and supply separately and then showing how demand and supply interact to determine both the prices of products and the quantities exchanged in the marketplace. We begin with the demand side of the market.

DEMAND

DEMAND

The amount of a product that individuals are willing and able to buy over a certain period of time.

Demand refers to the buyers' side of the marketplace. The **demand** for a product is the amount that individuals are willing and able to buy over a certain period of time. As such, demand is a statement of desires, of what individuals want to buy with their limited incomes rather than what they actually buy. We will see that consumers do not always buy what they want to buy.

Our ultimate interest is the *market demand* for any one product, the total amount demanded by all consumers of the product. When consumers in the United States decide that they want to buy 1 million compact discs each month, what factors influence their decision? The natural place to begin is with an individual's demand for the product, since each individual is deciding how much of the product to buy. The market demand is just the sum of all the individual demands. So think about a representative consumer buying some common, everyday product, and ask this question: What determines how much of that product the person wants to buy each week, or month, or year?

Demand and the Consumer's Economic Problem

The demand for any product arises from the three-part economic problem that all individuals must solve, consisting of objectives, alternatives, and constraints. Let's focus on the problem that individuals face as consumers of goods and services. Suppose that all decisions have been made with respect to how income is earned and that all income is spent on goods and services. There is no saving. Recall from Chapter 1 the structure of the individual's three-part economic problem under these assumptions.

The person's *objective* is to achieve the greatest possible utility, or satisfaction, from consuming goods and services.

The person's *alternatives* are the various goods and services that provide utility. Particular characteristics further distinguish one good or service from another. Consider, for example, all the attributes that distinguish one house from another or the numerous options that are available to you when you buy a new car.

The person's *constraints* are a combination of that person's limited income and the prices of the various goods and services. The constraints assure that the person cannot buy endless quantities of goods and services. People always want more than they can have.

The structure of the consumer's economic problem indicates that the demand for any one product depends on tastes or preferences, income, and prices.

Tastes or *preferences* determine how much satisfaction is achieved from consuming different amounts of each product. Does consuming some product make you feel good? Does it advance your knowledge? Does it cause your friends to look up to you? Do you prefer Pepsi or Coke? Tastes or preferences serve as a catch-all for every possible motive underlying consumption and for all the quality distinctions, real or imagined, that people perceive among various products.

Income is the scarce resource in this problem. What people want to buy depends on their available resources as well as their preferences. The income that is relevant is the income actually available to individuals for consumption. Taxes reduce the income available to spend on goods and services. Conversely, transfers received from governments or other family members increase available income. Therefore, taxes and transfers should be included in the list of factors that affect demand, along with income earned in the factor markets.

Prices include not only the price of the product itself, but prices of other products as well. For example, music lovers can satisfy their passion by purchasing cassette tapes or compact discs or by attending concerts. Since these products all provide a similar kind of satisfaction, the demand for any one of them depends on the prices of all the other options.

THE INDIVIDUAL DEMAND CURVE   Economists have a special interest in the effect of the price of a product on its quantity demanded because prices are the centerpiece of a free market system. As noted in Chapter 4, prices incorporate all relevant economic information and coordinate market exchanges between buyers and sellers. In order to understand how prices perform these functions, we need to isolate the effect of price on the quantity that buyers demand (and the quantity that sellers supply). However, tastes, income, and all the other factors are continually changing, and these changes simultaneously affect quantity demanded. Therefore, if we want to isolate the influence of price on quantity demanded, we must assume that all the factors influencing quantity demanded *except price* are held constant. Holding all other things equal, or constant, how do changes in the price of the product affect the quantity demanded? (In economics the other things equal assumption is often stated in its Latin version, *ceteris paribus*. We will use the English version, other things equal, throughout this text.)

TABLE 5.1   **A Consumer's One-Year Demand Schedule for Compact Discs**
(Hypothetical Data)

PRICE OF COMPACT DISCS	QUANTITY DEMANDED OF COMPACT DISCS
$24	3
20	5
16	6
12	7
8	8
4	10

INDIVIDUAL DEMAND SCHEDULE

The quantity of a good that an individual is willing and able to buy at each price, other things equal.

For most people and most products, most of the time, price and quantity demanded are inversely related, other things equal. The higher the price of a product, the smaller the quantity demanded; the lower the price of a product, the larger the quantity demanded. The inverse relationship between price and quantity demanded is illustrated by the hypothetical demand schedule for compact discs in Table 5.1. The **individual demand schedule** indicates, at different prices, how many compact discs a consumer wants to buy during the course of the year, other things equal. At the relatively high price of $24 the consumer wants to buy only 3 discs. As the price decreases to $16, the quantity of discs demanded increases to 6. A further decrease in price to $8 leads to a further increase in quantity demanded to 8 discs; and so on. Price and quantity demanded are inversely related.

INDIVIDUAL DEMAND CURVE

A graphical representation of the individual demand schedule, showing the quantity of a good that an individual is willing and able to buy at each price, other things equal.

A demand curve is the graph of a demand schedule. The line labeled d in Figure 5.1 is the **individual demand curve** for compact discs associated with the consumer's demand schedule in Table 5.1. Price is on the vertical axis, and the quantity demanded is on the horizontal axis. The demand curve is drawn as a solid line to allow for all possible combinations of price and quantity demanded, not just the few price-quantity combinations shown in Table 5.1. Notice how the line slopes downward and to the right, indicating that price and quantity demanded are inversely related.

LAW OF DEMAND

Other things equal, the lower the price of a product, the larger the quantity demanded; the higher the price of a product, the smaller the quantity demanded.

THE LAW OF DEMAND   The inverse relationship between price and quantity demanded holds with such regularity that it is elevated to the status of a law of human behavior, the Law of Demand. The **Law of Demand** says, *other things equal*, the lower the price of a product, the larger the quantity demanded; the higher the price of a product, the smaller the quantity demanded. In terms of the demand curve, the Law of Demand says that individuals' demand curves slope downward and to the right, just like the individual demand curve for compact discs does in Figure 5.1.

REFLECTION: Can you think of any product for which your demand curve is upward sloping? That is, you are willing to buy more of the product the higher its price, other things equal.

Laws of human behavior never hold as universally as physical laws such as the Law of Gravity. Situations arise for which the Law of Demand is violated. However, the force of the law is that these situations are quite rare, truly exceptional. We always *expect* price and quantity demanded to be inversely related. The same notion of expectation applies to any law of human behavior.

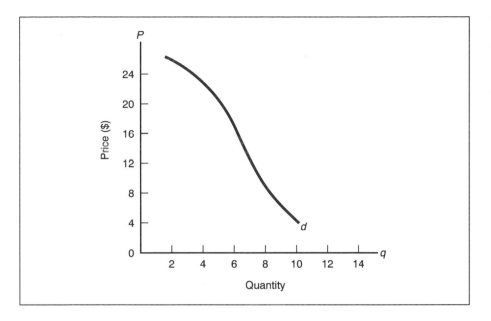

FIGURE 5.1

The Individual Demand Curve for Compact Discs

The individual demand curve for compact discs, *d*, is a graph of the hypothetical individual demand schedule for compact discs in Table 5.1. The demand curve is downward sloping in accordance with the Law of Demand; price and quantity demanded are inversely related. The higher the price the lower the quantity demanded and the lower the price the higher the quantity demanded, other things equal.

THE SUBSTITUTION AND INCOME EFFECTS   What lies behind the Law of Demand? Why are the individual demand curves for most products downward sloping? Economists have identified two separate effects of a change in price—the substitution effect and the income effect—to explain the Law of Demand.

The substitution effect of a price change is a relative price effect. It is based on the idea that consumers compare the prices of all products when deciding how much of each product they want to buy. As a result of the **substitution effect,** when prices change, consumers tend to purchase more of those products that have become relatively cheaper and fewer of those products that have become relatively more expensive.

Points along a demand curve are drawn on the assumption that only the price of the product is changing. The prices of all other products remain constant. Therefore, referring of Figure 5.1, when the price of compact discs declines from $16 to $8, compact discs have become cheaper relative to all other products. According to the substitution effect, the individual responds by substituting in favor of compact discs and against other products. The quantity of compact discs demanded increases. Therefore, when price decreases from $16 to $8, the substitution effect helps explain why quantity demanded increases from 6 to 8 discs.

The income effect of a change in price is an absolute price, or purchasing power effect. **Purchasing power** refers to the amount of goods and services consumers are able to buy with their limited incomes. Economists also refer to purchasing power as **real income.** Real income implicitly compares the dollar value of income with the prices of the goods and services that the income will be used to purchase.

Purchasing power increases when the price of any product decreases, other things equal, because consumers can buy more goods and services with their limited incomes. Conversely, purchasing power decreases when the price of

SUBSTITUTION EFFECT (OF A PRICE CHANGE)

The tendency to purchase more of those products that have become relatively cheaper and fewer of those products that have become relatively more expensive when relative prices change.

PURCHASING POWER

The amount of goods and services that consumers are able to buy with their limited incomes, given prices; also called *real income.*

REAL INCOME

A measure of income that compares the dollar value of income with the prices of the goods and services that the income will be used to purchase; also called *purchasing power.*

any product increases, other things equal. Refer again to Figure 5.1. The individual purchases 6 compact discs when the price is $16. The total expenditure on discs is $96 ($96 = $16 · 6). If the price of discs decreases to $8, the individual can purchase 6 discs for a total expenditure of only $48 ($48 = $8 · 6). The decrease in price has freed up $48 that can be used to buy more goods and services. The individual's purchasing power has increased.

INCOME EFFECT (OF A PRICE CHANGE)

The change in the quantity demanded of a good due to the effect that the change in its price has on an individual's purchasing power or real income.

As a result of the **income effect,** consumers tend to buy more of most goods and services when their purchasing power increases. Therefore, when the price of compact discs decreases from $16 to $8, the consumer responds by using some of the increased purchasing power to purchase more compact discs (and other products as well). The income effect of the price decrease helps explain why the quantity of discs demanded increases from 6 to 8.

In conclusion, when the price of a product decreases, other things equal, both the substitution and the income effects lead to an increase in quantity demanded. In our example, the combination of the two effects explains why the quantity of discs demanded increases from 6 to 8 when the price decreases from $16 to $8.

You should test your understanding of the substitution and the income effects by considering the case of a price increase. Why do the two effects, combined, lead to a decrease in the quantity of discs demanded from 6 to 5 when the price of compact discs increases from $16 to $20 in Figure 5.1?

The Market Demand Curve

Analyzing market events requires knowledge of market demand. The *market demand curve* for a product registers the *total* quantity demanded at each price by *all* consumers, other things equal. Table 5.2 and Figure 5.2 show how to construct the market demand curve for compact discs from the individual demand curves. For purposes of illustration the example assumes that the entire demand for compact discs comes from two individuals, person 1 and person 2.

Table 5.2 shows the individual demand schedules of the two people and the market demand schedule. Person 1 has the demand schedule for compact discs from Table 5.1, reproduced in the second column of the table. Person 2 has a different demand schedule for compact discs, shown in the third column of the table. Individual demand schedules for compact discs, or any other product,

TABLE 5.2   One-Year Individual Demand and Market Demand Schedules for Compact Discs (Hypothetical Data)

PRICE OF COMPACT DISCS	QUANTITY DEMANDED OF COMPACT DISCS		
	Person 1	Person 2	Total Market
$24	3	0	3
20	5	1	6
16	6	3	9
12	7	4	11
8	8	5	13
4	10	9	19

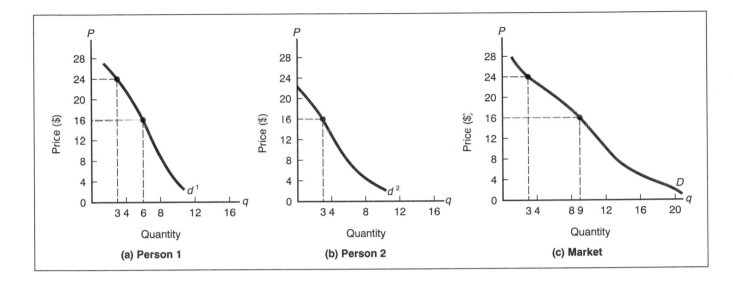

(a) Person 1   **(b) Person 2**   **(c) Market**

are likely to differ because people have different tastes and different incomes. The fourth column of the table records the **market demand schedule,** the total quantity demanded by all consumers at each price.

The market demand schedule is the sum of the individual demand schedules. (Column 4 = column 2 + column 3.) For example, at a price of $24 person 1 wants to buy 3 discs, but person 2 finds the price is too high and does not want to buy any discs at that price. Therefore, the total quantity demanded at $24 is 3 discs (3 = 3 + 0), as shown in the fourth column. Similarly, at a price of $16 person 1 wants to buy 6 discs, and person 2 wants to buy 3 discs. The total quantity demanded at $16 is 9 discs (9 = 6 + 3). The construction of the market demand schedule is the same whether the market consists of two or two million individual consumers. In either case the total (market) quantity demanded at each price is the sum of the quantities demanded by all the individuals.

The **market demand curve** is the graph of the market demand schedule, with price on the vertical axis and quantity on the horizontal axis. Figure 5.2 pictures the individual and market demand curves corresponding to the individual and market demand schedules in Table 5.2. The demand curve of person 1 is shown in Figure 5.2(a), and the demand curve of person 2 is shown in Figure 5.2(b). The market demand curve is shown in Figure 5.2(c).

As illustrated in Figure 5.2, the market demand curve is derived by adding the individual demand curves horizontally at each price. For example, at a price of $16, the quantity on the market demand curve (9) is equal to the sum of the quantities on the two individual demand curves (6 + 3). Notice that the market demand curve is downward sloping. This must be so, since the market demand curve is just the horizontal summation of the individual demand curves, each of which is downward sloping. Thus, the Law of Demand applies to the market demand curve.

In actual market situations total quantities demanded at any given price are enormously larger than each individual quantity demanded. For example, in the United States the market demand for compact discs is millions of times larger at every price than the average individual demand. Therefore, to distin-

FIGURE 5.2

The Market Demand Curve for Compact Discs

The individual and market demand curves for compact discs are graphs of the hypothetical demand schedules in Table 5.2. The market demand curve, *D*, in Figure 5.2(c) indicates the total quantity demanded at each price, other things equal. It is the horizontal summation of the two individual demand curves, assuming that Person 1 and Person 2 are the only two buyers in the market. The market demand curve is downward sloping, in accordance with the Law of Demand. Price and quantity demanded are inversely related, other things equal.

MARKET DEMAND SCHEDULE

The total amount demanded of a good by all the consumers at each price, other things equal.

MARKET DEMAND CURVE

A graphical representation of the market demand schedule, showing the total quantity demanded of a good by all consumers at each price, other things equal; the horizontal summation of the individual demand curves.

guish between individual and market demands we will use D to represent market demand curves and d to represent individual demand curves, as in Figure 5.2. Similarly, we will use Q to represent market quantity demanded and q to represent individual quantity demanded when we are not using actual numbers as in this example. Q is understood to be many times larger than q. Note, however, that prices are the same on the market and the individual demand curves. In both cases, price is measured as dollars per unit of the product. In our example price is the cost to each consumer of a single compact disc.

CHANGE IN QUANTITY DEMANDED VERSUS CHANGE IN DEMAND   The analysis of market events requires a very subtle distinction in terminology between a change in quantity demanded and a change in demand. A **change in quantity demanded** refers to movements along the demand curve as price changes, other things equal. Along the market demand curve in Figure 5.2(c), an increase in price from $16 to $20 causes a *decrease* in quantity demanded from 9 compact discs to 6 compact discs. Conversely, a decrease in price from $16 to $8 causes an *increase* in quantity demanded from 9 discs to 13 discs.

A **change in demand** refers to a shift in the entire demand curve. A change in demand occurs when one of the "other things" influencing quantity demanded, such as incomes, tastes, or the price of a related product, changes. These factors are not shown on the horizontal or vertical axis for the graph of a demand curve. They lie behind the demand curve, determining the position and slope of the curve. If one, or more, of these factors changes, the entire demand curve shifts to a new position.

In Figure 5.3 the shift in the demand curve up and to the right from D to D' is an *increase* in demand. The quantity demanded increases at every price. The shift in the demand curve down and to the left from D to D'' is a *decrease* in demand. The quantity demanded decreases at every price. Let's take a brief

CHANGE IN QUANTITY DEMANDED

A movement along the demand curve as price changes, other things equal.

CHANGE IN DEMAND

A shift in the entire demand curve.

FIGURE 5.3

Shifts in the Market Demand Curve

The entire market demand curve shifts when one of the factors that influences demand, other than the price of the product, changes. For example, an increase in consumers' incomes causes an increase in the demand for most products; the market demand curve shifts up and to the right, from D to D'. Conversely, a decrease in consumers' incomes causes a decrease in the demand for most products; the market demand curve shifts down and to the left, from D to D''.

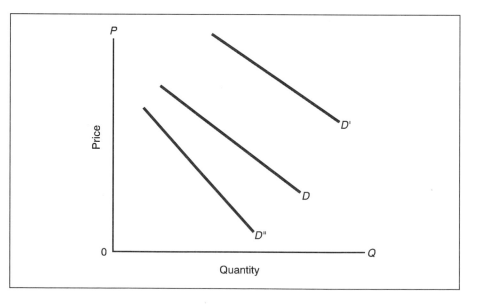

look at some of the more important factors that cause the demand curve to change.

INCOME   When consumers have more income, their ability to purchase goods and services increases. Therefore, an increase in consumers' incomes leads to an increase in demand for a wide range of products. Their demand curves shift upward and to the right, as from D to D' in Figure 5.3. Conversely, a decrease in consumers' incomes leads to a decrease in demand for most products. Their demand curves shift downward and to the left, as from D to D'' in Figure 5.3. Products whose demands respond to income in this way are called **normal** goods because this is how we expect changes in income to shift their demand curves.

For some products, however, changes in income shift the demand curve in the opposite direction. An increase in income decreases demand, and a decrease in income increases demand. An example is a less tender cut of beef such as chuck steak. As peoples' incomes increase, they tend to buy less chuck steak and more of the tender cuts of beef such as sirloin. Products such as chuck steak are called **inferior** goods because consumers clearly prefer other products. Families with very low incomes buy chuck steak only because they cannot afford to buy sirloin. If their incomes were to increase so that they could afford to buy sirloin, they would switch from chuck steak to sirloin.

TASTES OR PREFERENCES   Changes in consumers' tastes shift demand curves as well. We see this very clearly with the coming and going of fads. You may remember the Cabbage Patch doll craze when you were a youngster. Demand increased so rapidly that it outpaced the ability of producers to supply dolls. At the height of the craze anxious parents were willing to pay $100 or more to anyone who could supply them with a doll. The Cabbage Patch fad lasted for about two years, after which the demand curve shifted back down. The price of the dolls returned to a normal level for dolls of that type.

POPULATION   An increasing population tends to increase demand for all products simply because more and more individual demand curves are being added to the market demand curve. The market demand curve shifts to the right. Conversely, a decreasing population tends to decrease demand for all products. The market demand curve shifts to the left.

PRICES OF RELATED PRODUCTS: SUBSTITUTES AND COMPLEMENTS   Two products are said to be related if a change in the price of one of them changes the demand for the other. Related products can be either substitutes or complements. Two products are unrelated if a change in the price of one of them has no effect on the demand for the other.

Substitutes are products that provide the same general kind of service. Compact discs and cassette tapes are substitute products because each one provides a means of listening to recorded music. When two products are **substitutes,** a decrease in the price of one of them decreases the demand for the other. Conversely, an increase in the price of one increases the demand for the other. For example, if the price of compact discs decreases, they become more attractive to consumers relative to cassette tapes. The demand for cassette tapes decreases.

NORMAL GOOD

A good whose consumption rises as income rises.

INFERIOR GOOD

A good whose consumption goes down as income rises.

SUBSTITUTES

Products that provide the same general kind of services; specifically, two goods whose relationship is such that a decrease in the price of one good decreases the demand for the other good.

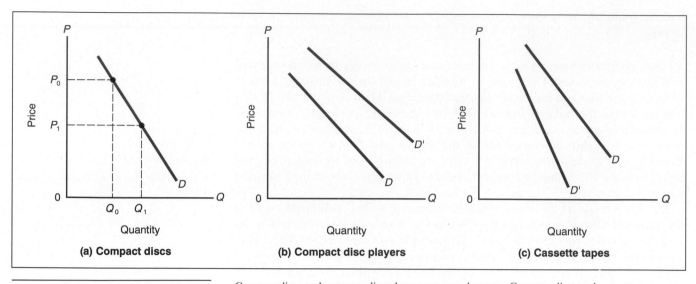

FIGURE 5.4

Complements and Substitutes

Compact discs and compact disc players are complements. Compact discs and cassette tapes are substitutes. Therefore, a decrease in the price of compact discs from P_0 to P_1 causes: a) an increase in the quantity demanded of compact discs from Q_0 to Q_1 in Figure 5.4(a); b) an increase in the demand for compact disc players—the demand curve shifts up and to the right from D to D' in Figure 5.4(b); and c) a decrease in the demand for cassette tapes—the demand curve shifts down and to the left from D to D' in Figure 5.4(c).

COMPLEMENTS

Products that are used together to provide a service; specifically, two goods whose relationship is such that a decrease in the price of one good increases the demand for the other.

Complements are products that are used together to provide a service. Compact discs and compact disc players are complements. When two products are complements, a decrease in the price of one of them increases the demand for the other. Conversely, an increase in the price of one decreases the demand for the other. For example, if the price of compact discs decreases, they become more attractive to consumers, and the demand for compact disc players increases.

A final example involving compact discs, cassette tapes, and compact disc players will highlight the important distinction between a change in quantity demanded and a change in demand. Figure 5.4 pictures the demand curves for the three products.

Suppose that the price of compact discs decreases. Figure 5.4(a) shows the demand curve for compact discs. The decrease in the price of compact discs from P_0 to P_1 results in an increase in the *quantity demanded* from Q_0 to Q_1. The decrease in price results in a movement along the demand curve for compact discs.

Figures 5.4(b) and 5.4(c) picture the demand curves for compact disc players and cassette tapes, respectively. A decrease in the price of compact discs shifts the demand curves in these markets because the price of compact discs does not appear in either panel. It is one of the factors in the background being held constant. Since compact discs and compact disc players are complements, the fall in the price of compact discs makes compact disc players more attractive to consumers. The *demand* for compact disc players increases from D to D', as shown in Figure 5.4(b). Since compact discs and cassette tapes are substitutes, the fall in the price of compact discs makes cassette tapes less attrac-

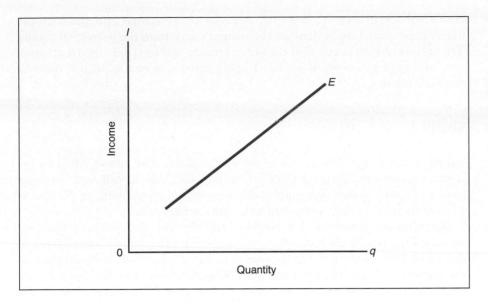

FIGURE 5.5

Engel's Curve

The Engel's curve for a product, *E*, shows the relationship between income and quantity demanded, other things equal. The Engel's curve for normal goods is upward sloping. An increase in income increases quantity demanded and a decrease in income decreases quantity demanded.

tive to consumers. The *demand* for cassette tapes decreases from *D* to *D'*, as shown in Figure 5.4(c).

Take care in distinguishing between a change in quantity demanded and a change in demand. They refer to very different phenomena.

GRAPHING OTHER DEMAND RELATIONSHIPS   A demand curve selects price, one of the many factors determining quantity demanded, and graphs it against quantity demanded, holding all other factors constant. As noted earlier, we have a special interest in the separate effect of price on quantity demanded. However, the separate effects of the other factors are also of interest in many applications. Any one of them could be selected and graphed against quantity demanded, holding all other factors constant *including price*. The resulting graph would picture the separate effect of that factor on quantity demanded, other things equal.

INCOME AND QUANTITY DEMANDED   For instance, suppose that we are interested in the relationship between a representative consumer's income and quantity demanded for some product. To graph this relationship, we place income on the vertical axis and quantity demanded on the horizontal axis, as shown in Figure 5.5. The graph of income against quantity demanded is called an **Engel's curve,** after the Prussian statistician Ernst Engel. Engel's nineteenth-century study of the effect of income on quantity demanded for a wide range of products is a landmark of economic analysis. For normal goods the relationship is upward sloping, as pictured in Figure 5.5. An increase in income increases quantity demanded, other things equal.

Engel's curves can apply to individual consumers or the entire market. A market Engel's curve shows the other things equal relationship between the total income available to consumers and the total quantity demanded for all consumers. The market Engel's curve is not the horizontal summation of each individual Engel's curve, however, because both income and quantity demanded are added when deriving the market curve from the individual curves. The relationship between total consumer income and total demand for all products, the aggregation of all market Engel's curves, is central to the study of macroeconomics.

SUPPLY

SUPPLY

The amount of a product that a firm is willing and able to sell over a certain period of time.

Supply refers to the sellers' side of the marketplace. The **supply** of a product is the amount that business firms are willing and able to sell over a certain period of time. Notice that supply, like demand, is a statement of desires, of what firms want to sell rather than what they actually sell.

Our ultimate interest is the *market supply* for any one product, the total amount supplied by all business firms producing the product. When firms in the United States decide that they want to supply 2 million compact discs to the market each month, what variables influence their decision? As with demand, we begin with the supply decision of an individual firm and then build the market supply from the individual firms' supplies.

Supply and the Firm's Economic Problem

The supply of any product arises from the three-part economic problem that all firms must solve, consisting of objectives, alternatives, and constraints. A firm's economic problem has the following structure.

The firm's *objective* is to achieve the maximum amount of profit, the difference between total revenue and total cost.

The firm faces two sets of *alternatives:*

1. What products to produce, and in what amounts; and
2. How to produce each product. (Recall from Chapter 1 that the How question involves the choice of a production technology along with the associated factors of production for that technology.)

The firm's *constraints* are threefold:

1. The production technologies available to the firm for producing each product;
2. The prices of the various factors of production associated with each technology; and
3. The demand for each product, which determines the price at which the firm can sell each product.

THE DETERMINANTS OF SUPPLY   The structure of the firm's economic problem indicates that its willingness to supply any one product depends on available production technologies, factor prices, the price of the product, and the prices of other products that the firm is able to produce.

The *production technologies* establish the physical link between the firm's inputs and outputs. They indicate the amounts of various factors of production needed to produce the quantities of each product supplied.

The **factor prices** include the prices of various kinds of labor; materials purchased from other firms, including energy; land and raw materials; and capital. The factor prices, along with the chosen production technology, determine the total cost of producing whatever quantity of product the firm chooses to supply.

The *price of the product* determines the total revenue received for whatever quantity of the product the firm chooses to supply. Total revenue is just price times quantity supplied.

The *price of all other products* the firm is capable of supplying determine the total revenue from supplying those products. Therefore, these prices help determine whether supplying the product is more profitable than supplying other products.

Taxes on firms also influence the supply decision because they add to the firms' production costs. For example, a sales tax causes firms to raise the prices of their products.

THE INDIVIDUAL FIRM'S SUPPLY CURVE   As with demand, we are interested in the relationship between the price of the product and the quantity supplied, holding constant all variables that influence quantity supplied *except price*. Other things equal, how do changes in the price of the product affect the quantity supplied?

For most firms and most products, most of the time, price and quantity supplied are directly related. The lower the price of a product, the smaller the quantity supplied; the higher the price of a product, the larger the quantity supplied. The direct relationship between price and quantity supplied is illustrated by the hypothetical supply schedule of a firm selling compact discs in Table 5.3.

The **individual firm's supply schedule** shows, at different prices, how many compact discs a firm is willing to supply throughout the course of a year, other things equal. At the relatively low price of $4 the quantity supplied is also relatively low. The compact disc firm is willing to supply only 10,000 discs each year. As the price rises to $16, the quantity the firm is willing to supply rises to 90,000 discs. As the price increases further to $24, the quantity supplied increases to 120,000 discs. Price and quantity supplied are directly related.

FACTOR PRICES

The prices of various kinds of labor, materials purchased from other firms, energy, land, raw materials, and capital, which determine the total cost of producing whatever quantity of product the firm chooses to supply.

INDIVIDUAL FIRM'S SUPPLY SCHEDULE

The quantity that the firm is willing and able to supply at each price, other things equal.

TABLE 5.3   One-Year Supply Schedule of an Individual Compact Disc Firm (Hypothetical Data)

PRICE OF COMPACT DISCS	QUANTITY SUPPLIED OF COMPACT DISCS (THOUSANDS)
$28	125
24	120
20	110
16	90
12	60
8	40
4	10

FIGURE 5.6

The Individual Firm's Supply Curve for Compact Discs

The individual firm's supply curve for compact discs, *s*, is a graph of the hypothetical supply schedule for compact discs in Table 5.3. The supply curve is upward sloping in accordance with the Law of Supply; price and quantity supplied are directly related. The higher the price the higher the quantity supplied and the lower the price the lower the quantity supplied, other things equal.

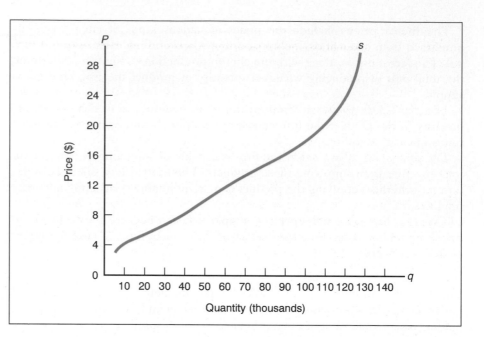

INDIVIDUAL FIRM'S SUPPLY CURVE

A graphical representation of the individual firm's supply schedule, showing the quantity that the firm is willing and able to supply at each price, other things equal.

An **individual firm's supply curve** is the graph of its supply schedule. The line labeled *s* in Figure 5.6 is the compact disc firm's supply curve associated with the firm's supply schedule in Table 5.3. Price is on the vertical axis, and quantity supplied is on the horizontal axis. The supply curve is drawn as a solid line to allow for all possible combinations of price and quantity supplied, not just the few price-quantity combinations shown in Table 5.3. Notice how the supply curve slopes upward and to the right, indicating that price and quantity supplied are directly related.

The Law of Supply

The direct relationship between price and quantity supplied occurs with such regularity that it is called the Law of Supply. The **Law of Supply** says, *other things equal*, the lower the price of a product, the smaller the quantity supplied; the higher the price of a product, the larger the quantity supplied.

LAW OF SUPPLY

Other things equal, the lower the price of a product, the smaller the quantity supplied; the higher the price of a product, the larger the quantity supplied.

SUPPLY CURVES AND MARGINAL COST   Why are supply curves upward sloping? Why must price rise in order to induce firms to supply more of a product? The answer lies in the pattern of the typical firm's cost of production, in particular, marginal cost. Recall from Chapter 2 that the margin in economics refers to the effects of small changes in economic activity. **Marginal cost** is the addition to total cost of producing an additional unit of output. At any given quantity it is the increase in total cost incurred by producing the last unit of output. For example, if a firm produces 50,000 compact discs, the marginal cost at 50,000 discs is the cost of producing the 50,000th disc. Notice that the concept of marginal cost is analogous to the concept of the marginal grade from the study example in Chapter 2. The marginal grade in that example referred to the increase in the student's test score for each additional hour of study.

MARGINAL COST

The addition to total cost of producing an additional unit of output.

Marginal cost is directly relevant to the supply decision because firms compare price with marginal cost when deciding whether to increase output. Price is the additional revenue a firm receives from supplying one more unit of output. Marginal cost is the additional cost to the firm of supplying one more unit of output. A firm will increase quantity supplied only if the price (additional revenue) is greater than the marginal cost (additional cost), so that the firm's profit increases. For example, the compact disc firm represented in Table 5.3 is willing to supply 90,000 discs when the price is $16. Therefore, the cost of producing each additional disc from 1 to 90,000, the marginal cost, must be less than $16, or the firm would not be willing to supply 90,000 discs. Also, the marginal cost of producing disc number 90,001 must be greater than $16 because the firm is not willing to supply it. The firm's willingness to supply discs stops when price and marginal cost are equal.

The key to the Law of Supply is that marginal cost tends to rise as output increases. For example, suppose that the compact disc firm decides to increase production from 50,000 discs to 51,000 discs. The additional costs of producing 1,000 more discs are likely to be greater than the additional costs incurred when the firm increased production by 1,000 discs from 49,000 to 50,000. The intuition behind the phenomenon of rising marginal cost comes from the production possibilities frontier of Chapter 3. Recall that the frontier bows outward because the opportunity costs of producing any one product increase as more and more of that product is produced. Business firms experience these rising opportunity costs directly in their cost of production. When they try to expand their own production, they find that the additional units of output are ever more costly to produce. Therefore, firms are willing to increase production only if they receive a higher price for their products to offset the higher marginal cost. Their supply curves are upward sloping.

The Market, or Industry, Supply Curve

Analyzing market events requires knowledge of market supply. The relationship between the market supply curve and the individual firms' supply curves is exactly analogous to the relationship between the market demand curve and the individual consumers' demand curves. The overall **market supply schedule** indicates the total quantity all firms in the market want to supply at each price, other things equal. It is the sum, at each price, of the individual firms' supply schedules. The **market supply curve** is the graph of the market supply schedule. Because an industry consists of all firms supplying a particular product, the market supply curve is also referred to as the *industry supply curve*. The market, or industry, supply curve is the horizontal summation of all the individual firms' supply curves, just as the market demand curve is the horizontal summation of all the individual consumers' demand curves. We will use S to represent the market, or industry, supply curve and s to represent an individual firm's supply curve. Similarly, we will use Q to represent the total quantity supplied by all firms in the market and q to represent the quantity supplied by an individual firm.

Finally, note that the market supply curve is upward sloping: The Law of Supply applies to the market supply curve. This must be so because the market supply curve is just the horizontal summation of the individual firms' supply curves, each of which is upward sloping.

MARKET SUPPLY SCHEDULE

The total quantity that all firms in the market are willing and able to supply at each price, other things equal.

MARKET SUPPLY CURVE

A graphical representation of the market supply schedule, showing the total quantity that all firms in the market are willing and able to supply at each price, other things equal; equal to the horizontal summation of the individual firms' supply curves; also called the *industry supply curve*.

CHANGE IN QUANTITY SUPPLIED VERSUS CHANGE IN SUPPLY   Using supply curves to analyze markets requires the same subtle distinction in terminology that we met with demand curves. You must keep straight the difference between a change in quantity supplied and a change in supply. A **change in quantity supplied** refers to movements along the supply curve as price changes, other things equal. A *change in supply* refers to a shift in the entire supply curve, as illustrated in Figure 5.7. A shift in the supply curve up and to the left from S to S' represents a decrease in supply. The quantity supplied has decreased at every price. A shift in the supply curve down and to the right from S to S'' represents an *increase* in supply. The quantity supplied has increased at every price.

CHANGE IN QUANTITY SUPPLIED
A movement along the supply curve as price changes, other things equal.

CHANGE IN SUPPLY
A shift in the entire supply curve.

A **change in supply** occurs when one of the "other things" influencing quantity supplied, such as the factor prices, the production technologies, the prices of other products, taxes, and the number of firms in the industry, changes or when special events, such as severe weather or a strike by a union, occur. These variables are not shown on the graph of a supply curve. They lie behind the supply curve, determining the position and slope of the curve. If one, or more, of these variable changes, the entire supply curve shifts to a new position.

Events that cause the supply curve to shift can be grouped into two categories: events that change the costs of production and events that change the total quantity supplied to the markets. The principal cost shifters are changes in factor prices, taxes, and the underlying production technology. The principal quantity shifters are changes in the prices of other products, changes in the number of firms in the industry, and special events such as severe weather or union strikes.

CHANGES IN SUPPLY

COST-INDUCED CHANGES IN SUPPLY   Anything that increases marginal cost shifts the supply curve up and to the left. Higher wage rates, rising fuel costs, and morale problems among the employees that reduce their productivity all increase marginal cost at every output and thereby decrease supply. They cause a shift in the supply curve from S to S' in Figure 5.7. Whether the shift from S to S' is viewed as an upward shift or a shift to the left is a matter of interpretation. The supply curve shifts up in the sense that firms require higher prices to supply any given quantity. For example, the price P_0 was sufficient to elicit an overall quantity supplied of Q_0 on the original supply curve S. Now P_2 is required to cover the higher marginal cost at Q_0 on the new supply curve S'. Alternatively, the supply curve shifts to the left in the sense that the willingness to supply decreases from Q_0 on S to Q_1 on S' at price P_0, and similarly at every price. The shift-up interpretation is perhaps the more natural one for cost-induced decreases in supply.

Conversely, anything that decreases marginal cost shifts the supply curve down and to the right. Reduced wage rates, declining fuel costs, and technological change that increases factors' (marginal) productivity all lower marginal cost at every output and lead to an increase in supply. They cause a shift in the supply curve from S to S'' in Figure 5.7. The price required to elicit an overall supply of Q_0 drops from P_0 to P_1 because of the decrease in marginal

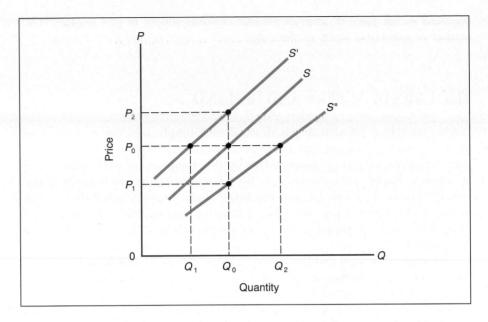

FIGURE 5.7

Shifts in the Market Supply Curve

The entire market supply curve shifts when one the factors that influences supply, other than the the price of the product, changes. For example, an increase in wages increases firms' marginal costs and causes a decrease in supply. The supply curve shifts up and to the left, from S to S'. Conversely, a decrease in wages decreases firms' marginal costs and causes an increase in supply. The supply curve shifts down and to the right, from S to S''.

cost (a shift down). Alternatively, at price P_0 the willingness to supply increases from Q_0 to Q_2 (a shift to the right).

Note that upward and downward shifts in demand and supply curves have opposite interpretations. An *upward* shift in a demand curve represents an *increase* in demand, whereas an *upward* shift in a supply curve represents a *decrease* in supply. Conversely, a *downward* shift in a demand curve represents a *decrease* in demand, whereas a *downward* shift in a supply curve represents an *increase* in supply. The left-right shifts have the same interpretation for each curve, however.

QUANTITY-INDUCED CHANGES IN SUPPLY Quantity-induced shifts in the supply curve may be either direct or indirect. Direct shifts in quantity supplied are caused by such events as widespread crop failures in agriculture or large numbers of firms leaving the industry because the market price is too low for them to earn a profit. Both events cause a decrease in supply to the market. The market supply curve shifts to the left, as from S to S' in Figure 5.7. Conversely, favorable weather conditions in agriculture or widespread entry into the industry by new firms responding to a high and profitable price causes an increase in supply to the market. The market supply curve shifts to the right, as from S to S'' in Figure 5.7.

Indirect quantity effects result from changes in the prices of other products that firms in the industry also supply or are capable of supplying. An increase in some other price *decreases* supply in this market as firms shift resources to the other product. The market supply curve shifts to the left. Conversely, a decrease in the price of another product *increases* supply in this market. The market supply curve shifts to the right.

THE LAWS OF SUPPLY AND DEMAND

We are now in a position to put demand and supply together and see how markets operate. Suppose that 1 million consumers of compact discs meet up with 100 firms supplying compact discs in the competitive marketplace. The consumers' market demand schedule for a few selected prices is given in the second column of Table 5.4, and the firms' market supply schedule is given in the third column of the table. The quantities represent the total number of discs demanded and supplied during the course of a year. All the numbers are hypothetical.

The market demand and the market supply curves, *D* and *S*, in Figure 5.8 correspond to the market demand and the market supply schedules in Table 5.4. The two curves are drawn as solid lines to show the total quantities demanded and supplied at prices other than those in the table. What will price and output be in the market for compact discs?

Our eye is naturally led to the point of intersection of *D* and *S* in Figure 5.8, at which the price of a disc is $16 and 9 million discs are exchanged between producers and consumers. This turns out to be the correct answer. Consumers in the aggregate purchase 9 million discs at a price of $16 per disc. Their total expenditures on discs, price times quantity, equal $144 million ($144 million = $16 · 9 million). The total expenditures are represented by the area of the rectangle 0*abc* in Figure 5.8. The height of the rectangle, 0*a*, is the price, $16. The base of the rectangle, 0*c*, is the quantity exchanged, 9 million. The area of the rectangle, base times height, is total expenditures. Conversely, the firms in the aggregate supply 9 million discs at a price of $16 per disc, receiving total revenues of $144 million.

MARKET EQUILIBRIUM

The intersection of the market demand and the market supply curves at which the quantity demanded equals the quantity supplied.

The intersection of the market supply and the market demand curves is referred to as the **market equilibrium**. In this market $16 is the equilibrium price, and 9 million discs is the equilibrium quantity.

TABLE 5.4 One-Year Market Demand and Market Supply Schedules for Compact Discs (Hypothetical Data)

PRICE OF COMPACT DISCS	QUANTITY DEMANDED OF COMPACT DISCS (MILLIONS)	QUANTITY SUPPLIED OF COMPACT DISCS (MILLIONS)	EXCESS SUPPLY OR EXCESS DEMAND (MILLIONS)	
$28	3	15	12	Excess
24	4	14	10	supply
20	6	11	5	.
16	9	9	0	Equilibrium
12	12	6	6	.
8	14	3	11	Excess
4	18	1	17	demand

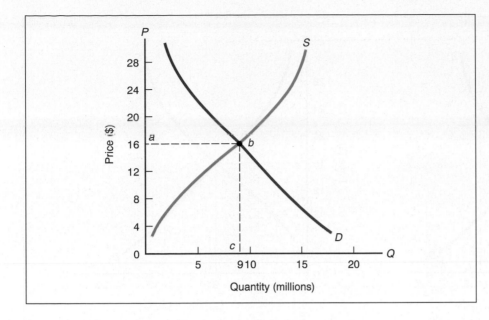

FIGURE 5.8

The Market for Compacts Discs

The market demand (*D*) and supply (*S*) curves are graphs of the hypothetical market demand and supply schedules in Table 5.4. The equilibrium occurs at the intersection of the demand and supply curves. The equilibrium price is $16, and the equilibrium quantity is 9 million compact discs.

Market Equilibrium

You should view the quantity-price combination of 9 million discs and $16 as something far more than a single point on a supply and demand diagram. To understand how markets operate, you must appreciate that the equilibrium price of $16 brings the demanders and suppliers of compact discs together in a manner shared by no other price.

An **equilibrium** is a state of rest or balance due to the equal action of opposing forces or influences. In the context of the marketplace the opposing forces are the Laws of Supply and Demand. They oppose one another in their responses to prices. The Law of Demand says that demand curves slope down and to the right. A higher price decreases the quantity demanded, and a lower price increases the quantity demanded. The corresponding Law of Supply says that supply curves slope up and to the right. A higher price increases the quantity supplied, and a lower price decreases the quantity supplied. At the equilibrium price of $16, and *only* at that price, do these opposing forces strike a balance: The quantity demanded by all the consumers exactly matches the quantity supplied by all the firms. Consumers *want* to buy 9 million discs, and firms *want* to supply 9 million discs at the equilibrium price of $16. Since both sides of the market are exchanging exactly the amount they want to exchange, the market is at rest, or in balance. No one has an incentive to change the market outcome.

An equilibrium does *not* imply that either the consumers or the business firms are necessarily happy with the result. Consumers no doubt wish that the price were lower than $16; firms would just as surely prefer a price higher than $16. Equilibrium is not about happiness, however. Rather, it is simply a matter of the equilibrium price matching desires on both sides of the market.

EQUILIBRIUM

A state of rest, or balance, due to the equal action of opposing forces or influences; in economics, a situation from which no one has any incentive to change.

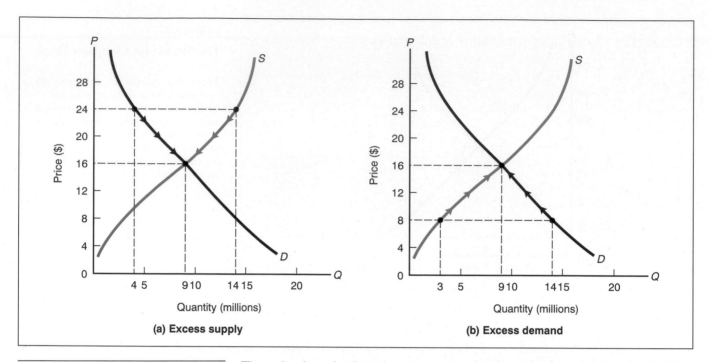

FIGURE 5.9

Excess Supply and Excess Demand in the Compact Disc Market

The market demand and supply curves correspond to the market demand and supply schedules in Table 5.4. In Figure 5.9(a), the market is in excess supply at a price of $24. The quantity supplied is 14 million compact discs and the quantity demanded is 4 million compact discs, for an excess supply of 10 million discs. A market is in excess supply at any price above the equilibrium price. The combined actions of the suppliers and demanders will automatically drive the price back down to the equilibrium price of $16. In Figure 5.9(b), the market is in excess demand at a price of $8. The quantity demanded is 14 million compact discs and the quantity supplied is 3 million compact discs, for an excess demand of 11 million discs. A market is in excess demand at any price below the equilibrium price. The combined actions of the suppliers and demanders will automatically drive the price back up to the equilibrium price of $16.

Excess Supply and Excess Demand

To appreciate this unique property of the equilibrium price, consider the state of the market at any price other than $16. For example, suppose that the price is greater than the equilibrium price—say, $24. Refer to Table 5.4 and Figure 5.9(a). The two graphs in the figure reproduce the market demand and the market supply curves from Figure 5.8. At a price of $24 firms in the aggregate want to supply 14 million discs. Consumers, however, want to buy only 4 million discs. The quantity supplied exceeds the quantity demanded. At a price of $24 the market is in **excess supply** in the amount of 10 million discs, the difference between the quantity supplied and the quantity demanded (10 million = 14 million − 4 million). Desires do not match, nor do they at any price above $16. The market is in excess supply at *any* price above the equilibrium. The fourth column of Table 5.4 records the amount of excess supply at all prices above $16. Excess supply reveals itself as a surplus of goods that firms are unable to sell.

EXCESS SUPPLY
The amount by which quantity supplied exceeds quantity demanded when price is above the equilibrium price.

Alternatively, suppose that the price is less than the equilibrium price—say, $8. Refer to Table 5.4 and Figure 5.9(b). At a price of $8 firms in the aggregate want to supply 3 million discs. Consumers, however, want to buy 14 million discs. The quantity demanded exceeds the quantity supplied. At a price of $8 the market is in **excess demand** in the amount of 11 million discs, the difference between the quantity demanded and the quantity supplied (11 million = 14 million − 3 million). Once again desires do not match, nor do they at any price less than $16. The market is in excess demand at *any* price below the equilibrium. The fourth column of Table 5.4 records the amount of excess demand at all prices below $16. Excess demand reveals itself as a shortage of goods available for consumers to buy.

EXCESS DEMAND

The amount by which quantity demanded exceeds quantity supplied when price is below the equilibrium price.

Two points from these examples deserve emphasis. First, the market conditions of equilibrium, excess supply, and excess demand must be associated with particular prices. In Figures 5.8 and 5.9 the same market is in equilibrium at a price of $16, in excess supply at a price of $24, and in excess demand at a price of $8. All three situations are possible in any market. The level of the market price determines which situation applies at any given time.

Second, the quantity purchased in the market *always* equals the quantity sold no matter what the price. The equality of purchases and sales is true by definition because a purchase and a sale are the opposite sides of any one market transaction. The amount bought and sold at any price is the lesser of the quantity supplied and the quantity demanded at that price. For example, in Figure 5.9(a), 4 million discs are bought and sold at a price of $24. Firms cannot force consumers to buy what they do not want to buy. In Figure 5.9(b), 3 million discs are bought and sold at a price of $8. Consumers cannot force firms to sell what they do not want to sell. The identity between purchases and sales is different from the concept of equilibrium, however, which is a matching of desires. Only at the equilibrium price of $16 is the amount bought and sold, 9 million discs, equal to the amount consumers and firms *want* to buy and sell.

Stability

The quantity-price combination of 9 million discs and $16 is more than an equilibrium. It is a *stable* equilibrium, meaning that the market will automatically return to the equilibrium from any other quantity-price combination. In other words, 9 million discs exchanged at a price of $16 is the only sustainable quantity-price combination in the market.

Think of the stability of an equilibrium in terms of a pendulum. The point at the bottom of the pendulum's swing is the only possible equilibrium, the only point of rest. Bring the pendulum to any other point and let go. As the pendulum swings back and forth, it is out of equilibrium, but the pendulum eventually returns to its equilibrium. The equilibrium point at the bottom is stable. The market's equilibrium is analogous to the pendulum's equilibrium in this respect. Whenever the desires of consumers and firms do not match, the economic self-interests of business firms and consumers cause price and output to change until desires do match, and the market returns to equilibrium.

To see why the equilibrium is stable, return to the case of the market in excess supply at a price of $24. Refer again to Figure 5.9(a). Let's begin with the firms' adjustments, since they make the production and pricing decisions. Firms produce 14 million discs with the expectation that they can sell this amount at a price of $24. The firms have misread the market, however. They are unable to sell all they would like to sell at $24. Consumers only want to buy 4 million discs. Unsold discs begin to accumulate at an annual rate of 10 million discs, the amount of the excess supply. Producing goods that cannot be sold is clearly unprofitable, the signal to the firms that the current market situation is not sustainable.

The firms will not continue to set their prices at $24 and supply 14 million discs year after year, knowing that consumers will only purchase 4 million discs. Rather, the firms can be expected to respond to the situation of excess supply in two ways. First, they sell off the unsold discs at special, one-time-only bargain prices. We have all seen these "inventory reduction sales." Once the discs have been produced, selling them at any price is more profitable than leaving them unsold. According to the demand curve in Figure 5.9(a), the price must fall all the way to $8 to induce consumers to purchase 14 million discs, the total amount of discs produced this year. Second, the firms assume that $24 is not a sustainable price, that the market price will soon decline. Because firms expect the price to fall, they lower their annual rate of production. Each firm moves back down its supply curve, with the result that both price and quantity supplied decline next year.

Firms make the production and pricing decisions, but consumers are equally important to the process of reaching the equilibrium. The fact that consumers only want to buy 4 million discs at a price of $24 contributes to the original excess supply. Then, as the price falls, consumers' economic self-interest of trying to maximize utility leads them to move down their demand curves. Their quantity demanded increases, further reducing the excess supply in the marketplace.

If some excess supply remains at the new lower price, firms adjust once again. Price continues to fall, quantity supplied decreases, and quantity demanded increases. The process of firms adjusting their sights downward continues until the price reaches the equilibrium price of $16, at which point all excess supply has been removed from the market. Firms are able to sell 9 million discs at a price of $16, exactly the amount they want to sell. The market has returned to equilibrium.

Choosing $24 as the starting price in this example is entirely arbitrary. The same argument applies for *any* price above the equilibrium price of $16. The profit motive of business firms, combined with consumers' desires to maximize utility, eventually drives all prices greater than $16 back down to $16. As a result, the quantity exchanged in the market returns to 9 million discs.

Prices below $16 are also not sustainable. They, too, will be driven back to equilibrium. Return to the case of the market in excess demand at a price of $8, shown in Figure 5.9(b). The firms believe the market price of $8 and plan to sell 3 million discs. The firms will soon realize that they have misread the market, however, this time being overly pessimistic. Eager consumers quickly remove all the product from the shelves. The quantity demanded, 14 million discs, exceeds the available supply of 3 million discs. Faced with a shortage of discs some customers offer to pay far more than the current market price of $8 "under the table." According to the demand curve in Figure 5.9(b), all 3 million discs can be sold at a price as high as $28.

The signals of empty shelves and "under the table" payments when the price is $8 are unmistakable. Firms know that they should increase both price and quantity supplied in order to increase their profits. Each firm moves up its supply curve. As the price increases, the self-interest of consumers leads them to decrease their quantity demanded, further reducing the amount of excess demand. The price continues to increase each period until it reaches the equilibrium price of $16, at which point all the excess demand is removed from the market. The same adjustment applies starting at any price below $16. The profit motive of business firms, combined with consumers' desires to maximize utility, eventually drives all prices less than $16 back up to $16. As a result, the quantity exchanged in the market returns to 9 million discs.

Of all the possible quantity-price combinations, therefore, only one need concern us—9 million discs and a price of $16, the point of intersection of the market supply and the market demand curves. If the market is there, it will stay there; if it is not there, it should quickly and automatically go there. By a happy coincidence, this is exactly the point our eye is led to on a supply and demand diagram.

The importance of a **stable market equilibrium** can hardly be overstated. If price and quantity could settle anywhere, no theory could possibly explain market events, past, present, or future. Economic analysis of a market economy would simply be impossible. Markets events become understandable, and predictable, only with the assurance that quantity and price will settle at their equilibrium values.

STABLE MARKET EQUILIBRIUM
A property of the market equilibrium such that the market automatically returns to the equilibrium from any other quantity-price combination.

Analyzing Markets Using Supply and Demand Curves

Prices and quantities in individual markets are forever changing. How can this be if the market quickly settles on one equilibrium price and quantity? The answer is that these changes in prices and quantities represent movements from one equilibrium to another.

The market equilibrium changes in response to *shifts* in the market demand curve, in the market supply curve, or in both. These shifts in turn are caused by changes in one or more of the variables determining quantity demanded or supplied, *other than the price of the product itself.* As we have seen, events causing the market demand curve to shift include changes in consumers' incomes (including changes in taxes and transfer payments), tastes, the prices of substitutes and complements, and the size and composition of the population. Events causing the market supply curve to shift include changes in production technologies, factor prices, and the prices of other products and direct changes in the quantity supplied resulting from crop failures or the presence of new firms in the industry. The following examples illustrate how shifts in the market demand and the market supply curves affect the equilibrium price and the equilibrium quantity.

SHIFTS IN THE DEMAND CURVE   Suppose that consumers' incomes increase. The increase in incomes increases the demand for all normal goods and services. Figure 5.10 shows the independent effect of the increase in incomes on the market equilibrium for a typical product.

FIGURE 5.10

A Shift in Demand

The market is originally in equilibrium at (Q_0, P_0), at the intersection of D and S. An increase in consumers' incomes increases demand, and the demand curve shifts up and to the right from D to D'. The new equilibrium is (Q_1, P_1), at the intersection of D' and S. An increase in demand tends to increase both the equilibrium price and the equilibrium quantity.

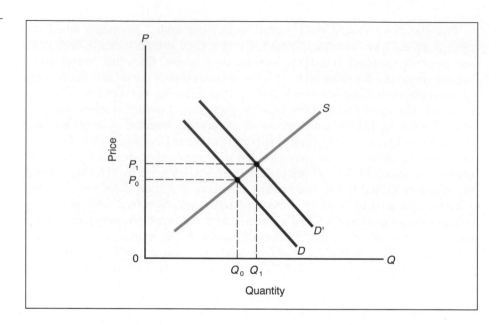

S is the market supply curve, and D is the market demand curve before the increase in incomes occurs. The original equilibrium is (Q_0, P_0), at the intersection of D and S. The increase in incomes shifts the market demand curve up and to the right from D to D'. The market establishes a new equilibrium (Q_1, P_1), at the intersection of D' and S. *The increase in demand increases both the equilibrium quantity and the equilibrium price.*

SHIFTS IN THE SUPPLY CURVE   Prices and quantities do not necessarily both increase over time, however; the computer industry is an obvious example of this fact. The use of computers has grown enormously over the past 20 years, while the price of a given amount of computing power has plummeted. Quantities have increased, and prices have decreased because the market for computers has been dominated by rapid technological change. The progression from vacuum tubes, to transistors, to silicon microchips, to microprocessors has substantially lowered the (marginal) cost of producing a given amount of computing power. The technological change has greatly increased supply. Figure 5.11 shows the independent effect of technological change on the market equilibrium in the computer market.

D is the market demand curve, and S is the market supply curve prior to the invention of the latest technology, the microprocessor. The original equilibrium is (Q_0, P_0), at the intersection of S and D. The technological change brought on by the invention of the microprocessor decreases costs and causes an increase in supply, shifting the market supply curve downward from S to S'. The new equilibrium is (Q_1, P_1), at the intersection of S' and D. *The increase in supply increases the equilibrium quantity and lowers the equilibrium price.* (The demand curve has also shifted out rapidly over time, but not by enough to overcome the even more rapid shift in the supply curve.) Thanks to technological progress, consumers can now buy personal computers for a few thousand dollars with computing power that, 10 years ago, was only available to businesses at prices of $100,000 and more.

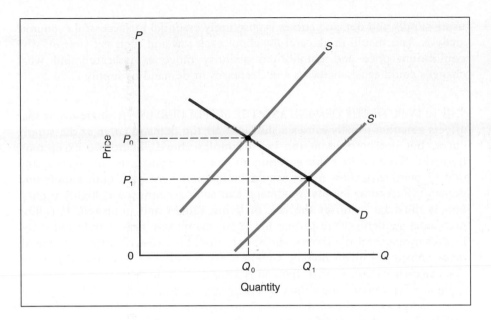

FIGURE 5.11

A Shift in Supply: Technological Change in Computers

Rapid technological change increases supply in the market for computers and drives down computer prices. The equilibrium in the computer market is (Q_0, P_0) before the latest technological change, at the intersection of D and S. The technological change increases supply, and the supply curve shifts down and to the right from S to S'. The new equilibrium is (Q_1, P_1), at the intersection of D and S'. An increase in supply tends to increase the equilibrium quantity and decrease the equilibrium price.

The first four rows of the Concept Summary table indicate the expected effects on equilibrium quantity and equilibrium price of all possible shifts in either the demand curve or the supply curve. The two examples above correspond to rows 1 and 3. Developing a facility for analyzing market events

CONCEPT SUMMARY

EFFECTS ON EQUILIBRIUM QUANTITY AND PRICE OF SHIFTS IN DEMAND AND SUPPLY CURVES

SHIFT	EFFECT ON EQUILIBRIUM QUANTITY	EFFECT ON EQUILIBRIUM PRICE
Demand increases Supply constant	Increases	Increases
Demand decreases Supply constant	Decreases	Decreases
Supply increases Demand constant	Increases	Decreases
Supply decreases Demand constant	Decreases	Increases
Demand increases Supply increases	Increases	?
Demand decreases Supply increases	?	Decreases
Demand increases Supply decreases	?	Increases
Demand decreases Supply decreases	Decreases	?

using supply and demand curves is absolutely essential to successful economic analysis. You should think carefully about each row and then ask yourself why equilibrium price and equilibrium quantity move as indicated and what changes could cause increases and decreases in demand or supply.

SHIFTS IN BOTH THE DEMAND AND THE SUPPLY CURVES   A single event that affects a market usually causes a shift in *either* the demand curve *or* the supply curve, but not both, as in the two examples above. There are exceptions, however. Suppose that the government were to legalize the production and sale of marijuana. This policy would undoubtedly increase both supply and demand. Regarding supply, producing and selling marijuana is highly profitable. It must be to offset the risk of being caught and punished. If selling marijuana suddenly were to become legal, many new firms would enter the market in search of the profits, and supply would increase. Regarding demand, many consumers might now be willing to try marijuana absent the legal sanctions against its use, so that demand is also likely to increase.

Figure 5.12 shows the effect of legalization on the market for marijuana. The market demand and the market supply curves before legalization are D and S. The market equilibrium before legalization is (Q_0, P_0), at the intersection of S and D. As a result of legalization, supply increases from S to S', and demand increases from D to D'. The new equilibrium is (Q_1, P_1), at the intersection of S' and D'. According to Figure 5.12, the equilibrium quantity of

FIGURE 5.12

Shifts in Both Supply and Demand: Legalizing Marijuana

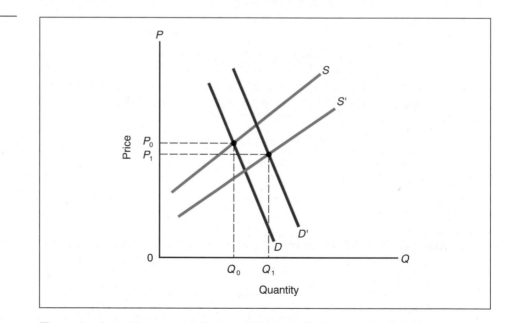

The market for marijuana is originally in equilibrium at (Q_0, P_0) before legalization, at the intersection of D and S. Legalizing marijuana would increase supply as more people grow marijuana for market. The supply curve shifts down and to the right from S to S'. Legalizing marijuana would also increase demand as more people are willing to use it. The demand curve shifts up and to the right from D to D'. The new equilibrium is (Q_1, P_1) after legalization, at the intersection of D' and S'. Increases in both supply and demand tend to increase the equilibrium quantity. The equilibrium price may increase, stay the same, or decrease depending on the relative size of the shifts in supply and demand.

marijuana increases substantially, but the equilibrium price of marijuana hardly changes at all.

The different amounts that quantity and price change illustrate an important general principle. *When both the supply and the demand curves shift, the direction of change in the equilibrium can confidently be predicted for quantity or for price, but not for both.* For example, legalizing marijuana would almost certainly increase the equilibrium quantity of marijuana exchanged in the market. Increases in supply and increases in demand tend to increase the equilibrium quantity. The effect on price is uncertain, however. The increase in demand tends to increase the equilibrium price; the increase in supply tends to decrease the equilibrium price. Therefore, whether the equilibrium price increases, decreases, or remains the same depends on the amount that each curve shifts. Figure 5.12 shows the supply shift slightly dominating the demand shift, so that the equilibrium price declines somewhat. But this does not necessarily have to be true. Were marijuana legalized, its price could rise if the increase in demand were strong enough to overcome the increase in supply.

The second four rows in the Concept Summary table indicate the predicted effects on equilibrium quantity and equilibrium price when both curves shift. Usually both curves shift as a result of two separate events, one event shifting each curve. A question mark (?) indicates that the predicted effect is uncertain. Once again, you should practice shifting demand and supply curves to make sure you understand the entries in each row.

Supply, Demand, and Inflation

A word of caution is in order about interpreting supply and demand diagrams during the inflationary times in which we live. A general price inflation poses a frame of reference problem for supply and demand analysis.

Supply and demand curves are drawn under the assumption that all the variables affecting quantity supplied and quantity demanded, other than the price of the product itself, are being held constant. The list of "other things equal" includes the prices of all other products. In other words, a supply and demand diagram implicitly assumes that there is no general price inflation. In fact, the prices of most goods and services are rising year by year. Therefore, a price change shown on a supply and demand diagram must be reinterpreted *relative* to the general rate of inflation. The price change is interpreted as a **real price change,** equal to the actual change in the price less the general rate of inflation.

For example, in 1992 the prices of goods and services purchased by consumers rose at an average rate of 2.9 percent. If a supply and demand analysis of some market shows that the price of the product increased during 1992, then the analysis is indicating that the price increased *relative* to the average of all other prices. Not only did the actual price of the product increase; it also increased by *more than* 2.9 percent. If the supply and demand analysis shows no change in the product's price during 1992, then the price did not change relative to the average of all other prices. The actual price increased by 2.9 percent, the overall rate of inflation. If the supply and demand analysis shows a decrease in price, then the price fell relative to the average of all other prices. The actual price may or may not have decreased. All the analysis indicates is that the price increased by *less than* 2.9 percent. Relative, or real, price de-

REAL PRICE CHANGE

The actual change in a price less the general rate of inflation.

HISTORICAL NOTE: A case of Budweiser sold for about $6.00 in the late 1960s when many of the parents of today's college students were in college. Today a case of Budweiser sells for about $15.00, two and a half times as much. But prices generally are over four times higher today than they were in the late 1960s, which means that the real price of Budweiser is much lower now than it was 25 years ago.

creases are common, even if actual price decreases are not. The prices of many products rise each year by less than the overall rate of inflation.

THE ELASTICITIES OF DEMAND AND SUPPLY

The preceding section showed the *direction* that equilibrium price and equilibrium quantity change in response to changes in demand and supply. We would like to know more than this, however, when analyzing market events. We would also like to have some idea *how much* the equilibrium price and the equilibrium quantity can be expected to change: A lot? A little? Hardly at all? The concept of elasticity tells us this. Elasticity is a measure of the responsiveness of quantity demanded or quantity supplied to a change in price. Let's begin with the elasticity of demand.

The Elasticity of Demand

(PRICE) ELASTICITY OF DEMAND

A measure of the responsiveness of quantity demanded to changes in the price of a product along a demand curve; specifically, the percentage change in quantity demanded divided by the percentage change in price (expressed as an absolute value).

The **price elasticity of demand** refers to the responsiveness of quantity demanded to a change in the price of the product along a demand curve. We will refer to the price elasticity of demand simply as the elasticity of demand, or demand elasticity, throughout the text. This is standard practice in economics. Elasticity always refers to price elasticity unless otherwise modified.

The elasticity of demand measures the responsiveness of quantity demanded by comparing the percentage change in quantity demanded with the percentage change in price. In particular, the elasticity of demand is the ratio of the percentage change in quantity demanded to the percentage change in price. The elasticity ratio is defined as an absolute number: Plus and minus signs are ignored when computing the percentage changes. In algebraic terms, the price elasticity of demand is

$$E_D = |\% \text{ change in quantity demanded}| \ / \ |\% \text{ change in price}|$$

where E_D is the price elasticity of demand. Demand is said to be elastic, unit-elastic, or inelastic depending on whether E_D is greater than, equal to, or less than 1.

1. If $E_D > 1$ demand is *elastic* between the prices. The percentage change in quantity exceeds the percentage change in price. Quantity demanded is relatively responsive to a change in price in percentage terms.
2. If $E_D = 1$, demand is *unit-elastic* between the prices.
3. If $E_D < 1$, demand is *inelastic* between the prices. The percentage change in quantity is less than the percentage change in price. Quantity demanded is relatively unresponsive to a change in price in percentage terms.

CALCULATING PERCENTAGE CHANGES   The following example illustrates the percentage change measure. Suppose that the quantity demanded of some product decreases from 600 to 300 units when the price of the product increases from $1 to $3. Is the demand for that product elastic, unit-elastic, or inelastic between $1 and $3?

Calculating the elasticity of demand runs into an immediate problem. Percentage changes are arbitrary numbers. A percentage change of any variable is the amount the variable changes divided by a base amount and multiplied by 100 to convert decimals to percentages. In our example quantity demanded decreases from 600 to 300 units. The change in the quantity demanded is 300 units (300 = 600 − 300). But what base quantity should we use in the denominator to divide into the change? In everyday practice the initial quantity of 600 is usually chosen as the base. Using this convention, the percentage change in quantity demanded is

$$|(\text{Change in quantity/base quantity}) \cdot 100| =$$

$$|(300/600) \cdot 100| = 50\%$$

The decrease in quantity demanded from 600 to 300 units is commonly represented as a 50 percent decrease.

Suppose, however, that the price returns to $1 and the quantity demanded to 600 units. By how much has the quantity demanded increased in percentage terms? Following the standard practice, 300 units would now be used as the initial base quantity. The 300-unit increase in quantity demanded would be represented as a 100 percent increase:

$$|(\text{Change in quantity/base quantity}) \cdot 100| =$$

$$|(300/300) \cdot 100| = 100\%$$

The two percentage changes are not symmetric, even though the actual change in quantity demanded is the same in each case.

To make increases and decreases symmetric, economists define the base quantity as halfway between the original and the new quantities. In our example the base would be 450 units (450 = (300 + 600)/2 = 900/2), and both the increase and the decrease in quantity demanded would be represented as a 67 percent change in quantity demanded.

$$|(\text{Change in quantity/base quantity}) \cdot 100| =$$

$$|(300/450) \cdot 100| = 67\%$$

The percentage change in price is calculated the same way. When the price increases from $1 to $3, the change in price is $2 ($2 = $3 − $1). The halfway point between the original and the new prices is $2($2 = ($1 + $3)/2 = $4/2). Therefore, the $2 increase in price is represented as a 100 percent increase:

$$|(\text{Change in price/base price}) \cdot 100| =$$

$$|(\$2/\$2) \cdot 100| = 100\%$$

The elasticity of demand between the two prices is the ratio of the percentage change in quantity to the percentage change in price.

$$E_D = 67\%/100\% = .67$$

Since the elasticity is less than 1, demand for the product is inelastic between $1 and $3. This method of calculating elasticity between two prices is called the arc elasticity of demand.[1]

A number of comments on the percentage change measure of elasticity are in order.

1. Absolute values are used to make all elasticity numbers positive. Otherwise, elasticity calculations along demand curves would be negative numbers because price and quantity are moving in different directions. When price increases (+), quantity demanded decreases (−); when price decreases (−), quantity demanded increases (+). Comparing negative numbers can be confusing.

2. The comparison between a change in price and the resulting change in quantity demanded must be made in percentage terms to avoid an "apples versus oranges" comparison between prices and quantities. Prices and quantities are measured in different units. Comparing actual changes in dollars with actual changes in units, or tons, or bushels is meaningless. For example, suppose that a $2.50 decrease in the price of compact discs increases the quantity demanded for the entire market by 60,000 discs per month. How can $2.50 be compared directly with 60,000 compact discs?

   Percentage changes are pure, unit-free numbers. In computing the percentage change in quantity, the units in which the quantity is measured appear in both the numerator and the denominator. Therefore, the units cancel in the calculation. Similarly, in computing the percentage change in price, dollars appear in both the numerator and the denominator. Therefore, dollars also cancel in the calculation. Since elasticity is the ratio of two pure, unit-free numbers, elasticity is also a pure, unit-free number.

3. Finally, the price elasticity of demand is an other things equal concept because it measures the responsiveness of quantity demanded to price along a demand curve. All other factors that might influence quantity demanded are assumed to be constant.

THE LIMITS: PERFECTLY INELASTIC AND PERFECTLY ELASTIC DEMAND   How large can demand elasticity be over a range of prices? How small can demand elasticity be? The reasonable limits are presented in Figure 5.13.

In Figure 5.13(a) the demand curve is vertical. The vertical line indicates that quantity demanded is totally unresponsive to changes in price: No matter what the price, quantity demanded remains at Q_0. When the demand curve is vertical, demand is *perfectly inelastic*. The percentage change measure of elasticity is zero.

The horizontal demand curve in Figure 5.13(b) represents the opposite extreme. Quantity demanded is as responsive to price changes as it can possibly be. Suppose that quantity demanded is originally at Q_0. Any increase in price

---

[1]Elasticity can also be measured at a point along a demand curve on the assumption that price changes by only a small amount. Write the ratio of the percentage change in output to the percentage change in price as $E_D = ((\Delta Q/Q)/(\Delta P/P))$. The Greek symbol Δ, called "delta," stands for "change in." Rearranging terms, $E_D = ((\Delta Q/\Delta P) \cdot (P/Q))$. The term $(\Delta Q/\Delta P)$ is the inverse of the slope of the demand curve at the given price and quantity, P and Q. E_D expressed this way is called the *point elasticity of demand*. Notice that E_D varies along a straight line demand curve. The slope is constant along a straight line demand curve, so that $(\Delta Q/\Delta P)$ is constant. But (P/Q) varies along the demand curve, falling as P decreases and Q increases. Therefore, E_D also falls along a straight line demand curve as P decreases and Q increases.

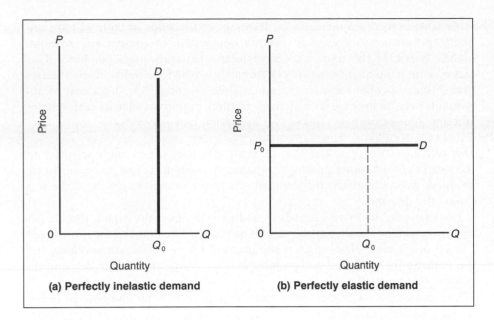

FIGURE 5.13

Perfectly Inelastic and Perfectly Elastic Demand

The extreme cases of demand elasticity are perfectly inelastic and perfectly elastic demand. The demand curve is vertical when demand is perfectly inelastic (Figure 5.13(a)). The quantity demanded is Q_0 no matter what the price. A change in price causes no change in quantity demanded. The demand curve is horizontal when demand is perfectly elastic (Figure 5.13(b)). The slightest increase in price above P_0 causes quantity demanded to fall to zero. The slightest decrease in price below P_0 causes quantity demanded to increase without limit.

above P_0 causes quantity demanded to go to zero. Any decrease in price below P_0 causes quantity demanded to grow without bound. When the demand curve is horizontal, demand is *perfectly elastic*. The percentage change measure of elasticity is infinitely large.

THE DETERMINANTS OF DEMAND ELASTICITY   What properties of goods and services determine whether their demands will be price elastic or inelastic? There are four principal factors that determine the elasticity of demand: whether the product is considered to be essential or inessential, whether it is expensive or inexpensive, the availability of substitute products, and the passage of time.

ESSENTIAL/INESSENTIAL   Do consumers consider the product essential or something of a luxury? The more essential the product, the more inelastic its demand; the less essential the product, the more elastic its demand. For example, we would expect the demand for food consumed at home to be far more inelastic than is the demand for food purchased in restaurants. Similarly, consumers' demand for automobiles is likely to be more inelastic than is their demand for air travel. Most people living in the suburbs consider the automobile a virtual necessity. In contrast, most people use air travel for vacations and visits to friends and relatives. If air fares increase significantly, this type of leisure travel can be postponed easily.

EXPENSIVE/INEXPENSIVE   As a general rule the less expensive a product, the more inelastic its demand; the more expensive a product, the more elastic its demand. Consumers are likely to be price sensitive to more expensive products for the simple reason that these products use more of their scarce incomes. The opportunity costs of consuming more expensive products are higher.

A pound of table salt costs about $.30 and seems to last for years. It is so cheap that most people probably do not know its price when they buy it. Even fairly large percentage increases or decreases in the price of table salt are unlikely to have much effect on quantity demanded. In comparison, an automobile is one of the more expensive items that consumers purchase. This factor alone tends to increase its price elasticity, which partially offsets the fact that so many people consider the automobile essential. The high cost of automobiles also helps explain why manufacturer incentives such as cash rebates and low-interest car loans succeed in increasing new car sales.

THE AVAILABILITY OF SUBSTITUTES   Demand elasticity is extremely sensitive to the number of substitute products available to consumers. The more substitute products, the more elastic the demand; the fewer substitute products, the less elastic the demand.

For example, the more narrowly a product is defined, the higher the elasticity is because the number of substitutes increases. The demand for a mid-sized Ford is much more elastic than is the demand for mid-sized automobiles, and the demand for mid-sized automobiles is more elastic than is the demand for automobiles generally.

Sometimes the three factors we have examined thus far combine to create a strong presumption that demand is either elastic or inelastic. At other times they give mixed signals. For example, the demand for table salt is presumably highly inelastic. Salt is considered essential by most people, it is inexpensive, and it does not have any close substitutes. Conversely, the demand for a Zenith 25-inch color television is presumably highly elastic. Owning a 25-inch color television set is hardly one of life's essentials. A 25-inch color television costs hundreds of dollars, and a Zenith 25-inch color television has many substitutes, the 25-inch color televisions of the other manufacturers. The characteristics of automobiles give mixed signals. The automobile is a necessity for many people, which tends to make its demand inelastic, but it is also very expensive, which tends to make its demand elastic. Public transportation and air and rail travel are substitutes in some uses, but in other uses the automobile has no reasonable substitutes. Because the signals are mixed, we cannot presume that the demand for automobiles is elastic or inelastic. In fact, researchers have found that the demand for automobiles is approximately unit-elastic.

THE PASSAGE OF TIME   The final determinant of demand elasticity is the passage of time. It differs from the other determinants because it applies to all products regardless of their characteristics. Demand becomes more elastic with the passage of time following a change in price simply because people need time to adjust to price changes. We are all creatures of habit to some extent and tend to resist change for any reason. Also, people may react to price changes by demanding different kinds of products, and business firms need time to change production to meet the new demands. In any event, demands that appear highly inelastic immediately following a price change may turn out to be fairly elastic after a year or so.

(PRICE) ELASTICITY OF SUPPLY

A measure of the responsiveness of quantity supplied to a change in price along a supply curve; specifically, the percentage change in quantity supplied divided by the percentage change in price.

The Elasticity of Supply

The **(price) elasticity of supply** measures the responsiveness of quantity supplied to changes in price along a supply curve. It shares the following properties with the elasticity of demand:

1. The elasticity of supply is defined as the ratio of the percentage change in quantity supplied to the percentage change in price:

$$E_S = \frac{(\% \text{ change in quantity supplied})}{(\% \text{ change in price})}$$

Unlike demand elasticity, however, supply elasticity does not use absolute values. Elasticity is always positive along an upward-sloping supply curve.

2. Supply is *elastic* if $E_S > 1$, unit-elastic if $E_S = 1$, and inelastic if $E_S < 1$.

3. The reasonable limits to supply elasticity are the same as for demand elasticity. A *vertical* supply curve is *perfectly inelastic*. Quantity supplied is completely unresponsive to changes in price, and $E_S = 0$. A *horizontal* supply curve is *perfectly elastic*. Quantity supplied is infinitely responsive to even the smallest change in price, and E_S is infinitely large.

THE DETERMINANTS OF SUPPLY ELASTICITY Four principal factors determine the elasticity of supply: the characteristics of the production technology, the ability of firms to switch production from one product to another, the amount of excess capacity in the industry, and the passage of time.

THE CHARACTERISTICS OF THE PRODUCTION TECHNOLOGY The production technology used to produce a product is central to the question of supply elasticity because the technology determines the relationship between the factor inputs and the output. When firms hire more factors of production to increase production, the production technology determines whether the resulting increase in output is large or small. The more labor, materials, fuel, and machines needed to produce a given increase in output, the higher the costs of producing the additional output, and the more inelastic (steeper) the firms' supply curves. Firms require higher prices to cover the higher costs. Conversely, the smaller the increase in factor inputs required to produce a given increase in output, the lower the costs of producing that output, and the more elastic (flatter) the firms' supply curves.

SUBSTITUTABILITY IN PRODUCTION In a production context, substitutability refers to the ability of firms to switch production among alternative products. As such, it relates to the production technologies of all the products a firm might produce. The more easily firms can shift production to other products, the more *elastic* the supply is; the more difficult it is for firms to shift production to other products, the more *inelastic* the supply is. Increases in the price of one product make it relatively more profitable than other products, whose prices remain constant. Firms want to shift resources from their other products to this product. Conversely, decreases in the price of one product make it relatively less profitable than other products, and firms want to shift resources toward their other products. The incentive to shift resources as prices change always exists. The substitutability among production processes determines how easily firms can respond to this incentive.

THE AMOUNT OF EXCESS CAPACITY IN THE INDUSTRY The elasticity of supply depends on how close the industry is operating to its full capacity, the limit of its production capability. The closer the industry is to full capacity, the more *inelastic* supply is; the farther the industry is from full capacity, the more *elastic* supply is. When firms have considerable excess capacity, some of their plant and equipment lies idle. If market conditions turn more favorable and if the firms hire additional workers in order to increase output, these workers can more fully utilize the idled plant and equipment. Output can be increased fairly easily and without large additional costs, since the firms have already purchased the idle resources. Near capacity, however, production is straining against the firms' plant and equipment, and output is more difficult and more costly to increase. The firms may be forced to pay workers overtime or to run more costly second and third shifts. Productivity also suffers if workers tire and the equipment breaks down more often, which reduces the additional output produced. The supply response becomes increasingly inelastic. Once firms reach their absolute maximum capacities the market supply curve becomes perfectly inelastic. Further increases in output are impossible regardless of the price.

THE PASSAGE OF TIME   The supply elasticities of most products increase with the passage of time following a change in price, just as the demand elasticities do. Firms, like consumers, are better able to respond to changing market conditions as time passes.

The following Concept Summary table summarizes the determinants of demand and supply elasticity.

CONCEPT SUMMARY
DETERMINANTS OF DEMAND AND SUPPLY ELASTICITY

A. DETERMINANTS OF DEMAND ELASTICITY

FACTOR	MORE ELASTIC	LESS ELASTIC
Essential/ inessential	Product considered inessential	Product considered essential
Expensive/ inexpensive	The more expensive the product	The cheaper the product
Availability of substitutes	Substitute products readily available	Substitute products not readily available
Passage of time	The longer the time from a price change	The shorter the time from a price change

B. DETERMINANTS OF SUPPLY ELASTICITY

FACTOR	MORE ELASTIC	LESS ELASTIC
Production technology	Fewer inputs required for a given increase in output	More inputs required for a given increase in output
Substitutability	Easy to switch to other products	Difficult to switch to other products
Capacity	Far from capacity	Close to capacity
Passage of time	The longer the time from a price change	The shorter the time from a price change

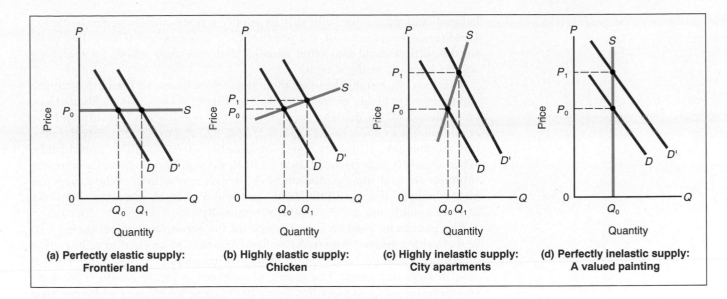

(a) **Perfectly elastic supply:**
    Frontier land

(b) **Highly elastic supply:**
    Chicken

(c) **Highly inelastic supply:**
    City apartments

(d) **Perfectly inelastic supply:**
    A valued painting

An increase in demand has different effects on the equilibrium quantity and equilibrium price depending on the elasticity of supply. In Figure 5.14(a), the supply of frontier land is perfectly elastic. The increase in demand for frontier land increases the equilibrium quantity from Q_0 to Q_1, but has no effect on the equilibrium price. In Figure 5.14(b), the supply of chicken is highly elastic. The increase in demand for chicken leads to a relatively large increase in the equilibrium quantity from Q_0 to Q_1, and a relatively small increase in the equilibrium price from P_0 to P_1. In Figure 5.14(c), the supply of city apartments is highly inelastic. The increase in demand for apartments leads to a relatively small increase in the equilibrium quantity from Q_0 to Q_1, and a relatively large increase in the equilibrium price (rent) from P_0 to P_1. In Figure 5.14(d), the supply of a famous painting is perfectly inelastic. The increase in demand for the painting increases the equilibrium price from P_0 to P_1, but has no effect on the equilibrium quantity.

FIGURE 5.14

Elasticities and Market Outcomes

Elasticities and Market Outcomes

Knowledge of demand and supply elasticities adds to our understanding of market outcomes because these elasticities determine, in part, the amount by which the equilibrium price and the equilibrium quantity change in response to changes in supply and demand. In the limiting cases of perfectly elastic or inelastic supply or demand, elasticity can override some of the expected effects on price and quantity listed in the Concept Summary on page 121.

The four graphs in Figure 5.14 show the effects of an increase in demand against four supply curves, ranging from perfectly elastic to perfectly inelastic. In each instance (Q_0, P_0), the intersection of the market supply curve, S, and the original market demand curve, D, is the original equilibrium. The new market demand curve after the increase in demand is D'.

When supply is perfectly elastic [Figure 5.14(a)], the increase in demand affects only the equilibrium quantity. Quantity increases, as expected, from Q_0 to Q_1. However, the equilibrium price remains at P_0 because suppliers are willing to supply any amount of the product at P_0. An example is the market for land on the frontier in colonial America. As the settlers pushed westward seeking new homesteads, the demand for frontier land increased. But uninhabited land was so plentiful that its supply was essentially perfectly elastic. Landowners could not raise the prices of their land because if they tried to do so, the settlers could find other plots of land that were selling for the going market price, P_0 in the diagram.

The next two graphs illustrate the intermediate cases. In Figure 5.14(b) the supply curve is highly elastic (very flat). In Figure 5.14(c) it is highly inelastic (very steep). When demand increase both the equilibrium quantity and the equilibrium price increase, as expected, from (Q_0, P_0) to (Q_1, P_1) in both cases. But the amounts of the price and the quantity increases differ considerably. When supply is high elastic [Figure 5.14(b)], the equilibrium quantity increases substantially, and the equilibrium price increases very little. When supply is highly inelastic [Figure 5.14(c)], the equilibrium quantity increases very little, and the equilibrium price increases substantially.

The market for chicken is an example of the second case. Over the past 20 years health-conscious Americans turned from beef to chicken to reduce their intake of fat and cholesterol. Fortunately for consumers, chickens are easy to raise in large quantities. The supply of chickens is highly elastic. Therefore, suppliers were able to meet the increased demand for chicken with very little increase in the price of chicken.

Apartments in urban areas illustrate the third case. As the population of the United States grew and became concentrated in the urban areas, the demand for apartments increased substantially. But urban land is scarce and highly valued for commercial and industrial uses. Increasing the supply of apartments is extremely costly because landlords have to bid the land away from potential industrial and commercial users. The supply of apartments is highly inelastic. Therefore, the increased demand for apartments has caused apartment rents to soar in many of the nation's cities.

Figure 5.14(d) shows the effect of an increase in demand when supply is perfectly inelastic. The equilibrium price increases, as expected, from P_0 to P_1, but the quantity remains at Q_0. Since the quantity supplied is Q_0 regardless of the price, it cannot respond to the price pressures resulting from an increase (or decrease) in demand. A good example of this case is the market for the famous paintings of the old masters. The demand for art has skyrocketed, but the supply of paintings cannot be increased. Consequently, the increase in demand has served only to bid up the prices to dizzying heights. Private art collectors now pay tens of millions of dollars for masterpieces such as Van Gogh's *Water Lilies*, much to the consternation of museum directors. The leading art museums are being bid out of the market for the best works of art.

The four graphs in Figure 5.14, and the examples, establish the following general principles: An increase or decrease in demand has a *larger* effect on the equilibrium *quantity* and a *smaller* effect on the equilibrium *price*, the *higher* the elasticity of supply. Conversely, an increase or decrease in demand has a *smaller* effect on the equilibrium *quantity* and a *larger* effect on the equilibrium *price*, the *lower* the elasticity of supply. In the limit of *perfectly elastic* supply, only *quantity* changes. Conversely, in the limit of *perfectly inelastic* supply, only *price* changes.

Using the same four graph technique, see if you can verify the corresponding general principles with respect to a shift in the supply curve:

An increase or decrease in supply has a *larger* effect on the equilibrium *quantity* and a *smaller* effect on the equilibrium *price*, the *higher* the elasticity of demand.

Conversely, an increase or decrease in supply has a *smaller* effect on the equilibrium *quantity* and a *larger* effect on the equilibrium *price,* the *lower* the elasticity of demand. In the limit of *perfectly elastic* demand (unlikely), only *quantity* changes. Conversely, in the limit of *perfectly inelastic* demand, only *price* changes.

Can you think of examples illustrating each case?

SUMMARY

Chapter 5 considered the Law of Supply and Demand. The chapter began with the demand side of the market.

1. The quantity demanded of a product is that amount that consumers are willing and able to buy over a certain period of time. The structure of the consumer's economic problem indicates that the quantity demanded is determined by the price of the product, the prices of related products, income, and tastes or preferences.

2. A demand schedule shows the quantity demanded at different prices, other things equal. A demand curve is a graph of a demand schedule. Demand schedules and demand curves obey the Law of Demand: The higher the price, the lower the quantity demanded, and vice versa.

3. The Law of Demand results from the substitution and the income effects of a price change. As a result of the substitution effect, consumers tend to substitute toward products that have become relatively cheaper. The income effect is a purchasing power effect that arises because a decrease in price increases purchasing power and therefore quantity demanded, and vice versa.

4. The market demand schedule is the sum of the individual consumers' demand schedules. Demand curves are graphical representations of these demand schedules. Thus, the market demand curve is the horizontal summation of the individual demand curves.

5. Market demand curves shift when one of the other variables influencing quantity demanded changes. The principal demand shifters are changes in income, population, tastes, and the prices of substitutes and complements.

6. An Engel's curve is the graph of the relationship between income and quantity demanded, other things equal, including the price of the product. Engel's curves are upward sloping for all normal goods.

The second section discussed the supply side of the market.

7. The quantity supplied of a product is the amount that firms are willing and able to sell over a certain period of time. The structure of the firm's economic problem indicates that the quantity supplied is determined by the price of the product, the prices of other products that the firm can supply, production technologies, factor prices, and taxes.

8. A supply schedule shows the quantity supplied at different prices, other things equal. A supply curve is a graph of a supply schedule. Supply schedules and supply curves obey the Law of Supply: The higher the price, the greater the quantity supplied, and vice versa.

9. The Law of Supply is based on the marginal cost of producing a product. Firms are willing to supply additional units of output only if price exceeds

marginal cost. Marginal cost rises as quantity supplied increases, so that firms require higher prices in order to increase supply.

10. The market supply schedule is the sum of the individual firms' supply schedules, and the market supply curve is the horizontal summation of the individual firms' supply curves.

11. Market supply curves shift when one of the other variables influencing quantity supplied changes. The principal supply shifters are changes in the prices of other products the firm supplies, the factor prices, the production technologies, and the number of firms in the industry and special events such as bad weather in agriculture.

The third section considered the interaction of supply and demand.

12. The equilibrium price and the equilibrium quantity occur at the intersection of the market demand and the market supply curves.

13. Any price greater than the equilibrium price causes excess supply. Any price lower than the equilibrium price causes excess demand. The market equilibrium is stable. The equilibrium price is the only sustainable price.

14. Equilibrium prices and equilibrium quantities change when either the market demand or the market supply curve shifts. When the market demand curve shifts, price and quantity move in the same direction; for example, an increase in demand increases both equilibrium price and equilibrium quantity. When the market supply curve shifts, price and quantity move in opposite directions; for example, an increase in supply decreases the equilibrium price and increases the equilibrium quantity.

15. The price changes shown on supply and demand diagrams are real price changes. A real price change is the actual price change less the overall rate of inflation.

The final section of the chapter discussed the price elasticities of demand and supply.

16. The (price) elasticity of demand (supply) is the ratio of the percentage change in quantity demanded (supplied) to the percentage change in price. Demand (supply) is elastic if the ratio is greater than 1, unit-elastic if the ratio equals 1, and inelastic if the ratio is less than 1. The price elasticity of demand is measured as an absolute value because price and quantity demanded change in opposite directions.

17. The principal determinants of demand elasticity are whether the product is considered to be essential or inessential, whether it is expensive or inexpensive, the availability of substitutes, and the passage of time.

18. The principal determinants of supply elasticity are the characteristics of the production technology, substitutability in production, the amount of excess capacity in an industry, and the passage of time.

19. An increase or decrease in demand has a larger (smaller) effect on the equilibrium quantity and a smaller (larger) effect on the equilibrium price, the higher (lower) the elasticity of supply. In the limit of perfectly elastic (inelastic) supply, only quantity (price) changes. A similar principle applies to an increase or decrease in supply.

KEY TERMS

Change in demand
Change in quantity demanded
Change in quantity supplied
Change in supply
Complements
Demand
(Price) Elasticity of demand
(Price) Elasticity of supply
Excess demand

Excess supply
Income effect (of a price change)
Individual demand curve
Individual firm's supply curve
Law of Demand
Law of Supply
Marginal cost
Market demand curve

Market equilibrium
Market supply curve
Purchasing power
Real price change
Stable market equilibrium
Substitutes
Substitution effect (of a price change)
Supply

QUESTIONS

1. a. What is the Law of Demand?
   b. How is it supported by the substitution and the income effects of a price change?
   c. What are the "other things equal" with respect to the demand curve?
2. a. What is the Law of Supply?
   b. What are the "other things equal" with respect to the supply curve?
   c. Why do we expect a firm's supply curve to be upward sloping?
3. Are the following pairs of goods likely to be complements, substitutes, or unrelated?
   a. baseball; California Angels ticket
   b. haircut; shampoo
   c. cream cheese; bagel
   d. golf clubs; tennis racquet
   e. Ford Taurus; Harley-Davidson motorcycle
4. Are the following goods likely to be inferior goods or normal goods?
   a. potatoes
   b. polyester suit
   c. Lincoln Town car
   d. butter
   e. compact discs
5. Suppose that the market demand and the market supply for compact discs (CDs) for various prices are as follows:

PRICE	QUANTITY DEMANDED	QUANTITY SUPPLIED
$32	0	56
28	5	48
24	9	38
20	14	28
16	18	18
12	23	9
8	28	0

   a. What is the equilibrium price? The equilibrium quantity?

   b. Are the market demand and the market supply schedules consistent with the Laws of Demand and Supply?
   c. Would you expect the equilibrium identified in part a to be a stable equilibrium?
6. Refer again to the data in question 5.
   a. Is the market in excess demand or excess supply when the price is $24? When the price is $12? For each case calculate the amount of excess demand or excess supply.
   b. What is the amount bought and sold when the price is $12? Why?
7. Three people have the following individual demand schedules for product A.

PRICE	PERSON 1	PERSON 2	PERSON 3
$1	5	8	7
2	4	8	7
3	3	8	2
4	2	6	0
5	1	6	0

   The numbers in columns two through four are the quantities demanded at each price in the first column.
   a. What is the market demand schedule for this product? (Assume that these three people are the only buyers.) Also draw the market demand curve.
   b. Why might the three people have different demand schedules?
   c. Is Person 1's demand elastic or inelastic between the prices of $1 and $2? Between the prices of $4 and $5? Answer the same questions for Person 2.
8. Would the following tend to increase or decrease the demand for American automobiles?
   a. A popular automotive magazine claims that American automobiles consume far more gasoline than do comparable foreign automobiles.
   b. Consumer incomes decrease by 5 percent.

c. The price of foreign automobiles decreases by 10 percent.

d. New technologies decrease the annual cost of maintenance on American cars by 20 percent.

e. The cost of producing American automobiles decreases by 20 percent.

9. Would the following tend to increase or decrease the supply of American automobiles?

a. The wages of American auto workers fall by 10 percent.

b. Consumers' incomes rise by 20 percent.

c. The use of robots on the American assembly line reduces the costs of production.

d. One of the major American auto manufacturers goes out of business.

e. The cost of automobile insurance decreases.

10. How will each of the following affect the equilibrium price and the equilibrium quantity of gasoline? Illustrate using demand and supply curves.

a. A million consumers this year purchase smaller, more fuel efficient cars.

b. A new outbreak of hostilities in the Persian Gulf leads to a sharp increase in the price of a barrel of crude oil.

c. Events a and b happen at the same time.

11. We know that over the last 10 years both the demand for and the supply of personal computers have increased dramatically. What factors might explain the huge increase in demand? What factors might explain the huge increase in supply? Which do you think has been greater, the increase in demand or the increase in supply? Why?

12. Rank the following items from least elastic to most elastic, and explain your ranking.

a. table salt

b. Ford Taurus

c. dental care (assume no dental insurance)

13. a. Discuss how the effects on the market equilibrium of a change (increase or decrease) in demand depend on the elasticity of supply.

b. Now apply your discussion to the economy as a whole. Suppose that the total demand for goods and services in the economy increases. Under which conditions is the supply of total goods and services likely to increase more? (1) The economy is currently operating far below its production possibilities frontier. (2) The economy is currently operating very close to its production possibilities frontier? Why?

Introduction to Macroeconomic Theory and Policy

6

The Macroeconomic Policy Goals I: Long-Run Economic Growth and Full Employment

LEARNING OBJECTIVES

CONCEPTS TO LEARN

The macroeconomic policy goals

Full employment

Cyclical unemployment

Frictional/search unemployment

Structural unemployment

The natural rate of unemployment

The Rule of 72

CONCEPTS TO RECALL

Long-run economic growth [3]

The circular flow of economic activity [4]

The Laws of Supply and Demand [5]

he United States has been the world's dominant economy in the last half of the twentieth century. In 1960, 40 percent of all the output produced for market worldwide was produced in the United States. As late as 1990, the figure was still impressive—27 percent.

There are some very dark clouds on the horizon, however. The United States has experienced a significant decline in long-run economic growth since 1973. The United States pushed its production possibilities frontier out at an average rate of 3 percent per year throughout the entire twentieth century up to 1974. Since then the growth in potential output has never been as high as 3 percent in any one year, and the average rate of growth over the past 20 years has been closer to 1 percent than to 3 percent.

A two-percentage-point decline in long-run economic growth may not seem like very much, but if the low rate of growth continues, it will eventually have disastrous consequences. Suppose that the U.S. economy grows at slightly more than 1 percent per year throughout the twenty-first century, as it has since 1974. By the end of the century the U.S. economy will be only about one-third as large as it would have been had it returned to its previous growth rate of 3 percent per year. The United States will also surely be a second-rate economic power.

A ROAD MAP FOR MACROECONOMICS

Chapter 6 begins our study of macroeconomics, which looks at the performance of the entire economy. The macroeconomics chapters of the text address the three fundamental questions of macroeconomic analysis:

1. What factors determine the circular flow of economic activity through a nation's product and factor markets, which we described in Chapter 4?

The circular flow behaves very erratically in all the developed market economies, expanding in some years and contracting in others. A far more sobering thought is that the ebbs and flows of the market economies occasionally become extreme and cause tremendous suffering. Unemployment reached 25 percent of the labor force in the United States in 1933, the worst year in the Great Depression of the 1930s. Prices rose 8 trillion percent in Germany in the early 1920s. What causes the circular flow to increase or decrease? How can the extremes of depression and rampant inflation happen, and how can they be avoided? Explaining the behavior of the circular flow of economic activity is the focal point of macroeconomic analysis.

The two remaining questions are policy questions, and they both involve the circular flow of economic activity.

2. How does the circular flow of economic activity relate to the four macroeconomic policy goals that we identified in Chapter 2: long-run economic growth, full employment (low unemployment), price stability (a low rate of inflation), and stability in economic relations with foreign countries (a balance between imports and exports and a stable value of the currency)?

The macroeconomic policy goals are vitally important because they determine the economic well-being of a nation. We want to understand how the performance of the economy affects each one of them.

3. How can the government influence the level and the composition of the circular flow and thereby help society achieve the macroeconomic policy goals?

We noted in Chapter 2 that the United States does not usually attack the policy goals directly by hiring the unemployed in make-work government programs, by using price controls to halt inflation, and so forth. Instead, the federal government tries to achieve the policy goals indirectly by influencing the overall performance of the economy. The two policies that the federal government relies on most are fiscal policy and monetary policy. Fiscal policy is budgetary policy. It refers to changes in the federal government's expenditures and taxes made for the specific purpose of changing the level or the composition of the circular flow. Monetary policy refers to changes in the nation's money supply made for the specific purpose of changing the level or the composition of the circular flow. How can the federal government use its fiscal and monetary policies to achieve the macroeconomic policy goals? This is the central macroeconomic policy question in the United States.

Chapters 6 and 7 begin our study of macroeconomics with a close look at the four macroeconomic policy goals in the context of the U.S. economy. The main purpose of studying macroeconomics is to gain an understanding of how a nation can best achieve these goals. Therefore, we must have a clear idea of what the goals are, what the government is trying to achieve, before analyzing the performance of the U.S. economy.

Chapter 6 discusses the goals of long-run economic growth and full employment. As noted in Chapter 3, these two goals have the greatest impact on the economic health of any nation. Chapter 7 then discusses the remaining goals of price stability and stability in U.S. economic relations with other countries. Achieving these goals is also important to the economic health of a nation, but not nearly as important as long-run economic growth and full employment are.

LONG-RUN ECONOMIC GROWTH

We discussed the fundamental principles associated with long-run economic growth in Chapter 3. You should have a firm understanding of the following four points from Chapter 3 as you begin your study of macroeconomics.

1. Long-run economic growth refers to *persistent increases in the potential of the economy to produce goods and services*. The words to emphasize in the definition are *persistent* and *potential*. Long-run economic growth is an ongoing process. Success or failure in achieving long-run growth is measured not over a period of years, but over decades, or generations, or even centuries. An economy that grows for a few years and then stops has not experienced long-run economic growth. Also, long-run economic growth refers to year-by-year increases in the *potential*, or *maximum*, *amount* of goods and services that could possibly move through the circular flow of economic activity, as opposed to increases in the *actual amount* of goods and services that move

through the circular flow. We pictured the process of long-run economic growth in Chapter 3 as an ever-expanding production possibilities frontier. The economy may or may not be operating on its frontier in any given year, but the actual performance of the economy is irrelevant in measuring long-run economic growth.

2. The economic constraints on a nation that determine its production possibilities are the quantity and the quality of its resources and the production technologies that are available for turning the resources into goods and services. In order to grow, therefore, a nation must continuously increase the quantity and the quality of its resources and place new, more productive technologies into production. Also, nations are ultimately interested in the growth in output per person rather than the growth in output itself. The amount of goods and services that an economy can deliver to each person, on average, determines a nation's standard of living.

3. Investment is the key to increasing the standard of living. Investment includes both investment in physical capital, such as plant and equipment, and investment in human capital, or education. Investment promotes long-run economic growth in every possible way. Investment in physical capital increases the stock of plant and equipment, which is one of the three primary factors of production. Also, new plant and equipment is usually better, higher-quality plant and equipment. New machines and factories embody the new production technologies that scientists and engineers have developed. Investment in human capital, which includes formal education in school and on-the-job training in businesses, is also essential to the process of long-run economic growth. For growth to continue, an economy needs scientists and engineers who can develop new production technologies, managers who are trained to operate large and complex businesses, and an educated labor force that can adapt to new technologies. In short, investment is the key to improving the productivity of all resources. A nation cannot enjoy an ever-higher standard of living unless its resources are becoming ever more productive over time.

4. The question of how fast an economy will grow lies at the heart of the Now versus the Future question, one of the four basic economic questions that all societies must answer. Business firms can produce only two kinds of final goods and services, investment goods and consumer goods. Therefore, more investment this year to promote economic growth implies less consumption this year. Future generations benefit from the more rapid economic growth made possible by a higher level of investment. Current generations bear the opportunity costs of growth because they are sacrificing consumer goods. They must save a higher percentage of their incomes to provide the funds for investment. Higher saving and higher investment go hand in hand.

Review the discussion of long-run economic growth in Chapter 3 if any of these points are unclear. We will only add to them a sense of the magnitudes involved with long-run economic growth in the United States.

How Fast Can the Economy Grow?

The process of economic growth requires an enormous amount of patience because countries can only push their production possibilities out very slowly over time. Most economists would place the upper limit of the long-run growth in output for the United States at 4 percent per year, and even 4 percent may be a little high. The average annual rate of growth in output in the United States throughout the entire twentieth century has been just a shade below 3 percent. A reasonable long-run growth report card for the United States might be as follows: 3.0–4.0 percent, excellent; 2.5–3.0 percent, good; 2.0–2.5 percent, fair; 2.0 percent or less, poor.

The potential growth in the U.S. standard of living, as measured by the growth in output per person, is even more modest. The growth in output per person is approximately equal to the growth in output minus the growth in population. Therefore, if population is growing at 1 percent per year, the figures on the growth scorecard must each be reduced by 1 percentage point to put them on an output-per-person basis.

The difference between rates of growth in output of 4 percent and 2 percent may not seem like much, but do not be fooled by the small numbers. Countries whose output grows at 4 percent per year will eventually be much better off than will countries whose output grows at 2 percent per year.

THE RULE OF 72   When thinking about rates of growth you should be aware of a handy rule of thumb known as the Rule of 72. The rule indicates how quickly something that grows at a certain annual percentage rate doubles in value. It works as follows. Divide 72 by the annual rate of growth, *g*, expressed as a percentage:

$$R_{72} = 72/g\%$$

The ratio R_{72} gives the number of years it takes for something growing at *g* percent per year to double in value.

For example, if the output of economy A is growing at 4 percent per year, then

$$R_{72} = 72/4 = 18$$

The output of economy A doubles in value every 18 years. If the output of economy B is growing at 2 percent per year, then

$$R_{72} = 72/2 = 36$$

The output of economy B doubles in value every 36 years.

Suppose that our two hypothetical economies, A and B, were the same size in 1900. Economy A grows at 4 percent per year throughout the twentieth century and beyond, while economy B grows at 2 percent per year throughout the twentieth century and beyond. By 2008, 108 years later, economy A will have doubled its capacity to produce output six times (6 = 108/18). In other words, it will be 64 times larger in 2008 than in 1900 (64 = 2·2·2·2·2·2). Economy B will have doubled its capacity to produce output only three times (3 = 108/36). It will be eight times larger in 2008 than in 1900 (8 = 2·2·2). Starting from the same point as economy B in 1900, economy A's two-percentage-point growth advantage allows it to be *eight times* larger than economy B by the beginning of the next century (8 = 64/8). Small percentage

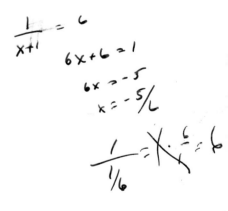

point differences in economic growth eventually make an enormous difference to the economic health of a nation.

The Recent U.S. Growth Report Card

How fast has the United States grown over the past few decades? This question is difficult to answer because long-run economic growth is difficult to measure. Remember that we are interested in the rate of growth of the *potential* or *maximum* output that the economy can produce, not in the actual rate of growth in output. Economists use two methods to estimate the rate of growth in potential output.

One method simply uses the actual rate of growth in output over a long period of time as the measure of long-run economic growth. The assumption is that the rate of growth in actual output approximates the rate of growth in potential output over the very long run. Our statement above that the U.S. economy has grown at a rate just shy of 3 percent per year throughout the twentieth century to 1974 made use of this method. The 3 percent growth rate refers to growth in actual output, not potential output, although the two were assumed to be one and the same over a 74-year period.

A second method attempts to measure long-run economic growth directly by building a simple model of the entire economy and then using the model to estimate what the level of national product (income) would be if the economy were operating on its production possibilities frontier. In other words, how much output could the economy produce if it were efficiently answering the How question, employing all its scarce resources and doing so as efficiently as possible? Changes in the estimated potential output year to year define the annual rate of economic growth.

Robert Gordon of Northwestern University used the second method to estimate the potential output of the U.S. economy every year since 1875. Part A of Table 6.1 records his estimates of long-run economic growth in the United States for each decade since 1950. The second column gives his estimate of the average annual rates of growth in total potential output for each decade; the third column records the average annual rates of growth in the U.S. population for each decade; the fourth column records the average annual rates of growth in potential output per person for each decade. Recall that the rate of growth in potential output per person is the best measure of the increase in a nation's standard of living. Notice that the rate of growth in potential output per person is approximately equal to the difference between the rate of growth in output and the rate of growth in population (within a few hundredths of a percentage point).

Gordon's estimates of potential output could well be inaccurate. No one can say for sure what the potential output of any economy is in any given year. Nonetheless, the estimates of the growth in potential output for the United States in Table 6.1 are the considered opinion of a recognized expert in macroeconomics, and we can safely assume that they are reasonably accurate. Gordon's estimates are also consistent with the pattern of long-run economic growth that most researchers find for the U.S. economy during the past 40 years.

We can see from the table that the rate of long-run economic growth in the United States has been steadily decreasing throughout the post–World War II

TABLE 6.1   **Long-Run Economic Growth in the United States**

A. AVERAGE ANNUAL RATES OF GROWTH BY DECADE, 1950–89

DECADE	GROWTH IN POTENTIAL OUTPUT %	GROWTH IN POPULATION %	GROWTH IN POTENTIAL OUTPUT PER PERSON %
1950–59	3.73	1.72	1.98
1960–69	3.51	1.27	2.21
1970–79	3.08	1.06	2.00
1980–89	2.36	0.98	1.37

B. AVERAGE ANNUAL RATES OF GROWTH BEFORE AND AFTER 1975

YEARS	GROWTH IN POTENTIAL OUTPUT %	GROWTH IN POPULATION %	GROWTH IN POTENTIAL OUTPUT PER PERSON %
1950–74	3.59	1.43	2.13
1975–90	2.54	1.02	1.50

SOURCE: R. Gordon, *Macroeconomics*, Fifth edition (Glenview IL: Scott, Foresman/Little, Brown, 1989), Appendix A, pp. A1–A7. Council of Economic Advisors, *Economic Report of the President, 1993* (Washington, D.C.: U.S. Government Printing Office, 1993), Table B-2, p. 351, Table B-3, p. 352, Table B-29, p. 381. The data on potential output for 1990 and 1991, in the table and in the text, are from R. Gordon, *Macroeconomics*, sixth edition (New York: Harper Collins, 1993), Appendix A, p. A6.

era. The decline in the rate of growth in the standard of living, as measured by the growth in output per person, was tempered somewhat by a corresponding decline in population growth.

Part B of the table shows that a distinct break in the rate of growth in output occurred in 1974, shortly after the Organization of Petroleum Exporting Counties (OPEC) engineered a fourfold increase in the price of oil. The annual rate of growth in potential output averaged 3.59 percent from 1950 through 1974, but only 2.54 percent since 1974. In fact, Gordon estimates that the rate of growth in potential output was 3 percent or better in *every* year between 1950 and 1974 and never again reached 3 percent in *any* year after 1974. For almost 20 years now the rate of long-run economic growth has been below the overall average rate of growth for the entire twentieth century.

The declining rate of growth is very troubling for the U.S. economy. Even a small decline in the rate of long-run economic growth, if it persists, has enormous implications for a nation's standard of living. For example, if the rate of long-run economic growth were to recover to its 1950–74 level and remain there, the U.S. economy would be 34 times larger 100 years from now than it is today. If, instead, the rate of long-run economic growth were to remain at its post-1974 level, the U.S. economy would be only twelve times larger 100 years from now than it is today. A permanent one-percentage-point decline in the rate of growth in output eventually has a very dramatic impact on the economy.

The first years of the 1990s were not at all encouraging, according to Gordon. He estimates that the growth in potential output fell to 1.02 percent in 1990 and 1991. With population growing at an annual rate of 1.01 percent, the growth in potential output per person was essentially zero.

These figures, and the comparison above of the hypothetical economies growing at 4 percent and 2 percent per year, point out a fundamental principle of macroeconomics: *Small changes in the rate of long-run economic growth have an impact on a nation's standard of living over the long run that dwarfs any other factor affecting the standard of living.* How a society answers the Now versus Future question is vitally important to the economic health of the nation over the long haul. We will look closely throughout the macroeconomics chapters at the factors that determine the levels of saving and investment in the economy. Since saving and investment are the most important determinants of long-run economic growth, they in turn are the single most important determinants of a nation's standard of living in the long run.

Every U.S. president since the mid-1970s has emphasized the need to save and invest more to increase the rate of growth. President Clinton is no exception. He stressed repeatedly during his campaign and while in office the need to "grow the economy," as he put it. The United States can certainly afford to bear the opportunity costs of growth, but one wonders if President Clinton will be any more successful in his quest for higher growth than his predecessors were. Citizens of the United States have apparently not been willing to give up any of their good life today to increase investment in physical capital or education for the benefit of future generations. As we saw in Chapter 3, saving and investment are low in the United States, both absolutely and relative to our major economic competitors such as Japan and Germany.

Actual Versus Potential Growth

One final point to note about economic growth is that an economy can grow faster than its rate of long-run economic growth if it starts from a position well below its production possibilities frontier. Output can grow very rapidly for a short while if producers are hiring workers who were unemployed and using machines that were lying idle. Once the economy reaches the frontier, however, the rate of growth in output year by year is limited by the rate of growth in potential output. For example, OPEC engineered a fourfold increase in the price of crude oil in 1973 that pushed the United States way below its production possibilities frontier in 1974 and 1975. The economy recovered starting in 1976 and moved rapidly back to the frontier. Output grew by 4.9 percent in 1976, 4.7 percent in 1977, and 5.3 percent in 1978. These rates of growth could not continue, however, once the economy reached the production possibilities frontier. In 1979, when the economy was essentially operating on its frontier, the rate of growth in output fell to 2.5 percent. This was approximately equal to Gordon's estimate of the rate of growth in potential output from 1976 to 1979.[1]

FULL EMPLOYMENT

Long-run economic growth is only half the prescription for a healthy economy. A nation must also realize its potential. It must make sure that its resources are fully employed so that the economy remains on or near its production

[1]Council of Economic Advisors, *Economic Report of the President, 1993* (Washington, D.C: U.S. Government Printing Office, 1993), Table B-2, p. 351.

possibilities frontier as the frontier shifts out over time. We turn next to the goal of full employment, concentrating on the full employment of labor.

The Employment Act of 1946 commits the federal government to pursue the goal of full employment. As part of its responsibility, the government goes to great lengths to determine how many people are unemployed, who the unemployed are, and why they have become unemployed.

Measuring the Unemployed

The Bureau of Labor Statistics (BLS), a division of the U.S. Department of Labor, surveys over 60,000 people each month to determine their labor market status. A survey of 60,000 people is large enough to be representative of the entire nation.

The people in the survey can be employed, unemployed, or not in the labor force. The **employed** are those who have worked at least one hour during the survey week. The **unemployed** are those who are actively seeking employment, but who are unable to find a job. In particular, a person is counted as unemployed if he or she (1) has not worked at all during the survey week and (2) is available for work and (3) either has searched for work within the previous four weeks or has been temporarily laid off and is waiting for recall by the employer. An economist would add, for those searching for work, that the search has to be appropriate. People must be seeking jobs consistent with their skills and must be willing to accept the going market wages for those jobs. An out-of-work blue-collar laborer cannot apply for a vacancy on the surgical staff of Columbia Presbyterian Hospital and claim to be unemployed. Similarly, a teen-ager who insists on a wage of $100 an hour to work at McDonald's is not unemployed. The BLS surveyors do not ask whether the unemployed are searching in an appropriate manner, they presume that their search is appropriate.[2]

The **labor force** is the sum of the people, aged 16 and older, who are either employed or unemployed.

$$\text{Labor force} = \text{employed} + \text{unemployed}$$

The remaining category of teen-agers and adults in the survey are those who are *not in the labor force*. They are not in the labor force because they are not interested in working at the time of the survey.

The **unemployment rate**, labeled U, is the ratio of the unemployed to the labor force, expressed as a percentage. It is the most widely reported statistic on overall labor market conditions.

Based on its surveys, the BLS estimated in 1992 that the U.S. labor force numbered approximately 127 million people, of whom 117.6 million were employed and 9.4 million were unemployed. (These data are for civilian workers; they exclude resident members of the Armed Services, approximately 1.6 million people.) The unemployment rate in 1992 averaged 7.4 percent throughout the year. Notice that, with a labor force of 127 million people, even very small changes in the unemployment rate affect a large number of people. Every one percentage point increase in the unemployment rate—say from 6 percent to 7

EMPLOYED

People who have worked for at least one hour during the week of the Bureau of Labor Statistics employment survey.

UNEMPLOYED

Those people who are actively seeking employment, but are unable to find a job.

LABOR FORCE

All people, aged 16 and older, who are either employed or unemployed.

UNEMPLOYMENT RATE

The ratio of the unemployed to the labor force, expressed as a percentage.

---

[2]For a more detailed description of how the BLS surveys and measures unemployment see J. Norwood, "The Measurement of Unemployment," *American Economic Review* 78, No. 2 (May 1988): 284–288.

TABLE 6.2 Unemployment in the United States

A. THE RATE OF UNEMPLOYMENT SINCE 1980

YEAR	RATE OF UNEMPLOYMENT %
1980	7.1
1981	7.6
1982	9.7
1983	9.6
1984	7.5
1985	7.2
1986	7.0
1987	6.2
1988	5.5
1989	5.3
1990	5.5
1991	6.7
1992	7.4

B. AVERAGE ANNUAL RATE OF UNEMPLOYMENT BY DECADE, 1950–92

DECADE	RATE OF UNEMPLOYMENT %
1950–59	4.5
1960–69	4.7
1970–79	6.2
1980–89	7.3
1990–1992	6.5

C. INCIDENCE OF UNEMPLOYMENT DURING THE 1980s

CATEGORY	AVERAGE ANNUAL RATE OF UNEMPLOYMENT %
All workers	7.3
Males	7.3
Females	7.0
Whites	6.3
Blacks	15.0
Teen-agers (16–19)	18.6
Black teen-agers (16–19)	39.8
Adult white males	6.4

SOURCE: Council of Economic Advisors, *Economic Report of the President, 1993* (Washington, D.C.: U.S. Government Printing Office, 1993), Table B-37, p. 390, Table B-38, p. 391.

percent—represents an additional 1.27 million people who want to work, but do not have a job.[3]

The BLS surveys have been ongoing since 1947. They have revealed a number of facts about unemployment in the United States that you should keep in mind as you think about the problem of unemployment. Table 6.2 presents some data illustrating these facts.

---

[3]*Economic Report of the President, 1993*, Table B-30, p. 382.

THE CYCLICAL NATURE OF UNEMPLOYMENT   The unemployment rate cycles inversely with the performance of the economy, rising when the circular flow of economic activity declines and falling when the circular flow increases. Part A of Table 6.2 records the annual unemployment rate during the 1980s. The unemployment rate tracks the performance of the economy very closely. When the economy went into a steep recession in 1982, the unemployment rate rose by two percentage points. As the economy recovered steadily throughout the remainder of the decade, the unemployment rate declined just as steadily, reaching a decade low of 5.3 percent by 1989. The recession starting off the 1990s increased the unemployment rate once again; it stood at 7.3 percent at the end of 1992.[4] The close inverse relationship between the unemployment rate and the performance of the economy has existed throughout the post–World War II era. It is one of the more important macroeconomic features of the U.S. economy.

THE WORSENING UNEMPLOYMENT RATE   Unemployment appears to be an ever-worsening problem in the United States, despite the government's commitment to reduce unemployment. Part B of Table 6.2 shows that the average unemployment rate has increased in every full decade since 1950. Moreover, the increases have been quite large. To put the numbers in perspective, suppose that the United States can reduce the unemployment rate from the 1980s average of 7.3 percent to the 1950s average of 4.5 percent. If so, an additional 3.5 million people who are currently unemployed would be able to find jobs.

Many economists have argued that the average unemployment rate will fall substantially during the 1990s for a number of reasons that we will discuss below. The first three years of the 1990s have not been particularly encouraging to that view, however. The unemployment rate increased steadily from 5.2 percent in January of 1990 to 7.3 percent by December of 1992, and averaged 6.5 percent from 1990 to 1992.[5]

THE UNEVEN INCIDENCE OF UNEMPLOYMENT   Unemployment does not strike all groups of people evenhandedly. Part C of Table 6.2 compares the average unemployment rates throughout the 1980s by gender, race, and age, relative to the unemployment rate for all workers. The data show that the chances of being unemployed vary tremendously by race and age. The unemployment rate for blacks was nearly 2½ times greater than the unemployment rate for whites was throughout the decade, 15 percent for blacks versus 6.3 percent for whites. Teen-agers also suffer very high unemployment rates. The teen-age unemployment rate for males was almost three times as high throughout the decade as the unemployment rate for adult white males was. The combined disadvantages of race and age are particularly damaging for black teen-agers. Nearly 40 percent of all black teen-agers in the labor force were unemployed during the 1980s.

---

[4]Council of Economic Advisors, *Economic Indicators, March 1993* (Washington, D.C.: U.S. Government Printing Office, 1993), 12.
[5]The unemployment rate for January 1990 is reported in Council of Economic Advisors, *Economic Report of the President, 1991* (Washington, D.C.: U.S. Government Printing Office, 1991), Table B-39, p. 330. The unemployment rate for December 1992 is reported in *Economic Indicators, March 1993*.

The relative disadvantages of blacks and teen-agers have been fairly constant over the past 40 years. The only major change in the incidence of unemployment has been among males and females. The female unemployment rate during the 1980s was slightly below the male unemployment rate. This is a reversal from past decades; the female unemployment rate typically exceeded the male unemployment rate prior to 1980.

UNDEREMPLOYED AND DISCOURAGED WORKERS   The unemployment rate may not be an accurate measure of how far society is from the goal of full employment. The Department of Labor attempts on occasion to estimate two other categories of people who are very dissatisfied with their labor market experiences, the underemployed and discouraged workers.

UNDEREMPLOYED

Workers who are counted as employed, but who are working below their full capacities, either part time when they want to work full time or at jobs below their skill levels.

The **underemployed** are workers who are counted as employed, but who are working below their full capacities. They may be working only part time when they want to work full time. Recall that a person need only work one hour during the survey week to be counted as employed. Or they may be working full time at a job below their skill levels, earning wages that are below their full earnings capacity. An example would be a high school teacher who has been let go after 20 years of teaching and is now driving a taxicab to try to make ends meet. A very large number of workers are underemployed in the United States. A 1986 Department of Labor study estimated that 6 million people were underemployed, about the same number of people who were unemployed at the time.

DISCOURAGED WORKERS

Those people who have become so discouraged trying to find an acceptable job that they have dropped out of the labor force.

Discouraged workers are people who have become so discouraged trying to find an acceptable job that they have dropped out of the labor force. A 1987 Department of Labor study estimated that approximately 1 million people were discouraged workers. This estimate is highly problematic, however, because many discouraged workers have only a loose attachment to the labor market. Over half of them had not searched for work within the past year. In any event the problem of underemployment appears to be far more serious than is the problem of discouraged workers in the United States.[6]

Some economists argue that the unemployment rate overstates the nation's employment problems. They point out that many unemployed workers refuse to take available jobs because they consider the jobs "beneath them," with wages that are unacceptably low. Should these people be counted as unemployed? The question is especially important because these same people may be eligible for unemployment insurance financed by working taxpayers. Should taxpayers support these people? These economists would answer no to both questions. They believe that people should be willing to accept underemployment over unemployment. In their view the economy is performing well enough if it generates a job for each person who wants to work. The economy cannot be expected to generate the "perfect" job for each person.

In summary, the unemployment rate as measured by the monthly BLS surveys may not give an entirely accurate picture of overall labor market conditions in the United States. Nonetheless, it is the primary statistic that government officials use when judging how well the economy is performing with respect to the goal of full employment.

---

[6]For a more complete discussion of underemployed and discouraged workers, and references for the Department of Labor Studies, see B. Kaufman, *The Economics of Labor Markets*, second edition (Chicago: The Dryden Press, 1989), 601–603.

Unemployment as a Macroeconomic Policy Problem

Despite the wealth of information on the unemployed, the nature of unemployment as a policy problem remains a slippery concept. We noted earlier that the United States does not attack the problem of unemployment directly by employing anyone who cannot find a job. Instead, the federal government directs its policies at the performance of the economy. The government attempts to reduce unemployment by using its fiscal and monetary policies to increase the circular flow of economic activity and create jobs in the private sector. Therefore, a key policy question is this: How much does the unemployment rate respond to fiscal and monetary policies?

In 1992, 7.4 percent of the labor force were unemployed, nearly 9 million people. Could the government have used fiscal and monetary policies to create decent private-sector jobs for some or all of these people? In trying to answer this question economists have found it useful to divide total unemployment into three distinct analytical categories: cyclical unemployment, frictional and search unemployment, and structural unemployment. Let's take a close look at each category.

Cyclical Unemployment

Cyclical unemployment is the only category of unemployment that is highly responsive to the performance of the economy and therefore to fiscal and monetary policies. The problem of cyclical unemployment arises because labor markets do not always operate according to the Laws of Supply and Demand. Wages tend to be sticky in many labor markets. When supply or demand shifts, wages do not adjust quickly to the new equilibrium level. The wage stickiness results in a pattern of unemployment that rises and falls with the overall performance of the economy.

Figure 6.1 compares what happens to measured unemployment in a competitive labor market [Figure 6.1(a)] versus a labor market with sticky wages [Figure 6.1(b)]. The demand curve for labor, D_L, indicates the amount of labor that firms want to hire at each wage. The supply curve for labor, S_L, indicates the number of people who want to work at each wage. In other words, S_L indicates the size of the labor force at each wage. The initial equilibrium in each graph is given by the labor-wage combination (L_0, W_0), at the intersection of D_L and S_L. Labor in this market is fully employed initially. L_0 people want to work at the equilibrium wage, W_0, and this is exactly the number who are working. The measured unemployment rate is zero.

Suppose that the economy goes into a recession and business falls off. Firms find that they cannot sell as many goods and services as they could before the economy softened. Consequently, they do not need as many workers, and their demand for labor falls from D_L to D_L' in both panels.

Figure 6.1(a) shows what would happen if the labor market were competitive and operated according to the Laws of Supply and Demand. The market quickly seeks a new equilibrium at the intersection of D_L' and S_L. The wage falls from W_0 to W_1, and the level of employment from L_0 to L_1. The labor force now consists of L_1 workers, those who want to work at the new equilibrium wage, W_1. Since L_1 is exactly the number of people who are working, unemployment remains at zero despite the recession.

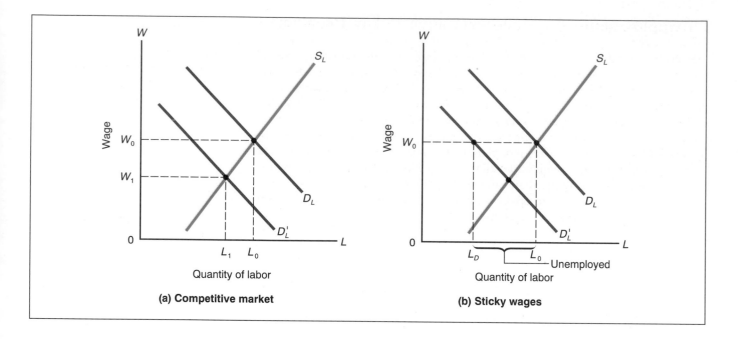

(a) Competitive market

(b) Sticky wages

FIGURE 6.1

Recessions, Competitive Labor Markets, and Sticky Wages

The figure compares how a labor market responds to a recession if it is competitive [Figure 6.1(a)] and if wages are sticky [Figure 6.1(b)]. The initial equilibrium is (L_0, W_0) in both graphs, at the intersection of D_L and S_L, and there is no unemployment. Then the economy experiences a recession and the demand for labor decreases to D'_L in each graph. If the labor market is competitive as in Figure 6.1(a), the new equilibrium is (L_1, W_1), at the intersection of D'_L and S_L. The L_1 workers who continue to work receive a lower wage, and $(L_0 - L_1)$ workers drop out of the labor force. No workers are unemployed. If wages are sticky at W_0 as in Figure 6.1(b), the decrease in demand causes an excess supply in the labor market. L_0 workers want to work, but firms are willing to hire only L_D workers. $(L_0 - L_D)$ workers are unemployed, equal to the amount of the excess supply at the sticky wage W_0. Sticky wages give rise to involuntary cyclical unemployment that rises and falls with the performance of the economy.

Workers do suffer because of the recession, but they take their losses in forms other than becoming unemployed. Some workers, $(L_0 - L_1)$ in number, drop out of the labor force; they are willing to work at the old wage, W_0, but not at the new, lower wage, W_1. Other workers, the L_1 people who continue to work, receive a lower wage.

Figure 6.1(b) shows what happens when wages are sticky. Suppose that workers resist a cut in their wages and employers agree to keep the wage at W_0. Now when the recession hits, the quantity of labor demanded by the firms falls to L_D at the **sticky wage**, W_0. The quantity of labor supplied remains the same as before the decline set in; L_0 workers still want to work at the wage W_0. The labor market is in excess supply at W_0 in the amount of $(L_0 - L_D)$. L_0 workers are looking for work, but the firms are willing to hire only L_D of them. The remaining $(L_0 - L_D)$ workers are unemployed. In other words, measured unemployment shows up as excess supply on a supply and demand diagram of a labor market.

When the economy recovers and the demand curve returns to D_L, the firms are once again willing to hire L_0 workers. Unemployment returns to zero. With sticky wages, therefore, the economy experiences **cyclical unemployment** that fluctuates with the state of the economy. Unemployment rises when the economy goes into recession and falls when the economy recovers and expands.

Cyclical unemployment does respond to fiscal and monetary policies. When an economy goes into decline and cyclical unemployment rises, the government can use fiscal and monetary policies to help the economy recover and reduce the level of employment. In terms of our example, proper fiscal and monetary policies can restore the demand for labor to D_L and return the economy to full employment at L_0. Moreover, the government has every incentive to reduce the level of unemployment because cyclical unemployment is involuntary. The $(L_0 - L_D)$ workers who are unemployed in our example want to work at a wage of W_0.

Wage stickiness is an important feature of the U.S. economy. Many wages and salaries do not respond quickly to changing labor market conditions. Twenty percent of all U.S. labor works under a three-year wage contract, which is the standard contract for labor unions in the United States. Not all of these workers are unionized, however; only 14 percent of the U.S. labor force belongs to a labor union. An additional 5 percent of the labor force works under two-year contracts. Some of these multiyear labor contracts contain provisions that adjust wages automatically for changes in inflation year by year, but they do not adjust wages automatically for changing labor market conditions. The vast majority of the remaining 75 percent of the labor force works under one-year contracts.[7] With most wages set for periods of one to three years, the ebbs and flows of the economy produce increases and decreases in the measured unemployment rate as represented by Figure 6.1(b).

WHY ARE WAGES STICKY?   The fact of wage stickiness in U.S. labor markets cannot be denied. What has long puzzled economists is why workers and firms have agreed to fixed-wage contracts over more flexible wage contracts. Why, for instance, do workers prefer to increase the risk of losing their jobs when the economy softens instead of accepting wage cuts so that more of them can keep their jobs? Referring to Figure 6.1, are workers on the whole necessarily better off at the sticky-wage equilibrium, (L_D, W_0), than at the flexible-wage equilibrium, (L_1, W_1)? The answers to these questions are not at all clear.

Sticky wages are hardly a new phenomenon, or peculiar to the United States. The great British economist John Maynard Keynes noticed that wages were sticky in the 1920s and 1930s in England. His observation led him to reject the existing theories of how the macro economy operates, which were all based on competitive labor markets with flexible wages. Keynes developed a new theory of the macro economy based on noncompetitive labor markets and sticky wages that remains one of the most widely embraced macroeconomic theories to this day—and one that we will develop in this text.

CONCERN FOR RELATIVE WAGES   Keynes believed that workers resist wage cuts because they want to maintain their relative position in the hierarchy of all wage earners. Their concern for relative wages leads them to prefer a 10 percent increase in the prices of goods and services to a 10 percent cut in their wages, even though each decreases their purchasing power by 10 percent. When prices rise, they know that all workers are affected similarly; when their wages are cut, they have no guarantee that everyone else's wages have also been cut.

THE INSIDER/OUTSIDER THEORY   More recent research on wage stickiness has explored a number of other possibilities. One of the more popular theories today is based on the control of decision-making power within unions and corporations. Consider the case of labor unions. The wage policies bargained for by union representatives must be approved by a majority vote of the union members. The older, more experienced members have more votes, and more political clout with the union representatives, than do the younger, less ex-

WAGE STICKINESS

The existence of impediments that prevent wages from moving to their equilibrium level at the intersection of the supply and demand curves for labor.

CYCLICAL UNEMPLOYMENT

Unemployment that fluctuates with the state of the economy because wages are sticky.

---

[7] J. Abraham, "Income Redistribution During a Disinflation," *Journal of Macroeconomics* 9, No. 2 (Spring 1987): 205.

perienced members. Small wonder, then, that the unions bargain for fixed-wage contracts, with layoffs determined by seniority. This is clearly the type of contract that the older, more experienced workers prefer. When a recession comes, they get to keep both their jobs and their incomes; the least experienced members get laid off and bear the entire brunt of the decline.

The same type of political maneuvering may take place among the managers of large corporations. The more experienced managers can secure their jobs and their incomes with a fixed-salary, layoff-by-experience strategy, which places all the risks of the ebbs and flows of the economy on the younger managers.

Economists refer to this politically determined wage policy as the **insider/outsider theory of wage setting.** The older, more experienced "insiders" have the decision-making power and use it to place all the risks of a business downturn on the younger, less experienced "outsiders."

EFFICIENCY WAGES Another popular explanation of wage stickiness relates to the long-term relationships that corporations have with many of their employees. Large corporations often make use of internal labor markets, in which they hire people into entry-level positions and then promote employees from within to higher-level positions in the corporation. Internal labor markets arose, in part, because corporations have to train new hires to turn them into productive employees. To the extent the training is specific to the firm, both the employees and the employers have an incentive to maintain their relationship after the training period ends. On the one hand, employees who receive firm-specific training are more productive to the firm that trains them than to any other firm, so they cannot earn as high a wage elsewhere. On the other hand, employers earn a return on their training programs only if the trained employees stay with the firm. If a trained employee leaves, the corporation loses the productivity of the employee and has to bear the costs of hiring and retraining a new employee. The practice of training new hires and promoting from within can lead to long-term employment relationships. Of all males over 40 in the United States 8 percent have worked for only one company.

The large corporations have adopted a number of salary and employment policies that are designed specifically to reduce turnover. For one, they have been willing to err on the high side and pay their experienced employees somewhat larger salaries than necessary in order to keep them. A higher-than-necessary salary policy has the added benefit of improving employee morale over the long haul, so that employees will remain happy and productive and not shirk their duties. These high salaries have been called **efficiency wages** because they are profitable (efficient) from the firms' point of view. The benefits of improved morale and reduced turnover more than offset the costs of paying higher-than-necessary salaries.

Corporations are also reluctant to cut salaries for fear that morale will suffer and their employees will begin to look elsewhere. Layoffs are much better than an across-the-board cut in salaries for maintaining morale if the corporation has to reduce its labor costs in the face of declining sales. Employees know that business is suffering when layoffs occur because the firm is obviously reducing its production and sales. In contrast, a cut in salaries is more difficult for employees to interpret. The firm may be cutting salaries to reduce costs in response to declining sales. But the firm may also be cutting wages simply to increase profits. A salary cut, then, is likely to breed suspicion and reduce

INSIDER/OUTSIDER THEORY

A theory of wage stickiness that says that the older, more experienced employees, the "insiders," have the decision-making power and use it to place all the risks of a business downturn on the younger, less experienced employees, the "outsiders."

EFFICIENCY WAGE

A wage that is higher than necessary to retain the employees, but that firms are willing to pay to improve the morale of the employees so that they will remain happy and productive and not shirk their duties; the wage that maximizes the profits of the firm.

morale. Also, the employees who avoid a layoff when times are bad are happy to have kept their jobs and their high salaries. Their emotional attachment to the corporation becomes stronger, if anything. When faced with a general economic decline, then, corporations would rather lay off some of their employees than cut salaries to reduce costs.

Long-term employment relationships through internal labor markets also foster the insider/outsider strategy of placing the employment and income risks on the least experienced employees. The entry level employees can most easily be replaced from outside the firm when the economic recovery occurs.

EVIDENCE ON STICKY WAGES   Two Princeton economists, Alan Blinder and Don Choi, recently surveyed the personnel directors and employees of 19 manufacturing firms in New Jersey and Pennsylvania to see if the more popular theories of wage stickiness were at all valid. Their survey results confirmed some of the theories. Nearly every employer gave the desire to avoid turnover as a reason for resisting wage cuts. They did not want to bear the costs of hiring and training new workers. Also, fairness in setting wages was very important to both employers and employees, and they agreed on what constituted a fair wage policy. The firms could cut wages only if it were necessary to stay in business or to place wages in line with the wages at comparable firms; cutting wages simply to increase profits was definitely seen as unfair. The personnel directors stressed that management was very reluctant to cut wages because this might be viewed as unfair by the employees. Gaining a reputation for treating employees unfairly is disastrous and must be avoided above all else. The best employees would leave, and the firm would not be able to attract good job applicants. Finally, when offered a choice between price increases and wage cuts that would have the same effect on their purchasing power, the employees overwhelming preferred the price increases, just as Keynes had surmised.[8]

If the attitudes expressed in this small survey are widespread, and one suspects that they are, then U.S. workers will have to live with cyclical unemployment. Firms have to lay off workers to reduce costs when their business falls off if they are not allowed to reduce wages. Sticky wages appear to have become socialized into employer-employee relationships.

THE REASONS FOR UNEMPLOYMENT   The cyclical pattern of unemployment is very evident in the official survey data. The BLS surveyors ask the unemployed how they became unemployed. They record the responses in one of four categories: job losers, job leavers, re-entrants, and new entrants. **Job losers** are those who have been laid off or fired by their employers. **Job leavers** are those who have voluntarily quit their jobs and are actively looking for another job. The **re-entrants** are those who were once employed, then dropped out of the labor force, and have now re-entered the labor force. The **new entrants** are those who are seeking employment for the first time; they have never worked before.

Table 6.3 records the percentages of unemployment accounted for by the four categories of unemployment, along with the total unemployment rate, for 1982, 1987, and 1992. The U.S. economy was mired in a deep recession in

JOB LOSERS

Those people who have been laid off or fired by their employers.

JOB LEAVERS

Those people who have voluntarily quit their jobs and are actively looking for other jobs.

RE-ENTRANTS

Those people who were once employed, then dropped out of the labor force, and have now re-entered the labor force.

NEW ENTRANTS

Those people who are seeking employment for the first time, having never worked before.

---

[8]A. Blinder and D. Choi, "A Shred of Evidence on Theories of Wage Stickiness," *Quarterly Journal of Economics* CV, Issue 4 (November 1990): 1003–1015.

TABLE 6.3   Reasons for Becoming Unemployed, 1982 and 1987, and 1992

CATEGORY	PERCENTAGE POINTS OF TOTAL UNEMPLOYMENT RATE		
	1982	1987	1992
JOB LOSERS	5.7	3.0	4.2
JOB LEAVERS	0.8	0.8	0.8
RE-ENTRANTS	2.2	1.6	1.8
NEW ENTRANTS	1.1	0.8	0.7
TOTAL UNEMPLOYMENT RATE[1]	9.7	6.2	7.4

[1]The numbers in the four categories do not always add to the total unemployment rate because of rounding error.

Source: Council of Economic Advisors, *Ecnomic Report of the President, 1993* (Washington, D.C.: U.S. Government Printing Office, 1993), Table B-39, p. 392.

1982, operating well below its production possibilities frontier. By 1987 the economy had undergone four years of rapid growth and was operating at or near the limits of its production possibilities frontier. The recession of 1990–91 sent the economy well below its frontier once again, where it remained in 1992.

The prospects of finding employment are obviously quite sensitive to the state of the economy. For example, the 3.5-percentage-point difference between the unemployment rates in 1982 and 1987 represents approximately 4 million additional people who were actively seeking employment and were unable to find a job in 1982. Moreover, the data show that the cyclical component of unemployment is highly concentrated among the job losers. They become unemployed against their wishes when the economy suffers, victims of the preference for sticky wages over flexible market clearing wages.

Fortunately, the government can reduce cyclical unemployment with its fiscal and monetary policies. The question that remains, though, is how much of the unemployment rate is accounted for by cyclical unemployment. In particular, how much of the 6.2 percent unemployment rate in 1987 was cyclical unemployment? The majority of economists would answer "Not too much, if any."

The data in Table 6.3 show that the other three categories of unemployment besides job losers are not as sensitive to the state of the economy. Also, job losers still accounted for about half of the unemployed in 1987, when the economy was near its production possibilities frontier. These data suggest that many factors other than the state of the economy determine the measured unemployment rate in the United States. These other factors explain the remaining two categories of unemployment, frictional and search unemployment and structural unemployment. They have very different causes than does cyclical unemployment and are not so responsive to fiscal and monetary policies.

Frictional and Search Unemployment

The concepts of frictional and search unemployment are so closely related that we have chosen to place them in a single category. They both result from imperfect information in labor markets.

A quick glance at the Help Wanted pages of your local newspaper will convince you that most people seeking employment have an enormous variety of options to choose from. There are many different occupations, and the various occupations differ considerably in their working conditions, their skill or educational requirements, and the wages that they offer. Wages may also differ from firm to firm within the same occupation. Matching people with available jobs is not a simple process, given all this variety. At the very least, people need to invest some time and effort to learn about their options. Even so, they may not have very good information about the job opportunities available to them.

Frictional and search unemployment both result from the need to obtain information. Roughly speaking, we can associate frictional unemployment with the job losers and search unemployment with the other three categories of the unemployed.

FRICTIONAL UNEMPLOYMENT   Frictional unemployment refers to the unemployment that inevitably exists in an economy as large, diverse, and dynamic as the U.S. economy. New job opportunities are forever being created, and other jobs eliminated, as consumers' tastes change from one set of products to another or as technological advances change the way that the goods and the services are produced. Labor markets remain in a constant state of flux, with workers losing their jobs in some sectors of the economy and being forced to find new jobs in other sectors. These sectoral shifts in the demand for labor occur independently of the overall state of the economy. For example, labor has been steadily shifting out of the manufacturing sector and into the service sector in the United States for the past 20 years, to the point where almost all new employment growth is in the service sector. The relative decline in manufacturing jobs is due primarily to labor-saving technological changes that have drastically reduced the amount of labor required to produce manufactured products. Increased competition from foreign manufacturers has also contributed to the job loss, although it is not nearly so important as labor-saving technological change. The percentage of U.S. national product accounted for by the manufacturing sector has held fairly steady at about 20 percent as the employment opportunities have fallen.

The movement of workers from sector to sector that goes on beneath the surface of the economy is sure to generate some measured unemployment, even if all labor markets are highly competitive and operate according to the Laws of Supply and Demand. The needs to gather information and to relocate act as frictions in the economy that produce the unemployment, which explains why this kind of unemployment is called **frictional unemployment.** Notice that frictional unemployment has nothing to do with sticky wages or with the overall state of the economy. Instead, the amount of frictional unemployment depends on two factors: the amount that the demand for labor shifts from product to product (sector to sector); and how quickly workers can move to new employment opportunities.

The unemployed are concentrated in two categories. One is the job losers who have been let go against their wishes. The other is the job leavers who voluntarily quit their jobs in the contracting sectors to seek out better jobs in the expanding sectors. Many economists would categorize the unemployment that the job leavers experience as search unemployment rather than frictional unemployment. The difference between frictional and search unemployment

FRICTIONAL UNEMPLOYMENT

Unemployment caused by the continuously shifting employment opportunities from sector to sector that go on beneath the surface of the economy; gathering information about job opportunities and relocating take time and act as frictions in the economy that generate unemployment.

is somewhat arbitrary, but the distinction between voluntary and involuntary unemployment is important in thinking about unemployment as a policy problem.

SEARCH UNEMPLOYMENT

Unemployment caused by employees who leave their jobs voluntarily and are looking for other jobs, or by re-entrants or new entrants to the labor force who are looking for a job.

SEARCH UNEMPLOYMENT   The concept of **search unemployment** rests on the simple idea that we are always trying to improve ourselves in all aspects of our lives. Part of our self-improvement is a continual search for better job opportunities once we decide to enter the labor force.

People who already have jobs are constantly on the lookout for better jobs. Changing jobs is commonplace in the United States; 25 percent of all U.S. workers move to a different industry every 3 years.[9] If job changers quit their jobs before searching for a new job, they are unemployed until they land the new job.

In fact, though, the vast majority of job changers never experience any unemployment. For example, when university professors search for better academic positions, they make contacts with colleagues throughout the profession. They may even apply to several faculties and arrange to give a number of seminars on their current research. But they do not have to give up their current positions to engage in the job search. If they do decide to join another university, they arrange to have their new contract begin the day after their old contract ends, so they are never unemployed. Similarly, managers can pick up the phone and discretely inquire about other job opportunities. They may even hire "headhunter" firms to search for them. Still, the data in Table 6.3 show that nearly 1 million people do quit their jobs before they have found a new position. Job leavers are an important component of the unemployed.

First-time entrants into the labor force and people who re-enter the labor force are also likely to experience some search unemployment. College graduates often engage in extensive searches before accepting their first permanent jobs. If their searches extend beyond graduation, they join the ranks of the unemployed until the searches end. Many teen-agers looking for summer or part-time employment experience short periods of unemployment. Teen-agers are also prone to become job leavers, searching yet again for another job. They stay with one job for less than three months, on average, in part because they are still in school and living at home, and in part because most of the jobs available to them are not very attractive.

Leaving and re-entering the labor force is much more common among women than men, at least among adults. Women spend an average of 31 percent of their potential work years away from work, compared with 3 percent for men. Nearly 70 percent of adult men who drop out of the labor force do so because they have become sick or disabled. Many of the sick and disabled men never return to work. Women, in contrast, tend to move between work at home and work in the marketplace. They most often drop out of the labor force to care for children or assume other household responsibilities. When the children have grown or the home responsibilities have lessened, women quite often return to work either part time or full time. When women do decide to re-enter the labor force, they are very likely to search for a while before accepting employment. In addition to seeking high-paying jobs, they may search

[9]R. Ehrenberg and R. Smith, *Modern Labor Economics: Theory and Public Policy*, fourth edition (New York: Harper Collins, 1991), 360.

for flexible working conditions that allow them to balance the various demands of the household and workplace.[10]

SEARCHING AS PRODUCTIVE ACTIVITY   Unemployment that results from voluntary search activity has very different policy implications from those of unemployment that results from being fired or laid off. Searching for better job opportunities is a type of investment in a person's future that is beneficial to both the individual and society alike.

Search unemployment arises because job leavers, labor force re-entrants, and new entrants do not necessarily take the first job available to them. No one wants to be unemployed, but both the individual and society gain from the search activity. The individual gains because searching uncovers valuable information about employment opportunities that leads to a higher-paying job. The higher pay more than compensates for the time spent unemployed. Society gains because searching produces a better match between workers and available jobs. The labor force overall is more productive despite the periods of unemployment while people are searching.

Search unemployment, like frictional unemployment, is not very sensitive to the overall state of the economy. An improving or declining economy pulls both ways on the amount of search activity. For instance, wages tend to increase more rapidly when the economy moves closer to its production possibilities frontier. The increase in wages increases the potential benefit of additional time spent searching. At the same time, however, the opportunity cost of additional time spent searching increases because the wages foregone while searching increase as well. With both the benefit and the cost of additional time spent searching increasing, the time spent searching may increase, decrease, or stay the same. The same argument applies in reverse when the economy is declining.

The data in Table 6.3 suggest that search unemployment does move somewhat with the economy. Unemployment among labor force re-entrants and new entrants was somewhat lower in 1987 than in 1982, while unemployment among re-entrants was somewhat higher in 1992 than in 1987. Even so, there are good reasons to believe that the government cannot affect the amount of search unemployment very much through fiscal and monetary policies. The primary cause of search unemployment is poor information about job opportunities, not the state of the economy. Therefore, efforts to reduce search unemployment have to focus on improving labor market information. A nationwide computerized job bank that helps match workers with jobs would be far more effective in reducing search (and frictional) unemployment than would fiscal and monetary policies.

In addition, many institutional factors within the economy have an important effect on search activity. The two-worker family sharply reduces the cost of searching for the second wage earner. Unemployment insurance, which replaces about half of the average worker's earnings for a period of 26 weeks, also reduces the cost of searching. Congress established the unemployment insurance program during the Great Depression to provide desperately needed

---

[10] The data in this paragraph are from B. Kaufman, *The Economics of Labor Markets*, third edition (Chicago: The Dryden Press, 1991), 336; and B. Shiller, *The Economics of Poverty and Discrimination*, fifth edition (Englewood Cliffs, N.J.: Prentice-Hall, 1989), Chapter 3.

income for people who had lost their jobs. Unemployment insurance is no doubt beneficial; it has prevented many families from falling into poverty while the breadwinner was unemployed. But it does have the unfortunate side effect of increasing the unemployment rate somewhat by reducing the cost of searching. One study estimates that every 10-percentage-point increase in the ratio of unemployment insurance to wages increases the average duration of a spell of unemployment by half a week. This is enough to have a noticeable effect on the measured rate of unemployment because the longer people search, the more likely a BLS surveyor will happen upon them when they are unemployed.[11]

A final point to remember is that search (and frictional) unemployment is not the policy problem that cyclical unemployment is. Search activity is voluntary and productive. It is also very short term. Sixty percent of all spells of unemployment last for a month or less, and much of the short-term unemployment is search (or frictional) unemployment.

Structural Unemployment

STRUCTURAL UNEMPLOYMENT

Unemployment caused by severe and lasting mismatches between people who are looking for work and the jobs that are available to them; the mismatches are typically geographic or skills-related.

Structural unemployment refers to severe and lasting mismatches between the people looking for work and the jobs that are available to them. The mismatches are most often geographic or skills-related.

Geographic mismatches can occur whenever a region is heavily dependent on one industry. Thirty years ago the classic example of structural unemployment was the Appalachian coal miner. Coal mines throughout the Appalachian Mountains had closed down as oil and natural gas had replaced coal as the preferred fuel for generating electricity and heating homes. Appalachia was so heavily dependent on coal that the unemployed miners were unable to find work in other occupations near their homes. The entire region remained chronically depressed for years on end, with unemployment rates much higher than the national average. Job opportunities were plentiful in other parts of the country, but the unemployed miners were understandably reluctant to pack up their families and head elsewhere. Appalachia was their home, after all. It had a culture and a lifestyle all its own. Many families chose to stay, even though the costs of staying were extremely high; they suffered chronic unemployment.

A more recent example of chronic regional unemployment is the state of Michigan with its unemployed automobile workers. For the past 10 to 15 years Michigan's unemployment rate has been at or near the top of the list among all industrial states, a distinction Michigan could do without. The auto workers who lost their jobs to foreign competitors know that job opportunities exist in other states, yet they do not want to leave their homes any more than the Appalachian coal miners did before them. They also know that they cannot duplicate the high wages they received as auto workers no matter where they move, which only increases their reluctance to move.

COMMENT: If the European consortium Airbus, which is heavily subsidized by a number of European governments, outcompetes McDonnell-Douglas and Boeing in international markets, this will cause an increase in structural unemployment in Seattle and St. Louis, where these companies have a major presence. California is also experiencing a sharp increase in structural unemployment with the cutbacks in defense spending.

Chronic skills mismatches most often result from educational failures or technological change or a combination of both. The increasing numbers of dropouts from the central-city high schools throughout the United States are an example of the former. The students who drop out often lack even the most

---

[11]R. Ehrenberg and R. Smith, *Modern Labor Economics: Theory and Public Policy*, second edition (Glenview, IL: Scott, Foresman, 1985), 617.

basic skills needed for steady employment—the ability to read and follow a set of instructions, write a short memo, do basic arithmetic, or show enough sense of responsibility just to report for work each day. Dr. Blanche Bernstein, the former head of public welfare in New York City, estimated that two-thirds of all teen-age welfare mothers in New York were simply unemployable for these reasons. No business would want to hire them, even if they were willing to work.[12]

Technological change can also lead to structural unemployment by changing the skill requirements of the labor force. A recent study of adult males tried to determine why men's labor force experiences have deteriorated markedly over the past 20 years. In 1970, 3.5 percent of adult men were either unemployed or had dropped out of the labor force. By 1990, before the recent recession hit, the percentage had risen to 5 percent. The study determined that almost all of the increase had occurred among the lowest-wage, lowest-skilled men. Technological change, such as the computer revolution, has reduced the overall demand for unskilled workers. Also, foreign competition in the manufacturing sector reduced the demand for unskilled blue-collar workers. The composition of unemployed men has definitely shifted over the past 20 years toward the unskilled workers.[13]

A new phenomenon that bears watching is a potential employment mismatch based on age. Faced with increasing international competition, many large corporations in the United States realized that they had too many middle managers. The first years of the 1990s witnessed a downsizing of managerial positions that occurred independently of the recession during that period. The downsizing targeted middle-aged managers, who were especially vulnerable on two counts: They had larger salaries than did the younger employees, and getting rid of them opened up the corporate structure to new blood. Many corporations did not simply fire the excess managers. They chose instead to buy them out with early retirement offers that were much more attractive financially than waiting and taking the normal retirement plan. The employees who accept the buyouts may decide after a few years that retiring at age 50 or 55 is too young and try to return to the labor force. If so, they are likely to have difficulty finding employment for the same reasons that they were offered the buyouts in the first place: Firms prefer to hire younger workers. The result would be an increase in structural unemployment on the basis of an age mismatch between job seekers and employers. Time will tell if this turns out to be an important phenomenon in the United States.

Structural unemployment, like search or frictional unemployment, is not very sensitive to the state of the economy. True, firms are more willing to hire and train unskilled (and older) workers when the economy is booming than when the economy is in a recession. Some of the decline in unemployment from 1982 to 1987 reported in Table 6.3 was no doubt due to a slight decline in mismatch, structural unemployment. Nonetheless, the government cannot hope to make a substantial dent in structural unemployment with its fiscal and monetary policies. Reducing structural unemployment requires entirely different strategies, such as relocation subsidies to the regionally unemployed, or

---

[12]B. Bernstein, "Welfare Dependency," in W. Bawden (ed.), *The Social Contract Revisited: Aims and Outcomes of President Reagan's Social Welfare Policy* (Washington, D.C.: Urban Institute Press, 1984), 125–156.
[13]W. Howe, "Labor Market Dynamics and Trends in Male and Female Unemployment," *Monthly Labor Review* 113, No. 11 (November 1990): 3–11.

subsidized job-training programs for the unskilled, or public-service jobs for the long-term unemployed.

The federal government did offer relocation subsidies under the Trade Adjustment Assistance Program, which was instituted in 1974. The subsidies were targeted at employees such as the auto workers whose jobs had been lost to foreign competition. The consensus opinion is that the program was generally ineffective. The unemployed were reluctant to move to other parts of the country, even with the benefit of a government subsidy. The federal government has also supported a variety of job-training programs since the 1960s, either directly or in partnership with private business, as part of its War on Poverty. These programs have been modestly successful. Job training is expensive, though, and the programs reached only a small minority of the structurally unemployed. Finally, as noted in Chapter 2, governments at all levels in the United States have been reluctant to offer public-service jobs to the long-term unemployed simply for the sake of employing them. In short, structural unemployment will remain an important feature of the U.S. economy for the foreseeable future.

Full Employment: The Natural Rate of Unemployment

The federal government has chosen to fight unemployment primarily through fiscal and monetary policies. Because of this, economists do not define the goal of full employment as achieving a zero rate of unemployment. Instead, they define full employment in terms of reaching the natural rate of unemployment, written U_{NR}, or, equivalently, the non-accelerating inflationary rate of unemployment, written U_{NAIR}.

The concept of the natural rate of unemployment relates to the fact that any large market economy will naturally experience some unemployment, whatever the state of the economy. The total rate of unemployment is the sum of cyclical unemployment, frictional and search unemployment, and structural unemployment.

$$U_{total} = U_{cyclical} + U_{frictional/search} + U_{structural}$$

Of the three components, we saw that only cyclical unemployment is highly responsive to the overall state of the economy and therefore to the government's fiscal and monetary policies. The remaining two components depend more on other inherent features within the economy, such as the amount of misinformation within labor markets, the natural frictions involved with changing jobs, the amount of voluntary job search people undertake, and mismatches between the unemployed and the available jobs. Therefore, the sum of frictional and search unemployment and structural unemployment comprises a **natural rate of unemployment** that cannot be reduced very much with fiscal and monetary policies.

$$U_{NR} = U_{frictional/search} + U_{structural}$$

The best the federal government can do is drive $U_{cyclical}$ down to zero with its fiscal and monetary policies. Its goal, in other words, is to reduce unemploy-

NATURAL RATE OF UNEMPLOYMENT

The sum of frictional and search unemployment and structural unemployment; the rate of unemployment that corresponds to production on the production possibilities frontier and that cannot be reduced very much by fiscal and monetary policies. Also called the *non-accelerating inflationary rate of unemployment.*

ment to U_{NR}. Setting $U_{cyclical}$ equal to zero, or U_{total} equal to U_{NR}, is a realistic meaning of full employment, given the policy choices of the federal government.

The equivalent concept of U_{NAIR}, the **non-accelerating inflationary rate of unemployment,** brings together the twin goals of full employment and price stability, with reference to the production possibilities frontier. The idea is this. All resources, including labor, are fully employed when the economy is on its production possibilities frontier. Also, we learned in Chapter 3 that a market economy must experience inflation if it tries to live beyond the boundaries of its production possibilities frontier. We will see in Chapter 19 that the inflation actually accelerates if the economy persists in trying to live beyond its means. A 10 percent inflation this year may become a 50 percent inflation next year, a 150 percent inflation the year after that, and then . . . who knows? Inflation can blow sky-high once it begins to accelerate.

The federal government clearly wants to avoid starting an accelerating inflation. It wants its fiscal and monetary policies to bring the economy to the production possibilities frontier, but no further. The question, then, is what level of unemployment constitutes being at full employment on the frontier, and the answer is the one just given. The economy has reached the frontier when

$$U_{cyclical} = 0 \quad \text{and} \quad U_{total} = U_{frictional/search} + U_{structural}$$

Any attempt to reduce the unemployment rate further runs the risk of starting an ever-accelerating inflationary process. Therefore,

$$U_{NAIR} = U_{frictional/search} + U_{structural} = U_{NR}$$

The natural rate of unemployment and the non-accelerating inflationary rate of unemployment are just alternative ways of defining the goal of full employment when it is to be pursued with fiscal and monetary policies.

Economists tend to prefer U_{NAIR} over U_{NR} because there is nothing truly natural about the natural rate of unemployment. It can be reduced by other policies such as cuts in unemployment insurance benefits to reduce the incentive to search or relocation subsidies to reduce geographic mismatches. Nonetheless, we will refer to full employment as U_{NR} in this text simply because U_{NAIR} is such a mouthful to say.

HOW LARGE IS U_{NR}?   How large is the natural rate of unemployment in the United States? This is a very important macroeconomic policy question, yet economists are not all in agreement on the answer. Estimates of U_{NR} vary widely, with most falling within the 4 percent to 7 percent range. Within these estimates, two to three percentage points are commonly attributed to structural unemployment, with the remainder attributed to frictional and search unemployment.

A range of three percentage points may not seem like much of a disagreement, but, remember, every percentage point of unemployment represents approximately 1.27 million workers. If the federal government targets its monetary and fiscal policies on a U_{NR} of 7 percent when the true U_{NR} is 4 percent, it may be unnecessarily forcing 3.8 million workers into involuntary cyclical

NON-ACCELERATING INFLATIONARY RATE OF UNEMPLOYMENT

The minimum that the rate of unemployment can be without starting an ever-accelerating inflationary process; also called the *natural rate of unemployment.*

unemployment. Conversely, if the federal government targets on a U_{NR} of 4 percent when the true U_{NR} is 7 percent, it risks starting a rampant inflationary process that may be very costly to stop. Clearly, a lot is riding on the estimate of U_{NR}.

Those economists who estimate a high U_{NR} point to the high-turnover nature of unemployment. Sixty percent of all spells of unemployment last for less than one month. This suggests that a great deal of unemployment is frictional or search unemployment, with a lot of short-term movement between jobs in different sectors of the economy and a lot of movement into and out of the labor force. High turnover also suggests that U_{NR} is quite high, since the rapid turnover occurs independently of the state of the economy.

Those economists who estimate a low U_{NR} look at the same unemployment data and notice a hard core of unemployment lying behind the turnover. Only 2.4 percent of the labor force suffers spells of unemployment that last six months or more, yet these workers account for 45 percent of the total weeks of unemployment experienced by all workers during the course of a year.[14] Also, 45 percent of all spells of unemployment end with the worker becoming discouraged and dropping out of the labor force. If discouraged workers re-enter the labor force, they appear to have suffered two relatively short spells of unemployment when they have actually been out of work for a fairly long period of time. The hard core of longer-term unemployment suggests that a significant percentage of unemployment is either cyclical or structural, not search or frictional. This in turn implies a lower estimate of U_{NR}, since $U_{structural}$ is unlikely to be more than two or three percentage points.[15]

IS U_{NR} RISING OR FALLING?   Another important question is whether U_{NR} is rising or falling, whatever its current level may be. We saw in Table 6.2 (part B) that total unemployment has been rising steadily in the United States over the past 40 years. Whether all the increase is due to an increase in the natural rate of unemployment is unclear. The 1970s and the 1980s each experienced a severe recession that drove cyclical unemployment way up for a few years. Unemployment reached a high of 8.3 percent during the recession of 1974–75 and 9.5 percent during the recession of 1981–82. The 1950s and the 1960s escaped recessions of these magnitudes.[16] Nonetheless, most economists believe that the U_{NR} was also increasing fairly steadily from the 1950s into the 1980s.

Four percent unemployment seemed like a reasonable "full employment" target for fiscal and monetary policies in the 1950s. In 1971 President Nixon's Council of Economic Advisers raised the full employment target to 5 percent. In 1981 President Reagan's Council of Economic Advisers raised the target once again to 6.5 percent. Economists may have disagreed with the numbers chosen for the U_{NR} by the president's advisers, but nearly everyone agreed that the U_{NR} was increasing during this period. There is less agreement on whether the U_{NR} is now rising, falling, or leveling off.

---

[14]The two sets of data are not inconsistent with one another, as the following simple example indicates. Suppose that nine workers experience 1 week of unemployment and one worker experiences 11 weeks of unemployment. Most spells of unemployment are short term, yet one worker experiences more than half of the 20 total weeks of unemployment. This is roughly the pattern of unemployment that we see in the United States.

[15]For a more complete discussion of the debate on the nature of unemployment see Kaufman, *Economics of Labor Markets*, 622–629.

[16]*Economic Report of the President, 1993*, Table B-37, p. 390.

Those economists who believe that U_{NR} is now falling point to a decline in the high-unemployment teen-age population and the more stable employment pattern of adult women, which has lowered their unemployment rate below that of adult men. Another factor arguing for a declining U_{NR} is the recent decrease in government transfer payments that support labor market searching, such as unemployment insurance and public assistance. Unemployment insurance benefits are now subject to federal income tax, and cash payments under public assistance programs have fallen sharply in real terms over the past ten years. They have not kept pace with the rate of inflation. These changes raise the costs of searching and reduce search unemployment.

The principal factors arguing for a steady or even a rising U_{NR} are the rapid pace of technological change and the increasing internationalization of the economy, both of which have contributed to the decline in low-skilled manufacturing jobs and raised the unemployment rate of adult males. Another possible factor increasing U_{NR} is the downsizing of managerial staffing in large corporations which, as noted above, may lead to an age-based increase in structural unemployment.

The net effect of these various factors on the U_{NR} is unclear. Economists are as divided on the trend in U_{NR} as they are on the size of U_{NR}.[17]

The Psychological Effects of Unemployment

The economic effects of unemployment on families and individuals are clear enough. Unemployment is one of the two main events that cause families to fall into poverty in the United States (along with separations of husbands and wives). What about the psychological effects of unemployment: Do spells of unemployment exact a large emotional toll as well?

Psychologists became extremely interested in the effects of unemployment on mental health during the Great Depression of the 1930s. The first systematic psychological study of unemployment followed a group of people who worked in a flax factory in Marienthal, Austria. The workers became unemployed when the factory closed in 1933. Since the factory was the main source of employment in Marienthal, most of the workers remained unemployed for a long time.

The Marienthal study spawned nearly 100 other psychological studies of unemployment during the Great Depression, mostly in the United States and Europe. The Great Depression studies generally uncovered a pattern of deteriorating mental health following unemployment that proceeded in a series of three stages. Workers initially reacted with shock to their unemployment. Once the shock wore off, they moved into a period of alternating optimism and pessimism. This second stage finally gave way to a sense of fatalism and resignation as the unemployment persisted. The psychologists attributed the deterioration of the workers' mental health to the loss of time structure and regular, habitual activity in their lives, which undermined their sense of purpose. Another important contributing factor was the reduction in social contacts following unemployment, which led to a loss of stature and identity. The Great

---

[17]For further discussion of the factors affecting U_{NR} see R. Krashevski, "What Is So Natural About High Unemployment?," *American Economic Review* 78, No. 2 (May 1988): 289–293; and Howe, "Labor Market Dynamics," 3–11.

Depression studies generally corroborated Freud's view that steady employment is a person's strongest tie to reality among people in the labor force.

Studies of the psychology of unemployment have continued to proliferate to this day. Psychologist Norman Feather undertook an exhaustive review of all the psychological research on unemployment in the 50-year period from the Great Depression to the mid-1980s.[18] Feather believes that two general conclusions have emerged from all the research, whatever else the individual studies may show: (1) Unemployment has a larger effect on mental health the greater the financial strain on the individual or family, and (2) unemployment acts primarily as a catalyst in the process of deteriorating mental health.

The relationship between financial strain and mental health explains why unemployment typically causes more psychological and emotional distress among middle-aged men than among teen-agers. The unemployed men are usually the breadwinners of the family, whereas unemployed teen-agers are often still attached financially to their families. Psychologists also see the relationship between financial strain and mental health as a powerful argument for unemployment insurance programs. Unemployment insurance provides both good financial insurance *and* good emotional insurance for the nation's labor force.

Unemployment is a psychological catalyst in the sense that it intensifies whatever psychological and emotional problems already exist when the unemployment occurs. There is very little evidence that emotionally healthy individuals suffer any lasting psychological effects from unemployment. When psychological stress is present, however, unemployment increases the stress by removing the structure in people's lives and threatening their sense of purpose. This finding is generally consistent with the earlier psychological studies during the Great Depression, with one important exception. The more recent research has not found the deterioration-by-stages pattern that was so prominent in the Great Depression studies.

No other general conclusions have emerged from the research as strongly as these two, according to Feather. The main reason why not is that psychologists have not been able to agree on the appropriate model for studying the effects of unemployment on mental health. The relationship between unemployment and mental health is obviously a varied and complex problem. Feather conjectures that psychological theory may not yet be developed enough to reach a general understanding of the emotional consequences of unemployment.

SUMMARY

The first section of Chapter 6 posed the three fundamental questions of macroeconomics.

1. What factors determine the circular flow of economic activity?
2. How does the circular flow of economic activity relate to the four macroeconomic policy goals that we identified in Chapter 2: long-run economic growth, full employment (low unemployment), price stability (a low rate of inflation), and stability in economic relations with foreign countries (a balance between imports and exports and a stable value of the currency)?

[18]N. Feather, *The Psychological Impact of Unemployment* (New York: Springer-Verlag, 1989). See, especially, his summary comments in Chapter 10, pp. 244–253. Feather discusses the Great Depression studies in Chapter 2, pp. 10–19.

3. How can the government influence the level and the composition of the circular flow with its fiscal and monetary policies and thereby help society achieve the macroeconomic policy goals?

The second section of the chapter discussed the macroeconomic goal of long-run economic growth.

4. Long-run economic growth refers to lasting increases in the potential of the economy to produce goods and services. It involves pushing the production possibilities frontier out continuously over time.

5. Investment is the key to long-run economic growth, both investment in physical capital and investment in human capital (education). Investment changes the quantity and the quality of the nation's resources and embodies new production technologies, all of which help promote long-run economic growth.

6. Countries must be patient when pursuing long-run growth. The outer limits of growth in the United States are on the order of 4 percent per year.

7. Long-run economic growth is the most important factor in determining the overall economic health of a nation over the long haul. Even one-percentage-point differences in the rate of growth can have an enormous effect on a nation's standard of living in the long run.

The final section of Chapter 6 discussed the goal of full employment/low unemployment.

8. People are unemployed if they are actively seeking employment, but are unable to find a job, or if they have been temporarily laid off and are waiting to be recalled.

9. The average rate of unemployment has increased every decade in the United States since 1950. Also, the incidence of unemployment varies considerably by race and age. Blacks have much higher unemployment rates than do whites, and teen-agers have much higher unemployment rates than do adults.

10. Economists distinguish three types of unemployment for the purposes of analysis: cyclical unemployment, frictional and search unemployment, and structural unemployment.

11. Cyclical unemployment is highly sensitive to the ebbs and flows of the economy and is therefore affected by fiscal and monetary policies. It exists because wages are sticky; workers and employers have settled on a sticky-wage policy with layoffs and recalls rather than a flexible-wage policy that would preserve workers' jobs when the economy goes into a recession. We considered three popular explanations why wages may be sticky: (a) Workers resist wage cuts because they want to preserve their position in the hierarchy of wages, (b) according to the insider/outsider theory, experienced workers prefer layoffs and rehires because the newer workers bear the burden of this system, and (c) employers with internal labor markets pay high wages and resist wage cuts to preserve worker morale and reduce costly turnover. Cyclical unemployment is concentrated among job losers.

12. Frictional unemployment and search unemployment are based on misinformation. Frictional unemployment refers to the unemployment resulting from the natural frictions of the economy as new jobs are forever being created and other jobs destroyed. Workers need time to discover the new job opportunities. Search unemployment is concentrated among the job leavers, re-entrants, and new entrants who search for the best job oppor-

tunity before accepting a job. Searching is voluntary and rational behavior for the individual. Some search unemployment is also desirable for society since it creates better matches between employer and employee.

13. Structural unemployment refers to severe mismatches between the unemployed and the jobs that are available. The most common mismatches are skills mismatches or geographic mismatches. Neither frictional/search unemployment nor structural unemployment is as sensitive to the performance of the economy as cyclical unemployment is.

14. The natural, or non-accelerating inflationary, rate of unemployment is the sum of frictional/search unemployment plus structural unemployment. It is the level of unemployment that exists when the economy is on its production possibilities frontier. Cyclical unemployment is zero on the frontier. The best that fiscal and monetary policies can hope to do is to reduce total unemployment to the natural rate of unemployment.

15. Unemployment has psychological costs as well as economic costs. Psychological studies of unemployment have shown that unemployment causes more emotional distress the more financial strain it puts on the family or the individual. Unemployment also intensifies whatever emotional problems are present at the time the unemployment occurs.

KEY TERMS

cyclical unemployment
discouraged workers
efficiency wage
employed
frictional unemployment
insider/outsider theory

labor force
natural rate of unemployment
non-accelerating inflationary rate of
unemployment
search unemployment

structural unemployment
underemployed
unemployed
unemployment rate
wage stickiness

QUESTIONS

1. a. What are the four main macroeconomic policy goals in the United States?
   b. Does the federal government try to achieve the goals directly for the most part?
   c. Briefly describe the two main policies that the federal government uses to try to achieve the four macroeconomic policy goals.
2. What is long-run economic growth? Would you expect the following to promote long-run economic growth?
   a. Firms invest heavily in research and development.
   b. Firms invest heavily in advertising to increase sales.
   c. The government establishes five new public universities.
3. Do you agree or disagree with the following statement? The decrease in long-run economic growth in the United States from an average of about 3 percent per year before 1973 to an average of about 1 percent per year since 1973 is too small a decrease to worry about.
4. a. How does the Bureau of Labor Statistics define and attempt to measure unemployment?
   b. What are the limitations of the rate of unemployment as an indication of the nation's employment problems?

5. a. What are the three categories of unemployment that economists have defined to help them analyze and understand the problem of unemployment?
   b. What government policies are needed to reduce each category of unemployment?
   c. Which of the categories of unemployment does each of the following headlines describe?
      (i) "College graduates are having difficulty finding that first job"
      (ii) "Auto sales depressed, 2000 autoworkers laid off"
      (iii) "High school drop-outs seen as unfit for today's computerized workplace"
      (iv) "The Home Shopping Network may replace the sales clerk by the year 2010"
6. a. What is wage stickiness, and why is it important to the problem of unemployment?
   b. What are some of the popular theories economists have developed to explain sticky wages? Which of these theories do you find most persuasive? Which least persuasive?
7. What are the advantages and the disadvantages of unem-

ployment insurance?

8. Do you agree or disagree with the following statement? Macroeconomic policy cannot be viewed as successful until we have achieved zero percent unemployment.

9. a. What is the natural rate of unemployment?
   b. Will the following policies undertaken by the government serve to reduce the natural rate of unemployment?
      (i) Tax relief for firms that relocate to economically depressed, high unemployment areas of the country

      (ii) Government training programs for unskilled workers
      (iii) Fiscal and monetary policies designed to restore the economy to full employment.

10. a. What factors may be causing the natural rate of unemployment to increase during the 1990s?
    b. What factors may be causing the natural rate of unemployment to decrease during the 1990s?

7

The Macroeconomic Policy Goals II: Price Stability and Stable International Economic Relations

LEARNING OBJECTIVES

CONCEPTS TO LEARN

Inflation	Imports and exports
Consumer price index	The balance of trade
Hyperinflation	Dollar depreciation/appreciation
Fisher equation	

CONCEPTS TO RECALL

The circular flow of economic activity [4]	The Laws of Supply and Demand [5]

I nflation is Public Enemy #1 in the United States according to the pollsters. The Gallup organization has asked the American public every year since 1935 to name the most pressing problem—military, social, economic, or otherwise—facing the country. The answer most often given during peacetime is inflation.

The federal government has certainly responded to the public's concern about inflation. The Employment Act of 1946 commits the administration and Congress to the goal of price stability, and the government goes to great lengths to measure and track the rate of inflation in the United States. The goal of price stability remains an elusive target, however. Prices have risen every year but two since the end of World War II (1949 and 1954).

The internationalization of the U.S. economy has been another major economic story of the past 25 years, and it will continue to be for the foreseeable future. From the end of World War II until the early 1960s the United States enjoyed a truly dominant position in the world economy, one without any important challengers. Since then, of course, Japan, Western Europe, and many other countries have risen up to become serious competitors to U.S. producers, both here and abroad. The overriding concern now among the American people is whether the United States can compete effectively in world markets. People worry about the loss of manufacturing jobs to foreign imports and about foreign ownership of U.S. businesses.

The Employment Act of 1946 does not commit the federal government to any particular international economic goals, nor has any subsequent legislation. Nonetheless, the unwritten "rules of the game" in international trade commit all nations to maintaining a reasonable balance between their imports and their exports and a stable exchange value of their currencies relative to other currencies. The United States has not always played by the rules, even though every administration and every Congress pays lip service to them. The United States' imports have greatly exceeded its exports every year since 1984. Also, the dollar has moved up and down considerably year by year against the Japanese yen, the German mark, the British pound, and the other major currencies ever since 1973, when the major currencies were set free from government support to seek their own levels in the foreign exchange markets.

Chapter 7 discusses the two remaining macroeconomic policy goals, price stability and stability in our economic relations with foreign countries.

PRICE STABILITY/LOW INFLATION

INFLATION

Continuing increases in the level of prices generally, usually expressed as a percentage rate of increase.

Inflation refers to a process of *continuing increases in the level of prices generally*, with particular emphasis on the words *generally* and *continuing*.

To say that prices *generally* are increasing means that the prices of a large number of goods and services must be increasing simultaneously to constitute an inflation from a macroeconomic perspective. For example, the price of medical care has been increasing rapidly every year for the past 20 years and more. If this were the only price that was rising, we could speak of an inflation in the price of medical care. But the United States would not be experiencing an

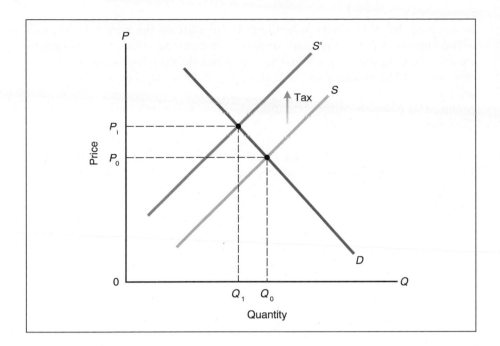

FIGURE 7.1

Taxes and Inflation

The price of some product is initially P_0 at the intersection of D and S, and there is no inflation. A tax on the product shifts the supply curve up by the amount of the tax from S to S'. The price of the product increases until it reaches its new equilibrium level P_1, at the intersection of D and S', at which point the price stops increasing. A tax causes a one time shift in the supply curve that leads to a permanently higher price level, but not to an inflation.

inflation as the term is properly understood. Medical care would just become ever more expensive relative to other goods and services year after year. In fact, though, most other prices have been rising as well, so that the rising price of medical care is contributing to the general price inflation in the United States.

To say that the price increases must be *continuing* indicates that inflation is an ongoing process, not just a temporary, one-time increase in prices. You must take care to distinguish between higher price *levels* and *continuous increases* in price levels when thinking about the problem of inflation. Figure 7.1 illustrates the distinction. Think of the figure as picturing the market for any representative good or service. The market is originally in equilibrium at the intersection of the market demand and supply curves, D and S. The equilibrium quantity and price are Q_0 and P_0, respectively.

We saw when studying the Laws of Supply and Demand that the price of a product tends to increase whenever demand increases or supply decreases. Suppose that the supply decreases because the government levies a tax on the product. The tax shifts the supply curve up by the amount of the tax, from S to S' in the figure. The new equilibrium is (Q_1, P_1), at the intersection of D and S'.

Tax increases are often considered inflationary because they drive up prices. The figure shows, however, that a tax increase does not cause an inflationary process in and of itself. The price increases for awhile after the government levies the tax as the market moves to its new equilibrium. But the increase in price would not be considered an inflation because the period when the price is increasing is only temporary. The price stops rising once it reaches P_1, the new equilibrium price level. There was no inflation in the original equilibrium, and there is no inflation at the new equilibrium.

True, the price is higher in the new equilibrium, and it will not come back down. A tax increase does drive up the price. But a higher price *level* does not constitute an inflation. Prices must be *continuously increasing* to term the process an inflation. In other words, something has to shift up the supply curve and/ or the demand curve continuously over time to cause an inflation, so that prices are continuously rising. A tax increase does not do this. It causes only a one-time shift in the supply curve and therefore only a one-time increase in the price level.

One final point about the definition of inflation is worth noting. Inflation is expressed as the percentage rate of change in a price over a period of time, most often a year. The annual rate of inflation is the ratio of the change in price during the year to the price at the beginning of the year, multiplied by 100 to convert the ratio into a percentage.

Annual rate of inflation
$$= [(P_{\text{end of year}} - P_{\text{end of previous year}})/P_{\text{end of previous year}}] \cdot 100$$

For example, suppose that the price of a gallon of milk was $2.00 at the end of 1992 and $2.20 at the end of 1993. Then the annual rate of inflation in the price of milk during 1993 was 10 percent:

$$\text{Annual rate of inflation}_{\text{milk}} = [(\$2.20 - \$2.00)/\$2.00] \cdot 100$$
$$= (\$.20/\$2.00) \cdot 100 = 10\%$$

The standard shorthand expression for the rate of inflation is $\Delta P/P$. Δ is the Greek symbol for "change," so that $\Delta P/P$ is the change in price divided by the price, or the rate of change in the price. The P in the denominator refers to the price level at the end of the previous period (1992 in our milk example). The term $\Delta P/P$ is understood to be the percentage rate of change in the price, even though the final multiplication by 100 is usually left out of the expression.

Computing a Price Index and an Overall Rate of Inflation

The federal government reported that the rate of inflation in the United States during 1992 was 2.9 percent. Calculating a single number to represent "the" overall rate of inflation requires some explanation because the prices of individual goods and services do not all rise at the same rate. In 1992 many prices rose by more than 2.9 percent, many prices rose by less than 2.9 percent, and the prices of some products even fell (personal computers and floppy discs, for example). The reported 2.9 percent rate of inflation is an average of many different price changes. The question, then, is this: What is a sensible way to compute an average overall rate of inflation from the individual rates of inflation of many different products?

THE REFERENCE MARKET BASKET   The standard method of computing an overall rate of inflation, and the one used by the federal government, is a two-step process. The government begins by defining a market basket of goods and services that is purchased by a typical member of some reference group. The reference group may consist of households (consumers), or business firms, or governments, or even all the purchasers of final goods and services in the entire economy. Next, the government determines how much the market basket of goods and services costs each month and converts the monthly costs into a price index. The annual rate of inflation is then calculated as the percentage increase in the cost of the market basket from year to year or, equivalently, the percentage increase in the price index from year to year. Each reference group has its own price index and rate of inflation, based on the relevant market basket for the group.

The most closely watched price index is the **consumer price index,** the CPI, which is based on a market basket of consumer goods and services purchased by the typical household. The rate of inflation refers to the annual percentage change in the CPI unless otherwise qualified, an example being the 2.9 percent rate of inflation for 1992 reported above. The CPI has very important economic consequences. It is used as the basis for adjusting wages in labor union contracts that contain annual *cost-of-living-adjustment clauses* (COLA clauses) and for adjusting government transfer payments, such as Social Security retirement benefits and public assistance. The adjustments are designed to protect workers and transfer recipients from increases in the cost of living caused by inflation. Some private pensions are also adjusted annually on the basis of the CPI.

CONSUMER PRICE INDEX

A price index based on a market basket of consumer goods and services purchased by the typical household.

CONSTRUCTING A PRICE INDEX   We can illustrate how to construct the CPI and the corresponding rate of inflation with a simple market basket consisting of two goods. The procedures for constructing the CPI, or any other price index, are the same no matter how many goods the market basket contains. Therefore, assume for the purposes of our example that every household purchases just two goods, a single kind of food and a single type of clothing.

Suppose that the typical household buys 10 units of the food and 20 units of the clothing during the year. Therefore, the market basket for consumers that we will use to compute our hypothetical CPI and the rate of inflation consists of 10 units of food and 20 units of clothing.

Let's assume that the price of the food was $12 per unit and the price of the clothing was $4 per unit on December 31, 1987. Therefore, the total cost of the market basket at the end of 1987 was $200:

$$\text{Cost of market basket}_{1987} = (\$12 \cdot 10) + (\$4 \cdot 20) = \$120 + \$80 = \$200$$

Suppose that the price of the food had risen to $18 and the price of the clothing had risen to $5 by December 31, 1988. Therefore, the total cost of the market basket at the end of 1988 is $280:

$$\text{Cost of market basket}_{1988} = (\$18 \cdot 10) + (\$5 \cdot 20) = \$180 + \$100 = \$280$$

The rate of inflation during 1988 is the percentage increase in the cost of the market basket from December 31, 1987, to December 31, 1988:

$$\begin{aligned}\text{Rate of inflation}_{1988} &= [(\$280 - \$200)/\$200] \cdot 100 \\ &= (\$80/\$200) \cdot 100 \\ &= 0.4 \cdot 100 = 40\%[1]\end{aligned}$$

---

[1]An equivalent way to compute the percentage change is to divide the cost of the market basket on December 31, 1988, by its cost on December 31, 1987, and subtract 1:

$$\begin{aligned}\text{Rate of inflation}_{1988} &= [(\$280/\$200) - 1] \cdot 100 \\ &= (1.4 - 1) \cdot 100 = .4 \cdot 100 = 40\%\end{aligned}$$

Working with the cost of an actual market basket is unwieldy because the market basket contains a large number of goods and services. For example, the actual expenditures on goods and services by a typical household may have been something like $20,590.15 at the end of 1987. Rather than publish numbers such as these, the government turns the annual costs of the market basket into a simpler price index. The only purpose of determining the costs of the market basket each year is to compute rates of inflation, and the simple price index is sufficient for this.

A price index is constructed by dividing the cost of the market basket every year by the cost of the market basket in the base year. The price index is multiplied by 100 to turn it into a percentage relative to the base year. Therefore, the CPI in our example is constructed by dividing the cost of the market basket in each year by the cost in 1987, the base year. The CPI for 1987 is arbitrarily set equal to 100:

$$\text{CPI}_{1987} = (\text{cost of market basket}_{1987}/\text{cost of market basket}_{1987}) \cdot 100$$
$$= (\$200/\$200) \cdot 100 = 1.0 \cdot 100 = 100$$

The consumer price index for 1988 is 140:

$$\text{CPI}_{1988} = (\text{cost of market basket}_{1988}/\text{cost of market basket}_{1987}) \cdot 100$$
$$= (\$280/\$200) \cdot 100 = 1.4 \cdot 100 = 140$$

The rate of inflation during 1988 is the percentage change in the CPI from 1987 to 1988:

$$\text{Rate of inflation}_{1988} = [(140 - 100)/100] \cdot 100 = 40\%$$

The percentage change in the CPI gives the same rate of inflation as the percentage change in the cost of the market basket. This must be so because the CPI simply divides the cost of the market basket each year by the same number, the cost of the market basket in the base year 1987. Therefore, the cost of the market basket in the base year cancels out when computing the percentage changes from one year to the next.

Continuing with our example, suppose that the cost of the market basket rises to $300 by December of 1989. The CPI for 1989 is

$$\text{CPI}_{1989} = (\text{cost of market basket}_{1989}/\text{cost of the market basket}_{1987}) \cdot 100$$
$$= (\$300/\$200) \cdot 100 = 1.5 \cdot 100 = 150$$

CPI_{1989} tells us that the cost of the market basket was 50 percent higher in 1989 than in the base year of 1987. The annual rate of inflation during 1989 is the percentage change in the CPI from 1988 to 1989:

$$\text{Rate of inflation}_{1989} = [(150 - 140)/140] \cdot 100$$
$$= (10/140) \cdot 100 = .071 \cdot 100 = 7.1\%$$

In general, the rate of inflation between any two years is the percentage change in the consumer price index between the two years. In our example, the rate of inflation between 1987 and 1989 is 50 percent.

INFLATION: A WEIGHTED AVERAGE OF PRICE INCREASES   Defining the rate of inflation as the percentage increase in the cost of a market basket of goods and services leads to an equivalent and very intuitive definition of the overall rate of inflation. The *overall rate of inflation* turns out to be a weighted average of the rates of inflation of each item in the market basket, where the individual weights reflect the importance of each item to the consumer in the base year. Specifically, the weights are the proportion of total expenditures devoted to each item in the base year. Deriving the weighted average interpretation of the rate of inflation is tedious, so we will just demonstrate it with the numbers in our simple example.

In 1987, our base year, the typical household spent 60 percent of its income on food [($120/$200) · 100 = 60%] and 40 percent of its income on clothing [($80/$200) · 100 = 40%]. Therefore, the rate of inflation in any one year is .6 times the rate of inflation in food during the year plus .4 times the rate of inflation in clothing during the year.

$$\text{Rate of inflation} = .6 \cdot (\Delta P/P)_{food} + .4 \cdot (\Delta P/P)_{clothing}$$

In 1988 the price of food rose from $12 to $18, a 50 percent in crease [($18 − $12)/$12 = $6/$12 = .5 = 50%]; the price of clothing rose from $4 to $5, a 25 percent increase [($5 − $4)/$4 = $1/$4 = .25 = 25%]. Therefore, the rate of inflation during 1988 was

$$\text{Rate of inflation}_{1988} = .6 \cdot (50\%) + .4 \cdot (25\%) = 30\% + 10\% = 40\%$$

the same answer obtained by using the percentage change in the CPI.

Notice that the overall rate of inflation is closer to the rate of inflation of food than that of clothing, since food is more important in the typical household's budget. This makes sense. An increase in the price of automobiles has a much greater impact on our cost of living than does an increase in the price of toothpicks. Therefore, a 10 percent inflation in the price of automobiles ought to get much more weight than a 10 percent inflation in the price of toothpicks when constructing an overall rate of inflation. Our simple example shows that the market basket/price index method of computing the rate of inflation does give more weight to products that are more important in consumers' budgets.

The Consumer Price Index

The CPI is constructed and published by the Bureau of Labor Statistics (BLS), the same agency that measures the rate of unemployment. The actual CPI contains many more than two items. Indeed, the BLS goes to great lengths to track the rate of inflation for consumer goods and services. The bureau sends representatives to over 19,000 retail establishments in 85 urban areas throughout the United States to sample the prices of a few thousand consumer products. The prices of food, fuel, and a few other items are sampled every month. All other prices are sampled at least every other month, and every month in the five largest urban areas. In all, the BLS representatives collect data on more than 100,000 individual prices every other month. These are actual prices, not the list or "manufacturer's suggested retail prices." For example, the representatives try to determine the actual prices of new cars sold during the month at the dealerships that they visit; they do not record the sticker prices posted on the car windows.

The market basket of goods and services to be sampled each month is based on detailed Consumer Expenditure Surveys undertaken by the Census Bureau every 10 years or so. The most recent Consumer Expenditure Survey was conducted from 1982 through 1984; approximately 57,000 households participated in the survey. The last Consumer Expenditure Survey before that was in 1972–73. The BLS used the results of the 1982–84 survey to construct a new base-year market basket of goods and services for 1987. The market basket applies to a "typical" household living in an urban area; urban households represent about 80 percent of all households. The previous base year had been 1981, based on the 1972–73 survey results.

Part A of Table 7.1 records the proportion of total expenditures accounted for by the seven major categories of consumer products in the 1987 market basket: food, housing, apparel and upkeep, transportation, medical care, entertainment, and other goods and services. These percentages are the combined weights given to the rates of inflation of the products within each category in constructing the overall rate of inflation. Part A of the table also records the average annual rates of inflation during the 1980s for each of the seven categories and for all products. We can see from the table that the rates of inflation varied considerably across the categories during the decade. The prices of medical care and other goods and services rose more than did the overall average, and the prices of food, apparel and upkeep, and transportation rose less than the average. Inflation in housing and entertainment was just about at the overall average.

Part B of Table 7.1 records the change in price over the entire decade for a selection of items. Hospital rooms had the highest rate of inflation of all the items recorded by the BLS, and televisions had the lowest rate of inflation. The negative 27 percent for televisions indicates that the price of televisions fell by 27 percent during the decade. Televisions experienced *price deflation*, the opposite of price inflation. The list of items contains good and bad news for college students. The bad news you no doubt already suspected: The price changes for college tuition and school books and supplies were among the 10 highest rates of inflation across all products. The good news is that sound equipment, interstate telephone calls, and televisions, each popular items among students, were the only broad categories of products whose prices fell during the 1980s.

CORE RATE OF INFLATION

The rate of inflation that is based on a restricted market basket of goods and services, which excludes items that have highly volatile prices and that have significant weight in computing the overall rate of inflation.

THE CORE RATE OF INFLATION   The BLS also publishes an underlying or **core rate of inflation,** which is based on a restricted market basket that excludes all items of food, shelter (within housing), and energy (within housing and transportation). The prices of these items are highly volatile, and each has a fairly high weight in the overall rate of inflation. Consequently, they have an undue influence on the monthly changes in the rate of inflation.

Food prices are highly volatile because they are determined by the Laws of Supply and Demand for the most part. They rise and fall with every shift in the market supply or the market demand curve. Food also has nearly an 18 percent weight in computing the overall rate of inflation (refer to part A of Table 7.1). The shelter category includes mortgage interest rates, which oc-

TABLE 7.1   The Consumer Price Index

A. THE SEVEN MAJOR CATEGORIES OF CONSUMER PRODUCTS IN THE 1987 CPI
MARKET BASKET

CATEGORY	PROPORTION OF TOTAL EXPENDITURES IN MARKET BASKET %	AVERAGE ANNUAL RATE OF INFLATION DURING THE 1980s %
Food	17.8	4.4
Housing	42.9	5.2
Apparael and upkeep	6.3	3.1
Transportation	17.2	4.3
Medical care	5.4	8.1
Entertainment	4.4	5.1
Other goods and services	6.0	7.9
All items	100.0	5.1
Core rate of inflation (excludes food, shelter, energy)		5.4

B. PERCENTAGE CHANGE IN PRICE DURING THE 1980s—SELECTED ITEMS

ITEM	PERCENTAGE CHANGE IN PRICE DECEMBER 1979–DECEMBER 1989 %
Hospital rooms	161.9
College tuition	149.0
School books and supplies	140.5
Automobile insurance	119.9
Cereal	117.4
Rent	75.5
Electricity	68.8
Snacks	65.4
Postage	64.2
Maintenance and repair services	63.2
Cosmetics	60.3
New Cars	44.0
Motor fuel	3.5
Women's suits	2.5
Coffee	2.1
Sound equipment	− 2.5
Telephone calls—interstate	− 14.7
Television	− 27.0
All items	64.0

SOURCES: M. Schmidt, "Comparison of the Revised and the Old CPI," *Monthly Labor Review* 110, No. 11 (November 1987): Table 1, p. 4; and P. Jackman, "Consumer Prices in the 1980's: the Cooling of Inflation," *Monthly Labor Review* 113, No. 8 (August 1990): Table 1, p. 20, Table 2, p. 22, and Table 3, pp. 23 25.

casionally increase or decrease by 5 to 10 percent within a month. Energy prices have been extremely volatile ever since 1973, when the Organization of Petroleum Exporting Countries (OPEC) first took control of the world oil market. OPEC used its market power to increase the price of crude oil eightfold from 1973 to 1980. Then, in 1981, OPEC fell into disarray and lost its grip on the world oil market countries. The price of crude oil plummeted, declining by almost one-third between 1981 and 1984. OPEC has never regained control of the market, and the price of oil has tended to fluctuate quite a bit.

By removing these three important and highly volatile items, the core rate of inflation gives a better indication of the month-by-month changes in the rates of inflation for all consumer products. For example, suppose that the price of food rises generally by 10 percent in one month, which has happened on occasion. This alone would increase the overall rate of inflation by 1.8 percentage points ($.18 \cdot 10\% = 1.8\%$) during the month.

The distinction between the core and the overall rates of inflation becomes less important over longer periods of time, however, because the ups and downs of food, shelter, and energy prices tend to cancel out over time. According to Table 7.1, the annual average core rate of inflation during the 1980s was 5.4 percent, just about the same as the annual average overall rate of inflation of 5.1 percent.

REFLECTION: The next time your morning newspaper reports a big increase or decrease in the rate of inflation from the preceding month, notice how much of the change is due to changes in the prices of food, or shelter, or energy.

Other Important Price Indexes

The federal government publishes a number of other price indexes and inflation rates for other reference groups besides households. Two of the more important are the producer price index (PPI) and the GDP deflator.

PRODUCER PRICE INDEX

A price index that is designed to track changes in the cost of production over time; it has three components derived from three separate market baskets: crude materials; intermediate materials, supplies, and components purchased from other firms; and finished manufactured goods.

THE PRODUCER PRICE INDEX   The **Producer Price Index** (PPI) is designed to track changes in the costs of production over time. It is derived from three separate market baskets: crude materials; intermediate materials, supplies, and components purchased from other firms; and finished manufactured goods. The finished goods prices in the PPI are wholesale prices, not retail prices. The BLS obtains information on producer prices from a monthly mail survey sent to thousands of firms, and publishes each component of the PPI as a separate index.

The components of the PPI are closely watched because they are considered to be good leading indicators, or predictors, of future changes in the CPI. Firms in the United States are quick to pass increases or decreases in their costs of production on to their customers by raising or lowering their prices. Therefore, changes in the PPI are typically followed by changes in the CPI within the next few months.

THE GDP DEFLATOR   The GDP deflator is derived from a very broad market basket of final goods and services purchased in all four sectors of the economy: the household sector, the business sector, the government sector, and the rest-of-world sector. GDP stands for gross domestic product; it refers to the value of all the final products that flow through the markets for goods and services.

The GDP deflator plays a very important role in tracking the growth of the economy over time. Suppose that the dollar value of the circular flow of economic activity in the United States increases by 10 percent during the year. The GDP deflator is used to determine how much of the 10 percent increase is due to increases in the flow of real goods and services through the product and the factor markets and how much is simply due to price increases. We will return to the GDP deflator in Chapter 8, which discusses how the government's accountants measure the circular flow of economic activity.

The Costs of Inflation

Inflation is undoubtedly Public Enemy #1 because of the common perception that inflation robs everyone of purchasing power. This perception is certainly understandable. We noted in Chapter 6 that most labor contracts set wages for anywhere from one to three years. Once people's wages have been set, they naturally hope for stable prices because every percentage point of inflation lowers the purchasing power of their paychecks.[2] Also, everyone feels the effects of inflation, whereas unemployment affects only a small percentage of the labor force. Most people are fairly secure in their jobs; they do not see unemployment as a serious threat to their well-being. Small wonder, then, that people most often select inflation as the leading problem facing the nation.

The notion that inflation robs everyone of purchasing power is not correct, however. It flies in the face of a fundamental principle of macroeconomics, the circular flow of economic activity. The dollar value of goods and services that flow through a nation's product markets must equal the dollar value of incomes earned in a nation's factor markets. Therefore, if inflation is driving up the prices of goods and services that people buy, it must also be increasing the wages, interest rates, and rents that are the sources of their incomes.

The only way that inflation can affect the overall purchasing power of a nation is through imports and exports, the one leak in the circular flow. Higher import prices caused by inflation translate into higher incomes for foreign citizens, not U.S. citizens. Therefore, inflation in import prices does transfer purchasing power to foreign countries. The United States lost hundreds of billions of dollars of purchasing power to the OPEC countries from 1973 to 1980.

The loss in purchasing power in imports is counterbalanced, however, by inflation in export prices, which transfers purchasing power from foreign citizens to U.S. citizens. The *net* transfer of purchasing power, therefore, depends on the relative sizes of imports and exports and the rates of inflation in each. This net transfer is not very important in the United States because the difference between imports and exports each year is always only a small percentage of the total national income and product. Throughout the 1980s, for example, the value of imports exceeded the value of exports by an average of $38 billion, less than 1 percent of the national product.

The people who see inflation robbing them of purchasing power forget that their wage increases each year depend in part on the underlying rate of inflation in the economy. Wage increases will be higher if the economy has been experiencing a 10 percent rate of inflation than if prices have been stable—in fact, about 10 percent higher, on average. The circular flow of economic activity

---

[2]Some of the three-year labor union contracts contain cost-of-living adjustment clauses, known as COLA clauses, that automatically increase wages each year to match the increases in the CPI. Most employee contracts do not have this built-in inflation protection, however.

naturally tends to protect the purchasing power of people's incomes during periods of inflation.

THE THREAT OF HYPERINFLATION   Inflation may not rob everyone of purchasing power, but economists consider inflation to be a very serious problem nonetheless. For starters, governments must take care to keep inflation under control because the process of inflation is driven by an internal dynamic that feeds upon itself. The following scenario can easily occur if governments are not careful. Prices begin rising at the rate of 10 percent per year, then 20 percent, then 100 percent, then 1,000 percent; finally, the process blows sky high into a **hyperinflation,** in which new higher prices are quoted every hour. The point at which hyperinflation sets in is the point at which people lose confidence in their currency. No one wants to hold the nation's money because they have no idea what they will be able to buy with it; the entire financial structure of the economy is threatened. During hyperinflations the political cartoonists draw consumers entering stores with shopping carts full of money and leaving with a single loaf of bread.

HYPERINFLATION

An inflation in which prices are increasing very rapidly, causing people to lose confidence in the currency.

With hyperinflation comes real economic hardship. Businesses go bankrupt, people lose their jobs, and many economic exchanges revert to barter, with goods and services traded directly for other goods and services. Economic growth grinds to a halt until the government takes steps to reissue a new money and restore people's confidence in it.

The United States has always managed to keep inflation under control and avoid the hardships of a hyperinflation. Not so other countries' economies, however. Prices exploded in the Central Powers of Europe during the early 1920s. Prices in Austria were 242 times higher in June 1924 than in January 1921; in Hungary, 504 times higher in March 1925 than in July 1921; and in Poland, 9,620 times higher in April 1924 than in January 1921. These inflations paled in comparison with the German hyperinflation, however. Prices in Germany were 80 *billion* times higher in June 1924 than in January 1921! A more recent hyperinflation occurred in Bolivia during 1985, when prices rose by 11,750 percent in that year alone.[3]

Many countries today have uncomfortably high rates of inflation. Poland and Yugoslavia are struggling with inflation as they try to convert their economies to capitalism. Prices rose over 580 percent in each country during 1990. Argentina and Brazil experienced four-digit inflation during 1990, 2,314% and 2,937%, respectively. These countries may not yet be in hyperinflations, but they are clearly flirting with financial disaster.

Experience has taught that even a moderate amount of inflation is very difficult to stop once it takes hold and that an inflationary process can blow up into a hyperinflation if the government does not keep inflation under control. The good news is that governments can easily control inflation if they want to. The bad news is that stopping an inflationary process can be very costly for a short period of time. Governments are sometimes unwilling to bear the costs, so they let the inflation feed upon itself and run out of control.

We will return to the internal dynamic that drives inflation in Chapter 19, after we understand how the macro economy operates. At this point we want

---

[3]T. Sargent, "The Ends of Four Big Inflations," in R. Hall, ed., *Inflation* (Chicago: University of Chicago Press, 1982), 51, 62–63, 70–71, 74–75. *International Financial Statistics Yearbook, 1992,* (Washington, D.C.: International Monetary Fund, 1992), pp. 189, 235, 243, 579, 749.

to focus on the costs associated with moderate and controlled amounts of inflation, such as the United States has been experiencing. The costs take the form of inefficiencies and redistributions of purchasing power.

THE COSTS OF MODERATE INFLATION   The costs of inflation depend on three factors: (1) whether the inflation is balanced or unbalanced, (2) whether economic contracts and institutions have adjusted to the inflation, and (3) whether the level of inflation each year is anticipated or unanticipated.

An inflation is **balanced** if the prices of all goods and services, including all factors of production, are rising at exactly the same rate. An inflation is **unbalanced** if prices are rising at different rates, some faster than and others slower than the overall average rate of inflation.

Economic contracts are adjusted to inflation if all the dollar values stipulated in the contracts, including all prices, increase and decrease automatically in proportion to the overall rate of inflation. Contracts with this feature are said to be *indexed*, or tied, to the CPI; if the CPI rises by 10 percent, then all dollar values in the contract automatically rise by 10 percent. One institutional feature of the economy that has an important effect on the costs of inflation is a nation's tax system. A tax is adjusted for inflation if the purchasing power of the taxes paid to the government, the so-called real tax payment, is independent of the rate of inflation. For example, suppose that you would owe $1,000 under an income tax if there were no inflation and $1,100 if prices were to rise by 10 percent. Your real tax payment is the same in either case; you owe 10 percent more in taxes when prices rise by 10 percent. The income tax is adjusted for inflation.

Inflation is **fully anticipated** if everyone always knows what the inflation rate will be, this year, next year, and forever after. Inflation is **unanticipated** if it catches people by surprise: Everyone expects a 5 percent inflation in the year 2000, and the actual rate of inflation turns out to be 10 percent. Inflations are always unanticipated to some extent; no one can peer into the future with an unerring crystal ball.

Notice that the three factors are interrelated. Inflation will be more balanced the more contracts are indexed to the CPI. Also, a balanced inflation with indexing is somewhat easier to anticipate than is an unbalanced inflation without indexing. Conversely, the better people can anticipate inflation, the more likely contracts and institutions are to be indexed to inflation, and the more balanced the inflation will be.

PURE INFLATION: BALANCED, ADJUSTED, AND ANTICIPATED   Let's begin the analysis of the costs of inflation with the purest type of inflation. Imagine an inflation that is balanced and fully anticipated, with all contracts and institutions adjusted to the inflation. Inflation has been 10 percent forever and will continue to be 10 percent forever. Everyone correctly anticipates that inflation will be 10 percent, so all contracts are indexed to the 10 percent inflation and the inflation is balanced. All goods and factor prices rise by 10 percent. This pure case is unrealistic, to be sure, but it gives us a baseline for comparing the costs of inflation under different assumptions about the three factors.

The costs of a balanced, fully adjusted to, and fully anticipated inflation would be extremely small so long as the inflation remained moderate—say, 10 percent of less. A pure inflation of this kind gives rise to only two kinds of

BALANCED INFLATION

An inflation in which the prices of all goods and services, including all factors of production, are rising at exactly the same rate.

UNBALANCED INFLATION

An inflation in which the prices of individual goods and services are rising at different rates, some faster than and others slower than the overall rate of inflation.

FULLY ANTICIPATED INFLATION

This exists if everyone knows what the inflation rate will be in all future years.

UNANTICIPATED INFLATION

This exists when people are unable to guess correctly what the rate of inflation will be in all future years.

inefficiencies: (1) the costs to consumers and businesses of reducing the amount of cash they hold and (2) the printing costs to businesses of continually updating the prices of products listed in catalogs, in brochures, and on restaurant menus.

The shoe-leather costs of inflation. The dollar bills and coins that we all carry as a matter of convenience for small day-to-day transactions become ever less attractive when prices are rising. They do not offer a rate of return, so they cannot be protected from inflation. Every percentage point of inflation erodes the purchasing power of our cash by a percentage point each year; a dollar bill buys 10 percent less each year when the rate of inflation is 10 percent. Consequently, we all have an incentive to reduce our cash holdings in favor of other assets that are protected from a pure inflation, such as savings accounts, certificates of deposit, stocks, and bonds. But this means that we have to make more trips to our bank to take money out of our savings accounts or make more calls to our broker to sell some stocks or bonds whenever we want to buy the small items that require payments in cash. Economists refer to the extra costs of managing our cash in this way as the *shoe-leather costs of inflation.*

The shoe-leather costs are not very large in the United States, in part because we already do economize on cash through the use of credit cards and checks. The most common estimate of the shoe-leather costs is approximately $0.5 billion for every one-percentage-point increase in the rate of inflation.[4] This is a minuscule cost in a $6 trillion economy.

The menu costs of inflation. The menu costs of having to continually update price lists because of inflation are also extremely small. Firms would update price lists fairly regularly even without an inflation as their demand and cost conditions changed. A moderate inflation would probably not change the pattern of updating price lists very much. Economists do not have good estimates on the *menu costs of inflation*, but they are undoubtedly smaller even than the shoe-leather costs of inflation.

A pure inflation would not have any important redistributional effects either. Everyone is treated symmetrically by the balanced inflation, and no one is caught by surprise with a sudden unexpected change in inflation, so there are no channels for realigning purchasing power throughout the population. The only loss in purchasing power is through the shoe-leather and the menu costs. The former is likely to be felt by everyone, and the latter is too small to be of any consequence.

In summary, then, a moderate pure inflation that is balanced, fully adjusted to, and fully anticipated is hardly a burden at all to an economy. The circular flow of economic activity largely protects the purchasing power of people's incomes, and nothing else happens of much consequence.

The costs of inflation rise sharply when the inflation is unbalanced, unadjusted to, and unanticipated, however. Let's look at some of the ways in which actual inflations give rise to inefficiencies and redistribute purchasing power.

UNBALANCED INFLATION   Inflation in the United States is typically highly unbalanced. We saw above that, throughout the 1980s, the price of hospital rooms rose over two and one-half times faster than the average rate of inflation, and the price of television sets actually fell.

---

[4]See, for example, S. Fischer, *Indexing, Inflation, and Economic Policy* (Cambridge, MA: MIT Press, 1986), 12. Fischer's book is widely cited on the costs of inflation. See, especially, the introduction and Chapters 1 and 2.

Most of the unbalance in measured inflation is due to differences in the demand and supply conditions across individual markets. For example, demand could be growing in some markets and declining in other markets. Nonetheless, inflation will tend to be unbalanced even when the impetus for inflation is an across-the-board increase in the demand for goods and services caused by an increase in the money supply. The reason why is that some firms respond quickly and others more slowly to changes in the average rate of inflation. David Stockton undertook a study of 91 industries in the United States to determine how quickly they respond to changes in inflation. His data covered 32 years, from 1949 to 1980. He found tremendous variation in the response to inflation. Eight of the industries reacted almost instantaneously to changes in inflation. These were highly competitive industries to which the Laws of Supply and Demand apply, including food products, textiles, home electric equipment, office machinery, and toys and sporting goods. At the other end of the spectrum were the regulated and highly concentrated final goods industries, including the electric utilities, capital equipment, and transportation equipment. These industries take two to three years to fully adjust to changes in inflation.[5]

Stockton's findings have important implications for the costs of inflation. An increase in inflation leads to more variation in *relative* prices when industries adjust at different rates to the inflation. Prices in the quick-to-adjust industries rise relative to prices in the slow-to-adjust industries, the more so the bigger the increase in inflation. In other words, the higher the inflation becomes, the more unbalanced it becomes. The increased variation in relative prices in turn generates inefficiencies and haphazard redistributions of purchasing power throughout the economy.

Inefficiency. An unbalanced inflation misallocates resources by knocking individual markets out of equilibrium and substituting a pattern of excess supplies and demands. The relatively higher prices in the quick-to-adjust industries induce producers to bring more resources into these markets and increase the quantities supplied. At the same time, the higher prices drive consumers to seek out substitute products and decrease the quantities demanded. The reactions of producers and consumers result in excess supply in the quick-to-adjust markets. Conversely, the relatively lower prices in the slow-to-adjust markets decrease the quantities supplied and increase the quantities demanded. The result is excess demand in the slow-to-adjust markets. The inflation-induced pattern of excess supplies and demands wastes society's scarce resources because the resources do not go to the markets where they are most highly valued.

Redistribution. An unbalanced inflation also redistributes purchasing power from consumers who favor the products of the relatively higher priced, quick-to-adjust industries to the consumers who favor the products of the relatively lower priced, slow-to-adjust industries. Whether this redistribution is likely to be pro-poor or pro-rich is difficult to say, however. The poor spend a higher percentage of their incomes than do the rich on the basic necessities—food, clothing, and shelter. If we knew that the basic necessities were mostly produced by the quick-to-adjust industries, then we could conclude that an unbalanced inflation redistributes purchasing power from the poor to the rich.

---

[5]D. Stockton, "Relative Price Dispersion, Aggregate Price Movement, and the Natural Rate of Unemployment," *Economic Inquiry* XXVI, No. 1 (January 1988): 1–22.

The reverse would be true if the basic necessities were mostly produced by the slow-to-adjust industries. Stockton's data do not show any consistent pattern along these lines, however. His quick-to-adjust industries are a mixture of basic necessities (food products, textiles) and luxury items (home electronics, toys and sporting goods). Also, his slow-to-adjust industries include electricity, a basic necessity.

Not surprisingly, studies of past U.S. inflations have not uncovered any definite pro-poor or pro-rich pattern to the purchasing power effects of the inflations. The redistributions of purchasing power are more or less haphazard. They tend to vary from one episode of inflation to the next, depending on which items are leading the overall rate of inflation and which are lagging behind.

UNADJUSTED INFLATION   As indicated above, economists are primarily interested in the extent to which two institutional features of the economy—contracts for products and factors of production and the nation's tax laws—are adjusted to inflation.

Unadjusted contracts. The analysis of unbalanced inflation has already indicated that most contracts are not indexed to the CPI. This is unfortunate because the economy would be much more efficient if all contracts were indexed. All prices would adjust immediately to changes in the rate of inflation, inflation would be balanced, and the economy would avoid the pattern of excess supplies and demands brought about by an unbalanced inflation.

Business firms and workers are reluctant to index contracts to the CPI, however, despite the economywide advantages to indexing. They would be comfortable indexing only if they were assured that everyone is indexing simultaneously. Otherwise, they know that inflation is sure to be unbalanced and the individual firms and workers that do index become vulnerable to changes in the overall rate of inflation in this situation.

Business firms are primarily concerned about two sets of prices: the prices they receive for their products and the prices of the inputs needed to produce their products. They are much less concerned about prices generally. Any firm that thinks about indexing the price of its products to the CPI would be wary of the following scenario. Suppose that the CPI rises by 10 percent, but that the prices of a firm's inputs rise by much less than 10 percent. This is entirely possible with an unbalanced inflation. Assume for the sake of discussion that the firm's input prices do not rise at all. The firm would be forced to raise the prices of its products by 10 percent if it is indexed to the CPI, even though its costs of production have not increased. The 10 percent price increases would put the firm at a severe disadvantage if its competitors were not indexed to the CPI because the competitors would not have raised their prices. A 10 percent *decrease* in the CPI might be even worse for the indexed firm; it could force the firm to lower its prices below its costs of production. Small wonder that firms are reluctant to index their prices to the CPI unless every firm indexes simultaneously.

Workers are equally wary of having their wages indexed to the CPI. Their big fear is a decrease in the CPI, which would lower their wages relative to other workers whose wages are not indexed. The unions that fought for COLA clauses in their contracts assumed that the CPI would only increase, not decrease. They would not have been so interested in COLA clauses if the CPI were equally likely to move up or down.

The costs to an economy of not having indexed contracts in times of inflation are the same as those noted in the previous section on unbalanced inflation. Unindexed prices generate a pattern of excess supplies and demands that misallocates scarce resources and causes haphazard redistributions of purchasing power.

Unadjusted taxes. Taxes in the United States are only partially indexed for inflation. The taxpayers who receive income from capital are the most vulnerable to inflation because income from capital is not indexed to inflation under either the federal personal or the federal corporation income taxes. The tax laws relating to income from capital are extremely complicated. We will illustrate the problem that inflation causes for income from capital with one example, the capital gain received on the sale of stock.

Suppose that you bought a share of stock in some company for $100 in 1980 and sold the stock in 1990 for $200. Your *capital gain* on the stock is $100, the difference between the price you sold it for in 1990 and the price you bought it for in 1980 ($100 = $200 − $100). The capital gain is counted as part of your taxable income in 1990 under the federal personal income tax. You would pay a tax of $28 on the capital gain if you were in the 28 percent tax bracket.

If prices remained the same between 1980 and 1990, your $100 capital gain represents an increase in purchasing power. After paying the $28 tax, you still have an increase in purchasing power of $72, which represents your real return on the stock. Suppose that prices doubled between 1980 and 1990, however. In this case your $100 capital gain has not increased your purchasing power at all because it takes $200 to buy in 1990 what $100 bought in 1980. The $172 remaining after paying the $28 tax does not buy as much in 1990 as the $100 bought in 1980. The return on your stock is actually negative; you have transferred purchasing power to the government.

The government can protect capital gains from inflation by indexing the purchase price of stocks to the CPI. Taxpayers would be allowed to increase the purchase price of a stock by the increase in the CPI since the time of purchase when computing their capital gains. In our example, you would increase the purchase price to $200 and show no taxable capital gain on the stock if the CPI doubled between 1980 and 1990. This calculation correctly indicates that the $100 capital gain merely protected your purchasing power. It did not represent an increase in purchasing power, and you should not pay a tax on it.

The government's failure to index capital gains and other sources of capital income is anti-rich because the rich own the vast majority of the nation's capital. It also artificially raises the cost of capital during times of inflation, which discourages investment and slows down economic growth. Reforming the tax laws to protect capital income from inflation would undoubtedly make the economy more productive and efficient.

UNANTICIPATED INFLATION   The inability to anticipate inflation correctly adds to the efficiency losses of an unbalanced and unadjusted inflation by increasing the overall uncertainty in the economy. People may react to the uncertainty by purchasing unproductive assets such as gold as a hedge against inflation. They may also be reluctant to enter into long-term contracts that lock them into a highly uncertain future. The federal government may have more difficulty issuing 30-year bonds, and banks may be unwilling to write 25- and 30-year mortgages to homeowners. The unexpected pattern of inflation has not had these effects in the United States, perhaps because inflation has moved within fairly narrow bounds. It has never been lower than −2.1 percent (1949) or higher than 18.1 percent (1946) since World War II. No one knows for sure how people would react if the swings in inflation year to year were quite a bit larger or what the additional costs would be.

The main cost of unanticipated inflation is distributional. It increases the likelihood of haphazard redistributions of purchasing power throughout the economy. We will illustrate with three of the more important redistributional effects: (1) redistributions among wage earners, (2) redistributions from people with unearned incomes to people with earned incomes, and (3) redistributions from lenders to borrowers.

Redistributions among wage earners. We noted in Chapter 6 that 5 percent of all employees in the United States work under two-year contracts, 20 percent work under three-year contracts, and most of the rest work under one-year contracts. The three-year contract is the standard union contract. The wage increases negotiated in these contracts would presumably take into account the average rate of inflation so long as the inflation is correctly anticipated. Suppose, though, that a spurt of inflation catches employees by surprise. Imagine that inflation has been zero for some time and that the employees negotiate their contracts expecting that inflation will continue to be zero. Suddenly inflation jumps to 10 percent per year and remains there. The employees are now saddled with negotiated annual wage increases that are too low each year by 10 percentage points. They lose some of the purchasing power that they expected to enjoy.

The sudden increase in inflation affects the employees differently depending on the length of their contracts. The employees with one-year contracts can adjust to the higher inflation next year. The other employees are locked into the wrong contracts for two and three years (we are ignoring COLA clauses to focus on the effects of unanticipated inflation). The result of the unexpected surge in inflation is a redistribution of purchasing power from the employees with longer contracts to the employees with shorter contracts. The amount of the redistribution among workers through this channel appears to be substantial. A recent study by Jesse Abraham suggests that every one-percentage-point increase in unexpected inflation may redistribute purchasing power equal to 1 percent of *total wages* among employees with contracts of different lengths.[6]

Unearned incomes versus earned incomes. People who rely on unearned sources of income are especially vulnerable to unexpected inflation. These include the elderly who are living off private pensions and Social Security retirement benefits and the poor who receive public assistance from the government. Pensions and public transfers are not naturally protected from inflation by the circular flow of economic activity as are sources of earned income, such as wages, interest income, and rents. Every one-percentage-point increase in inflation reduces purchasing power by one percentage point if these unearned sources of income are truly fixed.

The ability to anticipate inflation correctly is an important factor in determining how well unearned incomes are protected from inflation. Companies want to know how much their future pension commitments will be each year as they engage in long-range planning. They will be more willing to index the pensions to the CPI if they can anticipate future inflation than if inflation rises

---

[6]J. Abraham, "Income Redistribution During a Disinflation," *Journal of Macroeconomics* 9, No. 2 (Spring 1987): 218.

and falls unexpectedly. Similarly, administrators and legislators want to know what their future commitments will be under the various public transfer programs as they struggle to keep their budgets in balance. They, too, are more likely to index the transfers to the CPI if they believe that they can anticipate future inflation.

The record of protecting unearned incomes from inflation is mixed in the United States. Most private pensions are not indexed to the CPI, they are truly fixed sources of income to the retirees who receive them. The few private pensions that are indexed usually stipulate a maximum amount of inflation adjustment, such as 3 percent per year. Congress indexed Social Security retirement benefits to the CPI in the early 1970s. Social Security is the largest government transfer program and the main source of income for a large number of the elderly. The largest cash public assistance program for the poor, Aid to Families with Dependent Children (AFDC), is not indexed to the CPI, however. AFDC provides monthly cash benefits to single-parent families with children who are living in poverty. The monthly benefit levels are determined by the state governments, and the states have not been willing to protect the poor from inflation, in large part because they have been pressed to keep expenditures down to balance their budgets. The average monthly benefit level nationwide fell by 14 percent from 1975 to 1988 after adjusting for inflation.

Inflation in the United States almost certainly transfers purchasing power from unearned income to earned income, although the size of the transfer is unknown. Moreover, the transfer is just as certainly pro-rich and anti-poor because the poor rely much more on sources of unearned income than do the rich.

Redistributions from lenders to borrowers. Unexpected inflation transfers substantial amounts of purchasing power from lenders to borrowers. The following simple example illustrates why.

Suppose that your friend wants to borrow $100 from you for one year. Assume for the moment that the rate of inflation is zero, always has been zero, and is expected to remain at zero for the foreseeable future. You and your friend have to decide on the interest rate to charge for the loan. As a lender you think along the following lines. Your friend is asking you to give up $100 of purchasing power today. You are willing to do that, but only if you receive more than $100 of purchasing power when he pays you back one year from now. In other words, you want some return for your sacrifice. You decide that 5 percent is an appropriate return, so you ask him to pay you back $105 one year from now: the $100 that he borrowed plus 5 percent interest on the $100. Your friend agrees to the 5 percent interest charge. As the borrower, he understands that in order to receive $100 of purchasing power today he must be prepared to sacrifice even more purchasing power in the future. This is the opportunity cost of borrowing. So he is willing to sacrifice $105 of purchasing power one year from now. If all lenders and borrowers think along these lines, the interest rate on loans will be 5 percent in a world without inflation.

Now assume that everyone expects the rate of inflation to be 10 percent during the next year. You would no longer be willing to accept a 5 percent rate of interest on the loan. You need $110 one year from now to buy the same goods and services that $100 buys today, so you have to charge your friend a 10 percent rate of interest just to protect your purchasing power. Then, if you require an additional 5 percent in purchasing power to make the loan, you have to add five percentage points of interest on top of the 10 percent, for a total interest rate of 15 percent. You now ask your friend to pay you back $115 one year from now: $110 to protect your purchasing power and an additional $5 of purchasing power. Your friend will agree to the 15 percent rate of interest because he was willing to give up 5 percent more purchasing power one year from now than he borrowed today. He expects to have 10 percent more income with all prices, including factor prices, expected to rise by 10 percent. So paying back $115 in a world of 10 percent inflation is the same burden as paying back $105 in a world without inflation. If all borrowers and lenders think along these lines, the interest rate on loans will be 15 percent when the expected rate of inflation is 10 percent.

The situation we are interested in here is one in which the 10 percent inflation occurs, but catches people by surprise—everyone expected inflation to remain at zero. In this case you and your friend will agree to a 5 percent rate of interest because neither of you expects that the interest rate needs to be adjusted for inflation. At the end of the year, however, your friend turns out to have made a great deal and you a terrible deal. Your friend repays you $105, which is less than the purchasing power that you lent him one year ago now that prices are 10 percent higher. You have, in effect, paid your friend to lend him money. The effective interest rate on your loan is *minus* 5 percent once you adjust for inflation, equal to the loss in your purchasing power.

Our simple example illustrates the principle that an *unexpected* inflation redistributes purchasing power from lenders to borrowers. The reverse is also true: An unexpected deflation (reduction in inflation) redistributes purchasing power from borrowers to lenders (rework the above example with an unexpected 10 percent decrease in prices and see how you gain at the expense of your friend).

The redistribution of wealth through unanticipated inflation is the most important redistributional effect of inflation in the United States. Every 1 percent increase in unanticipated inflation redistributes approximately $60 billion of purchasing power from creditors (net lenders) to debtors (net borrowers), an amount equal to 1 percent of the national product.[7] The creditors are concentrated among the highest- and lowest-income families, and the debtors are in the middle of the distribution. Therefore, the redistribution of wealth favors the middle classes at the expense of both the rich and the poor in the United States. In addition, the federal government is a large net debtor. The federal debt exceeds $4 trillion. Therefore, unanticipated inflation transfers a substantial amount of purchasing power from the private sector to the federal government.

HISTORICAL NOTE: Many farmers in the United States went bankrupt in the early 1980s as inflation fell from 13 percent to less than 3 percent in three years. They were locked into high-interest loans taken out in 1979 and 1980 and could not make the principal and interest payments once the inflation subsided.

THE FISHER EQUATION

The relationship between observed, or nominal, interest rates and the underlying real interest rates that says that the observed interest rate on a financial security equals the real interest rate plus the expected rate of inflation.

THE FISHER EQUATION   Our simple example when the rate of inflation is expected illustrates a very important formula in macroeconomic analysis known as the Fisher equation, after economist Irving Fisher who first discovered it. The Fisher equation says that the observed, or nominal, interest rate on a loan equals the underlying real rate of interest plus the expected rate of inflation.

$$i_{\text{observed, nominal}} = r_{\text{real}} + \Delta P/P_E$$

The underlying real rate of interest, r_{real}, is the additional purchasing power that the lender requires and the borrower is willing to pay. r_{real} is 5 percent in our example. $\Delta P/P_E$ is the expected rate of inflation. $i_{\text{observed, nominal}}$ is the

[7]Fischer, *Indexing* Ch. 1, pp. 25–26.

interest rate that appears on the loan contract, that is, the actual amount of interest that the borrower pays the lender. $i_{observed, nominal}$ is 15 percent in our example when the expected rate of inflation is 10 percent; it is 5 percent when the expected rate of inflation is zero.

The Fisher equation says that observed or nominal interest rates consist of two components: the expected rate of inflation, which protects the purchasing power of the loan, and an underlying real rate of interest, which reflects the additional purchasing power that the lender requires and the borrower is willing to pay.

Notice another very important implication of the Fisher equation. *Interest rates increase and decrease point for point with increases and decreases in the expected rate of inflation.* Countries that are free of inflation have interest rates on the order of 5 percent. Countries that have been experiencing 20 percent inflation have interest rates on the order of 25 percent. And countries that have been experiencing triple-digit inflation of 300 percent have interest rates on the order of 305 percent. Interest rates have to adjust to the expected inflation in order to protect the purchasing power in loan contracts. The Fisher equation will play a central role in our analysis of inflation later on in the text.[8]

SUMMING UP: THE COSTS OF INFLATION Judging the costs of inflation ultimately depends on one's point of view. The University of Chicago's Robert Lucas argues that the only costs of inflation, per se, are the shoe-leather and the menu costs of a balanced, fully adjusted, and anticipated inflation. These costs are trivial, as we have seen. He attributes all the other inefficiencies and redistributional effects described above to other factors. Lucas blames the costs of an unbalanced inflation on the various institutional and political forces that prevent contracts and the tax system from being indexed to the CPI. Inflation itself is not the culprit. He also believes that the ebbs and flows of inflation, which make inflation so hard to anticipate, are the result of misguided fiscal and monetary policies that only serve to destabilize the economy. Lucas notes that these policies also cause changes in output and employment that are likely to be far more important than are any changes in the rate of inflation.

MIT's Stan Fischer disagrees with Lucas. Fischer argues that the costs of inflation have to be viewed within the existing institutional context of the economy. He would count all the costs described above as costs of inflation, which leads him to conclude that the costs of even a moderate amount of inflation are quite large in the United States. Fischer believes that a 10 percent rate of inflation would redistribute substantial amounts of purchasing power and generate efficiency losses on the order of 2 percent of the national product. Two percent of the national product is around $120 billion, or about $500 per person per year. Fischer does concede that the costs of inflation are mostly avoidable. He agrees with Lucas that most of the costs would disappear if prices and the tax system were indexed to the CPI and if the government maintained a steadier policy course.[9]

CURRENT ISSUE: Many of the industrialized market economies have had low rates of inflation in the 1990s and they want to keep inflation low. By the end of 1992, the central banks of Canada, Germany, Great Britain, Japan, and New Zealand had announced target rates of inflation of 2 percent or less. In mid-1993, Fed Chairman Alan Greenspan expressed concern about inflation even though the rate of inflation in the United States was less than 3 percent at the time. (*The Economist*, November 7, 1992, p. 23.)

---

[8]The point-for-point relationship between interest rates and expected inflation would not be expected to hold precisely because of real-world complications such as taxation, which our simple example ignores. Nonetheless, the point-for-point relationship is approximately true in the United States.

[9]Fischer, *Indexing*, p. 4; and R. Lucas, "Discussion," of S. Fischer, "Towards an Understanding of the Costs of Inflation," in K. Brunner and A. Meltzer, eds., *The Costs and Consequences of Inflation*, vol. 15 of *Carnegie-Rochester Conference Series on Public Policy* (Amsterdam: North Holland, 1981), 43–50.

Whatever their views on the costs of inflation, most economists agree that inflation is nowhere near as serious a problem as high levels of unemployment and slow economic growth are. The only caveat, and a crucial one, is the need to keep inflation tightly under control. A nation should never allow itself to start down the path of ever-increasing inflation and face the threat of a runaway hyperinflation. A modern economy cannot function without the use of money, and people will have confidence in the nation's currency only if they are assured that the government will act to keep inflation under control. We will see that governments can control inflation if they want to, and they really have no choice but to do so.

IMPORTS, EXPORTS, AND THE VALUE OF THE DOLLAR

Nations engage in trade with one another to increase their standards of living. We saw in Chapter 3 how international trade allows a nation to push its consumption possibilities beyond the limits of its own production possibilities frontier.

Imports are the key to the increase in living standards made possible by trade. Nations import to gain access to goods and services that they cannot produce at all, or at least not as well as other nations can. For example, the United States could grow bananas under tightly controlled hothouse conditions that artificially produce a tropical climate. But this would use a lot of scarce resources, and the bananas would be very expensive. Far better to let the tropical countries grow the bananas in their natural habitat and import the bananas. Consumers in the United States wind up with cheaper bananas, and the resources that would be needed to grow bananas in the United States can be put to much more productive uses.

Automobiles are a less clear-cut example than bananas, but the same principle applies. If Honda, Mitsubishi, and Toyota can build cars that the American public likes more cheaply than can General Motors, Ford, and Chrysler, then the United States should increase its imports of the Japanese cars and reduce its own production of cars. The American public resists the principle in the case of automobiles because more Japanese imports mean fewer jobs for American auto workers. In fact, imports generally have a bad name in the United States because people equate imports with loss of jobs. You can be sure that some politician will call for trade restrictions on imports whenever they threaten American producers. Bananas may not be a threat, but foreign automobiles certainly are.

The concern for jobs is understandable. The jobs lost by the American auto workers to foreign competition represent a big loss to each of the displaced auto workers and their families, and the loss of a job is highly visible. Moreover, the job losses tend to be concentrated geographically; witness the high unemployment among auto workers in Michigan.

Balanced against these losses, however, are the gains to the American consumers who are able to buy better and cheaper automobiles. These gains draw much less attention than do the losses because the benefits to each consumer are fairly small and not very visible. Moreover, the benefits are also not at all concentrated; they are shared broadly by millions of consumers throughout the United States. Make no mistake about it, though. Study after study shows that the small gains received by the millions of consumers are many times larger in the aggregate than are the large losses suffered by the tens of thousands of auto workers who lose their jobs. The losses to the auto workers are real. But the nation as a whole is far better off by importing automobiles and having the displaced auto workers seek employment elsewhere.

Always remember that imports are the ends of international trade. Gaining access to imported products is the sole purpose for engaging in trade with foreign nations. Imports are good, not bad, for a nation.

The Balance of Trade

If imports are the ends of international trade, then exports are the means to those ends. Countries are not willing to produce goods and send them to other countries unless they receive goods in exchange. In other words, a nation must export in order to be able to import. A nation's **balance of trade** is the difference between the value of its exports and the value of its imports. Most nations are forced by the unwritten rules of international trade to have a balance of trade approximately equal to zero: The value of their exports must equal the value of their imports. The following simple example will illustrate why this is so.

Suppose that all of U.S. trade consists of a single British importer selling wool sweaters in the United States and a single U.S. exporter selling food in London. The British importer sells $180 worth of sweaters. The U.S. exporter sells food valued at £100.

The importer is a British citizen. She does not want dollars; she wants pounds sterling that she can take back to England and spend there. Similarly, the exporter is a U.S. citizen. He does not want pounds sterling; he wants dollars that he can take back to the United States and spend there. So the importer and the exporter bring their currencies to the foreign exchange market, where the currencies of different nations are exchanged. The foreign exchange markets establish exchange rates at which the different currencies can be exchanged.

Assume that the exchange rate of dollars for pounds sterling is $1.80 per pounds sterling.

$$\text{Exchange rate} = \$1.80/\pounds$$

The importer and the exporter meet and exchange their currencies at this rate. The exchange is even. The importer gives her $180 to the exporter in exchange for his £100, and they both now have their own currencies.

Notice that before they exchange the currencies, we know the *dollar* value of the imported sweaters ($180) and the *pound sterling* value of the exported food (£100). The two values cannot be compared because they are denominated in different currencies. The exchange of currencies sets the *dollar* value of the food exports ($180), and we can now compare the dollar value of the exports with the dollar value of the imports. The two values are equal (at $180), indicating that England and the United States have made an even exchange of goods for goods, sweaters for food. The balance of trade in each country is zero.

Suppose, instead, that the foreign exchange market has established an exchange rate of $1.60 per pound sterling.

BALANCE OF TRADE

The difference between the value of a nation's exports and the value of its imports (merchandise exports and imports only; excludes trade in services).

Exchange rate = $1.60/£

At this rate, the exchange of currencies between the importer and the exporter is no longer even. The U.S. exporter gives the British importer his £100 and receives $160 from her in exchange. The importer has $20 left over. The dollar value of the imports remains at $180 as before, but the dollar value of the exports is only $160. From the U.S. point of view, the value of imports exceeds the value of exports by $20, exactly the amount that the British importer has left over after the exchange of currencies. The United States is said to have a **deficit** in its balance of trade because its balance of trade is negative $20. Conversely, England has a **surplus** in its balance of trade; the value of its exports exceeds the value of its imports.

A balance-of-trade deficit is a good deal for the United States and a bad deal for England. Citizens of the United States are receiving sweaters in part for pieces of paper, dollar bills. They are not required to exchange goods for goods, food for sweaters, even up. Conversely, British citizens are producing and sending sweaters to the United States and are not receiving an equal value of goods, food, in exchange. Part of their scarce resources used to produce the sweaters are being exchanged for pieces of paper, dollar bills. The British importer may be willing to place the dollars in U.S. financial securities as a form of saving (see below), but suppose that she does not want to. Then the trade imbalance cannot continue. The British will insist on an even exchange of goods for goods. Although our example is highly simplified, it shows why nations must export in order to import.

Stable Value of the Currency

Nations want their currencies to be stable in value relative to the currencies of other nations in addition to striving for a zero balance of trade. These two goals are closely related, as we will see in a moment.

Stable currency values create a more certain business environment for firms engaged in international trade. For example, firms exporting food to England know that sometime in the future they will be exchanging pounds sterling for dollars. They have to guess what the exchange rate of dollars for pounds will be six months, one year, two years from now as they plan their production and marketing strategies for the English market. The more stable the dollar is, the better they are able to predict the future exchange rates, and the more confidence they have in their business plans. A stable value of the dollar helps to promote international trade by reducing uncertainty.

In addition, movements in the value of a nation's currency generate a pattern of gainers and losers within the country that are best avoided. Let's begin with a few definitions before demonstrating this point.

A nation's currency is said to **depreciate** if its value falls relative to other currencies. For example, suppose that the dollar–pound sterling exchange rate changes from $1.80/£ to $2.00/£. The value of the dollar has fallen relative to the pound. It used to take $1.80 to buy one £; now it takes $2.00 to buy one £. The dollar has depreciated in value relative to the pound. A depreciating dollar is commonly referred to as a weaker dollar.

Conversely, a nation's currency is said to **appreciate** if its value rises relative to other currencies. For example, suppose that the dollar–pound sterling ex-

BALANCE-OF-TRADE DEFICIT
The value of a nation's imports exceeds the value of its exports.

BALANCE-OF-TRADE SURPLUS
The value of a nation's exports exceeds the value of its imports.

DEPRECIATION (CURRENCY)
The value of a nation's currency falls relative to the value of other currencies.

APPRECIATION (CURRENCY)
The value of a nation's currency rises relative to the value of other currencies.

change rate changes from $1.80/£ to $1.60/£. The value of the dollar has risen relative to the pound. It used to take $1.80 to buy one £; now it only takes $1.60 to buy one £. The dollar has appreciated in value relative to the pound. An appreciating dollar is commonly referred to as a stronger dollar.

The common terms *weaker dollar* and *stronger dollar* suggest that a depreciation of the dollar is bad for everyone in the United States and an appreciation of the dollar is good for everyone. This is not so. Some people gain and others lose when the dollar exchange rate moves in either direction. The three groups most directly affected by a change in the exchange rates are consumers, import-competing industries, and export industries. Import-competing industries are those that face direct competition from foreign imports. The U.S. automobile and textile industries are examples. The three groups are affected differently when the dollar depreciates or appreciates.

Suppose that the dollar depreciates in value from $1.80/£ to $2.00/£. This is bad for consumers, but good for exporters and import-competing industries. Consumers lose because British goods have become more expensive for them. A fine wool sweater priced at £100 in London used to cost U.S. consumers $180. Now they must pay $200 for it. Notice that the price rises to U.S. consumers even if the sweater is no more costly to produce and continues to sell for £100 in London. The depreciation of the dollar has made the sweater more expensive in the United States.

Import-competing industries, unlike consumers, gain from the depreciation. Consumers are more likely to buy domestically produced products because the imported products have become more expensive. Staying with our example, some consumers will refuse to pay $200 for the British sweater. They will buy a sweater from a U.S. producer instead. Similarly, the Big Three U.S. auto manufacturers have a much easier time selling their cars when the dollar depreciates against the Japanese yen.

Finally, U.S. exporters gain when the dollar depreciates. A depreciating dollar simultaneously makes imports more expensive to U.S. consumers and U.S. exports cheaper for foreign consumers. Suppose that an IBM personal computer sells for $1,800 in the United States. The computer cost a British citizen £1,000 before the dollar depreciated. After the dollar depreciates to $2.00/£, the same computer costs the British citizen less than £1,000 because £1,000 now exchanges for $2,000. IBM's sales of personal computers in England increase when the dollar depreciates relative to the pound, even though the dollar price of the computer, $1,800, has not changed.

The reverse is true when the dollar appreciates in value—say, from $1.80/£ to $1.60/£. Consumers gain because imported British goods are now cheaper for them. Import-competing industries lose because U.S. consumers are more likely to buy the relatively cheaper foreign imports. Exporters also lose because U.S. products are now more expensive to foreign customers. These points were driven home in the mid-1980s when the dollar appreciated sharply against most of the world's currencies. As a result, U.S. imports increased substantially, and import-competing manufacturers suffered badly; U.S. exports also fell sharply as exporters had great difficulty selling products that were suddenly much more expensive to foreign consumers and businesses. Complaints grew that U.S. manufacturing was unable to compete anymore with the foreign manufacturers. But productivity in U.S. manufacturing was not declining during that period, either absolutely or relative to foreign manufacturers. The import-competing and the export manufacturers simply had difficulty selling their products in the face of the appreciating dollar. Not surprisingly, the fortunes of the U.S. manufacturers improved when the dollar began depreciating against the major currencies in 1986. The dollar has continued to depreciate against most of the major currencies into the 1990s, and the fears of being outcompeted have subsided a bit.

The effects on consumers when the exchange rate depreciates or appreciates are much larger in the aggregate than are the effects on the import-competing and the export industries. This is why the labels "weaker dollar" for a depreciating dollar and "stronger dollar" for an appreciating dollar make sense. As we have just seen, a weaker (depreciating) dollar is bad for consumers, and a stronger (appreciating) dollar is good for consumers, and consumers' losses and gains are the most important.

The Value of the Dollar and the Balance of Trade

We noted above that the goals of a zero balance of trade and a stable value of the currency are closely related to one another. Let's return to our simple example of a single British importer and a single U.S. exporter to see why.

When the exchange rate is $1.80/£, both countries achieve a zero balance of trade, and the British importer's $180 trades even up for the U.S. exporter's £100. There is no pressure on the exchange rate to change, and the value of the dollar is stable relative to the pound. A zero balance of trade and a stable dollar go hand in hand. This is no accident. The dollar can be stable relative to the pound only if the two countries in our example have achieved a zero balance of trade.

Consider the situation when the exchange rate is $1.60/£. The dollar value of U.S. imports exceeds the dollar value of U.S. exports, and the British importer is holding $20 that she does not want. This situation cannot be an equilibrium period after period. The British importer will try to get rid of all her dollars and exchange them for pounds. Her desire to sell her excess dollars puts downward pressure on the value of the dollar, and the dollar begins to depreciate. The dollar continues to depreciate until the exchange rate reaches $1.80. At this point the importer's $180 trades even up for the exporter's £100. Moreover, the dollar value of U.S. imports equals the dollar value of U.S. exports, at $180; the depreciation of the dollar restores the equality of exports and imports.

This example gives us another perspective on the principle that countries have to export to be able to import. Suppose that a country's exports begin to lose out to foreign competition so that the value of the country's imports exceeds the value of its exports. The trade imbalance causes the currency to depreciate, which raises the costs of imports. Therefore, the loss of the export markets eventually makes the country's imports more expensive and reduces the gains from international trade.

The United States: An Exception to the Rule

The principle that a nation must achieve a zero balance of trade in order to stabilize the value of its currency holds for most nations of the world. The United States is one exception, however. The value of the dollar can be stable even if the values of U.S. imports and U.S. exports are very unequal. The reason why is that foreign citizens may be quite willing to hold dollars.

Return one last time to our simple example of the British importer and the U.S. exporter in the case when the exchange rate is $1.60/£ and the importer ends up with an additional $20. We assumed above that the importer does not want the $20; she only wants pounds sterling. Suppose that the importer were willing to hold the $20, however, by purchasing a certificate of deposit or a U.S. government bond. If so, there would be no pressure for the exchange rate to change. She would be willing to exchange $160 for the U.S. exporter's £100 and hold onto her remaining $20 as a form of saving. The exchange rate would remain stable at $1.60/£.

Why might the importer be willing to hold the $20? One reason is the special role of the dollar in international trade. The United States has been such an important player in international markets for so long that the dollar has gained the status of a worldwide money. People can use dollars to buy goods and services in almost any country. As a result, they are as willing to hold dollars as they are their own currencies. Our importer knows that she can always trade the dollars for goods and services anywhere. The same is not true of the Mexican peso or the Russian ruble. She would probably not be willing to hold these currencies.

A second reason why people might want to have dollars is that they look to U.S. financial markets as a good place to put their savings. Money managers of large corporations, banks, insurance companies, and pension trust funds are on the lookout worldwide for financial securities such as stocks, bonds, and certificates of deposit that will earn them a good rate of return. Consequently, U.S. financial securities are always an attraction. One reason is that the U.S. financial markets are the most highly developed in the world. Money managers can choose from a huge variety of financial securities, and exchanges of securities are easily accomplished. The United States is also very stable politically; the managers know their funds are relatively safe in the United States. Foreign money managers need dollars to invest in the U.S. financial markets, so there is always a demand for dollars that is independent of the trade in imports and exports. Our British importer may be willing to hold the $20 because she wants to save $20 and she believes that buying, say, a U.S. certificate of deposit is the best way for her to save.

In summary, the rules of international trade are somewhat different for the United States (and for the other industrialized nations with highly developed capital markets). The value of U.S. imports can exceed the value of U.S. exports, and the dollar can still be stable. The requirement for dollar stability is as follows: *The dollar is stable if the amount of dollars that foreign citizens are willing to hold is equal to the difference between U.S. imports and exports.*

This turns out to be a difficult condition to satisfy because the willingness to hold dollars in the United States is itself not very stable. Flows of funds into and out of the United States are very sensitive to conditions in financial markets worldwide. Funds flow in when interest rates rise in the United States. Funds flow out when interest rates rise in Europe. An inflow of funds causes the dollar to appreciate as money managers seek to buy dollars with Japanese yen and French francs and German marks; an outflow of funds causes the dollar to depreciate as the money managers sell their dollars for foreign currencies. Achieving a stable dollar is extremely difficult in the face of the worldwide flow of funds.

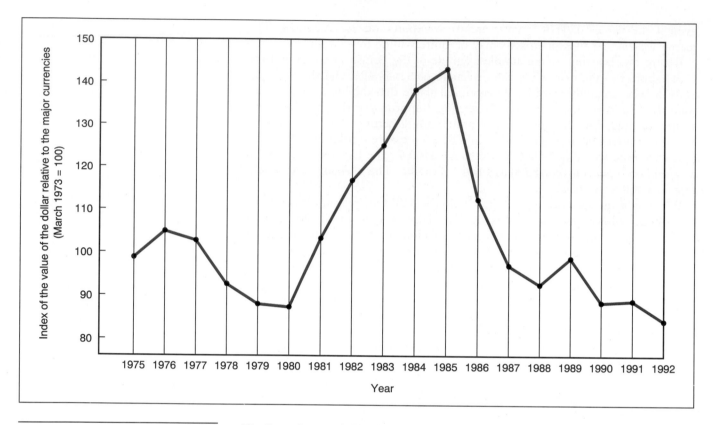

FIGURE 7.2

The Dollar versus Foreign Currencies, 1975–92

The figure shows an index of the value of the dollar relative to a weighted average of the currencies of a number of the industrialized market economies, from 1975–1992. The index sets the relative value of the dollar equal to 100 in March, 1973. The value of the dollar has not been stable since 1975. In particular, the dollar appreciated steadily and substantially against the major currencies from 1980 to 1985, and then depreciated steadily and substantially against the major currencies from 1985 to 1992.

SOURCE: Council of Economic Advisors, *Economic Report of the President, 1993* (Washington, D.C.: U.S. Government Printing Office, 1993), Table B-107, p. 470.

Figure 7.2 shows the value of the dollar relative to an index of the major currencies from 1975 to 1992. The figure indicates just how elusive the goal of a stable dollar has been for the United States.

The United States has also failed to achieve a zero balance of trade throughout most of the post–World War II period, although this goal is somewhat less important for the United States than for other countries. Table 7.2 records the average difference between the value of exports and the value of imports for each decade since 1950. We can see that the United States has switched from being a large net exporter of goods and services to being a very large net importer of goods and services. The switch occurred for many reasons that we will discuss in the remaining chapters of the text.

One final point is that even the United States cannot import more than it exports indefinitely. Foreign citizens will not save forever; they will eventually want to cash in their savings and consume. When they do, either the dollar will depreciate as they trade the dollars for their own currencies, or they will buy U.S. goods. Either way, U.S. exports will rise, and U.S. imports will fall,

TABLE 7.2   **Average Annual Value of the Difference Between Exports and Imports by Decade Since 1950**

DECADE	EXPORTS MINUS IMPORTS ($ BILLION)
1950s	$ 3.4
1960s	7.5
1970s	12.6
1980s	− 38.3
1990–92	− 40.4

SOURCES: Council of Economic Advisors, *Economic Report of the President, 1991* (Washington, D.C.: U.S. Government Printing Office, 1991), Table B-1, p. 287. Council of Economic Advisors, *Economic Report of the President, 1993*, (Washington, D.C.: U.S. Government Printing Office, 1993), Table B-1, p. 349. Council of Economic Advisors, *Economic Indicators, March 1993*, (Washington, D.C.: 1993), p. 1.

turning the balance-of-trade deficit into a surplus. Over time, therefore, even the United States must maintain an equality between its exports and its imports. It, too, has to export to be able to import.

SUMMARY

The first section of Chapter 7 discussed the problem of inflation.

1. Inflation refers to a process of continuous increases in the level of prices generally.
2. The federal government tracks inflation by defining a market basket of goods and services for some reference group. The annual rate of inflation is the increase in the cost of the market basket during the year. The government computes a price index by dividing the value of the market basket each year by its value in the base year, assigning the base year a value of 100. The rate of inflation is then the percentage change in the price index over time. This method of computing inflation makes the overall rate of inflation a weighted average of the rates of inflation of each item in the market basket. The weights are assigned to each item in proportion to expenditures on the item within the market basket. Three closely watched price indexes are the consumer price index (CPI), the producer price index (PPI), and the GDP deflator.
3. The consumer price index is based on a market basket of consumer goods and services. It is used to adjust for inflation in wage and pension contracts and to protect government transfer payments from inflation.
4. The producer price index is based on three market baskets of producer inputs: crude materials; intermediate materials, supplies and components; and finished manufactured goods sold at wholesale. Changes in the PPI lead to future changes in the CPI as producers pass their cost increases through to consumers.
5. The GDP deflator is based on a market basket of final goods purchased by all sectors of the economy. It is used to divide changes in the value of the circular flow of economic activity into real changes and price changes.

6. Governments should strive to keep inflation low for two reasons:
   a. An inflationary process has an internal dynamic that can feed upon itself if the government allows it to. A 10 percent inflation this year becomes a 100 percent inflation next year, and so on, leading to a hyperinflation in which prices are changing every hour. Hyperinflation goes hand in hand with loss of confidence in the currency and the financial system generally. Economic exchange reverts to a straight barter of goods for goods, and economic growth grinds to a halt.
   b. Even moderate amounts of inflation lead to efficiency losses and haphazard redistributions of purchasing power.

7. The inefficiencies and redistributions caused by a moderate amount of inflation depend on the extent to which the inflation is (a) unbalanced, (b) unadjusted to, and (c) unanticipated. An inflation is unbalanced if prices of individual goods and services are rising at different rates. An inflation is unadjusted to when economic contracts and/or the tax system are not indexed to the rate of inflation. An inflation is unanticipated when year-to-year changes in the rate of inflation catch people by surprise. The three conditions are interrelated. For example, a balanced, anticipated inflation is much easier to adjust to than is an unbalanced, unanticipated inflation. All three conditions are present in every inflation.

8. There would be only two very small costs to a balanced, fully adjusted to, fully anticipated inflation: the shoe-leather costs of managing cash more closely and the menu costs of firms having to change their prices more frequently. Neither cost is of much consequence.

9. An unbalanced inflation leads to inefficiencies by increasing the variation in relative prices. The high-inflation markets tend to be in excess supply, and the low-inflation markets tend to be in excess demand. An unbalanced inflation also leads to haphazard redistributions of purchasing power. People who favor the high-inflation products lose relative to people who favor the low-inflation products.

10. Inflations are unadjusted to because neither firms nor workers are interested in indexing their prices and wages to the CPI unless they can be assured that everyone is indexing to the CPI simultaneously. The failure to index economic contracts to inflation leads to potentially large efficiency losses. The U.S. tax system is also not fully indexed to inflation, which means that the amount of taxes people pay in relation to their incomes varies with the rate of inflation. Income from capital is particularly vulnerable to inflation.

11. The main effect of an unanticipated inflation is that it greatly increases the amount of haphazard redistributions of purchasing power through the economy. Workers on long-term labor contracts lose relative to workers on short-term labor contracts. People with fixed incomes lose relative to people with earned incomes. Debtors/borrowers gain at the expense of creditors/lenders. An unanticipated inflation also increases the efficiency costs of inflation by increasing the amount of uncertainty in the economy.

12. Economists disagree on the costs of a moderate inflation. One view holds that the costs of inflation, per se, are minuscule. They consist only of the shoe-leather and the menu costs. All the other costs are due not to the inflation, but to the factors that make the inflation unbalanced, unadjusted to, or unanticipated. Another view holds that the costs of inflation must be

counted within the institutional context of the economy. According to this view, the costs of a moderate inflation in the United States are substantial, but avoidable.

The second section of the chapter discussed the goals of an equality between imports and exports and a stable value of the currency.

13. Imports are the ends of trade: Countries import to gain access to goods that are produced better or more cheaply in foreign countries.

14. Exports are the means to the end. Countries have to export in order to import. Foreign countries will not send goods to a country unless they receive goods in exchange.

15. Most countries are forced to have a zero balance of trade, in which the value of their imports equals the value of their exports. If the value of their imports exceeds the value of their exports (a balance-of-trade deficit), the importers end up holding the other nation's currency, which they may not want to do.

16. A currency depreciates when its value falls relative to other currencies. A currency appreciates when its value rises relative to other currencies. Nations seek a stable value of their currency because a stable currency makes for a more certain environment for international trade and investment. Also, changes in the value of a nation's currency lead to a pattern of gains and losses that are best avoided. A depreciating currency is bad for consumers who buy imports and good for exporters and import-competing firms. The reverse is true of an appreciating currency.

17. The two goals of a zero balance of trade and a stable currency are related. For example, if the value of imports exceeds the value of exports for a small country, the value of its currency depreciates.

18. The United States does not have to have a zero balance of trade each year to maintain a stable dollar because people are willing to hold dollars. In any event, the United States has not achieved a zero balance of trade or a stable value of the dollar over the past 15 to 20 years.

KEY TERMS

appreciation (currency)	depreciation (currency)	inflation
balanced inflation	Fisher equation	producer price index
balance of trade	fully anticipated inflation	unanticipated inflation
consumer price index	hyperinflation	unbalanced inflation
core rate of inflation		

QUESTIONS

1. Describe how the federal government constructs the consumer price index (CPI).

2. Name two other price indexes published by the federal government other than the CPI. Indicate how they differ from the CPI and why they are useful.

3. The values of the CPI for the United States from December 1989 through December 1992 were

1989: 109.2
1990: 115.1
1991: 119.9
1992: 123.5

a. What were the rates of inflation in the United States as measured by the CPI in 1990, 1991, and 1992?

b. What was the cumulative rate of inflation from December 1989 through December 1992?

4. Suppose that you learn that inflation in a certain country is *balanced* and *fully anticipated*.

   a. What do the italicized terms mean?

   b. What are the economic costs of a balanced and fully anticipated inflation?

   c. Is inflation likely to be balanced? To be fully anticipated? Why or why not?

5. a. Why is it not true that inflation robs everyone of purchasing power?

   b. What is a hyperinflation, and why is it a policy problem?

6. To what extent is the U.S. economy indexed against inflation? Support your answer with some specific examples.

7. Discuss the following statement, making use of the Fisher equation where appropriate: Unanticipated inflation causes a redistribution from lenders to borrowers, whereas a fully anticipated inflation does not.

8. a. Has the dollar been stable relative to other currencies in the recent past?

   b. What are the advantages to the United States and to other countries of having a stable value of the dollar relative to other currencies?

9. a. What does it mean to say that the dollar has appreciated in value?

   b. Who gains and who loses in the United States from an appreciation of the dollar?

   c. Who gains and who loses in Germany from an appreciation of the dollar against the German mark?

10. a. Why must the value of imports equal the value of exports for most countries?

    b. Why do large industrialized countries like the United States not have to maintain an equal value of imports and exports every year? Why, though, must the value of their imports and their exports be approximately equal over time?

8

The National Income and Product Accounts

LEARNING OBJECTIVES

CONCEPTS TO LEARN

National income

Gross domestic product (GDP)

Value added

Consumption

Investment

Government purchases of goods and services

Net exports

The national income = national product accounting identity

The total saving − investment accounting identity

Disposable income

GDP deflator

CONCEPTS TO RECALL

The circular flow of economic activity [4]

arvard's Simon Kuznets is generally credited with giving birth to modern macroeconomics in the 1930s. His innovation? Kuznets invented the national income and product accounting system for the macro economy.

This may sound like a fairly mundane accomplishment, but Kuznets's national accounts were a tremendous breakthrough in economic analysis for policy makers and economists alike. For the first time, governments had a framework for collecting and organizing macroeconomic data that allowed them to monitor the performance of their economies. Likewise, Kuznets's national accounting system enabled economists to put various macroeconomic theories to the test against actual data. Before Kuznets's national accounts, individual statistics on various parts of the economy were just that—individual statistics. They had no coherent story to tell.

The national income and product accounts perform two tasks that are absolutely essential to the study of macroeconomics. They measure the overall level of economic activity during the course of a year in a consistent manner, and they identify various components within the economy, such as the consumption and saving of households, that have an important bearing on the overall performance of the economy.

Chapter 8 describes the national income and product accounts of the United States. We need to have a clear and coherent picture of the entire economy before we try to understand how the macro economy operates.

The national income and product accounts measure the overall level of economic activity in terms of the circular flow of economic activity. As such, the fundamental accounting problem is to ensure that the value of the circular flow is the same everywhere on the circle. The two natural places to measure the flow of economic activity are the factor markets and the product markets. The value of the labor, capital, and land exchanged in the nation's factor markets during the year is called the **national income.** The value of the final goods and services exchanged in the nation's product markets during the year is called the **national product.** The national income and product accounts must define the two so that they are always equal to one another. The fundamental accounting identity for the economy as a whole is that national income equals national product.

A secondary goal in describing the overall level of economic activity is to divide changes in national income or product into real changes and price changes. If national product increases by 10 percent during the year, what portion of the 10 percent represents increases in the amount of real goods and services exchanged, and what portion is the result of price increases? The national income and product accounts can give us the answer. This is important because we want to be able to monitor the real growth of the economy.

The national income and product accounts do much more than describe the overall level of economic activity. Economists and policy makers want to understand how consumption and saving by households, investment by business firms, government expenditures and taxes, and other components of the circular flow influence the macro economy and the four macroeconomic policy goals. The national income and product accounts help them think about these issues by showing how all the components fit together.

NATIONAL INCOME

The value of the labor, capital, and land exchanged in the nation's factor markets during the year.

NATIONAL PRODUCT

The value of the final goods and services exchanged in the nation's product markets during the year.

TABLE 8.1   Income Statement of a Hypothetical Corporation

Value of Sales	=	Cost of Goods Sold
Sales		Intermediate goods Compensation of employees Rental payments to persons Net interest paid Corporate profits

The national income and product accounts for the United States are compiled by the Bureau of Economic Analysis (BEA), a division of the U.S. Department of Commerce. Thanks to the BEA you can follow the U.S. economy very closely if you want to. The BEA publishes detailed statistics on national income and national product four times a year, and a selection of statistics every month, in the *Survey of Current Business*. The bureau has put together a consistent set of national accounts going all the way back to 1929. The BEA accountants have provided us with the framework and the language that we need to analyze the economy.[1]

Chapter 8 has four objectives:

1. to describe how the BEA accountants define national income and national product so that national income equals national product;
2. to define a number of the components of the circular flow that are important in understanding how the economy operates and to indicate how the components are related to one another;
3. to show how to divide changes in national product into real changes and price changes; and
4. to reflect upon what the national income and product accounts can tell us about a nation's standard of living.

NATIONAL INCOME AND NATIONAL PRODUCT

The Income Statement of the Firm

The fundamental accounting identity between national income and national product is best understood if we begin at the microeconomic level, with the income statement of a business firm. An **income statement** records the value of the output and the income generated by the firm during the course of the year. As such, the income statement is a miniature version of the national accounts.

Table 8.1 presents a highly simplified income statement of a hypothetical corporation. The left-hand side of the statement records the value of the firm's sales, the output of the firm. The right-hand side of the statement lists the

INCOME STATEMENT

A record of the value of the output and income generated by the firm during the course of the year; a record of a firm's sales and the cost of goods sold.

---

[1]An excellent reference on the national income and product accounts and other statistics published by the U.S. government is Albert Sommers, *The U.S. Economy Demystified*, revised edition (Lexington, MA: D. C. Heath, 1988).

costs of goods sold, the costs of purchasing the inputs needed to produce the goods (or services). The inputs are intermediate goods and the three primary factors of production, labor, land and capital. *Intermediate goods* include fuels, such as oil and gas; other raw materials, such as iron ore; and semi-finished products used in the production of the firm's product, such as tires and glass for automobiles. Firms purchase intermediate goods from other firms.

The costs to the firm of purchasing labor, land, and capital are simultaneously the incomes received by the households supplying these primary factors of production to the firm. **Compensation of employees** is the payment to, and income received by, labor. It includes wages, salaries, and fringe benefits, such as employer contributions to health insurance and pension plans. **Rental payments to persons** are combined payments to land and to capital. The rent paid for space in an office building is in part a payment for the use of the land that the building sits on and in part a payment for the use of the building itself. The portion of the rent allocated to the land is a source of income for the owner of the land. The portion of the rent allocated to the building is a source of income to those who supplied the funds to build the building. **Net interest paid** is the difference between any interest paid and any interest received by the firm. Firms receive interest when they place funds temporarily in certificates of deposit, government bonds, and other financial securities. Most of the interest paid by firms is interest on bonds that they have issued to raise funds for investment. Therefore, net interest paid is a source of income from borrowed capital. It represents a return to the firm's bondholders who have loaned funds to the firm for the purchase of capital. The final cost of goods sold is **corporate profits,** a payment to the firm's stockholders who own the firm. The owners supply funds for investment in return for stock certificates that entitle them to share in the profits of the firm. Therefore, corporate profits are a source of income from owner-supplied capital.

The income statement represents an accounting identity: *The value of sales always equals the cost of goods sold.* Corporate profits are the residual item that guarantees the two sides of the income statement balance. The profits are the funds remaining after the firm pays all its other costs of production out of the revenues from its sales. Profits can be positive, zero, or negative. For example, if profits are zero, then the firm pays nothing that year for owner-supplied capital, and the stockholders receive no income on the funds they have supplied to the firm. The principle that profits are the residual item in the cost of goods sold is very important to the structure of the national income and product accounts. We will see that all the adjustments made by the national income accountants to ensure that national income equals national product turn on the role of profits as the residual item in the firm's income statement.

National Income

National income is the sum of all payments to, or income received by, the primary factors of production—labor, land, and capital. It includes the four sources of income listed on the income statement—compensation of employees, rental income of persons, net interest paid, and corporate profits—summed over all the firms in the economy. Data on compensation of employees are gathered primarily from the states' unemployment insurance systems, which have detailed wage and salary data on almost all private-sector employees. The

COMPENSATION OF EMPLOYEES

The payment to, and the income received by, labor, including wages, salaries, and in-kind fringe benefits.

RENTAL PAYMENTS TO PERSONS

The combined payments to land and to capital in the form of rents.

NET INTEREST

The difference between interest paid and interest received by firms.

CORPORATE PROFIT

The difference between the value of sales and the cost of goods sold; the income received by the stockholders who own the firm.

other three items are compiled primarily from corporate tax returns, which list the sources of income separately as part of the costs of goods sold.

A fifth, and final, component of national income is **proprietors' income,** which is the income earned by noncorporate forms of business, principally partnerships and sole proprietorships. The data on proprietors' income are collected primarily from personal income tax returns, which often do not list the sources of income separately. For example, college professors who write text books often establish sole proprietorships so that they can deduct their home offices as an expense to reduce their income taxes. The income that they report to the U.S. Internal Revenue Service (IRS) as the "profit" from their textbooks is a mixture of the different sources of income. A portion of the income is really a salary for the time spent writing the text. Another portion is an implicit rental payment for the land on which the house was built. Still another portion is a return to capital, which includes the office and any equipment in the office, such as a personal computer. The BEA does not attempt to break down the income into its separate sources. Instead, it records proprietors' income as a separate component of national income.

To summarize:

National income = compensation of employees + rental income of persons
+ net interest paid + corporate profits + proprietors' income

These are the five payments to and sources of income received by the primary factors of production—labor, land, and capital.

Value Added

The next task is to see how the national income accountants define national product so that it equals national income. The best way to do this is not to proceed directly to the product markets. Instead, we will take an intermediate step and define a concept called the value added of a business firm (or other producer). Value added measures the circular flow of economic activity at the sites where the goods and the services are produced.

The concept of value added views the firm as beginning its production process with the intermediate goods purchased from other firms. The firm then adds the primary factors of production—labor, land, and capital—to the intermediate goods and produces its own products, which have a greater value than did the intermediate goods it started with. The value of its own products is equal to the sales of the firm. The difference between the value of its sales that it ends with and the cost of the intermediate goods that it starts with is the **value added** of the firm.

Value added = sales − cost of intermediate goods

The overall value added for the economy is the sum of the value added by each producer.

The value added by a firm derives from the addition of the primary factors of production. Notice that value added equals the sum of the four payments to the primary factors listed on our hypothetical income statement in Table 8.1. Sales equals the total cost of goods sold, which is the sum of all five items

PROPRIETORS' INCOME

Income or profit earned by unincorporated forms of business, principally partnerships and sole proprietorships.

VALUE ADDED

For a single producer, the difference between the value of sales and the cost of the intermediate goods that it buys from other producers; for the economy, the sum of the value added by each producer.

of cost on the right-hand side of the income statement. Value added, in effect, brings the cost of intermediate goods over to the left-hand side of the income statement, where it is subtracted from sales. Therefore, the value added by the firm must equal the sum of the remaining four items on the right-hand side, the payments to the primary factors of production. Also, the overall value added for the economy must equal national income (proprietors' income is also the difference between sales and the cost of intermediate goods for partnerships and proprietorships).

The concept of value added illustrates that national product is not equal to total sales of all goods and services. It includes only the sales of final or finished products, that is, products that are sold to final users and not to other firms as intermediate goods.

The following example will clarify the relationships among national income, value added, and national product. Imagine a very simple economy consisting of three producers: farmers who grow wheat, millers who grind the wheat into flour, and bakers who use the flour to bake bread. All the wheat grown is sold to the millers for flour. All the flour milled is sold to the bakers for bread. The bread is the final product. It is sold to the households, who consume it. Also, the only scarce primary factor of production in this economy is labor, so that wages are the only source of income. The land for growing wheat is so plentiful that it is free, and the producers somehow manage to produce their products without any capital.

Table 8.2 records the production activity of this economy, which begins with the growing of wheat. The wheat seeds are manna from heaven. They are simply lying on the ground for the farmers to pick up and plant, so that the cost of intermediate goods is zero for the wheat farmers. The farmers' labor is worth $5, according to the table. The value of the wheat sold is $5, equal to the cost of producing the wheat, and the farmers sell their wheat to the millers. The value added by the wheat farmers is also $5, the difference between the farmers' sales ($5) and the cost of intermediate goods, the wheat seeds ($0). Notice that the value added in wheat farming equals the income earned by the farmers.

The millers take the $5 worth of wheat, add $10 worth of labor, and produce $15 worth of flour, which they sell to the bakers. The $15 equals the cost of producing the flour. The value added by the millers is $10, the difference between their sales ($15) and the cost of intermediate goods, the wheat ($5). The value added in milling equals the income earned by the millers.

TABLE 8.2   Value Added, National Income, and National Product for a Hypothetical Economy

PRODUCTION ACTIVITY	COST OF INTERMEDIATE GOODS	LABOR	SALES	VALUE ADDED
FARMING WHEAT	$ 0	$ 5	$ 5	$ 5
MILLING FLOUR	5	10	15	10
BAKING BREAD	15	20	35	20
TOTALS	20	35	55	35
CONSUMPTION: $35 (BREAD)				

The bakers take the $15 worth of flour, add $20 worth of labor, and produce $35 worth of bread, which they sell to the households for consumption. The $35 equals the cost of producing the bread. The value added by the bakers is $20, the difference between their sales ($35) and the cost of intermediate goods, the flour ($15). The value added in baking equals the income earned by the bakers.

The national income in our simple economy is $35, the sum of the wages earned by labor at each stage of production [$35 − $5 (farmers) + $10 (millers) + $20 (bakers); column 3 of the table]. Remember, labor is the only primary factor of production in the economy. The value added in our simple economy is also $35, the sum of the value added at each stage of production [$35 = $5 (farming) + $10 (milling) + $20 (baking); column 5 of the table]. The value of national product that equals national income and value added is the $35 worth of bread sold as a *final* product to the households for consumption.

Notice that the national product is *not* equal to the total sales of product in the economy, which is $55 [$55 = $5 (wheat) + $15 (flour) + $35 (bread); column 4 of the table]. Adding the sales at each stage involves double-counting the intermediate goods. The $15 of flour includes the $5 of wheat, and the $35 of bread includes the $15 of flour. The $35 of bread is the sum of the value added at each stage of production, not the sum of the total sales at each stage. Equivalently, bread is the only *final* product that flows through the markets for goods and services and therefore the only component of national product.

CURRENT ISSUE: Many economists and policy makers are in favor of levying a new Federal tax on the value added of firms to help close the Federal budget deficit. The value added tax, called VAT, is widely used in Europe.

Gross Domestic Product

National income accountants use two different concepts to define the national product of a country, gross domestic product and gross national product. You have no doubt seen references to both measures in newspaper and magazine articles. The **gross domestic product** (GDP) is the value of final goods and services produced within a country, whether by the country's own citizens or by the citizens of a foreign country. The **gross national product** (GNP) is the value of final goods and services produced by the citizens of the country no matter where the citizens happen to live. Suppose, for example, that a British tax accountant moves to New York City and prepares tax returns for U.S. households and that a U.S. citizen moves to London and prepares tax returns for British households. The tax services provided by the British accountant are included in U.S. gross domestic product and excluded in U.S. gross national product. Conversely, the tax services provided by the U.S. accountant are excluded in U.S. gross domestic product and included in U.S. gross national product.

Fortunately, we need not be concerned about the distinction between GDP and GNP because they are almost equal in the United States. In 1992 GDP was $5950.7 billion, and GNP was $5961.9 billion. The difference between them, $11.2 billion, was only 0.2 percent of GDP. The distinction between GDP and GNP is more important for state and local governments in the United States. Subnational governments would naturally choose GDP as the measure of total economic activity because they want to measure the output produced within their borders.

The BEA used gross national product as the measure of U.S. national product until 1992, when it switched to gross domestic product. The changeover

GROSS DOMESTIC PRODUCT (GDP)

The value of final goods and services produced within a country during the year, whether by the country's own citizens or by the citizens of a foreign country.

GROSS NATIONAL PRODUCT (GNP)

The value of the final goods and services produced by the citizens of the country during the year no matter where the citizens happen to live.

to GDP brought the United States in line with the rest of the world; all but a handful of nations use gross domestic product as the measure of their national product. We will use GDP throughout the text to represent the national product.

GDP can be broken down into its components in two ways: by the sector that produces the output and by the sector that purchases the output. The most common breakdown, and the one most useful for economic analysis, is by the sector that purchases the final goods and services. From the expenditure point of view, GDP is comprised of the total expenditures by all the final demanders in the economy, those who purchase the final goods and services. Final demanders are found in all four sectors of the economy that we described in Chapter 4: the household sector, the business sector, the government sector, and the rest-of-world sector. GDP is the sum of consumption (C) by households, investment (I) by businesses, purchases of goods and services (G) by governments, and net exports [exports (Ex) minus imports (Im) to and from the rest of the world].

$$GDP = C + I + G + (Ex - Im)$$

Let's take a closer look at the expenditure components of GDP. Each one has an important effect on the overall performance of the economy.

CONSUMPTION

Aggregate purchases of final goods and services by households.

CONSUMPTION   **Consumption** by households is the dominant component of the U.S. national product, averaging between 60 and 65 percent of GDP. The fortunes of the overall economy rise and fall with the growth in consumption simply because consumption is such a large part of the total. Rapid economic growth can be sustained only if consumption demand is growing rapidly. Conversely, the economy stagnates whenever consumption demand stagnates. Explaining what determines consumption demand is one of the key elements in any macroeconomic theory of the economy.

The only anomaly associated with consumption expenditures is the BEA's accounting of consumer durables, those goods that are expected to last for more than a year. Suppose that you buy a new car for $10,000. You are not consuming the services of the car the instant that you buy it. Instead, you consume the services of the car over time as you drive it. In other words, the purchase of the car is a form of saving for future consumption from your point of view. You are buying a real asset that yields you a stream of services over time, analogous to the purchase of a financial asset such as a certificate of deposit that earns you a stream of interest income over time. Nonetheless, the BEA counts the entire $10,000 as part of total consumption expenditures when you purchase the car, rather than trying to estimate the stream of consumption services over time. Treating consumer durables as consumption expenditures at the time of purchase tends to overstate the amount of consumption in the economy and understate the amount of saving.

INVESTMENT   Investment by business firms is much smaller than consumption, averaging about 15 percent of GDP. Nonetheless, investment is a very important contributor to the performance of the economy. We have already seen that investment is the key to long-run economic growth. In addition, investment is the least stable component of GDP, and many economists believe that it is a major cause of the ebbs and flows of modern market economies.

The treatment of investment in the national accounts is very complicated. The BEA defines three separate categories of investment expenditures: (1) nonresidential fixed investment, (2) residential fixed investment, and (3) the increase in the final goods inventories of manufacturers. Each category is important to the study of macroeconomics and requires some comment.

NONRESIDENTIAL FIXED INVESTMENT **Nonresidential fixed investment** is what we normally think of as investment by business firms: purchases of new plant and equipment. The BEA accountants refer to the building of new plant as construction of nonresidential structures, which consist of factories, warehouses, office buildings, and retail outlets. They refer to machinery and other equipment as nonresidential producers' durable equipment.

NONRESIDENTIAL FIXED INVESTMENT

Purchases of new plant and equipment during the year.

Investment versus existing capital. The BEA counts only *new* construction activity and purchases of *new* equipment as part of investment. The purchase and sale of an *existing* structure or an *existing* machine is not counted as part of investment. The distinction between new and existing structures and equipment is essential in recording the flow of production activity during the year and in maintaining the equality between national income and national product.

Recall from Chapter 3 that investment is a flow variable and capital is a stock variable. Investment represents new production activity during the year, which is part of the overall circular flow of economic activity and generates income. In fact, the BEA records construction activity as part of investment while the construction activity is ongoing because an ongoing construction project is generating income at the same time. The BEA does not wait until the structures are completed to count them as part of investment.

In contrast, an existing building or machine was produced in some past year and generated income in the past. It is part of the existing stock of capital, but not part of investment. The purchase and sale of the building this year is just a transfer of part of the existing stock of capital from one owner to another. Therefore, to count the purchase and sale of existing buildings or machines as part of investment would overstate the current year's production activity. It would also break the equality between national income and national product; national product would increase without any corresponding increase in national income.

Investment versus intermediate goods. Businesses buy two kinds of goods from other businesses: intermediate goods and investment goods. Both kinds of goods are used as inputs in the production of goods and services. Yet intermediate goods are netted out of national product, whereas investment goods are counted as final goods and become part of the national product. What is the distinction between them? The answer is durability—how long they are expected to last—with a year's time being the dividing line. Intermediate goods are expected to be used up within the year; investment goods are expected to last for more than a year. An example of the distinction between them is the purchase of a new blast furnace to be used in the production of steel and the coal used to fire the furnace. The coal is used up immediately as it is purchased and counted as an intermediate good. The blast furnace is expected to last for more than a year, so it is counted as part of the investment of the firm.

Depreciation/capital consumption allowance. Business firms distinguish between intermediate goods and investment goods just as the national income accountants do. A steel producer would record the purchase of the coal as an intermediate good on the income statement of the firm. In contrast, the firm would count the value of the blast furnace as an addition to the firm's stock of capital and record it on the balance sheet of the firm, which lists the firm's assets and liabilities. The blast furnace would not appear as a cost of goods sold on the income statement, nor would any investment in plant and equipment.

Capital goods are used up in the process of producing goods and services, however. Blast furnaces, personal computers, and factories depreciate in value as they continue to produce goods and services no matter how well they are maintained. The process of depreciation can be very slow. Machines and equipment may remain productive up to 10 years, or even longer. Some structures may last 35 years and more. Eventually, though, every firm expects to replace its existing capital stock.

Firms set aside funds to replace their existing capital stock in an account called depreciation, which is recorded on the income statement as a cost of goods sold. The amount entered as depreciation is not an out-of-pocket expense. Rather, it is an estimate of how much the firm's capital stock has depreciated in value during the year. Table 8.3 reproduces the income statement of our hypothetical corporation from Table 8.1, with depreciation added on the right-hand side. Firms want to record an estimate of depreciation as part of their costs because every dollar of depreciation lowers their profits by one dollar. The smaller their profits, the smaller their tax liability.

ECONOMIC DEPRECIATION

The decline in the market value of a firm's capital stock over a given period of time.

Economists define **economic depreciation** as the decline in the market value of the firm's capital stock during the year. The depreciation could be due to wear and tear, or accidental damage, or obsolescence as a better technology is discovered, or simply aging. Notice that depreciation applies to the *entire* capital stock of the firm, not just to the investments of the current year.

The U.S. Internal Revenue Service (IRS) recognizes depreciation as a legitimate cost of production for tax purposes, but it does not ask each firm to estimate the economic depreciation of its capital stock. Instead, the IRS provides guidelines to firms for computing depreciation on different kinds of capital for ease of administration. The guidelines indicate how long each type of capital is expected to last.

The BEA accountants also recognize the depreciation of the capital stock as a legitimate cost of production. They do try to estimate the economic depreciation of the nation's capital stock, rather than relying on the IRS guidelines, however, because they want to generate the best possible estimate of the capital stock. They call their estimate of economic depreciation the **capital consumption allowance** (*CCA*).

CAPITAL CONSUMPTION ALLOWANCE

An estimate by the Bureau of Economic Analysis of the economic depreciation of the nation's stock of capital during the year.

Gross investment and net investment. The capital consumption allowance drives a wedge between national income and national product that has to be accounted for. To see why, refer to the income statement in Table 8.3. Re-

TABLE 8.3 **Income Statement of a Hypothetical Corporation**

Value of Sales	=	Cost of Goods Sold
Sales		Depreciation Intermediate goods Compensation of employees Rental payments to persons Net interest paid Corporate profits

member that whatever amount the firm enters for the depreciation of its capital stock reduces corporate profits by the same amount. Depreciation has no effect on the total cost of goods sold or on the value of sales. The same holds true at the national level. The BEA reduces corporate profits and proprietors' income by the amount of its estimate of capital consumption allowance. As a result, national income falls below gross domestic product by the amount of the capital consumption allowance.

The BEA corrects this discrepancy by distinguishing between gross investment (I_G) and net investment (I_N). **Gross investment** is value of new capital put in place during the year, the three categories of investment defined above. **Net investment** equals gross investment minus the BEA's estimate of the capital consumption allowance on the entire stock of capital.

$$I_N = I_G - CCA$$

In Chapter 3 we defined investment as the change in the stock of capital without distinguishing between gross and net investment. Now we can say that net investment is the better measure of the change in the value of the stock of capital. The value of a nation's capital stock changes in two ways: (1) it increases by the addition of new capital during the year, the amount of gross investment, I_G; and (2) it decreases by the depreciation of the existing stock of capital, the capital consumption allowance, CCA. Net investment captures both changes.

The difference between gross and net investment in the United States is substantial because the annual decline in the value of the capital stock is very large. In 1992, for example, I_G was $770.4 billion, and I_N was only $117.0 billion. The capital consumption allowance is so large primarily because the U.S. stock of capital is so large, in excess of $12 trillion. In other words, producers in the United States had to invest over $650 billion in 1992 just to maintain the value of the existing stock of capital.

Gross domestic product and net domestic product. The distinction between gross and net investment in turn leads to a distinction between gross domestic product and **net domestic product** (NDP). GDP includes gross investment, and NDP includes net investment. The difference in the treatment of investment is the only difference in these two measures of national product, so that GDP and NDP differ by the amount of the capital consumption allowance. NDP is the measure of national product that is conceptually equal to national income.

To summarize:

$$I_G = I_N + CCA$$
$$GDP = C + I_G + G + (Ex - Im)$$
$$NDP = C + I_N + G + (Ex - Im)$$

Therefore,

$$GDP = NDP + CCA$$

RESIDENTIAL FIXED INVESTMENT The BEA treats all purchases by households as consumption with one exception, purchases of new houses. A new house is a real asset so similar to an office building or any other business structure that

GROSS INVESTMENT

The value of new capital put in place during the year, equal to the sum of purchases of new plant and equipment, increases in firms' inventories, and purchases of new homes.

NET INVESTMENT

The difference between gross investment and the BEA's estimate of the capital consumption allowance (depreciation).

NET DOMESTIC PRODUCT (NDP)

The difference between gross domestic product and the BEA's estimate of the capital consumption allowance (depreciation).

the BEA counts the construction of new houses as part of total investment under the category of residential fixed investment. Residential fixed investment also includes apartments and condominiums, anything built for use as a residence.

The same accounting rules apply to residential construction as apply to non-residential construction. The value of the construction is counted as it is put in place to correspond to the income that is simultaneously being generated in building the house. Also, residential fixed investment includes only the purchase of newly constructed houses and other residences. The purchase and sale of existing houses is simply a transfer of ownership; it is not a current production activity that generates income.

Residential fixed investment accounts for about 30 percent of total investment and only 4 percent of total GDP. Nonetheless, the housing market is very important to the study of macroeconomics because the demand for new homes is very sensitive to the level of interest rates. Most new homes are purchased with the help of a mortgage, which is a loan to a home buyer that uses the house as collateral. If you default on your mortgage payments, you forfeit ownership of your home to the bank. The standard mortgage is paid back with level monthly payments over 15 to 30 years. Each percentage point increase in mortgage rates increases the monthly payment by $50 to $100 on a $100,000 mortgage, so that the demand for mortgages is very sensitive to the level of interest rates.

CHANGE IN INVENTORIES GDP and national income are designed to measure the overall level of economic activity. As such, they need to account for the change in manufacturers' inventories during the year.

Manufacturers and retailers often hold inventories of manufactured goods. For example, a toy manufacturer may ship the toys it produces to a warehouse and then sell the toys out of the warehouse to the retailers. General Motors, Ford, and Chrysler ship cars to their dealers that the dealers sell off their lots. The amount of toys in the warehouse and the amount of cars on the dealers' lots are the inventories of toys and cars. The value of a firm's inventory is one of the assets of the firm; it is considered part of the firm's stock of capital.

Suppose that the amount of inventories held by manufacturers increases during the year. For example, a toy manufacturer produces more toys than it sells during the year, so the amount of toys in the warehouse increases. Production activity has occurred; the firm has manufactured toys and generated income in the process. Yet none of the increase in inventory appears on the income statement of the firm. The toys are not reflected in the firm's sales on its income statements because they were not sold. Producing the toys did generate payments to factors of production that appear on the income statement; the firm bought some intermediate goods and paid wages, rents, and interest attributable to the production of the additional toys in its warehouse. But since the toys were not sold, all these costs of production simply decrease the firm's profits by the same amount. Therefore, the production of the additional toys does not change the firm's total cost of goods sold. Since the production of the additional toys is not reflected in either the firm's sales or its cost of goods sold, this production activity does not appear in either national product or national income. The BEA accountants adjust for this by (1) counting the increase in inventory as part of investment, which increases national product, and (2) adding the increase in inventory to corporate profits (or proprietors' income), which increases national income. The increase in inventory is considered to be a sale by the firm to itself on its investment account. The purchase of inventory represents an increase in the assets of the firm in the form of inventory capital.

Similarly, the BEA accountants subtract any decrease in inventories from investment and profits to more accurately reflect the amount of production activity during the year. Suppose that the toy manufacturer has sold more toys than it has produced during the year, so that its inventory has decreased from the beginning to the end of the year. The amount that the inventory decreased represents sales of toys that were produced in past years, not this year. Nonetheless, selling these toys increases the firm's sales and profits, so the toys appear in both national product and national income for the current year. The BEA accountants correct for this by adjusting investment and profits downward by the decrease in inventory, thereby preserving the national income and product accounts as a measure of production activity during the year.

The change in inventories is a very small component of total investment, less than 5 percent in most years. Even so, inventories play a central role in the study of macroeconomics. We will see that firms adjust their inventories in a manner that drives the economy to an equilibrium level of national income. Also, *changes* in inventories often account for the majority of *changes* in gross domestic product from year to year.

GOVERNMENT PURCHASES OF GOODS AND SERVICES   The government sector is central to the study of macroeconomics. After all, the federal government is responsible for pursuing the four macroeconomic policy goals through its fiscal and monetary policies.

The national income and product accounts record the various items in the budgets of the federal, state, and local governments. For the purposes of macroeconomic analysis it is useful to distinguish three broad categories within the governments' budgets: government purchases of goods and services, transfer payments, and taxes. Government purchases of goods and services and transfer payments are the two types of government expenditures. Taxes are the main source of government revenues.

Recall that fiscal policy is budgetary policy; it involves changes in government purchases of goods and services, or transfer payments, or taxes. We will see that changes in these three broad categories have very different effects on the economy. You will better understand why this is so once you understand how each category fits into the national income and product accounts.

GOVERNMENT PURCHASES   **Government purchases of goods and services** (G) are part of gross domestic product. We noted in Chapter 1 that governments play roles of both consumer and producer in the economy. When the government purchases goods or services in its role as a consumer, it is much like a household purchasing goods and services. For example, the purchase of a land-based missile can be thought of as an act of public consumption that contributes to the national security. As such, it belongs in both the national income and the national product. On the income side, the missile was produced by a private firm and generated income in the form of wages and salaries, rents, interest payments, and profits. On the product side, the missile is a final prod-

GOVERNMENT PURCHASES OF GOODS AND SERVICES

Aggregate purchases of final goods and services by the federal, state, and local governments; the services are primarily the labor services of government employees.

uct, and the government is the final demander. The missile will sit in its silo, one hopes never to be used.

The government's role as a producer is accounted differently from that of a private business firm. The only major source of income from government production is the compensation of government employees. Governments take land by eminent domain for schools, military bases, and the like. They rarely pay rent to anyone. The BEA counts the interest on the government debt as a transfer payment because most of the interest is not a payment for borrowed capital. The majority of government debt outstanding is federal debt, and most of the federal debt was issued to pay for past wars or for current transfer payments and operating expenses. Very little of the federal debt has been issued to finance public investments. Finally, government production is not-for-profit. Indeed, much of the output from government production is not even sold; for example, the operating expenses of local schools and military bases are covered out of tax revenues. Whenever the output is sold, the price is set to cover the operating expenses, so there is no return to capital. Therefore, all that is left to include in the circular flow of economic activity from government production is the compensation of government employees, which is part of national income. The BEA maintains the equality between national income and national product by counting the compensation of government employees as part of the governments' purchases of goods and services. In fact, nearly all of the services purchased by governments are the labor services of government employees.

TRANSFER PAYMENTS   Transfer payments are not counted as part of the national product because they do not correspond to any production activity during the year. People receive transfer payments because of who they are, not because they have provided a service to anyone during the year. Families on welfare receive monthly checks from the government because they are poor. Retirees receive Social Security monthly benefits because they contributed payroll taxes to the Social Security System during their working lifetimes. Their payroll contributions were made in the past, not the present. In contrast, a check paid to a public school teacher is a payment for services rendered during the current year.

Raising taxes to finance transfer payments redistributes resources within the private sector. It does not change the level of the circular flow or economic activity. Income leaves the private sector when the government collects the taxes and returns to the private sector when the government makes the transfer payments. In contrast, raising taxes to finance government purchases of goods and services does increase the circular flow of economic activity. People hired to teach in the public schools are engaged in productive activity, just as they would be if they were hired by a private firm.

TAXES   All taxes levied on the suppliers of labor, capital, and land are automatically included in national income and national product. This includes the federal and the state personal and corporation income taxes, the Social Security payroll tax, and the local property tax. These taxes are part of the circular flow because the BEA values labor, land, and capital at the cost to the firms of hiring these factors of production. The cost to the firm includes any taxes paid by these factors on the income earned.

For example, suppose that you begin to work for a corporation after college at a salary of $20,000. Your take-home pay is less than $20,000 because the firm deducts federal and state personal income taxes and the Social Security payroll tax from your paycheck. The BEA accountants record your entire

TABLE 8.4   **Income Statement of a Hypothetical Corporation**

Value of Sales	=	Cost of Goods Sold
Sales		Indirect business taxes
		Depreciation
		Intermediate goods
		Compensation of employees
		Rental payments to persons
		Net interest paid
		Corporate profits

$20,000 salary as part of the compensation for employees because that is what the firm pays to hire you. Although the firm may deduct in your behalf the income taxes that you owe, these deductions do not change the fact that the firm is paying you a salary of $20,000. Similarly, the rental payments to persons, net interest paid, corporate profits, and proprietors' income recorded in national income all include any taxes paid on these sources of income. Moreover, since the cost of goods sold on the income statement includes all income taxes, the value of sales also includes all income taxes. Income taxes are part of national product as well as national income. Finally, local property taxes are also included in national income because households pay these taxes out of their take-home pay.

Indirect business taxes (*IBT*) are the one exception to the rule that all taxes are included in national income and national product. **Indirect business taxes** are primarily the sales and excise taxes that firms pay on the sale of their products. Firms list indirect business taxes as a separate cost on their income statements, as illustrated in Table 8.4. As a result, these taxes drive a wedge between sales and the sources of income regardless of who bears the burden of the tax.

Suppose that the firm succeeds in passing the tax on to its customers by raising its prices. In this case the value of sales increases by the amount of the tax, and corporate profits remain the same. Suppose, instead, that the firm cannot raise its prices, and it bears the full burden of the tax. In this case the value of sales remains constant, and the firm's profits fall by the full amount of the tax. In either case the tax has driven a wedge between sales, which appear as part of the national product, and profits, which appear as part of the national income. Indirect business taxes are the main break in the equality between national income (*NI*) and net domestic product (NDP). The BEA adjusts by adding indirect business taxes to national income to maintain the equality.

To summarize:

$$\text{NDP} = NI + IBT$$
$$\text{GDP} = \text{NDP} + CCA = NI + IBT + CCA$$

INDIRECT BUSINESS TAXES

Sales and excise taxes that firms pay on the sale of their products.

NET EXPORTS   The increasing internationalization of the U.S. economy has been one of the major ongoing macroeconomic stories of the past 30 years. Exports and imports are now each approximately 11 percent of GDP; in 1965 they were only 5 percent of GDP. Exports and imports are now large enough to have a substantial impact on overall economic activity.

We saw in Chapter 4 that net exports are the one leakage in the circular flow of economic activity. The BEA accountants have to include net exports in GDP both to record the amount of production activity in the United States and to maintain the equality between national income and national product.

EXPORTS

Goods and services produced domestically and sold in foreign countries.

Exports (*Ex*) are goods and services that are produced domestically and sold in foreign countries. As such, they are part of the annual production activity in the United States and contribute to U.S. national income. But they are not included as part of the expenditures by U.S. final demanders because they are purchased by households, business firms, and governments in foreign countries. The BEA accountants adjust by adding exports to GDP.

IMPORTS

Goods and services produced in foreign countries and sold in the domestic country.

The reverse holds true for imports. Imports (*Im*) are goods and services that are produced in foreign countries and sold in the United States. As such, they are not part of the annual production activity in the United States, and they do not contribute to U.S. national income. But they are included as part of the expenditures by U.S. final demanders because they are purchased by U.S. households, business firms, and governments. The BEA accountants adjust by subtracting imports from GDP.

NET EXPORTS

The difference between exports and imports.

The adjustment for exports and imports is typically combined into one term, **net exports**, which is the difference between exports and imports.[2]

$$\text{Net exports} = Ex - Im$$

Summary: National Income and Product

This concludes our tour of the circular flow of economic activity as recorded in the national income and product accounts of the United States. The key concepts are national income, the value of the income earned by the labor, land, and capital exchanged in the nation's factor markets; gross (net) domestic product, the value of the final goods and services exchanged in the nation's product markets; and the fundamental accounting identity between national income and gross domestic product. The only differences between national income and gross domestic product are the capital consumption allowance and the indirect business taxes. Gross domestic product is more widely reported than is national income as the measure of the total economic activity.

DISPOSABLE INCOME, SAVING, AND INVESTMENT

We next want to look at two components of the circular flow of economic activity that are crucial to the study of macroeconomics: disposable income and saving. We also want to develop a second important accounting identity: total saving in the economy must equal the level of investment.

---

[2]Earlier we distinguished between gross domestic product (GDP) and gross national product (GNP) in terms of where the final goods and services are produced. The difference between GDP and GNP in terms of expenditures occurs in net exports. Net exports in GDP consist of all merchandise trade in goods and services. Net exports in GNP include merchandise trade plus the net flow of factor incomes to the United States from the rest of the world. The net income flow equals receipts of income by U.S. citizens earned in foreign countries minus receipts of income by foreign citizens earned in the United States. In terms of our previous example, the income earned by the U.S. tax accountant in London is an example of the former, and the income earned by the British tax accountant in New York is an example of the latter. Technically, only GNP corresponds to national income because the U.S. national income only includes income earned by U.S. citizens.

Disposable Income

Households earn all the income generated in the economy because they own all the labor, land, and capital supplied to the nation's factor markets. Households do not receive all the income that they earn, however. Some of their income is siphoned off by the government and business sectors before they have a chance to use it.

The income actually available to households for their own use is called **disposable income.** Macroeconomists are particularly interested in disposable income because households base their consumption and saving decisions on disposable income, not on national income.

The main difference between national income and disposable income results from the taxes and the transfers of the federal, state, and local governments. The taxes that households pay out of national income are not part of their disposable income. Federal and state personal income taxes and the Social Security payroll tax are often withheld from our wages and salaries even before we receive our paychecks. If we then pay a property tax to a local government or if the corporation in which we own stock pays federal or state corporation income taxes before paying us our dividends, these taxes further reduce the income available to us for our own spending and saving. Governments give as well as take, however. Transfer payments such as Social Security benefits and public assistance checks increase the disposable incomes of the households that receive them. Therefore, to go from national income to disposable income we must subtract all taxes paid to governments and add back in all transfer payments received from governments. The only exception to this rule is the amount of indirect business taxes paid by business firms. Indirect business taxes are not part of national income to begin with.

The second important difference between national income and disposable income is the retained earnings of business firms. *Retained earnings* are a portion of the profits that managers set aside to finance future investment projects. These funds are not available to households as disposable income.

The combined effect of taxes and retained earnings means that only a fraction of corporate profits and proprietors' income ends up as disposable income of households, even though they are both part of national income. Consider corporate profits. National income includes the corporate profits before any tax has been paid out of them. As we have just seen, the portion of the profits that corporations pay in corporation income taxes to federal and state governments is not available to households. The corporate profits that remain after the taxes have been paid have one of two destinations. The managers can pay out the after-tax profits as dividends to the stockholders, or they can retain these profits as retained earnings. Only the portion of corporate profits that is paid out in dividends becomes part of the disposable income of households. The retained earnings remain with the corporation.

Corporate profits − corporate income taxes = corporate after-tax profits
Corporate after-tax profits = dividends + retained earnings

Retained earnings are called **business saving** ($S_{business}$) because they are part of the national income that is saved to finance investment. Retained earnings can be thought of as saving that managers do on behalf of the stockholders. The stockholders/households own all the after-tax profits, but they let the man-

DISPOSABLE INCOME
The income available to households for their own use, to be consumed or saved.

BUSINESS SAVING
The portion of the profits that managers set aside to finance future investment projects; also called *retained earnings*.

agers keep part of the profits as retained earnings for further investment in the corporation.

To summarize, disposable income differs from national income because of taxes, government transfer payments, and retained earnings.

Disposable income (DI) = national income (NI)
  − all taxes (Tx) [except indirect business taxes]
  + government transfer payments (Tr)
  − retained earnings of business firms ($S_{business}$) [business saving]

$$DI = NI - Tx \text{ (except } IBT) + Tr - S_{business}$$

National income is quite a bit larger than disposable income is in the United States. In 1992 national income was $4,744.1 billion, and disposable income was $4,430.8, a $300 billion difference.

Finally, households can do two things with their disposable income: They can consume their income, or they can save it. Saving by households is called **personal saving** ($S_{personal}$).

$$DI = C + S_{personal}$$

PERSONAL SAVING

The portion of disposable income that households do not consume.

PERSONAL INCOME   The BEA publishes another measure of household income, personal income, that is closely related to disposable income. The only difference between them is that personal income includes personal taxes, which consist primarily of the federal and the state personal income taxes. Disposable income excludes these taxes.

$$\text{Personal income} = \text{disposable income} + \text{personal taxes}$$

Personal income in the United States was $5,058.1 in 1992, about $627 billion more than disposable income.

Personal income receives more attention in the news media than does disposable income because the BEA publishes estimates of personal income each month. The BEA can estimate disposable income only on a quarterly basis since some of the tax data needed to compute disposable income are not available on a monthly basis. Although personal income is more widely reported, disposable income is more relevant to macroeconomic analysis. Households base their spending and saving decisions on their disposable income, not on their personal income.

The Saving = Investment Accounting Identity

We have seen that the circular flow of economic activity causes an identity between national income and national product. The national income flowing through the nation's factor markets must equal the national product flowing through the nation's product markets. Lying beneath the surface of the circular flow is another accounting identity of fundamental importance to the study of macroeconomics, the identity between saving and investment. If the national income accountants define national income and national product so that the two are equal, then the total saving in the economy must equal the level of investment.

Deriving the equality between saving and investment from the equality between national income and national product is tedious, but well worth the effort. We saw in Chapter 3 that investment is the key to long-run economic growth. The identity between saving and investment indicates that saving and investment go hand in hand. Policies designed to stimulate investment are of little use if the level of saving cannot be increased. Conversely, policies designed to stimulate saving are of little use if firms do not increase their level of investment. We always have to think about saving and investment together. In addition, the equality between saving and investment highlights the interrelationships among three of the leading macroeconomic issues of the day in the United States: the low level of investment, the large federal budget deficit, and the trade imbalance between imports and exports. A little work now to understand the identity between saving and investment will pay great dividends in your study of macroeconomics.

Our goal is to begin with the equality between national income and national product and show that it implies the equality between saving and investment. We will begin with the equality between national income (NI) and net domestic product (NDP), which leads to an equality between total saving and net investment.

We know that national income (NI) and net domestic product (NDP) are not quite equal; they differ by the amount of indirect business taxes (IBT).

$$National\ income\ =\ national\ product$$

$$NI\ +\ IBT\ =\ NDP$$

Write NDP in terms of its components, the expenditures by final demanders.

$$NI\ +\ IBT\ =\ C\ +\ I_N\ +\ G\ +\ (Ex\ -\ Im)$$

Next, we want to replace national income with disposable income. To do this, we have to built up from disposable income to national income. We did the reverse above in going from national income to disposable income. To go from disposable income to national income, add taxes (except indirect business taxes) and retained earnings (business saving) to disposable income, and subtract government transfer payments from disposable income.

$$NI\ =\ DI\ +\ Tx\ [except\ IBT]\ -\ Tr\ +\ S_{business}$$

Therefore,

$$National\ income\ =\ national\ product$$

$$DI\ +\ Tx\ [except\ IBT]\ -\ Tr\ +\ S_{business}\ +\ IBT\ =\ C\ +\ I_N\ +\ G\ +\ (Ex\ -\ Im)$$

Combine the two tax terms of the left-hand side so that Tx refers to *all* taxes from now on.

$$DI\ +\ Tx\ -\ Tr\ +\ S_{business}\ =\ C\ +\ I_N\ +\ G\ +\ (Ex\ -\ Im)$$

Next, replace disposable income with the sum of its components, consumption plus personal saving.

$$C\ +\ S_{personal}\ +\ Tx\ -\ Tr\ +\ S_{business}\ =\ C\ +\ I_N\ +\ G\ +\ (Ex\ -\ Im)$$

Notice that consumption (C) appears on both sides of the equation, so that we can cancel it. Also, combine personal and business saving into one term.

$$(S_{\text{personal}} + S_{\text{business}}) + Tx - Tr = I_N + G + (Ex - Im)$$

We want net investment (I_N) by itself on the right-hand side. Therefore, bring government purchases of goods and services (G) and net exports ($Ex - Im$) over to the left-hand side, and combine all the government terms.

$$(S_{\text{personal}} + S_{\text{business}}) + (Tx - Tr - G) + (Im - Ex) = I_N$$

The three terms on the left-hand side show the three sources of saving in the economy from every sector of the economy. The first term is saving by the private sector, consisting of personal saving by the household sector and business saving by the business sector. The second term is saving by the government sector. The third term is saving by the foreign or rest-of-world sector.

$$S_{\text{private sector}} + S_{\text{government sector}} + S_{\text{foreign sector}} = I_N$$

The sum of the saving by each sector is the total saving in the economy. Therefore, we have shown that total saving equals net investment.

$$S_{\text{total}} = I_N$$

Some comments on each source of saving are in order.

PRIVATE-SECTOR SAVING

The sum of personal saving and business saving.

SAVING BY THE PRIVATE SECTOR   Personal saving and business saving are typically combined as saving by the private sector because the households own all the private business firms in the economy. Any after-tax profits earned by corporations and other businesses are really income earned by the stockholders of the firm. As indicated above, a decision to retain some of the profits for future investment is a saving decision by the managers of the firm on behalf of the stockholders. The stockholders presumably take into account any retained earnings saved on their behalf when deciding how much to save out of their own disposable income. Therefore, business saving and personal saving are closely linked.

GOVERNMENT SAVING

The difference between government revenues and government expenditures.

SAVING BY THE GOVERNMENT SECTOR   Saving by a government is the same as running a budget surplus. A government's budget is in surplus if its tax revenues (and other fees) exceed its total expenditures on transfer payments and purchases of goods and services (budget surplus: $Tx - Tr - G > 0$). Conversely, a government's budget is in deficit if its tax revenues (and other fees) are less than its total expenditures on transfer payments and purchases of goods and services (budget deficit: $Tx - Tr - G < 0$). A budget deficit represents negative saving, or dissaving, by a government. In other words, a budget deficit is a negative budget surplus. Saving by the government sector is the combined saving, or budget surpluses, of the federal, state, and local governments.

A budget surplus is a form of saving because a government disposes of excess tax revenues that it has not spent much as a household disposes of funds that it decides to save and not spend. The government's treasurer places the funds in checking and savings accounts, certificates of deposit, and other financial instruments that the government is allowed to buy. The funds then move through the financial markets to their ultimate destination, investment by business firms. (Appendix A discusses how funds flow through the nation's financial markets from savers to investors. The pathways are often very complex; funds can travel through many layers of financial institutions on their journey to the investors.)

SAVING BY THE FOREIGN SECTOR   To see why the difference in the value between imports and exports represents saving by the foreign sector, return to our simple example in Chapter 7 of the U.S. food exporter and the British clothing importer. Recall that the exporter sells 100£ worth of food in London, and the importer sells $180 worth of sweaters in the United States. Once the importer and the exporter exchange pounds sterling for dollars on the foreign exchange market, we know the dollar value of the food exports. We considered one example in which the exchange rate was $1.60/£. At this exchange rate the importer gives up $160 for the exporter's 100£, and the dollar value of the exports is $160. The dollar value of the imports ($180) exceeds the dollar value of the exports ($160) by $20, exactly the amount that the importer has left over after the exchange of currencies. The importer in our example has no choice but to hold the $20 in the United States. She may place the funds in a bank account or buy another kind of financial asset such as a certificate of deposit, a stock, or a bond. This is exactly what households do when they save and what governments do when they run a surplus.

Our simple example illustrates the following general principle: Whenever the dollar value of imports exceeds the dollar value of exports, importers are holding dollars that become part of the total saving in the economy. Dollars saved by foreign citizens finance U.S. investments just as do the dollars saved by U.S. households, businesses, and governments.[3]

FOREIGN SAVING

The difference between imports and exports.

TOTAL SAVING

The sum of personal saving, business saving, government saving, and foreign saving.

Accounting Identities and Economic Behavior

The saving = investment identity places before us the interrelationships among three of the leading macroeconomic stories in the United States: a disappointingly low level of net investment, large government budget deficits fueled by record federal deficits, and a huge trade imbalance of imports over exports. These stories have been ongoing in tandem since 1982, shortly after President Reagan first took office, and we will return to them time and again in the macroeconomic chapters that follow. Some of the key issues are evident from just looking at the accounting identity, however. For example, we can see that large budget deficits reduce total saving in the economy dollar for dollar. This may have a depressing effect on net investment if funds saved in the private sector end up buying government bonds rather than financing private investment. At the same time, the huge trade imbalance counteracts the budget deficits to some extent by providing a huge source of saving from foreign citizens. Foreign citizens have been buying some of the federal debt.

---

[3]$S_{\text{foreign sector}}$ also includes the net interest flows to and from the United States on assets held by U.S. citizens in foreign countries and assets held by foreign citizens in the United States.

They have also been directly financing investment by business firms in the United States. Investment in the United States might have been even lower without the influx of funds from abroad.

A word of caution is in order, however—*extreme* caution. Be sure you understand the equality between saving and investment for what it is, a national income accounting identity. Saving must equal investment by definition, given the circular flow of economic activity. The equality between saving and investment has no behavioral content in and of itself; it cannot explain cause and effect. For example, huge budget deficits may not cause a decrease in total saving or investment. Instead, the deficits may induce households and firms to save more if they believe that their taxes will be increased sometime in the future to pay off the debt. Households and firms may then increase their saving to have more funds available to pay the higher future taxes. Or the budget deficits may induce a trade imbalance as foreigners rush in to buy the safe, high-yielding federal bonds. The value of the dollar appreciates when foreign money managers with pounds and francs and yen are seeking dollars. An appreciating dollar causes imports to rise and exports to fall. These are just two of any number of possibilities. One cannot infer cause and effect from a national income accounting identity.

Nonetheless, the accounting identity must hold. Any explanation of macroeconomic events must be consistent with the fact that total saving from all sectors of the economy must equal the level of investment. We will return often to the equality of saving and investment in our study of macroeconomics.

Summary of the U.S. National Income and Product Accounts

Table 8.5 on pages 786–87 summarizes the relationships we have developed in the chapter and includes 1992 values of all items for the United States.

CONSTANT DOLLAR GDP AND THE GDP DEFLATOR

The BEA publishes two values of gross domestic product: current dollar, or nominal, GDP; and constant dollar, or real, GDP. **Current dollar or nominal GDP** is the actual dollar value of the GDP during the year. **Constant dollar or real GDP** measures the value of the GDP generated each year at the prices that existed in a given base year. The current base year is 1987. Therefore, the constant dollar or real GDP for each year is the value that the GDP would be had it been purchased at 1987 prices. Changes in the constant dollar GDP from year to year represent changes in the real quantities of goods and services flowing through the nation's product markets because the prices of the goods and services are held constant at their base year values. Constant dollar GDP removes the effect of inflation on the circular flow of economic activity.

The GDP Deflator

The BEA converts current dollar GDP to constant dollar GDP by means of a price index called the **GDP deflator.** The GDP deflator is constructed along the lines of the consumer price index (CPI) that we described in Chapter 7.

CURRENT DOLLAR (NOMINAL) GROSS DOMESTIC PRODUCT

The actual dollar value of the gross domestic product generated during the year.

CONSTANT DOLLAR (REAL) GROSS DOMESTIC PRODUCT

The value of the gross domestic product generated each year, evaluated at the prices that existed in a given base year.

GDP DEFLATOR

A price index based on a market basket of consumption goods, investment goods, government purchases, and net exports; used to convert current dollar GDP into constant dollar GDP.

The BEA accountants define a market basket of goods and services that are representative of the items in the GDP. The GDP market basket contains a selection of consumer goods and services, investment goods, goods and services purchased by governments, and net exports. The GDP deflator then tracks changes in the cost of purchasing the market basket over time.

The only difference between the GDP deflator and the CPI is that the GDP market basket changes each year to reflect the current components of the GDP. The CPI market basket is representative of a household's purchases in a chosen year and remains constant from year to year.

Changes in the CPI are most often used to represent the overall rate of inflation. The main purpose of constructing a GDP deflator is to convert the actual current dollar GDP to the constant dollar GDP. The conversion is simple: Divide the actual current dollar GDP by the GDP deflator (expressed as a decimal fraction) to compute the constant dollar GDP. Division by the GDP deflator is said to "deflate" the actual value of the GDP to its constant dollar value. For example, the actual current dollar GDP for 1992 was $5,951 billion, and the GDP deflator for 1992 was 120.9. Therefore, the constant value GDP was $4,922 billion.

$$\text{Constant value GDP}_{1992} = \text{current value GDP}_{1992}/\text{GDP deflator}_{1992}$$
$$= \$5,951 \text{ billion}/1.209 = \$4,922 \text{ billion}$$

Because the GDP deflator uses the current year's market basket, dividing actual GDP by the GDP deflator has the effect of computing the dollar value of GDP each year using the base year (1987) prices.[4]

Using constant dollar GDP rather than current dollar GDP to monitor the growth of an economy over time is important during times of inflation, such as the United States has been experiencing since World War II. The rate of growth in actual current dollar GDP is a combination of the rate of growth in real goods and services and the rate of growth in prices. Inflation can easily dominate the rate of growth in nominal current dollar GDP. For example, suppose that the U.S. economy is operating on its production possibilities frontier and that output is growing at its limit of 3 to 4 percent per year. Inflation happens to be 10 percent per year. Current dollar GDP would be growing at 13 to 14 percent per year (approximately), far more than the real growth of the economy. The majority of the growth in current dollar GDP is due to inflation.

The effect of inflation on the rate of growth in current dollar GDP increases over time. Compare the current and the constant dollar GDP figures for 1950 and 1992 (in $ billion):

	1950	1992
Current dollar GDP	$ 286	$5,951
Constant dollar GDP	1,400	4,922

---

[4]To see this, express the GDP deflator for 1992 as GDP deflator$_{1992} = (P_{92} \cdot Q_{92})/(P_{87} \cdot Q_{92})$. Notice that the quantities are the current year (1992) quantities. The actual current dollar GDP$_{1992} = P_{92} \cdot Q_{92}$. Therefore, dividing the current dollar GDP_{1992} by the GDP deflator$_{1992}$ to compute the constant dollar GDP_{1992} yields

$$\text{Constant dollar GDP}_{1992} = (P_{92} \cdot Q_{92})/[(P_{92} \cdot Q_{92})/(P_{87} \cdot Q_{92})] = P_{87} \cdot Q_{92}$$

$P_{87} \cdot Q_{92}$ is the dollar value of the 1992 components of the GDP using the 1987 prices.

TABLE 8.5　The National Income and Product Accounts of the United States, 1992 ($ billions)

A. NATIONAL INCOME AND NATIONAL PRODUCT

National Income

National income		$4,744.1
Compensation of employees	3,525.2	
+		
Rental income of persons	4.7	
+		
Net interest paid	415.2	
+		
Corporate profits	394.5	
+		
Proprietors' income	404.5	

Gross Domestic Product

Gross domestic product		5,950.7
Consumption	4,095.8	
+		
Gross investment	770.4	
+		
Government purchases of goods and services	1,114.9	
+		
Net exports		−30.4
Exports	636.3	
−		
Imports	666.7	

Gross and Net Investment

Gross investment		770.4
Net investment	117.0	
+		
Capital consumption allowance	653.4	

Net Domestic Product

Net domestic product		5,297.3
Gross domestic product	5,950.7	
−		
Capital consumption allowance	653.4	

Gross Domestic Product and National Income

Gross domestic product[a]		5,950.7
National income	4,744.1	
+		
Indirect business taxes	504.2	
+		
Capital consumption allowance	653.4	

[a]The three components listed do not add to gross domestic product because of the exclusion of minor items that we ignored in the chapter, and because of statistical discrepancies that arise in collecting the data.

(table continued on next page)

TABLE 8.5   The National Income and Product Accounts of the United States, 1992 ($ billions) (continued)

B. DISPOSABLE INCOME, PERSONAL INCOME, CONSUMPTION, AND PERSONAL SAVING

Disposable Income

Disposable income		4,430.8
National income	4,744.1	
−		
Taxes (except indirect business taxes)	918.4	
+		
Transfers (government + private)	866.1	
−		
Retained earnings	103.2	
+		
Other[b]	(−)157.8	

Personal Income

Personal income		5,058.1
Disposable income	4,430.8	
+		
Personal taxes	627.3	

Consumption and Personal Saving

Disposable income		4,430.8
Consumption (and other personal outlays)[c]	4,218.2	
+		
Personal saving	212.6	

C. INVESTMENT AND SAVING

Net Investment = Total Saving

Net Investment = Total Saving			117.0
Total saving			117.0
Saving: private sector		315.8	
Personal saving	212.6		
+			
Business saving (retained earnings)	103.2		
+			
Saving: government sector		(−)282.2	
+			
Saving: foreign sector[d]		83.4	

[b]The path from national income to disposable income is somewhat more complicated than represented in the chapter. The Other category includes portions of compensation of employees and net interest that households do not have at their disposal, and other minor items. It also includes some statistical discrepancies.

[c]Consumption here includes personal transfers of interest and other items that are in addition to the consumption of goods and services listed under gross domestic product.

[d]Saving by the foreign sector includes interest earned on assets held by foreign citizens in the United States and by U.S. citizens in foreign countries, as well as other minor transfers. These items are excluded from net exports listed under gross domestic product. Foreign saving also includes a large statistical discrepancy, which is inevitable when trying to account for transactions across international borders.

SOURCES: U.S. Department of Commerce, Economics and Statistics Administration, Bureau of Economic Analysis, *Survey of Current Business* 73, No. 3 (March 1993): Table 1.1, p. 6; Table 1.9, p. 8; Table 1.14, p. 9; Table 2.1, p. 10; and Table 5.1, p. 14. The historical data in the chapter are from Council of Economic Advisors, *Economic Report of the President, 1993*, (Washington, D.C.: U.S. Government Printing Office, 1993), unless otherwise noted (and earlier editions of the *Economic Report of the President* in some cases).

Current dollar GDP increased nearly 21-fold during the 42-year period (5,951/286 = 20.8), whereas constant dollar GDP increased only 3.5-fold (4,922/1400 = 3.5). The increase in the constant dollar GDP best measures the growth in real goods and services because both the 1950 GDP and the 1992 GDP are evaluated using 1987 dollars. We can see that much of the 21-fold increase in current dollar GDP was due to inflation. The lesson is clear: Use data on constant dollar GDP to track the real increases in the circular flow of economic activity over time.

REAL GDP AND THE STANDARD OF LIVING

Growth in real GDP per person is the best single measure available to economists for judging how much the standard of living has improved over time within a country. But how good a measure is it? For instance, real GDP per person in the United States was $9,194 in 1950 (1987 prices). By 1992 real GDP per person had grown to $19,274, slightly more than twice its value in 1950. These data tell us that the United States was producing and delivering two times as many goods and services to its citizens, on average, in 1992 than in 1950. Can we conclude from this that the average citizen in the United States was twice as well off in 1992 as in 1950? The answer is almost certainly no.

The main problem with attempting to link real GDP per person to economic well-being is that GDP is really not designed to measure economic well-being. GDP is primarily a measure of the amount of marketed activity that takes place within an economy during the course of a year: the value of final goods and services exchanged in a nation's product markets. As a result, real GDP per person misses a number of factors that affect the standard of living.

Imputing Values to Nonmarketed Activity

The first problem in trying to link real GDP per person with the standard of living is that GDP ignores a lot of nonmarketed activity that contributes to people's economic well-being. The BEA accountants do attempt to adjust GDP figures for some kinds of nonmarketed activity. The two most important adjustments are the value of food consumed on the farm that produced it and the value of housing services consumed by homeowners.

The BEA accountants try to estimate the market value of the food that farmers set aside for their own families. The estimated value of the food is counted simultaneously as a source of income for the farmer and as consumption by the family. Imputing a value of housing service to homeowners is an attempt to treat home ownership and renting symmetrically. If a family rents an apartment, the rent they pay is a source of rental income to the landlord and a form of consumption by the family. No such payment exists when a family owns its own home, yet the family is consuming housing services just as the renting family is. To maintain consistency between renting an apartment and owning a home, the BEA accountants impute a value of rent on the owned home equal to what an equivalent house would rent for. Homeowners are seen as paying the imputed value of the rent to themselves as income and using it to consume an equal amount of housing services. Notice that the imputed values of food or rent simultaneously increase one component of national income (farmers' income or rental income to persons) and one component of national product (consumption). Any adjustment to the national income and product accounts must maintain the equality between national income and national product.

The Underground Economy

The BEA adjustments for nonmarketed activity still miss a large amount of nonmarketed activity, both legal and illegal, that has come to be known as underground economy. The legal segment of the underground economy includes such activities as barter—the straight exchange of goods and services—and home production. The illegal segment of the underground economy includes criminal activities such as the drug trade and the more general problem of tax evasion.

Regarding the legal activities, suppose that I have a green thumb and my neighbor is an auto mechanic, so we agree to exchange our services without pay. I tend his gardens, and he fixes my car. If I were to hire a mechanic and he were to purchase a landscaping service, national income and product would rise by the value of each service. Given that we exchange the services in a barter arrangement, however, our services remain "underground" and are not recorded in the accounts, even though they are just as valuable to us as if we had purchased them. The same point applies to the child rearing, cooking, cleaning, and repair work that people do for themselves in their own homes and apartments. National income and product increase when people take the children to a daycare center, or go to a restaurant, or hire a domestic to clean the house, or hire a carpenter to repair the bathroom ceiling. These valued activities go unreported when people do them themselves.

Regarding the illegal activities, criminal behavior such as illicit drug dealing raises an interesting ethical question. Crime pays on average, sad to say. Criminal behavior contributes to the economic well-being of many who engage in it. But should the ill-gotten gains from crime be counted as part of society's well-being? If the answer is no, then income and consumption from the sale of illegal drugs does not belong in national income or national product.

Tax evasion, although illegal, is a somewhat different issue since it is often associated with legal activities. For example, operating a bar is largely a cash-run business, and hiding cash transactions from the tax authorities is much easier than hiding credit card transactions. Suppose that the otherwise law-abiding owners of a bar decide that the combined bite of the state sales tax, the federal and the state income taxes, and the federal payroll tax is just too much to bear, so they hide some of their sales from the tax authorities. The sale of drinks is legal and ought to be recorded as part of national income and national product, but the BEA accountants will not pick up the hidden sales and income. Domestics are another example. People who clean houses or do light repair work and yard chores often insist on being paid in cash so they can avoid paying taxes on the income. They, too, are part of the underground economy.

The size of the underground economy is an important issue for macroeconomic analysis. Consider the example of an increase in income taxes. Macroeconomic theory predicts that an income tax increase will lower the level of economic activity, as we will see. The presence of a large underground economy could well make the effect of the tax increase seem larger than it

REFLECTION: What routine, day-to-day services does your household provide for itself that your family could purchase in the market if it chose to do so?

really is, however. The problem is that tax increases drive more activity underground. Some people may quit their jobs and do more of the household chores themselves rather than hiring others to do them. In addition, tax evasion on marketed activities is likely to rise. Therefore, although the recorded level of national income and product decreases following an income tax increase, much of the decrease could be offset by increases in underground activities. Since economists cannot see the underground activities, they tend to overestimate the reaction of the economy to the tax increase.

CURRENT ISSUE: We have had tax accountants tell us that they estimate the underground economy to be about one-third of the GDP. Of course, many of their clients operate on the fringes of the underground economy.

Estimating the size of the underground economy is obviously a very difficult task. A recent study of the underground economy in Great Britain found it to be 3 to 5 percent of the recorded British GDP.[5] Whether this estimate is accurate, or whether it reflects the size of the underground economy in the United States, is anyone's guess.

Quality Changes and the GDP Deflator

Still another problem in linking changes in constant dollar GDP to changes in economic well-being is that the market basket used to compute the GDP deflator keeps changing over time. Earlier we compared the constant dollar GDPs for 1950 and 1992. The 1950 constant dollar GDP is based on a representative market basket of goods from 1950, and the 1992 constant dollar GDP is based on a representative market basket of goods from 1992. Those are very different market baskets. Just think about the consumer portion of the basket. Very few households had a television in 1950, and now our homes are filled with many other electronic gadgets that did not exist at all in 1950: CD players, microwave ovens, videocassette recorders, and so on.

The BEA accountants do try to account for quality changes in some of the more important products such as automobiles. If the price of a new car increases by 10 percent, the BEA tries to estimate how much of the 10 percent increase is the result of real quality improvements, such as air bags and anti-lock brakes, and how much is a pure price increase. Adjustments of this kind are limited though, and the accountants can hardly adjust adequately for quality changes when entirely new products appear and other products disappear. Just what is the appropriate 1987 price of a 1950 vacuum tube, 9-inch, black-and-white television? Constant dollar GDP comparisons are clearly less accurate the longer the time period being compared. This is unfortunate because we would like to be able to track real economic growth, and changes in the standard of living, over a very long period of time.

Pollution, Depleted Resources, and Other Economic Bads

Economic growth is somewhat of a mixed blessing. With growth and industrial development come a number of economic "bads": pollution of the environment, destruction of forests and wetlands, depletion of oil and mineral reserves, an increase in work-related accidents and fatalities, crowding and crime in major cities, and so forth. The national income and product accounts do not subtract out most of these bads.

---

[5]S. Smith, "European Perspectives on the Shadow Economy," *European Economic Review* 33 (1989): 592.

The treatment of pollution in the national accounts is especially one-sided. The costs of pollution are ignored, yet fighting pollution raises GDP, as when manufacturers buy scrubbers for their smokestacks to reduce pollution. The BEA accountants estimate the depreciation of the capital stock each year, but they do not bother to estimate the annual destruction or depletion of our natural resources. The costs of industrial accidents are also misrepresented in the national accounts. The working time lost because of accidents does reduce GDP, but the medical care required to treat the accidents increases GDP. Given the high cost of medical care, an industrial accident probably increases GDP!

The BEA's decision on these matters is undoubtedly pragmatic. How does one value the decline in health or, worse, the loss of life from pollution? What is the cost of destroying or depleting our irreplaceable natural resources? By how much does living in fear of crime reduce the quality of life? Any method of evaluating these costs would be fairly arbitrary. Nonetheless, ignoring the economic bads that are the inevitable consequences of growth clearly overstates the increase in economic well-being as measured by the growth in real GDP per person.

> HISTORICAL NOTE: The reverse is also true. Industrial air and water pollution has declined substantially in the United States since 1970. The gains in reduced pollution are missed in the GDP so the growth in GDP per person understates the increase in the U.S. standard of living since 1970 on this score.

Leisure Time

Valuing changes in leisure time is yet another difficult problem in trying to link the growth in real GDP to economic well-being. Manufacturing workers in the United States have enjoyed ever more leisure time throughout the twentieth century. The average workweek in manufacturing was 54.3 hours in 1900.[6] It had decreased to 38.6 hours by 1953 and has remained fairly constant since then. Increases in constant dollar GDP since 1900 clearly understate the growth in economic well-being by failing to include the value of the increased leisure time.

The value of leisure time can cut the other way, too. The past 35 years have witnessed a steady increase in the percentage of women in the labor force. Married women with families who work in the labor market no doubt have much less leisure time than did their counterparts of 35 years ago who worked only in the home. Two-earner families make real GDP grow more rapidly, but the growth in GDP overstates the growth in economic well-being because it misses the loss in leisure time that many women have suffered.

The Distribution of Income

One final point needs to be made about using real GDP as a measure of economic well-being. Suppose that we could somehow ignore all the measurement problems noted above. Even so, growth in real GDP per person is not all that societies care about. They also care how the additional output (income) is distributed.

The 1980s were hailed as a decade of steady economic growth in the United States. Indeed, the economy did enjoy over 100 months of uninterrupted growth in real GDP per person from the third quarter of 1982 onward, as the economy returned to the production possibilities frontier from the depths of the 1981–82 recession. On closer inspection, however, economists discovered

---

[6]R. Ehrenberg and R. Smith, *Modern Labor Economics: Theory and Public Policy*, Second edition, (Glenview, IL: Scott, Foresman, 1985) Table 6.3, p. 152.

that the economic growth was extremely unbalanced. The rising tide of growth did not lift all of the boats during the 1980s; the distribution of income became much more unequal. The people at the very top of the income distribution received a hugely disproportionate share of the income gains, while the people at the bottom of the distribution hardly gained at all. Economic growth in the 1980s had little effect on the number of people living in poverty.

Did the decade of the 1980s improve the overall economic well-being of the United States? Your answer to this question depends on how you weigh the size of the economic pie against the distribution of the pie, that is, the gains in real GDP per person against the increasing inequality of income. People have come out strongly on both sides of this question.[7]

A Concluding Comment

Let's end on a positive note. Real GDP per person may be a very imperfect measure of the standard of living, but it is the best measure available to us. And it tells the right story, by and large.

Economic historians have attempted to trace U.S. real GDP back to the early years of the nation. One study estimates that real GDP per person was $1,285.50 in 1820 (1987 prices). As noted earlier, it was $19,274 in 1992, 15 times larger than in 1820. The population of the United States was 28 times larger in 1992 than in 1820, but the real GDP was over 400 times larger![8]

Is the U.S. standard of living 15 times higher now than in 1820? Perhaps not. The GDP figures may overstate the improvement in the standard of living because of the increase in marketed activity since 1820 and the numerous economic bads associated with growth. Then again, the GDP figures may understate the improvement in the standard of living because we enjoy so much more leisure time than did our ancestors. Scratching out a living on the farms and the frontier in the early 1800s took backbreaking labor every waking hour of the day.

Whatever the truth of the matter, there can be no doubt that the U.S. standard of living has improved many times over since 1820. The GDP figures testify loud and clear to the stunning economic success of American capitalism.

SUMMARY

Chapter 8 described the national income and product accounts of the United States, which are compiled by the Bureau of Economic Analysis within the U.S. Department of Commerce. Table 8.5 summarized the most important accounting relationships. Some of the key principles underlying the accounts are the following.

---

[7]Economists also rely on GDP per person to compare the relative standards of living in different countries. Unfortunately, comparisons of GDP across countries may be a worse gauge of relative economic well-being than are comparisons of GDP within countries over time. We will consider these problems in Chapter 22, which discusses the low-income developing countries.

[8]The estimate of GDP per person in 1820 is from A. Maddison, *Phases of Capitalist Development* (Oxford: Oxford University Press, 1982), 8. (Conversion to 1987 prices for purposes of comparison was done by author.)

1. The national income and product accounts measure the circular flow of economic activity. As such, the fundamental accounting identity is that national income must equal national product.

2. If national income is defined to equal national product, then saving must equal investment. The three components of saving are
   a. saving by the private sector, consisting of the personal saving of households and business saving (or retained earnings out of profits);
   b. saving by the government sector, equal to the combined budget surpluses of the federal, state, and local governments. Government deficits represent negative government saving; and
   c. saving by the foreign sector, equal to the difference between imports and exports.

3. The value added by business firms measures the circular flow at the point of production. It is equal to total sales less the cost of intermediate goods.

4. A very important component of the circular flow is disposable income, which is the income available to households. Households base their consumption and saving decisions on their disposable income. Consumption is by far the most important component of gross domestic product, and personal saving helps finance the investment of business firms.

5. Current dollar or nominal GDP is the actual value of GDP in a given year. Constant dollar or real GDP evaluates the GDP in a given year using base-year prices. The current base year is 1987. The GDP deflator is a price index of final goods and services that is used to convert current dollar GDP to constant dollar GDP. Dividing the current dollar GDP by the GDP deflator has the effect of evaluating the GDP in the base-year prices.

6. The best available measure of the overall economic well-being of a nation is real GDP per capita. It is used to track improvements in a nation's standard of living over time and to compare relative standards of living across countries.

7. Even so, real GDP per capita is a flawed measure of economic well-being because it is not designed for that purpose. Its intent is to measure the amount of marketed activity during the year. As such, it misses or miscalculates the effects on economic well-being of all of the following:
   a. the underground economy, consisting of legal bartering of goods and services, household production, and illegal activities such as criminal behavior and tax evasion;
   b. many of the economic bads that inevitably accompany economic growth, such as air and water pollution, destruction and depletion of natural resources, the increase in industrial accidents, and crowding and crime in major cities;
   c. quality changes in goods and services, including the introduction of new products and the disappearance of other products over time;
   d. changes in leisure time; and
   e. changes in the distribution of income.

8. Real GDP per person in the United States has grown 15-fold since 1820. The standard of living in the United States may or may not be 15 times higher than in 1820, but the growth in real GDP per person clearly shows that American capitalism has been a stunning economic success.

KEY TERMS

capital consumption allowance
compensation of employees
constant dollar (real) gross domestic product
consumption
corporate profit
current dollar (nominal) gross domestic product
disposable income
economic depreciation
exports
foreign saving

government purchases of goods and services
government saving
gross domestic product
gross investment
gross national product
imports
income statement
indirect business taxes
national income
national product

net domestic product
net exports
net interest
net investment
personal saving
private-sector saving
proprietors' income
rental payments to persons
retained earnings
total saving
value added

QUESTIONS

1. a. Why must national income equal national product?
   b. What is value added, and why must it equal national income?
2. Which of the following are included in the measurement of GDP?
   a. An increase or decrease in firms' inventories during the year.
   b. Purchases of the products of one firm by another firm to be used as material inputs.
   c. Purchases of foreign cars by domestic citizens.
   d. Purchases of houses built 10 years ago.
   e. The decline in pollution from paper mills during the year.
3. What is the capital consumption allowance, and how might it differ from economic depreciation?
4. a. Can net investment ever be negative?
   b. Can gross investment ever be negative?
5. a. What is the difference between disposable income and national income?
   b. Why is each of these income concepts important to the study of macroeconomics?
6. a. What are the three components of total saving?
   b. Why must total saving equal investment for the entire economy?
7. Suppose that the national income accountants find the following data for an economy during 1992 (data in $ billion).

Consumption = $8,000
All taxes = $3,000
Disposable income = $12,000
Retained earnings = $2,000
Capital consumption allowance = $1,000

Government purchases = $1,000
Government transfers = $1,500
Exports = $3,000
Imports = $1,000

Compute the values of personal saving, gross domestic product, net domestic product, net and gross investment, and total saving.

8. You are given the following data on the current dollar GDP and the GDP deflator for some country:

YEAR	CURRENT DOLLAR GDP ($ BILLION)	GDP DEFLATOR (1987 = 100)
1991	$5,000	125
1992	6,000	200

Did constant dollar (real) GDP increase or decrease in 1992?

9. Suppose that a country had a real GDP per person of $10,000 in 1950 and now has a real GDP per person of $15,000. Can we conclude that the citizens of the country are better off now than they were in 1950?

10. The data in the table below refer to the same simple economy described in the chapter. Wheat is used to make flour, flour is used to make bread, and bread is sold to consumers as a final product. Labor is the only primary factor of production. Fill in the missing entries in the table.

	INTERMEDIATE MATERIALS	LABOR	SALES	VALUE ADDED
Wheat	0	10		
Flour		20		
Bread		50		

Also calculate the national income, total value added, total sales in the economy, and consumption of bread

9

Modeling the Macro Economy: New Classical and New Keynesian Perspectives

LEARNING OBJECTIVES

CONCEPTS TO LEARN

The business cycle

Fiscal policy

Monetary policy

New classical economics

New Keynesian economics

Aggregate demand and aggregate supply

Aggregate demand and aggregate supply shocks

CONCEPTS TO RECALL

The three-part economic problem [1]

The circular flow of economic activity [4]

The Laws of Supply and Demand [5]

The macroeconomic policy goals [6, 7]

  a. Long-run economic growth [6]

  b. Full employment [6]

  c. Price stability [7]

  d. Stable international economic relations [7]

The national income = national product accounting identity [8] *ill Clinton's victory over George Bush in the 1992 presidential election was more than a changing of the political guard in Washington. It was a profound changing of the economic guard as well.*

There are two main schools of macroeconomics today, new classical economics and new Keynesian economics. The new classical economists believe that the macro economy performs about as well as can be expected on its own in the short run. "Hands off" is their general advice to the government. In their view, doses of fiscal and monetary policies cannot expect to do much good and may actually be harmful. They tend to limit their policy prescriptions to long-run problems, such as policies to increase long-run economic growth. The new Keynesians, in contrast, believe that the economy can perform very badly in the short run if left on its own. They favor active intervention with fiscal and monetary policies to help the economy pursue the macroeconomic policy goals.

Presidents Reagan and Bush kept counsel with economists whose leanings were more toward the new classical view. They both agreed that the economy can best solve its own problems for the most part. President Clinton swept the new classical economists out of Washington and surrounded himself with some of the very best new Keynesian economists. The president made it quite clear in his first State of the Union address to Congress that he wants the federal government leading the way on any number of economic problems. The administration's economic policy stance is interventionist again, more so than at any time since the Nixon administration in the early 1970s.

Having discussed the four macroeconomic policy goals and described the national income and product accounts, we are now in a position to study the overall operation and performance of the U.S. economy.

Chapter 6 identified the three fundamental questions of macroeconomic analysis: (1) What factors determine the circular flow of economic activity? (2) How does the circular flow of economic activity relate to the four macroeconomic policy goals? (3) How can the government influence the level and the composition of the circular flow with its fiscal and monetary policies and thereby help society achieve the macroeconomic policy goals. Chapter 9 begins with some observations on these three questions that will serve as a guide to where we are heading in the chapters that follow.

Macro economists have not come close to reaching an agreement on how to answer the fundamental questions. One reason why they have not has to do with the size and the complexity of any modern economy. No one can hope to understand the U.S. economy in all its details. Instead, economists are forced to study the economy with highly simplified models, and they cannot agree on the best model for analyzing the economy.

Chapter 9 considers the all-important first step in macroeconomic analysis: how to build a model of the macro economy. The discussion includes an overview of the two leading macro models in use today, the new classical model and the new Keynesian model. We will make use of both models in our analysis of the U.S. economy.

THE CIRCULAR FLOW OF ECONOMIC ACTIVITY AND MACROECONOMIC POLICY

The Business Cycle

The central question that macro economists wrestle with is the determination of the circular flow: What factors determine the level and the composition of the circular flow of economic activity?

The study of the circular flow is interesting in its own right because the circular flow does not simply increase in a smooth and orderly fashion from year to year. Far from it. As we noted in Chapter 6, the circular flow of economic activity is highly erratic in all the world's developed market economies. In some years market economies perform well below their production possibilities frontiers. Resources lie idle, and the production of goods and services is much smaller than it could be. In other years market economies strain against their production possibilities frontiers. Resources are fully utilized, and the production of goods and services is as large as possible.

Furthermore, erratic behavior is the rule, not the exception. The circular flow of economic activity moves continually over time in a pattern of expansions and contractions, booms and busts, called the **business cycle.** The circular flow may grow for awhile, but each period of growth eventually comes to an end and is followed by a period of decline, a recession. Fortunately, each recession also eventually comes to an end and is followed by a period of growth.

The periods of growth and recession vary in duration and intensity. An economy may experience uninterrupted growth for a number of years or for just a few months; similarly, the recessions may last for years or months. When economies are growing, the rate of growth may be rapid or slow; when economies are in decline, the rate of decline may also be rapid or slow. Long or short, intense or mild, the business cycle is a fundamental macroeconomic fact of life in a market economy.

We can see these patterns in Figure 9.1, which illustrates the behavior of the circular flow of economic activity for the U.S. economy from 1977 through 1992. The horizontal axis lists each quarter (three-month period) from the beginning of 1977 to the end of 1992. For example, 1978:4 refers to the fourth quarter of 1978, the three-month period from October through December. The vertical axis records the real gross domestic product of the United States, in billions of dollars, using 1987 prices as the base year. The values of real gross domestic product listed for each quarter are annual rates, that is, the value that would result if the flow of domestic product during the quarter were maintained for an entire year. The solid line represents the production possibilities frontier for the economy during each quarter. It is an estimate of maximum value of real gross domestic product that the economy could sustain without causing any severe inflationary pressures.

The uneven performance of the U.S. economy, including the cyclical pattern of growth and recession, is evident from the figure. At the beginning of 1977 we see that the economy was operating below its production possibilities frontier. Large oil price increases in 1973–74 had pushed the economy into a deep recession. By 1977 the economy had entered a period of growth and was proceeding to march back to its frontier. The progress was temporarily halted by

BUSINESS CYCLE

The continuing pattern over time of expansions and contractions, booms and busts, in the circular flow of economic activity in capitalist economies.

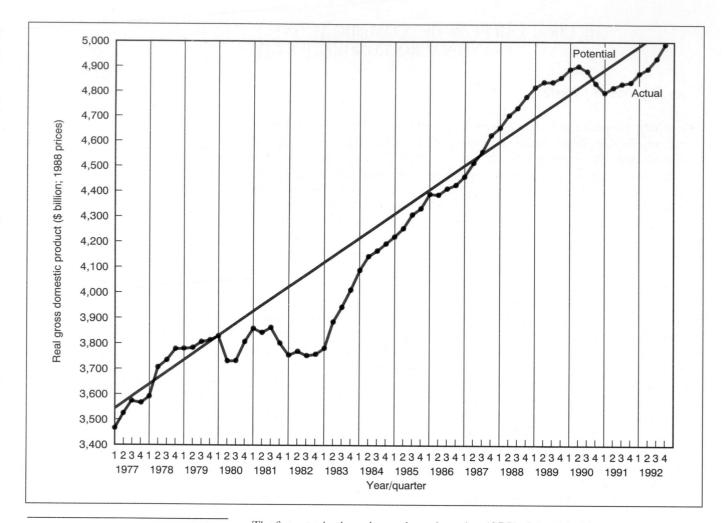

FIGURE 9.1

The United States Economy—1977–92

The figure tracks the real gross domestic product (GDP) of the United States in each quarter from 1977 to 1992. The straight line is an estimate of the sustainable productive capacity of the economy, corresponding to the production possibilities frontier. The performance of the U.S. economy during this period reflects the erratic, cyclical ebbs and flows that are typical of all the industrialized market economies. At times real GDP was increasing and at other times it was decreasing. Sometimes the economy strained against its productive capacity, and at other times it operated well below the production possibilities frontier.
SOURCE: R. Gordon, *Macroeconomics*, sixth edition (New York: Harper Collins, 1993), Appendix A, p. A6; and Council of Economic Advisors, *Economic Indicators, March 1993* (Washington, D.C.: U.S. Government Printing Office, 1993), 2. The potential GDP line was drawn as a straight line through Gordon's estimate of potential real GDP for 1977:1 and 1992:2 to serve as a simple visual approximation of Gordon's time series of estimated potential real GDP for each quarter.

a slight decline in fourth quarter of 1977, but the economy quickly recovered, reached the frontier in early 1978, and essentially remained at the frontier through the first quarter of 1980. At that point the period of prosperity came to an end, as the economy declined sharply during the second quarter of 1980. The economy began to recover over the next year, but before it could return to the frontier, it suffered a very sharp recession that lasted for over a year. By the middle of 1982 the U.S. economy was farther below its production possibilities frontier than at any time since the Great Depression of the 1930s. The economy finally reversed direction near the end of 1982 and entered a long period of virtually uninterrupted growth back to the frontier. The period of growth continued until 1990, when the economy experienced another brief recession that lasted through the first quarter of 1991. In summary, the period from 1977 to 1992 exhibited all the typical macroeconomic features of developed market economies: some years when the economy is straining at the limits of its capacity, other years when the economy is operating well below its capacity, and a cyclical pattern of growth and recession that varies considerably in duration and intensity. The study of macroeconomics tries above all else to understand why market economies behave in this erratic fashion.

HISTORICAL NOTE: In 1993 the U.S. economy was growing, but very slowly—not even fast enough to reduce the unemployment rate significantly.

The Circular Flow and the Macroeconomic Policy Goals

Economists are not interested in the question of what determines the circular flow of economic activity just for its own sake. The question is important because the ebbs and flows of the economy have a direct impact on each of the four macroeconomic policy goals. We talked about one obvious example in Chapter 6, the problem of cyclical unemployment. People have a much easier time finding good, high-paying jobs and avoiding unemployment if the economy is growing rapidly and pushing against its production possibilities frontier than they do if the economy is declining and operating far below its production possibilities frontier. Similarly, inflation is likely to increase when the economy moves close to the frontier and begins to strain against its productive capacity. Investment is also influenced by the performance of the economy. Business firms are more likely to invest if the economy is booming than if the economy is languishing in the depths of a recession. These are just a few of the ways that the level of the circular flow affects the macroeconomic policy goals.

The composition of the circular flow also has a direct impact on the macroeconomic policy goals. We noted in Chapter 3 that the only final goods an economy can produce are investment goods and consumer goods. The rate of long-run economic growth depends crucially on the investment/consumption mix within the economy. Another important compositional issue relates to the distinction between current dollar gross domestic product (GDP) and constant dollar GDP. What factors determine how much of the growth in current dollar GDP is growth in real GDP and how much of the growth is just price increases?

Part and parcel to understanding what determines the level and the composition of the circular flow is understanding the linkages between the circular flow and the macroeconomic policy goals. We will emphasize these linkages throughout the macroeconomics chapters of the text because the macroeconomic policy goals ultimately determine the overall economic health of a nation.

Fiscal and Monetary Policies

The national governments of all countries engage in macroeconomic policy. Broadly speaking, **macroeconomic policy** is an attempt to achieve the macroeconomic policy goals by intervening in some form in the operation of the economy. Macroeconomic policy is typically associated with the national gov-

MACROECONOMIC POLICY

An attempt to achieve the macroeconomic policy goals by intervening in some form in the operation of the economy.

ernment because only the national government can hope to influence the overall level of economic activity.

As noted in Chapter 2, the United States has generally been unwilling to pursue the macroeconomic goals directly. The federal government does not typically offer "make-work" government jobs to anyone who is unemployed, or control prices to prevent inflation, or commandeer people's savings to increase the level of investment, or block the flow of imports and exports to any great extent. The government would have to control economic activity with a very heavy hand to pursue the macroeconomic policy goals so directly, and this is inconsistent with the U.S. commitment to market capitalism. Instead, the United States has chosen an indirect approach to achieving the macroeconomic policy goals. The macroeconomic policies of the federal government target the economy itself, not the policy goals. The government attempts to influence the level and the composition of the circular flow of economic activity and thereby achieve the macroeconomic policy goals. This is why understanding what determines the circular flow of economic activity and how the circular flow links to the policy goals is so important. The federal government cannot possibly hope to conduct effective macroeconomic policy without this understanding, given the way it has chosen to proceed.

We noted in Chapter 6 that the two principal macroeconomic policies of the federal governments are fiscal policy and monetary policy. We will focus on these two policies throughout the text.

FISCAL POLICY

Changes in the federal budget made for the specific purpose of influencing the level and the composition of the circular flow of economic activity; includes changes in government spending on goods and services, changes in transfer payments, or changes in taxes.

FISCAL POLICY   Recall that **fiscal policy** refers to changes in the federal budget made for the specific purpose of influencing the level and the composition of the circular flow of economic activity. These budgetary changes could be changes in government spending on goods and services, or changes in transfer payments, or changes in taxes; in other words, they could be changes in any component of the federal budget. The conduct of fiscal policy is the joint responsibility of the administration and the Congress, since they have joint control over the federal budget.

A word on the motivation for budgetary changes is in order. The administration and the Congress undertake changes in the federal budget for all kinds of reasons, most of which have nothing to do with trying to affect the performance of the economy. In the early 1990s, for example, the administration proposed and the Congress approved large reductions in military expenditures following the disintegration of the Eastern European Communist bloc and the Soviet Union. These reductions were clearly motivated by strategic military considerations, the belief that the military threat to Western Europe and the United States had been substantially reduced. We would not tend to think of the military cutbacks as an act of fiscal policy. In contrast, when the Congress passes a temporary reduction in personal income taxes to stimulate the economy or extends the period that unemployed workers can collect unemployment insurance, these are clearly instances of fiscal policy.

Ascribing motives to individual budgetary changes is problematic, however. We will learn that changes in government expenditures and taxes affect the level and the composition of the circular flow regardless of why they were undertaken. Therefore, when the administration and the Congress are deciding on the appropriate fiscal policy stance, they have to take into consideration all the legislated budgetary changes that are expected to occur throughout the year for whatever reason. They may or may not decide to make additional changes in government expenditures or taxes for the sake of the economy. Whatever they decide, though, the total of all the changes in government expenditures and taxes during the year defines the fiscal policy stance of the government.

To give a recent example, the Clinton administration decided in 1993 that the projected cuts in military spending were not enough. President Clinton wanted to reduce the federal budget deficit considerably for reasons that we will explore in later chapters. So the administration proposed spending cuts in other areas to bring the total cut in spending to about $250 billion over a five-year period. The administration also proposed $250 billion in tax increases over the same five years. Congress approved these changes in the summer of 1993.

MONETARY POLICY   **Monetary policy** refers to changes in the money supply made for the specific purpose of influencing the level and the composition of the circular flow of economic activity. The two most important components of the money supply in the United States are the dollar bills of various denominations and the checking accounts in commercial banks and other depository institutions. The money supply has a direct effect on the circular flow because most economic transactions are paid for with dollars or checks.

The conduct of monetary policy in the United States is the responsibility of the Board of Governors of the **Federal Reserve Banking System,** which is the nation's central bank. The Federal Reserve is commonly referred to as the "Fed." Congress established the Fed in 1913 as a public agency separate from the administration and the Congress. The chairman of the Board of Governors is required to appear before the Congress each year to report on the board's intended monetary policy. But the Board of Governors is free to increase or decrease the money supply as it chooses.

Motivation is not an issue with monetary policy. The Fed is a non-profit institution whose primary responsibility is to manipulate the money supply in a manner consistent with achieving the macroeconomic policy goals. Virtually all changes in the money supply engineered by the Fed are motivated by a desire to affect the performance of the economy.

The Three-Part Economic Problem for the Entire Economy

The conduct of fiscal and monetary policies can be thought of as the government's attempt to solve the standard three-part economic problem for the entire macro economy, consisting of objectives, alternatives, and constraints.

Objectives: The objectives are the four macroeconomic policy goals. One might think that the government should try to reach each of the four goals simultaneously. Unfortunately, this is not always possible, given the choice to pursue the goals indirectly by manipulating the economy. Fiscal and monetary policies that move the economy closer to one of the goals often move the economy farther away from one or more of the other goals. For example, policies that stimulate the economy and move it closer to the production possibilities frontier create jobs for unemployed workers. They may also induce more investment by business firms, which increases long-run economic growth.

MONETARY POLICY

Changes in the money supply made for the specific purpose of influencing the level and the composition of the circular flow of economic activity.

FEDERAL RESERVE BANKING SYSTEM

The central bank of the United States, commonly referred to as the "Fed."

But policies that stimulate the economy are also likely to increase the rate of inflation, reduce the value of the dollar relative to other currencies, and increase the balance-of-trade deficit. The government is thus often forced to choose. The policy question is this: What set of policies provides the best compromise among the macroeconomic policy goals?

Alternatives: The alternatives are the policy options available to the government for achieving the macroeconomic policy goals, principally fiscal and monetary policies.

Constraints: The primary constraint in the macroeconomic policy problem is the economy itself, which determines how the application of fiscal and monetary policies affects each of the macroeconomic policy goals. The economy also determines the extent to which the four goals are compatible with one another. Suppose that the Fed increases the money supply. What effect does this have on unemployment? On long-run economic growth? On inflation? On the value of the dollar? The economy holds the answers to these questions. Understanding what determines the circular flow of economic activity simultaneously helps us define the menu of policy choices that are available to the government.

The study of macroeconomics can be thought of as an attempt to understand the structure of the three-part macroeconomic policy problem and to determine how best to solve it. This has not proved to be an easy task.

Economists are not at all in agreement about how to solve the macroeconomic policy problem. Divisions run deep. One source of disagreement is largely a matter of taste and centers on the objectives. Economists may disagree on the importance that policy makers should attach to each of the policy goals. Some economists may favor an all-out attack on unemployment; others may be concerned about holding down the rate of inflation. If so, their policy recommendations are likely to be quite different. A more important and fundamental disagreement centers on the constraint, that is, on the operation and the performance of the economy. Macro economists cannot agree on what factors are most important in determining the circular flow of economic activity. They have not settled on the best model for analyzing the economy. To understand why not, we have to think a bit about the problem of how to build a model of the entire economy.

THE NEED FOR A MACRO MODEL

Trying to understand the operation of a modern market economy is a truly daunting task. Nowhere is the need for the modeling approach to economic analysis more obvious than in the study of macroeconomics. Think back for a moment to the description of the U.S. economy in Chapter 4: more than 250 million consumers, 18 million business firms producing tens of thousands of products, $2 trillion of government expenditures, hundreds of billions of dollars of international trade with over 100 nations, $6 trillion worth of goods and services produced every year. No one can hope to understand such a huge and complex economy in all its details, and economists do not even try. They approach the study of macroeconomics by building highly simplified models of the macro economy that, they believe, capture the essential features of how the economy operates.

Macro economists understand that their models are much, much simpler than are the complex economies that they are trying to describe. They know that they are ignoring many aspects of the economy and that their models may sometimes be wide of the mark in predicting the unemployment rate, the level of inflation, or the pace of economic growth. Nonetheless, one has no choice but to think about the modern macro economy in an extremely simplified way. Building a model of the economy is the necessary first step in macroeconomic analysis.

Even highly simplified models of the economy can be extremely complicated. Private economic consulting firms, such as DRI–McGraw-Hill and Chase Econometrics, build huge mathematical models that are designed to forecast, or predict, various aspects of the economy. They sell their forecasts to businesses who want to know where the economy is heading in order to help them with their production and marketing plans. Many government agencies have also built large mathematical forecasting models to help them design fiscal and monetary policies that will best meet the macroeconomic policy goals. Agencies with their own forecasting models include the Federal Reserve, which is in charge of controlling the nation's money supply; the Congressional Budget Office, which offers economic analysis and advice to the Congress; the Council of Economic Advisers, which advises the president and writes the annual *Economic Report of the President;* and the U.S. Treasury and the states' departments of revenue, which are interested in forecasting future tax collections.

The private and the government forecasting models are exceedingly complex. The largest forecasting models contain hundreds of economic variables embedded in thousands of interrelated equations that only very large mainframe computers are capable of solving. Even so, these large forecasting models look very simple when set against the staggering complexity of the U.S. economy. They, too, miss much of the detail of the economy, with the result that they all have their good and bad years. At times one of the forecasting models may be right on the mark. At other times it may miss by a wide margin, as when it predicts a decrease in unemployment over the next six months and the unemployment rate actually rises.

Our goals in this text are much more modest than those of the giant forecasting models. We want to describe a few simple relationships that will give us a good first-pass understanding of how the U.S. economy operates. We are after a qualitative analysis of the key macroeconomic variables, such as national income, investment, interest rates, and the unemployment rate, not accurate quantitative predictions of their values. For instance, the models we will be using are far too simple to be able to predict the rates of unemployment and inflation to the nearest percentage point. They are detailed enough, however, to indicate what forces cause unemployment and inflation to rise or fall, and this is enough for our purposes.

Whether simple or complex, all models of the macro economy have the same basic goal in mind. They are all trying to explain what forces determine the level and the composition of the circular flow of economic activity. Why does the circular flow increase by 6 percent one year and not at all the next? Why is the level of saving and investment so low in the United States? Macro models are useful to business and the government only to the extent they can answer questions such as these. To give one example, the better we understand the circular flow of economic activity, the better we can answer the two fundamental macroeconomic policy questions: (1) How do the level and the composition of the circular flow affect the four macroeconomic policy goals? (2) How can the government help to achieve the macroeconomic policy goals through its monetary and fiscal policies?

Modeling the Circular Flow

Since all macro models are trying to explain the circular flow of economic activity, they all begin with the same relationship, one that describes the circular flow. The first relationship, or equation, of every macro model represents the circular flow through the market for goods and services. It is written

$$Y = C^d + I^d + G^d + (Ex^d - Im^d)$$

The Y on the left-hand side of the equation stands for national income. The terms on the right-hand side are the demands, or desired expenditures, of the four sectors of the economy. C^d is consumption demand by the household sector, I^d is investment demand by the business sector, G^d is the demand for goods and services by the government sector, and $(Ex^d - Im^d)$ is the demand for net exports [the demand for exports (Ex^d) minus the demand for imports (Im^d)] by the foreign sector.

The equation represents the supply and the demand sides of the product markets. The left-hand side of the equation indicates the total, or aggregate, value of final goods and services that producers are willing to supply to the product markets. Producers generate the national income in the process of producing their goods and services. Since national income equals national product, the value of the national income generated in production equals the value of all the final goods and services produced during the year. As noted above, the right-hand side of the equation indicates the total, or aggregate, demand for the final goods and services in the product markets by all four sectors of the economy.

The equation serves as a statement of equilibrium for the economy as a whole. It says that the circular flow of economic activity has achieved its equilibrium value when the total amount of final goods and services that producers are willing to supply is equal to the total amount of final goods and services that demanders are willing to buy. The equation is analogous to the equilibrium condition for a single market: A market is in equilibrium when the supply of the product equals the demand for the product.

The remaining task in building a macro model is to specify what economic variables determine each side of the equation. What variables determine how much total product the producers in the economy are willing to supply? What variables determine how much total product the final demanders are willing to buy? These turn out to be among the more controversial questions in all of economics. Economists have debated long and hard over the key variables that determine the circular flow of economic activity in a modern capitalist economy such as the United States, and the debate continues to rage. The professional economics literature contains at least five different basic models of the U.S. economy. The models differ in the emphasis they place on the supply and the demand sides of the product markets and on the variables that are most important in determining aggregate supply and demand. Macro economists cling tenaciously to their preferred models.

The debate among macro economists is difficult to resolve precisely because macroeconomic models are so simple relative to the economy they are trying to describe. Simplicity requires sweeping assumptions about how the economy operates. Every model of the economy contains some assumptions that are realistic and others that are unrealistic, with the result that each has its strong and weak points. At best, a macro model will be useful for explaining and predicting some events and not so useful for explaining and predicting other events. No one macro model can hope to explain and predict everything with unerring accuracy.

Everyone is striving toward the same end—a consensus best model of the macro economy. But finding that "best model" has proved to be an elusive goal. The truth is that macroeconomics is a much less settled discipline than is microeconomics. The vast majority of economists are in agreement about the basic principles of microeconomics. Macroeconomics, in contrast, has been perpetually in turmoil, no more so than today.

THE NEW CLASSICAL AND THE NEW KEYNESIAN PERSPECTIVES

Two models, the new classical model and the new Keynesian model, have emerged from the pack to become the leading macroeconomic models of the day. New classical economists and new Keynesian economists have very different views about the variables that determine the circular flow of economic activity. The differences between them are important because their models also have very different implications for government policy. New classical economists do not believe that the government can do much to improve the performance of the private economy in the short run. In their view, occasional doses of fiscal and monetary policies are bad medicine. These measures are unnecessary because they cannot bring the economy closer to the macroeconomic policy goals, on average. They are also undesirable because they cause the economy to behave erratically. The best course for the government is steady-as-she-goes. The government should announce its intended fiscal and monetary policies and stick to its plans so that the private economy knows exactly what the government is doing. This helps individuals and business firms perform more confidently and effectively.

The new Keynesians, in contrast, believe that fiscal and monetary policies have an important role to play in managing the economy. In their view market economies can perform very badly if left to their own devices, straying far from any one or all of the macroeconomic policy goals. Occasional doses of fiscal and monetary policies, correctly administered, are just the right medicine for an ailing economy. They can significantly improve the overall performance of the economy and help a nation achieve its macroeconomic policy goals.

We want to highlight the main differences between the new classical and the new Keynesian models because they will be featured throughout the macroeconomics chapters of this text. Unfortunately, a consensus between the two leading branches of macroeconomic analysis appears to be a long way off.

The New Classical Model

The so-called classical economists of the 1800s and early 1900s had one prevailing model of how individual product and factor markets operated—supply and demand. To the extent they thought about macroeconomics, they simply assumed that the overall level of economic activity was also governed by the Laws of Supply and Demand. They analyzed the exchanges in a nation's product markets as if these markets comprised a single competitive market blown up to encompass the entire economy. The new classical economists of today embrace the old classical view that the macro economy is best modeled as if it were competitive and governed by the Laws of Supply and Demand.

A reasonable case can be made for the assumption that the Laws of Supply and Demand determine the overall level of economic activity in the United States. Industrial organization economists who study individual product markets tell us that the majority of output in the U.S. economy is marketed under highly competitive conditions. A common estimate is that the Laws of Supply and Demand are a useful tool for analyzing how prices and quantities change in approximately 70 percent of all the product markets in the United States.

There also appears to be a substantial amount of competition in the markets for labor and capital, the two most important primary factors of production. Of all the workers in the United States, 25 percent (more than 31 million individuals) change the *industry* in which they work within every three-year period, and only one-half of all full-time workers have held the same job for more than 3½ years.[1] Workers in the United States are clearly willing and able to respond to market opportunities. Wages and salaries are also quite flexible and responsive to market conditions in a large number of labor markets. For example, the starting salaries of college graduates fell relative to salaries generally in the 1970s when the baby boom generation was graduating and flooding the job market. The starting salaries of college graduates are rising today relative to salaries generally as the first members of the small baby bust generation are now graduating and entering the job market.

Similarly, U.S. financial markets are responsive to the rates of return available on various financial securities. If the interest rate on government bonds rises slightly relative to the return available on common stocks, money tends to pour out of the stock market and into the government bond market. Also, the average level of interest rates in the financial markets rises and falls with the amount of money that the Federal Reserve makes available in the economy. The free flow of resources among markets and flexible prices that respond to market conditions are the hallmarks of competitive markets.

The point is that modeling the overall economy as if it were competitive and governed by the Laws of Supply and Demand ought to be a good approximation of reality if the majority of the nation's individual product and factor markets are highly competitive.

PREDICTIONS OF THE NEW CLASSICAL MODEL   Modeling the macro economy as competitive leads to a number of predictions about the behavior of prices and quantities, some of which are highly controversial.

---

[1] R. Ehrenberg and R. Smith, *Modern Labor Economics: Theory and Public Policy*, fourth edition (New York: Harper Collins: 1991), 360.

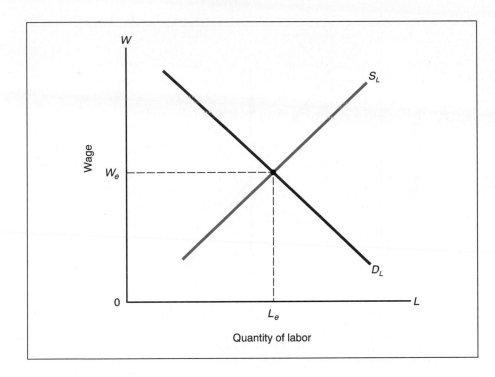

FIGURE 9.2

Full Employment in a Competitive Labor Market

A competitive labor market operates in accordance with the Laws of Supply and Demand. The supply curve S_L indicates how many people are willing to work at each wage and the demand curve D_L indicates how much labor the firms are willing to hire at each wage. The equilibrium is (L_e, W_e), at the intersection D_L and S_L. Everyone who wants to work at the wgae W_e is working, so there is full employment. Also, firms use the labor that they hire where it is most valued, so the output produced with the labor L_e is as large as possible. Therefore, if all labor (and other factor) markets were competitive, the economy would operate on its production possibilities frontier.

Perhaps the most striking prediction of the competitive new classical model is that the U.S. economy will almost always be on, or at least very near, its production possibilities frontier. This prediction follows from the assumption that factor markets are competitive. To see why, let's consider the simplest possible case in which there is only one kind of labor, and labor is the only primary factor of production. Figure 9.2 illustrates the market for labor.

D_L is the market demand curve for labor. It is the sum of the individual demand curves from all the producers in the economy. S_L is the market supply curve for labor. It is the sum of the individual supply curves from all the workers in the economy. The interaction of the market demand and the market supply curves establishes an equilibrium wage of W_e and an equilibrium quantity of labor exchanged of L_e. Each firm takes the share of L_e that it has purchased and produces the maximum amount of output that it can. Since no workers are unemployed and each firm is producing as much output as possible, the total output produced in the economy is as large as it can possibly be, given the amount of labor that the workers are willing to supply. The economy is operating on its production possibilities frontier.[2]

Figure 9.3 illustrates this result in terms of the overall markets for final goods and services. The graph is the analogue to the single-market supply and demand graph for the entire economy. The output, Q, on the horizontal axis represents the total flow of final goods and services through the nation's product markets. It is the real, or constant dollar, gross domestic product (or net domestic product), the value of the final goods and services expressed in 1987

---

[2]The conclusion remains the same if we add capital, land, and many different kinds of labor. Each firm takes the resources that it purchases in the factor markets and combines them to produce as much output as it possibly can. No resources are unemployed if the factor markets are competitive, so the economy is operating on its production possibilities frontier.

FIGURE 9.3

Aggregate Demand and Aggregate Supply in the New Classical Model

The aggregate demand curve, *AD*, indicates the total amount of output, *Q*, demanded by all final demanders in the economy at each overall price level, *P*. The aggregate supply curve, *AS*, indicates the total amount of output supplied by all producers at each overall price level. The new classical assumption that factor markets are competitive implies that *AS* is vertical at Q^*, the value of real gross domestic product (GDP) corresponding to the production possibilities frontier. Real GDP is entirely determined by the quantity and quality of a nation's resources and by the available production technologies, the same factors that determine the production possibilities frontier. The overall price level adjusts the aggregate quantity demanded to the frontier level of output. The equilibrium overall price level is P_0 at the intersection of *AD* and *AS*.

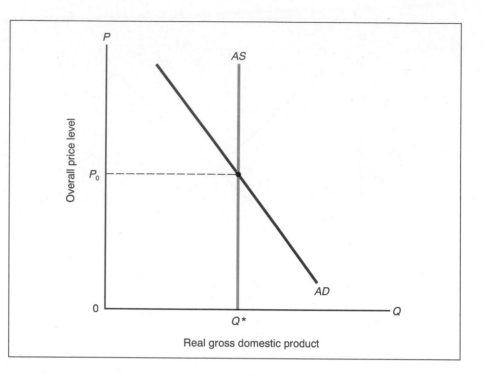

AGGREGATE DEMAND

The total quantity of final goods and services demanded at each overall price level by all the final demanders in the economy; the aggregate demand curve, labeled *AD*, is a graph of aggregate demand.

AGGREGATE SUPPLY

The total quantity of final goods and services supplied at each overall price level by all the producers in the economy; the aggregate supply curve, labeled *AS*, is a graph of aggregate supply.

prices. The price, *P*, on the vertical axis is the overall level of the prices of final goods and services as measured by a broad-based price index such as the GDP deflator. The demand and supply curves are labeled *AD* and *AS*, respectively, to indicate that they are the aggregate, or total, demand and supply curves for the economy as a whole. *AD*, **aggregate demand,** indicates the total quantity of final goods and services demanded at each overall price level by all the final demanders in the economy. *AS*, **aggregate supply,** indicates the total quantity of final goods and services supplied at each overall price level by all the producers in the economy.

We have drawn *AD* to be downward sloping in the usual manner for reasons that will be explained in Chapter 18. *AS* must be vertical as drawn, however, at the value of real gross domestic product that the firms produce with the resources they have purchased in the competitive factor markets. We are assuming that Q^* is the total amount of final goods and services that the producers supply, given the total amount of labor, L_e, made available to them (from Figure 9.2).

The vertical *AS* curve at Q^* is the one-dimensional representation of the nation's production possibilities frontier. It is the maximum amount of real or constant dollar gross domestic product that the economy can produce, given the quantity and quality of the resources supplied in the factor markets and the production technologies available to the producers. We have seen that the economy will actually produce Q^* and be on its production possibilities frontier if the factor markets are competitive.

Notice that the firms will supply Q^* once they have hired the amount of labor, L_e, no matter what the price level, *P*, is. The role of the price level is to adjust the aggregate quantity demanded to the aggregate supply of Q^*. The aggregate quantity demanded is Q^* when the price level is P_0. Therefore, the

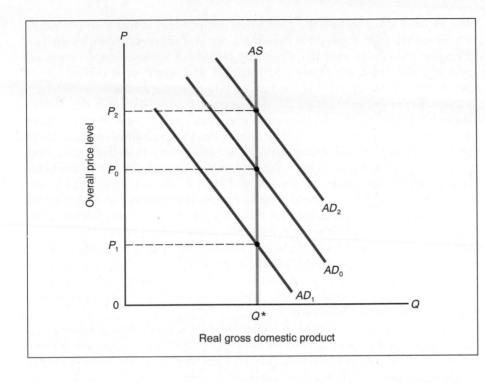

FIGURE 9.4

Changes in Aggregate Demand in the New Classical Model

In the new classical model, real gross domestic product (GDP) is the frontier level of output for all intents and purposes, Q^* in the figure, because of the assumption that factor markets are competitive. Therefore, changes in aggregate demand only affect the overall price level. A decrease in aggregate demand from AD_0 to AD_1 may briefly bring the economy below its production possibilities frontier. But the excess supplies in the product markets cause the overall price level to decrease from P_0 to P_1, which quickly brings the economy back to equilibrium on the frontier, at the intersection of AD_1 and AS. Similarly, an increase in aggregate demand from AD_0 to AD_2 causes excess demands in the product markets which increase the overall price level from P_0 to P_2. The economy quickly returns to equilibrium on the frontier, at the intersection of AD_2 and AS.

equilibrium for the competitive macro economy pictured in Figure 9.3 is an overall price level of P_0 and a real gross domestic product of Q^*.

Shifts in aggregate demand may move the economy above or below the frontier, but these situations can only be short-lived. We saw when studying the Laws of Supply and Demand that prices adjust quickly in competitive markets to restore equilibrium. Similarly, a competitive macro economy quickly returns to equilibrium on the production possibilities frontier. Figure 9.4 illustrates.

Aggregate demand is originally at AD_0, and the economy is in equilibrium at P_0 and Q^*, as in Figure 9.3. If aggregate demand should decrease to AD_1, producers can no longer sell Q^* at the price level P_0. The product markets are in excess supply at P_0, and the quantities purchased by the final demanders drop. The economy has moved below its production possibilities frontier. The situation will soon correct itself, however, because the excess supplies put downward pressure on the product prices and increase the aggregate quantity demanded. The overall price level continues to decrease until it reaches P_1, at which point equilibrium is restored on the production possibilities frontier. The quantity demanded along AD_1 equals Q^* when the overall price level is P_1.

Similarly, an increase in aggregate demand to AD_2 creates a situation of excess demands throughout the nation's product markets. This situation is also short-lived. The excess demands put upward pressure on the product prices. The overall price level continues to rise until it reaches P_2, at which point equilibrium is restored on the frontier.

The implications of the competitive new-classical model are clear: The United States should almost always be operating on, or very near, its production possibilities frontier. Therefore, real gross domestic product is determined entirely by the supply side of the economy, that is, by the quantity and quality of a nation's resources and the production technologies available to producers. These are the same factors that determine the production possibilities frontier. The new classical economists argue that periods of rising unemployment are primarily the result of increases in frictional and search or structural unemployment, that is, increases in the natural rate of unemployment.

New Keynesian economists do not agree. They believe that the United States has experienced many periods of very high cyclical unemployment when the economy is operating well below its production possibilities frontier. Moreover, the periods of high unemployment are not always short-lived. They can persist for years at a time. The U.S. economy remained in the grip of the Great Depression for the entire decade of the 1930s. Nothing so disastrous as the Great Depression has happened since. Even so, the economy remained below the production possibilities frontier for a few years during and following the recessions of the mid-1970s, the early 1980s, and the early 1990s. The problem of recurring periods of high and lasting cyclical unemployment plagues all the developed market economies. Indeed, a major weakness of capitalism as an economic system is that capitalist economies all too often waste scarce resources by allowing them to lie idle. The new Keynesian view is certainly the majority view among macro economists.

The competitive new classical model yields a second, closely related prediction that appears to be at odds with the facts: Changes in aggregate demand primarily cause changes in prices. Any changes in output caused by a change in aggregate demand are temporary and inconsequential. We saw this in Figure 9.4. The principal effect of the decrease in aggregate demand from AD_0 to AD_1 is a decrease in the overall level of prices from P_0 to P_1. Any resulting decline in output is fleeting; the economy quickly recovers to Q^* on the production possibilities frontier. Similarly, the principal effect of the increase in aggregate demand from AD_0 to AD_2 is an increase in the overall level of prices from P_0 to P_2.

Numerous studies have shown that the facts in the United States are quite different, unless the economy is operating right up against its production possibilities frontier. Changes in aggregate demand cause both prices and output to change at even modest levels of unemployment, and the changes in output persist for a very long time. The change in output is more pronounced, and longer lasting, the higher the level of unemployment.[3]

In addition, the pattern of the price and the quantity changes in response to a shift in aggregate demand is directly opposite to the pattern of the price and the quantity changes that we observe when demand shifts in a single competitive market. In individual competitive markets, prices and profits are the signals that show firms how they should change their output. Therefore, when demand shifts in a competitive market, prices and profits change first, and then firms respond by changing their output.

Figure 9.5 illustrates how prices and output respond to a shift in demand in a single competitive market. The market is initially in equilibrium at (Q_0, P_0), at the intersection of the initial demand curve, D_0, and the three supply curves shown in the graph. Suppose that demand increases suddenly to D_1.

---

[3]Of course, the new classical economists would argue that the economy is never much below its frontier. We will see in Chapter 18 that changes in aggregate demand can change aggregate output in the new classical model, but only if the change in demand leads to events that cause the frontier to move in or out as well. The links between demand and the frontier are problematic, however. In any case, the point remains that only changes in aggregate supply have any important impact on aggregate output in the new classical model.

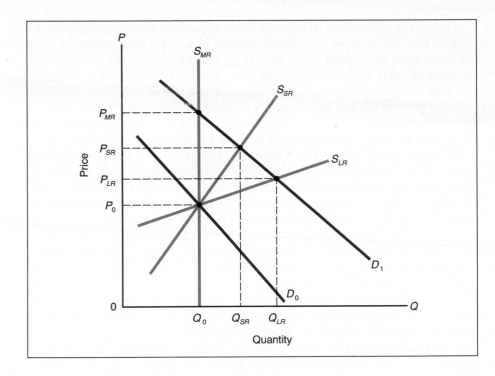

FIGURE 9.5

An Increase in Demand in a Single Competitive Market

The figure shows how a single competitive market responds over time to an increase in demand. The original equilibrium is (Q_0, P_0) at the intersection of D_0 and the three supply curves. Demand then increases from D_0 to D_1. In the momentary run, producers cannot adjust output and the vertical momentary supply curve S_{MR} applies. Price rises to P_{MR}, at the intersection of S_{MR} and D_1. As time passes, producers increase output along the short-run supply curve S_{SR}. The short-run equilibrium is (Q_{SR}, P_{SR}), at the intersection of D_1 and S_{SR}. As more time passes and the short-run becomes the long-run, the long-run supply curve S_{LR} applies. The final equilibrium is (Q_{LR}, P_{LR}), at the intersection of D_1 and S_{LR}. Over time, therefore, the increase in price moderates and the increase in output builds. This is exactly the opposite of how the macro economy responds to an increase in aggregate demand when there are unemployed resources. In such an economy the increase in the overall price level builds and the increase in real gross domestic product moderates over time.

The response to the increase in demand occurs in three stages, called the momentary run, the short run, and the long run.

The **momentary run** is the period immediately following the increase in demand. The firms are caught by surprise and have already decided to supply the quantity Q_0 to the market. They cannot change their production decisions for the moment. Therefore, the market supply curve during the momentary run, the curve labeled S_{MR} in the figure, is vertical at Q_0. The price rises sharply from P_0 to P_{MR} to restore equilibrium along the new demand curve, D_1. The firms' profits increase, since they are selling the same output as before at much higher prices.

The higher prices and profits are the signals to the firms to increase their output as soon as they can, when the momentary run becomes the short run. During the **short run** the firms can increase their output by varying some of their factors of production, but not all of their factors of production. For instance, the firms may be able to hire more labor, but they cannot build or buy new factories until more time has passed. So they respond by running second or third shifts in their existing factories. Now output increases along the short-run supply curve, labeled S_{SR}, and the market establishes a new equilibrium at (Q_{SR}, P_{SR}) for the duration of the short run. Notice that the increase in output has put downward pressure on the price, which falls from P_{MR} to P_{SR}. Nonetheless, the firms are still earning handsome profits at the price P_{SR}.

The short run gives way to the **long run** when firms can vary all their factors of production. They can now put new factories into operation, which should lower their costs of production and increase their profits even more. Also, new firms can enter the market, which they will do because the market is profitable. Now output increases along the flatter long-run supply curve, S_{LR}. In the final long-run equilibrium, output increases to Q_{LR}, and the price decreases further from P_{SR} to P_{LR}.

MOMENTARY RUN

The period immediately following a change in supply or demand when producers cannot change their output supplied to the market.

SHORT RUN

The period following a change in supply or demand over which firms can vary some of their factors of production, but not all of them.

LONG RUN

A period of time over which firms can vary all of their factors of production, and can enter or exit an industry.

In summary, an increase in demand in a competitive market causes price to increase first, followed by increases in output. Moreover, the increases in output build over time, from Q_0 to Q_{SR} to Q_{LR} in Figure 9.5. In contrast, the increases in price moderate over time, from P_{MR} to P_{SR} to P_{LR} in the figure. P_{LR} is not far above the original P_0. The same pattern of responses follows a decrease in demand, but in reverse. First prices and then profits fall, leading eventually to decreases in output. The decreases in output build over time, and the decreases in price moderate over time as the price moves back toward P_0.

The responses of price and output at the macro level to an increase in aggregate demand are exactly the opposite of the responses in Figure 9.5 when the economy is operating below its production possibilities frontier. It is as if the labels of the three supply curves were reversed. An increase in aggregate demand leads almost immediately to an increase in aggregate output, in real gross domestic product, whereas the overall price level increases very little at first. The increase in aggregate demand may not lead to a significant increase in prices for six months or more. As a general rule, prices are slower to rise the higher the initial rate of unemployment. In any event the output response precedes the price response at the macro level. Moreover, as time passes, the price increases build, and the output increases moderate. The aggregate supply curve, AS, becomes steeper, not flatter, over time.

The same pattern applies to a decrease in aggregate demand, but in reverse. Real gross domestic product decreases first, followed by decreases in the overall price level. As time passes, the price decreases build, and the decreases in real gross domestic product moderate.[4]

To summarize, the new classical competitive model does not do well in predicting how the U.S. economy responds to changes in aggregate demand. Aggregate output does change in response to changes in aggregate demand, and the changes in output can persist for a long time, perhaps five years or more. Also, the changes in aggregate output tend to precede the changes in the overall price level. These responses of output and price are directly opposite to the predictions of the competitive model.

The actual behavior of prices and output in the United States suggests that certain kinds of market imperfections have an important role to play in explaining the operation of the macro economy. The economy does not operate strictly in accordance with the Laws of Supply and Demand.

The New Keynesian Model

The new Keynesians come at the problem of explaining the ebbs and flows of the economy from the opposite direction. They believe that output responds to changes in aggregate demand because the economy is riddled with market imperfections. Market imperfections are the centerpiece of the new Keynesian model of the economy.

The great British economist John Maynard Keynes offered the first systematic challenge to the competitive model of the macro economy in the 1930s. The economies of Western Europe, Great Britain, and United States were caught in the throes of the Great Depression at the time. Unemployment in-

---

[4]For an excellent discussion of the behavior of aggregate prices and quantities in the United States, see R. Gordon, *Journal of Economic Literature* XXVIII, No. 3 (September 1990): 1115–1171.

creased to 25 percent of the labor force in the United States by 1933 and rose even higher in England. The story is that Keynes looked out his office window at the unemployed workers in the bread lines and concluded that the Laws of Supply and Demand were not operating in the British labor markets. He disagreed with the classical view that the unemployment was temporary and would disappear once wages and prices had adjusted to return the capitalist economies to their production possibilities frontier. Wages and prices fell substantially from 1929 to 1933, yet the unemployment persisted.

The events of the day led Keynes to reject the classical competitive model of the macro economy, which was essentially the only macro model of his day. He formulated an entirely new macroeconomic theory of a developed market economy which he set forth in *The General Theory of Employment, Interest, and Money*, published in 1936. Many consider Keynes's *General Theory* to be the greatest intellectual achievement in economics of the twentieth century. It introduced a completely new set of ideas about how the macro economy operates, ideas that his new Keynesian disciples believe have stood the test of time for the most part.

Keynes's theory of the macro economy came to be called Keynesian economics. The new Keynesian economists of the present day have mostly refined the basic ideas of Keynes's original theory to give them sounder theoretical underpinnings. We will consider four of Keynes's main ideas, which remain as central features of the modern-day new Keynesian model.

MAIN IDEAS OF THE NEW KEYNESIAN MODEL   *Idea 1: Wages and prices are sticky.* The most basic tenet of the new Keynesian model is that modern capitalist economies are riddled with market imperfections that cause many wages and prices to be sticky. Keynes focused on sticky wages and labor market imperfections. The new Keynesians are turning more of their attention to price stickiness and product market imperfections—why, for example, the overall price level does not respond quickly to changes in aggregate demand. They are also emphasizing imperfections in capital markets.

We discussed in Chapter 6 why wages appear to be sticky in many labor markets and why sticky wages generate a pattern of cyclical unemployment with layoffs and rehires. We will present the new Keynesian views on sticky prices and capital market imperfections in later chapters. It is enough at this point to note one of the fundamental assumptions of the new Keynesian model: Wages and prices are too sticky to serve the function of bringing the macro economy quickly to equilibrium when the economy is operating below its production possibilities frontier. In contrast to the new classical economists, the new Keynesians do not believe that wages and prices are the key variables determining the circular flow of economic activity in the short run. And the short run in macroeconomics can last for a considerable period of time, perhaps as long as five years.

What, then, is the key economic variable that drives the economy in the short run? The answer given by Keynes and his new Keynesian disciples is national income itself. In effect, the circular flow of economic activity feeds on itself. The amount of income generated today has a significant effect on the amount of income that will be generated tomorrow. Moreover, income changes with the ebbs and flows of the economy not because factor prices are changing, but because the amount of productive activity itself is changing. When aggre-

CURRENT ISSUE: Unemployment in Western Europe and Canada is higher, on average, than in the United States, and it responds less to an economic recovery. Economists are not sure why this is.

gate demand declines, firms do not immediately lower their wages and prices as the new classical competitive model suggests. Instead, firms lay off workers, vacate their factories and office buildings, and suffer a decline in profits. The income received by households declines because fewer people are working and because rental payments and profits decrease. Conversely, when aggregate demand increases, firms hire more workers, rent or build more factories and office buildings, and enjoy an increase in profits. Households have more income because the circular flow of real economic activity has increased, not because factor prices have risen.

Income affects the circular flow of economic activity through the demand side of the product markets. To see why, we need to turn to Keynes's second fundamental idea, that aggregate demand is a very important determinant of the circular flow of economic activity.

Idea 2: Aggregate demand is an important determinant of real gross domestic product. In the competitive new classical model the total output produced is completely determined by the supply side of the economy. The economy is always driven to the production possibilities frontier, so that the real gross domestic product depends on the quantity and the quality of the nation's resources and the production technologies available to the firms. The level of aggregate demand simply determines the overall price level; it has no important effect on total output.

In Keynes's view of the macro economy, the roles of aggregate supply and aggregate demand are essentially reversed. He argued that the total output in the economy was primarily determined by the level of aggregate demand, at least in the short run. The reason why turns on the fact that wages and prices are sticky.

Once firms choose to set their prices and wages, they essentially become passive actors in the economy and simply react to the demand for their products. The idea is that firms guess what the demand for their products will be and produce the output required to meet that demand. Should they happen to guess wrong the first time, they guess again and adjust their production accordingly. They keep adjusting production until their output just matches the actual demand for their products.

According to this view, the circular flow of economic activity is primarily determined by the level of aggregate demand. Aggregate supply passively adjusts to whatever the level of aggregate demand happens to be. If aggregate demand increases, firms hire more resources and increase production to meet the increase in demand. If aggregate demand decreases, firms lay off resources and reduce production to match the lower level of demand. Therefore, the level of real gross domestic output is primarily determined by the level of aggregate demand in the short run when wages and prices are sticky.

Notice that the Keynesian story is consistent with the fact that when aggregate demand changes, output changes first before price does. The firms' first reaction to a change in the demand for their products is to change their level of production. The firms may eventually change their prices, but the price changes come later.

We said earlier in the chapter that the first relationship in any macro model is the statement of equilibrium in the market for final goods and services:

$$Y = C^d + I^d + G^d + (Ex^d - Im^d)$$

The next step in building the new Keynesian model of the economy is to specify what factors determine the individual components of aggregate demand. According to the new Keynesian perspective, the better we understand what determines the components of aggregate demand, the better we will understand the performance of the macro economy in the short run. Therefore, all Keynesian macro models feature six key relationships: the statement of equilibrium plus five additional relationships that explain the determinants of aggregate demand, one each for consumption demand (C^d), investment demand (I^d), government demand for goods and services (G^d), export demand (Ex^d), and import demand (Im^d). The basic idea behind the new Keynesian model is that national income (or national product), Y, adjusts to meet the level of aggregate demand, $C^d + I^d + G^d + (Ex^d - Im^d)$.

A model of this form could be very simple. For instance, one factor that determines the government's demand for goods and services, G^d, is whether or not the country is fighting a war. Suppose that a war does break out and the government's demand for military weapons increases by $10 billion. According to the Keynesian view of the economy, the weapons manufacturers will increase their production by $10 billion to meet the increase in demand. The result is that national product and national income increase by $10 billion. A $10 billion increase in aggregate demand leads to a $10 billion increase in national income—very simple.

Unfortunately, the reaction of the economy to an increase in aggregate demand is not quite that simple because the level of national income is itself one of the more important determinants of aggregate demand. As a result, the circular flow of economic activity feeds on itself. A change in aggregate demand leads to a change in national income, which leads to a further change in aggregate demand, which leads to yet another change in national income, and so on, indefinitely.

Income is an important determinant of aggregate demand primarily because consumption demand is closely related to the level of national income, and consumption is the most important component of aggregate demand. An increase in national income leads to an increase in households' disposable income. The more disposable income households have, the more consumer goods they will want to buy. Conversely, a decrease in national income leads to a decrease in households' disposable income and a decrease in their consumption demand.

Let's return to our example of the $10 billion increase in the government's demand for weapons, keeping in mind the relationship between consumption demand and national income. As before, the weapons manufacturers increase their production by $10 billion, and national income increases by $10 billion. The $10 billion increase in national income is received by a large number of people: employees of the weapons manufacturers, employees of the firms that supply materials to the weapons manufacturers, stockholders of these firms, and so forth. The people who receive the additional income will spend some of it, not on weapons, of course, but on consumer goods and services—food, clothing, cars, medical care, movies, and the like. The producers of these consumer goods and services will increase their production to meet this new demand, so that national product and national income increase once again. But the increase in national income causes a further increase in consumption demand, which leads to yet another increase in national product and income, and so on, indefinitely. The $10 billion increase in the government's demand for weapons ultimately generates much more than a $10 billion increase in national income and national product.

Keynes argued that the process of national income feeding back on itself through aggregate demand is a dominant feature of the economy in the short run. In his view, income is much more important than are prices in explaining the short-term performance of the economy. And, remember, the short run can last for a considerable period of time. Understanding how national income affects each component of aggregate demand is obviously very important from a Keynesian perspective, since the relationship between national income and aggregate demand determines the nature of the feedback mechanism.

The final two ideas of Keynes that we want to consider relate directly to the question of economic policy. Keynes's macroeconomic theories gave birth to the notion that the government had an important role to play in improving the overall performance of the economy.

Idea 3: Left to its own devices, the macroeconomic performance of the economy may not be very desirable. An economy with highly competitive markets governed by the Laws of Supply and Demand, in which wages and prices are the key economic variables determining the circular flow of economic activity, is a highly desirable economy. Prices automatically drive the economy to its production possibilities frontier, so that society derives the maximum possible output from its scarce resources.

In contrast, an economy with sticky wages and prices—in which the circular flow of economic activity is driven by the level of aggregate demand, and national income itself is one of the more important variables determining the level of aggregate demand—can perform very poorly. Aggregate demand may lead the economy to a position well below its production possibilities frontier, with high levels of involuntary cyclical unemployment. Or aggregate demand may try to bring the economy beyond its production possibilities and fuel a serious inflationary process. Moreover, the economy can remain off its production possibilities frontier for a long time. Wages and prices are the variables that adjust to drive the economy to its frontier. If wages and prices are sticky, they cannot perform this task very well, and no other economic variables can take their place. Aggregate demand does not tend to return to the production possibilities frontier when it is driven by the overall level of economic activity instead of by prices.

The classical economists of the 1930s viewed the Great Depression as a temporary aberration that would quickly correct itself once wages and prices did their work. Keynes argued otherwise. He believed that the Great Depression would continue on for years unless governments acted to increase the level of aggregate demand. His fourth novel idea was that government policies could substantially improve the performance of the economy in the short run.

Idea 4: The government's fiscal and monetary policies can help achieve the macroeconomic policy goals. Keynes saw that fiscal and monetary policies can affect the performance of the economy because they change the level (and the composition) of aggregate demand. Fiscal policies involve changes in government spending on goods and services, or transfer payments, or taxes. Changes in government spending on goods and services have a direct effect on aggregate demand because they are part of aggregate demand. Changes in transfer payments and taxes affect aggregate demand indirectly by influencing the levels of consumption demand and investment demand. Monetary policy involves changes in the nation's money supply. It also affects aggregate demand indirectly by influencing the levels of consumption demand and investment demand.

The government's ability to manage the level of aggregate demand through its fiscal and monetary policies is very important in an economy with sticky wages and prices because aggregate demand affects the level of output. Keynes was among the first economists to appreciate the usefulness of fiscal and monetary policies. He argued that governments could lead their economies out of the Great Depression by using fiscal policies to increase the level of aggregate demand. Producers would respond to the increase in aggregate demand by hiring more resources and increasing production. Unemployment would fall, and the economies would move closer to their production possibilities frontier. The classical economists of his day missed this possibility because their competitive view of the macro economy led them to believe that aggregate demand had essentially no effect on the level of output. As we have seen, the competitive macro model suggests that an increase in aggregate demand increases only prices, not output.

Keynes was primarily interested in the question of how fiscal and monetary policies could be used to reduce unemployment because unemployment was the pressing issue of his day. In fact, the level (and the composition) of aggregate demand has a direct effect on all four macroeconomic policy goals. A primary objective in our study of macroeconomics is to understand how the government's fiscal and monetary policies relate to all four of the macroeconomic policy goals.

LIMITATIONS OF THE NEW KEYNESIAN MODEL   Keynes's views on the ability of fiscal and monetary policies to improve the performance of the economy were widely embraced by economists and policy makers. All of the highly developed capitalist nations try to manage their economies with fiscal and monetary policies. This does not mean that Keynes and his new Keynesian followers have completely won the day in macroeconomics, however. Far from it. The modern new Keynesian model remains a highly simplified model of the macro model, and, as such, it has its strengths and weaknesses. The competitive new classical macro model is better suited for many purposes.

We have argued that the Keynesian model outperforms the new classical model in explaining how the economy reacts in the short run to changes in aggregate demand. This is a considerable advantage because fiscal and monetary policies affect the economy by changing aggregate demand. The economy is often hit with other kinds of "shocks" to aggregate demand as well, such as a sudden burst of investment demand or a large decrease in defense spending. The Keynesian model has been very useful in explaining how the economy reacts to these demand-side events.

But the economy is also hit with shocks to aggregate supply, and in these cases the competitive new classical model may well have the advantage. An **aggregate supply shock** is any event that directly affects either firms' costs of production or their ability to supply output to the market. Common examples of cost-changing supply shocks are cost-reducing technological change, such as the introduction of robotics into the automobile assembly line, and changes in the prices of key inputs. The eightfold increase in oil prices engineered by the Organization of Petroleum Exporting Countries (OPEC) during

AGGREGATE DEMAND SHOCK

Any event that directly affects the total demand for goods and services at each overall price level.

AGGREGATE SUPPLY SHOCK

Any event that directly affects producers' costs of production or the quantity that they can supply to the market.

FIGURE 9.6

Aggregate Supply Shocks

The figure shows how the macro economy responds to aggregate supply shocks. The initial equilibrium is (Q^*, P_0), at the intersection of the aggregate demand and aggregate supply curves AD and AS_0. An adverse aggregate supply shock, such as an increase in oil prices or a severe drought, shifts the aggregate supply curve to the left, from AS_0 to AS_1. The new equilibrium is (Q_1, P_1), at the intersection of AD and AS_1. An adverse aggregate supply shock reduces real gross domestic product (GDP) and increases the overall price level. Conversely, a favorable aggregate supply shock, such as cost reducing technological change or exceptionally good weather for farming, shifts the aggregate supply curve to the right, from AS_0 to AS_2. The new equilibrium is (Q_2, P_2), at the intersection of AD and AS_2. A favorable aggregate supply shock increases real gross domestic product (GDP) and decreases the overall price level.

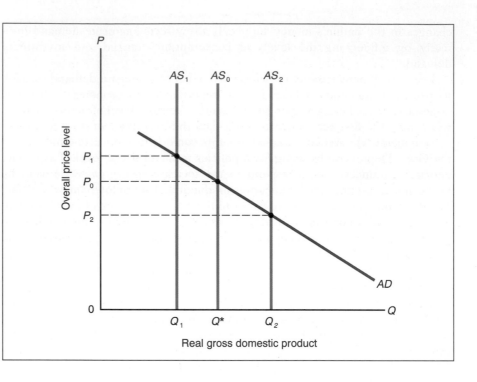

the 1970s was an enormously adverse supply shock to the U.S. economy. Conversely, the steep decline in oil prices in the early 1980s following the demise of OPEC's market power was a very favorable supply shock to the U.S. economy. Examples of output-changing supply shocks are a serious drought that affects crops and widespread strikes by labor unions that bring industries to a halt.

Cost-changing aggregate supply shocks are more important in the United States. Moreover, U.S. producers tend to pass cost changes through to the prices of their products very quickly, which is exactly what happens in competitive markets. Shifts up or down in the market supply curve quickly raise or lower the equilibrium price, respectively. This suggests that the competitive new classical macro model, with its flexible prices, is a good model for analyzing the effects of aggregate supply shocks. It is certainly better than the new Keynesian model, which is based on the assumption of sticky, sluggish price responses to market events.

Figure 9.6 illustrates the effects of aggregate supply shocks, using the competitive new classical model. Assume that the economy is originally in equilibrium at (Q^*, P_0), on its production possibilities frontier at the intersection of AD and AS_0, as in Figure 9.3.

An adverse supply shock, such as an oil price increase, shifts the aggregate supply to the left, from AS_0 to AS_1. The equilibrium quantity falls to Q_1, and the equilibrium price rises to P_1. An adverse supply shock is terrible for the economy. It simultaneously increases prices and lowers output, and it reduces the economy's production possibilities.

A favorable supply shock, such as productivity-enhancing technological change, shifts the aggregate supply to the right, from AS_0 to AS_2. The equilibrium quantity rises to Q_2, and the equilibrium price falls to P_2. A favorable supply shock is a blessing for the economy. It simultaneously lowers prices and increases output, and it increases the economy's production possibilities.

The effects pictured in Figure 9.6 are an accurate representation of how the U.S. economy actually responds to adverse and favorable supply shocks, even when the economy is operating below its production possibilities frontier. Prices and output respond quickly to supply shocks, as if the economy were highly competitive. The new classical model performs well in this instance.

New classical economists claim that aggregate supply shocks such as technological change affect the U.S. more often, and more substantially, than do aggregate demand shocks. This claim is controversial, but if it is correct, it is a strong argument in favor of using the new classical model to analyze the U.S. economy.

Another limitation of the new Keynesian model is a practical one. The potential to manage the economy in the short run with fiscal and monetary policies is quite different from the reality. Both fiscal and monetary policies take time to formulate and to work their way through the economy. As a result, knowing when to apply the policies can be a nasty problem. Also, fiscal and monetary policies are difficult, if not impossible, to coordinate because the Fed is independent of the Congress and the administration. We will see that the government is unlikely to be able to manage the economy very tightly in the short run.

The Long Run: Areas of Agreement

The competitive new classical model is an excellent model for analyzing long-run macroeconomic issues such as predicting the economic effects resulting from the aging of the U.S. population over the next 50 years, or describing the cumulative effects of the slowdown in productivity growth in the United States that began in 1973, or understanding how to control inflation. Most new Keynesian economists concede that wages and prices are reasonably flexible in the long run, so that the macro economy appears to be ever more competitive with the passage of time. Furthermore, long-run economic growth, the ability of the economy to push out its production possibilities frontier, dominates the economic landscape over the long haul. We saw in Chapter 3 that long-run economic growth requires increases in the quantity and the quality of a nation's resources and the development of new production technologies. These are all supply-side phenomena. Aggregate demand may pull the economy below its production possibilities frontier on occasion, but this is not very important when analyzing long-run issues. The actual growth in output over 25 or 50 years should be very close to the growth in potential output. Therefore, nothing much is lost by adopting the new classical assumptions that the economy is competitive and that it operates on its production possibilities frontier. In fact, economists almost always assume that the macro economy is competitive when analyzing long-run macroeconomic issues.

Consequently, the policy prescriptions of new classical and new Keynesian economists are often identical when they are addressing ways to promote long-run economic growth, or to keep a moderate inflation from gaining momentum and building to a runaway hyperinflation, or when analyzing the economic consequences of running large federal budget deficits year after year. The primary differences between them center on the short run.

WHERE TO BEGIN

We will begin our analysis of the macro economy from the new Keynesian perspective. Our first goals are to understand how the economy responds to changes in aggregate demand in the short run and how fiscal and monetary policies affect the level of aggregate demand. The new Keynesian model is the better model for these purposes.

To keep the analysis as simple as possible, we will assume that wages and prices are fixed rather than just sticky, so that any changes in national income or national product are changes in real income or output. We will also assume that the economy is operating well below its production possibilities frontier so that real income or output can both increase and decrease.

Our simple new Keynesian model will give us some important insights about how the performance of the economy affects three of the four macroeconomic policy goals: full employment, long-run economic growth, and the balance of trade and the dollar exchange rate. It is not useful for analyzing the problem of inflation.

Beginning with the new Keynesian model has an additional advantage. As noted in the introduction, new Keynesian thinking has swept into Washington following the Clinton election victory. All three members of Clinton's Council of Economic Advisers—Chairwoman Laura Tyson, Alan Blinder, and Joseph Stiglitz—received their graduate training at MIT, one of the centers of new Keynesian economics in the United States. Each one has made important contributions to the development of the new Keynesian perspective. The concepts that you will learn in the next few chapters are guiding the formulation of macroeconomic policy in Washington these days.

SUMMARY

Chapter 9 began with an overview of the three fundamental questions in macroeconomics.

1. The three fundamental questions are as follows:
   a. What determines the circular flow of economic activity?
   b. How do the level and the composition of the circular flow relate to the four macroeconomic policy goals of long-run economic growth, full employment, price stability, and stability in economic relations with foreign nations?
   c. How can the government help achieve the macroeconomic policy goals through its fiscal and monetary policies, which influence the level and the composition of the circular flow?
2. In all the developed market economies, the circular flow of economic activity moves through a pattern of booms and recessions over time called the business cycle. The periods of boom and recession vary both in intensity and in duration.
3. Fiscal policy is budgetary policy. It involves changes in government expenditures on goods and services, or transfer payments, or taxes to influence the level and the composition of the circular flow. Fiscal policy is the responsibility of the administration and the Congress.
4. Monetary policy involves changes in the money supply intended to influence the level and the composition of the circular flow. Monetary policy

is the responsibility of the Board of Governors of the Federal Reserve, the nation's central bank.

5. The conduct of macroeconomic policy can be thought of as an attempt to solve the three-part economic problem for the entire economy. The objectives are the four macroeconomic policy goals. The alternatives are fiscal and monetary policies. The constraint is the economy itself, which determines how the macroeconomic policies relate to the policy goals and the extent to which the four policy goals are compatible with one another.

Chapter 9 then turned to the problem of how to build a macroeconomic model of a highly developed market economy such as the U.S. economy. The second section of the chapter discussed the need for a macroeconomic model and the limitations of any such model.

6. A macroeconomic model of a highly developed market economy must be extremely simple relative to the economy it is trying to explain. It cannot hope to describe and predict every aspect of the economy. At best, a macro model will have both strengths and weaknesses. It will be useful for explaining and predicting some events and not so useful for explaining and predicting other events.

7. Even the largest mathematical forecasting models used by private firms and government agencies fail to capture many important details of the U.S. economy.

8. The primary goal of any macroeconomic model is to explain the forces that determine the circular flow of economic activity. As such, the first relationship or equation in all macro models is a representation of the circular flow through the product markets:

$$Y = C^d + I^d + G^d + (Ex^d - Im^d)$$

Y is national income and the terms on the right-hand side are the demands by each sector of the economy: household (C^d), business (I^d), government (G^d), and foreign ($Ex^d - Im^d$). The relationship describes the supply and the demand sides of the product markets. Firms generate the national income as they supply the final goods and services, the national product, which is equal in value to the national income. The right-hand side is the aggregate demand for the final goods and services.

9. Macro economists sharply disagree about how to complete the model. At least five different macro models appear in the professional literature. The models differ in the emphasis they give to the two sides of the product markets and in the variables they consider important in determining the supply and the demand of final goods and services.

The third section of the chapter contrasted and compared the two leading macroeconomic models of the day, the new classical model and the new Keynesian model.

10. The new classical economists have returned to the view of the classical economists of the late 1800s and early 1900s, that the macro economy is best modeled as if it is highly competitive and operates in accordance with the Laws of Supply and Demand. The model has a number of very strong implications:

a. Factor markets are highly competitive and automatically bring the economy to equilibrium on, or very near, its production possibilities frontier.

They do this without any significant amount of unemployed resources. Wages and prices are highly flexible.

b. Real gross domestic product is determined entirely by the supply side of the economy. The factors determining output are the quantity and the quality of the resources supplied in the factor markets and the production technologies available to producers. These are the same factors that determine the production possibilities frontier.

c. Changes in aggregate demand affect prices, but not output. Any change in output in response to a change in aggregate demand is temporary and of no consequence. Wages and prices soon adjust to return the economy to the production possibilities frontier.

d. Frequent doses of fiscal and monetary policies are uncalled for since the economy performs well enough on its own. Governments policies should be steady and predictable so that households and business firms can better plan their economic affairs.

11. Some of the predictions of the new classical model appear to be wide of the mark. Most economists would say that capitalist economies often operate below their production possibilities frontiers, with high levels of cyclical unemployment. Also, when economies are below their frontiers, changes in aggregate demand cause changes in output that can last for a number of years. Moreover, output responds first and then price to a change in aggregate demand. This is exactly the opposite of what happens in a single competitive market when demand changes.

12. The new Keynesian economists are disciples of John Maynard Keynes, who developed a completely different theory of how the macro economy operates. Keynes's thinking was motivated by the Great Depression, when unemployment in England exceeded 25 percent.

13. The chapter highlighted four of Keynes's main ideas.

a. The economy is riddled with imperfections that cause wages and prices to be sticky and prevent them from performing the function of returning the economy quickly to equilibrium on the production possibilities frontier. In the short run, which can last for many years, national income itself is a more important determinant of the circular flow than are wages and prices.

b. With wages and prices sticky, the supply side of the product markets becomes passive and simply reacts to changes in demand. If aggregate demand increases, producers hire more resources and increase their production. If aggregate demand decreases, producers lay off resources and decrease their production. Aggregate demand drives the economy in the short run, and income itself is one of the key determinants of aggregate demand. The economy feeds back on itself. An increase in aggregate demand increases production and national income, which leads to further increases in aggregate demand, and so on.

c. Aggregate demand may not lead the economy to a very desirable level of income. It may drive the economy well below its production possibilities at times and cause high levels of cyclical unemployment; at other times aggregate demand may try to bring the economy beyond its frontier and fuel an inflationary process. With wages and prices sticky, there is no mechanism to return the economy quickly to the frontier.

d. Fiscal and monetary policies change the level of aggregate demand. Since changes in aggregate demand affect output, frequent doses of fiscal and monetary policies can improve the performance of the economy. Keynes argued that governments should use fiscal policies to increase aggregate demand and lead the market economies out of the Great Depression.

14. The new Keynesian model appears to outperform the new classical model in explaining how the economy reacts to changes in aggregate demand in the short run. The new classical model has its own advantages, however. It does a better job of explaining how the economy reacts to aggregate supply shocks. An aggregate supply shock is anything that directly affects the costs of production or the ability to supply output to the market, such as technological change, or an increase in the price of an important input such as oil, or a drought. Supply shocks quickly affect both price and output at the macro level, exactly as one would expect if markets were highly competitive.

15. The disagreements between the two schools center on the short run. New Keynesians agree that the new classical model is appropriate for analyzing long-run macroeconomic issues, such as long-run economic growth, the need to keep inflation under control, and the dangers of running large federal budget deficits.

KEY TERMS

aggregate demand
aggregate demand shock
aggregate supply
aggregate supply shock

business cycle
Federal Reserve Banking System
fiscal policy
long run

macroeconomic policy
momentary run
monetary policy
short run

QUESTIONS

1. What is fiscal policy, and who is responsible for the conduct of fiscal policy in the United States?

2. What is monetary policy, and who is responsible for the conduct of monetary policy in the United States?

3. Why do economists need to build a model of the macro economy to think about how the economy operates?

4. What assumptions of the new classical model of the economy led to the conclusion that the economy always operates on or near the production possibilities frontier?

5. a. How do price and output respond to an increase in demand in a single market that operates according to the Laws of Supply and Demand? Consider the responses of price and output in the momentary run, the short run, and the long run.

   b. Is this the way that the overall price level and the national product respond to an increase in aggregate demand in the U.S. economy? If not, what are the differences between the macro responses and the single-market responses?

6. New Keynesian economists believe that wages and prices are sticky. How does this belief lead them to conclude that

aggregate demand determines national product (income) in the short run? What are some other important assumptions of the new Keynesian model?

7. a. Under what conditions, or for what events, does the new Keynesian model appear to be the better model for explaining the performance of the macro economy?

   b. Under what conditions, or for what events, does the new classical model appear to be the better model for explaining the performance of the macro economy?

8. Describe the different roles that aggregate demand and aggregate supply play in the new classical and the new Keynesian models of the economy.

9. Compare and contrast the new classical and the new Keynesian models in terms of their policy recommendations for achieving (a) the macroeconomic policy goal of full employment and (b) the macroeconomic policy goal of robust long-run economic growth.

10. Describe the macroeconomic policy problem in terms of the three-part economic problem consisting of objectives, alternatives, and constraints.

CASE

An International Comparison of Unemployment Rates*

H ow have unemployment rates in the United States compared with unemployment rates in the other industrialized market economies over the past twenty-five to thirty years? Table CS 2.1 lists the unemployment rates in the United States, Canada, Japan, Germany (formerly West Germany), France, Italy, and the United Kingdom for the years 1965–92. These countries are the seven industrial countries of the world with the highest per capita incomes. They are often referred to as the G7 (Group of Seven) countries. The table presents data on average annual unemployment rates over four subperiods: 1965–73; 1974–82; 1983–1989; and 1990–92. The period from 1974 to 1982 contained two large OPEC-induced oil price increases, one in late 1973 and the other in 1979, that threw most of the G7 countries into recessions in 1974 and again in 1981. The period from 1983–89 was generally a period of steady recovery and economic growth from the deep recession of 1981–82. The recovery lasted until 1990, when most of the G7 countries again experienced recessions followed, at best, by slow recoveries.

Comparing unemployment rates over a long period of time gives us a sense of the differences in the natural rates of unemployment among the G7 countries. Since the booms and recessions in these economies tend to move together, any large differences in average unemployment rates, or in the long-run trends in the unemployment rates, are likely to reflect differences in the underlying natural rates.

A number of facts stand out from the table.

*Provided by Manfred W. Keil, Northeastern University.

■ Japan is in a class by itself. It alone has experienced only a slight upward trend in unemployment since 1965, and its average unemployment rate over the entire period is much lower than that of any other G7 country. The United States and Canada have never had such low rates of unemployment since 1965.
■ European unemployment rates were somewhat comparable to Japan's until the first OPEC-induced oil price increase in 1973–74. Since then unemployment in Europe has exhibited a definite upward trend that economists refer to as Eurosclerosis. Notice that the period of recovery and growth from 1983 to 1989 did not push the European unemployment rates down, as it did in the United States. West Germany's upward trend was interrupted by the fall of the Berlin Wall and the subsequent unification of Germany, but the German unemployment rate has jumped sharply again above 8 percent in 1993.
■ The average rates of unemployment in the United States and Canada were approximately equal during the first two periods, after which a substantial gap has opened between the two countries.

What can account for these differences in the long-run behavior of unemployment rates among the G7 countries? One possible explanation is differences in the countries' unemployment insurance benefits. This is one likely reason why the Canadian unemployment rate has become so much higher than the U.S. rate. Canada's labor market looks remarkably similar to that of the U.S. as far as the composition of the labor force is concerned. There is more unionization in Canada, but the unions are concentrated in the public sector. The two countries also had similar unemployment

TABLE CS 2.1   Average Annual Unemployment Rates in the G7 Countries, 1965–1992 (percent)

United States	4.5	7.2	6.9	6.5
Canada	4.8	7.7	9.6	9.9
Japan	1.3	2.0	2.7	2.1
Germany	0.7	3.4	6.7	4.7
France	2.4	5.6	10.0	9.6
Italy	3.5	4.2	7.0	6.9
United Kingdom	3.2	6.7	10.3	8.5

SOURCE: Council of Economic Advisors, *Economic Report of the President 1993* (Washington, D.C.: U.S. Government Printing Office, 1993), Table B-106, p. 469. The 1992 unemployment data are through the third quarter of the year.

An International Comparison of Unemployment Rates (cont.)

insurance systems until 1971, when Canada considerably liberalized its program. The Canadian government raised the monthly unemployment benefits well above U.S. levels, and sharply reduced the time that people had to be previously employed to collect the benefits. The only puzzle is why the Canadian unemployment rate did not rise above the U.S. rate until 1976 (Canada's unemployment rate has been higher than the U.S. rate in every year since 1976, with the single exception of 1981, when it was .1 percent lower). The answer appears to lie in the fact that Canada is a raw material exporting country. Unlike the United States, Canada benefited from the two OPEC-induced oil price shocks of the 1970s. This same factor is now working against Canada, however, following the collapse of oil prices in the 1980s. Canada's more liberal unemployment insurance system and its heavier reliance on raw material exports may well be the principal reasons why Canada's unemployment rate has been two and three percentage points above the U.S. rate since 1983.

Unemployment benefits are also generally far more liberal in Europe than in the United States. The standard duration of unemployment benefits in the United States is 26 weeks, with occasional extensions to 39 and even 52 weeks in times of recession. In contrast, France pays unemployment benefits for almost 4 years, and Germany and the U.K. have no effective time limit on the duration of unemployment benefits. This may also explain another feature of European unemployment lying behind the data in the table. The European countries have been plagued by a very high percentage of long-term unemployment, people who have been unemployed for over a year. In 1988, the long-term unemployed accounted for only 7 percent of the total unemployed in Canada and the United States. The corresponding percentages in the European countries that year were: Germany, 47 percent; France, 45 percent; Italy, 69 percent; and the U.K., 45 percent. People who are unemployed for a long time tend to lose some of their skills, which makes them less likely to find employment. As a result, the Europeans experience an unemployment phenomenon called hysteresis, in which the unemployment rate does not return to the previous natural rate of unemployment once it rises above the natural rate. Instead, a period of high unemployment increases the underlying natural rate. We can see this phenomenon clearly in the period from 1983 to 1989, when the economic recovery in Europe did not reverse the upward trend in unemployment there.

How can we explain Japan's exceedingly low unemployment rates since 1965? The answer here may be that attitudes and institutions can have a substantial effect on unemployment. Japan is considered a corporatist economy (Germany was, too, until 1979). This term means that the unions, the employers, and the government work together to set national wage levels for each sector of the economy. National wage bargaining takes aggregate unemployment levels into account, which makes wages more responsive to cyclical situations. As a result, a corporatist economy such as Japan avoids large increases in unemployment following adverse aggregate demand or supply shocks to the economy.

ECONOMIC ADVISOR'S REPORT

Suppose that President Clinton hires you to advise him on unemployment insurance.

1. Explain to the president why most economists believe that increases in unemployment insurance benefits increase the natural rate of unemployment.
2. Suppose the economists are correct. Would you advise President Clinton to scrap the unemployment insurance program, or at least sharply curtail the monthly benefits (either their amount, or the duration for which unemployment benefits are paid, or both)?

National Income
Determination, Fiscal Policy,
and Unemployment

10

National Income Determination

LEARNING OBJECTIVES

CONCEPTS TO LEARN

Consumption function

Saving function

Marginal propensity to consume

Marginal propensity to save

Life-Cycle Hypothesis

Investment demand

Cost of capital

Equilibrium level of national income

The saving = investment equilibrium

CONCEPTS TO RECALL

The circular flow of economic activity [4]

New Keynesian economics [9]

Aggregate demand and aggregate supply [9]

The final decade of the twentieth century has gotten off to a disappointing start in the United States, economically speaking. The United States experienced a mild recession in 1990, which was then followed by a barely perceptible recovery. The recovery was so weak that the growth in output was not enough to lower unemployment throughout 1992 and the first half of 1993.

Economists all the while were bemoaning the lack of consumer confidence. Household surveys showed that people were not very confident about the future, and their lack of confidence made them hesitant to increase their spending. Economists knew that the economy could not pick up until consumers started spending because, as we saw in Chapter 8, consumption is almost two-thirds of GDP.

Investment was just as sluggish as consumption in the early 1990s. With consumers not spending, firms had little need to expand their production capacities. The low level of investment also bodes ill for the future because we know that investment is the key to long-run economic growth.

Consumption and investment hold center stage as we take our first look at the operation of the macro economy. They are the linchpins of macroeconomic analysis.

Chapter 10 analyzes the effects of aggregate demand on the circular flow of economic activity from the new Keynesian perspective. The analysis assumes that the economy is operating well below its production possibilities frontier, with lots of unemployed resources, so that changes in aggregate demand affect the real level of economic activity and not just the overall price level. Also, our focus is on the short run, when changes in real output and income are more important than are changes in prices. Therefore, we begin the analysis of the macro economy with a simplified version of the new Keynesian model in which wages and prices are not just sticky, but fixed.

Chapter 10 has one main goal: to explain how the economy operates when aggregate demand is the driving force behind the circular flow of economic activity. Government policy will come later. You must understand the operation of the economy before you can think about how the federal government might influence the economy through its fiscal and monetary policies. Therefore, the chapter develops the simplest possible macro model that can illustrate the operation of the macro economy.

THE SIMPLEST MACRO MODEL

A macro model must contain the household sector and the business sector at a bare minimum to illustrate how a market economy functions. The government and the foreign sectors can be added later; they do not change the fundamental principles relating to how the economy operates.

In the simplest possible economy the business sector hires all the primary factors of production supplied by the households and produces all the final goods and services supplied to the product markets. The two sources of demand for the final goods and services in the product markets are consumption by the household sector and investment by the business sector. Therefore, the statement of product market equilibrium for this economy is

$$Y = C^d + I^d$$

Recall that the left-hand side of the equation represents the supply side of the product markets. Y is the level of national income generated by the business firms in the process of producing the goods and the services that they supply to the product markets. The value of all the goods and the services supplied to the product markets, the national product, is equal to the value of the national income generated in production by virtue of the circular flow of economic activity. The right-hand side of the equation represents the demand side of the product markets, the sum of consumption demand by the households (C^d) and investment demand by the business firms (I^d). The product markets are in equilibrium when the aggregate supply of the final goods and services, Y, equals the aggregate demand for the final goods and services, $C^d + I^d$.[1]

Here are some points of review from earlier chapters to keep in mind as we build the simplest new Keynesian model.

Active Demand and Passive Supply

A major tenet of the new Keynesian perspective is that aggregate demand is the driving force that determines the circular flow of economic activity. Supply reacts passively to demand. Business firms set their wages and prices and then base their production decisions on their best guesses about what the demands for their products will be. The firms then adjust their production until the amount of goods and services supplied just equals the amount demanded. Therefore, the key to understanding the operation of the economy lies in understanding the factors that determine the level of aggregate demand, both consumption demand by the households and investment demand by the business firms. The aggregate supply of goods and services follows wherever aggregate demand happens to lead it. The second and third sections of the chapter describe the various factors that determine consumption demand and investment demand.

National Income and Aggregate Demand

A particularly important issue is how consumption demand and investment demand are themselves related to the level of national income or product.

---

[1]Gross domestic product (GDP), or national product, and national income are not quite equal. They differ by the sum of indirect business taxes and the capital consumption allowance on the stock of capital in the actual U.S. economy. Nonetheless, we can safely ignore these differences. In the first place, the simplest economy has no indirect business taxes because it has no government sector. In addition, the capital consumption allowance is an estimate of the depreciation of the *entire* stock of capital, most of which was put into place in previous years. As a result, the estimate of the capital consumption allowance by the Bureau of Economic Analysis (BEA) is essentially a constant that does not vary with the level of economic activity. Therefore, we can disregard it in distinguishing between GDP and national income. In fact, the text will ignore indirect business taxes even after we add the government sector, so that GDP (or national product) and national income will always be used interchangeably to refer to the circular flow of economic activity.

Also, Y is usually referred to as national income rather than as national product in macroeconomic analysis, a convention we will adopt in this text.

Chapter 9 described the dual relationship between aggregate demand and national income in which aggregate demand determines the level of national income and the level of national income in part determines aggregate demand. This dual relationship creates a feedback mechanism that magnifies the effects of changes in aggregate demand on the economy. The fourth section of the chapter puts consumption demand and investment demand together and shows how aggregate demand determines the equilibrium level of national income.

Saving, Investment, and Equilibrium

The final section of Chapter 10 develops an alternative and very useful way of describing the macro equilibrium, through saving and investment. We learned in Chapter 8 that if national income equals national product, then the total saving in the economy must equal the level of investment by business firms. Therefore, the circular flow of economic activity is in equilibrium when the amount that savers want to save is equal to the amount that producers want to invest.

Real Versus Nominal Values

Chapter 8 distinguished between the real, constant dollar, and nominal, current dollar values of macroeconomic variables. Macroeconomic theory attempts to explain the real, constant dollar value of the circular flow of economic activity and its various components. Since we are assuming that prices and wages are fixed, the nominal, current dollar value and the real, constant dollar value of the circular flow of economic activity are one and the same. Therefore, the values of all the economic variables—consumption, investment, national income, and so forth—are understood to be their real, constant dollar values, as required by the theory.

CONSUMPTION DEMAND

Think for a moment of the many factors that determine how much the members of your household choose to spend on consumer goods and services during the course of a year. Your list could be quite lengthy. It might include, at a minimum, your household's disposable income; its wealth in the form of stocks, bonds, savings accounts, and the value of your house if you own your home; the prices of the goods and services that you buy; interest rates; expectations about what prices, interest rates, and your household's disposable income and wealth will be in the future; the tastes and ages of every household member; and whether each member is employed or in college. Many factors shape each household's demand for goods and services, but one of the factors—disposable income—is far and away the most important for most households. The amount of goods and services that the typical household is willing and able to buy during the course of a year depends primarily on the amount of (real) disposable income that it receives during the year.

The Keynesian Consumption Function

John Maynard Keynes was the first economist to see that the link between consumption demand and disposable income had a substantial impact on the overall performance of the macro economy. He believed that a household's consumption demand has two components, a small component that is unrelated to the household's disposable income and a larger component that varies directly with the household's disposable income, although less than dollar for dollar. What is true for a representative household's consumption demand is true for the economy as a whole.

A HYPOTHETICAL CONSUMPTION FUNCTION   The hypothetical data in Table 10.1 are consistent with Keynes's views on the relationship between aggregate consumption and aggregate disposable income. The first column records the consumption demand at every level of disposable income in the second column. All data are real, constant dollar values in billions of dollars, to approximate the values of consumption and disposable income for the United States in the early 1990s.

Notice, first, that consumption demand equals disposable income when disposable income is $2,000. Thus, $2,000 is called the **break-even level of disposable income.**

Consumption demand is less than disposable income when disposable income is above $2,000. Since all that households can do is either consume or save their disposable incomes, households in the aggregate are saving over that range of disposable income. For example, consumption demand is only $4,400 when disposable income is $5,000. The amount of saving is $600, the difference between disposable income and consumption demand ($600 = $5,000

BREAK-EVEN LEVEL OF
DISPOSABLE INCOME

The level of disposable income at which households' consumption demand equals their disposable income.

TABLE 10.1   Consumption Demand: Consumption Function/Propensity to Consume ($ billion)

CONSUMPTION DEMAND (C^d)	DISPOSABLE INCOME (Y_d)	MARGINAL PROPENSITY TO CONSUME $(MPC = \Delta C^d/\Delta Y_d)$	AVERAGE PROPENSITY TO CONSUME $(APC = C^d/Y_d)$
$ 400	$ 0	—	—
1,200	1,000	.80 (= 800/1,000)	1.20
2,000	2,000	.80	1.00
2,800	3,000	.80	.93
3,600	4,000	.80	.90
4,400	5,000	.80	.88
5,200	6,000	.80	.87
6,000	7,000	.80	.86
6,800	8,000	.80	.85
7,600	9,000	.80	.84
8,400	10,000	.80	.84
9,200	11,000	.80	.84
10,000	12,000	.80	.83
10,800	13,000	.80	.83

— $4,400). Households can save in many ways, such as holding on to cash; depositing some of their disposable income in a savings account; buying financial assets such as stocks, bonds, and certificates of deposit; buying real assets such as a piece of land or a house; and paying back loans.

Consumption demand is greater than disposable income when disposable income is below $2,000. Households in the aggregate are dissaving over that range of disposable incomes; the amount of saving is negative. For example, consumption is $1,200 when disposable income is $1,000. Households in the aggregate are dissaving $200 (− $200 = $1,000 − $1,200). At these low levels of disposable income many households are trying to maintain their standards of living by dissaving. They may sell some stocks or real estate, draw down savings accounts, or borrow. These are all forms of dissaving that bring in money to households so that they can buy consumer goods and services that they could otherwise not afford out of their disposable incomes. Households cannot go on dissaving forever, but when their incomes fall sharply, they will dissave for awhile in an attempt to maintain their standards of living.

Note, finally, that consumption demand is $400 even when disposable income falls to zero. This is the amount of consumption demand that Keynes said was independent of disposable income and determined by all the other factors that influence consumption demand. You can think of this amount of consumption as being present at every level of disposable income. Households then increase their consumption demand above this base amount as they receive disposable income.

Figure 10.1 pictures the relationship between consumption demand and disposable income for the hypothetical data in Table 10.1. Aggregate (real) consumption demand, C^d, is on the vertical axis, and aggregate (real) disposable income, Y^d, is on the horizontal axis.

The 45° line is a frame-of-reference line that allows us to see each level of disposable income in the vertical direction. The distance from the origin to a given level of disposable income on the horizontal axis is equal to the height of the 45° line at that level of disposable income. For example, the point on the 45° line at a disposable income of $2,000 has a value of $2,000 measured in the vertical direction, the point on the 45° line at a disposable income of $5,000 has a value of $5,000 measured in the vertical direction, and so forth. Having a vertical measure of disposable income makes it easy to compare the levels of consumption demand and disposable income, since consumption demand is also measured in the vertical direction.

The line C^d is called the **consumption function,** or the *propensity to consume.* It shows the aggregate consumption demand during the year at each level of total disposable income, other things equal. The other things being held equal or constant are all the other factors that influence the households' demands for goods and services, such as wealth, tastes, and expectations about the future.

The consumption function, C^d, crosses the 45° line at the break-even level of disposable income, which is $2,000 in our example. The vertical distance to the 45° line at $Y_d^1 = \$2,000$ is the aggregate disposable income, $2,000. The vertical distance to C^d at $Y_d^1 = \$2,000$ is the aggregate consumption demand at that level of disposable income, also $2,000. Since the two lines intersect at $Y_d^1 = \$2,000$, aggregate consumption demand equals aggregate disposable income.

C^d is below the 45° line at all levels of disposable income above $2,000, indicating that households in the aggregate choose to save some of their dis-

CONSUMPTION FUNCTION

The relationship that indicates how much households in the aggregate are willing and able to consume during the year at every level of total disposable income, other things equal; also called *consumption demand.*

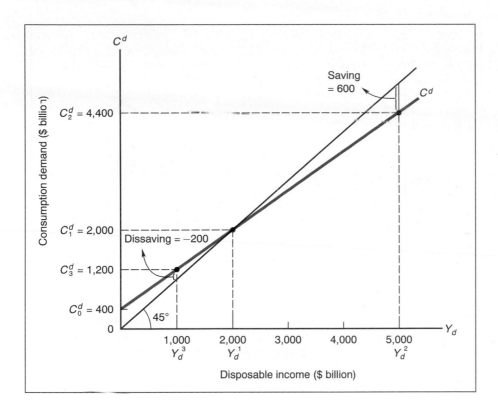

FIGURE 10.1

The Consumption Function

The consumption function, C^d, is a graph of the aggregate consumption demand by households at each level of disposable income, Y_d, from Table 10.1. Disposable income is on the horizontal axis and aggregate consumption demand is on the vertical axis. The consumption and income data are in real terms, billions of constant dollars. Points on the 45-degree line show the level of disposable income in the vertical direction. The break-even level of disposable income when households consume all their income is $2,000, at the intersection of C^d and the 45-degree line. Households save some of their disposable income at all income levels above $2,000. For example, when disposable income is $5,000, households consume $4,400 and save $600. The $600 of saving is the vertical distance between the 45-degree line and C^d. Households dissave at all income levels below $2,000. For example, when disposable income is $1000, households consume $1,200; their saving is ($-$)$200, the vertical distance between the 45-degree line and C^d.

posable income over this range. The amount of saving is the vertical distance between the 45° line and the consumption function at each level of disposable income. For example, at $Y_d^2 = \$5,000$, the vertical distance to C_2^d is $4,400, the aggregate consumption demand, and the vertical distance to the 45° line is $5,000, the aggregate disposable income. Aggregate saving is $600, the vertical distance between C_2^d and the 45° line. Both consumption demand and saving demand increase the farther disposable income rises above $2,000.

C^d is above the 45° line at all levels of disposable income below $2,000, indicating that households in the aggregate are dissaving over this range. The amount of dissaving is the vertical distance between C^d and the 45° line at each level of disposable income. For example, at $Y_d^3 = \$1,000$, the vertical distance to C_3^d is $1,200, the aggregate consumption demand, and the vertical distance to the 45° line is $1,000, the aggregate disposable income. Aggregate dissaving is $-\$200$, the vertical distance between C_3^d and the 45° line. The amount of dissaving increases the farther disposable income falls below $2,000.

C^d intersects the vertical axis at $C_0^d = \$400$. This is the amount of aggregate consumption demand that is independent of the level of disposable income.

THE MARGINAL PROPENSITY TO CONSUME   Our discussion of the consumption function so far has described how the level of consumption demand relates to the level of disposable income. Economists are also very interested in how consumption demand changes as disposable income changes with the ebbs and flows of the business cycle. Changes in consumption demand have a very important effect on changes in the circular flow of economic activity simply because consumption is around 60 to 65 percent of GDP.

FIGURE 10.2

The Marginal Propensity to Consume

The marginal propensity to consume, labeled MPC, is the slope of the consumption function, C^d. MPC = $\Delta C^d/\Delta Y_d$. The $MPC = 0.80$ at all levels of disposable income for the consumption function in Table 10.1. Households increase their consumption by $800 for every $1,000 increase in disposable income.

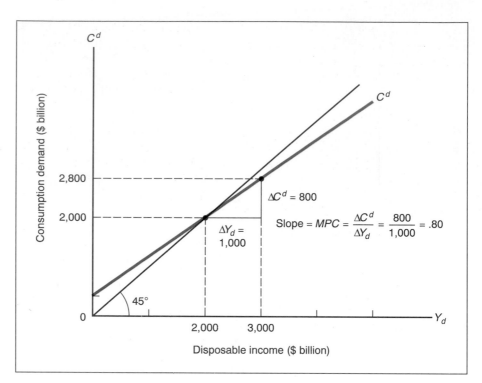

MARGINAL PROPENSITY TO CONSUME

The portion of each additional dollar of disposable income that households consume; the ratio of the change in consumption demand to the change in disposable income.

The relationship between changes in consumption demand and changes in disposable income is given by the slope of the consumption function. Refer to Figure 10.2. The slope of the consumption function is the rise over the run of C^d, the change in consumption demand divided by the change in disposable income. The slope of C^d is called the **marginal propensity to consume** and is usually referred to as the MPC.

$$MPC = \text{slope of } C^d = \Delta C^d/\Delta Y_d$$

The MPC indicates the portion of each *additional* dollar of disposable income that the household consumes. As such, the MPC must have a value between zero and one, inclusive, since a household can only consume or save each additional dollar of disposable income.

$$0 \leq MPC \leq 1$$

An MPC equal to one says that households consume all, and save none, of each additional dollar of disposable income. An MPC equal to zero says that households consume none, and save all, of each additional dollar of disposable income. An MPC between zero and one means that households both consume and save a portion of each additional dollar of disposable income, which is the realistic case.

The MPC for our hypothetical consumption function is .80, as indicated in the third column of Table 10.1. Households in the aggregate consume 80 cents and save 20 cents of each additional dollar of disposable income. For example, consumption demand increases from $2,000 to $2,800, an increase of $800, when disposable income increases from $2,000 to $3,000, an increase of $1,000.

MPC = \$800/\$1,000 = .80. Our hypothetical consumption function is consistent with Keynes's belief that consumption demand varies directly with disposable income, but less than dollar for dollar.

Note, finally, that the consumption function is flatter than the 45° line. The slope of the 45° line is 1, whereas the slope of C^d is the MPC, which is .80.

THE AGGREGATE U.S. CONSUMPTION FUNCTION   Does our hypothetical consumption function accurately reflect the relationship between aggregate consumption and aggregate disposable income over time in the United States? The answer is yes and no.

There have been innumerable studies of the aggregate U.S. consumption function because consumption is so important to the overall performance of the economy. The weight of the evidence from all the research is that our hypothetical consumption function is a reasonably accurate representation of the aggregate consumption function in the United States over the short run. The only wrinkle is that the aggregate consumption function becomes much steeper as time passes. The MPC in the short run, within a year or so, is on the order of .60 to .80. That is, every dollar increase or decrease in disposable income raises or lowers consumption spending by 60 to 80 cents within one year after the increase. Keynes was right: Consumption demand in any given year is very sensitive to the current level of disposable income being generated in the economy.

The research also consistently finds that the MPC builds over time. Permanent changes in disposable income that last for a number of years ultimately raise consumption spending over 90 cents on the dollar. The ratio of consumption spending to disposable income has averaged .91 each year since 1929, the first year that the Bureau of Economic Analysis collected data for the national income and product accounts. The .91 ratio is consistent with the estimates of the long-run MPC from the consumption function studies, which are on the order of .90 to .93. Our hypothetical MPC of .80 should therefore be viewed as a compromise between the short-run and the long-run MPCs in the United States. An MPC of .80 also happens to be a particularly easy number to work with in numerical examples. We will use it throughout the macroeconomics chapters of the text.[2]

Finally, the break-even level of aggregate disposable income is very low in the United States. Aggregate consumption equaled or exceeded aggregate disposable income only in the depths of the Great Depression, when unemployment was 20 to 25 percent of the labor force. Personal saving has been positive every year since 1940.

THE AVERAGE PROPENSITY TO CONSUME   The final column of Table 10.1 reports the **average propensity to consume (APC)** at each level of disposable income, which is the ratio of consumption to disposable income:

AVERAGE PROPENSITY TO CONSUME

The ratio of consumption demand to disposable income.

---

[2]For a summary of the research on the consumption function in the United States, and further discussion of the MPC in the short run and the long run, see R. Hall and J. Taylor, *Macroeconomics: Theory, Performance, and Policy*, 2nd edition (New York: W. W. Norton, 1988): 195–205. Hall and Taylor are among the more prominent macro economists in the United States. They place the short-run MPC at .76 and the long-run MPC at .91 (Table 8-1, p. 195).

$$APC = C^d/Y_d$$

Notice that the APC declines steadily as disposable income increases.

The declining APC for our hypothetical consumption function is consistent with the short-run aggregate consumption function in the United States. It is also consistent with the behavior of individual households throughout the United States in any given year. High-income households consume a lower portion of their disposable incomes than do low-income households. A declining APC is not consistent with the long-run aggregate consumption function in the United States, however. The APC has been essentially constant over the long run. As noted above, consumption has averaged about 91 percent of disposable income since 1929, even though real disposable income increased nearly sixfold from 1929 to 1990.

Take care to note the difference between the MPC and the APC. The MPC refers to the ratio of *changes* in consumption demand to *changes* in disposable income. The APC refers to the ratio of *levels* of consumption demand to *levels* of disposable income. The MPC is much more important to the study of the macro economy.

We will use the hypothetical consumption function in Table 10.1 and Figure 10.1 throughout the macroeconomics chapters of this text. Make sure that you understand its properties before proceeding.

Saving Demand

SAVING FUNCTION

The relationship that indicates how much households in the aggregate are willing and able to save during the year at every level of total disposable income, other things equal; also called *saving demand*.

The relationship between saving demand and disposable income follows immediately from the relationship between consumption demand and disposable income. The **saving function,** or the *propensity to save,* indicates how much households in the aggregate are willing and able to save at every level of total disposable income, other things equal. As we have already seen, the amount households save must always equal the amount they choose not to consume, since all that they can do with their disposable income is either consume it or save it. In other words, the aggregate saving function is the mirror image of the aggregate consumption function.[3]

Table 10.2 and Figure 10.3 present the hypothetical saving function that corresponds to our hypothetical consumption function. The first and third columns of Table 10.2 reproduce the hypothetical consumption and disposable income data from Table 10.1. Figure 10.3 also reproduces the hypothetical consumption function, C^d, from Figure 10.1 so that we can easily compare C^d with the saving function, S^d.

Notice, first, that consumption and saving in the first and second columns of Table 10.2 always add up to the disposable income in the third column. For example, when disposable income is $6,000, consumption is $5,200, and saving is $800 ($5,200 + $800 = $6,000).

Saving demand is zero at $2,000, the break-even level of disposable income when households in the aggregate are consuming all their disposable income. Therefore, the aggregate saving function, S^d, in Figure 10.3 cuts the horizontal axis at the disposable income of $2,000.

---

[3]The two potential sources of saving in our simplest economy are business saving, or retained earnings, and the personal saving of households. We will assume that the firms pay out all their profits as dividends, so that the only source of saving in our simplest economy is the personal saving of households.

TABLE 10.2   Saving Demand: Saving Funciton/Propensity to Save ($ billion)

CONSUMPTION DEMAND (C^d)	SAVING DEMAND (S^d)	DISPOSABLE INCOME (Y_d)	MARGINAL PROPENSITY TO SAVE (MPS = $\Delta S^d / \Delta Y_d$)	AVERAGE PROPENSITY TO SAVE (APS = S^d / Y_d)
$ 400	$(−) 400	$ 0	—	—
1,200	(−) 200	1,000	.20 (= 200/1,000)	(−) .20
2,000	0	2,000	.20	0
2,800	200	3,000	.20	.07
3,600	400	4,000	.20	.10
4,400	600	5,000	.20	.12
5,200	800	6,000	.20	.13
6,000	1,000	7,000	.20	.14
6,800	1,200	8,000	.20	.15
7,600	1,400	9,000	.20	.16
8,400	1,600	10,000	.20	.16
9,200	1,800	11,000	.20	.16
10,000	2,000	12,000	.20	.17
10,800	2,200	13,000	.20	.17

S^d is positive when disposable income is greater than $2,000. For example, when disposable income is $5,000, households in the aggregate are consuming $4,400 and saving $600.

S^d is negative when disposable income is below $2,000. This is the range of incomes when households are consuming more than their disposable incomes and dissaving. For example, when disposable income is $1,000, C^d is $1,200, and S^d is −$200.

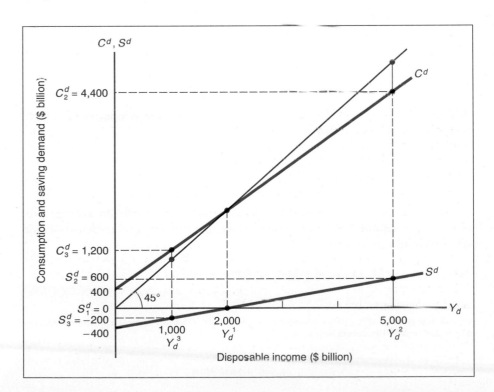

FIGURE 10.3

The Saving Function

The saving function, S^d, is a graph of the aggregate saving demand by households at each level of disposable income, Y_d, from Table 10.2. S^d is the mirror image of the consumption function, C^d, because households can either consume or save their disposable income. Saving is zero at the break-even level of disposable income, $2,000, when households consume all their disposable income. Saving is positive at all levels of disposable income above $2,000. For example, when disposable income is $5,000, households save $600. Saving is negative at all levels of disposable income below $2,000; households are dissaving. For example, when disposable income is $1,000, saving is (−)$200. The marginal propensity to save, labelled MPS, is the slope of the saving function. MPS = $\Delta S^d / \Delta Y_d$. The MPS = 0.20 for the saving function in Table 10.2

S^d hits the vertical axis at $-\$400$. This is the component of saving demand that is determined by the factors other than disposable income that influence the level of consumption demand and saving demand. The $-\$400$ of saving is the mirror image of the $\$400$ of consumption demand that is independent of disposable income.

THE MARGINAL PROPENSITY TO SAVE The slope of the saving function is the rise over the run of S^d, the change in saving divided by the change in disposable income. The slope of S^d is called the **marginal propensity to save** and is commonly referred to as the MPS.

MARGINAL PROPENSITY TO SAVE

The portion of each additional dollar of disposable income that households save; the ratio of the change in saving demand to the change in disposable income.

$$\text{MPS} = \text{slope of } S^d = \Delta S^d / \Delta Y_d$$

The MPS indicates the portion of each *additional* dollar of disposable income that the household saves. The MPS for our hypothetical saving function is .20. Every additional $\$1,000$ of disposable income increases saving by $\$200$ (refer to the fourth column of the table).

Notice that the MPC and the MPS add up to one for our hypothetical consumption and saving functions $(.80 + .20 = 1)$. In the aggregate the households in our simplest economy spend 80 cents and save 20 cents of each additional dollar of disposable income. The MPC and the MPS must always add up to one because each additional dollar of disposable income must be either consumed or saved.[4]

$$\text{MPC} + \text{MPS} = 1$$

We noted above that studies of the aggregate U.S. consumption function have found a short-run MPC in the range of .60 to .80 and a long-run MPC in the range of .90 to .93. Equivalently, these studies have found a short-run MPS in the range of .40 to .20 and a long-run MPS in the range of .10 to .07.

Also, the MPS must be between zero and one, inclusive, just as the MPC is.

$$0 \leq \text{MPS} \leq 1$$

AVERAGE PROPENSITY TO SAVE

The ratio of saving demand to disposable income.

The final column of Table 10.2 records the **average propensity to save (APS)** at each level of disposable income, which is the ratio of saving demand to disposable income:

$$\text{APS} = S^d / Y_d$$

The average propensity to save is also the mirror image of the average propensity to consume (APC) because the average propensities to consume and save must add up to one.

$$\text{APC} + \text{APS} = 1$$

---

[4]The derivation of the MPC, MPS relationship is as follows. $Y_d = C^d + S^d$. Therefore, in terms of changes, $\Delta Y_d = \Delta C^d + \Delta S^d$. Divide both sides by ΔY_d:

$$(\Delta C^d / \Delta Y_d) + (\Delta S^d / \Delta Y_d) = \Delta Y_d / \Delta Y_d = 1$$
$$\text{MPC} + \text{MPS} = 1$$

The APS rises steadily as disposable income increases for our hypothetical data, just the opposite of the APC. The MPS is much more important than the APS is to the study of the macro economy.

Other Factors Influencing Consumption Demand

The consumption function shows the independent, *other things equal* effect of disposable income on consumption demand. Changes in disposable income cause movements along the consumption function. The other factors that influence households' consumption demand—expectations about the future, prices, tastes, and so forth—are not pictured on the consumption function graph. They are lying behind the scene, determining the position of the consumption function. Changes in any of these other factors shift the entire consumption function up or down to a new position. Moreover, any change that shifts the consumption function must shift the saving function in exactly the opposite direction. Otherwise, consumption and saving would no longer add up to disposable income, which is unchanged.

For example, suppose that the households in our simplest economy have a change in tastes in favor of consumption. They want to consume $300 more at every level of disposable income. We would represent this by shifting C^d up by $300 in Figure 10.1 and adding $300 to the consumption data in Tables 10.1 and 10.2. C^d would now intersect the vertical axis at $700.

By deciding to consume $300 more at every level of disposable income, households have simultaneously decided to save $300 less at every level of disposable income. Therefore, we would also have to shift S^d down by $300 in Figure 10.3 and subtract $300 from the saving data in Table 10.2. S^d would now intersect the vertical axis at $-$700.

With these points in mind, let's take a look at some of the other factors that influence consumption demand and saving demand.

FUTURE EXPECTATIONS: THE LIFE-CYCLE HYPOTHESIS   Consumers do not base their consumption and saving decisions just on their current situations. Their future prospects also come into play. College students are a good example. Many students (or their parents) are spending far more than their current disposable incomes to attend college because they view a college education as a good investment in their future. They are borrowing and otherwise dissaving now with the expectation that their college degrees will gain them access to high-paying jobs after college.

The chief competitor to the Keynesian consumption function for explaining aggregate consumption assumes that consumers look far into the future, indeed over their entire lifetimes, in making their consumption and saving decisions. The competing model, called the **Life-Cycle Hypothesis,** was developed jointly in the late 1950s by Albert Ando of the University of Pennsylvania and Franco Modigliani of MIT.[5] We want to take some time with the Life-Cycle Hypothesis because it is one of the building blocks of the new classical model of the economy.

LIFE-CYCLE HYPOTHESIS

A theory of household consumption demand that attempts to explain the average pattern of lifetime income and consumption given by the age-earnings profile.

[5] A. Ando and F. Modigliani, "The Life-Cycle Hypothesis of Saving: Aggregate Indications and Tests," *American Economic Review* 53, No. 1, Part 1 (March 1963): 54–84. A precursor to the Ando, Modigliani paper was F. Modigliani and R. Brumberg, "Utility Analysis and the Consumption Function," in K. K. Kurihara, ed., *Post-Keynesian Economics* (New Brunswick, NJ: Rutgers University Press, 1954).

FIGURE 10.4

The Age-Earnings Profile and Lifetime Consumption

The figure shows the typical pattern of earnings and consumption over people's lifetimes. Age is on the horizontal axis, and consumption and income are on the vertical axis. The age-earnings profile, Y, indicates the average earnings of people at each age during their lives. Average earnings rise until middle age and then decline, falling sharply during retirement. The line C indicates the average consumption of people at each age during their lives. People smooth their consumption over their lifetimes to enjoy a fairly constant standard of living. They borrow when young, save during middle age to pay off their debts and build a nest egg for retirement, and dissave during their retirement. The Life-Cycle Hypothesis is based on this average pattern of lifetime earnings and consumption.

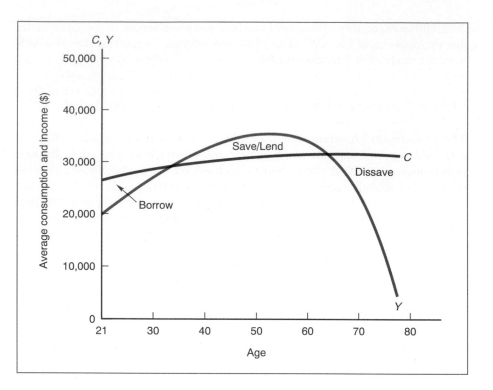

AGE-EARNINGS PROFILE

The average earnings per person at each age within the population.

The Life-Cycle Hypothesis was an attempt to explain the average pattern of lifetime income and consumption observed in the United States, which is illustrated in Figure 10.4. The horizontal axis lists each age within the population, starting with age 21. The vertical axis records the average values of earned income and consumption per person by all people of the corresponding age on the horizontal axis. The hump-shaped curve labeled Y is the **age-earnings profile** of the population, the average earnings per person at each age. Income rises steadily until late middle age and then begins to decline, falling sharply during the retirement years. The curve labeled C shows the average consumption per person at each age.

The figure shows that lifetime consumption is much smoother than is lifetime income. On average, people borrow when they are young to support a level of consumption above their annual incomes. Young adults may borrow heavily to buy big-ticket items, such as houses and cars, or to further their educations, or they may use credit card debt simply to increase their current standard of living. As people reach middle age, they consume less than their incomes and save. They pay back their earlier debts and begin to build up a nest egg for their retirement years. In their retirement years they once again consume more than their incomes, living off the accumulated savings during their high-income, middle-age years.

Modigliani and Ando hypothesized that this pattern of lifetime income and consumption is the result of people making consumption plans over their entire lifetimes and adjusting each year as new information becomes available. First, they project what their lifetime resources will be. The two main types of lifetime resources are their projected labor market earnings over their working lifetimes and inherited wealth. (Inherited wealth is inconsequential for most people, however.) They also take into account both current and projected future taxes and government transfers such as Social Security to calculate their projected disposable incomes. People then borrow and lend as necessary to smooth consumption so that they enjoy a fairly constant standard of living out of their lifetime resources.

The Keynesian and Life-Cycle views of the consumption and saving decision could hardly be more different. Keynes linked consumption demand to current disposable income each year. The Life-Cycle Hypothesis links consumption demand to lifetime resources. Not surprisingly, the two theories have very different implications.

For starters, the Life-Cycle Hypothesis suggests that the short-run MPC out of current disposable income ought to be very low. To see why, suppose that a household receives an increase in disposable income during the year. The change in income could have been anticipated or unanticipated, and it could be viewed as either permanent or temporary. Consider the expected reaction to each type of change under the Life-Cycle Hypothesis.

An anticipated change in disposable income—An example of a fully anticipated change in disposable income might be a 3 percent salary increase (after taxes) received by a tenured faculty member at a major university. The professor has taught at the university for 15 years, has always planned to stay there until retirement, and expects to receive after-tax salary increases on the order of 3 percent each year. Because the 3 percent salary increase was fully anticipated, it has already been factored into the professor's lifetime consumption plan. Therefore, it has absolutely no effect on his consumption; the short-run MPC out of the salary increase is zero. In general, only *unanticipated* changes in disposable income can change consumption under the Life-Cycle Hypothesis. The only remaining question is whether households view unanticipated changes as permanent or temporary.

An unanticipated change in disposable income, viewed as permanent—An example of this case might be a young executive who wins a promotion to vice-president in charge of marketing and receives a huge increase in salary along with the promotion. The executive was in competition with many other managers for the position; she could not assume that she would get the promotion so it could not have been fully anticipated. Having received the promotion, however, she views the salary increase as permanent. She now expects to receive much higher salaries in future years than she would have received without the promotion. The unanticipated, permanent increase in her annual salary shifts her age-earnings profile up by the full amount of the salary, so she increases her consumption by the full amount of the salary as well. The short-run MPC out of a *permanent*, but *unanticipated*, increase in annual income is one. (The short-run MPC would be even greater than one if the change in income this year suggests even bigger changes in future years, as it might in this example.)

An unanticipated change in disposable income, viewed as temporary—Unanticipated, temporary changes in disposable income would include one-time windfall gains such as gambling winnings, an unexpected tax rebate, or, in the other direction, a short spell of unemployment. The short-run MPC out of temporary changes in income such as these would be very low. They represent an increase or decrease in lifetime resources, but because they are one-time changes, people spread the consumption from these changes over their remaining lifetimes.

For young people the immediate effect on consumption is very low, probably little more than 5 percent of the change in disposable income. For example, suppose that a young adult wins a $1,000 prize in the state lottery for guessing most of the numbers correctly. If he is a Life-Cycle consumer, he will not consume the $1,000 immediately because he wants to smooth his consumption over his lifetime. Instead, he might place the $1,000 in a savings account earning 5 percent so that he can increase his consumption each year by $50. He may also consume a small portion of the $1,000 each year, but his short-run increase in consumption is likely to be very small.

In summary, only *unanticipated* changes in disposable income that are expected to be *permanent* generate a short-run MPC that is very much different from zero. Not all changes in disposable income are likely to be of this kind, however. Many unanticipated changes in disposable income are undoubtedly viewed as temporary, given the endless ebbs and flows of the business cycle. For instance, most spells of unemployment are temporary, and probably unanticipated. Also, many changes in disposable income are probably anticipated to a large extent, especially among those employees with long-term employment relationships. Therefore, the short-run MPC should be quite low if people behave according to the Life-Cycle Hypothesis.

How does the Keynesian consumption function stack up against the Life-Cycle Hypothesis? As with most models, they both have their strengths and weaknesses.

The biggest problem for the Life-Cycle Hypothesis is explaining the high short-run MPC of .60 to .80 in the United States. Consumption demand is highly sensitive to changes in current disposable income, in line with the Keynesian consumption function. Economists have long puzzled over why the short-run MPC is so high, and the issue is far from resolved.

The main advantage of the Life-Cycle Hypothesis is that it provides a theory for explaining why many factors other than disposable income might influence consumption demand. We will briefly mention a few of them to conclude the discussion of consumption demand.

HISTORICAL NOTE: A recent study found that blue collar workers reduce their consumption by one-fourth as much as white collar workers per dollar of income lost during a spell of unemployment. This is consistent with the Life-Cycle Hypothesis. Blue collar workers are likely to view a spell of unemployment as a temporary reduction in their incomes, whereas white collar workers are likely to view a spell of unemployment as leading to a permanent reduction in their incomes. M. Dywarski and S. Sheffrin, "Consumption and Unemployment," (*Quarterly Journal of Economics* CII, Issue 2 (May 1987): 411–428.)

WEALTH   Wealth should certainly have some effect on consumption. Suppose that two people each earn $25,000 per year, but one has recently inherited $10 million. The person with the inheritance would be expected to consume more each year because he has much greater lifetime resources to draw on.

A famous instance of wealth affecting aggregate consumption in the United States occurred after World War II. Many economists were expecting a return to the Great Depression once the war wound down and aggregate demand was no longer supported by enormous amounts of government military expenditures. Instead, the nation transformed itself fairly quickly back to a peacetime economy, and the economy performed very well. The savior was consumption demand, which turned out to be much stronger than anyone had expected. The federal government had financed the war by issuing large amounts of debt to the American public. After the war, when people were once again free to buy consumer goods and services, they viewed their holdings of the government's bonds as a huge increase in their wealth and went on a consumption binge. Their consumption had been low for many years because of the Great Depression and the War.

Changes in private wealth do not always have such a large effect on consumption demand, however. The stock market crashed on October 19, 1987; the Dow Jones Industrial Index lost 500 points on that day, fully 20 percent of its value. Some people feared that the crash would depress consumption demand and lead the economy into a recession, but consumption demand hardly changed at all. Economists are not sure why. One explanation is that most households own stocks indirectly through their pension funds. Only about 20 percent of households hold stocks directly. Another explanation is that the stock market had been rising rapidly during the previous year, so that the 500-point loss merely returned the Dow Jones to its level of the year before. In any event the crash of 1987 confirmed the widespread belief that changes in stock prices have little effect on consumption demand in the United States.

PRICES   The effect of prices on consumption demand has been incorporated into our analysis for the most part because we have been referring to real consumption and real disposable income. An increase in the consumer price index lowers real disposable income, other things equal. Prices also have wealth effects that can affect consumption demand, however. An increase in prices reduces the value of our money holdings and thereby reduces our real wealth. We also saw how unanticipated changes in the rate of inflation can transfer purchasing power between debtors and creditors. These wealth-induced price effects are likely to be quite small, however.

INTEREST RATES   Interest rates can affect the timing of consumption in the Life-Cycle model. Higher interest rates make saving more attractive, so people save more now and consume more later on in their lives. Conversely, lower interest rates discourage saving, so people consume more now and consume less later on in their lives. Many economists question whether these Life-Cycle effects are very important, however. Most studies do not find that consumption and saving are very sensitive to changes in interest rates.

THE AGE DISTRIBUTION OF THE POPULATION   The Life-Cycle Hypothesis suggests that aggregate consumption and saving ought to vary with the age distribution of the population. The reason is simply that the young and the old tend to dissave, and the middle-aged tend to save. This prediction, if true, could be a ray of sunshine for the United States.

Most economists believe that the United States needs to increase its saving and investment in order to increase productivity and long-run economic growth, yet personal saving has been abnormally low over the past 15 years. The huge baby boom generation that was born between 1947 and 1964 may have been largely responsible for the decline in personal saving. The baby boomers were in their young adult years for the most part over the past 15 years, a period of dissaving according to the Life-Cycle Hypothesis. They are now approximately 30 to 50 years of age, in or just entering their middle-age years. The Life-Cycle Hypothesis predicts that their saving should increase sharply as they pay off the debts of their youth and begin to build a retirement nest egg. If the Life-Cycle Hypothesis is correct, the baby boomers will usher in a new period of high saving and high investment in the United States and put an end to the low-saving, low-investment, low-growth scenario that the United States has been stuck in since 1974.

INVESTMENT DEMAND

Investment demand is the other component of aggregate demand in our simplest economy.

The most striking feature of investment is its volatility. Investment moves with the business cycle just as consumption does, increasing when national income is increasing and decreasing when national income is decreasing. But the swings in investment are much more pronounced than are the swings in consumption. Northwestern's Robert Gordon calculated the change in gross investment during eight business cycles in the United States from 1948 to 1982. Gross investment fell by an average of 20 percent during the downturns and rose by an average of 33 percent during the upturns. These percentage changes were about six times larger than the percentage changes in consumption, or any other component of GDP. And net investment is even more volatile than is gross investment.[6]

The volatility of investment makes it highly unpredictable. Economists have tried long and hard, and without much success, to pin down the factors that determine investment demand. How much does investment demand respond to changes in national income? Tax policy? Interest rates? Stock market prices? Corporate profits? To what extent is investment demand driven by technological change? Economists cannot agree on the answers to these questions, and their disagreements extend to all three components of investment—plant and equipment, inventories, and housing. Every component of investment is highly volatile and difficult to predict.

Our main concern in this chapter is whether investment demand is closely related to the current level of economic activity. We will focus on investment in plant and equipment in answering this question because it is the most important component of investment.

Investment in Plant and Equipment

Investment in plant and equipment increases and decreases with the business cycle, but it is *not* closely related to the level of economic activity. To understand why not, you must keep firmly in mind the distinction between capital and investment.

The stock of capital is the factor of production that firms combine with labor, land, and material inputs to produce their output. Investment is the *change* in the stock of capital during the year. Given this distinction, the investment decision can be viewed as a two-step process that takes place at the beginning of each year. First, firms determine their desired stock of capital, the amount of capital that they would like to have in place by the end of the year. Then they decide on a level of investment during the year that will increase their

---

[6]R. Gordon, *Macroeconomics*, fifth edition (Glenview, IL: Scott, Foresman/Little, Brown 1989), 579–581; Table 1, p. 580. Also, E. Prescott, "Theory Ahead of Business Cycle Measurement," Federal Reserve Bank of Minneapolis, *Quarterly Review* (Fall 1986), p. 9.

existing stock of capital either part way or all the way to the new desired stock of capital. Let's look at both parts of the decision, with an eye toward how each part is related to the current production or sales of the firm.

THE DESIRED STOCK OF CAPITAL   The desired stock of capital is certainly related to the level of output that the firm expects to be producing and selling in the future. A higher level of output requires more capital and all other factors of production; a lower level of output requires less capital and all other factors of production. Moreover, the output that the firm expects to be producing and selling in the future ought to bear some relationship to its current level of production and sales, which means that the desired stock of capital is related to the current level of production and sales.

The relationship between the desired stock of capital and the current level of production and sales may not be all that close, however, because capital is durable. Most equipment can be expected to last for anywhere from 3 to 10 years, and some structures may last for 30 years or even longer. Therefore, in deciding on their desired stock of capital, firms are not just going to consider their current level of sales. They will also try to guess what their sales will be for a number of years into the future. Guesses about the future are uncertain at best, but firms have to guess, and they are likely to consider much more than their current level of sales in making their guesses. For example, suppose that a firm's sales are 10 percent higher this year than last year. Does this mean that the firm's sales will remain at the new level next year, or increase by another 10 percent, or change by some other amount? The managers of the firm will bring more information to bear in answering the question than just the 10 percent increase in sales this year. They will consider the trend of sales over the past five years or so; they will also factor in their best guess about where the overall economy is heading in the near future.

Keynes believed that uncertainty about the future was the key element in the investment decision. He described investment demand as being driven by unpredictable "animal spirits," by which he meant waves of optimism and pessimism about future sales as managers peered into a highly uncertain future.

In any event, a firm's desired stock of capital may not be very closely related to its current level of sales.

THE INVESTMENT DECISION   Even if the desired stock of capital were closely related to the current level of sales, investment would not be. Investment is the *change* in the stock of capital. Therefore, if the desired stock of capital is related to the current *level* of sales, the rate of investment would be related to the *change* in the firm's sales. In other words, investment depends on the expected *growth* of sales *regardless* of what the current *level* of sales happens to be.

Any possible relationship between investment and the current level of production or sales is further clouded by the fact that many investment projects take a long time to complete. Firms cannot necessarily increase their existing stock of capital to the desired stock of capital within one year.

The time to completion has a substantial effect on the rate of investment in the United States. Firms in the aggregate complete only about one-third of their planned investment in plant and equipment in any one year.[7] The ma-

---

[7]Hall and Taylor, *Macroeconomics*, p 238.

jority of plant and equipment investment undertaken each year is the result of decisions made in previous years.

In summary, the rate of investment in plant and equipment does not bear a close relationship to the current level of production. Therefore, we will assume for simplicity that the plant and equipment component of investment demand is entirely unrelated to the level of national income.

A HYPOTHETICAL INVESTMENT DEMAND CURVE   Figure 10.5 illustrates the investment demand curve for plant and equipment for our simplest economy. Investment demand is on the vertical axis, and national income, labeled Y, is on the horizontal axis. The investment demand curve, I^d_{P+E} is horizontal at a level of $400 (as with consumption and saving, all data are in billions of constant dollars). In other words, we are assuming that firms in the aggregate want to invest $400 in plant and equipment during the year regardless of the level of national income.

You should not take this too literally. Investment demand would surely fall if national income were to fall to zero, and just as surely rise if national income were to triple in value. Interpret the investment demand curve as referring to a "reasonable" range of national income. If national income is currently at $6,000, it is unlikely to rise above $7,000 or fall below $5,000. Therefore, we are assuming that investment demand remains at $400 for all values of national income that are likely to occur.

The $400 of investment demand is determined by factors other than the current level of economic activity. Changes in these other factors shift I^d_{P+E} up and down. As we have already seen, one such factor is the expected change

FIGURE 10.5

Investment in Plant and Equipment and National Income

Firms' investment in plant and equipment is not closely related to the level of national income. It is determined, instead, by such factors as the projected growth in national income and the cost of capital. Therefore, our simplest model assumes that the demand for investment in plant and equipment is unrelated to the level of national income, Y. In particular, we are assuming that investment in plant and equipment is $400 over the range of values that national income is likely to have (in billions of constant dollars). Therefore, the graph of investment in plant and equipment, I^d_{P+E}, is horizontal at a value of $400. Changes in the other factors that influence plant and equipment investment shift I^d_{P+E} up or down.

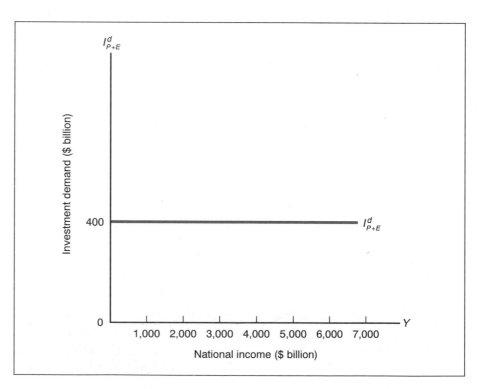

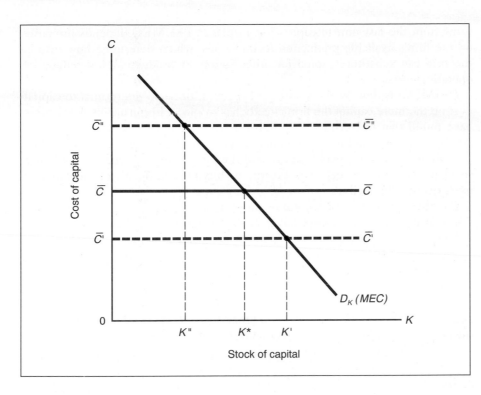

FIGURE 10.6

The Desired Stock of Capital and the Cost of Capital

The figure shows that a firm's desired stock of capital is inversely related to the cost of capital. The demand curve for capital, D_K, is called the marginal efficiency of capital (MEC). It indicates the returns to adding another unit of capital at each level of the firm's capital stock. The returns are the amount that the new unit of capital reduces the firm's costs of production. C is the cost of capital, which depends on four factors: the price of new capital, interest rates, the rate of depreciation of the capital stock, and the tax system. C is a constant, $\overline{C}$, because no one firm is large enough to affect the cost of capital. The firm's desired stock of capital is the amount of capital at which the marginal efficiency of capital equals the cost of capital, the intersection of D_K and $\overline{C}$. The desired stock of capital is K^* when the cost of capital is $\overline{C}$. A decrease in the cost of capital from $\overline{C}$ to $\overline{C}'$ increases the desired stock of capital to K'. An increase in the cost of capital from $\overline{C}$ to $\overline{C}''$ decreases the desired stock of capital to K''.

in the level of economic activity. Let's consider briefly some of the other factors that economists believe have an important effect on investment demand.

OTHER FACTORS AFFECTING INVESTMENT DEMAND   Most of the factors that affect investment demand do so by influencing the desired stock of capital. Earlier we said that firms base their desired stock of capital on their expected output or sales. The other factors affect the desired stock of capital by influencing the amount of capital that firms want to use to produce each unit of output, called the **capital/output ratio**. The two most important factors determining a firm's capital/output ratio are the production technologies available to the firm and the cost of capital.

THE DEMAND FOR CAPITAL, PRODUCTION TECHNOLOGY, AND THE COST OF CAPITAL When choosing their desired stock of capital, firms compare the returns from each additional unit of capital with the cost of the capital. Adding capital has value to the firm if it reduces the operating costs of producing the output. The returns to each additional unit of capital are the amount that the capital reduces the operating costs. The firm adds capital to the point at which the returns from the last unit of capital just equal the cost of the capital. The total amount of capital at that point is the desired stock of capital.

Figure 10.6 illustrates the capital decision. Dollars of return and cost are on the vertical axis, and the total amount of capital is on the horizontal axis. The demand curve for capital, D_K, is often referred to as the **marginal efficiency of capital**, labeled MEC. The marginal efficiency of capital refers to the re-

CAPITAL/OUTPUT RATIO

The amount of capital required to produce each unit of output.

MARGINAL EFFICIENCY OF CAPITAL

The returns to capital from the last unit of capital put in place; also, the demand curve for capital.

turns from the last unit of capital put in place. The MEC depends primarily on the firm's available production technologies, which determine how readily the firm can substitute capital for other factors of production and reduce its operating costs.

D_K (MEC) is downward sloping, as expected, because the returns to capital decline the more capital the firm already has in place. For instance, many firms have found that microcomputers drastically reduce the costs of various secretarial, accounting, and record-keeping activities by replacing more costly office personnel, secretaries, bookkeepers, and the like. Even so, a firm can only use so many microcomputers. The returns to buying additional microcomputers must eventually decline.

COST OF CAPITAL

The annual cost to a firm of purchasing an additional unit of capital.

$\overline{C}$ is the annual **cost of capital** to the firm. It is constant at $\overline{C}$ because each firm is usually an insignificant buyer in the overall national market for capital. A firm cannot influence its cost of capital no matter how much capital it buys.

The desired stock of capital, K^*, is at the intersection of the D_K (MEC) and $\overline{C}$. The returns to the last unit of capital at K^* as measured by the demand for capital, the MEC, just equal the cost of capital, $\overline{C}$.

THE COST OF CAPITAL AND THE DESIRED STOCK OF CAPITAL   The figure shows that the cost of capital has a direct effect on the desired stock of capital. A decrease in the cost of capital from $\overline{C}$ to $\overline{C}'$ induces the firm to increase its capital/output ratio, so that its desired stock of capital increases from K^* to K'. Conversely, an increase in the cost of capital from $\overline{C}$ to $\overline{C}''$ induces the firm to decrease its capital/output ratio, so that its desired stock of capital decreases from K^* to K''.

The cost of capital to a firm depends primarily on four elements: the prices of the capital goods, interest rates, the rate at which the capital depreciates, and the tax system.

The price of the capital. The price that the firm has to pay for a machine, a factory, or an office building is the obvious component of the cost of capital. The cost of microcomputers clearly depends on whether the firm pays $10,000 or $12,000 for each computer.

Interest rates. Suppose that a microcomputer costs a firm $10,000 and that the firm borrows the $10,000 to pay for it at an interest rate of 8 percent. The annual interest charge of $800 ($800 = 8% of $10,000) is part of the annual cost of the computer.

The firm is more likely to pay for the computer out of its retained earnings simply because the firms in the United States finance almost two-thirds of their investment from retained earnings. In this case the interest charge is no longer an out-of-pocket cost to the firm, but it remains an opportunity cost associated with the computer. The firm always has the option of giving the stockholders the $10,000, rather than buying a computer. If the stockholders can earn 8 percent on their savings, then $800 is the annual opportunity cost of investing $10,000 in a microcomputer.

Depreciation. All capital begins to depreciate as soon as it is placed into production, and the firm has to set aside funds in its depreciation account to replace capital as it wears out. The annual depreciation charges are part of the annual cost of capital. Suppose that the $10,000 microcomputer is expected to last for 10 years and depreciates in value at the constant rate of 10 percent per year over the 10 years. The annual depreciation charge is $1,000 ($1,000 = 10% of $10,000). The sum of the $800 interest charge and the $1,000 depreciation charge, $1,800, defines the basic annual cost of capital associated with the computer.

Tax policy. The tax system has a significant effect on the cost of capital. All returns to capital are subject to tax, either by the corporation income tax or by the personal income tax (for proprietorships and partnerships). These taxes raise the cost of capital by increasing the returns that firms require on their capital to cover the other components of the cost of capital.

Congress has used three main tax instruments to affect the cost of capital: corporation income tax rates, depreciation allowances, and investment tax credits. Congress can raise the cost of capital by increasing the corporation income tax rate or lower the cost of capital by reducing the corporation income tax rate. In addition, the U.S. Internal Revenue Service (IRS) determines how quickly firms can depreciate various kinds of capital for tax purposes. The faster the allowable rate of depreciation is, the less tax the firms have to pay and the lower the cost of capital is. An **investment tax credit** allows firms to deduct a portion of the total value of their investment during the year against their taxable profits. The most recent example was a 10 percent tax credit on certain equipment investment that was in effect from 1964 to 1986. An investment tax credit also lowers the cost of capital.

INVESTMENT TAX CREDIT

A tax credit under the federal corporation income tax that allows firms to deduct a portion of the total value of their investment during the year from their taxable profits.

INVESTMENT DEMAND AND THE COST OF CAPITAL   Economists are sharply divided on the question of whether the government can influence investment demand very much by changing the cost of capital through tax policies, at least in the short run. All economists would agree that the demand for *capital* is inversely related to the cost of capital as drawn in Figure 10.6, both for the individual firm and for the entire economy. The point of contention is the extent to which *investment* in plant and equipment is also inversely related to the cost of capital.

Refer to Figure 10.7, which relates the investment demand curve for plant and equipment, I_{P+E}, to the cost of capital. Is the investment demand curve quite steep, such as I^1_{P+E}, so that investment in plant and equipment is not very sensitive to changes in the cost of capital? Or is the investment demand curve relatively flat, such as I^2_{P+E}, so that investment in plant and equipment is quite sensitive to changes in the cost of capital?

Some economists think that the investment demand curve looks like I^1_{P+E}, very steep. They believe that investment in plant and equipment depends primarily on the expected growth in sales. Firms invest when they think their sales will grow, and they do not invest when they think their sales will be flat. The cost of capital makes very little difference beyond that. The link between investment and the cost of capital is weak because firms cannot easily substitute capital for other factors of production. In other words, the desired stock of capital itself is not very responsive to the cost of capital. Also, the delays associated with investing weaken the link between investment demand and changes in the cost of capital still further. Investment responds slowly to changes in the cost of capital, too slowly for tax policy to be an effective tool for spurring investment demand in the short run. So, for example, if the economy is languishing in a recession, tax policies that reduce the cost of capital do not induce firms to invest very much at all. Instead, the government should pursue policies to stimulate aggregate demand so that firms' sales will grow. A growing economy is the key to promoting a high level of investment.

Other economists think that the investment demand curve looks like I^2_{P+E}, relatively flat. They argue that firms can easily substitute capital for other fac-

FIGURE 10.7

Investment Demand and the Cost of Capital

Economists agree that the desired stock of capital is closely related to the cost of capital, C. They disagree on the extent to which investment in plant and equipment in a given year is determined by the cost of capital in the same year. Some economists believe that investment demand is not very sensitive to changes in the cost of capital, that the investment demand curve is very steep, like I^1_{P+E}. In their view, investment demand depends mostly on the growth in aggregate demand. Other economists believe that investment demand is quite sensitive to changes in the cost of capital, that the investment demand curve is relatively flat, like I^2_{P+E}. In their view, Congress can increase investment demand with tax policies, such as an investment tax credit, that lower the cost of capital.

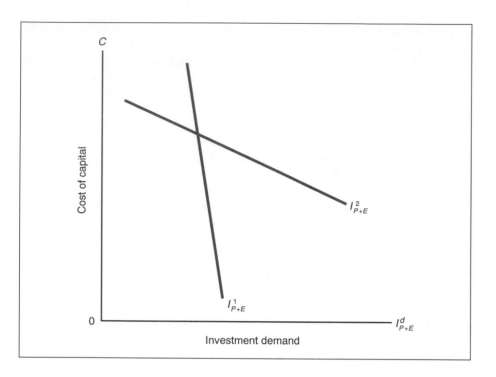

tors of production, so that the demand for capital is quite responsive to changes in the cost of capital. They also believe that the investment response is quick enough to make tax policy an effective spur to investment demand.

The differences between these two views have been difficult to resolve, in part because of the volatility in investment demand, and in part because of the lags in investment. So much of this year's investment in plant and equipment is the result of decisions made in past years that economists have difficulty untangling exactly what determines the level of investment each year.[8]

OTHER FACTOR PRICES   Our discussion of the cost of capital assumed that the prices of other factors of production are held constant. Changes in wages, the price of oil, and other factor prices also affect the firm's desired capital/output ratio because the other factors of production are either substitutes or complements to capital in the production. For instance, labor and capital tend to be substitutes in production. An increase in wages induces firms to substitute capital for labor, raising the desired stock of capital, and presumably the level of investment. High wages in the United States no doubt spurred the development of the fast-food restaurants such as McDonald's and KFC. The fast-food restaurants are much more capital intensive than are the diners and the family-style restaurants they replaced.

[8]Robert Eisner of Northwestern is a leading proponent of the view that the investment demand curve is more responsive to growth in demand than to the cost of capital. Robert Hall of Stanford and Dale Jorgenson of Harvard are leading proponents of the view that the investment demand curve is quite responsive to the cost of capital. Their seminal studies are: R. Eisner, *Factors in Business Investment* (Cambridge, MA: Ballenger, 1978) and R. Hall and D. Jorgenson, "Tax Policy and Investment Behavior," *American Economic Review* 57, No. 3 (June 1967): 391–414.

Investment in Inventory

Goods held in inventory are either goods in process that are being used as material inputs in production, such as the engines to be placed in the cars on the assembly line, or finished goods that are sitting in warehouses or on the shelves of the retailers. American manufacturers, wholesalers, and retailers hold an enormous amount of inventory, about 40 cents for every dollar of GDP.

The amount of goods in inventory at any given time is the stock of inventory capital. *Investment* in inventory is the amount that inventories *change* from the beginning to the end of the year. Unlike the stock of inventory, investment in inventory is quite small, usually less than 5 percent of total investment expenditures. Nonetheless, inventory investment is very important to the operation of the economy. Decreases in inventory investment accounted for 87 percent of the decreases in GDP, on average, during the eight recessions from the end of World War II to 1990. Inventory investment is also the most volatile component of investment demand.[9]

The analysis of inventory investment proceeds along the same lines as the analysis of plant and equipment investment. Firms first decide on their desired stock of inventory capital based on their expected sales during the year. Then they invest in inventory to adjust their current stock of inventory to the desired stock.

The only difference, and an important one, is that firms can adjust their inventories very quickly. The average investment in inventory is just a few days' worth of production in most industries. As a result, the desired stock of inventory is very closely related to the current level of production and sales, and the investment quickly adjusts the inventories to the desired stock. This does not mean, however, that investment in inventory is closely related to the level of production or sales. As with plant and equipment, it is the stock of inventories that is related to the current level of production or sales. Investment in inventory, the change in the stock, is related to the *change* in production or sales, whatever the *level* of production or sales may be.

There is no close relationship between inventory investment and the level of production or sales, either for the individual firm or for the economy as a whole.

Therefore, we will assume that investment demand for inventories, I_{INV}^d, is unrelated to the level of national income in our simplest economy. In other words, a graph relating I_{INV}^d to national income, Y, would be horizontal, just as the graph of I_{P+E}^d is in Figure 10.5. For the purposes of our model, we will assume that firms in the aggregate want their inventories to increase by $25 during the course of the year regardless of the overall level of economic activity. The $25 is determined by factors other than national product or income, such as the expected change in sales or the cost of capital.

The only wrinkle in inventory investment is that the desired investment in inventories could just as easily be zero or negative as positive. $I_{INV}^d = 0$ means that firms in the aggregate want their stock of inventories to remain the same. $I_{INV}^d < 0$ means that firms in the aggregate want to lower their stock of inventories during the year.

---

[9]A. Blinder and L. Maccini, "Taking Stock: A Critical Assessment of Recent Research on Inventories," *Journal of Economic Perspectives* 5, No. 1 (Winter 1991): 73–96. The data on inventory are on pages 73 through 75.

INVENTORY INVESTMENT AND NATIONAL INCOME   The ability of firms to adjust their inventories quickly plays a very important role in the operation of the macro economy. We will make the following assumption in our model: Once firms decide how much they want their inventories to change, they stick to that decision. They do not tolerate *unwanted* increases or decreases in their inventories.

This is a very realistic assumption. Firms monitor their inventories very closely because unwanted changes in inventory in either direction can be very costly. Think of a car dealer who happens to sell Buicks as an example. Detroit manufactures the cars and ships them to the dealer on a regular schedule. Suppose that the dealer's sales fall off, yet Detroit keeps shipping the cars. The inventory of cars on the lot begins to build up, and the dealer may eventually have to rent lot space from other firms to store the unsold cars. This situation obviously cannot continue. The dealer will eventually call the manufacturer and tell it to stop shipping the cars. If Detroit gets similar calls from a number of Buick dealers, it will lay off auto workers, cut production, and ship fewer Buicks to the dealers. The Buick dealers will sell the cars on their lots, that is, sell out of inventory, until their desired level of inventory is restored.

Suppose, instead, that the dealer's sales are greater than expected. The dealer begins to sell cars at a faster clip than Detroit is shipping them, and the dealer's inventory of cars on the lot begins to decline. This situation cannot continue either because no dealer wants to stock out of cars. The great fear of car dealers, and other merchants, is losing customers to competitors. Customers come in to buy mid-sized Buicks, but cannot find the cars they want on the lot. So they go to the Honda, Ford, and Dodge dealers to buy their mid-sized cars and never again purchase a mid-sized Buick. Therefore, the dealer, fearing lost sales, calls the manufacturer and asks it to ship more cars. If Detroit gets similar calls from a number of Buick dealers, it will hire more auto workers, increase production, and ship more Buicks to the dealers.

Car dealers are no different from most other sellers of manufactured goods. Unwanted changes in inventories lead to predictable changes in employment and production, as follows:

SITUATION	REACTION
Unwanted inventory accumulation	Lay off workers and cut production National income decreases
Unwanted inventory depletion	Hire more workers and increase production National income increases

We will see in the next section how the adjustment in inventories brings the economy to its equilibrium.

Investment in Housing

Most investment in housing is undertaken by households, not firms. As such, the decision to build a new home is part of the consumption decision. It is clearly a long-run decision, one that is determined by more than the current level of the household's disposable income. Therefore, we will assume that

REFLECTION: Your own experiences should convince you that firms do not want to stock out of inventory. How many times during the past year have you tried to buy something and not been able to because the item was temporarily out of stock? It happens, but not often.

the investment demand for housing, I_H^d, is also unrelated to the current level of economic activity. In other words, a graph relating I_H^d to national income, Y, would be horizontal, just as the graph of I_{P+E}^d is in Figure 10.5. For the purposes of our model, we will assume that investment demand for housing is $175 (billion) regardless of the level of national income.

Investment in housing is noteworthy because it is the one component of investment demand that everyone agrees is highly sensitive to the cost of capital, in particular, to mortgage interest rates. A one-percentage-point change in the interest rate on a 30-year, $100,000 mortgage changes the monthly payment by about $50 to $75. Changes of this magnitude are enough to trip the balance for many households on the decision of whether or not to take out a mortgage and buy a new home.

Total Investment Demand

The **total investment demand** is the sum of the three components of investment demand: investment demand for plant and equipment, investment demand for inventory, and investment demand for housing. Since we are assuming that each component of investment demand is unrelated to the current level of economic activity, total investment demand is also unrelated to the current level of economic activity.

$$I^d = I_{P+E}^d + I_{INV}^d + I_H^d$$
$$I^d = \$400 + \$25 + \$175$$
$$I^d = \$600$$

I^d is horizontal at $600 (billion) at every level of national income, as pictured in Figure 10.8. The $600 of investment demand is determined by factors other

TOTAL INVESTMENT DEMAND

The sum of the three components of investment demand: investment demand for plant and equipment, investment demand for inventory, and investment demand for housing.

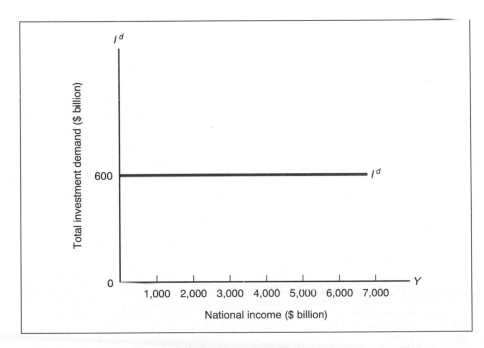

FIGURE 10.8

Total Investment Demand

Total investment demand, I^d, is the sum of the demands for investment in plant and equipment, in inventory, and in housing. Our simplest model assumes that each component of investment demand is independent of the level of national income, Y. We are assuming that total investment demand is $600 over the range of values that national income is likely to have. Therefore the graph of total investment demand, I^d, is horizontal at a value of $600. Changes in factors other than national income that influence any one of the components of total investment demand shift I^d up or down.

than the level of economic activity, such as expected future sales or the cost of capital. Changes in these factors shift I^d up or down.

THE EQUILIBRIUM LEVEL OF NATIONAL INCOME

Having described how consumption demand and investment demand are related to national income, we are now in a position to describe the equilibrium for the economy.

The equilibrium condition in our simplest economy is

$$Y = C^d + I^d$$

Firms guess what the demand for their products will be and produce to meet that demand. The total amount of final goods and services they produce is the national product, which is also equal to the national income received by the households for their factors of production. Our simplest economy is in equilibrium when the aggregate demand for the final goods and services equals the value of the national income that the firms have produced. The aggregate demand for the final goods and services is the sum of consumption demand and investment demand.

Table 10.3 and Figure 10.9 demonstrate the equilibrium for our simplest economy based on the hypothetical consumption demand and investment demand relationships from the previous two sections. The first column of Table 10.3 reproduces the hypothetical consumption function from Table 10.1. It records the consumption demand, C^d, at each national income listed in the fourth column of the table.[10] The second column of the table records the total investment demand, I^d, which is $600 regardless of the level of national income. The third column is aggregate demand, the sum of consumption demand and investment demand at every level of national income. For example, when national income is $4,000 (fourth column), consumption demand is $3,600, and investment demand is $600. Aggregate demand is $4,200, the sum of $3,600 ($C^d$) and $600 ($I^d$). As above, the data on consumption, investment, and national income are in real terms, in billions of constant dollars.

Figure 10.9 pictures aggregate demand at every level of national income, Y. The vertical axis measures aggregate demand, and the horizontal axis measures national income. The 45° line is again a frame-of-reference line that shows the value of national income in the vertical direction. Aggregate demand at each level of national income is measured by the line ADE, the sum of C^d (from Figure 10.1) and I^d (from Figure 10.8). Economists often use the letters ADE to represent the graph of aggregate demand in terms of national income to distinguish it from the aggregate demand curve labeled AD in Chapter 9, in which price is the variable determining aggregate demand. ADE stands for **aggregate desired expenditures** or **aggregate demand for expenditures**. Both terms are just different ways of describing aggregate demand. We will

AGGREGATE DESIRED EXPENDITURES (AGGREGATE DEMAND FOR EXPENDITURES)

The relationship between the aggregate demand for final goods and services and national income, other things equal.

---

[10]Consumption demand is related to disposable income, not national income, but disposable income and national income are equal in our simplest economy. Disposable income differs from national income by the amount of government taxes and transfers and the retained earnings of the business firms. Government taxes and transfers are zero in the simplest model, and we are assuming that firms pay out all profits as dividends, so that retained earnings are also zero.

TABLE 10.3   The Equilibrium Level of National Income for the Simplest Economy: Household and Business Sectors ($ billion)

CONSUMPTION DEMAND (C^d)	INVESTMENT DEMAND (I^d)	AGGREGATE DEMAND ($C^d + I^d$)	NATIONAL INCOME (Y)	INVENTORIES AND PRODUCTION RESPONSE
$ 400	$600	$ 1,000	$ 0	Unwanted inventory
1,200	600	1,800	1,000	depletion
2,000	600	2,600	2,000	Increase production
2,800	600	3,400	3,000	.
3,600	600	4,200	4,000	.
4,400	**600**	**5,000**	**5,000**	**Equilibrium**
5,200	600	5,800	6,000	.
6,000	600	6,600	7,000	.
6,800	600	7,400	8,000	Unwanted inventory
7,600	600	8,200	9,000	accumulation
8,400	600	9,000	10,000	.
9,200	600	9,800	11,000	.
10,000	600	10,600	12,000	.
10,800	600	11,400	13,000	Decrease production

continue to refer to *ADE* as aggregate demand, however, because aggregate demand is the standard terminology.

Geometrically, *ADE* is obtained by adding I^d vertically to C^d. Since I^d is constant at $600, *ADE* is just $600 larger than C^d at every level of Y. In other words, *ADE* has the same shape as C^d. Most important, the slope of *ADE* is

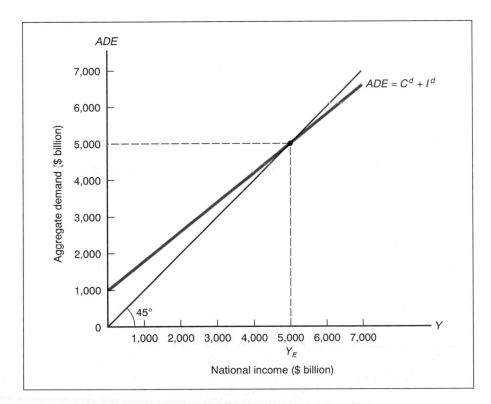

FIGURE 10.9

The Equilibrium Level of National Income

The figure is a graph of the equilibrium level of national income for our simplest economy from the data in Table 10.3. The line ADE indicates the aggregate desired expenditures, or aggregate demand, at each level of national income, *Y*. ADE in our simplest model is the sum of consumption demand by households, C^d, and total investment demand by business firms, I^d. National income is on the horizontal axis and aggregate demand is on the vertical axis. The aggregate demand and income data are in real terms, in billions of constant dollars. The equilibrium level of national income is at the intersection of the ADE line and the 45-degree line, $5,000 in our simplest model. At the equilibrium, national income equals aggregate demand. $Y_E = C^d + I^d$. The value of income, or output, generated by the producers equals the value of goods and services that the final demanders want to buy.

EQUILIBRIUM LEVEL OF NATIONAL INCOME

The level of national income at which aggregate demand equals national income; alternatively, the level of national income at which saving demand equals investment demand.

the same as the slope of C^d, the MPC, which is equal to .80 in our simplest economy. Refer again to Table 10.3, and notice that every $1,000 change in Y increases ADE by $800. For example, when Y increases from $2,000 to $3,000, ADE increases from $2,600 to $3,400, an increase of $800.

The **equilibrium level of national income,** labeled Y_E, occurs at the intersection of ADE and the 45° line in Figure 10.9, when national income is $5,000. The equilibrium level of national income is $5,000 because $5,000 is also the value of aggregate demand when Y is $5,000. The firms have guessed that the aggregate demand for their output will be $5,000, so they produce that level of GDP and generate that level of national income. The firms have guessed correctly. Refer to Table 10.3. When national income is $5,000, households want to buy $4,400 worth of consumer goods and services (first column of the table), and firms want to buy $600 worth of investment goods (second column of the table). In the aggregate, therefore, households and firms want to buy $5,000 worth of final products ($5,000 = $4,400 + $600), exactly the value of final products that the firms have produced.

The equilibrium condition for our simplest economy is satisfied:

$$Y = C^d + I^d \quad \text{at } Y = \$5,000$$

Aggregate supply in the product markets, the left-hand side, equals aggregate demand in the product markets, the right-hand side, so that nobody has any incentive to change their decisions. The economy stays at $5,000, the equilibrium level or Y_E, unless something causes the ADE line to shift.

Adjusting to Equilibrium

The economy automatically moves to the equilibrium if it does not happen to be there. Figure 10.10 and the fifth column of Table 10.3 illustrate why the economy always adjusts quickly to its equilibrium.

Consider, first, any level of national income above the equilibrium, $Y_E = \$5,000$. For example, suppose that firms guess the aggregate demand for their output will be $8,000, so they produce that level of output and generate that level of national income, labeled Y_1 in Figure 10.10(a). The firms have guessed wrong this time. Aggregate demand is only $7,400, equal to $6,800 of consumption demand and $600 of investment demand. Therefore, $8,000 cannot be an equilibrium level of income.

We have to return to the national income and product accounts to understand why firms do not continue to produce $8,000 worth of output. The national accounts tell us that the sum of *actual* consumption expenditures (C^A) and *actual* investment expenditures (I^A) must be $8,000 when national income is $8,000. National income equals the sum of expenditures by final demanders—this is a national income and product accounting identity that is true at *every* level of national income. $Y_1 = C_1^A + I_1^A = \$8,000$.

Therefore, aggregate *actual* expenditures are given by the height of the 45° line at $8,000 in the figure, equal to national income. But aggregate demand, or aggregate *desired* expenditures, is only $7,400, the height of the ADE line at $8,000. $ADE = C_1^d + I_1^d = \$7,400$. Someone is buying $600 worth of goods that they do not want to buy. That someone turns out to be the business firms. They are "buying" unwanted goods for their inventories.

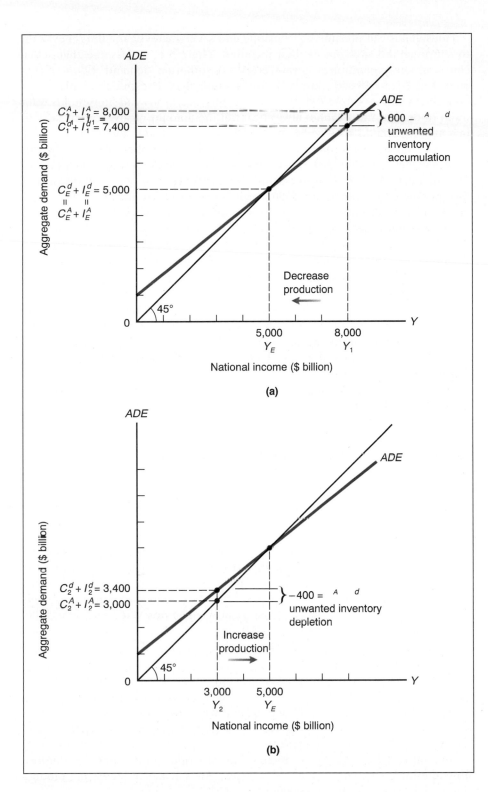

FIGURE 10.10

Adjusting to the Equilibrium Level of National Income

The figure shows how the economy automatically adjusts to the equilibrium level of income, $5,000 in our simplest model, at the intersection of the ADE and 45-degree lines. In Figure 10.10(a), the economy is initially above the equilibrium at $Y_1 = \$8,000$. Aggregate demand, $C_1^d + I_1^d$, is only $7,400. The difference between national income and aggregate demand, $600, is the vertical distance between the ADE and 45-degree lines at $8,000. The $600 is unwanted inventory accumulation; firms are not selling as much as they thought they would. The firms respond by cutting production to reduce their inventories until national income returns to $5,000, the equilibrium level. At the equilibrium, firms' actual and desired investment in inventory are equal. $I_E^d = I_A^d$. In Figure 10.10(b), the economy is initially below the equilibrium at $Y_2 = \$3,000$. Aggregate demand, $C_2^d + I_2^d$, is $3,400. The difference between national income and aggregate demand, $(-)\$400$, is the vertical distance between the ADE and 45-degree lines at $3,000. The $(-)\$400$ is unwanted inventory depletion; firms are selling more than they thought they would. The firms respond by increasing production to increase their inventories until national income returns to $5,000, the equilibrium level.

Households can presumably consume and save whatever amounts they want to consume and save out of their incomes. Therefore, we assume that actual consumption expenditures always equal consumption demand. $C_1^A = C_1^d = \$6,800$ at $Y_1 = \$8,000$. Similarly, we assume that investment in plant and equipment and investment in housing are whatever firms and households want them to be. But firms cannot always control the amount of investment in their inventories. Should they guess wrong about the demand for their products, they end up investing more or less in inventory than they want to. In this example they guessed that consumers and firms would buy \$8,000 worth of final products. In fact, consumers and firms only want to buy \$7,400 worth of final products. The remaining \$600 worth of unsold goods piles up in the firms' inventories, representing unwanted inventory investment.

Refer to the ninth line in Table 10.3. $I^d = \$600$, as always. When $Y = \$8,000$, $C_1^A = C_1^d = \$6,800$. Therefore, $I_1^A = \$1,200$, the difference between Y_1 and C_1^A ($\$1,200 = \$8,000 - \$6,800$). This is the national income and product accounting identity. Finally, $I_1^A - I_1^d = \$600$, the amount of the unwanted inventory investment ($\$600 = \$1,200 - \$600$).

This situation cannot continue because firms do not let unwanted goods pile up in their inventories. As we saw in the preceding section, they react by cutting production until the amount that they are investing in inventory is exactly what they want it to be. Lower production means a lower level of national income, so that Y falls below \$8,000.

Firms experience unwanted inventory accumulation whenever aggregate demand is less than national income. But ADE is less than Y for any value of Y greater than \$5,000. For example, at $Y = \$7,000$, aggregate desired expenditures are only \$6,600, and firms experience \$400 of unintended and unwanted inventory accumulation. Therefore, firms continue to cut production until $Y_E = \$5,000$, at which point $I^d = I^A = \$600$, and investment in inventory is exactly what firms want it to be.

To summarize: *At any Y greater than* Y_E, *ADE is below the 45° line, which means that aggregate demand is less than national income. Firms cut production to* Y_E *to avoid unwanted inventory accumulation.*

The reverse situation applies for any level of national income below the equilibrium level. Refer to Figure 10.10(b). Suppose that firms guess that the demand for their products will be \$3,000, so they produce $Y_2 = \$3,000$. Once again the firms have guessed wrong; only this time aggregate demand exceeds \$3,000. Households want to consume \$2,800, and firms want to invest \$600, for an aggregate demand of \$3,400. $ADE = \$3,400$ at $Y_2 = \$3,000$. The households and the firms are buying \$400 more worth of goods than the firms thought they would buy.

The national income and product accounting identity says that actual expenditures must equal \$3,000. $Y_2 = C_2^A + I_2^A = \$3,000$. But $C_2^A = C_2^d = \$2,800$. Therefore, $I_2^A = \$200$, the difference between Y_2 and C_2^A ($\$200 = \$3,000 - \$2,800$). The \$400 difference between the actual expenditures and the desired expenditures represents unwanted inventory depletion. $I_2^A - I_2^d = -\$400$ ($-\$400 = \$200 - \$600$). This situation cannot continue because firms do not want to stock out of inventory. They react by increasing production and Y increases above \$3,000.

Firms experience unwanted inventory depletion whenever aggregate demand is greater than national income. But ADE is greater than Y for any value of Y less than \$5,000. So firms increase production to \$5,000, the equilibrium level of income.

To summarize: *At any Y less than* Y_E, *ADE is above the 45° line, which means that aggregate demand exceeds national income. Firms increase production to* Y_E *to avoid unwanted inventory depletion.*

In conclusion, the *equilibrium* level of national income, *the point at which* ADE *cuts the 45° line*, is the only sustainable level of national income for the economy. The desire of firms to keep their inventories under control automatically drives the economy to its equilibrium.

EQUILIBRIUM IN TERMS OF SAVING AND INVESTMENT

The national income and product accounts teach us that if national income equals national product, then saving must equal investment. This implies that the equilibrium for the economy can be described in terms of saving and investment, which is called the leakages-and-injections approach to equilibrium.

Households receive all the national income, but they do not spend all their income. They save part of it. The amount they save represents a *leakage* from the product markets because the dollars of saving do not return directly to the firms as sales of consumer goods and services. The saving has to be made up by the investment of the firms, which the saving ultimately finances. The investment is the *injection* into the product markets that offsets the saving leakage. The circular flow of economic activity can only be in equilibrium if saving demand equals investment demand: The amount that the households want to save has to match the amount that the firms want to invest. In other words, the desired leakages from the circular flow equal the desired injections into the circular flow at the equilibrium.

The households do all the saving in our simplest economy, and the firms do all the investment (except for investment in housing), and households and firms have different motives for saving and investing. Households save to be able to consume more in the future. Firms invest to maximize their profits. Therefore, although *actual* saving must equal *actual* investment, saving demand, the amount that households *want* to save, does not necessarily equal investment demand, the amount that firms *want* to invest. We can see this in our simplest economy. Investment demand is $600 (billion) at all levels of economic activity. Saving demand varies with the level of economic activity, however. It equals $600 only at one level of national income—the equilibrium level.

Table 10.4 and Figure 10.11 represent the savings = investment equilibrium for our simplest economy. The first column of Table 10.4 records the level of saving at each level of national income listed in the third column. The saving data reproduce the data from Table 10.2 (remember that disposable income equals national income in our economy). The second column of the table records the constant investment demand of $600.

Saving and investment are on the vertical axis of Figure 10.11, and national income, *Y*, is on the horizontal axis. The saving function, S^d, reproduces the saving function from Figure 10.3. The investment demand curve, I^d, is horizontal at $600 as before. S^d reaches $600 and intersects I^d when *Y* equals $5,000, the equilibrium level of national income from the preceding section. (Refer to the sixth line of Table 10.4 to confirm that saving is $600 when national income is $5,000.) The equilibrium level of national income has to be the same as before because S^d corresponds to the consumption function, C^d, from the previous section.

TABLE 10.4   The Equilibrium Level of National Income for the Simplest Economy: Household and Business Sectors—Saving = Investment Approach—($ billion)

SAVING DEMAND (S^d)	INVESTMENT DEMAND (I^d)	NATIONAL INCOME (Y)	ACTUAL SAVING AND INVESTMENT ($S^A = I^A$)	UNWANTED INVENTORY DEPLETION ($-$) OR ACCUMULATION ($I^A - I^d$)
$(-) 400	$600	$ 0	$(-) 400	$(-) 1,000
(-) 200	600	1,000	(-) 200	(-) 800
0	600	2,000	0	(-) 600
200	600	3,000	200	(-) 400
400	600	4,000	400	(-) 200
600	**600**	**5,000**	**600**	**0 (Equilibrium)**
800	600	6,000	800	200
1,000	600	7,000	1,000	400
1,200	600	8,000	1,200	600
1,400	600	9,000	1,400	800
1,600	600	10,000	1,600	1,000
1,800	600	11,000	1,800	1,200
2,000	600	12,000	2,000	1,400
2,200	600	13,000	2,200	1,600

To summarize: *The equilibrium level of national income occurs at the intersection of* S^d *and* I^d.

No other level of national income can be an equilibrium. If the economy happens to be operating at some other level, the firms quickly adjust their production and return the economy to the equilibrium. The story is the same as before.

Suppose, for example, that Y is temporarily above the equilibrium, at $7,000. The level of saving demand is $1,000 when $Y_1 = \$7,000$, which is $400 more than the investment demand of $600. Households are saving more, and consuming less, than firms thought they would. The result is unwanted inventory accumulation that the firms do not allow to continue. They cut production and quickly return the economy to the equilibrium Y of $5,000.

We can see the unwanted inventory accumulation if we remember that *actual* saving (S^A) must equal *actual* investment (I^A). This is a national income and product accounting identity that is true at *every* level of national income. We are also assuming that the households save what they want to save. $S_1^A = S_1^d = \$1,000$. Therefore, actual investment must also equal $1,000, which is $400 more than the firms' intended investment of $600. $I_1^A = \$1,000$; $I^d = \$600$. $I_1^A - I^d = \$400$. Therefore, $400 is the unwanted investment in inventory (refer also to the fourth and fifth columns of the table).

At the equilibrium, when $Y = \$5,000$:

$$S_E^d = S_E^A = \$600 = I_E^A = I_E^d$$

The amount that households want to save equals the amount that firms want to invest. In particular, the firms are investing exactly what they want to in their inventories. The economy remains at $5,000 unless some event causes S^d or I^d to shift. (Refer to the fourth and fifth columns of the table.)

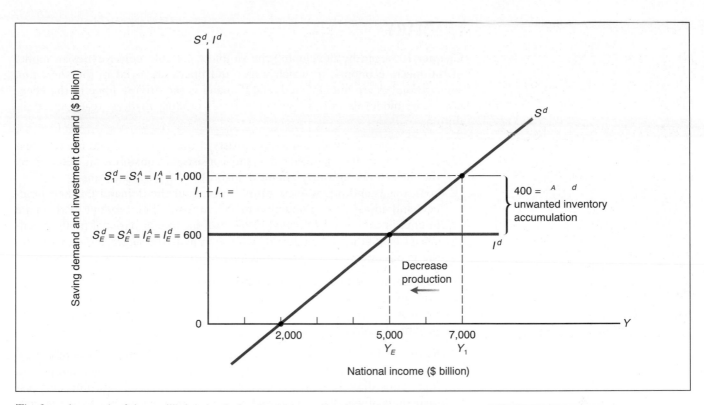

The figure is a graph of the equilibrium level of national income for our simplest economy from the data on saving and investment demand in Table 10.4. The economy is at its equilibrium level of national income when saving demand, S^d, the amount that households want to save, equals investment demand, I^d, the amount that business firms want to invest. The equilibrium level of national income is at the intersection of S^d and I^d in the figure, $5,000 in our simplest model. At Y_1 = $7,000, above the equilibrium, the actual level of saving and the actual level of investment both equal $1,000. Actual saving always equals actual investment; that is a national income accounting identity. But the actual investment of $1,000 is greater than the firms' desired investment of $600. The difference, $400, represents unwanted investment in inventory. The firms respond by cutting production until national income falls to the equilibrium level of $5,000. The equilibrium is the same as in Figure 10.9, because $S^d = I^d$ at the same level of national income for which $Y = C^d + I^d$.

FIGURE 10.11

Saving, Investment, and Equilibrium

Test your understanding of the equilibrium level of national income one last time by describing what happens in terms of saving and investment when the economy is operating below the equilibrium of $5,000—say, at Y = $4,000. Can you see that the firms are experiencing unwanted inventory depletion at Y = $4,000 and that they respond by increasing production until the economy returns to the equilibrium?

Looking Ahead

We are now ready to see how the economy moves from one equilibrium to another in response to changes in aggregate demand. This is one of the main topics of Chapter 11.

SUMMARY

Chapter 10 began by developing the simplest possible new Keynesian model of the macro economy, in which wages and prices are fixed in the short run, some resources are unemployed, and demand is the driving force in the economy. The model describes how the nation's product markets reach an equilibrium.

1. The simplest possible economy consists of the household and the business sectors, in which aggregate demand consists of consumption demand by the households and investment demand by the business firms.

2. With wages and prices fixed, firms guess about the demand for their products and adjust their production to the demand. The product markets are in equilibrium when the level of national income or national product generated in producing goods and services equals the aggregate demand for the goods and services, consumption demand plus investment demand.

The next two sections of the chapter discussed the determinants of consumption demand and investment demand, with particular emphasis on the extent to which national income is itself an important determinant of either component of aggregate demand.

3. Keynes believed that households' consumption demand consists of a small component that is unrelated to disposable income and a larger component that varies directly with the current level of disposable income, but less than dollar for dollar. The other things equal relationship between consumption demand and disposable income is the consumption function, or the propensity to consume. The other things being held constant are all the factors that influence consumption demand besides disposable income—wealth, expectations about the future, the age distribution of the population, and so forth. Changes in these variables increase or decrease consumption demand at every level of disposable income—they shift the consumption function up or down.

4. The marginal propensity to consume, labeled the MPC, is the slope of the consumption function, the ratio of the change in consumption demand to the change in disposable income. The MPC is a fraction between zero and one, inclusive.

5. The saving function, or the propensity to save, is the mirror image of the consumption function because all that households can do with their disposable income is either consume it or save it. The marginal propensity to save, labeled the MPS, is the slope of the saving function, the ratio of the change in saving demand to the change in disposable income. The MPS is also a fraction between zero and one, inclusive. Also, MPC + MPS = 1.

6. The Keynesian consumption function appears to be consistent with aggregate consumption over time in the United States. Research on consumption demand typically finds that the short-run MPC is between .60 and .80 and the long-run MPC is slightly above .90.

7. The chief competitor to the Keynesian consumption function is the Life-Cycle Hypothesis, which assumes that households plan their consumption over their lifetimes, borrowing and lending to smooth consumption relative to income. They adjust their lifetime consumption plans to changes in their

lifetime resources, which consist of current and expected labor market earnings and inherited wealth. They also take into account current and expected future government transfers and taxes, which affect their lifetime disposable incomes. The Life-Cycle Hypothesis is an important component of the new classical model of the economy.

8. A principal implication of the Life-Cycle Hypothesis is that the MPC out of changes in current disposable income is very low, close to zero, if the change is either anticipated or, if unanticipated, viewed as temporary. The MPC out of unanticipated changes in current disposable income that are viewed as permanent is close to one. In fact, the MPC out of temporary changes in disposable income does appear to be much smaller than the MPC out of permanent changes in disposable income in the United States, as predicted by the model. The Life-Cycle Hypothesis also provides a theory to explain how other factors, such as wealth and the age distribution of the population, affect consumption demand. Its main weakness is that it underpredicts the aggregate MPC in the United States.

None of the three components of investment demand—plant and equipment, inventory, and housing—is closely related to the level of national income. Therefore, we are assuming that each is a constant, independent of the level of national income in the simplest model. The third section of the chapter made the following additional points about each component of investment demand.

Plant and Equipment

9. The desired stock of *capital* is related to a firm's expected output or sales, which implies that *investment* in plant and equipment is related to the *change* in output or sales, not to the level. The desired stock of capital also depends on the firm's capital/output ratio, which is determined primarily by the firm's production technology, the cost of capital, and other factor prices.

10. The cost of capital depends primarily on four factors: the price of each unit of capital, interest rates, the rate of depreciation of the capital, and the tax system. Changes in corporate tax rates, depreciation allowances, and investment tax credits are the primary fiscal policy tools that Congress uses to influence the cost of capital.

11. Economists agree that changes in the cost of capital affect the desired stock of capital, but they do not agree on whether changes in the cost of capital have an immediate and important effect on investment demand. One problem in trying to estimate the effect of the cost of capital on investment demand is that many investment projects take such a long time to order, build, and put into place. The result is that much of the investment in any one year is the result of investment decisions made in past years, so that the relationship between the cost of capital and current investment is difficult to determine.

Inventory Investment

12. Unlike plant and equipment, firms can adjust their inventories quickly to their desired stock of inventory. An important assumption of the new Keynesian aggregate demand model is that firms do not tolerate unwanted inventory accumulation or depletion. If demand is higher than anticipated

and inventories are depleting, firms hire more workers and increase production. If demand is lower than anticipated and inventories are accumulating, firms lay off workers and decrease production.

Housing Demand

13. Investment in housing is the one component of investment demand that is highly sensitive to changes in the cost of capital, in particular, to changes in mortgage interest rates.

The fourth section described how the macro economy automatically seeks an equilibrium level of national income and national product.

14. The equilibrium occurs when aggregate demand equals the level of national income generated in production. In terms of the aggregate demand–45° line graph, the equilibrium occurs at the intersection of the aggregate demand line *ADE* and the 45° line.

15. When national income is above the equilibrium, aggregate demand is less than national income, and firms experience unwanted inventory accumulation. They cut production to the equilibrium. When national income is below the equilibrium, aggregate demand is greater than national income, and firms experience unwanted inventory depletion. They increase production to the equilibrium.

The final section of Chapter 10 described the equilibrium in terms of saving demand and investment demand.

16. The equilibrium level of national income occurs when saving demand equals investment demand. Actual saving always equals actual investment—this is a national income and product accounting identity. But the amount households *want* to save, saving demand, equals the amount firms *want* to invest, investment demand, only at the equilibrium.

KEY TERMS

age-earnings profile
aggregate desired expenditures
(aggregate demand for expenditures)
capital/output ratio
consumption function

cost of capital
equilibrium level of national income
Life-Cycle Hypothesis
marginal efficiency of capital

marginal propensity to consume
marginal propensity to save
saving function
total investment demand

QUESTIONS

1. What is the marginal propensity to consume? What is the marginal propensity to save? How are the two concepts related? Explain.
2. The text assumed that the demand for investment in plant and equipment is unrelated to the current level of national income, even though the demand for capital (the desired stock of capital) may be closely related to the current level of national income. Explain why there is a difference between the demand for capital and the demand for investment in this regard.
3. Answer the following questions about the cost of capital.

a. What is the cost of capital, and what are the principal components that make up the cost of capital?
b. How does the U.S. Congress attempt to influence the cost of capital?
c. Virtually all economists assume that the demand for capital (the desired stock of capital) is closely related to the cost of capital. Why? At the same time, economists disagree about whether investment demand is closely related to the cost of capital. Explain why there is a difference between the demand for capital and the demand for investment in this regard.

4. Name two events that might cause the consumption function to shift up (or down). Explain how, and why, they cause the consumption function to shift.

5. Answer the following questions about inventory investment.
   a. Can the demand for inventory investment be negative? Why or why not?
   b. What is happening to firms' investment in inventory when the level of national income is above the equilibrium level of income? In answering this question, distinguish between firms' actual investments in inventory and their desired investments in inventory (their investment demand).

6. Explain why the economy adjusts to one equilibrium level of national income for a given level of aggregate demand (that is, for a given *ADE* line in the *ADE*–45° line graph).

7. Compare and contrast the Keynesian consumption function and the Life-Cycle Hypothesis. Your answer should cover the following points, with appropriate explanations.
   a. What assumptions does each one make about how households form their consumption plans?
   b. What does each one imply about the relationship between aggregate consumption demand and current disposable income?
   c. How well does each one fit the facts about consumption demand in the United States?

8. Suppose that a star baseball player is scheduled to receive a $750,000 increase in salary next year according to the terms of his contract. Next year is the third year of his five-year contract with the club. The contract stipulates how much his salary is to be during each year of the contract. Would you expect his consumption to increase next year? Indicate how your answer to this question depends on whether he is a Life-Cycle consumer or a Keynesian consumer.

9. The baby boom generation, born between 1947 and 1964, is the largest group within the U.S. population. The baby boomers are now in their middle-age years.
   a. Why, and how, might the passage of the baby boomers through middle age affect the level of saving in the United States? Indicate how your answer depends on whether the baby boomers are likely to be Life-Cycle or Keynesian consumers. Which do you think they are likely to be? Why?

   b. Why is the level of saving an important issue in the United States (or in any nation)?

10. An economy has the following consumption data.

DISPOSABLE INCOME ($ BILLION)	CONSUMPTION DEMAND ($ BILLION)
0	200
1,000	1,100
2,000	2,000
3,000	2,900
4,000	3,800
5,000	4,700

Answer the following questions based on these data, giving appropriate explanations.
   a. What is the break-even level of disposable income? Over what range of disposable incomes are households saving? Over what range of disposable incomes are households dissaving?
   b. What is the marginal propensity to consume for this economy? What is the marginal propensity to save?
   c. Define the average propensity to consume. What happens to the average propensity to consume as disposable income increases in this economy? Is this pattern realistic?
   d. Name some events that might cause consumption demand to increase (or decrease) at every level of disposable income, and indicate why. For each event, explain also what is happening to saving demand.
   e. These data are reasonably consistent with the Keynesian consumption function. Are they likely to be consistent with consumption according to the Life-Cycle Hypothesis?

11. Suppose that our simplest economy has the consumption demand and the investment demand relationships pictured below. Show how you would combine the two relationships to determine the equilibrium level of national income for the economy.

   Also, select a level of national income different from the equilibrium level on your diagram. Discuss how and why the economy would automatically return to the equilibrium level of national income from the level of national income that you selected.

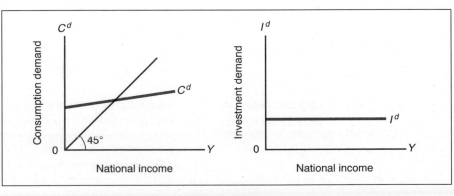

10
Algebraic Analysis of Equilibrium

This appendix shows how to derive the equilibrium in Chapter 10 algebraically, using both the aggregate demand and the saving = investment methods. It also shows what happens when the economy is out of equilibrium.

THE AGGREGATE DEMAND METHOD

The general form of the straight-line Keynesian consumption function used throughout Chapter 10 is

$$C^d = C_0 + \text{MPC} \cdot Y$$

C^d is consumption demand, and Y stands for either disposable income or national income in our simplest economy. C_0 is the intercept on the vertical axis, the value of consumption demand when $Y = 0$. MPC, the marginal propensity to consume, is the slope of the consumption function, the ratio $\Delta C^d / \Delta Y$. $C_0 = 400$, and MPC $= 0.8$ in the chapter, so that our hypothetical consumption function is

$$C^d = 400 + 0.8 \cdot Y$$

(All dollar values in the appendix are in billions of constant dollars.)

The general form of the total investment demand used throughout Chapter 10 is

$$I^d = \bar{I}$$

I^d is total investment demand, and $\bar{I}$ is a constant independent of the level of Y. $\bar{I} = 600$ in the chapter, so that our hypothetical investment demand is

$$I^d = 600$$

The equilibrium level of national income is the level that equals aggregate demand, the sum of $C^d + I^d$.

Equilibrium condition: $Y = C^d + I^d$

Substitute the equations for C^d and I^d on the right-hand side of the equilibrium condition:

$$Y = [400 + 0.8 \cdot Y] + 600$$
$$Y = 1,000 + 0.8 \cdot Y$$

Bring all Y terms to the left-hand side and solve for Y:

$$Y - 0.8 \cdot Y = 1,000$$
$$0.2 \cdot Y = 1,000$$
$$Y = 1,000/0.2 = 5,000$$

The equilibrium level of Y, or Y_E, is 5,000.
   To check that 5,000 is the equilibrium, add C^d and I^d at $Y = 5,000$:

$$C^d = 400 + 0.8 \cdot 5,000 = 400 + 4,000 \quad = 4,400$$
$$I^d = \quad\quad\quad\quad\quad\quad\quad\quad\quad\quad\quad\quad\quad\quad\quad \underline{600}$$
$$C^d + I^d = \quad\quad\quad\quad\quad\quad\quad\quad\quad\quad\quad\quad\quad\quad 5,000$$

THE SAVING DEMAND EQUALS INVESTMENT DEMAND METHOD

The general form of the straight-line saving function used throughout Chapter 10 is

$$S^d = S_0 + \text{MPS} \cdot Y$$

S^d is saving demand. S_0 is the intercept of the saving function on the vertical axis, the value of saving demand when $Y = 0$. MPS, the marginal propensity to save, is the slope of the saving function, the ratio $\Delta S^d/\Delta Y$. The saving function is the mirror image of the consumption function because households can only consume or save their incomes.

$$C^d + S^d = Y$$

at every level of Y, including $Y = 0$. Therefore, the intercepts of the two functions must add to zero. $C_0 + S_0 = 0$. Since $C_0 = 400$, $S_0 = -400$.
   Also, the proportions of any change in income that are consumed and saved must add to one. $\Delta C^d/\Delta Y + \Delta S^d/\Delta Y = 1$. Therefore, the slopes of the two functions must add to one.

$$MPC + MPS = 1$$

The MPS = 0.2 when the MPC = 0.8.

Therefore, our hypothetical saving function that corresponds to our hypothetical consumption function is

$$S^d = -400 + 0.2 \cdot Y$$

Investment demand is as above:

$$I^d = 600$$

The equilibrium level of national income is the level at which saving demand equals investment demand.

Equilibrium condition: $S^d = I^d$

Substitute the equations for S^d and I^d in the equilibrium condition:

$$-400 + 0.2 \cdot Y = 600$$

Isolate Y on the left-hand side, and solve for Y:

$$0.2 \cdot Y = 1,000$$
$$Y = 5,000$$

To check that 5,000 is the equilibrium, compared S^d and I^d at $Y = 5,000$:

$$S^d = -400 + 0.2 \cdot 5,000 = -400 + 1,000 = 600 = I^d$$

THE ECONOMY OUT OF EQUILIBRIUM

Let's consider one example of the economy out of equilibrium—say, at $Y = 7,000$.

Aggregate Demand Versus National Income

At $Y = 7,000$:

$$
\begin{aligned}
C^d &= 400 + 0.8 \cdot 7,000 = 400 + 5,600 &&= 6,000 \\
I^d &= &&\underline{600} \\
C^d + I^d &= &&6,600 < 7,000
\end{aligned}
$$

Aggregate demand is less than Y by 400, so the firms experience 400 of unwanted inventory accumulation. They cut production back to the equilibrium of 5,000.

Saving Demand Versus Investment Demand

At $Y = 7,000$:

$$S^d = -400 + 0.2 \cdot 7,000 = -400 + 1,400 = 1,000 > 600 = I^d$$

Saving demand exceeds investment demand by 400. The saving leakage from the product markets exceeds the investment injection into the product markets by 400, so the firms experience 400 of unwanted inventory accumulation. They cut production back to the equilibrium of 5,000.

QUESTIONS

Given the following information for an economy, find the equilibrium level of national income, Y_E.

$$C^d = 300 + 3/4 \cdot Y \qquad C^d = \text{consumption demand}$$
$$I^d = 40 \qquad\qquad I^d = \text{investment demand}$$
$$\qquad\qquad\qquad Y = \text{income (national and disposable)}$$

Also:

a. What is the value of the marginal propensity to consume?
b. Find the relationship between saving demand (S^d) and national income (Y). What is the value of the marginal propensity to save?

c. Show that $S^d = I^d$ at the equilibrium level of income computed above.
d. How large is aggregate demand when national income equals 1,000?
e. Describe how the economy will adjust to the equilibrium level of national income when national income is temporarily at 1,000.

11

The Spending Multiplier, Fiscal Policy, and Unemployment

LEARNING OBJECTIVES

CONCEPTS TO LEARN

The macroeconomic policy problem	Balanced budget multipliers
Spending multiplier	Recessionary and inflationary gaps
Tax multiplier	Practical limitations of U.S. fiscal policy
Transfer multiplier	

CONCEPTS TO RECALL

The production possibilities frontier [3]	Saving function [10]
The circular flow of economic activity [4]	Marginal propensity to consume [10]
Full employment [6]	Marginal propensity to save [10]
Fiscal policy [9]	Equilibrium level of national income [10]
Consumption function [10]	

he United States faced a mixed blessing in the early 1990s. The collapse of the Soviet Union reduced the threat of war in Europe and allowed the United States the luxury of making substantial cuts in defense spending. The defense cutbacks were doubly welcome because of the huge federal budget deficit, which was approaching $400 billion by 1992.

At the same time, however, the economy was mired in a recession. The timing of the defense cutbacks could not have been worse for the economy. Defense spending is almost entirely purchases of goods and services, and, as we will see in Chapter 11, reducing government purchases has the most powerful negative effect on the equilibrium level of national income of all possible budgetary changes. The large cuts in defense spending served to deepen the recession and slow down the recovery, especially in states such as California, Connecticut, Massachusetts, Texas, and Washington whose industries rely heavily on defense contracts.

Normally the federal government could have countered the effects on the economy of the military cutback by reducing taxes or increasing spending in other nondefense areas. Indeed, many people had long awaited the day when the government could divert some of its spending from defense to domestic purposes. But Ross Perot's presidential campaign had successfully hammered away on the evils of the large federal budget deficit, and Congress was not about to make any move that would increase the deficit.

President Clinton was extremely worried about the negative impact of the defense cutbacks. In his first months in office he pushed hard for a modest $16 billion package of spending increases to help boost the economic recovery. Most economists thought that Clinton's stimulus package was too small to make much of a difference to the economy, but it did not matter anyway. Congress refused to pass even $16 billion in spending increases and handed Clinton his first political defeat on economic policy.

Chapter 11 focuses on John Maynard Keynes's two great insights into macroeconomic policy that paved the way for government intervention into the macro economy. His first insight was that aggregate demand may not lead the economy to a very desirable equilibrium. The market economies of the United States, Great Britain, and Western Europe were operating way below their production possibilities frontiers during the Great Depression of the 1930s, when Keynes was formulating his ideas about how the macro economy operates. His second insight was that wages and prices could not be counted on to bring an economy to its frontier, at least not in any reasonable period of time. Nonetheless, Keynes argued that the capitalist countries did not have to wait for the Depression to run its course. The government could lead the economy back to the frontier with proper doses of fiscal and/or monetary policies.

Chapter 11 begins by describing the macroeconomic policy problem as Keynes and his new Keynesian disciples define it.

THE MACROECONOMIC POLICY PROBLEM

We saw in Chapter 10 how aggregate demand leads the economy to one equilibrium level of national income when wages and prices are sticky and firms react passively to the demand for their products. The policy problem is that the equilibrium determined by the level of aggregate demand may not be a very desirable equilibrium. Figure 11.1 illustrates two possibilities that have plagued all the developed market economies from time to time.

Figure 11.1 pictures both the production possibilities frontier for the economy and the aggregate demand–45° line graph from Chapter 10. The axes of the production possibilities frontier are consumer goods and services and investment goods, the two kinds of final products in our simplest economy.

Figure 11.1(a) represents the situation that Keynes saw during the Great Depression. Refer, first, to the aggregate demand–45° line graph. Aggregate demand at every level of national income is given by the solid aggregate demand line, ADE_0. ADE_0 intersects the 45° line at Y_0^A, the equilibrium level of national income for the economy. Unfortunately, Y_0^A is not a very desirable equilibrium, as illustrated by the production possibilities frontier graph. Y_0^A lies well inside the production possibilities frontier. Aggregate demand is not sufficient to fully employ all the resources in the economy; willing and able workers are unemployed, and machines lie idle. The economy is in a recession or worse, as in the 1930s.

Return once more to the aggregate demand–45° line graph. The line Y_{FE} is called the full-employment level of national income. It indicates the level of national income that would be necessary to fully employ all resources, so that the economy is operating on its frontier. In other words, Y_{FE} is the representation of the two-dimensional production possibilities frontier in one dimension, national income. Since Y_{FE} is drawn to the right of the equilibrium Y_0^A, the graph shows that the economy is operating inside its frontier.

Notice one important difference between the equilibrium and the full-employment levels of national income. The position of Y_0^A is determined by the level of aggregate demand. It must occur at the intersection of ADE_0 and the 45° line. In contrast, the position of Y_{FE} is somewhat arbitrary because we cannot be sure where to draw Y_{FE}. We do not know what the full-employment level of national income really is, just as we do not know how far out from the origin to draw the production possibilities frontier. Nonetheless, drawing Y_{FE} somewhere to the right of Y_0^A indicates that the economy is operating below its frontier. The farther Y_{FE} is to the right of Y_0^A, the farther the economy is below the frontier. Representing the state of the economy in this way is sufficient for our purposes.

Recessions and depressions are not the only undesirable possibilities. Market economies occasionally try to push beyond their means, which can only build up inflationary pressures that, at worst, lead the economy down the path to hyperinflation. Figure 11.1(b) illustrates the inflationary scenario. The equilibrium level of national income, Y_0^B, on the aggregate demand–45° line graph, at the intersection of the solid aggregate demand line ADE_0 and the 45° line, is beyond the production possibilities frontier. Y_{FE}, the one-dimensional representation of the frontier, is to the left of the equilibrium Y_0^B. Drawing Y_{FE} anywhere to the left of the equilibrium level of national income on the aggregate demand–45° line graph represents an economy trying to live beyond its means.

No economy can really live beyond its means, of course. Y_{FE} is the highest possible level of *real* or constant dollar national income. An equilibrium such as Y_0^B beyond Y_{FE} has to be interpreted as nominal or current dollar national income. The difference in dollar value between Y_0^B and Y_{FE} is all due to inflation which, as we will see later on in the text, accelerates if the economy continues to try to live beyond its means.

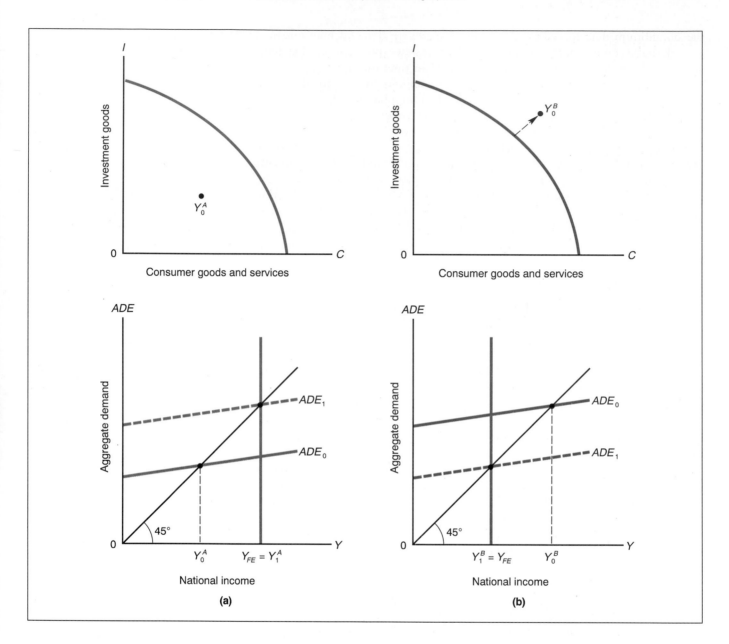

FIGURE 11.1

Unemployed Resources and Inflation

The figure shows two problems that afflict market economies, unemployed resources and inflation, analyzed from a new Keynesian perspective. In Figure 11.1(a), the equilibrium level of income is Y_0^A, at the intersection of ADE_0 and the 45-degree line in the bottom graph. The top graph shows that Y_0^A, is below the production possibilities frontier; the economy has unemployed resources. The vertical line Y_{FE} in the bottom graph represents the production possibilities frontier. It is the level of national income that would fully employ all resources and place the economy on the frontier. The government's policy problem is to increase aggregate demand from ADE_0 to ADE_1 through expansionary fiscal and/or monetary policies to bring the economy to equilibrium on the frontier. In Figure 11.1(b), the equilibrium level of income is Y_0^B, at the intersection of ADE_0 and the 45-degree line in the bottom graph. The top graph shows that Y_0^B is beyond the production possibilities frontier; the economy is trying to live beyond its means, which can only result in an inflation. The vertical line Y_{FE} in the bottom graph is the maximum real output that the economy can produce. Y_0^B is nominal, current dollar national income. The government's policy problem is to decrease aggregate demand from ADE_0 to ADE_1 through contractionary fiscal or monetary policies to bring the economy to equilibrium on the frontier.

Keynes's first policy insight was that, left to its own devices, an economy driven by aggregate demand could continue to operate above or below the frontier for a long time. In particular, Keynes disagreed with the prevailing classical theory of his day that wages and prices would quickly adjust to bring the economy back to the frontier. Keynes did not think wages and prices could be counted on to re-establish an equilibrium on the frontier in any reasonable period of time.

This led to Keynes's second policy insight, that the government could bring the economy to its frontier fairly quickly by means of fiscal and/or monetary policies. The production possibilities frontier is more or less fixed in the short run. Y_{FE} on the aggregate demand–45° line graphs in Figure 11.1 depends on the quantity and the quality of the nation's resources and on the available production technologies, which are difficult to change in the short run. But the government does not have to change the frontier. Instead, fiscal and monetary policies work by changing the level of aggregate demand, which changes the equilibrium level of national income. Aggregate demand can be changed fairly quickly. The short-run policy goal, then, is to change the equilibrium level of national income so that the equilibrium is on the frontier.

An economy in a recession, or depression, operating well below its production possibilities frontier, requires a dose of expansionary fiscal and/or monetary policy. **Expansionary** fiscal and monetary policies are policies that increase the level of aggregate demand. Refer to Figure 11.1(a). The short-run policy goal is to use expansionary fiscal and/or monetary policy to shift the level of aggregate demand up from the solid line, ADE_0, to the dotted line, ADE_1. ADE_1 intersects the 45° line at Y_{FE}, so that the new equilibrium level of national income, Y_1^A, coincides with Y_{FE} and the economy is now operating on its production possibilities frontier.

An economy trying to live beyond its production possibilities frontier requires a dose of contractionary fiscal and/or monetary policy. **Contractionary** fiscal and monetary policies are policies that decrease the level of aggregate demand. Refer to Figure 11.1(b). The short-run policy goal is to use contractionary fiscal and/or monetary policy to shift the level of aggregate demand down from the solid line, ADE_0, to the dotted line, ADE_1. ADE_1 intersects the 45° line at Y_{FE}, so that the new equilibrium level of national income, Y_1^B, coincides with Y_{FE} and the economy is now operating on its production possibilities frontier.

Economists refer to fiscal and monetary policies as *aggregate demand management* because they keep the economy operating on or near its production possibilities frontier by manipulating the level of aggregate demand. The economy always operates at its equilibrium. The short-run policy goal as Keynes described it is to match the equilibrium with the frontier.

EXPANSIONARY POLICY

A fiscal or monetary policy that increases the level of aggregate demand.

CONTRACTIONARY POLICY

A fiscal or monetary policy that decreases the level of aggregate demand.

The Steps in Doing Policy

Aggregate demand management is essentially a three-step process.

Step 1. Policy makers first have to decide on an appropriate target level of national income, Y_{Target}, that they want to establish as the equilibrium. Keynes naturally thought in terms of achieving the full-employment level of income, Y_{FE}, because unemployment was the overriding problem during the Great Depression. Policy makers always give full employment very high priority, but there are three other macroeconomic policy goals besides full employment: long-run economic growth, price stability, and a zero balance of trade and a stable dollar. We saw in Chapter 9 that the four macroeconomic policy goals are often conflicting, so that policy makers have to compromise. For example, increasing aggregate demand to reduce unemployment can make inflation worse and lower the value of the dollar. If unemployment is near the natural rate of unemployment, U_{NR}, but inflation is worsening, the government may decide that a lower equilibrium level of national income is desirable to fight inflation, even if it increases unemployment somewhat. The target level of national income that the policy makers choose is the one that they believe represents the best compromise or balance among the four policy goals.

Step 2. The second step for the policy makers is to build a reliable model of the economy. The model performs three essential functions. It tells the policy makers what the equilibrium level of national income would be without any government policies. It also indicates how the equilibrium changes in response to particular doses of fiscal and monetary policies. Finally, the model shows how different levels of national income affect each of the macroeconomic policy goals. Policy makers cannot set the target level of national income unless they understand the links between the macroeconomic policy goals and the economy. We have begun to build our own model of the economy, the model from Chapter 10, to help us understand the government's policy options.

Step 3. The third and final step for the policy makers is to design specific fiscal and/or monetary policies that will match the equilibrium level of national income, Y_E, with the target level, Y_{Target}.

One of the goals of this chapter is to see how fiscal policy affects the equilibrium level of national income. To do this, we need to understand how changes in aggregate demand affect the equilibrium through a process called the spending multiplier. This is best accomplished with our simplest model, before we add the government sector.

THE SPENDING MULTIPLIER

As noted in Chapter 9, an economy led by aggregate demand has a feedback nature to it. Firms respond to an increase in aggregate demand by increasing production and generating more income in the economy. The workers, landlords, and capitalists who receive the income consume some of it, which generates still more demand. Producers of consumer goods and services respond to the increase in consumption demand by increasing production, which generates more income, which leads to still more consumption, and so on. The result is that an initial change in aggregate demand leads to a much greater change in the equilibrium level of income. The feedback nature of the economy through consumption demand multiplies the effects of the increase in aggregate demand on the economy. A concept called the spending multiplier indicates the ultimate effect of the feedback process on the equilibrium.

Suppose that aggregate demand increases or decreases at every level of national income. In other words, *ADE* in the aggregate demand–45° line graph shifts up or down. The **spending multiplier,** labeled $M_{Spending}$, relates the change in the equilibrium level of national income to the initial change, or shift, in aggregate demand.

SPENDING MULTIPLIER

The ratio that relates the change in the equilibrium level of national income to an initial change, or shift, in aggregate demand.

Saving, Investment, and the Spending Multiplier

The saving = investment view of equilibrium is the easiest way to see the spending multiplier graphically. Figure 11.2 illustrates the spending multiplier.

The economy is originally in equilibrium at $Y_0 = \$5,000$, at the intersection of the saving function, S^d, and the original investment demand curve, I_0^d. S^d, I_0^d, and the original equilibrium are taken from our simplest economy in Chapter 10. The slope of S^d, the marginal propensity to save (MPS), is .20. I_0^d is $600 at every level of Y. (All data are in billions of constant dollars.)

Suppose that firms become more optimistic about the future and investment demand increases by $100, from $I_0^d = \$600$ to $I_1^d = \$700$. Y_0 can no longer be the equilibrium level of national income because I_1^d exceeds S^d at $Y_0 = \$5,000$. Now that demand has increased, firms would experience unwanted depletion of their inventories if they continued to produce $5,000 worth of goods and services. Instead, firms increase production in response to the increase in demand to rebuild their inventories. The new equilibrium occurs at $Y_1 = \$5,500$, at the intersection of S^d and the new investment demand curve, I_1^d.

Notice that the change in the equilibrium level of national income is $500, which is five times more than the $100 increase in investment demand ($Y_1 - Y_0 = \$5,500 - \$5,000 = \$500$). The feedback nature of the economy has multiplied the change in investment demand by a factor of five. How do we know that the new equilibrium is $500 greater than the original equilibrium? The answer lies in the marginal propensity to save, the MPS.

The ratio of the change in I^d to the change in Y_E is the rise over the run of the saving function S_d, the slope of S^d, or the MPS.

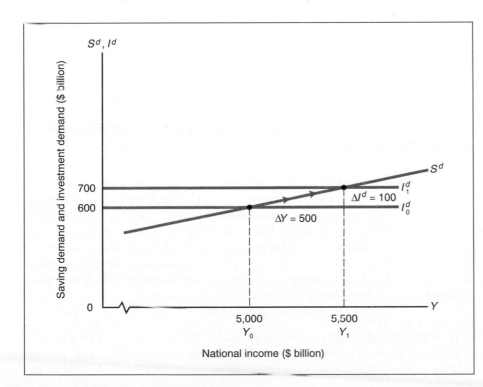

S^d, I^d

Saving demand and investment demand ($ billion)

700

600

S^d

$\Delta I^d = 100$

I_1^d

I_0^d

$\Delta Y = 500$

0

5,000
Y_0

5,500
Y_1

Y

National income ($ billion)

FIGURE 11.2

The Spending Multiplier

The economy is initially in equilibrium at $Y_0 = \$5,000$ in our simplest economy, at the intersection of the saving function, S^d, and investment demand curve I_0^d. The data are in billions of constant dollars. Then investment demand increases by $100, from $I_0^d = \$600$ to $I_1^d = \$700$. The new equilibrium is $Y_1 = \$5,500$, at the intersection of S^d and I_1^d. The $100 increase in investment demand leads to a multiplied $500 increase in the equilibrium level of national income. The value of the spending multiplier is [1/MPS]. MPS, the slope of S^d, equals 0.20. Therefore the value of the spending multiplier is 5 (= 1/0.20).

$$\text{Slope of } S^d = \text{MPS} = \Delta I^d / \Delta Y$$

The MPS is .20, and $\Delta I^d = \$100$. To solve for the change in national income, bring ΔY to the left-hand side of the equation and MPS to the right-hand side.

$$\begin{aligned} \Delta Y &= (1/\text{MPS}) \cdot \Delta I^d \\ &= (1/.20) \cdot \$100 \\ &= 5 \cdot \$100 \\ &= \$500 \end{aligned}$$

The term 1/MPS is the spending multiplier, M_{Spending}.

$$M_{\text{Spending}} = 1/\text{MPS}$$

M_{Spending} multiplies the change in investment demand to compute the change in the equilibrium level of national income. $M_{\text{Spending}} = 5$ when MPS = .20. Every $1 increase in investment demand increases the equilibrium level of national income by $5.

M_{Spending} can also be expressed in terms of the slope of the consumption function, the marginal propensity to consume (MPC). We know that MPC + MPS = 1, or MPS = 1 − MPC. Therefore,

$$M_{\text{Spending}} = 1/(1 - \text{MPC})$$

For example, when the MPS is .20, MPC = .80, the slope of the consumption function in our simplest economy.

$$M_{\text{Spending}} = 1/(1 - .80) = 1/.20 = 5$$

the same value of M_{Spending} as above. The spending multiplier is more commonly expressed in terms of the MPC than the MPS.

Properties of the Spending Multiplier

Two properties of the spending multiplier are worth noting before developing the intuition behind the multiplier process.

THE MPS, THE MPC, AND M_{SPENDING} *The higher the value of the MPC, the higher the value of* $M_{Spending}$. Alternatively, *the lower the value of the MPS, the higher the value of* $M_{Spending}$. Table 11.1 illustrates the different values of M_{Spending} for different values of the MPC and the MPS. When the MPC and the MPS are both .50, $M_{\text{Spending}} = 2$. As the MPC rises from .50 to .90 in the table (alternatively, as the MPS falls from .50 to .10), M_{Spending} increases from 2 to 10. The numbers in the table indicate that changes in aggregate demand can have a very powerful effect on the equilibrium level of national income.

THE SPENDING MULTIPLIER IS SYMMETRIC   *The feedback multiplier process is symmetric. Changes in aggregate demand have the same powerful effect on the economy whether aggregate demand is increasing or decreasing.* In our example a $100 de-

**TABLE 11.1   The Marginal Propensities to Save and Consume and the
Spending Multiplier**

MARGINAL PROPENSITY TO SAVE (MPS)	MARGINAL PROPENSITY TO CONSUME (MPC)	SPENDING MULTIPLIER $[M_{\text{Spending}} = 1/\text{MPS} = 1/(1 - \text{MPC})]$
.50	.50	2
.33(1/3)	.67(2/3)	3
.25	.75	4
.20	.80	5
.10	.90	10

crease in investment demand would lead to a $500 decrease in the equilibrium level of national income. To see why, return to Figure 11.2, and reverse the initial and the final equilibria in your mind's eye. Think of $I_1^d = \$700$ and $Y_1 = \$5,500$ as the initial equilibrium, and imagine that investment demand decreases by $100, from $I_1^d = \$700$ to $I_0^d = \$600$. The new equilibrium occurs at the intersection of S^d and I_0^d, at $Y = \$5,000$. The decrease in Y is $500, five times as large as the change in I^d.

Saving Demand and the Spending Multiplier

Why does a change in aggregate demand lead to a multiplied change in the equilibrium of national income? The intuition in terms of saving and investment is the following. Return to our first example of the $100 increase in investment demand.

The economy can be in equilibrium only if saving demand equals investment demand. Therefore, when investment demand increases by $100, saving must also increase by $100 to return the economy to equilibrium. What causes saving to increase? The answer is the increases in national income as firms respond to the increase in demand by increasing production. Households move upward along the aggregate saving function, S^d, in the direction of the arrows as they receive the additional income. The equilibrium is restored when national income increases enough to generate $100 more saving demand.

One dollar of additional national income does not generate one dollar of additional saving demand, however. It generates only $.20 of additional saving in our example, since the MPS is .20. Five dollars of additional national income are needed to generate one dollar of additional saving. Therefore, national income must increase by $500 to generate the additional $100 of saving.

In general, each additional dollar of national income generates only MPS times one dollar worth of additional saving. This means that 1/MPS dollars of additional national income are required to raise saving by one dollar. Therefore, each dollar increase in investment demand requires 1/MPS dollars of additional income to restore the saving demand = investment demand equilibrium. Thus, 1/MPS is the spending multiplier.

The same argument applies in reverse to a decrease in investment demand. Saving demand must decrease by the same amount as investment demand in order to restore the equilibrium. Therefore, national income must fall by

1/MPS times the decrease in investment demand to reduce saving demand by the required amount.

Consumption, National Income, and the Multiplier

The intuition behind the feedback multiplier process is most evident from the interrelationship between consumption demand and national income. Table 11.2 illustrates the round-by-round feedback between consumption and national income that generates the multiplied increase in national income. The MPC is .80, as above.

The first row of the table shows the immediate effect of the $100 increase in investment demand. The $100 change in investment demand appears in the second column. Producers of investment goods see the increase in demand, so they produce $100 more investment goods and generate $100 more national income. National income increases immediately by $100, as indicated by the fourth column.

The economy continues to expand, however. The workers, landlords, and capitalists associated with the investment goods industries now have $100 more income. They spend MPC times the $100, or $80 ($80 $= 0.80 \cdot$100), on consumer goods and services: food, clothing, entertainment, cars, and the like. Consumption demand in the second round has increased by $80 (third column, second row). Producers of these consumer goods and services see the increased consumption demand and increase their production by $80, generating $80 more national income in the process. The $80 increase in national income appears in the fourth column, second row of the table. National income has now increased by $180: $100 in the first round in the investment goods industries and $80 in the second round in the consumer goods industries.

The economy expands still further in the third round. The $80 of additional national income generated in the second round is received by workers, landlords, and capitalists associated with the consumer goods industries. They

TABLE 11.2   The Multiplier Process Round by Round ($ billion)

ROUND	CHANGE IN INVESTMENT DEMAND (ΔI^d)	CHANGE IN CONSUMPTION DEMAND (ΔC^d)	CHANGE IN NATIONAL INCOME (ΔY)
1	$100	$ —	$100
			+
2	—	$.80 \cdot$100 = 80	80
			+
3	—	$.80 \cdot$ 80 = 64	64
		.	+
4		.	.
.		.	.
.		.	.
.		.	+
.		.	
			Final $\Delta Y = 500

spend MPC times the $80, or $64 ($64 = 0.80 · $80) on consumer goods and services, the same kinds of goods and services that households bought in the second round. Consumption demand in the third round has increased by $64 (third column, third row). Producers of these consumer goods and services see the increased consumption demand and increase their production by $64, generating $64 more national income in the process. The $64 increase in national income appears in the fourth column, third row of the table. National income has now increased by $244: $100 in the first round in the investment goods industries; $80 in the second round in the consumer goods industries; and $64 in the third round, also in the consumer goods industries.

The process continues indefinitely as the households that receive more income each round spend MPC of it on consumer goods and services in the next round. The interaction between consumption demand and national income drives the round-by-round increases in national income. Notice, though, that each new round is only MPC, or .80, as large as the preceding round. The additions to national income become ever smaller, and the economy homes in on a new higher equilibrium level of national income.

The final change in national income in response to the initial $100 increase in investment demand is the sum of the changes listed in the fourth column of the table. The change in the equilibrium is

$$\Delta Y = \$100 + \$80 + \$64 + \dots$$

which can be written as

$$\Delta Y = \$100 + (0.80 \cdot \$100) + (0.80 \cdot 0.80 \cdot \$100) + \dots$$
$$\Delta Y = \$100 + (0.80 \cdot \$100) + [(0.80)^2 \cdot \$100] + \dots$$

Each successive round is smaller than the previous round by .80, the MPC. The sum of the round-by-round changes in the limit turns out to be

$$\Delta Y = \$100 \cdot [1/(1 - 0.80)] = \$100 \cdot [1/(1 - MPC)]$$
$$= \$100 \cdot M_{Spending} = \$100 \cdot 5 = \$500$$

$100 is the initial change in aggregate demand, the increase in investment demand; $1/(1 - MPC)$ is the spending multiplier. The change in income is $M_{Spending}$ times the initial change in aggregate demand, or $500, as expected.

REFLECTION: The spending multiplier gives us another perspective on why the marginal propensity to consume is less than one. What would the value of the spending multiplier be if the MPC were one or greater than one?

The Spending Multiplier, Recessions, and Expansions

The multiplier process explains why, when aggregate demand declines, the newspapers are filled for awhile with stories about the economy going from bad to worse. Recessions tend to build in strength before they bottom out, whether at the national level or the state level. Suppose, for example, that the U.S. automobile industry suffers a very bad year—car sales fall way off. As a result, General Motors, Ford, and Chrysler cut production and lay off auto workers, and unemployment begins to rise in Michigan. The decline of the Michigan economy spreads far beyond the auto industry, however. The unemployed auto workers have less income, so they spend less on consumer goods and services. Retailers see that the demand for their products has fallen, so they cut production and reduce their work forces. Income in the state falls still further, round by round, until the majority of the multiplier process has been completed. Within a year or so storefronts are boarded up, downtown office space lies vacant, new housing starts have declined, and the Michigan unemployment rate reaches 10 percent or more. The majority of the newly unemployed during the year are not even auto workers. The multiplier process magnifies the steep decline in new car sales into a statewide recession in Michigan.

That's the bad news. The good news is that the multiplier process helps the entire state economy recover when auto sales pick up again. The recovery begins with the auto workers being recalled and then spreads round by round as the increased income and consumption demand interact to produce a booming economy once again.

The Michigan story illustrates another very important point about the spending multiplier. The initial $100 increase in aggregate demand in our example does not have to be an increase in investment demand. The spending multiplier applies equally to all components of aggregate demand. The initial increase could have been a $100 increase in consumption demand, such as an increase in the demand for new cars. Or the $100 could have been a combined increase in investment demand and consumption demand totaling $100, such as a $75 increase in consumption demand and a $25 increase in investment demand. A $100 increase in aggregate demand generates a $500 increase in the equilibrium level of national income no matter what component or components of aggregate demand increase in the first round to start the process going. The interrelationship between consumption demand and disposable income takes over from the second round onward to add $400 of new national income and complete the multiplier process following the initial increase in aggregate demand in the first round.

THE SPENDING MULTIPLIER IN THE UNITED STATES

Our simplest economy is adequate for illustrating the round-by-round nature of the multiplier process. But the model is far too simple to capture some of the more important features of the actual spending multiplier in the United States.

We noted in Chapter 10 that the actual MPC in the United States increases over time, from around .75 in the short run to a value slightly above .9 in the long run. An MPC of .9 implies a spending multiplier of 10 in our simplest economy:

$$M_{\text{Spending}} = 1/(1 - \text{MPC}) = 1/(1 - .9) = 1/0.1 = 10$$

In fact, the actual spending multiplier in the United States is far below 10. Economists Gary Fromm and Lawrence Klein surveyed 11 of the leading forecasting models in the United States. Six of the models that have a distinct Keynesian orientation place the actual U.S. spending multiplier within a range of 1.0 to 3.0, far below 10. In addition, five of these six models show a hump-shaped pattern for the multiplier process, illustrated in Figure 11.3.

The horizontal axis records the passage of time, by quarters. The vertical axis indicates the change in national income in response to a $1 increase in

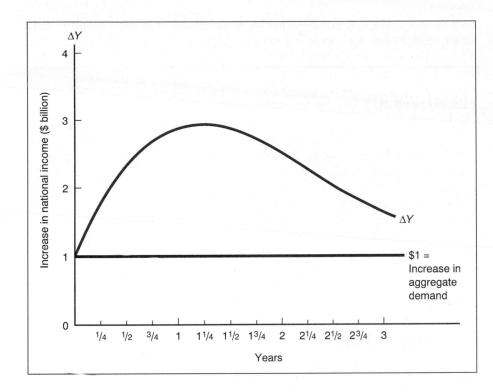

FIGURE 11.3

The Spending Multiplier in the United States

The figure illustrates the properties of the actual spending multiplier in the United States, as estimated by the large forecasting models that have a new Keynesian perspective. The horizontal axis records the passage of time, by quarters, after an increase in aggregate demand. The vertical axis records the increase in national income resulting from a $1 increase in aggregate demand. The spending multiplier is hump-shaped. The increase in national income builds to its peak value within 6 months to a year and three quarters after the increase in aggregate demand, and then declines to its final value between 1.0 and 2.5 after about three years.

aggregate demand. According to the forecasting models, the spending multiplier builds to its peak between 1.5 and 3.0 anywhere from six months to a year and three-quarters after the increase in aggregate demand. It then declines to a final value between 1.0 and 2.5 within three years. Our simplest model does not have this hump-shaped feature. The multiplier process described above builds continuously over time to its final value.[1]

Our simplest model is consistent with one feature of the U.S. spending multiplier, however: the speed of the multiplier process. The forecasting models suggest that the spending multiplier reaches its peak value fairly quickly. The same is true in our simplest model in the sense that the majority of the change in national income occurs in the early rounds. The change in national income in our example is $244 after only three rounds ($244 = $100 + $80 + $64), approximately half of the final change of $500. The change in national income is $336 after five rounds, two-thirds of its final value, and nearly $450 after 10 rounds, 90 percent of its final value. Three to five rounds of the multiplier would probably occur within six months of calendar time, and 10 rounds within a year, a time frame roughly consistent with the large forecasting models.

Nonetheless, we clearly have a way to go in building a model that adequately describes the operation of the U.S. economy, even qualitatively. Subsequent chapters will complicate the simplest model in a number of ways that both reduce the value of the spending multiplier and generate the hump-shaped pattern of Figure 11.3. A section on the U.S. spending multiplier will appear

[1]L. Klein and G. Fromm, "A Comparison of Eleven Econometric Models of the United States," *American Economic Review* 63, No. 2 (May 1973): 385–393. Table 5, p. 391 has a summary of the multipliers.

each time we add a new feature to the model that brings the spending multiplier more in line with its actual value.

FISCAL POLICY

We are now in a position to add the government sector to our model and explore the possibilities of fiscal policy. Recall that fiscal policy is budgetary policy. Fiscal policy refers to changes in the federal government's purchases of goods and services (G), and/or transfer payments (Tr), and/or taxes (Tx) undertaken for the specific purpose of changing the level or the composition of the circular flow of economic activity.

Can fiscal policy affect the level of aggregate demand and the equilibrium level of national income? Yes indeed. Changes in government purchases, transfer payments, and taxes each have a powerful, multiplied effect on the circular flow of economic activity. Let's consider each component of the federal budget separately.

Government Purchases of Goods and Services

Changes in government purchases of goods and services have a direct, dollar-for-dollar effect on aggregate demand because government purchases of goods and services are part of aggregate demand. With the government sector added to our model, aggregate demand is now the sum of the household sector's consumption demand (C^d), the business sector's investment demand (I^d), and the government sector's demand for goods and services (G^d). The new equilibrium condition in the product markets is

$$Y = C^d + I^d + G^d$$

The right-hand side of the equation is the aggregate demand for final goods and services by households, business firms, and the federal, state, and local governments. The left-hand side of the equation is the supply of final goods and services to the product markets by the producers, the value of the national product or national income. The product markets are in equilibrium when aggregate demand equals national income.

G^d AND NATIONAL INCOME   The first question to ask is whether government purchases are closely related to the current level of national income. The answer is no. Federal and state and local purchases of goods and services are primarily determined by factors other than the current level of economic activity.

Most federal purchases are for defense or are defense-related, about 80 percent of the total federal G. Defense purchases are clearly determined by national security and other military considerations, not the current level of national income.

State and local government purchases are larger than federal purchases in the United States, approximately 60 percent of total G, and cover a whole range of functions. Public education is the largest component of state and local G,

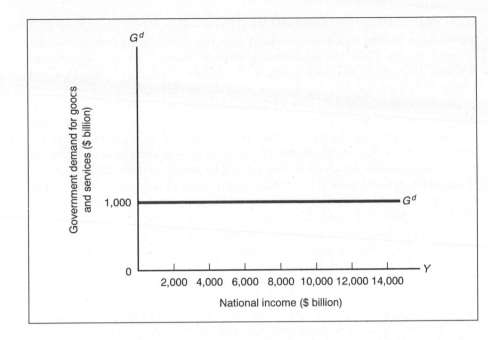

FIGURE 11.4

Government Spending on Goods and Services and National Income

Purchases of goods and services by the federal, state, and local governments are not closely related to the level of national income. They are determined, instead, by such factors as national security considerations and the number of children to be educated by the local public schools. Therefore, our simplest model assumes that government purchases are unrelated to the level of national income, Y. In particular, we are assuming that government spending on goods and services is $1,000 over the range of values that national income is likely to have (in billions of constant dollars). Therefore, the graph of government spending on goods and services, G^d, is horizontal at a value of $1,000. Changes in the other factors that influence government purchases shift G^d up or down.

about 35 percent of the total. Other important areas of state and local spending are the construction and maintenance of highways; public safety, including police, fire, and correctional institutions; the public hospitals; and general government, which covers the operating expenses of the administrative, legislative, and judicial branches of the governments.

Many factors besides income have an important influence on each of these components of state and local G. For example, local education expenditures are driven as much or more by the number of children to be educated than by a community's income. Expenditures on highway maintenance and construction depend heavily on weather conditions and the traffic density on the roadways. Police and correctional expenditures vary with crime rates. And so on. State and local income is just one of many factors determining the size of the state and local public sector, and probably not the most important factor.

Therefore, we will assume that the total government demand for goods and services is unrelated to the current level of national income, just as we did for investment demand. Figure 11.4 illustrates.

Government demand for goods and services is on the vertical axis, and the current level of national income, Y, is on the horizontal axis. G^d is horizontal, equal to $1,000 (billion) regardless of the level of Y. G was approximately $1,000 billion ($1 trillion) in the United States during 1992. The $1,000 of G^d is determined by factors other than the current level of national income. Changes in these other factors, such as more or fewer children to be educated, shift G^d up or down. We are also assuming that governments can buy what they want to buy, just as with consumption demand. The government demand for goods and services is the same as the actual government purchases of goods and services.

The assumption that G^d is unrelated to Y in the short run is very realistic for the United States. Even the huge private and government mathematical forecasting models assume that there is little or no feedback from the current level of national income to federal, state, and local government purchases.

EQUILIBRIUM WITH THE GOVERNMENT SECTOR   Since G^d is a constant, adding the government sector to our model does not change the properties of the simplest model. Only the equilibrium level of national income is different because government demand is added to aggregate demand. Table 11.3 and Figure 11.5 show the new equilibrium with the government sector.

The first two columns of Table 11.3 reproduce the hypothetical consumption function and the investment demand relationship from Chapter 10. (As before, all data are in billions of dollars.) The MPC = .80, and investment demand is constant at $600. The third column of the table records the constant $1,000 of government demand for goods and services. The fourth column shows the level of aggregate demand at each level of national income listed in the fifth column. Aggregate demand in the fourth column is the sum of the first three columns, C^d (first column) + I^d (second column) + G^d (third column).

The equilibrium level of national income is $10,000, when aggregate demand (fourth column) equals national income (fifth column). The reason why $10,000 must be the equilibrium is the same as in the simplest economy without a government sector. Firms guess about the demand for their products and produce to meet the demand. In this case $10,000 is the only level of national income at which firms guess right. The $10,000 worth of final goods and services that they produce is exactly equal to the value of final goods and services that households, firms, and governments in the aggregate want to buy. Therefore, no one has any incentive to change from the equilibrium.

The firms have guessed wrong about the demand for their products at any level of national income other than the equilibrium and experience unwanted inventory depletion or accumulation as a result. Firms quickly adjust their guesses about demand and their production to the equilibrium level, so that their inventories behave as they want them to. Refer to the sixth column of the table to see the adjustment to the equilibrium.

Figure 11.5 pictures the new equilibrium on the aggregate demand–45° line graph. The aggregate demand line, ADE, in Figure 10.9 for the simplest econ-

TABLE 11.3   The Equilibrium Level of National Income: Household, Business, and Government Sectors ($ billion)

CONSUMPTION DEMAND (C^d)	INVESTMENT DEMAND (I^d)	GOVERNMENT DEMAND (G^d)	AGGREGATE DEMAND $(C^d+I^d+G^d)$	NATIONAL INCOME (Y)	INVENTORIES AND PRODUCTION RESPONSE
$ 400	$600	$1,000	$ 2,000	$ 0	Unwanted inventory
1,200	600	1,000	2,800	1,000	depletion
2,000	600	1,000	3,600	2,000	Increase production
2,800	600	1,000	4,400	3,000	.
3,600	600	1,000	5,200	4,000	.
4,400	600	1,000	6,000	5,000	.
5,200	600	1,000	6,800	6,000	.
6,000	600	1,000	7,600	7,000	.
6,800	600	1,000	8,400	8,000	.
7,600	600	1,000	9,200	9,000	.
8,400	**600**	**1,000**	**10,000**	**10,000**	**Equilibrium**
9,200	600	1,000	10,800	11,000	
10,000	600	1,000	11,600	12,000	Unwanted inventory
10,800	600	1,000	12,400	13,000	accumulation
					Decrease production

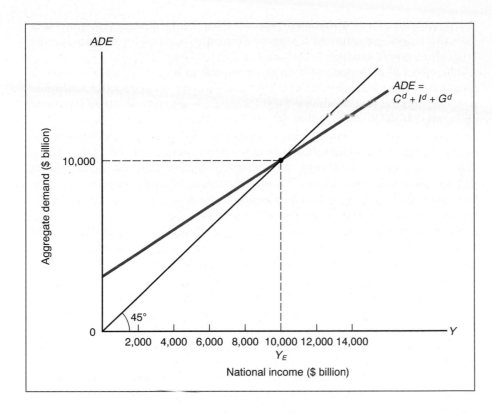

FIGURE 11.5

The Equilibrium Level of National Income with the Government Sector

The figure is a graph of the equilibrium level of national income for our economy from the data in Table 11.3. Adding the government sector to our model means that aggregate desired expenditures, *ADE*, or aggregate demand, is the sum of consumption demand by households (C^d), investment demand by business firms, (I^d), and government spending on goods and services by the federal, state, and local governments (G^d). $ADE = C^d + I^d + G^d$. Adding the government sector does not change the basic properties of our simplest model without a government sector from Chapter 29. The equilibrium level of national income is at the intersection of the *ADE* and the 45-degree lines, equal to $10,000 (in billions of constant dollars). Also, since G^d is a constant, the slope of the *ADE* line remains the marginal propensity to consume (MPC), and the value of the spending multiplier is still $M_{\text{Spending}} = 1/(1 - \text{MPC})$.

omy without the government was the vertical sum of the consumption function, C^d, from Figure 10.1 and the investment demand curve, I^d, from Figure 10.8. Because I^d is a constant, *ADE* had the same shape as C^d. The new *ADE* line in Figure 11.5 simply adds another constant in the vertical direction, the horizontal government demand curve, G^d, from Figure 11.4. Since I^d and G^d are both constant at every level of Y, *ADE* continues to have the same shape as C^d. *ADE* is now $1,600 above C^d, the sum of I^d ($600) and G^d ($1,000), but *ADE* still has the same slope as C^d, the MPC, equal to .80. Refer to the fourth and fifth columns of Table 11.3. Aggregate demand increases by $800 for every $1,000 increase in national income. For example, aggregate demand increases by $800 from $10,000 to $10,800 when national income increases by $1,000 from $10,000 to $11,000.

The equilibrium occurs at the intersection of *ADE* and the 45° line, just as in the simplest economy. The new equilibrium is $Y_E = $10,000$; Y_E used to be $5,000 without the $1,000 of government demand. Otherwise, the graphical analysis of the equilibrium is the same as in the simplest economy.

G^d AND THE SPENDING MULTIPLIER   The value of the spending multiplier remains the same with the addition of the government sector: $M_{\text{Spending}} = 1/(1 - \text{MPC})$ as before. Therefore, M_{Spending} is still equal to 5 because the MPC out of changes in national income is still equal to .80. Every $1 change, or shift, in aggregate demand leads to a $5 change in the equilibrium level of income. Furthermore, the spending multiplier applies to changes in G^d because G^d is part of aggregate demand. Every $1 increase or decrease in G increases or decreases aggregate demand by $1 and leads to a $5 increase or decrease in the equilibrium level of national income. Changes in government purchases give the federal government a very powerful tool indeed for influencing the level of economic activity.

The effect of a change in G^d on the equilibrium level of national income is most easily seen by referring to Table 11.2, which illustrated the multiplier process. Suppose that the initial $100 increase in aggregate demand had been an increase in G^d from $1,000 to $1,100 rather than a $100 increase in I^d. The analysis would carry through exactly as before. Rounds two and beyond are driven by the interrelationship between consumption demand and national income, which is unchanged by the addition of a constant level of government demand for goods and services. All that matters in the first round to start the multiplier process going is that producers of some type of goods and services see an increase in demand, increase production to meet the new demand, and generate $100 more national income. The demand for consumer goods and services takes over from there on to complete the multiplier process.

The same principle regarding the spending multiplier holds as before: The spending multiplier applies equally to initial changes, or shifts, in any and all components of aggregate demand, whether ΔC^d, or ΔI^d, or ΔG^d.

In conclusion,

$$\Delta Y_E = M_{\text{Spending}} \cdot \Delta G^d$$

Note, for example, that adding $1,000 worth of government purchases of goods and services to the simplest model increased the equilibrium level of national income by $5,000, from $Y_E = \$5,000$ to $Y_E = \$10,000$.

FINANCING GOVERNMENT EXPENDITURES   Any change in a government's budget always involves at least two separate steps because the government's total expenditures must be matched by the receipt of funds to finance them. For instance, an increase in government purchases has to be financed somehow. The first step is the increase in G^d. The second step is the financing, and the government has a number of options. One option is to "finance" the increase in G^d by decreasing other expenditures in the same amount, which keeps all the changes on the expenditure side of the budget. The other option is to increase government revenues, and here governments have three main choices: (1) print new money, (2) issue new debt, or (3) increase taxes.

Printing new money, dollar bills, to finance new expenditures is an option available only to the federal government because state and local governments do not issue their own money. The federal government has occasionally financed some of its expenditures by printing money, although the usual sources of revenue are new debt and taxes. In any event we will hold off analyzing the print-money option until the chapters on money and monetary policy. An increase in government expenditures financed by printing money is a combined fiscal and monetary policy. In contrast, an increase in government expenditures financed by issuing new debt or raising taxes is a pure fiscal policy.

DEBT FINANCING   Governments run a deficit when their expenditures exceed their revenues from tax collections and fees. They borrow to finance their deficits by issuing new debt in the form of promissory notes that they sell to the public. A *promissory note* is a promise to repay the face value of the note, usually $1,000, at some date in the future, called the maturity date. The note may or may not pay interest to the holder each year until the maturity date. The amount that the buyers/lenders are willing to pay for the notes is the amount of money borrowed to cover the deficit.

The U.S. Treasury issues three kinds of promissory notes: bills, notes, and bonds. Treasury bills mature within 1 year; Treasury notes mature within 1 to 10 years; and Treasury bonds mature anytime beyond 10 years, usually from 10 to 30 years. Treasury bills do not pay interest to the holders, whereas Treasury notes and bonds do.

The federal government has the luxury of borrowing to finance its expenditures because it can always find willing buyers for its debt. Treasury bills, notes, and bonds are highly desirable financial securities. They offer competitive rates of return and a variety of maturity dates. Savers can purchase anything from 180-day Treasury bills to 30-year Treasury bonds. The existing securities are also easily bought and sold, so that savers/lenders can switch the maturity of their debt holdings or exchange their Treasury debt for some other form of saving at any time and in virtually any amount. The final attraction is safety. U.S. Treasury securities are considered to be the safest of all financial securities worldwide: The federal government will be the very last institution to default on its debt payments. Safety is one reason why foreign citizens and institutions have been eager buyers of the federal debt. We noted in Chapter 4 that the federal government has exploited the attractiveness of its debt and has increased its reliance on debt financing ever since 1981, the first year of the Reagan administration. The record annual deficits have continued throughout the Bush administration and into the Clinton administration, with no end in sight.

Chapter 12 will take a close look at the economic implications of an expanding federal debt. Our concern in this chapter is the effect of debt financing on aggregate demand in the short run.

New debt can affect the level of aggregate demand only if it changes the level of saving by households and businesses. We will assume at this point that issuing new federal debt affects the *composition* of saving, but not the *level* of saving. Given the opportunity to buy new issues of Treasury bills, notes, and bonds, some households and businesses choose to buy the Treasury securities rather than placing their saving in bank accounts or purchasing other financial securities, such as stocks, corporate bonds, and certificates of deposit. But they do not increase their saving to buy the new debt. Therefore, issuing new debt has no affect on aggregate demand. Consumption demand and investment demand remained unchanged.

The effect of this assumption is that the spending multiplier applies to a debt-financed increase in government purchases of goods and services. In terms of our model, a $1 increase in G^d financed with new debt increases the equilibrium level of national income by $5, just as above. The spending multiplier also applies to a decrease in government purchases of goods and services if the government reduces its borrowing by the same amount. With less new debt being issued, households and businesses buy other financial securities with the portion of their saving that they would have used to buy the new debt. They do not decrease the level of their saving.

The assumption that increases or decreases in government borrowing have no effect on aggregate demand is an assumption of convenience at this point. It is useful for comparing the relative effects of government purchases, taxes, and transfers on aggregate demand. It is not an accurate assumption, however. Most economists believe that government borrowing does affect aggregate demand even in the short run because it changes the level of interest rates throughout the economy, and some components of aggregate demand are sensitive to interest rates. An analysis of interest rates goes hand in hand with the role of money in the economy, so we will wait until the money chapters of the text to analyze the effects of debt financing on aggregate demand.

The remaining option to finance government purchases, raising taxes, does have a powerful, multiplied effect on the economy. We turn next to the analysis of taxes.

Taxes

Taxes, unlike government purchases, are not part of aggregate demand because they are not a direct payment for a good or a service. Tax checks written to governments do not pass through the product or factor markets within the circular flow of economic activity. Therefore, increases or decreases in taxes have no *immediate* impact on the level of gross domestic product (GDP) or national income. Nonetheless, changes in taxes have a powerful, multiplied effect on the equilibrium level of national income through their indirect effects on consumption demand and investment demand.

An *increase* in taxes *decreases* aggregate demand by decreasing either consumption demand or investment demand, or both. The decrease in aggregate demand leads to a multiplied decrease in the equilibrium level of national income. Conversely, a *decrease* in taxes *increases* aggregate demand by increasing either consumption demand or investment demand, or both. The increase in aggregate demand leads to a multiplied increase in the equilibrium level of national income.

Let's look more closely at the relationships among taxes, consumption demand, and the equilibrium level of national income, using our model as an example. We will consider a $100 increase in taxes to compare the effects with the $100 increase in government purchases analyzed above.

TAX MULTIPLIER

The ratio that relates the change in the equilibrium level of national income to a change in taxes on households.

THE TAX MULTIPLIER   Our goal is to develop a tax multiplier along the lines of the spending multiplier. The **tax multiplier,** labeled M_{Tax}, relates the change in the equilibrium level of national income to a change in taxes on households. The derivation of the tax multiplier proceeds in four steps.

Step 1: Taxes, national income, and disposable income. The first step is to recall that taxes drive a wedge between national income and disposable income. We can no longer assume that the two are equal. In particular, although an increase in taxes has no immediate impact on national income, it does reduce households' disposable income dollar for dollar. Therefore, a $100 increase in taxes paid by households reduces their disposable income by $100.

$$\Delta Y_d = (-)\Delta Tx = (-)\$100$$

The minus sign indicates that disposable income and taxes change in the opposite direction. An increase in taxes decreases disposable income; a decrease in taxes increases disposable income.

Step 2: Consumption demand and disposable income. The second step relates the change in disposable income to the change in consumption demand. The two are related through the marginal propensity to consume (MPC). Every \$1 change in disposable income changes consumption demand by MPC times \$1. The MPC = .80 in our model.

$$\Delta C^d = 0.80 \cdot \Delta Y_d$$

The change in disposable income is equal to the change in taxes, but in the opposite direction. Therefore, every \$1 *increase* in taxes *reduces* consumption demand by MPC times \$1.

$$\Delta C^d = \text{MPC} \cdot (-)\Delta Tx = 0.8 \cdot (-)\Delta Tx = 0.8 \cdot (-)\$100 = (-)\$80$$

Consumption demand decreases by \$80 when taxes increase by \$100, equal to MPC times the change in taxes.

Step 3: Consumption demand and the equilibrium. The third step relates the change in consumption demand to the change in the equilibrium level of national income. The two are related through the spending multiplier.

$$\Delta Y_E = M_{\text{Spending}} \cdot \Delta C^d = [1/(1 - \text{MPC})] \cdot \Delta C^d$$

ΔY_E refers to the change in the equilibrium level of national income. $M_{\text{Spending}} = 5$ in our model.

$$\Delta Y_E = 5 \cdot (-)\$80 = (-)\$400$$

Step 4: The tax multiplier. The last relationship shows that a \$100 increase in taxes decreases the equilibrium level of national income by \$400. Therefore, the tax multiplier in our model is $(-)4$.

$$\Delta Y_E = M_{\text{Tax}} \cdot \Delta Tx$$
$$(-)\$400 = M_{\text{Tax}} \cdot \$100$$
$$M_{\text{Tax}} = (-)4$$

The minus sign indicates that taxes and the equilibrium move in opposite directions. Taxes are a *drain* on aggregate demand. An increase in taxes reduces consumption demand and decreases the equilibrium level of national income. Conversely, a decrease in taxes increases consumption demand and increases the equilibrium level of national income. A \$100 decrease in taxes increases the equilibrium level of national income by \$400.

Notice that the tax multiplier is not as large as the spending multiplier. In particular, the tax multiplier is MPC times the spending multiplier, as well as having the opposite sign.

$$M_{\text{Tax}} = (-)4; \quad M_{\text{Spending}} = 5; \quad (-)4 = (-)0.80 \cdot 5$$

Changes in taxes have a less potent effect on the equilibrium than do changes in aggregate demand because they work indirectly in changing aggregate demand. Every \$1 change in taxes changes consumption demand by only MPC times \$1. The remaining portion of the tax change changes saving demand by MPS times \$1. In our example consumption demand decreases by \$80, and saving demand decreases by \$20 in response to the \$100 increase in taxes. Therefore, aggregate demand changes, or shifts, by only \$80, not by the full \$100. The \$20 of the tax increase that comes out of saving would not have been spent in any case, so it has no effect on aggregate demand. In contrast, the \$100 change in government purchases in our earlier example changes aggregate demand by the full \$100.

In terms of the aggregate demand–45° line graph in Figure 11.5, a \$100 increase in government purchases of goods and services shifts *ADE* up by \$100. A \$100 increase in taxes decreases consumption demand by \$80, so *ADE* shifts down by \$80.

The relationship between the tax multiplier and the spending multiplier in our model is true for any value of the MPC. M_{Tax} is always MPC times M_{Spending} and has the opposite sign. The general expression for the spending multiplier is

$$M_{\text{Spending}} = 1/(1 - \text{MPC})$$

Therefore, the general expression for the tax multiplier is

$$M_{\text{Tax}} = (-)\text{MPC} \cdot M_{\text{Spending}}$$
$$= (-)[\text{MPC}/(1 - \text{MPC})]$$

For an MPC of .80,

$$M_{\text{Tax}} = (-)[0.80/(1 - 0.80)] = (-)[0.80/0.20] = (-)4$$

In conclusion, changes in taxes on households, such as a change in the federal personal income tax, have a powerful, multiplied effect on the equilibrium level of national income. Note, also, that the federal government can change taxes to affect the economy without having to change its expenditures. It can finance a tax cut by increasing its borrowing and issuing new debt, and it can raise taxes and simultaneously reduce its borrowing. The tax multiplier applies to all tax changes affecting households that are offset by changes in borrowing, just as the spending multiplier applies to changes in government purchases that are offset by changes in borrowing.

REFLECTION: Test your understanding of the tax multiplier by seeing if you can rework each step of our example for a \$100 decrease in taxes.

Transfer Payments

Changes in transfer payments are the third tool of fiscal policy, along with changes in government purchases and taxes. Transfer payments are analytically equivalent to negative taxes because the only difference between transfer payments and taxes is the direction in which the money flows. Households and businesses write checks to governments when they pay taxes; governments write checks to households and businesses when they make transfers to them. Otherwise, transfer payments and taxes are identical. Transfer payments, like taxes, are not direct payments for a good or a service, so transfer payments do not enter the circular flow of economic activity and are not part of aggregate demand. Therefore, changes in transfer payments, like changes in taxes, have no immediate impact on GDP or national income. They do, however, have the same powerful, multiplied effect on the equilibrium level of national income as do taxes through their indirect effects on consumption demand and investment demand. The only difference is the direction of the effect. Transfer payments are a contributor to aggregate demand. An *increase* in transfer payments *increases* aggregate demand and the equilibrium level of national income; a *decrease* in transfer payments *decreases* aggregate demand and the equilibrium level of national income.

THE TRANSFER MULTIPLIER   The **transfer multiplier,** labeled M_{Transfer}, relates the change in the equilibrium level of national income to a change in government transfer payments. The derivation of the transfer multiplier proceeds exactly as the derivation of the tax multiplier did. Only the direction of the effects changes. We will again consider a $100 increase in transfer payments and an MPC equal to 0.8. The four steps, briefly, are as follows.

Step 1: Transfers, national income, and disposable income. Although the $100 increase in transfer payments has no immediate impact on national income, it does increase households' disposable income by $100.

Step 2: Consumption demand and disposable income. Consumption demand increases by MPC times the $100 increase in disposable income, or $80. Equivalently, consumption demand increases by MPC times the $100 increase in the transfer payments.

Step 3: Consumption demand and the equilibrium. The equilibrium level of national income changes by M_{Spending} times the change in consumption demand. $M_{\text{Spending}} = 5$, and $\Delta C^d = \$80$. Therefore,

$$\Delta Y_E = 5 \cdot \$80 = \$400$$

Step 4: The transfer multiplier. A $100 increase in transfer payments leads to a $400 increase in the equilibrium level of national income. Therefore, the value of the transfer multiplier is $(+)4$.

$$M_{\text{Transfer}} = 4$$

M_{Transfer} is MPC times M_{Spending} and has the same sign. The transfer multiplier is smaller than the spending multiplier is because transfer payments work indirectly on aggregate demand. The $100 increase in transfer payments increases consumption demand by MPC times $100, or $80, not by the full $100. The remaining $20 of the transfer payments is saved and does not affect aggregate demand.

The general expression for the transfer multiplier is

$$M_{\text{Transfer}} = \text{MPC}/(1 - \text{MPC})$$

M_{Transfer} applies to all debt-financed changes in transfer payments.

Notice that M_{Transfer} is the same as M_{Tax} except for the sign. An increase in transfer payments increases the equilibrium, whereas an increase in taxes de-

TRANSFER MULTIPLIER

The ratio that relates the change in the equilibrium level of national income to a change in government transfer payments.

creases the equilibrium. Otherwise, the tax and the transfer multipliers are both MPC times the spending multiplier.

The Balanced Budget Multipliers

So far we have been considering changes in expenditures and tax revenues that are "financed" by changes in borrowing. A government can also increase or decrease its expenditures and tax revenues by the same amount. An equal change in expenditures and tax revenues is called a **balanced budget change** because it does not change the size of the government's deficit.

BALANCED BUDGET CHANGE

An equal change in government expenditures and revenues.

Balanced budget changes are particularly appealing to so-called fiscal conservatives who want to hold the line on government spending. They argue that debt financing makes it too easy to vote for new government programs, whereas balanced budget increases promote fiscal responsibility. Administrators and legislators are more likely to scrutinize proposals for new spending programs if they know that they have to raise taxes to pay for them.

Two kinds of balanced budget changes must be distinguished for macro economic purposes: (1) a change in the government's purchases matched by an equal change in taxes and (2) a change in transfer payments matched by an equal change in taxes. These two budgetary changes leave the government's budget deficit unchanged, but they have quite different effects on the economy.

$\Delta G^d = \Delta Tx$ A balanced budget change in government purchases and taxes changes the equilibrium level of national income. Our previous examples indicate why.

Earlier we considered a $100 increase in government purchases and a $100 increase in taxes. The net effect on the equilibrium of a $100 balanced budget change in G^d and Tx is the sum of the two changes taken individually.

The spending multiplier gives the change in the equilibrium level of national income resulting from a change in government purchases. Since $M_{\text{Spending}} = 5$ in our model, a $100 increase in G^d increases the equilibrium level of national income by $500.

$$\Delta Y_E = M_{\text{Spending}} \cdot \Delta G^d = 5 \cdot \$100 = \$500$$

The tax multiplier gives the change in the equilibrium level of national income resulting from a change in taxes. Since $M_{\text{Tax}} = (-)4$ in our model, a $100 increase in taxes decreases the equilibrium level of national income by $400.

$$\Delta Y_E = M_{\text{Tax}} \cdot \Delta Tx = (-)4 \cdot \$100 = (-)\$400$$

Therefore, the net change in the equilibrium from a $100 increase in G^d and Tx is $100.

$$\Delta Y_E = \$500 - \$400 = \$100$$

The increase in government purchases increases aggregate demand and increases the equilibrium level of national income. The increase in taxes decreases aggregate demand and decreases the equilibrium level of national income. The two effects do not cancel out, however, because the spending multiplier is greater than the tax multiplier is. Changes in government purchases have a greater effect on aggregate demand than do equal dollar changes in taxes, so the equilibrium level of national income increases.

Notice that the change in the equilibrium is exactly equal to the balanced budget change in government purchases and taxes, $100. This result is not peculiar to our model, with its MPC of .80. It holds for any MPC and the corresponding values of M_{Spending} and M_{Tax}. *Equal changes in* G^d *and* Tx *change the equilibrium level of national income by the same amount and in the same direction.* A $25 increase in G^d and Tx increases the equilibrium level of national income by $25, a $33 decrease in G^d and Tx decreases the equilibrium level of national income by $33, and so forth.

The **balanced budget multiplier** *for government purchases and taxes,* labeled $M_{\Delta G^d = \Delta Tx}$, relates the change in the equilibrium level of national income to a balanced budget change in G^d and Tx. Since the equilibrium changes in the same direction and amount as the balanced budget change, the value of the balanced budget multiplier is one.

BALANCED BUDGET MULTIPLIER
The ratio that relates the change in the equilibrium level of national income to a balanced budget change in government purchases and taxes.

$$M_{\Delta G^d = \Delta Tx} = 1$$

The algebra needed to derive this result for any MPC is messy and will be left to the appendix to Chapter 11.

$\Delta Tr = \Delta Tx$ Balanced budget changes in transfer payments and taxes leave the equilibrium level of national income unchanged. The *balanced budget multiplier for transfers and taxes,* labeled $M_{\Delta Tr = \Delta Tx}$, relates the change in the equilibrium level of national income to a balanced budget change in transfer payments and taxes. Since $M_{\text{Tax}} = (-)M_{\text{Transfer}}$, the value of the multiplier is zero. Our previous examples are once again instructive.

$M_{\text{Transfer}} = 4$ in our model. A $100 increase in transfer payments increases the equilibrium level of national income by $400. $M_{\text{Tax}} = (-)4$. A $100 increase in taxes decreases the equilibrium level of national income by $400. Therefore, a $100 balanced budget increase in transfer payments and taxes has no effect on the equilibrium.

$$\Delta Y_E = \$400 - \$400 = 0$$
$$M_{\Delta Tr = \Delta Tx} = 0$$

Summary: The Fiscal Policy Multipliers

The following Concept Summary table lists the five fiscal policy multipliers developed in this section. The multipliers are a convenient way of thinking about the effects of virtually any budgetary changes on the equilibrium level of national income.

> CONCEPT SUMMARY

THE FISCAL POLICY MULTIPLIERS

FISCAL POLICY	FISCAL POLICY MULTIPLIER
Change in government purchases (ΔG^d)	$M_{\text{Spending}} = 1/(1 - \text{MPC})$
Change in transfer payments (ΔTr)	$M_{\text{Transfer}} = \text{MPC}/(1 - \text{MPC})$
Change in taxes (ΔTx)	$M_{\text{Tax}} = (-)\text{MPC}/(1 - \text{MPC})$

Balanced Budget Multipliers:

a. Equal change in government purchases and taxes
  ($\Delta G^d = \Delta Tx$) $M_{\Delta G^d = \Delta Tx} = 1$

b. Equal change in transfer payments and taxes
  ($\Delta Tr = \Delta Tx$) $M_{\Delta Tr = \Delta Tx} = 0$

Following are some examples that show how the multipliers can help us understand some important fiscal policy issues. Our first example relates to the limitations of macroeconomic policy at the state level.

STATES' ECONOMIC POLICIES   State governors are always talking a good economic game. They claim that their administrations are pursuing economic policies to promote a healthy state economy, and they are quick to take credit when their economies perform well. Voters are just as quick to blame the governors when their states' economies turn sour. In fact, the idea that states can pursue effective macroeconomic policies is largely a myth. State governments have very little control over their economies.

The first problem governors face in trying to manage their economies is that the fate of their economies is largely determined by events happening beyond the states' borders. Suppose that we were to build a set of national income and product accounts for a state. The "national" income = "national" product accounting identity is

$$Y = C + I + G + (Ex - Im)$$

The main difference between a state's and the nation's accounts is that net exports are much more important at the state level. Much of what a state's own firms produce, especially the output of the large manufacturing corporations, is exported to citizens and firms in other states. Automobile manufacturers, computer companies, and the larger manufacturing firms sell most of their products out of state. Also, many firms depend greatly on federal defense contracts. Similarly, many of the goods and services that a state's own citizens buy are imported from firms located in other states. In effect, each state is like a small nation surrounded by large nations. Its economic destiny is largely tied to the economies of the other states and to the federal government.

In addition, states have a very limited set of policy options for managing their economies. They cannot isolate themselves from outside events. The Constitution of the United States prohibits states from using tariffs, quotas, export taxes, or any other commercial devices that would limit the free flow of goods and services across their borders. Monetary policy is also out because states do not issue their own money. So states are essentially left with fiscal policies as the only means of managing their economies, and they are limited to balanced budget moves, by and large.

All but a few states have laws that require their governors to submit balanced operating budgets each year, and the U.S. financial markets would force the states into balancing their operating budgets even if these laws did not exist. State debt is not as readily accepted as federal debt is. States can issue debt to finance specific capital projects, but, unlike the federal government, they cannot routinely issue debt to cover operating deficits. A state that persisted in running operating deficits would soon find its bond rating lowered to junk bond status, and the financial markets may eventually cut it off entirely from borrowing. States do run operating deficits on occasion, but they have to promise to raise taxes and/or cut expenditures to restore balance as a condition for continued access to borrowing.

The problem for state fiscal policies is that the balanced budget multipliers are too low. Suppose that a state government increases its expenditures to try to stimulate the economy. Since the majority of state expenditures are purchases of goods and service, G^d, the potential stimulus from increased spending is quite large. But the state also has to raise taxes to finance the new expenditures, so the best that it can hope for is a balanced budget multiplier of one. $M_{\Delta G^d = \Delta Tx} = 1$. Unfortunately, a multiplier of one is too low, given the current resistance to larger governments and higher taxes. State governments simply cannot raise spending and taxes by enough to have a significant effect on their economies.

Governors trumpet the job-creating benefits of policies to lure new business into the state. States commonly offer businesses space in government-subsidized industrial parks, complete with water, sewage, electricity, and ample parking. They may also throw in state and local tax abatements as an added inducement. The industrial parks no doubt do attract new business into the state, creating new jobs and stimulating the economy. But the governors conveniently ignore the depressing effect of the additional taxes needed to pay for these kinds of business subsidies. The net effect on the economy of the subsidies and new taxes combined is unlikely to be very large.

States are in a worse bind if the increased expenditures are transfer payments because the balanced budget multiplier for transfers and taxes is zero. $M_{\Delta Tr = \Delta Tx} = 0$. A state's public assistance expenditures naturally increase when the state economy goes into a recession, as some of the unemployed are eventually forced onto the welfare rolls. The increased transfer payments do give a boost to the economy. But the increase in taxes needed to finance the transfers exactly offsets the stimulating effect of the transfers.

In conclusion, state macroeconomic policy is vastly overrated. Only the federal government can hope to articulate and carry out policies to achieve the macroeconomic policy goals.

THE FISCAL POLICY OPTIONS   Our second example is a simple numerical exercise that illustrates the nature of the macroeconomic policy problem and the

CURRENT ISSUE: California is in the midst of taking a big hit with the decrease in defense spending, and Californians will no doubt turn to the state for help to create new jobs. The government may not be able to help very much, though. The immediate impact of the defense cutbacks is to throw the state's budget into deficit because California has a huge public assistance program. The state may have to raise taxes, which will cause more job loss.

various fiscal policy options that the federal government might use to solve the problem. The exercise uses our model of the economy from Table 11.3 and Figure 11.5, in which the MPC = .80.

SETTING THE TARGET LEVEL OF NATIONAL INCOME   As indicated in the first section of the chapter, the first step in solving the policy problem is determining a target level of national income that offers the best compromise among the four macroeconomic policy goals. To keep things simple, let's assume that the government's policy makers are concerned only about unemployment and they determine that the full-employment level of national income is $12,000 (billion).

BUILDING A MODEL OF THE ECONOMY   The next step in solving the policy problem is building a model of the economy that shows what the equilibrium level of national income is and how the economy would react to different kinds of policies. We already have a model. Figure 11.6 reproduces the aggregate demand–45° line graph from Figure 11.5. The equilibrium level of national income, Y_0, is $10,000, at the intersection of the solid aggregate demand line, ADE_0, and the 45° line. The full-employment level of national income, Y_{FE}, is $12,000, as indicated by the solid vertical line.

RECESSIONARY AND INFLATIONARY GAPS   The economy is experiencing a **recessionary gap:** The equilibrium level of national income, Y_E, is below the full-employment level of national income, Y_{FE}. The economy is operating below its production possibilities frontier, and resources are unemployed. For

RECESSIONARY GAP

Exists when the equilibrium level of national income is less than the full-employment level of national income; the size of the gap is the amount that aggregate demand has to increase to bring the equilibrium level of national income to the full-employment level of national income.

FIGURE 11.6

A Recessionary Gap

The economy is in equilibrium at Y_0 = $10,000, at the intersection of the aggregate demand line ADE_0 and the 45-degree line. Y_0 is less than the full-employment level of national income, Y_{FE} = $12,000, so the economy is experiencing a recessionary gap. The size of the gap is $400, the amount that aggregate demand has to increase to bring the economy to equilibrium at the full-employment level of income Y_{FE}. The size of the gap is the required change in national income, $2,000, divided by the spending multiplier, which is 5 is our model. [$400 = $2,000/5].

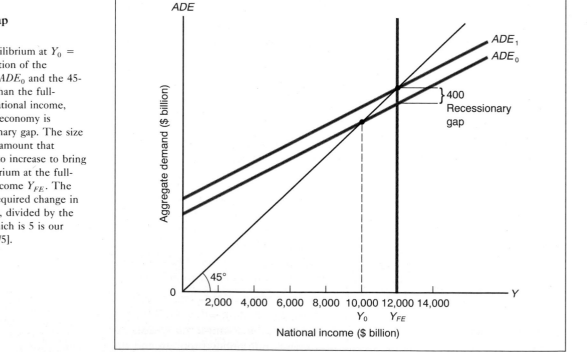

future reference, the reverse situation when the equilibrium level of national income, Y_E, is above the full-employment level of national income, Y_{FE}, is an **inflationary gap.** The economy is trying to push beyond its production possibilities frontier, leading to an inflation.

The *size* of the recessionary gap is *not* the difference between Y_E and Y_{FE}, however. Instead, it is the amount that aggregate demand has to increase to bring the equilibrium level of national income to the full-employment level of national income. In other words, the size of the recessionary gap is the vertical distance between ADE_0 and ADE_1 in Figure 11.6. As such, the size of the recessionary gap is the required change in income ($Y_{FE} - Y_E$) divided by the spending multiplier.

$$\text{Size of the recessionary gap} = (Y_{FE} - Y_E)/M_{\text{Spending}}$$

The required change in income ($Y_{FE} - Y_E$) is \$2,000 (\$2,000 = \$12,000 − \$10,000); $M_{\text{Spending}} = 5$ in our model. Therefore,

$$\text{Size of the recessionary gap} = \$2,000/5 = \$400$$

Government policies have to increase (shift) aggregate demand by \$400 to remove the recessionary gap. Once aggregate demand has shifted, the multiplier process increases national income by the additional \$1,600 necessary for Y_E to reach Y_{FE} at \$12,000.

FISCAL POLICY OPTIONS The final step is to design an expansionary fiscal policy that will increase aggregate demand by \$400 and thereby increase Y_E by \$2,000. A number of different expansionary fiscal policies can remove the recessionary gap. Here are three of them, each of which makes use of the fiscal policy multipliers summarized in the previous Concept Summary table.

1. *A debt-financed increase in government purchases of goods and services.* The spending multiplier applies to debt-financed increases in G^d. Therefore, the required increase in G^d is \$400.

$$\Delta Y_E = M_{\text{Spending}} \cdot \Delta G^d$$
$$\$2,000 = 5 \cdot \$400$$

Since G^d is part of aggregate demand, a \$400 increase in G^d does increase aggregate demand by \$400, as required to remove the recessionary gap.

2. *A decrease in taxes "financed" by an increase in debt.* The tax multiplier applies to the decrease in taxes. $M_{\text{Tax}} = (-)4$ in our model. Therefore, the required decrease in taxes is \$500.

$$\Delta Y_E = M_{\text{Tax}} \cdot \Delta Tx$$
$$\$2,000 = (-)4 \cdot (-)\$500$$

The \$500 cut in taxes increases consumption demand by MPC times \$500, or \$400 (\$400 = 0.8 · \$500). Since C^d is part of aggregate demand, a \$500 tax cut does increase aggregate demand by \$400, as required to remove the recessionary gap.

INFLATIONARY GAP

Exists when the equilibrium level of national income is greater than the full-employment level of national income; the size of the gap is the amount that aggregate demand has to decrease to bring the equilibrium level of national income to the full-employment level of national income.

REFLECTION: See if you can design still other expansionary fiscal policies to remove the recessionary gap. Try one or two fiscal policies involving changes in transfer payments.

3. *A balanced budget increase in government purchases of goods and services and in taxes.* $M_{\Delta G^d = \Delta Tx} = 1$. Therefore, G^d and Tx must increase by \$2,000 to increase Y_E by \$2,000. The increase in G^d increases aggregate demand by \$2,000. The \$2,000 tax increase reduces C^d by MPC times \$2,000, or \$1,600 (\$1,600 $= 0.80 \cdot$ \$2,000). The net increase in aggregate demand is \$400 (\$400 $=$ \$2,000 $-$ \$1,600), as required to remove the recessionary gap.

FISCAL POLICY IN PRACTICE

These simple numerical exercises demonstrate the theoretical possibilities for fiscal policy, what fiscal policy can achieve in principle. The actual conduct of fiscal policy is not quite so routine as these exercises make it seem, however. The government cannot just pick out a target level of national income and expect to reach it with a set of fiscal policies any time it wants to.

Economists ask: Can the government hope to fine tune the economy through countercyclical fiscal and monetary policies? **Fine tuning** means keeping the economy at or very near the target level of income. An obvious example is keeping the economy operating on or very near the production possibilities frontier at all times. **Countercyclical policies** are policies that counteract movements in aggregate demand that threaten to move the economy away from the target level of national income. An example is an expansionary fiscal policy that increases aggregate demand to counteract a fall in consumption demand that would otherwise plunge the economy into a recession. An opposite example is a contractionary fiscal policy that decreases aggregate demand to counteract a rise in consumption demand that would otherwise attempt to move the economy beyond its production possibilities frontier and build up unwanted inflationary pressures.

Can the government fine tune the economy? The answer is almost certainly no. Most economists agree that the best the government can hope to do is "lean against the wind," that is, prevent the economy from heading toward disaster. The government cannot prevent recessions, but it can prevent a recession from turning into another Great Depression. Similarly, the government cannot prevent occasional bouts of inflation, but it can prevent an inflation from developing into an explosive hyperinflation.

We can only consider the problems associated with fiscal policy at this point.

The Fiscal Policy Lags

The conduct of fiscal policy is fraught with practical difficulties. Foremost among them are the time lags involved with fiscal policy, the time required to enact a fiscal policy and have it take effect. The time lags occur in three stages, one right after another: (1) the recognition lag, (2) the administrative lag, and (3) the operational lag.

THE RECOGNITION LAG   The **recognition lag** is the time required for policy makers to realize that the economy is in trouble and needs a dose of countercyclical policy. The length of the recognition lag depends on the time required to collect reliable data on macroeconomic variables and on the ability to forecast

FINE TUNING

Using fiscal or monetary policies to keep the economy at or very near the target level of national income.

COUNTERCYCLICAL POLICY

A fiscal or monetary policy that counteracts the movements in aggregate demand whenever aggregate demand tends to move the economy away from the target level of national income.

RECOGNITION LAG (FISCAL OR MONETARY POLICY)

The time required for policy makers to realize that the economy is in trouble and needs a dose of countercyclical policy.

the future performance of the economy. Data on GDP, inflation, and unemployment are available with only about a one-month lag. As noted in Chapter 9, however, forecasting remains more an uncertain art than an exact science. The large macroeconomic forecasting models, private and government, have not been very successful at predicting recessions or inflations. Especially disconcerting was their utter failure to predict three of the more dramatic economic episodes of the past 20 years: the recession of 1974–75, the recession of 1981–82, and the abrupt recovery in 1983–84.

The 1974–75 recession was the deepest recession in the United States since the Great Depression of the 1930s, yet the forecasting models failed to see it coming in 1973. The average prediction of the large models at the time was that real gross national product (GNP) would *grow* by 2.2 percent from the first quarter in 1974 to the first quarter of 1975. Instead, real GNP *fell* by 3.8 percent.

The recession of 1981–82 supplanted the 1974–75 recession as the deepest since the Great Depression. Once again the forecasting models were wide of the mark. The average forecast was that nominal GNP would fall by 2.1 percent from the third quarter of 1981 to the third quarter of 1982. In fact, nominal GNP fell by 10.8 percent.

The forecasting models also missed the ensuing recovery. Unemployment had risen sharply during the recession and was still at 9.6 percent at the end of 1983. The average forecast in 1983 was that unemployment would remain above 9 percent in 1984. Instead, the recovery was much stronger than predicted, and unemployment fell to 7.5 percent by the end of 1984.[2]

The inability to forecast accurately is a serious handicap for fiscal (and monetary) policy. The government can hardly hope to fine tune the economy if it cannot predict where the economy will be over the next six months to a year. In truth, the economy is often far from its target before the policy makers recognize the nature of the problem.

THE ADMINISTRATIVE LAG   The **administrative lag** is the time required to enact legislation to change government purchases, or transfer payments, or taxes. The standing joke around Washington is that as soon as the policy makers recognize that the economy is in trouble, the government springs into inaction. The budgetary process is extremely cumbersome and time-consuming in the United States.

The budgetary cycle normally begins in the fall when the administration starts to put together its entire proposed budget for the next fiscal year, which begins the following October. The budget proposal incorporates the administration's forecasts for the economy over the next fiscal year. The budget is submitted to Congress in January. The House and the Senate then work from January to September to pass the legislation needed to authorize all the individual expenditure and revenue components of the budget and to appropriate the actual expenditures for each program. Committees in both houses hold hearings on the various parts of the budget, taking testimony from experts and

ADMINISTRATIVE LAG (FISCAL POLICY)

The time required to enact legislation to change government purchases, transfer payments, or taxes.

---

[2]The data in this section are taken from the discussion of macroeconomic forecasting difficulties in R. Gordon, *Macroeconomics*, fifth edition (Glenview, IL: Scott, Foresman/Little, Brown, 1989), 466–469. See, also, S. McNees, "Which Forecast Should You Use?", *New England Economic Review* (July/August 1985): 36–42. McNees is a recognized authority on the performance of the various forecasting models.

other interested parties. The committees then draft bills and send them to the full House and Senate for a vote.

The final House and Senate bills usually differ. If so, the bills relating to economic policy are sent to the Joint Economic Committee, which holds its own hearings and drafts a compromise bill. The compromise bill is then sent back to the House and Senate for another vote. The legislative process is never entirely completed by October, so parts of the budget each year are supported by temporary continuing resolutions until the final legislation is passed.

Needless to say, all this takes a considerable amount of time. One study of 10 major tax bills enacted from 1948 to 1965 found that the average time from administrative proposal to final passage was 8 months, with a range of 1 to 18 months.[3] The situation has hardly improved since then. The 1986 Tax Reform Act was signed in October of 1986. The Reagan administration published its first proposal for tax reform in November of 1984.

Any hope of fine tuning the economy with fiscal policy is clearly out of the question with such long administrative lags. The administrative lag has been a serious obstacle to the conduct of effective fiscal policies.

OPERATIONAL LAG (FISCAL POLICY)

The time period from the passage of new legislation to the final change in the equilibrium level of national income.

THE OPERATIONAL LAG   The final lag is the **operational lag,** the time period from the passage of new legislation to the final change in the equilibrium level of national income. The operational lag has two distinct stages: (1) the time required to change expenditures or taxes once the legislation to do so has been enacted and (2) the length of the multiplier process. Fiscal policies cannot affect the economy until the expenditures or taxes are actually changed. Once the changes occur, the multiplier process determines how quickly changes in government expenditures and taxes affect the circular flow of economic activity.

CHANGING EXPENDITURES AND TAXES   Government purchases, especially military and public works projects, are often very difficult to change quickly. Sophisticated military weapons systems and major construction projects such as highways or public office buildings take years to complete. Congress passes legislation that authorizes and appropriates the expenditures in one year, and then the actual expenditures take place over a period of years. Perhaps the outstanding example is the federal interstate highway system. Funds for the interstate system were appropriated in 1956, yet parts of the interstate are still not completed! The long operational lags involved with most government purchases virtually rule them out as a tool for fine tuning the economy.

The time required to change transfer payments depends on exactly what is being changed. Consider public assistance as an example. The lags could be quite long if the legislation changes the eligibility rules, which determine who qualifies for welfare. Each state or local welfare office would have to review both its existing caseload and potential new cases before new welfare checks could be written. In contrast, a simple increase in the monthly benefit levels could be enacted within a month.

A common anti-recession policy is the extension of the time period that the unemployed can receive unemployment insurance, typically from the standard period of 26 weeks to 39 weeks or even a year. Extending unemployment

[3]J. Pechman, *Federal Tax Policy* (Washington, D.C.: The Brookings Institution, 1966), Ch. 3 and Table 3.1, p. 32.

insurance can lead to increases in unemployment benefits within a month or two.

Changes in the personal income tax can also occur very quickly because the majority of taxpayers have taxes withheld from their paychecks. Payroll offices can easily change the amount of taxes withheld within a month or two after the legislation is enacted.

THE MULTIPLIER PROCESS The final lag in the conduct of fiscal policy is the multiplier process. We saw earlier in the chapter that the multiplier process is reasonably quick. The majority of the multiplier works its way through the economy well within a year's time.

Add up the recognition, administrative, and operational lags and the conclusion is clear: Fiscal policy is unlikely to be able to fine tune the economy. The best it can hope to do is "lean against the wind" to help prevent an economic disaster, and most economists are convinced that fiscal policy is flexible enough to do this.

A Long-Standing Tax Proposal

The most serious lag in the conduct of fiscal policy is the lengthy and cumbersome administrative lag. For this reason many economists have long proposed that Congress give the president the power to raise or lower the personal income tax rates temporarily according to some well-defined rule that is based on the performance of the economy. For example, the administration could cut the tax rates by any amount up to 10 percent for one year if real GDP falls for two consecutive quarters. Alternatively, the administration could raise the tax rates by any amount up to 10 percent for one year if inflation exceeds 10 percent. The idea is that an automatic tax rule would circumvent the administrative lag and be an effective countercyclical policy tool. The administration could act quickly in response to a problem, actual tax collections could be changed within a month or two, and these changes in taxes would have a powerful, multiplied effect on the economy.

Many economists now believe that an automatic tax rule would not be very effective. The issue turns on the last point, that changes in taxes have a powerful, multiplied effect on the economy. Tax changes do have a powerful, multiplied effect if they are viewed as permanent. But these tax changes are specifically designed to be temporary, and temporary tax changes may not change aggregate demand very much.

As we saw in Chapter 10, the Life-Cycle Hypothesis suggests that households distinguish between permanent and temporary changes in their disposable income. They increase their consumption by almost the full amount of a permanent change, whereas they hardly increase their consumption at all in response to a temporary change. Temporary increases or decreases in disposable income mostly lead to temporary increases or decreases in saving. In other words, the MPC from a temporary change in disposable income is very low, close to zero. If this is true, then the tax multiplier is also quite small. Temporary tax changes cannot change aggregate demand or the equilibrium level of national income very much at all.

The federal government has given economists two good opportunities to put the Life-Cycle Hypothesis to the test with regard to taxation. In 1968 the government enacted a 10 percent across-the-board increase in the personal income tax rates to counteract inflationary pressures that had been building in the economy. The increase took effect in July of 1968 and was to be removed at the end of 1970. In 1975, Congress enacted a one-time 10 percent rebate of 1974 tax payments with a ceiling of $200 to help pull the economy out of the recession. Taxpayers knew at the outset that both the 1968 tax surcharge and the 1975 tax rebate were temporary. Studies of these events strongly suggest that the MPC out of temporary tax changes is much less than the MPC out of permanent tax changes, as predicted from the Life-Cycle Hypothesis. The estimates range from MPC = 0 (temporary tax changes only affect saving) to MPC = 0.5 (half of a temporary tax decrease is consumed, half is saved), with the majority of the estimates near the low end.[4]

These studies suggest that giving the administration the discretion to change tax rates temporarily according to a set rule may not be an effective counter-cyclical policy tool. Suppose that the "temporary" MPC is only .20. Then the "temporary" tax multiplier is only $(-).25$ $[M_{Tax} = (-)MPC/(1 - MPC) = (-)0.20/(1 - 0.20) = (-)0.20/0.80 = (-).25]$. With a tax multiplier this low, temporary tax rate changes on the order of 5 to 10 percent would change the equilibrium level of national income by about $10 billion, a change hardly noticeable in a $6 trillion economy.

The issue is moot in any event, since Congress has never been willing to give up any of its tax powers to the administration. The United States will have to live with the long administrative lag associated with changes in tax policy.

SUMMARY

Chapter 11 began with a description of the macroeconomic policy problem that the federal government tries to solve with its fiscal and monetary policies.

1. The essence of the policy problem is that aggregate demand may not lead the economy to a very desirable equilibrium level of national income. For example, the equilibrium may be well below the production possibilities frontier, with high levels of unemployment. Alternatively, aggregate demand may try to bring the economy beyond its production possibilities frontier, leading to inflation.
2. The conduct of fiscal or monetary policy is a three-step process.
   a. First, policy makers must set a target level of national income that represents the best compromise among the four macroeconomic policy goals of long-run economic growth, full employment, low inflation, and a zero balance of trade and stable value of the dollar.
   b. Then policy makers need a model of the economy that indicates (i) what the equilibrium would be without any dose of policy, (ii) how the economy would respond to specific fiscal or monetary policies, and (iii) how changes in the equilibrium would affect the four macroeconomic policy goals.

---

[4]For a review of the literature on the different reactions to permanent and temporary changes in taxes and transfers, see R. Hall and J. Taylor, *Macroeconomics: Theory, Performance, and Policy*, second edition (New York: Norton, 1988), 211–212. Also: A. Blinder and A. Deaton, "The Time Series Consumption Function Revisited," *Brookings Papers on Economic Activity* 2 (1985): 465–511; J. Poterba, "Are Consumers Forward Looking? Evidence from Fiscal Experiments," *American Economic Review* 78, No. 2 (May 1988): 413–417.

c. The final step is designing fiscal and/or monetary policies to meet the target level of national income. Fiscal and monetary policies are called aggregate demand management because they change aggregate demand to move the equilibrium to the target level of national income. Expansionary fiscal and monetary policies increase aggregate demand. Contractionary fiscal and monetary policies decrease aggregate demand.

The second section of Chapter 11 described the spending multiplier.

3. The spending multiplier, labeled $M_{Spending}$, relates changes in the equilibrium level of national income to changes or shifts in aggregate demand. A change in aggregate demand leads to a multiplied change in the equilibrium level of national income because of the feedback between national income and consumption demand. An increase in national income increases disposable income, which increases consumption demand, which further increases national income, and so on, round by round. A change or shift in any component of aggregate demand can start the round-by-round multiplier process.

4. $M_{Spending} = 1/(1 - MPC)$ for the simplest economy. The higher the MPC is, the higher $M_{Spending}$ is, and vice versa. Also, the multiplier process is symmetric. Equal increases and decreases in aggregate demand lead to equal multiplied increases and decreases in the equilibrium level of national income.

The third section of the chapter added the government sector to the simplest model and explored the various options for fiscal policy.

5. Fiscal policy consists of changes in government demand for goods and services (government purchases), transfer payments, or taxes made with the intention of changing the equilibrium level of national income.

6. Government purchases are part of aggregate demand. The equilibrium condition for an economy consisting of the household, business, and government sectors is that the level of national income equals the sum of consumption demand, investment demand, and government demand for goods and services. $Y = C^d + I^d + G^d$.

7. The spending multiplier applies to changes in government purchases because government purchases are part of aggregate demand.

8. Taxes and transfers are not part of aggregate demand. Nonetheless, changes in taxes and transfers have a powerful, multiplied effect on the equilibrium level of national income because they affect consumption demand (and investment demand). The tax multiplier relates changes in the equilibrium level of income to changes in taxes. The transfer multiplier relates changes in the equilibrium level of income to changes in transfer payments. $M_{Tax} = (-)MPC/(1 - MPC)$; $M_{Transfer} = MPC/(1 - MPC)$. The tax and the transfer multipliers are smaller than the spending multiplier is because changes in taxes and transfers affect aggregate demand indirectly rather than directly, as in the case of changes in government purchases. The Concept Summary table on page 338 lists the various fiscal policy multipliers.

The final section of Chapter 11 discussed the three time lags involved with the actual conduct of fiscal policy: the recognition, administrative, and operational lags.

9. The recognition lag is the time required for policy makers to recognize that the economy is in trouble and needs a dose of fiscal (or monetary) policy. The length of this lag depends in part on the ability to forecast the future performance of the economy, which is an uncertain art at best.

10. The administrative lag is the time between the recognition of a problem and the passage of legislation that changes government purchases, transfer payments, or taxes. The administrative lag is very long for fiscal policy, often a year or more.

11. The operational lag is the time from the change in the legislation to the change in the equilibrium level of national income. It has two parts: (a) the time required to actually change government expenditures or revenues and (b) the length of the multiplier process. Government purchases often take years to change. The time required to change transfer payments and tax revenues depends on the nature of the legislated changes. Changes in tax rates, or extensions of unemployment insurance benefits, can occur within a month or two. Fundamental structural changes in transfer programs or taxes may take much longer. Once the fiscal changes are made, the multiplier process works fairly quickly.

12. The combined time lags are considerable, long enough to rule out fiscal policy as a means of fine tuning the economy, that is, keeping the equilibrium level of national income close to the target level at all times. The best fiscal policy can hope to do is "lean against the wind" and help prevent an economic disaster such as the Great Depression or a hyperinflation.

13. Tempoary changes in taxes and transfer payments intended to increase or decrease aggregate demand have been used on occasion in the United States. Research suggests that these policies have not been very successful because the MPC out of temporary tax changes appears to be very low, probably much less than one-half, in line with the prediction of the Life-Cycle Hypothesis. A low MPC implies a low tax multiplier and not much effect on aggregate demand.

KEY TERMS

administrative lag (fiscal policy)
balanced budget change
balanced budget multiplier
contractionary policy
countercyclical policy

expansionary policy
fine tuning
inflationary gap
operational lag (fiscal policy)
recessionary gap

recognition lag (fiscal or monetary policy)
spending multiplier
tax multiplier
transfer multiplier

QUESTIONS

1. What is expansionary fiscal policy? Contractionary fiscal policy? Give some examples of each. During his first year in office President Clinton proposed, and Congress approved, cutting government expenditures by about $250 billion and increasing taxes by about $250 billion over the five-year period from 1993 to 1998. Is this policy expansionary or contractionary?

2. a. Describe the steps involved in making macroeconomic policy.
   b. Why is making policy as much an art as a science? For example, why might two different policy makers with access to the same data on the economy reach different conclusions about what fiscal policy to pursue?

3. Use the spending multiplier to calculate the change in na-

tional income that would result from a $200 decrease in government spending. Assume that the MPC = 0.90.

4. Explain why an increase in aggregate demand of $1 leads to more than a $1 increase in the equilibrium level of national income.

5. a. Calculate the change in national income if the government increases its transfer payments by $500 and finances the transfers by issuing debt. Assume that the MPC = 0.75.

   b. How would your answer change if the transfers were financed by a $500 increase in taxes?

6. Suppose that the economy is at the full-employment level of national income and the federal government cuts defense spending by $100 billion. By how much must the government change taxes, and in what direction, to keep the economy at the full-employment level of national income? Assume that the MPC = 2/3.

7. Suppose that the equilibrium level of national income is $1,000 and the full-employment level of income is $1,500.

   a. Is the economy experiencing an inflationary gap or a recessionary gap?

   b. Represent this situation on the *ADE*–45° line graph, and show the size of the gap on your diagram.

   c. Calculate the size of the gap, assuming that the MPC = 0.80.

   d. Describe two fiscal policies that would close the gap, and indicate why they would work.

8. a. Describe the three lags in the conduct of fiscal policy.

   b. Why do these lags suggest that the federal government is unable to fine tune the economy with fiscal policies? Be sure to indicate what it means to fine tune the economy.

9. The text assumed that government spending on goods and services (*G*) is unrelated to the level of national income.

   a. Why is this a reasonable assumption for a macro model?

   b. What components of *G*, either federal or state/local, do you think might possibly be related to national income and why?

10. Why is it so much more difficult for state governments to control their economies than it is for the federal government to control the national economy?

11. You are given the following diagrams representing consumption demand (*Cᵈ*), investment demand (*Iᵈ*), and government spending on goods and services (*Gᵈ*). How would you put these diagrams together to find the equilibrium level of national income?

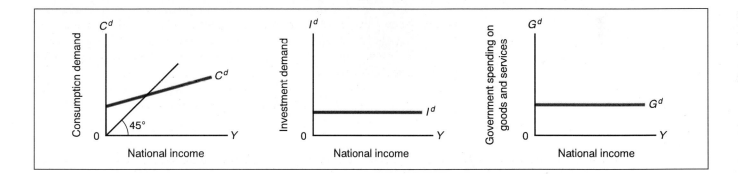

11

Algebra of the Spending Multiplier and the Fiscal Policy Multipliers

The appendix derives algebraically the various multipliers presented in Chapter 11.

THE SPENDING MULTIPLIER IN THE SIMPLEST ECONOMY

The equilibrium condition in the simplest economy with only the household and the business sectors is

$$Y = C^d + I^d$$

The Keynesian consumption function, C^d, is

$$C^d = C_0 + \text{MPC} \cdot Y$$

Investment demand is a constant independent of gross domestic product (GDP)/national income:

$$I^d = \bar{I}$$

Substitute the equations for C^d and I^d into the equilibrium condition, and solve for the equilibrium, Y_E.

$$Y = C_0 + (MPC \cdot Y) + \bar{I}$$
$$Y - (MPC \cdot Y) = C_0 + \bar{I}$$
$$Y \cdot (1 - MPC) = C_0 + \bar{I}$$
$$Y_E = [1/(1 - MPC)] \cdot (C_0 + \bar{I})$$

The spending multiplier relates changes in the equilibrium level of national income to changes, or shifts, in aggregate demand. Therefore, write the equilibrium equation in terms of changes.

$$\Delta Y_E = [1/(1 - MPC)] \cdot (\Delta C_0 + \Delta \bar{I})$$

ΔC_0 is the change or shift in the consumption function, $\Delta \bar{I}$ is the change or shift in investment demand, and the sum of $\Delta C_0 + \Delta \bar{I}$ equals the shift in aggregate demand. $M_{Spending} = 1/(1 - MPC)$. The MPC in our simplest economy is .80, so that $M_{Spending} = 5$ [$5 = 1/(1 - 0.8) = 1/0.2$]. The multiplier equation indicates that the spending multiplier applies equally to changes in consumption demand and investment demand.

THE FISCAL POLICY MULTIPLIERS

Adding the government sector to our model involves two changes. First, government purchases of goods and services, G^d, are part of aggregate demand. Therefore, the equilibrium condition with the government sector is

$$Y = C^d + I^d + G^d$$

We are assuming that G^d is a constant independent of national income.

$$G^d = \overline{G}$$

$\overline{G} = 1,000$ in our simple economy.

Second, taxes and transfers drive a wedge between national income, Y, and disposable income, Y_d.

$$Y_d = Y - Tx + Tr$$

Consumption demand is related to disposable income, not national income.

$$C^d = C_0 + (MPC \cdot Y_d)$$

Substituting the equation for disposable income into the consumption demand equation gives consumption demand in terms of *national income.*

$$C^d = C_0 + [\text{MPC} \cdot (Y - Tx + Tr)]$$

Also, I^d is a constant in our simple economy.

$$I^d = \bar{I} \ (= 600)$$

Substitute C^d, I^d, and G^d into the equilibrium condition, and solve for the equilibrium, Y_E. Note that C^d must be expressed in terms of national income, not disposable income.

$$Y = C_0 + [\text{MPC} \cdot (Y - Tx + Tr)] + \bar{I} + \overline{G}$$
$$Y = C_0 + (\text{MPC} \cdot Y) - (\text{MPC} \cdot Tx) + (\text{MPC} \cdot Tr) + \bar{I} + \overline{G}$$
$$Y - (\text{MPC} \cdot Y) = C_0 - (\text{MPC} \cdot Tx) + (\text{MPC} \cdot Tr) + \bar{I} + \overline{G}$$
$$Y \cdot (1 - \text{MPC}) = (C_0 + \bar{I} + \overline{G}) - (\text{MPC} \cdot Tx) + (MPC \cdot Tr)$$
$$Y_E = \{[1/(1 - \text{MPC})] \cdot (C_0 + \bar{I} + \overline{G})\}$$
$$+ \ \{[-\text{MPC}/(1 - \text{MPC})] \cdot Tx\} + \{[\text{MPC}/(1 - \text{MPC})] \cdot Tr\}$$

Write the equilibrium equation in terms of changes to determine the various fiscal policy multipliers.

$$\Delta Y_E = \{[1/(1 - \text{MPC})] \cdot (\Delta C_0 + \Delta \bar{I} + \Delta \overline{G})\}$$
$$+ \ \{[-\text{MPC}/(1 - \text{MPC})] \cdot \Delta Tx\} + \{[\text{MPC}/(1 - \text{MPC})] \cdot \Delta Tr\}$$

$M_{\text{Spending}} = 1/(1 - \text{MPC})$ and applies to changes in G^d, as well as to changes in consumption demand and investment demand.

$M_{\text{Tax}} = -\text{MPC}/(1 - \text{MPC})$ and applies to changes in taxes.

$M_{\text{Transfer}} = \text{MPC}/(1 - \text{MPC})$ and applies to changes in transfer payments. Note that M_{Tax} and M_{Transfer} are both MPC as large as M_{Spending} and that $M_{\text{Tax}} = (-) M_{\text{Transfer}}$.

For an MPC = .80,

$M_{\text{Spending}} = 1/(1 - \text{MPC}) = 1/(1 - 0.8) = 1/0.2 = 5$

$M_{\text{Tax}} = -\text{MPC}/(1 - \text{MPC}) = -0.8/(1 - 0.8) = -0.8/0.2 = -4$

$M_{\text{Transfer}} = \text{MPC}/(1 - \text{MPC}) = 0.8/(1 - 0.8) = 0.8/0.2 = 4$

The balanced budget multiplier, $M_{\Delta G^d = \Delta Tx} = 1$, combines the separate effects on Y_E of changes in G^d and Tx. The effect of ΔG^d on the equilibrium is

$$\Delta Y_E = M_{\text{Spending}} \cdot \Delta G^d = [1/(1 - \text{MPC})] \cdot \Delta G^d$$

The effect of ΔTx on the equilibrium is

$$\Delta Y_E = M_{\text{Tax}} \cdot \Delta Tx = [-\text{MPC}/(1 - \text{MPC})] \cdot \Delta Tx$$

The combined effect on the equilibrium is

$$\Delta Y_E = \{[1/(1 - \text{MPC})] \cdot \Delta G^d\} + \{[-\text{MPC}/(1 - \text{MPC})] \cdot \Delta Tx\}$$

But $\Delta G^d = \Delta Tx$ for a balanced budget change. Therefore, substitute ΔG^d for ΔTx in the equation for ΔY_E, and factor out ΔG^d.

$$\Delta Y_E = \{[1/(1 - MPC)] - [MPC/(1 - MPC)]\} \cdot \Delta G^d$$

Combine the two terms in the brackets, which have a common denominator.

$$\Delta Y_E - [(1 - MPC)/(1 - MPC)] \cdot \Delta G^d = 1 \cdot \Delta G^d$$

The balanced budget multiplier is one. The equilibrium level of national income changes by the same amount as the change in G^d ($= \Delta Tx$), and in the same direction.

QUESTIONS

a. Given the following information for an economy, find the equilibrium level of income, Y_E.

$C^d = 200 + 2/3 \cdot Y_d$ Y_d = disposable income
$I^d = 20$ Y = national income
$G^d = 70$ C^d = consumption demand
$T = 24$ I^d = investment demand
   G^d = government demand for goods and services
   T = taxes—transfer payments

b. What is the value of the spending multiplier for this economy? Of the tax multiplier? Of the $\Delta G^d = \Delta Tx$ balanced budget multiplier? (*Hint:* What is the MPC?)

c. If government spending on goods and services, G^d, decreases by 10, what will the change in Y_E be?

d. If the government matches the decrease in G^d by a cut in taxes of 10, how will your answer to part c change?

e. If the economy is at the full-employment level of income and the government increases G^d by 10, how can it change taxes to keep the economy at full employment? If government transfer payments increase by 12, by how much will the equilibrium level of income change? If the government increases taxes by 12 to finance the transfer payments, what will the net effect on Y_E be?

Suppose that the government decides that the target level of income is 900. Relative to the equilibrium computed in part a, is the economy experiencing a recessionary or an inflationary gap? What is the size of the gap? Design two government policies that will eliminate the gap.

12

Automatic Stabilizers, Net Exports, and Budget Deficits

LEARNING OBJECTIVES

CONCEPTS TO LEARN

Automatic stabilizers	Structural budget deficit
Marginal propensity to import	The burden of the federal debt
Cyclical budget deficit	

CONCEPTS TO RECALL

Dollar depreciation/appreciation [7]	Fiscal policy [9, 11]
Net exports [7, 8]	Marginal propensity to consume [10]
The total saving = investment accounting identity [8]	Equilibrium level of national income [10]

he great policy dilemma of the 1990s centers on the combination of a sluggish economy and large federal budget deficits.

Most economists believe that the large federal deficits are very bad for the economy. They reduce saving, investment, productivity, and long-run economic growth, and in doing so they place a tremendous burden on future generations who are helpless to defend themselves politically. Yet reductions in the deficit require either cuts in government spending or increases in taxes, or both. We just saw in Chapter 30 that both spending cuts and tax increases have powerful, multiplied depressing effects on the economy.

President Clinton opted for going after the deficit. His first major macroeconomic policy initiative was a five-year, $500 billion deficit reduction plan containing approximately equal amounts of spending reductions and tax increases. His deficit reduction plan just barely squeaked by the Senate and the House in the summer of 1993. Clinton's plan has merit; the deficit will have to be reduced sooner or later, and the benefits of reducing the deficit appear to be substantial over the long haul. But the members of Congress were a tough sell, in large part because they knew that deficit reduction of this magnitude would almost certainly increase unemployment and cause a fair amount of economic misery over the next five years. Is the nation willing to bear the short-run costs of unemployment for the long-run benefits of deficit reduction? This may well be the leading macroeconomic question in the United States today.

The dilemma will be turned around the other way on President Clinton's other large policy initiative, health care reform. Estimates of the annual cost of a comprehensive federal health care program are on the order of $100 to $150 billion. Will Congress enact such a program, given the large budget deficit? Time will tell whether the federal government stays the course on reducing the budget deficit.

Chapter 10 demonstrated the feedback nature of the new Keynesian model, which occurs through the relationship of consumption demand to disposable income. Consumption demand is not the only channel through which national income feeds back to aggregate demand, however. Changes in national income directly affect business saving in the business sector, tax collections and transfer payments in the government sector, and imports in the foreign sector.

These other three channels of feedback differ from the consumption feedback channel in one very important respect. The consumption demand channel makes national income highly sensitive to changes in aggregate demand. It is the basis of the spending multiplier by which an increase in aggregate demand leads to a multiplied increase in national income. The other three feedback channels have the opposite effect. They are called automatic stabilizers because they make national income less sensitive to changes in aggregate demand. They lower the value of the spending multiplier.

Chapter 12 develops the three remaining feedback channels from national income to aggregate demand. The most important of the three in the U.S. economy is the feedback through taxes and transfers in the government sector. Not only is this feedback the most important automatic stabilizer, but also it has a sizable impact on the federal government's budget deficit, one of the leading macroeconomic issues of the day.

The federal government began running huge budget deficits in the first years of President Reagan's administration and has continued to do so ever since. President Reagan inherited a public debt of approximately $1 trillion. By 1993 the public debt had surpassed $4 trillion and was increasing even more rapidly than during the Reagan years. Much has been written about the evils of the huge federal budget deficits and the ever-expanding public debt, some fact and some fiction. You cannot begin to separate fact from fiction until you understand how the economy feeds back into the federal budget deficit through its effect on taxes and transfers.

Chapter 12 begins with an analysis of the automatic stabilizers. In the process we will complete our new Keynesian model of the economy by adding net exports to aggregate demand.

AUTOMATIC STABILIZERS

An **automatic stabilizer** is any component of the economy that is related to the level of national income and lowers the value of the spending multiplier. As such, an automatic stabilizer stabilizes the economy by making it less responsive to aggregate demand shocks. The lower the value of the spending multiplier is, the less the equilibrium level of national income changes in response to an increase or a decrease in aggregate demand. Also, an automatic stabilizer is automatic in the sense that its stabilizing effect is built into the economy. It is not the result of any conscious decision by government policy makers or anyone else.

The four principal automatic stabilizers in the U.S. economy are taxes, transfer payments, business saving, and imports.

Taxes

The federal, state, and local governments collected nearly $1.8 trillion of taxes in 1992, approximately 38 percent of the national income. Whatever other economic effects these taxes may have, they are far and away the most important automatic stabilizer in the U.S. economy.

Our analysis of the tax multiplier in Chapter 11 assumed that governments can raise any given amount of tax revenue that they want to during the course of a year. The specific example in the chapter was a $100 billion federal tax increase. The hidden assumption we made there to illustrate the tax multiplier is that the federal government is continually adjusting the structure of its taxes behind the scenes to hit its revenue target. The **tax structure** consists of the tax rates and the tax base, that is, which items of income or output are subject to tax, and which are exempt from tax.

In fact, governments do not continually adjust the tax structure during the course of the year. They set the tax structure and let the tax revenues fall where they may. The result is that tax collections are directly related to the state of the economy. Tax revenues rise when national income increases and fall when national income decreases, as illustrated in Figure 12.1.

The horizontal axis records the level of national income, and the vertical axis records the total tax revenues collected by the federal, state, and local governments. The line, *Tx*, shows the total tax revenues collected at each level

AUTOMATIC STABILIZER

Any component of the economy that is related to the level of national income and lowers the value of the spending multiplier; automatic stabilizers make the economy less responsive to aggregate demand shocks.

TAX STRUCTURE

The tax rates and the tax base of any particular tax.

FIGURE 12.1

Tax Revenues and National Income

Four of the five major taxes in the United States—the federal and state personal income taxes, the payroll tax for Social Security, the federal and state corporation income taxes, and the state sales taxes—all tax components of the circular flow of economic activity. Therefore, tax revenues vary directly with the level of national income. The upward-sloping line, *Tx*, shows the direct relationship between tax revenues and national income. National income, *Y*, is on the horizontal axis and tax revenues, *Tx*, are on the vertical axis. An increase in national income increases tax revenues and a decrease in national income decreases tax revenues.

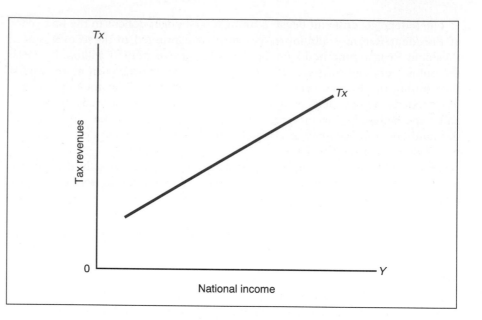

of national income. *Tx* is upward sloping to indicate that tax revenues rise and fall along with the state of the economy. The straight line, *Tx*, actually understates somewhat the sensitivity of tax revenues to the economy. A 1 percent increase in national income raises tax revenues by slightly more than 1 percent.

The reason why tax revenues vary directly with the sate of the economy is obvious just from listing the five major taxes in the United States (in order of importance): the federal and the state personal income taxes, the federal Social Security payroll tax, general sales and excise taxes (primarily state), the property tax (primarily local), and the federal and the state corporation income taxes. The personal income, payroll, and corporation income taxes are levied on all or part of the national income received in the factor markets, and the general sales and excise taxes are levied on sales in the product markets. The revenues collected by these taxes clearly depend on the circular flow of economic activity. The property tax is the one exception among the five taxes. It is not directly related to the circular flow because it is a levy on wealth, not income. Even so, property values do tend to rise and fall with the state of the economy.

Taxes act as an automatic stabilizer because they are a drain on aggregate demand. Suppose that aggregate demand increases and national income begins to increase round by round in the multiplier process. The additional tax dollars siphoned off by the government each round as national income increases reduce households' disposable income, which reduces their consumption demand. As a result, the increases in national income during each round of the multiplier process are less than they would be if tax collections were unrelated to national income. The value of the spending multiplier declines.

True, governments might spend the additional tax revenues on government purchases or transfer payments, but what governments do with the tax revenues is a separate issue. They might also choose to retire some of their debt. The point is that the tax revenues in and of themselves act as a drain on aggregate demand that reduces consumption demand and partially offsets the multiplier process.

TABLE 12.1   The Multiplier Process Round by Round ($ billion)

ROUND	CHANGE IN INVESTMENT DEMAND (ΔI^d)	CHANGE IN CONSUMPTION DEMAND (ΔC^d)	CHANGE IN NATIONAL INCOME (ΔY)	CHANGE IN TAX REVENUES ($\Delta Tx = .25 \cdot \Delta Y$)	CHANGE IN DISPOSABLE INCOME ($\Delta Y_d = \Delta Y - \Delta Tx$)
1	$100	$ —	$100	.25 · $100 = $25	$75
			+		
2	—	.80 · $75 = $60	60	.25 · $ 60 = $15	45
			+		
3	—	.80 · $45 = $36	36	.25 · $ 36 = $ 9	27
			+		
4		⋮		⋮	
⋮					
		FinalΔY = $250			

We can see how income and sales taxes act as an automatic stabilizer by expanding our round-by-round example of the multiplier process from Chapter 10, which was represented in Table 10.2. Recall that the example begins with a $100 (billion) increase in investment demand and that the marginal propensity to consume (MPC) is .80. We assumed in Chapter 10 that the government changed the tax structure behind the scenes to keep tax revenues constant. Table 12.1 represents the multiplier process under the more realistic assumption of a fixed tax structure and automatically changing tax revenues.

Columns two through four in the table are the same as in Table 10.2: the change in investment demand (second column), the change in consumption demand (third column), and the change in national income (fourth column). Table 12.1 adds the change in taxes (fifth column) and the change in disposable income (sixth column) each round. Our new example assumes that the change in taxes each round is 0.25 (25 percent) times the change in national income, which is roughly the case for all taxes combined in the United States. Twenty-five percent is called the *marginal tax rate*, the tax rate on additional income. The change in disposable income each round (sixth column) is the difference between the change in national income (fourth column) and the change in taxes (fifth column). The MPC out of *disposable income* is .80.

The multiplier process begins, as in our previous example, with a $100 increase in investment demand. Producers of investment goods increase production to meet the new demand, and national income increases by $100 in the first round, just as before (fourth column, first row). Rounds two and beyond are different, however. The government now takes 25 percent of the $100 increase in national income for taxes. Tax revenues increase by $25 (fifth column, first row) ($25 = .25 · $100). Households are left with a $75 increase in disposable income (sixth column, first row) ($75 = $100 − $25).

Households base their consumption demand in the second round on the increase in their *disposable income*, not on the increase in national income. Therefore, the increase in consumption demand in the second round is MPC · ΔY_d, or $60 (third column, second row) ($60 = 0.80 · $75). Producers of consumer goods increase production to meet the new consumption demand, and national income increases by $60 in the second round (fourth column, second row). The government takes 25 percent of the $60 increase in national income for taxes. Tax revenues increase by $15 (fifth column, second row)

(.25 · \$60 = \$15). Households are left with a \$45 increase in disposable income (sixth column, second row) (\$45 = \$60 − \$15).

Households' consumption demand in the third round increases by MPC · ΔY_d, or \$36 (third column, third row) (0.80 · \$45 = \$36). Producers of consumer goods increase production to meet the new consumption demand, and national income increases by \$36 in the third round (fourth column, third row). The multiplier process continues in this way indefinitely.

The change in national income after three rounds is the sum of the entries in the fourth column: ΔY = \$100 + \$60 + \$36 = \$196. Compare this with the \$244 change in national income after three rounds in our previous example without income and sales taxes: ΔY = \$100 + \$80 + \$64 = \$244. The 25 percent tax rate on additional national income substantially lowers the increase in consumption demand and national income from the second round on.

The final change in the equilibrium level of national income with a 25 percent marginal tax rate turns out to be \$250, compared with \$500 in our previous example. The income and the sales taxes are a very potent automatic stabilizer, indeed. They lower the value of the spending multiplier by 50 percent, from 5 to 2.5. National income is only half as responsive to the change in aggregate demand in our model with a built-in 25 percent marginal tax rate.

Transfer Payments

Government transfer payments, unlike taxes, are contributors to aggregate demand. Transfer payments increase households' disposable incomes and their consumption demand. Nonetheless, some government transfer payments act as an automatic stabilizer because they are inversely, or negatively, related to the level of national income, as shown in Figure 12.2.

The horizontal axis records the level of national income, and the vertical axis records the total amount of government transfer payments, most of which are federal. The line, *Tr*, shows the total level of government transfer payments at every level of national income. *Tr* is downward sloping to indicate that government transfer payments move inversely to the state of the economy. Transfer payments increase when national income decreases and decrease when national income increases.

The two most important transfer programs that vary with the economy are unemployment insurance and public assistance ("welfare"), particularly Food Stamps, Aid to Families with Dependent Children (AFDC), and Medicaid. Unemployment rises when the economy goes into a recession, and more people apply for unemployment insurance benefits. Conversely, unemployment falls when the economy is booming, and fewer people apply for unemployment insurance benefits. Unemployment insurance benefits rose to approximately \$25 billion during the depths of the 1981–82 recession. By 1987, when the economy had returned to its production possibilities frontier, unemployment insurance benefits had fallen to \$15 billion.[1]

Similarly, unemployment is one of the two events that is most likely to cause a spell of poverty in a family (separation of husband and wife is the other).

---

[1]Executive Office of the President of the United States, *Budget of the United States Government, Fiscal Year 1993, Supplement, February 1992* (Washington, D.C.: U.S. Government Printing Office, 1992), Part Five: Historical Tables, Table 11.1, p. 5–136.

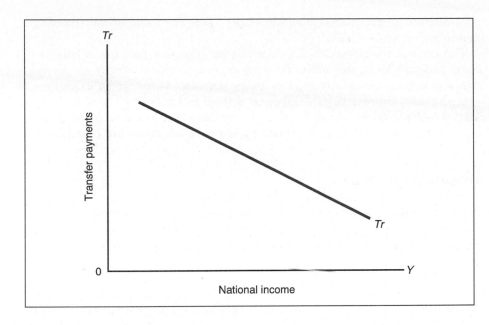

FIGURE 12.2

Transfer Payments and National Income

Some transfer programs, such as Unemployment Insurance and Public Assistance, are sensitive to the level of national income. When national income decreases and people lose their jobs, unemployment insurance benefits and public assistance payments increase. The reverse is true when national income increases and more people are employed. The downward-sloping line, *Tr*, shows the inverse relationship between transfer payments and national income. National income, *Y*, is on the horizontal axis and transfer payments, *Tr*, are on the vertical axis. An increase in national income decreases transfer payments and a decrease in national income increases transfer payments.

The poverty rate rises when the economy is in a recession, and more people apply for Food Stamps and AFDC. People who qualify for AFDC automatically qualify for Medicaid benefits, so Medicaid costs increase as well. The reverse is true when the economy recovers and the poverty rate falls. Public assistance does not respond to the state of the economy as strongly as unemployment insurance does, but public assistance is definitely inversely related to the level of national income.

To see why government transfer programs such as unemployment insurance and public assistance act as an automatic stabilizer, return to our multiplier example above with transfer payments substituted for taxes. Suppose that government transfer payments *decrease* by 25 percent of the *increase* in national income. In other words, when national income increases by $100 in the first round, unemployment insurance benefits, public assistance, and other income-sensitive government transfer payments decrease by a total of $25. The analysis carries through exactly as above. With transfer payments down by $25, households' disposable income has increased by only $75, equal to the $100 increase in earned national income minus the $25 decrease in transfer payments. Therefore, consumption in the second round increases by .80 · $75 = $60, and so on, as before. The final change in the equilibrium level of national income is once again $250.

The actual marginal transfer rate is much less than 25 percent in the United States. Government transfer payments are not nearly as important an automatic stabilizer in the United States as taxes are. The combined spending on unemployment insurance, public assistance, and other income-sensitive transfer payments was approximately $250 billion in 1992, far less than the $1.8 trillion of tax revenues.[2] Nonetheless, our example indicates why income-sensitive

---

[2]*Budget of the United States Government*, Part Five: Historical Tables, Tables 3.2, 11.1, and 11.2.

government transfer payments automatically lower the value of the spending multiplier.

The tax and transfer examples point out an important principle relating to automatic stabilizers: *Any drain on aggregate demand that is directly (positively) related to national income acts as an automatic stabilizer.* Taxes are an example.

Conversely, *any contributor to aggregate demand that is inversely (negatively) related to national income acts as an automatic stabilizer.* Government transfer programs such as unemployment insurance and public assistance are examples.

Business Saving

Business saving, the retained earnings of corporations, is another important automatic stabilizer in the U.S. economy. As with taxes, business saving is a drain on aggregate demand that is directly (positively) related to national income.

Corporate profits before taxes are the most volatile component of national income. Also, corporate profits are usually the first component to change when the growth in national income increases or decreases. For example, the current dollar value of national income increased each year throughout the 1980s, within a range of 3.1 percent (1981) to 11.4 percent (1984). In contrast, corporate profits before taxes increased in the five years when the rate of growth in national income was increasing and decreased in the five years when the rate of growth in national income was decreasing.

The corporation income taxes paid on corporate profits are an automatic stabilizer and have already been accounted for in the discussion of taxes. The after-tax corporate profits have one of two destinations: They are either paid out as dividends or held as retained earnings, business saving. The dividends become part of households' disposable income, but the retained earnings do not. Therefore, retained earnings are, like taxes, a drain on aggregate demand that reduces disposable income and consumption demand.

Retained earnings are also directly, and very dramatically, related to national income. Corporations do not often change their dividend payout policies, with the result that dividends do not fluctuate very much. Dividends increased steadily each year throughout the 1980s at an average annual rate of 8.5 percent. With dividends growing fairly steadily, retained earnings bear the brunt of the swings in corporate profits. Retained earnings exhibited the same pattern as did before-tax corporate profits during the 1980s, increasing when the rate of growth in national income was increasing and decreasing when the rate of growth in national income was decreasing. But the volatility of retained earnings was much greater than that of before-tax corporate profits. The average annual rate of change in before-tax corporate profits was 11.8 percent, plus or minus, during the 1980s. The average annual rate of change in business saving was a whopping 41.4 percent, plus or minus.[3] Therefore, although business saving is a minor component of national income, its extreme sensitivity to changes in national income makes it an important automatic stabilizer in the U.S. economy.

---

[3]Council of Economic Advisors, *Economic Report of the President, 1993* (Washington, D.C.: U.S. Government Printing Office, 1993), Table B-22, p. 373.

Net Exports

The United States is the least dependent on international trade of all the developed market economies and has been throughout the entire post–World War II era. Twenty years ago U.S. exports and imports were small enough, each less than 5 percent of gross domestic product (GDP), that their macro-economic effects could be ignored for the most part. This is no longer true. The increasing internationalization of the U.S. economy has been one of the leading economic stories over the past 30 years. Exports and imports are now about 11 percent of GDP and have a number of important effects on the U.S. economy.[4]

One of the more important is that the foreign sector has become the second largest automatic stabilizer in the United States behind taxes. The feedback from national income to aggregate demand through the foreign sector is now a significant feature of the U.S. economy. This feedback has always been important in the other developed market economies.

In order to understand why the foreign sector acts as an automatic stabilizer we need to take some time to add the foreign sector to our simple model of the economy. The demand for net exports, the difference between export demand (Ex^d) and import demand (Im^d), is the final component of aggregate demand. The foreign sector will play a key role in our analysis of the economy from here on.

NET EXPORTS AND AGGREGATE DEMAND   Aggregate demand is the sum of the demands for the national product by all four sectors of the economy: the household sector (C^d), the business sector (I^d), the government sector (G^d), and the foreign sector ($Ex^d - Im^d$). Therefore, the equilibrium condition in the product markets for the entire economy is

$$Y = C^d + I^d + G^d + (Ex^d - Im^d)$$

The product market for final goods and services is in equilibrium when the value of national income (national product) generated by the producers, Y, equals the aggregate demand for the national product by all four sectors of the economy.

The two principal determinants of the demand for both exports and imports are the level of national income and the exchange rates. Let's begin with the key question that we asked of the other components of aggregate demand: How are export demand and import demand related to the level of national income?

IMPORT DEMAND AND NATIONAL INCOME   The household and the business sectors both purchase a large amount of imported goods from foreign producers. Their demand for imports is such that the overall demand for U.S. imports is closely and directly (positively) related to the level of U.S. national income.

The demand for imported goods and services by U.S. households is part and parcel of their demand for consumer goods and services generally. When

[4]Council of Economic Advisors, *Economic Indicators, March 1993* (Washington, D.C.: U.S. Government Printing Office, 1993), 1.

TABLE 12.2   Import Demand ($ billion)

IMPORT DEMAND (Im^d)	NATIONAL INCOME (Y)
$ 50	$ 0
150	1,000
250	2,000
350	3,000
450	4,000
550	5,000
650	6,000
750	7,000
850	8,000
950	9,000
1,050	10,000
1,150	11,000
1,250	12,000
1,350	13,000

households have more disposable income, their demand for Sony televisions, German Audis, Irish sweaters, and other foreign products increases along with their demand for domestic products. Conversely, when households have less disposable income, their demand for foreign products decreases along with their demand for domestic products. Since national income and disposable income move together, the demand for U.S. imports of consumer goods and services is directly related to U.S. national income.

The link between U.S. import demand and U.S. national income is just as direct in the business sector. Approximately two-thirds of U.S. imports are raw materials, intermediate products, and capital goods purchased by U.S. producers. When U.S. firms increase production and generate more national income, they import more of these inputs from foreign firms. Conversely, when U.S. firms decrease production and generate less national income, they import fewer of these inputs from foreign firms.

In conclusion, the overall demand for U.S. imports by both U.S. households and U.S. business firms is closely and directly (positively) related to the level of national income. Table 12.2 and Figure 12.3 present a hypothetical import demand function for our simple economy.

The import demand function has the same general shape as our hypothetical consumption function from Chapter 10. It has one component that is unrelated to the level of national income and another component that is positively related to the level of national income. Refer to Table 12.2, which shows the level of imports demanded (first column) at every level of national income (second column). As before, all data are in billions of constant dollars.

Import demand is $50 when the level of national income is zero. This is the component that is unrelated to the level of national income. It is determined by other factors that affect import demand, such as exchange rates. Import demand then increases by $100 for every $1,000 increase in national income. For example, import demand is $150 when national income is $1,000; it increases by $100 to $250 when national income increases to $2,000.

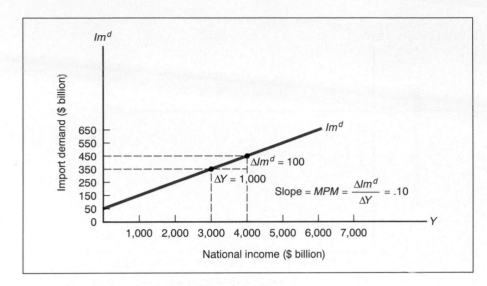

FIGURE 12.3

Import Demand and National Income

The figure is a graph of the hypothetical demand for imports in Table 12.2. National income, Y, is on the horizontal axis and the demand for imports, Im^d, is on the vertical axis. The data are in billions of constant dollars. The import demand function, Im^d, is upward sloping; imports vary directly with the level of national income. As national income rises, consumers buy more imported products and firms import more capital goods and intermediate products. The reverse is true as income falls. The slope of the import demand function is the marginal propensity to import (MPM). MPM = $\Delta Im^d/\Delta Y$. The MPM for our import demand function equals 0.10.

The **marginal propensity to import,** labeled the MPM, is analogous to the marginal propensity to consume. The MPM is the ratio of the change in import demand to the change in national income.

$$MPM = \Delta Im^d/\Delta Y$$

The MPM = .10 in our example, approximately its value for the U.S. economy.

Figure 12.3 pictures our hypothetical import demand function. The vertical axis records the level of import demand, and the horizontal axis records the level of national income. The straight line, Im^d, the import demand function, shows the level of import demand at every level of national income. Im^d intersects the vertical axis at $50, indicating that import demand is $50 when national income is zero. The slope of Im^d, the rise over the run, is .10, the MPM. Changes in factors other than national income that affect the demand for imports, such as exchange rates, shift Im^d up or down.

EXPORT DEMAND AND NATIONAL INCOME   The demand for U.S. exports is also closely related to the level of national income, but not to *U.S.* national income. U.S. exports are sales to consumers, producers, and governments in foreign countries. As such, the demand for U.S. exports is the same as the demand for U.S. imports within foreign countries. Consequently, the demand for U.S. exports is directly (positively) related to the national incomes of *foreign countries*. When the economies of Japan and Western Europe are booming, U.S. exporters find the demand for their food, computers, and airplanes increasing. Conversely, when the economies of Japan and Western Europe fall into a recession, the demand for these U.S. exports decreases.

Any connection between the demand for U.S. exports and *U.S.* national income occurs only indirectly through the effect of the U.S. economy on other economies. For instance, Canada is the leading trading partner of the United States. A booming U.S. economy tends to pull the Canadian economy along

MARGINAL PROPENSITY TO IMPORT

The additional amount of import demand resulting from a $1 increase in national income; the ratio of the change in import demand to the change in national income.

FIGURE 12.4

Export Demand and National Income

The demand for U.S. exports depends on the level of national income in foreign countries, but does not depend closely on the level of U.S. national income. Therefore, our model assumes that export demand is independent of the level of U.S. national income. In particular, we are assuming that export demand is $750 over the range of values that U.S. national income is likely to have (in billions of constant dollars). Therefore, the graph of export demand, Ex^d, is horizontal at a value of $750. Changes in factors that influence the demand for U.S. exports, such as a depreciation or appreciation of the dollar, shift Ex^d up or down.

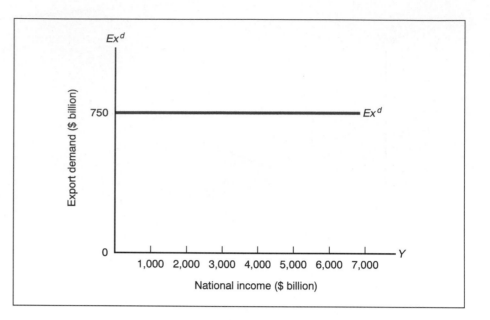

with it because Canadian exports to the United States increase, and an increase in Canadian exports increases Canadian aggregate demand and national income. The larger Canadian national income in turn feeds back to an increased demand for U.S. exports to Canada.

The indirect relationship between U.S. exports and U.S. national income is not nearly as strong as the direct relationship between U.S. imports and U.S. national income, however. Therefore, we will assume for simplicity that the demand for U.S. exports is unrelated to the level of U.S. national income, as illustrated in Figure 12.4.

The demand for U.S. exports is assumed to be $750 (billion) at every level of U.S. national income. The export demand line, Ex^d, is horizontal at $750. The $750 is determined by factors other than U.S. national income, such as exchange rates or foreign national incomes. Changes in these other factors shift Ex^d up or down.

EQUILIBRIUM WITH THE FOREIGN SECTOR   Figure 12.5 completes our model of the economy by adding net exports to the model of Chapter 11. All data are in billions of dollars, as before. The aggregate demand line, ADE, in Figure 11.5 for the simpler economy excludes the foreign sector. To build the new aggregate demand line from the old aggregate demand line we need to (1) add, vertically, the export demand line, Ex^d, from Figure 12.4; and (2) subtract, vertically, the import demand function, Im^d, from Figure 12.3.

Adding export demand geometrically to aggregate demand is straightforward. Since export demand is constant, $750, at every level of national income, adding Ex^d just shifts up the old ADE line by $750. In other words, Ex^d changes the position, but not the slope, of the ADE line.

Subtracting import demand vertically from aggregate demand is a bit trickier. Since import demand increases as national income increases, ever-larger amounts of import demand are subtracted from the old ADE line at higher

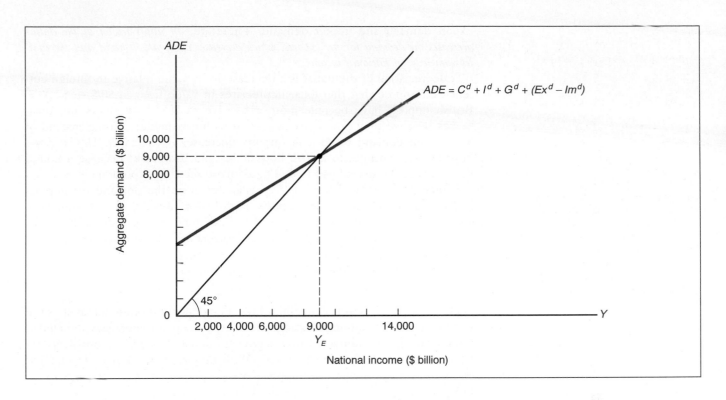

FIGURE 12.5

The Equilibrium Level of National Income in the Complete Model of the Economy

Adding the foreign sector completes the list of final demanders in the economy. *ADE*, or aggregate demand, is the sum of consumption demand by households (C^d), investment demand by business firms (I^d), government spending on goods and services by the federal, state, and local governments (G^d), and net exports in the foreign sector ($Ex^d - Im^d$). $ADE = C^d + I^d + G^d + (Ex^d - Im^d)$. As always, the equilibrium level of national income is at the intersection of the ADE and the 45-degree lines, $9,000 in our model (in billions of constant dollars). Adding the foreign sector flattens the ADE line somewhat because import demand is positively related to national income. As the level of national income increases, ever more important demand is subtracted from aggregate demand.

levels of national income. Refer to Table 12.2. At $Y = 0$, $Im^d = \$50$, so that the new *ADE* line is $50 below the old *ADE* line. At $Y = \$5,000$, $Im^d = \$550$, so that the new *ADE* line is $550 below the old *ADE* line. At $Y = \$12,000$, $Im^d = \$1,250$, so that the new *ADE* line is $1,250 below the old *ADE* line. Therefore, subtracting import demand both *lowers* and *flattens* the *ADE* line. The *ADE* line for the full economy has a smaller slope than did the *ADE* line for the simpler economy without a foreign sector. We will return to the slope of the *ADE* line below.

As always, the equilibrium level of national income is at the intersection of the aggregate demand line, *ADE*, and the 45° line. $Y_E = \$9,000$ according to Figure 12.5.

NET EXPORTS AND EXCHANGE RATES   We saw in Chapter 7 that changes in the dollar exchange rate for foreign currencies affect both export demand and import demand simultaneously. A brief review will be helpful.

Recall that an appreciation of the dollar is an increase in its value relative to foreign currencies. Suppose that the dollar appreciates in value from $1.80/£ to $1.60/£. British imports have become cheaper to U.S. households and businesses because they can now buy a pound sterling for only $1.60 instead of $1.80. The demand for British imports increases. Conversely, U.S. exports have become more expensive to British households and businesses because a pound now buys only $1.60 instead of $1.80. The demand for U.S. exports decreases.

In general, an appreciation of the dollar increases the demand for imports and decreases the demand for exports. It shifts Im^d upward in Figure 12.3, and it shifts Ex^d downward in Figure 12.4. Net exports are the difference between export demand and import demand. Therefore, *an appreciation of the dollar decreases the demand for net exports, which decreases aggregate demand and the equilibrium level of national income.*

A depreciation of the dollar is a decrease in its value relative to foreign currencies. Suppose that the dollar depreciates in value from $1.80/£ to $2.00/£. British imports have become more expensive to U.S. households and businesses because they now must pay $2.00 to buy a pound sterling instead of $1.80. The demand for British imports decreases. Conversely, U.S. exports have become cheaper to British households and businesses because a pound now buys $2.00 instead of $1.80. The demand for U.S. exports increases.

In general, a depreciation of the dollar decreases the demand for imports and increases the demand for exports. It shifts Im^d downward in Figure 12.3, and it shifts Ex^d upward in Figure 12.4. Therefore, *a depreciation of the dollar increases the demand for net exports, which increases aggregate demand and the equilibrium level of national income.*

Let's now return to the analysis of automatic stabilizers.

IMPORTS AS AN AUTOMATIC STABILIZER   The demand for imports satisfies the conditions for an automatic stabilizer. It is a drain on aggregate demand—import demand is subtracted from aggregate demand—and it is positively related to the level of national income. With imports now 11 percent of GDP and a marginal propensity to import of about .10, imports have become a very important automatic stabilizer for the U.S. economy.

Think back to the round-by-round multiplier process to see why imports act as an automatic stabilizer. Suppose that an initial increase in aggregate demand starts a round-by-round increase in national income, as in our previous examples. To the extent that households spend some of their increased income on imported goods, the increase in production to meet their demand increases national income in *foreign* countries, not in the United States. That additional income earned by foreign workers, landlords, and capitalists leaks out of the multiplier process. It is not available to U.S. households for consumption in the next round. The result is that the final change in U.S. national income is less than it would have been without the leakage of income to imports. The spending multiplier is smaller.[5]

HISTORICAL NOTE: In August of 1993 the Fed sold Japanese yen for dollars to depreciate the Yen relative to the dollar. It did this to help support the sagging Japanese economy, which was mired in a deep recession at the time. A depreciation of the Yen against the dollar encourages Japanese exports to the United States and discourages Japanese imports from the United States, thereby increasing aggregate demand in Japan.

THE INCREASINGLY IMPORTANT FOREIGN SECTOR   The increasing importance of the foreign sector in the United States was driven home in the 1980s, when the economy struggled to recover from the recession of 1981–82. The recovery took five years—the economy did not return to the production possibilities frontier until 1987—and the foreign sector played a key role in slowing down the pace of the recovery.

Part of the problem was the natural increase in import demand as national income increased, which acted as an automatic stabilizer. The increase in imports reduced the value of the spending multiplier and reduced the growth in national income.

---

[5]The only difference between imports and the other automatic stabilizers is that the leakage occurs in the first round of the multiplier process. Refer back to Table 12.1, and suppose that 25 percent of all U.S. purchases are imports. If so, then national income would only increase by $75 in the *first* round, since $25 of the initial increase in investment is purchased from foreign producers. The value of the spending multiplier would be slightly smaller than in our tax example.

The stabilizing effect of import demand is always present and, by itself, would not have slowed the recovery all that much. Taxes and transfers are much more important automatic stabilizers than is import demand. But a second factor kicked in that greatly increased the foreign sector's drag on the economy, a dramatic appreciation of the dollar. The dollar appreciated by 38 percent against the major currencies between 1981 and 1985, as the United States became the favored nation for savers and investors worldwide.[6] Foreigners were anxious to invest in U.S. real estate and private companies and to otherwise place their savings in all kinds of U.S. financial securities, including U.S. government bonds, certificates of deposit, and corporate stocks and bonds. They needed dollars to transact in the U.S. markets, so they offered their currencies for dollars in the foreign exchange markets and drove up the value of the dollar. As expected, the appreciation of the dollar simultaneously reduced export demand and increased import demand, further reducing net exports and holding down the growth of the economy.

The experience of the 1980s is likely to be repeated. We will see in later chapters that an increase in aggregate demand can cause an appreciation of the dollar, which reduces net exports and removes some of the increase in aggregate demand. The 1980s have taught us that the foreign sector is now large enough to exert a significant drag on aggregate demand when the dollar is appreciating.

The Overall Impact of Automatic Stabilizers

Automatic stabilizers offer the U.S. economy a fair amount of protection against aggregate demand shocks. Income and sales taxes, income-sensitive government transfer payments, business saving, and import demand combine to reduce the value of the spending multiplier by about 40 percent. In other words, a change in aggregate demand changes the equilibrium level of national income by only 60 percent as much as it would without the automatic stabilizers.

Geometrically, automatic stabilizers flatten ADE in the aggregate demand–45° line graph. We have already seen how import demand directly flattens ADE. Income and sales taxes, income-sensitive transfer payments, and business saving indirectly flatten ADE by making consumption demand less sensitive to changes in national income. They do so by causing disposable income to change by less than national income changes. Take the federal personal income tax as an example. Because income taxes increase when national income increases, households do not receive the full benefit of the increase in national income. The increase in their disposable income equals the increase in national income minus the increase in their federal income taxes. Since consumption demand depends on disposable income and not on national income, the change in consumption demand is smaller than it would be without an income tax.

Figure 12.6 shows that a change in aggregate demand produces a smaller change in the equilibrium level of national income the flatter ADE is. The steeper line, $ADE_0^{w/oAS}$, is the aggregate demand line without automatic stabilizers. The flatter line, $ADE_0^{w/AS}$, is the aggregate line with automatic stabilizers. The initial equilibrium level of national income is Y_0, at the intersection of each ADE_0 line and the 45° line.

---

[6]*Economic Report of the President, 1993*, Table B-107, p. 470.

FIGURE 12.6

Aggregate Demand with and without Automatic Stabilizers

The figure shows how automatic stabilizers flatten the aggregate demand line, *ADE*, and make the economy less sensitive to changes in aggregate demand. $ADE^{w/oAS}$ is the relatively steep aggregate demand line that would exist without automatic stabilizers. $ADE^{w/AS}$ is the actual, relatively flat aggregate demand line with automatic stabilizers such as income taxes and import demand. The equilibrium level of national income is initially Y_0; at the intersection of $ADE_0^{w/oAS}$, $ADE_0^{w/AS}$, and the 45-degree line. A decrease in aggregate demand in the amount *ab* shifts the two aggregate demand lines down to $ADE_1^{w/oAS}$ and $ADE_1^{w/AS}$. Without automatic stabilizers, the equilibrium level of national income would fall to $Y_1^{w/oAS}$, at the intersection of $ADE_1^{w/oAS}$ and the 45-degree line. With automatic stabilizers, the equilibrium level of national income falls to $Y_1^{w/AS}$, at the intersection of $ADE_1^{w/AS}$ and the 45-degree line. The automatic stabilizers reduce the decline in national income by about 40 percent.

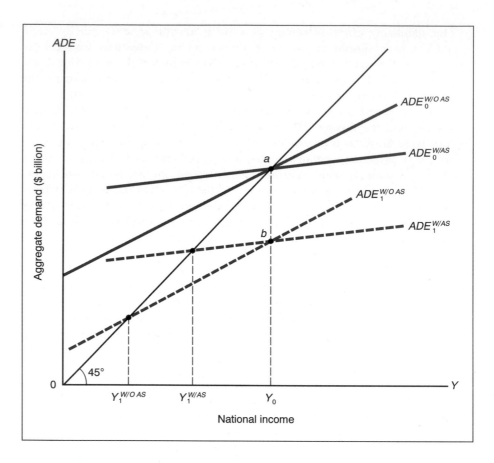

Suppose that aggregate demand decreases by the amount *ab*. The equilibrium level of national income falls to $Y_1^{w/AS}$ with automatic stabilizers, at the intersection of the dotted line $ADE_1^{w/AS}$ and the 45° line. In contrast, the equilibrium level of national income falls all the way to $Y_1^{w/oAS}$ without automatic stabilizers, at the intersection of the dotted line $ADE_1^{w/oAS}$ and the 45° line. The distance between Y_0 and $Y_1^{w/AS}$ is approximately 60 percent of the distance between Y_0 and $Y_1^{w/oAS}$ for the U.S. economy.

Automatic Stabilizers: Good or Bad?

Are automatic stabilizers good or bad for the U.S. economy? The answer depends on where the economy happens to be.

Automatic stabilizers are good when the economy is operating close to the target level of national income because the economy stays closer to the target when aggregate demand shifts up or down. Suppose that Y_0 is the target level of national income in Figure 12.6. When aggregate demand falls by *ab*, the economy stays closer to the target with automatic stabilizers than without automatic stabilizers.

Automatic stabilizers are definitely a blessing when the economy begins to go into a recession because they break the fall in national income. The annual unemployment rate reached 8.5 percent during the recession of 1974–75 and 9.7 percent during the recession of 1981–82. As bad as these figures were, the unemployment rate would have been several percentage points higher each time without the automatic stabilizers. More recently, import demand fell by $6 billion in 1991, which helped support aggregate demand during the recession of 1990–91. It had risen by $38 billion in 1990, and rose again by $47 billion in 1992 as the economy began to recover.[7]

Whenever the economy moves into a recession, you can bet that the news media will ask economists this question: Are we headed for another Great Depression? Almost all economists answer no for at least two good reasons.

The first is that the economy has much more automatic stability now to break the fall than it had during the Great Depression. When the Depression hit in 1930, income and sales taxes were minuscule compared with today, the federal government had no public assistance or unemployment insurance programs (they began with the passage of the Social Security Act of 1935), and imports were unimportant. Today, because of the automatic stabilizers, a recession is much less likely to snowball into another Great Depression.

According to Victor Zarnowitz of the National Bureau of Economic Research, a dollar increase in GNP led to a $.95 increase in disposable income in the period from 1912 to 1945, but only a $.39 increase in disposable income in the period from 1945 to 1982. As a result, he estimates that the spending multiplier has decreased from a range of 3.2 to 5.1 in the earlier period to a range of 1.8 to 2.5 in the latter period.[8]

A second reason is that most economists have faith that the federal government will use its fiscal and monetary policies to prevent a disaster like the Great Depression. In contrast, macroeconomics was not well developed in the 1930s, and policy makers at the time did not understand how to use fiscal and monetary policies to get the economy growing again. The fiscal policies that were tried were hardly expansionary at all, and monetary policy was disastrous. The Fed sat back and watched the money supply decrease by one-third in the first years of the Great Depression. Economists are confident that the government will not repeat those mistakes.

Automatic stabilizers are not so desirable if the economy is operating far from its target, however, because then a larger change in aggregate demand is necessary to bring the economy back to the target. Returning again to Figure 12.6, suppose that the target level of national income is $Y_1^{w/oAS}$, so that the economy is initially suffering an inflationary gap at Y_0. Without automatic stabilizers, contractionary policies have to shift aggregate demand down by ab to close the gap. With automatic stabilizers, contractionary policies have to shift aggregate demand down by much more than ab to close the gap. A decrease in aggregate demand of ab only brings the economy to $Y_1^{w/AS}$, about 40 percent above the target. The required change in aggregate demand with automatic stabilizers may be larger than is politically feasible if the economy strays from its target. Therefore, automatic stabilizers that are a blessing when the economy begins to move into a recession become something of a curse when the economy is trying to recover from the depths of a recession. As already noted, automatic stabilizers slowed the recovery from the deep 1981–82 recession. They also exerted a drag on the economy in the early 1990s as the economy struggled to recover from the recession of 1990–91.

---

[7] The unemployment data are from the *Economic Report of the President, 1993*, Table B-37, p. 390. The import data are from *Economic Indicators*, March 1993, 1.

[8] Victor Zarnowitz, "Facts and Factors in the Recent Evolution of Business Cycles in the United States," in *NBER Working Paper #2865* (Cambridge, MA: National Bureau of Economic Research, 1989), 26 and 28.

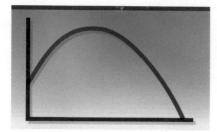

THE SPENDING MULTIPLIER IN THE UNITED STATES

The previous section on the spending multiplier in Chapter 11 noted that the simple models of Chapters 10 and 11 vastly overstated the value of the spending multiplier. $M_{\text{Spending}} = 1/(1 - \text{MPC})$ in those simple models. Since the long-run MPC for the United States is on the order of .90, those models predict an M_{Spending} of about 10, whereas the actual M_{Spending} in the United States is in the neighborhood of 1 to 3.

The automatic stabilizers bring us part of the way to the actual spending multiplier. By knocking out 40 percent of the value of the spending multiplier, the automatic stabilizers reduce M_{Spending} in our model from 10 to 6.

The appendix to this chapter presents the detailed algebra of the spending multiplier with automatic stabilizers. The basic idea is that M_{Spending} depends on the slope of the ADE line in the aggregate demand–45 ° line graph. The slope of ADE is called the **marginal propensity to spend** out of national income. It indicates what portion of the change in national income feeds back into a further change in aggregate demand during each round of the multiplier process.

MARGINAL PROPENSITY TO SPEND

The portion of the change in national income that feeds back into further changes in aggregate demand during each round of the multiplier process; the slope of the aggregate desired expenditures (ADE) line.

$$M_{\text{Spending}} = 1/(1 - \text{marginal propensity to spend})$$

The slope of ADE is the MPC in the simple models of Chapters 10 and 11 without automatic stabilizers. As we have seen, automatic stabilizers decrease the slope of ADE, the marginal propensity to spend; in the process they lower the value of M_{Spending}.

Automatic Stabilizers Versus Discretionary Policies

A final point about automatic stabilizers needs to be stressed: The government cannot rely on automatic stabilizers to keep the economy at a target level of national income. If a change (shift) in aggregate demand moves the economy off its target, the automatic stabilizers help by reducing the resulting change in the equilibrium. But this is all they can do. Automatic stabilizers cannot reverse the change (shift) in aggregate demand to return the economy to the target.

Return again to Figure 12.6, and assume that the initial equilibrium, Y_0, is the target level of national income. When aggregate demand decreases by ab, the automatic stabilizers help by breaking the fall of national income. The economy moves to $Y_1^{w/AS}$ instead of $Y_1^{w/oAS}$. But the economy will stay at $Y_1^{w/AS}$ unless the government responds with expansionary fiscal or monetary policies to shift the dotted line $ADE_1^{w/AS}$ back up to its initial position.

The fact that income-tax collections automatically decrease and unemployment insurance benefits automatically increase as national income decreases cannot reverse the direction of aggregate demand. Any changes in the federal budget that respond automatically to the level of national income, as well as the other automatic stabilizers, just flatten the ADE line; they do not shift ADE. Only discretionary fiscal and monetary policies can shift ADE up or down to match the equilibrium with the target level of national income.

BUDGET DEFICITS AND FISCAL POLICY

The president and the Congress have every political incentive to talk a good fiscal policy game. They often claim that they are pursuing expansionary fiscal policies to get the economy moving or contractionary policies to hold down the growth of aggregate demand—whatever is necessary to help achieve the macroeconomic policy goals. How can you put them to the test and judge for yourself the direction and the magnitude of fiscal policy?

The federal government publishes a wealth of information on fiscal policy. You might begin by reading through the federal budget line by line to see what has been appropriated for each agency. The Office of Management and Budget publishes the federal *Budget of the United States Government* each year, along with supporting *Special Analyses of the Federal Budget,* over a thousand pages of detailed information on the federal budget. You might also read the comments on fiscal policy in the annual *Economic Report of the President,* put together by the president's Council of Economic Advisers, as well as the numerous budget studies undertaken by the Congressional Budget Office, the research arm of the Congress.

Of course, neither you nor most anyone else has the time or the inclination to pore over all the published information on the government's fiscal policies. What you want instead is a simple, "quick and dirty" measure of the direction and the magnitude of the government's discretionary fiscal policy stance for any one year. At the very least, the measure should indicate whether fiscal policy is expansionary or contractionary and give a sense of how expansionary or contractionary. The simple measure of fiscal policy most often reported in the news media is the change in the federal budget deficit from one year to the next.

The change in the federal budget deficit would appear to be a reasonably good measure of the government's fiscal policy stance. The **budget deficit** is the difference between expenditures and revenues, that is, government purchases plus transfer payments minus taxes (and other fees):

$$\text{Deficit} = G + Tr - Tx$$

The change in the deficit is the change in these three items:

$$\Delta\text{Deficit} = \Delta G + \Delta Tr - \Delta Tx$$

Changes in government purchases, transfer payments, and taxes are the three main tools of fiscal policy. Therefore, the change in the deficit from one year to the next summarizes the net change in all three fiscal policy tools.

An increase in the deficit is commonly interpreted as an indication of expansionary fiscal policy. The deficit can increase only if the increase in government purchases and increase in transfer payments exceed the increase in taxes, which would tend to increase aggregate demand. The more the deficit increases, the more expansionary the fiscal policy is. Conversely, a decrease in the deficit is commonly interpreted as an indication of contractionary fiscal policy. The deficit can decrease only if the increase in government purchases plus the increase in transfer payments is less than the change in taxes, which would tend to decrease aggregate demand. The more the deficit decreases, the more contractionary the fiscal policy is.

ACTUAL BUDGET DEFICIT
The difference between government expenditures and government revenues.

Unfortunately, the change in the federal budget deficit is not a very reliable measure of the government's fiscal policy stance. The problem is that changes in the deficit depend on two factors: (1) discretionary changes in expenditure programs or taxes, which is what we want to measure; and (2) changes in the state of the economy, whether the equilibrium level of national income is increasing or decreasing. The deficit is very sensitive to the state of the economy because both taxes and transfer payments vary with the level of national income. When the economy moves into a recession and unemployment increases, tax collections automatically decrease and income-sensitive transfer payments automatically increase. The budget deficit increases. Conversely, when the economy is booming and unemployment decreases, tax collections automatically increase and income-sensitive transfer payments automatically decrease. The budget deficit decreases. Changes in the state of the economy have an enormous effect on the size of the federal deficit. Every one percentage point increase in the unemployment rate increases the deficit by approximately $50 billion.

The Structural Deficit

A single measure, the change in the deficit, cannot untangle the separate effects of these two factors on the budget deficit. The effect of the economy on the deficit has to be removed to assess the government's fiscal policy stance. In 1955 economists at the Bureau of Economic Analysis devised a deficit concept that does this; they called it the high-employment deficit. President Reagan's economic advisers changed the name of the high employment deficit to the structural deficit, which is the name more commonly used today.

The structural deficit standardizes the measure of the deficit at one level of national income. The natural choice is the full employment level of national income or, alternatively, the natural rate of unemployment, U_{NR}, which we will assume is 6 percent. Therefore, the **structural deficit** is an estimate of what the federal deficit would be *if* the economy were at the natural rate of unemployment, regardless of where the economy actually is. Having standardized the structural deficit measure at U_{NR}, changes in the structural deficit from year to year indicate the government's fiscal policy stance.

The structural deficit removes the effect of the economy on the deficit because the structural deficit is always measured at $U_{NR} = 6$ percent each year. The only way that the structural deficit can change is if the federal government makes discretionary changes in its expenditure or tax programs that increase or decrease the budget deficit at every level of national income, including the full employment level of national income. This is what fiscal policy is all about. Therefore, changes in the structural deficit are a reliable measure of the government's fiscal policy stance:

■ *An increase in the structural deficit indicates that fiscal policy has been expansionary.* The federal government has undertaken programmatic changes in its expenditure and tax programs that increase the budget deficit at every level of national income.

■ *A decrease in the structural deficit indicates that fiscal policy has been contractionary.* The federal government has undertaken programmatic changes in its expenditure and tax programs that decrease the budget deficit at every level of national income.

STRUCTURAL BUDGET DEFICIT

An estimate of what the government's budget deficit would be if the economy were at full employment (the natural rate of unemployment), regardless of where the economy actually is; it increases and decreases with discretionary changes in government spending on goods and services, transfer payments, or taxes; formerly referred to as the *high-employment budget deficit.*

Some Pitfalls With the Structural Deficit

The change in the structural deficit is not a perfect measure of the government's fiscal policy stance, however. An immediate problem is that the structural deficit is only an estimate, not an actual number. Different economists may arrive at different estimates of what the deficit would be *if* unemployment were at the natural rate.

Another problem is that the natural rate of unemployment is a moving target. The level of national income required to keep the unemployment rate at 6 percent increases as the production possibilities frontier expands over time and labor becomes more productive. The higher the full-employment level of national income is, the larger tax collections are and the smaller some of the transfer payments are. In other words, the structural deficit measured at U_{NR} = 6 percent has a natural tendency to decrease over time. A decrease in the structural deficit may be due to economic growth rather than a contractionary fiscal policy.

Still another problem is that changes in government purchases have a greater multiplied effect on the equilibrium level of national income than do changes in taxes or transfer payments. Suppose that the government's fiscal policy is a balanced budget change, consisting of equal increases in government purchases and taxes. The balanced budget multiplier is one; this fiscal policy is expansionary. Yet balanced budget changes leave the structural deficit unchanged, suggesting that fiscal policy has been neither expansionary nor contractionary.

Finally, many economists recommend computing the ratio of the structural deficit to the full employment level of national income or GDP and using changes in the ratio as the measure of fiscal policy. Changes in the ratio give a better indication of the *magnitude* of the government's fiscal policy initiatives than does the structural deficit itself.

These problems notwithstanding, the change in the structural deficit (or in the ratio of the structural deficit to national income) is a fairly reliable "quick and dirty" measure of the government's fiscal policy stance. It is far better than the change in the actual deficit. Unfortunately, the news media almost always report changes in the actual deficit rather than the structural deficit. You may have to search through government publications such as the *Economic Report of the President* to find data on the structural deficit.

The Cyclical Deficit

The **cyclical deficit** is the difference between the actual deficit and the structural deficit.

cyclical deficit = actual deficit − structural deficit

Since the structural deficit is measured at the natural rate of unemployment, the size of the cyclical deficit depends entirely on the state of the economy. It increases and decreases with the business cycle, hence the name cyclical deficit.

The cyclical deficit mirrors the performance of the economy:

■ *The cyclical deficit is positive when* U > U_{NR} *and becomes larger the farther* U *is above* U_{NR}. For example, at U = 8% the actual deficit is larger than the

CYCLICAL BUDGET DEFICIT

The component of the government's budget deficit that fluctuates with the state of the economy; the difference between the actual budget deficit and the structural budget deficit.

structural deficit, which assumes that U = 6%. The cyclical deficit is positive.

■ *The cyclical deficit is zero when* $U = U_{NR}$. If the actual unemployment rate were 6 percent, then both the actual deficit and the structural deficit would be equal. The cyclical deficit would be zero.

■ *The cyclical deficit is negative (a surplus) when* $U < U_{NR}$ *and becomes more negative the farther* U *is below* U_{NR}. Suppose that the unemployment rate is 3 percent and the actual deficit is in balance. Since the structural deficit is the deficit at U = 6%, it is positive. With the actual deficit = 0, the cyclical deficit is negative (a surplus).

Summary: The Structural and the Cyclical Deficits

To summarize, economists conceptually divide the actual federal budget deficit into two components, the structural deficit and the cyclical deficit.

$$\text{Actual deficit} = \text{structural deficit} + \text{cyclical deficit}$$

Therefore, changes in the deficit from year to year consist of changes in the structural and the cyclical deficits.

$$\Delta\text{Actual deficit} = \Delta\text{structural deficit} + \Delta\text{cyclical deficit}$$

The change in the structural deficit results from the government's discretionary fiscal policy. An increase in the structural deficit indicates an expansionary fiscal policy, and a decrease in the structural deficit indicates a contractionary fiscal policy. The change in the cyclical deficit results from automatic changes in tax collections and income-sensitive transfer payments as the level of national income increases and decreases. An expanding economy reduces the cyclical deficit, and a contracting economy increases the cyclical deficit.

HISTORICAL NOTE: Unemployment increased by two percentage points from 1990 to 1993. This alone has added over $100 billion each year to the federal deficit.

Budget Deficits During the 1980s

Table 12.3 presents the actual, structural, and cyclical federal budget deficits during the 1980s, when the federal deficit leaped to the forefront as a leading macroeconomic issue. The estimates of the structural deficit were made by Northwestern's Robert Gordon and assume that U_{NR} = 6 percent. The cyclical deficit is the difference between the actual deficit and Gordon's estimated structural deficit. The data illustrate a number of the principles about budget deficits discussed above.

THE CYCLICAL DEFICITS   Notice first how the cyclical deficits mirror the performance of the economy. The economy moved into the deepest recession since the Great Depression during 1981–82, and the unemployment rate rose briefly above 10 percent. The deep recession caused a dramatic increase in the cyclical deficit, as personal and corporation income tax collections fell off and income-sensitive transfer payments such as unemployment insurance benefits increased. Following the recession the economy began a long, slow recovery

TABLE 12.3 The Federal Budget Deficits, 1980–89 ($ billion)

YEAR	ACTUAL DEFICIT[a]	STRUCTURAL DEFICIT[b]	CYCLICAL DEFICIT	RATIO OF STRUCTURAL DEFICIT TO NATIONAL INCOME (%)
1980	$ 68.0	$ 35.4	$ 32.6	1.6
1981	96.0	42.5	53.5	1.7
1982	202.6	98.8	103.8	3.9
1983	169.2	105.4	63.8	3.9
1984	187.0	154.7	32.3	5.1
1985	212.2	192.3	19.9	5.9
1986	189.0	160.4	28.6	4.7
1987	164.3	176.0	(−) 11.7	4.8
1988	167.4	203.6	(−) 36.2	5.1
1989	137.0	180.2	(−) 43.2	4.3

[a]Actual deficit = structural deficit + cyclical deficit.
[b]Structural deficits assume U_{NR} = 6 percent.
SOURCE: R. Gordon, *Macroeconomics*, 5th edition (Glenview, IL: Scott, Foresman/Little, Brown, 1989), Appendix A, pp. A5–A7. Council of Economic Advisors, *Economic Report of the President, 1993* (Washington, D.C.: U.S. Government Printing Office, 1993), Table B-21, p. 371.

that continued through the remainder of the decade. The steady recovery led to a steady decrease in the cyclical deficit, as tax collections rose and income-sensitive transfer payments declined. The cyclical deficit turned negative (became a surplus) beginning in 1987, when the unemployment rate dipped below Gordon's assumed natural rate of 6 percent. The unemployment rate had fallen to 5.3 percent by 1989.

THE STRUCTURAL DEFICITS The structural deficits increased substantially each year from 1981 through 1985, indicating that fiscal policy was highly expansionary during that time. The increases were largely the result of a massive military buildup combined with a 23 percent cut in the personal income tax (more on these below). The expansionary fiscal policy was just the right medicine for an ailing economy trying to recover from a recession, according to the new Keynesian perspective. Indeed, many new Keynesian economists believe that the government's fiscal policy stance was the main reason for the recovery.

The structural deficit decreased somewhat in 1989, indicating that fiscal policy was mildly contractionary. This may have contributed to precipitating the mild recession of 1990.

ACTUAL DEFICITS AND FISCAL POLICY The data also reveal how changes in the actual deficit can be a misleading indicator of the government's fiscal policy stance, both its magnitude and its direction. Compare the changes in the actual and the structural deficits from 1987 to 1988. The actual deficit hardly changed at all, whereas the structural deficit increased by more than $27 billion. Using the change in the actual deficit as the measure of fiscal policy would suggest that fiscal policy was essentially neutral, whereas the increase in the structural deficit correctly shows that fiscal policy was somewhat expansionary.

Worse yet, changes in the actual deficit can misrepresent the direction of fiscal policy. Compare the changes in the actual and the structural deficits from

1986 to 1987. The actual deficit *decreased* by about $25 billion, suggesting that fiscal policy was contractionary. In contrast, the structural deficit *increased* by nearly $16 billion, correctly indicating that fiscal policy was mildly expansionary. The cyclical deficit column shows that the decrease in the actual deficit was due to the continued rapid growth of the economy. The lesson is clear: Use changes in the structural deficit, not in the actual deficit, to assess the government's fiscal policy stance.

LARGE STRUCTURAL DEFICITS AND THE BURDEN OF THE DEBT

The increased reliance on deficit financing that began during the Reagan/Bush administrations represented a major and an unprecedented shift in federal budgetary policy. The federal government had run very large budget deficits only once before, during World War II to finance the war effort. The World War II deficits were actually a much larger percentage of national income than were the Reagan/Bush deficits. The difference, though, is that the Reagan/Bush deficits were peacetime deficits, and the federal government had never before even considered running such large peacetime deficits for years on end.

Particularly noteworthy was the increase in the structural deficits, to $200 billion and more. When the deficits first began to appear, President Reagan assured the American public that the economy would grow its way out of the deficits as it returned to full employment. His economic advisers admitted, however, that economic growth would not reduce the projected structural deficits because the structural deficits are calculated *at* full employment.

To put the numbers in Table 12.3 in perspective, the average actual and structural deficits from 1970 to 1979 were $31.4 billion and $26.1 billion. The average actual and structural deficits from 1980 to 1989 were $159 billion and $135 billion, each five times as large as its 1970s counterpart.[9]

Each year that the government runs a deficit it increases the amount of public debt outstanding. The Reagan/Bush deficits were so large that the debt is growing faster than the growth in the national product. President Reagan inherited a public debt of $909 billion, equal to 34 percent of the gross national product (GNP). By 1992 the public debt had increased to $4002 billion, equal to 67 percent of the GDP.[10] The public debt continued to grow faster than did the national product into the Clinton administration.

The dramatic increase in deficit financing came about immediately after President Reagan took office in 1981. Reagan proposed three major budgetary changes:

1. A massive increase in defense expenditures to counter what he perceived to be a growing military threat from the Soviet Union.
2. A 23 percent cut in personal income tax rates, by far the largest federal tax cut ever, to stimulate the economy. The proposed tax cut was especially intriguing because it was based on a new supply-side theory of how the

---

[9]R. Gordon, *Macroeconomics*, fifth edition (Glenview, IL: Scott, Foresman/Little, Brown, 1989), Appendix A, pp. A5–A7.

[10]*Economic Indicators, March 1993*, 1, 32. *Economic Report of the President, 1993*, Table B-1, p. 348. Executive Office of the President of the United States, *Budget of the United States Government, Fiscal Year 1993, Supplement, February 1992* (Washington, D.C.: U.S. Government Printing Office, 1992), Part Five: Historical Table, Tables 7.1, p. 5–89.

CHAPTER 12   Automatic Stabilizers, Net Exports, and Budget Deficits   379

economy responds to tax policy that had nothing in common with the Keynesian tax multiplier theory of Chapter 11. We will explore the supply-side theory of tax policy in Chapter 19.

3. Huge cuts in nondefense purchases and transfer payments to keep the budget in balance. President Reagan was a staunch fiscal conservative who did not believe in running budget deficits. He also wanted to reduce federal social welfare expenditures, which had been growing rapidly since the early 1960s.

Congress agreed with President Reagan's assessment of the Soviet military threat and authorized the increase in defense spending. It also approved the income tax cuts. The economy was suffering from the double whammy of high unemployment and high inflation, and no one seemed to know what to do. In its frustration Congress considered the new supply-side theory and said in effect: "What the heck, let's give it a try." Congress balked at most of the cuts in social welfare expenditures and other nondefense purchases, however. It refused to slash the major social welfare programs such as Social Security, Medicare, Medicaid, and Aid to Families with Dependent Children. The net results were a huge increase in defense spending and a record tax cut, which meant a huge increase in the structural deficit. The structural deficits took awhile to reach their full value because the tax cuts were phased in over three years: a 5 percent cut in the first year, followed by 10 percent cuts in each of the next two years. The military spending increases were also phased in over time.

The tax cuts have never been restored. Defense spending was cut back significantly after the breakup of the Soviet Union, but not enough to counter the growth of federal expenditures in other areas, particularly social welfare programs, interest on the debt, and the savings and loan bailout. Consequently, the structural deficits continued to be in the $200 billion range in the 1990s, and the public debt is still growing faster than is the national product.

Are large structural deficits a problem? Is a large and growing public debt a burden on the economy? Before answering these questions, take note of the emphasis on structural deficits in the discussion so far. Economists always focus on the structural deficit when thinking about the economic implications of deficits and the public debt. The cyclical deficit responds automatically to the ebbs and flows of the economy and is essentially beyond the control of the government. It does serve as an important automatic stabilizer as we have seen, but it is otherwise irrelevant to an economic analysis of budget deficits and the public debt.

The question of whether structural deficits are a problem has a different answer in the short run and the long run.

Temporary Structural Deficits

Keynes taught economists and policy makers not to fear temporary, short-run structural deficits. On the contrary, running a deficit can be extremely beneficial if the economy is moving into a recession. Increasing government expenditures or cutting taxes increases aggregate demand, which can nip the recession in the bud and save millions of people their jobs.

Furthermore, the government will not always be running temporary deficits. Sometimes aggregate demand grows too rapidly and tries to bring the economy beyond its production possibilities frontier. When this happens, the government might respond by decreasing government expenditures or increasing taxes to decrease aggregate demand, which is likely to cause a temporary structural budget surplus.

The temporary structural deficits and surpluses may not cancel out over time, but the public debt would remain small and inconsequential. The ratio of public debt to national income would undoubtedly decline over time.

A BALANCED BUDGET?   President Bush pushed hard throughout his administration for an amendment to the Constitution that would require the administration to submit a balanced operating budget each year, just as most of the state governors are required to do. He had the support of many legislators as well. Proponents of the balanced budget amendment argue that it would bring much needed fiscal discipline to the budgetary process. The amendment would stop the rapid growth of the public debt immediately and force the administration and the Congress to be more careful in assessing new government expenditure programs.

The fiscal discipline argument has merit. Even so, the vast majority of economists oppose the balanced budget amendment on macroeconomic grounds. As a practical matter, any balanced budget legislation would have to be defined in terms of the actual budget, not the structural budget. Unfortunately, requiring the federal government to balance the actual budget each year has perverse macroeconomic consequences. It forces fiscal policy to become pro-cyclical rather than countercyclical.

Economists worry about the following scenario. Suppose that the administration and the Congress design a balanced budget for the year, as required. During the course of the year national income decreases unexpectedly, and the economy begins to move into a recession. The decrease in national income reduces tax collections and increases income-sensitive transfer payments, moving the budget from balance to a deficit. Since the administration and the Congress are forced to balance the budget, they have to respond to the deficit by decreasing government spending and/or raising taxes for the next year. But decreases in government spending and tax increases both lead to multiplied *decreases* in national income, which makes the recession worse.

The government needs to *increase* the deficit still further to fight the recession, not balance the budget. Instead, a balanced budget requirement forces the government into pro-cyclical fiscal policies that follow the economy and increase the ebbs and flows of the business cycle. Most economists believe that this is too high a price to pay for whatever fiscal discipline a balanced budget amendment may bring.

The balanced budget amendment has never gotten off the ground. Nonetheless, Congress became so exasperated with the large budget deficits that it enacted two separate pieces of legislation to force the government to balance the budget. The Gramm-Rudman-Hollings Act of 1985 (GRH) mandated a gradual reduction in the deficit each year, with a target of balancing the budget by 1991. GRH was essentially ignored, so Congress tried again in 1990 with the Omnibus Budget Reconciliation Act of 1990 (OBRA). The new law raised taxes somewhat and scheduled a series of reductions in expenditures each year, with a target of balancing the budget by 1996. OBRA is headed for the same fate as GRH. The budget deficit kept increasing in 1991 and 1992, and no one takes the 1996 target date seriously anymore.

President Clinton does not support a balanced budget amendment, but he did call for a $500 billion reduction in the deficit over five years. We will return to this policy below.

Perhaps these balanced budget laws are ineffective in part because the administration and the Congress instinctively respond to the macroeconomic implications of changes in the deficit. They are not willing to bear the short-run costs of deficit reduction.

Long-Run Structural Deficits

Large structural deficits that continue for years on end and build up a large public debt are a different matter entirely from temporary structural deficits that are responding to a recession. They can be a substantial burden to the economy. The analysis of continuing structural deficits differs as well. Economists assume that resources are fully employed when analyzing the long-run burden of a growing public debt. The short-run ebbs and flows of the business cycles are not so relevant in a long-run context.

PUBLIC INVESTMENT OR PUBLIC CONSUMPTION?   The first question to ask about a policy of continuing structural deficits is this: What are the deficits financing? Is the government issuing debt to finance investment in public capital, such as schools, highways, and hydroelectric projects? Or is the government issuing debt to finance the current operating expenses of the government agencies and transfer payments?

Issuing debt to finance public investment is perfectly sound. After all, the business sector is a net debtor. Businesses routinely issue debt to finance their investments, and governments can, too. The only issue in this case concerns the investments themselves: Are the investments productive?

A debt-financed private investment is productive if it brings in enough additional revenues to cover all the operating expenses of the project, pay off the principal and the interest on the debt, and have enough profit left over to give the stockholders an acceptable return on their investment. The same productivity test applies to debt-financed public investments, with one twist: Governments do not always sell the output of the public projects. Families with schoolchildren do not pay tuition to the local public schools, and most highways are toll-free. Instead, the government raises taxes to cover the expenses of building and maintaining public schools and highways. Nonetheless, public investments expand the nation's production possibilities frontier and increase the national income whether or not they bring in any revenues. If a public investment is productive, the government can raise taxes to cover the operating expenses of the project, pay off the principal and the interest on the debt, and still leave citizens with plenty of additional disposable income to enjoy. Indeed, public education may well have contributed more to long-run economic growth in the United States than has any comparable amount of private investment.

Issuing debt to finance annual operating expenses and transfer payments can be a burden, however. A business cannot issue debt year after year to finance its operating expenses and hope to survive. Governments can do this because of their power to tax, but they should avoid the temptation.

Unfortunately, this is essentially what the federal government has been doing since 1981. The government does not keep a separate capital budget, so it is difficult to know how much of federal purchases are public investments. The best estimates, though, are that gross federal investment is much less than $100 billion each year, and most of this is military investment. Net federal investment is probably on the order of $20 billion annually. The majority of the recent structural deficits have been supporting operating expenses and transfer payments.

The nature of the burden in this case depends on whether the public debt is external or internal. **External debt** is debt held by foreign citizens, businesses, and governments. **Internal debt** is debt held by U.S. citizens, businesses, and government agencies. Most of the federal debt is internal debt; foreign citizens and businesses own only about 20 percent of the privately held federal debt.

EXTERNAL DEBT   External public debt is analogous to private debt. Suppose that you go into debt to buy a stereo system. You purchase the stereo with a credit card and pay back the card company over the next two years. Borrowing to consume goods and services today involves a trade-off of future consumption for present consumption. In borrowing the money to buy the stereo system today, you have agreed to sacrifice even more purchasing power in the future because you have to pay interest on the debt. This is the burden of the debt to you.

External debt issued to pay for current operating expenses or transfer payments places a nation in the same position. The burden of the external debt is the transfer of purchasing power to foreign citizens in the future as the nation pays back the debt, with interest. One reason why debt financing is so tempting is that the present generations can enjoy the current consumption and place the payback burden on future generations.

INTERNAL DEBT   The burden of financing current operating expenses and transfers with internal debt is extremely subtle, far more so than is commonly understood. People are led astray in thinking about the burden of the public debt because they draw an analogy between public and private debt. The analogy holds true only for external public debt, however. Internal public debt is not at all analogous to private debt because the citizens owe the debt to themselves. It is as if one of your hands could borrow from and pay back the other hand.

The false analogy between private and internal public debt leads people to worry that the public debt will bankrupt the nation, but bankruptcy is not the problem. The government can always raise taxes to pay off its internal debt. The money leaves the private sector when the taxes are paid and returns to the private sector as the government buys back its debt with interest. No resources leave the country as they do when the government pays off its external debt.

The federal government is not about to retire its internal debt, however, because taxes reduce the efficiency of the market system. Raising taxes by about $3 billion to pay off the internal debt would entail enormous efficiency costs. In addition, retiring the internal debt would redistribute resources toward the wealthy who hold a disproportionate share of the debt. Still, bankruptcy is not the problem.

Instead, the potential problem with internal debt is that it can reduce private investment, leaving future generations with a smaller capital stock, a less pro-

EXTERNAL DEBT (PUBLIC)
Public debt that is held by foreign citizens, businesses, and governments.

INTERNAL DEBT (PUBLIC)
Public debt that is held by U.S. citizens, businesses, and government agencies.

ductive economy, and slower long-run economic growth. The deficit is said to crowd out private investment. This is a very serious problem because, as we have seen, long-run economic growth is the most important determinant of a nation's overall economic well-being.

To see the effect of debt financing on private investment, recall the investment = saving accounting identity from Chapter 8.

$$\text{Investment} = S_{\text{Private}} + S_{\text{Government}} + S_{\text{Foreign}}$$

The two sources of **national saving** are S_{Private}, saving by the household and the business sectors, and $S_{\text{Government}}$, saving by the government sector. We will ignore foreign saving, S_{Foreign}, for the moment, to concentrate on internal debt.

$S_{\text{Government}}$ is the government budget surplus, so that deficit financing reduces $S_{\text{Government}}$ dollar for dollar. Whether deficit financing also reduces national saving depends on how S_{Private} responds to the budget deficit. Most economists believe that S_{Private} does not increase dollar for dollar with the decrease in $S_{\text{Government}}$. Consequently, deficit financing reduces national saving, which must then reduce the level of investment. The reasoning is as follows.

The first point to understand is that the burden of the debt is a long-run problem. Therefore, when thinking about the debt burden economists typically assume a fully employed economy. Since the only final goods the economy can produce are consumer goods or investment goods, any increase in consumption must come at the expense of saving and investment at full employment. Economists also assume that households are making long-run consumption decisions in line with the Life-Cycle Hypothesis, and smoothing consumption over their lifetimes.

A growing public debt is likely to reduce national saving, and investment, under these two assumptions. The government cannot keep expanding public debt faster than the economy is growing, as has been the case since 1981, and still be able to sell its bonds. Eventually the government has to raise taxes again and reduce the resources of future generations. The effect of deficit financing in a Life-Cycle model is a redistribution of resources from older generations to younger generations under this scenario.

The net result of the transfer across generations is an increase in consumption and a decrease in saving and investment. The reason why is that older generations have a higher MPC than do younger generations. Suppose that the government cuts taxes by $100 today, issues $100 of new debt, and announces that it will increase taxes by enough 20 years from now to pay back the ensuing debt, with interest. Compare the reactions of two groups of people: the elderly, who expert to live only two more years, and the young, who expect to live 40 more years.

The elderly have a net increase in resources because they do not have to pay the future taxes. They also spend most of their tax cuts because they only have two years left to live.

The young buy the majority of the debt and adjust their consumption over the remainder of their lives, taking into account the new debt and the anticipated future tax increase. By buying the debt and receiving interest on it they obtain the funds that they will eventually need to pay the future tax increase. But they still lose on net because they have to pay back enough taxes to cover both their own tax cuts and the tax cuts of the elderly. Overall, their lifetime resources are reduced by the amount that the elderly gain, and they reduce their consumption as a result.

NATIONAL SAVING

The amount of saving generated by the domestic economy during the year, equal to the sum of saving by the private sector and saving by the government sector; the difference between total saving and foreign saving.

CURRENT ISSUE: President Clinton's $500 billion deficit reduction plan will not eliminate the federal budget deficits. But it may cause the debt to grow more slowly than GDP, in which case the burden of the debt will steadily diminish over time.

The increase in consumption by the elderly exceeds the decrease in consumption by the young because the elderly are spreading their gains over two years, whereas the young are spreading their losses over 40 years. Consequently, total consumption increases, and total saving and investment decrease.

Models designed to study these intergenerational consumption effects show that their impact on saving and investment can be very large when the government runs large structural deficits for 10 or 20 years, as is the case today. The current generation's consumption and transfer binge places an enormous burden on future generations through reduced productivity and long-run economic growth.[11]

FOREIGN SAVING AND INVESTMENT   So far we have been ignoring saving by the foreign sector, $S_{Foreign}$, to concentrate on the effects of internal debt. Purchase of the debt by foreigners, external debt, is a source of foreign saving. Therefore, deficit financing with external debt substitutes for the decrease in $S_{Government}$ dollar for dollar and does not decrease total saving or crowd out investment. Foreigners did purchase an increasing proportion of the government debt during the 1980s, which helped prevent U.S. investment from declining. Remember, though, that external debt is still a burden because it requires transfers of future resources out of the United States. Substituting external debt for internal debt just changes the nature of the burden on future generations.

The Great Policy Dilemma Once Again

President Clinton buys the argument that large structural deficits reduce long-run economic growth. He continually stresses the need to "grow the economy" and believes that deficit reduction is the place to start. At the same time, the sluggish economy argues strongly against large spending cuts and tax increases.

Many economists who dislike the structural deficits nonetheless argue that putting people back to work should be the first priority. They believe that the Congress and the administration should forget the deficit for the moment and engage in expansionary fiscal policies to stimulate employment. In their view deficit reduction can wait until the private sector is back on its feet and better able to take the spending cuts and tax increases.

The dilemma posed by the large structural deficits and a sluggish economy is a real one. The right course for fiscal policy is not at all clear. Although Congress did enact Clinton's deficit reduction plan, it remains to be seen whether Congress will actually reduce the structural budget deficit over the next five years.

---

[11]A minority of economists argue that structural deficits have virtually no effect on national saving and investment. Harvard's Robert Barro is the leading proponent of this view. Barro believes that the majority of households behave according to the Life-Cycle Hypothesis *and* that they are altruistic toward future generations. They will not let the government transfer resources from the future generations to the present generations through deficit financing. In particular, the elderly, because they are altruistic, do not increase their consumption. Instead, they buy government bonds with their tax cuts and bequeath the bonds so that their heirs are not burdened by the inevitable future tax increase. The result is that $S_{Private}$ increases by the same amount that $S_{Government}$ decreases. Deficit financing has no effect at all on national saving and investment.

Most economists doubt that Life-Cycle consumers are so altruistic toward future generations. They believe that deficit financing does transfer resources across generations, reduce national saving, and crowd out private investment as described above.

SUMMARY

Chapter 12 began with a discussion of automatic stabilizers in the U.S. nconomy.

1. National income feeds back to aggregate demand through four channels in addition to consumption demand. income and sales taxes, income-sensitive government transfer payments, business saving (retained earnings), and import demand. The feedback in each instance serves as an automatic stabilizer, which is defined as any component of the economy that is related to national income and lowers the value of the spending multiplier. As such, these automatic stabilizers make the economy less sensitive to changes in aggregate demand.

2. Income and sales taxes, income-sensitive transfer payments, and business saving act as automatic stabilizers because they cause disposable income to change by less than national income changes. Since consumption demand is related to disposable income, consumption demand changes by a smaller amount during each round of the multiplier process, which reduces the value of the spending multiplier.

3. Import demand acts as an automatic stabilizer because imports remove some of the round-by-round change in national income from the circular flow of economic activity during the multiplier process. Expenditures on imports become sources of income to foreign producers, not domestic producers.

4. Any drain on aggregate demand that is positively related to the level of national income acts as an automatic stabilizer. Income taxes, business saving, and import demand are examples. Any contributor to aggregate demand that is negatively related to the level of national income also acts as an automatic stabilizer. Income-sensitive government transfer payments are an example.

5. The four automatic stabilizers reduce the value of the spending multiplier in the United States by about 40 percent.

6. Automatic stabilizers are helpful if the economy is operating close to its target level of national income because changes or shocks to aggregate demand do not move the economy as far away from the target. They are a hindrance if the economy is far from the target because larger increases in aggregate demand are needed to return to the target. For example, automatic stabilizers break the fall of an economy heading into a recession, but they make it more difficult for the economy to recover from a recession.

The first section of the chapter also added the foreign sector to our model to complete the new Keynesian aggregate demand model of the macro economy.

7. Aggregate demand for the complete economy, which consists of the household, business, government, and foreign sectors, is the sum of consumption demand, investment demand, government demand for goods and services, and net export demand. Net export demand is the difference between export demand and import demand. The product markets are in equilibrium when aggregate demand equals the level of national income generated in production.

8. Export demand depends on the levels of national income in foreign countries, not on the level of domestic national income. Import demand is directly related to the level of domestic national income, in part because

some of consumption demand is for imports and in part because businesses import some of the raw materials, intermediate products, and capital goods used as inputs in production. This is why import demand is an automatic stabilizer.

The second section of the chapter discussed how changes in the federal budget deficit can be used to measure the direction and the magnitude of discretionary fiscal policy.

9. Changes in the deficit from year to year result from two factors: (a) any discretionary or programmatic changes in government purchases, transfer payments, or taxes, which is what discretionary fiscal policy means; and (b) changes in the state of the economy.

10. Economists conceptually divide the actual budget deficit into two components, the structural budget deficit and the cyclical budget deficit, in order to measure the independent effects of these two factors. The structural budget deficit is an estimate of what the deficit would be if the economy were operating at the natural rate of unemployment. The cyclical deficit is the difference between the actual deficit and the estimated structural deficit.

11. Changes in the structural deficit year to year measure the direction and the magnitude of discretionary fiscal policy during the course of the year. An increase in the structural deficit indicates that the government undertook an expansionary fiscal policy. A decrease in the structural deficit indicates that the government undertook a contractionary fiscal policy. Changes in the cyclical deficit mirror the state of the economy, which affects the deficit through taxes and income-sensitive transfer payments. For example, the cyclical deficit increases when the economy enters a recession because tax collections fall and income-sensitive transfer payments rise.

One of the more striking features of the Reagan/Bush presidencies was the increased reliance on debt financing, which led to very large structural deficits and caused the public debt to grow more rapidly than did national income. The large structural deficits continued into the Clinton administration. The final section of Chapter 12 analyzed the effects of large structural deficits and a growing public debt.

12. Incurring a temporary structural deficit to head off a recession can be very useful. It supports aggregate demand and can save millions of workers their jobs. For this reason most economists oppose a balanced budget amendment to the Constitution, which would force the federal administration to submit balanced (actual) budgets each year as most state governors are required to do. A balanced budget amendment would no doubt promote fiscal discipline, but at the cost of causing fiscal policy to be pro-cyclical, amplifying the ebbs and flows of the business cycle.

13. A policy of long-run structural deficits can be a serious burden to the economy, however. The first question to ask is this: What are the deficits financing? Issuing debt to finance public investments in school buildings, highways, and the like is a sound budgetary practice, equivalent to businesses issuing debt to finance their private investments. The only issue in this case is whether or not the public investments are productive.

14. The burden arises if the structural deficits are primarily financing current operating expenses and transfer payments, as the recent deficits have been.

The nature of the burden depends on whether the debt is external (owed to foreigners) or internal (owed to the country's own citizens). Most of the privately held U.S. debt is internal debt.

15. External debt is analogous to private debt. The burden lies in the fact that the nation eventually has to transfer purchasing power to foreign citizens in order to pay back the debt, with interest. Public debt cannot grow faster than national income forever.

16. Internal debt is not analogous to private debt because citizens owe the debt to themselves. The burden with internal debt lies in the fact that it can crowd out private investment, thereby lowering productivity and long-run economic growth. National saving consists of the saving by the private sector and the government sector. Deficit financing reduces saving by the government sector dollar for dollar. Most economists believe that saving by the private sector increases by less than the deficit, so that national saving decreases, and investment along with it. Issuing external debt is a source of foreign saving, which supports investment. But external debt still results in a burden because of the future transfer of purchasing power that is required.

KEY TERMS

actual budget deficit
automatic stabilizer
cyclical budget deficit

external debt (public)
internal debt (public)
marginal propensity to import

marginal propensity to spend
national saving
structural budget deficit

QUESTIONS

1. Taxes are a drain on aggregate demand, and government transfer payments are a contributor to aggregate demand. Yet they both act as automatic stabilizers. How can this be?

2. Suppose that the consumption expenditures of U.S. citizens shift from domestic goods to imported goods, while leaving the total demand for goods and services unchanged. What effect does this change in tastes have on the equilibrium level of national income? On the balance of trade (= exports minus imports)?

3. Show the effect of a depreciation of the dollar on the import demand and export demand functions. Explain how the depreciation of the dollar affects net export demand and the equilibrium level of national income.

4. The following table gives the value of import demand at each level of national income.

IMPORT DEMAND	NATIONAL INCOME
100	1,000
150	2,000
250	3,000
400	4,000
600	5,000

Calculate the marginal propensity to import (MPM) for each $1,000 change in national income. Is the slope of the import demand function constant? Would you expect households' MPM to rise as their incomes rise?

5. Suppose that the government announces that the federal budget deficit increased by $10 billion last year. Based on this information can you decide whether the government pursued an expansionary fiscal policy last year? Why is the change in the federal budget deficit not a reliable measure of fiscal policy?

6. a. Why is the change in the structural federal budget deficit a better measure of the government's fiscal policy stance than is the change in the actual federal budget deficit?

   b. Why is the change in the structural budget deficit not a perfect measure of the government's fiscal policy stance?

7. Assume that a country has a balanced budget initially. The country's economic structure has automatic, built-in stabilizers in the form of taxes and government transfers. Suppose that national income decreases as a result of a decrease in consumption demand.

   a. What is the effect of the decrease in consumption demand on the actual budget deficit? On the structural budget deficit?

   b. If the government is required by law to maintain a balanced (actual) budget, what further impact would this law have on aggregate demand and national income as the government tries to re-balance the budget?

8. a. How does the burden of an external public debt differ from the burden of an internal public debt?

   b. Are there any conditions under which neither external debt nor internal debt is a burden to a nation?

9. In a certain economy, transfer payments by the government increase by $0.30 for every $1 decrease in the national income. Also, total tax revenue increases by $0.40 for every $1 increase in national income. The MPC = 0.8. Suppose that something causes aggregate demand to increase by $10,000, so that national income increases by $10,000 in the first round of the multiplier process.

   a. Given the above tax and transfer structure of the econ-omy, what is the increase in national income in the second round of the multiplier process?

   b. How would your answer to part a change if national income had decreased by $10,000?

10. *Extra credit:* Suppose that the government cuts taxes, issues new debt, and announces that it will raise taxes in the future to pay back this debt. There are only two generations in the economy: the young and the old. There are more old people than young people. What will happen to total saving and investment as a result of this tax cut? How would your answer change if all the old people had bequest motives and wanted to leave as much inheritance as possible to their children and grandchildren?

12

Algebraic Analysis of Income Taxes and Net Exports

The appendix contains two sections. The first section presents an algebraic treatment of income taxes as an automatic stabilizer. The second section completes the new Keynesian aggregate demand model of the economy by adding net exports to aggregate demand.

INCOME TAXES AS AN AUTOMATIC STABILIZER

The algebraic model of the economy in the appendix to Chapter 11 assumed that tax revenues were a constant that was independent of the level of national income. As we saw in Chapter 12, tax revenues vary directly with the level of national income. A more realistic tax equation is

$$T = T_0 + t \cdot Y$$

T_0 is a constant representing the portion of tax revenues that is independent of national income; t is the marginal tax rate, the slope of the Tx line in Figure 12.1; and Y is national income. The text assumed a value of $t = .25$.

Taxes affect consumption demand by reducing disposable income below national income. Consumption demand is

$$C^d = C_0 + \text{MPC} \cdot Y_d$$

where Y_d is disposable income.

$$Y_d = Y - T$$

Substituting the income tax equation for T

$$Y_d = Y - (T_0 + t \cdot Y)$$

Substituting the equation for disposable income into the consumption demand equation gives consumption demand in terms of *national income.*

$$C^d = C_0 + \text{MPC} \cdot [Y - (T_0 + t \cdot Y)]$$
$$= C_0 + \text{MPC} \cdot Y - \text{MPC} \cdot T_0 - \text{MPC} \cdot t \cdot Y$$

Combining the Y terms,

$$C^d = C_0 + \text{MPC} \cdot (1 - t) \cdot Y - \text{MPC} \cdot T_0$$

The two remaining components of aggregate demand are investment demand and government purchases, which are both unrelated to the level of national income.

$$I^d = \bar{I}$$

$$G^d = \bar{G}$$

The equilibrium condition is

$$Y = C^d + I^d + G^d$$

Substitute the equations for the three components of aggregate demand in the right-hand side of the equilibrium condition, and solve for Y.

$$Y = C_0 + \text{MPC} \cdot (1 - t) \cdot Y - \text{MPC} \cdot T_0 + \bar{I} + \bar{G}$$
$$Y - \text{MPC} \cdot (1 - t) \cdot Y = (C_0 + \bar{I} + \bar{G}) - \text{MPC} \cdot T_0$$
$$Y \cdot [1 - \text{MPC} \cdot (1 - t)] = (C_0 + \bar{I} + \bar{G}) - \text{MPC} \cdot T_0$$
$$Y = [1/[1 - (1 - t) \cdot \text{MPC}]] \cdot (C_0 + \bar{I} + \bar{G})$$
$$- [\text{MPC}/[1 - (1 - t) \cdot \text{MPC}]] \cdot T_0$$

The change in the equilibrium in response to changes in the components of aggregate demand or T is

$$\Delta Y = [1/[1 - (1 - t) \cdot \text{MPC}]] \cdot (\Delta C_0 + \Delta I + \Delta G)$$
$$- [\text{MPC}/[1 - (1 - t) \cdot \text{MPC}]] \cdot \Delta T_0$$

The spending and the tax multipliers with an income tax are

$$M_{\text{Spending}} = 1/[1 - (1 - t) \cdot \text{MPC}]$$
$$M_{\text{Tax}} = -\text{MPC}/[1 - (1 - t) \cdot \text{MPC}]$$

An income tax reduces the values of both multipliers. To see this, compare M_{Spending} without and with an income tax.

WITHOUT AN INCOME TAX	WITH AN INCOME TAX
$M_{Spending} = 1/(1 - MPC)$	$M_{Spending} = 1/[1 - (1 - t) \cdot MPC]$

The income tax increases the value of the denominator and lowers the value of the spending multiplier. For example, the text assumed an MPC of .80 and a marginal tax rate, t, of .25. $M_{Spending}$ without the income tax is 5. With the income tax

$$
\begin{aligned}
M_{Spending} &= 1/[1 - (1 - .25) \cdot .80] \\
&= 1/[1 - (.75 \cdot .80)] \\
&= 1/(1 - .60) \\
&= 1/.40 = 2.5
\end{aligned}
$$

The 25 percent marginal tax rate reduces the value of the spending multiplier by half. The income tax is a powerful automatic stabilizer.

THE COMPLETE MODEL WITH THE FOREIGN SECTOR

The demand for net exports, exports minus imports, is the final component of aggregate demand.

Export demand in the United States is independent of U.S. national income.

$$Ex^d = \overline{X}$$

Import demand in the United States is directly related to U.S. national income, according to the relationship

$$Im^d = M_0 + MPM \cdot Y$$

M_0 is the portion of import demand that is unrelated to the level of national income, and MPM is the marginal propensity to import.

The equilibrium condition for the full model is

$$Y = C^d + I^d + G^d + (Ex^d - Im^d)$$

Substitute the equations for all the components of aggregate demand into the right-hand side of the equilibrium condition, and solve for Y.

$$
\begin{aligned}
Y &= C_0 + MPC \cdot (1 - t) \cdot Y - MPC \cdot T_0 + \overline{I} + \overline{G} + [\overline{X} - [M_0 + MPM \cdot Y]] \\
Y &- MPC \cdot (1 - t) \cdot Y + MPM \cdot Y = \\
&\qquad (C_0 + \overline{I} + \overline{G} + \overline{X} - M_0) - MPC \cdot T_0 \\
Y &\cdot [1 - MPC \cdot (1 - t) + MPM] = (C_0 + \overline{I} + \overline{G} + \overline{X} - M_0) - MPC \cdot T_0 \\
Y &= [1/[1 - (1 - t) \cdot MPC + MPM]] \cdot (C_0 + \overline{I} + \overline{G} + \overline{X} - M_0) \\
&\qquad - [MPC/[1 - (1 - t) \cdot MPC + MPM]] \cdot T_0
\end{aligned}
$$

The change in the equilibrium in response to changes in the components of aggregate demand or T_0 is

$$\Delta Y = [1/[1 - (1 - t) \cdot \text{MPC} + \text{MPM}]]$$
$$\cdot (\Delta C_0 + \Delta \bar{I} + \Delta \bar{G} + \Delta \bar{X} - \Delta M_0)$$
$$- [\text{MPC}/[1 - (1 - t) \cdot \text{MPC} + \text{MPM}]] \cdot \Delta T_o$$

The value of the spending multiplier is now

$$M_{\text{Spending}} = 1/[1 - (1 - t) \cdot \text{MPC} + \text{MPM}]$$

Imports lower M_{Spending} still further because MPM increases the value of the denominator. For example, the text assumed MPM = .10. The value of M_{Spending} with MPC = .80, t = .25, and MPM = .10 is

$$M_{\text{Spending}} = 1/[1 - (1 - .25) \cdot .80 + .10]$$
$$= 1/[1 - (.75 \cdot .80) + .10]$$
$$= 1/(1 - .60 + .10)$$
$$= 1/.5 = 2$$

Compare this with M_{Spending} = 2.5 above, with an income tax, but no import demand.

Taxes and import demand act as automatic stabilizers because they reduce the *marginal propensity to spend out of national income* from .80 (the MPC) in the simplest model of the economy to .50 in the complete model. The income tax takes $.25 of every $1 of national income generated out of the circular flow of economic activity during each round in the multiplier process, leaving consumers with a $.75 increase in disposable income. They spend .80 (the MPC) of their disposable income, or $.60 of the $1 increase in *national income*, in the next round of the multiplier process ($.60 = .80 \cdot $.75). But $.10 of their spending is on imports, which leaks out of the circular flow of economic activity into the pockets of foreign producers. Therefore, the increase in *domestic* aggregate demand and national income is $.50 in the next round of the multiplier process for every $1 of *national income* generated in the preceding round. The marginal propensity to spend out of national income is .50, which is the denominator of the spending multiplier.

QUESTIONS

1. a. Given the following information for an economy, find the equilibrium level of national income, Y_E.

$C^d = 200 + .8 \cdot Y_d$ Y_d = disposable income
$I^d = 10$ Y = national income
$G^d = 70$ C^d = consumption demand
$T = 100 + .3 \cdot Y$ I^d = investment demand
     G^d = government demand for goods and services
     T = income taxes (transfer payments are zero)

b. What is the value of the spending multiplier for this economy?

2. Now add net exports to the economy in question 1.

$Ex^d = 50$ Ex^d = export demand
$Im^d = 10 + .2 \cdot Y$ Im^d = import demand

a. Find the new equilibrium level of national income, Y_E.
b. What is the value of the marginal propensity to import?
c. What is the value of the spending multiplier for this economy?

13

Business Cycles: The Multiplier-Accelerator Model and the Real Business Cycle

LEARNING OBJECTIVES

CONCEPTS TO LEARN

The business cycle	Multiplier-accelerator model
Indexes of cyclical indicators	Real business cycle model

CONCEPTS TO RECALL

Laws of Supply and Demand [5]	Equilibrium level of national income [10]
Gross domestic product (GDP) [8]	Investment demand [10]
Aggregate demand and aggregate supply [9]	Life-Cycle Hypothesis [10]

e saw in Chapter 4 that there is no such thing as a perfect economic system. The centrally planned socialist economies of Eastern Europe and the Soviet Union collapsed under the weight of oppressive central bureaucracies and grossly misallocated resources that made their economies highly unproductive. Their citizens believed that capitalism was the better alternative.

Capitalism is not a perfect economic system either, however. The Achilles' heel of capitalism is the business cycle, the continual ebbs and flows of economic activity that at times throw people out of work and at other times send prices spiraling upward. Capitalist countries live perpetually in the shadows of the Great Depression of the 1930s and the hyperinflations in Western Europe following each of the world wars.

Understanding the causes of business cycles has always been the number one research goal of modern macroeconomics, yet economists are still a long way from reaching that goal. The business cycle is perhaps the least understood and most controversial topic in all of economics.

You certainly will not find a definitive answer to the question of what causes business cycles in this text. Chapter 13 turns to an analysis of the business cycle with two more modest goals in mind. The chapter begins with a discussion of how economists and policy makers monitor the performance of the economy and what they have learned about business cycles in the United States. We then consider two popular models of the business cycle. One, called the multiplier-accelerator model, is widely embraced by new Keynesian economists. The other, called the real business cycle, has become the principal model used by new classical economists to explain how the macro economy operates.

MONITORING THE BUSINESS CYCLE IN THE UNITED STATES

Most economic historians credit Wesley C. Mitchell with being the founding father of modern research on the business cycle. Mitchell's treatise *Business Cycles*, published in 1913, was the first detailed, systematic study of the macroeconomic performance of the developed market economies. Then, in 1920, Mitchell was instrumental in forming the National Bureau of Economic Research (NBER), whose primary research agenda in the beginning was to monitor the economic performance of the United States and 16 other developed market economies. The NBER quickly became recognized as the center of business cycle research in the United States, a position it holds to this day.

The Traditional View of the Business Cycle

Mitchell and his colleagues at the NBER established the traditional view of macroeconomic fluctuations. They pictured the developed market economies as moving through a recurring series of temporary expansions and contractions that cycle around a more permanent trend rate of growth in real national prod-

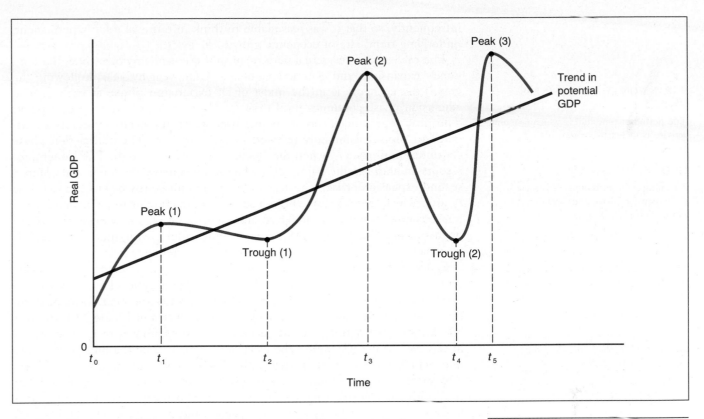

The figure illustrates the different phases of the business cycle. Time is on the horizontal axis and real GDP is on the vertical axis. The straight line represents the production possibilities frontier, the maximum sustainable level of real GDP, which is assumed to grow at a constant rate over time. At time t_0 the economy is an expansion phase of the cycle, which ends at time t_1 when the cycle reaches its peak. Then the economy moves into the contraction phase of the cycle which lasts until t_2, when the cycle reaches its trough. A new expansion phase begins after t_2 and continues until the cycle reaches another peak at t_3. The economy continues to cycle indefinitely. The figure shows two complete peak-to-peak business cycles. The length of the first business cycle is $(t_3 - t_1)$, and the length of the second cycle is $(t_5 - t_3)$. The first of the two business cycles is both longer and shallower than the second business cycle.

FIGURE 13.1

The Phases of the Business Cycle

uct; hence the term *business cycles.* This is the view we used when describing the performance of the U.S. economy since 1977 in Chapter 6. The NBER's view of the macro economy was essentially unchallenged until the new classical real business cycle theory came along in the 1980s.

Figure 13.1 illustrates the traditional view. Real gross domestic product (GDP) is on the vertical axis, and time is on the horizontal axis. The straight line through the cycles is the permanent, trend rate of growth in potential GDP. It represents the rate at which the production possibilities frontier is moving out over time, or the rate of long-run economic growth. We saw in Chapter 3 that increases in potential GDP require changes in the quantity or the quality of a nation's resources and changes in production technologies. Mitchell and his colleagues at the NBER presumed that these changes occur fairly slowly, and fairly steadily, over time. They recognized that the rate of long-run economic growth could change over time, as it did in the United States after 1973. But they believed that these changes would happen only

EXPANSION PHASE (BUSINESS CYCLE)

The period of time during which economic activity is increasing; commonly referred to as a *boom.*

PEAK (BUSINESS CYCLE)

A turning point in the business cycle when the expansion phase ends and the contraction phase begins.

CONTRACTION PHASE (BUSINESS CYCLE)

The period of time during which economic activity is declining; commonly referred to as a *recession.*

TROUGH (BUSINESS CYCLE)

A turning point in the business cycle when the contraction phase ends and the expansion phase begins.

CYCLICAL INDICATOR

A monthly or quarterly data series that contains reliable and significant information concerning the performance of the economy over time and that moves in a pattern consistent with the movement of the overall business cycle.

infrequently, so that it was reasonable to think in terms of a fairly permanent, underlying trend rate of economic growth.

The cycles track the actual performance of the economy over time, the temporary expansions and contractions of real GDP year by year. Following the graph, the economy is in the midst of an **expansion phase** at time t_0. The expansion phase continues until time t_1, when the economy reaches a **peak.** The peak represents a turning point, after which the economy enters a **contraction phase,** commonly referred to as a *recession.* The contraction phase continues until time t_2, when the economy reaches a **trough.** The trough represents another turning point, after which the economy rebounds and enters a second expansion phase. The second expansion phase reaches its peak at time t_3, after which the economy enters a second contraction phase. The contraction phase continues until the trough at time t_4, after which a new expansion phase begins again. The pattern continues on indefinitely, with alternating periods of expansion and contraction cycling around the permanent trend line.

Economists describe business cycles in terms of their length and severity, both of which can vary considerably from cycle to cycle. The *length* of one complete business cycle is the time from one peak to the next.[1] The peak-to-peak measure identifies two complete business cycles in Figure 32.1, the first one lasting from t_1 to t_3 and the second one lasting from t_3 to t_5. The *severity* of the cycle is the distance of the peaks and troughs from the underlying trend line, which can vary within each cycle. For example, economists speak of a shallow or a deep recession, depending how far the trough of the cycle is below the production possibilities frontier. The first business cycle in the figure is both longer and shallower than is the second business cycle.

CYCLICAL INDICATORS   Mitchell and the other NBER economists pioneered a method of monitoring the performance of the overall economy by following over time a large number of data series, which they called cyclical indicators. A **cyclical indicator** is a data series that meets three criteria: economic significance, current availability and reliability, and timing.

A data series can satisfy the criterion of economic significance in one of two ways. It can be an important component of one of the four elements of the economy that the NBER monitors over time: output, income, employment, or trade (both domestic and international). Or it can be something that macro economists believe has a significant influence on one or more of these elements, such as the nation's money supply. The NBER has never just monitored the growth of GDP alone.

The criterion of current availability and reliability means that the data are available periodically over a very short period of time, preferably monthly, but no longer than quarterly. The data also must be of good quality, collected from reputable and reliable sources and comparable over a long period of time. A data series is not useful for monitoring the performance of the economy if the information contained in the series keeps changing over time.

The third criterion, timing, is the heart of the matter. The data series must move over time in a pattern consistent with the movement of the overall business cycle. Most important, the peaks and the troughs of the data series must bear a reasonably consistent relationship to the peaks and the troughs of the business cycle.

---

[1]A complete cycle could also be measured from trough to trough, which would identify a different business cycle, with a different length, from the peak-to-peak measure. The peak-to-peak measure is the one commonly used.

The NBER began publishing its list of cyclical indicators in 1938, and the list has since grown to include over 100 series. The U.S. Department of Commerce elevated the NBER to semi-official status as the monitor of the economy when the department agreed, in 1961, to publish the NBER's cyclical indicators each month in its *Business Conditions Digest*. That publication remained in existence until 1990; the department now incorporates the cyclical indicators within its monthly *Survey of Current Business*.[2]

THE INDEXES OF CYCLICAL INDICATORS   The Department of Commerce pushed the method of cyclical indicators one step further in 1968 when it developed and began publishing three indexes based on the cyclical indicators: the index of leading indicators, the index of coincident indicators, and the index of lagging indicators. Each index is a composite of cyclical indicators that have similar timing, but that cover different sectors of the economy or different types of economic activities. The department chooses the "best" cyclical indicators for each of the indexes according to the three criteria mentioned above.

The **index of leading indicators** is designed to forecast aggregate economic activity and to predict the turning points of the business cycle, both the peaks and the troughs. Therefore, the peaks and the troughs of the cyclical indicators chosen for this index must precede the peaks and the troughs of the business cycle. The index consists of the 11 cyclical indicators listed in Table 13.1.

The **index of coincident indicators** is designed to track the expansion and the contraction phases of the business cycle, and its turning points, as they occur. The index consists of the four cyclical indicators listed in Table 13.1. Notice that each cyclical indicator corresponds to one of the four elements of the economy that the NBER attempts to monitor: employment, income, output (production), and trade.

The **index of lagging indicators** is designed to confirm the existence of the various phases of the business cycle and its turning points. As such, it is expected to move over time in the same pattern as the index of coincident indicators, with a few months' delay. The peaks and the troughs of the cyclical indicators chosen for this index must come after the peaks and the troughs of the business cycle. The index consists of the seven cyclical indicators listed in Table 13.1.

The leading, coincident, and lagging indexes are the most closely watched indicators of overall economic activity in the United States. They are widely reported each month in the news media because they are generally perceived to be a reasonably accurate gauge of the current state of the economy and where it is heading. The Department of Commerce has revised the composition and the construction of the indexes frequently since 1968 in a continuing effort to improve their ability to track the business cycle. The last revision was in January of 1989.

DATING THE PEAKS AND THE TROUGHS   The Department of Commerce has left to the NBER the task of dating the peaks and the troughs of each business cycle. The NBER's reputation in U.S. business cycle research is such that its estimates of the peaks and the troughs are virtually the only estimates ever published or cited.

INDEX OF LEADING INDICATORS
An index of 11 cyclical indicators that is designed to forecast aggregate economic activity and predict the turning points of the business cycle.

INDEX OF COINCIDENT INDICATORS
An index of four cyclical indicators that is designed to track the expansion and the contraction phases of the business cycle, and its turning points, as they are occurring.

INDEX OF LAGGING INDICATORS
An index of seven cyclical indicators that is designed to confirm the existence of the various phases of the business cycle and its turning points with a few months' delay.

---

[2]The early history of the National Bureau of Economic Research and its approach to describing business cycles can be found in D. Zerwitz, "Business Cycles," *NBER Reporter: Program Report* (Spring 1989).

TABLE 13.1 The U.S. Department of Commerce Indexes of Leading, Coincident, and Lagging Indicators, as of January 1989

INDEX OF LEADING INDICATORS
1. Average weekly hours of production for nonsupervisory workers, manufacturing
2. Average weekly initial claims for unemployment insurance, state programs
3. Manufacturers' new orders in 1982 $, consumer goods and material industries
4. Contracts and orders for plant and equipment in 1982 $
5. Index of new private housing units authorized by local building permits
6. Index of stock prices, 500 common stocks
7. Money supply (M2) in 1982 $[1]
8. Vendor performance, percentage of companies receiving slower deliveries
9. Change in sensitive materials prices, weighted moving average, smoothed
10. Change in manufacturers' unfilled orders in 1982 $, durable goods industries, smoothed
11. Index of consumers' expectations, compiled by the University of Michigan Survey Research Center

INDEX OF COINCIDENT INDICATORS
1. Employees on nonagricultural payrolls
2. Personal income less transfer payments in 1982 $
3. Index of industrial production
4. Manufacturing and trade sales in 1982 $

INDEX OF LAGGING INDICATORS
1. Average duration of unemployment in weeks (inverted)
2. Ratio, manufacturing and trade inventories to sales in 1982 $
3. Average prime rate charged by banks
4. Commercial and industrial loans outstanding in 1982 $
5. Ratio, consumer installment credit outstanding to personal income
6. Change in index of labor cost per unit of output, manufacturing, smoothed
7. Change in CPI for services, smoothed

[1]M2 is a broad measure of the money supply that will be discussed in Chapter 14.

SOURCE: M. Hertzberg and B. Beckman, "Business Cycle Indicators: Revised Complete Indexes," *Business Conditions Digest* 29, No. 1 (1989): 97–102.

The NBER formalized the process of dating peaks and troughs in 1980 when it established an ongoing Business Cycle Dating Committee. The sole function of the committee is to meet on occasion to decide if a peak or a trough in the business cycle has occurred.

The committee does not use any simple objective rule to select a peak or a trough. Instead, it relies heavily on the NBER's cyclical indicators, and its decisions are ultimately quite subjective. For example, the committee reported that it identified a trough in November of 1982 by looking at data series on real GNP, real retail sales, real personal income, industrial production, and unemployment, "among others." The problem with this approach is that the cyclical indicators reach their own peaks or troughs at different times, so that the committee has to make a best-judgment call on whether the overall business cycle has reached its peak or trough.

A widely used simple rule of thumb is that the economy is in a recession if real GDP declines for two consecutive quarters. Presumably a recession is over by this rule as soon as real GDP grows for one quarter, since it has then no longer declined two quarters in a row. The Business Cycle Dating Committee could easily reach a different conclusion by looking at an entire set of cyclical indicators, however, as it did during the recession of the early 1990s.

The committee had identified July 1990 as the peak of the long expansion phase that began following the trough of November 1982. Real GDP subsequently fell during the last two quarters of 1990, a recession by the common rule of thumb. Real GDP then grew briefly during the first half of 1991, signaling the end of the recession by the common rule of thumb. The committee disagreed that the recession had ended, though, arguing that it would not want to identify a trough until the cyclical indicators it was following had returned to their previous peaks. Only then could the committee be sure, in retrospect, that the economy had entered an expansion phase. In fact, the recovery stalled in mid-1991, and the cyclical indicators stayed well below their previous peaks. Consequently, the committee declined to identify a business cycle trough at that time; in its judgment it was too early to tell if the economy had reached a trough. Finally, the committee met in December of 1992 and announced, with the advantage of hindsight, that the trough had occurred in March of 1991. As of mid-1993 the economy was still in a mild expansion phase heading toward the next peak.[3]

Evidence on Business Cycles in the United States

The NBER has identified nine peaks and nine troughs from the first post–World War II peak of December 1948 to the last trough in March 1991, eight full peak-to-peak U.S. business cycles over that 42 year period. Table 13.2 lists all the post-war peaks and troughs.

Victor Zarnowitz, a professor at the University of Chicago Business School and a senior research associate of the NBER, has recently completed a study that compared the six complete peacetime business cycles in the United States from 1912 to 1945 with the six complete peacetime business cycles from 1945 through 1982.[4] His study uncovered some very good news.[5]

For starters, the U.S. economy has become far more stable since World War II. Business cycles are much less severe in the more recent period, both the expansions and the contractions. As one example, Zarnowitz compared the changes in industrial activity and employment during the expansion and the contraction phases of the cycles during both periods. Industrial activity increased by 50 percent and employment by 22 percent, on average, during the expansion phases of the earlier period. The comparable figures for the later period are 26 percent for industrial activity and 11 percent for employment, roughly half as large. The decrease in the severity of the contraction phases has been even more pronounced. Industrial activity decreased by 27 percent and employment by 18 percent, on average, during the contraction phases of the earlier period. The comparable figures for the later period are 11 percent for industrial activity and only 3 percent for employment.

[3]For further discussion of the methods of the business cycle dating committee see R. Hall, "The Business Cycle Dating Process," *NBER Reporter: Program Report* (1991/92).

[4]The peacetime cycles exclude the two cycles that occurred during the world wars in the earlier period and the two cycles that occurred during the Korean and Vietnam wars in the later period.

[5]V. Zarnowitz, "Facts and Factors in the Recent Evolution of Business Cycles in the United States," *NBER Working Paper # 2865* (February 1989). See, especially, Tables 2 and 3. For an exhaustive study of the business cycle, see V. Zarnowitz, *Business Cycles: Theory, History, Indicators and Forecasting*, NBER Studies in Business Cycles, 27 (1990).

TABLE 13.2   Peaks and Troughs of U.S. Business Cycles Since World War II
(year: quarter)

PEAK	TROUGH
1948:4	1949:4
1953:2	1954:2
1957:3	1958:2
1960:2	1961:1
1969:4	1970:4
1973:4	1975:1
1980:1	1980:3
1981:3	1982:4
1990:3	1991:1

SOURCE: V. Zarnowitz, "Facts and Factors in the Recent Evolution of Business Cycles in the United States," *NBER Working Paper #2865* (February 1989): Table 8. R. Hall, "The Business Cycle Dating Process," *NBER Reporter: Program Report* (Winter 1991/92): 1–3. Also, a telephone conversation with the NBER to determine the 1991:1 trough.

Zarnowitz offers a number of plausible explanations of why the economy has become so much more stable. Foremost among them is one that we noted in Chapter 12, a dramatic rise in the impact of automatic stabilizers, particularly within the government sector. He also believes that the shift to services in the later period has been stabilizing because the demand for services is much less sensitive to the business cycle than is the demand for manufactured products.

Another piece of good news is that the average proportion of time spent in the expansion phase during a complete business cycle has increased dramatically. In the earlier period 53 percent of the average cycle was spent in the expansion phase and 47 percent in the contraction phase. In the later period 75 percent of the average cycle was spent in the expansion phase and only 25 percent in the contraction phase.

The only characteristic that has not changed is the average length of a complete business cycle, which was 45 months in both periods. One wonders if this conclusion would stand had Zarnowitz extended the later period to the 1990s. The most recent peak-to-peak cycle ran from July 1981 to July 1990, 108 months, one of the longest complete cycles ever. The more recent data do appear to be consistent, however, with Zarnowitz's finding that the expansion phases are becoming longer and the contraction phases shorter. The expansion phase from November 1982 to July 1990 was among the longest expansion phases of the entire twentieth century.

A final comment concerns the ability of the index of leading indicators to forecast the business cycle. We noted in Chapter 9 that the large macroeconomic forecasting models have not done particularly well in forecasting the business cycle. In truth, the index of leading indicators has not fared any better. The index is an accurate predictor in the limited sense that since the index was first published in 1968, each peak and trough of the business cycles has been preceded by corresponding peaks and troughs in the index. This is hardly surprising, since the cyclical indicators in the index are chosen in large part because their turning points precede the turning points in the business cycle. But the forecasting value of the index of leading indicators is diminished because the lead time of the index has been highly variable. At times the index turning point is a month or two ahead of the business cycle turning point, at other times six months or more ahead. The index also has the distressing habit of issuing false signals in the form of extra turning points. The index has reached a peak or a trough four more times than the business cycle has since 1968, each time predicting a turning point that did not come. The Department of Commerce's frequent revisions notwithstanding, the index of leading indicators is not a dependable forecasting tool. This is hardly surprising, given that both the length and the severity of the business cycles are so variable in the United States.

Internal Versus External Business Cycles

Having now taken a look at the pattern of business cycles in the United States, let's return to the fundamental question of macroeconomics that we posed in the beginning of the chapter. Why do market economies have such a strong inherent tendency to move in cycles over time, through an endless succession of expansions and contractions? The aggregate demand models of Chapters 10 through 12 are not well equipped to answer this question because they are inherently static rather than dynamic. They show how the economy tends to move automatically to a single equilibrium level of national income for a given level of aggregate demand. They are not designed to show how the level of national income tends to move in cycles over time.

The equilibrium level of national income can change in these models, but only in one way—through shocks to aggregate demand. An aggregate demand shock is any event that causes aggregate demand to increase or decrease at every level of aggregate demand. In terms of the aggregate demand–45° line graph, an aggregate demand shock shifts the aggregate demand line *ADE* up or down. Increases or decreases in aggregate demand kick in the multiplier process, which causes the level of national income to increase or decrease for awhile until national income reaches its new equilibrium.

Economies are continually bombarded by aggregate demand shocks of all kinds, and these shocks certainly play a role in pushing national income up and down. Changes in consumer confidence often trigger large increases or decreases in consumption demand. Government purchases increase whenever nations enter into wars with other nations and then decrease when the wars end. Depreciations and appreciations of the dollar cause net export demand to rise and fall. Expansionary and contractionary fiscal and monetary policies can cause many or all of the components of aggregate demand to shift up and down simultaneously. Indeed, we noted in Chapter 7 that the University of Chicago's Robert Lucas, a leading new classical economist, believes that misguided fiscal and monetary policies have been a major cause of instability in the U.S. economy.

Our earlier models can analyze only aggregate demand shocks, but economies are also continually buffeted by aggregate supply shocks that directly affect production. Especially good or bad weather often has a dramatic impact on agricultural production. Strikes in a key industry such as steel can cripple production in a number of industries for awhile. Inventions and innovations often lead to long waves of investment demand as firms replace their outmoded capital. An obvious example has been the computerization of production after World War II following the invention of the analog computer. An earlier example was the electrification of both households and business firms in the late

POLITICAL BUSINESS CYCLE

A theory that attributes the business cycle to attempts by the incumbent administration to manipulate the economy to increase its chances of re-election, consisting of expansionary pre-election policies and contractionary post-election policies.

1800s. Aggregate supply shocks must also play an important role in explaining economic fluctuations.

Some economists even believe that they have found evidence of a **political business cycle,** in which the incumbent administration manipulates the economy to increase its chances of re-election. According to this theory, the administration engages in expansionary fiscal and monetary policies right before the election to reduce unemployment because it knows that jobs mean votes. Then, after the election, the administration engages in contractionary fiscal and monetary policies to offset the inflationary pressures that have built as a result of its pre-election expansionary policies. Most economists find this theory unpersuasive, however, if only because an administration is unlikely to be able to fine tune the economy in this manner, even if it were inclined to do so. The fiscal and monetary policy lags are simply too long and too uncertain for this strategy to work.

Aggregate demand and supply shocks may well play the leading role in explaining the economic fluctuations of the market economies. Even if this were so, however, a theory of the business cycle based entirely on these shocks is not entirely satisfactory. Aggregate demand and supply shocks are, by their nature, events that hit the economy in a largely random, unpredictable fashion. Yet the inherent tendency for market economies to move in cycles is so pronounced that any theory of the business cycle based solely on these shocks would have a gravity/anti-gravity feel to it: What goes up must come down, and what goes down must come up.

For this reason economists have long searched for internal mechanisms built into the economy that inherently cause the economy to move in cycles over time. The problem with built-in mechanisms is that they tend to predict business cycles that are far more regular and smooth than are actual business cycles. The idea, though, is that the internal mechanisms generate a tendency for regular cycles, and then outside aggregate demand and supply shocks upset the regular pattern somewhat. The combination of the internal mechanisms and the outside shocks generates the highly irregular business cycles that we observe.

Most of the early theories of the business cycle in the era of modern macroeconomics stressed internal mechanisms over outside shocks. The theories of the past 10 years or so have switched their primary emphasis to the role of outside shocks in explaining business cycles. We will look at one model of each type for the remainder of the chapter.

THE MULTIPLIER-ACCELERATOR MODEL

MULTIPLIER-ACCELERATOR MODEL

An internal model of the business cycle that is based on the instability of investment demand and its relationship to national income through both the demand side and the supply side of the economy.

One of the most successful and influential of the internal-mechanism business cycle models was also one of the first, the **multiplier-accelerator model** of investment demand developed by MIT's Paul Samuelson in 1939. Samuelson set out to modify Keynes's new theory of the macro economy so that it would generate business cycles.[6]

Samuelson reasoned that investment demand is likely to be an important cause of business cycles because it is by far the most volatile component of

---

[6]P. Samuelson, "Interactions between the Multiplier Analysis and the Principle of Acceleration," *Review of Economic Statistics* 21, No. 2 (May 1939): 75–78.

aggregate demand. The volatility of investment demand is to be expected. It is inherent in the stock-flow relationship between capital and investment. A small change in the demand for capital leads to a much larger change in investment demand.

To see why, suppose that a small firm has been using a stock of 100 personal computers and that the computers last an average of five years before they have to be replaced. Twenty computers wear out each year. Therefore, the firm has to invest in 20 new computers each year just to maintain the stock of computers at 100.

This year the firm decides to expand and determines that it will now need 110 computers. As a result, it has to invest in 30 computers this year, 20 to replace the worn-out computers and 10 to increase the stock to 110. Notice what has happened. A 10 percent increase in the firm's demand for capital, from 100 to 110 computers, has resulted in a 50 percent increase in the firm's investment demand, from 20 to 30 new computers.

In addition to the inherent instability of investment demand, Samuelson saw that investment demand for plant and equipment is related to national income in two ways, one through the demand side of the economy and one through the supply side. Investment is related to national income through the demand side of the economy because investment demand is one of the components of aggregate demand. Investment is related to national income through the supply side of the economy because firms need capital to produce goods and services, and they increase their stock of capital by investing in plant and equipment. The two-way relationship between investment and national income generates an inherent tendency for the economy to move in cycles. The theory is as follows.

The expansion phase—Suppose that the economy is initially in equilibrium. Consumers then become more confident about the future and increase their consumption demand. The increase in consumption demand begins to generate a multiplied increase in national income. The firms that produce consumer goods have to increase their production capacity to meet the increase in consumption demand, so they increase investment to increase their stock of capital. This is the supply side relationship between investment and national income that we have ignored in our previous analysis of the multiplier process.

The increase in investment demand leads to a further increase in aggregate demand and propels the economy to an even higher multiplied level of national income. The economy is going through its expansion phase. Samuelson saw the increase in investment demand as accelerating the multiplier process that was started by an increase in the consumption demand. This is why he called his theory the multiplier-accelerator model of the business cycle.

The peak—The expansion cannot continue indefinitely, however. Once firms increase their investment they are increasing the rate at which they are adding to their stock of capital. Remember, investment is the change in the stock of capital.

$$I = \Delta K$$

At some point they will decide that the *level* of investment, that is, the *rate of increase* in their stock of capital, is sufficient. Once they do, investment demand stops increasing and so does aggregate demand. The economy homes in on an equilibrium level of income, the peak of the business cycle.

The contraction phase—The economy cannot stay at the peak because the capital stock eventually catches up to the amount required to produce the peak level of goods and services. When it does, the firms do not need to invest at all. Investment demand declines to zero, which decreases aggregate demand and leads to a multiplied decrease in national income. The decrease in investment demand brings the economy into its contraction phase.

The trough—The economy homes in on a new equilibrium level of national income, the trough of the business cycle. Fortunately, the recession must end as well for the simple reason that capital depreciates as it is used in production. At some point enough capital will wear out that firms do not have enough capital left to produce even the recession-level of goods and services. Firms need to invest to replenish their capital stocks. The increase in investment demand increases aggregate demand and leads to a multiplied increase in national income. The economy is back in an expansion phase once again.

The pattern of expansions and contractions continues indefinitely. Notice that the cycles are internally generated by the dual demand—and supply-side relationships between investment and national income. The only outside shock to the economy was the initial increase in consumption demand at the beginning of the story.

Other Applications of the Theory

INVENTORY INVESTMENT   In 1941, shortly after Samuelson published his theory, the University of Chicago's Alan Metzler discovered that the two key relationships underlying the multiplier-accelerator model applied to inventory investment as well.[7] Metzler's extension of Samuelson's theory was important. It showed that economies have at least one built-in mechanism that tends to keep recessions short because stocks of inventory are depleted very quickly once firms stop investing in inventory. In addition, changes in inventories tend to be a very large component of the changes in national income in the United States, especially during the contraction phase. Decreases in inventories accounted for 87 percent of the decreases in GDP, on average, during the eight contractions from World War II to 1990.[8]

CONSUMER DURABLES   The multiplier-accelerator model also applies to consumer durables such as automobiles and major appliances because they have essentially the same attributes as capital goods. The stock of consumer durables and the purchase of new consumer durables bear the same stock-flow relationship to each other as do capital and investment. Not surprisingly, consumer durables are the most unstable component of consumption demand. Also, the stock-flow relationship leads to the same dynamic over time described above for investment demand.

For example, car sales are likely to move in cycles. A run of a few good years of car sales is almost certain to be followed by a bad year. As the stock

---

[7] L. A. Metzler, "The Nature and Stability of Inventory Cycles," *Review of Economic Statistics* 23 (August 1941): 113–129.

[8] A. Blinder and L. Maccini, "Taking Stock: A Critical Assessment of Recent Research on Inventories," *Journal of Economic Perspectives* 5, No. 1 (Winter 1991): 73–74. This is an excellent overview of the economic research on inventory investment.

of cars becomes ever newer, large numbers of consumers will eventually decide that they do not need to buy a new car. Conversely, a run of a few bad years of car sales is almost certain to be followed by a good year. Consumers can hold off their purchases of new cars only so long. As the stock of cars ages and their cars spend more time in the repair shop, large numbers of consumers will eventually decide that the time has come to buy a new car. This appears to have been the case in 1993, a particularly good year for the auto manufacturers. The average age of the cars on the road at the beginning of 1993 was about as high as it ever gets. Consumers could not delay buying those new cars any longer.

INVESTMENT, AGGREGATE DEMAND, AND THE COST OF CAPITAL   The multiplier-accelerator theory rests on the notion that firms invest only if they see the demand for their products growing. As such, the theory is favored by those economists who believe that the growth in aggregate demand, and not the cost of capital, is the key to investment demand. These economists also tend to be new Keynesians because the multiplier-accelerator theory offers an important reason to worry about the level of aggregate demand. Remember, investment is the key to long-run economic growth. The multiplier-accelerator theory suggests that a high level of investment demand can occur only in an environment of rapidly growing aggregate demand.

EMPIRICAL RELEVANCE   Samuelson's multiplier-accelerator theory has stood up pretty well to the test of time. As noted in Chapter 10, economists have had great difficulty isolating the factors that determine investment demand. Nonetheless, many economists have had some success predicting investment demand in both plant and equipment and in inventories using models based on the multiplier-accelerator theory. Moreover, whatever success the theory has in explaining inventory investment translates directly into an ability to track the U.S. business cycles, since changes in inventory investment account for such a large portion of the changes in national income. The overall weight of the investment research has convinced a large number of economists that the multiplier-accelerator mechanism is an important feature of the U.S. economy and an important force driving U.S. business cycles.

At the same time, many economists, especially those of the new classical persuasion, disagree with this position. The new classical economists have developed a completely different theory to explain the business cycle called the real business cycle, which we turn to next. The real business cycle model challenges virtually every aspect of the new Keynesian view of the macro economy, from how to interpret the business cycle, to how the economy operates, to whether fiscal and monetary policies can hope to improve the overall performance of the economy.

THE REAL BUSINESS CYCLE THEORY

New classical and new Keynesian economists have completely different explanations of the business cycle. Their differences begin with two fundamentally different assumptions about how the macro economy operates that we discussed in Chapter 9. The new classical economists assume that the economy is essentially competitive, with flexible wages and prices; the new Keynesian economists assume that the economy is riddled with market imperfections that give rise to sticky wages and prices. In addition, the new classical economists assume that consumers are Life-Cycle consumers for the most part; the new Keynesian economists assume that the typical consumer is a Keynesian consumer.

Recall that the new classical assumption of competitive factor markets implies that all resources are fully and efficiently employed so that the economy operates on its production possibilities frontier. Therefore, only one level of real GDP is possible in equilibrium, the full employment level of real GDP on the production possibilities frontier. The AS curve in the product markets is vertical at that output. Furthermore, only changes in aggregate supply can change the equilibrium level of output in the economy. These are changes in the quantity and quality of the nation's resources, or changes in production technologies, the same changes that cause the production possibilities frontier to shift out over time. Changes in aggregate demand, in and of themselves, only affect the equilibrium price level.

The study of the business cycle is inherently a long-run exercise because it follows the performance of the economy over a long period of time. Consistent with the long-run perspective, the new classical economists assume that households are forward-looking consumers who behave according to the Life-Cycle Hypothesis. They smooth their consumption over their entire lives in order to maximize their lifetime utility or satisfaction out of what they perceive to be their lifetime resources. Households adjust their consumption year by year as they receive new information about their lifetime resources, but always in a way that smooths lifetime consumption. An important implication of the Life-Cycle Hypothesis is that the marginal propensity to consume out of temporary changes in current disposable income is very low. In contrast, the Keynesian consumption function assumes that the marginal propensity to consume out of all changes in disposable income, temporary or permanent, is quite high.

Shocks Versus Internal Mechanisms

In addition to their different assumptions about the macro economy, the new classical economists have shifted the emphasis on what drives the economic fluctuations in market economies. They de-emphasize internal mechanisms, such as the multiplier-accelerator theory, and emphasize the role of outside shocks to the economy. According to the new classical view, market economies are driven by continual shocks to the fundamental structure of the economy, which consists of household preferences, resources, and production technologies. These are shocks to the real side of the economy as opposed to the monetary or the financial side; hence the term **real business cycle** to describe their theory.

An example of a shock to preferences is a shift against saving and in favor of current consumption, such as appears to have occurred in the United States over the past 20 years. Examples of resource shocks are natural disasters, such as floods and hurricanes that destroy crops and property, and changes in the prices of imported raw materials, such as the dramatic increases and decreases in crude oil prices that buffeted the U.S. economy in the 1970s and 1980s. The most common type of technology shock is a technological change that increases the productivity of the nation's resources, particularly the productivity

REAL BUSINESS CYCLE THEORY
A theory to explain the business cycle developed by new classical economists that is based on outside shocks to the fundamental structure of the economy, which consists of household preferences, resources, and production technologies.

of labor because labor is the most important resource. Technological change can lead to the development of new products or to new, less costly ways of producing existing products. Also, the technological changes can arise in either the domestic economy or the foreign economies. If foreign firms are leading the way in technological change, the domestic firms may lose their markets to the foreign competitors, forcing resources to shift to new industries. An obvious example is the technological and competitive edge that Japanese firms have recently enjoyed over U.S. firms in many consumer electronic products, such as television and stereo equipment. Production in some of these areas has virtually ceased in the United States.

These real shocks may be temporary or permanent. Even if they are temporary, however, their effects on the economy persist for awhile and cause a period of expansion or contraction that has the appearance of a business cycle. New classical economists do not like the term *business cycle*, however, because it implies an underlying regular pattern to the expansions and contractions that they do not believe exists. Instead, the shocks are random and unpredictable and lead to the highly irregular pattern of expansions and contractions that we observe in all market economies. For this reason they prefer to call the irregular ups and downs of the economy *economic fluctuations* to remove any connotation of a regular cycle. The name *real business cycle theory* is something of a misnomer in this regard.

Technological Change and Economic Fluctuations

The real business cycle theory is still relatively new, having first appeared in the early 1980s. The theory to date has emphasized continuing, random productivity shocks in all sectors of the economy as the primary engine that drives economic fluctuations. In addition, the productivity shocks are assumed to result primarily from technological change, both domestic and foreign. The productivity shocks are positive, on average, so that the economy grows over time, but there is considerable variation around the average. This explains why the pattern of expansions and contractions is so irregular.

The emphasis on productivity shocks is understandable, given that only changes in aggregate supply can change real output in the competitive new classical macro model. A productivity shock is an aggregate supply shock that shifts the vertical *AS* curve to the right for a favorable shock and to the left for an unfavorable shock. A favorable shock makes the nation's resources more productive, thereby expanding the nation's production possibilities frontier. National product and national income also increase as the competitive economy remains on the frontier. Conversely, an unfavorable shock makes the nation's resources less productive, thereby decreasing the nation's production possibilities frontier. National product and national income also decrease as the competitive economy remains on the frontier.

Productivity shocks generate economic fluctuations in the new classical competitive model that are consistent with two well-documented facts about economic fluctuations in the United States:

1. *All the aggregate real variables in the private sector tend to move together.* Output, consumption, investment, and employment all tend to increase during an expansion. Conversely, output, consumption, investment, and employment all tend to decrease during a contraction.

2. *Real wages are pro-cyclical.* Real wages refer to purchasing power, the ratio of wages to the prices of the goods and the services that workers buy with their wages.

$$W_{real} = W/P$$

Where W is the wage and P is a broad price index of goods and services such as the consumer price index (CPI) or the GDP deflator. Real wages tend to increase during expansions and decrease during contractions, although only slightly.

A theory of economic fluctuations ought to be consistent with these two facts, and the new classical real business cycle theory is. Let's consider the standard real business cycle story of an expansion driven by a positive productivity shock as an example.

Suppose that some new technological change leads to a temporary increase in labor productivity throughout the economy. The increase in labor productivity increases the production possibilities frontier and allows output and income to expand. Also, because labor is more productive, it commands a higher real wage, and households' real disposable incomes rise. The households do not consume all of their additional income, however, because they are Life-Cycle consumers. They realize that the increase in disposable income is only temporary, so they consume only a small part of it and save the rest. The saving allows them to spread the consumption gains over their lifetimes.

The increase in saving finances an increase in investment. Remember, the only two final products that firms can produce are consumption goods and investment goods, and the competitive factor markets keep the economy on its production possibilities frontier. Therefore, the saving by households translates directly into more investment by firms.

The increase in investment increases the capital stock and allows firms to increase production. The investment alone cannot increase output very much, however, because it is only a small percentage of the capital stock. For example, net investment in the United States in 1992 was approximately $120 billion, which represented less than a 1 percent increase in the $14 trillion stock of capital.[9] Employment has to increase to get a significant increase in output because labor is by far the more important factor of production. The workings of the labor market are crucial in any analysis of economic fluctuations.

Real business cycle theory assumes that labor markets are competitive, operating according to the Laws of Supply and Demand. The temporary, productivity-enhancing technological change does increase employment, as illustrated in Figure 13.2.

The vertical axis records the real wage, not the nominal wage, and the horizontal axis the quantity of labor. People base their labor supply decisions on the real wage because they know that the real wage defines how much purchasing power they have to buy goods and services. They do not jump at a 10 percent wage increase if they know that prices are also rising by 10 percent.

---

[9]Board of Governors of the Federal Reserve System, *Balance Sheets for the U.S. Economy, 1945–92* (Washington, D.C: U.S. Government Printing Office, 1993), Table 11.1. U.S. Department of Commerce, Economics and Statistics Administration, Bureau of Economic Analysis, *Survey of Current Business* 73, No. 3 (March 1993): Table 1.1, p. 6 and Table 1.9, p. 8.

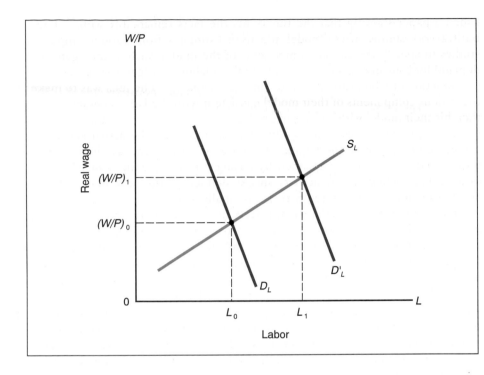

FIGURE 13.2

Competitive Labor Markets and the Real Business Cycle

Real business cycle theory assumes that labor markets are competitive for the most part, as in the figure. The quantity of labor is on the horizontal axis. The real wage, W/P, is on the vertical axis because firms base their hiring decisions on the real wage and workers base their labor supply decisions on the real wage. The initial equilibrium is $(L_0, (W/P)_0)$, at the intersection of the labor demand and supply curves D_L and S_L. An increase in labor productivity increases the firms' demand for labor from D_L to D_L^1. The new equilibrium is $(L_1, (W/P)_1)$, at the intersection of D_L^1 and S_L. Workers increase the amount of labor they supply from L_0 to L_1 in response the higher real wage, and the larger labor supply allows firms to increase production. Measured unemployment is always at the natural rate of unemployment when labor markets are competitive. The new classical economists argue that any reduction in measured unemployment as the economy expands is primarily due to a decrease in voluntary search unemployment or in frictional unemployment.

Similarly, employers base their hiring decisions on the real wage, which they compare to the productivity of the workers. They, too, think in real terms, comparing wages to the prices of their products. The original equilibrium before the technological change occurs at $[L_0, (W/P)_0]$, at the intersection of D_L and S_L.

The technological change makes workers more productive to firms, so their demand for labor shifts from D_L to D_L'. The new equilibrium is $[L_1, (W/P)_1]$, at the intersection of D_L' and S_L. Both the real wage and employment rise, and the increase in employment is the primary reason why firms are able to increase their output.

In summary, the standard real business cycle story of an economic expansion driven by technological change is entirely consistent with the two basic facts about economic expansions in the United States. Output, consumption, investment, and employment all increase, and the real wage rises. Also, the desire of households to smooth consumption and increase saving, which increases investment, provides a mechanism for the expansion to continue after the immediate impact of the technological change ends. Firms will be increasing the capital stock and expanding output and income for quite some time after the technological change occurs.

REFLECTION: You should think through the opposite case of a decrease in productivity by reversing all the steps of the story above. See how it generates a contraction in which output, consumption, investment, and employment all decrease and the real wage falls.

Does Real Business Cycle Theory Fit the Facts?

How well does real business cycle theory fit the facts of economic fluctuations in the United States? It has the direction right; how about the magnitudes?

Two leading new classical economists, Finn Kydland and Edward Prescott, gave real business cycle theory a tremendous boost in 1982 when they pub-

portant features of developed market economies. New Keynesian research is focused on the question of how very different kinds of households and firms react in different kinds of market settings. New classical research is focused on the question of how representative households and competitive firms respond to changing economic conditions. The new Keynesians believe that the new classical research agenda is the wrong agenda for understanding the U.S. economy.

MONEY MATTERS   Finally, the new Keynesians ask the new classical real business cycle proponents to explain why real GDP appears to be so responsive to changes in the money supply, which is a financial shock to the economy rather than a real shock.

The New Classical Counterattack

The new classical economists are not without their defenses against the charges and can mount an impressive counterattack on a number of points as well.

PRODUCTIVITY SHOCKS   They argue that aggregate productivity changes are not the result of large, visible events, but rather the cumulation of thousands of small changes in industries throughout the economy. On average, the economy experiences technological progress and grows, but there is much variation around the average.

MICRO VERSUS MACRO LABOR SUPPLY RESPONSES   Regarding the working of the labor markets, they would argue that the empirical estimates of labor supply responsiveness are misleading. The labor market research has been focused at the micro level, on the labor supply response of individuals. Most of the change in hours of work during expansions and contractions, however, is the result of a relatively small number of people making large, all-or-none, 40-hour-per-week movements in and out of the labor force. This explains why the macro employment response to small changes in real wages is large, whereas the micro individual response appears to be quite small. Real wages change enough over the cycle to drive a fair number of people over the all-or-none line, so that total hours of work change substantially.

MONEY FOLLOWS OUTPUT   New classical economists concede that changes in the money supply and changes in real GDP are highly correlated. Both increase and decrease together. But they argue that the new Keynesians have cause and effect reversed. The money supply follows and accommodates changes in output; it does not cause changes in output. We will have to wait a few chapters to pursue this issue. Suffice it to say that the Barsky/Miron study of the seasonal cycle comes down strongly on the new classical side here. The money supply typically surges in the fourth quarter, along with the surge in Christmas sales. The government is clearly increasing the money supply to accommodate the Christmas demand. The increase in the money supply is certainly not causing the Christmas demand.

WHERE ARE THE NEW KEYNESIAN MICRO FOUNDATIONS? When they go on the attack, the new classical economists argue that the new Keynesians are simply assuming wage and price stickiness. The new Keynesians, they say, have not yet been able to explain convincingly how wage and price stickiness is compatible with the idea that households and firms are trying to solve their economic problems as best they can by engaging in exchange. How do sticky prices and wages, and involuntary unemployment, maximize the economic interests of either households or firms? The new classical economists charge that the new Keynesians have not been able to answer this fundamental question. In contrast, competitive markets with flexible prices do maximize their economic interests, which is why it is a good assumption.

REAL BUSINESS CYCLE THEORY IS MUCH LESS DEVELOPED   Finally, the new classical economists point out that Keynesian theory is over 60 years old, whereas real business cycle theory is little more than 10 years old. They believe that the real business cycle is a good and proper benchmark model for understanding the U.S. economy and that the best research agenda is to continue to develop and refine the model.

A Reconciliation?

Are you confused about how the economy operates and what policies the government should undertake to manage the economy, if any? If you are, be assured that you are not alone. The new Keynesian and the new classical economists have put forth completely different views about the nature of economic fluctuations, how the macro economy operates, and whether fiscal and monetary policies are useful. Moreover, the two views are a long way from a reconciliation. Listen to what some of the leading economists from each school have to say.

Charles Plosser of the University of Rochester is a strong proponent of the real business cycle model. He chides the new Keynesians for their lack of convincing and consistent micro foundations based on the choices people make to solve their economic problems, which leads the new Keynesians into ad hoc theorizing, such as the multiplier-accelerator model. He sees this as an "essential flaw," a "fundamental problem" with the new Keynesian theory, so essential and fundamental that "the underpinnings of our understanding of economic fluctuations are likely to be found somewhere other than a suitably modified version of the Keynesian model."

New Keynesians Gregory Mankiw and Lawrence Summers, both of Harvard University, are just as strident on the other side.

Mankiw: "[Real business cycle theory] will, I predict, ultimately be discarded as an explanation of observed fluctuations."

Summers: "[Real business cycle theory] has no ability to explain economic fluctuations in the United States or other capitalist economies."

Plosser, Mankiw, and Summers do not sound like economists who are about to reconcile their differences, do they?[13]

---

[13]C. Plosser, "Understanding Real Business Cycles," *Journal of Economic Perspectives* 3, No. 3 (Summer 1989): 51–77. The quotes are on pp. 51 and 52. N. G. Mankiw, "Real Business Cycles: A New Keynesian Perspective," *Journal of Economic Perspectives* 3, No. 3 (Summer 1989): 79–90. The quote is on p. 89. L. Summers, "Some Skeptical Observations on Real Business Cycle Theory," *Quarterly Review*, Federal Reserve Bank of Minneapolis (Fall 1986): 23–27. The quote is on p. 24.

Unfortunately, empirical research using aggregate macroeconomic data is unlikely to be able to resolve the differences between the new Keynesian and the new classical economists in a convincing fashion. Bits and pieces of evidence supporting one side or the other of the kinds mentioned above will undoubtedly continue to emerge; but decisive evidence one way or the other, probably not. The conclusion is inescapable: Macroeconomics these days is truly in a state of turmoil when it comes to explaining the short-run ebbs and flows of the economy and what to do about them.

SUMMARY

Chapter 13 began with a discussion of how economists and policy makers monitor the performance of the economy and what they have learned about business cycles in the United States.

1. The National Bureau of Economic Research (NBER) has been recognized as the center of research on the U.S. business cycle since its founding in 1920. The NBER established the traditional view of the business cycle as a temporary, recurring series of expansions and contractions moving around a more or less permanent, trend rate of growth in potential real GDP. The trend rate of growth is the rate at which the production possibilities frontier moves out over time.

2. The NBER also pioneered the technique of monitoring the performance of the economy by means of a broad set of cyclical indicators. Cyclical indicators are data series that are reliable, are currently available, are economically significant, and reflect the timing of the overall business cycle to some degree. The NBER has traditionally monitored the behavior of output, income, employment, and trade.

3. The Department of Commerce publishes three indexes that are composites of the NBER's cyclical indicators.
   a. *The index of leading indicators* is designed to forecast aggregate economic activity and predict the peaks and the troughs of the business cycle.
   b. *The index of coincident indicators* is designed to track the expansion and contraction phases of the business cycle, and the peaks and the troughs, as they are occurring.
   c. *The index of lagging indicators* is designed to confirm the existence of the phases of the business cycle and its turning points.

These three indexes are the most closely watched indicators of overall economic activity in the United States.

4. The Business Cycle Dating Committee of the NBER is charged with identifying the peaks and the troughs of the business cycle in the United States, and everyone uses its estimates. The committee relies on a broad set of cyclical indicators, and a fair amount of judgment, in determining the peaks and the troughs. The NBER has identified nine peaks and nine troughs since the first post–World War II peak in December of 1948, eight complete peak-to-peak business cycles in all.

5. A recent study by the NBER's Victor Zarnowitz compared the U.S. business cycles from 1945 to 1982 with the cycles from 1912 to 1945. He found that the business cycle has become much less severe in the recent period,

on average, due in large part to the increased automatic stability in the economy. Zarnowitz also found that the expansion phase has increased substantially relative to the contraction phase. The average length of the complete cycle has not changed; it was 45 months in each period. Business cycles are highly irregular, however. There is considerable variation around the average length and severity of the cycles.

The second section of the chapter presented Samuelson's multiplier-accelerator model of investment demand.

6. The multiplier-accelerator model is an example of an internal mechanism built into the economy that tends to generate business cycles.

7. Investment demand is inherently unstable because of the stock-flow relationship between capital and investment. A small percentage change in the demand for capital leads to a much larger percentage change in the demand for investment.

8. Investment demand bears a dual relationship to national income, one operating through the demand side of the economy and one operating through the supply side of the economy. The demand-side relationship is that investment demand is part of aggregate demand. The supply-side relationship is that firms need capital to produce goods and services, and they increase their stock of capital by investing.

9. Investment "accelerates" the expansion phase of the cycle because firms need to invest in order to increase their production capacity to meet the growing demand. Investment also brings about and accelerates the contraction phase of the cycle because firms do not need to add to their production capacity when the economy is at its peak, or when the economy is declining. Investment demand falls at these times. The economy eventually recovers from the recession as capital depreciates and firms have to increase investment again to replenish their capital stocks.

10. Many new Keynesian economists believe that the multiplier-accelerator mechanism is an important driving force behind the business cycle in the United States.

The final section of Chapter 13 presented the new classical real business cycle theory of economic fluctuations, which is now the main branch of the new classical school.

11. Real business cycle theory stresses outside shocks to the real structure of the economy as the driving force behind economic fluctuations. The real structure consists of preferences, resources, and production technologies. The models of the past 10 years have assumed that the principal shocks are productivity shocks caused by technological change.

12. The basic real business cycle story of an expansion is that a temporary technological change expands the production possibilities frontier and increases households' incomes by increasing the real wage. Households are Life-Cycle consumers. They save most of the temporarily higher real wage, which leads to an increase in investment. They also increase their labor supply because of the higher real wage, which increases employment and allows output to expand. The story is consistent with the two main facts of economic fluctuations in the United States: Output, consumption, investment, and employment all tend to increase (and decrease) simultaneously, and real wages are pro-cyclical.

13. Since the new classical economists assume that the economy is competitive, they do not view economic fluctuations in the traditional way (that is, as temporary cycles around a permanent trend). There is no permanent trend in potential real GDP distinct from the actual performance of the economy. The shocks expand and contract the production possibilities frontier, and the competitive economy remains on its frontier for all intents and purposes.

14. The economic fluctuations result when households and business firms react as well as they can to the continuing random shocks to the economy. Furthermore, their reactions are as efficient as can be expected because markets are essentially competitive. Therefore, fiscal and monetary policies cannot improve the performance of the economy in the short run.

15. The new Keynesians challenge the real business cycle theory on a number of grounds. They believe that wages and prices are sticky, that much unemployment is involuntary, and that changes in involuntary unemployment explain why all the real economic variables move together over the cycle. They also believe that the swings in labor productivity are the result of labor hoarding, not technological change. They refuse to believe that economic downturns are efficient responses to economic shocks and see the need for corrective fiscal and monetary policies.

16. The principal new classical counterargument is that the new Keynesians have been unable to explain how their assumptions of wage and price stickiness are compatible with the economic interests of households and firms who are trying to solve their economic problems through exchange.

KEY TERMS

contraction phase (business cycle)
cyclical indicator
expansion phase (business cycle)
index of coincident indicators

index of lagging indicators
index of leading indicators
multiplier-accelerator model
peak (business cycle)

political business cycle
real business cycle theory
trough (business cycle)

QUESTIONS

1. What are some reasons why the U.S. economy has become more stable in the second half of the twentieth century than it was in the first half of the twentieth century?

2. What are some of the difficulties that economists at the NBER face in trying to determine the peaks and the troughs of a business cycle?

3. Is each of the following events an aggregate demand shock or an aggregate supply shock to the economy, or both?
   a. OPEC countries increase the price of oil.
   b. The U.S. government sends military troops to Somalia for a relief operation.
   c. Scientists discover a new form of energy that decreases production and transportation costs.
   d. The Clinton administration increases public investment in infrastructure throughout the country.

4. Why must both the contraction phase and the expansion phase of a business cycle eventually come to an end, according to the multiplier-accelerator model of the business cycle?

5. a. Suppose that producers believe that an increase in demand for their goods will be followed by an even larger increase in demand in the future. What would be the effect of such a demand increase on net investment, according to the multiplier-accelerator theory of the business cycle?
   b. Suppose, instead, that producers believe that the increase in demand will last only for one year and then return to its current level. How would this affect net investment?

6. Discuss the major differences between the multiplier-accelerator theory and the real business cycle theory in their attempts to explain the persistence of business cycles.

7. Suppose that an economy enters a recession; national output decreases, and unemployment increases. The government asks two economists for policy advice. One of the economists is a proponent of new Keynesian theory, and the other one is a devoted new classical economist. Based on your knowledge of these two theories, explain what policy advice you think that each economist would give.

8. a. What are the main points of the new Keynesian critique of real business cycle theory?
   b. What are the main points of the new classical critique of the new Keynesian theories?

9. What is the major difference between the traditional view (represented by the NBER) and the new classical view of the business cycle? In particular, how do they differ in interpreting the cyclical changes in output?

10. How do the new classical economists explain large fluctuations in employment accompanied by small changes in real wages?

CASE

Hard Times in California*

The U.S. standard of living sagged over the three years from 1989 to 1992, reflecting four years of recession and slow economic growth. The national unemployment rate rose from 5.3 percent in 1989 to 7.4 percent in 1992, and income per person dropped by $170 in constant 1992 dollars.

Californians bore more than their share of the downturn. Their income per person fell by $960 in constant 1992 dollars, the largest decrease suffered by any state, and their unemployment rate soared from 5 percent to 9 percent. From 1990 to 1991 alone, California employers shed over half a million workers from their payrolls.

One major blow to the California economy was the cutback in national defense spending. In 1988, federal spending on military contracts in California was double the national average on a per person basis. But as the United States spent less on aircraft and munitions after the fall of the Soviet Union, defense workers found pink slips in their pay envelopes. For example, over 150,000 California aerospace workers lost their jobs.

A second large shock hit the construction sector. Developers across the nation built thousands of office towers and shopping malls in the early 1980s in response to special incentives in the Economic Recovery and Tax Act of 1981. Just as it was becoming clear that they had overbuilt, the Tax Reform Act of 1986 knocked out the tax incentives that were propping up the commercial construction sector, and

*Provided by David Denslow, University of Florida.

the worsening savings and loan crisis removed much of its funding. The construction sector collapsed nationwide. The collapse was particularly severe in California because it was accompanied by slowing population growth. Knowing that jobs were unavailable in California, fewer people moved into the state and ever more people moved out. The slower population growth meant reduced demand for new houses, as well as for offices and shopping malls.

Battered by the defense cutbacks and the collapse of its construction sector, California would have plunged into depression, not merely a recession, were it not for the presence of a considerable amount of automatic stability in the California economy. One major source of automatic stability is "import" demand, where imports refer to purchases from other states. When Californians buy fewer automobiles, part of the impact is felt in Michigan. When they buy fewer carpets and less furniture, the profits of factories in the Carolinas decline. Consequently, some of the multiplier effect from reduced defense and construction activity is felt by other states, not California.

The second important automatic stabilizer for the California economy is federal taxes and transfer payments. As Californians were becoming poorer relative to the rest of the country, they sent smaller amounts from their paychecks to the U.S. Treasury. They also received more federal transfers in the form of public assistance and unemployment compensation. As a result, while the average income of Californians fell by $960 over three years, their average *disposable* income fell by only about $460, nearly $500 less. Much of

(continued on next page)

Hard Times in California (cont.)

the difference came from lower federal taxes and higher federal transfers.[1]

Every state, not just California, has the advantage of being partially insured against severe regional recessions by federal taxes and transfers. For example, the Midwest economy suffered during the early 1980s as the soaring value of the dollar overseas slashed the demand for American food and industrial products. Other regions of the country shared their losses as the proportion of national taxes paid by the Midwest fell and the proportion of federal transfers received increased. When the turn came for the East and West coastal regions to tumble in the late 1980s and early 1990s, the Midwest helped out by paying a larger fraction of national taxes and receiving a smaller share of federal transfers.

The nationwide scope of our insurance against regional downturns intrigues Europeans, as they attempt to move toward a single currency. If Europe adopts a single currency, then no nation will have an independent monetary policy. Just as California cannot fight its recession by expanding its money supply to cut interest rates, so France would be unable to push its interest rates below those in the rest of Europe. With a single currency, all the Western European nations would have the same interest rates.

The Europeans know that if California were a separate country, it might enjoy some advantages from having its own

[1]The California income data are from U.S. Bureau of Economic Analysis (BEA) diskettes, May 1993 release. The employment data are from recent BEA county diskettes, which also contain state data.

monetary policy. Also, the California dollar could float against the U.S. dollar, just as the Canadian dollar does now, and help cushion shocks to the economy. But any such gains would be more than offset by the loss of the insurance against local recessions through federal taxes and transfers. Knowing this, some economists are questioning whether Europe would be wise to adopt a single currency if the European nations are unwilling to forge a community-wide system of taxes and government transfer payments.

ECONOMIC ADVISOR'S REPORT

Suppose that the governor of California hires you to advise him on how the state government can help fight the recession in California.

1. What policies that you might recommend to President Clinton to fight a national recession would be unavailable to the governor to fight the California recession?
2. Do you think that the governor has any highly effective policy tools for getting the state's economy back on its feet? If yes, what are they and why are they effective? If no, why not?
   Now suppose that you are advising the European Community (EC) in the year 2000, and assume that they have adopted a single currency.
3. Would you advise the EC to adopt a community-wide unemployment insurance program financed by an EC income tax? What are the advantages and disadvantages of such a plan?

IV

Money and Monetary Policy

14

The Nature of Money and Banking: First Principles

LEARNING OBJECTIVES

CONCEPTS TO LEARN

U.S. money supply	The properties of money
Balance sheets, assets, and liabilities	The Fed
Demand for money	Commercial banks (depository institutions)
Velocity of circulation	Open Market Operation
The equation of exchange	

CONCEPTS TO RECALL

The circular flow of economic activity [4]	Hyperinflation [7]

C hapters 14, 15, and 16 turn to a topic that is near and dear to all of us—money. Money is the magical, mystical side of economics. It is not a resource or factor of production like labor, capital, or land. The dollar bills that you carry with you are just pieces of paper with no inherent value of their own. They are not backed by anything—you cannot turn them in at the nearest bank for gold or silver or anything else. Your checking account balance that you write checks against to buy things is nothing more than a configuration of electrons on some computer storage disk. Yet most economists believe that the amount of dollar bills and checking account balances has a profound effect on the circular flow of **real** goods and services. We want to understand why and how this can be so in the next three chapters.

Chapter 14 begins our study of money with two specific goals in mind. We want to understand the nature of money and to see why money is so important to the functioning of the macro economy.

The study of money and monetary policy is chock full of details about financial institutions and financial markets that are unfamiliar to most beginning students of economics. Rather than dive right in, Chapter 14 begins with some general principles relating to money that apply to all market economies regardless of their particular financial arrangements. Institutional details of the U.S. monetary system are kept to a bare minimum. These general principles will prepare us for the various institutional details relating to the supply of money in the United States that appear in Chapters 15 and 16.

WHAT IS MONEY?

The natural starting point in our analysis of money is to pin down what it is that we are talking about. What exactly is money? This turns out to be a difficult question to answer. Many things have served as money throughout history, and the nature of money tends to change and evolve within a country over time.

We have to begin somewhere, though, so let's accept for now the most common definition of money. **Money** is anything that is routinely used to pay for goods and services and to pay off debts. According to this definition, the money supply in the United States and in all the other developed market economies consists of three items: currency, checking accounts with unlimited checking privileges (providing the account has sufficient funds), and traveler's checks.

Table 14.1 lists the average daily amount of each item in the United States during 1992. The table indicates that currency and checking accounts are the only two components of the money supply of any consequence. We can safely ignore traveler's checks in our analysis of money.

Currency refers to the dollar bills and coins of various denominations circulating throughout the economy. Dollar bills are called Federal Reserve Notes because they are issued by the **Federal Reserve Banking System,** the "Fed" for short, which is the central bank of the United States. (Take out a bill, and notice that "Federal Reserve Note" appears along the top of the face side.) Economists usually refer to dollar bills as **Federal Reserve Notes,** labeled

MONEY

Anything that is routinely used to pay for goods and services or to pay off debts.

CURRENCY

The dollar bills and coins of various denominations circulating in the economy.

FEDERAL RESERVE BANKING SYSTEM

The central bank of the United States.

FEDERAL RESERVE NOTE

A dollar bill of any denomination that is the paper currency of the United States.

TABLE 14.1   **The Money Supply in the United States, 1992 (Average Daily Amount)**

COMPONENT		AMOUNT (BILLIONS)
Currency		$279.4
Transactions deposits		679.1
Demand deposits	319.2	
Other checkable deposits	359.9	
Travelers checks		8.1
	Total money supply	$966.6

SOURCE: Council of Economic Advisors, *Economic Indicators, March 1993* (Washington, D.C.: U.S. Government Printing Office, 1993), 26–27.

FRN, a practice we will follow in this text. The issuing of paper currency today is controlled by the central banks in all the developed market economies.

Coins used to be an important component of all currencies, but they are relatively unimportant today. Pennies, nickels, dimes, and so on amount to only a few billion dollars in the United States.

Checking accounts with unlimited checking privileges are called **transactions deposits.** They include *regular checking accounts* that do not pay interest and the various kinds of *NOW and Super NOW* accounts that do pay interest. NOW stands for negotiable order of withdrawal.

The U.S. government's publications list the regular checking accounts as "demand deposits" because the balances in these accounts are payable to the owners on demand. In contrast, banks have the right to hold up payment on NOW accounts for a few days, although they almost never exercise the right. The government lists them as "other checkable deposits."

Businesses own most of the regular checking accounts in the United States because they are not allowed to hold NOW accounts. Households own most of the NOW accounts. The vast majority of transactions deposits are held with commercial banks.

You or someone in your family may have a deposit account at a bank with limited checking privileges, such as a money market deposit account with a three- or a six-check limit per month. These accounts are not considered to be part of the money supply because they are not *routinely* used to pay for goods and services or to pay off debts.

Notice, also, that credit card transactions are not part of the money supply. You may buy something with a credit card, but you do not literally *pay* for it with the card. A credit card transaction is really a short-term loan from a merchant to you, with the credit card company standing in the middle. Your credit card allows you to take possession of goods and services before you pay for them. The credit card company pays the merchant with a check at the end of the month, and you then pay the credit card company, usually by check. Most credit card companies allow you to spread the payment over a number of months with an interest charge, at which point they become the lenders, not the merchant. The point is that the actual payment for goods and services in credit card transactions in made by check, not by credit card.

TRANSACTIONS DEPOSIT
A checking account with unlimited checking privileges.

Two final words of caution are in order when thinking about money because of the way that the term *money* is used in everyday speech. First, people tend to think of money only in terms of currency, as in "I have to get some 'money' out of my NOW account." Don't fall into that trap. Balances in NOW accounts and regular checking accounts are money, too. Indeed, as Table 14.1 shows, they are the most important component of the money supply. You do not increase the amount of money that you have when you go to the bank and write a $50 check for "Cash" against your NOW account to get $50 worth of Federal Reserve Notes (FRN). Instead, you are merely changing the form of your money, substituting $50 of FRN for $50 in your NOW account. Get used to thinking of checking account balances as money.

In addition, take special care to distinguish between money and income. They are very different concepts, yet they tend to be used interchangeably in everyday speech. The confusion arises because we are paid in money for our work. For instance, suppose that you have a work-study job and your friend asks you: "How much money did you make last semester?" Everyone understands the meaning of this question. Still, "making money" refers to printing new money in economic analysis, and private citizens cannot do this, at least not legally. Better to ask: "How much income did you earn last semester?"

Income is a flow variable, such as the amount earned over a given period of time—an *hourly* wage, an *annual* salary, or work-study earnings over a *semester*. Money is a stock variable; it does not have a time dimension. The data in Table 14.1 were computed by measuring the amount of money in the economy at the end of each business day during 1992 and then calculating the average of the daily amounts for the year. The average amount of currency, checking accounts, and traveler's checks held by the public in 1992 is a very different concept from the flow of national income received by the public in the nation's factor markets during 1992. The distinction between money and income is crucial in macroeconomic analysis.

THE CIRCULAR FLOW AND THE EQUATION OF EXCHANGE

The importance of money to the operation of the economy can best be understood with reference to the circular flow of economic activity. Chapter 8 presented three different measures of the circular flow: national income, national product, and value added. They calculate the circular flow at three different points on the circle. National income measures the flow of activity through the nation's factor markets. National product measures the flow of activity through the nation's product markets. And value added measures the contribution to overall economic activity by the producers in the economy.

National income, national product, and value added essentially measure the total amount of *marketed* activity within the economy during the year. This suggests that the circular flow can also be measured in terms of money because money is the second part of all market exchanges. Goods and services (including factors of production) pass from the sellers to the buyers in exchange for money, which passes from the buyers to the sellers. Therefore, the circular flow of (marketed) economic activity must be equal to the product of two terms: the average amount of money in the economy multiplied by the number of times that money changes hands from buyers to sellers during the course of a year.

The measure of the circular flow in terms of money is called the **equation of exchange,** written

$$M \cdot V = Y$$

Y is the current dollar value of the national income; M is the average amount of money in the economy; and V is the **velocity of circulation,** or velocity for short, the number of times that money changes hands to pay for final goods and services (or, alternatively, for primary factors of production) during the year.

The equation of exchange is another national income accounting identity because the velocity of circulation is defined as the ratio of the national income to the money supply:

$$V = Y/M$$

In other words, the velocity of circulation converts the average *stock* of money, the money supply, into a *flow* of national income during the course of a year.

For example, in 1992 the average money supply (M) in the United States was \$966.6 billion, and the national income (Y) was \$4,744.1 billion.[1] Therefore, the velocity of circulation in1992 was 4.91.

$$V = Y/M = \$4{,}744.1/\$966.6 = 4.91$$

Alternatively,

$$Y = M \cdot V = \$966.6 \cdot 4.91 = \$4744.1$$

Viewed from the perspective of the equation of exchange, the U.S. economy generated a national income of \$4,744.1 in 1992 because the money supply of \$966.6 changed hands between buyers and sellers 4.91 times during the year.

The equation of exchange is also commonly represented in terms of the national product and written

$$M \cdot V = P \cdot Q$$

The right-hand side of the equation represents the current dollar value of the national product as prices times the quantities: the prices of the goods and services times the quantities of the goods and services flowing through the nation's product markets. The national product version of the equation of exchange has the advantage of separating out price changes (inflation) from quantity changes within the circular flow from year to year.

Velocity and the Demand for Money

The velocity of circulation depends on the demand for money by households, businesses, and government agencies. To understand the connection between

EQUATION OF EXCHANGE

The measure of the circular flow of economic activity in terms of money; a national income accounting identity, which says that the dollar value of national income or national product equals the product of the money supply times the velocity of circulation.

VELOCITY OF CIRCULATION

The ratio of the dollar value of national income or national product to the money supply; the number of times the money supply changes hands during the year to buy final goods and services (or primary factors of production).

[1]Council of Economic Advisers, *Economic Indicators, March 1993* (Washington, D.C.: U.S. Government Printing Office, 1993), 4, 26, and 27.

velocity and the demand for money you must understand what the demand for money means.

Our demand for money is *not* the answer to this question: Would we like more money? (Sure we would, in unlimited amounts!) Instead, the **demand for money** is the amount of money that we want to hold at any one time and not spend. This is a tricky concept, however, because we do not want money for its own sake, unlike any other good or service. Money is useful to us only because we can get rid of it in exchange for goods and services. Also we do not tend to hold a given amount of money. Quite the contrary; our money holdings vary considerably over time. The amount of money that we have increases when we cash or deposit our paychecks and then decreases as we spend our money. Consequently, the demand for money has to be interpreted as an average amount of money held over a period of time.

The following simple example illustrates the concept of demand for money. Suppose that you earn $200 each month from a work-study job and get paid once a month. You place your entire work-study check in your NOW account at the beginning of the month and write checks on your account during the month to buy goods and services, drawing your account down to zero on the last day of the month. You then replenish your account with another $200 work-study check on the first day of the next month and proceed to write checks as before, drawing the account down to zero at the end of the month. The same pattern continues each month. To keep the example simple, assume also that you do not use Federal Reserve Notes. The balance in your NOW account is the only money that you have.

The amount of money that you hold in this example varies from $200 to zero and is hardly ever constant for more than a day at a time. Therefore, your demand for money has to be interpreted as the average of your money holdings each day during the month. You hold relatively large amounts of money during the first days of the month, near $200, and relatively small amounts of money during the last days of the month, nearer to zero. Suppose that you spend your money evenly over the month, the same amount each day. In this case, the average of your daily money holdings would be $100, the midpoint between the beginning-of-month $200 balance and the end-of-month zero balance. The $100 average balance is your demand for money.

Interpreting the demand for money as an average amount held establishes the link between velocity and the demand for money. Your personal velocity of circulation in our example is equal to 2 (measured on a monthly basis). You support $200 of income or spending each month with an average of $100 of money.

$$V_{\text{Personal}} = \text{monthly income/average amount of money held}$$
$$= \$200/\$100 = 2$$

Turning the ratio upside down, your demand for money, an average daily balance of $100, is equal to one-half of your monthly income of $200. In other words, velocity is just the inverse of the demand for money expressed as a proportion of income. The velocity is 2; the demand for money as a proportion of income is one-half. The inverse relationship between velocity and the demand for money is an important link in understanding how money affects the economy.

DEMAND FOR MONEY
The average amount of money that a person or an institution wants to hold and not spend.

The Importance of Money in the Economy

The equation of exchange is a simple, yet powerful, tool for seeing the potential economic effects of money on the economy. For example, suppose that the velocity of circulation happened to be a constant equal to $\overline{V}$. All households, businesses, and government agencies want to hold an amount of money that is a constant proportion of their incomes for some reason. The equation of exchange in this case is

$$M \cdot \overline{V} = P \cdot Q$$

We can see that monetary policy has a very potent effect on the economy with V constant. A change in the money supply must lead to a change in prices, P, or to a change in real output, Q, or to both. And therein lies the magic of money. Money, after all, is nothing more than pieces of paper, in the case of Federal Reserve Notes and configurations of electrons stored on computer disks, in the case of checking accounts. Yet changes in the money supply can directly affect the circular flow of economic activity. That the amount of money in the economy can affect the prices of goods and services is not so surprising. What is surprising, though, is that money can affect the real side of the economy. This substance called money can determine whether or not someone has a job! Other pieces of paper and other configurations of electrons stored on computer disks do not have this power. Call them money, however, and they are able to affect the rate of inflation and unemployment, two of society's macroeconomic policy goals. We want to understand why money has such power.

Let's stay with the example of constant velocity to explore further the potential consequences of money for the real side of the economy. Chapters 10 through 12 analyzed the effects of changes in aggregate demand on the economy without any mention of the money supply. When economists do not mention an economic variable, they are implicitly assuming that the variable is constant, the other things equal assumption. Therefore, the analysis in those chapters implicitly assumed that the money supply was constant. We also assumed that prices were constant in order to focus on changes in real income or output when there are lots of unemployed resources. If velocity is constant as well, then the equation of exchange implies that real income or output must also be constant. Constant M, V, and P imply a constant Q. Remember, the equation of exchange is a national income accounting identity; it has to be true at all times.

But a constant Q means that the value of the spending multiplier (and all the other fiscal policy multipliers) must be zero because real income or output cannot change. A change in one component in aggregate demand must necessarily be completely offset by equal changes in aggregate demand in the opposite direction to maintain the economy at a constant equilibrium level of real income. Fiscal policy is useless; only monetary policy can affect the economy.

Don't worry, though. All that you learned in Chapters 10 through 12 has not been for naught. The point of the constant velocity example is simply to show that the presence of money in the economy has an impact on all aspects of the economy. In fact, the velocity of circulation is not constant; it varies somewhat from year to year.

For example, velocity defined in terms of national income ranged from a high of 5.60 to a low of 4.71 between 1980 and 1990. The average annual change in velocity, plus or minus, during the 1980s was only 0.22, or 4.2 percent of its average value. Velocity fell steadily from 1981 to 1986, with the exception of one upward tick in 1984, and then rose steadily from 1986 to 1990.[2]

Velocity tends not to be highly variable in normal times because it is largely determined by institutional factors that change only slowly, such as how often people are paid and how they pay for goods and services. We will see in Chapter 16 that the demand for money, and thus velocity, also responds to changes in economic variables such as the level of national income and interest rates.

Changes in aggregate demand can affect real national income or output if velocity can change, even if money and prices are constant. Indeed, the equation of exchange gives us a whole new perspective on aggregate demand. It indicates that changes in aggregate demand affect the equilibrium level of real national income *because* they change the velocity of circulation. No other possibility exists if money and prices are constant.

For instance, an increase in aggregate demand increases the equilibrium level of real national income by activating idle money that was being held and not spent and by getting that money to change hands. The demand for money has to decrease so that velocity can increase. An example is a debt-financed increase in government purchases. The federal government induces people to reduce their money holdings in exchange for Treasury bonds and then activates the money with its purchases. The result is that the money supply turns over more rapidly. Velocity increases, which increases the equilibrium level of real national income.

In conclusion, looking at the economy through the equation of exchange teaches us two valuable lessons. The first is that the federal government can affect the macro economy with both monetary and fiscal policies. Monetary policies work by changing the money supply. Fiscal policies work by changing the velocity of circulation against a constant money supply (as do all changes in aggregate demand). The second is that the impact of money reaches far beyond the narrow confines of monetary policy. Money affects all aspects of the macro economy, including how the economy responds to changes in aggregate demand.

THE NATURE OF MONEY

Now that we have seen the power of money, let's look more closely at the nature of money to understand the source of its power and how its power is maintained.

The Various Forms of Money

The first point to understand is that the power of money has no necessary connection with the form that it takes. All kinds of substances have served as money throughout history.

---

[2]Council of Advisers, *Economic Report of the President, 1993* (Washington, D.C.: U.S. Government Printing Office, 1993), Table B-22, p. 372 and Table B-65, p. 423.

The earliest monies were *full-bodied coins* made of precious or semi-precious metals. Full-bodied means that the face value of a coin is equal to the value of the metal in the coin. A full-bodied 10 cent coin, for example, would have 10 cents worth of metal in it. The Chinese were using full-bodied coins as early as the twenty-second century B.C.. The coins were made of bronze and fashioned into an oblong, knife like shape. The coins that developed later on in the West were usually made of gold, silver, or copper and had the more rounded shape that we are used to.

Full-bodied coins are not a very convenient form of money. They are heavy and bulky to transport and are vulnerable to theft and debasement. *Debasing* a coin means substituting cheaper alloys for the more precious metals in the coin. People were forever taking their coins to assayers to certify the value of their money. In addition, full-bodied coins quickly lose their value as money whenever the market value of the metal in the coin exceeds the face value of the coin. People melt down the coins and sell the metal for its market value. This problem eventually led to the use of *token coins* made of inexpensive alloys whose market value is only a tiny fraction of the face value of the coin. Very few coins today contain any precious metals.

The most recent U.S. example of the problem with using precious metals in coins occurred in the 1960s. Dimes and quarters had always contained some silver. In the 1960s, however, the market price of silver rose to the point that the dimes and quarters contained more than $.10 and $.25 worth of silver, respectively. Sure enough, dimes and quarters began to disappear as enterprising folk melted them down to sell the silver. The government had no choice but to mint new dimes and quarters out of cheaper alloys from then on.

The many disadvantages of coins have always led people to search for different kinds of money. Trading merchants during the Renaissance discovered the convenience of checking accounts, and deposit banking flourished in trading centers such as Venice and Florence. Renaissance banking was more primitive than modern banking, though, because all transfers of deposits occurred within one bank. Merchants could only write checks to other merchants who kept deposits at the same bank. Transfers of deposits by check from one bank to another did not appear until the eighteenth century in England.

The use of paper currency on a widespread scale also developed in England during the eighteenth century when the Bank of England, a private bank at the time, began issuing paper notes. The notes were truly substitutes for the gold coins that were also in use because the notes were *fully convertible* into gold. The bank agreed to take back its notes in exchange for an amount of gold equal to the face value of the notes anytime a holder of its notes wanted to make that trade.

Money in the United States

The United States has used a wide variety of monies throughout its history. When the early colonists were trading with the Native American Indians, many different substances served as money, including furs, tobacco, bullets, and wampum. Wampum was a bead that the Native Americans fashioned out of shells. They used both black and white beads, with the black beads having twice the value of the white beads. The use of wampum as money was so common that the term has survived to this day in the United States as a slang term for money.

Once the colonies broke from England, the new United States relied largely on coin, paper currency called bank notes issued by private state banks, and checking account deposits as money. The colonies had issued a paper currency called the Continental dollar during the Revolutionary War to help pay for the war. They borrowed the term *dollar* for their currency from the Dutch word *thaler*, which was a silver coin minted in Bohemia during the sixteenth century. The Continental dollar quickly became worthless, however, even before the war had ended. Chastened by the fate of the Continental, Congress did not authorize a national paper currency until 1863 when it passed the National Banking Act of 1863. The new currency, called "greenbacks," replaced the private state bank notes by law. Only national banks could issue the greenbacks.

A national paper currency has been in use in the United states ever since 1863. The currency was convertible at various times into gold or silver from 1879 to 1961, most recently into silver. Convertibility ended in 1961, when the Fed replaced the "silver certificates" with the Federal Reserve Notes. All you can get for a dollar bill now is another dollar bill.

Today, as we have seen, virtually all of the money in the United States is in one of two forms, a nonconvertible national currency, the Federal Reserve Notes, and checking account balances. The same is true in all the developed market economies.[3]

The Properties of Money

If the form that money takes is not the source of its economic power, what is? The answer lies in the properties of money. The power of money derives from what money does rather than from what money is. Money has three main properties or functions. It serves as the medium of exchange, the unit of account, and a store of value.

MEDIUM OF EXCHANGE

Anything that people are routinely willing to accept in exchange for goods and services (and factors of production).

THE MEDIUM OF EXCHANGE   The medium of exchange is the defining property of money. Something serves as a **medium of exchange** if people are routinely willing to accept it in exchange for goods and services (including factors of production). Anything that has this property is money; anything without this property is usually not considered money. The medium of exchange property is the basis of the common definition of money given in the beginning of the chapter. The three items listed in Table 14.1 are money because they do routinely serve as the medium of exchange.

The medium-of-exchange property is the source of money's power to move the economy. The amount of Federal Reserve Notes and checking account balances in the economy affects aggregate demand precisely because people are willing to accept FRN and checks in exchange for goods and services, for real resources. Conversely, other pieces of paper and configurations of electrons on computer disks cannot affect aggregate demand because they are not accepted as a medium of exchange. The source of money's power is as simple as that.

---

[3]Much of the historical information on money in this chapter and the following chapters is taken from T. Simpson, *Money, Banking, and Economic Analysis*, third edition (Englewood Cliffs, NJ: Prentice-Hall, 1987), Chapter 2, pp. 11–34.

The line distinguishing money from nonmonies in terms of the medium-of-exchange property is difficult to draw with any precision. Checks written on money market demand deposits with limited checking privileges are accepted as a medium of exchange as commonly as checks written on regular checking or NOW accounts. Is the limit on the number of checks allowed per month really an important distinction? Furthermore, most savings accounts without checking privileges are highly **liquid,** meaning that they are easily converted to money. If households and businesses consider them as good as money, should they not be considered part of the money supply?

These questions have no hard and fast answers. For this reason the federal government publishes three different versions of "the money supply" in the United States, labeled M1, M2, and M3. **M1** is the narrowest transactions definition of money, the most common definition, and the one we have been using. It consists of the items in Table 14.1, those financial securities that are routinely used for transactions. **M2** consists of M1 plus limited-checking money market deposit accounts and various kinds of very highly liquid small savings accounts with balances under $100,000, such as money market mutual funds, passbook savings accounts, and certificates of deposit. It also includes some very short-term deposit accounts in European financial institutions held by U.S. citizens. M2 is much larger than M1, $3,473.6 billion on average in 1992, compared with $966.6 billion for M1. **M3,** the broadest definition of money, consists of M2 plus various kinds of large deposit accounts with balances exceeding $100,000, including institutional money market mutual funds and European accounts held by U.S. citizens. M3 in 1992 was $4,177.4 billion. Table 14.2 summarizes the three different versions of the U.S. money supply.

Many economists favor M2 over M1 as the better definition of money because money market deposit accounts are used for transactions and small savings accounts are routinely converted into Federal Reserve Notes or checking accounts for spending purposes. Also, the velocity of circulation defined in terms of M2 is slightly more stable than is the velocity defined in terms of M1. The average annual change in M2 velocity during the 1980s, plus or minus, was 3.6 percent, compared with 4.2 percent for M1.[4] This implies that controlling the amount of M2 has more predictable effects on national income than does controlling the amount of M1. In contrast, only a few economists favor M3 as the definition of money because large savings accounts are seldom converted directly into Federal Reserve Notes or checking accounts. We will continue to use the narrow M1 definition in this text because it is most closely tied to the defining characteristic of money as the medium of exchange.

THE UNIT OF ACCOUNT   The **unit of account** is the standard that defines the value of goods and services in exchange. The dollar is the unit of account in the United States; the value in exchange of each good or service is its price expressed in terms of dollars. All the developed market economies use their currencies as the unit of account. The yen is the unit of account in Japan, the franc in France, and so forth.

Having a unit of account is absolutely essential to the operation of a modern developed economy. Economic agents have to know the relative values of goods and services when deciding how much of any one good to buy or sell.

LIQUID ASSET

A financial asset that is easily converted into money.

M1

The narrowest definition of money, consisting of those financial securities that are routinely accepted for transactions; the sum of currency and balances in checking accounts with unlimited checking privileges.

M2

A definition of money, consisting of M1 plus limited-checking money market deposit accounts and various kinds of very highly liquid small savings accounts with balances under $100,000.

M3

A broad definition of money, consisting of M2 plus various kinds of large deposit accounts with balances exceeding $100,000, including institutional money market mutual funds and European accounts held by U.S. citizens.

UNIT OF ACCOUNT

The standard that defines the value of goods and services in exchange.

---

[4]The data for M2 velocity are from the same sources as M1 velocity on page 427.

charge 9 percent interest on car loans, yet pay only 4 percent interest on their NOW accounts.

The practice of banks lending the funds deposited with them is reputed to have started with the goldsmiths in England during the eighteenth century. Before the reign of Charles I, merchants in England stored the full-bodied gold coins that they received from selling their wares in the Tower of London for safekeeping. Charles I broke the trust by expropriating some of the gold, at which point the merchants began storing their gold with private goldsmiths. The goldsmiths originally earned their profit by charging a fee for storing the coins. They soon realized, however, that they did not have to keep all the gold coins in storage because not all the depositors would seek to withdraw their coins at the same time. They could greatly increase their profits by lending some of the gold coins, with interest, to other merchants. All they had to do was keep some coins on hand to meet day-to-day requests for withdrawal. The result was that more gold coins circulated throughout the economy; the money supply increased.

Modern banks follow the same principle as the goldsmiths. They keep only a small fraction of the funds deposited with them on hand for day-to-day transactions and lend the rest. The result is that the amount of checking account balances increases.

LENDING TO INCREASE THE AMOUNT OF CHECKING ACCOUNT BALANCES   The easiest way to see that bank loans create new checking account balances is to consider the line-of-credit arrangement that banks commonly have with businesses. A line of credit means that the bank stands willing to lend to the business any amount up to some maximum amount, the line of credit. In return, the business may agree to keep a certain checking account balance with the bank, on average.

Suppose that a business negotiates a $10 million loan with the loan officer of a bank as part of its $50 million line of credit. The loan transaction begins just as in the borrower-lender transaction described above. The bank draws up a loan contract that stipulates the terms of the loan, which is simultaneously a new asset for the bank/lender and a new liability for the business/borrower. The second half of the transaction differs from the earlier example, however. Instead of transferring funds that it has on hand, the loan officer goes to her computer terminal and simply creates a new $10 million checking account balance for the business. The business can then write checks on the $10 million account. The $10 million account is quite literally a new configuration of electrons created and stored on a computer disk.

Table 14.7 illustrates how the line-of-credit loan affects the balance sheets of the bank and the business. The $10 million loan, as indicated, is simultaneously an asset for the bank and a liability for the business. The newly created $10 million checking account balance is simultaneously an asset of the business and a liability of the bank. Remember the rule: Money is an asset to anyone who holds it and a liability to the bank that issues it. The money in this case is the checking account. The money supply has increased by $10 million as a result of the bank loan.

Central banks in other countries increase the amount of their nations' currencies in essentially the same way. They make loans and give the borrowers newly printed currency—francs, yen, deutsche marks—which is simultaneously an asset of the borrower and a liability of the central bank.

TABLE 14.7   Commercial Bank Loans and Checking Accounts: Creating a New Checking Account Balance by Making a Loan

COMMERCIAL BANK		BUSINESS BORROWER	
Assets	Liabilities	Assets	Liabilities
Loan $10 million (+)	Checking account $10 million (+)	Checking account $10 million (+)	Loan $10 million (+)

Most loans to individuals are not line-of-credit loans. A bank does not create a new checking account for us when we take out a home mortgage or a car loan.[5] Instead, the bank gives us a cashier's check. Even so, the loan creates new checking account balances. We immediately give the check to the seller of the house or to the car dealer, and he or she deposits the check in his or her bank. New checking account balances are created as soon as the seller deposits the cashier's check.

Remember this whenever you have doubts that bank loans create new money in the form of checking account balances: Checking account balances are the most important component of the U.S. money supply, more than twice as large as the amount of Federal Reserve Notes in the United States. Banks do not simply lend FRN. We will take a closer look at the money creation process in Chapter 15. Our purpose here is just to establish the principle that bank loans create new money.

CALLING IN LOANS TO DECREASE THE AMOUNT OF CHECKING ACCOUNT BALANCES   The mortgage or the car loan that we take out is *secured* by the house or the car that is being financed; that is, the bank assumes ownership of our house or car if we default on the loan. In contrast, many business loans are *unsecured* loans. The bank cannot take ownership of any particular asset of the business if the business defaults on the loan. In return for getting unsecured loans, businesses often have to accept a *call feature* in the loan contract, which means that the bank has the right to call for immediate and full repayment of the loan at any time. Calling in unsecured loans decreases the amount of checking account balances as the loan is paid back.

The balance sheet implications of calling in a $10 million loan are exactly the reverse of the entries in Table 14.7. Just reverse all the signs. Calling in the loan *subtracts* both the loan and the checking account balances from the balance sheets of both the bank and the borrower. The checking account balances *decrease* by $10 million.

Calling in loans is a drastic measure that banks do not take under normal business conditions. When loans and checking account balances decrease in the banking system, they usually do so by a process of attrition. Old loans are being repaid and new loans issued all the time. Banks reduce the amount of their loans and checking account balances when they decide not to issue new loans as the old loans are repaid. The point is that the total amount of bank loans outstanding largely determines the total amount of checking account balances in the banking system. Similarly, central banks in other countries can

---

[5]An exception is the home equity loan, in which we receive a line of credit to write checks up to a maximum amount.

14. Commercial banks and the other depository institutions primarily use the borrower-lender transaction to increase and decrease the amount of their checking account balances. Banks create new checking account balances when they make loans. Banks reduce the amount of checking account balances when they call in loans or decide not to write new loans as old loans are repaid. Central banks in other countries primarily use the borrower-lender transaction to increase and decrease their currencies because, unlike the Fed, they do not have anything as convenient as the outstanding Treasury debt to trade.

15. Money is an asset to anyone who holds it; it is a liability of the bank that issues it.

KEY TERMS

asset
balance sheet
bank run
currency
demand for money
equation of exchange
Federal Reserve Banking System

Federal Reserve Note
liability
liquid asset
M1
M2
M3
medium of exchange

money
net worth
open market operation
store of value
transactions deposit
unit of account
velocity of circulation

QUESTIONS

1. a. Who owns most of the regular checking accounts, and why do they use them? Who owns most of the NOW accounts, and why do they prefer them over regular checking accounts?
   b. Why are credit card transactions not classified as part of the money supply?

2. What is the difference between money and income?

3. a. What is the velocity of circulation, and how is it related to the national product?
   b. Suppose that the velocity of circulation is 5 and the dollar value of the economy's national product (national income) is $6 trillion. How large is the money supply in the economy?

4. a. How would you measure your demand for money?
   b. What are some of the reasons why you and others hold money? Do your motives differ somewhat for Federal Reserve Notes and for checking account balances?

5. What are the main functions of money? Does money have competitors (actual or potential) for any or all of these functions? If yes, give an example of a competitor.

6. a. What is the difference between the M1 and M2 definitions of money?
   b. Why do some economists favor M2 over M1 as the better definition of money?
   c. What arguments can be made for using M1 as the definition of money?

7. a. Are Federal Reserve Notes backed by anything tangible?

b. Why are Federal Reserve Notes considered to be part of the money supply?
   c. Are they the most important component of the money supply?
   d. Why has paper currency replaced full-bodied coins made of precious metals as the primary form of currency throughout the world?

8. Show how the following transactions affect the balance sheets (assets and liabilities) of Joe and Sue.
   a. Joe initially has $5,000 of Federal Reserve Notes, and Sue initially has 1,000 shares of stock valued at $25 per share. Joe then buys 100 shares of stock from Sue.
   b. Joe initially has $5,000 of Federal Reserve Notes. Instead of selling her stock, Sue borrows $3,000 from Joe.

9. a. How does the Fed increase or decrease the amount of Federal Reserve Notes outstanding through Open Market Operations? Show how the balance sheets of the Fed and the securities dealers are affected by these Open Market Operations.
   b. How do central banks in other countries that do not have large amounts of government debt increase and decrease their money supplies?

10. Why does the money supply increase when a commercial bank makes a loan to a business customer as part of a line-of-credit agreement? Show how the balance sheets of the commercial banks and the business customers are affected by these loans.

15

The Monetary System
of the United States

LEARNING OBJECTIVES

CONCEPTS TO LEARN

Federal Reserve Banking System	Money multiplier
Reserves	Savings and loan associations
The reserve requirement	

CONCEPTS TO RECALL

U.S. money supply [14]	Open Market Operation [14]
The Fed [14]	Balance sheet, assets, and liabilities [14]
Commercial banks (depository institutions) [14]	

hapter 15 considers the institutional details of the U.S. monetary system that play a role in determining the growth of the money supply. Most beginning economics students have very little knowledge of the U.S. monetary system. They have heard of the Fed and the depository institutions, but the world of money and finance is one big puzzle to them. If this is true of you, keep in mind as you begin that there are three main pieces to the puzzle: the Federal Reserve Banking System (the Fed), the depository institutions, and the nonbank public.

The Fed is the nation's central bank. It is in charge of issuing the nation's currency, the Federal Reserve Notes, and of conducting monetary policy. The depository institutions are the hub of the monetary system, standing in the middle between the Fed and the nonbank public. They are private-sector firms that issue the largest component of the U.S. money supply that the Fed is charged with controlling, the transaction deposits or checking accounts. The households, businesses, and government agencies within the nonbank public are the direct link between the money supply and the overall performance of the economy. They hold the money and use it to finance purchases of goods and services and of various kinds of financial securities, such as stocks and bonds.

After reading Chapter 15 you will understand the basic functions of the Fed and the depository institutions. You will also see how the three pieces of the monetary puzzle fit together in such a way that the Fed is able to gain control over the amount of checking account balances in the depository institutions. The Fed cannot hope to control the growth of the money supply and conduct an effective monetary policy if it cannot limit the depository institutions' ability to make loans and create new checking accounts.

Our tour of the U.S. monetary system begins with the Federal Reserve Banking System, the nation's central bank, which sits at the top of the system.

THE FEDERAL RESERVE BANKING SYSTEM

Federal Banking Legislation

The Federal Reserve Banking System evolved to its current structure and functions in a series of distinct steps since its founding in 1913. The three main pieces of legislation relating to the Fed are the Federal Reserve Act of 1913, the National Banking Acts of 1933 and 1935, and the Depository Institutions Deregulation and Monetary Control Act of 1980.

FEDERAL RESERVE ACT OF 1913

An act of Congress that established the Federal Reserve Banking System, the first true central bank in the United States.

THE FEDERAL RESERVE ACT OF 1913   The Congress established the nation's first true central bank with the passage of the **Federal Reserve Act of 1913.** Its motives for having a central banking system were essentially twofold. The Treasury wanted a central bank to serve as its financial agent in international transactions and currency exchanges with England and the rest of Western Europe. Trade between the United States and these countries was increasing, and most of them had central banks. Closer to home, and far more important,

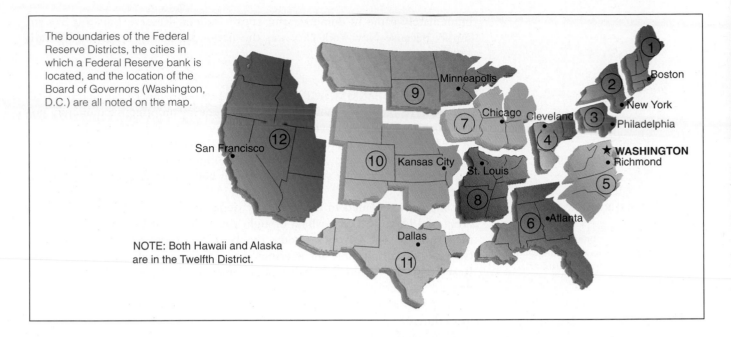

The boundaries of the Federal Reserve Districts, the cities in which a Federal Reserve bank is located, and the location of the Board of Governors (Washington, D.C.) are all noted on the map.

NOTE: Both Hawaii and Alaska are in the Twelfth District.

the Congress wanted a central bank that would act as a lender of last resort to the nation's private banks to prevent runs on the banks.

The United States had just been through a serious run on its banks that resulted in the Panic of 1907, the latest in a series of financial panics that had plagued the country throughout its history. Bank runs can easily feed on themselves and cause widespread bank failures without a central bank. If one major bank gets into financial trouble, its depositors begin a run on the bank as they rush to close their deposit accounts in exchange for currency. The bank is then sure to fail because it cannot meet all the depositors' claims for currency. Depositors in other healthy banks see what is happening, become nervous, and begin runs of their banks, which also cannot met the depositors' claims. So other banks begin to fail. Finally, sheer panic sets in when enough large banks have failed, and the entire banking system is threatened with a domino-like collapse.

A central bank can prevent the bank runs by standing ready to lend currency to any private bank threatened by a run. Once nervous depositors realized that they can exchange their deposits for currency, the bank runs are nipped in the bud, calm is restored, and the nation avoids a financial panic. Congress envisioned in 1913 that preventing bank runs would be the primary function of the Fed.

The Congress set up the Federal Reserve Banking System as a separate and independent nonprofit governmental body that was not subject to the direct control and oversight of either the Congress or the administration. The United States was divided into 12 geographic regions, each with its own Federal Reserve Bank located in a major city within the region. Figure 15.1 shows the current regional structure of the Federal Reserve Banking System and indicates where the 12 Federal Reserve Banks are located.

The 12 Federal Reserve Banks operated more or less as separate entities in the beginning, responsible only to their own regions. The banks even carried on their own Open Market Operations. The result was that the New York Fed

FIGURE 15.1

The Federal Reserve System

The Federal Reserve Banking System is divided into twelve geographic districts throughout the United States. Each district is served by a Federal Reserve Bank located in one of the major cities within each district. The map indicates the geographical boundaries of each Federal Reserve district and the location of the twelve Federal Reserve Banks.

SOURCE: Reprinted by permission from *Economics*, second edition, by Roger A. Arnold. Copyright © 1992 by West Publishing Company. All rights reserved.

ELABORATION: Most diehard conservatives who are extremely skeptical of government intervention in the economy concede the need for a central bank to take control of the money supply. The supply of money could be determined privately by the Laws of Supply and Demand, but this arrangement tends to make financial markets highly unstable. The frequent financial panics in the United States before 1913 are testimony to the need for a guiding hand over the money supply.

immediately came to dominate the entire Federal Reserve Banking System, simply because New York City was the nation's financial center in the early 1900s.

THE NATIONAL BANKING ACTS OF 1933 AND 1935   Having 12 autonomous Federal Reserve Banks was not conducive to operating an effective monetary policy. The arrangement proved disastrous at the onset of the Great Depression in 1929. The Federal Reserve Banks stood by and let bank after bank fail within their regions from 1929 to 1933. The money supply fell by one-third at a time when the money supply should have been increasing to support aggregate demand.

Congress responded to the monetary debacle with the **National Banking Acts of 1933 and 1935,** which brought the 12 Federal Reserve Banks under the control of one governing body, the **Board of Governors.** The Board of Governors is responsible for overseeing the operations of the entire Federal Reserve Bank System. It consists of seven members appointed by the president to 14-year terms, with one member replaced every two years. The long-term appointments are designed to keep the Board of Governors free of political influence.

The National Banking Acts also established the **Federal Open Market Committee (FOMC)** to formulate and execute a single, nationwide Open Market policy. The FOMC is made up of the seven members of the Board of Governors plus five presidents of Federal Reserve Banks, one of whom is the president of the New York Fed. Today the FOMC meets about eight times each year to set the course of monetary policy consistent with the four macroeconomic policy goals. As noted in Chapter 14, the Trading Desk at the New York Fed conducts the purchases and sales of Treasury securities on behalf of the FOMC.

Finally, the National Banking Acts gave the Board of Governors a number of financial regulatory powers, including the ability to set interest rate ceilings on various savings and time deposits and margin (borrowing) limits on purchases of common stock on the stock exchanges.

THE DEPOSITORY INSTITUTIONS DEREGULATION AND MONETARY CONTROL ACT OF 1980   The final landmark piece of legislation in the evolution of the Federal Reserve Banking System was the **Depository Institutions Deregulation and Monetary Control Act of 1980 (DIDMCA).** DIDMCA brought all financial institutions that accept deposit accounts of any kind, the **depository institutions,** under the control of the Fed. The depository institutions include the commercial banks and the so-called thrifts, which consist of the savings and loan associations, savings banks, and credit unions. In return, the depository institutions receive all the banking services offered by the Fed, including lender-of-last-resort protection. Before 1980 the Fed's control extended only to the commercial banks, and then only to those commercial banks that chose to be members of the Federal Reserve Banking System.

DIDMCA also phased out all interest rate ceilings on savings accounts and other time deposits, such as certificates of deposit, between 1980 and 1986. The only important restrictions on deposit accounts today are the two noted in Chapter 14: Depository institutions cannot offer an interest rate on regular checking accounts, and most businesses cannot own interest-bearing NOW accounts.

NATIONAL BANKING ACTS OF 1933 AND 1935

Acts of Congress that brought the 12 Federal Reserve Banks under the control of one governing body, the Board of Governors.

BOARD OF GOVERNORS (FEDERAL RESERVE)

The seven-member governing body that oversees and controls the Federal Reserve Banking System.

FEDERAL OPEN MARKET COMMITTEE (FOMC)

A 12-member committee of the Fed that formulates and executes the Fed's purchases and sales of Treasury securities on the Open Market in the conduct of monetary policy.

DEPOSITORY INSTITUTIONS DEREGULATION AND MONETARY CONTROL ACT OF 1980 (DIDMCA)

An act of Congress that brought all depository institutions under the control of the Fed.

DEPOSITORY INSTITUTION

A financial institution that accepts deposit accounts of any kind.

The Functions of the Federal Reserve Bank System

The Federal Reserve Banking System performs a number of important functions and services as the nation's central bank. The Fed

1. issues the national paper currency, the Federal Reserve Notes.
2. acts as a lender of last resort to prevent runs on banks.
3. supervises the depository institutions to ensure that they engage in sound banking practices.
4. operates 48 clearinghouses nationwide that keep track of the entire stream of payments among the depository institutions. For instance, the clearinghouses inform every institution at the end of each day of the volume of checks written against its deposit accounts and the volume of checks deposited to its accounts. Having large clearinghouses keep track of the flow of checks is much cheaper than having each institution keep track of its own deposit accounts.
5. acts as the fiscal agent of the U.S. Treasury. The Treasury maintains its own checking accounts at the Federal Reserve Banks. It deposits checks from taxes and fees into these accounts as they come in and writes checks against these accounts to finance government purchases and transfer payments. The Federal Reserve Banks also engage in exchanges of international currencies with other central banks and hold gold certificates that are backed by the gold owned by the federal government. The gold certificates are a holdover from the days prior to 1971 when the federal government stood willing to convert dollars held by foreign citizens into gold certificates. Until 1993 the Fed also served as the broker for selling all new issues of Treasury securities. Now securities dealers perform this function.
6. holds reserves against deposits for the depository institutions (these reserve accounts are described below).
7. is fully responsible for formulating and conducting the nation's monetary policy. The Fed's Open Market Operations are the primary means that it uses to control the growth of the money supply.

The rest of the chapter will focus on the first, sixth, and seventh functions, which are closely related and lie at the heart of increases and decreases in the nation's money supply.[1]

CURRENT ISSUE: The volume of transactions recorded by the Fed's clearinghouse system, called CHIPS, equals the value of the GDP, approximately $6 trillion, every 2½ days. (*The Economist*, October 17, 1992, p. 95.)

The Depository Institutions

The commercial banks hold the lion's share of all the transactions deposits, both the regular checking accounts and the NOW accounts, so we will concentrate on them in describing the U.S. monetary system. The appendix to Chapter 15 discusses the widespread failures of the savings and loan associations during the 1980s and the subsequent taxpayer bailout of their depositors. The savings and loan failures were a serious matter because they ended up wasting a lot of resources on bad investments. They had little effect on the U.S. money supply, however.

[1]For a booklet that describes the history, structure, and functions of the Federal Reserve System, see Board of Governors of the Federal Reserve System, *The Federal Reserve System: Purposes and Functions* (Washington, D.C.: U.S. Government Printing Office, 1984). Another excellent source on the history of the Federal Reserve System is T. Simpson, *Money, Banking, and Economic Analysis*, third edition (Englewood Cliffs, NJ: Prentice-Hall, 1987), chapter 10, pp. 195–215.

TABLE 15.2

Assets

RESERVE REQUI

The minimum aver
deposit account bala
banks (and other de
must maintain over
period.

16

Monetary Policy

LEARNING OBJECTIVES

CONCEPTS TO LEARN

Transactions demand for money

Precautionary demand for money

Speculative demand for money

Loan markets

Practical limitations of U.S. monetary policy

Interest rates

CONCEPTS TO RECALL

Long-run economic growth [3, 6]

Laws of Supply and Demand [5]

New Keynesian economics [9]

Monetary policy [9, 15]

Equilibrium level of national income [10]

Balance sheet, assets, and liabilities [14]

Demand for money [14]

Open Market Operation [14, 15]

Money multiplier [15]

he chairmanship of the Fed may well be the most powerful economic position in the world. The current chairman, Alan Greenspan, controls the money supply of the world's largest economy and does so without having to answer directly to the Congress, the administration, or anyone else.

Most economists believe that changes in the money supply affect both the circular flow of goods and services and the interest rates in U.S. financial markets. This means that Greenspan has considerable influence over each of the four macroeconomic policy goals in the United States. It also means that the whole world hangs on Greenspan's every word about U.S. monetary policy. Imports by the United States are nearly 20 percent of all the world's imports. The economic fate of most nations is closely tied to that of the United States; it has been said that the world sneezes when the United States catches a cold. Also, money flows into and out of U.S. financial markets from all corners of the earth as U.S. interest rates rise and fall.

The power of the chairmanship has its limitations, however. Paul Volcker, chairman of the Fed under Presidents Carter and Reagan, is often credited with helping to bring down inflation from 13 percent in 1979 to 3.8 percent by 1982 when he clamped down on the growth of the money supply. He is also credited with plunging the economy into the recession of 1981–82, the worst recession in the United States since the Great Depression. The chairman of the Fed cannot overcome the inherent conflicts among the macroeconomic policy goals, the power of the chairmanship notwithstanding. We will also see that monetary policy cannot hope to fine tune the economy any more than fiscal policy can.

Chapter 16 analyzes the effects of monetary policy on the economy. The Fed has full responsibility for the conduct of monetary policy in the United States.

Any discussion of monetary policy must begin by acknowledging that monetary policy lies at the center of the controversy between the new Keynesian and the new classical economists. The new Keynesian economists believe that monetary policy has a significant impact on the circular flow of goods and services. In their view, changes in the money supply affect the level and the composition of aggregate demand, which in turn affects real national income and influences each of the four macroeconomic policy goals. The new classical economists believe that the causal link between the money supply and the real side of the economy is just the reverse. In their view, changes in the money supply follow, rather than cause, the circular flow of real goods and services for the most part. They argue that monetary policy has a direct and a significant causal effect only on the rate of inflation in both the short run and the long run.

Our analysis of monetary policy in Chapter 16 continues with the new Keynesian assumptions employed in Chapters 10 through 13. The policy horizon is the short run. Wages and prices are fixed, and the economy is operating far below its production possibilities frontier with lots of unemployed resources, so that changes in aggregate demand affect real national income. Macro economists agree that monetary policy does have short-run effects described in this chapter under these assumptions. The issue that divides the new Keynesian and the new classical economists is whether these are the proper assumptions for modeling the economy in the short run.

Chapter 19 will consider the effects of monetary policy over the long run when wages and prices are flexible, as the new classical economists believe. Macro economists agree that the primary effect of monetary policy is on inflation under these conditions.

Our main goal in Chapter 16 is to understand the short-run effects of monetary policy on two key economic variables, the equilibrium level of (real) national income and interest rates (and other rates of return on assets). Chapter 16 brings interest rates into our analysis of macroeconomics for the first time. They are not one of the four macroeconomic policy goals, but they have a direct impact on many of the goals.

THE ECONOMIC EFFECTS OF MONETARY POLICY

The economic effects of monetary policy depend to some extent on the nature of the financial sector within a country: the kinds of financial institutions and markets it has, how they are structured, and how they operate. The financial sectors of the developed market economies differ considerably from one another. For instance, we noted in Chapter 14 that the Fed alone among the world's central banks relies primarily on the exchange-of-assets method to increase or decrease the money supply. In addition, the United States has far and away the largest and most highly developed financial sector. It has the largest number of banks and other financial institutions positioned between the ultimate savers and the ultimate investors in the economy, and by far the largest volume and the widest variety of financial securities are traded on its financial markets. Another difference among the developed market economies is the degree of independence between their financial and their nonfinancial business sectors. For example, many of the leading financial institutions in Japan are closely aligned with leading manufacturing firms, whereas in the United States the financial sector operates far more independently from the manufacturing sector.

These differences notwithstanding, the principal economic effects of monetary policy are essentially the same in all the developed market economies. For this reason we want to begin our analysis of monetary policy in a simple way that abstracts from the particular institutional details of the U.S. financial sector. This will allow us to see the fundamental principles of monetary policy that apply to any developed market economy. With the fundamental principles in hand, we can then add some of the important institutional details that influence the conduct and the effectiveness of monetary policy in the United States.

A Money Rain: Expansionary Monetary Policy

The abstract device that economists use to understand the main economic effects of expansionary monetary policy is called a **money rain.** The idea is this. Imagine that the economy is initially in complete equilibrium. Supply equals demand in *all* markets, real or financial, every product market, every factor market, and the markets for every financial security, including money. Suddenly the central bank decides to engage in an expansionary monetary policy and inject new money into the economy. It prints the money and loads

MONEY RAIN

An abstract device used by economists to represent an increase in the money supply that imagines the new money falling from the sky.

it into helicopters, which fly over the countryside dropping the money. The skies are filled with a rain of money, and people from households and business firms rush out to grab the money as it falls to the ground.

Another less dramatic way of imaging a money rain is to think of the central bank mailing the newly printed money to some households and businesses that it has selected at random. This then gives us a simple way of describing a contractionary monetary policy that decreases the money supply. The central bank could write to randomly selected households and businesses and require them to send back some of their money.

The rain of new money upsets the initial equilibrium in the economy as the households and businesses react to the infusion of new money. Their immediate reaction centers on the asset side of their balance sheets because money is an asset to households and businesses. Every household and business firm had the exact composition of assets that it wanted as part of the overall equilibrium in the economy before the money rain. The new money upsets the composition of their assets; they now have too much money and too few of all other assets. The economic effects of the expansionary monetary policy result when households and businesses try to restore the proper proportions of assets on their balance sheets. Let's take a look at the assets held by households and businesses to see exactly what happens.

THE ASSETS HELD BY HOUSEHOLDS AND BUSINESS FIRMS Table 16.1 lists the more important assets that appear on the balance sheets of households and business firms. The assets are both real and financial assets. Each household or business firm might not have every asset listed, but these are the assets that we would find on the aggregate balance sheets of the household and the business sectors.

We will begin with the households. Their real assets are houses, other real estate, and consumer durables, such as automobiles and the major household appliances—refrigerators, washing machines, and the like. These real assets are

TABLE 16.1 Assets of Households and Business Firms

| | HOUSEHOLDS | | | BUSINESS FIRMS | |
	Assets			Assets	
Financial assets	FRN Checking accounts Savings deposits Certificates of deposit Money market accounts Stocks Corporate bonds Treasury bonds State and local bonds Insurance		Financial assets	FRN Checking accounts Savings deposits Certificates of deposit Money market accounts Stocks Corporate bonds Treasury bonds State and local bonds Insurance Accounts receivable	
Real assets	Consumer durables Houses Other real estate		Real assets	Plant and equipment Inventories	

all goods that are expected to last more than a year. As noted in Chapter 8, the purchase of a consumer durable is really a form of saving, even though it is counted as a component of consumption expenditures in the national accounts and is a part of aggregate demand. Households buy real assets today to receive and consume a future stream of services associated with using the asset—transporation from their cars, the storage of food in their refrigerators, and so forth. The purchase of a house is also a form of saving. Once again, households are trading consumption today when they buy houses in exchange for future consumption in the form of housing services. The purchase of a new home is simultaneously considered to be part of investment in the national accounts and part of aggregate demand.

The purchase or holding of financial assets is the other way in which households save. They have a lot of choices—money, various kinds of savings and time deposits such as passbook savings accounts and certificates of deposit, stocks, corporate and government bonds, and insurance. The items listed in the table are just a partial menu of the kinds of financial securities available to households as a means of saving some of their current income for future consumption.

Turn next to the business firms. The real assets are the productive capital of the firms, that is, the plant, equipment, and inventories that they use in producing and selling their products. Purchases of new plant and equipment and increases in inventories represent investment in physical capital, which is part of aggregate demand.

The financial assets are the various ways in which businesses can save to finance their future investments. Their choices are generally the same as for households, with a few exceptions. The most notable difference is *accounts receivable*, which refers to the value of goods that a firm has sold, but has not yet received payment for. Accounts receivable are an important financial asset for many firms, whereas they would seldom appear on households' balance sheets. In addition, corporations are restricted in the types of stocks that they can hold in other corporations, and corporations hold most of the non-interest-bearing regular checking accounts.

Households and business firms tend to hold a variety of assets for two reasons. The first is that different assets offer different kinds of services. Each real asset provides a future stream of specific consumption services to households or a future stream of specific productive services to business firms. In contrast, financial assets usually provide a future stream of income that can be used to purchase a variety of goods and services. Many financial assets offer their own distinctive services as well. Money provides transactions services in its role as the medium of exchange. Savings deposits are very safe and highly liquid short-term assets. Corporate stocks provide equity in the form of a share in the profits of the firm. The future income stream with stocks is fairly uncertain, but has the potential for very large gains in some instances. Corporate and government bonds, in contrast, yield a known stream of future income if they are held until they mature. Insurance provides financial protection against ill health, an accident, or an untimely death much more cheaply than do other kinds of assets. In short, households and firms can buy a variety of valued services by spreading their saving over a broad range of assets. They are said to diversify their portfolios of assets in this way.

Diversifying assets has the additional advantage of reducing risk. Buying assets is inherently risky because the future returns on most assets cannot be known with certainty. We do not know for sure what interest rates or stock prices will be a year from now, or whether the roof on our house will leak and cost $6,000 to replace. Savers can reduce the risk they expose themselves to by purchasing a variety of assets whose returns are uncorrelated with one another. Roughly speaking, two assets are uncorrelated if the economic conditions that tend to make the returns on one of the assets exceptionally high (exceptionally low) are different from the economic conditions that tend to make the returns on the other asset exceptionally high (exceptionally low). A portfolio containing a mixture of money, deposits of various kinds, stocks, bonds, and real estate is less risky than is a portfolio with the same average rate of return that contains only one kind of stock. In short, people know that they should not put all their eggs in one basket.

Households have to determine the proper size and composition of their asset holdings as part of solving their economic problems. How much do they want to save for the future? What kinds of services do they want from their assets, both real and financial? What trade-offs are they willing to accept between risk and return? The answers to these questions determine the level and the composition of the assets on their balance sheets.

The same point applies to business firms. Firms have to decide how much and what kinds of capital to use in producing and selling their goods and services. This is the how-to-produce part of their economic problem, and the decisions they make determine the level and the composition of the real assets on their balance sheets. They also have to decide how much they should save for future investment and in what form—how much money they should hold, what kinds of insurance they need and how much of each, and how many accounts receivable they are willing to carry. These decisions determine the level and the composition of the financial assets on their balance sheets.

ADJUSTING TO NEW MONEY   The central bank's money rain upsets the equilibrium that households and firms have achieved on the asset side of their balance sheets. They now have more money than they had planned on holding, and their reaction is entirely predictable. They will get rid of some of the money and buy other assets to restore the proper composition of assets on their balance sheets. Each person might not buy more of every asset. Some people may use the new money to buy a car; others may buy more insurance or a certificate of deposit; still others may exchange the money for a mix of assets. The same holds true for each business firm. In the aggregate, though, the demand for all other assets increases. The excess supply of money creates an excess demand for all other assets, real and financial, throughout the economy. The effects of monetary policy result when people and firms exchange the new money for other real and financial assets.

Notice, though, that the new money gives rise to an apparent paradox. People and firms are trying to get rid of the money, but in the aggregate they cannot succeed. The new money does not disappear. The only way that the economy can return to equilibrium is if the demand for money increases to meet the new higher supply of money. For example, suppose that the money supply was initially $100 and the money rain increases the money supply to $150. The demand for money must have been $100 before the money rain for the economy to be in equilibrium. Immediately after the money rain the supply of money is $150, but the demand still only $100. Money is in excess supply, which is what leads households and firms to seek out other assets.

The equilibrium in the economy can be restored only when the demand for money rises to $150 to meet the new supply of $150. But the demand for money is the amount of money that households and firms are willing to *hold*, and not spend on other assets. In other words, the process of trying to get rid of money has to generate economic effects that simultaneously increase the demand for money so that households and firms are eventually willing to hold the new money.

The study of monetary policy, then, raises two questions:

1. What are the effects of an expansionary monetary policy? What happens in the economy as households and firms try to get rid of the new money and buy other assets?
2. How do the effects of an expansionary monetary policy feed back into the demand for money so that households and firms are eventually willing to hold the new money and stop trying to buy other assets? In other words, how does the economy return to equilibrium with a new, higher money supply?

THE DEMAND FOR REAL ASSETS   The first important effect of an expansionary monetary policy is that it increases the demand for real assets. Some households use their new money to buy houses and other consumer durables. They may also buy nondurable goods and services—food, entertainment, and so forth—that would not appear on a balance sheet, in which case their net worth decreases. In either event, the increase in money leads to an increase in consumption demand.

Similarly, some firms use their new money to buy new capital goods. They invest in plant and equipment or increase the level of their inventories. The increase in money also leads to an increase in investment demand.

The increase in consumption demand and investment demand represents an increase in aggregate demand, which increases the equilibrium level of income. Figure 16.1 illustrates.

Aggregate demand before the money rain is ADE_0, and the equilibrium level of national income is Y_0, at the intersection of ADE_0 and the 45° line. (We are ignoring the foreign sector at this point to keep the analysis as simple as possible.) The injection of new money into the economy through the money rain increases aggregate demand to ADE_1, as consumption demand increases from C_0^d to C_1^d and investment demand increases from I_0^d to I_1^d. The increase in aggregate demand leads to a multiplied increase in national income through the spending multiplier. The new equilibrium level of national income is Y_1, at the intersection of ADE_1 and the 45° line.

The analysis indicates that the amount of money in the economy is one of the "other things equal" that determines the level of aggregate demand on the *ADE*–45° line graph. The more money in the economy, the higher the level of aggregate demand, which is certainly what our intuition would suggest. The analysis also reveals the first important effect of an expansionary monetary policy on the economy: *An increase in the money supply increases aggregate demand and the equilibrium level of national income.*

NATIONAL INCOME AND THE DEMAND FOR MONEY   The increase in national income also increases the demand for money, which is necessary to restore

FIGURE 16.1

The Money Rain, Aggregate Demand, and National Income

A "money rain" that increases the supply of money increases aggregate demand as households and businesses exchange their excess money for real assets. The initial equilibrium level of national income is Y_0 before the money rain, at the intersection of ADE_0 and the 45° line. Households buy more consumer durables, which increases consumption demand from C_0^d to C_1^d. Households also buy new houses, and firms increase their purchases of plant and equipment and inventory, which increases invest demand from I_0^d to I_1^d. Therefore, aggregate demand increases to ADE_1 as a result of the money rain, and the new equilibrium level of national income is Y_1, at the intersection of ADE_1 and the 45° line. An increase in the money supply increases the equilibrium level of national income.

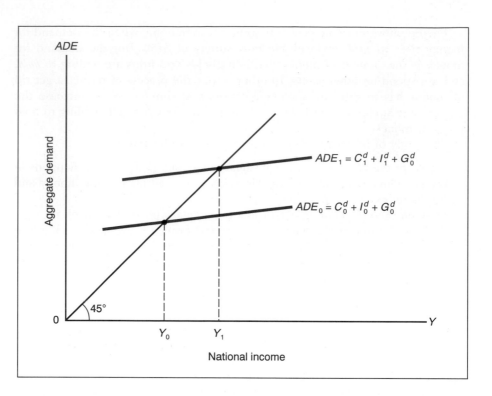

equilibrium to the households' and firms' balance sheets. The reason why is that money is the medium of exchange.

The primary motive supporting the demand for money is a transactions motive, to facilitate the purchases of goods and services. Households and businesses would have to take money out of other deposit accounts or call their brokers to sell stocks and bonds every time they wanted to buy something if they did not hold money. These transactions take time and energy and may even require the payment of fees such as bank service charges or brokerage fees. The value of holding money is that it avoids these transactions costs.

Money would not be an attractive asset if it were not the medium of exchange. Federal Reserve Notes and regular checking accounts do not offer a rate of return. NOW accounts do pay interest, but other equally safe and highly liquid assets such as passbook savings accounts, short-term certificates of deposit, and Treasury bills typically offer slightly higher rates of return than do NOW accounts.

Furthermore, the value of holding money increases the more that households and businesses spend. This is why high-income, high-spending individuals carry more FRN and keep larger checking account balances, on average, than do low-income, low-spending individuals. People can economize on money to some extent. Credit cards allow people to hold less money because they can pay off their credit card balances as soon as they deposit their paychecks. To the extent they do this, they do not have to hold money at all to pay for credit card transactions. Not all transactions use credit cards, however, so that the demand for money varies directly with households' spending and income. Similarly, larger businesses hold more money on average than do smaller businesses.

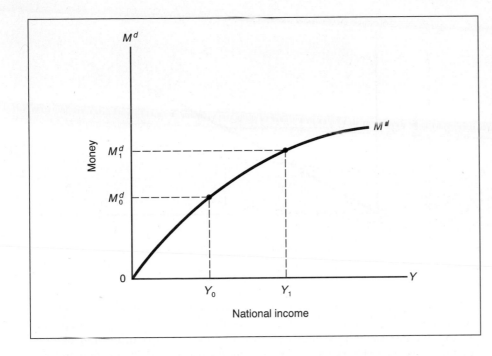

FIGURE 16.2

The Transactions Demand for Money

Households and businesses have a transactions demand for money because money is the medium of exchange for purchasing goods and services and factors of production. The quantity of money demanded for transactions purposes is directly related to the level of real national income as indicated by the transactions demand for money curve M^d. Real national income is on the horizontal axis and the transactions demand for money is on the vertical axis. The curve M^d is bowed downward because households and businesses can economize on their holdings of money as income increases. The money rain in our example increases the equilibrium level of national income from Y_0 to Y_1, which increases the quantity of money demanded for transactions purposes from M_0^d to M_1^d. The increase in the quantity of money demanded helps to restore the equilibrium between the supply of money and the demand for money following the money rain.

What is true for individual households and business firms applies to the entire economy. Refer to Figure 16.2. The demand for money is on the vertical axis, and (real) national income is on the horizontal axis. The figure shows that the demand for money varies directly with the level of national income. The quantity of money demanded is larger the higher national income is, and the quantity of money demanded is smaller the lower national income is. The direct relationship between the demand for money and national income is called the **transactions demand for money** because it derives from money's role as the medium of exchange. More national income means more spending in the nation's factor and product markets, and more spending causes households and firms to hold more money to facilitate the spending.

Notice that the demand for money is not a straight line. It bows downward to reflect the ability to economize on money as income and spending rise. Empirical studies suggest that the demand for money is nowhere near proportional to national income. A 1 percent increase in national income increases the quantity of money demanded by only about 0.6 percent in the United States.[1]

The two income levels pictured in Figure 16.2 are the same as those in Figure 16.1. Y_0 is the equilibrium level of national income before the money rain, and Y_1 is the equilibrium level of national income after the money rain. The increase in national income in turn increases the quantity of money demanded for transactions purposes from M_0^d before the money rain to M_1^d after the money rain. The transactions demand for money increases because households and firms are spending more at the new equilibrium.

TRANSACTIONS DEMAND FOR MONEY

The fundamental motive for holding money that derives from money's role as the medium of exchange; it says that the aggregate demand for money is directly related to real national income, directly related to the overall price level, and inversely related to interest rates and rates of return on other assets.

[1]This is the income elasticity reported in D. Jaffe, *Money, Banking, and Credit* (New York: Worth Publishers, 1989), 395.

FIGURE 16.3

The Overall Price Level and the Transactions Demand for Money

The quantity of money demanded for transactions purposes is directly proportional to the overall price level as indicated by the straight line M^d because money is denominated in nominal terms. A doubling of the overall price level from P_0 to P_1 on the horizontal axis doubles the quantity of money demanded from M_0^d to M_1^d on the vertical axis.

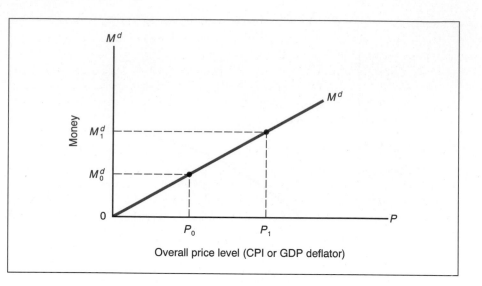

Overall price level (CPI or GDP deflator)

In conclusion, one of the important effects of the expansionary monetary policy, the increase in national income, simultaneously serves to increase the demand for money. The higher demand for money helps bring households' and firms' balance sheets back into an equilibrium in which the demand for money matches the new higher supply, so that the desire to get rid of the new money eventually ends.

One final point about the transactions demand for money needs to be stressed. The levels of national income pictured in Figures 16.1 and 16.2 refer, as always, to *real* or *constant dollar* national income. The transactions demand for money, however, is determined by the *nominal* or *current dollar* level of national income because Federal Reserve Notes and checking accounts are denominated in nominal dollar amounts. Figure 16.2 relates the demand for money to real income and spending, to the *number* of transaction that are made in the economy. But the demand for money also depends on the *dollar value* of those transactions, on the *prices* of the goods and services. Suppose, for example, that you are forced to spend twice as much to buy the same goods and services because the prices of all goods and services double. The doubling of prices doubles your transaction demand for money because you need twice as much money to pay for the same goods and services.

Figure 16.3 pictures the relationship between the transactions demand for money and a broad-based index of prices for goods and services, such as the consumer price index (CPI) or the gross domestic product (GDP) deflator. The level of real income or spending, the number of transactions, is being held constant in the figure. The relationship is a straight line because the demand for money increases in direct proportion to the increase in the price index, for a given number of transactions. For example, the quantity of money demanded for transactions purposes doubles from M_0^d to M_1^d when the price level doubles from P_0 to P_1.

THE DEMAND FOR FINANCIAL ASSETS   The new money in the economy also increases the demand for financial assets of all kinds, as households and business firms seek to exchange their money for other financial assets. The increase in the demand for financial assets decreases the interest rates and other rates of return on these assets. The decrease in interest rates and other rates of return on financial assets is the second important economic effect of an expansionary monetary policy.

We will illustrate the relationship between the demand for assets and their rates of return for two assets that households and businesses hold—savings deposits and corporate and government bonds—since this is the first time we have talked about rates of return on assets.

SAVINGS DEPOSITS   The following simple example shows why an increase in the demand for savings deposits decreases the interest rate on these deposits. Suppose that a commercial bank decided just before the money rain to attract $10 million in new saving deposits in order to increase its reserves so that it can make new loans. The bank managers figure that they have to offer an interest rate of 7 percent on the accounts to reach their $10 million target. The money rain occurs just as they are about to announce the 7 percent rate.

The money rain causes the bank managers to change their thinking about the interest rate needed to attract the $10 million of new savings deposits. They realize that households and businesses now have an excess supply of money that they are eager to exchange for other assets, including savings deposits. Consequently, they should be willing to accept a lower return on the deposits. So the bank managers decrease their interest rate offer to 6 percent, confident that 6 percent is now sufficient to attract $10 million of new deposits.

The example of savings deposits applies to any financial security that offers a rate of interest, such as money market deposit accounts and certificates of deposit. The attempt to get rid of the new money puts downward pressure on the interest rates of all interest-bearing financial securities.

CORPORATE OR GOVERNMENT BONDS   The increased demand for corporate and government bonds also lowers the rate of return available on them. We have to understand how to compute the rate of return on a bond to see why.

The standard bond contract between a borrower and a lender stipulates three conditions: the face value or principal on the bond, the annual interest *payment* on the bond (*not* the interest *rate)*, and the date that the bond matures. The *face value,* usually $1,000, is the amount the borrower agrees to pay back to the lender on the date when the bond matures. The annual interest payment is an additional payment that the borrower agrees to make each year to the lender until the maturity date. These three conditions never change throughout the life of the bond.

The *price* of the bond is the amount that someone pays for the bond contract with the three stated conditions. The price is a variable, even at issue when the contract is written. The price at issue is the amount of money the lender loans to the borrower, either a corporation or the government. It can be equal to, more than, or less than the face value of the bond, the amount of money that the borrower agrees to repay the lender when the bond matures. Once most corporate and government bonds are issued, they are traded on a secondary market through bond brokers and securities dealers, where the price is again a variable. The purchase and sale of an existing bond just changes the person to whom the borrower owes the annual interest payment and the $1,000 principal at the maturity date.

The rate of return available to a bondholder is inversely related to the price of the bond. To see why, suppose that today you purchase a $1,000 bond (the face value), which offers an annual interest payment of $80 and matures one year from now. You plan to hold the bond until it matures.

Your return on the bond during the year has two components. The first is the $80 interest payment. The second is the difference between the $1,000 that you will receive one year from today and the amount that you pay for the bond today. Call the purchase price today P_{Today}. The return on the bond is

$$\text{Return} = \text{interest payment} + (\text{face value} - P_{Today})$$
$$= \$80 + (\$1,000 - P_{Today})$$

Dividing the return by the purchase price today converts the return into a rate of return, labeled R_{Bond}.

$$R_{Bond} = [\text{interest payment} + (\text{face value} - P_{Today})]/P_{Today}$$
$$= [\$80 + (\$1,000 - P_{Today})]/P_{Today}$$

For example, suppose that you pay $995 for the bond. Then your rate of return during the year is 8.5 percent (to the nearest tenth of a percent).

$$R_{Bond} = [\$80 + (\$1,000 - \$995)]/\$995$$
$$= (\$80 + \$5)/\$995$$
$$= \$85/\$995 = .085 = 8.5\%$$

The rate of return on the bond decreases the higher the price of the bond. P_{Today} appears in both the numerator and the denominator in the rate-of-return calculation. The larger P_{Today}, the smaller the numerator and the larger the denominator, both of which decrease R_{Bond}. Conversely, the lower the price of the bond, the higher its rate of return.

For example, we saw that the rate of return is 8.5 percent if you pay $995 for the bond. The rate of return on this bond drops to 8 percent if you pay $1,000 for the bond.

$$R_{Bond} = [\$80 + (\$1,000 - \$1,000)]/\$1,000$$
$$= \$80/\$1,000 = .08 = 8\%$$

The rate of return on the bond falls below 8 percent if you pay more than $1,000 for the bond. For example, at a price of $1,025, the rate of return is 5.4 percent.

$$R_{Bond} = [\$80 + (\$1,000 - \$1,025)]/\$1,025$$
$$= (\$80 - \$25)/\$1,025$$
$$= \$55/\$1,025 = .054 = 5.4\%$$

You may wonder why anyone would pay more than $1,000 for a $1,000 bond. As the last example indicates, however, bonds priced at more than their face value still can yield a positive rate of return. You might be quite willing to pay $1,025 for this bond if the rates of return on other assets were in the 4 percent range.[2]

---

[2]If you plan to sell the bond before it matures, then the expected sales price replaces the $1,000 face value in the calculation, and the rate of return is an expected rate of return.

Many short-term bond contracts, such as Treasury bills that mature within one year, do not even have an interest payment. They just stipulate the $1,000 face value and a maturity date—say, six months from the date of issue. The price on Treasury bills must always be below $1,000 to yield a positive rate of return.

To summarize: *The price of a bond and the rate of return on a bond are inversely related.* The higher the price of a bond, the lower its rate of return; the lower the price of a bond, the higher its rate of return. This makes sense intuitively: The more you have to pay for a bond (or any asset), the less it is worth to you, other things equal.

Now return to our example of the money rain. Some households and firms with the new money are looking to exchange the money for corporate and government bonds. The increased demand for these bonds drives up their prices and decreases their rates of return to the new buyers.

You may have noticed that the sellers of the bonds after the money rain, those who had purchased the bonds sometime in the past, experience an increase in their rate of return as the bond prices rise. But the return to the sellers is irrelevant because it is a return on decisions made in the past. The relevant rate of return is the prospective return to the purchasers, the rate of return available to the households and firms that are trying to exchange their new money for bonds. The rate of return from their point of view decreases. Indeed, the sellers of the bonds are now in the same position. Having sold the bonds, they now have money to spend. If they try to buy other bonds with the money or put it is savings deposits, they will find that the rates of return on these assets have decreased.[3]

EXPANSIONARY MONETARY POLICY AND RATES OF RETURN   The examples of the savings deposits and bonds illustrate the general principle that an increase in demand for any financial asset lowers the rate of return on the asset to the purchasers. The money rain, by creating an excess supply of money and an excess demand for all other financial assets, lowers the rates of return on the financial assets. In conclusion: *An expansionary monetary policy lowers interest rates and other rates of return on financial assets.*

We will usually refer to the rates of return on financial securities as interest rates from here on, even though many rates of return are not in the form of interest rates, as we have just seen for bonds.

INTEREST RATES AND THE DEMAND FOR MONEY   The decline in interest rates following the money rain feeds back into the demand for money. It increases the quantity of money demanded and helps the economy return to equilibrium with the new, higher money supply.

The transactions demand for money is sensitive to the interest rates available on other financial assets because those interest rates define the opportunity cost of holding money. The higher the interest rates, the higher the opportunity cost of holding money, and the lower the interest rates, the lower the opportunity costs of holding money. For example, if one-year certificates of deposit offer a 10 percent rate of return, every $100 held as Federal Reserve Notes or deposited in a regular checking account sacrifices $10 of interest in-

---

[3]The same analysis applies to common stocks. The money rain increases the demand for stocks, which drives up stock prices and lowers the rate of return available on stocks to the new purchasers.

come that could have been earned on the certificate of deposit. In contrast, if one-year certificates of deposit offer only a 3 percent rate of return, holding $100 as Federal Reserve Notes or in a regular checking account sacrifices only $3 of interest income.

When deciding how much money to hold for transactions purposes, households and businesses have to compare the interest available on other assets with the time and the expense of converting these other assets to money whenever they want to buy something. The $10 of interest income offers more compensation for the time and the expense of converting to money than does the $3 of interest income. Therefore, the transactions demand for money is inversely related to interest rates on other financial assets. The higher the interest rates, the less money held for transactions purposes, and the lower the interest rates, the more money held for transactions purposes.

The opportunity cost of holding money in a NOW account is less than these examples indicate because NOW accounts pay interest. Interest rates on NOW accounts are typically less than interest rates on other liquid assets, however, because of their advantage as a medium of exchange. Therefore, the opportunity cost of holding a NOW account is still positive, so that the demand for NOW accounts is also inversely related to interest rates on other financial assets.

Economists have described two other motives for holding money besides the transactions motive; the precautionary motive and the speculative motive. These other motives also suggest an inverse relationship between the demand for money and interest rates.

PRECAUTIONARY DEMAND FOR MONEY

The motive for holding money to cover temporary and unexpected expenses or losses of income.

The **precautionary motive** says that households and businesses may keep some money on hand to cover temporary and unexpected expenses or losses of income, such as a medical emergency, a temporary spell of unemployment, or an unexpected increase in the price of heating oil. Money held for these purposes is undoubtedly quite small. These situations happen only infrequently, and households and firms can find many safe, highly liquid short-term assets to hold as a precautionary reserve that yield higher rates of return than does money. Money market mutual funds, U.S. Treasury bills, and passbook savings accounts are three such assets. To the extent a precautionary demand for money exists, however, the demand is likely to be highly sensitive and inversely related to interest rates on other highly liquid assets.

SPECULATIVE DEMAND FOR MONEY

The motive for holding money based on expectations of future interest rates.

Keynes proposed a **speculative motive** for holding money based on expectations of future interest rates. His idea was that people have a notion about what the "normal" or average rate of interest is on various financial assets. Interest rates move in cycles over time, just as national income and employment do. When interest rates rise above the "normal" range, people see this as a temporary situation because they expect interest rates to return to the "normal" levels. Therefore, they reduce their money holdings in exchange for the other assets in order to take advantage of the opportunity. Conversely, when interest rates fall below the "normal" range, people also see this as a temporary situation. They hold more money because they do not want to lock themselves into other financial assets when interest rates are unusually low. Instead, they are content to sacrifice some interest now and wait until the interest rates return to "normal." The speculative motive therefore also generates an inverse relationship between the demand for money and interest rates.

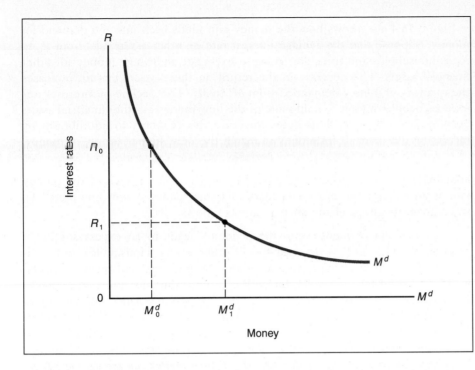

FIGURE 16.4

Interest Rates and the Demand for Money

The interest rate available on other financial assets defines the opportunity cost of holding money. Therefore, the demand for money is inversely related to the level of interest rates on other financial assets, as indicated by the demand for money curve M^d. The quantity of money demanded is on the horizontal axis and the average interest rate on other financial assets is on the vertical axis. The money rain in our example lowers the average interest rate on other financial assets from R_0 to R_1, which increases the quantity of money demanded from M_0^d to M_1^d. The increase in the quantity of money demanded helps to restore the equilibrium between the supply of money and the demand for money following the money rain.

The speculative motive may have been important in the recession of the early 1990s. Interest rates on money market funds, certificates of deposit, and other highly liquid assets fell to very low levels in 1991 and 1992, in the 2 to 4 percent range. Such low interest rates had not been observed for 20 years or more. At the same time, the demand for money skyrocketed, especially the demand for NOW accounts, which grew at annual rates in excess of 10 percent.[4] Households may have been waiting for interest rates to rise and were willing to sacrifice the small interest advantage of staying in other liquid assets. Interest rates on these assets were only about one percentage point above the interest rates on NOW accounts, so the sacrifice of holding NOW accounts in the meantime was not very large.

Figure 16.4 illustrates the inverse relationship between the demand for money and interest rates. Interest rates are on the vertical axis, and the demand for money is on the horizontal axis. For Federal Reserve Notes and regular checking accounts, interpret the interest rate on the vertical axis as the average interest rate on other liquid assets. For NOW accounts, interpret the interest rate as the difference between the average interest rate on other liquid assets and the interest rate on the NOW accounts. Notice that the quantity of money demanded remains fairly low for medium and high values of interest rates. Households and business firms prefer other liquid assets to money when interest rates are in this range because the opportunity cost of holding money is high. The quantity of money demanded increases substantially at very low interest rates, however, consistent with Keynes's speculative motive for holding money and the experience of 1991 and 1992.

---

[4]Council of Economic Advisers, *Economic Indicators, March 1993* (Washington, D.C.: U.S. Government Printing Office, 1993), 26.

Figure 16.4 also shows how the money rain feeds back into the demand for money. Suppose that the average interest rate on other assets falls from R_0 to R_1 as households and firms are trying to exchange their new money for other financial assets. The decrease in the return on these assets in turn increases the quantity of money demanded from M_0^d to M_1^d. The decline in interest rates induces people to want to hold more of the new money as other financial assets become less attractive. This helps to return the economy to equilibrium by increasing the demand for money to match the new, higher supply of money.

SUMMARY: AN EXPANSIONARY MONETARY POLICY   Our analysis of the money rain as an example of an expansionary monetary policy is now complete. To summarize, the steps of the analysis are as follows:

1. The injection of money into the economy leads to an excess supply of money and an excess demand for all other assets. Households and businesses want to exchange the new money for both real and financial assets.
2. The demand for real assets, for both consumer durables and capital goods, increases. The result is an increase in consumption demand and investment demand, which increases aggregate demand and the equilibrium level of national income. The demand for financial assets also increases, which decreases interest rates (and other rates of return) on these assets. Therefore, *an expansionary monetary policy has two important effects on the economy: It increases the equilibrium level of national income and reduces the average level of interest rates.*
3. The two effects of the expansionary monetary policy feed back into the demand for money and return the economy to equilibrium. The increase in national income increases the quantity of money demanded for transactions purposes because there is more spending on goods and services in the aggregate. The decrease in interest rates decreases the opportunity cost of holding money and further increases the quantity of money demanded.
4. The economy returns to equilibrium when national income increases by enough, and interest rates fall by enough, to increase the demand for money to the new, higher supply of money. Households and businesses are content to hold the new money at this point and they stop trying to exchange money for other real and financial assets. Their portfolio of assets is once again in equilibrium.

A Contractionary Monetary Policy

The analysis of a contractionary monetary policy, in which the central bank reduces the money supply, follows the analysis of an expansionary monetary policy step for step, with all the results reversed. Suppose that the Fed asked all households and businesses to mail some of their money back to the Fed. The reaction of the households and the businesses, and the return to equilibrium, would be as follows:

1. The reduction of money upsets the equilibrium that households and businesses had achieved in their portfolio of assets. They now have too little money and too much of all other assets. Money is in excess demand, and all other assets are in excess supply. Therefore, households and businesses

want to exchange real and financial assets for money to build up their money holdings.

2. The demand for real assets, both consumer durables and capital goods, decreases. This results in a decrease in consumption demand and investment demand, which decreases aggregate demand and the equilibrium level of national income. The demand for financial assets also decreases, which raises interest rates (and other rates of return) on these assets. Households and businesses are now taking money out of other deposit accounts and trying to sell assets such as corporate and government bonds. Interest rates on the deposit accounts rise as bank managers are forced to offer higher interest to hold on to these accounts. Bond prices fall in the sell-off, which raises the rates of return available on these assets to new purchasers.

Therefore, *a contractionary monetary policy has two important effects on the economy: It decreases the equilibrium level of national income and increases the average level of interest rates.*

3. The two effects of the contractionary monetary policy feed back into the demand for money and return the economy to equilibrium. The decrease in national income decreases the quantity of money demanded for transactions purposes because there is less spending on goods and services in the aggregate. The increase in interest rates increases the opportunity cost of holding money and further decreases the quantity of money demanded.

4. The economy returns to equilibrium when national income decreases by enough, and interest rates rise by enough, to decrease the demand for money to the new, lower supply for money. Households and businesses are content to hold the reduced amount of money at this point and they stop trying to exchange other real and financial assets for money. Their portfolio of assets is once again in equilibrium.

The following Concept Summary table summarizes the effects of expansionary and contractionary monetary policies on the equilibrium level of national income and interest rates.

CONCEPT SUMMARY

THE EFFECTS OF MONETARY POLICY ON REAL NATIONAL INCOME AND INTEREST RATES

MONETARY POLICY	REAL NATIONAL INCOME	INTEREST RATES
Expansionary (Fed buys Treasury securities on the Open Market)	Increase Y	Decrease R
Contractionary (Fed sells Treasury securities on the Open Market)	Decrease Y	Increase R

We are now in a position to consider the institutional details of how monetary policy works its way through the economy in the United States.

MONETARY POLICY IN THE UNITED STATES

The Fed does not drop money from helicopters or ask households and firms to mail money back to the Fed. We saw in Chapter 14 that the primary method of conducting monetary policy is the Open Market Operation in which the Fed buys and sells existing Treasury securities. The Fed *buys* Treasury securities from securities dealers to *increase* the money supply and *sells* Treasury securities to securities dealers to *decrease* the money supply.

The ultimate effects on the economy of the Fed's Open Market Operations are the same as those summarized above. The Fed's method of conducting monetary policy simply changes somewhat the pathway that the economy takes to reach those effects. The same holds true for any of the developed market economies. The effects of monetary policy are the same; the pathway to the effects depends on the particular monetary and financial institutions within the country.

The Open Market Operation changes the story about the money rain in two ways. The first is that the commercial banks (and other depository institutions) become key players in bringing about the two effects. The Fed's Open Market Operations are designed, first and foremost, to throw the commercial banks' portfolios of assets out of line. It is the commercial banks' reactions that are counted on to change the level of national income and the interest rates. The second is that the effects on national income and interest rates do not occur simultaneously. Instead, the Fed sets off a causal chain of events in which its Open Market Operation first changes interest rates, which then change the levels of aggregate demand and national income. Moreover, the key interest rate is the interest rate on commercial bank loans to households and businesses.

The causal chain of events is as follows:

■ *Expansionary monetary policy*

Fed's purchase of Treasury securities $\rightarrow R \downarrow \rightarrow C^d \uparrow$ and $I^d \uparrow \rightarrow Y_E \uparrow$

■ *Contractionary monetary policy*

Fed's sale of Treasury securities $\rightarrow R \uparrow \rightarrow C^d \downarrow$ and $I^d \downarrow \rightarrow Y_E \downarrow$

Expansionary Monetary Policy

EXPANSIONARY MONETARY POLICY

An increase in the money supply undertaken by the Fed for the purpose of increasing aggregate demand; the Fed buys Treasury securities on the Open Market.

Let's consider an **expansionary monetary policy** in the United States.

THE OPEN MARKET OPERATION   As we saw in Chapters 14 and 15, the policy begins when the Trading Desk at the New York Fed calls the securities dealers at a few large commercial banks, brokerage houses, and investment banks and announces its intention to buy some of its Treasury securities. The securities dealers offer prices at which they are willing to sell, and the Fed buys from the dealers offering the lowest prices.

Suppose that the Fed buys entirely from the securities dealers at Merrill Lynch in order to keep the story simple. No money or checks change hands in most of these transactions. Instead, the Fed takes ownership of the Treasury securities and, in return, has one of its clearinghouses adjust the balance sheet

TABLE 16.2   The Fed's Open Market Purchase of Treasury Securities

THE FED		COMMERCIAL BANK OF MERRILL LYNCH		MERRILL LYNCH	
Assets	Liabilites	Assets	Liabilities	Assets	Liabiliites
Treasury (+) securities	Reserves (+)	Reserves (+)	Checking account (+) of Merrill Lynch	Checking (+) account	
				Treasury (−) securities	

of the commercial bank that Merrill Lynch uses. The clearinghouse increases the bank's reserves by the amount of the Open Market purchase on the asset side of the bank's balance sheet and also increases Merrill Lynch's checking account with the bank by the same amount on the liability side of the bank's balance sheet. Table 16.2 records the effects of the Open Market purchase on the balance sheets of Merrill Lynch, the commercial bank, and the Fed.

Merrill Lynch exchanges Treasury securities for an equal increase in its checking account balance on the asset side of its balance sheet. The commercial bank's reserves and checking accounts increase on the asset and the liability sides of its balance sheet, respectively. The Fed's holdings of Treasury securities increase on the asset side of its balance sheet, matched by an equal increase in reserves due commercial banks on the liability side of its balance sheet. The money supply increases immediately by the amount of the Open Market purchase, in the form of the increase in Merrill Lynch's checking account balance.

The increase in the money supply has almost no immediate impact on aggregate demand and the equilibrium level of national income. Merrill Lynch receives the new money, yet the composition of its assets is not necessarily thrown out of equilibrium. The Merrill Lynch securities dealers have willingly exchanged some of their Treasury securities for the checking account. Also, Merrill Lynch and the other financial institutions that the Fed trades with on the Open Market use very little real capital. So even if their portfolios were out of line, they would not purchase much more real capital with the new checking account balance and cause a noticeable increase in investment demand.

THE COMMERCIAL BANKS AND THEIR LOANS   The commercial banks (and other depository institutions) are the key to the real effects of monetary policy in the United States because it is their portfolios of assets that are thrown out of equilibrium most dramatically by the Fed's Open Market Operations. In our example the Open Market purchase by the Fed gives the commercial bank excess reserves. The bank now has too many reserves and too few loans. This position is costly to the bank because reserves do not offer a rate of return, whereas the return on bank loans is the principal source of revenue for the bank.

The Fed counts on the fact that commercial banks have a strong incentive to seek out new borrowers and to exchange their excess reserves for new loans. The market for bank loans occupies center stage in the conduct of monetary policy in the United States.

Figure 16.5 illustrates the market for bank loans. The interest rate on bank loans is on the vertical axis, and the quantity of loans to households and busi-

FIGURE 16.5

Expansionary Monetary Policy and the Market for Bank Loans

In the market for bank loans the commercial banks are the suppliers/lenders and the households and businesses are the demanders/borrowers. The quantity of bank loans is on the horizontal axis and the interest rate on bank loans is on the vertical axis. The supply curve, S, is upward sloping because banks are willing to lend more money the higher the interest rate. The demand curve, D, is downward sloping because households and businesses are willing to borrow more money the lower the interest rate. The initial equilibrium in the loan market is (L_0, R_0), at the intersection of D^0 and S^0. An expansionary monetary policy increases banks' excess reserves, which the banks want to lend. The supply of bank loans increases from S^0 to S^1, and the new equilibrium is (L_1, R_1), at the intersection of D^0 and S^1. The expansionary monetary policy lowers the interest rate on bank loans, which induces households and businesses to increase their borrowing and spending.

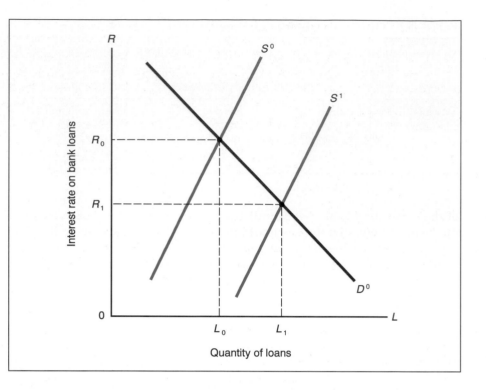

nesses is on the horizontal axis. The market supply and the market demand curves, S^0 and D^0, represent the initial situation before the Fed's Open Market purchase. The supply curve represents the banks' willingness to lend at various interest rates. S^0 is upward sloping, as usual. The interest rate on loans represents the rate of return on the loan to the bank. The higher the loan interest rate is, the more the banks are willing to lend; the lower the loan interest rate is, the less the banks are willing to lend. The demand curve, D^0, represents the households' and business firms' willingness to borrow at various interest rates. D^0 is downward sloping, as usual. The interest rate on loans represents the cost of borrowing to the borrowers. Therefore, the higher the loan interest rate is, the less the households and the firms are willing to borrow; the lower the loan interest rate is, the more the households and the firms are willing to borrow. The initial equilibrium is at the intersection of S^0 and D^0. L_0 bank loans are written at an interest rate of R_0.

A general point about loan markets is worth noting before continuing. In any supply and demand diagram of a loan market, the *supplier* is always the *lender*, for whom the loan is an asset, and the *demander* is always the *borrower*, for whom the loan is a liability. Only the identity of the lenders and the borrowers changes from market to market. For instance, when you open a passbook savings account, you are lending money to a bank. The savings account is your asset and the bank's liability. Therefore, in a supply and demand graph of passbook savings accounts, the households are the lenders, and the banks are the borrowers.

Return to the market for bank loans in Figure 16.5, in which the banks are the lenders and the households and the firms are the borrowers. The increase in reserves because of the Fed's Open market purchase increases the banks' willingness to lend at every interest rate. The supply curve shifts down and to the right, from S^0 to S^1. The banks' increased willingness to supply puts downward pressure on the interest rate. Banks are anxious to find new borrowers to get rid of their non-interest-bearing excess reserves, and they are willing to offer lower rates to borrowers. The loan interest rate falls from R_0 to R_1, which induces households and firms to move downward along their demand curves and increase their borrowing. The quantity of loans increases from L_0 to L_1.

THE INCREASE IN AGGREGATE DEMAND   The decrease in the interest rate on bank loans is the key interest rate effect that the Fed hopes for. A primary goal of an expansionary monetary policy is to increase aggregate demand and the equilibrium level of national income. The mechanism for increasing aggregate demand is the increase in bank loans. Households and firms borrow from commercial banks and other depository institutions primarily to finance purchases of real assets. Households borrow to buy big-ticket items, such as houses, cars, and major appliances. Firms borrow to pay for investment in plant and equipment and in inventory. Therefore, the downward-sloping demand curve for bank loans implies that the demand for consumer durables and for investment is also sensitive to the interest rate on bank loans.

Figure 16.6 illustrates. Figure 16.6(a) shows the demand for consumer durables, and Figure 16.6(b) shows investment demand. Both demands are related to the interest rate on bank loans, which is on the vertical axis. According to the graphs, the decrease in the interest rate on bank loans from R_0 to R_1 increases the quantity of consumer durables demanded from C_0^{Dur} to C_1^{Dur} and increases the quantity of investment demanded from I_0^d to I_1^d. The combined increase in consumption spending and investment spending demanded by households and firms corresponds to the increase in their borrowings from L_0 to L_1 in Figure 16.5.

Chapter 10 discussed the extent to which the demand for consumer durables and investment demand are sensitive to interest rates on bank loans. The

FIGURE 16.6

The Interest Rate on Loans, Consumer Durables, and Investment

Households borrow to finance consumer durables and new houses, and businesses borrow to finance their investments in plant and equipment and inventory. Therefore, the demands for consumer durables and investment are inversely related to the interest rates on bank loans, as shown by the curves C^{Dur} and I^d in Figure 16.6(a) and Figure 16.6(b), respectively. An expansionary monetary policy that reduces the interest rate on bank loans from R_0 to R_1 increases the quantity of consumer durables demanded from C_0^{Dur} to C_1^{Dur} in Figure 16.6(a). It also increases the quantity of investment demanded from I_0^d to I_1^d in Figure 16.6(b). The increase in spending on consumer durables and investment as a result of an expansionary monetary policy increases aggregate demand and the equilibrium level of national income.

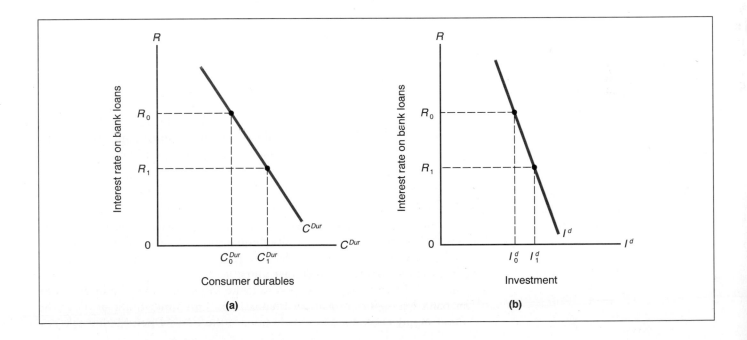

(a)

(b)

conclusion was as follows. The demand for mortgage loans to finance new homes appears to be quite sensitive to mortgage interest rates. The purchase of new homes is part of investment demand. The demand for consumer durables, particularly the demand for automobiles, also appears to be fairly sensitive to loan rates. The relationship between interest rates and investment in plant and equipment and in inventories is a source of controversy among economists. Everyone agrees that the demand for *capital* is related to interest rates, but economists disagree sharply on whether investment in plant and equipment and in inventories is sensitive to interest rates.

In any event, the Fed hopes to stimulate consumption demand and investment demand by pumping reserves into the banking system and inducing banks to reduce the interest rates on loans so that they can turn the reserves into loans. We saw in Chapter 15 that the money supply increases ultimately by a multiple of the Fed's Open Market purchase of Treasury securities as the banks make the new loans. The new money being created by the bank loans supports the increase in consumer demand and investment demand. Aggregate demand increases and leads to a multiplied increase in the equilibrium level of national income, as illustrated in Figure 16.1.

Our analysis of an expansionary monetary policy is now complete. To summarize, the pathway from the Fed's Open Market purchase of Treasury securities, to the lowering of interest rates, to the increase in national income proceeds in the following steps:

1. The Open Market purchase creates excess reserves in the commercial banks and throws their holding of assets out of equilibrium. The banks want to exchange the non-interest-bearing excess reserves for loans.
2. The banks' desire to make loans drives down the interest rate on bank loans, which induces households and firms to increase their borrowing in order to finance increases in consumer durables and investment. The increase in consumption demand and investment demand increases aggregate demand, which increases the equilibrium level of national income.
3. In conclusion: *An expansionary monetary policy increases national income and decreases interest rates on assets.* This is the same conclusion that we reached for the money rain.

Contractionary Monetary Policy

CONTRACTIONARY MONETARY POLICY

A decrease in the money supply undertaken by the Fed for the purpose of decreasing aggregate demand; the Fed sells Treasury securities on the Open Market.

The Fed begins a **contractionary monetary policy** by having the Trading Desk at the New York Fed sell some of its Treasury securities, mostly Treasury bills, to the securities dealers that it trades with. The Open Market sale works its way through the economy exactly as the Open Market purchase, except in reverse. Make sure that you understand the following step-by-step summary of the effects of a contractionary monetary policy.

1. The Open Market sale drains reserves from the commercial banks and throws their holdings of assets out of equilibrium. The banks are now below their reserve requirements and have to reduce the amount of their loans in order to build up their reserve accounts.
2. The banks' decreased willingness to make loans drives up the interest rate on bank loans. Refer again to Figure 16.5. This time, think of S^1 as the initial supply curve for loans made prior to the Fed's Open Market sale and

the initial equilibrium as (L_1, R_1), at the intersection of D^0 and S^1. The banks' decreased desire to lend shifts the supply curve up and to the left to S^0 and establishes a new equilibrium at (L_0, R_0), at the intersection of D^0 and S^0. The increase in the interest rate from R_1 to R_0 induces households and firms to decrease their borrowing to finance increases in consumer durables and investment. Borrowing decreases from L_1 to L_0. In Figure 16.6, the quantity of consumer durables demanded decreases from C_1^{Dur} to C_0^{Dur}, and the quantity of investment demanded decreases from I_1^d to I_0^d in response to the higher interest rate on loans. The decreases in consumption demand and investment demand decrease aggregate demand, which decreases the equilibrium level of national income.

3. In conclusion: *A contractionary monetary policy decreases national income and increases interest rates on assets.* This is the same conclusion that we reached if the Fed asked people at random to mail in some of their money.

The previous Concept Summary table summarizes how expansionary and contractionary monetary policies in the United States affect the equilibrium level of national income and interest rates.

Practical Problems with U.S. Monetary Policy

In Chapter 11 we noted that the administration and the Congress cannot fine tune the economy with their fiscal policies because of the many practical difficulties that arise in the conduct of fiscal policy. The best that fiscal policy can hope to do is "lean against the wind" and help prevent the economy from straying too far from whatever target level of national income the administration may set. The same is true of monetary policy. The conduct of monetary policy is plagued with its own set of practical difficulties that prevent the Fed from being able to fine tune the economy.

THE POLICY LAGS   For starters, the Fed's Board of Governors faces the same three policy lags as the administration does in the conduct of fiscal policy: the recognition lag, the administrative lag, and the operational lag.

RECOGNITION LAG   The **recognition lag** is the time required for the Board of Governors to recognize that the economy is in trouble and needs a dose of expansionary or contractionary monetary policy. Recall that the length of the recognition lag depends on the ability to collect reliable data and forecast the future performance of the economy. As noted in the discussion of fiscal policy, forecasting is the problem. The Board of Governors is no better at economic forecasting than anyone else is. Monetary and fiscal policies suffer an equal handicap here.

ADMINISTRATIVE LAG   The **administrative lag** is the time required to change the course of monetary policy once the Board of Governors decides to do so. Here the Board of Governors has a decided advantage over the administration and the Congress. We saw that the administrative lag was an enormous problem in the conduct of fiscal policy; the budgetary process is lengthy and cumbersome. Not so in the conduct of monetary policy. The administrative lag is extremely short, virtually non-existent. The Board of Governors instructs the

RECOGNITION LAG (MONETARY POLICY)

The time required for the Board of Governors to recognize that the economy is in trouble and needs a dose of expansionary or contractionary monetary policy.

ADMINISTRATIVE LAG (MONETARY POLICY)

The time required to change the course of monetary policy once the Board of Governors decides to do so.

Fed's Open Market Committee (FOMC) on its goals for monetary policy, and the FOMC meets almost monthly to discuss the state of the economy in relation to the Board of Governors' goals. Should the FOMC decide that a dose of monetary policy is required, all it need do is call the Trading Desk at the New York Fed with instructions to begin an Open Market Operation. The Trading Desk then places calls to the securities dealers it trades with and begins to execute either a purchase or a sale of Treasury securities on the Open Market. The whole process takes only a day or two.

OPERATIONAL LAG   Recall that the operational lag in fiscal policy has two parts. The first is the time from the passage of legislation to the actual change in government purchases, transfer payments, or tax collections. The second is the multiplier process, the time required for the changes in spending or taxes to affect the equilibrium level of national income.

OPERATIONAL LAG (MONETARY POLICY)

The time required for a change in the money supply to affect the equilibrium level of national income.

The first half of the corresponding **operational lag** under monetary policy does not exist because the money supply increases or decreases simultaneously with the Open Market Operation. The Fed's purchase of Treasury securities increases the money supply by the amount of the purchase. The Fed's sale of Treasury securities decreases the money supply by the amount of the sale.

The operational lag that matters for monetary policy is the time required for the change in the money supply to affect the equilibrium level of national income. Here is where the conduct of monetary policy suffers its main practical problems. The consensus among economists is that the lag between the change in the money supply and the change in the equilibrium level of national income is very long, at least a year to a year and a half on average. What is worse, the lag is highly variable, both in timing and in effect. In truth, the Fed never has a very clear idea of when its Open Market Operations will affect the economy, and with what force. The operational lag is every bit the practical difficulty for the conduct of monetary policy that the administrative lag is for the conduct of fiscal policy.[5]

The Fed's difficulties with the operational lag stem from two main sources: uncertainties about the size of the money multiplier and uncertainties about the demand for money.

THE SIZE OF THE MONEY MULTIPLIER   Chapter 15 noted the uncertainties with respect to the size of the money multiplier, which relates the final change in the money supply to the Fed's initial Open Market Operation. Recall that the problem here is the commercial banks (and other depository institutions). They are not the passive economic agents that they are represented to be in the simple money multiplier exercise. Instead, they are profit-maximizing business firms whose actions tend to make the growth of the money supply pro-cyclical rather than countercyclical. The Fed has not always been able, or even willing, to counteract the pro-cyclical tendencies of the banks. (Review the discussion of the commercial banks at the end of Chapter 15 if you are unclear about these points.)

UNCERTAINTIES ABOUT THE DEMAND FOR MONEY   The Fed must be able to predict the demand for money accurately in order to conduct an effective mon-

---

[5]For further discussion of the operational lag associated with monetary policy, see R. Hall and J. Taylor, *Macroeconomics: Theory, Performance, and Policy*, second edition (New York: Norton, 1988), 350–351.

etary policy because the demand for money determines how the economy reacts to a change in the money supply. As we have seen, a change in the money supply causes national income and interest rates to change, which in turn feeds back into the demand for money. The economy returns to equilibrium when national income and interest rates change by enough so that the change in the demand for money matches the change in the money supply. Therefore, the Fed has to know how the demand for money is related to national income and interest rates in order to be able to predict how its monetary policies will affect national income and interest rates.

Unfortunately, the demand for money has been hard to pin down. The money demand curves in Figures 16.2 and 16.4 shift around quite a bit over time, and the Fed has not always foreseen the shifts. Two celebrated cases of the Fed misreading the demand for money occurred 10 years apart, in 1981 and 1991.

Paul Volcker was chairman of the Board of governors during the Carter administration and the first term of the Reagan administration. Volcker decided, in October of 1979, to clamp down on the growth of the money supply over the next few years to fight inflation. The CPI had increased by 13.3 percent in 1979. Then in 1980 Congress passed the Depository Institutions Deregulation and Monetary Control Act of 1980 (DIDMCA), which authorized the interest-paying NOW checking accounts nationwide, beginning in 1981. NOW accounts had been available in only a few states before DIDMCA. The NOW accounts became part of the money supply and were an instant hit among households.

The result was a huge, and unanticipated, increase in the demand for money, which is also contractionary. Households reduced their demand for houses and consumer durables, and sold other financial assets, to build up their NOW accounts. The increase in the demand for money following DIDMCA made Volcker's contractionary monetary policy far more contractionary than it would otherwise have been. Many economists believe that the combination of the contractionary monetary policy and the large increase in the demand for money was largely responsible for bringing on the recession of 1981–82, the deepest recession in the United States since the Great Depression. The combination also helped to produce record-high short-term interest rates, in the 17 to 20 percent range. Volcker certainly did not want either of these results.

In 1991 Alan Greenspan, the chairman of the Board of Governors under President Bush, decided to increase the money supply to pull the economy out of the recession. The money supply as measured by M1 increased at an annual rate of 10 percent throughout 1991 and 1992. Many economists thought this was the appropriate policy at the time and predicted that the economy would begin to grow sometime in 1992 before the presidential election. Instead, the economy remained stagnant until the last quarter of 1992 and contributed to President Clinton's victory over President Bush that November. The problem again was an unexpected increase in the demand for money.

The increase in the money supply drove down interest rates on short-term assets to levels that had not been seen in the United States for 20 years or more. As noted earlier, NOW accounts, savings deposits, money market funds, and short-term certificates of deposit were paying interest rates in the 2 to 4 percent range in October of 1992. Households and businesses responded by increasing their holdings of regular and NOW checking accounts and by pulling out of the other short-term financial assets. M1 grew rapidly, whereas M2 hardly grew at all. The quantity of money demanded had grown much more rapidly than the Fed had foreseen, and the monetary policy was not nearly as expansionary as anticipated.

These two episodes are obviously instances when the demand for money changed very dramatically. The demand for money is normally more stable than it was at these times, but it is never entirely predictable. As a consequence, the Fed can never be certain just how expansionary or contractionary its monetary policies will be.

CONTRACTIONARY VERSUS EXPANSIONARY MONETARY POLICY[6]   Many economists believe that a contractionary monetary policy is more immediately effective than is an expansionary monetary policy. They argue that the Fed can stop a booming economy from overheating with contractionary monetary policy, but that the Fed might not be able to bring an economy out of a recession with expansionary monetary policy. They liken the economy to a train moving along a track dragging a long rope. The Fed's contractionary policy can pull on the rope and halt the economy in its tracks, but the Fed's expansionary policy can only push on the rope and cannot thereby move the economy forward.

The commercial banks may actually help the Fed with its contractionary monetary policy, assuming the Fed does remove reserves from the banking system. The banks make the policy even more contractionary if they engage in credit rationing at high interest rates, and many economists believe that they do. Figure 16.7 illustrates the effects of credit rationing.

Figure 16.7(a) shows the traditional explanation of how a contractionary monetary policy affects the market for bank loans, the explanation given above. The loan interest rate is on the vertical axis, and the quantity of loans is on the horizontal axis. The initial equilibrium prior to the contractionary policy is (L_0, R_0), at the intersection of the initial supply and demand curves, S^0 and D^0. The Fed sells some of its Treasury securities on the Open Market and drains reserves from the banking system. The banks have to reduce their loans to meet the reserve requirements, so the supply curve shifts up and to the left from S^0 to S^1. The new equilibrium is (L_1, R_1), at the intersection of S^1 and D^0. The decrease in the supply of loans increases the loan interest rate and decreases the quantity of loans. Less borrowing means less spending on consumer durables and investment and a lower level of aggregate demand.

Banks, however, may not let the interest rate on loans rise by enough to clear the market, to R_1 in our example. They worry that very high interest rates are likely to attract more and more loan applications for highly risky projects. The high interest rates force households and firms into riskier projects that have higher average rates of return, but also a higher likelihood of failure and default on the loan. Therefore, rather than granting a loan to any borrower who is willing to pay the high rate, R_1, banks hold the line on the increase in the interest rate and engage in credit rationing.

Figure 16.7(b) illustrates the loan market with credit rationing. Supply decreases from S^0 to S^1, as in Figure 16.7(a), when the Fed drains reserves from the banking system. Instead of letting the interest rate rise to R_1 and clear the market, banks refuse to let the interest rate rise above R_2. Households and firms want to borrow an amount L_2^D at the interest rate R_2, whereas the banks are only willing to lend an amount L_2^S. The market for loans is in excess demand in the amount $L_2^D - L_2^S$.

CREDIT CRUNCH

A condition of excess demand in the loan markets in which potential borrowers complain that they cannot get loans even when they are willing to pay the quoted interest rate for the loans.

---

[6]The material in this section is more advanced and may be skipped in shorter courses with no loss in continuity.

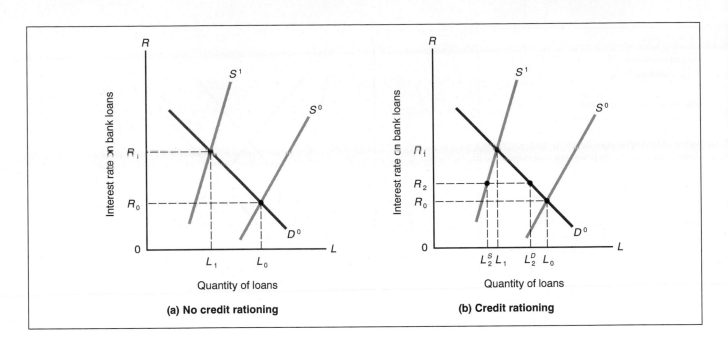

(a) No credit rationing

(b) Credit rationing

The advantage to the banks of holding down the interest rate is that they can review and compare the relative risks of the L_2^D loan requests and ration the L_2^S loans they are willing to make to the best customers. What they lose with the lower interest rate they more than make up by screening out the worst customers and lowering the default rate on their loans. Notice that credit rationing reduces the amount of loans relative to the market-clearing solution from L_1 to L_2^S, which means that spending on consumer durables and investment is lower as well. Credit rationing makes the contractionary monetary policy even more contractionary.

The evidence that commercial banks and other depository institutions do engage in credit rationing is fairly substantial. The economy is said to experience a **credit crunch** when potential borrowers complain that they cannot get loans even when they are willing to pay the quoted interest rate for the loans. Credit crunches have been fairly common in the United States. They occurred in 1966, 1969–70, 1974–75, and 1980, and the Fed was undertaking a contractionary monetary policy in each instance. The commercial banks (and other depository institutions) do appear to ration credit when reserves are scarce.

The commercial banks cannot be so helpful to the Fed during an expansionary monetary policy. The problem during a recession is on the demand side of the loan market, as illustrated in Figure 16.8.

The supply and demand curves, S^0 and D^0, represent the state of the market for bank loans prior to both the recession and the expansionary monetary policy. The pre-recession, pre-policy equilibrium is (L_0, R_0). The recession occurs first and decreases the demand for loans from D^0 to D^1. Workers are laid off, and businesses see little or no growth in the demand for their products. Consequently, the demands for consumer durables and investment decrease, along with the demand for loans to finance these goods. Notice, too, that the demand curve has become steeper as well as shifting down and in. Laid-off workers and managers who see little growth in demand become less responsive to the interest rates on loans. Lower interest rates do not increase the quantity of loans demanded as much during a recession as they do in a healthier economy.

FIGURE 16.7

Credit Rationing and Contractionary Monetary Policy

Figure 16.7(a) shows how the market for bank loans would respond to a contractionary monetary policy without credit rationing. The initial equilibrium is (L_0, R_0), at the intersection of the demand curve for loans D^0 and the supply curve for loans S^0. The contractionary monetary policy drains reserves from the commercial banks, which decreases the supply of loans from S^0 to S^1. The new equilibrium is (L_1, R_1) at the intersection of D^0 and S^1. Banks do not let the interest rate rise to R_1, however, because that high an interest rate induces borrowers to finance very risky projects and increases the default rate on the loans. Instead, the banks engage in credit rationing as shown in Figure 16.7(b). They set the interest rate at R_2, which creates an excess demand for loans equal to $(L_2^D - L_2^S)$. The excess demand allows the banks to screen out the riskiest borrowers and reduces the default rate of the loans. The quantity of loans drops from L_1 without credit rationing to L_2^S with credit rationing, which makes the monetary policy even more contractionary.

FIGURE 16.8

Expansionary Monetary Policy in a Recession

The figure shows why the Fed might not be able to bring the economy out of a recession with expansionary monetary policy. The initial equilibrium in the market for bank loans before the recession is (L_0, R_0), at the intersection of D^0 and S^0. A recession reduces the demand for loans by households and businesses and makes their demand for loans more inelastic. The demand curve shifts down from D^0 to D^1. The equilibrium in the market for bank loans during the recession, but before the expansionary monetary policy, is (L_1, R_1), at the intersection of D^1 and S^0. The expansionary monetary policy creates excess reserves in the commercial banks and increases the supply of bank loans from S^0 to S^1. The final equilibrium after the expansionary monetary policy is (L_2, R_2), at the intersection of D^1 and S^1. The expansionary monetary policy causes a relatively large decrease in the interest rate on bank loans from R_1 to R_2, but only a modest increase in loans from L_1 to L_2. The modest increase in borrowing by households and businesses means that aggregate demand does not increase very much, and the economy remains in a recession.

The equilibrium in the loan market during the recession, but before the expansionary monetary policy, is (L_1, R_1), at the intersection of S^0 and D^1.

Suppose that the Fed tries to counteract the recession with an expansionary monetary policy. It buys some Treasury securities on the Open Market and injects more reserves into the banking system. The new reserves increase the bank's willingness to lend, and the supply curve shifts out and down from S^0 to S^1. The new equilibrium is (L_2, R_2), at the intersection of S^1 and D^1.

The expansionary monetary policy mostly affects the interest rates on loans and not the quantity of loans. The interest rate decreases substantially, from R_1 to R_2; the equilibrium quantity of loans increases only slightly, from L_1 to L_2. Spending on consumer durables and investment also increases only slightly, which means that aggregate demand increases only slightly, and the economy remains in a recession.

The problem is that the decline in interest rates does not induce much additional borrowing from households and firms. This is exactly what happened in 1991 when the Fed undertook an expansionary monetary policy to pull the economy out of the recession. Banks took the new reserves created by the Fed and bought financial securities, mostly Treasury securities, from other financial institutions and from the government. They did not write many new loans because there just was not much demand for loans. The financial institutions that sold the securities to the banks simply held on to their newly created checking account balances.

The pull on a rope, push on a rope analogy goes back at least as far as John Maynard Keynes. Keynes believed that monetary policy could not pull the market economies out of the Great Depression because new bank reserves would not lead to much more borrowing. He argued that expansionary fiscal policies were needed because they increase aggregate demand directly. In fact, U.S. commercial banks had large amounts of excess reserves during the Great Depression. The banks could not find borrowers for these funds, as Keynes had predicted. And, since interest rates on short-term financial securities were near zero, they simply chose to hold excess reserves.

WHAT TO TARGET?   The practical problems discussed above raise an interesting question for the Fed: What economic variable or variables should the Fed try to control with its Open Market Operations? An ideal target variable would have two properties. It would be a variable that the Fed could control very tightly and one that has a well-defined relationship to national income and interest rates, particularly national income. Unfortunately, there does not appear to be such an ideal target variable.

The Fed can most closely control the monetary base, the sum of Federal Reserve Notes plus reserves, with its Open Market purchases and sales. The monetary base is, in turn, closely related to the narrow M1 transactions definition of the money supply. As we have just seen, however, increasing or decreasing M1 does not always have highly predictable effects on the level of national income. Some economists argue that the Fed should target M2 instead because the velocity of circulation is somewhat more stable with respect to M2 than to M1. In other words, changes in M2 have the more predictable effect on national income through the equation of exchange, $M \cdot V = P \cdot Y$. The drawback to this suggestion is that the Fed probably cannot control the level of M2 very tightly just with Open Market Operations.

The Fed has never resolved the target variable problem and has shifted targets often throughout its history. The Fed currently looks at a broad range of financial indicators in setting its monetary policy, including broad money aggregates such as M2 and M3, the amount of reserves borrowed from the discount window, and a wide spectrum of interest rates. One implication of this broad-based approach is an admission that monetary policy cannot fine tune the economy. The Fed knows that the best it can hope to do is "lean against the wind."

REFLECTION: According to the newspapers, what are the Fed's policy intentions, and why? Do you agree with the chairman's statements about the nature of the economy's problems? Do you have the same priorities as the chairman does regarding the macroeconomic policy goals?

INTEREST RATES AS A MACROECONOMIC POLICY VARIABLE

Chapter 16 has added a second layer of complexity to our study of the macro economy by bringing interest rates into the analysis. We had been concerned with a single policy variable, the level of (real) national income, before this chapter. From now on, though, we will keep track of two policy variables simultaneously, the level of (real) national income and interest rates.

Interest rates certainly capture the attention of the public throughout the world. Big-city newspapers publish daily the interest rates and rates of return on a large number of financial securities. Small changes in key interest rates, such as the Fed's discount rate or the commercial banks' prime lending rate, often cause a flurry of excitement worthy of front-page headlines.

The attention given interest rates is hardly surprising. Households and business firms have an obvious interest in the behavior of interest rates. Changes in interest rates affect the return on their assets and the cost of their debt and other liabilities. Interest rates are important from a broader social perspective as well. They have a direct impact on some of the macroeconomic policy goals and on other goals that societies care about.

Should interest rates be low or high from a social perspective? The question has no clear-cut answer. Some of society's goals argue for low interest rates, whereas others argue for high interest rates. The usual arguments for keeping interest rates low are that low interest rates promote long-run economic growth, encourage home ownership, and help the poor. The counterargument for keeping interest rates high is that high interest rates protect and strengthen the value of the dollar relative to foreign currencies. One suspects that the arguments for low interest rates have won the day in the United States, judging from the uproar that always accompanies a sharp increase in interest rates. Let's take a brief look at the arguments on each side.

The Benefits of Low Interest Rates

LONG-RUN ECONOMIC GROWTH   The connection between interest rates and long-run economic growth runs through investment in plant and equipment and in human capital (education). We have seen that investment in both physical and human capital is the most important determinant of long-run economic growth. In addition, many economists believe that investment demand is inversely related to the cost of capital, and interest rates are an important component of the cost of capital. The higher interest rates are, the higher the cost of capital is, and the lower investment demand is; the lower interest rates are, the lower the cost of capital is, and the higher investment demand is.

The argument, then, is that low interest rates stimulate investment demand and promote long-run economic growth. Low interest rates encourage firms to borrow or use their retained earnings to finance investment in plant and equipment. Similarly, low interest rates encourage people to borrow to further their educations.

The connection between interest rates and long-run economic growth is a powerful argument for favoring low interest rates, simply because long-run economic growth is so crucial to the overall economic well-being of any nation. The call for lowering interest rates to promote economic growth is especially compelling for the United States. We saw in Chapter 6 that the United States has been stuck in a low-investment, low-growth profile ever since 1973. Nothing would improve U.S. living standards more than an increase in investment and growth. In addition, long-term interest rates have been exceedingly high by historical standards throughout the 1980s and into the 1990s. As a result, the cost of capital in the United States is very high, among the highest of the industrial market economies. This may explain in part why the United States devotes a lower percentage of its resources to investment than do nearly all the other industrial market economies.

Politicians and economists have been advocating higher investment and growth as a top economic priority for the past 20 years. Many economists believe that the government cannot hope to achieve that goal unless long-term interest rates are substantially reduced.

The only caveat in the lower-interest-rate argument concerns the presumed relationship between interest rates and investment in plant and equipment. As noted in Chapter 10, economists disagree on the sensitivity of plant and equipment investment to interest rates, and to the cost of capital generally. Some economists believe that demand for plant and equipment investment is highly sensitive to interest rates. Other economists disagree. The latter believe that plant and equipment investment is determined primarily by the rate of growth in aggregate demand and that interest rates play only a minor role in the investment decision. Still, virtually all economists would agree that low interest rates are more conducive to investment and long-run economic growth than are high interest rates. The only disagreement is over how low interest rates would need to be to stimulate investment.

HOME OWNERSHIP   Owning a home is part of the American dream, and the federal government has tried a number of different approaches to help people achieve that dream.

During the Great Depression, Congress established and initially funded the savings and loan associations (S&Ls) and the savings banks, the so-called thrifts, whose sole function at the time was to accept deposits and issue home mortgages. The thrifts operated under the auspices of the Federal Home Loan Bank Board, which bore roughly the same relationship to the thrifts as the Fed did to the commercial banks.

Congress also offers numerous incentives for home ownership through the federal personal income tax. For example, homeowners can deduct both the interest paid on their mortgages and their local property taxes from their incomes in computing their taxable incomes. In addition, homeowners are not taxed on the capital gains from selling a house if they buy another house of equal or greater value. Renters are not given any comparable tax advantages.

Finally, the government has tried to keep interest rates low to encourage home ownership. Most homes are bought with the aid of a mortgage loan, and the demand for mortgages is highly sensitive to mortgage interest rates. For this reason, investment in new homes is the most interest-sensitive component of investment demand.

Congress tried at first to ensure low mortgage interest rates through direct regulation. It authorized interest-rate ceilings on the savings deposits of thrifts shortly after the thrifts began operation. The theory behind the ceilings was that low interest rates on deposits would permit the thrifts to offer low interest rates on their mortgages. One problem with this theory is that it required a whole host of additional interest-rate ceilings on other financial securities to ensure that households would keep their deposits at the thrifts. The Depository Institutions Deregulation and Monetary Control Act of 1980 finally removed all the interest-rate ceilings and allowed other financial institutions to write mortgages. The point still holds, though, that lower interest rates encourage households to take out mortgages and invest in new homes.

HELPING THE POOR   The distributional argument for low interest rates is based on a perception that, on average, high-income people are net lenders, or creditors, and low-income people are net borrowers, or debtors. Therefore, low interest rates are pro-poor because they help debtors by reducing the cost of borrowing and hurt creditors by reducing the return to lending.

The perception is not quite accurate for the United States. The people in both the top 20 percent of the income distribution and the bottom 20 percent of the income distribution are net lenders or creditors, on average. The 60 percent of the people in between are net borrowers or debtors, on average. Therefore, low interest rates redistribute income from the top and the bottom of the income distribution to the middle.

The reason that the people at the bottom of the distribution are net lenders, on average, is that this group contains a large percentage of the nation's elderly, who are living off the savings accumulated during their working years. Low interest rates really hurt the elderly because interest income is a major component, often the main component, of their total income. The elderly took a very big hit during the early 1990s when interest rates on their certificates of deposit and other savings accounts plummeted in response to the Fed's expansionary monetary policy.

Concern for the poor has often been used as a justification for low interest rates, the misperception about the distribution of net lenders and net borrowers notwithstanding.

The Benefits of High Interest Rates

The primary argument for keeping interest rates high is that high interest rates support the value of the dollar. The connection between interest rates and the value of the dollar arises because financial markets no longer honor national boundaries. They are truly international in scope. Money managers in large manufacturing corporations, insurance companies, commercial banks, and other financial institutions search worldwide for financial securities that offer the best rate of return and other financial services. Moreover, financial markets are always open for business in some part of the world, so that financial transactions can be made around the clock.

The worldwide linking of financial markets has meant that small changes in U.S. interest rates generate a huge flow of funds across U.S. borders that affects the dollar exchange rate. Suppose, for example, that the Fed undertakes a contractionary monetary policy that raises U.S. interest rates. Money managers in London, Bonn, Paris, and Tokyo react immediately by selling financial securities in their own markets and buying financial securities in the United States to take advantage of the higher U.S. interest rates. They need dollars to buy securities in the U.S. financial markets, however, so they first have to exchange their currencies for dollars. Their offerings of pounds sterling, deutsche marks, francs, and yen for dollars in the foreign exchange markets drive up the value of the dollar against all these currencies. Therefore, an increase in U.S. interest rates very quickly causes the dollar to appreciate. The "stronger" dollar in turn helps U.S. consumers because imported goods are now cheaper to them. (The stronger dollar hurts U.S. exporters and import-competing firms, however. Review the analysis in Chapter 7 of the gains and losses from changes in the dollar exchange rate if you are unclear on these points.)

Conversely, a decrease in U.S. interest rates leads to an immediate outflow of funds from the United States. The dollar depreciates as money managers trade dollars for foreign currencies in the foreign exchange markets so that they can buy financial securities in London, Tokyo, and other foreign markets. If the dollar is already "weak," the government may be reluctant to pursue monetary or fiscal policies that lower interest rates and weaken the dollar still further, despite the many arguments for lowering interest rates.

The Concept Summary table summarizes the relationship between interest rates and the various policy goals.

CONCEPT SUMMARY
INTEREST RATES AND POLICY GOALS

ADVANTAGES OF LOWER INTEREST RATES
—Promote long-run economic growth (through investment in plant and equipment and in education)
—Promote home ownership (through lower mortgage rates)
—Improve the distribution of income (helps net debtors, hurts net creditors)

ADVANTAGES OF HIGHER INTEREST RATES
—Increase the value of the dollar (dollar appreciates relative to foreign currencies)

SUMMARY

The first section of Chapter 16 explored the economic effects of monetary policy in terms of a money rain that abstracts from the institutional details of a nation's financial sector. The analysis is short run and assumes a new Keynesian policy environment of sticky wages and prices and unemployed resources.

1. Households and businesses hold a variety of real and financial assets. The real assets of households include consumer durables, houses, and other real estate. The real assets of businesses are their productive capital—plant, equipment, and inventories. The financial assets held by both households and businesses include money, other deposit accounts, stocks, bonds, and insurance; businesses also hold accounts receivable.

2. The injection of new money into the economy upsets the composition of assets on the balance sheets of households and businesses. They now have too much money and too few of all other assets.

3. The economic effects of an expansionary monetary policy result when households and businesses exchange the new money for both real and other financial assets. The economy returns to equilibrium because the economic effects that result from trying to get rid of the money eventually cause the demand for money to rise to match the new, higher supply of money.

4. The desire to buy real assets with the new money increases consumption demand and investment demand, which increases aggregate demand and leads to a multiplied increase in real national income.

5. The increase in national income increases the transactions demand for money. The primary motive for holding money is related to its function as the medium of exchange. The larger national income is, the more households and businesses spend, and the larger their transactions demand for money is. A 1 percent increase in national income increases the quantity of money demanded by 0.6 percent.

6. The quantity of money demanded for transactions purposes also increases in direct proportion to the overall level of prices because FRN and checking account balances are denominated in nominal dollar values.

7. The desire to buy financial assets with the new money decreases interest rates (and rates of return) on these assets. For example, the increase in demand for corporate or government bonds drives up their prices. The prices of bonds are inversely related to their (expected) returns.

8. The demand for money is inversely related to interest rates because the interest rates on financial assets define the opportunity cost of holding money. Therefore, the decrease of interest rates as a result of the new money in the economy further increases the quantity of money demanded.

9. An expansionary monetary policy increases (real) national income and decreases interest rates on financial assets. The economy returns to equilibrium when national income increases by enough, and interest rates decrease by enough, that the demand for money increases to equal the new, higher supply of money.

10. Conversely, a contractionary monetary policy decreases (real) national income and increases interest rates on financial assets. The economy returns to equilibrium when national income decreases by enough, and interest rates increase by enough, that the demand for money decreases to equal the new, lower supply of money.

The second section of the chapter explained the institutional details associated with the conduct of monetary policy in the United States, in which the commercial banks and the market for bank loans play the major role.

11. *Expansionary monetary policy:* The Fed buys Treasury securities, which increases excess reserves in the banking system and allows banks to make more loans. The increased supply of loans lowers the interest rate on bank loans and induces households and businesses to borrow more. They borrow to finance purchases of consumer durables and investment goods, so that the increased borrowing increases aggregate demand and national income. Interest rates, especially interest rates on bank loans, decrease first, and then aggregate demand and real national income increase.

12. *Contractionary monetary policy:* The Fed sells Treasury securities, which decreases reserves in the banking system and forces banks to reduce their lending. The decreased supply of loans raises the interest rate on bank loans and induces households and businesses to borrow less. They purchase fewer consumer durables and investment goods, so that the decreased borrowing decreases aggregate demand and national income. Interest rates, especially interest rates on bank loans, increase first, and then aggregate demand and real national income decrease.

13. The Fed cannot fine tune the economy with its monetary policies. The operational lag is a major stumbling block in the conduct of monetary policy. The time from the Fed's Open Market Operation to the change in national income is very long, more than a year on average, and highly variable. Two practical problems for the Fed are uncertainty about the value of the money multiplier and uncertainty about the demand for money. Also, the Fed is better able to slow down the growth in aggregate demand with a contractionary policy than to increase the growth in aggregate demand with an expansionary policy.

14. The Fed currently looks at a broad range of financial indicators in setting its monetary policies, including broad money aggregates such as M2 and M3 and a large number of interest rates.

The final section of Chapter 16 considered the advantages of higher or lower interest rates from a social perspective.

15. The main advantages of low interest rates are that they promote investment and long-run economic growth, promote home ownership, and help net debtors who are perceived to be among the poorer citizens.

16. The main advantage of high interest rates is that they increase the value of the dollar against foreign currencies.

KEY TERMS

administrative lag (monetary policy)
contractionary monetary policy
credit crunch
expansionary monetary policy

money rain
operational lag (monetary policy)
precautionary demand for money

recognition lag (monetary policy)
speculative demand for money
transactions demand for money

QUESTIONS

1. a. What are some of the financial and the real assets held by households? By businesses?
   b. Why do households and businesses hold such diversified portfolios of assets?
2. a. What effect does an increase in the supply of money have on the equilibrium level of national income, and why?
   b. What effect does an increase in the supply of money have on interest rates and other rates of return on assets, and why?
3. Why does a money rain eventually cause an increase in the demand for money that matches the new, higher supply of money?
4. Suppose that you buy a corporate bond in the secondary market that has exactly one year left until it matures. The bond has a face value of $1,000 and pays an annual interest of $100. You pay $1,050 for the bond and plan to hold it until it matures. Calculate your rate of return on the bond.
5. a. Suppose that you buy a share of stock whose price is currently $50. You plan to sell the stock one year from now, and you expect the price of the stock to be $60 when you sell it. The stock pays an annual dividend of $3. Calculate your expected rate of return on the stock.
   b. Given the other savings options available to you today, would you actually be interested in buying this stock?
   c. How would your answers to parts (a) and (b) change if the current price of the stock is $60?

6. The demand for money in the economy is closely related to three economic variables: real national income, the overall level of prices, and interest rates on financial assets. Why is the demand for money related to each of these variables? Name one other factor besides these three that might affect the demand for money, and indicate why it would do so.
7. Most economists believe that expansionary and contractionary monetary policies in the United States first affect interest rates and then affect the equilibrium level of national income. Why is this?
8. Discuss the various motives behind the demand for money. What are some of the disadvantages of holding money as an asset?
9. Identify the three main lags in the conduct of monetary policy. Compare and contrast these lags with the three main lags in the conduct of fiscal policy. To what extent are the lags similar? To what extent are they different? Can the Fed expect to be able to fine tune the economy with its monetary policies?
10. Discuss this statement: The Fed conducts the monetary policy in the United States, but the commercial banks are largely responsible for the success or failure of monetary policy.

17

Fiscal Policy, Monetary Policy, and the Macroeconomic Policy Goals

LEARNING OBJECTIVES

CONCEPTS TO LEARN

Crowding out:

1. through consumer durables and investment

2. through net exports

Short-run Phillips Curve

Okun's Law

CONCEPTS TO RECALL

n 1992, the United States had not succeeded in reaching any of the four macroeconomic policy goals. Personal saving was 5 percent of disposable income, and net investment was less than 2 percent of gross domestic product (GDP). The United States remained stuck in its low-saving, low-investment, low-growth scenario of the past 20 years. Unemployment was 7.3 percent, at least one percentage point above the natural rate of unemployment, and maybe more. Inflation was 2.9 percent. The balance-of-trade deficit was $84 billion, and the dollar depreciated 3.5 percent against the yen and a number of the other major currencies, continuing a pattern that began in 1986.[1]

Everyone is striving toward the same macroeconomic goals, Democrat, Republican, and independent, liberal and conservative alike. We all want higher long-run economic growth in the 3 to 4 percent range, unemployment no higher than 5 or 6 percent, stable prices, a near-zero balance of trade, and a stable dollar in the foreign exchange markets. The outstanding macroeconomic policy question, though, is this: How do we get there?

Chapter 17 pulls together the new Keynesian analysis of the macro economy that began in Chapter 10. The chapter describes how the government can use its fiscal and monetary policies to pursue the four macroeconomic policy goals over the short run, in an economy with sticky wages and prices and unemployed resources. We will see that there is not necessarily any one best policy.

The chapter begins by tying up one loose end before turning to the macroeconomic policy goals. Our analysis of monetary policy in Chapter 16 showed how expansionary and contractionary monetary policies affect both national income and interest rates. To complete the analysis of the macro economy, we need to see how increases and decreases in aggregate demand, which include expansionary and contractionary fiscal policies, affect the level of interest rates. Previous chapters considered the effect of changes in aggregate demand on the equilibrium level of national income, but not on interest rates.

AGGREGATE DEMAND, FISCAL POLICY, AND INTEREST RATES

Our previous analysis of aggregate demand and fiscal policy described how changes in aggregate demand affect the equilibrium level of national income. To review briefly, the multiplier analysis in Chapter 11 showed that changes or shifts in aggregate demand lead to a multiplied change in the equilibrium level of national income. An increase in any component of aggregate demand leads to a multiplied increase in the equilibrium level of national income, and a decrease in any component of aggregate demand leads to a multiplied decrease in the equilibrium level of national income. Moreover, the increases and the decreases in aggregate demand could result from expansionary or contrac-

---

[1]U.S. Department of Commerce, Economics and Statistics Administration, Bureau of Economic Analysis, *Survey of Current Business* 73, No. 3 (March 1993): Table 2.1, p. 10 (personal saving); Table 1.1, p. 6 and Table 1.9, p. 10 (net investment). Council of Economic Advisers, *Economic Indicators, March 1993* (Washington, D.C.: U.S. Government Printing Office, 1993), 12 (unemployment), 24 (inflation), and 35 (balance of trade).

tionary fiscal policies, which involve changes in the government's purchases of goods and services, or transfer payments, or taxes.

We need to ask how changes in aggregate demand affect interest rates to complete the analysis of aggregate demand. The answer is that an *increase* in aggregate demand, including an expansionary fiscal policy, *increases* interest rates, and a *decrease* in aggregate demand, including a contractionary fiscal policy, *decreases* interest rates. Note the difference in fiscal and monetary policies with regard to interest rates. Expansionary fiscal and monetary policies both increase aggregate demand and the equilibrium level of national income. This, after all, is the definition of an expansionary policy. But an expansionary fiscal policy increases interest rates, whereas an expansionary monetary policy decreases interest rates. Similarly, contractionary fiscal and monetary policies decrease both aggregate demand and the equilibrium level of national income. But a contractionary fiscal policy decreases interest rates, whereas a contractionary monetary policy increases interest rates. The different effects on interest rates turn out to be crucial to the government's ability to hit whatever targets it sets for national income and interest rates.

Consumption Demand and Interest Rates

AN INCREASE IN CONSUMPTION DEMAND   Let's use changes in consumption demand to illustrate how changes in aggregate demand affect interest rates. Any component of aggregate demand will do, so we may as well begin with the one that we are most familiar with. Begin with an increase or shift up in consumption demand. We want to see why an increase in consumption demand increases interest rates.

The key to the analysis lies in the adjustments to the households' balance sheets that are necessary to accommodate the increase in consumption demand. Table 17.1 reproduces the typical household's balance sheet from Table 16.1, with loans added on the liability side. The loans represent borrowing from

TABLE 17.1   Balance Sheet of Households

	ASSETS	LIABILITIES
Financial assets	FRN Checking accounts Savings deposits Certificates of deposit Money market accounts Stocks Corporate bonds Treasury bonds State and local bonds Insurance	Loans
Real assets	Consumer durables Houses Other real estate	

banks, or from other financial institutions such as credit unions, or borrowing against credit cards.

When households decide to buy more consumer durables and other consumer goods and services, they have to obtain money somehow to finance their increased expenditures. The balance sheet in Table 17.1 shows that they have three ways of getting the money:

1. They can use their own money that they have on hand;
2. They can reduce their holdings of other financial assets, exchanging them for money; or
3. They can borrow the money.

What they cannot do is finance the new spending with new income that they may have earned because an increase in consumption demand means an increase in demand at *every* level of income. They have to match the increase in consumption demand with a decrease in their saving demand, which means either reducing their holdings of money and other financial assets or increasing their borrowing.

USING MONEY Suppose that all households just used their money on hand to finance their increased consumption demand. This would have no effect on interest rates because no one would ever enter the financial markets.

REDUCING OTHER FINANCIAL ASSETS Not all households will be able, or willing, to finance the entire increase in their consumption demand with their own money, however. They have to seek money from other sources, and this is what drives up interest rates.

One way households can raise the money is to reduce their holdings of other financial assets. For example, a household seeking money may call up its broker and place an order to sell some of its bonds. The broker finds someone else who is willing to buy the bonds and arranges the sale and purchase. The household and the other party engage in a trade of assets through the broker, as illustrated in Table 17.2.

Household 1 wants the money to finance new spending and exchanges some of its bonds for money. Household 2 is willing to exchange money for the bonds. Household 1 then takes the money and spends it on consumer goods.

Selling bonds is not the only possibility, of course. Households may get the money they need by drawing down their savings accounts and money market deposit accounts, cashing their certificates of deposit, and calling their brokers to sell some stocks as well as bonds. The transactions increase the interest rates and rates of return on all these assets.

The situation is the reverse of the analysis of the money rain in Chapter 16, when households were trying to get rid of the new money and increase their holdings of other financial assets. Now, with households drawing down their savings accounts, money market deposit accounts, and certificates of deposit,

TABLE 17.2 An Exchange of Existing Assets: Money for Corporate Bonds

HOUSEHOLD 1			HOUSEHOLD 2		
Assets		Liabilities	Assets		Liabilities
M	(+)		Corporate bonds	(+)	
Corporate bonds	(−)		M	(−)	

TABLE 17.3   Borrowing from a Credit Union

CREDIT UNION			EMPLOYEE		
Assets		Liabilities	Assets	Liabilities	
Checking account	$(-)$		Checking account $(+)$	Loan	$(+)$
Loan	$(+)$				

bank managers have to offer higher interest rates to maintain the dollar balances that they want in these accounts. Likewise, households are now entering the stock and the bond markets looking to sell. The desire to sell stocks and bonds decreases stock and bond prices and increases the rates of return on these assets to prospective buyers. After all, the household that buys the bonds in our example above, Household 2, will buy only at a "good" price, that is, a lower price. The lower price raises the expected return on the bond, which is what induces Household 2 to give up some of its money for the bonds. Remember that the demand for money is inversely related to the interest rates on competing assets. The higher return on the bonds reduces the amount of money that households want to hold. Those with money will exchange their money for other financial assets only if those other financial assets become more attractive.

In conclusion: *The desire to reduce holdings of financial assets in order to finance an increase in consumption demand raises the interest rates and rates of return on these assets.*

BORROWING THE MONEY   Still other households will choose to borrow the money needed to finance their increase in consumption demand. Most loans to households are made by banks, automobile finance corporations, credit unions associated with their places of employment, and credit card companies. Table 17.3 illustrates a loan from a credit union. It is a common example of the borrower-lender relationship described in Chapter 14.

An employee applies to his credit union for a loan. Once the credit union approves the loan, it writes a loan contract that is simultaneously an asset of the credit union/lender and a liability of the employee/borrower. The credit union issues a check drawn on its checking account at a bank in the amount of the loan and gives it to the employee who deposits it in his bank. The transfer of money from lender to borrower is the transfer of checking account balances between the two. The employee then writes checks against the deposit to finance the new spending.

The increased demand for borrowing by households drives up interest rates in the loan markets, as illustrated in Figure 17.1.

The figure represents the market for loans from all sources. The interest rate on loans is on the vertical axis, and the quantity of loans is on the horizontal axis. The market supply and the market demand curves are S^0 and D^0 prior to the increase in consumption demand. The banks, credit unions, credit card companies, and the like are the suppliers/lenders, and the households are the demanders/borrowers (along with the business firms).[2] The loan market is initially in equilibrium at (L_0, R_0), at the intersection of S^0 and D^0.

_____

[2]The figure lumps all the lenders together, even though they charge different interest rates. The main reason the rates differ is that the terms of the loans—for example, the payback period and the level of security—differ. Think of the interest rate as an average of the various loan rates charged by the different lenders.

FIGURE 17.1

Consumption Demand and the Market for Loans

The figure pictures the market for loans to households from the main institutions that lend to households—banks, automobile finance companies, credit unions, and credit card companies. S is the supply curve of loans from these lenders and D is the demand curve for loans by households. The initial equilibrium is (L_0,R_0), at the intersection of D^0 and S^0. An increase in consumption demand increases the demand for loans from D^0 to D^1 as some households borrow to finance their increased consumption expenditures. The new equilibrium is (L_1,R_1), at the intersection of D^1 and S^0. An increase in consumption demand increases the interest rate on loans, as does an increase in any component of aggregate demand, including an expansionary fiscal policy.

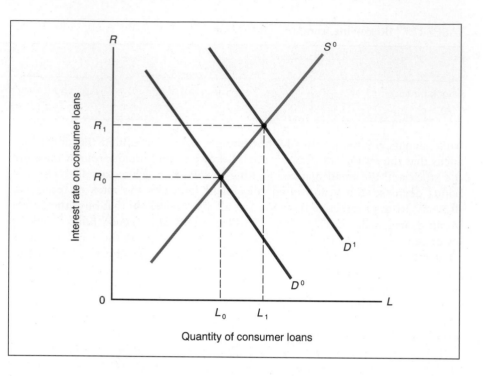

The increase in consumption demand increases the demand for borrowing by some of the households and shifts the demand curve up and to the right from D^0 to D^1. The new equilibrium is (L_1, R_1), at the intersection of S^0 and D^1. The increased demand for loans puts upward pressure on interest rates as the lenders realize that they can make more loans at higher rates. The loan rate increases from R_0 to R_1. Also, the quantity of loans written increases from L_0 to L_1 to support the increase in consumption demand.

In conclusion: *An increase in the demand for loans increases the interest rate on loans.*

To summarize, an increase in consumption demand leads some households to reduce their holdings of financial assets or borrow to raise money in order to finance the new consumption spending. Either method of obtaining money increases interest rates.

A DECREASE IN CONSUMPTION DEMAND   A decrease in consumption demand lowers interest rates. The analysis is exactly the opposite of an increase in consumption demand. A decrease in consumption demand is equivalent to an increase in saving demand. Households want to buy fewer consumer goods and increase their saving. They can increase saving by holding more money, increasing their holdings of other financial assets, or paying back their loans and reducing their borrowing.

Interest rates would not change if all the households decided just to hold more money. But this is unlikely. Households will undoubtedly use some of the funds saved from the reduced spending to increase their holdings of other financial assets. They will place some of the funds in savings and money market deposit accounts, buy certificates of deposit, and tell their brokers to buy more stocks and bonds. The increased demand for financial assets reduces the interest rates and rates of return on these assets, as we saw in the case of the money rain. Other households will pay back loans and reduce their borrowing. The demand for loans decreases and lowers the interest rate on loans.

Refer again to Figure 17.1 to see how the decrease in the demand for loans affects the interest rate on loans. This time, think of (L_1, R_1) as the initial equilibrium, at the intersection of D^1 and S^0. The decrease in consumption demand decreases the demand for loans and shifts the demand curve down and to the left, from D^1 to D^0. The decreased demand for loans puts downward pressure on interest rates as the lenders have difficulty finding borrowers. The loan rate decreases from R_1 to R_0, and the quantity of loans written decreases from L_1 to L_0 along with the decrease in consumption demand.

To summarize, a decrease in consumption demand leads some households to increase their holdings of financial assets or reduce their borrowing. Either form of increased saving decreases interest rates.

The analysis of consumption demand illustrates this principle: *An increase in any component of aggregate demand increases interest rates, and a decrease in any component of aggregate demand decreases interest rates.* There is nothing special about consumption demand. Any increase in aggregate demand from any source has to be financed, which means that some people or institutions are reducing their holdings of financial assets or borrowing to obtain money and are putting upward pressure on interest rates. Conversely, any decrease in aggregate demand from any source increases saving in the economy, which means that some people or institutions are increasing their holdings of financial assets or reducing their borrowing and are putting downward pressure on interest rates.

Fiscal Policy and Interest Rates

Fiscal policy affects the economy by directly changing or shifting aggregate demand. Therefore, the effects of fiscal policy on interest rates must be the same as for changes in aggregate demand: *An expansionary fiscal policy increases aggregate demand and raises interest rates. A contractionary fiscal policy decreases aggregate demand and lowers interest rates.*

EXPANSIONARY FISCAL POLICY   We saw in Chapter 11 that a debt-financed increase in government purchases is highly expansionary. It increases the equilibrium level of national income by the spending multiplier times the increase in government purchases. A debt-financed increase in government purchases also increases interest rates because the Treasury is borrowing more from the public to raise the money it needs to pay for the new purchases.

Borrowing by the Treasury is a standard borrower-lender transaction of the kind described in Chapter 14. The loan contracts in this case are the Treasury bills, notes, and bonds, which the Treasury creates and issues for sale to the public in return for money. The newly issued Treasury bills, notes, and bonds are simultaneously a new liability of the Treasury, the borrower, and an asset to whoever purchases them, the lender. The Treasury receives a check from the lender, which it then uses to finance the new government purchases. As we have seen, once the Treasury securities are issued, they are actively traded in the secondary Open Market by the Fed and others.

The increased borrowing by the Treasury adds to the overall demand for loans in the economy and increases the interest rates on loans. The effects on the nation's loan markets are identical to those described in Figure 17.1. The demand curve for loans shifts up and to the right, and both the interest rate and the quantity of loans increase. The intuition for the increase in interest rates is that the Treasury has to offer the lenders a higher return so that the lenders will accept the new debt. It does this by offering to sell the new Treasury bills, notes, and bonds at lower prices, which raises the rate of return on these securities to the buyers/ lenders. The higher returns on the Treasury securities raise interest rates in all markets as borrowers compete for the increasingly scarce funds.

What is true for this example holds for all expansionary fiscal policies. An expansionary fiscal policy increases interest rates.[3]

CONTRACTIONARY FISCAL POLICY   All contractionary fiscal policies have the opposite effect—they reduce interest rates. For example, suppose that the federal government reduces its purchases and matches the reduction in expenditures with a reduction in borrowing. We saw in Chapter 11 that this fiscal policy is highly contractionary. The equilibrium level of national income decreases by the spending multiplier times the decrease in government purchases.

The reduction in government spending also lowers interest rates because the Treasury is decreasing its borrowing from the public and reducing the demand for loans in the economy. The demand curve for loans in Figure 17.1 shifts down and to the left, and both the interest rates on loans and the quantity of loans decline. The direct intuition for the decrease in interest rates is that the Treasury can sell its bills, notes, and bonds at higher prices because it is not offering as many of them. The higher prices lower the rate of return on the Treasury securities. The lower returns on the Treasury securities reduce interest rates in all loan markets because more funds are available to borrowers.

The same analysis applies to all contractionary fiscal policies. A contractionary fiscal policy decreases interest rates.

Aggregate Demand and the Velocity of Circulation

The equation of exchange

$$M \cdot V = P \cdot Q = Y$$

gives us another perspective on why an increase in aggregate demand increases interest rates and a decrease in aggregate demand decreases interest rates.

Changes in aggregate demand occur against a background of a constant money supply. Only a given amount of money is available to finance whatever amount of spending is desired in the aggregate by the household, business,

---

[3]A balanced budget increase in government purchases and taxes also increases interest rates even though the Treasury is not increasing its borrowing. The reason is that households are paying a portion of their taxes out of their savings, an amount equal to MPS times the increase in their taxes. Some households have to sell assets or borrow to meet their tax liabilities, which increases interest rates in the financial markets.

government, and foreign sectors. We have also been assuming that prices are constant. With money (M) and prices (P) constant, the equation of exchange indicates that any increase in aggregate demand, including an expansionary fiscal policy, increases real national product or income (Q or Y) by increasing the velocity of circulation (V). The constant supply of money turns over at a faster rate, and national product or income increases. Conversely, any decrease in aggregate demand, including a contractionary fiscal policy, decreases real national product or income by decreasing the velocity of circulation (V). The constant supply of money turns over at a slower rate, and national product or income decreases. The rquired increases and decreases in the velocity of circulation are brought about by the increases and the decreases in interest rates.

Consider an increase in aggregate demand. Since not everyone who wants to spend more has the money on hand, money has to change hands from those who have money that they are not going to spend on goods and services to those who do not have enough money to buy all the goods and the services they want to buy. Those without money attempt either to sell financial assets to those with the money or to borrow from them. The increase in interest rates induces those with the money to reduce their holdings of money and either buy the assets being offered or lend. The money is now in the hands of those who want to spend it, and aggregate demand increases as the money is spent. Transferring the money in this way gets the constant money supply to turn over faster, and the higher velocity of circulation allows for the multiplied increase in national income.

The same analysis applies in reverse to a decrease in aggregate demand. Interest rates falls as the demand for financial assets increases and the demand for loans decreases. The decrease in interest rates increases the quantity of money demanded, the constant money supply turns over more slowly, and the lower velocity of circulation allows for a multiplied decrease in national income.

Crowding Out, Interest Rates, and the Spending Multiplier

Our analysis of the spending multiplier and the various fiscal policy multipliers in Chapter 11 ignored the change in interest rates that results from a change in aggregate demand. We need to correct this oversight because the change in interest rates feeds back into aggregate demand in a way that substantially reduces the value of the multipliers. The interest rate feedback occurs through two distinct channels. One channel is through the demands for consumer durables and investment in the domestic economy. The other channel is through net exports in the foreign sector. The change in interest rates is said to **crowd out** these components of aggregate demand and lower the value of the multipliers. In effect, the constant supply of money constrains the amount that aggregate demand can change.

CROWDING OUT: CONSUMER DURABLES AND INVESTMENT   Consider first the crowding out of consumer durables and investment. Suppose that the federal government increases its purchases of goods and services and finances the increase by issuing debt. Chapter 11 analyzed a debt-financed increase in government purchases with the aggregate demand–45° line graph, as follows.

Crowding Out: Consumer Durables and Investment

The initial equilibrium level of national income is Y_0, at the intersection of ADE_0 and the 45° line. A debt financed increase in government purchases increases G^d from G_0^d to G_1^d, and aggregate demand shifts up from ADE_0 to ADE_1. The new equilibrium level of national income would be Y_1, at the intersection of ADE_1 and the 45° line, if interest rates did not rise. The increase in aggregate demand does increase interest rates, which increases the cost of borrowing to households and firms. As a result, households reduce their purchases of consumer durables and new houses, and firms reduce their purchases of plant and equipment and inventory. Consumption demand increases from G_0^d to C_1^d, investment demand decreases from I_0^d to I_1^d, and aggregate demand shifts down from ADE_1 to ADE_2. The final equilibrium level of national income is Y_2, at the intersection of ADE_2 and the 45° line. The rise in interest rates crowds out consumer durables and investment, which reduces the value of the spending multiplier.

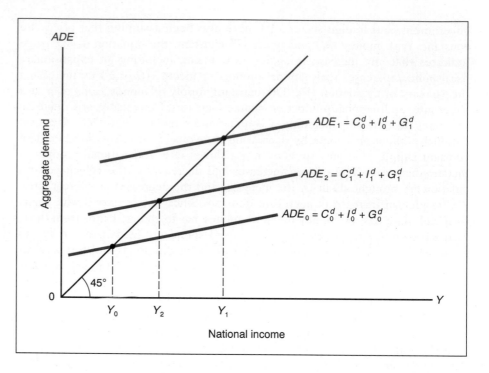

Refer to Figure 17.2. The equilibrium level of national income is initially Y_0, at the intersection of aggregate demand line ADE_0 and the 45° line. The increase in government purchases increases G^d from G_0^d to G_1^d, which shifts up the aggregate demand line from ADE_0 to ADE_1. The new equilibrium level of national income is Y_1, at the intersection of ADE_1 and the 45° line.

Our previous analysis assumed that the change in G^d was the only change (shift) in aggregate demand because it ignored the increase in interest rates that accompanies the increase in aggregate demand. In fact, the increase in interest rates feeds back into the demands for consumer durables and investment and shifts these two components of aggregate demand down.

Figure 17.3 illustrates the interest rate feedback. The figure reproduces Figure 16.6, which indicated how the demands for consumer durables and investment are related to interest rates. Figure 17.3(a) shows the relationship between interest rates and the demand for consumer durables, C^{Dur}. Figure 17.3(b) shows the relationship between interest rates and investment demand, I^d. Both demands are downward sloping, inversely related to interest rates, because interest rates are an important component of the cost of buying consumer durables, new houses, plant and equipment, and inventory.

Suppose that interest rates were initially R_0 before the increase in government spending. At R_0 the demand for consumer durables is C_0^{Dur}, and the investment demand is I_0^d. C_0^{Dur} is the consumer durables component of the initial consumption demand, C_0^d, in Figure 17.2, and I_0^d is the same as I_0^d in Figure 17.2. The increase in government spending raises interest rates to R_1 as the Treasury increases its borrowing. The increase in interest rates raises the cost of borrowing to households and firms. Households respond by reducing their spending on consumer durables to C_1^{Dur} in Figure 17.3(a). Firms respond by reducing their investment spending to I_1^d in Figure 17.3(b).

Return again to Figure 17.2. The increase in interest rates reduces consumption demand from C_0^d to C_1^d and investment demand from I_0^d to I_1^d. There-

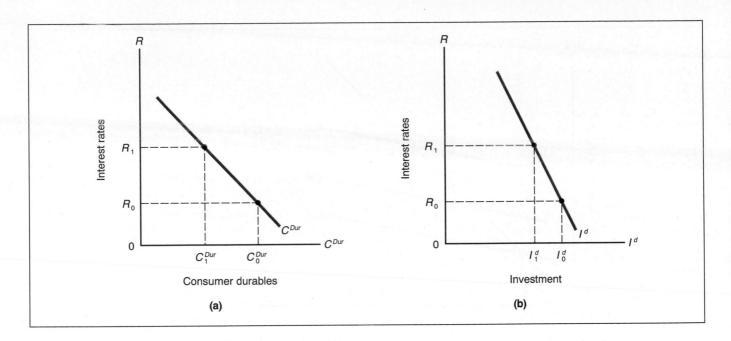

fore, aggregate demand shifts down from ADE_1 to ADE_2. The final equilibrium level of national income is Y_2, at the intersection of ADE_2 and the 45° line. The increase in interest rates feeding back into consumption demand and investment demand has reduced the value of the spending multiplier. The increase in government purchases increases the equilibrium level of national income from Y_0 to Y_2, instead of from Y_0 to Y_1 without the interest rate feedback.

The increase in government purchases crowds out consumption demand and investment demand because the money supply is constant and there is only so much money to go around. The government, by borrowing money to finance its expenditures, leaves less money available for households and businesses to borrow. Interest rates rise to reflect the increasing scarcity of funds and choke off some consumption demand and investment demand.

The interest rate feedback through consumption demand and investment demand is symmetric. It also reduces the impact of a decrease in aggregate demand. To see why, suppose that the federal government decreases its purchases and borrows less as a result. The Treasury's reduced demand for loans decreases interest rates, which induces households to spend more on consumer durables and housing and induces firms to buy more plant and equipment and more inventory. Refer again to Figure 17.3, and think of R_1 as the initial interest rate and R_0 as the new lower interest rate. C^{Dur} and I^d both increase in response to the lower rates. The higher demand for consumer durables and investment increases aggregate demand relative to what it would be without the interest rate effect and reduces the multiplied decrease in national income brought on by the decrease in government purchases.

CROWDING OUT: NET EXPORTS   The crowding out of net exports occurs because interest rates have a substantial impact on the value of the dollar. We saw in Chapter 16 that an increase in U.S. interest rates causes funds to flow into the United States from abroad in search of U.S. securities and increases the value of the dollar. The dollar appreciates relative to the other major currencies. Conversely, a decrease in U.S. interest rates causes funds to flow out

FIGURE 17.3

Interest Rates, Consumer Durables, and Investment

The increase in aggregate demand in Figure 17.2 increases interest rates from R_0 to R_1. As a result, households reduce their purchases of consumer durables and houses and firms reduce their purchases of plant and equipment and inventory. Figure 17.3(a) pictures the demand curve for consumer durables, C^{Dur}, in terms of the interest rate on loans, which is on the vertical axis. The increase in interest rates from R_0 to R_1 reduces households' purchases of consumer durables from C_0^{Dur} to C_1^{Dur}. Figure 17.3(b) pictures the investment demand curve, I^d, in terms of the interest rate on loans. The increase in interest rates from R_0 to R_1 reduces purchases of investment goods from I_0^d to I_1^d. The reduction in consumer durables and investment is one source of the crowding out effect as interest rates change in response to a change in aggregate demand.

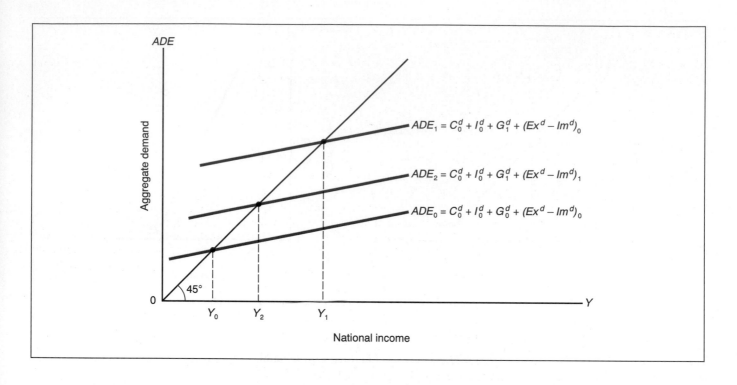

FIGURE 17.4

Crowding Out: Net Exports

The initial equilibrium level of national income is Y_0, at the intersection of ADE_0 and the 45° line. As in Figure 17.2, an increase in government purchases increases G^d from G_0^d to G_1^d, and the equilibrium level of national income would rise to Y_1, at the intersection of ADE_1 and the 45° line, if interest rates did not rise. The increase in interest rates attracts funds from foreign countries into the United States, which appreciates the value of the dollar. An appreciation of the dollar increases import demand, from Im_0^d to Im_1^d, and reduces export demand, from Ex_0^d to Ex_1^d. The demand for net exports decreases from $(Ex^d - Im^d)_0$ to $(Ex^d - Im^d)_1$, and aggregate demand shifts down from ADE_1 to ADE_2. The final equilibrium level of national income is Y_2, at the intersection of ADE_2 and the 45° line. The rise in interest rates crowds out net exports, which lowers the value of the spending multiplier.

of the United States in search of foreign securities and decreases the value of the dollar. The dollar depreciates relative to the other major currencies. An appreciation or depreciation of the dollar in turn feeds back into net exports.

Figure 17.4 illustrates the crowding out of net exports. The figure reproduces the initial shift in aggregate demand from ADE_0 to ADE_1 in Figure 17.2, resulting from the increase in government demand. As before, the equilibrium level of national income would increase from Y_0 to Y_1 without the interest rate feedback to aggregate demand. The increase in aggregate demand increases U.S. interest rates, however, so that funds flow into the United States and the dollar appreciates relative to the other major currencies. The appreciation of the dollar makes imports cheaper to U.S. consumers and U.S. exports more expensive to foreign consumers.

For example, suppose that the dollar appreciates in value from $1.80/£ to $1.60/£. British goods priced at 1£ used to cost U.S. consumers $1.80. Now they cost only $1.60. The lower price of imports to U.S. consumers increases the quantity of imports demanded. Conversely, U.S. goods priced at $1.80 used to cost British consumers 1£. Now they cost more than 1£ because 1£ buys only $1.60 in the foreign exchange markets. The higher price of U.S. exports to British consumers decreases the quantity of U.S. exports demanded.

The increased demand for imports and the reduced demand for U.S. exports both reduce the demand for net exports. Net exports shift down from $(Ex^d - Im^d)_0$ to $(Ex^d - Im^d)_1$ in Figure 17.4, which shifts aggregate demand down from ADE_1 to ADE_2. The reduction in net exports induced by the appreciation of the dollar reduces the value of the spending multiplier. The increase in government purchases increases the equilibrium level of national income from Y_0 to Y_2, instead of from Y_0 to Y_1.

The interest rate feedback through net exports is also symmetric; it reduces the impact of a decrease in aggregate demand. To see why, suppose that the government reduces its purchases of goods and services and borrows less. The chain of events that follows is exactly the reverse of the above. Because the Treasury is borrowing less, U.S. interest rates fall, and funds flow out of the United States in search of higher returns in foreign markets. The outflow of funds depreciates the dollar—say, from $1.60£ to $1.80/£—which makes imports more expensive to U.S. consumers and U.S. exports cheaper to British consumers. The decreased demand for imports and the increased demand for U.S. exports both increase the demand for net exports. The higher demand for net exports increases aggregate demand relative to what it would be without the interest rate/exchange rate feedback and reduces the multiplied decrease in national income brought on by the decrease in government purchases.

The two crowding-out channels are either/or propositions to some extent; the more one occurs, the less the other occurs. For example, suppose that aggregate demand increases and funds really pour into the United States as U.S. interest rates begin to rise. The increased supply of foreign funds represents an increase in saving by the foreign sector and increases the total saving in the economy. As such, it makes more funds available to those who are selling assets or borrowing to raise money, and it mitigates the increase in interest rates. The less interest rates rise, the less consumer durables and investment are crowded out. At the same time, however, the more foreign funds that enter the United States, the greater the appreciation of the dollar. The more the dollar appreciates, the more net exports are crowded out. Conversely, suppose that the United States were totally isolated from the rest of the world, so that net-export crowding out is impossible. Then U.S. rates would rise by the maximum amount and enhance the crowding out of consumer durables and investment.

Twenty-five years ago net-export crowding out was essentially ignored in the macroeconomic analysis of the U.S. economy. Not so any more. The increasing internationalization of the U.S. economy has made net-export crowding out an important phenomenon for policy makers to consider. Net-export crowding out may be even more important today than consumer durable–investment crowding out is.

Net-export crowding out was certainly a significant factor in slowing down the recovery of the economy from the deep recession of 1981–82. As noted in Chapter 12, the government undertook an extremely expansionary fiscal policy to pull the economy out of the recession. The economy responded, but did not return to the production possibilities frontier until 1987. A major reason for the long recovery period was that the dollar appreciated 23 percent against the major currencies from 1982 through 1985, in part because U.S. interest rates were very high.[4] The large appreciation of the dollar decreased net exports and held down the growth of aggregate demand as the economy was trying to recover. At the same time, the influx of foreign funds supported investment and consumer durables. These two components of aggregate demand grew at their usual pace during the recovery.

CROWDING OUT AND THE POLICY OPTIONS   The crowding-out phenomenon has some interesting implications for the timing of fiscal and monetary policies.

CROWDING-OUT EFFECT

Changes in the demands for consumer durables, investment, and net exports that are induced by the change in interest rates following a change (shift) in aggregate demand, and that lower the value of the spending multiplier.

CURRENT ISSUE: The United States is lobbying hard to make its economy even more internationalized. President Clinton is pressing other nations to open up government contracts for telecommunications equipment to worldwide competitive bidding. At present, most European governments require that this equipment be purchased from domestic producers.

---

[4]Council of Economic Advisers, *Economic Report of the President, 1993* (Washington, D.C.: U.S. Government Printing Office, 1993), Table 107, p. 470.

Fiscal policy tends to stimulate the economy more rapidly than does monetary policy because it directly affects aggregate demand. But the crowding-out phenomenon ultimately reduces the ability of fiscal policy to stimulate or slow down the economy regardless of whether crowding out occurs through the consumer durables–investment channel or the net export channel. Crowding out does not apply to monetary policy, however. For example, an expansionary monetary policy reduces interest rates, and the reduction in interest rates stimulates consumer durables demand and investment demand. It does not crowd them out. Also, the reduction in interest rates leads to an outflow of funds from the United States, which depreciates the dollar and stimulates net export demand. Therefore, sustaining a recovery from a recession may well require a dose of expansionary monetary policy at some point to counteract the crowding-out problem with fiscal policy.

The same point holds in reverse. If the federal government really wants to hold down the growth of aggregate demand, it might start with a contractionary fiscal policy. But it should also consider slowing down the growth of the money supply at some point in order to shore up interest rates. Higher interest rates help to reduce spending on consumer durables and investment. They also support the value of the dollar, which reduces net export demand as well.

The need for monetary policy to help maintain the growth in aggregate demand is even more compelling now that the U.S. economy has become more international in scope. Net-export crowding out can significantly reduce the effectiveness of fiscal policy without some help from monetary policy.

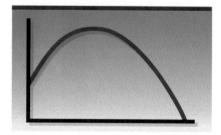

THE SPENDING MULTIPLIER IN THE UNITED STATES

Chapter 11 introduced the spending multiplier in the context of the simplest possible economy as

$$M_{\text{Spending}} = 1/(1 - \text{MPC})$$

We noted at the time that although the simple spending multiplier captures the idea of the multiplier process, it is unrealistic in two respects. First, it greatly overstates the actual value of the spending multiplier in the United States. The MPC is approximately .9 in the long run, which implies a spending multiplier of 10. In fact, the actual spending multiplier is on the order of 1 to 3. In addition, the multiplier process is hump-shaped, as illustrated in Figure 11.3. A change in aggregate demand produces a multiplied change in national income that builds continuously for about a year and a half, after which the change in national income begins to decline and settle in on its final value.

We saw in Chapter 12 that automatic stabilizers reduce the value of the simple spending multiplier by approximately 40 percent, from a value of 10 to a value of 6. The automatic stabilizers result when national income feeds back into aggregate demand through taxes, transfer payments, business saving, and import demand. Now we have seen that interest rates also feed back into aggregate demand, crowding out consumer durables, investment, and net exports and reducing the spending multiplier still further. Adding the crowding-out phenomenon to automatic stabilizers brings the actual spending multiplier most of the way down into the 1 to 3 range.

The crowding-out phenomenon also explains the hump-shaped pattern of the multiplier process. Refer again to Figures 17.2 and 17.4. The movement of the economy from Y_0 to Y_2 can be thought of as occurring in two steps over time, first from Y_0 to Y_1 and then from Y_1 to Y_2. The increase in government spending starts a multiplier process going that builds continuously to a peak of Y_1. Then, after about a year and a half, the increase in interest rates begins to take effect. The rise in interest rates eventually decreases consumption demand and investment demand, as represented in Figure 17.2, and net export demand, as represented in Figure 17.4. National income declines from its peak of Y_1 and settles on its final value of Y_2. The multiplier process is hump-shaped, as required.

AGGREGATE DEMAND MANAGEMENT: THE POLICY OPTIONS

The federal government attempts to control aggregate demand over the short run through its fiscal and monetary policies. The Concept Summary table lists the short-run effects of fiscal and monetary policies on two key economic policy variables, (real) national income and interest rates.

CONCEPT SUMMARY

THE EFFECTS OF FISCAL AND MONETARY POLICIES ON REAL NATIONAL INCOME AND INTEREST RATES

FISCAL POLICY	REAL NATIONAL INCOME	INTEREST RATES
Expansionary (increase G, Tr; decrease Tx)	Increase Y	Increase R
Contractionary (decrease G, Tr; increase Tx)	Decrease Y	Decrease R

MONETARY POLICY	REAL NATIONAL INCOME	INTEREST RATES
Expansionary (Fed buys Treasury securities on the Open Market)	Increase Y	Decrease R
Contractionary (Fed sells treasury securities on the Open Market)	Decrease Y	Increase R

To review:

- *An expansionary fiscal policy increases both national income and interest rates.* Expansionary fiscal policies include increases in government purchases of goods and services, increases in transfer payments, and decreases in taxes. Fiscal policy is the responsibility of the administration and the Congress.
- *A contractionary fiscal policy decreases both national income and interest rates.* Contractionary fiscal policies include decreases in government purchases of goods and services, decreases in transfer payments, and increases in taxes.
- *An expansionary monetary policy increases national income and decreases interest rates.* The Fed conducts an expansionary monetary policy by buying Treasury securities on the Open Market from securities dealers at a few large commercial banks, brokerage houses, and investment banks. The Fed's purchase of Treasury securities increases the reserves in the commercial banks, which allows them to make more loans and create new checking account balances.
- *A contractionary monetary policy decreases national income and increases interest rates.* The Fed conducts a contractionary monetary policy by selling some of its Treasury securities on the Open Market to the securities dealers. The Fed's sale of Treasury securities decreases the reserves in the commercial banks, which forces them to reduce their loans and checking account balances.

Notice that expansionary and contractionary fiscal and monetary policies have the same effect on national income, but the opposite effect on interest rates. An easy way to remember the different interest rate effects is to recall how the policies affect the market for loans. Fiscal policy changes the *demand* for loans, whereas monetary policy changes the *supply* of loans.

For example, an expansionary fiscal policy increases the demand for loans, as in Figure 17.1, primarily because of increased borrowing by the Treasury. The increased demand for loans increases the average interest rates on loans. In contrast, an expansionary monetary policy increases the supply of loans, as in Figure 16.5, because it gives banks excess reserves to lend. The increased supply of loans decreases the average interest rates on loans. The quantity of loans increases with both policies and the economy expands, but with opposite effects on interest rates. Test your understanding of these points by thinking about how contractionary fiscal and monetary policies affect the market for loanable funds.

Hitting National Income and Interest Rate Targets

Chapter 12 concluded with a simplified example of the government's economic policy problem in which the government used different kinds of fiscal policies to reach the full-employment level of national income. Now we are in a position to consider a more complex policy problem in which the government uses two economic policies, fiscal policy and monetary policy, to manipulate two economic policy variables, national income and interest rates. Let's briefly review the nature of the economic policy problem before proceeding.

Recall that solving the economic policy problem is a three-step process. The government's policy makers first have to decide what goals they are trying to achieve. The four macroeconomic policy goals are long-run economic growth, full employment, price stability, and a balance of trade approximately equal to zero along with a stable value of the dollar. These goals are often conflicting, and the federal government does not pursue them directly in any case. Instead, it pursues them indirectly, primarily by managing aggregate demand through its fiscal and monetary policies. Changes in aggregate demand directly affect the equilibrium level of national income and interest rates, which in turn influence the four macroeconomic policy goals. Therefore, the second step is to set target values for national income and interest rates that the policy makers believe represent the best possible compromise in terms of achieving the four macroeconomic policy goals. The third and final step is to design a combination of fiscal and monetary policies to hit the national income and interest rate targets.

The different interest rate effects of fiscal and monetary policies are crucial to hitting both targets because they give the federal government two independent policy instruments for managing aggregate demand. With two independent policy instruments, the federal government has the flexibility it needs to manipulate both national income and interest rates as it desires. In principle, the federal government can simultaneously hit whatever target values of national income and interest rates it has set with a suitable combination of fiscal and monetary policies.

In practice, the possibilities for fiscal and monetary policies are far more limited. We have seen that the federal government cannot fine tune the economy with either fiscal or monetary policy. The best either policy can hope to do is "lean against the wind" and nudge the economy in the right direction. Nonetheless, the independence of fiscal and monetary policies is still useful because it allows the government to "lean" independently on national income and interest rates. The government can decide whether it would like national income to increase, stay about the same, or decrease and whether it would like interest rates to increase, stay about the same, or decrease. Then, it can use its fiscal and monetary policies, either alone or in combination, to achieve simultaneously any one of the three choices for national income and any one of the three choices for interest rates. Manipulating the direction of national income and interest rates is not the same as hitting exact target values for national income and interest rates, to be sure. But it is enough to give the federal government a considerable amount of influence over the four macroeconomic policy goals.

The following eight examples indicate how the federal government can manipulate the direction of national income and interest rates with its fiscal and monetary policies. The first four examples are the simplest; they require only one policy, either fiscal policy or monetary policy. The last four examples are more complex; they require a combination of fiscal and monetary policies.

When thinking about these examples, you may want to refer back to the Concept Summary table on page 527, which summarizes the effects of fiscal and monetary policies on national income and interest rates.

SINGLE POLICIES   Four desired directional targets for national income and interest rates are possible with single policies.

1. *Increase national income and decrease interest rates.* Suppose that the government's policy makers decide that they want to increase aggregate demand and national income in order to reduce unemployment. They also want to decrease interest rates to spur investment demand and long-run economic growth. An

expansionary monetary policy produces the desired result. The Fed should buy Treasury securities on the Open Market to increase reserves in the commercial banks. An expansionary monetary policy simultaneously increases aggregate demand and national income and decreases interest rates.

The remaining examples will indicate the directional targets for national income and interest rates without indicating why the government might want these targets. The next section of the chapter looks closely at how changes in national income and interest rates influence the four macroeconomic policy goals.

2. *Increase national income and increase interest rates.* Expansionary fiscal policy moves the two variables in the desired direction. The administration and the Congress should increase government purchases, increase transfer payments, or cut taxes, either singly or in combination. An expansionary fiscal policy simultaneously increases aggregate demand and national income and increases interest rates.

3. *Decrease national income and decrease interest rates.* Contractionary fiscal policy is the answer if the government wants to decrease aggregate demand and national income while simultaneously decreasing interest rates. The administration and the Congress should decrease government purchases, decrease transfer payments, or raise taxes, either singly or in combination. A contractionary fiscal policy simultaneously decreases aggregate demand and national income and decreases interest rates.

4. *Decrease national income and increase interest rates.* The correct policy in this case is a contractionary monetary policy. The Fed should sell Treasury securities on the Open Market to drain reserves from the commercial banks. A contractionary monetary policy simultaneously decreases aggregate demand and national income and increases interest rates.

COMBINATION POLICIES   The following four examples require a combination of fiscal and monetary policies. They illustrate the principle that the government has the flexibility to hit national income and interest rate targets simultaneously with a suitable combination of fiscal and monetary policies.

5. *Increase national income and keep interest rates about the same.* Suppose that the government's policy makers decide that they want to increase aggregate demand and national income, but that they are satisfied with the level of interest rates. Conducting only one of the policies changes both national income and interest rates. Therefore, these two targets require a combination of fiscal and monetary policies.

A combination of expansionary fiscal policy and expansionary monetary policy produces the desired result. Expansionary fiscal policy increases both national income and interest rates. Expansionary monetary policy increases national income and decreases interest rates. The two policies both serve to increase aggregate demand and national income. At the same time, they pull in opposite directions on interest rates and tend to cancel each other out. Therefore, a suitable combination of expansionary fiscal policy and expansionary monetary policy can increase aggregate demand and national income while leaving interest rates just about the same.

6. *Decrease national income and keep interest rates about the same.* The proper policy this time is a combination of contractionary fiscal policy and contractionary monetary policy. The contractionary fiscal policy decreases both na-

tional income and interest rates. The contractionary monetary policy decreases national income and increases interest rates. The two policies serve to decrease national income while pulling in opposite directions on interest rates. Therefore, a suitable combination of the two can decrease aggregate demand and national income while leaving interest rates just about the same.

7. *Leave national income about the same and increase interest rates.* These two targets require a combination of expansionary fiscal policy and contractionary monetary policy. The expansionary fiscal policy increases both national income and interest rates. The contractionary monetary policy decreases national income and increases interest rates. The two policies pull in opposite directions on national income. At the same time, they both serve to increase interest rates. Therefore, a suitable combination of the two can leave aggregate demand and national income just about the same while increasing interest rates.

8. *Leave national income about the same and decrease interest rates.* These two targets require a combination of contractionary fiscal policy and expansionary monetary policy. The contractionary fiscal policy decreases both national income and interest rates. The expansionary monetary policy increases national income and decreases interest rates. Once again, the two policies pull in opposite directions on national income. This time, though, they both serve to decrease interest rates. Therefore, a suitable combination of the two can leave aggregate demand and national income just about the same while decreasing interest rates.

These combination policy strategies suggest other possibilities. For example, suppose that the government's policy makers want aggregate demand and national income to increase substantially. They also want interest rates to increase, but only a little. The proper policy response might be a very expansionary fiscal policy coupled with a mildly expansionary monetary policy. The mildly expansionary monetary policy keeps aggregate demand and national income growing while counteracting somewhat the increase in interest rates brought on by the expansionary fiscal policy.

REFLECTION: What combination of fiscal and monetary policies would help drive interest rates down substantially while increasing national income only slightly?

Coordinating Fiscal and Monetary Policies

The attempt to manipulate national income and interest rates with a combination of fiscal and monetary policies encounters one serious practical problem that we have not stressed previously, the problem of coordinating the two policies. Fiscal and monetary policies are not conducted under one umbrella. Fiscal policy is the responsibility of the administration and the Congress, and monetary policy is the responsibility of the Fed. Moreover, Congress established the Federal Reserve Banking System as a separate and independent government agency. The Fed is not under the direct oversight of either the Congress or the administration. The chairman of the Fed's Board of Governors does have to appear before Congress twice a year to indicate the Fed's views on the state of the economy and its intentions regarding monetary policy. Other than this, the federal government makes no specific attempt to coordinate its fiscal and monetary policies.

The result of the Fed's independence is that fiscal and monetary policies can, and often do, work at cross-purposes. An outstanding example occurred in response to the deep recession of 1981–82. The administration and the Congress embarked on the most expansionary fiscal policy in the nation's history. The Fed, meanwhile, was still pursuing a very tight monetary policy that it had begun in 1979 to squeeze inflation out of the economy. The combination of a very expansionary fiscal policy and a very tight monetary policy served to slow down the recovery from the recession. It also produced very high interest rates, much higher than the nation wanted, given its concern about low levels of investment and sluggish long-run economic growth.

Congress has been willing to bear the occasional costs to macroeconomic policy of an independent Fed. It had good reasons for wanting the central bank to operate without undue political influence from the administration or the Congress, and few in Washington are seriously proposing that the Fed give up its independence.

AGGREGATE DEMAND MANAGEMENT: THE POLICY GOALS

Now that we have seen how the government can use its fiscal and monetary policies to manipulate the direction of national income and interest rates, one final policy question remains: How do changes in national income and interest rates relate to the four macroeconomic policy goals of long-run economic growth, full employment, price stability, and a zero balance of trade along with a stable value of the dollar?

The following Concept Summary table defines the menu of choices that are available to policy makers over the short run. It pulls together all that we have said in the previous chapters about the relationship of national income and

CONCEPT SUMMARY

NATIONAL INCOME (Y), INTEREST RATES (R), AND THE MACROECONOMIC POLICY GOALS (SHORT-RUN)

	LONG-RUN ECONOMIC GROWTH (INVESTMENT)	FULL EMPLOYMENT	PRICE STABILITY	BALANCE OF TRADE, STABLE DOLLAR
Increase Y	Increase investment multiplier accelerator model	Decrease unemployment	Increase inflation	Increase imports Worsen balance of trade
Decrease Y	Decrease investment (multiplier accelerator model)	Increase unemployment	Decrease inflation	Decrease imports Improve balance of trade
Increase R	Decrease investment (increase cost of capital)			Inflow of foreign currencies Dollar appreciates in value
Decrease R	Increase investment (decrease cost of capital)			Outflow of dollars Dollar depreciates in value

interest rates to the macroeconomic policy goals. Understand that the table is a menu of policy choices under a very particular set of assumptions. It assumes that the changes in national income and interest rates are the result of the government's fiscal and monetary policies. As such, the changes are driven by changes in aggregate demand. It also assumes a new Keynesian policy environment in which wages and prices are sticky in the short run and the economy may be operating far beneath its production possibilities frontier with lots of unemployed resources.

Let's run through each entry in the table to recall what we have learned so far.

National Income and the Policy Goals

Changes in national income have a significant impact on all four of the macroeconomic policy goals.

LONG-RUN ECONOMIC GROWTH   Investment in plant and equipment is a key determinant of long-run economic growth, and the link between national income and investment is the multiplier-accelerator model of Chapter 13. The main insight of that model is that firms invest only when they project an increasing demand for their products. Otherwise, they do not need to expand their production capacity. Therefore, rapid growth in aggregate demand is absolutely essential in order to have a high-investment economy. Firms simply will not invest very much if aggregate demand is stagnating and the economy is suffering from high unemployment and excess capacity. This is true no matter how low the cost of capital may be, either because interest rates are low or because the federal government is offering firms special tax incentives to invest.

Some economists believe that investment in plant and equipment is determined more by the growth of aggregate demand than by the cost of capital. Although this point is controversial, most economists would agree that a stagnating economy is not especially conducive to investment in plant and equipment.

Many new Keynesian economists would also argue that the crowding-out phenomenon does not apply when the economy is far from full employment. They believe that an increase in aggregate demand in this situation stimulates investment demand through the multiplier-accelerator mechanism, rather than crowding it out. They talk about investment being "crowded in" when unemployment is very high.

FULL EMPLOYMENT/LOW UNEMPLOYMENT The connection between national income and unemployment is very direct in a world of sticky wages and prices. The unemployment rate rises and falls with the ebbs and flows of the business cycle. A decrease in aggregate demand and national income leads firms to reduce production and lay off workers, which increases the unemployment rate. An increase in aggregate demand and national income leads firms to increase production and hire more workers, which decreases the unemployment rate. We saw in Chapter 6 how the involuntary job losers category of the unemployed swings with the business cycle. In response to the business cycle, workers and firms in the United States appear to have adopted a policy of layoffs and rehires instead of a flexible wage policy that would maintain full employment at all times.

PRICE STABILITY/LOW INFLATION   The previous chapters have said little about inflation because they were assuming fixed wages and prices in order to capture the essence of the new Keynesian view of the economy in the short run. A full analysis of price inflation appears in Chapter 19. Controlling inflation is by its very nature a long-run policy problem, and new Keynesian and new classical economists agree on how to keep inflation under control in the long run.

Changes in aggregate demand do change the rate of inflation even in the short run, however, and in the way that one would expect. An increase in aggregate demand increases the rate of inflation, and a decrease in aggregate demand decreases the rate of inflation. The basic insight into why comes from the Laws of Supply and Demand. An increase in aggregate demand places more product markets and factor markets in a state of excess demand and fewer in a state of excess supply. The results are upward pressure on prices generally throughout the economy and a higher rate of inflation. Conversely, a decrease in aggregate demand places more product markets and factor markets in a state of excess supply and fewer in a state of excess demand. The results are downward pressure on prices generally throughout the economy and a lower rate of inflation.

THE SHORT-RUN PHILLIPS CURVE   Notice that the goals of full employment and price stability are in direct conflict with one another in the short run. An increase in aggregate demand reduces the unemployment rate, but increases the rate of inflation. A decrease in aggregate demand reduces the rate of inflation, but increases the unemployment rate.

The inverse relationship between unemployment and inflation in response to changes in aggregate demand was first documented by British economist A. W. Phillips for the British economy. Subsequent research by U.S. economists verified the same inverse relationship for the U.S. economy. The relationship, pictured in Figure 17.5, became known as the short-run Phillips Curve.

The rate of inflation is on the vertical axis, and the unemployment rate is on the horizontal axis. The vertical line highlights the natural rate of unemployment, U_{NR}, the unemployment rate when the economy is operating on its production possibilities frontier. U_{NR} is assumed to be 6 percent in the graph. The **short-run Phillips Curve** shows how the rate of inflation and the unemployment rate respond to a change in aggregate demand in the short run. Note that the curve is quite flat at high unemployment rates, becomes steeper as the unemployment rate approaches the natural rate, and then becomes very steep as the unemployment rate reaches and falls below the natural rate. The shape of the curve indicates that the inflation and the unemployment rates respond quite differently to changes in aggregate demand depending on the state of the economy when aggregate demand changes.

For example, suppose that the government undertakes expansionary fiscal and monetary policies that increase aggregate demand in order to reduce the unemployment rate. According to the figure, the increase in aggregate demand can reduce the unemployment rate substantially with only a slight increase in

SHORT-RUN PHILLIPS CURVE

A curve that shows how the rate of inflation and the unemployment rate respond to a change in aggregate demand in the short run.

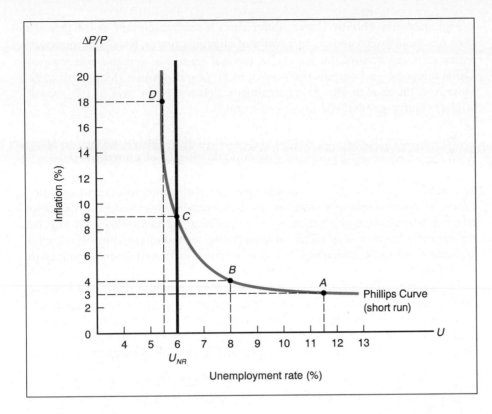

FIGURE 17.5
The Short-Run Phillips Curve

The short-run Phillips Curve shows how unemployment and inflation respond to a change in aggregate demand in the short run. The unemployment rate, U, is on the horizontal axis, and the inflation rate, $\Delta P/P$, is on the vertical axis. An increase in aggregate demand has different effects on unemployment and inflation depending on the state of the economy. The movements from A to B, B to C, and C to D are the result of equal increases in aggregate demand. The increase in aggregate demand at point A, when the unemployment is 11.5 percent, reduces unemployment by 3.5 percentage points to 8 percent, and increases the rate of inflation by only 1 percentage point, from 3 percent to 4 percent. As the economy moves closer to and even beyond its production possibilities frontier represented by the natural rate of unemployment, U_{NR} (= 6 percent), the same increase in aggregate demand generates a smaller reduction in unemployment and a larger increase in inflation. For example, starting at point C, when unemployment is 6 percent, the same increase in aggregate demand as at point A reduces the unemployment rate by only half a percentage point, from 6 percent to 5.5 percent, and increases the rate of inflation by 9 percentage points, from 9 percent to 18 percent.

inflation in the short run if the unemployment rate is very high to begin with. Fiscal and monetary policies reduce the unemployment rate from 11.5 percent at point A to 8 percent at point B with only a one-percentage-point increase in inflation, from 3 percent to 4 percent. The same expansionary fiscal and monetary policies reduce the unemployment rate less and the inflation rate more in the short run if the unemployment rate is nearer the natural rate to begin with. The movement from B to C assumes the same increase in aggregate demand as for the movement from A to B. This time, however, the unemployment rate declines by only two percentage points, from 8.0 percent to 6.0 percent, while the rate of inflation increases by five percentage points, from 4 percent to 9 percent. Finally, suppose that the same expansionary fiscal and monetary policies are applied when the economy is on its sustainable production possibilities frontier and the unemployment rate is at 6 percent, the natural rate. Now most of the increase in aggregate demand simply causes higher inflation. The unemployment rate drops by only a half of a percentage point, from 6 percent at point C to 5.5 percent at point D, while the rate of inflation increases by nine percentage points, from 9 percent to 18 percent. The numbers are hypothetical, but they illustrate how a given dose of expansionary policy has a very different impact on unemployment and inflation in the short run, depending on the state of the economy.

The same analysis applies in reverse to contractionary fiscal and monetary policies. The same dose of contractionary policy reduces inflation more, and increases unemployment less, the lower the unemployment rate is to begin with.

The short-run Phillips Curve underscores a very important point that we have not emphasized earlier. In a world of changing prices, fiscal and monetary policies directly control the growth of *nominal* aggregate demand and *nominal* national income and output, the growth of $P \cdot Q$ and not just the growth of Q. Moreover, the growth of nominal aggregate demand is the *sum* of the growth in prices (inflation) and the growth in output.

$$\text{Rate of growth in } P \cdot Q = \text{rate of growth in } P + \text{rate of growth in } Q$$
$$= \text{rate of inflation} + \text{rate of growth in } Q$$

OKUN'S LAW

An observed relationship between output growth and unemployment, which states that every 2.5-percentage-point increase in the rate of growth of output reduces the unemployment rate in the United States by 1 percentage point.

The rate of growth in Q determines how much the unemployment rate declines. A common rule of thumb for the U.S. economy is called **Okun's Law:** Every 2.5-percentage-point increase in Q reduces the unemployment rate by 1 percentage point. Okun's Law is named after economist Arthur Okun, who first described the relationship between output growth and unemployment in the 1970s.

The short-run Phillips Curve indicates that the growth in nominal aggregate demand is split differently between inflation and growth in real output, depending on the state of the economy. Suppose that the increase in the growth of nominal aggregate demand in our example is 10 percent. The implied breakdown into inflation and growth in output in Figure 17.5 is roughly as follows:

	RATE OF INFLATION	RATE OF GROWTH IN Q
A to B	1%	9%
B to C	5	5
C to D	9	1

The numbers on each line must add up to 10 percent, the growth in nominal aggregate demand. The unemployment numbers and the rate of growth in output numbers in the example are roughly in accord with Okun's Law. For instance, the 5 percent increase in Q from B to C reduces unemployment by two percentage points (from 8 percent to 6 percent), exactly as Okun predicted ($5\%/2.5 = 2\%$). The other rate-of-growth numbers are not exactly right, but close.

We cannot stress strongly enough that the short-run Phillips Curve applies only in the short run, as its name suggests, and only in response to changes in aggregate demand. The long-run analysis of inflation in Chapter 19 will show that the inverse relationship between inflation and unemployment breaks down over time and disappears entirely in the long run. There is no long-run relationship at all between inflation and unemployment. In addition, inflation and unemployment respond very differently in the short run to a change in aggregate supply. An adverse aggregate supply shock, such as an increase in the price of crude oil, increases both inflation and unemployment. A favorable aggregate supply shock, such as an improvement in productivity, decreases both inflation and unemployment. Inflation and unemployment bear a direct relationship to one another in the short run when changes in national income are being driven by the supply side of the economy.

THE BALANCE OF TRADE AND THE VALUE OF THE DOLLAR   The balance of trade is the difference between the values of imports and exports. National income and the balance of trade are connected through the marginal propensity to import, which as we saw in Chapter 12, is approximately equal to .1 in the United States. An increase in national income increases imports of consumer goods, raw materials, intermediate inputs, and capital goods and worsens the balance of trade. A decrease in national income decreases imports of these goods and improves the balance of trade.

The change in imports also feeds back somewhat into the value of the dollar. Consider the case of an increase in national income leading to an increase in imports. The importers who sell their goods in the United States are foreign citizens who eventually want to exchange the dollars that they receive into their own currencies. The desire to exchange dollars for foreign currencies lowers the value of the dollar; the dollar depreciates. Conversely, a decrease in imports reduces the exchange of dollars for foreign currencies and raises the value of the dollar; the dollar appreciates.

Interest Rates and the Policy Goals

Changes in interest rates have a significant impact on two of the macroeconomic policy goals, long-run economic growth and the value of the dollar.

LONG-RUN ECONOMIC GROWTH   Interest rates influence long-run economic growth through their impact on investment demand. Interest rates are a major component of the annual cost of capital to business firms. The lower interest rates are, the lower the cost of capital is, and the higher the firms' desired stock of capital is. The presumption is that the increase in the desired stock of capital induces firms to increase their annual rate of investment. Conversely, the lower interest rates are, the higher the cost of capital is, and the lower the firms' desired stock of capital is. Presumably investment demand also decreases.

Economists cannot agree on whether interest rates and investment demand are closely related in the short run. Nearly all economists would agree, however, that low interest rates are more conducive to investment than are high interest rates over the long run, which is the relevant horizon for long-run economic growth. Economists have been uniformly critical of the high long-run interest rates in the United States that have persisted throughout the 1980s and into the 1990s. They believe that the high interest rates have contributed to the nation's low rate of economic growth. The main reason why most economists favor reducing the federal government's structural budget deficit is to reduce interest rates and stimulate investment demand.

THE BALANCE OF TRADE AND THE VALUE OF THE DOLLAR   The relationship between interest rates and the value of the dollar is strong and immediate. We have seen that an increase in U.S. interest rates leads to an immediate inflow of foreign funds, which increases the value of the dollar. The dollar appreciates relative to the world's major currencies. Conversely, a decrease in U.S. interest rates leads to an immediate outflow of funds to foreign financial markets, which decreases the value of the dollar. The dollar depreciates relative to the world's major currencies. The impact of interest rates on the dollar exchange rate is much stronger and more immediate than is the impact of national income, which operates indirectly through import demand.

What Should the Targets Be?

The menu of policy choices in the Concept Summary table indicates that choosing target levels of national income and interest rates over the short run is never an easy decision. The table is full of conflicts among the goals. For instance, the federal government may want to increase national income in order to reduce unemployment and to spur investment and growth, but then it has to live with a higher rate of inflation and a worsening balance of trade. Or the government may want to decrease interest rates to encourage investment, but lower interest rates weaken the value of the dollar and make imports more expensive to consumers. The choice of national income and interest rate targets is always a judgment call. Which goals are the most important to pursue at the moment? Which combination of national income and interest rates represents the best possible compromise among the goals? Reasonable people can reasonably disagree on the best answers to these questions.

Political considerations also enter into the policy decision and lead to their own set of compromises. A good recent example occurred in 1991. The Bush administration desperately wanted to pull the economy out of the recession in time for the 1992 election. Most economists would agree that the quickest way to get the economy moving is with expansionary fiscal policy, since it directly increases aggregate demand. The large budget deficit had tied the administration's hands, however. Increasing the deficit even more in 1991 was considered political suicide by both the administration and the Congress. So the Bush administration relied on expansionary monetary policy, which increases aggregate demand only indirectly and much more slowly. As we saw in Chapter 16, the lags from increases in the money supply to increases in aggregate demand during a recession can be very long, well over a year. This appeared to be the case in 1991–92. The Fed began pumping reserves into the commercial banks in the second quarter of 1991, but the economy did not show any signs of life until the third quarter of 1992, too late to save the Bush presidency.

Add together the conflicts among the macroeconomic policy goals, the practical difficulties in conducting fiscal and monetary policies, and the various political considerations that appear from time to time, and the recipe for concocting just the right short-run policy mix is an exceedingly tricky one indeed.

REFLECTION: The introduction mentioned that the United States has been having problems meeting all four macroeconomic policy goals. Which ones would you give highest priority to, and what policies would you recommend to pursue them? What would be some of the costs of your policies?

SUMMARY

Chapter 17 pulled together the analysis of the macro economy in Chapters 10 through 16, which looked at the operation of the economy in the short run from a new Keynesian perspective of sticky wages and prices and unemployed resources.

The first section of the chapter considered how changes in aggregate demand affect interest rates. It began with a change in consumption demand.

1. An increase in consumption demand increases interest rates because some households have to reduce their holdings of financial assets or borrow to obtain the money they need to buy goods and services. Both transactions increase interest rates. For example, the desire to sell stocks and bonds lowers their prices and raises their rates of return. An increased demand for loans increases interest rates on loans.

2. Conversely, a decrease in consumption demand is an increase in saving demand. Households increase their demand for financial assets and reduce their borrowing, both of which decrease interest rates.

3. An expansionary fiscal policy increases aggregate demand directly, so it increases interest rates. Increased deficit financing requires the Treasury to borrow more, which increases the demand for loans throughout the economy.

4. Conversely, a contractionary fiscal policy decreases aggregate demand directly, so it decreases interest rates. Reducing the deficit results in less borrowing by the Treasury, which decreases the demand for loans throughout the economy.

5. The change in interest rates following a change in aggregate demand crowds out consumer durables, investment, and net exports and lowers the value of the spending multiplier. For example, an increase in aggregate demand increases interest rates, which reduces the demand for consumer durables and investment. Higher interest rates also increase the value of the dollar as funds flow into the United States, seeking the higher returns. An appreciation of the dollar reduces the demand for exports and increases the demand for imports, both of which reduce the demand for net exports.

6. Crowding out through interest rates also explains the hump-shaped pattern of the multiplier process. For example, an increase in aggregate demand causes national income to increase rapidly at first, but then the increase in interest rates reduces the demand for consumer durables, investment, and net exports, and national income declines to its final value.

The second section of the chapter showed how the government can, in principle, hit target values of national income and interest rates with a suitable combination of fiscal and monetary policies.

7. Fiscal and monetary policies give the government two independent policy tools to hit national income and interest rate targets because they have opposite effects on interest rates. Expansionary fiscal and monetary policies both increase aggregate demand and national income, but expansionary fiscal policy increases interest rates, whereas expansionary monetary policy decreases interest rates. Contractionary fiscal and monetary policies both decrease aggregate demand and national income, but contractionary fiscal policy decreases interest rates, whereas contractionary monetary policy increases interest rates.

8. The best the federal government can hope to do is influence the direction of national income and interest rates, rather than hitting target values exactly. The chapter considered a number of possibilities. For example, a desire to increase both national income and interest rates requires an expansionary fiscal policy. A desire to increase national income, but leave interest rates about the same, requires a combination of expansionary fiscal policy and expansionary monetary policy.

The final section of Chapter 17 summarized how national income and interest rates relate to the four macroeconomic policy goals.

9. Changes in national income influence all four goals in the short run. For example, increases in aggregate demand and national income
   a. promote investment demand and long-run economic growth through the multiplier-accelerator process,
   b. lower unemployment,

    c. increase inflation, and

    d. worsen the balance of trade by increasing the demand for imports.
Decreases in aggregate demand and national income have the opposite effects.

10. The short-run Phillips Curve illustrates the inverse relationship between inflation and unemployment in response to a change in aggregate demand. The relationship varies, depending on the state of the economy. For example, an increase in aggregate demand decreases unemployment less and increases inflation more the lower the initial rate of unemployment, and vice versa.

11. Changes in interest rates primarily affect long-run economic growth and the value of the dollar. For example, a decrease in interest rates

    a. stimulates investment demand and long-run economic growth because interest rates are an important component of the cost of capital, and

    b. causes the dollar to depreciate in value as funds flow out of the United States, seeking higher returns elsewhere.

An increase in interest rates has the opposite effects.

KEY TERMS

crowding-out effect   Okun's Law   short-run Phillips Curve

QUESTIONS

1. What effect does each of the following policies have on the rate of inflation and the unemployment rate in the short run?
   a. a 10 percent tax cut
   b. a 12 percent rise in government expenditures
   c. a 5 percent cut in government transfer payments

2. Why does an increase in aggregate demand cause interest rates to rise?

3. a. Explain what is meant by the crowding out of consumer durables and investment and by the crowding out of net exports.
   b. Discuss the role of interest rates in the crowding-out phenomenon.
   c. What effect does crowding out have on the value of the spending multiplier?

4. What is Okun's Law? Suppose that output is $1,000, and the unemployment rate is 6 percent initially. If output increases to $1,050, what does Okun's Law predict the new rate of unemployment will be?

5. Draw the short-run Phillips Curve, and explain why you drew it as you did. What appears on the axes? What do points along the short-run Phillips Curve represent?

6. Discuss the directional effects on the equilibrium level of national income and the level of interest rates in the short run when the government engages in the following policies:
   a. Congress passes a 6 percent increase in all personal income tax rates.

   b. The Fed sells $200 million of Treasury debt on the Open Market.
   c. The Fed increases the reserve requirement on checking account deposits by one percentage point.
   d. The federal government increases government spending on goods and services by $5 billion, financed by increasing the debt.
   e. Both (a) and (b) occur simultaneously.
   f. Both (c) and (d) occur simultaneously.

7. Suppose that the government is satisfied with the current level of interest rates (rates of return) throughout the economy, but is dissatisfied with the growth in national income. Design a set of monetary and fiscal policies that will increase national income, but leave interest rates unchanged. Be specific about your policy choices, and indicate why your policies would work.

8. Suppose that the federal government undertakes the following combination of fiscal and monetary policies. Congress raises all personal income tax rates by 5 percent, and the Fed buys $20 million of Treasury debt on the Open Market. Discuss what qualitative effects this combination of policies has on each of the four macroeconomic policy goals in the short run.

9. Suppose that the federal government wants to increase output growth without worsening the balance of trade. What fiscal and monetary policies should the government undertake?

10. Suppose that the federal government is interested in increasing investment demand. Answer the following questions.
    a. Why might the government want to increase investment demand?
    b. Which of the following four policy options is the best for increasing investment demand, and why: expansionary fiscal policy, expansionary monetary policy, contractionary fiscal policy, or contractionary monetary policy?
    c. Describe one possible undesirable side effect of the policy option that you chose in part (b). (*Note:* Your answers to parts (a) and (c) should relate to the macroeconomic policy goals.)

11. Suppose that
    (i) prices are rising at the rate of 6 percent per year,
    (ii) output is rising at the rate of 3 percent per year, and
    (iii) the money supply is rising at the rate of 4 percent per year.
    a. What must be happening to the income velocity of circulation (*V*)? Why?
    b. What must be happening to the demand for money? Why?

CASE

The Accord of 2006: The End of Fiscal Policy?*

This case takes you into the future and asks you to consider the ramifications of a drastic change in federal economic policy.

In 2005, Andrew Mackintosh was appointed Chairman of the Board of Governors of the Federal Reserve System, having served as a board member since 2003. Although Mackintosh's background is in academia rather than banking, he comes from a new generation of economists that is tired of the theoretical debates between new Keynesian and new classical economists. Mackintosh favors a more pragmatic approach to monetary and fiscal policy.

It comes as a surprise, then, when in 2006 the President of the United States (who had just appointed the Chairman the previous year) and Mackintosh agree that the United States Treasury will stop selling new issues of Treasury securities to the public. Instead, as old Treasury bills, notes, and bonds mature, the government will have two options. It can redeem the maturing securities with funds received from taxes or other revenues, or it can redeem them by issuing new securities. But—and here is the shocker—it must sell the new securities only to the Federal Reserve, not to the public.

Furthermore, whenever the Treasury seeks to turn over old, maturing securities, the Fed will be obligated to buy the newly issued replacement securities. But the Fed will have the discretion to buy, or not to buy, newly issued Treasury securities that represent additional indebtedness as the result of a federal budget deficit. If the Fed chooses not to buy the new offerings, then there can be no new debt and no new increase in government spending over its revenues for any given fiscal year.

These new stipulations regarding the issuing and purchase of Treasury securities are referred to as "The Accord of 2006."

Under the Accord of 2006, it is theoretically possible that after 15 years, in 2021 (when most of the pre-2006 indebtedness would have matured), either the national debt will have been lowered toward zero with payoffs from government revenues, or (more likely) the national debt will be owned entirely by the Federal Reserve System, itself a government agency. In effect, the national debt will be owed by the government to itself.

The Accord of 2006 is a pragmatic attempt to end, or at least reduce, the huge structural federal budget deficits that the government has been running ever since 1981. The Gram-Rudman-Hollings Act of 1985, the Omnibus Budget Reconciliation Act of 1990, and the 1993 passage of President Clinton's $500 billion deficit reduction plan all failed to reduce the deficits. President Clinton's plan failed because of the enormous increases in federal expenditures for health care following the passage of the National Health Care program. Providing 37 million Americans with quality health care turned out to be far more expensive than the administration and Congress had anticipated, and they were unwilling to raise taxes to pay for the program. The current President and Chairman Mackintosh feel it is time for a more drastic approach to reducing the deficit, one which gives the Fed the power to limit deficit spending by the administration and Congress.

---

*Provided by James J. McLain, University of New Orleans

(continued on next page)

The Accord of 2006: The End of Fiscal Policy? (cont.)

ECONOMIC ADVISOR'S REPORT

Suppose that you are the economic advisor to the Assistant Secretary of the Treasury for Central Bank Affairs, and are asked to lead a team that will consider several questions raised by the Accord of 2006.

1. The first question Treasury wants you to answer is this: What interest rate should the Fed pay for any Treasury securities that it buys? How was the interest rate determined before the Accord, and should the Fed try to duplicate the results of that system?
2. Is the Accord of 2006 better than the old system of essentially independent fiscal and monetary policies for:
   (a) Holding down aggregate demand when the economy is booming and straining against its production possibilities frontier?
   (b) Increasing aggregate demand when the economy is operating far below its production possibilities frontier, with lots of unemployed resources?

Indicate how your answers to these questions depend on the following possible choices by the Fed:

(i) The Fed will not buy newly issued Treasury securities if they are intended to finance a federal budget deficit.
(ii) The Fed will buy newly issued Treasury securities if they are intended to finance a federal budget deficit, but only up to a limit of $150 billion each year.
(iii) The Fed will buy all newly issued Treasury securities regardless of why the Treasury is selling them.

3. The Employment Act of 1946 made the President responsible for promoting non-inflationary, full-employment economic growth.
   (a) Will the federal government's attempt to reach these goals be freer from political pressures under the Accord of 2006?
   (b) Does the Accord remove fiscal policy as a means of fulfilling the goals of the Employment Act of 1946?
   (c) Does the Accord allow the Fed to conduct a monetary policy that is independent of federal budgetary policy?

4. Does it matter whether the national debt is owned by the Fed or by private U.S. citizens?

The Role of Prices and the
Problem of Inflation

18

Aggregate Supply and Aggregate Demand

LEARNING OBJECTIVES

CONCEPTS TO LEARN

Aggregate demand curve

Short-run aggregate supply curve

Long-run aggregate supply curve

Stagflation

CONCEPTS TO RECALL

Laws of Supply and Demand [5]

Aggregate demand and aggregate supply [9]

New Keynesian economics [9]

New classical economics [9]

Aggregate demand and aggregate supply shocks [9]

Real business cycle model [13]

il has been one of the leading macroeconomic stories of the past 20 years. It is the prime example of the tremendous effect that supply shocks can have on an economy.

When the Organization of Petroleum Exporting Countries (OPEC) increased the price of crude oil eightfold from 1973 to 1979, it threw the industrialized market economies into turmoil. They suffered the double whammy of rising unemployment and rising inflation and were helpless to do much about it. In 1980, inflation in the United States was 12.5 percent and unemployment was 7.1 percent. Congress in its exasperation passed the largest tax cut in U.S. history on the basis of a new and untried supply-side theory of how tax cuts work, which the media dubbed Reaganomics. The Western European nations were so panicked by the specter of inflation that they tied their currencies to the German mark. They knew that the Germans feared inflation more than anyone and would do everything in their power to hold down the growth of their money supply to keep the mark strong and prevent inflationary pressures from building. The other nations of Western Europe were not sure they had the resolve to fight the inflation on their own. The oil price increases also brought enormous hardships to the low-income developing nations. Many were forced to borrow heavily at very high interest rates in order to finance their imports, and a number of them eventually defaulted on their debt.

OPEC lost its market power in 1980, and the price of oil came tumbling down almost as sharply as it had risen in the 1970s. The collapse of the oil prices ushered in a new period of prosperity. Inflation in the United States fell to 3.7 percent by 1982, and the economy grew steadily from December 1982 to July 1990, one of the longest periods of uninterrupted growth in the United States during the twentieth century. Inflation also ceased to be a serious threat in Western Europe, and many of the Western European economies enjoyed rapid growth as well. Oil was not solely responsible for the reversal of fortunes in the United States and Europe, but it certainly deserved a large part of the credit. By the end of the 1980s the debt problem had also subsided a bit for the developing nations, except for countries like Mexico that rely heavily on oil exports. For the Mexicans the earlier rise in oil prices was a blessing, and the subsequent collapse of oil prices was a curse. Most nations, though, are very thankful that oil prices are not expected to rise rapidly anytime in the near future.[1]

Chapters 18 and 19 explore the role of prices in the macro economy. Chapter 18 describes how prices help to bring the economy to an equilibrium in both the short run and the long run. Chapter 19 then concludes our study of macroeconomics with a discussion of some current policy issues. Its main focus, though, is on the problem of keeping inflation under control.

Chapter 18 begins by developing the aggregate supply–aggregate demand (AS–AD) model of the macro economy that we introduced in Chapter 9. The AS–AD model highlights the role of prices in bringing the economy to its

---

1. Council of Economic Advisers, *Economic Report of the President, 1993* (Washington, D.C.: U.S. Government Printing Office, 1993), Table 37, p. 390 (unemployment) and Table 58, p. 415 (inflation).

equilibrium. We will then use the AS–AD model to compare and contrast the new Keynesian and new classical perspectives on how the macro economy operates.

AGGREGATE DEMAND AND AGGREGATE SUPPLY: AN OVERVIEW

We began our study of the macro economy in Chapter 9 with the observation that the first relationship in every macro model is

$$Y = C^d + I^d + G^d + (Ex^d - Im^d)$$

The relationship describes the overall equilibrium in the nation's product markets in terms of supply and demand. The left-hand side of the relationship represents aggregate supply. Y is the (real) national income or national output generated by producers in supplying goods and services. The right-hand side of the relationship represents the aggregate demand for goods and services, broken down into its four components by sector of the economy. Aggregate demand is the sum of consumption demand (C^d) by the household sector, investment demand (I^d) by the business sector, demand for goods and services (G^d) by the government sector, and net export demand ($Ex^d - Im^d$) by the foreign sector. The relationship says that the nation's product markets are in equilibrium when the aggregate supply of goods and services equals the aggregate demand for goods and services.

Our analysis of supply and demand for a single product in the introductory chapters of the text emphasized the role of price in bringing a competitive market to equilibrium because the price is what draws suppliers and demanders together in exchange. The price of each good and each service is the one variable that households and firms share in common as they try to solve their economic problems through exchange. For the same reason, prices also play a crucial role in bringing the overall macro economy to its equilibrium.

Nonetheless, our analysis of the macro economy following Chapter 9 kept prices in the background by assuming that they are constant. We did this to highlight the new Keynesian view of how the economy operates over the short run when lots of resources are unemployed and prices (and wages) are fairly sticky. The new Keynesians argue that national income or national output is primarily determined by aggregate demand in that environment and that aggregate supply responds passively to aggregate demand. They also believe that national income is more important than are prices in determining the level of aggregate demand in the short run.

New Keynesian economists do not ignore prices, however. They acknowledge that prices vary more and become more important in the short run as the economy nears or reaches its production possibilities frontier and that prices are flexible enough in the long run to bring the macro economy to its long-run equilibrium. New Keynesian economists also acknowledge that the economy is occasionally hit by significant aggregate supply shocks that change firms' costs of production and feed through quickly to prices.

The new classical economists argue that prices are always the most important variable bringing the macro economy to its equilibrium, both in the short run and in the long run. In their view the vast majority of product markets and

FIGURE 18.1

The Aggregate Demand Curve

The aggregate demand curve, *AD*, is a graph of the aggregate demand schedule, which indicates the aggregate quantity of final goods and services demanded by all the final demanders—households, businesses, governments, and the foreign sector—at each overall price level. Real national product, *Q*, is on the horizontal axis, measured in $billions, and the overall price level, *P*, represented by the GDP deflator, is on the vertical axis. *AD* is downward sloping. In the figure, an increase in the GDP deflator from 100 to 110 decreases the aggregate quantity of final goods and services demanded from $5,000 to $4,800. A decrease in the GDP deflator from 100 to 90 increases the aggregate quantity of final goods and services demanded from $5,000 to $5,300. The inverse relationship between the aggregate quantity demanded and the overall price level arises principally because the quantity of money demanded for transactions purposes is directly related to the overall price level.

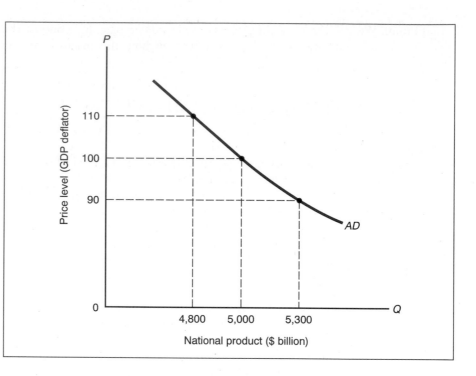

factor markets are highly competitive and operate roughly in accordance with the Laws of Supply and Demand. Prices (and wages) are flexible for the most part, not sticky. Therefore, the best model of the macro economy is one in which prices equate aggregate supply and aggregate demand at all times as a natural by-product of equating supply and demand in each individual market.

We need to develop the AS–AD model of the economy in order to compare and contrast the new Keynesian and the new classical views of the economy. The development here extends the earlier introductory presentation of the model in Chapter 9 and pulls together some material from other chapters. Let's begin with aggregate demand because it is not a source of controversy between new Keynesian and new classical economists.

AGGREGATE DEMAND

AGGREGATE DEMAND SCHEDULE

A schedule that indicates the quantity of national output demanded by the four sectors of the economy at each overall level of prices.

AGGREGATE DEMAND CURVE

A graph of the aggregate demand schedule that shows the quantity of national output demanded by the four sectors of the economy at each overall level of prices.

An **aggregate demand schedule** describes the quantity of national output demanded by the four sectors of the economy at each overall level of prices. The **aggregate demand curve,** labeled *AD*, is a graph of the aggregate demand schedule. It is downward sloping, as illustrated in Figure 18.1.

P on the vertical axis represents the overall or average level of the prices of all products. It is a broad-based price index of goods and services, such as the gross domestic product (GDP) deflator. *Q* on the horizontal axis is a measure of real national product, such as constant dollar GDP, in billions of dollars. It represents the real quantities of goods and services demanded in the nation's product markets by the household, business, government, and foreign sectors combined. The aggregate demand curve, *AD*, shows that price and aggregate quantity demanded are inversely related, as expected. The national product demanded is $5,000 when the GDP deflator is 100. The national product demanded decreases to $4,800 when the GDP deflator rises to 110; the national product demanded increases to $5,300 when the GDP deflator falls to 90. (The numbers are hypothetical.)

The aggregate demand curve and the demand curve for a single product are both downward sloping, but the similarity between the two ends there. They are very different concepts.

The downward-sloping, single-market demand curve is a picture of the Law of Demand. It describes the relationship between the quantity demanded and the price of the product under the assumption of *other things equal*. In particular, the single-market curve assumes that all other prices and consumers' incomes are being held constant. Therefore, when the price rises, the product becomes more expensive relative to all other products, and the purchasing power of the consumers' incomes falls. When the price falls, the product becomes cheaper relative to all other products, and the purchasing power of the consumers' incomes rises. The changes in relative prices and purchasing power are the sources of the substitution and income effects that support the Law of Demand.

The aggregate demand curve, *AD,* in contrast, does not hold other things equal. The GDP deflator on the vertical axis is a broad-based price index. When it rises from 100 to 110, the assumption is that the prices of *all* goods and services are changing simultaneously. Some prices may be rising by more than 10 percent and some by less than 10 percent, but the overall level of all prices is increasing by 10 percent, on average. Moreover, the aggregate demand curve allows for the possibility that all factor prices are changing as well, even though many factor prices are not part of the GDP deflator. The standard assumption lying behind the aggregate demand curve is that factor prices always change by the same percentage as product prices do, so that the purchasing power of the national income generated in the nation's factor markets does not change. For example factor prices are assumed to increase by an average of 10 percent when the GDP deflator increases from 100 to 110. Therefore, the standard substitution and income effects of a single price change do not apply at the aggregate level. When all product and factor prices change simultaneously by the same percentage, neither relative prices nor the purchasing power of national income changes.

The downward slope of the *AD* curve results from the relationship between the overall price level and the transactions demand for money. We saw in Figure 16.3 that the transactions demand for money is directly proportional to the overall price level. A 10 percent increase in the overall level of prices causes a 10 percent increase in the transactions demand for money. The reason why is that Federal Reserve Notes and checking account balances are denominated in nominal terms. Therefore, if the prices of goods and services rise by 10 percent on average, people need 10 percent more money to buy the same amount of goods and services as before the price increase.

The 10 percent increase in the overall price level forces people to readjust their balance sheets. They need to obtain the extra money, setting off the chain of events described in Chapter 17. They draw down their deposits in savings and money market accounts and sell other financial assets, such as stocks and bonds, which drives up interest rates and rates of return on these financial assets. The higher interest rates in turn decrease the interest-sensitive components of aggregate demand, principally consumer durables and investment, especially investment in housing. In other words, the increased demand for money causes people to hold fewer real assets as well as fewer financial assets. The higher interest rates also attract foreign funds, which drives up the value of the dollar. The appreciating dollar in turn increases the demand for imports and decreases the demand for exports; the demand for net exports decreases. The decreased demand for consumer durables, investment, and net exports reduces the aggregate quantity demanded.

To summarize:

$$P \uparrow \rightarrow \text{transactions demand for money} \uparrow \rightarrow R \uparrow \rightarrow$$
$$C^{Dur}, I^d, (Ex^d - Im^d) \downarrow \rightarrow \text{aggregate quantity demanded} \downarrow$$

The same argument applies in reverse. A decrease in the overall price level causes a proportionate decrease in the transactions demand for money, which causes people to adjust their balance sheets in the opposite direction. They add to their savings and money market accounts and buy more stocks and bonds, which drives down interest rates on these financial assets. The decrease in interest rates increases interest-sensitive components of aggregate demand, such as consumer durables and investment. People buy more real assets as well as more financial assets. The decrease in interest rates also leads to an outflow of funds to foreign markets, which causes the dollar to depreciate and increases the demand for net exports.

To summarize:

$$P \downarrow \rightarrow \text{transactions demand for money} \downarrow \rightarrow R \downarrow \rightarrow$$
$$C^{Dur}, I^d, (Ex^d - Im^d) \uparrow \rightarrow \text{aggregate quantity demanded} \uparrow$$

A number of other factors support the inverse relationship between aggregate demand and the overall price level as well. For instance, corporate and government bonds are also denominated in nominal terms. Therefore, the purchasing power of bondholders' wealth decreases when prices rise, which may reduce consumption demand and investment demand. In addition, many pensions are not indexed to a broad-based price index such as the consumer price index (CPI) or the GDP deflator. The retirees with unindexed pensions do lose purchasing power when the overall price level increases, which lowers their consumption demand. The same holds true for many of the poor who receive public assistance transfers. Their welfare checks have not kept pace with the CPI over the past 20 years in the United States. None of these other factors is nearly so important as the transactions demand for money, however, in producing a downward-sloping aggregate demand curve.

AD and the *ADE*–45° Line Graph

The aggregate demand line, *ADE*, on the *ADE*–45° line graph that we have been using up to now shows the other things equal relationship between aggregate demand and (real) national income or output. It assumes that the overall price level is constant, one of the "other things" being held equal that fix the position of the curve. Increases and decreases in the overall price level shift the *ADE* line up and down. Figure 18.2 illustrates the relationship between the aggregate demand curve, *AD*, specified in terms of prices, and *ADE*, specified in terms of national income. It uses the hypothetical numbers in Figure 18.1.

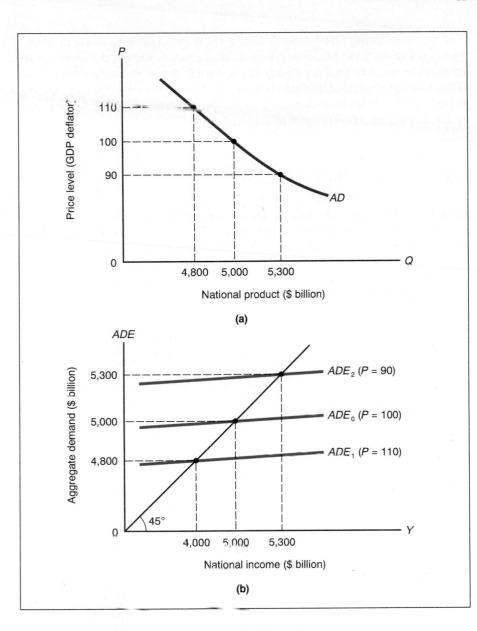

FIGURE 18.2

The *AD* Curve and *ADE*-45° Line

Figure 18.2(a) pictures the aggregate demand curve, *AD*, from Figure 18.1. Figure 18.2(b) pictures aggregate desired expenditures, *ADE*, which are determined by the level of real national income, *Y*. Real national product and real national income are assumed to be equal. Every *ADE* line corresponds to one value of the GDP deflator. For example, ADE_0 shows aggregate desired expenditures at every level of national income when the GDP deflator is 100. Conversely, every point on the *AD* curve corresponds to an intersection of the *ADE* and 45° lines in Figure 18.2(b), because aggregate demand equals real national product (national income) only at the equilibrium level of national income. Therefore, when the GDP deflator is 110, the *ADE* line is ADE_1, and the equilibrium level of national income is $4,800. When the GDP deflator is 90, the *ADE* line is ADE_2, and the equilibrium level of national income is $5,300.

AD is in Figure 18.2(a), and *ADE* is in Figure 18.2(b). *Q* in Figure 18.2(a), national product, has the same value as *Y* in Figure 18.2(b), national income. The values of *Q* and *Y* are in billions of dollars. Each *ADE* line in Figure 18.2(b) is associated with one value of the GDP deflator on the vertical axis in Figure 18.2(a). ADE_0 is the relationship between aggregate demand and national income (national output) when the GDP deflator is 100. Also, each level of national product on the *AD* curve corresponds to the equilibrium level of national income in Figure 18.2(b), the intersection of *ADE* and the 45° line. National income (national product) is equal to aggregate demand only at the equilibrium. Figure 18.2(a) indicates that aggregate demand is $5,000 when the GDP deflator is 100. Therefore, the equilibrium level of national income (national product) in Figure 18.2(b) associated with ADE_0 is $5,000.

An increase in the GDP deflator to 110 shifts the ADE line down to ADE_1. The equilibrium level of national income decreases to \$4,800, the corresponding level of national product on AD in Figure 18.2(a). A decrease in the GDP deflator to 90 shifts the ADE line up to ADE_2. The equilibrium level of national income (national product) increases to \$5,300, the corresponding level of national product on AD in Figure 18.2(a).

AGGREGATE SUPPLY

AGGREGATE SUPPLY SCHEDULE

A schedule that indicates the quantity of national output supplied by all producers at each overall level of prices.

AGGREGATE SUPPLY CURVE

A graph of the aggregate supply schedule that shows the quantity of national output supplied by all producers at each overall level of prices.

An **aggregate supply schedule** describes the quantity of national output supplied by all producers at each overall level of prices. The **aggregate supply curve,** labeled AS, is a graph of the aggregate supply schedule.

Aggregate Supply: The Long Run

The disagreement between the new Keynesian and the new classical economists centers on the aggregate supply curve, and then only in the short run. Both sides agree that wages and prices are flexible enough that markets essentially operate according to the Laws of Supply and Demand in the long run. In Chapter 9 we discussed the following macroeconomic implications of assuming that the economy is competitive.

1. Competitive factor markets automatically bring the economy to the production possibilities frontier. Consequently, the long-run aggregate supply curve, AS_{LR}, is vertical, as pictured in Figure 18.3. Q_0 is the frontier level of national product.
2. The national product is entirely determined by the supply side of the economy. Producers generate the frontier output, Q_0, in Figure 18.3 regardless of the overall price level for the goods and services. Aggregate demand simply determines the overall price level at the frontier, P_0, in Figure 18.3. The long-run equilibrium is (Q_0, P_0), at the intersection of AD and AS_{LR}.

Review the discussion in Chapter 9 if you are unclear about any of these points.

This consensus among economists underscores why long-run economic growth is ultimately the most important of the four macroeconomic policy goals. Refer again to Figure 18.3. A nation must shift AS_{LR} to the right and increase output to improve its standard of living over the long run. But shifting AS_{LR} is possible only if the nation can push out its production possibilities frontier through the process of long-run economic growth. As we saw in Chapter 3, expanding the frontier requires investment in physical and human capital, both of which make the nation's resources more productive. Without long-run economic growth, AS_{LR} stays put, and the standard of living stagnates. Nations must be patient, however, because long-run economic growth is a slow process. For example, the United States can shift out AS_{LR} only about 3 to 4 percent per year, at best.

Both new Keynesian and new classical economists advocate government policies to promote investment and long-run growth. Common proposals include increasing public investment in the nation's transportation and communications networks; reducing the structural budget deficits to keep interest rates low and

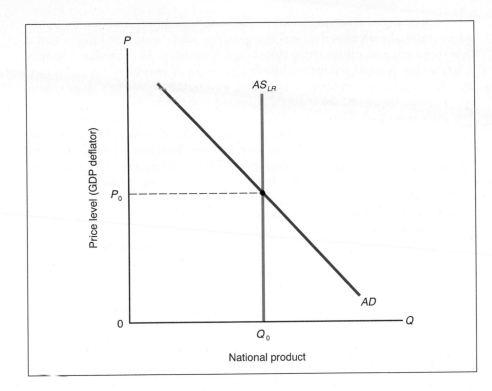

FIGURE 18.3

Aggregate Supply in the Long Run

The aggregate supply curve is a graph of the aggregate supply schedule, which indicates the aggregate quantity of final goods and services supplied by all producers in the economy at each overall price level. Real national product, Q, is on the horizontal axis, and the overall price level, P, represented by the GDP deflator, is on the vertical axis. New Keynesian economists agree with new classical economists that markets are competitive enough, and prices are flexible enough, to bring the economy to its production possibilities frontier in the long run. Both schools agree that the long-run aggregate supply curve, AS_{LR}, is vertical at Q_0, the frontier level of real national product. The role of the overall price level in the long run is to adjust the aggregate quantity demanded along the aggregate demand curve, AD, to the frontier output, Q_0. The long-run equilibrium is (Q_0, P_0), at the intersection of AD and AS_{LR}.

encourage investment demand; subsidizing education of all kinds, from training programs for unskilled high school drop-outs to student loans and grants for higher education; supporting research and development for new products and new production technologies; and easing the tax burden on saving and investment, the most radical suggestion being to replace the federal personal and corporation income taxes with a personal consumption tax that exempts saving and investment from taxation.

The Clinton administration has embraced all these proposals for promoting long-run economic growth, with the single exception of the tax reforms. President Clinton does support tax credits for investment. Yet he also supported, and Congress passed, an increase in the top federal personal income tax rate from 31 percent to 39.6 percent, to ensure that the burden of reducing the budget deficit falls disproportionately on the rich. This will tend to reduce saving and investment, because the high-income taxpayers do most of the saving in the United States.

People joke that all they hear from macro economists these days is "invest, invest, invest." Maybe so—the need to stimulate investment to promote long-run economic growth is one of the few macroeconomic policies that new Keynesian and new classical economists agree on—that, and the need to control inflation, another long-run policy issue.

Aggregate Supply: The Short Run

New Keynesian and new classical economists disagree completely about the behavior of prices and output in the short run. Their disagreement centers on the nature of the aggregate supply curve in the short run.

New Keynesian economists look at the macro economy and see a market system riddled with imperfections that produce sticky wages and prices and a short-run aggregate supply curve that is far from vertical. In their view, changes in aggregate demand produce substantial changes in output in the short run, especially when the economy is operating well below its production possibilities frontier. Moreover, the changes in output can persist for a very long time, five years and more. The long-run adjustment back to AS_{LR} is so slow that the government should not wait for the economy to return to the production possibilities frontier on its own. Instead, it should use fiscal and monetary policies to change the level of aggregate demand and bring the economy back quickly to the frontier. This is especially imperative in times of recession and high unemployment.

New classical economists look at the macro economy and see a highly competitive market system in which wages and prices are flexible in the short run as well as the long run. In their view there are no important differences between the long-run and the short-run aggregate supply curves, at least none that have any relevance for policy. Fiscal and monetary policies cannot hope to improve the performance of the economy in the short run, and they can actually do some harm. The economy functions as well as can be expected on its own over the short run.

AS_{SR}: THE NEW KEYNESIAN PERSPECTIVE   Figure 18.4 pictures the new Keynesian view of the short-run aggregate supply curve, AS_{SR}. The curve is fairly flat when the economy is far below its production possibilities frontier represented by AS_{LR}, becomes steeper as the economy approaches the frontier, and becomes very steep as the economy reaches and moves beyond its sustainable, long-run frontier. The shape of AS_{SR} mirrors the shape of the short-run Phillips Curve described in Chapter 17 and for the same reason. The economy is never completely in equilibrium, according to the new Keynesians. Some individual markets are in excess supply, and others are in excess demand at any one time. The markets in excess supply put downward pressure on the overall price level, and the markets in excess demand put upward pressure on the overall price level.

When the economy is at point A, well below the frontier, many markets are in excess supply, and relatively few markets are in excess demand. An increase in aggregate demand at that point removes much of the excess supply without causing much upward pressure on wages or prices. Most of the increase in aggregate demand results in an increase in output, and the economy moves from A to B. A similar increase in aggregate demand starting at point B causes more of an increase in prices and less of an increase in output than at point A. More markets are already in excess demand, so that there is more upward pressure on prices throughout the economy. The upward pressure on prices becomes especially strong as the economy reaches the sustainable frontier at point C. Supply is difficult, if not impossible, to increase in most markets. Many firms experience supply bottlenecks for key resources; they want to buy more to expand production, but the resources are temporarily unavailable. The result is that a similar increase in aggregate demand at point C generates a relatively large increase in prices and very little increase in output. New Keynesians also believe that market economies often operate in the A to B range with lots of unemployed resources.

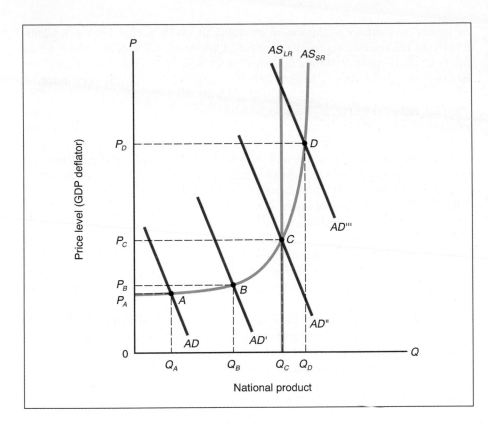

FIGURE 18.4

The Short-run Aggregate Supply Curve: New Keynesian Perspective

The figure shows how new Keynesian economists view the short-run aggregate supply curve, AS_{SR}. AS_{SR} is relatively flat at low levels of real national product when there are a lot of unemployed resources, and then becomes steeper as the economy approaches its production possibilities frontier represented by Q_C and the long-run aggregate supply curve AS_{LR}. AS_{SR} becomes very steep as the economy tries to push beyond Q_C, which is the maximum sustainable level of real national product in the long run. Consequently, increases in aggregate demand have different effects in the short run depending on the state of the economy. An increase in aggregate demand from AD to AD' increases real national product substantially from Q_A to Q_B, with only a slight increase in the overall price level from P_A to P_B. In contrast, an increase in aggregate demand from AD'' to AD''' increases real national product only slightly from Q_C to Q_D, but causes a big increase in the overall price level from P_C to P_D. The shape of AS_{SR} mirrors the shape of the short-run Phillips curve in Figure 17.5.

The wage and price stickiness that underlies new Keynesian theory has two sources. One is a set of noncompetitive labor market institutions that cause *real wages* to be sticky and generally set above the equilibrium level. The other is a set of product market imperfections that cause *nominal prices* to be sticky. The combination of real wage stickiness and nominal price stickiness produces the flat and then upward-sloping AS_{SR} in Figure 18.4. It explains why output responds to changes in aggregate demand in the short run.

REAL WAGE STICKINESS When new Keynesian economists look at the labor market, they focus their attention on labor market institutions in the so-called primary sector of the labor market, in which turnover is fairly low and employees and employers are likely to engage in long-term employment relationships. We discussed in Chapter 6 why workers and firms in the primary labor markets have generally chosen a system of rigid wages, which leads to layoffs and rehires as the economy ebbs and flows, rather than a system of highly flexible wages, which would ensure full employment at all times. The explanations turn on such concepts as internal labor markets, efficiency wages, insider/outsider theories of wage setting, and workers' concern for their relative position in the hierarchy of wages.

Review the discussion in Chapter 6 if you are unclear about these explanations. Rigid (real) wages are a crucial underpinning of the new Keynesian theory because they explain the existence of cyclical unemployment, which is involuntary and ebbs and flows with the economy. Always keep in mind that some kind of factor market imperfections, such as those just described, must lie behind any theory of the macro economy in which output responds significantly to changes in aggregate demand. Otherwise, with competitive factor markets, the economy always operates on or near its production possibilities frontier, and changes in aggregate demand cannot affect output very much.

NOMINAL PRICE STICKINESS   Real wage stickiness can cause output to respond to changes in aggregate demand by increasing and decreasing involuntary unemployment. A more direct reason why output responds to changes in aggregate demand, according to the new Keynesians, is that prices themselves are sticky. This is especially true of the prices of final manufactured goods, which constitute approximately 20 percent of the gross domestic product.

Markets tend to become more concentrated and dominated by very large firms as manufactured products move up through the production hierarchy from semi-finished products to the final products that are part of gross domestic product. The final goods manufacturers at the top of the hierarchy are often huge and complex firms that produce a wide range of products and buy inputs from hundreds and even thousands of suppliers. IBM and General Motors are examples.

The giant corporations are far removed from the small firms operating in highly competitive market environments whose prices are essentially dictated to them by the Laws of Supply and Demand. The large final goods manufacturers are price setters, not price takers. In addition, the very complexity of their operations makes their prices somewhat sticky. They are likely to react to an increase in demand at first by hiring more workers and increasing production, while leaving their prices unchanged. They may eventually increase price, but only if they perceive that the increase in demand is permanent. Similarly, they first react to a decrease in demand by laying off workers and decreasing production, while leaving their prices unchanged. In contrast, an increase in demand in a highly competitive market drives up price almost immediately, and a decrease in demand drives price down almost immediately.

The price stickiness of the large firms in response to changes in demand is the result of two factors. One is that changing their prices is not costless. The other is that they may not have the information they need to determine if they should change their prices.

Regarding the costs of changing prices, the large firms typically publish catalogs that list the prices of their products. A decision to change their prices means that they have to publish new price catalogs and inform their customers of the price changes. Economists refer to these as the **menu costs** of changing prices. The menu costs are not very large, to be sure. But they do exist, so the firms need to be sure that their demand and cost conditions have changed sufficiently to warrant changing the prices of their products.

MENU COSTS

The costs to producers of publishing new price catalogs and informing customers of price changes.

Regarding the information requirements, the key issue for macroeconomics is how quickly the final goods manufacturers change their prices after a change in aggregate demand. Their price response could be fairly slow simply because of the sheer complexity of their operations. Firms care about the relationship between the demands for their own products and the costs of producing their own products. They do not care directly about aggregate demand or aggregate supply. Suppose that the Fed increases the money supply, which increases aggregate demand. The increase in aggregate demand puts upward pressure on prices throughout the economy, yet the large final goods manufacturers may be slow to see the price trend developing. On the demand side, the demands for their products may not increase immediately with the increase in aggregate demand. On the cost side, the increase in aggregate demand drives up prices on semi-finished inputs and increases firms' costs. But the input price increases percolate slowly and haphazardly up through the production hierarchy. Since the final goods manufacturers buy from hundreds of suppliers, they may not be aware for awhile that their input costs are increasing. Some firms may not even experience much of a cost increase at first, especially if some of the firms' suppliers are reluctant to increase prices to their largest and most loyal customers. In addition, many of the final goods manufacturers make use of internal labor markets and unionized labor, which means that their wages are also somewhat sticky. Labor and material inputs comprise the vast majority of most firms' total production costs. Therefore, sticky wages and slow-to-respond input costs make for sticky overall costs of production that do not increase immediately with an increase in aggregate demand.

Combine the menu costs of changing prices with sticky production costs and a pattern of product demands that may not follow aggregate demand, and it becomes clear why the final goods manufacturers are often slow to increase their prices when aggregate demand increases. Instead, they hold the line on their prices for awhile and simply increase production to meet whatever increase they see in the demands for their own products.

The same argument applies in reverse. A decrease in aggregate demand puts downward pressure on prices throughout the economy. But the downward price pressure may not immediately lower these firms' costs. Nor do the demands for their individual products necessarily decrease in step with the decrease in aggregate demand. As a result, firms are reluctant to bear the menu costs of lowering their prices. Instead, they react by laying off workers and reducing production if the demands for their own products fall off.

THE COSTS OF STICKY WAGES AND PRICES   Sticky real wages and nominal prices are very costly to society precisely because they cause such large changes in output as aggregate demand changes. Figure 18.5 illustrates.

The GDP deflator on the vertical axis represents the overall price level; national product is on the horizontal axis. Suppose that the economy is initially in equilibrium on the production possibilities frontier at the intersection of AD^0 and AS_{LR}. The GDP deflator is 100, and GDP is Q_0, the output on the frontier. Aggregate demand then decreases from AD^0 to AD^1, which happens to be a 10 percent decrease. Because real wages and prices are sticky, the economy moves down along the short-run aggregate supply curve, AS_{SR}. The GDP deflator declines only slightly to 98, and GDP falls substantially from Q to Q_1 in the short run. The economy has moved below its production possibilities frontier, and unemployment increases.[2]

Suppose, instead, that all wages and prices were indexed to the growth in nominal aggregate demand. Now, as aggregate demand falls by 10 percent to AD^1, all wages and prices fall in lockstep by 10 percent. With all wages and prices (and therefore costs) falling by the same amount, neither workers nor firms have any incentive to change their employment or production decisions. The economy remains on AS_{LR} at the frontier, Q, instead of moving down along

---

2. We will draw AS_{SR} as a straight line from now on to make the graphs easier to read, unless the more realistic curved AS_{SR} curve is essential to the analysis.

FIGURE 18.5

The Social Costs of Sticky Wages and Prices

The figure illustrates the social costs of sticky wages and prices. The economy is initially in its long-run equilibrium on the production possibilities frontier at the intersection of AD^0, AS_{LR}, and AS_{SR}. The frontier level of real national product is Q_0 and the overall price level is 100. Then aggregate demand decreases to AD^1. With flexible wages and prices, the overall price level would fall to 90 and the economy would remain on its production possibilities frontier at Q_0, at the intersection of AD^1 and AS_{LR}. With sticky wages and prices, the overall price level falls only to 98. Real national product decreases to Q_1, at the intersection of AD^1 and AS_{SR}. The sticky wages and prices cause society to lose output ($Q_0 - Q_1$) in the short run, and the losses in output continue as the economy slowly returns to its long-run equilibrium on the frontier.

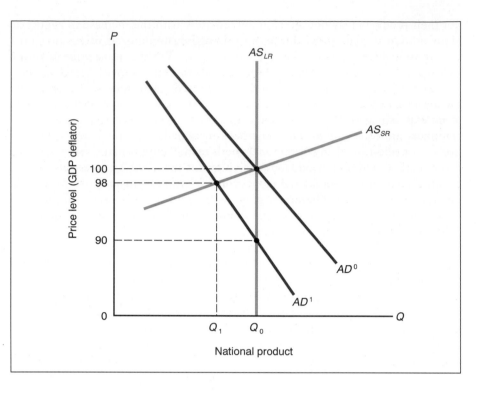

AS_{SR}. The GDP deflator eventually falls by 10 percent, equal to the decrease in nominal aggregate demand, in order to maintain the equilibrium on the frontier.

The loss of output and employment due to the sticky real wages and nominal prices when aggregate demand decreases is an enormous cost for society to bear. The economy would operate much more efficiently and generate far more output over time if all wages and prices were indexed to the GDP deflator. The problem, though, is that no one firm is willing to index its wages and prices to the growth in nominal aggregate demand unless it can be assured that all firms are indexing. Otherwise, each firm wants to control its own prices and set them in relation to its own demands and costs.

We discussed in Chapter 7 why firms and workers are unwilling to index their prices and wages to the overall price index. The reason is a coordination problem. No one firm or group of workers is willing to index its prices or wages unless it can be assured that all firms and workers are indexing their prices or wages. Review that discussion if you are unclear about this point. The unwillingness to index prices is another crucial underpinning of the new Keynesian model in the short run.

THE PROBLEMS WITH GOVERNMENT INDEXING Only the government would be able to coordinate an indexing to the overall price level by forcing all firms and workers to index together. The federal government has not been willing to do this, however, nor should it. Indexing wages and prices to nominal aggregate demand would prevent relative prices from changing and would generate its own set of inefficiencies.

To see why, suppose that a change in tastes shifts consumers' demands in favor of some products and against other products without changing the value of nominal aggregate demand. Consumers spend as much as before; they just allocate their expenditures differently. Efficiency requires that the prices of the favored products rise and the prices of the out-of-favor products fall. But with all prices indexed to nominal aggregate demand, no prices would change. The result would be excess demands in the favored markets and excess supplies in the out-of-favor markets. This is inefficient because resources are not shifting to the favored markets where they are most valued. Aggregate supply shocks would cause similar problems because they change costs differently for different products. For instance, a huge increase in oil prices does not increase the costs of production equally for all products. Relative prices have to vary to reflect the cost differences in order to maintain efficiency and to prevent excess supplies and demands from developing.

Any government-imposed indexing policy would have to grant exceptions based on individual market conditions in order to avoid creating excess demands and supplies. Experience has taught that this is not practicable, however. The Nixon administration tried to index wages and prices in the early 1970s in an attempt to control inflation directly. The commission in charge of implementing the indexing rule received thousands of petitions from firms seeking special considerations based on their individual market conditions, and many firms simply ignored the rule. The administration abandoned indexing within two years on the grounds that it was unworkable and unenforceable.

The only pricing system that is fully efficient is one of completely flexible wages and prices that are determined by the Laws of Supply and Demand. The Laws of Supply and Demand keep the economy on its production possibilities frontier and allow relative prices to change as needed whenever supplies and demands change in individual markets. They also cause wages and prices to move in lockstep together when nominal aggregate demand changes.

THE NEW CLASSICAL ATTACK   The high costs of the swings in output and employment are the point of attack by the new classical economists against the new Keynesian theory of sticky wages and prices. The new classical economists ask, quite reasonably, why individuals and firms accept wage and pricing policies that are so costly to them. Why should workers accept rigid real wages when flexible real wages would keep them fully employed? Why should firms maintain sticky prices in the face of falling demand and lose sales and customers? If flexible real wages and nominal prices are so much more efficient, why haven't they become the norm? The new Keynesian theories about why real wages and nominal prices are sticky are simply not convincing to the new classical economists because they entail such enormous individual and social costs.

The new Keynesian economists counter by stressing the coordination problem. Their theories described above about sticky real wages and nominal prices make sense from the perspective of the individuals and the firms that have adopted them. True, society would be far better off with more flexible wage and price setting. But, as noted above, no individual or firm has any incentive to adopt the broader social perspective on its own, and the government has no good method of achieving the broader social perspective.

New Keynesian economists also believe that the facts are incontrovertible—markets are riddled with imperfections, workers are often involuntarily unemployed, and changes in aggregate demand generate substantial shifts in aggregate output when resources are unemployed. If their theories in support of these facts are not entirely convincing, then they believe that they simply have to work harder on the underlying theory. One cannot change the facts.

The new classical economists counter that the new Keynesian "facts" are not, in fact, true, as we saw in Chapter 13 and will discuss further below. For the moment, though, let's pursue some additional implications of the new Keynesian theory.

FROM THE SHORT RUN TO THE LONG RUN The new Keynesian assumptions of fairly sticky wages and prices in the short run and fairly flexible wages and prices in the long run have one very important implication. Output responds to a change in aggregate demand in the pattern of a business cycle. Figure 18.6 illustrates.

The economy is initially in equilibrium on the frontier at (Q_0, P_0) in each graph, at the intersection of AD^0, AS^0_{SR}, and AS_{LR}. Figure 18.6(a) shows how the economy reacts to a decrease in aggregate demand—say, as the result of a contractionary monetary policy. AD shifts down and to the left from AD^0 to AD^1. The economy moves down along AS^0_{SR} to its short-run equilibrium at the intersection of AD^1 and AS^0_{SR}. As expected, the decrease in aggregate demand decreases both price and quantity. The overall price level falls from P_0 to P_1, and the output falls from Q_0 to Q_1. The economy is now operating below its production possibilities frontier, with unemployed resources.

The economy does not stay at the short-run equilibrium, however, because the product markets (and labor markets) are in excess supply overall. The excess supply puts downward pressure on prices (and wages), which lowers firms' costs of production and shifts the short-run aggregate supply curve down and to the right. AS_{SR} keeps shifting until it reaches AS^2_{SR}, and the economy returns to equilibrium on the frontier. The final long-run equilibrium is (Q_0, P_2), at the intersection of AD^1, AS^2_{SR}, and AS_{LR}. In the long run, therefore, a decrease in aggregate demand cannot affect output. It just lowers the overall price level, from P_0 to P_2 in this example. In the meantime, though, output moves in a business-cycle pattern. It first falls from Q_0 to Q_1 after the decrease in aggregate demand and then rises back to Q_0.

The same conclusion applies to an increase in aggregate demand—say, as the result of an expansionary monetary policy. Figure 18.6(b) shows how the economy reacts to an increase in aggregate demand.

AD shifts up and to the right from AD^0 to AD^1. The economy moves up along AS^0_{SR} to its short-run equilibrium at the intersection of AD_1 and AS^0_{SR}. As expected, the increase in aggregate demand increases both price and quantity. The overall price level rises from P_0 to P_1, and the output temporarily rises above the sustainable frontier from Q_0 to Q_1.

The economy does not stay beyond its production possibilities frontier in the long run. Product markets (and labor markets) are in excess demand overall. The excess demand puts upward pressure on prices (and wages), which raises firms' costs of production and shifts the short-run aggregate supply curve up and to the left. AS_{SR} keeps shifting until it reaches AS^2_{SR}, and the economy returns to equilibrium on the frontier. The final long-run equilibrium is (Q_0, P_2), at the intersection of AD^1, AS^2_{SR}, and AS_{LR}. In the long run, therefore, an increase in aggregate demand cannot affect output. It just raises the overall price level, from P_0 to P_2 in this example. Once again, though, output moves

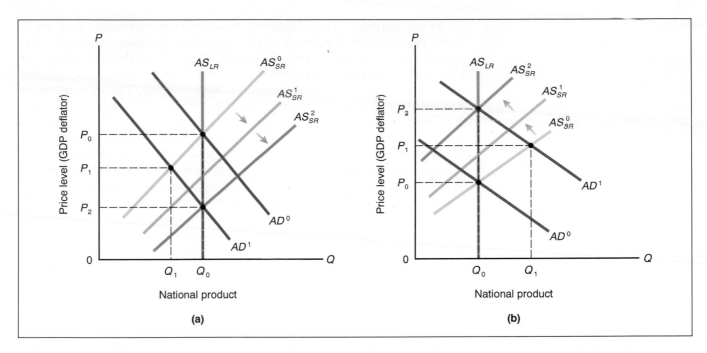

(a)

(b)

The figure illustrates how the economy moves in a business-cycle pattern in response to a change in aggregate demand, under new Keynesian assumptions. Figure 18.6(a) shows how the economy responds to a decrease in aggregate demand and Figure 18.6(b) shows how the economy responds to an increase in aggregate demand. The economy is initially in its long run equilibrium (Q_0, P_0) on the production possibilities frontier in both graphs, at the intersection of AD^0, AS_{LR}, and AS_{SR}^0. In Figure 18.6(a), aggregate demand decreases from AD^0 to AD^1. The economy moves to the short-run equilibrium (Q_1, P_1) below the frontier, at the intersection of AD^1 and AS_{SR}^0. With more goods and factor markets in excess supply, prices and wages drop and reduce firms' costs of production. The short-run aggregate supply curve shifts down and to the right from AS_{SR}^0 to AS_{SR}^1 to AS_{SR}^2. The economy returns to a long-run equilibrium (Q_0, P_2) on the frontier, at the intersection of AD^1, AS_{LR}, and AS_{SR}^2. Output first decreases from Q_0 to Q_1 and then increases from Q_1 to Q_0, in a business-cycle pattern. In Figure 18.6(b), aggregate demand increases from AD^0 to AD^1. The economy moves to the short-run equilibrium (Q_1, P_1) above the frontier, at the intersection of AD^1 and AS_{SR}^0. With more goods and factor markets in excess demand, prices and wages rise and increase firms' costs of production. The short-run aggregate supply curve shifts up and to the left from AS_{SR}^0 to AS_{SR}^1 to AS_{SR}^2. The economy returns to a long-run equilibrium (Q_0, P_2) on the frontier, at the intersection of AD^1, AS_{LR}, and AS_{SR}^2. Output first increases from Q_0 to Q_1 and then decreases from Q_1 to Q_0 in a business-cycle pattern.

FIGURE 18.6

The Adjustment From the Short Run to the Long Run

in a business-cycle pattern. It first rises from Q_0 to Q_1 after the increase in aggregate demand and then falls back to Q_0.

In conclusion, a decrease in aggregate demand that brings on a recession is followed by a period of falling prices and rising output as the economy moves back to the frontier. Citizens can expect some good economic news for awhile following a recession.

Similarly, an increase in aggregate demand that increases output and pushes hard against the production possibilities frontier is followed by a brief period during which prices rise and output declines. Citizens can expect some bad economic news for awhile following a boom period.

POLICY IMPLICATIONS   The adjustment from the short run to the long run in either case is not very relevant to new Keynesian economists, however. Regarding the decrease in aggregate demand, they believe that the adjustment back to the long-run equilibrium is very slow if the economy falls far below the production possibilities frontier into a deep recession. The recovery period may be five years, or even longer. Therefore, the sensible strategy is to intervene with expansionary fiscal and monetary policies that shift up aggregate demand and return the economy to the frontier much more quickly. Why wait for the economy to recover and allow people to suffer in the meantime?

Indeed, Keynes believed that the adjustment would never occur. He argued that falling wages and prices would hurt debtors and keep aggregate demand below the frontier level. For example, suppose that someone borrows $100 and agrees to pay it back next year. Meanwhile, wages and prices fall by half. Now paying back the $100 involves the sacrifice of twice as much purchasing power as did the original $100 given to the borrower. Many debtors may well go bankrupt at the lower prices, in which case their consumption demand would certainly decrease. Although some new Keynesian economists still follow Keynes in this respect, most believe that falling prices and wages do eventually bring the economy back to the frontier. The disagreement is not important, though, because all new Keynesians agree that the use of expansionary fiscal and monetary policies in order to increase output and reduce unemployment is the proper response to a recession.

New Keynesians believe that the adjustment to the frontier is much quicker in the case where aggregate demand increases beyond the frontier. Most markets are thrown into excess demand, firms experience supply bottlenecks for many of their inputs, and prices rise rapidly throughout the economy. Still, why allow price pressures to build? Once again, the sensible strategy is to respond to the increase in aggregate demand with contractionary fiscal and monetary policies that bring *AD* back to its original position and remove the price pressures.

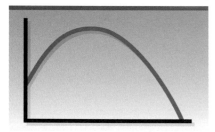

THE SPENDING MULTIPLIER IN THE UNITED STATES

The price changes that follow a change in aggregate demand are the final chapter in our story about the spending multiplier in the United States. Recall that the value of the multiplier is in the range of one to three after a period of a few years. Moreover, the multiplier process is hump-shaped. National income increases steadily for about one and a half years following an increase in aggregate demand and then decreases to its final value of one to three.

Our simple model of the economy in Chapter 10 predicted a very high value of the spending multiplier, around 10, based on a marginal propensity to consume (MPC) that builds to about 0.9 over a few years. Chapter 12 introduced the automatic stabilizers, such as income taxes and income-sensitive transfer payments, and noted that they reduce the spending multiplier by about 40 percent. Chapter 17 added the interest rate changes that follow a change in aggregate demand and argued that they reduce the spending multiplier still further by crowding out consumer durables, investment, and net exports. The interest-rate effect also generates the hump-shaped pattern of the multiplier process.

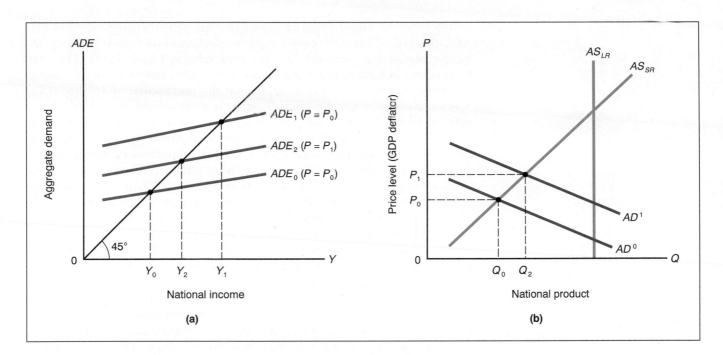

The figure shows how changes in the overall price level lower the value of the spending multiplier. Figure 18.7(a) pictures the ADE-45° line diagram, with aggregate desired expenditures determined by the level of real national income, Y. Figure 18.7(b) pictures aggregate demand and aggregate supply, AD and AS, with real national product, Q, on the horizontal axis and the overall price level, P, on the vertical axis. The economy is initially in a short-run equilibrium at Y_0 ($=Q_0$) on both graphs, at the intersection of ADE_0 and the 45° line in Figure 18.7(a), and at the intersection of AD^0 and AS_{SR} in Figure 18.7(b). In Figure 18.7(a), an increase in aggregate demand shifts the ADE line from ADE_0 to ADE_1, and the economy heads to a new equilibrium level of national income, Y_1, at the intersection of ADE_1 and the 45° line. But the increase in aggregate demand increases the overall price level from P_0 to P_1, as illustrated in Figure 18.7(b). Aggregate demand shifts from AD^0 to AD^1, and the new short-run equilibrium is (Q_2,P_1), at the intersection of AD^1 and AS_{SR}. The increase in the overall price level shifts the ADE line down from ADE_1 to ADE_2 in Figure 18.7(a). The final short-run equilibrium level of national income is Y_2 ($=Q_2$), at the intersection of ADE_2 and the 45° line. The rise in the overall price level has reduced the value of the multiplier; the equilibrium level of national income increases to Y_2 instead of Y_1.

FIGURE 18.7

Changes in the Overall Price Level and the Spending Multiplier

The price changes that follow a change in aggregate demand also reduce the value of the spending multiplier and contribute to its hump-shaped pattern. Figure 18.7 illustrates, for an increase in aggregate demand.

Figures 18.7(a) presents the ADE–45° line graph that we have been using to illustrate the spending multiplier. Figure 18.7(b) shows the AS–AD representation of the economy. The two graphs assume that the economy is initially in a short-run equilibrium well below its production possibilities frontier with lots of unemployed resources. In Figure 18.7(a), aggregate demand is ADE_0, and the equilibrium level of national income is Y_0, at the intersection of ADE_0 and the 45° line. The corresponding aggregate demand curve in Figure 18.7(b) is AD^0. The economy is in equilibrium at the intersection of AD^0 and AS_{SR}. National output is Q_0, corresponding to national income, Y_0, and the overall price level is P_0.

Refer again to Figure 18.7(a). Suppose that aggregate demand increases from ADE_0 to ADE_1. The new equilibrium level of national income is Y_1, at the intersection of ADE_1 and the 45° line. Now refer to Figure 18.7(b). The corresponding increase in aggregate demand is to AD^1, and the economy moves to a new short-run equilibrium, (Q_2, P_1), at the intersection of AD^1 and AS_{SR}. The equilibrium national output, Q_2, does not correspond to the equilibrium national income, Y_1, because ADE_1 in Figure 18.7(a) assumes that the overall price level remains at P_0. We had been assuming constant prices in our previous analysis of the spending multiplier. The increase in price to P_1 shifts down the ADE line from ADE_1 to ADE_2 and establishes a new equilibrium level of national income at Y_2. Y_2 corresponds to national output, Q_2, in Figure 18.7(b).

The price increase following the increase in aggregate demand reduces the value of the spending multiplier. National income increases from Y_0 to Y_2, rather than from Y_0 to Y_1 without the price increase. Also, the price increase contributes to the hump-shaped pattern of the multiplier process. The economy begins building to Y_1, but then backs down to Y_2 as prices increase and choke off some of the aggregate demand.

The value of the spending multiplier must be zero in the long run because the economy always operates on its production possibilities frontier in the long-run equilibrium. As we have seen, a change in aggregate demand changes only prices in the long run. The spending multiplier is inherently a short-run concept, however, that is meant to apply when the economy is operating well below its production possibilities frontier. Showing how the economy responds to a change in aggregate demand under these conditions over a period of three years or so is useful information to new Keynesian economists. It helps them determine what fiscal and monetary policies achieve the best balance among the four macroeconomic policy goals.

AGGREGATE SUPPLY SHOCK

Any event that directly affects firms' costs of production or the quantity that they can supply to the market.

AGGREGATE SUPPLY SHOCKS The new Keynesian theory allows for **aggregate supply shocks** once the assumption of constant wages and prices is dropped.

Recall that an adverse supply shock is any event that increases production costs or reduces output directly. Examples are an increase in the price of crude oil engineered by OPEC and a widespread drought that destroys crops. An adverse supply shock shifts AS_{SR} up and to the left. It may also shift AS_{LR} to the left if it is a lasting event that reduces the nation's production possibilities. A permanent increase in oil prices would affect AS_{LR}; a one-year drought would not. Figure 18.8(a) illustrates the effects of an adverse supply shock. It assumes that the supply shock is lasting and has long-run effects, to be as general as possible.[3]

The economy is initially in equilibrium on the frontier where AD^0, AS_{SR}^0, and AS_{LR}^0 intersect. The overall price level is P_0, and the output is Q_0, the frontier output. A lasting adverse supply shock shifts AS_{SR} from AS_{SR}^0 to AS_{SR}^1, and AS_{LR} from AS_{LR}^0 to AS_{LR}^1. The price level rises to P_1, and the output falls to Q_1 in the short run.

The economy is in overall excess supply in the short run relative to the new long-run supply curve, AS_{LR}^1. Therefore, the price level falls to P_2, restoring equilibrium on the new frontier at output Q_2 in the long run. The economy

---

3. We are assuming that AS_{SR} shifts more than AS_{LR} because producers are better able to adjust to a supply shock as time passes.

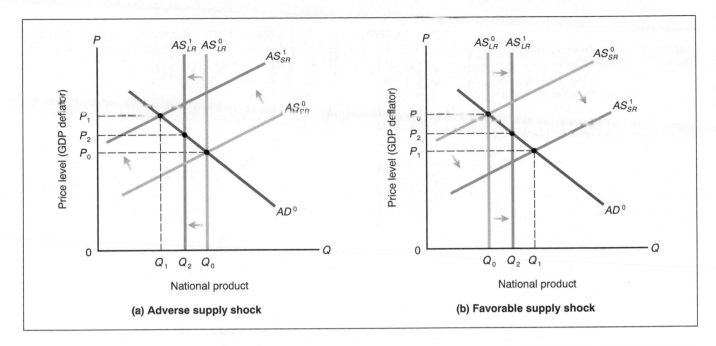

(a) Adverse supply shock   **(b) Favorable supply shock**

The figure shows how the economy responds in a business-cycle pattern to an aggregate supply shock. Figure 18.8(a) pictures an adverse aggregate supply shock and Figure 18.8(b) pictures a favorable aggregate supply shock. The economy is initially in its long-run equilibrium (Q_0, P_0) on the production possibilities frontier in both graphs, at the intersection of AD^0, AS^0_{LR}, and AS^0_{SR}. In Figure 18.8(a), the adverse supply shock shifts both AS_{LR} and AS_{SR} to the left, from AS^0_{LR} to AS^1_{LR}, and from AS^0_{SR} to AS^1_{SR}, respectively. The new short-run equilibrium is (Q_1, P_1), at the intersection of AD^0 and AS^1_{SR}. With the economy now below its frontier and more markets in excess supply, prices and wages drop and reduce firms' costs of production. AS_{SR} shifts back down and to the right. The economy eventually returns to a long-run equilibrium (Q_2, P_2) on its new frontier, at the intersection of AD^0 and AS^1_{LR}. Output at first decreases from Q_0 to Q_1 and then increases from Q_1 to Q_2 in a business-cycle pattern. In Figure 18.8(b), the favorable supply shock shifts AS_{LR} and AS_{SR} to the right, to AS^1_{LR} and AS^1_{SR}. The new short-run equilibrium is (Q_1, P_1) at the intersection of AD^0 and AS^1_{SR}. Wages and prices rise and AS_{SR} shifts back to the left. The long-run equilibrium is (Q_2, P_2) at the intersection of AD^0 and AS^1_{LR}. Output increases from Q_0 to Q_1, and then decreases from Q_1 to Q_2, in a business-cycle pattern.

FIGURE 18.8

Aggregate Supply Shocks

would return to a long-run equilibrium at (Q_0, P_0) if the adverse supply shock were temporary and only affected AS_{SR}.

A favorable supply shock is any event that decreases production costs or increases output directly. Examples are a cost-reducing technological change such as the ongoing improvements in computer technology and particularly favorable weather that increases crop yields. A favorable supply shock shifts AS_{SR} down and to the right. As with an adverse supply shock, it may also shift AS_{LR} to the right if it is a lasting event that increases the nation's production possibilities. Cost-reducing technological changes shift AS_{LR}; favorable weather for one year does not. Figure 18.8(b) illustrates the effects of a favorable supply shock. It also assumes that the supply shock is lasting and has long-run effects, to be as general as possible.

The overall price level is initially P_0, and the output is Q_0, the frontier output, as in Figure 18.8(a). A lasting favorable supply shock shifts AS_{SR} from AS^0_{SR} to AS^1_{SR}, and AS_{LR} from AS^0_{LR} to AS^1_{LR}. The price level falls to P_1, and output rises to Q_1 in the short run.

ELABORATION: New classical economists would argue that the business cycle pattern as the economy adjusts to its frontier is the only important internal mechanism within the economy that contributes to the ebbs and flows of economic activity over time. Even so, they see the business cycle as resulting primarily from an endless series of outside aggregate demand and aggregate supply shocks, mostly the latter.

FIGURE 18.9

Aggregate Supply Shocks and the Short-Run Phillips Curve

The economy is initially in equilibrium at point A on the short-run Phillips Curve PC_{SR}^0, with an unemployment rate of U_0 and a rate of inflation of $(\Delta P/P)_0$. Point A is below the production possibilities frontier represented by the natural rate of unemployment, U_{NR}. An adverse supply shock shifts the short-run Phillips Curve up and to the right from PC_{SR}^0 to PC_{SR}^1, and the economy moves to point B on PC_{SR}^1. The adverse supply shock causes stagflation, as unemployment increases from U_0 to U_1 and inflation increases from $(\Delta P/P)_0$ to $(\Delta P/P)_1$. A favorable supply shock shifts the short-run Phillips Curve down and to the left from PC_{SR}^0 to PC_{SR}^2, and the economy moves to point C on PC_{SR}^2. The favorable supply shock brings the double blessing of lower unemployment and lower inflation. Unemployment decreases from U_0 to U_2 and inflation decreases from $(\Delta P/P)_0$ to $(\Delta P/P)_2$.

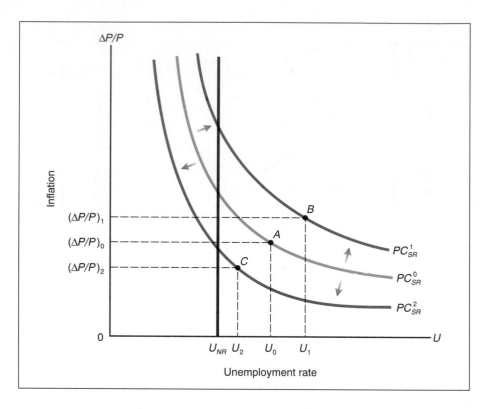

The economy is in overall excess demand in the short run relative to the new long-run supply curve, AS_{LR}^1. Therefore, the price level rises to P_2, restoring equilibrium on the new frontier at output Q_2 in the long run. The economy would return to a long-run equilibrium at (Q_0, P_0) if the favorable supply shock were temporary and only affected AS_{SR}.

Notice that adverse supply shocks such as an increase in oil prices are a double whammy for the economy. They both increase prices and reduce output. Conversely, favorable supply shocks such as cost-reducing technological changes are a double blessing. They both reduce prices and increase output. Also, output responds in a business-cycle pattern to aggregate supply shocks, just as it does to changes in aggregate demand.

Aggregate supply shocks also affect the short-run Phillips curve described in Chapter 17. Refer to Figure 18.9. The rate of inflation is on the vertical axis, and the unemployment rate is on the horizontal axis. The initial short-run Phillips Curve before the aggregate supply shock is PC_{SR}^0. Assume that the economy is at point A, with an inflation rate of $(\Delta P/P)_0$ and an unemployment rate of U_0.

An adverse aggregate supply shock such as an OPEC-engineered increase in oil prices shifts the short-run Phillips Curve up and to the right, from PC_{SR}^0 to PC_{SR}^1 in the figure. The Phillips Curve representation illustrates the double whammy of an adverse supply shock directly in terms of the macroeconomic policy goals of inflation and unemployment. An adverse supply shock tends to increase both inflation and unemployment in the short run. For example, suppose that the economy moves from point A on PC_{SR}^0 to point B on PC_{SR}^1. The adverse supply shock has increased the inflation rate from $(\Delta P/P)_0$

to $(\Delta P/P)_1$, and it has also increased the unemployment rate from U_0 to U_1. MIT's Pául Samuelson dubbed the situation of increasing inflation and increasing unemployment a situation of **stagflation.**

A favorable aggregate supply shock such as the cost-reducing technological change in computers shifts the short-run Phillips Curve down and to the left, from PC_{SR}^0 to PC_{SR}^2 in the figure. A favorable supply shock has the happy effect of decreasing both inflation and unemployment in the short run. For example, suppose that the economy moves from point A to point C on PC_{SR}^2. The favorable supply shock has decreased the inflation rate from $(\Delta P/P)_0$ to $(\Delta P/P)_2$, and it has also decreased the unemployment rate from U_0 to U_2. No one has yet coined a phrase for this double blessing.

We can see why the OPEC-induced oil price increases in the 1970s were such a curse and why the collapse of oil prices in the 1980s was such a blessing for all oil-importing countries. Oil prices are a very important aggregate supply shock, undoubtedly the single most important aggregate supply shock of the past 20 years.

AS_{SR}: THE NEW CLASSICAL PERSPECTIVE   The new classical economists believe that the new Keynesian analysis of the U.S. economy is dead wrong. They especially disagree with the Keynesian analysis of how the economy responds to changes in aggregate demand.

When they look at the labor markets, they see the high turnover of the American workforce, the substantial amount of wage flexibility in many markets, and the frequent spells of short-term unemployment that they interpret as increases and decreases in search or frictional unemployment.

When they look at the product markets, they point to the research of industrial organization economists, which concludes that as many as 70 percent of all products in the United States are marketed under reasonably competitive conditions. The new classical economists are convinced that the macro economy should be viewed as if it operates according to the Laws of Supply and Demand at all times. They know that this is not entirely accurate (just as the new Keynesians know that their model is not entirely accurate). But the new classical economists believe that it is the most reasonable representation of the macro economy.

REAL BUSINESS CYCLE THEORY   The prevailing view of the economy among new classical economists is the real business cycle model, which we described in Chapter 13. To review briefly, the theory is securely anchored to the long-run aggregate supply curve. It sees the economy as competitive enough that it is always operating on or very near its production possibilities frontier, that is, on or very near AS_{LR}. The ebbs and flows of the economy represent movements in the frontier itself for the most part, as the frontier is buffeted by increases and decreases in productivity. The erratic behavior of productivity shifts AS_{LR} to the right and left and causes the business-cycle-like changes in output and employment that we observe. In other words, the economy is driven by the supply side, not the demand side as in new Keynesian theory.

In addition, real business cycle theory assumes that households adopt the most extreme long-run point of view in solving their economic problems. They behave according to the Life-Cycle Hypothesis and plan both their consumption and their labor supply decisions over their entire lifetimes.

STAGFLATION

A period of increasing inflation, falling output, and rising unemployment that follows an adverse aggregate supply shock.

Any notion of a short-run aggregate supply curve different from AS_{LR} is essentially unimportant in a world of competitive markets, life-cycle consumers, and production that is continually buffeted by increases and decreases in productivity. Only shifts in AS_{LR} can significantly affect the real side of the economy.

Real business cycle theorists concede that a change in aggregate demand can have real effects, even over the short run, *but only if it simultaneously causes* AS_{LR} *to shift as well, so that the nation's production possibilities change.* Otherwise, a change in aggregate demand can affect only prices. Moreover, as we saw in Chapter 13, changes in output over the short run require changes in people's decisions to supply more or less labor. Producers can significantly increase production in the short run only if people are willing to supply more labor to them. Conversely, producers must cut production if the supply of labor falls. Also, what looks like a short-run aggregate supply response is really a shift in the long-run aggregate supply curve. More labor supply expands the nation's production possibilities frontier by giving producers more resources; it shifts AS_{LR} to the right. Less labor supply contracts the nation's production possibilities frontier by giving producers fewer resources; it shifts AS_{LR} to the left. Finally, voluntary employment and output move hand in hand according to the real business cycle theory. The changes in the rate of unemployment over time measured by the Bureau of Labor Statistics surveys are virtually all changes in frictional or voluntary search unemployment. The natural rate of unemployment ebbs and flows along with the production possibilities frontier.

The requirement that a change in aggregate demand must shift AS_{LR} to affect output means that the source of the change in aggregate demand matters. An increase or a decrease in one of the components of aggregate demand can have real effects. This includes expansionary and contractionary fiscal policies. A change in the money supply cannot have real effects. Let's compare the two cases to see why they have different effects.

A direct change in aggregate demand. The link between changes in aggregate demand and the nation's production possibilities runs through interest rates, according to real business cycle theory. Consider an increase in aggregate demand. We saw in Chapter 17 that an increase in any component of aggregate demand increases interest rates as some people (or firms, or the government) have to sell financial assets or borrow to finance the increase in expenditures. Here is yet another way to think about why interest rates rise in the competitive new classical environment. An increase in any one component of aggregate demand must crowd out other components of aggregate demand, since the economy is already on its production possibilities frontier and there are only so many resources to go around. Therefore, interest rates have to rise to crowd out consumer durables, or investment, or net exports.

The crowding out is not complete, however. The increase in interest rates increases the supply of labor, which expands the frontier and allows total output to increase to meet some of the increase in demand. The link between interest rates and labor supply arises because of the assumption that people plan their labor supply decisions over their lifetimes. They are continually reassessing how much they want to work in total throughout their lives and when they want to work. The increase in interest rates gives them an incentive to change the timing of their employment toward the present. The reason is that any income earned now and saved earns a higher rate of return right away,

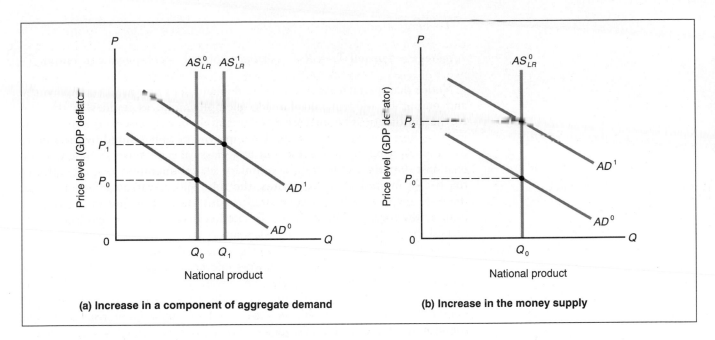

(a) Increase in a component of aggregate demand   **(b) Increase in the money supply**

The new classical economists concede that an increase in aggregate demand can increase real national product, but only if the increase causes the production possibilities frontier to shift out as well. Figure 18.10(a) shows that an increase in a component of aggregate demand, such as that caused by an expansionary fiscal policy, can increase output. The initial equilibrium is (Q_0, P_0) on the frontier, at the intersection of AD^0 and AS^0_{LR}. An expansionary fiscal policy increases aggregate demand from AD^0 to AD^1 and causes interest rates to rise. The increase in interest rates induces people to supply more labor, which shifts out the production possibilities frontier from Q_0 to Q_1 and allows firms to increase production. The new equilibrium is (Q_1, P_1) on the new frontier, at the intersection of AD^1 and AS^1_{LR}. In contrast, Figure 18.10(b) shows that an increase in the money supply cannot increase output. Aggregate demand increases from AD^0 to AD^1 following the increase in the money supply, which places markets in excess demand and causes prices to rise. The increase in prices increases the quantity of money demanded for transactions purposes in direct proportion to the price increase, so the households and businesses just hold the new money. Output remains at Q_0, and the new equilibrium is (Q_0, P_2), at the intersection of AD^1 and AS^0_{LR}. An increase in the money supply only increases the overall price level.

FIGURE 18.10

Changes in Aggregate Demand: New Classical Perspective

so that people choose to work more now and less in the future in order to take advantage of the higher interest rates. The increase in labor supply in turn allows firms to expand production. Therefore, the increase in aggregate demand increases both employment and output as the production possibilities frontier expands.

Figure 18.10(a) shows the effects of the increase in aggregate demand in terms of the aggregate demand and the aggregate supply curves. The initial equilibrium before the increase in aggregate demand is (Q_0, P_0), at the intersection of AD^0 and AS^0_{LR}. The increase in aggregate demand shifts the aggregate demand curve up and to the right, from AD^0 to AD^1. Simultaneously, the rise in interest rates increases the supply of labor and shifts the long-run aggregate supply curve to the right, from AS^0_{LR} to AS^1_{LR}. The new equilibrium is at (Q_1, P_1), at the intersection of AD^1 and AS_{LR} along the new expanded production possibilities frontier.

To summarize:

Aggregate demand $\uparrow \rightarrow R \uparrow \rightarrow$ labor supply $\uparrow \rightarrow$ employment, output $\uparrow$

Notice that the increase in aggregate demand does not increase employment and output by reducing involuntary unemployment, as it does in the new Keynesian theory. The increase in labor supply in response to the increase in interest rates is entirely voluntary. Unemployment as measured by the Bureau of Labor Statistics may decrease, but new classical economists assume that this is almost entirely a reduction in voluntary search unemployment. People see the rise in interest rates and reduce the time spent searching for jobs, since they are more willing to accept employment. The reduction in search time reduces the measured unemployment rate because people are less likely to be picked up as unemployed by the BLS surveyors.

A decrease in aggregate demand has exactly the opposite effect on labor supply. The decrease in demand lowers interest rates as people buy financial assets and reduce their borrowings. The lower interest rates induce people to postpone employment to the future, since the returns to saving are lower. Both employment and output fall, and measured unemployment rises as people spend more time searching for jobs.

To summarize:

Aggregate demand $\downarrow \rightarrow R \downarrow \rightarrow$ labor supply $\downarrow \rightarrow$ employment, output $\downarrow$

The main problem with this theory is that the connection between interest rates and labor supply is very weak. Our intuition tells us that interest rates do not have much of an impact on how much we decide to work, and empirical research bears this out. Labor economists have not been able to find any significant relationship between interest rates and labor supply.

New classical economists are not particularly troubled by this research, however, because they do not believe that changes in aggregate demand are an important cause of changes in output and employment in any event. They believe output and employment are primarily driven by changes in productivity that directly shift the long-run aggregate supply curve. The aggregate quantity demanded follows shifts in AS_{LR}, and not the other way around for the most part.

A change in the money supply. A change in the money supply does not affect aggregate supply at all. It changes only prices. To see why, suppose that the Fed doubles the money supply. The new money shifts up the aggregate demand curve and creates excess demand in all markets. The excess demands increase prices, but this is all that happens.

The reason why has to do with the demand for money. Recall from Chapter 16 that the transactions demand for money is directly proportional to the overall price level because Federal Reserve Notes and the checking account deposits are denominated in nominal terms. Therefore, the demand for money increases in step with the prices as they rise. Eventually all prices double, which doubles the demand for money to match the doubling of the money supply. At this point the economy is once again in equilibrium.

The expansionary monetary policy is ineffective because every household and every firm simply accepts the new money into their balance sheets to cover the doubling of the prices. No one attempts to buy other financial or real assets with the new money, as they would in a new Keynesian environment of sticky prices. Consequently, the increase in the money supply has no effect whatsoever on the real side of the economy. Output, employment, interest rates, consumption, and all other real economic variables remain unchanged.

Figure 18.10(b) shows the effect of a doubling of the money supply in terms of the aggregate demand and the aggregate supply curves. The initial equilibrium before the increase in the money supply is (Q_0, P_0), at the intersection of AD^0 and AS^0_{LR}, just as in Figure 18.10(a). The new money shifts the aggregate demand curve up from AD^0 to AD^1. The new money does not shift the long-run aggregate supply curve. Therefore, the new equilibrium is (Q_0, P_2), at the intersection of AD^1 and AS_{LR}. Output remains the same, and the overall price level doubles from P_0 to P_2.

Similarly, a decrease in the money supply only lowers prices. The decrease in the money supply shifts aggregate demand down and creates excess supplies throughout the economy. The excess supplies lower prices, and the demand for money falls in step with the fall in prices. Eventually the decrease in the demand for money matches the decrease in the money supply, and equilibrium is restored without any effect on the real side of the economy.

The new Keynesian economists see this analysis and ask: How can one ignore the strong correlation between the money supply and output? Output increases when the money supply increases, and output decreases when the money supply decreases. In their view changes in the money supply clearly cause changes in output.

The new classical economists answer: True, output and the money supply move together over time. But the new Keynesians reverse cause and effect. Most of the money supply consists of checking account deposits, which are created by banks making loans. When a favorable productivity shock causes output to expand, businesses and consumers come to the banks seeking loans. More bank loans are issued, and checking account deposits expand. When an unfavorable productivity shock causes output to contract, businesses and consumers are less interested in borrowing. Fewer bank loans are issued, and checking account deposits contract. Output drives the money supply, not the other way around.

In conclusion, real business cycle theory rejects virtually all of the new Keynesian analysis of Chapters 10 through 17. Changes in aggregate demand do not have a significant effect on real national income and output precisely because economies never operate far from their production possibilities frontier. The spending multiplier is close to zero, even in the short run. More to the point, fiscal and monetary policies have *no* role to play in keeping the economy on its frontier. The competitive market economy does this job, and does it well. Fiscal and monetary policies cannot improve the performance of the economy in the short run.

Fiscal and monetary policies can affect output only to the extent that they can change the quantity and the quality of resources or induce firms to develop and adopt new technologies. These are the only things that can affect the real side of the economy because they alone determine the production possibilities frontier. They are also long-run, not short-run, phenomena.

For example, an expansionary fiscal policy that increases interest rates may increase output in the short run by increasing the supply of labor. But new classical economists are more likely to argue for a mix of fiscal and monetary policies that keep interest rates low in order to stimulate investment and long-run economic growth. Long-run growth is far more important than is any short-run increase in output that the higher interest rates may induce. The government must also keep inflation under control, another long-run policy problem that, as we will see in Chapter 19, is accomplished by keeping the growth of the money supply under control.

SUMMARY

Chapter 18 explored the role of prices in bringing the macro economy to equilibrium, using the aggregate supply–aggregate demand (AS–AD) model. The chapter also compared and contrasted the new Keynesian and the new classical theories on how the economy operates, using the AS–AD model as the basis for comparison.

The first section of the chapter developed the aggregate demand curve.

1. The aggregate demand curve, AD, shows the aggregate quantity demanded by all four sectors of the economy at each overall price level.
2. AD is downward sloping primarily because of the effect of prices on the demand for money. An increase in the overall price level increases the transactions demand for money, which in turn increases interest rates as people sell financial assets to increase their money holdings. The higher interest rates reduce the demand for consumer durables, investment, and net exports, which reduces aggregate demand. The opposite analysis applies to a decrease in the overall price level.

The second section of the chapter developed the aggregate supply curve.

3. The aggregate supply curve shows the aggregate quantity of output supplied by all producers at each overall price level.
4. New Keynesian and new classical economists agree that the economy is competitive enough, and wages and prices flexible enough, over the long run that the long-run aggregate supply curve, AS_{LR}, is vertical at the output corresponding to the production possibilities frontier. Competitive factor markets guarantee that the economy operates on its frontier. Real national product (national income) is determined entirely by the supply side of the economy in the long run. Aggregate demand serves only to set the overall level of prices; prices adjust so that the aggregate quantity demanded equals the frontier output.

The disagreement between the two schools centers on the nature of aggregate supply in the short run.

The New Keynesian View of Aggregate Supply in the Short Run:

5. The short-run aggregate supply curve, AS_{SR}, is distinctly different from AS_{LR}. AS_{SR} is relatively flat when the economy is far below the frontier, becomes steeper as the economy approaches the frontier, and becomes quite steep as the economy moves beyond its sustainable frontier. Therefore, changes in aggregate demand change real national product (national income) in the short run, and the short run can persist for quite a long time.

6. AS_{SR} is relatively flat because of a combination of sticky real wages and sticky nominal prices. Sticky real wages result from labor market institutions such as internal labor markets and labor unions, which lead to layoffs and rehires in response to the ebbs and flows of the economy, rather than leading to a flexible wage policy that maintains full employment at all times. Sticky nominal prices result from a combination of the menu costs of changing prices and the size and the complexity of the final goods manufacturers. Firms care about the relationship of their demands to their costs, and they do not always move in line with aggregate demand. The result is that the final goods manufacturers are often slow to adjust their prices.

7. The economy eventually adjusts to the production possibilities frontier in the long run. A decrease in aggregate demand that leads to a short-run equilibrium output below the frontier creates excess supplies in markets generally, which lower prices and costs of production. AS_{SR} shifts down and to the right until equilibrium is restored on the frontier. Conversely, an increase in aggregate demand that leads to a short-run equilibrium output above the frontier creates excess demands in markets generally, which raise prices and costs of production. AS_{SR} shifts up and to the left until equilibrium is restored on the frontier. In either case, output moves in a business-cycle pattern.

8. The adjustment to the long-run equilibrium is so slow when there are unemployed resources that the government should not wait for it to happen. Instead, the government should use fiscal and monetary policies to keep the economy operating on or near its production possibilities frontier.

9. The change in prices that follows a change in aggregate demand reduces the value of the spending multiplier and contributes to the hump-shaped pattern of the multiplier process.

10. An adverse aggregate supply shock such as an increase in oil prices increases firms' costs of production, which increases prices and reduces output in the short run. It produces a stagflation—both unemployment and inflation increase. A favorable aggregate supply shock such as cost-reducing technological change has the opposite effects.

The New Classical View of Aggregate Supply in the Short Run:

11. The economy is highly competitive, wages and prices are flexible, and the economy always operates on or near its production possibilities frontier. There is no essential difference between the short-run and the long-run aggregate supply curves, at least none that has any relevance to policy in the short run. The government cannot improve the performance of the economy in the short run. Real business cycle theory is now the prevailing theory of the new classical school. It says that real national product (national income) is determined by the supply side of the economy and can change only if the production possibilities frontier itself (AS_{LR}) shifts in or out.

12. Changes in aggregate demand can change output, but only if they affect the nation's production possibilities. This means that the source of the change in aggregate demand matters.

13. An increase in any component of aggregate demand does affect production possibilities because it causes interest rates to change, and the change in

interest rates changes the supply of labor. For example, an increase in aggregate demand increases interest rates, which causes people to supply more labor today. The increased supply of labor lowers real wages, firms hire more workers, and output expands. A decrease in any component of aggregate demand has the opposite effects. The problem with this theory is that economists cannot find any evidence that interest rates influence the supply of labor. This is not troublesome to new classical economists, however, because they believe that most changes in output are due to changes in productivity, and not to changes in aggregate demand.

14. A change in the money supply changes aggregate demand, but it has no effect on the real side of the economy. For example, a doubling of the money supply simply doubles prices. People's demand for money doubles along with the prices, so that they just hold on to the new money and nothing else happens.

KEY TERMS

aggregate demand curve
aggregate demand schedule
aggregate supply curve

aggregate supply schedule
aggregate supply shock

menu costs
stagflation

QUESTIONS

1. a. Draw a reasonable aggregate demand curve with the overall price level and national product on the axes, and explain why you drew it as you did.

   b. How does an aggregate demand curve for the economy as a whole differ from an aggregate demand curve for an individual market?

2. a. Draw a reasonable aggregate supply curve with the overall price level and national product on the axes.

   b. Is the curve that you drew a short-run aggregate supply curve or a long-run aggregate supply curve, or could it be both the short-run and the long-run aggregate supply curves?

   c. How does an aggregate supply curve for the economy as a whole differ from an aggregate supply curve for an individual market?

3. Consider the following aggregate demand schedule.

GDP Deflator	Aggregate Demand
105	4,900
100	5,000
95	5,200

   a. Draw the aggregate demand curve for this aggregate demand schedule.

   b. Next, represent this aggregate demand schedule using the ADE–45° graph with national income on the horizontal axis and aggregate desired expenditures on the vertical axis.

   c. Comment on the relationship between the aggregate demand curves in the two graphs.

4. Compare and contrast the principal assumptions of the new Keynesian and the new classical theories of macroeconomics, as well as their theories about how the macro economy operates. Be sure to highlight areas of agreement between the two schools as well as areas of disagreement.

5. Draw reasonable-looking aggregate supply curves for the short run and the long run, using new Keynesian assumptions. Explain why you drew them as you did. How would each curve change, if at all, under new classical assumptions?

6. Some aggregate supply shocks shift both the long-run and the short-run aggregate supply curves, and some aggregate supply shocks shift only the short-run aggregate supply curve. Give one example of each type of aggregate supply shock, and explain why they have different effects on the long-run aggregate supply curve.

7. Consider the aggregate supply–aggregate demand framework under new Keynesian assumptions. Assume the economy is in long-run equilibrium where output is 5,000 and the price level is 100.

   a. If the government undertakes a combination of contractionary fiscal and monetary policies, what effects will these policies have on output and prices?

   b. How would your answer change as the economy moves from the short run to the long run following the policy changes?

8. What is meant by nominal price stickiness? What are the causes of nominal price stickiness, according to the new Keynesian school?

9. a. Give some examples of adverse aggregate supply shocks.
   b. Demonstrate graphically the effects of these shocks, using the AS–AD framework under new Keynesian assumptions. Consider both the short-run and the long-run reactions to the shocks.
   c. Give some examples of favorable aggregate supply shocks, and repeat the analysis in part (b) for the favorable shocks.

10. a. What is stagflation?
    b. What type of shocks to the economy might cause a period of stagflation?
    c. Depict stagflation graphically, using the AS–AD framework and also using the Phillips Curve framework.
    d. What policies might new Keynesian economists recommend in response to the problem of stagflation?
    e. What policies might new classical economists recommend in response to the problem of stagflation?

11. Why does the economy respond to aggregate demand or supply shocks in the pattern of a business cycle under new Keynesian assumptions about the macro economy?

CHAPTER

19

Controlling Inflation
and
Other Policy Issues

LEARNING OBJECTIVES

CONCEPTS TO LEARN

Rational expectations	Supply-side economics
Long-run Phillips Curve	Policy credibility

CONCEPTS TO RECALL

Laws of Supply and Demand [5]	Aggregate demand and aggregate supply [9, 18]
Inflation [7]	Aggregate supply shock [9, 18]
Fisher equation [7]	The equation of exchange [14]
New Keynesian economics [9, 18]	Short-run Phillips Curve [17]
New classical economics [9, 18]	

here is a standing joke among economists about their worst professional nightmare. It is being cornered at a party and asked a macroeconomic policy question: What should the government do about _____? Everything hangs on the blank at the end of the question.

The situation becomes especially uncomfortable if the blank is a short-run issue such as reducing unemployment. The economist stammers a bit to buy some time as he begins thinking about the rift between the new Keynesian and the new classical schools over the short run. His thoughts turn down the new Keynesian path for awhile, and he ponders the various policy options that we discussed in Chapter 17. Coming up with policies to reduce unemployment is easy enough, but he knows that before he blurts out an answer, he has to worry about how each policy affects the other macroeconomic policy goals. His thoughts then turn down the new classical path, and he is tempted to answer: "Why nothing, of course. The government's fiscal and monetary policies cannot hope to improve the performance of the economy over the next year." The poor economist becomes completely tongue-tied as the guests drift away.

The nightmare is avoided if the blank at the end of the question refers to a long-run policy issue such as increasing investment and growth, or reducing the burden of the ever-increasing public debt, or keeping inflation under control. New Keynesian and new classical economists are pretty much in agreement on these issues. The economist breathes a heavy sigh of relief and quickly offers an opinion with some degree of confidence.

Chapter 18 emphasized the sharp disagreement between the new Keynesian and the new classical economists about the operation of the macro economy in the short run. They do not disagree about everything, however. Chapter 19 concludes the macroeconomic section of the text with an analysis of three policy issues that the two schools agree on. The first is the nature of inflation and how to keep it under control. The second is whether the government has any effective leverage over the supply side of the economy in the short run. The third is the need for consistent and believable government policies.

THE NATURE OF INFLATION AND HOW TO CONTROL IT

Few economic variables are watched as closely as is inflation in the United States. Chapter 7 described how the Department of Commerce samples nearly 100,000 prices of goods and services every month and uses these price data to update broad-based price indexes such as the consumer price index (CPI) and the gross domestic product (GDP) deflator. The department's monthly announcements of the rate of inflation as measured by these indexes receive a great deal of attention in the news media.

What determines the rate of inflation in the United States? Economic research on inflation has focused mostly on the average rate of inflation during the course of a year rather than on the monthly inflation rates reported by the Department of Commerce. This research has shown that the annual rate of inflation depends primarily on four factors: the growth in nominal aggregate demand, the state of the economy relative to the production possibilities frontier, the presence of aggregate supply shocks, and people's expectations about the future rate of inflation.

A word on perspective is in order before analyzing how each of these factors affects the rate of inflation: The distinction between the short run and the long run is crucial to the analysis of inflation. Tracking the rate of inflation month by month as the Department of Commerce does is a clear case of statistical overkill. Even a year is too short a time horizon to get an accurate picture of an underlying inflationary process.

Remember, inflation refers to *sustained* increases in prices generally, with emphasis on the word *sustained*. An inflationary process is inherently a long-run phenomenon, a pattern of general price increases that is projected to continue year after year after year. An increase in prices of 5 percent on an annual basis that lasts for a few months, or even a year or two, and then stops altogether hardly constitutes an inflationary process, at least not one that has any relevance for government policy.

The important question is this: What can *sustain* an inflationary process more or less indefinitely? The four factors listed above all push the rate of inflation up and down from one year to the next or even from one month to the next. As such, they all have some influence on the underlying inflationary process because the short-run pattern of inflation can feed into inflation over the longer run. But we will see that only two of the factors—the growth in nominal aggregate demand and people's expectations of inflation—can truly sustain an inflation over the long run. These two factors are the twin engines that drive an inflationary process and are therefore the keys to the problem of keeping inflation under control.

Chapters 17 and 18 described how the first three factors affect the rate of inflation over the short run. Let's briefly review what we have said about these factors and consider whether their effects on inflation over the short run carry over the long run. The review in hand, we can then add the fourth factor—people's expectations of inflation—and move from the short run to the long run, where the analysis of inflation properly belongs.

Our analysis of the first three factors is based on the new Keynesian view of the short run. We will briefly indicate in each instance how the new classical real business cycle theory would modify the analysis. The differences between the two schools are unimportant, however, because they reach essentially the same conclusions about the nature of inflation in the short run.

The Growth of Nominal Aggregate Demand

The final section of Chapter 17 described how a 10 percent increase in nominal aggregate demand affects the rate of inflation; the growth in real national product, or output; and unemployment in the short run. The short-run Phillips curve, pictured in Figure 17.5, shows how the increase in aggregate demand is split between an increase in inflation and a decrease in unemployment.

Our analysis at the time did not consider whether the 10 percent growth in aggregate demand was a one-shot increase that would last for only a year or a steady rate of growth that would continue indefinitely. The distinction between a one-shot increase and continuous steady growth in aggregate demand is crucial to the analysis of inflation, however. A one-shot increase in aggregate

FIGURE 19.1

A One-time Increase in the Money Supply and Inflation

The figure shows that a one time increase in the money supply causes a higher price level but not a sustained inflation. The initial long-run equilibrium before the increase in the money supply is (Q_0, P_0) on the production possibilities frontier, at the intersection of AD^0, AS_{LR}, and AS_{SR}^0. There is no inflation. The increase in the money supply increases aggregate demand from AD^0 to AD^1 and prices start to rise as the economy moves to the short run equilibrium (Q_1, P_1), at the intersection of AD^1 and AS_{SR}^0. Markets are generally in excess demand at Q_1 so prices and wages rise further, which increases firms' costs of production. AS_{SR} shifts up and to the left until it reaches AS_{SR}^2 and removes the excess demand. The new long-run equilibrium is (Q_0, P_2) on the frontier, at the intersection of AD^1, AS_{LR}, and AS_{SR}^2. Prices stop rising once they reach P_2. The increase in the money supply raises the overall price level from P_0 to P_2 but does not cause a sustained inflation.

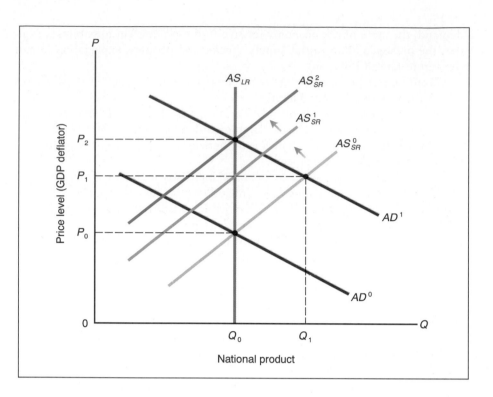

demand cannot sustain an inflation, whereas a steady growth in aggregate demand is absolutely essential for sustaining an inflation. The distinction between the two is best seen with reference to the aggregate supply–aggregate demand (AS–AD) framework pictured in Figure 19.1.

Suppose that the economy is initially in long-run equilibrium on its production possibilities frontier at the intersection of AD^0, AS_{LR}, and AS_{SR}^0. The frontier output is Q_0, and the overall price level as measured by the GDP deflator is P_0. The rate of inflation is zero. Suddenly the Fed increases the money supply and keeps it at its new higher *level* indefinitely. The result is a one-time increase in aggregate demand from AD^0 to AD^1.

The one-time increase in aggregate demand produces some fairly dramatic effects for awhile, but it cannot sustain an inflationary process in and of itself. At first, prices and output rise, and unemployment falls, as the economy heads to the temporary short-run equilibrium, (Q_1, P_1), at the intersection of AD^1 and AS_{SR}^0. The Department of Commerce's monthly price data begin to show an inflation developing, since prices are now rising from P_0 to P_1.

The short-run equilibrium cannot maintain itself, however, because the economy is now beyond its sustainable production possibilities frontier. The excess demand in the economy continues to drive up prices of both goods and factors, and the increase in factor prices increases firms' costs of production. The rising production costs act as a series of adverse aggregate supply shocks that shift the short-run aggregate supply curve up and to the left. AS_{SR} shifts from AS_{SR}^0 to AS_{SR}^1 to AS_{SR}^2, returning the economy to a long-run equilibrium on the frontier. The economy experiences a period of stagflation as the economy returns to the frontier. Prices continue to rise from P_1 to P_2, output falls from Q_1 to Q_0, and unemployment increases.

Notice, though, that all the action ends when the economy returns to the frontier. The inflation stops once the price level rises to P_2, and the unemployment rate returns to the natural rate at the frontier output, Q_0. The one-time increase in aggregate demand has increased the price *level* from P_0 to P_2, but it has not generated a lasting inflation.

The new classical real business cycle analysis of the one-time increase in the money supply reaches the same conclusion. The only difference is that real business cycle theory assumes that the economy moves immediately to the new long-run equilibrium, (Q_0, P_2), without all the short-run drama of the new Keynesian analysis.

Both schools agree that the inflation can continue only if the *growth* in aggregate demand is *maintained*, if there is a 10 percent increase year after year, indefinitely. With aggregate demand growing steadily year by year, the *AD* curve continues to shift up and to the right every year, and the overall price level never settles down to a new higher equilibrium *level*. Instead, the overall price level increases steadily year after year, which is the definition of an inflationary process. We will return to the role of aggregate demand growth in sustaining an inflation later on in the analysis.

The State of the Economy

The state of the economy relative to the production possibilities frontier affects the rate of inflation in the short run because it determines whether markets generally are in excess demand or excess supply throughout the economy. The state of the economy is embodied in the shape of the short-run Phillips Curve. We saw that the Phillips Curve is quite flat when the economy is operating far beneath the production possibilities frontier, with high unemployment and markets generally in excess supply. An increase in nominal aggregate demand under those conditions mostly increases output and decreases unemployment. It causes only a small increase in the rate of inflation. The Phillips Curve becomes steeper as the economy approaches the frontier, and very steep as the economy reaches and exceeds the frontier in the short run. The steepening of the Phillips Curve indicates that a given increase in nominal aggregate demand increases inflation more and more, and reduces unemployment less and less, as the economy approaches and exceeds the frontier. Output becomes ever more difficult to expand near the frontier, since most of the nation's resources are already employed. Under those conditions the increase in nominal aggregate demand translates mostly into an increase in inflation.

The independent, other things equal effect of the state of the economy on inflation should wash out over the long run as the economy moves through the ebbs and flows of the business cycles. At times the economy will be below the frontier, which tends to lower the rate of inflation; at other times the economy will be near or even above the frontier, which tends to increase the rate of inflation. These periods of upward and downward pressure on inflation should essentially cancel one another out over the long run. The one exception, as we will see below, is if the government tries to keep the economy permanently above or below the frontier. But this is really a decision about how fast the government will let nominal aggregate demand grow. The growth in nominal aggregate demand determines the state of the economy in the long run, and not the other way around.

Real business cycle theory would deny that the state of the economy has any relevance to inflation because the economy is always operating on or near its production possibilities frontier. New classical economists believe that the economic research on inflation has "discovered" this effect only because it has mismeasured the position of the frontier. In any event, both schools agree that the state of the economy is not an essential factor in explaining inflation over the long run.

Aggregate Supply Shocks

Aggregate supply shocks have a pronounced effect on inflation in the short run because they change the costs of production, and firms in the United States are quick to pass cost changes through to price changes. An adverse supply shock, such as the increase in the price of crude oil induced by the organization of Petroleum Exporting Countries (OPEC), quickly leads to higher prices. The quadrupling of the price of crude oil in late 1973 and early 1974 was largely responsible for the jump in inflation from 3.4 percent in 1972 to 8.7 percent in 1973 to 12.3 percent in 1974. Similarly, a favorable supply shock, such as the collapse of OPEC in 1980, leads just as quickly to lower prices. The price of crude oil fell from over $30 a barrel to around $10 a barrel during 1980 and 1981 and was a major contributor to the decrease in inflation from 12.5 percent in 1980 to 8.9 percent in 1981 to 3.8 percent in 1982.[1]

The changes in oil prices in the 1970s and in the early 1980s were one-time events, and the same point applies to a one-time-only aggregate supply shock as to a one-time-only increase in aggregate demand. A one-time-only aggregate supply shock can affect the rate of inflation in the short run, but not in the long run. Figure 19.2 illustrates.

The economy is initially in long-run equilibrium on its production possibilities frontier at the intersection of AD^0, AS_{LR}, and AS_{SR}^0. The frontier output is Q_0, and the overall price level is P_0. There is no inflation. Then a one-time-only adverse aggregate supply shock, such as an increase in oil prices, hits the economy. The supply shock shifts the short-run aggregate supply curves up and to the left, to AS_{SR}^1. The economy experiences stagflation for awhile as prices rise, output falls, and unemployment increases. The stagflation ends, however, when the economy reaches the new short-run equilibrium, (Q_1, P_1), at the intersection of AD^0 and AS_{SR}^1.

The period of stagflation is then followed by a period of deflation and increasing output as the economy adjusts back to its long-run equilibrium on the frontier. The reason why is that markets throughout the economy are generally in excess supply at the short-run equilibrium, (Q_1, P_1). The excess supply puts downward pressure on prices and costs, and the short-run aggregate supply curve begins to shift back down and to the right. It keeps shifting until it returns to AS_{SR}^0, and the initial long-run equilibrium, (Q_0, P_0) is restored on the frontier.

We noted in Chapter 18 that an adverse supply shock shifts the short-run Phillips Curve up and to the right, increasing both inflation and unemployment. This is the initial period of stagflation. Eventually, however, the effect of the shock wears off if it is a one-time-only event, and the short-run Phillips Curve tends to shift back down to its original position.

---

[1]Unless otherwise noted, all data on U.S. inflation rates and unemployment in this chapter are from the Council of Economic Advisers, *Economic Report of the President, 1993* (Washington, D.C.; U.S. Government Printing Office, 1993), Table B-58, p. 415 (inflation) and Table B-37, p. 390 (unemployment).

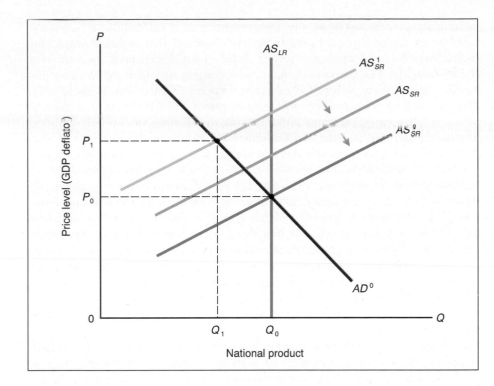

FIGURE 19.2

An Adverse Supply Shock and Inflation

The figure shows that an adverse supply shock causes prices to rise for a short time but has no lasting effect on the overall price level. The initial long-run equilibrium before the adverse supply shock is (Q_0, P_0) on the production possibilities frontier, at the intersection of AD^0, AS_{LR}, and AS_{SR}^0. There is no inflation. The adverse supply shock shifts the short-run aggregate supply curve up and to the left from AS_{SR}^0 to AS_{SR}^1. Prices start to rise as the economy moves to the short run equilibrium (Q_1, P_1), at the intersection of AD^0 and AS_{SR}^1. Markets are generally in excess supply at Q_1 so prices and wages begin to fall, which decreases firms' costs of production. AS_{SR} shifts back down and to the right until it reaches AS_{SR}^0 and removes the excess supply. The economy returns to its original long-run equilibrium (Q_0, P_0) on the frontier, at the intersection of AD^0, AS_{LR}, and AS_{SR}^0. The adverse supply shock does not change the long-run equilibrium price, P_0.

In conclusion, the inflationary effect of the adverse supply shock is very short-lived, as it is with a one-time increase in aggregate demand.[2] Aggregate supply shocks have to continue year after year to have a continuing effect on the rate of inflation. An example would be the continuing technological change in the production of personal computers that has driven the prices of these computers steadily downward for over a decade. Many supply shocks, especially adverse supply shocks, are of the one-time-only variety, though, in which case the above analysis applies. The one-time shocks have no lasting impact on inflation. Real business cycle theory agrees with the new Keynesian analysis of aggregate supply shocks.

Expected Inflation

The one factor we have left out so far in our analysis of inflation is the role played by people's expectations of what the rate of inflation will be in the future. The role of expected inflation turns out to be crucial because the interplay between actual and expected inflation is one of the twin engines that drive and sustain an inflationary process.

Economists might be better off if expected inflation were not such an important determinant of inflation because it makes the future course of inflation somewhat difficult to predict. One problem created by expectations is that an

---

[2]The example assumes that the supply shock does not affect the production possibilities, so that it shifts only AS_{SR}. A one-time-only shock that shifted both AS_{SR} and AS_{LR} would still have only a short-run effect on the rate of inflation. The only difference is that the period of deflation and increasing output when the economy returns to the long-run equilibrium would be shorter or non-existent because AS_{LR} would have shifted to the left.

inflationary process takes on the characteristics of a self-fulfilling prophecy. Inflation increases this year *because* people expected that inflation would increase, or inflation decreases this year *because* people expected that inflation would decrease. The markets for financial securities are much the same in this respect. Stock prices will rise if everyone expects them to rise because then everyone will be trying to buy stocks; stock prices will fall if everyone expects prices to fall because everyone will be trying to sell their stocks. Self-fulfilling prophecies can lead to large and unpredictable swings in the behavior of economic variables over time, and this is certainly true about the path of inflation.

A second problem is that economists are not sure how people form future expectations about anything, including future inflation. People's recent experience with inflation no doubt influences their predictions about future inflation. They are likely to expect a higher rate of inflation next year if inflation has averaged 10 percent over the past three years than if it has averaged only 2 percent. At the same time, people almost certainly do more than simply extrapolate past rates of inflation into the future. Their expectations about future inflation are undoubtedly forward-looking as well. At the very least, they will give some thought to the following question: Are future economic conditions expected to remain about the same as today, or are they expected to change significantly?

For example, suppose that inflation has been 2 percent per year for as long as people can remember, yet the Fed is about to announce a dramatic change in its monetary policy. Most people have a rough idea that an increase in the money supply increases prices and that a decrease in the money supply decreases prices. Therefore, they are likely to wait until the Fed announces its new policy before forming their expectations about next year's inflation. If the Fed announces that it plans to double the money supply next year, people are likely to expect a rate of inflation much higher than 2 percent next year. Similarly, if the Fed announces that it will cut the money supply in half next year, people might well expect a deflation, even though prices have recently been rising. Expecting the rate of inflation to remain at 2 percent following either of these announcements would not be reasonable.

RATIONAL EXPECTATIONS

The assumption that rational individuals consider all relevant information (past, present, and future) currently available when forming expectations of the future.

RATIONAL EXPECTATIONS   Almost all *theoretical* research in macroeconomics assumes that people are forward-looking in forming their expectations about the future values of all economic variables, including inflation. Macro economists assume that people have **rational expectations,** meaning that they consider all relevant information currently available to them when forming their expectations of the future. In terms of predicting future inflation, the relevant information might include the rate of inflation over the recent past, the current state of the economy, whether the economy has just been hit with significant aggregate demand or supply shocks, and the government's announced intentions for fiscal and monetary policies in the near future.

The key implication of rational expectations is that people's predictions of the future are correct *on average* over time. This does *not* mean that they always guess right about future inflation (or anything else): indeed, they could guess wrong all the time. To say that people are correct *on average* just means that they are equally likely to overestimate inflation or to underestimate inflation, so that their prediction errors tend to cancel out over time. In other words, they do not predict future inflation in such a way that they systematically overestimate or underestimate the rate of inflation year after year.

Rational expectations is certainly a reasonable presumption. After all, why would people continue to predict the future in ways that they know are wrong? Suppose that you were using a method of predicting future inflation that always underestimated next year's actual rate of inflation and that your predictions were about 3 percent too low on average. You would naturally adjust your predictions up by 3 percent to correct for the underestimation. After the adjustment, you are now as likely to overestimate next year's rate of inflation as to underestimate it. Of course, some new information may come to light that suggests a different adjustment is appropriate in the future. Whatever you do, however, you will not stick with a method that has proven to underestimate inflation systematically year after year.

Empirical research on how people form expectations of inflation has not entirely supported the rational expectations assumption. People appear to extrapolate past rates of inflation rather more in forming their expectations of future inflation than rational expectations would suggest. They make too little use of current and forward-looking information, such as the current state of the economy or the Fed's announcements on the future growth of the money supply. Nonetheless, people do appear to consider the government's policy announcements to some extent in predicting the future course of inflation. This is important because we will see that it can reduce the costs of stopping an inflationary process.

FROM EXPECTED INFLATION TO ACTUAL INFLATION   Economists may not know how people form their expectations of inflation, but they do know that the expectation of inflation feeds back into actual inflation and helps to sustain an inflation. The feedback from expected to actual inflation occurs through the supply side of economy by driving up the costs of production. We will illustrate the feedback with two components of costs, wages and interest rates.

EXPECTED INFLATION AND WAGE RATES   Imagine union leaders and management sitting down at the bargaining table to negotiate the next union contract, which will stipulate the wage rate over the next three years, among other things. The union leaders are interested in increasing their members' real wages, or purchasing power. As such, the annual wage increases they bargain for depend on their expectation of the annual rate of inflation over the next three years. For example, suppose that they want the members' purchasing power to increase by 3 percent per year. In this case the annual wage increases in the contract would have to be three percentage points higher than the union leaders' expectation of inflation. If they expect no inflation over the next three years, they would be willing to settle for 3 percent annual wage increases. If they expect inflation to average 10 percent per year, however, they will bargain for 13 percent annual wage increases. The members need a 10 percent wage increase just to match the expected inflation and an additional three percentage points to give them the 3 percent increase in their purchasing power.

Management, meanwhile, is thinking along much the same lines. It, too, is concerned about the relationship between wages and prices—in this case the wages it pays relative to the prices of the firm's products. Suppose that it is willing to grant a wage increase three percentage points higher than the increase in its prices because it projects that the union members will be 3 percent more productive each year. As such, the annual wage increase they are willing to offer also depend on their expectation of the annual rate of inflation over the next three years, assuming that they believe their prices will change the same as prices generally. Management would be willing to offer annual 3 percent wage increases if it expects no inflation over the next three years. It would be willing to offer annual 13 percent wage increases if it expects inflation to average 10 percent per year.

Therefore, with the union leaders and management both thinking in terms of the real wage, wages adjust point for point with expected inflation. Wage increases that would be 3 percent with no expected inflation jump to 13 percent when expected inflation is 10 percent and jump to 53 percent when expected inflation is 50 percent. Moreover, there is nothing special about unionized labor. All employees expect to receive wage increases that protect their purchasing power by building in the expected rate of inflation, and employers are willing to offer such wage increases. The expectation of inflation increases all firms' actual labor costs point for point with the expected inflation.

EXPECTED INFLATION AND INTEREST RATES   We have already seen in Chapter 7 that interest rates also adjust point for point with the expected rate of inflation. Recall the Fisher equation, which says that

$$i_{\text{nominal}} = r_{\text{real}} + \Delta P/P_E$$

i_{nominal} is the nominal interest rate, the interest rate that we actually observe on financial securities. r_{real} is the real interest rate, the purchasing power of the annual interest payment. $\Delta P/P_E$ is the expected rate of inflation.

Interest rates adjust point for point with the expected rate of inflation for the same reason that wage rates adjust. Lenders and borrowers both think in terms of purchasing power when deciding on the interest rate on a loan. Lenders insist on adding the expected rate of inflation to the interest rate in order to protect the purchasing power of the interest they receive. They want to ensure that the interest payment truly increases their purchasing power relative to the purchasing power of the money they are lending today. Borrowers are willing to pay the additional interest if they believe that their incomes will rise by the expected rate of inflation. In that case, the higher nominal interest rate does not increase the purchasing power that they sacrifice in paying back the loan with interest. Review the example in Chapter 7 if you are unclear about this.

Interest rates are an important component of the firms' costs of capital. Therefore, the expectation of inflation drives up firms' actual costs of capital point for point with the expected inflation.

With the expectation of inflation increasing their wage costs and interest costs, firms are forced to raise their prices to cover the higher costs of production.[3] This has the added effect of driving up the costs of material inputs, the semi-finished products that firms buy from other firms. The expected inflation has fed into the actual inflation and serves to keep the inflation going.

Expected inflation acts as a *continuing* adverse aggregate supply shock that shifts the short-run aggregate supply curve up and to the left over time, as illustrated in Figure 19.3. Once people expect an inflation, the expectation

---

[3]We will see in Chapter 21 that an expected inflation also depreciates the nation's currency point for point, so that firms also have to pay more for the raw materials, material inputs, and capital goods that they import from foreign producers.

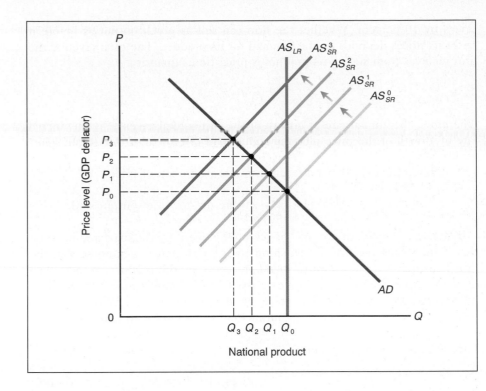

FIGURE 19.3

Expected Inflation, Actual Inflation, and Aggregate Supply

The economy is initially in a long-run equilibrium without any inflation or any expectation of inflation. The initial long-run equilibrium is (Q_0, P_0) on the production possibilities frontier, at the intersection of AD, AS_{LR}, and AS_{SR}^0. Once people begin to expect an inflation their expectations feed into an actual inflation through the supply side of the economy. An expected inflation increases wages, interest rates, and the prices of material inputs, all of which increase firms' costs of production. The short-run aggregate supply curve shifts up and to the left continuously, from AS_{SR}^0 to AS_{SR}^1, AS_{SR}^2, AS_{SR}^3, indefinitely, which causes prices to rise from P_0 to P_1, P_2, P_3, indefinitely. The expectation of inflation is one of the twin engines (the other being an increase in the money supply) that drives and sustains an inflation.

drives up production costs at the same rate as the expected inflation and shifts AS_{SR} up continuously from AS_{SR}^0 to AS_{SR}^1 to AS_{SR}^2 to AS_{SR}^3. The difference between inflation and our earlier example of a one-time-only aggregate supply shock is that AS_{SR} never stops shifting. AS_{SR} continues to shift up indefinitely as long as people continue to expect a positive rate of inflation. The economy never settles down to one short-run equilibrium, and prices never stop increasing either. Instead, the expectation of inflation drives the actual inflation indefinitely through the supply side of the economy.

Notice, too, that expected inflation shifts only AS_{SR} and not AS_{LR}. AS_{LR} represents the nation's production possibilities frontier, which is determined by the quantity and the quality of a nation's resources and its production technologies. None of these is affected by an inflation.

Nominal Aggregate Demand Growth Once Again

Expected inflation increases production costs and forces firms to raise their prices. But this cannot be the end of the inflation story because it leaves one question unanswered: Can firms sell their products at the new higher prices? The answer depends on the demand for the firm's products, which takes us back to the growth in nominal aggregate demand. The supply-side engine of the expected inflation is not enough to sustain an inflation by itself. The demand-side engine of continued growth in nominal aggregate demand must also be present to pull the prices ever upward.

Look at the problem first from the point of view of an individual firm. Assume that the expected annual rate of inflation is 10 percent, which increases the firm's costs of production by 10 percent and forces the firm to raise its prices by 10 percent. Whether the firm can sell as much output as before it raises its prices depends on the demand for its product. The total revenue the firm receives from selling its product is price times quantity:

$$TR = P \cdot q$$

Therefore, the annual rate of growth of the firm's total revenue is the annual rate of growth of the price plus the annual rate of growth of the output sold:

Rate of growth of total revenue = rate of growth of price
+
rate of growth of output sold

The rate of growth of the price is set at 10 percent by the expected inflation that is increasing the firm's production costs by 10 percent. Suppose that the firm's customers do not want to spend any more on the product, in total, than they had been spending. In that case the total revenue received by the firm is constant, and the rate of growth of total revenue is zero. With the firm's prices growing at 10 percent, the output sold must fall by 10 percent:

Rate of growth of total revenue (0%) = rate of growth of price (+10%)
+
rate of growth of output sold (−10%)

Customers have to be willing to spend 10 percent more on the firm's product for the firm to sell as much output as it did before the price increase:

Rate of growth of total revenue (10%) = rate of growth price (+ 10%)
+
rate of growth of output sold (0%)

All firms are in the same position when the expected inflation is 10 percent. Therefore, aggregate demand has to grow at the expected rate of inflation for aggregate output, the national product, to remain the same.

Figure 19.3 shows what happens when aggregate demand is not growing in the context of an expected inflation. The short-run aggregate supply curves are shifting up and to the left along the same aggregate demand curve, AD. Prices are continuously rising, but notice that output is continuously falling as well, from Q_0 to Q_1 to Q_2 to Q_3, indefinitely. This situation obviously cannot continue. People will not continue to expect a 10 percent inflation after output has fallen far below the production possibilities frontier, markets are generally in excess supply, and more and more workers are becoming unemployed. The only way the inflation can sustain itself is if aggregate demand grows as well in step with the expected inflation, 10 percent per year in our example. Figure 19.4 illustrates.

The short-run aggregate supply curve, AS_{SR}, shifts up by 10 percent each year, indefinitely, as in Figure 19.3, driven by the 10 percent expected inflation. This time, however, AD also shifts up by 10 percent each year, from AD^0 to AD^1 to AD^2 to AD^3, indefinitely, to match the shifts in the short-run aggregate supply curve. As a result of the aggregate demand shifts, the economy

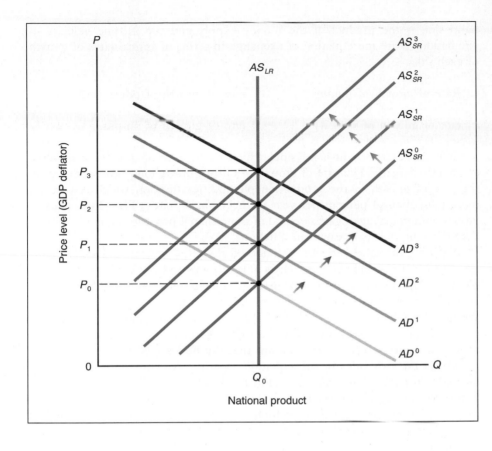

FIGURE 19.4

Increases in the Money Supply and Inflation

The figure shows how the twin engines of expected inflation and increases in the money supply drive and sustain an inflation. The initial long-run equilibrium is (Q_0, P_0) on the production possibilities frontier, at the intersection of AD^0, AS_{LR}, and AS_{SR}^0. Then people come to expect a 10 percent inflation, which begins to shift the short-run aggregate supply curve up by 10 percent indefinitely, from AS_{SR}^0, to AS_{SR}^1, AS_{SR}^2, etc. The inflation would eventually stop without an increase in aggregate demand above AD^0, however. People would not continue to expect an inflation with output falling and unemployment rising. To sustain the inflation, the government has to increase the money supply continuously so that aggregate demand increases by 10 percent indefinitely from AD^0 to AD^1, AD^2, etc. With both AS_{SR} and AD shifting up continuously by 10 percent, the economy remains on the frontier at Q_0, and the price level continues to increase by 10 percent, from P_0 at the intersection of AD^0 and AS_{SR}^0, to P_1 at the intersection of AD^1 and AS_{SR}^1, and so forth, indefinitely.

remains on the frontier at output Q_0, at each intersection of the corresponding AD and AS_{SR} curves; all resources remain fully employed; and the inflation can sustain itself indefinitely. Growth in nominal aggregate demand is clearly an essential ingredient of an inflationary process. Moreover, the growth in nominal aggregate demand must be (approximately) equal to the rate of inflation. A 10 percent inflation requires growth in nominal aggregate demand of (approximately) 10 percent; a 50 percent inflation requires growth in nominal aggregate demand of (approximately) 50 percent; and so forth.

MONEY AND INFLATION   The government ultimately determines the growth in nominal aggregate demand with its fiscal and monetary policies, which means that the government has the ability to control inflation. In fact, *controlling inflation means controlling the growth of the money supply.* Nobel Laureate Milton Friedman has said that inflation is always and everywhere a monetary phenomenon, and virtually all economists would agree with him, at least for any significant amount of inflation that is sustained over the long run. The reason why money and inflation are so tightly linked can be seen from the equation of exchange:

$$M \cdot V = P \cdot Q$$

The right-hand side of the equation is nominal aggregate demand. The left-hand side is the product of the money supply and the income velocity of circulation. Write the equation of exchange in terms of annual rates of growth of each side:

Rate of growth of money   rate of growth of prices (inflation)
+   =   +
rate of growth of velocity   rate of growth of output

Look first at the right-hand side, which is the rate of growth of nominal aggregate demand. The rate of growth of output in the long run is limited by the rate of growth in the production possibilities frontier, which can be no more than about 4 percent per year in the United States. Therefore, rates of growth in nominal aggregate demand of more than 4 percent that are sustained over the long run must cause an inflation.

Regarding the left-hand side, the rate of growth of velocity is largely determined by institutional factors, such as how often people are paid and how they pay for goods and services. Consequently, velocity changes very little year by year in normal times, sometimes rising a bit and at other times falling a bit. We noted in Chapter 14 that velocity changed by an average of only 4.2 percent per year, plus or minus, throughout the 1980s. The rate of growth in the money supply, in contrast, can be any amount that the Fed wants it to be.

Putting the two sides of the equation together, we can see that the large increases in nominal aggregate demand needed to sustain a high rate of inflation require correspondingly large increases in the money supply. And this is exactly what happens in times of high inflation in all countries. If a country has been experiencing a 20 percent inflation for some time, you can be sure that its money supply has been increasing by nearly 20 percent per year. If another country has been experiencing a 300 percent inflation, you can be sure that its money supply has been increasing by nearly 300 percent per year. It cannot be otherwise.

Large increases in nominal aggregate demand without large increases in the money supply would require large increases in velocity, and this is not going to happen. For example, an ever more expansionary fiscal policy by itself would eventually crowd out consumer durables, investment, and net exports and have little impact on nominal aggregate demand. This is just another way of saying that velocity can only increase slowly in normal times. The need to have money in order to spend constrains the growth in nominal aggregate demand unless the money supply itself is growing.

THE PRESSURES TO MAINTAIN AN INFLATION   Economists have long advised government officials that controlling the growth of the money supply is the key to controlling inflation. Why, then, do governments occasionally let the money supply grow rapidly and support a very high level of inflation? After all, stopping the growth of the money supply is easy to do, and high inflations are dangerous. They can easily turn into hyperinflations, which destroy faith in the currency and threaten a nation's entire financial structure.

The answer is that governments come under tremendous pressures from all sides to keep an inflation going once it gets started. Figure 19.3 illustrates the short-run costs of halting the growth in aggregate demand. Think of the government as halting the growth in aggregate demand by halting the growth in the money supply and holding aggregate demand at AD in the figure. The short-run problem is that, having just experienced inflation, people continue to expect inflation for awhile, which shifts AS_{SR} up and to the left, as in Figure 19.3. The shifting AS_{SR} curve against the now-constant AD curve reduces output below the frontier; firms go bankrupt, and workers lose their jobs. Neither business nor labor wants this result, so the business and labor leaders petition the government to keep pumping more money into the economy to maintain the growth in aggregate demand. They much prefer the result pictured in Figure 19.4, in which nominal aggregate demand grows by enough to keep the economy on its frontier, the firms in business, and the workers employed.

Worse still, additional pressure to keep the inflation going comes from within the government itself. High inflations are invariably associated with periods of high budget deficits, during which the government resorts to issuing large amounts of debt to finance its expenditures. Once an inflation is established, and people come to expect it, the interest rates that the government has to pay on its debt rise point for point with the expected rate of inflation. This is the lesson of the Fisher equation.

For example, suppose that the inflation rate has settled in at 50 percent per year and everyone expects it to continue at that rate. The government has to offer interest rates of 55 or 60 percent to issue its debt—and now has a strong incentive to keep the inflation going. If it stops printing money and ends the inflation, it would face *real* interest rates of 55 and 60 percent on its outstanding debt, which it cannot honor unless it cuts spending or raises taxes significantly. The far simpler alternative is to keep printing the money and maintain the inflation. Indeed, the government even has an incentive to *increase* the rate of inflation steadily over time so that it can pay off the interest on its debt with dollars that have less purchasing power than did the dollars it borrowed from the public. Keeping the actual inflation running ahead of the expected inflation transfers purchasing power from the private sector to the government sector when the government is debt financing.

The government's incentive to maintain and even increase inflation once it begins to debt finance its expenditures is so powerful that the University of Chicago's Robert Lucas has termed inflation a fiscal phenomenon. Lucas appreciates that growth in the money supply is what sustains an inflation. But he believes that the temptation for deficit spending is what really causes governments to give in to inflation.[4] Moreover, deficit spending gives the central bank an easy avenue for increasing the money supply. It simply buys the new Treasury debt issues with newly printed money, so that the government is effectively financing its expenditures by printing money. (The Fed is not allowed to buy new Treasury issues, but it could buy the debt in the secondary market immediately after it is issued, which would amount to the same thing. Economists call this "monetizing the debt.")

FROM INFLATION TO HYPERINFLATION   Once the government decides to print whatever amount of money is necessary to sustain an inflationary process, it creates a highly unstable circular dynamic that can easily blow apart into a

[4]R. Lucas, "Discussion" of S. Fischer, "Towards an Understanding of the Costs of Inflation: II," in K. Brunner and A. Meltzer, eds., *The Costs and Consequences of Inflation*, vol. 15 of the *Carnegie Rochester Conference Series on Public Policy* (Amsterdam: North Holland Publishing Company, 1981), 43–50. The inflation-is-a-fiscal-phenomenon statement is on p. 46.

hyperinflation. Actual inflation feeds the expectation of future inflation, which feeds back into the actual inflation, which feeds into expected inflation, and so on, indefinitely. And the vicious circle is continually validated and maintained by pumping ever more money into the economy. People may eventually lose faith in the government's ability to keep the inflationary process under control. The instant this happens they lose faith in the money as a medium of exchange and refuse to hold it. The institutional factors that normally hold down the growth of velocity are overwhelmed as people become desperate to get rid of their money. Velocity skyrockets, and the inflation becomes a runaway hyperinflation. The rate of inflation increases much more rapidly than does the growth of the money supply once the hyperinflation sets in because it is fueled by the runaway growth in velocity as well as the growth in the money supply.

In conclusion, the analysis of inflation yields both good news and bad news. The good news is that governments can always stop an inflation. All they have to do is halt the growth in the money supply. The bad news is that governments may not always have the will to stop the inflation because they do not want to bear the short-run costs that go along with it. Some firms will go bankrupt, some workers will lose their jobs, and the government will be forced to cut spending or raise taxes. The tight relationship between money supply growth and inflation now cuts the other way. Governments can easily avoid these short-run costs by printing whatever money is required to sustain or even increase the inflation. But refusing to face the short-run costs of stopping an inflation runs the risk of a devastating hyperinflation down the road.

Governments are well advised to keep a tight rein on the growth of the money supply over the long run and to avoid the temptation of debt-financing current expenditures. No government wants the political headache of deciding between short-run economic hardships and the long-run risk of a hyperinflation. Yet the combination of even moderate inflation and large budget deficits is a potentially explosive mixture that creates precisely these kinds of headaches.

HISTORICAL NOTE: The reunification of Germany forced the government into making large social expenditures and weakened somewhat its longstanding resolve to hold down inflation as its number one priority. The weakened resolve was short-lived, however. By 1992 Germany was once again holding fast against the build-up of inflationary pressures.

THE SHORT-RUN AND LONG-RUN PHILLIPS CURVES Chapter 17 first described the costs of fighting an inflation in terms of the short-run Phillips Curve. Recall that the short-run Phillips Curve shows the inverse relationship between inflation and unemployment when the government manipulates aggregate demand with its fiscal and monetary policies. Expansionary fiscal and monetary policies, which increase aggregate demand, increase inflation and decrease unemployment in the short run. Contractionary fiscal and monetary policies, which decrease aggregate demand, decrease inflation and increase unemployment in the short run. We now know that contractionary monetary policy is necessary to squeeze inflation out of the economy, and the short-run Phillips Curve shows that the cost is an increase in unemployment in the short run.

At the same time, our analysis of inflation indicates that the cost of fighting inflation really is a short-run cost. The economy does not have to suffer increased unemployment forever as the cost of fighting inflation. In other words, the short-run Phillips Curve cannot be a stable relationship as time passes and the short run turns into the long run.

Economists generally agree that markets are competitive enough, and wages and prices flexible enough, that the economy eventually moves to its production possibilities frontier. The only long-run equilibrium output is the frontier

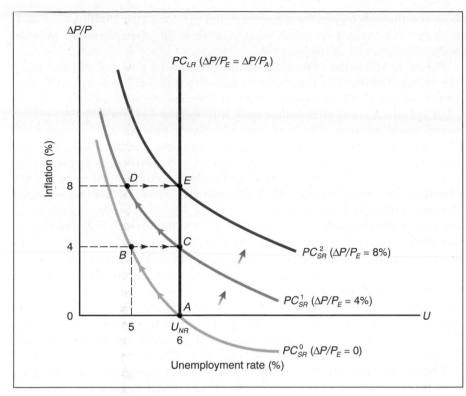

FIGURE 19.5

The Long-run Phillips Curve

The figure shows that there is no trade-off between inflation and unemployment in the long run. This is because each short-run Phillips Curve is associated with a given expected inflation and the expected inflation adjusts in the long run to the actual inflation. The economy is initially in long-run equilibrium at point A on the production possibilities frontier. Both actual and expected inflation are zero, and unemployment is at the natural rate, U_{NR}. Then an increase in the growth of aggregate demand moves the economy to point B along the short-run Phillips Curve PC_{SR}^0, which is consistent with zero expected inflation. Unemployment drops below U_{NR} to 5 percent and inflation rises to 4 percent. Eventually people come to expect a 4 percent inflation, which shifts the short-run Phillips curve up and to the right to PC_{SR}^1. PC_{SR}^1 is consistent with a 4 percent expected inflation. The economy returns to point C at U_{NR}, with an actual inflation of 4 percent. A further increase in the growth of aggregate demand moves the economy to point D on PC_{SR}^1. Unemployment again falls to 5 percent, and inflation increases to 8 percent. Eventually people come to expect an 8 percent inflation, which shifts the short-run Phillips Curve up and to the right to PC_{SR}^2. PC_{SR}^2 is consistent with an 8 percent expected inflation. The economy returns to point E at U_{NR}, with an actual inflation of 8 percent. The long-run Phillips curve, PC_{LR}, is vertical at U_{NR}. The economy is in long-run equilibrium on its frontier at U_{NR} when the actual inflation equals the expected inflation. This condition can hold at any rate of inflation: positive, zero or negative.

output, which is completely determined by the supply side of the economy. Aggregate demand just determines the overall price level in the long run, and any price level is consistent with the long-run equilibrium.

Now translate these results into a Phillips Curve diagram such as Figure 19.5, which has inflation on the vertical axis and unemployment on the horizontal axis. The natural rate of unemployment, U_{NR}, corresponds to the frontier level of output. Therefore, the only long-run equilibrium for the economy is at U_{NR}. Also, just as any price level is consistent with the frontier output, any rate of inflation is consistent with the natural rate of unemployment. The ver-

LONG-RUN PHILLIPS CURVE

A curve representing the idea that the economy tends to the natural rate of unemployment in the long run and that there is no long-run trade-off between inflation and unemployment; shows that any rate of inflation is compatible with the natural rate of unemployment in the long run.

tical line through U_{NR} in the figure is called the **long-run Phillips Curve.** It indicates that there is no relationship, inverse or otherwise, between inflation and unemployment in the long run.

Figure 19.5 illustrates the relationship between the long-run and the short-run Phillips Curves. The key to the relationship is that every short-run Phillips Curve assumes a given expected rate of inflation. In contrast, the long-run Phillips Curve applies after people have adjusted their expectations of inflation to the actual inflation. The story goes as follows. The economy is initially in long-run equilibrium at point A. Inflation is zero and has been zero for some time, so that expected inflation is also zero. Unemployment is at the natural rate, U_{NR}, assumed to be 6 percent. Suddenly the government increases the growth of the money supply, which increases the growth in nominal aggregate demand. Prices (and wages) rise at the rate of 4 percent per year. People did not expect the change in policy, however, so that they continue to expect zero inflation. The economy moves along the short-run Phillips Curve, PC_{SR}^0, which assumes zero expected inflation. The reduction in unemployment (increase in output) occurs because workers and bondholders have locked themselves into one-year or longer contracts that assumed zero inflation. As the inflation ensues, firms find their prices rising, but not their costs, so they hire more workers and increase output. The new short-run equilibrium is at point B; inflation rises from zero to 4 percent, and unemployment falls below the natural rate to 5 percent.

The short-run equilibrium cannot maintain itself, forever. Once people realize that the government is allowing the money supply to grow and that actual inflation is 4 percent, they come to expect a 4 percent inflation. The increase in expected inflation from zero to 4 percent causes wages and interest rates to rise and acts as an adverse aggregate supply shock that shifts the short-run Phillips Curve up and to the right to PC_{SR}^1. The economy returns to the frontier and U_{NR} at point C, with an inflation rate of 4 percent. The actual and expected rates are once again equal, at 4 percent, as required for long-run equilibrium.

If the government wants the unemployment rate to return to 5 percent, it has to increase the growth of the money supply even faster, so that actual inflation outstrips expected inflation once again. Suppose that the government does this and generates an 8 percent inflation. This time the economy moves along the short-run Phillips Curve, PC_{SR}^1, to point D. The economy cannot remain at this short-run equilibrium, however. Once people understand that the government has increased the growth of the money supply and that the actual inflation is 8 percent, they adjust their expected inflation up from 4 percent to 8 percent. The increase in expected inflation shifts the short-run Phillips Curve up and to the right once again to PC_{SR}^2, and the economy returns to the frontier and U_{NR} at point E. The actual and expected rates are once again equal, at 8 percent, as required for long-run equilibrium.

The relationship between the short-run and the long-run Phillips Curves leads to a number of interesting conclusions.

INFLATION IN THE LONG-RUN EQUILIBRIUM Any rate of inflation is consistent with the long-run equilibrium on the production possibilities frontier. The equilibrium condition is only that actual inflation equals expected inflation, which can be satisfied at any rate of inflation: zero, 200 percent, 430 percent, or anything else. This explains why economies can function with inflations of 300 percent and more. Economies can always return to their frontiers once people have adjusted to the inflation.

ACCELERATING INFLATION   The only sensible unemployment target in the long run is the natural rate of unemployment. Trying to drive unemployment permanently below the natural rate does not just generate an inflation; it generates an *ever-accelerating* inflation that must ultimately become a hyperinflation. Refer again to Figure 19.5. Suppose that the government tries to keep the unemployment rate permanently at 5 percent. It can reach the target at first by generating a 4 percent inflation. But as people's expectations adjust to the new inflation, the economy begins to move back to the frontier. So the government has to increase the money supply even more rapidly and generate an 8 percent inflation. Once again expectations adjust, so the government has to increase the money supply even faster, generating, say, a 12 percent inflation. In short, the government has to keep actual inflation continually ahead of expected inflation. But expected inflation always adjusts to actual inflation, which means that still higher inflation is needed to keep unemployment at 5 percent. The cycle never ends as the short-run Phillips Curves keep shifting upward continuously. The result is an accelerating inflation that can only lead eventually to a runaway hyperinflation.

The only possible justification for trying to lower the unemployment rate is to test where the natural rate really is. Some economists believe that the natural rate of unemployment is around 4 percent. The more commonly accepted rate is in the 5 to 6 percent range. Their conjecture may well be worth testing. If they are correct, then maintaining the unemployment rate at 5 or 6 percent may be keeping 1 or 2 million people unemployed unnecessarily. If they are wrong, pushing the unemployment rate down to 4 percent for awhile would not be too costly in terms of the extra inflation it would cause.

DECELERATING INFLATION/ACCELERATING DEFLATION   Perhaps the most surprising conclusion of the analysis is that keeping the unemployment rate permanently above the natural rate generates an ever-decelerating inflation or an ever-accelerating deflation. The analysis is exactly the reverse of the accelerating case.

Slowing down the growth of the money supply in order to generate a higher rate of unemployment lowers the actual rate of inflation as the economy moves along its short-run Phillips Curve. Then expected inflation adjusts to the new lower actual inflation, the short-run Phillips Curve shifts down, and the economy attempts to return to the frontier and U_{NR}. To hold the unemployment rate above U_{NR}, the government has to reduce the growth of the money supply still further, which lowers actual inflation. The lower actual inflation causes people to lower their expected inflation, the short-run Phillips Curve shifts down again, and the process continues. Inflation continues to decelerate, eventually leading to an accelerating deflation if the government persists in keeping the unemployment rate above U_{NR}.

ELIMINATING AN INFLATION   The government might want to keep unemployment above U_{NR} temporarily because this is the only way economists know to squeeze inflation out of an economy. Figure 19.6 illustrates.

Suppose that the economy is initially in long-run equilibrium at point A on the long-run Phillips Curve. Unemployment is at the natural rate, U_{NR}. The rate of inflation is 12 percent and has been for some time, so that it is also the expected rate of inflation.

The government decides that 12 percent inflation is unacceptable and wants to lower inflation from 12 percent to zero. The quickest way to do this is to

FIGURE 19.6

Reducing an Inflation With a Deep Recession

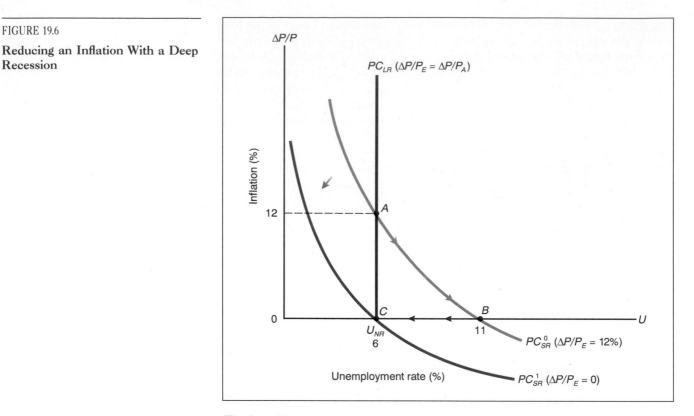

The figure illustrates how the government can reduce an ongoing inflation with monetary policy by generating a deep recession for a short period of time. The figure assumes that the economy is initially in long-run equilibrium at point A, at the intersection of PC_{LR} and PC_{SR}^0. Unemployment is at the natural rate, U_{NR}, and both the actual and expected inflation are 12 percent. PC_{SR}^0 is consistent with an expected inflation of 12 percent. To reduce the inflation to zero the government halts the growth of the money supply and brings the economy to point B on PC_{SR}^0. Unemployment rises to 11 percent and inflation falls to zero. By keeping the economy at point B, and the actual inflation at zero, people eventually come to expect zero inflation. The reduction of expected inflation from 12 percent to zero percent shifts the short-run Phillips Curve down and to the left to PC_{SR}^1. PC_{SR}^1 is consistent with zero expected inflation. The economy can then return to a long run equilibrium on the frontier at point C with zero inflation, at the intersection of PC_{LR} and PC_{SR}^1.

generate a short, but very deep, recession. Stop the growth of the money supply completely, or even reduce the money supply, and inflation will drop to zero right away. The economy moves to point B along the short-run Phillips curve, PC_{SR}^0, which is associated with the expected 12 percent inflation. Unemployment rises sharply to 11 percent as inflation falls to zero.

This move is costly in terms of higher unemployment, but the economy does not have to stay there for long. Once people realize that the government has decreased the growth of the money supply and that the actual inflation is zero, they adjust their expected inflation down to zero. The reduction in expected inflation acts as a favorable aggregate supply shock that shifts the short-run Phillips Curve down to PC_{SR}^1. The economy moves back to its long-run equilibrium at point C. Unemployment is once again at U_{NR}, and inflation is zero.

Another possibility is to move more slowly with a longer, shallower recession—to have the government generate, say a 7 percent unemployment rate and a 9 percent inflation in the short run. Then it would keep the unemployment rate at 7 percent as expected inflation adjusts downward until it equals zero. At this point the economy can return to its frontier with zero inflation.

Both the quick fix and the longer, slower fix are costly in the short run, but these are the only sure-fire ways of squeezing inflation out of the economy.

HISTORICAL NOTE: The Fed has kept a vigilant guard against the buildup of inflationary pressures. For example, in mid-1993 the economy was growing very slowly, yet Chairman Greenspan considered slowing down the growth of the money supply because inflation appeared to be inching up beyond the 3 percent mark.

New Keynesian and New Classical Perspectives

New Keynesian and new classical economists essentially agree with the preceding analysis of the relationship between the short-run and the long-run Phillips Curves. Their only disagreement is over the length of the short run. New Keynesians argue that an equilibrium on a short-run Phillips Curve can last for a fairly long time. Actual inflation differs from expected inflation not so much because people are fooled, but rather because wages and prices are sticky for reasons given in Chapters 6 and 18. Businesses are reluctant to change prices, and workers agree to wage and salary contracts of one year and more, so that the adjustment to changes in expected inflation is necessarily slowed down.

New classical economists argue that an equilibrium on a short-run Phillips Curve is short-lived. Wages and prices are flexible even in the short-run. Moreover, people have rational expectations; they quickly take into account what the government is doing and adjust their expectations accordingly. The result is that expected inflation adjusts quickly to match actual inflation whenever actual and expected inflation diverge, and the economy returns quickly to the frontier.

One important policy implication of their different opinions relates to how quickly the government can squeeze inflation out of the economy. The new Keynesians argue that reducing inflation requires either a deep, short recession or a prolonged, shallow recession. The new classical economists argue that inflation can be squeezed out almost immediately.

The evidence appears to favor the new Keynesians on this point. For example, inflation fell sharply from 12.5 percent in 1980 to 3.8 percent in 1982. But the new Keynesians point out that it took the deepest recession since the Great Depression to accomplish this. Unemployment rose to 9.7 percent by 1982. And there were still other favorable supply side shocks that helped reduce the inflation as well, such as the collapse of oil prices. Also, the more mild recession of the early 1990s reduced the rate of inflation more slowly. Inflation fell from 6.1 percent in 1990 to 3.1 percent by 1991 and then fell only slightly to 2.9 percent in 1992.

Stan Fischer of MIT, a leading new Keynesian economist, estimates that the cumulative costs in lost output of reducing inflation from 10 percent in 1980 to 4 percent by 1985 amounted to 25 percent of one year's national product.[5] This is an enormous cost and argues strongly for not letting inflationary pressures build if at all possible.

---

[5]S. Fischer, "Real Balances, the Exchange Rate, and Indexation: Real Variables in Disinflation," *The Quarterly Journal of Economics* CIII, Issue 1 (February 1988): 28. The 1992 inflation rate is from Council of Economic Advisers, *Economic Indicators, March 1993* (Washington, D.C.: U.S. Government Printing Office, 1993), 24.

Interest Rates One Last Time

A final point about inflation concerns the behavior of interest rates in an inflationary environment. We said in Chapter 16 that an increase in the money supply decreases interest rates. The analysis then was referring to the effects of a *one-time* increase in the money supply on the underlying *real* interest rates, the interest rates on which savers and investors base their decisions. The analysis was also short run and in a new Keynesian policy environment of sticky wages and prices.

The analysis in this chapter refers to a sustained increase in the rate of growth of the money supply, which maintains an inflation over the long run. The Fisher equation indicates that the nominal, or observed, interest rates must increase under these conditions. The continued expectation of inflation dominates any short-run decrease in interest rates brought about by an initial increase in the money supply.

Suppose, for example, that the economy has been experiencing no inflation and no growth in the money supply for some time and that both real and nominal interest rates average 5 percent. Then the Fed allows the money supply to grow by 10 percent per year, indefinitely.

Both the real and the nominal interest rates may drop below 5 percent immediately after the money supply begins to increase. Eventually, though, the nominal interest rate must rise. The continued growth in the money supply must increase both actual and expected inflation to 10 percent in the long run (approximately). Once the economy returns to the frontier and expected inflation is 10 percent, the real interest rate returns to 5 percent, and the nominal interest rate increases to 15 percent. The sustained growth in the money supply ultimately increases nominal interest rates point for point with the increase in expected inflation that it brings.

Always keep the Fisher equation in mind in an inflationary environment, especially in periods when the rate of inflation is increasing or decreasing. Interest rates tend to move in the same direction as inflation because expected inflation tends to adjust to actual inflation.

MANAGING THE ECONOMY THROUGH THE SUPPLY SIDE

Adverse aggregate supply shocks, such as an increase in oil prices, are nasty events for an economy; they increase both inflation and unemployment. Worse yet, economists are not convinced that the government has any effective remedy for them in the short run. Figure 19.7 illustrates the nature of the government's short-run policy problem.

Suppose that the economy is initially in long-run equilibrium on its production possibilities frontier at the intersection of AD^0, AS_{LR}, and AS_{SR}^0. Output is Q_0, the frontier output, and the overall price level is P_0. Suddenly the economy is hit with an adverse supply shock that shifts the short-run aggregate supply curve up and to the left from AS_{SR}^0 to AS_{SR}^1. A period of stagflation sets in with rising prices, falling output, and rising unemployment as the economy moves to a new short-run equilibrium at the intersection of AD^0 and AS_{SR}^1. Output falls to Q_1 and the overall price level rises to P_1 in the shot run. (The

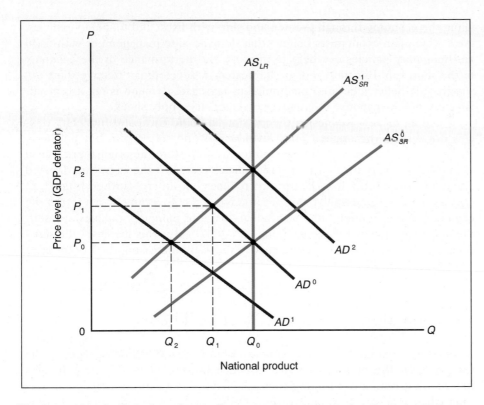

FIGURE 19.7

Responding to an Adverse Aggregate Supply Shock

The figure shows the limitations of responding to an adverse aggregate supply shock with fiscal and monetary policies, which manipulate aggregate demand. The initial long-run equilibrium before the adverse supply shock is (Q_0, P_0) on the production possibilities frontier, at the intersection of AD^0, AS_{LR}, and AS_{SR}^0. The adverse supply shock shifts the short-run aggregate supply curve up and to the left from AS_{SR}^0 to AS_{SR}^1, which reduces output and increases prices. The new short-run equilibrium is (Q_1, P_1), at the intersection of AD^0 and AS_{SR}^1. The government can restore the initial price level P_0 in the short-run with contractionary fiscal and monetary policies that decrease aggregate demand from AD^0 to AD^1. The new equilibrium would be (Q_2, P_0), at the intersection of AD^1 and AS_{SR}^1. But contractionary policies reduce output even further from Q_1 to Q_2. Alternatively, the government can return the economy to the frontier output Q_0 in the short run with expansionary fiscal and monetary policies that increase aggregate demand from AD^0 to AD^2. The new equilibrium would be (Q_0, P_2), at the intersection of AD^2 and AS_{SR}^1 (and AS_{LR}). But expansionary policies increase prices even further from P_1 to P_2. Neither policy response is entirely satisfactory.

supply shock may also shift AS_{LR}, but we are ignoring that possibility to focus on the short-run policy problem.)

New Keynesian and new classical economists would agree that the ideal policy response would be through the supply side of the economy. The government would like to have a set of policy tools that could quickly shift AS_{SR}^1 back down and out to AS_{SR}^0 and restore the original equilibrium on the frontier. The question is whether such supply-side policy tools exist. At the moment the answer appears to be no.

New classical economists have a natural interest in developing effective short-run supply-side policies. They believe that the economy is buffeted mostly by aggregate supply shocks, and they do not place much stock in managing the economy through the demand side with fiscal and monetary policies. New Keynesian economists believe that demand-side management with fiscal and monetary policies can help to improve the performance of the economy in the short run. But they, too, are interested in developing effective short-run supply-side policies because manipulating aggregate demand is not a very satisfactory policy response to an adverse aggregate supply shock.

According to new Keynesian theory, demand-side fiscal and monetary policies can restore the original price level *or* the original output, but not both. Refer again to Figure 19.7. The government can restore the original price level with contractionary fiscal or monetary policies that shift the aggregate demand curve down from AD^0 to AD^1. But this reduces output still further, from Q_1 to Q_2, and increases unemployment. Alternatively, the government can return the economy to the frontier with expansionary fiscal or monetary policies that shift the aggregate demand curve up from AD^0 to AD^2. But this increases the inflationary pressures of the aggregate supply shock by increasing the overall price level from P_1 to P_2.

Reaganomics: A Supply-Side Tax Theory

The issue of manipulating the economy from the supply side was put to the test in 1981, the first year of the Reagan administration. President Reagan inherited an economy suffering from stagflation resulting primarily from one-time adverse aggregate supply shock—OPEC had doubled the price of crude oil in 1979. Inflation rose from 9.0 percent in 1978 to 12.5 percent by 1980, and the unemployment rate rose from 6.0 percent to 7.0 percent. The administration's policy response to the stagflation ushered in one of the more interesting episodes of fiscal policy in the entire history of the United States.

The Reagan administration argued that the government could manipulate the economy through the supply side in the short run with income tax policy. In their view a cut in income taxes increases aggregate supply in the short run, shifting AS_{SR} down and to the right. Conversely, an increase in income taxes decreases aggregate supply in the short run, shifting AS_{SR} up and to the left. Therefore, they proposed a large tax cut to increase aggregate supply and effectively combat both the rising inflation and the rising unemployment simultaneously. The tax cut proposal was dubbed Reaganomics, or supply-side economics.

The tax cut proposal was particularly interesting because the theory behind it was directly counter to the prevailing view of taxes at the time, which was Keynesian. Keynes argued that tax increases and decreases affect the economy in the short run by shifting aggregate demand, not aggregate supply. Only a proverbial handful of economists believed that a tax cut could have any significant effect on aggregate supply in the short run, whether they labeled themselves new Keynesian or new classical. Nonetheless, Congress was willing to give supply-side economics a try. It passed the largest income tax cut in U.S. history, a 23 percent reduction in the personal income tax rates phased in over three years.

The Keynesian and supply-side views of tax cuts could hardly be more different. Keynes argued that a tax cut stimulates the economy by increasing people's disposable income, which increases consumption demand. The supply-side theory argued that a tax cut stimulates the economy by lowering input prices, particularly wages and interest rates, which increases aggregate supply.

TAX CUTS, LABOR SUPPLY, AND SAVING   We laid out the Keynesian theory of income tax cuts in Chapter 11. The heart of the supply-side theory is that an income tax cut increases the supply of labor and saving for investment, both of which increase aggregate supply. Regarding labor, a cut in income tax rates increases the after-tax wages that workers receive—the workers' take-home pay—and encourages people to work harder, so that the supply of labor increases. The increased supply of labor puts downward pressure on the wages that firms pay their workers, which induces firms to hire more workers. Regarding saving and investment, an income tax cut increases the after-tax return that people receive on their saving, which encourages them to save more. The increase in personal saving puts downward pressure on interest rates in the financial markets, which induces firms to invest in more capital and increase production. The increase in employment and investment increases production. AS_{SR} shifts down and to the right.

SUMMARY: KEYNESIAN VERSUS SUPPLY-SIDE TAX THEORY   The battle lines between the prevailing Keynesian theory and the new supply-side theory were firmly drawn in 1981 around the tax cuts.

Keynesian theory:

Income tax cut $\rightarrow$ disposable income $\uparrow$ $\rightarrow$ consumption demand $\uparrow$ $\rightarrow$ aggregate demand $\uparrow$ $\rightarrow$ real national output and income $\uparrow$

Supply-side theory:

Income tax cut $\rightarrow$ after-tax wages, interest rates $\uparrow$ $\rightarrow$ labor supply, savings $\uparrow$ $\rightarrow$ employment, investment $\uparrow$ $\rightarrow$ real national output and income $\uparrow$

ASSESSING THE SUPPLY-SIDE THEORY   The main problem that the vast majority of economists had with the supply-side theory at the time was factual, not theoretical. The supply-side effects on labor supply and saving are possible in theory, but did not appear to be very likely. Research on labor supply had suggested that changes in wage rates have little or no short-run effect on the overall supply of labor in the United States. The same was true of interest rates and saving. Interest rates change quite a bit over time, but even large changes in interest rates appear to have very little effect on how much people save in the short run. Economists simply had no reason to believe that the tax cuts would have much effect on either labor supply or private saving in the short run, and therefore, on aggregate supply. Subsequent research since 1981 has reached essentially the same conclusions.[6]

---

[6]For a review of the economic research on the effects of income taxes on labor supply and saving, see: J. Hausman and J. Poterba, "Household Behavior and the Tax Reform Act of 1986," *Journal of Economic Perspectives* 1, No. 3 (Summer, 1987): 101–119; B. Bosworth and G. Burtless, "Effects of Tax Reform on Labor Supply, Investment, and Saving," *Journal of Economic Perspectives* 6, No. 1 (Winter 1992): 3–25.

Also, the tax cuts in and of themselves lower the government budget surplus (increase the budget deficit), which is the government component of saving. *National saving* is the sum of the private-sector saving and government saving. If the tax cuts do not increase personal saving, then they will reduce national saving.

THE EVIDENCE   The economy recovered steadily from the recession of 1981–82 following the tax cut, most of which was phased in during 1982 and 1983. Unemployment fell from 9.7 percent in 1982 and 9.6 percent in 1983 to 7.5 percent in 1984 and to 7.2 percent in 1985. Was the recovery demand led or supply led? The majority of economists believe that the recovery was demand led rather than supply led. The tax cut appeared to have no effect at all on the supply of labor, exactly as most economists had predicted. Also, private saving decreased instead of increasing. How, then, did the tax cuts propel the supply side of the economy if the labor supply and private saving did not increase? These are, after all, the key components of the supply-side tax theory. Finally, federal personal income tax collections fell sharply as a result of the tax cuts, so that national saving fell sharply as well. The tax cuts appeared to stimulate the economy by increasing consumption demand, in line with the Keynesian theory.

In summary, the events following the Reagan tax cut did not convince very many economists that government tax policy is an effective tool for manipulating the economy through the supply side in the short run. What, then, can the government use to offset adverse aggregate supply shocks if tax policy cannot do it? Macro economists do not have an answer to this question. Unless they come up with something, the economy will have to suffer the occasional adverse aggregate supply shock and the stagflation that accompanies it. The only pleasant thought to offset this unhappy conclusion is that the economy will occasionally receive favorable aggregate supply shocks, as it did when the oil prices collapsed in the 1980s.

Tax Policy in the Long Run

This does *not* mean, however, that tax policy has no effect on aggregate supply in the long run. Quite the opposite is true, especially with regard to saving and investment. Changes in tax policy usually change both the after-tax rate of return to savers and the cost of capital to business firms. Saving and investment may respond only slightly in the short run to changes in the rate of return to saving and in the cost of capital. But the small short-run effects tend to build over time and can have a substantial impact on saving and investment over the long run. Since saving and investment are the key to long-run economic growth and since long-run economic growth is the most important determinant of a nation's standard of living, tax policy can make a big difference to a nation's economic well-being.

A number of economists have built simple models of the U.S. economy that are designed to track the effects of tax and other budgetary policies over very long periods of time, 50 to 100 years and more. These models always reach the same conclusions about tax policy. Tax reforms that lower tax rates on saving and investment and that raise tax rates on consumption in order to keep total tax revenues constant over time lead to much more saving and investment in the long run. The additional saving and investment increase productivity and push out the production possibilities frontier, so that the economy is eventually able to produce much more output. Completely replacing the federal personal income tax with an equal revenue expenditures tax that only taxes consumption may increase the national product by as much as 10 to 20 percent after 20 years or so, according to these models. A 20 percent increase in the national product translates into an additional $4,800 for every person every year in the United States.

These models reach the same general conclusion about budget deficits. We have seen that government borrowing to finance large structural deficits raises interest rates and the cost of capital. Large structural deficits also transfer resources from future to current generations because the government must eventually raise taxes or cut spending to reduce the deficits. All these effects significantly reduce saving, investment, productivity, and long-run economic growth over the long haul. The long-run economic models suggest that a policy of running structural deficits on the order of $200 billion for 10 to 15 years, as the federal government has been doing, may eventually reduce the national product by 10 percent or more[7].

Virtually all economists would recommended that the federal government keep taxes on saving and investment low and reduce the structural budget deficits if it is serious about promoting saving, investment, and long-run economic growth. They would also say that nothing is more important than long-run economic growth to the overall economic well-being of a nation. New Keynesian and new classical economists are in complete agreement here. So is President Clinton and a (bare) majority of Congress. In the summer of 1993, Congress passed Clinton's proposed $500 billion reduction in the deficit from 1993 to 1998.

POLICY CREDIBILITY: STEERING A STEADY COURSE

New Keynesian and new classical economists generally agree that governments need to develop a reputation for consistency and credibility. They should get in the habit of announcing their policy intentions well in advance, doing what they say they are going to do, and staying the course until their policy goals have been met. Governments that continually shift their policies may lose their credibility and end up causing quite a bit of harm.

Let's take a look at the issue of policy credibility from a new Keynesian perspective, since the new Keynesians are the ones who are prone to advise the government to intervene in the economy. The new classical economists would naturally favor a steady and credible policy stance because they see the need for policy only in a long-run context.

The new Keynesians believe that active intervention with fiscal and monetary policies can improve the performance of the economy in the short run. They strongly disagree with the current new classical view that the economy

---

[7]Two excellent sources on the long-run effects of tax policy and budget deficits are L. Kotlikoff, "Taxation and Savings: A Neoclassical Perspective," *Journal of Economic Literature* XXII, No. 4 (December 1984): 1576–1629; and L. Kotlikoff, "Economic Impact of Deficit Financing," *International Monetary Fund Staff Papers* 31 (September 1984): 549–582.

remains on or near its production possibilities frontier at all times. Nonetheless, the majority of New Keynesians support a steady and credible policy stance. They see a number of advantages from their own perspective.

In the first place, new Keynesians recognize the practical limitations of conducting fiscal and monetary policies. They realize that the government cannot fine tune the economy by reacting immediately to every blip in aggregate demand or aggregate supply. The best these policies can hope to do is "lean against the wind" by nudging the economy back on track when it goes astray and preventing a bad situation from turning into a disaster. "Leaning against the wind" implies a steadier course for fiscal and monetary policies than does fine tuning right from the outset.

A steady and credible policy course also has a number of advantages in terms of the allocation of resources simply because it reduces uncertainty within the economy. Three that we have talked about in previous chapters are reducing unemployment, encouraging investment, and reducing the short-run costs of fighting inflation.

A major component of unemployment is search unemployment, in which the unemployed spend time searching out various job opportunities before accepting a job. A steady and credible set of policies would generate less confusion than do sudden stop-and-go policies about what the job opportunities are, both now and in the future. People would be able to reduce their search time, which would reduce the natural rate of unemployment and expand the economy's production possibilities. (New classical economists stress this point because they believe that measured unemployment is almost entirely search or frictional unemployment at all times.)

A more certain economic environment is also conducive to investment demand. We first made this point when discussing why a stable value of the dollar is one of the four macroeconomic policy goals. The idea is that stable exchange rates promote international trade and investment by reducing uncertainty. Businesses are more willing to invest and ship goods abroad the more confidence they have in the rate at which they can convert foreign currencies earned abroad back into dollars. The same general point applies to domestic investment.

The federal government offered a good counterexample of what not to do in the first half of the 1980s. The Reagan tax cut of 1981 affected more than the personal income tax. Congress also made substantial changes in the corporation income tax that, overall, sharply reduced the cost of capital for corporations. Then, in 1982, Congress had a change of heart and passed a substantial "correction" to the 1981 law that took away many of the 1981 tax advantages and increased the cost of capital. Congress changed the corporate tax rules yet again in the Tax Reform Act of 1986 (TRA86), removing the investment tax credit and introducing a number of other features that increased the cost of capital. TRA86 was particularly tough on the real estate industry, closing a number of tax advantages that had been in existence for decades. By the end of 1986 businesses were complaining that all these changes in the tax laws had made them hesitant to invest because they no longer had any confidence about the tax implications of their investments. Their complaints had more than a ring of truth to them, and Congress called a moratorium on major tax changes for a number of years. Wrenching businesses around like that is not the kind of thing the government ought to be doing.

Finally, a credible policy stance is very useful for fighting inflation. We saw that the expectation of inflation feeds an inflation through the supply side and that the government has to convince people not to expect inflation in order to eliminate inflation. Unfortunately, the only way to do this is to generate a recession to reduce actual inflation and let expected inflation come down with actual inflation. People's expectation of inflation should adjust downward quickly if they believe that the government means business and will stick with the recession until the inflation ends. Expected inflation appears to adjust downward only slowly in the United States, however, which is why squeezing inflation out of the economy is so costly. The reason why expected inflation adjusts so slowly may well be a lack of government credibility.

People know that jobs mean votes in national elections and that the administration and the Congress are unlikely to maintain a contractionary policy stance during an election year. Therefore, they have no reason to expect inflation to fall if they believe the federal government will shortly change to an expansionary stance. We noted in Chapter 13 that the evidence for an engineered political business cycle is not very convincing. Still, fiscal and monetary policies have both changed course frequently. Thus, U.S. citizens have very little reason to believe that the federal government will ever truly stay the course.

Stanford's Robert Hall has recommended that the federal government abandon its stop-and-go policy stance of the past and commit to a policy of constant growth in nominal aggregate demand—say, 5 percent per year. Hall's recommendation is noteworthy because he is firmly associated with the new Keynesian school.[8]

To see the implications of Hall's policy recommendation, recall that nominal aggregate demand is the product of prices times quantities:

$$Y = P \cdot Q$$

Also, the rate of nominal aggregate demand is the sum of the rates of growth in prices and quantities:

Rate of growth of Y = rate of growth of P (inflation)

+

rate of growth of Q

Suppose that output grows at 3 percent per year on average, equal to the rate at which the production possibilities frontier moves out over time. Then Hall's policy allows an average inflation of 2 percent per year over the long run.

The government would announce this policy and stick to it, so that it would have all the advantages of a steady and credible policy noted above. And the policy would always respond to aggregate demand and aggregate supply shocks in a set manner.

The government would simply offset any aggregate demand shocks with the appropriate fiscal and monetary policies in order to keep nominal aggregate demand growing at 5 percent year. For example, the government would

---

[8]Hall's proposal is presented in R. Hall and J. Taylor, *Macroeconomics: Theory, Performance, and Policy*, Second edition (New York: Norton, 1988), 498–501.

counter a decrease in the growth of consumption demand with expansionary fiscal and monetary policies that would keep the growth in aggregate demand at 5 percent.

The policy response to an adverse aggregate supply shock would be a slow and balanced offset to the price and the output effects of the shock. For example, suppose that an adverse aggregate supply shock drives up inflation to 5 percent and reduces the growth of output to zero. The government would not change the rate of growth in nominal aggregate demand, since prices and output are still growing at the rate of 5 percent combined. The result would be a shallow and prolonged recession in which the economy would return slowly to the frontier and inflation would be gradually reduced. Hall argues that a long and shallow recession is the best demand-side response to an adverse aggregate supply shock. He, like other economists, does not know how to respond quickly to the shock through the supply side.

A growing number of new Keynesian economists agree with Hall that steady growth in nominal aggregate demand is the best strategy for the government's fiscal and monetary policies. Having agreed on an overall growth target to manage output and inflation, the government can then adjust the mix of fiscal and monetary policies to increase or decrease interest rates.

Recall that interest rates primarily effect two other macroeconomic policy goals, long-run economic growth and the value of the dollar relative to foreign currencies. Lower interest rates stimulate investment and long-run economic growth and cause the dollar to depreciate in value. Higher interest rates retard investment and long-run economic growth and cause the dollar to appreciate in value. The government would presumably opt for low interest rates these days in the name of promoting growth. But a swing to high interest rates may be necessary on occasion to protect the dollar.

SUMMARY

Chapter 19 concluded the macroeconomic section of this text with a discussion of three policy issues on which new Keynesian and new classical economists are pretty much in agreement: controlling inflation, responding to adverse aggregate supply shocks, and meeting the need for consistent and credible government policies.

The first section of the chapter analyzed the process of inflation and how to keep it under control.

1. The rate of inflation year to year is determined primarily by four factors: the growth in nominal aggregate demand, the state of the economy, aggregate supply shocks, and the expectation of future inflation.
2. Inflation is inherently a long-run policy problem. Of the four factors, the growth in nominal aggregate demand and the expectation of inflation are the twin engines that drive an inflation over the long run.
3. A one-time change in aggregate demand and a one-time-only aggregate supply shock both change the rate of inflation in the short run, but they cannot sustain an inflation by themselves over the long run. Prices stop changing, and the inflation ends, when the economy returns to its long-run equilibrium on the production possibilities frontier.

4. The short-run Phillips curve indicates how the state of the economy affects the rate of inflation in the short run. Inflation tends to be lower the farther the economy is beneath its frontier, and vice versa. The effect of the state of the economy on inflation essentially washes out over the long run, however.

5. The expectation of inflation drives an inflationary process through the supply side of the economy because it increases firms' costs of production. Expected inflation feeds point for point into actual wage increases and into nominal interest rates, which affect firms' cost of capital. The increase in production costs acts as a continual adverse aggregate supply shock that shifts up the short-run aggregate supply curve, AS_{SR}, continually over time.

6. Economists assume that people have rational expectations. They are forward-looking in forming their expectations about the future course of inflation, or anything else, and take into consideration all information available to them, including the government's announced intentions for fiscal and monetary policies. The main implication of rational expectations is that people's guesses about the future course of inflation are correct, on average. They do not systematically over- or underestimate future inflation.

7. The growth in nominal aggregate demand is the other engine that drives inflation in the long run. Firms can sell their output after raising their prices because of inflation only if the demand for their products is continually growing.

8. The government ultimately controls the growth in nominal aggregate demand through its fiscal and monetary policies. The equation of exchange indicates that the key to preventing large increases in prices is to control the growth of the money supply. In that sense inflation is a monetary phenomenon.

9. Governments can easily stop the growth of the money supply in order to stop an inflation, but they may not have the will to do so. Stopping inflation entails short-run costs: Some firms go bankrupt, and workers lose their jobs. Also, governments nearly always run deficits during high inflations, so they would have to cut spending and/or raise taxes to meet the higher real interest payments on their debt. Governments sometimes choose to avoid the short-run costs and continue printing money to keep the inflation going. This runs the risk of turning a high inflation into a runaway hyperinflation.

10. There is no long-run trade-off between inflation and unemployment. The long-run Phillips Curve is vertical at the natural rate of unemployment, U_{NR}, which corresponds to the production possibilities frontier. The economy always returns to the frontier when expected inflation adjusts to the actual inflation. Each short-run Phillips Curve assumes a given expected inflation, so the short-run Phillips Curves keep shifting over time as expected inflation adjusts to actual inflation.

11. The economy can be in long-run equilibrium with any rate of inflation; all the long-run equilibrium requires is that actual inflation equal expected inflation. The only sensible long-run target for unemployment is the natural rate of unemployment. An attempt by the government to keep unemployment permanently below U_{NR} leads to an accelerating inflation. An attempt by the government to keep unemployment permanently above U_{NR} leads to an accelerating deflation.

12. The only way the government can squeeze inflation out of an economy is to engineer a recession with unemployment greater than U_{NR}, wait until expected inflation falls to zero, and then return the economy to the frontier. The costs of doing this appear to be quite high in the United States.

The second section of the chapter considered whether the government has any good short-run policy response to an adverse aggregate supply shock.

13. The Reagan administration cut the federal personal income tax rates by 23 percent across the board in 1981 in an attempt to stimulate the economy through the supply side. The goal was to combat the high inflation and the high unemployment that followed the 1979 OPEC-induced increase in oil prices. The supply-side theory was that a tax cut would increase the supply of labor and saving, which would lower costs of production and increase aggregate supply. The evidence following the tax cut suggested that it had little or no effect on either labor supply or saving. Instead, the short-run effect was to increase demand, in line with the Keynesian analysis of an income tax cut. Economists are still looking for an effective short-run response to an adverse aggregate supply shock.

14. Tax policy can have an enormous impact on saving, investment, and economic growth over the long run, however. Simple long-run models of the economy suggest that replacing the personal and the corporation income taxes with a consumption tax would promote saving, investment, and productivity and would raise the U.S. national product by as much as 20 percent. Reducing the federal budget deficit in order to reduce interest rates appears to have similar long-run benefits.

The final section of the chapter discussed the emerging consensus among all economists that the government should avoid surprises and pursue consistent and credible policies.

15. A consistent and credible government policy stance reduces uncertainty in the economy, which has a number of advantages. It reduces the search component of unemployment, promotes investment, and sharply reduces the short-run costs of squeezing inflation out of the economy.

KEY TERMS

long-run Phillips Curve   rational expectations

QUESTIONS

1. What are the principal factors that determine the rate of inflation? Which of these factors are more likely to drive the rate of inflation over the long run?
2. a. What does it mean to say that people have rational expectations? In particular, does having rational expectations mean that people always guess right about the future?
   b. Discuss some of the problems that expectations cause the government as it tries to formulate its fiscal and monetary policies.
3. a. Draw the short-run Phillips Curve and the long-run Phillips Curve. Indicate why you drew the curves as you did. Be sure to label the axes on your graph.
   b. Suppose that the government uses monetary and fiscal policies to decrease sharply the level of aggregate demand and thereby increase unemployment well above the natural rate of unemployment. Show how you would represent the short-run effect of that policy change on your graph.

c. Suppose that the government continues to keep the unemployment rate at that high level for 10 years in a row. Show what effect this long-run policy stance would have on each Phillips Curve that you drew in part (a), and explain your answer.

4. Indicate whether the following items will improve or worsen the short-run Phillips Curve (shift it down or up) or not affect the short-run Phillips Curve at all.

   a. Expected inflation rises from 5 percent to 10 percent per year.

   b. The growth in labor productivity increases from 2 percent to 4 percent per year.

   c. More people enter the labor force in search of part-time employment.

5. Describe some of the channels through which a change in the expected rate of inflation can affect the actual rate of inflation.

6. Consider an economy in long-run equilibrium at a natural rate of unemployment of 4 percent. Suppose that expected inflation is 3 percent. Using Phillips Curve analysis, show the effects of

   a. a rise in expected inflation to 5 percent.

   b. a rise in the natural rate of unemployment to 6 percent.

   c. both (a) and (b) together.

7. Suppose that Congress passes a 10 percent across-the-board increase in the personal income tax rates. Compare the effects of the tax increase on output and national saving, using Keynesian and supply-side tax theory.

8. Consider an economy with a constant velocity of circulation and sticky prices. The economy is currently in recession. If the central bank begins a policy of expanding the money supply by 4 percent per year, what can we say about the growth of output in the short run? In the long run? How does your answer change if the economy is at full employment initially?

9. What are the advantages of having the federal government follow a steady course with its fiscal and monetary policies, in which it announces its policy intentions and then maintains its policies as it said it would?

What Caused the Inflation of the 1970s?*

A side from times of war, the worst inflation experienced by the United States was in the 1970s. From 1970 to 1980 the consumer price index more than doubled. Retirees who had invested their savings in bonds or who had fixed pensions, and who had expected to live comfortably, had to scrape by instead.

Most people blame the 1970s inflation on OPEC, the oil cartel. Following the oil embargo of 1973 that was triggered by the Yom Kippur war in October 1972, the price of oil quadrupled, roughly from $3 a barrel to $12. After the fall of the Shah of Iran in 1979, the price doubled again. Consumer prices rose at the same time. Inflation as measured by the CPI jumped from 3.4 percent in 1972 to 8.7 percent in 1973 and to 12.3 percent in 1974. Similarly, inflation jumped from 9.0 percent in 1978 to 13.3 percent in 1979 and to 12.5 percent in 1980.

Food prices also soared twice during the 1970s, and at the same times as the oil prices. Drought hit the corn crop in the United States and the wheat crop in the Soviet Union. In earlier decades silos bursting with surplus grain stored by the U.S. government dampened swings in food prices, but new agricultural policies aimed at conserving soil instead of storing grain had depleted the surpluses.

The conventional wisdom that the inflation of the 1970s arose from the oil and food markets is correct in one sense. The sharp increases in the prices of oil and food were extremely adverse aggregate supply shocks that shifted the aggregate supply curve to the left and caused brief periods of stagflation in which prices rose and real GDP fell.

There may have been a more fundamental cause of the two bursts of inflation, however. The money supply, as measured by M2 (approximately currency, checkable deposits, and time deposits under $100,000), rose rapidly in 1971–72 and again in 1975–77, periods preceding the bursts of inflation. Could it be that the rapid monetary growth was the more important cause of the inflation, but that it operated with long delays?

A useful equation for thinking about this question is the equation of exchange, which can be written $P = MV/Q$. P is the price level, M is the quantity of money, V is the velocity of circulation, and Q is output. Suppose that V and Q are constant. Then a ten percent increase in M raises prices by 10 percent.

*Provided by David Denslow, University of Florida.

But V and Q are not constant. When an expansionary monetary policy by the Fed induces the commercial banks to create money, the velocity of circulation typically drops immediately following the increase in the money supply. Then after six months or so velocity snaps back and output starts to rise. Prices may rise significantly over a year or more later. The causes of these delays, or lags, are poorly understood.

Consequently, rapid growth of the money supply, not the oil cartel or the crop failures, may have been the true cause of the inflation of the 1970s. Why, then, did oil and food prices rise so much more than most other prices? OPEC and the crop failures are certainly part of the answer. Also important, though, are the elasticities of demand and supply for oil and food, both of which are very low. Given the low elasticities, an increase in the money supply that boosted overall economic activity and raised the demands for oil and food would promote large increases in oil and food prices. The price effect is amplified if there are cutbacks in supply at the same time, as there were in oil and food.

Therefore, an alternative explanation of the inflation of the 1970s is that the Fed caused it. By increasing the money supply too rapidly, the Fed increased aggregate demand and, later, prices. Oil and food prices rose especially rapidly because of the interaction of rising demand, OPEC, crop failures, and low elasticities. Indeed without the demand boost caused by the rapid monetary growth of 1971–72, OPEC might not have become an effective cartel.

There is a potential flaw in the alternative explanation, however. It does not explain how an increase in the U.S. money supply caused *global* oil and food prices to shoot up. The 1970s was a decade of inflation in most industrial economies, not just here. How can U.S. monetary policy be blamed for that?

A plausible answer is that speculators knew that prices in the United States would go up sooner or later after the increase in the U.S. money supply. They also knew that the rise in U.S. prices would depreciate the value of the dollar in the foreign exchange markets. For example, the dollar price of a pound sterling might rise from $1.60/£ to $1.80/£. Therefore, the speculators sold dollars with the idea of buying the dollars back later on when they were cheaper. The sale of dollars by speculators drove the value of the dollar down against foreign currencies even before U.S. prices rose.

The falling dollar hurt European export industries. With U.S. prices (relative to European prices) rising less rapidly

What Caused the Inflation of the 1970s? (cont.)

than the dollar was falling in 1972 and again in 1977–78, European exporters found it hard to compete with American producers. The Europeans central banks were forced to buy dollars to try to break the free fall of the dollar. The purchases of dollars with their own currencies expanded their money supplies. In this way an inflation that began in the United States spread across the Atlantic.

Another potential flaw in the monetary explanation of the inflation of the 1970s is that the rule that inflation follows rapid growth of M2 broke down in the 1980s. But this can be explained by the passage of the Depository Institutions Deregulation and Monetary Control Act of 1980 (DIDMCA), which deregulated the banking and thrift industries and increased the demand for interest-bearing NOW accounts. Another factor breaking the previously tighter link between the growth of M2 and inflation were a number of technological changes in handling financial transactions that spread through financial markets world-wide.

ECONOMIC ADVISOR'S REPORT

Suppose that the Fed's Board of Governors hires you to advise them on the problem of keeping inflation under control following an adverse supply shock to the economy such as the oil and food price increases of the 1970s. They ask you the following questions. How would you respond?

1. Is an adverse supply shock likely to cause a difficult policy problem for the Fed?
2. Can an adverse supply shock sustain in inflationary process by itself?
3. Should the Fed increase the growth of the money supply following an adverse supply shock, or reduce the growth of the money supply to zero, or follow a policy course somewhere between the two?
4. Do the nations of Western Europe care about how the Fed responds to an adverse supply shock?

SOURCE: Council of Economic Advisers, *Economic Report of the President 1993* (Washington, D.C.: U.S. Government Printing Office, 1993) Table B-59, pp. 415.

VI

International Economic Issues

20

International Trade
and
Barriers to Trade

LEARNING OBJECTIVES

CONCEPTS TO LEARN

The three principal models for explaining the pattern of international trade:	The economic effects of tariffs, quotas, and other trade restrictions
1. Ricardo's comparative advantage model	The North American Free Trade Agreement (NAFTA)
2. The factor endowments model	
3. The product differentiation/economies of scale model	The European Community
	GATT (General Agreement on Tariffs and Trade)

CONCEPTS TO LEARN

Opportunity cost [1]	The principle of comparative advantage [4]
The production possibilities frontier [3]	The Laws of Supply and Demand [5]

*T*ake a moment to look at Table 20.1. The table records the imports and the exports for the United States during 1992, by commodity and by the country of origin (for imports) and the country of destination (for exports).

The power of international trade fairly leaps from the table. It shows that U.S. citizens and businesses exchange commodities of every description with foreign citizens and businesses, and in both directions: agricultural produce, natural resources such as oil, a broad range of consumer goods and services, and both capital goods and semi-finished products that firms sell to other firms to be used as inputs in production. In addition, the United States trades with nations that are at every stage of economic and social development: the industrialized market economies, the oil-rich Organization of Petroleum Exporting Countries (OPEC), the Eastern European economies in transition, and the middle- and low-income developing nations of Central and South America, Asia, and Africa.

These international exchanges of imports and exports are voluntary exchanges between private citizens and businesses for the most part. As such, they must be mutually beneficial to buyers and sellers in the United States and elsewhere, or they would not occur. Table 20.1 reveals that the gains from international trade are very broad indeed. They are not limited to a narrow set of commodities or available to just a few countries.

Citizens and businesses in the United States have clearly recognized that international exchanges can help them solve their economic problems. Imports and exports are each about 11 percent of the gross domestic product (GDP) of the United States. Yet this is the lowest percentage of all the industrialized market economies, and a far lower percentage than for most of the world's middle- and low-income nations. Citizens of all nations understand that international trade can improve their economic well-being.

International exchanges help people solve their economic problems in the same way that domestic exchanges do. They exploit the division of labor and economies of scale that allow people to specialize in production while remaining generalists in consumption. The only difference is that the specialization occurs on a global scale.

Imports are the ends of international trade, the motivation behind specializing and trading. Nations import to gain access to goods and services that they cannot produce at all or that other nations produce better than they can, either more cheaply or with more desirable qualities. Exports are the means to these ends. Nations have to export to be able to import because foreign citizens insist on receiving real goods and services in exchange for the real goods and services they are sending abroad.

International exchanges are somewhat more limited than are domestic exchanges. The transactions costs of international exchanges tend to be higher because goods typically have to travel longer distances and pass through one or more border crossings. International transactors also have to bear the effort and the expense of exchanging their own currencies for foreign currencies in the foreign exchange markets. Political considerations may limit international exchanges as well. For example, government agencies are often required to purchase the majority of their capital and material inputs from domestic suppliers. These limitations notwithstanding, international trade has contributed greatly to improving standards of living throughout the world.

Chapters 20 through 22 conclude the text with a discussion of the global economy. Chapter 20 begins by developing the fundamental principles relating to the pattern of international trade. We want to understand why nations import or export certain goods; what the gains from international trade are; and why, despite the gains from trade, all nations choose to restrict international trade with such devices as tariffs and quotas. Chapter 21 then turns to the financial side of international trade, taking a close look at the flow of funds through the foreign exchange markets. Chapter 22 closes by analyzing the special economic problems of the low-income developing nations as they try to push out their production possibilities frontiers and improve their standards of living.

THE PATTERN OF INTERNATIONAL TRADE

The central question concerning international trade is why it is as broad as it is. People in the United States worry that U.S. industries will not be able to compete against the much lower wages of the low-income developing countries of Southeast Asia and Central and South America. At the same time people in the developing countries worry that their industries will not be able to compete against the superior technologies of the high-income industrialized nations. Yet neither low wages nor superior technologies have been a barrier to trade. To the contrary, international trade flourishes between the developing nations and the industrialized nations, to the benefit of each. Why is this? Another fact to be explained is the considerable amount of two-way trade in highly similar products. We see in Table 20.1 that two-thirds of U.S. trade is with the other industrialized nations. The majority of this trade involves the simultaneous import and export of semi-finished products and capital goods among firms— electrical equipment, machinery, computers, and the like. Another large component of this trade is in very similar consumer goods, such as beer, wine, and automobiles, which are also simultaneously imported and exported. Why do nations trade for minor variations of products that they can produce themselves?

Economists have developed three basic models to explain the variety of trade that we observe. The first is David Ricardo's theory of comparative advantage, which we met in Chapter 4. Ricardo's theory is based on differences in technologies and is useful for explaining interindustry trade between nations in different stages of economic development.

The second model stresses differences in factor endowments rather than differences in technologies as the basis for international trade. Some countries are blessed with large amounts of fertile land and natural resources and have a highly educated and skilled labor force. Other nations are resource-poor and have mostly an uneducated and low-skilled labor force. These differences in factor endowments can generate gains from trade. This model is particularly useful for seeing the distributional implications of trade. Some people gain, and other people lose from trade, even though the nation as a whole benefits. The losers from trade are the ones who fight for trade restrictions such as tariffs and quotas.

The third, and most recent, model focuses on international trade generated by the rivalry between large corporations that are competing for markets both domestically and internationally. These multinational corporations compete by

TABLE 20.1   U.S. Merchandise Exports and Imports, 1992 ($ billion)

	VALUE	PERCENTAGE OF TOTAL[a]	TOTAL
I. BY COMMODITY			
Exports			$448.1
Foods, feeds, beverages	$ 40.2	9.0	
Industrial supplies, materials	109.1	24.3	
Capital goods	176.7	39.4	
Autos and auto parts	46.7	10.4	
Other consumer goods	50.4	11.2	
Other	25.0	5.6	
Imports			$532.4
Foods, feeds, beverages	27.9	5.2	
Industrial supplies, materials	138.0	25.9	
Capital goods	134.4	25.2	
Autos and auto parts	91.5	17.2	
Other consumer goods	70.0	13.1	
Petroleum and petroleum related products	53.0	10.0	
Other	17.6	3.3	

[a]Percentages may not total 100 percent because of rounding error.

SOURCE: Council of Economic Advisers *Economic Report of the President 1993* (Washington, D.C.: U.S. Government Printing Office, 1993), 465, Table B-102. Council of Economic Advisers, *Economic Indicators*. (Washington D.C.: Government Printing Office, March 1993), 35.

trying to develop new products through research and development. A firm that successfully markets a new product gains a cost advantage over its rivals because of the economies of scale associated with developing and producing a narrowly defined product. This is the basic model used to explain the trade in similar products among the industrialized nations. It has also been used as a justification for trade restrictions to protect domestic industries while they are researching and developing new products.

Let's now take a closer look at each theory, beginning with Ricardo's theory of comparative advantage.

The Theory of Comparative Advantage

David Ricardo's fundamental insight about international trade was that both the pattern of trade and the gains from trade depend on differences in the opportunity costs of producing goods and services. Ricardo attributed the differences in opportunity costs to differences in the technologies used to produce the goods and the services. The newer models offer other reasons why opportunity costs of production might differ across countries, but differences in opportunity costs are still the basis for specialization and trade in these models.

The simple model that we developed in Chapter 4 to explain Ricardo's theory is useful for explaining many of the fundamental principles of international trade. Recall that we had two countries, the United States and England, each producing two goods, food (F) and clothing (C), before they trade. Labor is the only factor of production, and each country has 100 units of labor.

TABLE 20.1   U.S. Merchandise Exports and Imports, 1992 ($ billion) (cont.)

	VALUE	PERCENTAGE OF TOTAL[a]	TOTAL
II. BY COUNTRY[b]			
Exports			
Industrial countries			$263.8
Canada			
Japan	90.4	34.2	
Western Europe	47.2	17.9	
Australia	114.4	43.4	
New Zealand, South Africa	8.3	3.1	
	3.5	1.3	
Other countries			171.2
OPEC	20.7	12.1	
Eastern Europe	5.3	3.1	
Other countries[c]	145.2	84.8	
Imports			
Industrial countries			$309.1
Canada	100.2	32.4	
Japan	94.0	30.4	
Western Europe	108.1	35.0	
Australia	3.7	1.2	
New Zealand, South Africa	3.1	1.0	
Other countries			217.1
OPEC	32.5	15.0	
Eastern Europe	2.0	0.9	
Other countries	182.6	84.1	
Trade Balance (Exports − Imports)			
Industrial countries			(−)$45.2
Canada	(−) 9.8		
Japan	(−)46.8		
Western Europe	6.3		
Australia	4.6		
New Zealand, South AFrica	0.4		
Other countries			(−)45.9
OPEC	(−)11.8		
Eastern Europe	3.3		
Other countries	(−)37.4		

[b]Data by country are preliminary data for the first three quarters of 1992, annual rate.
[c]Includes Latin America, other Western Hemisphere countries, and other countries in Asia and Africa.

The United States is the more productive economy. A unit of labor in the United States produces 4 units of food and 3 units of clothing. A unit of labor in England produces 2 units of food and 2 units of clothing. Table 20.2 summarizes the production technologies in each country.

The black lines in Figure 20.1 show the production possibilities frontiers within each country, Figure 20.1(a) for the United States and Figure 20.1(b) for England.

The United States can produce 400 units of food if it puts all its labor into food production, 300 units of clothing if it puts all its labor into clothing production, and the other combinations of food and clothing along the black line frontier. The example in Chapter 4 assumed that, before trade, the United

TABLE 20.2   Production Technologies for Food and Clothing: Output per Unit of Labor

	FOOD	CLOTHING
United States	4F	3C
England	2F	2C

States allocates 55 units of labor to food production and 45 units of labor to clothing production, producing 220F and 135C at point A in Figure 20.1(a) $(220 = 4 \cdot 55; 135 = 3 \cdot 45)$.

England can produce 200 units of food if it puts all its labor into food production, 200 units of clothing if it puts all its labor into clothing production, and the other combinations of food and clothing along the black line frontier. The example in Chapter 4 assumed that, before trade, England allocates 72 units of labor to food production and 28 units of labor to clothing production, producing 144F and 56C at point A' in Figure 39.1(b) $(144 = 2 \cdot 72; 56 = 2 \cdot 28)$.

Both countries can gain from international trade because the opportunity cost of producing food is lower in the United States and the opportunity cost of producing clothing is lower in England. To produce 1 more unit of food, England must sacrifice 1 unit of clothing; to produce 1 more unit of food, the United States must sacrifice only ¾ of a unit of clothing. The United States has the comparative advantage in producing food; that is, it has the lower opportunity cost. Conversely, to produce 1 more unit of clothing, the United States must sacrifice ⁴/₃ units of food; to produce 1 more unit of clothing, England must sacrifice only 1 unit of food. England has the comparative advantage in producing clothing; that is, it has the lower opportunity cost.

Another useful way to state the comparative advantage of each country is in terms of the relative prices of food and clothing. The relative prices must reflect the opportunity costs of production along the production possibilities frontier. Therefore, the ratio of the price of food to the price of clothing in the United States is ¾, the inverse of the food-for-clothing trade-off along the frontier ($P_F/P_C = ¾ = .75$). The ratio of the price of food to the price of clothing in England is 1 ($P_F/P_C = 1$). Food is relatively cheaper in the United States, and clothing is relatively cheaper in England, reflecting their comparative advantages.

As we saw in Chapter 4, Ricardo's theory of comparative advantage says that both countries can gain if they specialize in the good for which they have a **comparative advantage** and trade at any ratio of food to clothing between 4F/3C and 1F/1C, the trading ratios along each country's production possibilities frontiers. The United States exports food and imports clothing, and England exports clothing and imports food. In terms of the price ratios, producers in the United States are willing to export food at any relative price greater than .75 ($P_F/P_C > .75$), and producers in England are willing to export clothing at any relative price less than 1 ($P_F/P_C < 1$; that is, so long as clothing is more expensive than food).

We assumed that the two countries specialize their production and trade at the rate of 5F for 4C. Equivalently, they trade at a relative price of .8, the inverse of the 5F for 4C trading ratio ($P_F/P_C = 4/5 = .8$).

COMPARATIVE ADVANTAGE

The principle that a country should specialize its production in those goods that it can produce with lower opportunity costs than other countries and trade for those goods that other countries can produce with lower opportunity costs.

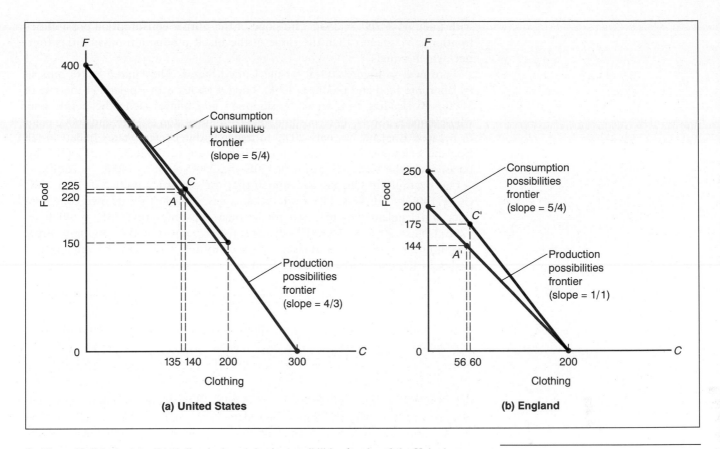

FIGURE 20.1

Comparative Advantage and the Gains From International Trade

In Figure 20.1(a), the inner black line is the production possibilities frontier of the United States, along which it can exchange food (F) for clothing (C) at the rate of $4F$ for $3C$. The U.S. produces and consumes at point A ($220F$, $135C$) without trade. By specializing its production in food, in which it has a comparative advantage, and trading with England for clothing, the U.S. can exchange food for clothing at the better rate of $5F$ for $4C$. Specialization and trade places the U.S. on the outer purple consumption possibilities frontier. At point C ($225F$, $140C$), the United States consumes both more food and more clothing than at point A without trade. In Figure 20.1(b), the inner black line is the production possibilities frontier of England, along which it can exchange food (F) for clothing (C) at the rate of $1F$ for $1C$. England produces and consumes at point A' ($144F$, $56C$) without trade. By specializing its production in clothing, in which it has a comparative advantage, and trading with the United States for food, England can exchange clothing for food at the better rate of $5F$ for $4C$. Specialization and trade places England on the outer purple consumption possibilities frontier. At point C' ($175F$, $60C$), England consumes both more food and more clothing than at point A' without trade. Both countries gain by specializing their production in the good in which they have a comparative advantage and trading for the other good.

CONSUMPTION VERSUS PRODUCTION POSSIBILITIES   Specialization and trade at 5F for 4C increases the consumption possibilities of both countries beyond their production possibilities frontiers, as illustrated by the purple lines in Figure 20.1. Refer, first, to Figure 20.1(b) for England. England puts all its labor into clothing and produces 200C. Then it trades with the United States at the rate of 4C for 5F, leading to a set of consumption possibilities along the purple line. For instance, if it traded all its clothing for food, it would be able to consume 250F, the other end-point of its consumption possibilities frontier with trade [($\frac{5}{4} \cdot 200 = 250$]. The slope of the purple consumption possibilities frontier is $\frac{5}{4}$, greater than the slope of the black production possibilities frontier, which equals 1.

Turn next to Figure 20.1(a) for the United States. The United States puts all its labor into food and produces 400F. Then it trades with England at the rate of 5F for 4C, leading to a set of consumption possibilities along the purple line, whose slope is also $\frac{5}{4}$. The consumption possibilities stop at 150F and 200C, point C, because England has only 200C to trade. If the United States traded for all England's clothing, it would give up 250F in return (250F/200C = 5F/4C). This trade leaves the United States with 150F and 200C (150F = 400F − 250F).

Our example in Chapter 4 assumed that the countries trade 175F for 140C (175F/140C = 5F/4C). The United States has 225F left for its own consumption, and England has 60C left for its own consumption (225F = 400F − 175F; 60C = 200C − 140C). They consume at points C and C' on their purple consumption possibilities frontiers. Both countries gain from specializing and trading; each one consumes more food *and* more clothing.

	WITH TRADE	WITHOUT TRADE
United States	225F, 140C	220F, 135C
	(point C)	(point A)
England	175F, 60C	144 F, 56C
	(point C')	(point A')

PRODUCTIVITY VERSUS OPPORTUNITY COSTS   The theory of comparative advantage explains why the low-income developing nations do not have to fear the superior technologies of the high-income countries. In our example the United States is more productive in producing *both* goods, yet England can gain from trading with the United States. Differences in opportunity costs, not differences in productivity, determine the pattern and gains from trade.

To underscore this point, suppose that labor in the United States were twice as productive in producing both goods, so that 1 unit of labor produced 4 units of food and 4 units of clothing. The opportunity costs of producing food and clothing are now the same in each country. One more unit of either good entails a sacrifice of one unit of the other good in both the United States and England. Neither country can gain from trade because they would only be willing to trade at the ratio 1F for 1C, which is the same ratio that they can trade in their own countries.

Another way to see why trade is not helpful is to think in terms of the relative prices. The relative price of food to clothing would equal 1 in both countries before trade ($P_F/P_C = 1$). The United States is willing to specialize in and export food only if the relative price of food rises, or $P_F/P_C > 1$. England is willing to specialize in and export clothing only if the relative price of clothing rises, or $P_F/P_C < 1$. There is no room to maneuver. The relative price of food to clothing must remain equal to 1, and each country can do as well by producing on its own as it can by specializing and trading.

The inability to gain from trade in this case has nothing to do with superior U.S. productivity. The same would be true if the United States were equally as productive as England in producing both goods, or half as productive in both. The problem is that the opportunity costs of production are the same in both countries; no country has a *comparative advantage* in either good.

Fortunately, the equally productive case is not realistic. All nations are certain to have a comparative advantage in producing some goods no matter how unproductive they may be in an absolute sense. In other words, all nations can gain from specializing their production and trading.

THE GAINS FROM TRADE AND THE TERMS-OF-TRADE   The *pattern* of trade in Ricardo's model depends only on the opportunity costs of production. Each country exports the good that it can produce relatively more cheaply. The *gains* from trade for each country depend on the **terms-of-trade,** the rate at which food and clothing are exchanged. The terms-of-trade in our example is 5F for 4C.[1]

Both countries gain from trade if the terms-of-trade is between the trading ratios available in each country without trade. This is the case in our example. The terms-of-trade, 5F for 4C, is between the trading ratio of 4F for 3C along the U.S. production possibilities frontier and the trading ratio of 1F for 1C along the British production possibilities frontier. Conversely, only one country gains if the terms-of-trade is at one of the country's trading ratios. For example, only England can gain if the terms-of-trade is 4F for 3C. England can only get 3F for 3C on its own. Trading 4F for 3C makes it better off. In contrast, the United States can get 3C for 4F whether it trades for the clothing or produces the clothing itself. It does not gain from trade. International trade cannot occur outside the boundaries of the within-country trading ratios.

The actual terms-of-trade depends on the relative demands for the two products. The greater the demand for food is, the higher the relative price of food (P_F/P_C) is, the more clothing trades for each unit of food, and the more the United States gains from trade. Conversely, the greater the demand for clothing is, the lower the relative price (P_F/P_C) is, the more food trades for each unit of clothing, and the more England gains from trade.

Returning to our example, suppose that the United States wants 120C and England wants 110C. The British are willing to trade only 90C for food, so that the United States is forced to produce some of its own clothing. This means that the terms-of-trade has to be at 4F for 3C, the U.S. ratio without trade, and $P_F/P_C = .75$. The U.S. clothing producers would switch to producing food at any higher price ratio. As a result, England receives all the gains from trade.

England specializes, produces 200C, and exports 90C to the United States in exchange for 120F (120F/90C = 4F/3C). It could only have 90F without trade if it produced both food and clothing and consumed 110C.

	WITH TRADE	WITHOUT TRADE
England	120F, 110C	90F, 110C

The United States does not specialize and cannot gain from trade. The United States wants 120C, yet receives only 90C in trade from England. Therefore, it uses 10 of its labor units to produce an extra 30C [30 = 3 · 10; 120C = 90C (from England) + 30C (own production)]. This leaves 90 units of labor

TERMS-OF-TRADE

The rate of exchange between imported goods and exported goods; alternatively, the ratio of a nation's export prices to its import prices.

---

[1]The terms-of-trade for a nation is usually defined as the ratio of the nation's export prices to its import prices. In our example, the terms-of-trade from the U.S. point of view is $P_F/P_C = .8$, and the terms-of-trade from the British point of view is $P_C/P_F = 1.25 = (5/4)$.

to produce 360F ($360 = 4 \cdot 90$). Having exported 120F to England, the United States is left with 240F ($240F = 360F - 120F$). But the United States can produce 240F and 120C on its own by allocating 60 labor units to food production and 40 labor units to clothing production ($240 = 4 \cdot 60$; $120 = 3 \cdot 40$). The United States does not gain from trade.

	WITH TRADE	WITHOUT TRADE
United States	240F, 120C	240F, 120C

To summarize, our example illustrates two fundamental principles about the gains from international trade. The first is that *the gains from international trade arise because trade changes a nation's terms-of-trade between goods and services.* The second is that *the gains from international trade are greater the better a nation's terms-of-trade is.*

COMPARATIVE ADVANTAGE AND EXCHANGE RATES   International transactions require exchanges of one nation's currency for another nation's currency. The exchanges of currency take place in the **foreign exchange markets,** in which the exchange rates between all nations' currencies are established.

The real and the financial sides of international trade are closely linked. Differences in opportunity cost, comparative advantage, determine not only the pattern of international trade, but also the range of values that an exchange rate between two currencies can have. Our simple example can also illustrate this fundamental principle of international exchange. To do so, however, we have to add actual prices to the example.

Suppose that the wage rate in England is 2£ per unit of labor. Since labor is the only factor of production, the prices of food and clothing in England must equal the labor cost of producing them. (We are assuming competitive markets.) In England, 1 unit of labor can produce either 2F or 2C. Therefore, 1 unit of food or clothing requires ½ unit of labor, or a labor cost of 1£. The prices of food and clothing must each be 1£ ($P_F = 1$£; $P_C = 1$£). Notice that $P_F/P_C = 1£/1£ = 1$, as above.

Suppose that the wage rate in the United States is \$12 per unit of labor. In the United States, 1 unit of labor can produce 4F. Therefore, 1 unit of food requires ¼ unit of labor, or a labor cost of \$3. $P_F = \$3$. Similarly, 1 unit of labor can produce 3C. Therefore, 1 unit of clothing requires ⅓ unit of labor, or a labor cost of \$4. $P_C = \$4$. Notice that $P_F/P_C = \$3/\$4 = .75$, as above.

The pound and the dollar prices of food and clothing in England and the United States determine the range of values for the dollar-pound exchange rate. In particular, the exchange rate must be equal to or between the ratios of the price of food in both countries and the price of clothing in both countries.

$$P_F^{US}/P_F^{Eng} \leq \$/£ \leq P_C^{US}/P_C^{Eng}$$

$$\$3/1£ \leq \$/£ \leq \$4/£$$

To see why this must be, consider the maximum possible value of the dollar in our example, \$3/1£. England is just indifferent to trade at this exchange rate, and the United States receives all the gains from trade. English citizens can buy 1 unit of food in England for 1£, or they can exchange the pound for \$3 and buy food in the United States. But \$3 only buys 1 unit of food in the

United States as well. The English neither gain nor lose by importing food from the United States, rather than producing it themselves.

Citizens in the United States are eager to import clothing from England at this exchange rate, however. Clothing costs $4 per unit in the United States. Its citizens can do better by exchanging $3 for 1£ and buying 1 unit of clothing from the British for 1£. Importing clothing from England saves $1 per unit of clothing. The British are willing to exchange clothing for food when the exchange rate is $3/1£, but the United States captures all the gains from trade.

Suppose that the dollar happened to appreciate in value to $2/1£ for some reason. The dollar is said to be **overvalued** at this rate because everyone will prefer to buy food and clothing in England. British citizens can buy either 1 unit of food or 1 unit of clothing in England for 1£. If they exchange 1£ for $2, they will not have enough dollars to buy either 1 unit of food or 1 unit of clothing in the United States. Citizens of the United States will also prefer to buy in England. A unit of food costs them $3, and a unit of clothing costs them $4 in the United States. They can do better by exchanging $2 for 1£ and buying either 1 unit of food or 1 unit of clothing for 1£ in England. An overvalued dollar prices U.S. producers out of all markets in which goods are traded.

Similarly, the dollar cannot fall lower than $4/1£. Suppose that the dollar happened to depreciate in value to $5/1£. The dollar is said to be **undervalued.** Now everyone wants to buy in the United States. Citizens in the United States will not exchange $5 for 1£ to buy food or clothing in England because food costs only $3 and clothing only $4 in the United States. Conversely, British citizens are eager to exchange pounds for dollars at this rate. Why pay 1£ for food or clothing in England when they can exchange 1£ for $5 and buy more than 1 unit of food or clothing in the United States? In this case the pound is the overvalued currency, and it prices British producers out of the market.

We assumed in our original example above that the United States and England exchange at the rate of 5F for 4C and trade 175F from the United States for 140C from England. This requires an exchange rate of $3.75/1£ at the wage rate and prices given above. To see why an exchange rate of $3.75/1£ is a trading ratio of 5F for 4C, note that $3.75 for 1£ is the same as $15 for 4£ ($15 = $3.75 · 4). In the United States $15 buys 5 units of food at a price of $3 per unit; in England 4£ buys 4 units of clothing at a price of 1£ per unit. Therefore, an exchange rate of $3.75/1£ allows U.S. and English citizens to trade 5F for 4C.

Both nations gain from trade at this exchange rate. Citizens in the United States used to pay $3 for food and $4 for clothing. They still pay $3 for food, but they can now buy clothing in England for $3.75, by exchanging $3.75 for 1£ and buying the clothing for 1£. Similarly, British citizens used to pay 1£ each for a unit of food and/or clothing. They still pay 1£ for clothing, but they can now buy more than 1 unit of food in the United States for 1£, by exchanging 1£ for $3.75 and buying the food for $3 per unit.

THE VALUE OF IMPORTS EQUALS THE VALUE OF EXPORTS   Note, finally, that the values of imports and exports are equal in our example. Let's compute the values in terms of dollars. We assumed that 175F exchanged for 140C. The price of food is $3 in the United States. Therefore, the dollar value of the food exports is $525 ($525 = $3 · 175). The clothing costs 140£ in England. The

OVERVALUED CURRENCY

The value of a nation's currency relative to other currencies is greater than its equilibrium value determined by the Laws of Supply and Demand in the foreign exchange markets.

UNDERVALUED CURRENCY

The value of a nation's currency relative to other currencies is less than its equilibrium value determined by the Laws of Supply and Demand in the foreign exchange markets.

dollar value of the clothing imports at an exchange rate of $3.75/£ is also $525 ($525 = $3.75 · 140).

The principle that the value of a nation's imports must equal the value of a nation's exports is another fundamental principle of international trade. The values may not be equal in any one year as they are in our simple example. In fact, the dollar value of U.S. exports generally exceeded the dollar value of its imports by a wide margin in the 1950s and 1960s, and the reverse has been true since the early 1980s. Nonetheless, the value of imports and exports must eventually balance out over time. An excess of imports must eventually be followed by an excess of exports, and an excess of exports must eventually be followed by an excess of imports.

The reason for this is simply that nations will not export resource-using goods and services to other nations without receiving goods and services in return. For example, when the dollar value of U.S. imports exceeds the dollar value of U.S. exports, as it does now, someone is sending the United States real goods and services in exchange for dollars (or U.S. financial securities). Eventually they will want to turn these dollars into real goods and services, and when they do, the dollar value of U.S. exports must rise. We will look more closely at the financial side of international trade in Chapter 21. As we do, though, keep in mind the fundamental principle that the value of a nation's imports must eventually equal the value of its exports.

CHEAP LABOR AND INTERNATIONAL TRADE   Our simple example illustrated that the low-income developing nations need not fear the superior technologies and productivity of the high-income industrial nations. Lower productivity is not a barrier to specialization and trade. The opposite side of this principle is that the industrialized nations need not fear the lower wages of the developing nations. Higher wages are not a barrier to specialization and trade either. Our simple example illustrates this important principle as well.

The 2£ wage rate in England translates into a wage rate of $7.50 at the exchange rate of $3.75/1£ ($7.50 = 2£ · $3.75/£). Although $7.50 is well below the $12 wage rate in the United States, the difference in wage rates between the countries has no effect on the pattern of trade or the gains from trade. The low wages in England do not drive out the U.S. food producers. All that matters is that the dollar-pound exchange rate stay somewhere between the ratios of the food prices and clothing prices in the two countries. So long as it does, the United States exports foods, England exports clothing, and both countries can gain from trade.

The chief threat to a nation's standard of living is stagnating productivity growth, not competition from other low-wage or high-productivity nations. Remember that long-run economic growth is the most important determinant of a nation's standard of living. Whether wages are high or low, growing or stagnating, depends on a nation's ability to increase productivity and push its production possibilities frontier out over time.

Economic growth always causes disruptions to the economy in the short run. In the context of international trade, unbalanced productivity growth across industries can change the pattern of comparative advantage and force nations to reallocate their resources. In our example, a doubling of labor productivity from 3C to 6C in the U.S. clothing industry would give the United States the comparative advantage in clothing. The United States would have to switch

CURRENT ISSUE: Many U.S. citizens are concerned about the large U.S. trade deficit with Japan. There is no need for a nation's imports and exports to be equal with each of its trading partners, however. The equality of imports and exports applies to total imports and exports with all nations combined. The U.S.-Japanese trade deficit would not seem so troublesome if the United States had an equally large trade surplus with all other nations combined.

food. Consumers in the United States decrease their quantity demanded from Q_E^0 to Q_D^1 units of food. $(Q_S^1 - Q_D^1)$ is the amount of food exported to England.

We have not shown the clothing market, but the reverse is happening there. A falling price ratio, P_F/P_C, in England is a rising price ratio, P_C/P_F. English clothing producers respond by increasing the quantity supplied, and English consumers respond by decreasing the quantity demanded. England exports clothing. Conversely, a rising P_F/P_C in the United States is a falling P_C/P_F. U.S. clothing producers respond by decreasing the quantity supplied, and U.S. consumers respond by increasing the quantity demanded. The United States imports clothing. The United States also continues to produce clothing, so that specialization is incomplete in the United States as well.

The expanded model shares a number of features with the simple Ricardo model of comparative advantage:

1. The pattern of trade is determined by differences in opportunity costs. The original high-price, high-cost producer of food, England, imports food from the original low-price, low-cost producer of food, the United States.

2. Both countries gain from trade. The gains on a supply-demand graph can be seen as follows. The demand curve shows, at every quantity, the amount that consumers are willing to pay to consume the last unit. Therefore, consumers get a surplus in the market that can be represented as the area beneath the demand curve and above the price they have to pay, up to the quantity demanded. The supply curve shows, at every quantity, the marginal cost of producing the last unit. Therefore, producers get a surplus in the market that can be represented as the area above the supply curve and below the price they receive, up to the quantity supplied.

Refer to the market for food in England in Figure 20.2(a). Consumers gain and food producers lose as the price falls from $P_F/P_C = 1$ to $P_F/P_C = .8$. The consumer surplus increases by the shaded areas labeled 1 and 2. These areas reflect the gain of consuming more food and paying a lower price for it. At the same time, the producer surplus decreases by the area labeled 1. This area reflects the loss of producing less food and receiving a lower price for it. The net gain is the area labeled 2. There will always be a net gain for the importing country because the demand curve is to the right of the supply curve over the range of prices that lead to imports.

Now refer to the market for food in the United States in Figure 20.2(b). Consumers lose and food producers gain as the price rises from $P_F/P_C = .75$ to $P_F/P_C = .8$. The consumer surplus decreases by the shaded area 1. Consumers buy less food and pay a higher price for it. At the same time, the producer surplus increases by the areas 1 plus 2. Domestic firms produce more food and receive a higher price for it. The net gain is the area 2. There will always be a net gain for the exporting country because the supply curve is to the right of the demand curve over the range of prices that lead to exports.

3. Resources are reallocated from the clothing industry to the food industry in the United States and from the food industry to the clothing industry in England. The only difference is that specialization is incomplete in both countries.

4. Although we have not shown the clothing markets, the value of imports must equal the value of exports in both countries. The intuition behind this result is that the same price ratio, $P_F/P_C = .8$, applies in both markets in each country.

The model of rising marginal costs is much richer than is the simple Ricardo model, however. In particular, it allows us to explore the important distribu-

GAINS FROM TRADE

The amount that a nation gains through international trade relative to producing itself all the goods and the services that it consumes; alternatively, the increase in consumer surplus plus producer surplus resulting from international trade.

tional implications of international trade. Although both countries gain from trade, the gains are not shared equally by all. Some factors of production gain, while others lose. To see these distributional implications we have to understand why countries might have different marginal (opportunity) costs.

FACTOR ENDOWMENTS AND COMPARATIVE ADVANTAGE   Why are the costs of producing certain products lower in some countries than in others? The Ricardo model points to differences in technologies across countries. The factor endowments model points to differences in factor endowments across countries. The United States has amassed an enormous stock of sophisticated capital, is blessed with huge amounts of fertile land, and has a highly educated, highly skilled labor force for the most part. Relative to its total resources, the United States has a higher proportion of capital, land, and highly skilled labor than does almost any other country in the world. The larger the supply of a factor the lower its price, other things equal. Therefore, the United States has a cost advantage, and hence a comparative advantage, in products that use relatively large amounts of capital, land, and highly skilled labor. At the same time, most other countries have more unskilled labor relative to their other resources than does the United States. Therefore, the wages of unskilled labor tend to be lower in other countries, so that they have a cost advantage, and a comparative advantage, in products that use relatively large amounts of unskilled labor.

Furthermore, we saw in Figure 20.2 that international trade increases the producer surplus in the export industries (food in the figure). Some of this additional surplus is captured by the factors of production that are used relatively more in these industries. Therefore, international trade increases the returns to capital, land, and highly skilled labor in the United States. Conversely, international trade decreases producer surplus in the import-competing industries (clothing in the figure), and the factors that are used relatively more in these industries suffer some of the loss in the producer surplus. Therefore, international trade lowers the wages of unskilled workers in the United States. One can understand why U.S. labor unions tend to support trade restrictions.

What is true for the United States is true generally throughout the world. *The relatively abundant factors, those used more intensively in the export goods, gain from trade. The relatively scarce factors, those used more intensively in the goods that compete with the imported goods, lose from trade.*[2]

THE NORTH AMERICAN FREE TRADE AGREEMENT   The factor endowments model is the one that has been used to debate the merits of including Mexico in the North American Free Trade Agreement (NAFTA). NAFTA is an agreement to remove all trade barriers among Canada, the United States, and Mexico. After a long and bitter political debate, Congress voted in November 1993 to include Mexico in NAFTA.

FACTOR ENDOWMENTS MODEL OF INTERNATIONAL TRADE

A model developed to explain the pattern of international trade that is based on differences in factor endowments across countries; countries specialize their production in and export those goods that use factors of production that are relatively abundant, and they import those goods that use factors of production that are relatively scarce.

---

[2]The factor endowments model also shows that trade tends to equalize the returns to factors worldwide. This is because the returns to factors in other countries are changing in the opposite direction to that in the United States. In the other countries, international trade decreases the returns to capital, land, and highly skilled labor, and increases the wages of unskilled labor. Advanced textbooks demonstrate that international trade would equalize the returns to all factors everywhere if factor markets were competitive worldwide. International trade substitutes for factor mobility in this sense. Barriers to factor mobility such as immigration laws, other trade restrictions, and the use of different technologies worldwide prevent returns to factors from equalizing in the real world.

Critics who wanted to exclude Mexico from NAFTA fear that expanding trade with Mexico will lower the wages of unskilled workers in the United States. The average wage of manufacturing workers in Mexico is only ⅛ the average wage of manufacturing workers in the United States. With all trade barriers removed, firms in Mexico, the United States, and elsewhere that produce goods using relatively large amounts of unskilled labor have a strong incentive to produce in Mexico and export to the United States. Unskilled U.S. workers in the import-competing industries will find their wages falling as the increased production in Mexico raises wages there. This will further increase the earnings inequality between high-wage and low-wage employees in the United States, which has been rapidly increasing since the late 1970s.

The issue takes on added emotion because of Mexico's lax environmental laws. The Mexican government has virtually no standards regarding the use of underground storage tanks, or the disposal of hazardous wastes, or the cleanup of abandoned hazardous waste sites. So U.S. firms that migrate to Mexico can also avoid the costs of complying with the U.S. environmental laws.

The movement of U.S. firms to Mexico has already begun. In the early 1980s, following the collapse of oil prices, the Mexican government established a policy called the Maquiladora program to encourage exports in order to replace the lost oil export revenues. The program allows firms, called *maquilas*, to import equipment and parts duty-free into Mexico so long as the final products are exported. By 1991 there were more than 2,000 maquilas operating in Mexico, employing 600,000 workers. More than half of the maquilas are auto parts or electronic equipment assemblers, both of which use primarily unskilled labor, and many of the maquilas are U.S. firms. The fear is that including Mexico in NAFTA will only accelerate the movement of U.S. firms into Mexico as they seek low-cost unskilled labor.

The fear that freer trade with Mexico will lower the wages of unskilled U.S. workers must be tempered by a number of considerations. First and foremost is the sheer size of the U.S. economy relative to the Mexican economy. One study critical of NAFTA estimated that investment by U.S. firms in Mexico would total $53 billion by the year 2000, an average of about $5 billion per year. This may seem like a lot until we remember that total investment in the United States exceeded $770 billion in 1992 alone. The projected investment in Mexico is less than 1 percent of total U.S. investment, a percentage much too small to have a noticeable impact on the overall U.S. market for unskilled workers, or anything else at the macro level.

In addition, suppose that the United States continues to restrict trade with Mexico in order to protect its unskilled workers. Restricting trade simply encourages unskilled Mexican workers to emigrate to the United States to seek the higher wages available here. And this has already happened, of course. No one knows for sure how many Mexican workers have entered the United States illegally to work, but one study estimates that 22 percent of the entire Mexican labor force is working in the United States.[3] The influx of Mexican workers

---

[3] The data on the maquilas and the projected U.S. investment in Mexico are from T. Koechlin and M. Larudee, "The High Cost of NAFTA," *Challenge* 35, No. 5 (September–October 1992): 19–26 (see, particularly, Table 1, p. 19, and p. 21). Mexico's pollution standards are described in S. Friedman, "NAFTA As Social Dumping," *Challenge* 35, No. 5 (September–October 1992): 27–32. The estimate of the percentage of the Mexican labor force in the United States is reported in W. Enders and H. Lapan, *International Economics: Theory and Policy* (Englewood Cliffs, N.J.: Prentice-Hall, 1987), 209.

has probably already lowered the wages of U.S. unskilled workers about as much as they are going to fall from the competition with Mexican labor.

A final point is that Mexico has a comparative advantage relative to the United States in products that use unskilled labor, NAFTA or no NAFTA. If U.S. firms are prevented from entering Mexico, then firms from other nations will take their place and export to the United States. Proponents of NAFTA argue that it is in the best interest of United States to allow the U.S. firms in.

On balance, including Mexico in NAFTA would not appear to have much of an effect on the wages of unskilled U.S. workers.

Product Differentiation and Economies of Scale

The third, and most recent, model of international trade attempts to explain why the high-income industrial nations both import and export very similar products. We saw in the introduction to the chapter that the two-way trade of similar products constitutes the majority of trade by the United States, and the same is true for all the industrial nations. This trade cannot be explained very well by comparative advantage or differences in factor endowments. The industrialized nations all have large stocks of sophisticated capital and highly educated and skilled labor, and their firms produce similar products using much the same technologies. A different model is clearly needed to explain this trade.

MULTINATIONAL CORPORATION

A corporation that has offices and/or factories in more than one country.

Over the past 15 years or so economists have come to understand this two-way trade as the result of competition among the large corporations of the industrialized nations. The large corporations are most often **multinational firms** with production facilities in a number of countries, and they compete on a global scale. The principal competition among them takes the form of research and development into new varieties of products, such as cars with better gas mileage, faster computer chips, beers with different tastes and alcohol content, and the like. Most of the innovation arising in large multinational corporations is product-related, not production/process-related. Each corporation is trying to carve out a niche for itself in the international marketplace.

PRODUCT DIFFERENTIATION/ ECONOMIES OF SCALE MODEL OF INTERNATIONAL TRADE

A model specifically developed to explain the two-way trade in similar products between the industrialized countries; based on the idea that multinational corporations compete with each other through the research and development of new products and successful products enjoy economies of scale, which gives them a niche in the international marketplace.

Two-way trade results from this competition in the following manner. A corporation's research and development staff works on generating new varieties and refinements of the company's products. The corporation test-markets each new product idea in the home market at first in order to save on transportation and marketing costs and to give it more flexibility to vary the products as needed. Once the corporation finds a successful product variation, economies of scale come into play. The research and development costs associated with any one product are usually an important component of the overall costs of producing the product. Furthermore, research and development costs are foregone or sunk costs that become spread over ever-larger quantities as a successful product expands its market. Consequently, the unit costs of producing the product steadily decline as sales increase, and the product gains a cost advantage through these economies of scale.

The firm expands to foreign markets once the product is a proven success at home, spreading the sunk research and development costs even further. The unit cost advantage from the economies of scale allows the corporation to compete successfully in the foreign markets against other varieties of the product. The product does find its niche in the international marketplace.

Two-way trade occurs because large corporations everywhere are playing the same game. Suppose that a U.S. corporation successfully develops one variety of a product and a German corporation successfully develops another variety of the same product. Then the U.S. firm exports its product variety to Germany, and the German firm exports its product variety to the United States. The United States and Germany engage in a two-way trade of highly similar products, which is exactly what we observe among the industrial nations.

Notice that only corporations in the industrial nations can easily play this game because only the industrial nations have economies large enough to allow them to develop their products first in their home markets and realize the economies of scale. Corporations in the smaller, middle- and low-income nations would have great difficulty developing and test-marketing new products in larger foreign markets.[4]

THE EUROPEAN COMMUNITY   The product differentiation/economies of scale model is the principal model that economists have used to assess the potential economic gains from the European Community (EC), which began operation on December 31, 1992. The EC is the culmination of a 35-year effort to remove trade barriers throughout Western Europe. The effort began in 1957 when six countries—Belgium, France, Italy, Luxembourg, the Netherlands, and West Germany—signed the Treaty of Rome to form the European Economic Community (EEC). Among other goals the six nations pledged to remove all internal tariffs between them within 12 years, a goal that they achieved by 1968. Six more nations joined the EEC between 1973 and 1983—Denmark, Ireland, and the United Kingdom in 1973; Greece in 1981; and Portugal and Spain in 1983.

Then, in 1985, Jacques Delors, the president of the European Commission, authored a White Paper entitled *Completing the Internal Market,* which outlined the steps necessary to achieve complete freedom of movement for all goods and factors throughout the 12 EEC nations.[5] The EEC formally adopted Delors's recommendations in July of 1987 with the passage of the Single European Act and established December 31, 1992, as the target date for the new European Community.

Even though the internal tariffs had long since disappeared, trade within the EEC was still severely restricted in 1985. In addition to the costs and the delays of border crossings, manufacturers trying to sell in other countries encountered a host of nontariff barriers in the form of highly specific product and technical standards, local content laws, and various kinds of marketing regulations. These barriers gave local producers a significant amount of protection from foreign competitors. For example, Italy had a law requiring that all pasta sold there be made from durum wheat, which no one in Western Europe grows besides the Italians; the French required that tile meet certain specifications, which effectively excluded the German and Italian tile manufacturers; the entire EEC required that the noise from lawn mower engines be less than 90 decibels,

---

[4]A small portion of the two-way trade has more conventional origins. Tourism is one example. Ski lovers in the United States head to South America in July and August, while South American surfers pass them in the airports heading to the U.S. beaches. Also, large countries whose natural resources are concentrated geographically are likely to both export and import the resources. The United States exports its Alaskan oil to the Pacific rim countries, while the Eastern seaboard states import oil from OPEC. The high costs of transporting oil explain this two-way trade.

[5]Commission of the European Communities, *Completing the Internal Market, White Paper from the Commission to the European Council* (Luxembourg: Office for Official Publications of the European Communities, 1985).

which kept the larger U.S. tractor mowers out of Europe. Delors's White Paper set down nearly 300 directives that would eliminate all regulations and restrictions of these kinds, and most of the directives were in effect by the end of 1992. The 12 EEC nations also eliminated all border inspections among themselves.

A study undertaken by the European Commission in 1987, commonly referred to as the Cecchini Report, estimated that the gains from "completing the internal market" would be considerable, on the order of 4.3 to 6.8 percent of the EC's combined national product.[6] Most economists who have independently studied the potential gains believe that the Cecchini Report is much too optimistic. Independent estimates typically place the gains at 1 to 2 percent of the European national product. But all economists agree that the majority of the gains, 60 percent and more, will come from greater competition and reduced costs through economies of scale. The reason is that four countries, France, Germany, Italy, and the United Kingdom, account for 70 percent of the population and 80 percent of the national product within the EC. Their economies are very much alike, so that fully 80 percent of all the trade within the EC is two-way trade of similar products.

The chief inefficiencies within Western Europe prior to the EC stemmed from each country having too many small, localized firms that were protected from competition. The average European firm in 1990 was much smaller than was its counterpart in the United States, and often much too small to realize the cost-saving economies of large-scale production. Two outstanding examples were railroad locomotives and industrial boilers. Western Europe had 16 firms producing locomotives and 12 firms producing industrial boilers. The United States had two of each. The localized firms were able to charge artificially high prices to cover their higher costs, however, because of all the market and the product regulations that protected their markets. One study found enormous differences in the prices of similar products throughout Western Europe. Pharmaceuticals were 10 times more expensive in some countries than in others, new car prices varied as much as 93 percent for the same models, and telecommunications equipment prices differed by as much as 40 percent across countries. Price differences of this order of magnitude are a sure sign that markets are segmented and protected from foreign competition.

Economists predict that the EC will lead to a substantial consolidation of industries within Western Europe. They see a smaller number of multinational firms emerging and competing with one another for markets throughout Europe. The multinational firms will realize the economies of large-scale production and drive out many of the smaller, higher-cost localized firms. The increased competition for markets will also lower prices, so that consumers will capture much of the cost savings of large-scale production. The large firms will also compete with one another primarily through the research and development of new product lines as described above, so that most of the increase in trade will be two-way trade in similar products.

In summary, the majority of the gains from opening up the markets of Europe will come from cost-reducing economies of scale and increased intra-industry competition among firms producing similar products. They will not

---

[6]M. Emerson and others, *The Economics of 1992: The EC Commission's Assessment of the Economic Effects of Completing the Internal Market* (Oxford: Oxford University Press, 1988). Paul Cecchini was a principal investigator on the study.

be the traditional gains to trade achieved through comparative advantage and the specialization of production in particular industries.[7]

TARIFFS AND NONTARIFF BARRIERS TO TRADE

The three principal models used to explain international trade create an extremely strong presumption for free trade. Each model concludes that a nation can significantly improve its overall economic well-being by opening up its borders to trade.

Nonetheless, all nations restrict the flow of imports and exports to some extent through tariffs and a variety of nontariff barriers. A **tariff** is a tax on a good or a service entering a country. Nontariff barriers take many forms. The most common nontariff barrier is the **quota,** which directly limits the quantity of a good or a service that can enter a country. Quotas are the main form of trade restriction used by the United States to reduce imports. Another popular nontariff barrier is the **voluntary export restriction,** in which one country asks a second country to voluntarily restrict its exports. For example, Japan agreed to voluntarily restrict its exports of automobiles into the United States beginning in 1981. Still other nontariff barriers are the various product and marketing regulations that existed in Europe before the establishment of the European Community. Other countries also resort to these kinds of trade restrictions.

Why are countries willing to sacrifice some of the potential gains from trade by implementing these types of trade restrictions, and what harm do they cause? The remainder of Chapter 20 attempts to answer these questions. Let's begin with tariffs.

TARIFF

A tax on a good or a service entering a country.

QUOTA

A government-imposed limit on the quantity of a good or a service that can be imported into a country.

VOLUNTARY EXPORT RESTRICTION

An agreement between two nations in which one nation voluntarily limits the quantity of its exports to the other nation.

A Brief History of Tariffs

Tariffs were originally imposed by the United States and other nations as the most convenient and reliable way of raising revenues to finance government expenditures. In 1792 the federal government collected $3.43 million in tariff revenues; total federal revenues at the time were only $3.67 million. Tariff revenues remained the single most important source of federal revenues as late as 1900, when they amounted to 41 percent of total federal revenues. The advent of income taxes in the early 1900s established a far more potent source of revenues than did tariffs, and tariffs steadily diminished to insignificance as a revenue raiser. By 1980 tariff revenues were only 1.4 percent of total federal revenues.[8]

The Great Depression of the 1930s led nations to discover a new use for tariffs. They saw tariffs as a means of protecting jobs and even of stimulating

---

[7]An excellent economic analysis of the EC, on which much of this section is based, is H. Flam, "Product Markets and 1992: Full Integration, Large Gains?," *Journal of Economic Perspectives* 6, No. 4 (Fall 1992): 7–30. The price differences are on p. 10, and an overview of the independent estimates of the economic gains is on p. 27. Another excellent source on the economics of the EC is the "Symposium on Europe 1992," along with the invited papers, in *Brookings Papers on Economic Activity* 2 (1989): 277–381. For the micro issues, see M. Peck, "Industrial Organization and the Gains from Europe 1992," 277–299. For the macro issues, see R. Dornbusch, "Europe 1992: Macroeconomic Implications," 341–362.

[8]Enders and Lapan, *International Economics*, 132, 134.

the economy by increasing domestic demand. Modern aggregate demand theory does teach us that tariffs can stimulate the economy, at least over the short run. Remember that import demand subtracts from aggregate demand. Therefore, tariffs, by lowering import demand, raise aggregate demand and the equilibrium level of income. The increase in aggregate demand leads firms to hire more workers. The hope in the 1930s was that tariffs could help reduce the staggering levels of unemployment that existed at the time.

The U.S. Congress bought the jobs protection and unemployment arguments and passed the Smoot-Hawley tariff, which raised the average tariff on U.S. imports to 50 percent, far above what it had ever been before (or has been since). Supporters of the Smoot-Hawley tariff overlooked two points, however. The first is the principle that the value of imports must equal the value of exports. Substantially reducing U.S. imports must eventually reduce U.S. exports as well because other countries cannot export as much to the United States. The reduction in their exports lowers their aggregate demand and income and prevents them from importing as much from the United States. This point was vaguely understood. The Smoot-Hawley tariff was viewed as a **beggar-thy-neighbor policy,** a blatant attempt to export U.S. unemployment to other nations. But the supporters did not make the connection that the eventual reduction in export demand would destroy jobs in the export sector and lower U.S. aggregate demand. A beggar-thy-neighbor policy does not work in the long run.

This fundamental principle quickly became moot, however, because of a second point that the supporters of the tariff overlooked: Other nations would not stand by and let the United States attempt to export its unemployment to them. They immediately retaliated with enormous tariffs of their own, and the predictable result was a disastrous reduction of trade worldwide that only served to deepen and prolong the Great Depression.

General Agreement on Tariffs and Trade

Chastened by the experience of the Great Depression, 23 countries met in 1947 and signed a **General Agreement on Tariffs and Trade,** commonly referred to as GATT. GATT commits the signatories to come together periodically in extended meetings called Rounds to negotiate reductions in tariffs and other trade restrictions. The negotiations must honor the **most-favored-nation principle,** meaning that any reduction in tariffs or other trade restrictions that is negotiated between any two nations automatically applies to all the nations under GATT. (That is, all nations must be treated as the most-favored nation is treated.)

There have been eight Rounds of negotiations since 1947, with each Round typically lasting for a number of years. The most recent Round is the Uruguay Round, which began in 1986 and still had not been completed as of November 1993. Also, GATT membership has grown from the original 23 members to nearly 100.

GATT has met with mixed success in reducing trade restrictions. It has been spectacularly successful in reducing tariffs, as Table 20.3 indicates. The average level of tariffs among GATT nations has fallen steadily since World War II; the days of retaliatory tariffs are far behind. At the same time, GATT has not succeeded in reducing quotas and other nontariff barriers. Quite the contrary;

BEGGAR-THY-NEIGHBOR POLICY

A government policy that attempts to export domestic unemployment abroad by means of tariffs and other restrictions on imports.

GENERAL AGREEMENT ON TARIFFS AND TRADE (GATT)

A treaty originally signed by 23 capitalist nations in 1947 that commits the signatories to reduce tariffs and other trade barriers; membership in GATT has grown to nearly 100 nations.

MOST-FAVORED-NATION PRINCIPLE

A fundamental principle of GATT that states that any reduction in tariffs or other trade restrictions that is negotiated between any two nations automatically applies to all nations.

TABLE 20.3 **Average Tariff Rates on Manufactured Goods for Industrialized Countries Within GATT**

YEAR	AVERAGE TARIFF RATES
1940	40%
1950	25
1960	17
1970	12
1980	8
1990	5

GATT ROUNDS	
Geneva	1947
Annecy	1948
Torquay	1950
Geneva	1956
Dillon	1960–61
Kennedy	1964–67
Tokyo	1973–79
Uruguay	1986–

SOURCE: "World Trade Survey," *The Economist* (September 22, 1990): 7.

these other forms of trade restrictions have mushroomed since World War II and have replaced tariffs as the main form of trade restriction. The proliferation of nontariff barriers is discouraging because GATT specifically forbids quotas and export subsidies and encourages the signatories to use tariffs rather than direct quantity restrictions if they feel that they must restrict trade.

GATT has faced two major handicaps in eliminating tariffs completely and in halting the growth of the nontariff barriers. The first is that GATT is riddled with exceptions that were necessary to be able to forge the original agreement in 1947. Agricultural products have always been exempt from the provisions of GATT, as are products considered essential to national security. GATT members are permitted to arrange "voluntary" restrictions, such as the Japanese agreement to limit auto exports to the United States. Trade restrictions are also permitted to correct balance-of-payment deficits (to be described in Chapter 21). The most sweeping exception, though, is the so-called Escape Clause, which allows a nation to withdraw previous concessions and protect a domestic industry if it can show that imports have or would substantially damage domestic producers. The Escape Clause essentially gives nations free rein to restrict trade as they please because import-competing industries are almost certain to be substantially damaged by a reduction in trade restrictions. The second handicap is that GATT is unenforceable. The original 23 GATT signatories failed in their attempt to establish a supernational agency to impose sanctions on nations that violate the letter or the spirit of GATT.

These two handicaps have led the authors of a best-selling textbook in international economics to conclude that "Despite GATT agreements, the ability of governments to restrict trade is virtually unlimited."[9] And the means that governments have increasingly chosen are quotas and other direct quantity restrictions.

CURRENT ISSUE: One major issue preventing the completion of the Uruguay Round has been the practice of subsidizing domestic agriculture. The United States, a major food exporter, has been strenuously pushing for a reduction in agricultural subsidies. Many of its competitors, France in particular, have been resisting just as strenuously.

[9]Enders and Lapan, *International Economics*, 132, 134.

FIGURE 20.3

The Social Cost of Tariffs

The figure shows that tariffs reduce the quantity of imports and, in doing so, throw away some of the gains from trade. Without a tariff, the price of food in England is .8£ as in Figure 20.2 (assuming $P_C = 1£$), and England imports an amount of food equal to $(Q_D^0 - Q_S^0)$. A tariff of .1£ per unit of food raises the price of food to .9£. At the higher price, domestic producers increase their quantity supplied from Q_S^0 to O_S^1 and consumers reduce their quantity demanded from Q_D^0 to Q_D^1. Imports fall to $(Q_D^1 - Q_S^1)$. Consumer surplus decreases by the sum of areas 1 + 2 + 3 + 4, because consumers now buy less food and pay a higher price. Producer surplus increases by area 1, because domestic producers supply more food and receive a higher price. The government collects tariff revenue equal to area 3. Tariff revenue = .1 · $(Q_D^1 - Q_S^1)$. The net loss to society from the tariff is the sum of areas 2 + 4, the amount of consumer surplus lost that no one else gains.

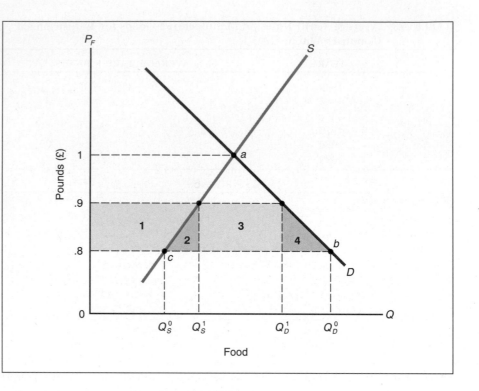

The Economic Costs of Tariffs and Quotas

Trade restrictions toss away some of the gains from trade that we described in Figure 20.2. Let's return to that example and consider a tariff levied by the British on imports of food in order to protect British farmers. This is a highly realistic example; agricultural products are commonly protected from free trade.

Figure 20.3 reproduces Figure 20.2(a). This time we will assume that the price of clothing is 1 ($P_C = 1£$), so that $P_F/P_C = P_F$.

The price of food is .8£ before the tariff. The quantity demanded at the free-trade price is Q_D^0. Domestic farmers Supply Q_S^0, and imports of food in the amount $(Q_D^0 - Q_S^0)$ provide the remaining quantity demanded. Suppose that the British impose a tariff of .1£ on each unit of food imported. The tariff raises the price of food in England to .9£. The higher price reduces the quantity demanded by consumers to Q_D^1 and increases the quantity supplied by domestic farmers to Q_S^1. Imports fall to $(Q_D^1 - Q_S^1)$.

We saw in Figure 20.2 that importing food without restriction gained society the triangular area *abc*. The tariff reduces some of the gain from trade as follows. Consumers lose the areas of surplus labeled 1, 2, 3, and 4 because they now pay a higher price for food and reduce their consumption. The domestic food suppliers gain the area of surplus labeled 1 that consumers lose because they now receive a higher price for food and increase their production. This is the protection effect of the tariff and represents a transfer from the consumers to the producers. The government also captures some of the area that consumers lose in the form of tariff revenue. The tariff revenue equals the height of the tariff times the amount of the imports under the tariff. This is the rectangular area labeled 3 in the figure:

$$\text{Tariff revenue} = \text{tariff} \cdot \text{imports}$$
$$= 0.1\pounds \cdot (Q_D^1 - Q_S^1) = \text{area 3}$$

The government presumably does something useful with the revenue, so that area 3 represents a transfer from the consumers to the government. Therefore, the net loss to society from the tariff is the sum of areas 2 and 4, the losses suffered by the consumers that no one captures. They are the portion of area *abc*, the gains from free trade, that society chooses to toss away by restricting trade with a tariff.

The economic effects of quotas and other types of direct quantity restrictions are much the same as those of tariffs. Under a quota the government issues quota licenses to individual foreign firms that place a limit on the quantity each firm can import into the country. Returning to our food example in Figure 20.3, suppose that instead of a tariff the government issues import licenses that, in total, restrict food imports to the amount $(Q_D^1 - Q_S^1)$, the same amount of imports as under the tariff. With imports limited to this amount, the domestic farmers can establish a price of .9£, the same price as with the tariff. With the price the same, the domestic supply and demand responses are the same. Domestic suppliers increase their quantity supplied to Q_S^1, and consumers reduce their quantity demanded to Q_D^1. The gains to domestic producers and the losses to consumers are also the same as with the tariff.

The only potential difference between the quota and the tariff is the tariff revenue, area 3 in Figure 20.3. The government would collect the same revenue under the quota if it auctions the quota licenses to the importers. Under the tariff, importers were willing to pay tariff revenue equal to area 3 and import $(Q_D^1 - Q_S^1)$ of food. Therefore, they would also be willing to pay the same amount for the quota licenses to import $(Q_D^1 - Q_S^1)$ food. Auctioning the quota licenses makes the quota identical to the tariff.

The common practice in the United States and in many other countries, however, is just to give the quota licenses to the importers free of charge. In this case the foreign importers capture area 3 as a pure economic profit, which economists call a **quota rent**. The quota rent arises because the quota allows the importers to sell their products at higher prices. Giving the licenses away adds area 3 to the overall economic loss, so that the total loss is the sum of areas 2, 3, and 4 in Figure 20.3.

A final point is that the economic effects of a quota are the same whether the quota is imposed by the government of the importing country or achieved by a voluntary agreement of the exporting country. Japan's agreement to voluntarily restrict exports of their automobiles to the United States is fully equivalent to a U.S.-imposed quota of the same amount on Japanese automobile imports. The voluntary export restriction raises the price of automobiles in the United States, thereby protecting U.S. auto makers and auto workers, hurting U.S. consumers, and increasing the profits of the Japanese auto makers in the form of a quota rent.

QUOTA RENT

The economic profit earned by foreign importers under a quota when the quota licenses are given away (or sold at less than their full market value).

The Politics of Trade Restrictions

Why do nations choose to sacrifice some of the gains from trade in this way? The answer lies in the distribution of the gains and the losses from trade in combination with the politics of trade. The import-competing industries lose from free trade, along with the factors of production specific to those industries. Moreover, the losses suffered by the individuals associated with these industries are large and concentrated. The farmers who are driven off their farms by food imports or the U.S. auto workers who lose their jobs to Japanese and German imports are big losers, and they tend to be concentrated in specific regions of the country. They have every incentive to lobby politicians for protection from trade to save their farms and their jobs. They may even be able to elicit sympathy from other citizens who understand the pain of losing one's livelihood.

In contrast, the gains from free trade are individually small and diverse. They accrue to millions of consumers in the form of cheaper or better products—for example, cheaper food and better cars. The gains to each individual consumer are minuscule compared with the losses suffered by the individual farmers or auto workers who lose their farms or jobs. But as Figures 20.2 and 20.3 show, the combined gains to the millions of consumers far exceed the combined losses to a few thousand farmers or auto workers. Even so, the millions of consumers have little individual incentive to lobby for free trade, and organizing them is difficult in any case. Therefore, the political outcome is predictable. The farm and automobile lobbies carry the day, the tariffs are imposed, and the nation as a whole loses.

The Costs of Trade Restrictions

A group of economists at the Federal Trade Commission (FTC) analyzed the overall costs of U.S. tariffs and quotas in 1983 and found the costs to be considerable. The U.S. tariff rates at the time averaged only 3.7 percent, yet the FTC estimated that removing all the tariffs would bring a net gain of $10.5 billion. The four largest direct quantity restrictions in 1983 were quotas on sugar, textiles, and steel and the Japanese voluntary export restraint on automobiles. The FTC economists concluded in each case that the losses to consumers far exceeded the gains to the domestic industries being protected. For example, the Japanese voluntary export restraint on automobiles cost consumers $1.1 billion in return for a $115 million gain to the U.S. auto industry. The biggest gainers were the Japanese producers, who received $824 million in quota rents. Consumers lost over $241,000 for every job saved in the U.S. auto industry. The pattern of gains and losses from the three quotas was much the same: large consumer losses, a much smaller protection gain to domestic producers, and very large quota rents to foreign producers. The overall estimated cost of the four trade restrictions was $2.2 billion, and the combined quota rents to the foreign producers were $1.9 billion. Restricting trade and then giving away the quota rents is very costly indeed![10]

Are There Any Good Trade Restrictions?

Can tariffs and quota ever be good for the nation as a whole? Economists would seriously consider only one case in which restricting trade may be beneficial

---

[10]D. Tarr and M. Morkre, *Aggregate Costs to the United States of Tariffs and Quotas on Imports: General Tariff Cuts and Removal of Quotas on Automobiles, Steel, Sugar, and Textiles*, Bureau of Economics Staff Report to the Federal Trade Commission, December 1984 (Washington, D.C.: U.S. Government Printing Office, 1984), Table 1, p. 2 and Table 4, p. 8.

for a large industrial nation such as the United States, the so-called **strategic tariff** or quota. Designing strategic tariffs or quotas that are actually beneficial is very difficult, however.

STRATEGIC TARIFFS The possibility of a strategic tariff arises in the context of the third model of international trade described above, which is based on the research and development of new product lines and economies of scale. The basic idea is that large domestic firms cannot easily protect themselves from foreign competitors while they are trying to develop new markets. They may have no believable strategy or threat to fend off the competitors. The government does have a believable threat, though: It can protect the domestic firms with tariffs and quotas (or give them direct subsidies). So the government becomes a partner in a strategy of trying to gain a first-mover advantage for its firms. Firms that are the first to develop successful products with the help of the government can then take advantage of economies of scale and gain penetration into foreign markets. The strategic tariffs (or quotas or subsidies) shift profits from foreign to domestic firms and promote exports.

A classic recent example of this strategy was the Japanese takeover of the market for computer memory chips. Texas Instruments, Intel, and National Semiconductor were among the U.S. firms that invented and developed the technology for making dynamic random access memory (DRAM) computer chips and had the semiconductor market to themselves in the early 1980s. The Japanese decided that they wanted to develop their own semiconductor memory chips, so they protected their producers from U.S. exports and went furiously to work developing and refining the chips on their own. Their research and development efforts were successful, and soon their firms were producing the most reliable memory chips. By the end of the decade NEC, Toshiba, and Hitachi had become the leading producers of the memory chips and had gained almost total control of the market.

Playing the strategic tariff or subsidy game successfully is extremely problematic, however. It typically requires enormous amounts of protection or subsidy. It also requires that the government select winners in advance, and it is not at all clear that governments can do this, especially in highly fertile, rapidly changing technological environments. Careful attempts by economists to estimate the benefits and costs of these strategies always conclude that they are losers.

The Japanese takeover of the memory chip market is a perfect case in point. It is generally considered to be a spectacular success story, so successful that it has led a number of politicians to call for further trade sanctions on the Japanese in order to encourage them to open up their markets. These politicians do not want a repeat of the memory chip "fiasco" in other industries. But MIT's Paul Krugman determined that the Japanese would have been much better off to leave this industry alone and import the chips that they needed from the original U.S. manufacturers. The costs of developing their own chips were just too large.

Krugman's study does not even take into consideration the fact that the Japanese have essentially lost the memory chip market to the U.S. firms in the 1990s. A new and faster computer architecture called reduced instruction set computing, or RISC, requires a completely redesigned memory chip. U.S. firms such as Sun Microsystems, MIPS, IBM, and Digital have taken the lead in developing and producing the new chip. This time the Japanese firms have

STRATEGIC TARIFF

A tariff that is designed to protect domestic firms from competition while they are attempting to research and develop successful new products.

CURRENT ISSUE: Laura Tyson, chairwoman of President Clinton's Council of Economic Advisers, is one economist who has argued in the past for trade restrictions against Japan if the Japanese refuse to open their markets further to U.S. products. In 1993 the Japanese agreed to allow more imports from the United States.

reacted by forming partnerships with the U.S. producers to market the chips; they will not try to develop and refine the new chip technology on their own.

The European Airbus Consortium is another case in point. It receives huge subsidies from a number of European governments to compete with the U.S. airframe manufacturers. One of its first planes was a mid-range commercial jet that it built to compete with Boeing's mid-range 767. Once again, a careful economic study shows that Europe would have been much better off simply buying the Boeing 767.

Picking winners in a high-tech environment is just too uncertain to be done with any confidence. Also, most of the potential gains from strategic tariffs are just shifts in profits from foreign producers to domestic producers. Consumers may not gain much from a successful strategic tariff. MIT's Krugman was a pioneer in developing the theory behind the potential gains from strategic tariffs and subsidies. Yet actual experience with these policies has led him back to the presumption for free trade. He concludes: "The economic cautions about the difficulty of formulating useful intervention and the political economy concerns that interventionism may go astray combine into a new case for free trade."[11]

SUMMARY

Chapter 20 began with a discussion of the three basic models that economists use to explain the variety of international trade that we observe: Ricardo's theory of comparative advantage, the factor endowments model, and the product differentiation/economies of scale model.

1. Ricardo's theory of comparative advantage shows that the pattern and the gains from trade depend on differences in opportunity costs in producing goods across countries. Ricardo attributed the cost differences to differences in technologies. His theory of comparative advantage says that countries can gain from trade if they specialize their production in the goods in which they have a comparative advantage (lower opportunity costs) and trade for goods in which other countries have a comparative advantage. International trade gives a country a consumption possibilities frontier beyond its production possibilities frontier.
2. Ricardo's model demonstrates many additional fundamental principles of international trade:
   a. A country gains more from specialization and trade the more that its terms-of-trade, defined as the ratio of the prices of the export goods to the prices of the import goods, improves. The terms-of-trade depends on the relative demands for the traded goods in Ricardo's model.
   b. The value of a nation's exports must equal the value of a nation's imports. Exports may not equal imports each year as in the model, but they must eventually be equal over time because nations insist on receiving real goods in exchange for their goods.

[11]Krugman quote in R. E. Baldwin, "Are Economists' Traditional Trade Policy Views Still Valid?" *Journal of Economic Literature* XXX, No. 2 (June 1992): 826. Baldwin's article is an excellent treatment of the benefits and the pitfalls of strategic trade restrictions, and cites the Airbus Study. For an analysis of the computer memory chip market, see W. Taffel, "Advantageous Liaisons," *Technology Review* 96, No. 4 (May/June 1993): 28–31, 34–36.

    c. The real and the financial sides of international trade are closely linked. The exchange rate must be between the price ratios of the traded goods in each country. An exchange rate outside these ratios will price the goods of the nation with the overvalued currency out of the market.

    d. Developing countries need not fear the superior technologies of the industrialized countries, and the industrialized countries need not fear the lower wages of the developing countries. Differences in opportunity costs, not in technology or wages, are the key to the gains from trade. Indeed, Ricardo's model is most useful for explaining trade between the developing and the industrialized nations.

3. The factor endowments model allows for increasing marginal costs and incomplete specialization, with a country continuing to produce the good that it imports. Countries have lower costs and a comparative advantage in producing goods that use factors that they have a relative abundance of. These are the goods that they export. For example, the United States has a comparative advantage in goods that use relatively large amounts of capital, land, and highly skilled labor. It has a comparative disadvantage in goods that use relatively large amounts of unskilled labor.

4. The factor endowments model highlights the distributional implications of trade. Trade increases the returns to the relatively abundant factors used in the export goods and lowers the returns to the relatively scarce factors used in the import-competing goods. For the United States, trade increases the returns to capital, land, and highly skilled labor and lowers the wages of unskilled workers.

5. The fear in bringing Mexico into NAFTA is that expansion of trade with Mexico will lower the wages of unskilled U.S. workers. This fear is exaggerated because the Mexican economy is so much smaller than the U.S. economy is and because so many Mexican workers are already working in the United States and have presumably already lowered the wages of unskilled U.S. workers.

6. The product differentiation/economies of scale model is used to explain the two-way trade of highly similar goods and inputs among the industrialized nations. The trade is the result of large multinational corporations competing for markets through research and development of new product varieties. Successful products enjoy economies of scale that give them a cost advantage and a niche in the international marketplace. With corporations in all countries playing this game, similar products are both imported and exported.

7. Most of the gains from the European Community will come from large multinational corporations driving out higher-cost local producers who were protected from international competitors by a host of barriers to trade in the form of product standards and marketing regulations. Most of the increase in trade will be two-way trade of similar products. The potential gains from the European Community appear to be about 1 percent of total European national product.

   The second section of Chapter 20 discussed the most common barriers to trade.

8. Barriers to trade include tariffs, quotas, and other nontariff barriers. A tariff is a tax on an imported good. A quota directly restricts the quantity of an

imported good. Other nontariff barriers include the various kinds of product standards and marketing regulations that existed in Western Europe before the European Community, and voluntary export restrictions.

9. Tariffs raise the price of imported goods, resulting in losses to consumers, gains to the import-competing industries and the workers in these industries, and increased tariff revenues for the government. Quotas are identical to tariffs if the quota licenses are auctioned off to the importers. Giving the licenses away turns the government revenues into quota rents received by the foreign importers. The main political argument for trade restrictions is to protect jobs in import-competing industries.

10. Studies of trade restrictions show that the aggregate losses to consumers usually far exceed the gains to the protected industries and the tariff revenues. Yet countries restrict trade because the losses from free trade to the import-competing industries and their workers are individually large and concentrated, whereas the gains to consumers are individually small and diverse. The narrow interests of the import-competing industries and their workers carry the day politically.

11. The General Agreement on Tariffs and Trade (GATT) is an international agreement to reduce tariffs and trade restrictions that was signed in 1947 by 23 nations. It now includes nearly 100 nations. GATT has been successful in reducing tariff rates, but unsuccessful in preventing the spread of quotas and other nontariff barriers.

12. The one tariff that might possibly benefit a large industrial nation as a whole is the strategic tariff. A strategic tariff protects large multinational corporations while they try to develop new product varieties through research and development. This strategy is costly, however, and picking winners in advance is chancy. Most studies show that strategic tariffs and other direct subsidies are losers; they cost more than their benefits.

KEY TERMS

beggar-thy-neighbor policy
comparative advantage
factor endowments model of international trade
foreign exchange markets
gains from trade
General Agreement on Tariffs and Trade (GATT)

most-favored-nation principle
multinational corporation
overvalued currency
product differentiation/economies of scale model of international trade
quota
quota rent

Ricardo's model of comparative advantage
strategic tariff
tariff
terms-of-trade
undervalued currency
voluntary export restriction

QUESTIONS

1. a. To what extent do Ricardo's comparative advantage model and the factor endowments model yield similar predictions about the pattern of international trade and the gains from international trade?

   b. In what ways does the factor endowments model expand on Ricardo's comparative advantage model?

2. Why might a quota make a country worse off than does a tariff, assuming that they both restrict imports by the same amount?

3. Why does a country impose tariffs, quotas, and other trade restrictions, even if the country as a whole becomes worse off?

4. Why might similar products be both imported and exported by a country? Give some examples of two-way trade in similar products that involve the United States.

5. Suppose that in Japan 1 unit of labor is used to make 2 videocassette recorders (VCRs) and 1 unit of labor is used to make 3 television sets (TVs). In the United States 1

unit of labor is used to make 1 VCR and 1 unit of labor is used to make 1 TV. Assume that labor is the only factor of production and that each country has 200 units of labor.

a. Which country has the comparative advantage in VCRs? In TVs?

b. Show that both countries can be made better off by specializing their production in one of the products and trading.

c. Given the trading ratio of VCRs to TVs that you chose for your answer to part (b), compare the production possibilities without trade and the consumption possibilities with trade in each country.

6. What factors determine how much a country gains from international trade?

7. Switzerland exports cheese (Swiss cheese, of course) to France for $2 a pound. Without trade, the equilibrium price in Switzerland would be $1.50 a pound, and the equilibrium price in France would be $2.50 a pound.

a. Draw reasonable-looking supply and demand curves for cheese in Switzerland and France. Show on your graph the gains from international trade for both Switzerland and France.

b. Suppose that France places a $.20 a pound tariff on cheese. Show on your graph the gains from international trade that are lost in France and the tariff revenue that is collected by the French government.

8. Citizens in the United States are often urged to "Buy American." Do you think that "Buy American" is good advice for the United States?

9. a. What is a strategic tariff, and why might it benefit a nation?

b. Who tends to gain more from a strategic tariff, domestic consumers or domestic producers?

c. Why are beneficial strategic tariffs so difficult to design?

d. Might a country like the United States be interested in strategic tariffs? If so, why? If not, why not?

10. What were the arguments in favor of and against allowing Mexico to join in NAFTA with the United States and Canada?

11. In what ways do the nations of Western Europe stand to gain from the European Community?

21

International Finance

LEARNING OBJECTIVES

CONCEPTS TO LEARN

The balance of payments

Flexible exchange rates

Fixed exchange rates

The Bretton Woods fixed exchange rate system

Fiscal and monetary policies under flexible and fixed exchange rates

CONCEPTS TO RECALL

The Laws of Supply and Demand [5]

Fiscal policy [9, 11, 12]

Monetary policy [9, 15, 16]

he distinctive feature of international transactions is that they require an exchange of one nation's currency for another nation's currency in the foreign exchange markets. The fundamental issue of international finance is how nations will arrange for the exchange of their currencies. They have two basic choices, a system of fixed exchange rates or a system of flexible, or floating, exchange rates.

In a system of **fixed exchange rates** the nations agree to fix the relative values of their currencies at one set of exchange rates. Then the nations' central banks agree to buy and sell foreign currencies as needed to maintain the exchange rates at the set values. In a system of **flexible,** or **floating, exchange rates** the exchange rates are determined in the free market according to the Laws of Supply and Demand. Moreover, the supplies and the demands for currencies are those of private individuals and firms. The central banks have no role to play in a pure flexible exchange rate system.

Both exchange rate systems have their advantages and disadvantages. The ambivalence in deciding which is the best system is evident in the history of international finance since World War II. In 1944, 44 nations met at Bretton Woods, New Hampshire, and established a fixed exchange rate system based on the dollar and gold. The dollar was pegged to gold at $35 per ounce, and the United States agreed to exchange dollars for gold on demand. All other currencies were then pegged to the dollar or to gold. The Bretton Woods arrangement lasted until 1973, when most of the developed market economies decided to switch to a flexible exchange rate system and allow their currencies to float on the free market.

The 1973 arrangement lasted until the 1976 Jamaica Agreements, which allowed nations to choose one of three options: adopt a flexible exchange rate, peg the exchange rate to one currency, or peg the exchange rate to a market basket of currencies. These options have remained in effect ever since, with the result that there is now quite a mixture of exchange rate systems in effect. For example, the United States and Japan have maintained flexible exchange rates, whereas most of the Western European nations have pegged their exchange rates to the German mark since 1979.

FIXED EXCHANGE RATE

An exchange rate that is set at a fixed value.

FLEXIBLE EXCHANGE RATE

An exchange rate that is determined by the Laws of Supply and Demand in the foreign exchange markets.

The primary goal of Chapter 21 is to explain the economic implications of choosing fixed versus flexible exchange rates. The chapter begins with a close look at the main kinds of international transactions that give rise to the supplies and the demands for currencies in the foreign exchange markets. A knowledge of these transactions will help us understand the issues involved with choosing an exchange rate system.

THE BALANCE OF PAYMENTS

BALANCE OF PAYMENTS

The double-entry accounting system that nations use to record their international transactions during the course of a year.

The accounting structure that nations use to record their international transactions during the course of a year is called the **balance of payments.** The Bureau of Economic Analysis of the U.S. Department of Commerce compiles and publishes the balance of payments for the United States. The balance of payments records international transactions by means of a double-entry system of international credits and debits. An **international credit** is any transaction that gives rise to a demand for dollars in the foreign exchange markets (alternatively, a supply of foreign currency). An **international debit** is any transaction that gives rise to a supply of dollars in the foreign exchange markets (alternatively, a demand for foreign currency). Double-entry bookkeeping means that every credit entry has a corresponding and offsetting debit entry, and every debit entry has a corresponding and offsetting credit entry. Consequently, the sum of the international credit transactions during the year must equal the sum of the international debit transaction during the year. In other words, the balance of payments must net to zero overall.

The balance of payments contains three main subsections: the current account, the capital account, and the official settlements account. The credits and debits in each of the subaccounts do not necessarily net to zero. A subaccount is in *surplus* if credits exceed debits and in *deficit* if debits exceed credits. Let's take a closer look at each of the subaccounts.

The Current Account

The most important entries in the **current account** are the exports and the imports of manufactured goods, called merchandise exports and imports. These are the exports and the imports that were listed in Table 20.1. When U.S. exporters of food, computers, and aircraft sell their products, they receive foreign currencies—for example, Japanese yen, German marks, and English pounds—which they eventually want to exchange for dollars. Therefore, merchandise *exports* give rise to a demand for dollars; they are recorded as *credits* in the balance of payments. When foreign importers of automobiles, cameras, and wines sell their products, they receive dollars, which they eventually want to exchange for their own currencies—for example, yen, marks, and French francs. Therefore, merchandise *imports* give rise to a supply of dollars; they are recorded as *debits* in the balance of payments. The **balance of trade** is the difference between merchandise exports and merchandise imports. The word *balance* refers to the difference between the credits and the debits within each subaccount.

The current account balance also includes services and flows of factor income into and out of the country. The most important services involved in international trade are tourism, travel, and financial services directly associated with exports and imports, such as insurance policies taken out on goods shipped abroad.[1] Most services that we routinely consume, such as haircuts, restaurant meals, and doctor visits, are local services that are not traded internationally. The flows of factor income are primarily interest and dividends received from saving and investment in foreign countries.

The accounting of the services and the factor income flows as debits and credits works just like the accounting of exports and incomes. For example, interest and dividend income received by U.S. residents from their saving and investment abroad gives rise to a demand for dollars as the income returns to the United States. Therefore, the *receipt of factor income by U.S. residents* is a *credit* in the balance of payments. Conversely, interest and dividend income received by foreign residents on their saving and investment in the United

INTERNATIONAL CREDIT

Any international transaction that gives rise to a demand for dollars in the foreign exchange markets, such as an export or a capital inflow.

INTERNATIONAL DEBIT

Any international transaction that gives rise to a supply of dollars in the foreign exchange markets, such as an import or a capital outflow.

CURRENT ACCOUNT (BALANCE OF PAYMENTS)

The subaccount in the balance of payments that records the exports and the imports of goods and services, the receipts of factor incomes by domestic and foreign residents, and net unilateral transfers.

BALANCE OF TRADE

The difference between a nation's merchandise exports and merchandise imports.

---

[1]The purchase and sale of military goods by the federal government is also included under services in the current account.

States gives rise to a supply of dollars as the income leaves the United States. Therefore, the *payment of factor income to foreign residents* is a *debit* in the balance of payments.

The **balance of goods and services** is the sum of the balance of trade plus net exports of services (exports − imports) plus net receipts of factor income (receipts by U.S. citizens − payments to foreign citizens).

The final entries in the current account balance are unilateral transfers into and out of the country by persons, firms, and governments. A *transfer by a foreign "resident" to the United States* gives rise to a demand for dollars and is a *credit* in the balance of payments. A *transfer by a U.S. "resident" to a foreign country* gives rise to a supply of dollars and is a *debit* in the balance of payments. Net unilateral transfers are the difference between transfers out of (debits) and transfer into (credits) the United States. The **current account balance** equals the balance of goods and services minus net unilateral transfers.

Net unilateral transfers are typically a small item and are usually ignored, so that the current account balance is often used interchangeably with the balance of goods and services in discussions of the balance of payments. In 1991, however, net unilateral transfers decreased by over $40 billion as foreign countries paid their share of expenses for the Gulf War to the United States. They helped drive the U.S. current account balance to near zero ($4 billion deficit) for the first time since 1981. The current account balance returned to a substantial deficit (debits greater than credits) in 1992.[2]

To summarize:

<u>CREDITS</u>　　　　<u>DEBITS</u>

Merchandise exports − merchandise imports = *balance of trade*

\+

Services exports − services imports

\+

Receipts of factor − payments of factor　= *balance of goods*
income　　　　　income　　　　　　　 *and services*

−

Net unilateral transfers　= *current account*
(debit)　　　　　　　　*balance*

The Capital Account

The **capital account** records the flow of capital into and out of a country. Capital flows across international borders whenever a resident of one country buys a financial security of a foreign country or makes a loan to a resident of a foreign country. As above, the "resident" could be an individual, a firm, or a government agency other than the central bank. The financial securities include bank deposit accounts, certificates of deposit, corporate and government bonds, corporate stocks—any financial security that represents a claim against a resident of a foreign country.

Purchases of U.S. financial securities and loans to U.S. residents by foreign residents are **capital inflows.** Since foreign residents need dollars to buy U.S.

BALANCE OF GOODS AND SERVICES

The sum of the balance of trade plus net exports of services plus net receipts of factor incomes.

CURRENT ACCOUNT BALANCE

The balance of goods and services minus net unilateral transfers.

CAPITAL ACCOUNT (BALANCE OF PAYMENTS)

The subaccount in the balance of payments that records capital inflows and outflows.

CAPITAL INFLOWS

Purchases of domestic financial securities or loans to domestic residents by foreign residents.

---

[2]Council of Economic Advisers, *Economic Indicators* (Washington, D.C.: U.S. Government Printing Office, March 1993), 36.

financial securities or lend in the United States, *capital inflows* give rise to a demand for dollars. They are recorded as *credits* in the balance of payments. Purchases of foreign financial securities or loans to foreign residents by U.S. residents are **capital outflows.** Since U.S. residents need foreign currencies to buy foreign financial securities or lend in foreign countries, *capital outflows* give rise to a supply of dollars. They are recorded as *debits* in the balance of payments.

Purchases of financial securities and issues of loans with more than one year to maturity are called *long-term* capital inflows and outflows. Other purchases and loans are considered *short-term* capital inflows and outflows. Stocks are considered long-term investments and checking accounts short-term investments no matter how long someone intends to keep them. Also, purchases of stock or other assets that give the foreign buyer a controlling interest in a firm are called **direct foreign investment.** All other international capital flows are considered to be *portfolio investments.*

The **capital account balance** equals the capital inflows minus the capital outflows.

To summarize:

CREDITS		DEBITS		
Capital inflows	−	Capital outflows	=	*capital account balance*
(purchases of U.S.		(purchases of foreign		
financial securities or		financial securities or		
loans to U.S. residents		loans to foreign resi-		
by foreign residents)		dents by U.S. residents)		

The Official Settlements Account

Central banks hold part of their assets in the form of international reserves, consisting primarily of foreign currencies, other very short-term financial securities denominated in foreign currencies such as 180-day government bonds, and gold. They also hold, as part of their liabilities, some of the international reserves of other central banks. The entries in the **official settlements account** are purchases and sales of these international reserves. We will be concerned with their purchases and sales of foreign currencies for the most part.

A *sale of foreign currency* by the Fed in exchange for dollars is a *credit* in the U.S. balance of payments. A loss of foreign currency may seem like an unusual credit, but it satisfies the rule of representing an increase in either the demand for dollars or the supply of a foreign currency. Conversely, *a purchase of foreign currency* by the Fed in exchange for dollars is a *debit* in the U.S. balance of payments. It represents an increase in either the supply of dollars or the demand for foreign currency.[3]

CAPITAL OUTFLOWS

Purchases of foreign financial securities or loans to foreign residents by domestic residents.

DIRECT FOREIGN INVESTMENT

The purchase of domestic stock or other assets by foreign residents that give them a controlling interest in a domestic firm.

CAPITAL ACCOUNT BALANCE

The difference between a nation's capital inflows and capital outflows.

OFFICIAL SETTLEMENTS ACCOUNT

The subaccount in the balance of payments that records transactions between a nation's central bank and the central banks of other nations.

---

[3]Most individuals and businesses do not deal directly with central banks. Instead, they exchange currencies at large commercial banks (and other private financial institutions). Even so, the Fed is likely to become involved in the transaction. For example, suppose that a commercial bank buys pounds from a U.S. exporter and pays with a cashier's check. The cashier's check reduces the bank's reserve account with the Fed. If the bank does not want its reserve account to decrease, it will sell the pounds to the Fed in exchange for more reserves. So the Fed ends up buying the pounds. We will speak of foreign currency purchases and sales directly with the Fed and other central banks to simplify the complexities of these transactions.

To summarize:

<table>
<tr><td>CREDITS</td><td></td><td>DEBITS</td><td></td></tr>
<tr><td>Sales of foreign currency and other international reserves by the Fed (or increases of foreign central bank deposits or securities at the Fed)</td><td>−</td><td>Purchases of foreign currency and other international reserves by the Fed (or increases of the Fed's bank deposits or securities at other central banks)</td><td>= *official settlements balance*</td></tr>
</table>

OFFICIAL SETTLEMENTS ACCOUNT BALANCE

The difference between international credit and debit transactions between a nation's central bank and the central banks of other nations.

Double-Entry Bookkeeping

The majority of capital flows and official settlements in the balance of payments result directly from exports and imports and from other entries in the current account. They are the second half of the current account transactions, the second entry in the double-entry method of bookkeeping, which guarantees that the overall international credits and debits must be equal.

For example, suppose that a U.S. resident buys a Nissan Maxima for $15,000 from a Japanese car dealer. The purchase of the car is an import and a debit in the current account balance. The offsetting credit entry depends on what the car dealer does with the $15,000. The dealer may deposit the customer's check in its checking account at a U.S. bank or buy other U.S. financial securities such as stocks or bonds. Each of these options is a capital inflow, an offsetting credit in the capital account. Or the car dealer may have lent the customer the $15,000. The loan is also a capital inflow, an offsetting credit in the capital account. Another possibility is that the car dealer exchanges the $15,000 for yen at the Fed to sent the funds back to Japan. The loss of $15,000 worth of yen is a loss of international reserves, an offsetting credit in the official settlements account.

The same offsetting entries in the capital and the official settlements accounts apply in reverse for U.S. exports. A sale of food in London by a U.S. exporter is an export and a credit in the current account. The exporter receives payment in pounds. If the exporter chooses to place the pounds in a London bank or purchase other financial securities in London, these transactions are capital outflows and offsetting debits in the capital account. A loan by the exporter to a British customer is also a capital outflow and an offsetting debit in the capital account. If the exporter exchanges the pounds for dollars at the Fed, the purchase of the pounds by the Fed is an offsetting debit in the official settlements account.

For small, low-income countries with poorly developed capital markets, most of the offsets to exports and imports are in the official settlements accounts. Exporters selling goods in Thailand do not want to hold many deposits in Thai banks or other financial securities denominated in the Thai currency, the bhat. They exchange most of the bhat they receive from selling their products for their own currency at the Thai central bank. This is another way of seeing why nations have to export in order to be able to import. Small nations such as Thailand have to maintain a near-equality between their exports and their imports on current account. Their exports generate the foreign currency, the international reserves, that they will need to sell to the foreign exporters selling in Thailand. They would soon run out of international reserves if they ran a large deficit on their current account, with imports exceeding exports. In other words, their official settlements account also remains in near equality as the central bank buys foreign currencies from the exporters and sells the foreign currencies to the importers in approximately equal amounts. The capital account transactions are relatively unimportant.

In contrast, a large percentage of the offsets to the current account in the industrial market economies such as the United States are in the capital account. Foreign exporters selling goods in the United States are quite willing to hold U.S. financial securities, just as U.S. exporters are willing to hold the financial securities of Japan, England, Germany, and so forth. In addition, the capital inflows and outflows can have a life of their own. They are not necessarily just offsets to the current account. The act of placing savings, or investing, in the securities of foreign countries for its own sake is called an **autonomous capital inflow** or **outflow.**

For example, the managers of a U.S. pension fund may decide to place some of their fund's portfolio in Japanese stocks. The managers need yen to purchase stocks on the Tokyo exchange, so they exchange dollars for yen at the Fed and then purchase the Japanese stocks in Tokyo. The purchase of the stock is an autonomous capital outflow, a debit in the capital account. The offsetting credit is the sale of yen by the Fed, which appears in the official settlements account.

Another example of an autonomous capital flow is a loan by a U.S. government agency to a developing nation, which the nation uses to buy food. Suppose that the nation buys food from the United States. The loan is an autonomous capital outflow and a debit in the capital account. The U.S. export of food to the nation is the offsetting entry in the balance of payments. It is a credit in the current account. This is an example of the **transfer mechanism,** in which first the money flows and then the goods follow. The transfer mechanism was an important feature of the Marshall Plan following World War II. The federal government poured money into Europe to help the Europeans recover from the war. Much of the money distributed through Marshall Plan grants and loans came right back to the United States through purchases of U.S. exports.

The transfer mechanism is incomplete if the receiving government spends the money elsewhere. For example, suppose that the government buys some of the food from France and the French exporter holds the dollars in an account at a French bank denominated in dollars. Dollar-denominated accounts in foreign banks are called **Eurodollar accounts,** and they have grown very rapidly over the past 20 years. An increase in a Eurodollar account is recorded as a short-term capital inflow in the U.S. balance of payments, the offsetting credit to the original capital outflow.

The fact that capital account transactions can be offsets to current account transactions means that the industrial market economies do not have to maintain a near-equality in their current account balances each year. They have the luxury of running a current account deficit for awhile, with imports exceeding exports. As noted earlier, the United States has been running large deficits in its current account every year since 1983, with the single exception of 1991. There is a limit to how long the United States or any other nation can run current account deficits, however. A deficit in the current account means that the combined capital and official settlements accounts are in surplus. Remember, overall the balance of payments must net to zero. A surplus in the official

AUTONOMOUS CAPITAL INFLOW (OR OUTFLOW)

A capital inflow (or outflow) undertaken for its own sake and not as an offset to some other transaction in the balance of payments.

TRANSFER MECHANISM (INTERNATIONAL TRADE)

A grant or a loan to a foreign country that is then used to buy exports from the country that gave the grant or the loan; in other words, a mechanism in which first the money flows and then the goods flow.

EURODOLLAR ACCOUNT

Any dollar-denominated account in a foreign bank.

settlements balance means that the nation is losing international reserves, and it certainly cannot do this forever and maintain its trading relationships. A surplus in the capital account means that capital inflows exceed capital outflows. On net, foreign residents are willing to hold the nation's financial securities. Eventually, though, the foreign residents will want to "cash in" and consume real goods and services; they will not go on saving forever. When they do decide to cash in, the deficit in the current account will have to turn into a surplus, with exports exceeding imports, so that the nation can earn the foreign currency that will be demanded. This is why even the modern industrial nations have to export in order to import despite the attractiveness of their capital markets. A deficit in the current account must eventually become a surplus. The day when the United States has to turn its current account deficit into a surplus may not be too far in the future.

The U.S. Balance of Payments

Table 21.1 shows the U.S. balance of payments for 1992. The pattern for 1992 was typical of every year since 1986, with the single exception of 1991 noted earlier. The current account had a large deficit, offset by large surpluses in the

TABLE 21.1   U.S. Balance of Payments, 1992 ($ billion)

CURRENT ACCOUNT	
Exports	439.3
Imports	(−)535.5[a]
Balance of trade	(−) 96.3
Net services	55.1
Receipts of factor income	109.2
Payments of factor income	(−) 99.1
Balance of goods and services	(−) 31.1
Net unilateral transfers	(−) 31.3
Current account balance	(−) 62.4
CAPITAL ACCOUNT	
U.S. private capital outflows	(−) 48.7
Foreign private capital inflows	80.1
Capital account balance	31.4
OFFICIAL SETTLEMENTS ACCOUNT	
U.S. official reserve outflows	3.9
Foreign official reserve inflows	40.3
Official settlements account balance	44.2
SUMMARY	
Current account balance	(−) 62.4
Capital account balance	31.4
Official settlements account balance	44.2
Statistical discrepancy	(−) 13.2
Overall Balance of Payments	0

[a]Debits (−)

SOURCE: Council of Economic Advisers, *Economic Indicators* (Washington, D.C.: Government Printing Office, March 1993), 36–37.

capital account and the official settlements account. The current account deficits and the capital account surpluses have been large ever since 1983.

The current account deficit resulted primarily from a $96 billion balance of trade deficit, which was split fairly evenly between the industrialized market economies ($-\$48$ billion) and all other countries ($-\$49$ billion). Nearly all of the balance of trade deficit with the industrialized countries was accounted for by Japan ($-\$50$ billion). Otherwise, the United States had a small trade deficit with Canada ($-\$11$ billion) and small trade surpluses with Western Europe ($\$6$ billion) and Australia, New Zealand, and South Africa ($\$11$ billion, combined). The main difference in this breakdown over the preceding seven years was with Western Europe. The United States had a small trade deficit with Western Europe through 1989 and a small trade surplus since 1990.

Regarding the other countries, the United States had balance of trade deficits with both the members of the Organization of Petroleum Exporting Countries (OPEC) ($-\$12$ billion) and all the other middle- and low-income countries ($-\$37$ billion). This has also been true since 1986.

The large, offsetting net capital inflows since 1983 have turned the United States from a large creditor nation into the largest debtor nation. A nation is a **creditor** if the market value of assets that its citizens hold abroad exceeds the market value of assets that foreign citizens hold in the nation. Conversely, a nation is a **debtor** if the market value of assets that its citizens hold abroad is less than the market value of assets that foreign citizens hold in the nation. In 1983 the market value of assets that U.S. citizens held abroad totaled $1,069 billion, and the market value of assets that foreign citizens held in the United States totaled $801 billion. The United States was a creditor in the amount of $268 billion ($268 = $1,069 − $801). By 1991 the market value of assets that U.S. citizens held abroad had grown to $2,107 billion. But the market value of assets that foreign citizens held in the United States had grown even more because of the huge annual capital inflows, to $2,489 billion. The United States was a debtor in the amount of $382 billion ($382 = $2,489 − $2,107).[4]

Foreign residents have clearly been willing to hold dollar assets in the United States. The outstanding question though, as noted above, is how much longer they will be willing to accumulate these assets before they cash them in to consume goods and services. The U.S. current account deficit and capital account surplus will reverse themselves when the foreign residents decide to cash in.

CREDITOR NATION

A nation for which the market value of the assets that its citizens hold abroad exceeds the market value of the assets that foreign citizens hold in the nation.

DEBTOR NATION

A nation for which the market value of the assets that its citizens hold abroad is less than the market value of the assets that foreign citizens hold in the nation.

EXCHANGE RATE SYSTEMS

Having described the main kinds of international transactions, we are now in a position to compare and contrast how fixed and flexible exchange rate systems coordinate these transactions. The exchange of foreign currency is part and parcel of all international transactions, and the exchange rate systems that nations choose dictate how the foreign exchange markets operate. Let's begin with the flexible exchange rate system, since this is the system that the United States has used to exchange dollars for foreign currencies ever since 1973.

---

[4]The historical data on the balance of payments, and the asset holdings, are from Council of Economic Advisers, *Economic Report of the President 1993* (Washington, D.C.: U.S. Government Printing Office, 1993), Table B-99, p. 461 (asset holdings), and Table B-100, p. 462 (balance of payments).

Flexible Exchange Rates

Foreign exchange markets are highly competitive by nature. Large numbers of buyers and sellers meet in these markets, and the individual markets located in the major cities throughout the world are all interconnected electronically to form one worldwide market. Transactors have excellent, up-to-the-minute information about the exchange rates between any two currencies. As a result, exchange rates are determined by the Laws of Supply and Demand so long as central banks choose not to intervene. This is precisely what happens under a flexible, or floating, exchange rate system in its purest form. The supplies and the demands for any one currency are those of private individuals and business firms and of government agencies other than central banks. The central bankers agree to let their currencies take on whatever values are consistent with the equilibrium between supply and demand.

Figure 21.1 illustrates how the Laws of Supply and Demand determine the exchange rate between dollars and British pounds. The quantity of pounds is on the horizontal axis, and the exchange rate in terms of dollars per pound is on the vertical axis.

The demand curve for pounds, $D_£$, comes from people with dollars who want to exchange them for pounds. They might be British exporters to the United States who want to exchange the dollars that they receive from their U.S. customers for pounds so that they can return the funds to England. Or they might be U.S. pension fund managers who want pounds to buy British financial securities or real estate in London. The demand curve is downward sloping in terms of dollars per pound. The more dollars that people have to exchange

FIGURE 21.1

Flexible Exchange Rates

The value of exchange rates is determined by the Laws of Supply and Demand in a flexible exchange rate system. In the figure, the quantity of pounds sterling exchanged, $£$, is the horizontal axis and the exchange rate in terms of dollar per pound, $\$/£$, is on the vertical axis. The demand curve for pounds, $D_£$, comes from sources such as British importers selling in the United States who want to convert the dollars they receive into pounds, or U.S. citizens who want pounds to buy British financial securities. The supply curve for pounds, $S_£$, comes from sources such as U.S. exporters selling in England who want to convert the pounds they receive into dollars, or from British citizens who want dollars to buy U.S. financial securities. The equilibrium exchange rate is $\$1.60/£$, at the intersection of $D_£$ and $S_£$, and $£_0$ pounds are exchanged for dollars in the foreign exchange markets.

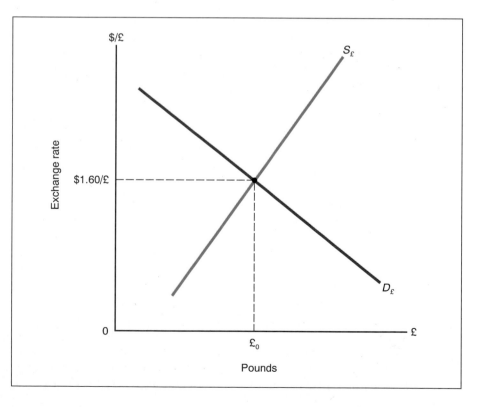

per pound—that is, the greater the dollar price of a pound—the smaller the quantity of pounds demanded. The fewer dollars that people have to exchange per pound—that is, the lower the dollar price of a pound—the larger the quantity of pounds demanded.

The supply curve for pounds, $S_£$, comes from people with pounds who want to exchange them for dollars. They might be U.S. exporters to London who want to exchange the pounds that they receive from their British customers for dollars so that they can return the funds to the United States. Or they might be British pension fund managers who want dollars to buy U.S. financial securities or real estate in New York City. The supply curve is upward sloping in terms of dollars per pound. The more dollars that people receive per pound—that is, the greater the dollar price of a pound, the larger the quantity of pounds supplied. The fewer dollars that people receive per pound—that is, the lower the dollar price of a pound, the smaller the quantity of pounds supplied.

The equilibrium value of the exchange rates occurs at the intersection of the demand and the supply curves. According to Figure 21.1, the equilibrium exchange rate is \$1.60/£, with $£_0$ pounds exchanged in the foreign exchange markets.

A word on point of view is in order before continuing. The demand curve for pounds is equivalent to the supply curve of dollars because anyone with dollars who wants to buy pounds is simultaneously a supplier of dollars in the foreign exchange markets. Similarly, the supply curve of pounds is equivalent to the demand curve for dollars because anyone who wants to supply pounds for dollars is simultaneously a demander of dollars in the foreign exchange markets. Therefore, we could have represented the exchange between dollars and pounds in terms of the supply and demand for dollars. The quantity of dollars exchanged would be on the horizontal axis, and the exchange rate in terms of pounds per dollar would be on the vertical axis. The analysis of the dollar-pound exchange rate would be the same with either diagram. For example, the diagram in terms of dollars would establish an equilibrium exchange rate of .625£/\$, the inverse of \$1.60/£. We will continue to use Figure 21.1 to analyze exchange rates under a flexible exchange rate system.

The analysis of a single exchange rate is somewhat misleading because exchange rates are not free to take on any values whatsoever. The exchange rates between different currencies must bear a particular relationship to one another. Exchange rates must also reflect the relative prices of traded goods within each country.

RELATIVE EXCHANGE RATES: ARBITRAGE   Regarding the relationship between exchange rates, suppose that the exchange rate between dollars and pounds is \$2/£ and the exchange rate between the German mark (DM) and the dollar is 2DM/\$. Then the exchange rate between the German mark and the pound must be 4DM/£. A mark-pound exchange rate at any other value would make arbitrage possible.

Arbitrage refers to buying and selling commodities whose prices are out of line in such a way as to guarantee a profit. It is not a gamble. To see how arbitrage works, suppose that the mark-pound exchange rate were 5DM/£, with the other exchange rates as listed above. Anyone could make a sure-fire profit. For example, a U.S. citizen could take \$2.00 and buy 1£, then sell the pound

ARBITRAGE

The buying and selling of commodities whose prices are out of line in such a way as to guarantee a profit.

for 5DM, and then sell the 5DM at 2DM/1$ for $2.50. The round trip in currencies has turned $2.00 into $2.50, guaranteed. These arbitrage transactions increase the demand for pounds and the supply of marks, both of which decrease the value of the mark relative to the pound. The possibility for arbitrage ends when the mark-pound exchange rate falls to 4DM/£.[5]

Most large financial institutions such as brokerage houses and commercial banks employ arbitrageurs whose job is to keep a close watch on exchange rates throughout the day and engage in arbitrage transactions when any two exchange rates are out of line. The actions of the arbitrageurs serve to keep all exchange rates tightly related to one another at all times. Profitable opportunities from misaligned exchange rates are immediately competed away.

RELATIVE EXCHANGE RATES: PURCHASING POWER PARITY   Regarding the relationship between exchange rates and the prices of traded goods, exchange rates should reflect the principle of purchasing power parity (PPP). The idea is that traded goods must cost the same in all countries where they are sold, except for transactions and transportation costs. For example, suppose that a traded good has a price of $1.50 in the United States and 1£ in England. Assuming that the good is costless to transport from one country to the other, the dollar-pound exchange rate must be $1.50/£. Any other exchange rate would lead to arbitrage in the good; anyone could make a profit by purchasing the good in one country and selling it in the other.

To see why, suppose that the exchange rate was $2/£. A U.S. citizen could buy the good in the United States for $1.50, ship it to England and sell it there for 1£, then sell the £ for $2 in the foreign exchange market. The original $1.50 has grown to $2. The demand for the good in the United States would raise its price there until it was $2. Now the relative prices of the good in the United States and England match the exchange rate, $2/£, and arbitrage is no longer possible.

Many goods are traded between countries. Also, the relationship between traded and nontraded goods ought to be approximately the same in every country. Therefore, **purchasing power parity** relates to an overall price index of goods in two countries, such as the GDP deflator. It says, for example, that the overall U.S. price index, P_{US}, must equal the overall British price index, P_{Eng}, multiplied by the dollar-pound exchange rate, e.

$$P_{US} = e \cdot P_{Eng}$$

Purchasing power parity ties down the absolute value of exchange rates, and not just their relative values. For example, it says that a doubling of prices in the United States must depreciate the dollar by half its value (that is, double the amount of dollars needed to buy a pound).

Purchasing power parity cannot be expected to hold as tightly as does the relationship between two or more exchange rates described above. Any number of economic events cause exchange rates to move up and down, as we will see in a moment. Goods prices also change over time, but they are much stickier than exchange rates are, which can change frequently even during the course

PURCHASING POWER PARITY

The principle that the overall price index of one country must equal the overall price index of any other country multiplied by the exchange rate of the first country's currency to the second country's currency.

---

[5]The dollar-mark and dollar-pound exchange rates may also change because of the arbitrage and establish a final equilibrium between the three currencies at different ratios than in our example. We have ignored this possibility to illustrate as simply as possible how arbitrage restores the proper equilibrium.

of a day. Also, the relationship between traded and nontraded goods might not be the same in every country. Finally, arbitrage in goods is more costly, more time consuming, and less certain than is arbitrage in exchange rates.

For all these reasons, economists expect purchasing power parity to hold approximately over the long run, but not necessarily in the short run. This appears to be the case. Recent studies have found that purchasing power parity holds reasonably well for the major currencies over a long run of about three to five years' duration, but not at all for shorter time periods.[6]

CHANGES IN EXCHANGE RATES   The exchange rate in Figure 21.1 changes whenever anything causes the demand curve or the supply curve to shift. The principal shifters of currency demand and currency supply curves are changes in factors that directly affect the demand or the supply of exports or imports, changes in the state of the economy, changes in interest rates in either country, and changes in the expected future values of the exchange rate.

FACTORS AFFECTING EXPORTS AND IMPORTS   Two obvious factors that have a direct impact on a nation's imports and exports are changes in tastes for traded goods and productivity changes that lower the costs and the prices of traded goods.

Suppose that British clothing becomes the new fad in the United States, so that the demand for imports from England increases. Refer to Figure 21.2(a). The curves $D_£^0$ and $S_£^0$ are the demand and the supply curves before the fad hits. The original exchange rate is \$1.60/£, just as in Figure 21.1. Once the fad hits the United States, the British clothing exporters selling in the United States have many more dollars, some of which they want to exchange for pounds to bring the funds to England. The demand for pounds increases from $D_£^0$ to $D_£^1$, and the new equilibrium exchange rate is at the intersection of $D_£^1$ and $S_£^0$. The dollar depreciates in value from \$1.60/£ to \$1.80/£.

In general, *an increase in the demand for imports increases the demand for foreign currency and depreciates the value of a nation's currency.* A clear example of this principle has been the great increase in demand for Japanese cars and consumer electronic products in the United States. The result has been a steady depreciation of the dollar against the yen over time. In 1972 a dollar traded for 303 yen in the foreign exchange markets; by the summer of 1993 a dollar traded for just over 100 yen.[7]

Productivity changes have a direct impact on the demand for traded goods. For example, rapid technological change in the production of personal computers has sharply lowered the costs of a given amount of computing power. The cost-reducing technological changes have increased the demand for U.S. personal computers in England. Figure 21.2(b) shows effects of the technological change on the dollar-pound exchange rate.

$D_£^0$ and $S_£^0$ are the demand and the supply curves for pounds before the technological change. The original exchange rate is \$1.60/£, as in Figure 21.2(a). This time U.S. exporters selling personal computers in England have

[6]See J. Whitt, Jr., "The Long-Run Behavior of the Real Exchange Rate: A Reconsideration," *Journal of Money, Credit and Banking* 24, No. 1 (February 1992): 72–81 (3-year estimate); and M. Manzer, "An International Comparison of Prices and Exchange Rates: A New Test of Purchasing Power Parity," *Journal of International Money and Finance* 9 (1990): 75–91 (5-year estimate).
[7]*Economic Report of the President 1993*, Table B-107, p. 470.

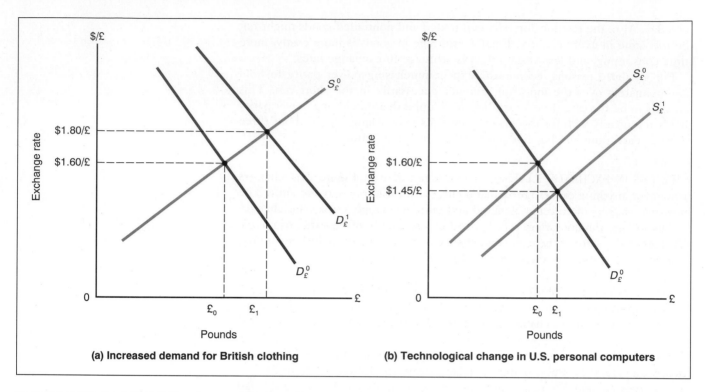

(a) Increased demand for British clothing

(b) Technological change in U.S. personal computers

FIGURE 21.2

The Demand for Imports, Technological Change, and Exchange Rates

The figure illustrates two events that would change the exchange rate between the dollar and the pound, an increase in the demand for British clothing by U.S. consumers, and technological change in the production of U.S. personal computers. The initial equilibrium in each figure before the events occur is at the intersection of $D_£^0$ and $S_£^0$. The exchange rate is \$1.60/£ and $£_0$ pounds are exchanged for dollars in the foreign exchange markets. In Figure 21.2(a), the increased demand for British clothing in the U.S. increases the demand for pounds from $D_£^0$ to $D_£^1$, as British importers in the United States have more dollars that they want to exchange for pounds. The new equilibrium is at the intersection of $D_£^1$ and $S_£^0$. The increase in the demand for British imports causes the dollar to depreciate to \$1.80/£, and increases the quantity of pounds exchanged to $£_1$. In Figure 21.2(b), the technological change in U.S. personal computers makes them more desirable to British consumers, so exports of U.S. personal computers to England increase. The supply of pounds increases from $S_£^0$ to $S_£^1$, as U.S. exporters in England have more pounds that they want to exchange for dollars. The new equilibrium is at the intersection of $D_£^0$ and $S_£^1$. The technological change causes the dollar to appreciate to \$1.45/£, and increases the quantity of pounds exchanged to $£_1$.

more pounds that they want to exchange for dollars in order to bring the funds back to the United States. The supply of pounds increases from $S_£^0$ to $S_£^1$, and the new equilibrium exchange rate is at the intersection of $D_£^0$ and $S_£^1$. The dollar appreciates in value from \$1.60/£ to \$1.45/£.

In general, *an increase in the demand for a nation's exports increases the supply of foreign currency and appreciates the value of the nation's currency.* Increases in productivity are an important factor tending to increase the demand for exports. The purchasing power parity principle indicates that the increases in productivity do not have to be specifically in the export goods in order to appreciate the currency. Productivity changes that reduce costs and prices in any industry have the same effect. In the PPP relationship above a reduction in P_{US} reduces e, the dollar per pound exchange rate.[8]

CHANGES IN AGGREGATE DEMAND   Changes in aggregate demand change the level of real national income or output and the rate of inflation. Both effects feed back into the value of the exchange rate.

For example, an increase in aggregate demand increases real national income. It also increases the rate of inflation as the economy moves along the short-run Phillips Curve. Both effects tend to depreciate the value of the currency.

The increase in national income increases the demand for imports through the marginal propensity to import. The higher income induces consumers to buy more foreign goods and induces producers to buy more foreign material inputs and capital goods in order to increase production. We have just seen that an increase in the demand for imports increases the demand for foreign currency and depreciates the value of a nation's currency.

The increase in inflation simultaneously makes imports more attractive and exports less attractive. The increased demand for imports increases the demand for foreign currency, and the decreased demand for exports decreases the supply of foreign currency. The nation's currency depreciates in value as both the demand curve and the supply curve shift up. This is another instance of the purchasing power parity principle at work. Any change in the overall price level must feed directly through to the exchange rate.

CHANGES IN INTEREST RATES   Changes in interest rates have an immediate impact on the exchange rate. We described this effect in the macroeconomic chapters of the text. The idea is that money managers shop worldwide for the best returns on their funds. When U.S. interest rates rise, money managers in London, Tokyo, and Bonn want to place more funds in U.S. financial securities. To do this, however, they must first obtain dollars on the foreign exchange market, so the demand for dollars increases and the dollar appreciates in value. Figure 21.2(b) applies to the increase in U.S. interest rates. An increase in demand for dollars by British money managers is equivalent to an increase in the supply of pounds because they want to exchange pounds for dollars. The supply curve, S, shifts out, as in the figure, and the dollar appreciates in value.

Conversely, a decrease in U.S. interest rates depreciates the value of the dollar. This time Figure 21.2(a) applies. Money managers want to shift their funds out of U.S. financial securities and into British, Japanese, and German financial securities. The demand for pounds and other foreign currencies increases, and the dollar depreciates in value.

EXPECTED FUTURE CHANGES IN EXCHANGE RATES   Some people enter the foreign exchange markets as speculators. They try to earn a profit by guessing what the value of exchange rates will be sometime in the future.

Speculation differs from arbitrage in two ways. First, arbitrage is guaranteed to earn a profit, whereas speculation is a gamble. Speculators win if they guess

---

[8]Recall, also, the U.S./British example illustrating Ricardo's model of comparative advantage in Chapter 20 where we showed what values the exchange rates could have. If U.S. labor were twice as productive, so that the goods' prices were half as large, the values of the exchange rates would also be half as large. The dollar would appreciate in value.

right and lose if they guess wrong. Second, arbitrage keeps exchange rates in the proper alignment with one another and thereby stabilizes foreign exchange markets. Speculation may also help to stabilize foreign exchange markets. But it can just as easily destabilize foreign exchange markets by causing large, volatile swings in exchange rates. For this reason, exchanges of currency motivated by speculation are commonly referred to as "hot" money.

To see the possibilities of stabilizing and destabilizing speculation, return to the example above of an increase in the demand for British imports, illustrated by Figure 21.2(a). The increased demand for imports shifts up the demand for pounds, and the dollar depreciates from $1.60/£ to $1.80/£. The speculators see the dollar depreciating and try to guess what it will do in the future—say, one year from now. Suppose that they believe that the surge in import demand is temporary, so they guess that the dollar will appreciate back to $1.60/£ one year from now. The way to earn a profit based on this guess is to exchange pounds for dollars now at $1.80/£ when the dollar is relatively cheap. Then they can sell the dollars back for pounds one year from now at $1.60/£ when the pound is relatively cheap. The $1.80 received for each pound now will buy more than 1£ one year from now if the speculators have guessed correctly.

This speculation is stabilizing. It creates a demand for dollars, or a supply of pounds, now when the dollar is depreciating. The supply curve for pounds, S_L, shifts out, and the exchange rate quickly moves back to $1.60/£. The speculation has kept the dollar close to its initial value. Notice, also, that the speculation becomes a self-fulfilling prophecy. The guess that the dollar will appreciate in the future generates the demand for dollars (supply of pounds) that causes the dollar to appreciate.

Unfortunately, the self-fulfilling prophecy of speculation can also be tremendously destabilizing. Continuing with the same example, suppose that when the speculators see the dollar depreciating from $1.60/£ to $1.80/£, they guess that the dollar will continue to depreciate—say, to $2.00/£ one year from now. This time the way to make a profit on the guess is to buy pounds with dollars for $1.80/£ when the pound is relatively cheap. Then they can sell the pounds back for dollars one year from now at $2.00/£ when the dollar is relatively cheap. The $1.80 used to buy each pound now will grow to $2.00 one year from now if the speculators have guessed correctly.

This speculation is destabilizing. It adds to the increased demand for pounds by the British importers, shifts D_L up further, and causes the dollar to depreciate beyond $1.80/£. Having seen the dollar depreciate even more, what do the speculators guess now? They could revise their expectations upward beyond $2.00/£, which increases the demand for pounds even more and further depreciates the dollar. There is no natural stopping point to the speculation. The upward revision of expectations could easily feed on itself and drive the dollar-pound exchange rate wildly upward.

MANAGED EXCHANGE RATES   The possibility of destabilizing speculation is an extremely serious threat to a flexible exchange rate system. International trade cannot flourish in an environment of wildly fluctuating exchange rates driven by the psychology of speculation. It is for this reason more than any other that central banks have chosen to intervene in the foreign exchange markets from time to time, creating a hybrid exchange rate system called the **managed,** or **"dirty," float.**

MANAGED EXCHANGE RATE ("DIRTY" FLOAT)

A variation of a flexible exchange rate system in which an exchange rate is determined by the Laws of Supply and Demand within a band of values selected by the central banks; alternatively, a variation of a flexible exchange rate system in which the central banks occasionally intervene in the foreign exchange markets in order to prevent their currencies from appreciating or depreciating "too much."

In one version of a managed float the central banks allow the exchange rates of the major currencies to move within a fairly wide band—say, plus or minus 10 percent of their current values—in order to take advantage of the Laws of Supply and Demand. Once an exchange rate hits either the upper or the lower limit of the band, however, the central banks intervene to keep the exchange rate within the band. The intervention prevents a destabilizing speculative psychology from taking hold of the foreign exchange markets.

In terms of our example, suppose that the Fed and the Bank of London agree to allow the dollar to depreciate from $1.60/£ to $1.80/£, but no further. Thus, $1.80/£ is the upper limit on the dollar-pound exchange rate band. At this point both central banks agree to supply whatever amount of pounds is needed to keep the exchange rates from rising above $1.80/£. The message to the speculators is clear: Do not expect a further depreciation of the dollar in the future. Now that the speculators have no reason to buy pounds, D_L does not increase further, and the exchange rate stays at $1.80/£.

The central banks do not need anything as formal as an announced band to prevent destabilizing speculation. All they need do to forestall a destabilizing speculation is to make clear their intention to intervene to prevent exchange rates from moving "too far" in either direction. An occasional intervention from time to time gives the central banks credibility. This more casual form of the managed float is the one that the Fed and the other central banks have employed since 1973 when the dollar was set free to fluctuate.

A key issue is how wide the bands should be or, alternatively, how far is "too far" under the more casual managed float. Allow the exchange rates to fluctuate within a wide range and the managed float is not much different from a pure flexible exchange rate system. The exchange rates between the major currencies may fluctuate quite a bit. Alternatively, set a narrow band explicitly or implicitly and the managed float is not much different from a fixed exchange rate system. It will require frequent interventions by the central banks.

The Fed has allowed the dollar to fluctuate substantially since 1973. Table 21.2 shows the average value of the dollar each year relative to an index of the major currencies. The data in the table are expressed as an index, with the relative value

TABLE 21.2 **Index of Dollar Exchange Rate Against the Major Currencies**[a]
(March 1973 = 100)

1973	98.9	1983	117.3
1974	99.4	1984	128.8
1975	94.1	1985	132.4
1976	97.6	1986	103.6
1977	93.3	1987	90.9
1978	84.4	1988	88.2
1979	83.2	1989	94.4
1980	84.9	1990	86.0
1981	100.9	1991	86.5
1982	111.8	1992	83.3

[a]The value of the dollar is a trade-weighted average of exchange rates against a broad range of currencies, adjusted by changes in consumer prices.

SOURCE: Council of Economic Advisers, *Economic Report of the President 1993* (Washington, D.C.: U.S. Government Printing Office, 1993), 470, Table B-107.

of the dollar in March 1973 chosen as the benchmark and set equal to 100. The relative values are in real terms; they correct for changes in consumer prices within each country in line with the purchasing power parity idea.

The table shows that the dollar has been quite volatile since 1973. It has undergone three long swings: depreciating fairly sharply in the late 1970s, then appreciating even more sharply through 1985, and then depreciating sharply again through 1992. It has also danced around a lot from year to year; annual changes of 10 percent and more have been fairly common.

Changes of this magnitude are somewhat surprising, given that the international economy is riddled with trade restrictions. We saw in Chapter 20 how nations have tried to restrict imports through tariffs and other nontariff barriers to prevent deficits in their current accounts. The industrial nations have also resorted to various kinds of capital controls to restrict the movement of destabilizing "hot" money through the foreign exchange markets. The capital controls most commonly take the form of preventing foreign financial institutions from operating in domestic capital markets. The industrial nations have also resorted to special taxes on capital outflows to try to discourage them. Nonetheless, neither the restrictions on trade and capital flows nor the occasional intervention of the central banks has prevented the dollar from fluctuating widely against the other major currencies. The other factors that influence exchange rates—changes in tastes, worldwide productivity growth, the state of the industrial economies, interest rates, and speculation—appear to have dominated the various trade restrictions and central bank interventions in determining the value of the dollar in the foreign exchange markets.

Many economists believe that changes in the dollar of these magnitudes are not healthy for international trade. Although world trade has grown considerably since 1973, they point out that world trade grew even more rapidly under the Bretton Woods fixed exchange rate system. They prefer a return to fixed exchange rates, which we turn to next.

Fixed Exchange Rate System

Under a fixed exchange rate system the nations agree to fix the exchange rates at a given set of values. Then the central banks intervene in the foreign exchange markets as need be to maintain the fixed values. The official settlements account becomes a crucial part of a nation's balance of payments transactions.

Figure 21.3 illustrates how a fixed exchange rate system operates. It is based on the earlier examples illustrated in Figure 21.2. Refer, first, to Figure 21.3(a).

Suppose that the dollar-pound exchange rate is fixed, or pegged, at \$1.60/£ and that this exchange rate is consistent with the demand for and the supply of pounds in the foreign exchange markets. The initial demand and supply curves, $D_£^0$ and $S_£^0$, intersect at \$1.60/£, as before. The quantity of pounds exchanged is $£_0$.

An increase in the demand for British clothing increases the demand for pounds from $D_£^0$ to $D_£^1$, also as before. Under a fixed exchange rate system, however, the dollar cannot depreciate in value to clear the foreign exchange market. Instead, the Fed is committed to supply whatever pounds are necessary to meet the increased demand at the fixed, \$1.60/£ exchange rate. The

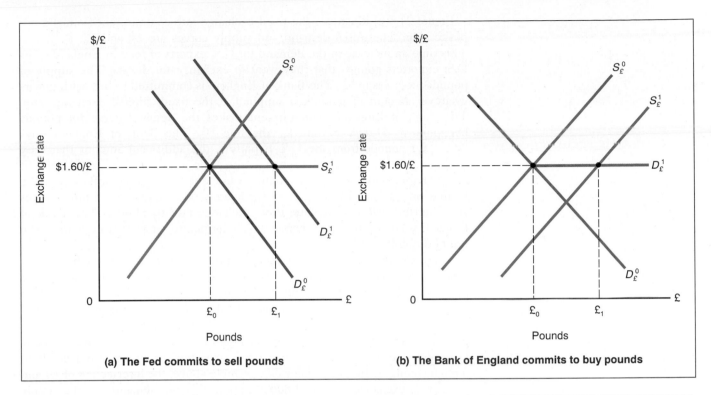

(a) The Fed commits to sell pounds   (b) The Bank of England commits to buy pounds

Under a fixed exchange rate system, nations agree to fix the exchange rates between their currencies and the central banks make a commitment to buy or sell currencies as needed to maintain the values of the exchange rates. The figure assumes that the United States and England have agreed to fix the dollar-pound exchange rate at $1.60/£, which is the current value of the exchange rate in the private foreign exchange markets. The private demand curve for pounds, $D_£^0$, and the private supply curve for pounds, $S_£^0$, intersect at $1.60/£. In Figure 21.2(a), an increase in the demand for British imports in the United States increases the demand for pounds from $D_£^0$ to $D_£^1$, which would depreciate the value of the dollar. The Fed is commited, however, to supply whatever pounds are needed in exchange for dollars to keep the dollar at $1.60/£. The Fed's commitment makes the supply of pounds perfectly elastic at $1.60/£, the supply curve $S_£^1$. $£_1$ pounds are exchanged for dollars in the foreign exchange markets, at the intersection of $D_£^1$ and $S_£^1$, with the Fed supplying $(£_1 - £_0)$ pounds. In Figure 21.2(b), an increase in the demand for U.S. exports in England increases the supply of pounds from $S_£^0$ to $S_£^1$, which would appreciate the value of the dollar. The Bank of England is commited, however, to buy whatever pounds are needed with dollars to keep the exchange rate at $1.60/£. The Bank of England's commitment makes the demand for pounds perfectly elastic at $1.60/£, the demand curve $D_£^1$. $£_1$ pounds are exchanged for dollars in the foreign exchange markets, at the intersection of $D_£^1$ and $S_£^1$, with the Bank of England buying $(£_1 - £_0)$ pounds.

FIGURE 21.3

Fixed Exchange Rates

Fed's commitment makes the supply curve horizontal at $1.60/£ beyond $£_0$, the line $S_£^1$. The Fed sells the importers $(£_1 - £_0)$ pounds, the additional amount that they demand at the fixed, $1.60/£ exchange rate. The same analysis would apply if the increase in the demand for pounds were due to a capital outflow from the United States to England or to speculators betting that the United States and England will soon revalue their exchange rate to $1.80/£. The Fed is committed to exchange pounds for dollars at $1.60/£ no matter who wants the pounds.

Figure 21.3(b) illustrates the fixed exchange rate commitment from the opposite side. The initial demand and supply curves are $D_\pounds^0$ and $S_\pounds^0$, as above. This time an increase in the demand for U.S. exports of food in England gives U.S. exporters pounds that they want to exchange for dollars. The supply of pounds increases to $S_\pounds^1$. The Bank of England is committed to buy with dollars whatever amount of pounds is supplied at the fixed, $1.60/\pounds$ exchange rate. The Bank of England's commitment makes the demand curve for pounds horizontal at $1.60/\pounds$ beyond $\pounds_0$, the line $D_\pounds^1$. The Bank of England buys $(\pounds_1 - \pounds_0)$ pounds from the U.S. exporters, the additional amount that they supply at the fixed, $1.60/\pounds$ exchange rate. The same analysis would apply if the increase in the supply of pounds were due to a capital inflow into the United States from England or to speculators betting that the United States and England will soon revalue their exchange rate to $1.40/\pounds$. The Bank of England is committed to exchange dollars for pounds at $1.60/\pounds$ no matter who wants the dollars.

These examples reveal two immediate problems with a fixed exchange rate system. First, nations must hold large amounts of foreign currencies to be able to honor their commitment to the fixed exchange rate. Second, the level at which the exchange rates are fixed or pegged is crucial to the continued operation of the system. We saw in Chapter 20 how an overvalued exchange rate can literally price a nation's goods out of international markets. Everyone in the nation wants to import foreign goods, and the nation's exporters cannot sell their goods in foreign countries. In terms of our first example above, the intersection of $D_\pounds^1$ and $S_\pounds^0$ is at an exchange rate of $1.80/\pounds$. Suppose that the demand and the supply curves remain there. The fixed exchange rate of $1.60/\pounds$ overvalues the dollar and forces the Fed to supply pounds forever. Something has to give because the Fed obviously cannot supply pounds forever.

We will uncover still another problem with fixed exchange rates below: Committing to a fixed exchange rate system sacrifices control of the domestic economy. The history of the United States under the Bretton Woods arrangement is instructive on all these points.

THE BRETTON WOODS SYSTEM   As noted in the introduction, 44 nations met at Bretton Woods, New Hampshire, in 1944 and agreed to a fixed exchange rate system centered on the dollar and gold. The dollar was pegged to gold at $35 per ounce. The United states had accumulated a huge stock of gold during the 1930s and agreed to exchange gold for dollars on demand at the pegged rate. The other nations then pegged their currencies either to the dollar or to gold. All nations wanted to avoid the chaos in international trade and finance that existed during the 1930s. Bretton Woods marked the first time that the leading capitalist nations were able to agree formally on an exchange rate system.

Another notable accomplishment of the Bretton Woods meeting was the establishment of the **International Monetary Fund (IMF)** to act as a forum for resolving exchange rate and balance of payments problems. The IMF had to approve all changes in exchange rates greater than 10 percent. The IMF also took on the role of helping smaller nations through temporary current account deficits by lending them dollars and other currencies. The IMF never had enough lending authority to help one of the industrialized nations through a balance of payments crisis, however.

The Bretton Woods system worked beautifully at first. The United States poured military and economic assistance into Western Europe and elsewhere

INTERNATIONAL MONETARY FUND (IMF)

An international agency established in 1947 by the capitalist countries that acts as a forum for resolving exchange rate and balance-of-payments problems.

immediately after World War II. The aid generated huge deficits in the capital account and the military portion of the current account in the U.S. balance of payments. But the transfer mechanism worked well because the U.S. economy was virtually the only industrial economy unscathed by the war. Most of the aid dollars came right back to the United States through sales by U.S. exporters. The capital and military account deficits were offset by a huge surplus in the U.S. balance of trade. This situation persisted throughout the 1950s.

Once Western Europe (and Japan) started to recover from the war, the transfer mechanism worked less well. The U.S. aid and military dollars were increasingly spent in other countries, and the U.S. balance-of-trade surplus began to shrink. There was still no pressure on the Fed's international gold and currency reserves, however, because everyone was happy to have the dollars. The dollar had gained acceptance as an international currency that could be spent anywhere. Therefore, the injection of aid and military dollars had the effect of increasing the international supply of money, which gave the industrial nations much needed liquidity as their economies were recovering and growing. International trade flourished under the Bretton Woods system well into the 1960s.

We might also note that the IMF was reasonably successful in helping the smaller nations with their balance-of-payments problems. It even created a new reserve currency in 1967 called a **special drawing right (SDR),** which all central banks agreed to accept as an international reserve in their settlement accounts. Nations could buy SDRs with their currency and then trade the SDRs with central banks for dollars and other major currencies that they needed to settle current account deficits. The SDRs were originally valued at 1SDR = $1. Starting in 1974 their value was set at a weighted average of the dollar, pound, franc, mark, and yen. The IMF has changed the weights periodically since 1974.

SPECIAL DRAWING RIGHT (SDR)

A reserve currency created by the IMF and accepted by all central banks as an international reserve in their official settlement accounts; countries can purchase SDRs with their own currencies and then trade them to central banks for dollars and other major currencies as needed to settle current account deficits.

The first problems with the Bretton Woods system appeared in the late 1960s. The U.S. balance of trade surplus continued to shrink, and the Vietnam War brought another huge injection of dollars into the international economy. For the first time the supply of dollars exceeded the demand for dollars, and some nations began to exchange their dollars for their own currencies and for U.S. gold. The other industrialized nations also began to resent the political power that the dollar's role as an international currency gave to the United States. The United States could send dollars anywhere with impunity.

By 1970 it was clear that the dollar was highly overvalued. It also became clear that there are no really good options under a fixed exchange rate system when a key currency becomes overvalued.

"SOLUTIONS" TO MISALIGNED CURRENCIES   One obvious "solution" was to devalue the dollar relative to gold—say, to $70 an ounce. The devaluation would immediately depreciate the dollar relative to all other currencies, which would make U.S. exports more competitive again and at the same time reduce U.S. imports. The improvement in the balance of trade would relieve some of the pressure on the dollar. The problem with this solution is that it creates the closest thing to a sure bet for the speculators. Upon learning that the United States was about to devalue, the speculators would try to buy up all the Fed's international reserves with dollars and then sell the reserves back to the Fed for dollars after the devaluation. The rush to buy international reserves would force the devaluation and earn enormous profits for the speculators. No one wanted to play into the hands of the speculators, so this "solution" was essentially ruled out.

Another "solution" that no one wanted was to increase trade restrictions and capital controls. The General Agreement on Tariffs and Trade (GATT) was pushing for freer trade and capital movements. The international economy already had too many trade restrictions and capital controls.

A third solution was for the United States to rein in its economy by lowering aggregate demand. This would reduce U.S. imports and improve the balance of trade, thereby lessening the pressure on the Fed's international reserves.

The reduction in aggregate demand begins automatically when the Fed exchanges gold or foreign currencies for dollars and dollar deposits. The sale of these assets for dollars or checks written against deposit accounts held by foreigners in U.S. banks removes dollars from circulation and reduces bank reserves. The effect is the same as a sale of Treasury securities by the Fed on the Open Market. The U.S. money supply decreases in either case, which leads to a decrease in aggregate demand.

The Fed may not want U.S. international transactions dictating the course of overall aggregate demand, however. If not, it can counter the decrease in the money supply caused by the loss of international reserves by purchasing an equal amount of Treasury securities on the Open Market. This is called a **sterilizing transaction** by the Fed because it is designed to leave the money supply constant. But if the Fed sterilizes the loss of international reserves, aggregate demand remains constant, the balance of trade does not improve, and the pressures on the Fed's international reserves continue apace.

Still another option is for the other industrial nations with balance of trade surpluses to stimulate their economies, which would increase U.S. exports. It would also reduce the other nations' exports if stimulating aggregate demand increases their rates of inflation. The other nations have no particular incentive to stimulate their economies, however. Under a fixed exchange rate system, only the deficit nations are under pressure to adjust their economies or risk losing all their international reserves. The surplus nations are gaining international reserves. They do not have to stimulate their economies if they do not want to. The purchase of international reserves by their central banks does automatically increase their money supplies and stimulate their economies. But they can also sterilize this effect just as easily as the Fed can sterilize in the other direction.

In any event, the United States decided by the early 1970s that the Bretton Woods system was no longer tenable. President Nixon unilaterally suspended convertibility of the dollar into gold in 1971 and then set the dollar free to float in 1973. Most economists believe that the fixed exchange rate system would not have survived the OPEC increase in oil prices that began in 1974 no matter what the United States had chosen to do.

Macroeconomic Policy and Exchange Rate Systems

The final point to make about choosing an exchange rate system is that the macroeconomic policy options are quite different under fixed and flexible exchange rates. Under flexible exchange rates, monetary policy is effective in controlling aggregate demand, whereas fiscal policy is relatively ineffective. Under fixed exchange rates, fiscal policy is effective in controlling aggregate

STERILIZING TRANSACTION

A transaction by a central bank that is designed to offset the effect on the money supply caused by any transaction on the official settlements account; an example is the Fed's sales of Treasury securities on the Open Market to offset its purchases of foreign currencies.

demand, whereas monetary policy is completely ineffective. These statements assume a Keynesian world of sticky wages and prices and unemployed resources in the short run.

FLEXIBLE EXCHANGE RATES

FISCAL POLICY We saw in Chapter 17 that the effectiveness of fiscal policy in controlling demand is greatly reduced by the crowding-out effect through net exports. To review, an expansionary fiscal policy increases aggregate demand and interest rates. The increase in interest rates attracts foreign funds, which have to be converted into dollars to enter the U.S. financial markets. The increased demand for dollars causes the dollar to appreciate in value, which reduces the demand for exports and increases the demand for imports. The reduction in net exports (exports − imports) reduces aggregate demand and offsets some or all of the stimulating effect of the expansionary fiscal policy.

The analysis applies in reverse for a contractionary fiscal policy. The reduction of interest rates leads to an outflow of dollars, which depreciates the dollar and increases net exports. The increase in net exports offsets some or all of the contractionary fiscal policy.

MONETARY POLICY Monetary policy is effective in controlling aggregate demand because interest rates move in the opposite direction from fiscal policy. An increase in the money supply increases aggregate demand and decreases interest rates. The decrease in interest rates drives funds out of the United States to foreign markets looking for higher returns. The exchange of dollars for foreign currency causes the dollar to depreciate in value, which increases the demand for exports and decreases the demand for imports. The increase in net exports supports the initial increase in aggregate demand instead of offsetting it.[9]

Conversely, a decrease in the money supply decreases aggregate demand and increases interest rates. The increase in interest rates attracts funds into the United States, which causes the dollar to appreciate in value. The appreciation of the dollar in turn causes a decrease in net exports, which supports the initial decrease in aggregate demand. Therefore, both increases and decreases in the money supply are effective in controlling aggregate demand in the short run.

FIXED EXCHANGE RATES

FISCAL POLICY Fiscal policy is effective in controlling aggregate demand under fixed exchange rates. The analysis begins the same way as under flexible exchange rates. The expansionary fiscal policy increases aggregate demand and increases interest rates. The increase in interest rates attracts foreign funds as before, but this time the Fed cannot let the dollar appreciate in value. Instead, it buys all the foreign currency offered with dollars at the fixed exchange rate. The purchase of the currencies increases the U.S. money supply, which sup-

---

[9]We saw in Chapter 19 that continued increases in the money supply at full employment, when real aggregate demand cannot increase, simply cause price inflation. The dollar depreciates point for point with the rate of inflation.

ports the initial increase in aggregate demand and returns the interest rates to their initial levels. There is no crowding-out effect through net exports (or through consumer durables and investment). The expansionary fiscal policy, combined with the induced increase in the money supply, leads to a multiplied increase in national income.

The same analysis applies in reverse. A contractionary fiscal policy reduces aggregate demand and begins to decrease U.S. interest rates. Funds leave the United States as investors seek higher returns elsewhere, and people sell dollars to the Fed for foreign currencies. The U.S. money supply decreases and drives interest rates back up to their initial levels. The contractionary fiscal policy, combined with the induced decrease in the money supply, leads to a multiplied decrease in national income. The key to the analysis is that the supply of funds to financial markets worldwide is perfectly elastic under fixed exchange rates (assuming no capital controls). Interest rates must be the same in all financial markets.

MONETARY POLICY Monetary policy is completely ineffective under fixed exchange rates. Suppose that the Fed increases the money supply by purchasing Treasury securities on the Open Market. An increase in the money supply begins to decrease interest rates, which drives funds out of the United States. People sell dollars to the Fed for foreign currencies, which reduces the money supply and restores the initial level of interest rates. The net result is no change in the money supply, no change in interest rates, and no change in aggregate demand. All the Fed has done is exchange Treasury securities for some of its international reserves. The same analysis applies in reverse. Under fixed exchange rates the Fed cannot increase or decrease the money supply if it is the central bank that buys and sells foreign currency to maintain the fixed exchange rate.

The only wrinkle in the analysis occurs if other central banks buy and sell foreign currency in order to maintain the fixed exchange rate. Return again to an increase in the money supply. This time, however, suppose that the Bank of England supplies the pounds that U.S. money managers want for their dollars in order to buy financial securities in London. The purchase of the dollars by the Bank of England increases the British money supply as it removes the dollars from circulation. The Bank of England will not want to keep the dollars, however, since they do not earn a rate of return. So the bank ships the dollars back to the Fed and instructs the Fed to buy Treasury securities on its behalf. Once the Fed buys the securities, the dollars return to circulation in the United States. The final effect is that both the U.S. and British money supplies have increased. The U.S. monetary policy is effective in increasing aggregate demand only if the British also increase their aggregate demand.

The general principle is that *the growth of the money supply must be the same in all countries that are tied together under fixed exchange rates.* No one country can independently change its money supply. Furthermore, we saw in Chapter 19 that the growth of the money supply determines the rate of inflation in the long run. Therefore, with the growth of the money supply equal everywhere under fixed exchange rates, *every country must have the same rate of inflation in the long run.*

In conclusion, governments have much more control over their internal economies with fiscal and monetary policies under a flexible exchange rate system than under a fixed exchange rate system. Under flexible exchange rates, monetary policy remains effective in controlling aggregate demand, and fiscal policy is partially effective. Under fixed exchange rates, fiscal policy remains effective in controlling aggregate demand, but governments lose independent control of their monetary policies. Also, without independent control of the money supply, governments cannot control the rate of inflation. Macroeconomic policies have to be coordinated across countries in the long run under fixed exchange rates.

These differences in macroeconomic policy options arise because of the different ways that the two exchange rate systems react to imbalances in international transactions. Under flexible exchange rates the exchange rate itself responds to current account or capital account surpluses or deficits according to the Laws of Supply and Demand. The appreciation and depreciation of the currencies protect the internal domestic macro economy somewhat from the international economy. In contrast, the entire economy has to adjust to current account or capital account surpluses or deficits when governments commit to fixed exchange rates.[10]

These policy differences are consistent with the philosophies underlying the two exchange rate systems. The fixed exchange rate system presumes that nations should first stabilize the international economy, which then forces them to keep their internal domestic economies in order and coordinated with one another. The flexible exchange rate system presumes that nations will strive to keep their internal domestic economies in order, which then tends to stabilize the exchange rates. Neither system is foolproof, as we have seen.

The ambivalence over which exchange rate system is best is reflected in the mix of fixed and flexible exchange rates in use throughout the world today. In 1984, 91 nations had pegged their exchange rates either to another currency or to a market basket of currencies, and 55 nations had flexible exchange rates. Generally speaking, the smaller, lower-income nations favor fixed exchange rates supported by strict controls on capital inflows and outflows. The larger, higher-income nations favor flexible exchange rates.[11]

The majority of economists believe that the larger industrial nations will continue to operate under flexible exchange rates. Pegging the major currencies at an appropriate level is chancy at best, and revaluing the major currencies once they have been pegged is difficult. Also, most of the industrial nations are not willing to give up the control over their internal domestic economies as they must under a fixed exchange rate system. The one exception has been the Western European nations of the European Community.

Exchange Rates within the European Community

The ambivalence toward exchange rate systems has been especially evident in Western Europe. The Western European nations floated their exchange rates in 1973 when the United States did. The flexible exchange rates lasted until

---

[10]The domestic economies are not entirely protected from the international economy under flexible exchange rates, however. We saw in earlier chapters how an appreciation of the dollar helps consumers because it makes imports cheaper, but hurts exporters and import-competing industries. Conversely, a depreciation of the dollar hurts consumers because it makes imports more expensive, but helps exporters and import-competing industries. These might be called the "micro" effects of flexible exchange rates.

[11]W. Enders and H. Lapan, *International Economics: Theory and Policy* (Englewood Cliffs, N.J.: Prentice-Hall, 1987), Table 23.1, pp. 510–511.

EXCHANGE RATE MECHANISM (ERM)

The dominant feature of the European Monetary System (EMS),which pegged the currencies of the Western European nations to the German mark.

1979, when they agreed to form a new European Monetary System (EMS). The heart of the EMS was the **Exchange Rate Mechanism,** which, for all intents and purposes, pegged all the currencies of Western Europe to the German mark.

OPEC had doubled the price of oil in 1979, setting off a surge of inflation throughout Europe and the United States. The Western Europeans feared that they would not have the discipline to fight the buildup of inflationary pressures and would lose control of their money supplies. They knew, however, that the Germans feared inflation more than did any other country, having experienced a disastrous hyperinflation following World War I. West Germany would certainly retain tight control of its money supply and fight off the inflation. Also, West Germany was by far the largest economy in Europe. Therefore, by pegging their currencies to the mark, the other nations were essentially pegging the growth in their money supplies to the growth in the German money supply. The West Germans' stand against inflation would force the other nations into the same posture. Pegging their currencies to the mark had the additional advantage of reducing exchange rate volatility throughout Europe, which had been considerable following the collapse of the Bretton Woods system.

The Exchange Rate Mechanism worked quite well. West Germany did hold fast against the inflationary pressures as expected, so that inflation remained under control in Europe throughout the 1980s. There were very few currency realignments until the early 1990s (see below).

Jacques Delors went even further in his 1985 White Paper. He envisioned a complete monetary union within the European Community by the turn of the century, with all nations using a single currency controlled by a Community-wide central bank, a true United States of Europe. The members of the European Community met in Maastricht in 1991 and set down a specific plan for moving to a single currency. Broadly speaking, the central bank of each nation would bear approximately the same relationship to the Community-wide central bank as the 12 Federal Reserve districts in the United States bear to the Board of Governors in Washington. At Maastricht the members also established economic conditions within each country that, if met, would allow them to join in the monetary union by 1996. The monetary union was to be completed by January 1, 1999, under any conditions.[12]

Most economists believe that the gains to moving from the Exchange Rate Mechanism to a single currency will be fairly small because the nations' macroeconomic policies are already closely coordinated and their currencies are fairly stable. The main benefit will come from eliminating the costs of currency exchanges, which are minor.

The issues connected with forming a monetary union may be moot, however. Many observers believe that the union will never come to pass, especially since Europe appears to be moving in the opposite direction.

The worldwide recession of the 1990s has brought severe strains to the Exchange Rate Mechanism. England and Italy dropped out of the EMS entirely in September of 1992. The precipitating event for them was Germany's decision in 1991 to reduce the growth of its money supply and increase interest rates in an effort to combat the inflationary pressures that had been building in the German economy following reunification. England and Italy did not

---

[12]This section is based on the excellent discussion of the plan for a monetary union in C. Bean, "Economic and Monetary Union in Europe," *Journal of Economic Perspectives* 6, No. 4 (Fall 1992): 31–52.

want to be forced to reduce the growth of their money supplies at a time when their economies were in the midst of a recession.

The German resolve to fight inflation put extreme pressure on the other countries as well. In August of 1993, the nations still in the EMS agreed to allow their currencies to float against the mark within a band of 15 percent in an attempt to gain more control over their economies. The original band had been just 2.25 percent. In short, Western Europe appears to be headed more in the direction of independent, floating exchange rates than in the direction of a monetary union.

CURRENT ISSUE: Norman Lamont, English Chancellor of the Exchequer in September 1992 when England dropped out of the EMS, believes that the dream of a monetary union is finished. Immediately following the loosening of the exchange rate band he was quoted as saying: "Maastricht is now dead. The prospects of a single currency have gone out the window." (*The Globe and Mail*, Toronto, August 3, 1993, B8.)

SUMMARY

Chapter 21 began with a discussion of the balance of payments, the accounting system that nations use to record their international transactions.

1. The balance of payments is a double-entry accounting of international credits and debits that must net to zero overall. An international credit (for the United States) is anything that gives rise to a demand for dollars (a supply of foreign currency). Examples are exports, capital inflows, and sales of foreign currency by the Fed. An international debit is anything that gives rise to a supply of dollars (a demand for foreign currency). Examples are imports, capital outflows, and purchases of foreign currency by the Fed.

2. The three subaccounts in the balance of payments are the current account, the capital account, and the official settlements account.

3. The current account records the flow of exports and imports of goods and services, the receipts and payments of factor incomes, and net unilateral transfers.
   a. The balance of trade is the difference between merchandise exports and imports.
   b. The balance of goods and services is the balance of trade plus exports minus imports of services plus receipts minus payments of factor income.
   c. The current account balance is the balance of goods and services minus net unilateral transfers.

4. A current account deficit means that foreign residents and central banks are accumulating dollars and dollar assets. A current account surplus means that U.S. residents and the Fed are accumulating foreign currencies and assets. Since people will not accumulate financial assets forever, a current account deficit must eventually become a current account surplus, and vice versa.

5. The capital account balance is the difference between capital inflows and capital outflows. Capital inflows are purchases of U.S. financial securities or loans to U.S. residents by foreign residents. Capital outflows are purchases of foreign securities or loans to foreign residents by U.S. residents.

6. The official settlements balance is the difference between the sale and the purchase of international reserves by the Fed. International reserves include foreign currencies, gold, and very short-term financial securities held by central banks.

7. Many of the entries in the capital account and the official settlements account are offsets to exports and imports in the current account.

8. The United States in recent years has had large current account deficits offset by large capital account and official settlement account surpluses. As a result, the United States has become the largest debtor nation; the value of U.S. assets held by foreign residents greatly exceeds the value of foreign assets held by U.S. residents.

The second section of Chapter 21 compared and contrasted the two basic exchange rate systems, flexible exchange rates and fixed exchange rates.

9. Under a flexible exchange rate system, a nation's exchange rate is determined by the Laws of Supply and Demand. The main factors determining the demands and the supplies of foreign currencies are tastes for traded goods and worldwide productivity changes, the state of the economy, interest rates, and speculation based on expectations of the future values of exchange rates.

10. Arbitrage of exchange rates keeps currencies in proper alignment with one another. Purchasing power parity fixes the absolute value of the exchange rates. It says that the exchange rate should reflect the ratio of prices within each country.

11. The United States has had a flexible exchange rate since 1973. The dollar has been quite volatile despite numerous trade and capital restrictions and despite occasional interventions by the Fed and other central banks to prevent the dollar from fluctuating "too much." A system of flexible exchange rates with occasional central bank intervention is called a managed, or "dirty," float.

12. Under a fixed exchange rate system, nations set their exchange rates at a given value, and the central banks commit to intervene in the foreign exchange markets in order to maintain the exchange rates at the set values.

13. The market economies agreed to adopt a fixed exchange rate system in 1944 at a meeting in Bretton Woods, New Hampshire. The dollar was pegged to gold at $35 an ounce, and the other currencies were pegged to the dollar or to gold. The Bretton Woods system survived until 1973 when the United States decided to switch to a flexible exchange rate.

14. Flexible and fixed exchange rates have very different macroeconomic implications. Under flexible exchange rates, fiscal policy is relatively ineffective, and monetary policy is effective in controlling aggregate demand in the short run. Under fixed exchange rates, fiscal policy is effective in controlling aggregate demand in the short run, but nations cannot pursue independent monetary policies or have separate rates of inflation.

15. The world today consists of a variety of exchange rates. Some nations have chosen a flexible exchange rate, some have pegged their currency to a major currency, and some have pegged their currency to a market basket of major currencies. For example, the United States and Japan have flexible exchange rates, whereas most of the Western European nations have pegged their exchange rates to the German mark within a narrow band.

KEY TERMS

arbitrage
autonomous capital inflow (or outflow)
balance of goods and services
balance of payments
balance of trade
capital account (balance of payments)
capital account balance
capital inflows
capital outflows

creditor nation
current account (balance of payments)
current account balance
debtor nation
direct foreign investment
eurodollar account
exchange rate mechanism
fixed exchange rate
flexible exchange rate

international credit
international debit
International Monetary Fund (IMF)
managed exchange rate ("dirty" float)
official settlements balance
purchasing power parity
special drawing right (SDR)
sterilizing transaction
transfer mechanism (international trade)

QUESTIONS

1. Indicate what balance-of-payments entries result from each of the following transactions, what subaccount each would appear in, and whether the transaction is a credit or a debit.
   a. IBM buys $500,000 worth of superconductors from a Japanese firm.
   b. A German investor buys $1 million worth of U.S. Treasury notes.
   c. The U.S. government loans the Indian government $10 million.
   d. An American tourist exchanges $1,000 for French francs at her local Federal Reserve Bank.
   e. An American firm sends $1 million worth of VCRs to Saudi Arabia in exchange for $1 million worth of oil.
2. Suppose that an American appliance dealer buys $500,000 worth of television sets from a Japanese firm. Name three possible credit transactions that might offset these imports in the balance-of-payments accounts, two in the capital account and one in the official settlements account.
3. a. Describe how the Bretton Woods system was instituted and how it operated.
   b. Instead of abandoning its fixed exchange rate in the early 1970s, why didn't the United States choose to devalue the dollar to improve its balance of trade?
   c. Why did the United States decide to abandon the Bretton Woods fixed exchange rate system in 1973?
4. Explain how the effectiveness of a nation's fiscal and monetary policies depends on whether it has a fixed or a flexible exchange rate.
5. Suppose that the exchange rates between the dollar, German mark, and British pound are as follows:

   $1/£   2DM/$ 4DM/£

   a. Describe how a U.S. arbitrageur can make a sure profit by buying and selling the three currencies.
   b. Next, describe how and why the arbitrage transactions restore equilibrium among the exchange rates. In particular, assuming that the first two exchange rates remain the same, what must be the equilibrium value of the German mark–British pound exchange rate?
6. How will an increase in the interest rate affect a nation's exchange rate under a flexible exchange rate system?
7. Use supply and demand analysis to show how each of the following events affects the dollar-franc exchange rate. Put the quantity of francs on the horizontal axis in your supply and demand graph.
   a. French wines become more popular in the United States.
   b. The French government purchases $1 million worth of U.S. Treasury notes.
   c. American automobile workers become more productive.
8. Suppose that wine costs 160 francs per bottle and cheese costs 2 dollars a pound. If the relative price of cheese in terms of wine is 10 pounds of cheese per bottle of wine, what is the dollar-franc exchange rate? What is the dollar price of wine? What is the franc price of cheese?
9. Describe what would happen if there is a difference in the rates of inflation between two countries that have a fixed exchange rate.
10. Why do most economists believe that the gains in moving from the Exchange Rate Mechanism to a single currency for the European Community would be small?

22

Developing Nations

LEARNING OBJECTIVES

CONCEPTS TO LEARN

Developing countries

The determinants of long-run economic growth in developing countries

The relationship between income distribution and economic development

The supply of and the demand for children

Outward-oriented versus inward-oriented strategies for economic development

CONCEPTS TO RECALL

Opportunity cost [1]

Long-run economic growth [3]

The Laws of Supply and Demand [5]

T he standard of living achieved in the Western industrial democracies—the United States, the countries of Western Europe, Canada, Japan, Australia, and New Zealand—is truly astounding from a global perspective. Unfortunately, most of the world's countries and people are not part of this high-income group.

In 1993 the world's population was 5.5 billion people. The vast majority of these people have far fewer creature comforts than are available to the average American, Western European, or Japanese citizen. Indeed, the standard of living throughout most of the world is appallingly low by comparison with the high-income countries. More than 3 billion people live in conditions of severe poverty, with annual incomes below $600 per person.

These people are not poor from lack of effort. They generally work long and hard throughout their lives. Work starts early in life in much of the world's rural areas. Children of six and seven weed in the fields or tend to livestock. Women play an important role in tending to crops, gathering firewood and water (often at great distance), cooking, and caring for young children. The men may work in the fields or migrate long distances seeking work in mines, plantations, or factories. In the cities young children sift through garbage dumps for bottles or cardboard that can be recycled. The sad truth is that life is very hard for most people.

Chapter 22 describes the economic circumstances that exist for most of the world's peoples who do not live in developed countries. It also examines some of the theories that seek to explain the process of economic development and analyzes a number of policy options that enhance the process of economic development.

With few exceptions, economic development is a long-term endeavor that takes place over many generations. It is also a complex process affected by cultural values, environmental constraints, political factors (both internal and external), and, not the least, economic institutions and policies.

OVERVIEW OF THE DEVELOPING NATIONS

Table 22.1 displays selected demographic and economic data by income group and region of the world for 1990.

We can see that the differences in living standards between the rich and the poor countries are enormous. The average citizen in the high-income, developed world enjoyed an income of $20,170 in 1990, which was 58 *times* that of the average citizen of the low-income, developing world ($350). Furthermore, there is every indication that this gap between the very rich and the very poor nations will continue and widen in the future. Persons from rich countries are also likely to live about 15 years longer, on average, than are their counterparts born in the lowest-income countries.

TABLE 22.1   World Economics by Income and Region

	POPULATION, MID-1990 (MILLIONS)	POPULATION GROWTH RATE, 1980–90 (%)	GNP PER CAPITA, 1990 ($)	LIFE EXPECTANCY AT BIRTH, 1990 (YEARS)	ADULT LITERACY, 1990 (%)
DEVELOPING ECONOMIES	4,146	2.0	840	63	74
Low income	3,058	2.0ᶜ	350	62ᶜ	60ᶜ
Lower middle income	629	2.0	1,530	65	75
Upper middle income	458	1.7	3,410	68	84
High income*a*	17	1.8	12,773	75	73
DEVELOPING ECONOMIES BY REGION					
South Asia	1,148	2.2	330	58	47
Sub-Saharan Africa	495	3.1	340	51	50
East Asia & Pacific	1,577	1.6	600	68	76
Latin America	433	2.1	2,180	68	84
Europe	200	0.1	2,400	70	85
DEVELOPED ECONOMIES*b*	777	0.6	20,170	77	96

*a*Israel, Singapore, Hong Kong, United Arab Emirates, and Kuwait. Kuwait's GNP was approximated from 1989 data.
*b*Western Europe, United States, Canada, Japan, Australia, and New Zealand.
*c*Excluding China and India, the population growth rate in this group rises to 2.6 percent, the life expectancy falls to 55 years, and the literacy rate falls to 55 percent.
SOURCE: The World Bank, *World Development Report 1992* (New York: Oxford University Press, 1992), Table 1, pp. 218–219.

Economic Development Defined

DEVELOPED COUNTRIES

Countries that have achieved, on average, a high standard of living, with a per capita income of at least $7,620 (as of 1990).

The Western democracies that have achieved high standards of living are called economically **developed countries.** These countries, with a combined population of less than 800 million people, comprise only 15 percent of the world's population.

Also considered developed, although struggling to adapt to free enterprise and private markets, are some of the former communist countries of Eastern Europe that were industrialized (Poland, the Czech and Slovak Republics, and Hungary) and some of the republics of the former Soviet Union (such as Russia and the Ukraine).

DEVELOPING COUNTRIES

Countries that range from the nearly developed to the very poor, with a per capita income of less than $7,620 (as of 1990); also called *less developed countries (LDCs).*

All other countries, where average incomes range from the nearly developed to the very poor, we will refer to as economically **developing countries** or, as they are often called, the **less developed countries (LDCs).**

These terms may be somewhat offensive to citizens of these countries. They are not meant to imply that people in rich countries are "advanced" in terms of human development compared to those in poor countries. Indeed, some of the poorest countries economically, such as India and China, have a much richer cultural and religious heritage than do countries with far higher incomes. Rather, this term refers to the means by which human lives can be bettered by access to economic resources—for raising life expectancy, improving literacy rates, and the like.

We might also note that some cultures would not see progress as coming from material betterment. In the Buddhist religion, which is practiced throughout much of East Asia, human advancement is spiritual in nature and comes from right living in harmony with nature. Economic growth that threatens this harmony would be a negative element in human advancement.[1]

The developing countries are also called *Third World countries*. This term arose during the Cold War to distinguish developing countries from the industrial capitalist democracies of the West (the First World) and the industrial communist countries of the Soviet bloc (the Second World).

A Geographical Comparison

There are enormous differences within the group of developing countries. For starters, recall from Table 3.2 that the World Bank groups the developing countries into three income categories: (1) low income (per capita income under $610), (2) lower middle income (per capita income between $611 and $2,465), and (3) upper middle income (per capita income between $2,466 and $7,619 (1990 figures).

The highest concentrations of world poverty are located in the rural areas of South Asia, sub-Saharan Africa, and parts of Southeast Asia. In much of Africa and South Asia, the picture of absolute poverty is bleak and pervasive.

In North Africa only Libya (with its large oil reserves) has a high per capita income; in sub-Saharan Africa only Gabon (with oil) and South Africa (with mining and manufacturing) have achieved an upper middle level of income per capita. In South Africa this accomplishment has been marred by the apartheid system of racial segregation and discrimination. In the rest of Africa average incomes are very low and have actually been falling.

There are many causes of Africa's declining per capita income over the past decade. Chief among these are war, political turmoil, self-serving authoritarian rulers, bad economic policies, drought, high population growth rates, and a colonial legacy of poor transportation systems and geographic boundaries that divide tribal groups.

South Asia has a similarly unpleasant economic situation and faces enormous challenges. Countries such as Afghanistan, Bangladesh, India, Laos, and Myanmar (Burma) are confronting internal and external political conflicts, environmental disasters, and high population growth rates. The very low incomes there provide little surplus that can be used to raise living standards. As in sub-Saharan Africa, what little surplus exists is often appropriated by a corrupt political system.

China is coping with the world's largest population of 1.1 billion people and a very low per capita income of $370 in 1990. Yet China's per capita income has grown by an astounding 5.8 percent a year over the period of 1965–90.[2] At this rate its per capita income will double every 12 years. In the twenty-first century China will catapult to the level of a significant world economy.

Although 60 percent of the world's peoples are living in poverty as measured by the World Bank, significant progress has been made in a number of countries over the last 50 years. Mainly this progress has come about through rapid industrialization, which has generated fast economic growth.

CURRENT ISSUE: The HIV (AIDS) virus is the latest scourge to hit the developing countries of Africa and Asia. The virus has gained a potentially devastating stranglehold in central Africa, particularly in Zaire, and it is spreading at an alarming rate in the major cities of Southeast Asia, particularly in Bangkok.

CURRENT ISSUE: Per capita income is rising by more than 10 percent annually in the southeastern coastal cities of China where the Chinese leaders have permitted free enterprise on a limited scale. The Chinese experiment with capitalism appears to be a smashing success, and it is fast spreading to the cities in the middle and northern parts of the country.

---

[1]For an interesting discussion of this point, see "Buddhist Economics" in E. F. Schumacher, *Small Is Beautiful: Economics as If People Mattered* (New York: Harper and & Row, 1974).
[2]*The World Bank Development Report* 1992, 218.

NEWLY INDUSTRIALIZING COUNTRIES (NICs)

Countries in East Asia that are rapidly industrializing and approaching or surpassing the living standards in the lower tier of developed countries.

In particular, the **newly industrializing countries (NICs)** of East Asia—the Pacific rim countries of South Korea, Taiwan, Hong Kong, and Singapore—are rapidly approaching and surpassing living standards in the lower-tier developed countries of Western Europe, such as Portugal and Greece. Fast on their heels are other Pacific rim countries, such as Malaysia and Thailand.

In Latin America a number of countries have industrialized rapidly, creating a large middle class. This is the case in Brazil, Uruguay, Venezuela, Mexico, Chile, and Argentina. However, most of these countries also face daunting social and political problems that have resulted in high inflation, huge government budget deficits, and overwhelming foreign debts. These factors lower their potential future growth by restricting the funds available for investment.

We have been making some broad comparisons of per capita gross domestic product (GDP) between countries and regions. It is appropriate at this point to examine some of the difficulties with such comparisons.

Problems in Comparing Incomes

Comparisons of income between countries can be a very tricky affair. First, there is a *measurement* problem, since each country accounts for gross domestic product (GDP) in a somewhat different way. For example, household production of subsistence crops for the family tends to be quite significant in very poor rural countries, yet this activity is probably underestimated in the GDP.

Second, calculating GDP *per capita* requires dividing the GDP estimate by the population. Population estimates can be highly inaccurate in countries with a rapidly growing population because it is expensive and difficult to carry out a nationwide census.

A third difficulty is the *conversion* problem. In order to compare GDPs between countries, these data must first be converted to a common currency such as the U.S. dollar. Using official exchange rates to convert poses a problem, since, as will be discussed later in this chapter, many governments maintain artificially high exchange rates. This distorts the true value of output produced. In addition, the value of a country's currency could rise or fall, depending on the demand for its exports. Most of what consumers buy may not be traded on the world market, however. Thus, the real purchasing power of income may be overstated or understated.

INTERNATIONAL COMPARISONS PROGRAM (ICP)

A program undertaken by the United Nations to correct for the problem of converting a country's gross domestic product (GDP) to another currency; it solves this problem by calculating a purchasing power parity exchange rate for each country.

The United Nations has an **International Comparisons Program (ICP)** to correct for the conversion problem by calculating a purchasing power parity exchange rate. The exchange rate is adjusted to reflect the costs of living in different countries and better reflects the true standards of living in different countries. Table 22.2 shows what a difference this adjustment can make.

For example, in 1990 the unadjusted gross national product (GNP) per capita of Japan ($25,430) surpassed that of the United States ($21,790) by a significant amount. But a visitor to Japan quickly notices that the typical Japanese consumer is less well off than the average American, despite Japan's supposedly higher average income level. The price of beef in Japan is $30 per pound, and the price of a very modest home in Tokyo suburbs could approach $1 million!

The higher measured GNP per capita in Japan is simply the result of the rise in the value of Japanese currency (the yen), caused by trade surpluses with the rest of the world and particularly with the United States. Thus, when Japan's entire yen economy is converted into dollars at the prevailing exchange

TABLE 22.2   **Purchasing Power Parity (PPP) Estimates of GNP Per Capita**[a]

COUNTRY	GNP PER CAPITA (NOMINAL $ 1990)	
	GNP Not Adjusted for PPP	GNP Adjusted for PPP[b]
Switzerland	32,680	$21,690
Japan	25,430	16,950
United States	21,790	21,360
Brazil	2,680	4,780
Bangladesh	210	1,050
Somalia	120	540

[a]GNP represents gross national product. The difference between GNP and GDP was explained in Chapter 27. Use of GNP rather than GDP is of little importance here.
[b]The 1990 PPP data were extrapolated from 1985 PPP estimates.

SOURCE: The World Bank, *The World Bank Development Report 1992* (New York: Oxford University Press, 1992) Table 30, 276–277.

rate (about 100 yen to the dollar in 1993), it appears as if Japan's standard of living is higher. But a nation's standard of living reflects the purchase of many products that are not traded on the world market. To reflect real living standards, the differences in purchasing power must be accounted for in making international comparisons.

The third column of Table 22.2 provides these purchasing power parity (PPP) comparisons. We see that, after accounting for differences in the costs of living, GNP per capita in Japan falls quite dramatically. It is now lower than in the United States by about 20 percent. In Bangladesh, by contrast, real per capita income rises fivefold to $1,050. This reflects the fact that Bangladesh is producing many nontradable goods. What little Bangladesh exports does not generate a strong demand for its currency. Therefore, when all the nontradable goods and services are converted to dollars at a low currency value, its GNP per capita is a low $210. Valuing what Bangladesh produces at a purchasing power parity exchange rate significantly increases the estimate of its standard of living.

Keep in mind that some heroic assumptions were made to reach these final numbers. These numbers also do not correct for the first two measurement problems of household production and population growth. In short, there is no easy or perfect method for making international comparisons, which is why they must always be done with sensitivity and caution.

Income Distribution

Even after adjusting for purchasing power parity, GDP per capita alone could give a very misleading picture of how an average family lives. This is because average income of a country can be high, yet most of that income could be going to just a small percentage of wealthy families. Some countries whose per capita incomes are very high are still considered less developed because of the unequal distribution of income. Hence, Saudi Arabia is still considered less developed despite its relatively high per capita income, since most of this income accrues to the royal family. Taking account of the *relative* income distribution is important. Later in this chapter we examine the connection between income distribution and development.

Other Measures of Development

Even if income distribution were not a large problem, GDP is by no means a perfect indicator of a nation's standard of living. GDP measures aggregate market activity, yet the quality of life depends on many factors besides marketed activity. Alternative measures of social well-being have been devised that attempt to assess directly the "quality of life." These measures include variables such as the infant mortality rate; the life expectancy rate; the literacy rate; the share of families with access to clean water; the share of families with access to electricity, gas, and the like; and the degree of political freedom, human rights, and so on.

In some cases GDP per capita is a poor indicator of the quality of life. China has a per capita income of just $370. Yet its life expectancy is 70 years, far in excess of the average of 55 years for other countries in this income group. Its adult literacy rate is 73 percent, again far superior to the average of 55 percent for countries with similar per capita incomes. Alternative measures of development are useful complements to GDP in suggesting differences in quality of life.

In many cases, though, GDP per capita is highly correlated with these alternative measures of development. Therefore, used with appropriate care, GDP can still serve as a starting point for examining social welfare and development.

THE DETERMINANTS OF LONG-RUN ECONOMIC GROWTH IN DEVELOPING COUNTRIES

Why are some countries rich and other countries poor? In some cases it is relatively easy to single out primary causes of economic success or failure. For instance, according to World Bank tables the country with the world's highest per capita income in 1990 was Kuwait (prior to the invasion by Iraq). Kuwait's high standard of living can be easily explained by its enormous oil reserves coupled with a tiny population of only 2.1 million. By contrast, the world's poorest country is Mozambique, with a per capita income of $210. Its abysmal situation can also be readily explained by decades of violent civil war.

In most cases, however, it is not possible to separate out single causes of economic success. Even for the examples given, the single explanations alone are not complete. Kuwait was a very poor nomadic sheikdom a hundred years ago with all its oil undiscovered underground. Only with the systematic application of the physical and mental capital (oil-drilling equipment, port facilities, and engineers) has Kuwait's living standard skyrocketed. Nor can Mozambique's low living standard be attributed solely to internal political strife. Mozambique was a pawn in the game of European colonization. The conditions imposed by the Portuguese colonial power led to a prolonged and bloody war for independence, which lasted until 1974. The revolutionary winners (backed by China in their independence struggle) then imposed a communist economy.

Seen from this perspective, the political and economic turmoil in Mozambique is the result of external, as well as internal, forces.

Indeed, no single variable or model can explain all the variation in income and wealth that we find around the world; rather, a complex mix of variables seems best suited to yielding useful interpretation and prediction.

Some of these variables are clearly economic and affect the long-run aggregate supply. We focus on the supply side because the factors limiting the production possibilities frontier are supply constraints. Four factors that are particularly important to expanding the frontiers of the developing countries are the labor force participation rate, the level of saving and its link to productive investment, the choice of production technologies, and the rate of population growth. Our analysis in this section will highlight these four factors.

Labor Force Participation Rate

The **labor force participation rate** is the size of a nation's labor force in relation to its total population. The rate of labor force participation depends on cultural, environmental, economic, and political forces.

To see why labor force participation might vary, let's consider life in the humid tropics. In tropical climates it makes no sense to work beyond what is necessary to satisfy one's immediate needs for food, shelter, and safety. Any excess food produced or collected would spoil in the heat and humidity. Moreover, since seasonal variation is minimal, food is readily obtained in the future whenever needed. Thus, there is no incentive to save.

With the slash-and-burn agricultural system used in the tropics, the soil is thin, and plots wear out quickly, leading to migration every few years. Therefore, basic needs are obtained very simply, and no culture of accumulation for the future tends to develop. The labor supply is brief and intermittent, intended to satisfy minimal, immediate needs only. Free time is spent in highly significant ritualized activities, which provide spiritual meaning. These culturally ingrained practices do not change overnight with the introduction of industrialized goods.

By contrast, colder climates are subject to months of freezing and difficult hunting and gathering conditions. Habits of saving become culturally ingrained, such as storing grains for use in the winter months. This leads to labor force participation not just on the basis of current needs, but also on the basis of future needs.

People generally work long and hard in the developing countries, as noted in the introduction. Yet despite their efforts, their standards of living remain abysmally low for the most part. The reason why is that their labor is not very productive.

LABOR FORCE PARTICIPATION RATE

The size of a nation's labor force relative to its entire population.

Saving, Investment, and Productivity

We saw in Chapter 3 that investment in physical and human capital (education) is the key to increases in productivity. The problem for the developing countries is the opportunity cost of investment. A higher rate of investment requires a higher rate of saving, and more saving means less consumption. With consumption at little more than subsistence levels in many of these countries, sacrificing consumption to increase investment is extremely costly.

Saving encounters additional cultural, institutional, and political impediments as well. One consequence of these additional barriers is that some of the saving that does occur does not end up financing productive investments.

So, for example, a peasant farmer in Africa might know that crop yields would rise if only irrigation water could be obtained from a river several miles away. But pipes and pumps to carry this water must be purchased at great expense. This farmer has no savings with which to purchase the pump, nor are there financial markets that would lend her the money. Even if savings were available for investment in terms of the local currency, the pumps must be imported from Europe, the United States, or Japan, and there is probably a shortage of foreign exchange needed to buy these imports. Furthermore, irrigation pumps run on electricity, which is not available in this area. Should a pump break down, obtaining spare parts, and the skills of a technician to install them, could be nearly impossible. Thus, while conceptually the problem of raising productivity is quite simple—just increase saving and investment—in practice there are innumerable roadblocks to be overcome.

For this reason, development does not happen overnight. Indeed, it took Western Europe three centuries of industrialization to achieve its current living standards. Increases in productivity must be sustained over a long period of time for a country to reach high levels of living. For example, if productivity grew by the relatively high rate of 2 percent a year, it would take more than a generation—36 years—for income to double. Thus, for a very poor country like India, with a per capita income of about $350 in 1990, it would still take slightly more than a hundred years for it to reach a per capita income of $2,800. A slower growth in productivity of 1 percent a year would mean achieving this income level only in the year 2206.[3]

Let's now take a closer look at some of the more common impediments to saving.

INSTITUTIONAL IMPEDIMENTS: SAVING AND FINANCIAL MARKETS   We discussed earlier how environmental factors might lead certain cultures, but not others, to acquire a habit of saving for the future. Institutional factors can also affect the savings rate and whether the funds that are saved are used to finance productive investments that increase economic growth.

In the developed world, financial markets exist to link savers and investors. Financial institutions such as banks are readily available and are a way of life for paying bills, saving for a college education, and storing up a retirement nest egg. Banks, savings and loans, stock and bond markets, insurance companies, and pension funds are all mechanisms whereby funds from savers are made available to borrowers seeking to invest. The efficiency with which financial institutions do this can be measured by the spread between the interest rate (or return) paid to savers and the interest rate (or return) charged to borrowers. In a market setting, competitive forces will ensure that a very small spread will be earned by financial institutions for linking savers and borrowers.

The process by which savings are translated into investments is not perfect in the developed world, but by and large financial institutions are successful

---

[3]The doubling time is easily found by the Rule of 72: Take the percentage growth rate, and divide this into the number 72. This result is the number of years needed for that variable to double. For the relatively low growth rates found in economics, this formula reasonably estimates the doubling time. In this example we are also assuming that the labor force participation rate stays constant, so that as the population grows, the labor force grows at the same rate.

at achieving their functions. Occasionally there have been dramatic failures, as in the Great Depression, when bank panics caused runs on the banks. Those persons lucky enough to get their savings out before a bank failed were likely to keep their bank notes hidden in their mattress, thus breaking the link between saving and productive investment.

In many parts of the developing world, saving is carried out in traditional ways that preserve cultural values. In North Africa and the Middle East, for example, Moslems present each bride with a very valuable gift, such as a gold bracelet. This bracelet is worn by the wife her entire life and represents a significant store of wealth. Should anything happen to her husband, the Moslem wife will always have this gold bracelet to sell.

This bracelet serves the valuable economic function of a safety net for the wife. Yet savings used to buy assets such as gold bracelets and other jewelry are not available for productive investments that would increase economic growth. Although less romantic, a husband could buy a bride a savings account in her name for $5,000, to be used only in the event of separation or the death of the husband. In this case these savings would be lent out to a business seeking to invest, thereby expanding the growth rate of the economy. In addition, the woman could see her wealth grow as interest on these savings is earned.

Yet in many poor areas the old ways persist. A woman can feel her gold jewelry pressed against her flesh. She feels safe since theft is very rare. She and her husband know little of what a financial market is, nor would they feel safe entrusting her life savings to strangers to care for. Thus, the least risky thing to do is to keep saving in the old-fashioned way.

There are other institutional roadblocks to developing the link between saving and productive investment. Financial institutions like banks pay interest to depositors and charge interest to lenders. But in Moslem countries, usury ("excessive" interest) is forbidden by the holy book of Islam, the Koran. (There were similar injunctions in the Christian church in the Middle Ages.) Private financial institutions could not survive if these religious rules were strictly enforced. In some cases this is overcome by changing the rules: A depositor to a bank could "buy" a deposit, and the bank could agree to "buy it back" in the future at an agreed-on higher price. The depositor thus earns a capital gain on this deposit, not an interest payment, and has obeyed the Islamic law.

POLITICAL IMPEDIMENTS: FINANCIAL REPRESSION   Sometimes governments weaken the savings–productive investment link through misguided policies that create **financial repression.**

Savers will use financial markets only if the benefits outweigh the costs. Quite often government policies have unintentionally made financial instruments (like savings deposits) very unattractive to savers. What results is disintermediation in which financial institutions lose deposits, thereby restricting the investment loans that can be made.

One policy that creates financial repression is an *interest rate ceiling.* By setting a maximum legal interest rate, government officials hope to prevent banks and other financial institutions from taking advantage of borrowers. The theory is that if banks have a cheap source of funds, they can offer lower interest rate loans to borrowers, thereby encouraging investment. In practice these ceilings are self-defeating, as demonstrated in Figure 22.1.

FINANCIAL REPRESSION

A reduction in the supply of savings caused by government policies, such as a government-imposed interest rate ceiling in financial markets.

FIGURE 22.1

An Interest Rate Ceiling

The figure shows the effects of an interest rate ceiling in the market for loanable funds, which governments in developing countries often impose in an attempt to reduce their firms' costs of borrowing to invest. The quantity of loans is on the horizontal axis and the nominal interest rate is on the vertical axis. S is the supply curve for loans by the savers/lenders, and D is the demand curve for loans by the investors/borrowers. Without government intervention, the equilibrium would be at the intersection of D and S. The interest rate would be 10 percent, and the quantity of loans L_1. An interest rate ceiling of 8 percent generates an excess demand for loans equal to $(L_2 - L_0)$. Instead of encouraging investment, the policy leads to a financial repression as the amount of saving (lending) available to finance investment decreases from L_1 to L_0. The policy also encourages corruption because the amount of funds available to investors, L_0, has to be rationed to investors who want L_2 loans at the artificially low interest rate.

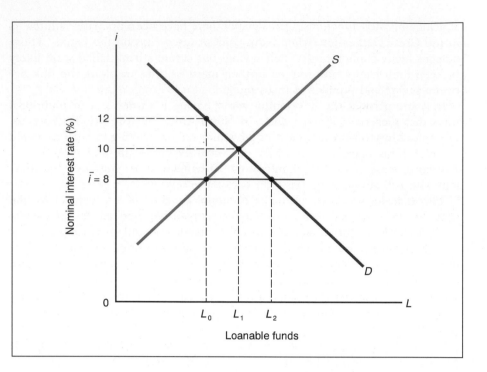

FIGURE 22.1

An Interest Rate Ceiling

The interest rate on loans is on the vertical axis, and the quantity of loans is on the horizontal axis. Savers generate the supply of funds to be loaned, and investors generate the demand for funds to be borrowed. The supply curve, S, indicates the savers' (lenders') supply of loans at each interest rate. The demand curve, D, indicates the investors' (borrowers') demand for loans at each interest rate. In this example the supply and demand equilibrium occurs at a nominal interest rate of 10 percent and a volume of funds loaned equal to L_1.

Suppose that the government imposes an interest rate ceiling at 8 percent. As interest rates fall from 10 percent to 8 percent, savers will search for alternative ways to store their wealth, such as speculation in real estate, stamps, rare paintings, or foreign currencies. Savers will cut back the supply of funds to L_0, thereby reducing the funds available for investment and lowering the rate of economic growth. The fallacy of an interest rate ceiling policy is that it ignores the fact that savers have options.

Moreover, the artificially low interest of 8 percent charged to borrowers will create a *shortage* of available funds equal to $(L_2 - L_0)$. More people will want to borrow at the artificially low interest rate than there are funds available. There is a queuing up for investment loans, and months, even years, may go by before investment funds become available. Or, worse, banks (and/or the government) may distribute these scarce funds via credit rationing to favorite industries. Corruption and bribery are ways of life in countries whose governments manipulate market prices and overregulate economic activity. There is no guarantee that the industries picked by the government to receive funds will provide the largest return, since the criteria for selection are often based on political favoritism.

The firms that are shut out of the market for loans are usually small businesses and small farmers. They are forced to borrow funds on the black market at very high interest rates, if they can obtain loans at all. These are also the business firms that tend to provide the most jobs, so that the lack of investment funds has a depressing effect on output and employment.

INFLATION, SAVINGS, AND CAPITAL FLIGHT   Savers care about the *real rate of interest*, which takes into account the expected inflation. The *real* rate of interest is the nominal rate of interest minus the expected inflation rate. If the nominal rate of interest is set at 8 percent and the expected inflation rate is 5 percent, then the *real* interest rate earned by the depositors is 3 percent.

Suppose that the inflation rate rises to 10 percent. The real interest earned is now *negative* 2 percent when the nominal rate is set at 8 percent (real rate of interest = 8 − 10 = −2). Said differently, at the end of the year the depositor will get back interest and principal that can buy 2 percent less than at the beginning of the year because of the rise in prices. If nominal interest rates are not allowed to rise with inflation (due to interest rate ceilings), then rising inflation will destroy the returns to saving, with negative consequences for the effective savings rate.

Rapid inflation in a currency will generally erode the value of all financial assets denominated in that currency. As domestic prices rise faster than foreign prices due to inflation, it becomes harder to sell exports, and imports become ever more attractive. This inevitably pushes down the value of the domestic currency and lowers the real wealth of those owning financial assets denominated in this currency.

As a hedge against losing wealth in a country with rapid inflation, people buy foreign currencies (such as the U.S. dollar). These dollars can be hoarded (thereby earning a rate of return equal to the depreciation of the local currency), or they can be invested in the United States or Europe. This is known as **capital flight.** Although the saving rate of a country may be high, the savings available to finance productive investments may be much lower because of capital flight.

In these last few sections we have identified various ways in which a country's savings do not find their way into productive investments. This decreases a country's growth rate, and, as we saw in Chapter 3, even a small reduction in the rate of long-run economic growth has a substantial effect on a nation's standard of living. For example, a permanent decline in the annual growth rate from 3 percent to 2 percent lengthens the time it takes income to double from 24 years to 36 years.

DIRECT FOREIGN INVESTMENT, LOANS, AND AID   One way in which a country with a low savings rate can grow faster is to acquire foreign savings through direct foreign investment, loans, or gifts. Direct foreign investment occurs when a foreign firm brings in financial capital to buy or build a factory. The foreign firm also generally supplies needed foreign exchange, technological know-how, administration, product design, and marketing. It may have a local partner if required by law.

Many LDCs encourage direct foreign investment as an easy way to acquire capital and technology and to create jobs. In the last 40 years U.S. multinational corporations have set up many manufacturing plants overseas. This was done for various reasons: to "jump over" tariff walls in Europe and Latin America, to be closer to final customers and reduce transportation costs, to be closer to sources of raw materials, to utilize less expensive labor, and to gain tax advantages.

CAPITAL FLIGHT

The purchase of foreign currencies or securities by domestic residents as a hedge against rapid domestic inflation.

Foreign multinational corporations are involved not just in manufacturing, but also in large-scale mining and agribusiness in LDCs. For example, multinational food companies operate plantations for growing and processing pineapples in the Philippines and bananas in Honduras. Aluminum companies maintain bauxite mines in Jamaica. Oil companies engage in drilling and pumping petroleum in Kuwait.

Most of these resource concerns engage in **export-enclave production.** What is produced is usually not consumed locally, but is exported to the First World. These exports of primary products constitute the bulk of foreign exchange earnings for many poor countries. By bringing in capital, along with advanced techniques for mining and agriculture, these firms create jobs and vital exports.

Direct foreign investment is a mixed blessing to many LDCs, however. Foreign ownership of factories, farms, and mines introduces a powerful political force, which can in some cases dominate the domestic political scene and may skew the distribution of income. Political domination may be matched by a cultural domination as well. With vast advertising budgets and mass-marketing techniques, foreign producers can overwhelm small local producers. Coca-Cola and television shows like "Dallas" become symbols of progress and advancement, while local cultures and traditions wither. The breakup of local cultures destroys the traditional economic system, which employs far more people than does the "modern" sector, leading to rising unemployment.

Foreign loans or gifts operate in much the same way as direct foreign investment. They raise the effective savings rate available to stimulate growth. In the 1950s and 1960s, loans to LDCs were generally made by multilateral government agencies such as the World Bank or by single government agencies such as the U.S. Agency for International Development (AID). In the 1970s private commercial banks became involved in "recycling petrodollars" to developing nations, resulting in the world debt crisis of the 1980s. The debt crisis is discussed later in this chapter.

EXPORT-ENCLAVE PRODUCTION
Refers to production by resource-using firms in the developing countries, typically multinational corporations, whose output is not consumed locally, but is exported to the First World, thereby earning foreign exchange and creating new jobs and export opportunities.

The Choice of Production Technologies

In a free market system the amount of capital used in production is determined by the available production technologies and the prices of factors of production. In developed countries such as the United States, the price of labor has risen steadily over several centuries. This has provided an incentive for using *labor-saving* technology that substitutes capital for labor in production. A car company that builds a new factory in the United States or Japan in the 1990s will use far more capital per car—for example, robots—than Henry Ford did at the turn of this century. The reason for this is simple: The cost of labor is relatively higher now, and the cost of capital is relatively cheaper. The cost of labor to a business is not only the wage paid, but also the fringe benefits (such as health care), unemployment compensation, expenses for health and safety regulations, sick leave, and vacations and holidays. Robots require none of these!

In the developing countries where labor is plentiful and capital is scarce, one would expect to find that efficient businesses will use *more* labor and *less* capital in production. That is generally what one finds. In India it is common to see large construction projects using hundreds of day laborers, carrying sacks of cement or earth on their backs. This is cheaper than any alternative because widespread unemployment holds down wages and because capital equipment is very expensive. By contrast, in the West this same project might be done with one or two large earth diggers (costing several hundred thousand dollars each) with a skeleton crew of only a few workers.

These differences in production technique are quite appropriate if they reflect the real scarcities of labor, capital, and other factors used in production. Unfortunately, the prices of resources in a market are often distorted in LDC countries, thereby giving false signals as to scarcity. These distorted factor prices may lead to an inappropriate use of resources, thereby slowing the country's growth rate.

DISTORTED FACTOR PRICES   Factor prices are distorted if the prices of resources used in production do not reflect the true scarcity of these resources. When this happens, profit-maximizing businesses may design and build factories that use a non-optimal combination of inputs in the production process. We say "may" because some techniques of production do not afford much substitution between labor and capital in production, even in the long run. For example, the manufacture of hazardous chemicals requires machinery rather than human contact. Also, many factories require a fairly fixed combination of labor and capital in the short run. Therefore, our discussion centers on the long run in which all resources in production become variable and refers specifically to the production of goods in which it is fairly easy to substitute capital for labor, as in the earth-moving example above.

Distorted factor prices mean that the economy is not producing efficiently because it is not using enough resources that are plentiful and cheap, and instead it is using resources that are scarce and expensive. This implies that the same output could be produced at a lower cost to society.

Despite the desire of most governments in the developing nations to increase jobs, they often adopt policies that distort factor prices in ways that reduce the attractiveness of hiring workers and increase the attractiveness of buying machinery as a substitute.

DISTORTIONS IN THE COST OF LABOR   Effective minimum wage laws, health and safety laws, family leave laws, and other laws that artificially raise the wage or benefits package of employees send a distorted signal to the marketplace as to the scarcity of labor. The message is that labor is a scarce commodity, and hence its cost is rising compared to other inputs in production. In the short run business firms may still hire the same number of workers as before, as long as they can pass on to customers the higher costs or absorb some loss in profits to maintain output and market share.

Generally, politicians who pass such laws might believe that there are fixed factors required in production and that greedy businesses have plenty of profit to share with workers. But in the long run, as new factories are built to replace old ones, the new factories (if they are built in the same labor market as before) generally use more automated equipment, which substitutes for labor.

DISTORTIONS IN THE COST OF CAPITAL   Governments unwittingly encourage businesses to substitute capital for labor in a number of ways. Usually this occurs because governments wish to industrialize quickly. To encourage the

FIGURE 22.2

An Overvalued Currency

The figure shows what would happen if the Mexican government overvalues the peso in an attempt to reduce the costs to Mexican firms of buying capital equipment from the United States. The quantity of dollars exchanged for pesos is on the horizontal axis, and the peso-dollar exchange rate in terms of pesos/$ is on the vertical axis. The equilibrium value of the exchange rate without the Mexican government's intervention is 3 pesos/$, at the intersection of $D_\$$ and $S_\$$, the demand curve and the supply curve for dollars. B dollars are exchanged for pesos in the foreign exchange markets. By setting a ceiling on the peso-dollar exchange rate of 2 pesos/$, the government overvalues the peso and generates an excess demand for dollars equal to $(C - A)$. With fewer dollars available, Mexican firms cannot buy as much capital equipment from the United States. An overvalued peso also encourages corruption as the A dollars available have to be rationed among the demanders who want C dollars. Finally, the firms who do obtain the scarce dollars have an incentive to use production techniques that are too capital intensive because they are buying the capital at an artificially low price.

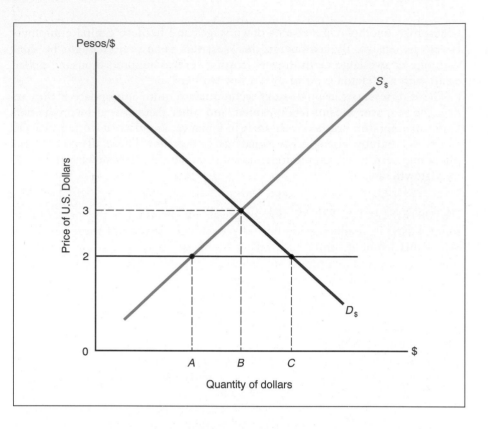

building of factories, governments often provide loans at below-market interest rates, or provide tax breaks on capital investments, or sell foreign exchange needed to buy important capital equipment at below-market rates. These programs all distort the true cost of capital, which is usually quite high in most developing countries because capital is so scarce. Yet to the business firms that receive these subsidies the most profitable way to build and operate the factory becomes more *capital-intensive*. Society loses because the capital-output ratio is higher than it otherwise would be, and many workers will not be employed.

Let's examine the last policy—manipulating the exchange rate. What would happen if a country such as Mexico decides to overvalue its own currency? It might do this in order to sell dollars more cheaply to firms wishing to industrialize.[4] Refer to Figure 22.2, which shows the supply and the demand for the U.S. dollar in foreign exchange markets. Dollars are supplied by Americans wishing to buy goods or assets in Mexico. Dollars are demanded by Mexicans wishing to buy goods or assets inside the United States. The exchange rate is on the vertical axis, and the quantity of dollars exchanged is on the horizontal axis. The exchange rate is expressed in terms of pesos per dollar.

The equilibrium exchange rate is 3 pesos to 1 dollar according to the figure. At this exchange rate the supply of dollars just equals the demand for dollars. The total number of dollars bought is the amount B. And, since the dollars are exchanged for pesos, the supply of pesos just equals the demand for pesos. The total number of pesos bought equals $3 \cdot B$.

---

[4]Mexico did this extensively in the past. Currently its exchange rate is floating and is no longer overvalued.

A company in Mexico seeking to import a $1 million machine from the United States would have to pay 3 million pesos at the equilibrium exchange rate. However, suppose that the Mexican government set a *price ceiling* of 2 pesos to the dollar. At this price the imported machine would cost the Mexican firm only 2 million pesos—a substantial savings. This is why governments set prices of foreign exchange too low or, alternatively, set their own currency price too high. The dollar is *undervalued,* and the peso is *overvalued.*

The harmful effects of an overvalued peso are twofold. By making imported capital equipment cheaper, it encourages use of more capital in production than is desirable, given the true scarcity of capital and labor. In addition, the overvalued peso creates a *shortage* (excess demand) of foreign exchange (dollars) equal to $(C - A)$. At the lower price of 2 pesos to the dollar, Mexicans want to buy more from the United States (amount C), and Americans want to buy less from Mexicans (amount A). The total amount of dollars that the Mexicans can buy drops to the amount A. Hence, less imported capital equipment can be bought than before, slowing the growth rate.

Because of the shortage of dollars, the Mexican central bank engages in rationing this scarce foreign exchange. Favoritism, bribery, and corruption are all problems that arise when the government sets a price ceiling on foreign exchange. There is no guarantee that firms with the best potential for promoting economic growth will get the funds.

The government has better means of promoting industrialization. For example, it could subsidize each unit of output produced. Business firms receive a subsidy, but only on the condition that they use technology appropriate to the actual resource conditions. Alternatively, if job creation is desired, governments could subsidize businesses for each job created. Either policy would encourage businesses to develop *capital-saving* production techniques and use more labor. Of course, these subsidies would be sensible only if unemployment were so widespread as to make the opportunity cost of labor close to zero. In this case the extra labor used would not reduce production somewhere else in the economy.

OTHER FACTORS CAUSING AN OVERUSE OF CAPITAL   Even if factor prices in LDCs truly reflected scarcity conditions, factories built in these countries might be too capital-intensive for other reasons. First, most capital equipment is designed and built in the First World. Naturally the type of capital equipment built reflects the scarcity conditions existing in the developed world, not those in the developing world. Only if the LDC market for this capital equipment is large enough to encourage First World companies to redesign it will it reflect technology appropriate for the LDCs.[5]

Second, multinational companies often build similar factories in various places around the world. With design and start-up costs comprising a large part of total investment costs, it may be cheaper overall for a multinational to have one factory design, whether that factory is built in Belgium (where labor costs are high) or Brazil (where labor costs are lower).

Third, new labor-saving technology invented in the First World often comes packaged with computerized equipment that allows for a better product to be produced. Automated scanners that check for manufacturing errors can do this

---

[5]This can be overcome somewhat through the purchase of used equipment in the First World. The older vintage equipment would be more labor-intensive.

better and faster than can any combination of human workers. To produce a higher-quality product the LDC factory may have no choice but to automate.

Finally, new labor-saving equipment is a status symbol in many LDCs. A modern tractor may yield social status, even if it entails a loss of profits in the short run.

DEVELOPMENT FROM THE "BOTTOM UP" Unemployment is very high in most of the developing world. This is due partly to the overuse of capital-intensive production technologies noted above and partly to rapid population growth and rapid urbanization. In the 1970s a movement grew up to alter the technology of production in ways that would favor the creation of jobs and thereby lower unemployment rates. Instigated by the publication in 1974 of E. F. Schumacher's book *Small Is Beautiful*, the *appropriate technology movement* was born. Schumacher advocated that LDCs utilize the labor resources at hand, rather than relying on capital equipment imported from abroad. He encouraged capital-saving technological innovation. Development, he argued, should happen from the bottom up, not the top down.

For example, suppose that rural peasants in India need energy for cooking. A top-down approach would use modern imported technology (paid for with foreign loans) to dam a river so that a huge hydroelectric plant could be built. Electric lines would then be run throughout rural areas. The cost of such a project could run into the tens of billions of dollars, creating a huge foreign debt. Moreover, India would be dependent on foreigners to run the electric plant until Indians could be trained and to supply critical spare parts over the life of the equipment. Rural peasants would need to earn hard currency to pay for electricity. Collection costs would be high, given the low literacy levels.

As an alternative, Schumacher proposed a bottom-up strategy that would use local resources and lead to local self-sufficiency. This is much like Mahatma Ghandi's famous walk to the sea, which liberated India from the mindset of buying imported salt from the British colonial masters when the oceans provided all the salt Indians would need. In terms of energy, a bottom-up approach would look for energy from a local, but overlooked, source—cow dung. Given the Hindu tradition of the "sacred cow," these animals are quite plentiful and useful in production. Abundant cow manure is thus available for free on the farm. Manure can be placed in a hole in the ground and covered with a sheet of scrap metal. An inexpensive pipe from the top runs into the peasant's hut. As manure is broken down by microorganisms, methane gas is given off. This naturally produced gas can be burned cleanly as a fuel. The decomposed cow dung can later be spread on the fields as fertilizer.

The bottom-up approach uses little capital and no scarce foreign exchange. It does require more labor to collect manure every few days. But the peasant has no electric bills to pay, and the country has no foreign debt. In India today methane stoves are common. Yet it took appropriate capital-saving technology to make it available to the masses. While such an approach would not be satisfying to the average American, with a per capita income of $21,790 in 1990, it is appropriate for the average Indian peasant, with a per capita income of $350. Because India does not use scarce savings to build a hydroelectric plant, these funds become available for other investment projects that help to increase India's potential rate of growth.

The choice of technology also has important ramifications for the distribution of income in society. Aside from the important objective of making the economy more efficient, appropriate technology can reduce social tensions that might arise if capital-intensive technology leads to greater unemployment in a labor-abundant country.

The Population Growth Rate

The fourth factor that has an important impact on economic growth in the developing countries is the population growth rate. A rising population provides a larger work force, which increases the potential level of output. However, this is a two-edged sword. If population grows faster than output, *per capita* income will fall.

High population growth rates found in the poorest developing nations are troubling because they put severe strains on the limited savings available for investment in human capital. For new workers to be productive they must have food, health care, education, housing, and other types of infrastructure. Poor countries have little by way of savings to begin with. High population growth rates mean that what little savings are available must be spread over an ever-greater number of workers.

A country's population growth rate is determined by many cultural, economic, and political variables. We will consider a few of the more important variables.

POPULATION AND THE STAGE OF ECONOMIC DEVELOPMENT   The richest countries contain an ever-smaller proportion of the world's population, and the poorest countries contain an ever-larger proportion. This is one of the reasons why population is a controversial topic. Efforts to curb population growth rates raise cries of racism, since the rich countries are predominantly white, while the poor countries are predominantly nonwhite.

Table 22.1 showed population growth rates by income group. The highest population growth rates are found in the poorest countries, which averaged 2.6 percent per year in the 1980s (excluding China and India). The lowest population growth rates are found in the richest developed countries, which averaged just 0.6 percent per year over the same period. Population growth rates vary widely within each category, however. In China, government laws raised the age at which young people could marry and provided severe economic penalties for those who had more than one child. China's population growth rate was only 1.4 percent per year in the 1980s. Kenya had a population growth rate almost three times that high, although it has an identical per capital GDP of $370.

A country's population growth rate is calculated as the difference between its birth rate and its death rate. (We are ignoring net immigration here.) For most of the world's history, birth rates and death rates were both high, so that population growth rates were low. Death rates fell dramatically all over the world in the twentieth century with the discovery of modern methods of inoculation against childhood diseases. In high-income countries this was accompanied by falling birth rates. In developing countries birth rates are beginning to fall, but death rates have fallen much faster. Therefore, the high population growth rates that we observe in the developing countries are the result of high birth rates and low death rates.

Does a high population growth rate *cause* a low per capita income? Or does a high per capita income *cause* a low population growth rate? Which is the horse pulling the cart? The evidence is that cause and effect runs in both directions. We have already indicated how a high population growth rate lowers the potential growth rate because investment must be spread over more workers. In the model below we examine how a higher per capita income could lead to a lower birth rate.

Families have children for a variety of reasons: love, companionship, custom, accident, religious principles, and so on. Economic factors also help determine the outcome. It may appear strange to talk about the supply of and the demand for children, yet both factors are at work in determining the population growth rate.

THE SUPPLY OF CHILDREN   Supply factors look at a couple's ability to control how many offspring they will have. Genetic factors of both men and women play an important role in determining fertility and hence the potential supply. Cultural and political values also determine the age at which people marry and govern accepted practices for frequency of sexual intercourse, types of acceptable contraceptives, the legality of abortion, and so on. In some cultures males migrate seasonally in search of work, thus lowering the frequency of sexual contact.

Economics also plays a role. Poor families may lack money or information about contraceptives or sterilization procedures, and, thus, even if they wanted to limit pregnancy, they may lack the means to do so (except through abstinence). Rich families can enhance their fertility using fertility drugs, in vitro fertilization, and other methods.

Thus, the supply of children is determined by genetics, cultural habits, laws, technology, and economics.

Yet supply factors alone are not enough to explain population growth rates. For many years population control experts disseminated birth control information and free contraceptives in poor rural areas. It was assumed that high birth rates were caused by the absence of technology or income for controlling the supply of children. By making these available, birth rates were expected to decline. In reality, birth rates did not decline in many rural areas. These families desired (demanded) more children, and they threw away the contraceptives.

THE DEMAND FOR CHILDREN   The demand for children refers to the desire to have children. Culture plays an important role in determining the desired family size. In some cultures children provide spiritual links to the world, so families want the most children possible. In many poor countries children have important economic functions also. They work in the fields or tend to livestock from an early age, providing food for the family. And they are the primary source of food and shelter when parents become too old to work. Having many children (especially sons) is desired to provide for security in old age.

Children are not very costly to raise in poor developing countries. Births are done at home by midwives. Babysitting is done for free by elderly relatives. Education in rural areas is limited, and out-of-pocket expenses are few. Thus, given the important benefits of children, and the limited cost, it is easy to see why in poor countries the desire to have more children is strongly ingrained.

In rich countries, by contrast, governments have outlawed child labor (except in rural areas affecting a small fraction of families). In addition, government and private pensions provide for retirement. Social Security and welfare programs provide for persons without adequate means. Hence, the economic benefits of children are greatly reduced in developed countries. The out-of-pocket costs of having children are high, including medical expenses, shelter, clothing, food, and education (including college).

Perhaps the largest expense of having children in developed countries is an "implicit" one—the time required to raise children. As economic opportunities increase for women in developing countries, so does the opportunity cost of their time. With a mobile society, nuclear families often live far away from relatives who could help with babysitting. Day care must be purchased at a high price.

In developed countries, therefore, the economic cost of having children is relatively high and the economic benefit relatively low. It is not surprising that the demand for children is lower as a consequence. Meanwhile, we have already indicated that wealthier countries can control the supply of children better as well.

Our supply and demand analysis is by no means the entire explanation for lower population growth rates in the developed countries. However, it does provide a strong theoretical model for explaining the existing evidence.

There are some important policy implications that derive from this analysis. One of these is that the best way to lower population growth rates is to raise incomes. A rising income will reduce both the demand for and the supply of children. But we should be careful to remember that per capita income is not a good measure of how the average family is living because the distribution of income is often quite unequal in the developing countries. That is why the distribution of income plays an important role in determining population growth rates, just as it does in determining the overall rate of saving. We need to consider the relationship between income distribution and economic development in order to understand the economic prospects of the developing countries.

INCOME DISTRIBUTION AND ECONOMIC DEVELOPMENT

Table 22.3 presents the 1990 distribution of income in five countries at different stages of economic development. The distribution of income in society can be measured in several ways. In Table 22.3 the population of a country is divided into five groups or quintiles. Each quintile comprises 20 percent of the total population. The percentage of income going to each quintile is shown also.

For example, the poorest 20 percent of households in Brazil earned just 2.4 percent of total household income. The second poorest 20 percent earned 5.7 percent of household income. The third and fourth quintiles earned 10.7 and 18.6 percent of household income, respectively. The richest 20 percent earned 62.6 percent of household income.

Since these data refer to shares of household income, not household income itself, these data are measures of *relative* income distribution. They do not measure absolute income differences. Thus, even though the poorest 20 percent in Bangladesh earn a greater share of household income than does the comparable group in Brazil, the *absolute* income level for the poorest 20 percent in Brazil may be higher.

TABLE 22.3   Measures of Income Distribution

COUNTRY	GDP PER CAPITA ($1990)[a]	YEAR	PERCENTAGE SHARE OF TOTAL HOUSEHOLD INCOME BY QUINTILE[b]					RATIO OF BOTTOM 40 TO TOP 20[c]
			Lowest 20 Percent	Second Quintile	Third Quintile	Fourth Quintile	Highest 20 Percent	
Bangladesh	1,050	1985–86	10.0	13.7	17.2	21.9	37.2	23.7/37.2
Malaysia	5,900	1987	4.6	9.3	13.9	21.2	51.2	13.9/51.2
Brazil	4,780	1983	2.4	5.7	10.7	18.6	62.6	8.1/62.6
United States	21,360	1985	4.7	11.0	17.4	25.0	41.9	15.7/41.9
Japan	16,950	1979	8.7	13.2	17.5	23.1	37.5	21.9/37.5

[a]GDP is calculated on the basis of purchasing power parity, using the United Nations International Comparisons Program.
[b]These estimates should be treated with caution. In Bangladesh the data refer to per capita expenditure. In Malaysia the data refer to per capita income.
[c]This is income going to the poorest 40 percent of households (the lowest two quintiles) compared to income going to the richest 20 percent of households.

SOURCE: The World Bank, *World Development Report 1992* (New York: Oxford University Press, 1992), Table 30, 276–277.

The Kuznets Curve

KUZNETS CURVE

A curve that shows the relationship between the income distribution and the per capita income for countries in different stages of economic development.

The data in the table suggest an interesting relationship between income distribution and per capita income known as the **Kuznets curve,** named after Simon Kuznets, who first described it. The Kuznets curve appears in Figure 22.3. Countries with very low per capita incomes tend to have relatively equal distributions of income (point *A*). Countries with high per capita incomes also tend to have relatively equal distributions of income (point *C*). Countries that are in the middle, however, tend to have income distributions that are much more unequal (point *B*). There are important exceptions to this rule, which are discussed below. And it is important to note that no country has or would desire to have a perfectly equal distribution of income.

The explanation for the hump in the Kuznets curve is not entirely clear, but there are some general tendencies that we can observe. The poorest countries of the world have a subsistence-based agricultural economy, which creates little by way of economic income. Consequently, the income distribution is relatively equal because just about everyone is very poor. As countries industrialize and income rises, however, not everyone is equally lifted out of poverty. Contrary to the axiom "A rising tide lifts all boats," in economic development some boats are anchored and flooded by the rising tide! In a growing market economy, those with the skills and the aptitudes valued by the market succeed. With access to education limited to a few, the rising demands for skilled labor cause a sharp rise in the relative wages and incomes of some and a decrease in the relative or absolute incomes of others.

This tendency toward inequality is often exacerbated by government policies that benefit industrial development at the expense of the poor in rural areas. Examples of government policies that result in a widening income distribution include overvaluing the exchange rate, which hurts the agricultural export sector in which many poor work; subsidizing credit for certain industries, which hurts the poor who are usually denied credit; and providing government education, health, and other programs only in cities, while most of the poor live in rural areas.

Inequality in land ownership (especially in Latin America) virtually precludes any chance for upward mobility in rural areas. Since colonial times in

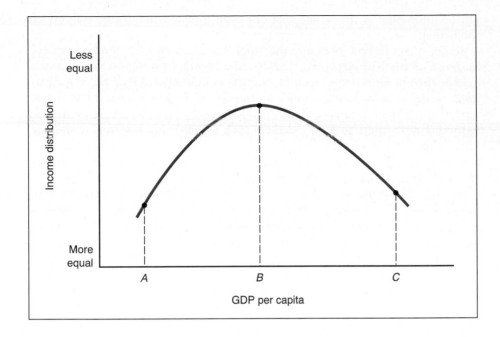

FIGURE 22.3

The Kuznets Curve

The Kuznets Curve shows the relationship between the distribution of income and per capita GDP for countries in different stages of development. GDP per capita is on the horizontal axis, and the income distribution is on the vertical axis. The income distribution tends to be most equal in the very poor and the very rich countries, and becomes much more unequal in the middle income countries that are undergoing rapid industrialization. The newly industrializing countries (NICs) of Asia are an exception to this tendency, however. They are maintaining a relatively equal distribution of income as they industrialize their economies.

Latin America, for example, most land has been held in a few large family estates called *latifundios*. Land is held often for purposes of prestige, not just income, and poor peasants cannot buy land even if someone would lend them the money to buy. There are some exceptions to this general picture. In Costa Rica land is more evenly distributed. It is no accident that Costa Rica also has one of the most stable democracies in Latin America. Since the revolution of 1917, Mexico has engaged in land reform, with mixed success.

Whatever its cause, the rise in inequality in many newly industrializing countries has proved to be a vexing problem. Those at the bottom of the socioeconomic ladder are the last to benefit from economic growth and the hardest hit during the inevitable economic downturns. Most developing countries have little by way of a social safety net for such emergencies. The terrible and grueling conditions of life at the bottom give rise to hundreds of millions of youths who are disaffected, disillusioned, and alienated from society. As England was industrializing in the nineteenth century, the masses of poor flowing into the industrial cities led to miserable and polluted living conditions—much as you find today in the megapoles of Mexico City, Rio de Janeiro, Cairo, Calcutta, and Jakarta. This gave rise to socialism and communism in England and other European countries because capitalism was not seen as a desirable system for human advancement. The anti-capitalist ideology was utilized by the communist regime in Russia following the revolution of 1917 and also was later adopted by Mao Zedong during and after his successful revolution in China in 1949.

Throughout the twentieth century, revolutionary movements sprang up around the world wherever young people had lost faith in the capitalist system. Revolutions in Cuba, Angola, Mozambique, Vietnam, and Nicaragua all led (at least initially) to the establishment of command economies that redistributed wealth and income. Communist guerrilla insurgencies to overthrow capitalism are still under way with various degrees of success in Guatemala, Peru, and the Philippines. Thus, the rise in inequality brings with it a social cost that can be quite high at times, and that can even threaten the overall stability of the nation.

As per capita income rises into the "high" range, inequality tends to lessen, as shown on the Kuznets curve. This is caused by many different factors, some market driven, others the result of political compromise. Over many generations, wages in a market may tend to equalize as higher wages in one sector attract new entrants and lower wages in another sector discourage new entrants. Assuming no barriers to entry, workers seek to better themselves by moving into higher-paying industries, and the greater supply of labor in these industries tends to depress wages in those industries and raise wages in the industries that are losing workers.

But the transition to a more equal income distribution may also require public action. Government laws help lessen income inequalities in numerous ways, for example, by creating universal public education, outlawing child labor and requiring compulsory school attendance, establishing a minimum wage, providing a legal basis for the creation of unions (as a countervailing power to monopsony), creating a progressive income tax, establishing the Social Security System, creating the G.I. bill (for educating veterans), providing for federally guaranteed student loans, and creating federal health, housing, and welfare programs, to name just a few.

The Asian NICs.

The rise in inequality is not a necessary condition for economic growth, however. In recent years the success of the Asian model has been widely noted. The Asian model is based on the success stories of the newly industrializing countries (NICs) of South Korea, Taiwan, Singapore, and Hong Kong. This basic strategy calls for redistribution of land into productive hands, redistribution and development of human capital via universal public education, and creation of labor-intensive, export-oriented industries. These economies have grown very successfully in an egalitarian way after an initial period of slow growth. Thus, the Kuznets hypothesis that a rise in inequality occurs with a rise in per capita income (up to a point) is not universally valid. However, the price to pay may be the greater authoritarian and paternalistic nature of these governments, which regulate human behavior to a greater degree than Westerners are comfortable with.

The unequal distribution of income and wealth in developing countries continues to be a source of great social tension. This social tension reduces the potential standard of living for the masses as more and more scarce resources are put into armaments to protect those who have from those who have not.

INWARD VERSUS OUTWARD GROWTH STRATEGIES

The Asian NICs represent outstanding success stories in contrast to the developing countries that pursued a diametrically opposite strategy. The NICs' strategy was outward-oriented. Its success hinged on achieving economies of scale through exports and gaining access to foreign markets (principally the United States). Other developing countries, by contrast, pursued an inward-oriented strategy. This inward strategy is called **import-substituting indus-trialization (ISI).**

The impetus for ISI was sound. Prior to the 1950s, developing countries exported raw materials (agricultural and mineral products) and imported fin-ished manufactured goods. As world incomes grew, the demand for manufac-tured goods grew much faster than did the demand for raw materials.[6] Devel-oping countries needed to produce more value added to their raw materials in order to prevent a fall in their terms-of-trade. The *terms-of-trade* is the ratio of export prices to import prices.

Industrialization was thus seen as the key to development. The question was which goods to produce? The Asian NICs chose to industrialize by pro-ducing goods desired in the United States. They had little choice, since their internal populations were very small and provided a limited internal market. They picked labor-intensive goods for which they had a comparative advantage in production.

The ISI countries, following a different approach, decided to produce man-ufactured goods that they themselves needed. In other words, they produced goods that they had previously imported—hence the term *import-substituting industrialization.* On one level this method appears logical. If a good is de-manded and imported, why not produce it domestically? The economist's an-swer is that it may be more costly to produce it domestically and cheaper to import it. Comparative advantage should dictate which products are imported and which are exported. ISI, however, did not proceed on the basis of com-parative advantage.

The Latin American Experience

ISI was the dominant strategy followed in Latin America in the 1950s and 1960s. As automobiles were a key part of the transportation system and as automobiles had been imported, the manufacture of automobiles became the leading edge of this movement. In the first phase automobiles were assembled using imported parts. In the next phase (called backward linkages) the parts themselves—steel, tires, windshields, radios, engines, transmissions, ball bear-ings, and so on—were manufactured.

At each stage high tariffs (sometimes over 100 percent) were placed on the imported item that was being manufactured domestically. In addition, many subsidies were provided in the form of tax breaks, low-interest-rate loans, and overvalued exchange rates. These high tariffs and subsidies were meant to be temporary to protect the "infant industry." However, domestic manufacturers, protected from competition from abroad and enjoying a near monopoly do-mestically, exerted significant pressure to maintain these tariffs and subsidies.

The results were quite good initially, as these economies grew substantially. The long-term effects were quite disastrous, however. Industrial products were being produced very inefficiently, with minimal economies of scale and little competition. The prices of domestic cars were far higher than were the prices of better-made imports. The overvalued exchange rates caused continual balance-of-payments problems, often requiring bailouts from the International

IMPORT-SUBSTITUTING
INDUSTRIALIZATION (ISI)

A strategy for economic growth and development in which a developing country produces goods that it had previously been importing.

---

[6]In more technical terms, the income elasticity of demand for manufactured goods is much higher than it is for raw materials.

Monetary Fund. The traditional agricultural export sector suffered, and income distribution became more unequal. Government subsidies led to large budget deficits that were financed by printing money, thereby causing high inflation rates. The low-interest-rate loans caused financial repression, resulting in a lower effective savings rate and capital flight. To provide capital and technology, foreign multinational companies were invited in with tax breaks. These companies often exerted significant political pressures that distorted the political process.

Petrodollar Recycling and the Debt Crisis

The failure of import-substituting industrialization became evident in the 1970s. The oil price shocks of 1973–74 and 1979 led many countries (mainly in Latin America) to borrow heavily from private banks in the developed countries in order to keep their industrial economies operating. Banks were flush with deposits to loan because many members of the Organization of Petroleum Exporting Countries (OPEC) could not spend all the oil revenues they were earning. Latin American countries historically had provided high returns to investors, and bankers were eager to earn these high returns. This funneling of oil deposits to developing countries was called **petrodollar recycling.**

PETRODOLLAR RECYCLING

The practice among financial institutions of lending to the developing countries the funds that they receive from the oil-producing countries.

In the early 1980s this system collapsed under the weight of rising interest rates and economic recession in developed countries. Borrowing countries could not earn the foreign exchange needed to pay the interest on the foreign debt, which by this time totaled over $800 billion. Latin American countries experienced a debt crisis that threatened the stability of the world's financial markets. Economic progress ground to a halt throughout Latin America as new investment funds dried up.

In the 1980s most of these countries went through painful economic adjustments in order to make their economies more competitive and to get out from under the debt overload. These economic reforms are discussed in the final part of this chapter.

Economic Reform in the 1980s and 1990s

The pervasive mismanagement of economies, leading to large fiscal deficits, runaway inflation, overvalued exchange rates, and current account deficits, inevitably generates a maze of piecemeal bureaucratic regulations that give way to bribery and corruption. The incentive structure in production is distorted, and financial markets, if they exist at all, do not work well. Add to this a fair amount of political instability and it is not hard to see why many developing countries lurch from one crisis to the next.

Against this backdrop there have been some real reform measures that should pay off in the 1990s. The collapse of the Soviet empire, and its economic reform known as *perestroika* is being echoed in various other parts of the world. Governments are making serious efforts at economic reform. In broad outline this involves

1. Cutting government spending. Especially necessary are cuts in subsidies to producers and subsidies to consumers that create surpluses of unwanted goods and shortages of desired goods, respectively.

2. Privatization of industry. The selling of inefficient state-owned companies reduces the fiscal deficit.

3. Setting realistic exchange rates. Exports are encouraged by lowering exchange rates to realistic levels, which leads to an improvement in the current account balance.

4. Reducing barriers to trade. Becoming part of the world trading system ensures that domestic manufacturers cannot hide behind tariff walls. Companies that do not produce efficiently know that they will fail.

5. Reforming financial markets. Allowing savers to earn a positive real rate of return boosts the savings rate and reduces capital flight. Elimination of credit rationing ensures that these savings find their way into productive investments.

These reforms, often carried out with the advice and financial backing of the International Monetary Fund, have produced success stories in Mexico, Chile, Ghana, and other countries. All across Latin America democratic governments have replaced authoritarian military rulers and are replacing closed, inefficient economies with more open, competitive economies.

As vital as these reforms are for long-run success, they bring immediate hardship to those at the bottom of the economic ladder. The social strain of adjustment is the Achilles' heel that could be the undoing of these governments and their programs.

SUMMARY

The first section of Chapter 22 examined the standards of living in the developing countries.

1. The developing countries include the nations of Latin America, Africa, and Asia, excluding Japan. Their populations make up about four-fifths of the world's population.

2. The poorest countries of the world are located in sub-Saharan Africa, Southeast Asia, and Central Asia. Their economics are largely agriculturally based.

3. It is difficult to compare GDPs between countries due to differences in measurement and problems with converting to a common currency. Incomes adjusted for purchasing power parities can significantly improve the reliability of cross-country comparisons. All comparisons should be used with care, however, because GDP is an imperfect measure of the quality of life.

4. Economic development is a complex process that occurs over many generations. It is difficult to pinpoint a single variable that explains success or failure in any one country. Economic institutions and policies can aid or hinder this process.

The second section of the chapter explored four key determinants of economic growth in the developing countries: labor force participation, the saving rate and the link between savings and productive investment, the choice of production technologies, and the population growth rate.

5. Labor force participation is generally very high in the developing countries. These countries remain poor because labor is not very productive.

6. A country must raise its savings rate in order to invest more and increase its potential growth rate. However, numerous cultural, institutional, and political factors hinder the channeling of savings into productive investments in many developing countries.

7. A country can grow faster by acquiring savings from abroad in the form of direct foreign investment, loans, or gifts.

8. The choice of technology affects the efficiency of the capital used. Distorted factor prices for labor and capital often lead to the wrong market signals being sent and cause businesses in the developing countries to use technologies that are too capital-intensive. Inappropriate capital-intensive technologies drain scarce savings and lower the rate of growth.

9. Population growth is very rapid in the poorest developing countries. This puts severe strains on the limited savings that are available for investment. High population growth rates are the result of both a high supply of children and a high demand for children.

The third section of the chapter looked at the relationship between the distribution of income and economic development.

10. The distribution of income is often most equal in the very poor and very rich countries and most unequal in the middle-income countries that are undergoing rapid industrialization. The Asian NICs have demonstrated that rising inequality is not a necessary condition for economic growth, however.

The final section of Chapter 22 compared and contrasted the outward-oriented and inward-oriented strategies for economic growth and development.

11. The Asian NICs followed a labor-intensive, outward-oriented export strategy for economic development that is based on the principle of comparative advantage and that proved to be highly successful. This strategy also mitigated the tendency toward a more unequal distribution of income.

12. The Latin American countries followed an inward-oriented import-substituting industrialization (ISI) strategy in which they tried to produce the goods that they had previously imported. This proved to be very costly in terms of economic efficiency and generated a number of macroeconomic problems, including high inflation, large budget deficits, current account trade deficits, and huge foreign debts.

13. Many developing countries are undertaking economic reforms to correct these problems. Protecting those at the bottom of the income distribution remains a serious problem for the future, however.

KEY TERMS

capital flight
developed countries
developing countries (LDCs or third world countries)
export-enclave production

financial repression
import-substituting industrialization (ISI)
International Comparisons Program (ICP)

Kuznets curve
labor force participation rate
newly industrializing countries (NICs)
petrodollar recycling

QUESTIONS

1. What are the strengths and the weaknesses of using per capita gross domestic product as a measure of how well off a particular country's citizens are?
2. Why do governments in developing countries often impose interest rate ceilings? Are interest rate ceilings a good policy?
3. As a country's per capita income rises, will the population tend to rise or fall? Explain.
4. Describe some of the factors that hold down the rate of saving in developing countries or prevent the saving that does occur from financing productive investments.
5. a. Discuss the differences between the outward-oriented growth strategy used by the Asian NICs and the inward-oriented growth strategy used by many of the Latin American countries.
   b. Why did each set of countries choose the growth strategy that it did?
   c. Which type of strategy has worked out better in practice, and why?

6. Are the gross domestic products of different countries comparable when they are all converted to one currency by their exchange rate with that currency? If yes, why? If no, why not?
7. Discuss the advantages and the disadvantages of direct foreign investment for developing countries.
8. What is the Kuznets curve, and why is it hump-shaped?
9. a. Why does it make sense for developing countries to use labor-intensive technologies rather than capital-intensive technologies?
   b. What incentives lead businesses in developing countries to use capital-intensive technologies?
10. Comment on the following statement: The demand for children is higher in developed countries than in developing countries because parents in developed countries have more resources to take care of their children.

CASE

The "Flipper" Factor in International Trade*

Dolphins swim above schools of tuna in the eastern tropical Pacific Ocean. Therefore, when fishing vessels catch the tuna in their nets, they invariably catch and kill a large number of dolphins as well. The U.S. Marine Mammal Protection Act of 1972, as amended in 1988, set a maximum level of dolphin mortality for U.S. tuna vessels fishing in this area. The Act also stipulated that tuna are not to be imported from any country whose fisherman have destroyed more than 1.25 times as many dolphins as the American fishing fleet did in the same year (from 1990 on).

The United States banned the import of yellowfin tuna products from Mexico in February, 1991 at the urging of environmentalists, and extended the ban to Venezuelan yellowfin tuna products in March, 1991. The United States also imposed a secondary ban on imports of yellowfin tuna products from France, Italy, the U.K., and Spain if the products used tuna imported from Mexico and Venezuela.

Mexico protested the U.S. ban before the Council of the General Agreement on Trade and Tariffs (GATT). In September 1991, a GATT dispute-resolution panel ruled that

both the primary ban and the secondary ban were in violation of GATT rules. The ruling was never formally adopted by the GATT Council, and the dispute died down when Mexico voluntarily took steps to protect the dolphins. Nonetheless, this episode illustrates a potential conflict between the enforcement of varying environmental standards in different countries and the promotion of free trade. Specifically, should a country be allowed by GATT to impose unilateral sanctions against its trading partners for having less stringent environmental standards? The killing of dolphins by tuna fishing vessels is a particularly interesting case in point.

Killing dolphins is objectionable to many Americans who have been brought up watching the "Flipper" television series, and who have enjoyed watching dolphins perform at dolphin shows such as Florida's Sea World. But is this an environmental issue that merits a trade embargo? The dolphin is not an endangered species and thus is not protected by the International Convention on Trade in Endangered Species. Also, how can Mexican tuna fishermen know in advance what the American dolphin kill will be? Finally, the GATT ruling against the United States was not arbitrary. It

*Provided by K. K. Fung, Memphis State University.

continued on next page

The "Flipper" Factor in International Trade (cont.)

was based on a reasonable principle that the way an imported product is produced is not a good reason to discriminate against it. Many U.S. health and enviornmental laws directly regulate production in order to promote safety in the workplace and to protect the environment. The GATT principle simply states that such laws cannot be applied unilaterally to other countries in restraint of trade.

To be generally applicable, GATT requires that health, safety, and environmental laws be necessary and least trade restrictive. This means that such laws should achieve their objectives with regulations that are least costly to comply with and that do not unduly impose higher compliance costs on foreign than domestic producers. The North American Free Trade Agreement (NAFTA) further specifies that these laws be based on scientific principles and risk assessment. The provisions of the Marine Mammal Protection Act on the killing of dolphins may be inconsistent with these GATT and NAFTA principles.

Non-tariff trade barriers have dominated discussions in the current Uruguay Round of GATT because they are the main form of trade restriction imposed by the industrialized nations. Many domestic policies which were never intended to protect domestic producers from foreign competition have inadvertently become significant non-tariff barriers to imports. The "flipper" dolphin-tuna incident is a notable example.

ECONOMIC ADVISOR'S REPORT

Suppose that you have been hired by GATT to advise them on the application of domestic environmental standards to international trade. They ask you the following questions. How would you respond?

1. If imports are cheaper because they have lower environmental costs, should nations be allowed to impose "anti-dumping" tariffs that reflect the higher environmental costs faced by domestic producers? Would your answer be the same if the imports were cheaper because of lower wages in the exporting country?
2. Environmental concerns were an important obstacle to the U.S. ratification of NAFTA. Mexico's conciliatory gesture in the dolphin/tuna dispute was largely designed to avoid jeopardizing NAFTA. If environmental safeguards are not built into NAFTA, will Mexico become a haven for heavily-polluting U.S. industries in search of lax environmental regulations?
3. In your opinion, what is the least trade-restrictive way for the United States to limit the importation of tuna products from Mexico that is consistent with the GATT principles on this issue?

SOURCES: "EC Spokesman Condemns U.S. For Marine Mammal Protection, Act," *ENA International Environment Daily*, February 19, 1992; "Environmentalists Against GATT," *Wall Street Journal*, March 19, 1993; "Free Trade vs. Law," *The National Law Journal*, March 29, 1993; "Mexico Announces a Dolphin Protection Plan," *Los Angeles Times*, September 25, 1993, D6; "The Greening of Protectionism," *The Economist*, February 27, 1993; "We Can Have Free Trade and Clean Environment," *The Houston Chronicle*, April 6, 1993, A13.

Government in the U.S. Economy

23

The Role of Government in the U.S. Economy and Government Expenditures

LEARNING OBJECTIVES

CONCEPTS TO LEARN

Natural monopoly	Moral hazard
The economics of information	Externalities
The principal-agent problem	Non-exclusive public goods
Adverse selection	

CONCEPTS TO RECALL

Equality of opportunity [2]	The for whom or distribution question [3]
Horizontal equity [2]	The macroeconomic policy goals [2,6,7]

overnment spending in the United States exceeds $2 trillion, approximately 35 percent of the total national output produced each year. Why does a society that is fundamentally committed to free market capitalism, and distrustful of government intervention, tolerate such massive government expenditures? The answer is that U.S. citizens are of two minds regarding the proper role of the government in the economy. They distrust the government, yet they willingly turn to the government to solve pressing economic problems. These two mind sets have been very much in evidence in recent presidential politics.

The distrust of government intervention in the economy runs deep in the United States. Ronald Reagan correctly sensed the growing disenchantment with ever-expanding government programs and rode a promise to "get the government off our backs" to a landslide victory in the 1980 presidential election. His administration failed to keep this promise, however. President Reagan inherited a federal budget of $600 billion, equal to 22.5 percent of the national output. In the final year of his administration, expenditures by the federal government had grown to $1.1 trillion, equal to 22.8 percent of the national output. President George Bush also campaigned on a promise to streamline the federal budget. He believed that the United States should rely more on the private sector to solve social problems and likened private initiatives to "a thousand points of light." President Bush was even less successful than President Reagan was in keeping his campaign promise. The growth in federal spending accelerated under his administration. By 1992 federal expenditures were nearly $1.5 trillion, equal to 24.4 percent of the national output.

Presidents Reagan and Bush were unable to reduce federal spending for many political and economic reasons. One of the more important economic reasons is that a market economy needs a strong government sector. Markets often fail to perform satisfactorily. When this happens, the American public has been quite willing to set aside its distrust of the government and accept government intervention into economic affairs.

President Bill Clinton rode this other mind set to victory in 1992. He campaigned on the need for change in the United States. Far from "getting the government off our backs," he saw the federal government leading the way in a frontal assault on a broad range of economic problems: reducing unemployment, reforming health care, cleaning up the environment, restoring quality in education, rebuilding the nation's infrastructure, and addressing a host of other issues. In 12 short years presidential policies had come full circle, tugging at the ambivalence that the people of the United States feel toward their government.

Chapters 23 and 24 discuss the economic role of the government sector in a market economy, with particular emphasis on the United States. Chapter 23 begins with the legitimate economic functions of the government in a market economy.

Governments have a very important economic role to play in a market economy. We noted in Chapter 4 that a market economy can hardly function at all without a government-imposed legal structure that, at a minimum, defines the property (ownership) rights to capital and land and enforces contracts between buyers and sellers. The government must also ensure that there is enough money available to "grease the wheels of commerce." Economic development would come to a halt without the use of money that people have confidence in.

The federal, state, and local governments in the United States have expanded their economic responsibilities far beyond these basic functions, however. We also saw in Chapter 4 that the government sector has been one of the leading growth sectors of the U.S. economy since World War II.

Even so, the distrust of government places an absolute condition on when the government can legitimately become involved in economic affairs. Government intervention is justified *only* on the basis of market failure in the United States. The American public clearly believes that the free market economy is the natural mechanism for answering the four basic economic questions outlined in Chapter 3: What? How? For Whom? Now versus the Future? Government intervention is justified only when the market system performs badly, or not at all. People may disagree in a particular instance about whether the market is performing sufficiently badly to warrant government intervention. But few people in the United States would support government intervention without evidence of significant market failure.

The belief in the market system also places limits on the appropriate forms of government intervention. Government policies must try to facilitate the operation of the market economy, not undermine it. The idea is that government economic policy should steer the free market back on the path toward efficiency and equity, not replace the market entirely with a set of government institutions. In some cases replacing the market is the only possible option, but this is definitely not the option of first choice.

The first section of Chapter 23 considers the economic problems that plague a market economy and lead to a call for government intervention. We want to understand how and why markets fail, how the government should respond to each instance of market failure, and how the government's policies can help promote efficiency and equity. The second section of the chapter then looks at actual government expenditures in the United States and shows that they are consistent with the legitimate functions of government. All the major U.S. government programs can be viewed as a response to market failure.

MARKET FAILURES JUSTIFYING GOVERNMENT INTERVENTION

Chapter 5 described the market system working as well as it possibly can, when markets are competitive and operate according to the Laws of Supply and Demand. Competitive markets have an impressive set of strengths:

1. Competitive markets give individuals and business firms the *freedom* to pursue their own self-interests and to solve their economic problems as they see fit.
2. Competitive market exchanges are *orderly* rather than chaotic, even though no one is directing the exchanges. Competitive markets move naturally to their equilibrium price and quantity.

3. Competitive markets are *responsive* to the desires of consumers. Prices and profits guide firms to produce the goods and services that consumers want. For example, we saw that an increase in the demand for a product increases its price. The increase in price is profitable for firms and induces them to increase the quantity supplied to meet the increase in demand.

4. Finally, the microeconomic chapters of the text show that competitive markets promote society's twin goals of *efficiency* and *equity*. The macroeconomic chapters give one example relating to efficiency. They show how competitive labor markets automatically bring the economy to its production possibilities frontier.

Freedom, order, responsiveness, and the potential for efficiency and equity—those are certainly impressive qualities arguing in favor of letting the free market economy solve society's economic problems. Where, then, does the market system go wrong? What problems justify a substantial economic role for the government as a corrector of market failure?

The truth of the matter is that a fair number of things go wrong, and all the capitalist nations have chosen to combat the ills afflicting their market economies with heavy doses of government intervention. Some nations intervene more aggressively than others, but no nation is anywhere close to the textbook ideal of pure market capitalism.

THE GOVERNMENT SECTOR IN THE INDUSTRIALIZED MARKET ECONOMIES

The World Bank publishes a selection of data on government spending and taxation for all nations. The data for the industrialized market economies reveal a number of similarities and differences among them.

The clearest indication of the relative sizes of the government sectors are the ratios of general government consumption by all levels of government to gross domestic product (GDP). General government consumption includes only the resources-using government purchases of goods and services; it does not include transfer payments. Therefore, these ratios indicate the percentage of a nation's resources that are allocated to the public sector.

The ratios reported for 19 of the industrialized market economies in 1989 were remarkably similar. Fourteen were within a range of 15 to 20 percent, including the United States at 20 percent. Denmark and Sweden were the exceptions on the high end, with ratios of 25 percent and 26 percent, respectively. Japan was the outstanding exception on the low end, with a ratio of 9 percent. The other low-end countries were Ireland, New Zealand, and Switzerland, at 14, 14, and 13 percent respectively. The message from these ratios is that the industrialized market economies have all chosen a mixed capitalist system. Their economies are predominantly private, but their commitment to capitalism has not precluded the development of substantial government sectors.

The World Bank also publishes data on total expenditures by the central governments, which include both government purchases and transfer payments. Data on transfer payments by lower-level governments are not widely available. The ratios of total central government expenditures to GDP, when set against the ratios of government consumption to GDP, give a sense of the willingness to redistribute purchasing power nation-wide through taxes and transfer payments, either cash or in-kind. Here we see much more variation among the industrialized market economies. In 1989, the ratios ranged from a high of 57.9 percent in Ireland to a low of 16.5 percent in Japan. The high-transfer countries, with ratios above 40 percent, were: Ireland (57.9); the Netherlands (54.5); Belgium (50.7); Italy (47.9); New Zealand (45.9); Norway (42.7); France (42.6); Denmark (41.8); and Sweden (40.6). The low-transfer countries, with ratios below 30 percent, were: Finland (29.3); Germany (29.0); Canada (23.1); United States (23.0); and Japan (16.5).

The World Bank data also show that only the United Kingdom and the United States devoted more than 10 percent of their central government expenditures to defense. The United States was the major outlier by far in 1989, at 24.6 percent, which explains why its government consumption ratio was relatively high. The United Kingdom was much closer to the rest of the pack, at 12.5 percent.

A word of warning is in order on using government data to judge a nation's commitment to free enterprise. Japan would appear to be the most committed to free enterprise on the basis of the government data. It is the low-end outlier on both government purchases and central government transfer payments. Yet Japan has long had a policy of targeting and subsidizing particular industries that it wants to develop. It also permits huge business combines among firms in the manufacturing and financial sectors that would be considered anticompetitive and illegal under U.S. antitrust laws. In fact, many observers have concluded that Japan is much less committed to unfettered free enterprise than the United States is, despite its much smaller government sector.[1]

Distributional, Allocational, and Stabilization Functions

Economists classify market failures, and the government policies designed to correct them, in three broad categories: distributional, allocational, and stabilization. The **distributional** problems and policies relate to the goal of achieving fair and evenhanded market exchanges and an acceptable distribution of income. The **allocational** problems and policies relate to the goal of achieving an efficient use of society's scarce resources. The **stabilization** problems and policies relate to achieving the macroeconomic goals of long-run economic growth, full employment, price stability, and satisfactory economic relations with foreign countries.

Keep in mind that the three categories are highly interdependent. For instance, any major government policy designed to correct perceived distributional inequities is likely to have important allocational and macroeconomic effects as well. Nonetheless, the three-way classification is a useful way of describing the various functions of government in a market economy.

DISTRIBUTIONAL POLICIES

Government economic policies that respond to market failures relating to the goals of achieving fair and evenhanded market exchanges and an acceptable distribution of income.

ALLOCATIONAL POLICIES

Government economic policies that respond to market failures relating to the goal of achieving an efficient use of society's scarce resources.

STABILIZATION POLICIES

Government economic policies that respond to market failures relating to the macroeconomic policy goals of achieving long-run economic growth, full employment, price stability, and satisfactory economic relations with foreign countries.

---

[1]The World Bank, *World Development Report 1991: The Challenge of Development* (Oxford, England: Oxford University Press, 1991), Table 9, p. 221 and Table 11, p. 225.

Distributional Problems

The government has a fundamental role to play in resolving the distribution question. The problem for a market economy concerns the distribution of income.

Left to its own devices, a market economy completely determines the distribution of income. The factor markets set values for all factor prices—the wage rates and salaries for every occupation, the rates of return on all forms of saving, and the rental values for every parcel of land. These factor prices combine with the quantities of factors that individuals supply to the marketplace to determine the income each person receives.

Unfortunately, the market system cannot guarantee that the distribution of income will be acceptable from society's point of view, even if all markets operated according to the Laws of Supply and Demand. The sticking point surrounds the ownership of resources. By and large, a market economy takes the initial ownership of resources as a given. Those who are able to bring large amounts of highly valued resources to the factor markets earn high incomes. Conversely, those with meager amounts of property, little savings, and few marketable skills earn low incomes. Unequals can be treated very unequally. Is this fair?

Unfortunately, the ownership of resources happens to be far from equal in any of the world's market economies. People begin the race for economic success each year at very different starting lines. Some people inherit large amounts of wealth; others are born into poverty. Some people are blessed with great intelligence or coordination; others are rather dull or uncoordinated. Some people are fortunate enough to have received college and even graduate educations; others are high school drop-outs. Not surprisingly, the results in the marketplace also tend to be very unequal. The distribution of income is highly unequal in the United States and the distribution of wealth is even more unequal. Also, large numbers of people are simply left behind in the economic race. It is estimated that over 35 million people in the United States live under conditions of poverty.

Suppose that society wants to change the distribution of income. A market system has no way of responding to this desire because significant changes in the personal distribution of income require significant changes in the current distribution of resources. Only the government can be counted on to change the distribution of resources in line with society's preferences. In a free market economy, changes in the distribution of resources are best accomplished by a policy of broad-based taxes and transfer payments that take income from some and give it to others.

PROBLEMS WITH GOVERNMENT INTERVENTION   Saying that the government *can* achieve a desirable distribution of income through general tax and transfer policies is a far cry from saying that government policies will actually achieve a desirable distribution of income. Government redistributional policies are sure to encounter a number of difficulties.

The first problem is that political debate may fail to reach a consensus on the distribution question, especially if public opinion is sharply divided. Resolving differences of opinion is especially problematic under democratic voting procedures, a point we will discuss in Chapter 24. In addition, those who are taxed may resent being taxed, especially if they disagree with the majority's views on the distribution. Finally, both taxes and transfers introduce inefficiencies into the market economy. Society, therefore, is faced with yet another tough question: What is the best trade-off between equity and inefficiency in redistributing income? The need to preserve efficiency may prevent society from redistributing income as much as it would like.

For all these reasons, governments are unlikely to achieve an entirely satisfactory solution to the distribution question. Nonetheless, only the government has any hope of succeeding. Left to its own devices, the market system simply cannot resolve the distribution question, *even if all markets are competitive and operate according to the Laws of Supply and Demand.*

Allocational Problems

Free market economies are particularly effective at allocating society's scarce resources, but all is not smooth sailing. Market economies encounter two kinds of obstacles along the way, market problems and technical problems. The two can occur independently, but they are often closely related. The technical problems are usually the source of the market problems.

The market problems relate to the fact that some markets are not very competitive. Approximately 25 percent of all goods and services in the United States are produced in noncompetitive markets that do not operate according to the Laws of Supply and Demand. The two most common reasons why markets become noncompetitive are that (1) a few very large firms come to dominate the market and (2) buyers and sellers do not all have access to the same information. Noncompetitive markets give rise to inefficiencies.

In addition to noncompetitive markets, capitalism suffers from a number of technical problems that lead to a call for government intervention. We will consider three of the more important technical problems in this section: incomplete markets, with reference to insurance; externalities; and public goods.

NONCOMPETITIVE MARKETS AND ECONOMIES OF SCALE   Markets become dominated by large firms not because the managers of these firms are smarter than the managers of smaller firms are. Rather, their market power most often has a technological basis, the presence of significant economies of scale. Production on a very large scale is often much cheaper, per unit of output, than is production on a small scale.

Economies of large-scale production pose a dilemma for supporters of a free market economy. On the one hand, economies of scale conserve society's scarce resources by reducing the overall costs of production. On the other hand, big firms with market power do not necessarily behave in a manner that transfers the cost savings through to consumers. Consumers gain only if the lower costs translate into lower prices. But large firms often set their prices well above their per-unit costs and capture an undue proportion of the cost savings as increased profits. Some people consider this unfair as well as inefficient.

Noncompetitive markets pose a very difficult question for society: Are the inefficiencies and inequities sufficiently harmful to warrant government action? The existence of market power creates a potential role for the government, but reasonable people can and do disagree on the question of whether government intervention can improve matters. The uncertainty of how to react to the market power of large firms has been reflected in the United States' antitrust posture. Tough antitrust laws that attempt to limit the market power of the large firms have been on the books since the early 1900s, but enforcement of the laws has varied considerably over time. The Reagan administration ushered in a much more relaxed stance against market power than had been true in the previous two decades. The U.S. Justice Department approved a number of mergers between large firms in the 1980s and 1990s that it would not have allowed in the 1960s and 1970s.

NATURAL MONOPOLIES The call for government intervention in the United States has been more persuasive when economies of scale lead to a **natural monopoly,** in which a single firm can supply the entire market demand most cheaply. Natural monopolies tend to arise when the start-up costs of production are very large relative to the operating costs of providing a good or a service once the production facilities are in place. Examples include the public utilities (electricity, water, sewage, and telephone), highway transportation, subways, recreational facilities such as parks and beaches, and radio and television broadcasting. Let's take a brief look at highway transportation since it is a major component of government spending in the United States.

HIGHWAY TRANSPORTATION Highways, bridges, and tunnels have the cost characteristics of a natural monopoly because the construction costs are such a high percentage of the total costs. Think of the output on a highway as the number of vehicles using the highway over a given period of time. Once the highway has been built, the cost of another car or truck using the roadway is minimal, at least up to the point of congestion. (Congestion is an example of an externality, another technical problem to be discussed below.) In northern climates even a substantial portion of the ongoing maintenance costs is due to weathering, not roadway usage. Therefore, the per-unit cost of highway transportation steadily declines as the fixed construction and maintenance costs are spread over an ever-larger number of vehicles.

The case for government provision of highways is especially compelling because large parts of a nation's highway network would never be provided by the private sector. Travel is so light in many rural areas that no private investor could charge a toll that would cover the full cost of the roadway. Charging tolls is not even feasible on most local streets. Therefore, if a nation desires a complete highway network, the government must provide it.

U.S. POLICY RESPONSES TO SCALE ECONOMIES The United States uses four principal strategies to maintain efficiency and equity in the presence of giant firms and natural monopolies: antitrust legislation, windfall profits taxes, direct regulation, and government provision of services. The microeconomic chapters of the text discuss each of these strategies.

NONCOMPETITIVE MARKETS AND IMPERFECT INFORMATION The free flow of information, equally available to all, is very important to the proper functioning of a market economy. This may seem like a fairly innocuous requirement, but the truth is that parties to market transactions often have very poor information. Since people who lack information are extremely vulnerable in a

NATURAL MONOPOLY

A market situation in which economies of scale are so large that a single firm can supply the entire market demand at the lowest cost.

market setting, informational problems are a common justification for government intervention.

THE ECONOMICS OF OBTAINING INFORMATION   Business firms often have an informational advantage over their customers regarding the products and the services they sell. Will the product do what it is supposed to do? Will it last? Firms usually know the answers to such questions, but consumers may not, short of buying the product and learning after the fact. More important, consumers may not be willing to obtain full information about a product prior to purchase. They are not just being lazy. To the contrary, their ignorance is most often a rational solution to an economic problem, in this case the problem of obtaining information.

The benefit of obtaining information is clear enough. The more information consumers have, the greater their knowledge is about the qualities of the product prior to purchase. But consumers may not acquire complete information because the process of obtaining information on products or services is costly. At the very least, consumers must spend time asking other consumers about a product's qualities. At worst, properly testing a product may require special equipment, perhaps even a laboratory setting, that individual consumers are unlikely to own or have easy access to. As a result, firms retain their informational advantage, and consumers are vulnerable to being disappointed.

Governments have a distinct advantage over individuals in obtaining information on products. One reason is that the process of obtaining information is subject to considerable economies of scale. Once any one person obtains the relevant information, no one else need duplicate that person's efforts. The information can be published and made available fairly cheaply to all. Having a single government agency test products and monitor services, and then publish the findings, is much less costly than having all consumers do their own testing and monitoring.

Another advantage to government testing is that the benefits of testing are millions of times greater from the government's perspective than from the individual's perspective. The government takes the broad social perspective and sees that testing can benefit everyone. Individuals, in contrast, are interested only in the benefits to themselves. Consequently, the government will bear the additional costs of obtaining full information about products and services, whereas an individual may not.

These are the reasons why governments establish various agencies to test products and monitor services, such as the Food and Drug Administration and the Bureau of Standards.

INCOMPLETE INSURANCE MARKETS   Uncertainty is an unavoidable fact of life. No one can know for sure what the future might bring. This is unfortunate, since most of us dislike uncertain situations, especially those that can have a significant impact on our lives. In the jargon of economics, we are *risk adverse*. We would gladly give up some income to turn an uncertain, risky environment into a certain, riskless environment.

The desire to avoid risks leads to a demand for insurance against the random misfortunes of life: accidents, sickness, untimely death, loss of job, and the like. Firms are willing to provide insurance against risky events if three conditions hold: (1) They can insure large numbers of people, (2) the probability that any one individual will suffer misfortune is unrelated to the probability that any other individual will suffer misfortune, and (3) the firm has good information about the people being insured. These conditions are not always satisfied, however, and when they are not, insurers cannot profitably insure against the risks. The private insurance markets are incomplete—a demand exists for a product that no one is willing to supply. When this happens, people naturally turn to the government to fill in the gaps with public insurance programs financed by tax dollars.

The two most common problems in insurance markets are that the events being insured against are not independent of one another and that the insurers cannot obtain all the information about those being insured that they need to write profitable policies.

DEPENDENT EVENTS Unemployment insurance and flood insurance are good examples of the first problem. Workers want to insure themselves against spells of unemployment, but unemployment tends not to be an independent event. When the economy experiences a recession, large numbers of workers lose their jobs more or less at the same time. When the economy improves, large numbers of the unemployed return to work. In other words, the probability that one worker will lose his or her job is not independent of the probability that other workers will lose their jobs.

The same is true of flooding. People living along a river want insurance against the possibility of a flood. But when the river overflows its banks, they all suffer together.

If everyone suffers misfortune at once, the insurance company is exposed to the same risk as any one individual, but the losses are magnified if the misfortune occurs. No company could profitably supply insurance under these conditions.

THE PRINCIPAL-AGENT PROBLEM The informational difficulties are more subtle. Insurance markets suffer from a condition of unequal access to information known as the **principal-agent problem.** The *principal,* the insurance company, would like to know everything about the risks of the *agents,* those being insured, so that they can write profitable insurance policies. But the insurers usually have only limited information about those being insured. The more incomplete the information about those being insured, the more vulnerable the insurer is to the problems of moral hazard and adverse selection.

Moral hazard. **Moral hazard** arises when the individuals being insured can influence the probability of the event being insured against, unbeknownst to the insurer. In the case of unemployment insurance, for example, insurance companies would be willing to offer policies only against the event that workers are laid off by the employer. Companies could not possibly write policies that paid off if a worker quit because any worker could then decide to quit and collect on the policy.

If companies attempted to write unemployment insurance policies against layoffs, however, they would be extremely vulnerable to moral hazard. Quitters could falsely claim that they were temporarily laid off and therefore were eligible for insurance. An insurance company might have no way of learning the truth, especially if employers agreed to go along with the workers' story in return for a kickback on the payout. If enough workers lied about their status,

PRINCIPAL-AGENT PROBLEM

An informational problem in which one individual (the principal) tries to monitor and control the behavior of another individual (the agent), but does not have enough information to do so, and the two individuals have different goals.

MORAL HAZARD

In the context of insurance, arises when individuals who are being insured can influence the probability of the event being insured against, unbeknownst to the insurer.

the actual payout on the policies could far exceed the expected payout, and the insurance companies would lose money.

Medical insurance is also vulnerable to moral hazard because people's behavior can influence the probability of their becoming ill. Insurance companies may not be able to monitor the behavior of their policyholders sufficiently to protect themselves from smokers, heavy drinkers, and the like. Contrast this with the case of suicide under life insurance policies. Insurance companies are not willing to pay if death is self-inflicted, but they are protected because suicides are fairly easy to detect. Moral hazard is not much of a problem for life insurance. The extent to which ill health is self-induced is obviously much more difficult to determine.

Adverse selection. The group of people covered by a particular kind of insurance policy varies in the risk each member of the group represents to the insurance company. For instance, any group of insured drivers includes good and bad drivers, and the bad drivers are more likely to make claims against their insurance policies. The differences in risk are not a problem by themselves. If the insurance company can distinguish among those being insured on the basis of risk, it can vary the premiums by risk. The automobile insurers are an example. They use the accident records of individual drivers to divide the drivers into normal and high-risk pools and then charge the accident-prone high-risk drivers a higher premium.

The problem of **adverse selection** occurs when insurance companies are unable to distinguish high-risk individuals from low-risk individuals. In this case the companies are forced to charge one premium to everyone despite the differences in risk. Insurance markets become shaky whenever this happens because the single premium discriminates against the low-risk individuals in favor of the high-risk individuals. If the premium is more than the low-risk individuals are willing to pay, they drop out and try to form an insurance pool with other low-risk individuals. The company is left with a more adverse (high-risk) pool and may experience losses because of excessive payouts.

Adverse selection may prevent an insurance market from ever developing. Forming a pool of only low-risk individuals may be impossible if the information problems are severe. Moreover, if low-risk individuals do drop out, companies stuck with ever-increasing percentages of high-risk individuals may be forced to charge higher premiums than the high-risk individuals are willing to pay. So high-risk individuals, too, may be forced out of the private insurance market. The normal market incentives that bring suppliers and demanders together are clearly absent in this instance.

Medical insurance is particularly vulnerable to the problem of adverse selection. The medical profession's understanding of the factors that predispose individuals to many kinds of illness is rudimentary at best. And even if the factors were better known, insurance companies might well have great difficulty in detecting some of them, such as genetic predispositions to disease.

ADVERSE SELECTION

In the context of insurance, arises when the insurance company is forced to set one premium because it cannot distinguish between high-risk and low-risk individuals, with the result that low-risk individuals cancel their policies.

ADDITIONAL MOTIVES FOR PUBLIC INSURANCE   Public insurance programs for the elderly in the United States have been motivated, in part, by two additional concerns that are not strictly allocational in nature. One is distributional and the other is paternalistic.

The distributional concern is suggested by the adverse selection problem. Certain individuals that the private insurers can identify as high risk may not be able to afford the premiums required to insure against their risks. The leading example is comprehensive medical care for the elderly. The risk of ill health obviously increases with age, so insurance companies require a higher premium to cover the elderly. Yet many of the elderly simply do not have enough income to pay the higher premium.

If the government steps in and provides the insurance, its motive is partly distributional. Medical insurance is being viewed as a **merit good,** a good that society considers a virtual necessity, but that is beyond the means of those with low incomes. The public insurance program acts as an in-kind transfer to the elderly.

The paternalistic motive applies to public pensions. People can save throughout their working lives to provide income for their retirement years. Large numbers of people may choose to live for the present, however, and not save enough for their retirement. These people risk becoming wards of the state after they retire. To remove this possibility, society asks the government to establish a public pension plan and force all workers to participate. The government has to force everyone to participate if its motive is paternalistic because it cannot tell in advance who will save enough for retirement and who will not.

PUBLIC INSURANCE IN THE UNITED STATES The various problems that undermine private insurance markets are among the more serious problems afflicting a market economy, if the United States is any indication. Governments in the United States have become major providers of insurance. For example, unemployment insurance, medical insurance for the aged, and public pensions that protect the aged against the loss of income at retirement are each among the largest programs in the federal budget. Taken together, public insurance represents the biggest single category of government expenditures, bigger even than defense. Citizens of the United States have been quite willing to call on the government when private insurance markets fail.

EXTERNALITIES When a buyer and a seller engage in a market transaction, they normally experience all the value and the cost associated with the transaction. Occasionally, though, some of the value or cost spills over onto third parties who have no direct role in the transaction. When this occurs, the transaction is said to involve an externality.

An **externality** is a third-party effect of a transaction that directly affects either consumers' satisfaction or firms' production possibilities. For example, you, your fellow students, and millions of other consumers and firms have an ongoing demand for paper products, a demand that paper manufacturers are quite willing to supply. In the process of producing paper, however, the paper companies pollute both water and air.

Air pollution ruins the paint on people's houses and cars and may cause health problems. Water pollution alters the recreational qualities of streams and lakes. They may no longer be fit for swimming, or game fishing, or pleasure boating. Polluted water may also pose a hazard to health. People suffer third-party losses that have no direct connection to the purchase and sale of paper.

POLLUTION Externalities such as air and water pollution create serious allocational problems for all economic systems. A market economy is particularly vulnerable to externalities because markets have no way of accounting for them. Consequently, no incentives exist to correct for them. Industrial pollution is a perfect case in point.

Air and water are **common-use resources,** meaning that no one owns the rights to them. Since no one owns them, no private market can exist for air and water. They are available to everyone free of charge, including the paper companies.

COMMON-USE RESOURCE

A resource such as water or air that no one owns.

Paper companies minimize their costs of production by using water and air for every conceivable purpose they can think of, since these resources are costless to them. Water and air are particularly convenient disposals for the companies' waste products. Paper companies also use the water to transport logs. If they happen to pollute the water or air in the process, no matter. They will not receive a bill for the third-party damages they have caused because no one owns these resources.

Can we expect paper companies to be public spirited and voluntarily choose not to pollute? Not at all. The normal market incentives argue against any public-spirited impulses that firms might have. Suppose that one public-spirited paper company decides to produce in a nonpolluting manner. Unless it can be assured that other paper companies will do the same, it will soon think better of the idea. The firm raises its costs of production by not polluting, which puts it at a competitive disadvantage relative to other firms that continue to pollute. Also, one paper company acting alone may have very little effect on the overall level of pollution if a number of companies are polluting. In this case the company's public-spirited impulse is not only costly; it is also futile.

POLLUTION AND ECONOMIC EFFICIENCY   Externalities do serious damage to the goal of economic efficiency. The best a market economy has to offer for promoting efficiency is the competitive market that operates according to the Laws of Supply and Demand. But even competitive markets are inefficient when market transactions give rise to externalities. They select the wrong output.

To see this, suppose that the Laws of Supply and Demand apply to the market for paper, as represented by Figure 23.1. D is the market demand curve of the consumers of paper. It reflects, at each quantity, the marginal value of paper to consumers in the sense of indicating the price they are willing to pay for the last unit of paper consumed. The market supply curve, S^{priv}, indicates at each quantity the marginal cost experienced by the paper companies in producing the paper. Left to its own devices, the market equilibrium is Q_0, at the intersection of D and S^{priv}.

Q_0 is not the efficient output, however, because it ignores the external damage caused by the pollution. The full social marginal cost of producing paper is given by the supply curve S^{soc}. S^{soc} adds to S^{priv}, at every output, the **marginal cost of pollution,** which is the additional cost of pollution experienced by all third parties combined when an additional unit of paper is produced.

MARGINAL COST OF POLLUTION

The additional cost of pollution experienced by all third parties combined when a polluting activity is increased by one unit.

The efficient allocation is Q_1, the intersection of D and S^{soc}. At Q_1 the marginal value of consuming paper equals the full social marginal cost of producing paper. The market goes beyond that point because it only takes into account the direct marginal cost that paper firms experience in producing the paper.

The government can correct for the pollution by taxing the paper companies based on the amount of damage that their pollution causes third parties. A

FIGURE 23.1

Pollution and the Market for Paper

At every output, the demand curve D indicates the marginal value of paper to consumers, and the supply curve S^{priv} indicates the marginal cost to the paper companies of producing paper. The equilibrium in the market for paper would be (Q_0, P_0), at the intersection of D and S^{priv}, without government intervention. The supply curve S^{soc} indicates the full social marginal cost of producing paper at every output. It adds to S^{priv} the marginal cost to all third parties combined of the pollution generated when the paper companies produce additional paper. The optimal output of paper is Q_1, at which the marginal value of paper equals the full social marginal cost of producing paper. The government can achieve Q_1 by means of a pollution tax on the paper companies which raises their effective market supply curve to S^{soc}. The higher price P_1 at the intersection of D and S^{soc} encourages consumers to conserve on their use of paper.

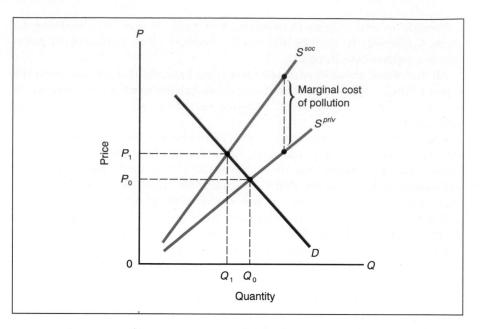

REFLECTION: Do you favor public primary and secondary education, or would you prefer that the government get out of the education business? A longstanding proposal in the United States that has broad support calls for a private education system in which the government's only role would be to provide tuition vouchers (subsidies) to children of low-income families so that they would be as free to choose among the private schools as anyone else. Is this a good idea?

NONEXCLUSIVE (PUBLIC) GOOD

A good such as national defense that is consumed by everyone once any one person or the government buys it; no one can be excluded or exclude themselves from consuming the good.

pollution tax has the effect of setting a price on the use of the scarce, and valued, clean air and water. A properly designed pollution tax shifts S^{priv} up to S^{soc} from the firms' perspective, so that they supply their paper along the correct social supply curve.

EDUCATION: AN EXTERNAL ECONOMY Pollution is an example of a harmful externality. Economists refer to such harmful third-party effects as *external diseconomies*. Third-party effects can also be beneficial, in which case they are referred to as *external economies*.

Education is a good example of an external economy. A democratic society can function effectively only if all voters have a minimum level of education. They must be literate and able to understand issues of social policy. Therefore, the education of each person makes everyone else better off, at least up to a point.

Left to its own devices, however, a free market economy is likely to produce too little education. People would decide how much education to buy on the basis of their personal gains from the education. They would have no incentive to consider the external benefits that their education gives to others because the market has no way of rewarding them for these benefits.

In the mid-1800s the United States chose to attack educational externalities directly by establishing the local public school system and mandating a minimum level of primary and secondary education for all its citizens. Government provision of education is not the only way to correct for the externality; subsidizing private education is another possible approach. Nonetheless, the United States obviously felt that an educated citizenry is so important that it was willing to replace the market with the government in this instance.

NONEXCLUSIVE GOODS   The final important allocational problem for a market economy involves **nonexclusive goods,** of which defense is the classic example.

Most goods and services are **exclusive goods.** When you purchase a hamburger, it is yours alone to eat and enjoy. The hamburger is *exclusive* to you. Defense expenditures are quite different, however. When the government buys a new missile, the services provided by that missile, whatever they may be, are entirely nonexclusive. The government cannot exclude anyone from consuming the services. Moreover, individuals cannot exclude themselves from consuming the services even if they would want to. In effect, nonexclusive goods such as missiles are the ultimate externality. Purchase of the good by anyone directly affects everyone.

Markets are helpless in the presence of nonexclusive goods. If society wants them, they must be purchased collectively through a government agency. This is why nonexclusive goods are usually referred to as *public goods.*

THE FREE-RIDER PROBLEM   To see why the market system has difficulty with nonexclusive goods, imagine that you are a member of a small island nation that is continually being harassed by other nations. One day a salesman visits the island offering a missile so destructive that, he claims, the mere threat of using it will deter others from ever bothering your country again. The salesman is very persuasive, and everyone wishes that the country owned the missile. Furthermore, the missile happens to be inexpensive; each person can afford it. Will anyone step forward and buy the missile? The chances are they will not.

Suppose that you buy the missile. This is exactly what the others want you to do. Once you buy it, they can enjoy the same services you do, and it does not cost them a dime. They become **free-riders** on your purchase, and you end up being the sucker. Better to let someone else be the sucker and free-ride on his/her purchase. But if everyone thinks alike, no one ends up buying the missile, *even though everyone wants it.* The incentive to free-ride destroys the normal incentive to engage in market transactions.

The free-rider problem exists for all nonexclusive goods. Lighthouses are another example. No one shipping company wants to pay for a lighthouse, given that all shipping companies will have equal access to its warning signal free of charge. This is why lighthouses are usually publicly provided.

Notice that the free-rider problem is absent with exclusive goods. If consumers want the services of exclusive goods, they must purchase the goods for themselves. This is the basis of the normal incentive to engage in market transactions.

EFFICIENT ALLOCATION OF NONEXCLUSIVE GOODS   Having the government purchase nonexclusive goods such as defense by no means solves the problem of properly allocating these goods. Deciding how much defense to purchase is one of the most difficult economic questions a government must wrestle with, even ignoring the thorny question of what services defense expenditures actually provide for a nation in the nuclear age. The basic problem is an information problem. The government must know the value that each consumer places on additional units of defense expenditure in order to allocate defense efficiently. Unfortunately, the government has no good way of obtaining this information.

Suppose that people sense that there is a direct connection between their stated preferences and their tax payments in support of a good such as defense. If so, the free-rider problem reappears. Defense enthusiasts have an incentive

EXCLUSIVE GOOD

A good whose benefits are received only by the person who consumes it.

FREE-RIDER

A person who consumes a nonexclusive (public) good without paying for any of the costs of the good.

to understate their preferences. If there is no direct connection between preferences and tax payments, the more likely case, defense enthusiasts may well have an incentive to overstate their enthusiasm. Those who dislike defense should overstate their displeasure no matter how they are asked to pay. The government cannot easily force people to reveal their true preferences.

A nonexclusive good such as defense is certain to breed disagreements, as indeed it does. The crux of the matter from an economic perspective is that everyone is forced to consume the same amount. Whatever quantity the government chooses, some people are sure to want more spent on defense and others less spent on defense.

Macroeconomic Stabilization Problems

Free market economies are not always capable of achieving the four macroeconomic policy goals of long-run economic growth, full employment, price stability, and satisfactory economic relations with other nations. We noted in Chapter 2 that the U.S economy has not performed particularly well with respect to any of these goals since the early 1970s.

The macroeconomic chapters of the text describe how government intervention through monetary and fiscal policies can help guide free market economies toward each of these goals. We would only note here that many of the nation's macroeconomic problems result from various kinds of market failure. For instance, the macro economy would operate much more effectively if firms and workers indexed their prices and wages to the overall price level. But no one firm or worker is willing to do this unless they can be assured that all other firms and workers are indexing their prices and wages too. The market failure here is an externality, a coordination problem. Also, unemployment would not be a serious problem if all labor markets were competitive.

GOVERNMENT EXPENDITURES IN THE UNITED STATES

What do governments in the United States actually do? By and large, exactly what you would expect them to do. Table 23.1 shows the composition of expenditures for the federal government in fiscal year 1992 and for state and local governments in fiscal year 1991. The major expenditure items correspond very closely to the legitimate functions of government discussed in the preceding section. Governments in the United States are clearly responding to instances of market failure. Moreover, the primary economic functions of the federal, state, and local governments have changed very little since World War II. The growth in the government sector has been more an increase of support within existing functions than an expansion of the government into new areas.

The Federal Government

Federal expenditures are concentrated in three areas that pose very difficult problems for market economies: national defense, insurance, and the distribution of income.

DEFENSE   We noted in Chapter 4 that the federal government is primarily a tax and transfer operation, with the single exception of national defense. Defense and defense-related activities account for approximately 70 percent of the federal government's expenditures on goods and services, the resource-using component of the federal budget. The remaining nondefense expenditures on goods and services largely pay the operating expenses of the various federal transfer agencies.

Most of the federal transfers to persons fall into one of three categories: (1) public insurance and pensions, (2) subsidies to farmers and veterans, and (3) public assistance.

REFLECTION: The recent cutbacks in defense spending are providing the United States with a long-awaited "peace dividend." How would you prefer that the dividend be used: Give it back to the private sector in the form of tax cuts? Use it to fund other domestic public services? If the latter, which public services?

SOCIAL INSURANCE AND PENSIONS   Table 23.1 shows that public insurance and retirement pensions dominate the transfer component of the federal budget. In fact, they account for approximately 70 percent of all transfer payments to persons by all governments in the United States. The transfers under these programs are mostly cash payments made directly to individuals. Also, eligibility under these programs is independent of a person's income. Consequently, most of the insurance and pension transfers go to the nonpoor. Their intent is to prevent people from falling into poverty when they are particularly vulnerable economically, such as when they retire or suffer a spell of unemployment.

The three major insurance and pension programs are Social Security, other federal pensions, and unemployment insurance.

SOCIAL SECURITY   Social Security is the largest domestic expenditure program in the entire U.S. fiscal system. Employees, and their employers, contribute to the Social Security System throughout their working lives by means of a payroll tax on wages and salaries. These tax payments entitle employees (and their dependents) to two kinds of support:

1. retirement pensions, life insurance, and disability insurance under OASDI (Old Age, Survivors, and Disability Insurance); and
2. medical insurance covering hospitalization, physicians' services, medicines, and supplies under Medicare. Coverage begins at age 65. Nearly all people working in the private sector participate in the Social Security System.

CIVILIAN AND MILITARY PENSIONS   Federal civil service and military employees have a separate retirement pension plan, as do many state and local government employees. The federal pensions are one of the largest items in the entire federal budget.

UNEMPLOYMENT INSURANCE   Unemployment insurance provides cash payments to workers who have been laid off by their employers, but not to those workers who have quit their jobs. The maximum length of time workers may receive unemployment payments varies by state, but most states have adopted a 26-week maximum. Unemployment insurance is financed by a payroll tax. Unlike the Social Security payroll tax, however, the tax is levied only on employers.

SUBSIDIES TO FARMERS AND VETERANS   The federal government has singled out two groups for special subsidies, farmers and veterans.

AGRICULTURAL PRICE SUPPORTS The market economy has not been particularly kind to U.S. farmers, either in the long run or in the short run. The long-run problem is that farm prices and farm incomes have not kept pace with prices and incomes generally throughout the twentieth century. Rapid technological change in the form of better fertilizers, pesticides, hybrid crops, and farming techniques has led to huge increases in supply over time that have outpaced the more modest increases in demand. The result is steadily downward pressure on prices, which has been particularly damaging to small farmers. The short-run problem is price instability caused by yearly changes in the weather. Good weather increases supply, which, because demand is highly inelastic for most crops, sharply reduces crop prices. Conversely, bad weather decreases supply, which sharply increases crop prices.

The federal government first responded to these problems during the Great Depression of the 1930s. The government chose to implement a price-support strategy that set a price floor for the major crop prices. The price-support programs have been modified on occasion since the Great Depression, but price supports remain the primary means of subsidizing farmers' incomes.

The agricultural price-support programs combine insurance and income-support motives. By stabilizing prices, they provide insurance to all farmers against the short-run variability of prices caused by good and bad weather. By supporting prices above the market price, they provide income support for the small-scale, lower-income farmers (although the majority of the support payments are received by the large-scale, higher-income farmers).

VETERANS BENEFITS All veterans are eligible for a number of in-kind transfers, such as subsidized education and housing. Disabled veterans receive additional cash allowances and subsidized health care.

PUBLIC ASSISTANCE The other set of transfer programs listed in part A of Table 23.1 (pp. 728–729) is comprised of the public assistance or "public welfare" programs. They constitute the remaining 30 percent of all government transfers to persons. The public assistance programs differ from the public insurance and pension programs in three respects: They are means-tested, that is, targeted to the poor; much of the assistance is distributed in kind rather than in cash; and many of the programs are jointly financed by the federal and state governments (and the local governments in some states). The four largest public assistance programs are Aid to Families With Dependent Children (AFDC), Supplemental Security Income (SSI), Food Stamps, and Medicaid.

AID TO FAMILIES WITH DEPENDENT CHILDREN The Social Security Act of 1935 established three categorical public assistance programs: Old Age Assistance, Aid to the Blind, and Aid to Families With Dependent Children. A fourth categorical program, Aid to the Disabled, was added in 1950. The assistance under these programs came in two forms, monthly checks paid directly to recipients and payments to physicians, hospitals, and other medical vendors for medical care provided to recipients and their families. The programs were administered by the state governments. The Federal government set guidelines for determining who was eligible to receive aid under each program, but the states had complete freedom to determine the amount of aid. The Federal government reimbursed the states for a portion of the aid through a grant-in-aid formula that gave a somewhat higher proportion of aid to poorer states.

Aid to Families with Dependent Children gives aid to poor families headed by a single parent. Two-parent families with an unemployed parent are also eligible for aid under certain conditions relating to the parents' efforts to find a job (although about half the states have for many years routinely given aid to these families). The number of recipients under AFDC exploded in the 1960s and 1970s, and AFDC became the program that most people associate with "welfare" in the United States. It is the largest cash public assistance program, and remains a joint federal-state effort, with the states responsible for administering AFDC and the federal government reimbursing the states for slightly more than half of the costs.

SUPPLEMENTAL SECURITY INCOME (SSI)   In January of 1974, Congress consolidated Old Age Assistance, Aid to the Blind, and Aid for the Disabled into one program, Supplemental Security Income. SSI is federally administered and financed, but states are free to supplement the federal payments and many do so. As a result, SSI retains some of the federal-state flavor of the three programs it replaced. Aid under these programs is targeted to poor individuals and their families who are age 65 or older, or blind, or disabled, as the names of the three original programs indicate.

FOOD STAMPS   The federal government broke new ground in 1971 when it added a food stamp program to the arsenal of public assistance programs. It marked the first time that Congress was willing to assist the nation's poor on a noncategorical basis. All poor families (and some nonpoor families who are close to the poverty line) are eligible to receive food stamps. The food stamp program is also entirely administered and financed by the federal government, unlike any of the other main public assistance programs.

MEDICAID   Medicaid came into being along with Medicare as part of the 1965 amendments to the Social Security Act. It consolidated all medical payments under the four federal-state public assistance programs and greatly expanded the available medical coverage. Otherwise, it retained the basic elements of the former medical assistance programs. The states administer the program and pay the medical providers, and the federal government reimburses the states for a share of the costs. Medicaid quickly became the largest public assistance program as medical costs skyrocketed after 1965. Some states provide Medicaid for "medically needy" families, those with large medical expenses who do not qualify for the public assistance programs.

OTHER PUBLIC ASSISTANCE   The federal government funds an additional 50 to 60 smaller public assistance programs in the areas of food, education, job retraining, housing assistance, medical care, veterans benefits, and other social services.

State and Local Governments

For the most part state and local expenditures are responding to two kinds of allocational market failure: externalities and natural-monopoly, decreasing-cost production. The major expenditure categories provide examples of each.

TABLE 23.1   Expenditures by Federal, State, and Local Governments in the United States

			EXPENDITURES (BILLIONS)	PERCENTAGE OF TOTAL EXPENDITURES
A. FEDERAL GOVERNMENT (FISCAL YEAR, 1992)[a]				
Government expenditures on goods and services			$478.1	32.4
	Expenditures (Billions)	*Percentage of Subcategory*		
Defense and defense related	$341.5[b]	71.4		
Non-defense expenditures	136.6	28.6		
Domestic transfers to persons (direct expenditures)			616.3	41.8
Social insurance and pensions				
Social Security benefits (OASDI)	288.3	46.8		
Medicare	129.2	21.0		
Civilian and military retirement	59.5	9.7		
Unemployment insurance	34.7	5.6		
Agricultural support payments	14.7	2.4		
Veterans benefits[c]	32.4	5.3		
Public Assistance				
Food and nutrition (Food stamps: 21.1)	21.3	3.5		
Supplemental Security Income (SSI)	18.3	3.0		
Net interest payments			198.8	13.5
Grants-in-aid			182.2	12.3
Payments to individuals	114.6	62.9		
AFDC	15.1	8.3		
Medicaid	72.5	39.8		
Other	67.6	37.1		
Total Expenditures			1475.4	100.0

[a]The data for the federal government are estimated outlays.   (continued)
[b]Includes national defense; general science, space, and technology; and international affairs.
[c]Includes education benefits; medical benefits; insurance benefits; and compensation, pension and burial payments.

EDUCATION   Recall that education found its way into the public sector in the nineteenth century because of the externality component of education: All citizens in a democracy benefit from any one person's education. State governments mostly provide higher education through state colleges and universities. The localities concentrate on primary and secondary education.

POLICE AND FIRE PROTECTION   Local police protection and fire protection also have significant externality components. The police externality is much

TABLE 23.1   **Expenditures by Federal, State, and Local Governments in the United States** (continued)

			EXPENDITURES (BILLIONS)	PERCENTAGE OF TOTAL EXPENDITURES
B. STATE GOVERNMENTS (FISCAL YEAR, 1991)[d]				
Direct Expenditures			442.3	70.3
Public welfare	100.1	22.6		
Education	80.5	18.2		
Highways	38.9	8.8		
Health and hospitals	38.5	8.7		
Other	184.3	41.7		
Grants-in-aid			186.5	29.7
Total General Expenditures			628.8	100.0
C. LOCAL GOVERNMENTS (FISCAL YEAR, 1991)[d]				
Education			229.2	36.8
Utilities			70.8	11.4
Health and hospitals			43.5	7.0
Police and fire protection			41.7	6.7
Public welfare			26.9	4.3
Highways			26.0	4.2
Other			185.3	29.6
Total General Expenditures			623.4	100.0

[d]Data for state and local governments were available through fiscal year 1991 only.

SOURCES: Part Five: Historical Tables, Executive Office of the President of the United States *Budget of the United States Government, Fiscal Year 1993, Supplement, February 1992.* (Washington D.C.: U.S. Government Printing Office, 1992), Table 3.1, p. 5–42; Table 3.2, pp. 5–46, 47; Table 11.1, p. 5–136; Table 11.2, pp. 5–143, 161, 162; Table 12.1, p. 5–165; Table 12.3, pp. 5–199, 200. U.S. Department of Commerce, Economics and Statistics Administration, Bureau of Census, *Government Finances: 1990–91 (Preliminary Report),* (Washington, D.C.: U.S. Government Printing Office, 1993), Series GF/91-5P, p. 1.

like the defense externality, only on a smaller scale. Fire protection also generates external economies: Protecting your house from fire protects your neighbors' houses to some extent as well.

PUBLIC UTILITIES, HIGHWAYS   We noted in the previous section that public utilities and highways are prime examples of decreasing-cost services.

OTHER   The "Other" category in state and local budgets is comprised of a wide range of services, including parks and recreation, natural resources, water and sewage, nonhighway transportation, correctional facilities, and general government. Either externalities or decreasing costs of production have driven all these services into the public sector.

State and local governments also participate in the nation's efforts to protect people from poverty, mostly through the provision of public assistance and public hospitals.

PUBLIC ASSISTANCE   The states' commitment to Medicaid, AFDC, and SSI (in some states) is substantial enough to make public welfare the largest category of states' own general expenditures.

Public welfare is also the fifth-largest category in local budgets, although this figure is a bit misleading. Most states do not require local contributions to the state's share of public assistance, although a few of the largest states do, most notably California and New York. Since these two states also have the largest welfare programs, their welfare expenditures end up being a noticeable percentage of total local government expenditures. For most local governments, though, public welfare is not a major item of expenditure.

HEALTH AND HOSPITALS   The health and hospitals component of state and local budgets can be viewed as a form of in-kind public assistance. A majority of these expenditures finance state mental and psychiatric hospitals or municipal general hospitals, which primarily serve patients who cannot afford private hospital care.

Our tour of the government sector in the United States concludes with two observations, one related to federal regulation and one related to the relationship between public transfer programs and private transfer payments.

The Federal Regulatory Agencies

The budget data in Table 23.1 hide the many regulatory functions of the federal government because expenditures by each regulatory agency are fairly small. Make no mistake about it, though. Regulation has been a principal response to market failure in the United States ever since the Great Depression of the 1930s. Forty-one new federal regulatory agencies came into being in the 40-year period from 1930 through 1979. The Carter and Reagan administrations finally called a halt to the growth in regulation.

Federal regulation is concentrated in five broad areas: banking and finance, competition and trade, employment and discrimination, energy and the environment, and safety and health. The regulatory agencies in each of these areas are responding to particular kinds of market failure, most of which we discussed in the preceding section. Familiar examples from each area include the Federal Reserve Banking System (control of the money supply), the Federal Trade Commission (antitrust and consumer protection from deception and fraud), the National Labor Relations Board (union and business labor practices), the Environmental Protection Agency (pollution control), and the Occupational Safety and Health Administration (worker health and safety).

Private Transfers and Public Transfers

Our discussion of public transfers ignored the role of private transfers as a means of income support in the United States. Private transfers include aid given by religious institutions, private charities, and within families. The extent of private transfers is difficult to determine because often individuals do not report transfers made to other family members. No one doubts, however, that

TABLE 23.2   Private and Public Transfers Among Income Classes (hypothetical data)

INCOME CLASS	PRE-TRANSFER EARNED INCOME	INCOME AFTER PRIVATE TRANSFERS	EXPECTED INCOME AFTER PUBLIC TRANSFERS	ACTUAL INCOME AFTER PUBLIC TRANSFERS
Rich	$60,000	$57,000	$57,000	$60,000
Middle Class	30,000	30,000	27,000	27,000
Poor	6,000	9,000	12,000	9,000

private transfers are an important component of income support. The best guess is that private transfers are at least a fifth as large as public transfers in the United States.

Economists have recently become interested in understanding how private transfers respond to public transfers because private transfers can easily undermine the intent of public transfer programs. The following simple example illustrates the problem that governments might face in trying to transfer income when private transfers also exist.

Suppose an economy consists of three classes of families, the rich, the middle class, and the poor. Each class contains the same number of families and all families within one class earn the same income. The earned incomes are listed in the first column of Table 23.2: $60,000 (rich), $30,000 (middle), and $6,000 (poor).

Suppose, at first, that there are no government transfer programs, only private transfers. Each rich family voluntarily transfers $3,000 to each poor family. The incomes of the three classes of families after these private transfers are listed in the 2nd column of Table 23.2: $57,000 (rich); $30,000 (middle); and $9,000 (poor).

The government notices that the income of the poor is still below the poverty line of $12,000 and decides to enact a public transfer program to lift the poor out of poverty. The government program transfers $3,000 to each poor family, paid for by taxes of $3,000 levied on each middle class family. The government expects the distribution of income after the public tax-transfer program to be that listed in the third column of Table 23.2: $57,000 (rich); $27,000 (middle); $12,000 (poor). But this is not what happens. Upon learning that the government is transferring $3,000 to the poor, the rich withdraw their private transfers to the poor. The net result is the distribution of income listed in the fourth column of the table: $60,000 (rich); $27,000 (middle); $9,000 (poor).

The rich have completely undermined the intentions of the government. The government intends to tax the middle class to transfer income to the poor. Instead, the government program has the effect of taxing the middle class to transfer income to the rich, and the poor remain in poverty. The government transfers are said to slide from the poor to the rich, and the poor remain in poverty. The government transfers slide from the poor to the rich as the result of the rich adjusting their private transfers in response to the government program.

Our simple example is not entirely unrealistic. Some recent research suggests that sliding private transfers may offset the redistributional effect of the Social Security system to some extent. As noted earlier, Social Security amounts to a massive transfer of income from the working young to the retired elderly. Some of the elderly, knowing that the younger generations are supporting them through payroll taxes, may transfer income back to their children and grandchildren by paying for part of their educations, or helping them with the rent, or leaving them larger bequests. Working parents may also be more willing to support their children, and save less for their own retirement, if they are counting on receiving Social Security benefits when they retire. The net redistribution of income from younger to older generations under the Social Security system is much less than it appears to be if private transfers respond in this way.

The effect of Social Security on private transfers is highly speculative at this point. Research on the relationship between private and public transfers is in its infancy. The early returns suggest that an increase in public transfers to some group does cause a reduction in private transfers to that group. The "slide" is nowhere near a dollar for a dollar as in our simple example, however, which means that government transfer programs can redistribute income at least somewhat as they intend. We will learn a lot more about the relationship between private and public transfers in the next ten years as this new line of research continues.

SUMMARY

The first section of Chapter 23 described the market failures that lead to a call for government intervention. The section began by reviewing the strengths of a market economy when markets are perfectly competitive and work as well as they possibly can. These are strengths that government policies should try to emulate and preserve.

1. Competitive markets that operate according to the Laws of Supply and Demand give individuals freedom to do as they wish, bring order to economic exchanges, are responsive to the desires of consumers, and promote society's twin goals of efficiency and equity.

Despite these strengths, the government has an important economic role to play in a free market economy. The market system fails in a number of ways that require government intervention to correct. All capitalist countries have chosen a system of mixed capitalism, with the market system and the government working hand in hand in the quest for efficiency and equity. Market failures fall into three broad categories—distributional, allocational, and macroeconomic stabilization.

2. *Distributional:* Markets generate a distribution of income in the process of setting prices in the factor markets for labor, land, and capital. But no market economy can guarantee that the resulting distribution of income is satisfactory, even if all markets are competitive. By and large, the factor markets take the ownership of resources as a given. Those who begin with a lot of valuable resources end up with a lot of goods and services, and

vice versa. Government intervention is necessary to correct perceived distributional imbalances, and general tax and transfer policies are the best way to redistribute purchasing power.

3. *Allocational:* Market economies are vulnerable to a number of market and technical problems that give rise to inefficiencies and that the government has to correct. The market problems arise because of economies of scale and imperfect information, which tend to make markets noncompetitive.

4. *Economies of scale:* Economies of scale can lead to markets dominated by large firms with considerable market power who do not pass the cost savings on to consumers by lowering their prices. Economies of scale sometimes give rise to a natural monopoly, in which one firm can supply the entire market most cheaply. Examples include the public utilities, highway transportation, parks and recreation facilities, and radio and television broadcasting. Governments have tried to curb the exercise of market power through windfall profits taxes, regulation, government provision of services, and antitrust legislation.

5. *Imperfect information:* Market imperfections arise when certain economic agents enjoy informational advantages over other agents. People lacking information are extremely vulnerable in a market economy and are hesitant to engage in market exchanges. Government agencies that test and monitor products are examples of government intervention motivated by informational problems.

Market economies are plagued by other technical allocational problems that only the government can resolve. The section considered three of the most important: incomplete insurance markets, externalities, and nonexclusive public goods.

6. *Incomplete insurance markets:* Consumers want insurance against the misfortunes of life, and private insurers are only partially willing to fulfill this need. Private insurers are reluctant to write policies when the events being insured against do not occur independently from one another. Unemployment insurance is a leading example. Insurance markets are also afflicted with the principal-agent problem—insurers (the principals) cannot know all they need to know about those being insured (the agents) in order to write profitable policies. The principal-agent information problem leaves insurers vulnerable to the twin problems of moral hazard and adverse selection. Medical insurance is a prime example. The government also provides public insurance for distributional and paternalistic reasons. Medical insurance for the elderly is an example of the former motive; it is viewed as a merit good. Public pensions are an example of the latter motive; society fears that people will not adequately provide for their retirement unless they are forced to.

7. *Externalities:* Even competitive markets lose their efficiency properties in the presence of external third-party effects. Markets end up exchanging the wrong quantities because they have no way of taking the external effects into account. Industrial pollution is a prime example of a harmful external effect. Education generates beneficial external effects. Only government policies such as taxes and subsidies can force consumers and producers to account for the external effects of their transactions when large numbers of people are affected.

8. *Nonexclusive goods:* Non-exclusive goods such as defense are the ultimate externalities: Purchase of a nonexclusive good by anyone directly affects everyone. Nonexclusive goods are vulnerable to the free-rider problem and are therefore virtually impossible to market. Government provision is the only viable option.

9. *Macroeconomic stabilization:* A free market economy does not always achieve the macroeconomic policy goals of long-run economic growth, full employment, price stability, and stability in a country's economic relations with foreign countries. Government fiscal and monetary policies can help achieve these goals. The need for fiscal and monetary policies results from various kinds of market failure, particularly noncompetitive labor markets and a coordination problem that prevents firms and workers from indexing their prices and wages to the overall price level.

The final section of Chapter 23 offered an overview of federal, state, and local expenditures. Government expenditures in the United States are primarily a response to the market failures identified in the first section of the chapter.

10. The federal government concentrates its spending in three areas: defense, redistribution, and public pensions and insurance. It also performs a number of necessary regulatory functions. The state and the local governments concentrate their spending on a wide range of allocational problems caused by externalities and economies of scale—the most important being education (externality) and the public utilities and highways (economies of scale). They also provide aid to the poor by participating with the federal government in the public assistance programs and by operating both psychiatric and general hospitals for those who cannot afford private hospital care.

11. Federal regulation is concentrated in five areas: banking and finance; competition and trade; employment and discrimination; energy and the environment; and safety and health.

12. Private transfers are about one-fifth as large as public transfers in the United States.

13. Private transfers are large enough to undermine the redistributional intentions of public transfers if private tansfers respond to public transfers. The section illustrated this point with a simple example in which the government taxes the middle class to pay for transfers to the poor. The rich respond by cutting their private transfers to the poor, so the net effect of the government's program is to tax the middle class to transfer to the rich. The public transfers are said to "slide" from the poor to the rich through the private response.

14. Evidence suggests that private transfers to charitable organizations decline when public transfers to the poor increase, but at nowhere near the dollar-for-dollar rate we used in our simple example.

KEY TERMS

adverse selection	externality	natural monopoly
allocational policies	free-rider	nonexclusive (public) good
common-use resource	merit good	principal-agent problem
distributional policies	moral hazard	stabilization policies
exclusive good		

QUESTIONS

1. What are the desirable attributes of competitive markets that operate according to the Laws of Supply and Demand? Answer from society's point of view.

2. If all markets operated according to the Laws of Supply and Demand, there would be no need for a government to solve economic problems in a capitalist economy. Do you agree or disagree with this statement? If you disagree, give some examples of remaining economic problems that the government would have to solve and why the problems would exist.

3. Economists classify market failures into three broad categories. What are they? Give an example of a market failure within each category that is important in the U.S. economy.

4. Match the following list of publicly provided goods and services with one (or more) of these categories of allocational problems: nonexclusive (public) good, natural monopoly, externality, economies of scale, information problem.
   a. public water and sewage
   b. education
   c. national defense
   d. the interstate highway system
   e. public health insurance

5. Why can a market system not be expected to solve the for whom or distribution question?

6. a. Give two examples of market problems that are caused by poor information, and explain briefly the nature of the problem.
   b. What can the government do to help overcome the problems that you described? Will government intervention necessarily be effective in either case?

7. Name five major areas of expenditure in the federal budget, and indicate how each can be viewed as a response to market failure. Then do the same for any three major areas of expenditure in state and local budgets.

8. An ardent environmentalist might argue that the optimal amount of industrial air and water pollution is zero pollution. Do you agree or disagree? Might your answer differ for different kinds of pollutants?

9. Many environmentalists believe that the Brazilian rain forests provide a significant portion of the earth's oxygen supply, and they express concern about the ongoing destruction of these forests.
   a. What kind of good is a rain forest?
   b. Why are the rain forests being destroyed if they are such an important source of the oxygen that we need to live?

10. In 1980 Ronald Reagan promised to "get the government off our backs." In terms of government expenditures, did he accomplish that goal? What significant changes have taken place in government spending in the United States over the past 10 to 15 years? What do you foresee as likely changes over the next 10 years?

24

Government Revenues, the Principles of Taxation, and the Economics of Democracy

LEARNING OBJECTIVES

CONCEPTS TO LEARN

The five major U.S. taxes

Debt financing

The normative criteria for tax design

Progressive, proportional, and regressive taxes

The theory of public choice

Arrow's Impossibility Theorem

Special-interest lobbying

CONCEPTS TO RECALL

Horizontal equity [2]

n the late 1970s a Californian named Howard Jarvis became the new hero of the fiscal conservatives when he led a successful property tax revolt in protest against ever-increasing government spending and taxes. Jarvis and his followers collected enough signatures to place a referendum on the ballot; called Proposition 13, this proposal placed a cap on local property taxes equal to 1 percent of property values. California voted yes on Proposition 13, and conservatives everywhere hailed the vote as a landmark victory. Jarvis proved that the people had the power to hold the government in check.

Enthusiasm for tax limitation swept through the country on the heels of Proposition 13. Similar property tax limitations quickly followed in Texas, Massachusetts, and a number of other states. On the national scene Ronald Reagan rode the sentiment for tax limitation to a landslide victory over Jimmy Carter in the 1980 presidential election. Shortly after taking office Reagan joined with conservative Congressman Jack Kemp of New York in persuading Congress to cut the personal income tax by 23 percent across the board. This was the largest tax cut of any kind in the history of the United States.

Liberals complained that Jarvis and his conservative followers had switched the debate over the role of the government from the expenditure side to the tax side in order to play on people's emotions. Rather than debating the proper role of government and what expenditures this role required, the conservatives simply painted taxes as an evil that took away people's spendable incomes. People naturally prefer to pay lower taxes, but that is not the issue according to the liberals. They should think first about what kinds of public services they want and then ask themselves whether they are willing to pay the taxes needed to finance the services.

Conservatives countered that public officials do not behave responsibly. They do not think in terms of the public's interest in efficiency and equity and what the government can do to achieve these goals. Instead, they use the government to pursue their own self-interest, and their self-interest is to keep raising taxes and spending. Only by limiting and even cutting taxes can citizens curb public officials' insatiable appetite for more spending.

The liberal-conservative debate over the government sector continues to rage in the United States.

Our discussion of the government's role in a market economy in Chapter 23 focused almost exclusively on government expenditures. Chapter 24 begins with a look at the revenue side of federal, state, and local budgets. The chapter then concludes our discussion of the government sector on a political note. The United States and most of the industrialized capitalist nations have chosen a representative democracy as their form of government. The final section of the chapter asks the practical question raised by the conservatives: To what extent is government economic policy really able to improve the efficiency and equity of the economy under a representative democracy? The answer is by no means clear.

THE PRINCIPAL SOURCES OF GOVERNMENT REVENUES

Governments in the United States use four main sources of revenue to finance their expenditures: (1) taxes; (2) direct charges to users of public services; (3) debt; and (4) grants-in-aid received from higher-level governments in the hierarchy of the federal, state, and local governments.

Tax collections are by far the most important source of revenues in the United States. They have financed between 70 percent and 75 percent of total government expenditures since 1981. Also, five taxes account for nearly all the tax revenue collected. They are, in order of importance, (1) the federal and the state personal income taxes, (2) the federal payroll tax earmarked for the Social Security Trust Fund, (3) general sales and excise taxes (primarily state), (4) property taxes (primarily local), and (5) the federal and the state corporation income taxes.

Grants-in-aid differ from the other three revenue sources because they are transfers of funds among governments rather than transfers of funds from the private sector to the public sector. Therefore, the ultimate sources of funds for financing public-sector programs are taxes, direct user charges, and debt. Grants-in-aid net out to zero for the fiscal system as a whole.

Table 24.1 lists the principal revenue sources of the federal government for 1992, and the state and local governments for 1991. The table shows that the governments have chosen very different means of financing their expenditures.

The Federal Government

The federal government relies almost entirely on two of the four revenue sources, taxes and debt. Tax collections account for 96 percent of all nondebt receipts. The federal government makes use of all of the taxes listed above, with the exception of property taxes, but the federal personal income tax and the Social Security payroll tax predominate. These two taxes account for approximately five-sixths of total federal tax revenues, and they are the two most important taxes in the entire U.S. fiscal system.

The use of debt financing requires some explanation. Governments issue debt to finance their budget deficits. A government's budget is in **deficit** when the government's expenditures exceed its revenues from taxes, direct user charges, and grants-in-aid. Conversely, a government's budget is in **surplus** when the government's revenues from these three sources exceed its expenditures. Governments finance their deficits by borrowing money from private and foreign citizens, business firms, and other governments. They issue new debt to the lenders in the form of government bonds in exchange for the money. A **government bond** is a promissory note that pays the bondholder (the lender) an amount equal to the principal or face value of the bond at a specified future date. The bond may also pay the lender interest on the principal each year until the government repays the principal.[1] The total amount of debt (borrowing) outstanding is the sum of all past budget deficits, less all

BUDGET DEFICIT

Exists when a government's expenditures exceed its revenues from taxes, direct user charges, and grants-in-aid.

BUDGET SURPLUS

Exists when a government's revenues from taxes, direct user charges, and grants-in-aid exceed its expenditures.

GOVERNMENT BOND

A promissory note issued by a government that pays the bondholder (the lender) an amount equal to the principal, or face value, of a bond at a specified future date.

---

[1]The federal government distinguishes among Treasury bills, notes, and bonds, depending on when it repays the principal. A Treasury bill repays the principal within 1 year, a Treasury note repays the principal within 1 to 10 years, and a Treasury bond repays the principal more than 10 years in the future.

TABLE 24.1 Revenue Sources of Federal, State, and Local Governments

	REVENUES (BILLIONS)	PERCENTAGE OF TOTAL EXPENDITURES
A. FEDERAL GOVERNMENT (FISCAL YEAR 1992)[a]		
Total receipts: Tax revenues and charges	$1075.7	72.9%

	REVENUES (BILLIONS)	PERCENTAGE OF TOTAL RECEIPTS
Personal income tax	478.7	44.5
Contributions for social insurance	410.9	38.2
Corporation income tax	89.0	8.3
Other taxes and charges	97.1	9.0

	REVENUES (BILLIONS)	PERCENTAGE OF TOTAL EXPENDITURES
Debt financing	399.7	27.1
Total expenditures	1475.4	100.0

B. STATE GOVERNMENTS (FISCAL YEAR 1991)[b]

	REVENUES (BILLIONS)	PERCENTAGE OF GENERAL REVENUE
Federal grants-in-aid	$ 134.9	24.5
Total taxes	310.5	56.3

	REVENUES (BILLIONS)	PERCENTAGE OF TOTAL TAXES
General sales and excise taxes	$153.5	49.4
Personal income tax	99.3	32.0
All other taxes	57.7	18.6

	REVENUES (BILLIONS)	PERCENTAGE OF GENERAL REVENUE
Direct user charges and miscellaneous revenues	106.3	19.2
Total general revenue	551.7	100.0

[a]The data for the federal government are estimated receipts and expenditures.
[b]Data for state and local governments were available through fiscal year 1991 only.

(continued)

past surpluses that were used to retire some of the debt. In other words, debt is a stock variable defined at a point in time, and a deficit is a flow variable defined over the course of a year, as are expenditures and revenues.

TABLE 24.1   Revenue Sources of Federal, State, and Local Governments (continued)

	REVENUES (BILLIONS)	PERCENTAGE OF GENERAL REVENUE
C. LOCAL GOVERNMENTS (FISCAL YEAR 1991)[2]		
Grants-in-aid	$201.9	37.3

	REVENUES (BILLIONS)	PERCENTAGE OF TOTAL GRANTS
From federal government	19.1	9.5
From state governments	182.7	90.5

	REVENUES (BILLIONS)	PERCENTAGE OF GENERAL REVENUE
Total taxes	214.7	39.6

	REVENUES (BILLIONS)	PERCENTAGE OF TOTAL TAXES
Property tax	161.7	75.3
Other taxes	53.0	24.7

	REVENUES (BILLIONS)	PERCENTAGE OF GENERAL REVENUE
Direct user chargers and miscellaneous revenues	125.2	23.1
Total general revenue	541.8	100.0

SOURCES: Executive Office of the President of the United States, *Budget of the United States Government, Fiscal Year 1993, Supplement, February 1992,* (Washington D.C.: U.S. Government Printing Office, 1992), Part Five: Historical Tables, Table 1.1, p. 5–14; Table 2.1, p. 5–22. U.S. Department of Commerce, Economics and Statistics Administration, Bureau of Census, *Government Finances: 1990–91 (Preliminary Report),* (Washington, D.C.: U.S. Government Printing Office, 1993), Series GF/91-5P, p. 1.

Heavy reliance on debt financing to fund annual expenditures was new to the Reagan administration and has continued ever since. The amount of federal debt held by the public was $709 billion at the end of 1980, right before President Reagan took office. The debt had grown to $2,050 billion by the end of 1988, Reagan's last year in office. By 1992, at the end of the Bush presidency, the federal debt held by the public was $2,687 billion, and it climbed above $3 trillion in 1992.

Even though President Clinton has made deficit reduction one of his top economic priorities, the debt will continue to grow rapidly. The projected federal deficit for 1993 is over $300 billion, and the President's deficit reduction plan, which congress just barely approved, will only reduce the deficit by $100 billion per year from 1993 to 1998.[2]

---

[2]The data on the public debt in this section are in Table 7.1, p. 5–89 of the February, 1992 *Supplement* to the *Budget of the United States Government, Fiscal Year 1993,* referenced in Table 24.1.

Previous administrations had also routinely issued new debt to help finance expenditures; the federal budget has been in deficit in all but two years since World War II. But the annual federal deficits were in magnitudes of billions and tens of billions of dollars, not hundreds of billions of dollars. Prior to the Reagan administration, the federal government relied almost exclusively on taxes to finance its expenditures.[3]

The State and Local Governments

State and local governments raise their revenues quite differently than does the federal government. They do not routinely use debt to finance their annual expenditures, and they rely much less on taxes than does the federal government.

Unlike the federal government, state and local governments ran surpluses every year throughout the 1980s. The recession of 1990–91 threw some of the large state governments into a deficit position as tax collections fell off. But these states are now raising taxes and user charges, and cutting expenditures, in order to bring their budgets into balance. Most state constitutions prohibit the use of debt to finance state or local operating expenditures (as opposed to capital expenditures).

Tax collections accounted for only 56.3 percent of state revenues and 39.6 percent of local revenues in 1991. As Table 24.1 indicates, these governments make up the revenue shortfall from two main sources, grants-in-aid from higher-level governments and direct user charges for public services. The most notable difference between the local and the state governments is their choice of taxes. Local governments collect three-fourths of all tax revenues from property taxes, and the property tax is the only significant source of tax revenue for most communities. By contrast, states make use of a number of taxes. They rely most heavily on the general sales tax and the personal income tax, but neither tax dominates, as the property tax does at the local level. The category "All other taxes" listed in Table 24.1 consists primarily of excise taxes earmarked to special state funds, such as the state gasoline taxes and motor vehicle excise taxes that are earmarked to state highway funds.

Let's now take a brief look at each of the major revenue sources.

The Five Major Taxes

FEDERAL AND STATE PERSONAL INCOME TAXES

THE FEDERAL PERSONAL INCOME TAX   The federal personal income tax is the largest single source of revenue in the entire U.S. fiscal system. It accounts for over 80 percent of total federal and state personal income tax revenues and serves as the model for most of the state personal income taxes.

---

[3]The one exception was during World War II, which was primarily debt financed. The war years from 1941 to 1945 brought about the largest increase in the federal debt as a percentage of national product in U.S. history. In 1946, the federal debt held by the public stood at 114 percent of the national product, compared with 53 percent of the national product in 1992.

A personal income tax is a tax on income received, levied either on individuals or on married couples. Married couples may file either one joint tax return or two individual tax returns. The federal personal income tax embodies the following general principles:

1. All factor income is subject to taxation, whether it derives from labor, capital, or land. As such, it represents a tax on the supply of these factors. (There are some important exceptions to this principle, to be noted below.)
2. The tax protects individuals and families with very low incomes by exempting a certain level of income from taxation. All taxpayers receive a personal exemption for themselves and for each family member and an additional standard deduction that is independent of family size.[4] Only income in excess of the exempt income is subject to tax. Income subject to tax is referred to as *taxable income*.

   In 1992 taxpayers received a personal exemption of $2,300 for each family member and an additional standard deduction of $6,000 (for married couples filing jointly). Therefore, a family of four paid tax only on income in excess of $15,200 ($15,200 = (4 · 2,300) + 6,000 = 9,200 + 6,000). The exemptions and standard deduction increase automatically each year with the rate of inflation.
3. In 1992, income was taxed at three different rates, 15, 28, and 31 percent, depending on the level of income. The rate schedule for married couples filing jointly in 1992 was as follows:

TAXABLE INCOME	MARGINAL TAX RATE
$0–35,800	15%
$35,801–86,500	28
Above $86,500	31

The tax rates are said to be *graduated*, meaning that they increase as income increases. Each income range is referred to as the *tax bracket* for the applicable marginal rate. For example, the 28 percent tax bracket includes the portion of taxable income ranging from $35,801 to $86,500.

Beginning in 1993, taxable incomes from 140,001 to 250,000 are subject to a marginal tax rate of 36 percent, and taxable income above 250,000 is taxed at a rate of 39 percent. The limits for the 15, 28, and 31 percent brackets increase from their 1992 amounts by the rate of inflation in 1993.

STATE PERSONAL INCOME TAXES   Forty-three states levy personal income taxes. Most of these taxes embody the three principles just described, including the graduated rate schedule. The most important difference between the federal and the state taxes is that the state tax rates are much lower, ranging in 1991 from 0.4 percent on the lowest level of taxable income in Iowa to 12 percent on the highest level of taxable income in North Dakota. (Massachusetts also taxes income from capital at a 12 percent rate.) This is why the federal tax looms larger in the economic decisions of most people than does their own state's income tax.

HISTORICAL NOTE: The Tax Reform Act of 1986 significantly increased the amount of low income protection from taxation. The exemption for each family member increased immediately from $1080 to $2000, and the standard deduction for married couples filing joint returns increased from $3600 to $5000. As a result, the level of income exempt from taxation for a family of four jumped nearly $5100, from $7920 to $13,000.

MARGINAL TAX RATE

The rate of tax applied to additional income received under a personal income tax.

HISTORICAL NOTE: The Tax Reform Act of 1986 replaced an eleven-bracket structure of graduated rates ranging from 11 percent to 50 percent with a four-bracket rate structure of 15–28–33–28 percent. The new rate structure was the culmination of a series of reforms over a 25 year period designed to reduce the number of tax brackets and lower the rates. In 1963 there were 24 tax brackets, with rates ranging from 20 percent to 91 percent. The rate structure was changed again in 1990 to 15–28–31 percent, and again in 1993.

---

[4]Taxpayers may itemize deductions for certain expenditures instead of taking the standard deduction if itemizing increases the amount of the deduction. Most low-income taxpayers do not choose to itemize, however.

THE SOCIAL SECURITY PAYROLL TAX   When Congress established the Social Security System in 1935, it decided to fund the system with a separate payroll tax on the wage incomes of all covered employees. Half of the tax is levied on the employee and half on the employer. In 1992 employees and employers each paid a tax of 6.2 percent on wage income up to a limit of $55,500 to provide for retirement and other cash benefits. Income in excess of the limit is untaxed. Hence, the maximum payroll tax liability for employees (and their employers) in 1992 was $3,441 (= 0.062 · $55,500). There is also now a separate payroll tax earmarked for the Medicare program. In 1992 the Medicare tax rate was 1.45 percent on all wage income up to a limit of $130,000. The upper limit will be removed in 1994.

The growth in payroll tax revenues has kept pace with the growth in Social Security benefits since 1935, to the point where the payroll tax is now the second most important tax in the U.S. fiscal system. For the majority of taxpayers the payroll tax is the most important tax; their payroll tax liability exceeds their federal personal income tax liability.

Congress adjusts the payroll tax revenues by periodically changing both the rate of tax and the income limit. The most recent set of adjustments resulted from the 1983 amendments to the Social Security Act. The 1983 amendments were designed to forestall an impending crisis that threatened to undermine the entire Social Security System. By the late 1970s annual benefit payments began to exceed annual payroll tax collections. Beyond that, the system was heading for disaster down the road when the huge baby boom generation, those people born between 1947 and 1964, retired.

The 1983 amendments made substantial changes in both the benefit schedules and the payroll tax that were designed to build up a huge surplus of funds until the baby boomers begin to retire. The surplus would then be drawn down to cover the baby boomers' retirement benefits. Included in the reforms was a series of increases in the payroll tax rates and income limits during the five-year period from 1983 to 1988.

The income limit on the retirement benefits portion of the tax increases each year with the rate of inflation. But with no new tax rate increases scheduled beyond 1988, the future growth in payroll tax revenues should be less rapid than it has been in the recent past.

GENERAL SALES AND EXCISE TAXES   An excise tax is a tax on the sale of a single commodity. A general sales tax is levied on a broad range of commodities, usually at a common rate.

General sales taxes have long been the leading source of tax revenue at the state level, although personal income taxes may soon overtake them. Forty-five states make use of the general sales tax. In 1991 the tax rates varied from a low of 3 percent in Wyoming to a high of 7 percent in New Jersey and Rhode Island.

The primary appeal of sales (and excise) taxes is that they are easy to administer. Most businesses keep careful records of sales receipts for their internal accounting purposes, and state departments of revenue can use these records as a basis for determining a business's sales tax liability.

Ease of collection is another reason why the low-income, developing countries rely heavily on sales taxes rather than personal income taxes. A broad-based personal income tax is just not possible for a developing country because such a large percentage of the population is illiterate. The burden of operating a personal income tax falls largely on the people; individuals must keep accurate records of their income and file a tax return. People cannot be expected to keep records and file tax returns if they cannot read or write. Consequently, the developing countries have to tax their businesses, and the sales tax has been a popular choice.

The principal complaint against the sales tax is the perception that it unduly burdens those with low incomes. Low-income people spend a higher percentage of their incomes on consumer goods and services than do high-income people. Thus, they suffer a disproportionately higher tax burden under a general sales tax. Twenty-eight states have attempted to reduce the burden of the sales tax on their poorer citizens by exempting food purchased for home consumption from taxation.

THE LOCAL PROPERTY TAX   Local property taxes account for 96 percent of all property tax revenues in the United States. Only a handful of states use the property tax as a major source of revenue, and the federal government does not tax property at all except after death as part of an estate tax.

The property tax is the only major tax that is not levied on a component of the circular flow of economic activity. It is a tax on a component of wealth, not on the expenditures or incomes that flow through goods and factor markets. The majority of property tax revenue is raised from local taxes on residential housing, although taxes on commercial and industrial property also raise substantial amounts of revenue. Taxes on other forms of personal property, such as cars, home furnishings, and pleasure boats, are far less common and are unimportant in terms of the total revenue they collect.

Survey after survey reveals that the property tax is the least popular of the major taxes. If the tax on residential property is so universally disliked, why do all local governments use it? They use it because the property tax is the only tax that is fairly easy to levy and administer at the local level. The value of residential property within a community offers every local government a natural, broad tax base. In contrast, sales taxes may not raise sufficient amounts of revenue in towns with little commercial or industrial activity.

The property tax is also easy to administer because property stays put, certainly relative to income. If localities levied income taxes, problems would arise over the issue of where the income was earned. If localities tried to tax the incomes of their residents, they would have difficulty collecting taxes on income earned outside their jurisdiction. If the localities tried to tax income earned within the community, they would have difficulty tracking down and collecting taxes from individuals who earn their incomes within the community, but live elsewhere. Residential property is so much easier to keep track of than income is.

Finally, sales and income taxes might well drive businesses and workers to neighboring communities without such taxes. Because existing residential property stays put, there is less risk of losing the tax base with a property tax. True, raising or lowering the property tax rate may affect the amount of new construction in the community and therefore the value of the tax base. But, more than any other tax, the property tax gives local governments the independence they need to finance the public services desired by the community.

REFLECTION: Does your state have a property (or other) tax cap? If so, have you noticed a decline in public services—for example, cutbacks in the curriculum or extracurricular programs at the high school or less frequent garbage collection? Even if your state does not have a tax cap, have public services declined over the past five years because of budgetary pressures?

FEDERAL AND STATE CORPORATION INCOME TAXES

THE FEDERAL CORPORATION INCOME TAX As the name implies, the federal and the state corporation income taxes are levied only on the income earned by corporations. The earnings of proprietors and partnerships are considered to be regular factor income received by the owners of these firms and are taxed under the federal and the state personal income taxes.

Corporate "income" or "profit" subject to the federal tax is roughly equivalent to the returns to capital invested in the corporation by the stockholders (owners), but only roughly. The actual tax base is extremely complex and varies by type of business. Broadly speaking, though, taxable profit is the difference between revenues from sales and two categories of costs, operating expenses and depreciation. The operating expenses of the corporation include out-of-pocket expenses for factors of production such as the wages and salaries of the firm's employees and the costs of material inputs and fuels, the sales and excise taxes paid on the sale of the products, and the interest paid to holders of corporate bonds who have loaned the corporation money for investment. Depreciation is an estimate of how much the value of the firm's stock of plant and equipment declines during the year, based on guidelines established by the U.S. Internal Revenue Service.

The federal corporation income tax employs a three-step graduated rate schedule, much like that for personal income tax. The corporate rates are 15, 25, and 34 percent. However, the 34 percent rate takes effect at only $75,000 of taxable income, so that virtually all corporate income is taxed at the 34 percent rate.[5]

STATE CORPORATION INCOME TAXES Forty-three states levy corporation income taxes, most of which are modeled after the federal tax. The main difference between the state and the federal taxes is the tax rate. The state tax rates are much lower, just as they are with the personal income taxes. In 1991, the tax rates ranged from a low of 1 percent in Alaska to a high of 12.25 percent in Pennsylvania. States are naturally reluctant to raise their corporate tax rates for fear that business firms will leave for states with lower tax rates. This reluctance has prevented the corporation income tax from becoming a major source of state revenues.[6]

Tax collectors like the corporation income tax because it is an easy source of revenue. Economists, on the other hand, generally dislike the tax. They were not pleased when the Tax Reform Act of 1986 increased federal corporation income tax revenues at the expense of personal income tax revenues.

Economists complain that the corporation income tax introduces a whole host of distortions into capital markets that would otherwise function fairly closely to the perfectly competitive ideal. The tax distorts capital markets by causing different kinds of assets to be taxed at very different rates. Demanders and suppliers of capital have a natural incentive to gravitate toward relatively lightly taxed assets and shy away from highly taxed assets. As a result, the

---

[5]In 1993 Congress increased the marginal tax rate to 35 percent on corporate income in excess of $10 million.
[6]All data on state taxes are from U.S. Advisory Commission on Intergovernmental Relations, *Significant Features of Fiscal Federalism 1992* (Washington, D.C.: U.S. Government Printing Office, February 1992), Table 22, pp. 68–72 (State personal income tax rates); Table 25, pp. 76–78 (State corporation income tax rates); and Table 29, pp. 89–90 (State sales tax rates and exemptions).

allocation of capital is quite different, and far less efficient, than it would be if all assets were taxed at the same rate.

For example, the tax encourages investment in the noncorporate sector at the expense of the corporate sector because only corporate income is taxed. The tax also encourages firms to engage in debt financing because they can deduct interest from the tax base, but not dividends. With more debt outstanding, firms become riskier than they otherwise would be. Firms can lay off workers to save on costs if business turns sour, but the obligation to repay their debts, with interest, remains no matter what happens. Finally, the complexities of the tax base happen to generate a very strong bias in favor of short-term investments, such as equipment, and against longer-term investments, such as physical plant.

Direct User Charges for Public Services

Direct user charges for public services go by many names: *rates* charged by the electric and water utilities, *tolls* on bridges and highways, *fares* on bus and rail transit, and admission *fees* to parks and beaches. The state gasoline *tax* is also considered by many to be a charge for the use of the state's roadways, especially since these taxes are earmarked to the state highway funds.

Call them what you will, direct user charges are extremely popular. They appeal to a deeply held principle of equity in the collection of government revenues, the **benefits received principle of taxation.** The benefits received principle says, simply, that taxes and other means of payment are fair if they bear a direct relationship to the benefits people receive from the public services being financed. The principle dates from seventeenth-century England, when landowners paid taxes to the king in return for the state's promise to maintain public order.

Direct user charges honor the benefits received principle as closely as possible. Users pay for the services, and nonusers do not; more-intensive users pay more for the service than do less-intensive users. This is exactly what the benefits received principle is all about.

The benefits received principle is bound to appeal to a capitalistic society because the market system operates on the same principle. Buyers pay only for those goods and services that give them benefit. They are not forced to buy anything that they do not want. Since user charges are nothing more than prices set by a public agency, they bear the same relationship to benefits received as do market prices.

Direct user charges would undoubtedly be used even more if they could be, but they are often not a practical option. The majority of public expenditure programs are just not amenable to payment according to benefits received. Paying for the nation's defense is one example. Any attempt to levy taxes for defense on the basis of benefits received would be undermined by the free-rider problem. People would refuse to reveal their true preferences if they thought that their tax payments would bear any close relationship to their stated preferences.

Pinning down the benefits of many public goods and services is problematic even without the free-rider problem. Public education is justified because of the external benefits it confers. But does anyone seriously believe that citizens could be taxed accurately on the basis of the external benefits that they receive

BENEFITS RECEIVED PRINCIPLE OF TAXATION

The principle that the taxes and other means of payment for public services are fair if they bear a direct relationship to the benefits people receive from the public services.

REFLECTION: Is your town substituting direct user charges for the property tax in order to pay for town services, such as contracting out garbage collection to private firms and charging fees to participate in town recreation programs or high school sports; is it relying on hidden user charges, as when parents volunteer to coach town soccer teams that used to be coached by town recreation personnel?

from public education? Trying to use the benefits received principle to pay for highways also raises difficult questions. How much benefit does each member of a community receive from the local roadways? What fraction of the benefits accrue to people outside the jurisdiction? Can outsiders be made to pay for these benefits, given that tolls are impractical for most local roadways? Even if tolls could be charged, should they be? If the marginal costs of traveling on the road are (near) zero, economic efficiency dictates that the price should be (near) zero. In this case the dictates of equity and efficiency are inconsistent with one another.

Redistributional transfer payments are still another category of expenditures that cannot be financed according to the benefits received principle. The primary beneficiary of a transfer payment is the person who receives it. Therefore, taxing to pay for transfers according to the benefits received principle would result in no net transfer at all.

We can now see why the federal government makes so little use of user charges. With defense, transfers to the poor, interest payments on the debt, and grants-in-aid dominating federal expenditures, the federal government must rely on general taxes such as the personal and the corporation income taxes that offer taxpayers no direct connection between the taxes they pay and the benefits they receive.

The only possible exception at the federal level is the Social Security payroll tax. The Social Security System was not a true pension plan prior to the 1983 amendments. It was essentially a pay-as-you-go, tax-transfer scheme that transferred income each year from the young to the elderly. The payroll tax revenues collected from employers and employees did not accumulate in an investment pension fund to pay for future retirement benefits. Instead, the tax revenues were immediately paid out to current retirees. Still, some economists argued that the payroll taxes came with an implied promise of future pension benefits and medical insurance and were therefore consistent with the benefits received principle. The 1983 amendments tightened the benefits received justification for the payroll tax by allowing for a surplus to accumulate to pay for the baby boomers' retirement years. By accumulating a surplus, the Social Security System now operates more like a standard private pension plan. The system is scheduled to return to a pay-as-you-go, tax-transfer scheme, however, after the baby boomers retire.

State and local governments also have to rely on general taxes to finance the majority of their expenditures, including each of the five major categories identified in Chapter 23: education, highways, public welfare, health and hospitals, and local police and fire protection.

Once the link between taxation and benefits received is broken, judging the merits of taxes requires a completely different set of principles. We will consider the principles governing the design of general taxes in the next section of this chapter.

Debt Financing

Issuing government bonds to raise funds is appropriate for only one purpose in the normal course of events: to finance public capital expenditures, such as school buildings, highways, and other public works construction projects. Governments are not supposed to issue bonds to finance the annual operating expenses associated with government programs. In this respect the accepted rules of public finance are similar to the rules of private business finance. Corporations routinely issue bonds to finance their investments in plant and equipment, but not to finance their annual production expenses.

The main difference between public and private debt is that most government projects are not expected to generate revenues to pay back the principal and interest on the bonds, although some projects are financed on that basis. High schools and rural highways do not generate revenues, whereas a debt-financed college dormitory at a state university might be able to pay back bondholders from student room fees.

When no revenues are expected from a capital project, governments issue **full faith and credit bonds** that are backed by the power to tax. The full faith and credit guarantee is that the government will raise sufficient tax revenues in future years to pay back the principal and interest on the debt. Bonds used to pay for self-financing projects such as college dormitories are called **revenue bonds.**

Raising taxes to repay full faith and credit bonds is perfectly legitimate. Highways and schools may not generate any revenues directly. But they do expand the nation's production possibilities frontier and allow national income to grow if they are productive. Taxing some of the additional income to repay the debt is appropriate, just as firms set aside some of their revenues to repay debt that was used to finance productive private investments.

Most economists recognize two other extraordinary circumstances in which the federal government can appropriately issue debt, wars and recessions. The first large infusion of public debt in the United States occurred during World War II. The government felt it had little choice but to borrow from the public at the time, with military expenditures running as high as 25 percent of total national output. The federal government may also issue debt whenever the circular flow of economic activity slows down and the economy experiences a recession. The macroeconomic chapters of this text show that requiring a balanced budget during a recession can make the recession worse. Moreover, debt-financed government expenditures, or tax cuts with tax revenues replaced by issuing debt, can help pull the economy out of a recession. But debt financing of operating expenses or transfer payments during a recession comes with the understanding that revenues from nondebt sources will meet or exceed these expenditures once the economy recovers.

State and local governments do follow the accepted rules of debt financing for the most part. Nearly all state governors and local administrators are required by state law to submit balanced operating budgets. Projected revenues from taxes, direct user charges, and grants-in-aid must be sufficient to cover all projected operating expenses during the upcoming year. State and local debt is used primarily for capital expenditures.

THE REAGAN-BUSH-CLINTON DEFICITS   The same cannot be said of the federal government. The huge federal budget deficits that began in 1981 have forced the government to issue debt to finance operating expenses as well as capital expenditures, and the debt cannot be justified by either of the extraordinary circumstances noted above. The deficits came about when President Reagan persuaded Congress to pass two large programs that sharply increased expenditures and reduced tax revenues. The expenditure program was a huge

FULL FAITH AND CREDIT BOND

Government bonds issued to finance capital projects that are not expected to bring in revenues; the bonds are backed by the government's power to tax.

REVENUE BOND

Government bonds that are used to pay for self-financing capital projects.

military buildup to counter a perceived threat to the nation's security from the Soviet Union. The tax program was the 23 percent reduction in the personal income tax that we mentioned in the introduction. The purpose of the tax cut was to help stimulate the economy. The Reagan deficits began when the economy was in the throes of a deep recession, but the administration itself projected that the huge deficits would continue once the economy had recovered to full employment. And, of course, the Reagan-Bush-Clinton deficits have been peacetime deficits.

Chapter 12 considers the various macroeconomic issues associated with large ongoing deficits and a large public debt.

NORMATIVE CRITERIA FOR TAX DESIGN

What principles should apply to the design of general taxes, those for which there is no necessary connection between tax payments and benefits received? Economists judge general taxes on the basis of five criteria: (1) ease of administration, (2) simplicity, (3) flexibility, (4) efficiency, and (5) equity.

The Properties of "Good" Taxes

EASE OF ADMINISTRATION   Ease of administration is really the foremost requirement of any general tax. Above all else, revenue departments have to be able to collect large amounts of revenue fairly easily. If a general tax is difficult to administer, a government simply will not use it.

We noted above that ease of administration was a principal appeal of three of the major U.S. taxes: general sales and excise taxes, local property taxes, and corporation income taxes. Personal income taxes and the Social Security payroll tax are also easy to administer. They have to be, or they would not have become the two leading U.S. taxes.

SIMPLICITY   Simplicity and ease of administration are closely related. The difference is that the simplicity criterion adopts the taxpayers' point of view. Taxpayers must understand the nature of their tax liability and be able to compute and pay their taxes with a minimum of time and effort. In particular, complying with the tax should not require taxpayers to maintain a detailed set of records that they would not otherwise keep.

The more complex a tax is, the more taxpayers will evade paying their proper tax liability, out of either ignorance or spite. Once tax evasion becomes widespread, the tax is no longer a useful source of revenue. Revenue departments cannot chase down everyone. This is why simplicity and ease of administration are so closely linked.

FLEXIBILITY   The flexibility criterion refers to the ability of a tax to respond appropriately to market failure. For general taxes this boils down to (1) flexibility in the pursuit of equity and (2) flexibility in the conduct of macroeconomic policy. As such, the flexibility criterion applies mostly to the design of federal taxes.

The federal personal income tax is potentially very flexible in both respects. Regarding equity, personal income taxes have a natural advantage over all the other major taxes in that they can be tailored most easily to the personal circumstances of the taxpayer. For instance, protecting poor families from the burden of taxation under a personal income tax is easily achieved by personal exemptions that remove the first dollars of income from taxation and vary by family size. Protecting the poor from tax burden is much more difficult under a payroll or property tax and virtually impossible under sales and excise taxes.

Flexibility in the conduct of macroeconomic policy refers to how quickly the government can change tax collections in response to changes in the state of the economy. The government must be able to change the structure of a tax quickly, for example, by adjusting tax rates up or down. Then the change in the tax structure must translate quickly into changes in actual tax collections.

The federal personal income tax is potentially a very flexible macroeconomic policy tool. Congress can enact temporary across-the-board surcharges or cuts in the tax rates in response to economic conditions. Then, given that the tax is withheld from workers' paychecks, the change in actual tax liabilities occurs with only about a month's delay. Workers see an almost immediate increase or decrease in their take-home pay.

In fact, the macroeconomic flexibility of the tax has not been exploited very often. Congress has usually been reluctant to change the tax structure without undertaking a full set of time-consuming congressional hearings. Chapter 11 discusses this point, along with other macroeconomic issues of federal tax policy.

EFFICIENCY   Tax policy can contribute to the efficient operation of the economy in certain situations. For instance, taxing polluters is an efficient, least-cost solution to the problem of pollution externalities. Tax policy can help achieve the macroeconomic policy goals.

For the most part, however, general broad-based taxes impede the efficient operation of a market economy. Sales taxes cause inefficiencies by forcing competitive markets for goods and services away from their natural supply and demand equilibriums. Income and property taxes also cause inefficiencies, the only difference being that they do their damage in the factor markets for labor, capital, and land. All major taxes inevitably cause some efficiency loss.

The amount of efficiency loss resulting from a broad-based tax depends on two factors, the level of the tax rate(s) and the elasticities of supply and demand in the markets that are taxed. These are the two factors that determine how much a tax changes the quantity in a market relative to the no-tax equilibrium. In general, a tax causes a larger change in quantity and a greater efficiency loss the higher the tax rate and the more elastic the supply and demand.

Therefore, the efficiency criterion takes on a negative slant when applied to tax policy. The goal is to select and design taxes that minimize the efficiency losses per dollar of revenue raised. The way to minimize efficiency loss is to keep tax rates low or to tax markets whose supplies or demands are highly inelastic.

EQUITY   What is the fairest way to raise general tax revenue? Since the benefits received principle is inoperable for general taxes, society must develop a whole new set of equity norms to guide the design of tax policy. No one can give a definitive answer to the question of what the fairest general tax is. As in all matters of equity, people are free to believe whatever they want to believe. Nonetheless, we can say that economists would vote overwhelmingly for one of two taxes as being the most fair: the personal income tax or a tax on personal consumption expenditures. The equity principles favoring these taxes trace their ancestry to the writings of Adam Smith and John Stuart Mill in the late 1700s and early 1800s.

THE ABILITY-TO-PAY PRINCIPLE OF TAXATION   Smith and Mill argued that citizens should view the payment of general taxes as a necessary sacrifice for promoting the common good. The key equity question as they saw it was this: What is the fairest way to ask people to sacrifice? They both concluded that the government should ask citizens to sacrifice in accordance with their *ability to pay*. In addition, they believed that taxes levied according to taxpayers' ability to pay should honor the principles of horizontal equity and vertical equity. **Horizontal equity** requires equal treatment of equals. **Vertical equity** says that unequals may be treated unequally.

As principles guiding tax design, horizontal and vertical equity raise two very important questions. First, in what sense are people to be considered equals, or unequals? In other words, what is the best measure of a person's ability to pay taxes? Both principles require an answer to these questions. Second, just how unequally may unequals be treated? The answer to this question defines society's notion of vertical equity.

The answer to the first question is directly tied to the choice of the tax base. The reason is that any tax is levied by applying a tax rate to a tax base. Two people whose tax bases have the same value are necessarily subjected to the same rate of tax and therefore pay the same tax. They are treated equally. So the tax base implicitly defines the sense in which two people are considered equal, in line with horizontal equity. By the same token, two people whose tax bases have different values are necessarily unequal. So differences in the tax base implicitly define the extent to which people are unequal for the purposes of applying the principle of vertical equity.

Having determined the proper tax base, satisfying the principle of vertical equity relates to the structure of the tax. The two elements of the tax structure that primarily determine just how unequally society intends to treat unequals are (1) the tax rates to be applied to different levels of the tax base and (2) the manner in which portions of the tax base are exempt from taxation.

HORIZONTAL EQUITY: CHOOSING THE TAX BASE   Let's turn first to the problem of choosing the tax base. Which tax base best measures a taxpayer's ability to pay? Most economists would answer either income or consumption. Proponents of an income tax argue that income earned during the course of a year is the best measure of a person's utility or economic well-being. Therefore, two people with equal income are equally well off and should pay the same tax. The income subject to tax should include all sources of income because people's well-being depends on how much income they have, not how it was received. Income received from all factors of production, income received from transfer payments, and **capital gains** or losses received from assets should all be part of the tax base. A capital gain on a stock or bond or other asset is the difference between the value of the asset at the end of the year and its value at the

---

HORIZONTAL EQUITY (TAXATION)

The principle that two people with equal levels of utility before a tax should have equal levels of utility after a tax.

VERTICAL EQUITY (TAXATION)

The principle that unequals may be treated unequally, that is, two people with different values of a tax base may legitimately pay different amounts of tax.

CAPITAL GAIN (ANNUAL)

The difference between the value of an asset at the end of the year and its value at the beginning of the year.

beginning of the year. Income defined broadly in this way is commonly referred to as the **comprehensive tax base** (CTB). Finally, the Internal Revenue Service should not care how people use their incomes, whether they save or consume, or how they save or consume.

Proponents of a consumption tax argue that consumption is the best measure of utility or well-being because it is the act of consumption that actually yields utility. Furthermore, people's well-being should be judged over their entire lifetimes, not from year to year. The vast majority of people lead self-contained economic lives. They inherit very little wealth at the beginning of their lives and bequeath very little wealth to their heirs when they die. Once people become adults, they make decisions about how to earn income throughout their lives, and they eventually consume virtually all their income before they die. For those few individuals who do bequeath a significant amount of wealth, the bequest can be viewed as a final act of consumption for the purposes of taxation.

When interpreted in the context of individuals' lifetimes, horizontal equity requires that two people with equal utility *over their lifetimes* before tax should have equal utility *over their lifetimes* after tax. Since the act of consumption is the best measure of utility, the pattern of lifetime consumption is the best surrogate measure for lifetime utility. Therefore, lifetime horizontal equity translates into the following proposition for taxation: Two people with the same amount of consumption each year of their lives should pay the same tax each year. This requirement can be met only with a personal consumption tax when taxes are collected annually.

For example, two people with equal consumption each year would pay equal taxes under a personal consumption tax, but not necessarily under a personal income tax. The problem with the income tax is that two people with the same pattern of lifetime consumption might not receive the same amount of income every year. Through saving and borrowing, many different patterns of income can result in the same pattern of consumption. If the two people's incomes do differ and if income is the tax base, then their tax payments would also differ year by year. Lifetime horizontal equity would not be achieved.

A personal consumption tax would be administered much as the personal income tax is now, with taxpayers filing once a year and tax payments withheld from each paycheck. The main difference is that taxpayers would deduct all saving from their income in determining the tax base. Since income can only be consumed or saved, the difference between income and saving is consumption.

The idea of changing the federal personal income tax into a personal consumption tax received a serious hearing in the debates leading up to the Tax Reform Act of 1986. The debate considered more than just the equity implications of switching the tax base. Efficiency and administrative issues were also involved. In the end, both the administration and the Congress decided in favor of retaining the personal income tax.

VERTICAL EQUITY: CHOOSING THE TAX STRUCTURE   Exactly how unequally should unequals be treated? This is a fundamental question of end-results equity, and no attempt to answer it has ever come close to gaining widespread acceptance. The best that the United States has been able to do is to recast the question in fairly general terms: Should taxes be progressive, proportional, or regressive? A consensus appears to exist that taxes should be at least mildly progressive.

COMPREHENSIVE TAX BASE

A broad-based measure of the personal income subject to tax under a personal income tax that includes all income received from factors of production, all transfer payments received, and net capital gains on assets received during the year.

The terms *progressive, proportional,* and *regressive* refer to the general pattern of tax burdens as income rises. The idea for an income tax is to compute the ratio of income taxes paid to income for each family (or unrelated individuals). The ratio defines the average tax burden (ATB) for each family:

$$ATB = T / Y$$

where T is the tax payment by the family and Y is the family's (comprehensive) income. Now observe what happens to the ATB as family income increases:

1. The tax is **progressive** if the ATB increases as income increases. Taxpayers not only sacrifice more income as their ability to pay increases; they also sacrifice an ever-increasing proportion of their income.
2. The tax is **proportional** if the ATB remains constant as income increases. Taxpayers sacrifice more in absolute amount as their ability to pay increases, but the proportion of income sacrificed remains constant.
3. The tax is **regressive** if the ATB declines as income increases. Taxpayers may or may not sacrifice more in absolute amount as their ability to pay increases, but the proportion of income they are asked to sacrifice declines.

The terms *progressive* and *regressive* are laden with emotion. A progressive tax is presumably good in that it contributes to society's attempt to redistribute income from rich to poor. It takes a *relatively* larger bite out of the rich. By the same token a regressive tax is presumably bad because it is counter to society's redistributional efforts. The poor sacrifice *relatively* more than do the rich. Similarly, a proportional tax is considered to be distributionally neutral, since rich and poor suffer tax burdens in the same proportion to their income.

VERTICAL EQUITY: THE U.S. TAX SYSTEM The consensus among public-sector economists is that the U.S. tax system is approximately proportional throughout all but the lowest, poverty-level income range, where it is mildly progressive. The proportionality results from the offsetting effects of the five major taxes, some of which are progressive, others regressive, and still others proportional.

The two major federal taxes somewhat offset one another. The federal personal income tax is among the more progressive of the major taxes. It is sharply progressive at the low end because of the personal exemptions and the standard deduction, and then it becomes mildly progressive to nearly proportional as income increases. The progressive effect of the graduated rate schedule is largely offset by the many deductions available to the middle- and high-income taxpayers. State personal income taxes follow the same pattern because they are modeled after the federal tax for the most part. Overall, they are slightly less progressive than is the federal tax. The federal and the state personal income taxes are so large that their low-end progressivity makes the entire U.S. tax system mildly progressive at the lowest income levels.

The Social Security payroll tax, in contrast, is the most regressive of the major taxes. The income cutoff in the tax base earmarked for cash benefits means that taxpayers with very high income pay the same tax as do taxpayers in the $50,000 to $60,000 income range, a very regressive feature. The payroll tax also hits low-income families very hard because it does not exempt any wage income from the tax.

Sales and excise taxes are proportional to mildly regressive. As noted earlier, they are perceived to be highly regressive because, in any one year, low-income

PROGRESSIVE TAX

A tax for which the average tax burden increases as the taxpayer's income increases.

PROPORTIONAL TAX

A tax for which the average tax burden remains constant as the taxpayer's income increases.

REGRESSIVE TAX

A tax for which the average tax burden declines as the taxpayer's income increases.

families consume a much higher percentage of their incomes than do high-income families. From a lifetime perspective, though, the tax becomes roughly proportional as the vast majority of people consume virtually all the income that they earn over their entire lives.

Economists are divided on the local property tax. The tax used to be viewed as highly regressive because economists thought that landlords could pass the tax on to renters, who have lower incomes than do homeowners. A newer, and emerging, view is that property owners bear most of the burden of the tax. If so, the tax is quite progressive because property is owned disproportionately by the rich. Still a third, and decidedly minority, view holds that the property tax is essentially a payment for local services in line with the benefits received principle. This is so because people seek out the communities that best match their preferences for local services and taxes. Issues of progressivity, proportionality, and regressivity are irrelevant for benefits received taxes because taxpayers get what they pay for. Benefits received taxes are distributionally neutral.

The federal and the state corporation income taxes are generally considered to be progressive. The majority of economists believe that corporate stockholders bear most of the burden of the tax, and income from capital is highly concentrated among the rich.

To summarize, the consensus is that the personal and the corporation income taxes are progressive, the state sales and excise taxes are proportional to mildly regressive, and the Social Security payroll tax is highly regressive. No one knows what to conclude about the local property tax, but this does not matter so much because the property tax is among the smaller of the major taxes. Overall, the mix of progressive, proportional, and regressive taxes makes the U.S. tax system roughly proportional throughout all but the lowest income ranges, where it is slightly progressive.

DEMOCRACY AND THE THEORY OF PUBLIC CHOICE

The political choices that nations make have important economic consequences. The final section of Chapter 24 analyzes the economic consequences of representative democracy, the form of government chosen by the United States and by most of the industrialized capitalist countries.

Chapter 23 discussed the appropriate economic role of the government as a corrector of market failures. The practical question, though, is whether government economic policy can actually hope to realize its potential for correcting market failures. Most economists were fairly confident 20 to 30 years ago. They taught that government policy could help an economy become more efficient and more equitable. Since that time, however, economists have become increasingly skeptical of government intervention.

The skeptics are rallying around an emerging economic view of political behavior known as the **theory of public choice,** whose central idea is that people behave the same way in the political arena as they do in the economic arena. The traditional view holds that people are self-motivated in their economic activities, but public spirited in their political activities. Not so, according to the new view. People do not suddenly change their stripes when they enter the political arena; they continue to pursue their own self-interests. In politics as in the market, people act to maximize their own utility.

THEORY OF PUBLIC CHOICE

A theory of government based on the premise that people behave in the same self-interested manner in the political arena as they do in the economic arena.

Self-interest is fine in the economic sphere. We have seen how self-interested economic behavior can lead to market transactions that are both efficient and equitable. Public choice theorists are much less sanguine about self-interested political behavior, however, especially in democratic forms of government. They believe that democratic political institutions and procedures can be a major stumbling block to the conduct of effective economic policy when behavior is self-motivated. The theory of public choice helps us understand why democratic forms of government so often encounter difficulties with the conduct of economic policy.

In Chapter 1 we noted that the traditional lines between the social sciences have become increasingly blurred of late. The theory of public choice is a leading example of this trend. A number of economists, led by Nobel laureates Kenneth Arrow and James Buchanan, have applied standard economic principles to political behavior, with fairly striking results. Foremost among them is the conclusion that democratic political institutions and procedures may hinder the quest for economic efficiency and equity.

Economic Efficiency and Democratic Voting Rules

The economic problems with democracy begin with the fact that democratic voting rules are not necessarily consistent with the pursuit of economic efficiency. Democratic voting rules come in many forms, from unanimous consent down to a simple (50 percent) majority. Of all the possible voting rules, only unanimity is fully consistent with economic efficiency.

Government policies clearly promote economic efficiency if they make some people better off without making anyone else worse off. Only unanimity can assure that all such policies, and only those policies, will be adopted. Under unanimous voting, any policy that makes some people better off without making anyone else worse off would pass. Those who stand to gain would vote in favor of the policy. Those who would not be any worse off would presumably abstain from voting. Conversely, any policy that generated losses for some would be blocked by the potential losers. In principle, then, government policy can achieve efficiency under a unanimous voting rule. The electorate would adopt all efficiency-improving policies until such opportunities were exhausted.

Democratic societies never choose unanimity, however, because the costs of obtaining unanimous agreement on a course of action are just too high. Voting by unanimous consent works well only with very small groups. Once the number of voters becomes fairly large, designing policies in which no one loses is virtually impossible. Since potential losers can always defeat a policy under unanimous voting, the unanimity requirement leads to political paralysis. This is why democracies choose less-stringent majority voting rules, such as a simple or a two-thirds majority.

Notice, though, that any voting rule short of unanimity introduces a cost into the political process, the cost of being on the losing side. These costs have not prevented societies from choosing majority voting rules, but majority voting can wreak havoc on economic policy formation under self-motivated behavior.

The economic problems with majority voting rules arise because majority voting is not fully consistent with economic efficiency. Policies that generate both gainers and losers cannot be judged by the efficiency criterion alone, yet such policies can pass under majority voting. This is not necessarily a bad outcome. Virtually all economic policies generate gains and losses, and voters in a democracy have to accept the possibility that they may be on the losing side of a vote. What is troubling, though, is that under majority voting rules voters can accept policies that reduce the overall level of economic well-being and reject policies that just as clearly increase the overall level of economic well-being.

To see these possibilities, suppose that everyone has the same income and is viewed by society as equally deserving, so that distributional considerations are not an issue. Imagine that a vote is taken on a policy in which voters totaling 51 percent of the electorate each receive small benefits and voters totaling 49 percent of the electorate each suffer substantial losses. The policy would pass under a simple majority vote, even though the aggregate losses greatly exceed the aggregate gains. Overall economic well-being has diminished.

Now reverse the situation. Imagine a policy in which voters totaling 51 percent of the electorate each suffer small losses and voters totaling 49 percent of the electorate each receive enormous benefits. The policy would fail a majority vote, even though the aggregate gains greatly exceed the aggregate losses. In this instance, majority voting rules cause voters to miss an opportunity to improve overall economic well-being.

Arrow's Impossibility Theorem

The potential efficiency problems with majority voting rules pale in comparison to a second problem uncovered by Nobel laureate Kenneth Arrow. He showed that majority voting rules might not generate a consistent set of social priorities when people disagree about what those priorities should be. His result, known as **Arrow's Impossibility Theorem,** stands as one of the foremost intellectual achievements of the twentieth century. It was especially disheartening to those who believe that personal freedom is best safeguarded by a democratic form of government. Arrow showed that majority voting procedures can come apart at the seams when social priorities are inconsistent.

ARROW'S IMPOSSIBILITY THEOREM

The proposition that individuals' preferences for particular government policies might not aggregate into a consistent set of social preferences for those policies under democratic voting rules.

We will illustrate Arrow's theorem with a simple example of choosing a policy that affects the distribution of income. Despite its simplicity, our example cuts right to the heart of the For Whom or distribution question, one of the four fundamental questions that any society must answer. The example shows why democracies might not be able to resolve the distribution question. The economic problems with democracy are certainly not limited to the pursuit of efficiency.

SOCIAL INCONSISTENCY   Suppose that three individuals, 1, 2, and 3, are considering three different policies for transferring $100 among the three of them. The policies A, B, and C are listed in Table 24.2.

The rows in the table indicate how much each individual receives under each policy. For instance, policy A transfers $50 to individual 1, $20 to individual 2, and $30 to individual 3; policies B and C are similar.

Suppose that the three people vote their own self-interest in line with the theory of public choice, so that their preferences for the three policies depend only on the size of the transfer they receive under each policy. Their self-interested preferences are as follows:

TABLE 24.2   Distribution of $100 Under Three Different Policies

POLICY	INDIVIDUAL 1	INDIVIDUAL 2	INDIVIDUAL 3
A	$50	$20	$30
B	30	50	20
C	20	30	50

- Person 1 prefers A to B, B to C, and A to C.
- Person 2 prefers B to C, C to A, and B to A.
- Person 3 prefers C to A, A to B, and C to B.

Although all three people know exactly what they prefer, the social preferences determined by a majority vote on the three policies are muddled. Two of the three individuals (1 and 3) prefer policy A to policy B. Two of the three (1 and 2) also prefer B to C. Since society prefers A to B and B to C under majority voting, consistency requires that society prefer A to C. Instead, two of the three (2 and 3) prefer C to A. Majority voting cannot determine which is the best policy, given the inconsistency.

The important conclusion to draw from this example is that majority voting cannot be expected to resolve the distribution question when voting behavior is self-interested. Democracies *may* be able to resolve the question if there is a broad consensus on what to do. No social inconsistency arises if everyone has the same preferences. But notions about what constitutes a fair distribution of income are likely to breed sharp disagreements. So attempts to reach a political consensus on the distribution question are especially prone to Arrow's social inconsistency problem.

Representative Governments

Our discussion so far relates to direct democracies such as the local town meeting, in which people vote directly on government policies. In fact, all democratic nations have chosen representative forms of government over direct democracies for the simple reason that direct democracies become unwieldy with large numbers of people. Unfortunately, representative forms of government are as vulnerable to inefficiencies and to Arrow's inconsistency problem as direct democracies are. With respect to Arrow's inconsistency problem, the three individuals in our example could have been legislators representing three equal-sized constituencies, with the dollar amounts referring to the amount received by each member of the constituency. None of the results change, so long as the legislators vote in the best interests of their constituencies.

Elected representatives can also vote for inefficient policies and defeat efficient policies. These possibilities are enhanced by two features that come into play with representative governments, special-interest lobbying and logrolling.

SPECIAL-INTEREST LOBBYING AND LOGROLLING   Representative government encourages special-interest lobbying because it drastically reduces the number of people voting. Lobbyists can much more easily target their efforts to sway the vote than they can under direct democracy. Special-interest lobbying is made even easier if the legislators engage in logrolling, in which one legislator votes for another member's pet project providing the second member agrees to return the favor. Special-interest groups only have to persuade a handful of legislators to get what they want when a system of logrolling is in place.

Special-interest lobbying generates a political bias in favor of small, well-organized groups with much to gain or lose and against large, poorly organized groups, the members of which stand to gain or lose only a small amount. Since this bias exists regardless of the merits of the positions taken, it can do severe damage to the quest for efficiency. Under the representative form of government, the gainers from a policy do not even have to be in the majority.

A favorite example among economists of the harmful economic effects of lobbying is tariff policy, which we discuss in detail in Chapter 20. Briefly, a tariff is a tax levied on goods imported into the country. Tariffs protect the investors and the workers in import-competing industries, such as automobiles, that produce products similar to those being imported. By raising the price of imports, tariffs allow these industries to charge higher prices and employ more workers. At the same time, tariffs hurt all consumers by forcing them to pay higher prices for the protected goods.

Study after study reaches the same conclusion regarding tariffs (and other forms of trade restriction): The costs to consumers, in the aggregate, far exceed the benefits to the protected industries. Tariffs reduce the overall efficiency of the economy. Nonetheless, tariffs pass because the protected industries and their workers have much to gain and are easily organized. They have well-heeled special-interest groups in Washington who lobby intensely for the tariffs. In contrast, each consumer loses only a relatively small amount from a tariff, and the millions of individual consumers are much less well represented in Washington. The political cards are stacked against both the consumer and economic efficiency.

To be fair, special-interest lobbyists do perform a useful informational function in a representative system of government. Lobbying helps overcome a nasty political problem that arises in all large democratic societies: Self-interested citizens have little or no incentive to become actively involved in the political process, or even to vote. Learning about issues, conveying preferences to elected officials, and voting are all costly endeavors, in time and effort if nothing else. Unfortunately, the expected benefits of a citizen's time and effort are negligible because one voice or one vote just does not count for very much. Therefore, the standard economic marginal benefit–marginal cost calculation tells self-interested voters not to bother becoming involved with political issues or voting.

Special-interest groups offer citizens a means of conveying their desires to public officials that has some political clout, much as the labor union gives individual workers market power that they would otherwise not have. Whether this informational advantage more than offsets the harm that these groups can do is an open question.

Bureaucrats

The theory of public choice also questions the motives of the bureaucrats who control the various governmental agencies. Bureaucrats are supposed to operate their agencies in the public interest, promoting efficiency and equity. But public choice theorists argue that they might not do so because bureaucrats have plenty of leeway to pursue their own self-interests.

For starters, government agencies often have a virtual monopoly on the services they provide. Only government agencies provide for the nation's defense, or supply water to communities, or build the nation's roadways. The bureaucrats who run these agencies do not have to worry about competing in the marketplace. All they need do is convince the legislature to provide them with funding.

Moreover, the legislators may be easy prey for the bureaucrats because the bureaucrats usually have a decided informational advantage. The provision of public services suffers from the same general principal-agent problem that plagues the insurance industry. In this case the legislature is the principal, and the bureaucrat is the agent. The legislature (the principal) presumably tries to monitor the bureaucrats (the agents) to ensure that they are behaving in the public interest. But legislatures may not be able to monitor the bureaucrats very effectively because only the bureaucrats know for sure what it costs to provide the services of the bureau.

If bureaucrats have personal objectives other than serving the public interest, they may well be able to use their informational advantage for their own personal gain. For example, they may overstate the costs of providing the service. If the legislature gives them sufficient revenues to cover the inflated cost estimates, they and their subordinates can pocket the difference between the revenues and the true costs. Simply overstating the salaries required to retain the top managers would do the trick if legislators do not have much knowledge of the market for managers. The excessive revenues may be used for expensive perquisites such as meals in fancy restaurants, plush offices, vacation jaunts during supposed business trips, and the like.

To give one other example of possible bureaucratic inefficiency, bureau chiefs may obtain some satisfaction from the sheer size of the agencies they run. If so, they can satisfy their desire for a larger agency by overstating the amount of labor required to provide the services. Since the legislature is unlikely to know the actual labor requirements, it may well agree to finance excessive amounts of labor. These are just some of the ways that bureaucrats can waste scarce resources for their own personal gain if they are self-interested rather than public spirited.

The Political Process: A Concluding Assessment

How damaging is the political process to the conduct of economic policy? This is a difficult question to answer. The theory of public choice has uncovered a number of potential problems, and many of its predictions ring true. Democracies do have trouble resolving sharp differences of opinion. Special-interest lobbying is a major industry in Washington, logrolling is commonplace, and we do suffer foolish policies by catering to narrow interests. Stories of outrageous bureaucratic excesses surface from time to time. Yet the evidence is not entirely one-sided. Much political behavior runs counter to the theory of public choice, as the following examples illustrate.

U.S. distributional policy— We know that people disagree sharply about redistributional policy, yet their disagreements have not appeared to generate much social inconsistency about the appropriate policy stance. To the contrary, U.S. redistributional policy has been remarkably stable since the 1930s, when the federal government entered the picture for the first time. The Social Security Act of 1935 instituted social security, unemployment insurance, and the federal-state public assistance programs. The combined strategy of public insurance and public assistance remains the foundation of the government's income-support policy to this day.

Special-interest lobbying— Special interest groups do not always have their way with elected officials. The special interest bias in policy making was notably absent in the deregulation of the trucking industry during the late 1970s. Trucking deregulation occurred despite vehement lobbying by the trucking industry and the Teamsters union, and the fact that the benefits of the deregulation to each consumer were minimal. Also, the United States has generally been a champion of free trade despite intense lobbying pressure for trade restrictions.

Civic-minded behavior— There is much evidence of civic-minded behavior. Many citizens do take the trouble to study the issues and cast their votes. Top-level federal bureaucrats often agree to serve the president at great sacrifice to their personal incomes. In truth, many people do appear to change their stripes and become public spirited when they enter the political arena.

Bureaucratic inefficiency— The alleged inefficiencies of bureaucracies are difficult to pin down. If bureaucrats can hide inefficiencies from their legislative overseers, they can also hide them from economic researchers. In any event, the empirical evidence on bureaucratic inefficiency is mixed.

Overall, there can be little doubt that the U.S. economy is more efficient and more equitable because of government intervention. To cite some of the most obvious examples, the market system would hardly be able to provide an adequate level of national defense or the network of roadways that we enjoy. And government income-support programs protect millions of families from slipping into poverty.

At the same time, however, the theory of public choice has introduced a proper note of caution about expecting too much from government policy. Remember, too, that the political difficulties that we have discussed ignore the considerable resource costs of government policy. These costs take two forms, the direct costs of operating the various government programs and the indirect costs of raising tax revenues in the form of administrative costs, taxpayer compliance costs, and efficiency losses.

President Reagan's conservative administration succeeded in driving home to the American public the caution about expecting too much from the government. Reagan laid to rest the old liberal notion, born during Franklin Roosevelt's administration, that the government is a sure-fire panacea for the ills of the marketplace. This is all to the good. Yet Reagan's announced intention to "get the government off our backs" just as surely overstated the case. A market economy cannot operate efficiently and equitably without a large dose of government intervention. The Clinton administration seems determined to sell the public on the potential value of government intervention when appropriately applied.

SUMMARY

The first section of Chapter 24 offered an overview of the principal sources of revenue used by the federal, state, and local governments.

1. The federal government relies primarily on two revenue sources, taxes and debt financing. The personal income tax and the payroll tax earmarked for Social Security are the two most important federal taxes, and by far the largest revenue raisers in the entire U.S. fiscal system.

2. State governments raise revenue from a variety of taxes, with general sales taxes and personal income taxes the most important. Grants-in-aid from the federal government and direct user charges for public services are also important sources of state revenues.

3. Local governments rely on three main revenue sources: local property taxes, federal and state grants-in-aid, and direct user charges for public services.

4. Direct user charges are popular among state and local governments because they are consistent with the benefits received principle of paying for public services. Users pay for the services, and nonusers do not pay, exactly as in free market exchanges. Most people consider this the fairest method of paying for public goods and services.

5. Issuing debt to finance public capital expenditures is appropriate. Issuing debt to finance government operating expenditures is not. The federal government may issue debt to fight wars or overcome a recession.

Unfortunately, the benefits received principle cannot be applied to many important government expenditures—for example, defense, education, many roadways, and redistributional transfer programs. These goods and services must be paid for with general taxes, such as the personal income tax. The second section of the chapter discussed the economic principles relating to the design of general taxes, with emphasis on the personal income tax.

6. The five economic norms applied to general taxes are ease of administration, simplicity, flexibility, efficiency, and equity.

7. Equity in general taxation requires that taxes be levied in accordance with a taxpayer's ability to pay. The two guiding subprinciples within the ability-to-pay principle are (a) horizontal equity—equal treatment of equals; and (b) vertical equity—unequals may be treated unequally.

8. Most economists divide into two camps with respect to what best measures a person's ability to pay taxes, income or consumption. Whichever measure is chosen as the best measure of ability to pay is necessarily the ideal tax base under horizontal and vertical equity. In the deliberations preceding the Tax Reform Act of 1986, the federal government chose income over consumption as the best tax base.

9. Ideally, the income subject to tax should be broad-based and include (a) all income from supplying factors of production; (b) all transfers received, whether public or private; and (c) capital gains. The sum of these three sources of income is called the comprehensive tax base (CTB) and is considered to be the best measure of utility, or ability to pay, by proponents of the income tax.

10. No consensus exists on the question of vertical equity. All one can say is that the United States appears to prefer a mildly progressive tax system, meaning that average tax burdens rise slightly as incomes rise.

11. The U.S. tax system is roughly proportional throughout the entire range of incomes except at the lowest income levels, where it is mildly progressive. The consensus opinion among economists is that the federal and the state personal and corporation income taxes are progressive, the general

sales and excise taxes are proportional to mildly regressive, and the Social Security payroll tax is highly regressive. Economists are not sure whether to view the property tax as a benefits received tax or a general tax. If the latter, the emerging view is that it is a progressive tax borne by property owners.

The final section of Chapter 24 discussed the economic pitfalls of democratic political institutions.

12. The theory of public choice argues that people tend to pursue their own self-interests in their political affairs, just as they do in their economic affairs.

13. Majority voting rules are not necessarily consistent with economic efficiency. A majority vote can pass economic policies that reduce economic efficiency and defeat policies that would improve economic efficiency.

14. Majority voting rules are also susceptible to Arrow's Impossibility Theorem, which says that a consistent set of social preferences on policy issues may not emerge when citizens disagree on the issues. Redistributional policies are especially prone to social inconsistencies.

15. Representative government is as vulnerable to promoting economic inefficiency as direct democracy is. Special-interest lobbying of elected representatives enhances the possibility of accepting inefficient policies by giving undue political influence to a small minority of voters. At the same time, special-interest lobbying improves economic decision making by giving a collective voice to individual voters. If self-interested voters are forced to act independently, the standard marginal benefit–marginal cost calculation argues against voting at all.

16. The theory of public choice also cautions that any political system is vulnerable to the whims of bureaucrats who run the public agencies. They may care far more for their own personal objectives than for the public's interest in efficiency and equity, and they also have considerable leeway to pursue their own interests. Bureaucrats do not face the usual competitive market pressures that automatically direct private-sector managers toward the public interest. Moreover, they have a decided informational advantage over the legislators who are trying to monitor their behavior. Only the bureaucrats know the true costs of running their agencies.

17. Although the theory of public choice has raised some troubling points, not all the evidence supports the theory. Redistributional policy in the United States has been remarkably consistent since the 1930s. Special-interest lobbyists do not always get their way. Public officials often display public-spirited behavior that appears to run counter to their narrow economic self-interests. Research shows that public agencies are not always inefficient.

KEY TERMS

Arrow's Impossibility Theorem
benefits received principle of taxation
budget deficit
budget surplus
capital gain (annual)
comprehensive tax base

full faith and credit bond
government bond
graduated tax rates
horizontal equity (taxation)
marginal tax rate
progressive tax

proportional tax
regressive tax
revenue bond
theory of public choice
vertical equity (taxation)

QUESTIONS

1. A government had the following expenditures and revenues in 1993 (billions of dollars):

YEAR	EXPENDITURES	TAX RECEIPTS	GRANTS-IN-AID	USER CHARGES
1993	1224.4	886.0	103.2	200.8

a. Was the government's budget in surplus or deficit in 1993, and by how much?

b. Was the government adding to its outstanding debt in 1993?

c. Are these data more likely to apply to a national government or to a state government?

2. What are the five major taxes in the United States, and which governments use them to raise a significant percentage of their tax revenues?

3. a. What does it mean to say that a tax is progressive? Proportional? Regressive?

b. Of the five major taxes in the United States, select the tax that you think is the most progressive and the tax that you think is the most regressive, and explain your choices.

4. a. Under what conditions might it be appropriate for a government to run a deficit? Why?

b. Are the recent federal budget deficits justified by any of the conditions you mentioned in part a?

5. Some politicians are proposing that Congress exclude capital gains from taxation under the federal personal income tax.

a. Is this proposal consistent with the principle of horizontal equity under an income tax?

b. Would excluding capital gains make the federal income tax more or less progressive?

c. What arguments can be made for excluding capital gains from taxation?

6. In 1993, Congress raised the highest marginal tax rate under the federal personal income tax from 31 percent to 39.6 percent for taxable incomes above $250,000. What are the equity and efficiency implications of increasing the highest marginal tax rate?

7. a. What is the main assumption about people's behavior that underlies the theory of public choice?

b. Why does the theory of public choice suggest that the government might not realize its potential to correct market failures? Give a few examples by way of illustration.

8. a. What democratic voting rule is entirely consistent with the goal of economic efficiency? Why is this voting rule not often used?

b. Why might a simple majority voting rule lead to inefficient government policies?

c. Why does the Arrow's Impossibility Theorem cast doubt on the ability of democratic societies to answer the for whom or distribution question?

9. a. How might special-interest lobbying undermine the goal of economic efficiency? Give an example.

b. What useful role does special-interest lobbying play in a representative democracy? Give an example.

10. *Extra credit:* Suppose that Rhonda, Steven, and Theresa use a majority voting rule to decide how to divide $12. They must choose among the options listed below.

	R	S	T
Option 1:	5	4	3
Option 2:	3	5	4
Option 3:	4	3	5

For example, option 1 would give $5 to Rhonda, $4 to Steven, and $3 to Theresa. The voting rules are that two of the options are pitted against each other and then the winner goes up against the remaining option.

Suppose that Steven ends up with the most money. Which of the two options were pitted against each other first?

CASE

A Free Ride to Cross-border Shopping*

The Peace Bridge over the Niagara River connecting Fort Erie, Ontario, Canada with Buffalo, New York, is packed with so many returning Canadian shoppers on weekends that a two-hour wait to clear customs is not unusual. Similar congestion occurs at most of the major border crossings between Canada and the United States. In 1991 Canadians made over 50 million U.S. border crossings, an average of two per person, double the 1986 level.

The border crossings are motivated by Canadians seeking bargains in the United States. Canadian prices for most goods and services are much higher than are the prices for the same items in the United States, sometimes two to three times higher. Even Canadian-made goods are often cheaper in the U.S. stores.

There are many reasons why prices are higher in Canada. One of the more important is that wages are a bigger expense in Canada because the minimum wage is higher in Canada and labor unions are stronger there. The higher wages are a major reason why the cost of doing business in Canada is 20 percent to 30 percent higher than in the U.S., on average. Indeed, the wholesale cost in Canada exceeds the retail cost in the United States for many goods. In addition, a number of government policies serve to raise production costs or prices. Canadian retailers are forced by law to re-label U.S.-made goods in both French and English. Canada has higher import duties on consumer goods than the United States. The tariffs on shoes, for example, make the price of imported shoes twice as high in Canada. Stiff production quotas on dairy and poultry products raise their prices by 60 percent. Extremely high "sin taxes" on gasoline, alcohol, and cigarettes make them two to three times more expensive in Canada. Many Canadians cross the border just to fill up their gas tanks. The 7 percent federal goods and services tax (GST) that went in effect on January 1, 1991 further increased the Canadian-U.S. price differences.

The U.S. price advantage might be less enticing to Canadians if transportation costs to the United States were higher. But 90 percent of Canada's 26.6 million people live within a 90-minute drive of the 3,000–4,000 mile long border.

The price differences are considerably narrowed after Canadians pay taxes and duties on their purchases at Canadian customs. But this is true only if Canadians declare all their purchases at customs, and many items are easily smuggled across the border. The Canadian government has imposed penalties to increase the voluntary declaration of purchases. Customs officials confiscate smuggled cigarettes or alcohol and impose heavy fines on offenders. Fines are also imposed on other undeclared goods, if they are discovered. But Canadian customs agents are too overwhelmed by the volume of traffic at the major border crossings to undertake a careful search of every car crossing back into Canada.

Some price differences would remain even if all the taxes and duties were collected. The much lower distribution costs of stateside factory outlets, discount warehouses, and megastores, coupled with less restrictive U.S. government regulations and lower sales taxes, remain formidable competitive advantages for the U.S. retailers. Moreover, the inconvenience of not being able to shop on Sundays in Canada (it is illegal for stores to be open on Sundays in many communities) would still attract cross-border shoppers, as would the greater variety of goods available in the U.S. stores.

Total spending by cross-border Canadian shoppers reached an estimated $5 billion (U.S. $4.3 billion) in 1991, an average of $100 per trip. Many new stateside shopping facilities have been set up to cater to Canadian shoppers. Bonwit Teller, one of the anchor stores in Buffalo's Galleria Mall, attributed 45 percent of its 1991 sales to Canadian shoppers. Some Canadian merchants are quietly expanding their operations in the United States to serve Canadian shoppers while others are closing down their operations in Canada. Forty percent of the retail space in Windsor, Ontario, Detroit's neighboring city, was vacant by the summer of 1993. One study estimated that Ontario residents spent $2.2 billion in the United States in 1991 and cost the province 14,000 jobs. The businesses and jobs that are lost in Canada are gained on the U.S. side.

Other related businesses have also prospered in the United States, such as hotels and restaurants. Canadians receive a $100 duty-free exemption on U.S. goods brought back to Canada if they stay in the United States for at least 48 hours. U.S. hotels offer special discounts to Canadians to encourage them to stay and claim the exemption, and Canadians have responded to the discounts. The hotel occupancy rate in Buffalo was 18 percent higher than the U.S. national average in 1991, matching occupancy rates in the popular U.S. vacation cities.

Cutting Canada's taxes to stem the flow of cross-border shoppers would not be easy because Canada needs the tax revenues to fund its universal health care system and the

*Provided by K. K. Fung, Memphis State University.

(continued on next page)

A Free Ride to Cross-border Shopping (continued)

many other government services that Canadians enjoy. One of the reasons that the government is so concerned about cross-border shopping is that the shoppers are free riding on the government services by avoiding the federal and provincial sales taxes. Changing government regulations to reduce production costs or prices would arouse fierce opposition from vested interests. Removing the high tariffs, or the diary and poultry production quotas, or the French/English labeling requirement would all be very risky politically.

ECONOMIC ADVISOR'S REPORT

Suppose that the Canadian government hires you to advise them on cross-border shopping. The government officials ask your advice on the following policies that they are considering to reduce cross-border shopping:

a. Impose higher tariffs, or levy special sales taxes, on imported goods;
b. Reduce the number of customs agents at the major crossings to increase the wait time for returning shoppers;
c. Increase the penalties for undeclared goods;
d. Remove the federal GST and replace the lost tax revenues with higher federal personal income taxes.

1. Give your assessment of each policy. In particular, will the policy reduce cross-border shopping? Will it have any other desirable or undesirable effects? Which policy, if any, do you favor?
2. The government officials have noted that many states in the U.S. are relying less on their sales taxes and more on their personal income taxes to raise tax revenues. They ask you how this shift in states' tax revenues will affect cross-border shopping. How would you answer?
3. In general, the government officials wonder how much freedom the Canadian government has to set its own economic and social policies when shoppers can vote with their feet (or cars) and travel to a neighboring country with different policies to avoid paying taxes. What would you say to them? How can the Canadian government increase its freedom to pursue its own economic and social policies?

Sources: "Border Shopping Becomes a Habit," *The Globe and Mail,* Toronto, August 9, 1993, A1 and A4.
"Fear and Clothing in Canada. Surge in Cross-border Shopping Alarms Government," *Chicago Tribune,* May 27, 1991, 1.
"Invasion of the Booty Snatchers," *Business Week,* June 24, 1991, 66–69.
"No End in Sight for Canadians' U.S. Shopping Spree," *The Reuter Business Report,* January 27, 1992.
"Shopping Smugglers May Face Stiff Fines," *The Toronto Star,* June 8, 1991, A1.
"Smugglers Face Stiffer Penalties," *The Toronto Star,* June 11, 1991, A1.
"Think-Tank Blames Sin Taxes, Unions for Cross-border Sales," *The Vancouver Sun,* August 19, 1992, D2.

A

The Flow of Funds from Savers to Investors in the United States

The flow of funds from savers to investors through a nation's financial markets is very complex. Funds do not travel in a simple, direct line from households to businesses. Rather, the flow of funds involves all four sectors of the economy—household, business, government, and foreign—and individuals and institutions within each sector can be either suppliers or demanders of funds. Also, dollars of saving often pass through many layers of institutions called financial intermediaries along their journey to the investors. To understand how the financial markets work we have to understand what kinds of transactions take place in the financial markets and the special role of the financial intermediaries in channeling funds from savers to investors.

Internal Financing

The majority of the total saving in the economy is channeled directly to investment by the business firms themselves. For example, in 1992, firms in the United States raised $770.4 billion to finance current and future investment projects. Of this total, $735.9 billion (95.5 percent) consisted of their own funds generated by the production and sale of their products. Although internal funding of investment may not seem like saving by individuals, remember that all businesses are owned by individuals, the stockholders of the firm. If the managers had not used these internal funds for investment, they would have distributed the funds to the stockholders as dividends, a source of income. Therefore, when managers set aside funds for investment, the stockholders are essentially allowing the managers to save in their behalf a portion of the income earned from the business.

Internal funding of investment comes from two sources of saving by business, capital consumption allowances and retained earnings. *Capital consumption allowances* are funds that firms set aside to replace equipment and structures as they age and lose their productive capacity. Capital consumption allowances for each unit of capital are supposed to match the *depreciation* of the capital, defined as the decline in the capital's economic value during the course of a year. In practice, firms estimate the depreciation of their capital stock based on guidelines established by the U.S. Internal Revenue Service (IRS). In principle, capital consumption allowances enable the firm to maintain its existing stock of capital without having to resort to outside funding. The firm replaces each unit of capital using funds accumulated from the capital consumption allowances on that unit while it was part of the production process.

Retained earnings are part of the accounting profits of the firm, the difference between total revenues and total operating expenses. Accounting profits end up as one of three things: as taxes, as dividends, or as retained earnings. Corporations pay taxes on their profits under the federal and state corporate income taxes. Partnerships and proprietors pay taxes on their profits under the federal and state personal income taxes. The profits remaining after taxes are either distributed to the firm's stockholders as dividends or retained in the company as retained earnings. The retained earnings are earmarked for future investment projects. Since capital consumption allowances are designed to replace existing capital, the retained earnings finance additions to the firm's stock of capital. In other words, retained earnings are funds set aside to help finance the continued expansion of the firm.

Capital consumption allowances are by far the more important source of internal funding for the firm and the single most important source of funds for investment. In 1992, for example, capital consumption allowances in the United States were $653.4 billion and retained earnings only $82.5 billion. Thus, capital consumption allowances accounted for 88.8 percent of all internal funds and 84.8 percent of all funds raised to finance U.S. investment in 1992.[1]

External Financing and the Financial Markets

Not all the funds for investment come from the firms themselves. As the figures for 1992 illustrate, U.S. firms raised $34.5 billion of the financing for their investments from external sources of saving. This is where the nation's financial markets enter the picture. The role of the **financial markets** is to transfer money throughout the economy from surplus agents to deficit agents. The **surplus agents** are the savers, or lenders, the suppliers of funds in financial markets. Surplus agents have more income than they desire to spend in any

FINANCIAL MARKETS

Markets that play the role of transferring money from surplus agents to deficit agents throughout the economy.

SURPLUS AGENTS

Economic agents who are the savers, or lenders, or the suppliers of funds in financial markets because they have more income than they desire to spend in any one year.

---

[1]U.S. Department of Commerce, Economics and Statistics Administration, Bureau of Economic Analysis, *Survey of Current Business*, 73, No. 3 (March 1993): Table 5.1, p. 14.

one year. The **deficit agents** are the borrowers, the users of funds in financial markets. Deficit agents have less income than they desire to spend in any one year. Investment is one of the uses of funds, but not the only one.

EQUITY AND DEBT   The transfer of money from surplus agents to deficit agents occurs in one of two ways: either through the creation of equity or debt, or through trades of money for existing equity or debt.

In an equity-creating transaction, a surplus agent transfers funds to a business firm in exchange for new shares of common stock. The agent becomes one of the owners of the firm, and the stock, or *equity*, entitles the agent to share in the profits of the firm. Transferring funds through equity is a gamble for surplus agents. They earn a return on their saving only if the firm is successful.

Transferring funds through debt is somewhat less of a gamble. In a debt-creating transaction, a deficit agent and a surplus agent form a borrower-lender relationship. The debt instrument can take one of two forms, a promise to repay or an order to repay. A *promise to repay* may take many different forms, but it always stipulates that the borrower will repay the lender certain amounts of money at specific dates in the future. One example is a corporate bond, which firms can use instead of issuing stock to raise funds for investment. The saver (lender) transfers funds to the corporation (borrower) in return for the corporate bond. The typical corporate bond includes a face value, an interest payment, and a date of maturity. The face value, often $1,000 or multiples of $1,000, is the principal on the bond, the amount the firm repays at the date of maturity. If the date of maturity is 10 years in the future, the bond is said to be a 10-year bond. The interest payment is an amount the firm pays the holder of the bond each year until the bond matures, for example, $80 per year for 10 years. The annual interest payments are in addition to the repayment of the principal when the bond matures. Holders of corporate bonds are not owners of the firm. They have no claim on the profits of the firm other than the principal and interest stipulated on the bond.

A variation of the standard bond is the *Treasury bill*, which the U.S. government uses to borrow money for less than a year's time. Treasury bills specify only a face value and a date of maturity. They do not pay interest. For example, you might lend the government $950 today in return for a Treasury bill that pays you $1,000 (the face value) in 180 days (the date of maturity). Still another variation of a promise to repay that consumers are familiar with is *installment debt*, the form used for automobile loans and home mortgages. In an installment contract the borrower repays the lender both principal and interest in equal monthly installments until the principal is entirely repaid. The monthly installments are computed by a complicated formula that takes into account the interest owed on the principal remaining after each installment.

An example of an *order to repay* is a checking account at a bank. You might not think of a checking account as a loan, but it is. When you place money in a checking account, you are lending the bank your money in return for an order to repay. When you write a check on your account, the bank must transfer the funds to whomever you have made the check payable. Checking accounts may or may not pay interest. Even if they do not, the account yields a return in the form of a service, the convenience of being able to pay for goods and services by check. Also, checking accounts have no specific date of maturity.

DEFICIT AGENTS

Economic agents who are the borrowers or the users of funds in financial markets because they have less income than they desire to spend in any one year.

You may close your account at any time, thereby terminating your loan to the bank.

Financial markets give rise to another type of transaction in which two agents trade existing equity and debt. Once common stock, corporate bonds, Treasury bills, and mortgages have been created, or issued, they can be traded. For example, you might have some money that you want to exchange for shares of common stock in IBM. Someone else, unknown to you, owns shares of IBM common stock and wants to exchange the stock for money. So the two of you exchange money for the IBM stock through a broker who has a license to trade stock on the New York Stock Exchange. In fact, most exchanges of stock are trades of existing stock, not issues of new stock that transfer funds directly from savers to firms. Stocks are not unique in this respect. There are also active markets for trading most existing debt instruments, such as the corporate and the government bond markets. Exchanges of existing equity and debt affect the rates of return available to savers on these financial instruments, but they do not transfer funds from savers to investors.

Equity and debt instruments are assets from a surplus agent's (lender's) point of view. An *asset* (credit) is something an agent owns or a claim the agent has against someone. Equity and debt instruments are debits or liabilities from a deficit agent's (borrower's) point of view. A *liability* is a something an agent owes, a financial claim against the agent due someone else. The difference between an agent's assets and its liabilities is its *net worth*, also referred to as *wealth*. An agent's wealth at any one time is the result of all its past lending and borrowing decisions up to that point. Notice that net worth or wealth need not be positive. An agent has negative net worth if its liabilities exceed its assets.

FINANCIAL INTERMEDIARY

Any institution involved in the process of transferring funds from suppliers to users that positions itself between the ultimate suppliers and the ultimate users of funds in financial markets, such as a commercial bank.

FINANCIAL INTERMEDIARIES   Financial markets give rise to many different kinds of financial intermediaries. A **financial intermediary** is any institution involved in the process of transferring funds from suppliers to users that positions itself between the ultimate suppliers and the ultimate users of funds. An example is a commercial bank, which borrows funds from households in exchange for checking or savings deposits and then lends the funds to businesses to help them finance their investment projects. In this set of transactions the holders of the checking and savings deposits are the ultimate suppliers of funds (lenders), the businesses are the ultimate users of funds (borrowers), and the commercial bank is the financial intermediary, serving to channel the funds from households to businesses.

Besides commercial banks, the most important financial intermediaries in the U.S. economy are savings banks, insurance companies, pension funds, and automobile finance companies. In the broadest sense these other financial intermediaries all operate in the same way as commercial banks when they transact with ultimate suppliers and ultimate users of funds. They accept funds from ultimate suppliers in exchange for which they offer a range of financial services that may or may not include a rate of return for the use of the funds. They then lend the funds to ultimate users. The rate of return they receive on their loans allows them to cover the costs of providing the financial services that they specialize in and to earn an acceptable return on their capital. (Financial intermediaries also transact with other financial intermediaries, but we will ignore that possibility for now as an unnecessary complication. Suffice it to note that many layers of financial intermediation can separate the ultimate suppliers and ultimate users of funds.)

Financial intermediaries provide three important services to savers and investors. They increase the options available to savers, they serve as brokers between savers and investors, and they sharply reduce the cost of transferring funds. These services increase the total amount of saving and investment by facilitating the transfer of funds from savers to investors. Let's look briefly at each of them.

INCREASING THE OPTIONS FOR SAVERS Most households do not offer all their saving directly to business firms by purchasing corporate bonds or stocks. Instead, they seek a variety of financial services from their saving. Households want checking accounts that offer the convenience of paying by check, pension plans that will provide a steady income throughout the retirement years, and life insurance policies that offer the combination of a savings account and a large payment to loved ones in the event of death. Commercial and savings banks, pension funds, and insurance companies come into being because they can profitably offer these kinds of services. Not surprisingly, the profit motive works just as well in financial markets as it does in nonfinancial markets to encourage the supply of financial services that households want to buy.

Table A.1 illustrates the importance of the various services offered by financial intermediaries. The table shows the distribution of financial assets held by U.S. households at the end of 1992. Notice that corporate and noncorporate equities and bonds amounted to only 33 percent of the total financial assets, excluding government securities. Households have chosen to place the majority of their saving over time with the financial intermediaries, particularly in

TABLE A.1   Financial Assets Held by Households, End of Year 1992

ASSET	VALUE (BILLIONS)
DEPOSITS	$ 3,351
PENSION FUND RESERVES	4,586
EQUITY IN NONCORPORATE BUSINESS	2,264
EQUITY IN CORPORATIONS	2,535
LIFE INSURANCE RESERVES	434
CORPORATE AND FOREIGN BONDS	131
OTHER NONGOVERNMENT SECURITIES	1,630
SUBTOTAL: FINANCIAL ASSETS OTHER THAN GOVERNMENT SECURITIES	$14,931
GOVERNMENT SECURITIES	1,250
TOTAL FINANCIAL ASSETS	$16,181

SOURCE: Board of Governors of the Federal Reserve System, *Balance Sheets for the U.S. Economy, 1945–92* (Washington, D.C.: U.S. Government Printing Office, 1993), Report C.9, Table B.100.

deposits at commercial and savings banks and in pension funds. Households presumably would save a lot less each year if their only savings options were to purchase corporate and noncorporate stocks and bonds.

SERVING AS BROKERS Financial intermediaries also promote saving and investment by serving as brokers between savers and investors. As we saw in Chapter 4, a broker is an agent who brings buyers and sellers together in a market. Stock brokers bring buyers and sellers of stock together in well-organized stock exchanges such as the New York Stock Exchange. Investment banks serve the same function in the market for corporate bonds. When a corporation issues bonds to raise money for investment, it does not bother to seek out people and institutions who are willing to hold the bonds. Instead, it relies on an investment bank to act as the broker. Investment banks bid for the bond issue, and the firm sells the bonds to the highest bidder. The investment bank that purchases the bonds then resells them to the economic agents who ultimately want to hold the bonds as part of their assets. The bank earns its profit by selling the bonds at a higher price than it paid for them. Stock exchanges and investment banking are just two examples of the many brokerage services provided by financial intermediaries.

REDUCING THE COST OF TRANSFERRING FUNDS Financial intermediaries promote saving and investment in yet a third way, by greatly reducing the costs of transferring funds from savers to investors. Suppose that a firm wants to borrow $10 million to finance an investment project and that each of 10,000 households wants to save $1,000, for a total saving of $10 million. Without the existence of financial intermediaries, the firm would have to seek out each household and write 10,000 separate loan contracts of $1,000 each in order to raise the $10 million. Financial intermediaries such as commercial banks can effect the transfer of funds from the households to the firms at a much lower cost. For example, each of the households might choose to open a $1,000 checking account at a commercial bank, so that the bank receives the $10 million in saving. Then the firm and the loan officers of the bank can negotiate a single $10 million loan contract to finance the investment. True, opening 10,000 checking accounts and negotiating the bank loan entail some costs. But transferring the $10 million from the households to the firm through the commercial bank is obviously much less costly and time-consuming than directly negotiating 10,000 loan contracts between the firm and the households.

A final point to note about financial intermediaries relates to the way in which individuals earn income from capital. A large portion of their capital income derives from the assets they hold with the financial intermediaries, such as interest earned on checking and savings accounts and pension annuities received during the retirement years. The income does not all come directly from the business firms whose capital is the ultimate source of the income. Financial intermediaries channel some of the income from capital from businesses to individuals in the process of channeling some of the saving of individuals to businesses for investment.

THE SUPPLIERS AND DEMANDERS OF FUNDS We are now in a position to trace the flow of funds from savers to investors through the financial markets. As we do, we will see that a substantial amount of the funds potentially available to finance investment is diverted to other uses and never reaches the business firms. The diversion of funds begins in the household sector.

HOUSEHOLD SECTOR   When consumers save, they do not just buy financial assets. They also buy real assets in the form of houses or consumer durables, such as automobiles and major appliances. Houses and consumer durables are considered real assets because they are similar to plant and equipment, the real assets of business firms. The house or automobile or stove purchased today generates a stream of housing or automotive or cooking services well into the future, just as plant and equipment purchased today generates a stream of goods or services for many years to come. Therefore, purchases of houses and consumer durables are more like a simultaneous act of saving and investment than an act of consumption, analogous to the financing of investment by business firms out of retained earnings. In fact, the purchase of a new home is so similar to the purchase of business capital that residential structures are included as part of the nation's stock of physical capital. All other real assets purchased by the household sector are considered to be consumer goods in the form of consumer durables, and not part of the capital stock.

Purchases of real assets are an important component of household saving. In 1992, for example, households increased their holdings of financial assets by $471.3 billion. In that same year households increased their holdings of real assets by $258 billion, consisting of a $189 billion increase in owner-occupied homes and a $69 billion increase in the stock of consumer durables (these figures are net of depreciation on these assets).[2] Furthermore, the purchase of real assets feeds back directly into the nation's financial markets because households often borrow to finance these purchases. They take out mortgages on new homes, borrow from banks or finance companies to purchase automobiles, and borrow on their credit cards to finance purchases of major appliances. In other words, the household sector is not only a supplier of funds to a nation's financial markets; it is also an important demander of funds.

For example, in the latter half of the 1980s households took advantage of newly created home equity loans, which allow them to borrow against the equity they have built up in existing homes. They have used the home equity loans to finance such things as home improvements, major appliances, cars, and their children's college educations. As a result, the increase in their mortage debt in recent years has far exceeded the increase in the stock of housing.

GOVERNMENT SECTOR   The federal, state, and local governments are also important players in the financial markets, and they can be either net demanders or net suppliers of funds. Governments levy taxes and fees to pay for their expenditures. If these revenues are used to purchase public investment goods, such as schools, highways, and office buildings, then they are in effect forced saving that increases the nation's stock of capital. Otherwise, government expenditures are either acts of public consumption or transfer payments that simply return the tax dollars to the private sector.

---

[2] Board of Governors of the Federal Reserve System, *Balance Sheets for the U.S. Economy, 1945–92* (Washington, D.C.: U.S. Government Printing Office, 1993), Report C.9, Table B.100.

If the taxes and fees of a government exceed its expenditures during the year, the government budget is in surplus, and the government becomes a supplier of funds to the financial markets. Government officials want to earn a rate of return on the excess revenues, so they place their funds in bank deposits and buy other interest-bearing financial assets, just as households do when they save. If expenditures exceed taxes and fees during the year, the government budget is in deficit, and the government has to borrow to cover the revenue shortfall. It becomes a net demander of funds in the financial markets. Each year since 1981 the federal government has run substantial deficits 'and has been a large net demander of funds. By contrast, the state and the local governments ran surpluses and were net suppliers of funds until the end of the decade, when obligations to their retirement accounts drained the operating surpluses and made them slight net demanders of funds. The federal government's annual deficits were always far greater than were the state and the local governments' annual surpluses, so that the government sector has been a large net demander of funds since 1981. In 1992, for example, the overall government sector was a net demander of funds in the amount of $407.7 billion.

REST-OF-WORLD (FOREIGN) SECTOR   U.S. households, businesses, and governments place some of their funds in foreign businesses and financial intermediaries. Similarly, foreign households, businesses, and governments place some of their funds in U.S. businesses and financial intermediaries. If the flow of funds out of the United States exceeds the flow of funds into the United States, the foreign sector is a net demander of funds in the U.S. financial markets. Conversely, if the flow of funds into the United States exceeds the flow of funds out of the United States, the foreign sector is a net supplier of funds to the U.S. financial markets. The latter has been the case throughout the 1980s and into the 1990s. The foreign sector was a very important supplier of funds and played a major role in financing the nation's investment. In 1992, for example, the net supply of funds into the United States totaled $68.9 billion.

ALL SECTORS COMBINED   Table A.2 summarizes the net flow of funds into the U.S. financial markets from the four nonfinancial sectors of the economy in 1992. The net flow of funds to financial markets (column 4) is the difference

TABLE A.2   Net Flow of Funds by Sector of the Economy 1992

SECTOR	NET ACQUISITION OF FINANCIAL ASSETS (BILLIONS)	NET ACQUISITION OF FINANCIAL LIABILITIES (BILLIONS)	NET INCREASE IN FINANCIAL WEALTH (BILLIONS)
HOUSEHOLD[a]	$471.3	$221.6	$249.7
NONFINANCIAL BUSINESS	165.5	88.5	77.0
STATE AND LOCAL GOVERNMENT	1.9	48.4	−46.5
U.S. GOVERNMENT	−31.0	330.2	−361.2
FOREIGN (REST-OF-WORLD)	179.1	110.2	68.9

[a]The household sector includes personal trusts and nonprofit institutions.

SOURCE: Board of Governors of the Federal Reserve System, *Flow of Funds Accounts: Flows and Outstandings, Fourth Quarter 1992* (Washington, D.C.: U.S. Government Printing Office, 1993), Report Z.1, Tables F.100, F.101, F.105, F.106, F.109.

between the net acquisition of financial assets, or lending (column 2), and the net increase in financial liabilities, or borrowing (column 3). The aggregate net flow of funds is the total amount of saving that is available to finance investment by business firms. The table shows that the household, business, and foreign sectors were net suppliers of funds and that the government sector was a net demander of funds. It also shows very clearly the important role of households as both suppliers and demanders of funds in the U.S. financial markets. Households were both the largest lenders *and* the second-largest borrowers of funds among all the sectors. Finally, the table indicates that the federal government's inability to balance its budget is a serious potential drain on investment. Funds borrowed to finance government deficits are not available to business firms for investment in plant and equipment. Fortunately, the foreign sector replaced some of the funds drained off by the government sector in 1992. This same pattern held true throughout most of the 1980s as well. Investment in the United States might well have been much lower over the previous decade had foreigners not placed large amounts of their saving in U.S. financial markets.

REFLECTION: Is internal financing of investments necessarily cheaper for firms than external financing is?

National Net Worth and the Income from Capital

Our overview of the flow of funds concludes with a look at the net worth of the United States. **National net worth,** the net worth of an entire nation, is the market value of the nation's real, or tangible, assets plus the market value of its land, less any claims against these assets held by foreigners. The real assets include all consumer durables and all capital goods owned by the household, business, and government sectors. The capital goods consist of residential structures (homes), nonresidential plant (factories, office buildings) and equipment (computers, desks), and inventories (goods that have been produced, but not yet sold). The real assets and the land are net worth for the nation as a whole because they are the nonlabor resources that produce goods and services for the benefit of the nation's citizens.

NATIONAL NET WORTH

The net worth or wealth of an entire nation, equal to the market value of the nation's real, or tangible, assets plus the market value of its land, less any claims against these assets held by foreigners.

In contrast, the financial assets owned by individuals and institutions do not produce anything. They are merely claims against the income generated by the real assets. Equity in the form of corporate stock is net worth to the individuals who hold the stock, but the market value of financial equity matches the market value of the capital that the equity has purchased. Therefore, to include financial equity as well as capital in national net worth would represent double counting. Financial debt instruments do not give rise to net worth at all because one lender's credit or asset is another borrower's debit or liability. For instance, when a firm issues corporate bonds to finance purchases of capital, the bonds are simultaneously an asset to the bondholders and a liability to the firm. This point is worth remembering when you read alarmist statements that U.S. consumers and businesses are awash in a sea of debt. A sea of debt is also a sea of credit. Being awash in a sea of credit does not sound quite so threatening.

Table A.3 shows the national net worth of the United States at the end of 1992. Saving in the U.S. economy over time has resulted in the accumulation of over $18 trillion of productive real assets, nearly $72,000 per person. Moreover, most of the saving has come from U.S. citizens. Foreign citizens held

TABLE A.3   Net Worth of the United States, End of Year 1992

TANGIBLE ASSETS	VALUE (BILLIONS)
RESIDENTIAL STRUCTURES	$ 5,188
NONRESIDENTIAL PLANT AND EQUIPMENT	5,538
INVENTORIES	1,101
CONSUMER DURABLES	2,191
SUBTOTAL OF REPRODUCIBLE ASSETS	$14,018
LAND AT MARKET VALUES	4,289
TOTAL TANGIBLE ASSETS	$18,307
U.S. GOLD AND SDRs[a]	20
NET CLAIMS ON FOREIGN ASSETS	−618
TOTAL CONSOLIDATED DOMESTIC NET ASSETS	$17,709

[a]SDRs refer to Special Drawing Rights that are used in international transactions. Gold and SDRs are considered assets because they can be used in international trade to purchase real goods and services from foreign countries.

SOURCE: Board of Governors of the Federal Reserve System, *Balance Sheets for the U.S. Economy, 1945–92* (Washington, D.C.: U.S. Government Printing Office, 1993), Report C.9, Table B.11.

claims to less than 4 percent of the real assets in 1992. A succinct statement of the productive activity in the U.S. economy in 1992 would read as follows: Producers in the United States combined $14 trillion of capital, $4.3 trillion of land, and a labor force of 127 million workers to produce $6 trillion worth of final goods and services.

SUMMARY

1. The majority of funds for investment are provided by the businesses themselves in the form of capital consumption allowances and retained earnings. Capital consumption allowances are funds set aside to replace existing capital as it depreciates in value. Retained earnings are the profits left over after the payment of taxes and dividends. These forms of internal busines saving are done by the firm's managers with the permission of the stockholders.

2. Businesses' need to finance some investment from external funds causes them to use the nation's financial markets. Funds are transferred from lenders to borrowers through equity or debt instruments. An equity instrument, such as a share of corporate stock, gives the lender a share of the profits of the business. A debt instrument, such as a corportae bond or a bank account, is a promise or an order that the borrower will repay the lender certain amounts of money at some future date(s).

3. Financial intermediaries are institutions such as banks, insurance companies, and pension funds, that position themselves between the ultimate savers and investors. Financial intermediaries promote saving and investment in three ways: by offering savers a wide variety of choices for their saving; by acting as brokers between lenders and borrowers; and by greatly reducing the costs of transferring funds from savers to investors.

4. All four sectors of the economy transact in the nation's financial markets. The houshold sector is the largest lender and the second largest borrower of funds. Households borrow primarily to finance their purchases of homes and consumer durables. Governments are net borrowers of funds if they run budget deficits (revenues less than expenditures) and net lenders of funds if they run budget surpluses (revenues exceed expenditures). The foreign sector is a net lender of funds if foreign citizens place more savings in the U.S. than U.S. citizens place abroad, and a net borrower of funds if the reverse is true. The household sector is a net lender of funds and the business sector is usually a net borrower of funds. The foreign sector has been a net lender of funds and the government sector has been a net borrower of funds since 1981. Total investment equals the aggregate net flow of funds to financial markets (aggregate net lending) plus the internal financing provided by business firms.

Ability to Trade The rate at which consumers can trade one good for another in their budgets, equal to the price ratio of the two goods.

Actual Budget Deficit The difference between government expenditures and government revenues.

Administrative Lag (Fiscal Policy) The time required to enact legislation to change government purchases, transfer payments, or taxes.

Administrative Lag (Monetary Policy) The time required to change the course of monetary policy once the Board of Governors decides to do so.

Adverse Selection In the context of insurance, arises when the insurance company is forced to set one premium because it cannot distinguish between high-risk and low-risk individuals, with the result that low-risk individuals cancel their policies.

Age-Earnings Profile The average earnings per person at each age within the population.

Aggregate Demand Curve A graph of the aggregate demand schedule that shows the quantity of national output demanded by the four sectors of the economy at each overall level of prices.

Aggregate Demand The total quantity of final goods and services demanded at each overall price level by all the final demanders in the economy; the aggregate demand curve, labeled *AD*, is a graph of aggregate demand.

Aggregate Demand Schedule A schedule that indicates the quantity of national output demanded by the four sectors of the economy at each overall level of prices.

Aggregate Demand Shock Any event that directly affects the total demand for goods and services at each overall price level.

Aggregate Desired Expenditures (Aggregate Demand for Expenditures) The relationship between the aggregate demand for final goods and services and national income, other things equal.

Aggregate Supply Curve A graph of the aggregate supply schedule that shows the quantity of national output supplied by all producers at each overall level of prices.

Aggregate Supply The total quantity of final goods and services supplied at each overall price level by all the producers in the economy; the aggregate supply curve, labeled *AS*, is a graph of aggregate supply.

Aggregate Supply Schedule A schedule that indicates the quantity of national output supplied by all producers at each overall level of prices.

Aggregate Supply Shock Any event that directly affects producers' costs of production or the quantity that they can supply to the market.

Allocational Efficiency Achieved in a product market when the quantity exchanged in the market maximizes the net value of producing and consuming a good; the market test is price equal to short-run marginal cost.

Allocational Policies Government economic policies that respond to market failures relating to the goal of achieving an efficient use of society's scarce resources.

Alternatives The part of the economic problem that refers to the necessity of making choices.

Appreciation (Currency) The value of a nation's currency rises relative to the value of other currencies.

Arbitrage The buying and selling of commodities whose prices are out of line in such a way as to guarantee a profit.

Arrow's Impossibility Theorem The proposition that individuals' preferences for particular government policies might not aggregate into a consistent set of social preferences for those policies under democratic voting rules.

Asset Something that is owned, real or financial; a claim against someone or some institution.

Automatic Stabilizer Any component of the economy that is related to the level of national income and lowers the value of the spending multiplier; automatic stabilizers make the economy less responsive to aggregate demand shocks.

Autonomous Capital Inflow (or Outflow) A capital inflow (or outflow) undertaken for its own sake and not as an offset to some other transaction in the balance of payments.

Average Fixed Cost At every output, the firm's fixed cost divided by its output.

Average Propensity to Consume The ratio of consumption demand to disposable income.

Average Propensity to Save The ratio of saving demand to disposable income.

Average Revenue Curve An individual firm's demand curve.

Average (Total) Cost At every output, the firm's total cost divided by its output.

Average Variable Cost At every output, the firm's variable cost divided by its output.

Balanced Budget Change An equal change in government expenditures and revenues.

Balanced Budget Multiplier The ratio that relates the change in the equilibrium level of national income to a balanced budget change in government purchases and taxes.

Balanced Inflation An inflation in which the prices of all goods and services, including all factors of production, are rising at exactly the same rate.

Balance of Goods and Services The sum of the balance of trade plus net exports of services plus net receipts of factor incomes.

Balance of Payments The double-entry accounting system that nations use to record their international transactions during the course of a year.

Balance of Trade The difference between the value of a nation's exports and the value of its imports (merchandise exports and imports only; excludes trade in services).

Balance-of-Trade Deficit The value of a nation's imports exceeds the value of its exports.

Balance-of-Trade Surplus The value of a nation's exports exceeds the value of its imports.

Balance Sheet A listing of a person's or an institution's assets, liabilities, and net worth.

Bank Run An attempt by large numbers of depositors to close their checking (and savings) accounts in exchange for currency.

Barrier to Entry or Exit Anything that restricts or prevents the free flow of resources into or out of an industry.

Barter An exchange of goods directly for other goods.

Beggar-Thy-Neighbor Policy A government policy that attempts to export domestic unemployment abroad by means of tariffs and other restrictions on imports.

Behavioral Barrier to Entry A strategic decision on the part of a firm that is specifically designed either to deter entry entirely or to accommodate entry by forcing new firms to enter on a smaller scale

Benefits-Received Principle A pricing principle for public services, which says that citizens should pay for public services in accordance with the benefits they receive from them.

Benefits Received Principle of Taxation The principle that the taxes and other means of payment for public services are fair if they bear a direct relationship to the benefits people receive from the public services.

Bilateral Monopoly A market situation consisting of one buyer confronting one seller.

Board of Governors (Federal Reserve) The seven-member governing body that oversees and controls the Federal Reserve Banking System.

Break-Even Level of Disposable Income The level of disposable income at which households' consumption demand equals their disposable income.

Break-Even Point A market situation in which a firm's total revenue equals its long-run total cost (price equals long-run average cost), so that economic profit is zero.

Budget Constraint The maximum combination of goods and services that a consumer is able to purchase, given the consumer's income and the prices of the goods and services.

Budget Deficit Exists when a government's expenditures exceed its revenues from taxes, direct user charges, and grants-in-aid.

Budget Line A graphical representation of the consumer's budget constraint.

Budget Surplus Exists when a government's revenues from taxes, direct user charges, and grants-in-aid exceed its expenditures.

Business Cycle The continuing pattern over time of expansions and contractions, booms and busts, in the circular flow of economic activity in capitalist economies.

Business Saving The portion of the profits that managers set aside to finance future investment projects; also called *retained earnings.*

Business Sector The sector of an economy that consists of all the private business firms and is the major producer of final goods and services.

Capital The plant and equipment required to produce goods and services; one of the primary factors of production.

Capital Account (Balance of Payments) The subaccount in the balance of payments that records capital inflows and outflows.

Capital Account Balance The difference between a nation's capital inflows and capital outflows.

Capital Consumption Allowance Funds that firms set aside to replace equipment and structures as they age and lose their productive capacity, equal in principle to the economic depreciation of capital.

Capital Flight The purchase of foreign currencies or securities by domestic residents as a hedge against rapid domestic inflation.

Capital Gain (Annual) The difference between the value of an asset at the end of the year and its value at the beginning of the year.

Capital Inflows Purchases of domestic financial securities or loans to domestic residents by foreign residents.

Capital Outflows Purchases of foreign financial securities or loans to foreign residents by domestic residents.

Capital/Output Ratio The amount of capital required to produce each unit of output.

Cartel An organization of some or all of the firms in an industry established for the purpose of maximizing the total profits of the cooperating firms.

Categorical Assistance Public assistance that is based on some personal characteristic of a family or unrelated individual in addition to low income, such as whether the person is living in a family headed by a single parent.

Centralized Economy An economic system in which an agency of the national government has authority over all economic decisions and full access to all relevant economic information.

Centrally Planned Socialism An economic system characterized by centralized decision making, the use of a national economic plan to process information and coordinate exchange, public ownership of capital and land, and the use of both moral and material incentives.

Change in Demand A shift in the entire demand curve.

Change in Quantity Demanded A movement along the demand curve as price changes, other things equal.

Change in Quantity Supplied A movement along the supply curve as price changes, other things equal.

Change in Supply A shift in the entire supply curve.

Circular Flow Diagram A graphical representation of the circular flow of economic activity through the nation's product and factor markets.

Circular Flow of Economic Activity The flow of goods and services and factors of production through the product and the factor markets of the economy that results from the interactions of individuals and business firms; the flow is circular because firms sell products to individuals in the product markets and individuals sell factors of production to firms in the factor markets.

Closed Shop A labor union rule that requires a worker to join an established union upon being hired.

Collective Bargaining A process in which elected union representatives bargain with management on behalf of the members of the union over pay and other terms of employment.

Common-Use Resource A resource such as water or air that no one owns.

Comparative Advantage The principle that a country should specialize its production in those goods that it can produce with lower opportunity costs than other countries and trade for those goods that other countries can produce with lower opportunity costs.

Compensation of Employees The payment to, and the income received by, labor, including wages, salaries, and in-kind fringe benefits.

Competitive Market A market in which a large number of firms sell very similar or identical products, consumers are well informed about the price that each firm charges for its product, and resources move easily into and out of the market in response to profits and losses.

Complements Products that are used together to provide a service; specifically, two goods whose relationship is such that a decrease in the price of one good increases the demand for the other.

Complete Ordering of Preferences The ability to provide an ordering of all alternative combinations of goods and services potentially available to the consumer.

Compounding The process of computing the equivalent future value of current dollars.

Comprehensive Tax Base A broad-based measure of the personal income subject to tax under a personal income tax that includes all income received from factors of production, all transfer payments received, and net capital gains on assets received during the year.

Conglomerate Merger A merger between firms operating in different product markets.

Constant Cost Industry An industry in which the minimum long-run average cost of the firms remains constant no matter how much output is supplied to the market, so that the long-run market supply curve is horizontal.

Constant Dollar (Real) Gross Domestic Product The value of the gross domestic product generated each year, evaluated at the prices that existed in a given base year.

Constant Returns to Scale

- *In terms of long-run total cost:* the region of the long-run total cost curve along which the percentage change in total cost is equal to the percentage change in output.
- *In terms of the production function:* an equal proportionate increase in all the firm's inputs by an amount k leads to a proportionate increase in the firm's output equal to k (for example, a doubling of all the firm's inputs leads to a doubling of the firm's output).

Constraints The part of the economic problem that refers to the limitations that prevent economic agents from achieving their objectives.

Consumer Durables Manufactured goods that typically last more than one year.

Consumer Equilibrium A situation in which the marginal rate of substitution between any two goods equals the ratio of their prices; the consumer is maximizing utility.

Consumer Nondurables Manufactured goods that typically last less than one year.

Consumer Price Index A price index based on a market basket of consumer goods and services purchased by the typical household.

Consumer Sovereignty The principle that individuals are best able to judge their own self-interests.

Consumer Surplus At any quantity exchanged in the market, the difference between the total value to consumers and the total market value.

Consumers Economic agents who consume goods and services and who supply the primary factors of production—labor,
capital, and land—to producers.

Consumption Aggregate purchases of final goods and services by households.

Consumption Function The relationship that indicates how much households in the aggregate are willing and able to consume during the year at every level of total disposable income, other things equal; also called *consumption demand.*

Contestable Market A market structure in which the existing firm or firms have market power and are subject to the possibility of hit-and-run entry by new firms.

Contraction Phase (Business Cycle) The period of time during which economic activity is declining; commonly referred to as a *recession.*

Contractionary Fiscal Policy Decreases in government purchases or transfer payments, or increases in taxes, for the purpose of decreasing aggregate demand.

Contractionary Monetary Policy A decrease in the money supply undertaken by the Fed for the purpose of decreasing aggregate demand; the Fed sells Treasury securities on the Open Market.

Contractionary Policy A fiscal or monetary policy that decreases the level of aggregate demand.

Contrived Scarcity The market situation generated by a pure monopolist (or any firm with market power), in which the monopolist (firm) consciously reduces its output below the efficient level of output to maximize its profit.

Controlled Experiment The scientific method of analysis for determining cause-and-effect relationships that studies the effects of changing one element in an environment at a time while holding constant all the other elements in the environment.

Cooperative Behavior Collusion by two or more firms in which they explicitly agree not to compete with one another.

Core Rate of Inflation The rate of inflation that is based on a restricted market basket of goods and services, which excludes items that have highly volatile prices and that have significant weight in computing the overall rate of inflation.

Corporate Profit The difference between the value of sales and the cost of goods sold; the income received by the stockholders who own the firm.

Corporation A form of business that is a recognized legal entity distinct from the owners of the firm, allows owners to transfer their shares of stock, allows owners to delegate authority and responsibility to a group of managers, has a potentially
unlimited life, and has limited liability for business losses.

Cost-Benefit Analysis The analysis of government investment projects.

Cost of Capital The annual cost to a firm of purchasing an additional unit of capital.

Countercyclical Policy A fiscal or monetary policy that counteracts the movements in aggregate demand whenever aggregate demand tends to move the economy away from the target level of national income.

CR4 The four-firm concentration ratio, equal to the percentage of total domestic sales accounted for by the four largest firms in the industry.

Craft Union A labor union in which every member of the union is engaged in one particular craft or trade.

Creative Destruction The process by which invention, innovation, and diffusion cause drastic changes in the economic environment, simultaneously destroying markets and bankrupting some firms while creating new markets and profitable opportunities for other firms.

Credit Crunch A condition of excess demand in the loan markets in which potential borrowers complain that they cannot get loans even when they are willing to pay the quoted interest rate for the loans.

Creditor Nation A nation for which the market value of the assets that its citizens hold abroad exceeds the market value of the assets that foreign citizens hold in the nation.

Cross-Price Elasticity of Demand The percentage change in the demand for one good divided by the percentage change in the price of a related good.

Crowding-Out Effect Changes in the demands for consumer durables, investment, and net exports that are induced by the change in interest rates following a change (shift) in aggregate demand, and that lower the value of the spending multiplier.

Currency The dollar bills and coins of various denominations circulating in the economy.

Current Account (Balance of Payments) The subaccount in the balance of payments that records the exports and the imports of goods and services, the receipts of factor incomes by domestic and foreign residents, and net unilateral transfers.

Current Account Balance The balance of goods and services minus net unilateral transfers.

Current Dollar (Nominal) Gross Domestic Product The actual dollar value of the gross domestic product generated during the year.

Current Market Discrimination In the context of labor markets, unequal treatment of people on the basis of personal characteristics, such as race or gender, that are unrelated to differences in their productivity, taking the form of unequal pay for the same work, unequal access to jobs, and unequal access to training programs and promotions.

Current Population Survey An annual survey of approximately 60,000 families and unrelated individuals compiled by the U.S. Bureau of the Census, which is used to obtain information on income and other personal characteritics.

Cyclical Budget Deficit The component of the government's budget deficit that fluctuates with the state of the economy; the difference between the actual budget deficit and the structural budget deficit.

Cyclical Indicator A monthly or quarterly data series that contains reliable and significant information concerning the performance of the economy over time and that moves in a pattern consistent with the movement of the overall business cycle.

Cyclical Unemployment Unemployment that fluctuates with the state of the economy because wages are sticky.

Debtor Nation A nation for which the market value of the assets that its citizens hold abroad is less than the market value of the assets that foreign citizens hold in the nation.

Decreasing Cost Industry An industry in which the minimum long-run average cost of the firms decreases as output supplied to the market increases, so that the long-run market supply curve is downward sloping.

Deficit Agents Economic agents who are the borrowers or the users of funds in financial markets because they have less income than they desire to spend in any one year.

Demand The amount of a product that individuals are willing and able to buy over a certain period of time.

Demand for Money The average amount of money that a person or an institution wants to hold and not spend.

Demand Pull Inflation Price inflation resulting from the attempt to purchase more goods and services than the economy is capable of producing.

Depository Institution A financial institution that accepts deposit accounts of any kind.

Depository Institutions Deregulation and

Monetary Control Act of 1980 (DIDMCA) An act of Congress that brought all depository institutions under the control of the Fed.

Depreciation The decline in the market value of the firm's stock of capital during the year.

Depreciation (Currency) The value of a nation's currency falls relative to the value of other currencies.

Derived Demand The principle that the demand for labor depends in part on the market for the product that the workers are producing; the higher the price of the product, the higher the wages, other things equal.

Developed Countries Countries that have achieved, on average, a high standard of living, with a per capita income of at least $7,620 (as of 1990).

Developing Countries Countries that range from the nearly developed to the very poor, with a per capita income of less than $7,620 (as of 1990); also called *less developed countries (LDCs)*.

Diffusion The final post-research stage of the process of invention and innovation in which firms are actually using a new production technology or producing and selling a new product.

Direct Foreign Investment The purchase of domestic stock or other assets by foreign residents that give them a controlling interest in a domestic firm.

Discount Factor The factor by which future dollars are multiplied to determine their present value; it is equal to $1/(1 + r)^n$, where r is the discount rate and n is the time in the future when the dollars are received or spent.

Discount Rate The interest rate used to calculate the present value of future dollars; alternatively, the interest rate used to compound current dollars to their future value.

Discount Rate (Federal Reserve) The rate of interest that the Fed charges commercial banks for loans of reserves to help the banks meet their reserve requirements.

Discounting to Present Value The process of computing the current value of future dollars.

Discouraged Workers Those people who have become so discouraged trying to find an acceptable job that they have dropped out of the labor force.

Diseconomies of Scale
- *In terms of long-run total cost:* the region of the long-run total cost curve along which the percentage change in total cost is

greater than the percentage change in output.
- *In terms of the production function:* an equal proportionate increase in all the firm's inputs by an amount k leads to a proportionate increase in the firm's output by less than k (for example, a doubling of all the firm's inputs leads to less than a doubling of the firm's output); also called decreasing returns to scale.

Disposable Income The income available to households for their own use, to be consumed or saved.

Distributional Policies Government economic policies that respond to market failures relating to the goals of achieving fair and evenhanded market exchanges and an acceptable distribution of income.

Dividends The portion of after-tax profits that managers of the firm pay to the stockholders.

Division of Labor As an economy grows and as business firms become larger, the process by which factors of production tend to become ever more specialized, performing highly specific tasks associated with only one small part of the production process.

Dynamic Efficiency The reduction in firms' costs of production over time due to technical change and increased productivity.

Economic Depreciation The decline in the market value of a firm's capital stock over a given period of time.

Economic Problem A three-part problem consisting of objectives, alternatives, and constraints.

Economic Profit The difference between total revenue and total (economic) cost.

Economic Rent The difference between the wage a worker receives and the wage required to attract the worker to the job.

Economic System The set of decision-making mechanisms, organizational arrangements, and rules for allocating society's scarce resources and determining the appropriate distribution of income.

Economics The study of the allocation of scarce resources through the process of exchange.

Economies of Scale
- *In terms of long-run total cost:* the region of the long-run total cost curve along which the percentage change in total cost is less than the percentage change in output.
- *In terms of the production function:* an equal proportionate increase in all the firm's inputs by an amount k leads to a proportionate increase in the firm's output by more than k (for example, a doubling

of all the firm's inputs leads to more than a doubling of the firm's output); also called increasing returns to scale.

Effectively Competitive Product Market   A product market in which individual firms have very little control over price and other market outcomes.

Effective Market (Monopoly) Power   The ability of a firm to maintain an economic profit in the long run.

Efficiency   A criterion for judging the solution to an economic problem that refers to making the choices that best meet the objectives; if the economic problem has a single objective, then efficiency means coming as close to the objective as possible; if the economic problem has more than one objective, then efficiency means that the Law of Substitution holds. A solution is efficient if moving closer to one objective requires moving farther away from at least one other objective.

Efficiency Wage   A wage that is higher than necessary to retain the employees, but that firms are willing to pay to improve the morale of the employees so that they will remain happy and productive and not shirk their duties; alternatively, the wage at which the marginal benefits and the marginal costs to the firm of further increases in the wage are equal; the wage that maximizes the firm's profit within the range of wages it could pay.

Employed   People who have worked for at least one hour during the week of the Bureau of Labor Statistics employment survey.

End-Results Equity   A criterion for judging the solution to an economic problem that asks whether economic outcomes are fair.

Engel's Curve   A graphical representation of the relationship between income and quantity demanded, other things equal.

Entrepreneurs   Imaginative individuals who bring new ideas to the business world and who are willing to take the risks of starting new ventures or businesses.

Equality of Opportunity   A principle of process equity that requires that individuals have equal access to whatever economic opportunities they are willing and able to pursue so that they can develop their economic potential to the fullest; in the context of product markets, all investors have equal access to profitable market opportunities because of the absence of barriers to entry and equal access to all relevant market information.

Equalizing Wage Differential   A difference in the wages for different jobs that just compensates workers for the relative attractiveness of the jobs.

Equation of Exchange   The measure of the circular flow of economic activity in terms of money; a national income accounting identity, which says that the dollar value of national income or national product equals the product of the money supply times the velocity of circulation.

Equilibrium   A state of rest, or balance, due to the equal action of opposing forces or influences; in economics, a situation from which no one has any incentive to change.

Equilibrium Level of National Income   The level of national income at which aggregate demand equals national income; alternatively, the level of national income at which saving demand equals investment demand.

Equity   In the context of product markets, the presence of equality of opportunity and horizontal equity; the inability of firms to maintain economic profits in the long run.

Eurodollar Account   Any dollar-denominated account in a foreign bank.

Excess Demand   The amount by which quantity demanded exceeds quantity supplied when price is below the equilibrium price.

Excess Reserves   The difference between a commercial bank's total reserves and its required reserves; the amount of reserves that a commercial bank can lend and still be able to satisfy the reserve requirement.

Excess Supply   The amount by which quantity supplied exceeds quantity demanded when price is above the equilibrium price.

Exchange   The trading of goods, services, and factors of production among the key players in the economy.

Exchange Rate Mechanism (ERM)   The dominant feature of the European Monetary System (EMS), which pegged the currencies of the Western European nations to the German mark.

Exclusive Good   A good whose benefits are received only by the person who consumes it.

Exhaustible Resource   A resource available in a finite amount whose quantity diminishes as it is used in production, such as the natural resources.

Expansion Phase (Business Cycle)   The period of time during which economic activity is increasing; commonly referred to as a *boom*.

Expansionary Fiscal Policy   Increases in government purchases or transfer payments, or decreases in taxes, for the purpose of increasing aggregate demand.

Expansionary Monetary Policy   An increase in the money supply undertaken by the Fed for the purpose of increasing aggregate demand; the Fed buys Treasury securities on the Open Market.

Expansionary Policy   A fiscal or monetary policy that increases the level of aggregate demand.

Explicit Monetary (Operating) Costs   The firm's out-of-pocket payments for its factors of production plus the general sales and excise taxes paid by the firm on the sale of its products.

Export-Enclave Production   Refers to production by resource-using firms in the developing countries, typically multinational corporations, whose output is not consumed locally, but is exported to the First World, thereby earning foreign exchange and creating new jobs and export opportunities.

Exports   Domestically produced goods and services, and factors of production, sold to foreign individuals, businesses, and governments.

Externality   A third-party effect of a transaction that directly affects either consumers' satisfaction or firms' production possibilities.

External Debt (Public)   Public debt that is held by foreign citizens, businesses, and governments.

Factor Endowments Model of International Trade   A model developed to explain the pattern of international trade that is based on differences in factor endowments across countries; countries specialize their production in and export those goods that use factors of production that are relatively abundant, and they import those goods that use factors of production that are relatively scarce.

Factor Indivisibility   The inability to use a fraction of a particular factor of production, as when a self-employed catering service owner has to use at least one truck.

Factors of Production   The resources or inputs that producers use to produce goods and services, consisting of labor, capital, land, and material inputs.

Featherbedding   A work rule in which firms are forced to hire workers who are of no value to them.

Federal Deposit Insurance Corporation (FDIC)   A public agency established by Congress that insures deposit accounts at commercial banks (and other depository institutions).

Federal Funds Rate The rate of interest that banks charge other banks on loans of excess reserves.

Federal Open Market Committee (FOMC) A 12-member committee of the Fed that formulates and executes the Fed's purchases and sales of Treasury securities on the Open Market in the conduct of monetary policy.

Federal Reserve Act of 1913 An act of Congress that established the Federal Reserve Banking System, the first true central bank in the United States.

Federal Reserve Banking System The central bank of the United States, commonly referred to as the "Fed."

Federal Reserve Note A dollar bill of any denomination that is the paper currency of the United States.

Financial Intermediary Any institution involved in the process of transferring funds from suppliers to users that positions itself between the ultimate suppliers and the ultimate users of funds in financial markets, such as a commercial bank.

Financial Markets Markets that play the role of transferring money from surplus agents to deficit agents throughout the economy.

Financial Repression A reduction in the supply of savings caused by government policies, such as a government-imposed interest rate ceiling in financial markets.

Fine Tuning Using fiscal or monetary policies to keep the economy at or very near the target level of national income.

Firm's How Problem The goal of producing the maximum output for a given total cost spent on factors of production; alternatively, the goal of producing a given output for the minimum total cost spent on factors of production.

Fiscal Policy Changes in the federal budget made for the specific purpose of influencing the level and the composition of the circular flow of economic activity; includes changes in government spending on goods and services, changes in transfer payments, or changes in taxes.

Fisher Equation The relationship between observed, or nominal, interest rates and the underlying real interest rates that says that the observed interest rate on a financial security equals the real interest rate plus the expected rate of inflation.

Fixed Cost The cost associated with the fixed factors of production in the short run.

Fixed Exchange Rate An exchange rate that is set at a fixed value.

Flexible Exchange Rate An exchange rate that is determined by the Laws of Supply and Demand in the foreign exchange markets.

Flow Variable A variable that can be measured only with reference to a period of time.

For Whom or Distribution Question Asks who will receive the various goods and services that are produced; one of the four fundamental economic questions that every society must answer.

Foreign Exchange Markets The markets in which nations' currencies are exchanged and the exchange rates between all nations' currencies are established.

Foreign Saving The difference between imports and exports.

Formal Education Refers to all schooling received in institutions outside the labor force, from elementary school through graduate school, and includes general vocational training by institutions established for that purpose and not associated with any one business firm.

Free-Rider A person who consumes a nonexclusive (public) good without paying for any of the costs of the good.

Frictional Unemployment Unemployment caused by the continuously shifting employment opportunities from sector to sector that go on beneath the surface of the economy; gathering information about job opportunities and relocating take time and act as frictions in the economy that generate unemployment.

Full Employment The condition when all people who want to work have a job.

Full Faith and Credit Bond Government bonds issued to finance capital projects that are not expected to bring in revenues; the bonds are backed by the government's power to tax.

Full Price The price of a product plus the value of the time spent shopping for and actually consuming the product.

Fully Anticipated Inflation This exists if everyone knows what the inflation rate will be in all future years.

Fully Decentralized Economy An economic system in which individuals and business firms make all economic decisions and are responsible for generating and processing all relevant economic information.

Gains from Trade The amount that a nation gains through international trade relative to producing itself all the goods and the services that it consumes; alternatively, the increase in consumer surplus plus producer surplus resulting from international trade.

GDP Deflator A price index based on a market basket of consumption goods, investment goods, government purchases, and net exports; used to convert current dollar GDP into constant dollar GDP.

General Agreement on Tariffs and Trade (GATT) A treaty originally signed by 23 capitalist nations in 1947 that commits the signatories to reduce tariffs and other trade barriers; membership in GATT has grown to nearly 100 nations.

General Training In a labor market context, the training people receive that teaches basic skills—reading, writing, arithmetic, analytical thinking, familiarity with computers, and so forth—that are useful in a number of occupations and that workers can take with them whenever they change jobs.

GINI Coefficient A common measure of the degree of inequality of income or wealth, equal to the area between the Lorenz curve and the diagonal of the square containing the Lorenz curve, divided by the entire area beneath the diagonal.

Government Bond A promissory note issued by a government that pays the bondholder (the lender) an amount equal to the principal, or face value, of a bond at a specified future date.

Government Purchases of Goods and Services Aggregate purchases of final goods and services by the federal, state, and local governments; the services are primarily the labor services of government employees.

Government Saving The difference between government revenues and government expenditures.

Government Sector In the United States, the economic activities of the federal government, the state governments, and all local governments.

Gross Domestic Product (GDP) The value of final goods and services produced within a country during the year, whether by the country's own citizens or by the citizens of a foreign country.

Gross Investment The value of new capital put in place during the year, equal to the sum of purchases of new plant and equipment, increases in firms' inventories, and purchases of new homes.

Gross National Product (GNP) The value of the final goods and services produced by the citizens of the country during the year no matter where the citizens happen to live.

Gross-of-Tax Price The price including the tax, which is the price that the consumers pay under an excise or sales tax.

Herfindahl-Hirschman Index (HHI) An index of industry concentration, equal to the sum of the squares of each firm's market share within the industry.

Horizontal Differentiation A form of product differentiation in which a firm distinguishes its product from the products of other firms in the industry by choosing where to locate its place of business.

Horizontal Equity A principle of end-results equity that requires that equals receive equal treatment; in the context of product markets, all owners of firms earn the same return to their capital in the long run (standardizing for risk).

Horizontal Equity (Taxation) The principle that two people with equal levels of utility before a tax should have equal levels of utility after a tax.

Horizontal Merger A merger between firms selling the same product.

Household Sector The sector of the economy that consists of individuals in their dual roles as consumers of final goods and services and as suppliers of factors of production to business firms.

How or Input Question Asks how the economy produces its goods and services; one of the four fundamental economic questions that every society must answer.

Human Capital The market value of all accumulated knowledge and skills.

Human Capital Theory A theory that analyzes the relationship between education and earnings, on the assumption that education increases people's earnings by making them more productive.

Hyperinflation An inflation in which prices are increasing very rapidly, causing people to lose confidence in the currency.

Impact of a Tax Refers to the levying of the tax; that is, who actually writes the tax check to the government.

Imports Goods and services, and factors of production, purchased from foreign individuals and business firms for domestic use.

Import-Substituting Industrialization (ISI) A strategy for economic growth and development in which a developing country produces goods that it had previously been importing.

Incentive-Based Pay A method of payment used by employers that relates pay directly to the results of an employee's work, such as the commissions received by salespeople.

Incidence of a Tax Refers to the true burden of the tax; that is, how the burden of the tax is split between demanders and suppliers.

Income Effect (of a Price Change) The change in the quantity demanded of a good due to the effect that the change in its price has on an individual's purchasing power or real income.

Income Elasticity of Demand A measure of the responsiveness of quantity demanded to a change in income; specifically, the percentage change in quantity demanded divided by the percentage change in income.

Income Statement A record of the value of the output and income generated by the firm during the course of the year; a record of a firm's sales and the cost of goods sold.

Increasing Cost Industry An industry in which the minimum long-run average cost of the firms increases as output supplied to the market increases, so that the long-run market supply curve is upward sloping.

Index of Coincident Indicators An index of four cyclical indicators that is designed to track the expansion and the contraction phases of the business cycle, and its turning points, as they are occurring.

Index of Lagging Indicators An index of seven cyclical indicators that is designed to confirm the existence of the various phases of the business cycle and its turning points with a few months' delay.

Index of Leading Indicators An index of 11 cyclical indicators that is designed to forecast aggregate economic activity and predict the turning points of the business cycle.

Indifference Curve A graphical representation of the different combinations of goods and services that an individual is indifferent to because they yield the same level of utility.

Indifference Map The set of all the indifference curves.

Indirect Business Taxes Sales and excise taxes that firms pay on the sale of their products.

Individual Demand Curve A graphical representation of the individual demand schedule, showing the quantity of a good that an individual is willing and able to buy at each price, other things equal.

Individual Demand Schedule The quantity of a good that an individual is willing and able to buy at each price, other things equal.

Individual Firm's Supply Curve A graphical representation of the individual firm's supply schedule, showing the quantity that the firm is willing and able to supply at each price, other things equal; equal to a competitive firm's marginal cost curve above the minimum of its average variable cost curve.

Individual Firm's Supply Schedule The quantity that the firm is willing and able to supply at each price, other things equal.

Industrial Union A labor union organized according to industry rather than the tasks that the workers perform within the industry.

Industry The collection of all firms producing the same product.

Inexhaustible Resource A resource whose quantity does not diminish as it is used in production, such as land.

Inflation Continuing increases in the level of prices generally, usually expressed as a percentage rate of increase.

Inflationary Gap Exists when the equilibrium level of national income is greater than the full-employment level of national income; the size of the gap is the amount that aggregate demand has to decrease to bring the equilibrium level of national income to the full-employment level of national income.

In-Kind Gift A charitable donation or transfer in the form of a particular good or service.

Innovation The process of recognizing the practical uses of an invention and understanding the steps required to make it commercially viable.

Insider/Outsider Theory A theory of wage stickiness that says that the older, more experienced employees, the "insiders," have the decision-making power and use it to place all the risks of a business downturn on the younger, less experienced employees, the "outsiders."

Intangible A benefit or a cost that cannot be evaluated in dollar terms.

Interdependence The principle that economic decisions are interrelated such that the consequences of a decision always spread beyond the immediate objectives of the decision.

Internal Debt (Public) Public debt that is held by U.S. citizens, businesses, and government agencies.

Internal Labor Market A method of hiring and promotion in which firms hire new employees from outside the firm only into the lowest-level jobs within the corporate hierarchy and then promote from within to all higher-level jobs.

Internal Yield on an Investment The rate of discount that just sets the present value of an investment equal to zero.

International Comparisons Program (ICP) A program undertaken by the

United Nations to correct for the problem of converting a country's gross domestic product (GDP) to another currency; it solves this problem by calculating a purchasing power parity exchange rate for each country.

International Credit   Any international transaction that gives rise to a demand for dollars in the foreign exchange markets, such as an export or a capital inflow.

International Debit   Any international transaction that gives rise to a supply of dollars in the foreign exchange markets, such as an import or a capital outflow.

International Monetary Fund (IMF)   An international agency established in 1947 by the capitalist countries that acts as a forum for resolving exchange rate and balance-of-payments problems.

Investment   A flow variable that refers to the increase in the stock of capital during the year.

Investment in Human Capital   Expenditures on education, both formal education received in school and on-the-job training provided by business firms.

Investment Tax Credit   A tax credit under the federal corporation income tax that allows firms to deduct a portion of the total value of their investment during the year from their taxable profits.

Job Leavers   Those people who have voluntarily quit their jobs and are actively looking for other jobs.

Job Losers   Those people who have been laid off or fired by their employers.

Known Reserves   The amount of a natural resource that the U.S. Geological Survey estimates is profitable to extract at current prices and with current production technologies.

Kuznets Curve   A curve that shows the relationship between the income distribution and the per capita income for countries in different stages of economic development.

Labor   A catch-all term referring to all the different kinds of skills and occupations found in the work force; one of the primary factors of production.

Labor Force   All people, aged 16 and older, who are either employed or unemployed.

Labor Force Participation   The percentage of the population that joins the labor force.

Labor Productivity   The amount of output produced per worker.

Land   The property on which business firms build their factories and office buildings; includes the fertile soil and natural resources contained within the land; one of the primary factors of production.

Law of Demand   Other things equal, the lower the price of a product, the larger the quantity demanded; the higher the price of a product, the smaller the quantity demanded.

Law of Diminishing Marginal Rate of Substitution   The more of a good that consumers have, the fewer units of another good they are willing to trade to consume an additional unit of the good.

Law of Diminishing Marginal Utility   The marginal utility of consuming a product decreases as the amount of the product consumed increases.

Law of Diminishing Returns   As increasing amounts of a variable factor of production are added to one or more fixed factors of production, the marginal product of the variable factor eventually declines.

Law of Diminishing (Marginal) Willingness to Trade   For a consumer, the marginal willingness to trade one good for some other good decreases as more and more of the one good is exchanged for the other good.

Law of Large Numbers   A property of statistics, which says that the average behavior of a large group of firms (or people) becomes highly predictable, even if the behavior of individual members of the group is highly unpredictable.

Law of Scarcity   The principle that resources are not sufficient to achieve all the objectives, or goals, of an economic problem.

Law of Substitution   A test of efficiency with more than one objective that says that moving closer to one objective is possible only by moving farther away from at least one other objective.

Law of Supply   Other things equal, the lower the price of a product, the smaller the quantity supplied; the higher the price of a product, the larger the quantity supplied.

Lease-Cost Production Rule   The solution to the firm's How problem, in which the firm equalizes the ratio of marginal product to price across all factors of production.

Legal Barrier to Entry   Any government policy, such as an exclusive franchise or a patent, that restricts or prevents the free flow of resources into or out of an industry.

Levered Investment   An investment that is financed in part with borrowed funds.

Liability   Something that is owed; a claim against someone by some other person or institution.

Licensing   A type of government regulation that restricts entry into an industry as a means of assuring service quality and standards or as a means of controlling the spread of socially undesirable activities.

Life-Cycle Hypothesis   A theory of household consumption demand that attempts to explain the average pattern of lifetime income and consumption given by the age-earnings profile.

Liquid Asset   A financial asset that is easily converted into money.

Long-Purse Theory   The theory that, in the absence of perfect capital markets, large firms have an advantage over new entrants in undertaking investment, since they can finance their investment out of past profits retained by the firms, whereas new entrants have to borrow to invest; this advantage acts as a barrier to entry.

Long Run   A period of time long enough that the firm is able to vary all factors of production and firms can enter or leave the industry.

Long-Run Economic Growth   A persistent increase in the economy's potential for producing goods and services.

Long-Run Phillips Curve   A curve representing the idea that the economy tends to the natural rate of unemployment in the long run and that there is no long-run trade-off between inflation and unemployment; shows that any rate of inflation is compatible with the natural rate of unemployment in the long run.

Long-Run Total Cost Curve   The other things equal relationship between output and total cost in the long run.

Lorenz Curve   A graph of the distribution of income that relates the cumulative percentage of all families, ordered by income from lowest to highest, to the cumulative percentage of the total income (wealth) that they receive.

Macroeconomic Policy   An attempt to achieve the macroeconomic policy goals by intervening in some form in the operation of the economy.

Macroeconomics   The study of the economy "in the large"; analyzes the overall performance of the economy.

Managed Exchange Rate ("Dirty" Float)   A variation of a flexible exchange rate system in which an exchange rate is determined by the Laws of Supply and Demand within a band of values selected by the central banks; alternatively, a variation of a flexible exchange rate system in which the central banks occasionally intervene in the foreign exchange markets in order to prevent their currencies from appreciating or depreciating "too much."

Margin   Refers to the effects of a small change in an economic variable.

Marginal Benefit   The additional benefit, in terms of the objectives, of the next unit of an activity.

Marginal Cost   The addition to total cost of producing an additional unit of output; in general, the change in total cost divided by the change in output.

Marginal Cost Curve   A graphical representation of marginal cost, showing at each output the addition to total cost of producing an additional unit of output.

Marginal Cost of Pollution   The additional cost of pollution experienced by all third parties combined when a polluting activity is increased by one unit.

Marginal Efficiency of Capital   The returns to capital from the last unit of capital put in place; also, the demand curve for capital.

Marginal (Physical) Product of Labor   The additional output produced by each additional unit of labor.

Marginal Product of Labor   The additional output produced by hiring one more unit of labor, holding all other factors of production constant.

Marginal Propensity to Consume   The portion of each additional dollar of disposable income that households consume; the ratio of the change in consumption demand to the change in disposable income.

Marginal Propensity to Import   The additional amount of import demand resulting from a $1 increase in national income; the ratio of the change in import demand to the change in national income.

Marginal Propensity to Save   The portion of each additional dollar of disposable income that households save; the ratio of the change in saving demand to the change in disposable income.

Marginal Propensity to Spend   The portion of the change in national income that feeds back into further changes in aggregate demand during each round of the multiplier process; the slope of the aggregate desired expenditures (*ADE*) line.

Marginal Rate of Substitution   The rate at which an individual is willing to trade one good for another so as to leave utility unchanged; the slope of an indifference curve.

Marginal Revenue   The increase in total revenue from selling one more unit of output; equal to price for a competitive firm.

Marginal Revenue Product of Labor   The marginal revenue from hiring an additional worker, equal to the product of the marginal (physical) product of labor and the marginal revenue from selling the output produced by that labor.

Marginal Tax Rate   The rate of tax applied to additional income received under a personal income tax.

Marginal Utility   The increase in utility obtained from consuming one more unit of a good.

Marginal Value   The value of the last good consumed by each consumer.

(Marginal) Willingness to Trade   The rate of trade between any two goods that leaves the consumer's level of utility unchanged; also called the *marginal rate of substitution* between the two goods.

Market   Any institutional arrangement through which buyers and sellers engage in the voluntary exchange of goods, services, and factors of production.

Market Demand Curve   A graphical representation of the market demand schedule, showing the total quantity demanded of a good by all consumers at each price, other things equal; the horizontal summation of the individual demand curves.

Market Demand Schedule   The total amount demanded of a good by all the consumers at each price, other things equal; the summation of the individual demand schedules.

Market Equilibrium   The intersection of the market demand and the market supply curves at which the quantity demanded equals the quantity supplied.

Market Power (Monopoly Power)   A market situation in which an individual firm faces a downward-sloping demand curve for its product.

Market Share   The ratio of a firm's sales (total revenue) to the total industry sales.

Market Supply Curve   A graphical representation of the market supply schedule, showing the total quantity that all firms in the market are willing and able to supply at each price, other things equal; equal to the horizontal summation of the individual firms' supply curves; also called the *industry supply curve.*

Market Supply Curve—Long run—the total quantity supplied by the firms in the market at each price, when each firm is producing at the MES, the minimum of its long-run average cost.

Market Supply Curve—Short run—the horizontal summation of the individual firms' supply or marginal cost curves, above the minimum of average variable cost.

Market Supply Schedule   The total quantity that all firms in the market are willing and able to supply at each price, other things equal; the sum of the individual firms' supply schedules.

Marketable Permit (Pollution)   A government-issued allowance to emit a certain amount of a pollutant that firms can buy and sell; used in the United States to control the emission of sulfur dioxide by the electric utilities under the Clean Air Act.

Mark-Up Pricing   A rule-of-thumb method of pricing in which a firm sets its price at a constant percentage above its unit or average cost.

Material Incentives   Incentives that appeal to economic self-interest by allowing individuals and business firms to keep the gains from their exchanges.

Material Inputs   Semi-finished products purchased by firms and used as a factor of production.

Means-Tested   Refers to public assistance that is given to families or individuals only if their incomes are below some predetermined amount.

Median Income   The income of the family in the middle of the income distribution (half the families have incomes higher than the median and half have incomes lower than the median).

Medium of Exchange   Anything that people are routinely willing to accept in exchange for goods and services (and factors of production).

Menu Costs   The costs to producers of publishing new price catalogs and informing customers of price changes.

Merit Good   A good that society considers a virtual necessity, but that is priced beyond the means of those with low incomes.

Microeconomics   The study of the economy "in the small"; analyzes the economic problems of individual economic agents and the exchanges between them.

Minimum Efficient Scale of Operation (MES)   The minimum of the long-run average cost curve; alternatively, the output at which economies of scale end and diseconomies of scale begin.

Minimum Wage (Federal)   A wage floor legislated by the federal government, set at $4.25/hour in 1993, which is the lowest wage that firms can pay their workers.

Model   A simplified description of some real-world situation that isolates one particular aspect of the situation and studies the effects on that one aspect as different elements are changed one at a time.

Momentary Run The period immediately following a change in supply or demand when producers cannot change their output supplied to the market.

Monetary Base The sum of Federal Reserve Notes plus bank reserves.

Monetary Policy Changes in the money supply made for the specific purpose of influencing the level and the composition of the circular flow of economic activity.

Money Anything that is routinely used to pay for goods and services or to pay off debts.

Money Multiplier The ratio that relates the total change in the money supply to the value of Treasury securities that the Fed purchases or sells on the Open Market.

Money Rain An abstract device used by economists to represent an increase in the money supply that imagines the new money falling from the sky.

Monopolistic Competition A product market characterized by a large number of firms producing slightly differentiated products, with easy entry and exit, and in which strategic behavior is unimportant.

Monopsony Power Market power in labor markets (or in any factor markets) such that firms are able to set the wage of the workers (or cost of the factors) they hire.

Moral Hazard In the context of insurance, arises when individuals who are being insured can influence the probability of the event being insured against, unbeknownst to the insurer.

Moral Incentives Incentives that encourage behavior for the good of society and may be enforced with legal sanctions.

Most-Favored-Nation Principle A fundamental principle of GATT that states that any reduction in tariffs or other trade restrictions that is negotiated between any two nations automatically applies to all nations.

Multinational Corporation A corporation that has offices and/or factories in more than one country.

Multiplier-Accelerator Model An internal model of the business cycle that is based on the instability of investment demand and its relationship to national income through both the demand side and the supply side of the economy.

M1 The narrowest definition of money, consisting of those financial securities that are routinely accepted for transactions; the sum of currency and balances in checking accounts with unlimited checking privileges.

M2 A definition of money, consisting of M1 plus limited-checking money market deposit accounts and various kinds of very highly liquid small savings accounts with balances under $100,000.

M3 A broad definition of money, consisting of M2 plus various kinds of large deposit accounts with balances exceeding $100,000, including institutional money market mutual funds and European accounts held by U.S. citizens.

National Banking Acts of 1933 and 1935 Acts of Congress that brought the 12 Federal Reserve Banks under the control of one governing body, the Board of Governors.

National Economic Plan A plan developed by the central authority that sets national economic objectives regarding the four fundamental economic questions and instructs lower-level decision-making units on how to carry out the plan.

National Income The value of the labor, capital, and land exchanged in the nation's factor markets during the year.

National Net Worth The net worth or wealth of an entire nation, equal to the market value of the nation's real, or tangible, assets plus the market value of its land, less any claims against these assets held by foreigners.

National Product The value of the final goods and services exchanged in the nation's product markets during the year.

National Saving The amount of saving generated by the domestic economy during the year, equal to the sum of saving by the private sector and saving by the government sector; the difference between total saving and foreign saving.

Natural Barrier to Entry Features inherent in production or supply, such as economies of scale and limited access to a vital factor of production, that restrict or prevent the free flow of resources into or out of an industry.

Natural Monopoly A market situation in which the MES (the minimum of the long-run average cost curve) of a single firm is at or beyond the entire market demand for the product.

Natural Rate of Unemployment The sum of frictional and search unemployment and structural unemployment; the rate of unemployment that corresponds to production on the production possibilities frontier and that cannot be reduced very much by fiscal and monetary policies. Also called the *non-accelerating inflationary rate of unemployment.*

Negative Income Tax A subsidy given to families or individuals whose income is below some predetermined amount and administered as part of the federal personal income tax.

Net Domestic Product (NDP) The difference between gross domestic product and the BEA's estimate of the capital consumption allowance (depreciation).

Net Exports The difference between exports and imports.

Net Interest The difference between interest paid and interest received by firms.

Net Investment The difference between gross investment and the BEA's estimate of the capital consumption allowance (depreciation).

Net-of-Tax Price The price excluding the tax, which is the price that producers receive to cover their costs under an excise or sales tax.

Net Value At any quantity exchanged in the market, the difference between the total value as perceived by the consumers and the total cost as experienced by the firms.

Net Worth The difference between a person's assets and liabilities; also called *wealth.*

Newly Industrializing Countries (NICs) Countries in East Asia that are rapidly industrializing and approaching or surpassing the living standards in the lower tier of developed countries.

New Entrants Those people who are seeking employment for the first time, having never worked before.

Non-Accelerating Inflationary Rate of Unemployment The minimum that the rate of unemployment can be without starting an ever-accelerating inflationary process; also called the *natural rate of unemployment.*

Noncompetitive Product Market A product market in which individual firms have considerable control over price and other market outcomes.

Noncooperative Behavior Independent decision making by firms in which they openly compete with one another.

Nonexclusive (Public) Good A good such as national defense that is consumed by everyone once any one person or the government buys it; no one can be excluded or exclude themselves from consuming the good.

Nonmonetary Operating Costs Costs of production that do not involve out-of-pocket payments for factors of production, the most important being an estimate of the depreciation of the firm's stock of capital.

Nonresidential Fixed Investment Purchases of new plant and equipment during the year.

Normal Good   A good whose consumption rises as income rises, other things equal.

Normative Economic Analysis   The study of what ought to be; attempts to determine appropriate norms or criteria for judging the results of economic behavior and activity.

Now Versus the Future Question   Asks whether society will favor the current generation over future generations, or the reverse; one of the four fundamental economic questions that every society must answer.

Objectives   The part of the economic problem that refers to the goals that economic agents try to achieve.

Official Settlements Account   The subaccount in the balance of payments that records transactions between a nation's central bank and the central banks of other nations.

Official Settlements Account Balance   The difference between international credit and debit transactions between a nation's central bank and the central banks of other nations.

Okun's Law   An observed relationship between output growth and unemployment, which states that every 2.5-percentage-point increase in the rate of growth of output reduces the unemployment rate in the United States by 1 percentage point.

Oligopoly   A product market dominated by a few large firms.

On-the-Job Training   Training offered by firms to their employees that teaches them skills that make them more productive to the firm.

Open Market Operation   A purchase or sale of Treasury securities by the Fed for the purpose of controlling the money supply.

Operating Expenses   The total accounting costs incurred by the firm in producing and selling its output, including the explicit monetary costs and certain nonmonetary costs.

Operational Lag (Fiscal Policy)   The time period from the passage of new legislation to the final change in the equilibrium level of national income.

Operational Lag (Monetary Policy)   The time required for a change in the money supply to affect the equilibrium level of national income.

Opportunity Cost   The economic meaning of cost; the value, in terms of the objectives, of the next best alternative.

Opportunity Cost of Capital   The return that the owners of the firm could earn if the value of the capital they own were invested in their next best investment alternatives.

Opportunity Cost of Labor   The wage or salary available to the employees of a firm in their next best employment alternatives.

Ordering of Preferences   When faced with two combinations of goods and services, the ability to determine either that one combination is preferred to the other or that the two combinations give the same level of utility; an ordering must also satisfy the condition of transitivity.

Overvalued Currency   The value of a nation's currency relative to other currencies is greater than its equilibrium value determined by the Laws of Supply and Demand in the foreign exchange markets.

Parity   The ratio of prices received by farmers for their output to the prices farmers pay for their inputs.

Partnership   A form of business with two or more owners who have total control over the operation of the business and who jointly determine how to transfer funds into and out of the business.

Payoff Matrix   A listing of the present values or the internal yields of an investment under every possible future environment.

Peak (Business Cycle)   A turning point in the business cycle when the expansion phase ends and the contraction phase begins.

Perfect Competition   A product market characterized by a large number of firms, identical products, perfect information, no strategic behavior, a free flow of resources into and out of the industry, and prices and quantities determined by the Laws of Supply and Demand.

Personal Saving   The portion of disposable income that households do not consume.

Petrodollar Recycling   The practice among financial institutions of lending to the developing countries the funds that they receive from the oil-producing countries.

Political Business Cycle   A theory that attributes the business cycle to attempts by the incumbent administration to manipulate the economy to increase its chances of re-election, consisting of expansionary pre-election policies and contractionary post-election policies.

Positive Economic Analysis   The study of what is; attempts to determine what actually exists in the real world and to describe the consequences of economic decisions.

Poverty Gap   The minimum total amount of income that all poor families and unrelated individuals would have to be given to reach the poverty line and escape poverty.

Poverty Line   The amount of income that allows a family or unrelated individual to purchase the bare necessities for a minimally adequate standard of living; anyone with income below the poverty line is considered to be living in poverty.

Precautionary Demand for Money   The motive for holding money to cover temporary and unexpected expenses or losses of income.

Predatory Pricing   A strategy used by an incumbent firm to deter entry in which the firm sets its price so low that a new entrant could not possibly make a profit.

Present Value   The equivalent current value of future dollars, equal to the future dollars multiplied by the relevant future discount factor.

Present Value of an Investment   The difference between the discounted stream of net returns on the investment and the initial investment cost.

Pre-Market Discrimination   Denying people equal opportunities to develop their natural abilities to the fullest extent possible in their formative years before they enter the labor market, as when children are denied access to the best schools because of their race or gender.

Price Ceiling   A legislated amount above which the market price is not allowed to rise.

Price Discrimination   Charging different customers different prices that are unrelated to differences in the cost of serving the customers.

(Price) Elasticity of Demand   A measure of the responsiveness of quantity demanded to changes in the price of a product along a demand curve; specifically, the percentage change in quantity demanded divided by the percentage change in price in absolute value.

(Price) Elasticity of Supply   A measure of the responsiveness of quantity supplied to a change in price along a supply curve; specifically, the percentage change in quantity supplied divided by the percentage change in price.

Price Floor   A legislated amount below which the market price is not allowed to fall.

Price Inflation   A persistent increase in

the prices of most goods and services.

Price Stability   Prices in general are neither rising nor falling.

Price Taker   A firm or individual who has no influence over the market price.

Principal-Agent Problem   An informational problem in which one individual (the principal) tries to monitor and control the behavior of another individual (the agent), but does not have enough information to do so, and the two individuals have different goals.

Prisoners' Dilemma   In the context of an industry cartel, a game played among the member firms in which the equilibrium outcome is for the firms to cheat and destroy the profits made possible by the cartel.

Private-Sector Saving   The sum of personal saving and business saving.

Process Equity   A criterion for judging economic activity that asks whether the rules under which the economy operates are fair.

Producer Price Index   A price index that is designed to track changes in the cost of production over time; it has three components derived from three separate market baskets: crude materials; intermediate materials, supplies, and components purchased from other firms; and finished manufactured goods.

Producer Surplus   At any quantity exchanged in the market, the difference between the total market value and the total cost of production.

Producers   Economic agents who produce goods and services by receiving factors of production from consumers and other producers.

Product Differentiation   A situation in which buyers distinguish or identify products by the firms that produce them; also refers to firms' attempts to distinguish their products from similar products produced by other firms in the industry, by either real or illusory means.

Product Differentiation/Economies of Scale Model of International Trade   A model specifically developed to explain the two-way trade in similar products between the industrialized countries; based on the idea that multinational corporations compete with each other through the research and development of new products and successful products enjoy economies of scale, which gives them a niche in the international marketplace.

Production Function   The relationship between a firm's outputs and its inputs that indicates the maximum output attainable

from all possible combinations of inputs that the firm might use.

Production Possibilities   The economy's capacity for producing goods and services, assuming that it produces them efficiently.

Production Possibilities Frontier   A graphical representation of the economy's capacity for producing goods and services, assuming that it produces them efficiently.

Production Technology   A blueprint or method for transforming inputs into outputs.

Production (Technical) Efficiency   Achieved when the output supplied to the market uses the least amount of society's scarce resources; the market test is that each firm produces in the long run at the minimum of its long-run average cost curve, the minimum efficient scale of operation (MES).

Profit   The difference between the revenue obtained from selling goods and services and the cost of producing them.

Profit-Maximizing Output Rule   A firm produces the output at which marginal revenue equals marginal cost (and charges the price on its demand curve corresponding to this output).

Profit-Maximizing Supply Rule   A perfectly competitive firm supplies the output at which price equals marginal cost as long as price is greater than (short-run) average variable cost.

Profit Satisficers   Large corporations that are interested in profit only to the point of achieving a satisfactory level of profit and then pursue other objectives.

Progressive Tax   A tax for which the average tax burden increases as the taxpayer's income increases.

Property Rights   The ownership of the factors of production.

Proportional Tax   A tax for which the average tax burden remains constant as the taxpayer's income increases.

Proprietors' Income   Income or profit earned by unincorporated forms of business, principally partnerships and sole proprietorships.

Purchasing Power   The amount of goods and services that consumers are able to buy with their limited incomes, given prices; also called *real income.*

Purchasing Power Parity   The principle that the overall price index of one country must equal the overall price index of any other country multiplied by the exchange rate of the first country's currency to the second country's currency.

Pure Market Capitalism   An economic system characterized by fully decentralized decision making, the use of markets to

process economic information and coordinate exchange, private ownership of capital and land, and the use of material incentives.

Pure Monopoly   A product market in which a single firm comprises the entire industry and has complete control over all supply decisions.

Pure Monopsony   The limiting case of monopsony power in which one firm is the only buyer of a particular kind of labor (or of any factor).

Quota   A government-imposed limit on the quantity of a good or a service that can be imported into a country.

Quota Rent   The economic profit earned by foreign importers under a quota when the quota licenses are given away (or sold at less than their full market value).

Rational Expectations   The assumption that rational individuals consider all relevant information (past, present, and future) currently available when forming expectations of the future.

Real Business Cycle Theory   A theory to explain the business cycle developed by new classical economists that is based on outside shocks to the fundamental structure of the economy, which consists of household preferences, resources, and production technologies.

Real Price Change   The actual rate of change in a price less the general rate of inflation.

Recessionary Gap   Exists when the equilibrium level of national income is less than the full-employment level of national income; the size of the gap is the amount that aggregate demand has to increase to bring the equilibrium level of national income to the full-employment level of national income.

Recognition Lag (Fiscal or Monetary Policy)   The time required for policy makers to realize that the economy is in trouble and needs a dose of countercyclical policy.

Re-Entrants   Those people who were once employed, then dropped out of the labor force, and have now re-entered the labor force.

Regressive Tax   A tax for which the average tax burden declines as the taxpayer's income increases.

Rent Control   A price ceiling on the rents that landlords can charge low-income tenants.

Rent Seeking   The pursuit of profitable market opportunities by entrepreneurs that is directed toward unproductive, socially wasteful ends.

Rental Payments to Persons   The combined payments to land and to capital in the form of rents.

Required Reserves   The minimum amount of reserves against deposit accounts that commercial banks (and other depository institutions) are required to keep in an account at the Fed; equal to the reserve requirement times the amount of deposit account balances.

Reserve Requirement   The minimum average ratio of reserves to deposit account balances that commercial banks (and other depository institutions) must maintain over every two week period.

Reserves   A non-interest-bearing account against deposits that commercial banks (and other depository institutions) must keep with the Fed; used by the Fed to control the amount of loans and deposits that banks can create.

Rest-of-World Sector   The sector of an economy that consists of a country's economic relations with foreign countries.

Retained Earnings   The portion of the accounting profits of the firm that is not paid out as taxes or as dividends to stockholders, but is set aside to help finance the continued expansion of the firm.

Revenue Bond   Government bonds that are used to pay for self-financing capital projects.

Rivalry   The name commonly used to describe nonprice competition among oligopolistic firms.

Sales Maximization   The goal of maximizing total revenue or sales by producing the output at which marginal revenue is zero.

Saving Function   The relationship that indicates how much households in the aggregate are willing and able to save during the year at every level of total disposable income, other things equal; also called *saving demand*.

Search Unemployment   Unemployment caused by employees who leave their jobs voluntarily and are looking for other jobs, or by re-entrants or new entrants to the labor force who are looking for a job.

Segmentation Theory   In the context of labor markets, the theory that businesses teach their employees all they need to know in order to perform the various tasks within

a company, so that on-the-job training is the only form of investment in human capital that determines a worker's productivity.

Segmented Labor Market   A labor market in which workers who are qualified for a particular job are denied access to that job.

Services   Purchases by consumers that are not manufactured, but that provide them with something useful.

Short Run   The period following a change in supply or demand over which firms can vary some of their factors of production, but not all of them.

Short-Run Phillips Curve   A curve that shows how the rate of inflation and the unemployment rate respond to a change in aggregate demand in the short run.

Short-Run Total Cost Curve   The other things equal relationship between output and total cost in the short run.

Shut-Down Point   A market situation in which a firm's total revenue equals its variable cost (price equals average variable cost), so that the firm is indifferent between producing and not producing.

Single Proprietorship   A form of business in which a single owner has total control over the operation of the business and has complete freedom to transfer funds into and out of the business.

Social Mobility   The extent to which families change their position over time within the personal distribution of income.

Socialism   An economic system with public ownership of capital and land.

Special Drawing Right (SDR)   A reserve currency created by the IMF and accepted by all central banks as an international reserve in their official settlement accounts; countries can purchase SDRs with their own currency and then trade them to central banks for dollars and other major currencies as needed to settle current account deficits.

Specific Training   In a labor market context, the skills that employees learn during on-the-job training that are useful only to the firm offering the training, such as learning how to operate highly specialized equipment used only by that firm.

Speculative Demand for Money   The motive for holding money based on expectations of future interest rates.

Spending Multiplier   The ratio that relates the change in the equilibrium level of national income to an initial change, or shift, in aggregate demand.

Stabilization Policies   Government economic policies that respond to market failures relating to the macroeconomic policy goals of achieving long-run economic growth, full employment, price stability, and

satisfactory economic relations with foreign countries.

Stable Dollar   The value of the dollar remains constant relative to the currencies of other nations.

Stable Market Equilibrium   A property of the market equilibrium such that the market automatically returns to the equilibrium from any other quantity-price combination.

Stagflation   A period of increasing inflation, falling output, and rising unemployment that follows an adverse aggregate supply shock.

Statistical Discrimination   Attributing to each member of a group the average characteristics of the entire group of people, which become the basis for hiring, training, or promoting any one individual within the group.

Sterilizing Transaction   A transaction by a central bank that is designed to offset the effect on the money supply caused by any transaction on the official settlements account; an example is the Fed's sales of Treasury securities on the Open Market to offset its purchases of foreign currencies.

Stock Variable   A variable that can be measured at a given point in time.

Store of Value   A means of holding wealth from one period to the next.

Strategic Behavior   Any decision by a firm that considers how other firms will react to the decision.

Strategic Tariff   A tariff that is designed to protect domestic firms from competition while they are attempting to research and develop successful new products.

Structural Budget Deficit   An estimate of what the government's budget deficit would be if the economy were at full employment (the natural rate of unemployment), regardless of where the economy actually is; it increases and decreases with discretionary changes in government spending on goods and services, transfer payments, or taxes; formerly referred to as the *high-employment budget deficit*.

Structural Unemployment   Unemployment caused by severe and lasting mismatches between people who are looking for work and the jobs that are available to them; the mismatches are typically geographic or skills-related.

Substitutes   Products that provide the same general kind of services; specifically, two goods whose relationship is such that a decrease in the price of one good decreases the demand for the other good.

Substitution Effect (of a Price Change)   The tendency to purchase more of those products that have become relatively cheaper and fewer of those products that have become relatively more expensive when relative prices change.

Sunk Cost   A firm's fixed cost in the short run, arising from decisions about factors of production that were made in the past.

Supply   The amount of a product that a firm is willing and able to sell over a certain period of time.

Supply Rule for Maximizing Profit   A competitive firm should produce the output at which price (marginal revenue) equals marginal cost.

Surplus Agents   Economic agents who are the savers, or lenders, or the suppliers of funds in financial markets because they have more income than they desire to spend in any one year.

Tacit Collusion   An implicit agreement among the large corporations in an oligopoly, most often in the form of an agreement not to compete in terms of prices.

Target Efficiency   In the context of public assistance, transfer payments that are given only to the poor and remove them from poverty at the lowest possible expense.

Tariff   A tax on a good or a service entering a country.

Tax Multiplier   The ratio that relates the change in the equilibrium level of national income to a change in taxes on households.

Tax Structure   The tax rates and the tax base of any particular tax.

Terms-of-Trade   The rate of exchange between imported goods and exported goods; alternatively, the ratio of a nation's export prices to its import prices.

Theory of Public Choice   A theory of government based on the premise that people behave in the same self-interested manner in the political arena as they do in the economic arena.

Time-Based Pay   A method of payment used by employers that consists of a straight payment per unit of time independent of the results of the employee's work, such as a manager's annual salary.

Total Cost Curve   The best possible relationship between a firm's total cost and its output; it indicates either the minimum total cost of producing each level of output the firm might choose to produce or the maximum output obtainable for each given amount of total cost.

Total Economic Cost   For any given output, the total opportunity cost of the factors of production used in producing and selling that output.

Total Investment Demand   The sum of

the three components of investment demand: investment demand for plant and equipment, investment demand for inventory, and investment demand for housing.

Total Market Value   The dollars exchanged between the consumers and the producers in the market, equal to the total expenditures paid by the consumers and the total revenues received by the firms.

Total Saving   The sum of personal saving, business saving, government saving, and foreign saving.

Transactions Demand for Money   The fundamental motive for holding money that derives from money's role as the medium of exchange; it says that the aggregate demand for money is directly related to real national income, directly related to the overall price level, and inversely related to interest rates and rates of return on other assets.

Transactions Deposit   A checking account with unlimited checking privileges.

Transfer Mechanism (International Trade)   A grant or a loan to a foreign country that is then used to buy exports from the country that gave the grant or the loan; in other words, a mechanism in which first the money flows and then the goods flow.

Transfer Multiplier   The ratio that relates the change in the equilibrium level of national income to a change in government transfer payments.

Transfer Payment   The redistribution of existing income from one economic agent to another.

Transitivity   A condition on an ordering of consumer preferences requiring that all pairwise rankings of alternative combinations be consistent with one another.

Trigger Strategy   A punishment strategy within the context of a tacit collusion to maintain prices above average cost, in which the rival firms threaten to cut their prices to average cost forever if one of the firms cheats on the pricing agreement.

Trough (Business Cycle)   A turning point in the business cycle when the contraction phase ends and the expansion phase begins.

Ultimate Recovery Reserves   The amount of a natural resource that the U.S. Geological Survey estimates could conceivably be profitable to extract at any time in the future.

Unanticipated Inflation   This exists when people are unable to guess correctly what the rate of inflation will be in all future years.

Unbalanced Inflation   An inflation in which the prices of individual goods and services are rising at different rates, some faster than and others slower than the overall rate of inflation.

Underemployed   Workers who are counted as employed, but who are working below their full capacities, either part time when they want to work full time or at jobs below their skill levels.

Undervalued Currency   The value of a nation's currency relative to other currencies is less than its equilibrium value determined by the Laws of Supply and Demand in the foreign exchange markets.

Unemployed   Those people who are actively seeking employment, but are unable to find a job.

Unemployment   The condition when people are actively looking for work, but are unable to find a suitable job.

Unemployment Rate   The ratio of the unemployed to the labor force, expressed as a percentage.

Union Shop   A labor union rule that requires a worker to join a union within 30 days after being hired.

Unit of Account   The standard that defines the value of goods and services in exchange.

Utility   The value that a consumer derives from the consumption of goods and services.

Utility-Maximizing Decision Rule   Utility is maximized when the ratios of marginal utility to price are equal for all goods.

Value Added   For a single producer, the difference between the value of sales and the cost of the intermediate goods that it buys from other producers; for the economy, the sum of the value added by each producer.

Value of Labor's Marginal Product   The marginal revenue from hiring an additional unit of labor in a competitive labor market, equal to the marginal (physical) product of labor times the price of the good or service that the labor is producing.

Value of Marginal Product of Capital (VMP_K)   The present value of the additional revenue received over time from adding one more unit of capital to the existing capital stock.

Variable Cost   The cost associated with the variable factors of production.

Velocity of Circulation   The ratio of the dollar value of national income or national product to the money supply; the number of times the money supply changes hands during the year to buy final goods and services (or primary factors of production).

Vertical Differentiation A form of product differentiation in which a firm distinguishes its product from the products of other firms in the industry on the basis of quality.

Vertical Equity A principle of end-results equity that asks how unequals should be treated; specifically, how much redistribution should society undertake among people with different amounts of income or wealth.

Vertical Equity (Taxation) The principle that unequals may be treated unequally, that is, two people with different values of a tax base may legitimately pay different amounts of tax.

Vertical Merger A merger between firms that operate in different stages in the production and marketing of a single product.

Voluntary Export Restriction An agreement between two nations in which one nation voluntarily limits the quantity of its exports to the other nation.

Wage Stickiness The existence of impediments that prevent wages from moving to their equilibrium level at the intersection of the supply and demand curves for labor.

Wealth The difference between a person's assets and liabilities; also called *net worth*.

What or Output Question Asks what goods and services the economy will produce and in what quantities; one of the four fundamental economic questions that every society must answer.

Windfall (Excessive) Profit A return to capital over and above the opportunity cost of capital that society considers to be excessive.

Workfare A state-administered program in which the state welfare office identifies the poor who are able to work, helps them find a job, and then makes work a prerequisite for receiving public assistance.